Exchange 2000 .NET Server

Black Book

Phillip G. Schein
Evan Benjamin
Cherry Beado

CORIOLIS™

President and CEO
Roland Elgey

Publisher
Al Valvano

Associate Publisher
Katherine R. Hartlove

Acquisitions Editor
Charlotte Carpentier

Development Editor
Jessica Choi

Product Marketing Manager
Tracy Rooney

Project Editor
Greg Balas

Technical Reviewer
Carl Burnham

Production Coordinator
Todd Halvorsen

Cover Designer
Jody Winkler

CD-ROM Developer
Michelle McConnell

Exchange 2000 .NET Server Black Book

The Coriolis Group, LLC
14455 N. Hayden Road
Suite 220
Scottsdale, Arizona 85260

(480) 483-0192
FAX (480) 483-0193
www.coriolis.com

Library of Congress Cataloging-in-Publication Data
Schein, Phillip G.
Exchange 2000 .NET server black book / Phillip Schein and Evan Benjamin.
p. cm.
Includes index.
ISBN 1-57610-997-6
1. Microsoft Exchange Server (Computer file). 2. Client/server computing. I. Benjamin, Evan. II. Title.
QA76.9.C55 S345 2001
005.7'13769--dc21

2001042170
CIP

CORIOLIS™

Printed in the United States of America
10 9 8 7 6 5 4 3 2 1

The Coriolis Group, LLC • 14455 North Hayden Road, Suite 220 • Scottsdale, Arizona 85260

A Note from Coriolis

Coriolis Technology Press was founded to create a very elite group of books: the ones you keep closest to your machine. In the real world, you have to choose the books you rely on every day *very* carefully, and we understand that.

To win a place for our books on that coveted shelf beside your PC, we guarantee several important qualities in every book we publish. These qualities are:

- *Technical accuracy*—It's no good if it doesn't work. Every Coriolis Technology Press book is reviewed by technical experts in the topic field, and is sent through several editing and proofreading passes in order to create the piece of work you now hold in your hands.
- *Innovative editorial design*—We've put years of research and refinement into the ways we present information in our books. Our books' editorial approach is uniquely designed to reflect the way people learn new technologies and search for solutions to technology problems.
- *Practical focus*—We put only pertinent information into our books and avoid any fluff. Every fact included between these two covers must serve the mission of the book as a whole.
- *Accessibility*—The information in a book is worthless unless you can find it quickly when you need it. We put a lot of effort into our indexes, and heavily cross-reference our chapters, to make it easy for you to move right to the information you need.

Here at The Coriolis Group we have been publishing and packaging books, technical journals, and training materials since 1989. We have put a lot of thought into our books; please write to us at **ctp@coriolis.com** and let us know what you think. We hope that you're happy with the book in your hands, and that in the future, when you reach for software development and networking information, you'll turn to one of our books first.

Coriolis Technology Press
The Coriolis Group
14455 N. Hayden Road, Suite 220
Scottsdale, Arizona
85260

Email: ctp@coriolis.com
Phone: (480) 483-0192
Toll free: (800) 410-0192

To my parents:
You do not ask me for anything; I will always owe you my life.

To Adrienne:
You do not ask me for anything; you heard what I neglected to say.

To Nicole:
I asked you for time to finish what I needed to do:
A book, a bell, an extinguished candle.
—Phillip G. Schein

❧

This book is dedicated to my parents who have contributed their support,
as well as all the fine people at New Horizons in New York City,
who have helped me learn so much.
To all my friends and family, I say thanks.
—Evan Benjamin

❧

To my family, the Beado's, for everything that I am, to my MISNet family,
for everything that I learned, and to all my friends, for believing in me.
—Cherry Beado

❧

About the Authors

Phillip G. Schein is a certified technical trainer specializing in Web application development, courseware design and publishing, and project management. Phil has written the *Exchange 2000 Administration Exam Prep*, *Windows 2000 Security Design Exam Cram*, and the *MCSE Windows 2000 Security Design Personal Trainer* for The Coriolis Group. He has also written articles about the computer industry for more than ten years. Mr. Schein has led corporate training seminars for Fortune 100 publishing companies, agricultural research firms, insurance reinvestment concerns, and business leaders in the insurance industry.

In addition to being a Master Certified Internet Webmaster (CIW) Designer and Certified CIW Instructor, Microsoft Certified Systems Engineer/Trainer (MCSE/MCT), and Novell Certified Network Engineer (CNE), The Chauncey Group International recognizes Phil as a Certified Technical Trainer (CTT). He has CompTIA A+ Certification (A+) in both Windows/DOS and Macintosh, and the latest CompTIA i-NET+ (i-NET+) certification. Mr. Schein is also a Microsoft Office User Specialist (MOUS) and Product Specialist (MCP+I) in several Microsoft products.

A native New Yorker, Mr. Schein completed undergraduate studies at the University of Rochester, in New York state, and graduate course requirements for a doctoral degree in physiological psychology at Indiana University in Bloomington. Formerly a staff instructor and interim network administrator at a college in New York, and training site manager for a national retail company, Phil has recently delivered several programs as an adjunct professor of E-Commerce at the University of Richmond in Virginia. Prior to his career in the computer industry, he also spent more than ten years as an accounting manager in the transportation industry. He has served on the Board of Trustees for two not-for-profit organizations.

Evan Benjamin is a computer consultant and trainer in New York City. He has worked with the Microsoft operating system for almost 10 years in various capacities, including network administrator and power user. Evan is a Certified Microsoft Trainer, as well as an MCSE. He has also earned certifications with Novell and Checkpoint Software. Evan received his B.S. in mathematics from Washington University in St. Louis, and his MBA from Southern Illinois University in Edwardsville, Illinois. His current functions include teaching advanced technical courses for New Horizons Computer Learning Center in the heart of New York City.

Cherry A. Beado, is a senior technical consultant at MISNet, Inc., a Microsoft Certified Systems Engineer, and Microsoft Certified Trainer. Her bias is messaging and collaboration software. Cherry has managed numerous Microsoft Exchange implementations and migrations, from small to several thousand users with different architecture. She is a contributor for OutlookExchange.Com, and had several articles under her name.

Having been in the IT Industry for more than seven years now, Ms. Beado has worked for several companies, including a CD-ROM publishing company, an Internet Service Provider, and currently, the third largest software company in the Philippines.

A computer engineering graduate of Adamson University, Cherry considers herself lucky to have landed jobs that not only challenged her intellect, but also allowed her to constantly hone her skills.

Acknowledgments

We want to thank acquisitions editor, Charlotte Carpentier, for the opportunity to contribute to the Coriolis collection of Black Books, and for help when the road got a little rocky. I personally do apologize and am embarrassed that you lost your bet! Along with her, we wish to thank Todd Halvorsen, production coordinator; April Nielsen, interior designer; Laura Wellander, cover designer; Tracy Rooney product marketing manager; and Michelle McConnell, the CD-ROM developer for performing critical roles with quiet dignity and grace on the book. We also want to thank project editor Dan Young for his brief, but significant stint, in editing some of our manuscript. I promise, Dan, to always use a green highlight in the future!

We are also indebted to our copyeditor, Julie McNamee, for carefully reading and improving our text. In addition, we need to thank Carl Burnham, our technical editor, for very strong, insightful technical support and candid remarks.

I personally want to thank my coauthor, Evan Benjamin. We both have journeyed together down a long and remarkable road that was meant for neither agnostic nor skeptic. Given all that has happened in the life cycle of this and the last book, we have to pause for a moment and focus just on the sweet air filling our lungs. Sometimes <LOL>, that's all a person has! Nevertheless, we are privileged to be alive. Without pain, there is no passion; without passion, no yearning to endure. I guess that's what Faulkner was talking about; the choice of enduring rather than just surviving. I also want to thank Cherry Beado for gracefully filling the breach and contributing her work under difficult conditions. Your students at home, and in Korea, as well as your coworkers, are lucky people to have the opportunity to work with you every day…in the flesh. I haven't forgotten that I promised you an extra hot viente mocha in Manila. Not too many people in this hemisphere can say that and mean it.

Finally, I want to acknowledge and sincerely thank Greg Balas, our project editor, for patiently dealing with missed deadlines, and the many frustrations that I, and my coauthors, caused. We needed and were thankful for your support throughout a project that, like most, was filled with many ups and downs.

Contents at a Glance

Part I An Introduction to Microsoft Windows 2000 Platform and Messaging Systems

Chapter 1 Messaging and Collaboration 3

Part II Planning for Exchange 2000 Implementation

Chapter 2 Understanding Messaging Systems 41

Chapter 3 The Envisioning Stage 65

Chapter 4 Planning the Implementation 97

Chapter 5 Planning Recipient Objects 133

Chapter 6 Planning Site Topology 171

Chapter 7 Planning Services 203

Part III Installing and Configuring Exchange 2000

Chapter 8 Security, Disaster, and Recovery 259

Chapter 9 Exchange Server Issues 315

Chapter 10 Installing Core Components 375

Chapter 11 Developing a Routing Strategy 431

Chapter 12 Client Installation 481

Part IV Managing and Optimizing Exchange 2000

Chapter 13 System Administration 523

Chapter 14 Maintenance and Troubleshooting 565

Chapter 15 Connecting to Other Messaging Systems 615

Chapter 16 Web Storage System and Dashboards 665

Chapter 17 Outlook Forms and Exchange Workflows 703

Chapter 18 Collaboration Data Objects (CDOs) and Process 743

Table of Contents

Introduction xxxi

Part I An Introduction to Microsoft Windows 2000 Platform and Messaging Systems

Chapter 1
Messaging and Collaboration 3
Scalable Services 5
.NET Initiative 5
A Paradigm Shift toward Knowledge Management 8
Design 13
Administration Tools: Server Access 14
Distributed Services 16
Physical Topology 17
Storage Infrastructure 18
The Database Layer 19
Multiple Databases 20
Distributed Configuration 21
Clustering 21
Web Storage System 22
OWA Architecture 26
OWA Protocol Support 29
Extensibility 32
Web Services 33
Realtime Collaborative Services (RTC) 34
Microsoft Exchange Chat Service 35
Instant Messaging 36

Part II Planning for Exchange 2000 Implementation

Chapter 2
Understanding Messaging Systems 41
The Primary Functions of Exchange 2000 Server 41
What Exchange Server Can Do for You 42
Exchange 2000: An Overview 42

The Ideal Messaging Server 43
How Exchange 2000 Meets the Criteria 45
Advantages of Exchange 2000 52
The Case for Exchange 2000 55
Cautious Optimism 56
Some Final Thoughts 60
Windows 2000 Guidelines and Planning Points 61

Chapter 3
The Envisioning Stage 65

In Depth 66

A Vision Statement 67
Corporate Objectives 67
The Problem Statement 68
The Proposed Solution 69
The Risk Analysis 69
The Project Scope 70
Planning Guidelines 70
Using a Process Model 70
An Operational Framework 72
Contingency Management 72
Contingency Countermeasures 74
Service Management 75
Change Management 75
Problem Management 77
Needs Assessment 78
Define Consumer Needs 79
Assessing Current Resources and Infrastructure 80
Planning Deployment 83
Design an Organizational Plan 83
Design the Hardware Infrastructure 83
Determining Pilot Study Objectives 86

Immediate Solutions 88

Outlining Project Management Steps 88
Performing a Business-Impact Analysis 88
Performing a Risk-Assessment Analysis 89
Evaluating the Cost/Benefit of SLAs 90
Maintaining Recovery Capabilities 90
Designing a Pilot Study 91
Conducting a Gap Analysis 91
Building a Contingency Plan 92

Building a Help Desk Workflow Protocol 93
Constructing a Disaster-Recovery Plan 93
Assessing the Environment 94
Planning Steps Prior to Deployment 94
Planning Public Folders 95
Calculating Hardware Storage Space 95

Chapter 4
Planning the Implementation 97

In Depth 98

A Project Management Methodology 98
- Planning Objectives 99
- Perceived Benefits 101

Determining Pilot Study Objectives 102
Implementing the Plan 103
- Basic Management Tools 105
- Physical Structure 105
- Application Server Software 106
- Network Infrastructure 107
- Directory Service Components 108
- AD Logical Structure 109
- AD Logical Components 114
- Administrative Roles 116
- AD Groups 116
- Policies 117
- Default Recipient Policies 118

Exchange 2000 Structure 118
- Recipient Management 118
- Naming Standards 119
- Public Folders 120
- Foreign Mail Systems 122
- RTC Services 123

Immediate Solutions 125

Identifying Pre-Installation Tasks 125
Determining the Scope of AD Groups 125
Planning a DNS Namespace 126
Planning Naming Contexts 127
Managing the Configuration Container 128
Planning Recipient Management 128
Configuring Recipient Settings 129
Removing Recipient Policy 130

Defining a New Recipient Policy 130
Determining the Scope of Groups 131
Creating Security and Distribution Groups 131
Performing a Foreign Mail System Audit 132

Chapter 5
Planning Recipient Objects 133

In Depth 134

New Concepts in Exchange 2000 134
Directory Objects in Exchange 2000 136
Administrative Models for Recipient Objects 145
Legacy Recipients in Exchange 2000 147
The Importance of ADC for Recipient Management 147

Immediate Solutions 150

Creating a Mailbox-Enabled Recipient Object 150
Adding Mailbox Information to Existing Users 151
Creating a Mail-Enabled User Recipient Object 153
Mail-Enabling a Security or Distribution Group 156
Planning Recipient Access to Exchange 2000 Using Only a MAPI-Based Client 157
Mail-Enabling Groups in a Multidomain Environment 160
Optimizing Replication Traffic for Mail-Enabled Groups 160
Planning a Postmaster Mailbox 161
Planning Dedicated Mailboxes with Disabled User Accounts 161
Determining the Number of Mailboxes You Can Add to a Single Exchange 2000 Server 162
Setting Storage Limits for Recipient Objects 163
Using Recipient Policies for Recipient Objects 165
Updating Recipient Objects Using the Recipient Update Service 167
Implementing Administrative Groups and Assigning Permissions to Them 168
Administrative Groups You Created Are Not Visible in System Manager 170

Chapter 6
Planning Site Topology 171

In Depth 172

Enterprise Organization 172
Creating a Physical Structure 174
Network Structure 174
Protocols 175
Virtual Servers 179
Exchange Components 179
Transport Core 179
How Components Work Together 182

Planning Routing Groups 185
Creating a Routing Group 186
The Role of the Routing Group Master 186
Routing Information in the AD and DNS 187
Message Routing and Group Expansion 187
Link State Routing 187
Site Links 189
Summary 190
Immediate Solutions 191
Planning an OU Structure 191
Accessing Knowledge Resources Using a Browser 191
Considering AD Group Types 192
Determining AD Group Scopes 192
Creating Groups in Mixed Mode 194
Creating Mail-Enabled Groups 194
Planning AD Security Groups 195
Planning AD Distribution Groups 195
Planning Site Boundaries 195
Determining the Number of GC Servers 196
Estimating GC Database Sizing 196
Determining GC Server Sizing 198
Planning GC Server Placement 198
Selecting Attributes to Replicate to the GC 199
Planning Routing Strategies 199
Planning System Message Flows between Sites 200
Planning How Sites Are Linked 201
Testing whether ESMTP Is Enabled 201
Enabling ESMTP Support 202
Requesting ETRN/TURN from a Different Server 202

Chapter 7
Planning Services 203
In Depth 204
Enrolling Users via AD Instead of KM Services 204
Microsoft Frameworks and TCO 207
Administrative Tools 207
The Interplay of Roles 208
Recipient Management 214
Domain Structure 215
Administrative Models 216
Specialized Tools for Recipient Management 217
Permission Management 218
Policies 219

Server Management 220
- Administrative Models 221
- Tools That Support Server Management 223
- System Policies and Groups 224

Other Administrative Areas 224
- Security and Distribution Groups 225
- Public Folders 225

RTC 226
- Collaboration Technologies and Concepts 226
- KM Service in Exchange 2000 231

Outsourcing Collaborative Services 234

Immediate Solutions 235

Connecting to an Exchange Server for Services 235
Creating a MMC 236
Creating an Emergency Repair Disk (ERD) 237
Modifying the MMC **RestrictAuthorMode** Registry Key 239
Modifying the MMC **RestrictToPermittedSnapins** Registry Key 240
Installing and Managing Certificate Services 240
Installing a CA 241
Installing KM Services 242
Granting Manage Permissions to KM Services 244
Enrolling Users in KM Services 244
Creating a Chat Community 245
Creating a Chat Channel 246
Creating a Restricted Chat List 247
Disabling without Removing a Chat Community 249
Removing a Chat Community 249
Troubleshooting IM 249
Creating a New Chat Community 250
Installing an IM Service 251
Changing the Password Policy for an IM Server 251
Limiting the Number of IM Connections 252
Providing IM Service Access 252
Configuring IM Channel Defaults and Language Options 253
Creating a Chat User Class 253
Creating a User Ban from an IRC Channel 254
Enrolling Users Using AD Rather Than KM Services 255

Part III Installing and Configuring Exchange 2000

Chapter 8
Security, Disaster, and Recovery 259

In Depth 260

Why Security Is Important 260
Security Measures Protect Your Network 261
Security Measures Help Prevent Disasters 267
The Ultimate Disaster Recovery Plan? 274
The Underlying Technology 275
A Note on Exchange 2000 Clusters 276
Backup-and-Restore Strategies 277
Using **ESEUTIL** and **ISINTEG** for Database Consistency 286

Immediate Solutions 288

Protecting Your Mission-Critical Mailbox Stores 288
Deleting a Mailbox in Exchange 2000 288
Configuring a Deleted Items Retention Period 290
Configuring a Deleted Mailbox Retention Period 291
Reconnecting a Deleted Mailbox to a New User Object 292
Recovering a Mailbox from a Backup 293
Changing the Legacy Distinguished Name for a Recovery Server 296
Creating a SMTP Virtual Server 297
Configuring Authentication for SMTP Virtual Servers 300
Restricting Connections via IP Address or Domain for SMTP Virtual Servers 301
Creating a GPO for a Domain 304
Installing the Security Analysis and Configuration Snap-In 306
Planning an Optimal RAID Configuration 308
Disabling EFS for All Users in a Domain 309
Running **ISINTEG** and **ESEUTIL** to Check Your Databases for Inconsistencies 311
Troubleshooting the Inability to Apply Security Permissions Because of Missing Security Tab 314

Chapter 9
Exchange Server Issues 315

In Depth 316

Server Issues Related to Security 317
Using Message-Based Security 318
Content Management 323
Virus Management 325
Server Issues Related to DNS and TCP/IP 328
DNS Used for AD Queries 328
DNS Used for FE/BE Configuration 329

Integrating AD Service with Existing DNS Servers 329
Exchange 2000 and TCP/IP 331
Server Issues Related to Delegation of Rights 334
It All Began with the Design of AD 334
Then Came Exchange System Management 334
Delegating Control 335
Even More Granular Control for Exchange 2000 336
Server Issues Related to Migration from Exchange 5.5 Server 337

Immediate Solutions 346

Configuring Message Formats for the POP3 Virtual Server 346
Configuring Overriding Message Formats for Individual Users 348
Configuring MIME Formats for the Default Internet Message Format 350
Using the Rules Wizard in Outlook 2000 for Content Management 351
Using the Junk and Adult Content Filters with the Outlook Client 356
Finding Appropriate Content-Management Software 357
Dealing with Mail Abuse Prevention on Exchange 2000 358
Working with the Email Security Update in Outlook 2000 360
Connecting Exchange 2000 to the Internet Using a Static IP Address 362
Setting TCP/IP Port Numbers for Firewalls in Mixed-Mode Exchange Environments 364
Using the Delegation of Control Wizard to Assign Permissions 365
Restricting Access to Public Folders in the Outlook 2000 Client 367
Converting Universal Distribution Groups to Universal Security Groups to Secure Access to Public Folders 369
Installing the ADC with a Connection Agreement in a Mixed-Mode Exchange Server Environment 370

Chapter 10
Installing Core Components.. 375

In Depth 377

Storage Groups (SGs) 377
Internet Connectivity 378
Additional SMTP Virtual Servers 378
Mail Gateway 378
SMTP Connector 379
Domain Name System (DNS) Configuration 379
Active Directory (AD) 380
Set Up Forests 381
Set Up Domains 386
Set Up Mailboxes 388
Install Exchange 2000 390
Components for Exchange 2000 390
Exchange System Management Tools 391
Realtime Collaboration (RTC) 391

Immediate Solutions 392

Installing Exchange 2000 Components 392
Installing Exchange 2000 in a Forest without Earlier Versions 393
Installing Exchange 2000 in a Forest with Earlier Versions of Exchange 394
Installing Additional Exchange 2000 Servers 396
Installing Exchange 2000 on Windows 2000 Member Servers 397
Installing Exchange 2000 Unattended 397
Transferring the Schema Master 398
Transferring the Schema Master Role when the Schema Master Fails 398
Setting Schema Write Operations in the Registry 400
Configuring the Exchange 2000 System Attendant 402
Configuring the Information Store 404
Setting Mailbox Properties 406
Creating a New Public Folder Tree 407
Adding a Public Folder Store 410
Setting Public Folder Store Properties 410
Changing Public Folder Home Servers 412
Replicating Public Folders 413
Scheduling Replication for All Folders in a Database 413
Scheduling Replication for a Single Folder 414
Installing IM Service 414
Configuring IM 415
Enabling a User for IM 416
Installing the MSN Messenger Service Client 417
Configuring Exchange 2000 Chat Service 417
Creating a Chat Community for Selected Administrative Groups 418
Connecting a Chat Community to a Server 419
Removing a Chat Community from the Server 420
Disabling a Chat Community Temporarily 420
Deleting a Chat Community from the Server 421
Creating Channels 421
Configuring an Internet Connection 422
Creating Additional SMTP Virtual Servers 422
Creating an SMTP Connector 423
Configuring a NNTP Connection 423
Configuring a NNTP Virtual Server 424
Creating Newsgroups 425
Configuring Message Tracking 426
Adding a Configuration Item Using MMC 426
Configuring a Console Taskpad 427
Determining Workload Using Load Simulator 428
Benchmarking Using LoadSim 429
Creating the LoadSim Topology 430

Chapter 11
Developing a Routing Strategy 431

In Depth 432

Transport Components in Exchange 2000 432
Phase 1—Your Current Environment 436
Phase 2—Planning Routing Groups 437
Exchange 5.5 Routing and Coexisting with Exchange 2000 438
Developing Routing Groups and Routing Boundaries 439
Phase 3—Message Flow in Exchange 2000 Using Connectors 442
Message Flow Topology in Exchange 2000 442
Message Flow Architecture in Exchange 2000 444
Implementing Messaging Connectors 445
Optimizing and Troubleshooting Message Routing in Exchange 2000 450
Troubleshooting Tools Used in Exchange 2000 452

Immediate Solutions 455

Understanding Message Routing in Exchange 5.5 455
Planning Single Routing Groups in Your Organization 455
Planning Multiple Routing Groups in Your Organization 456
Deploying Public Folder Replicas in Remote Routing Groups 457
Designing Routing Group Strategies Based on Administrative Models 458
Selecting the RGM within a Routing Group 459
Creating a New Routing Group Using System Manager 461
Moving Servers between Routing Groups Using System Manager 462
Using Link State Routing with All Connectors in Exchange 2000 463
Resolving Target Bridgehead Addresses Using the SMTP Connector 463
Creating an RGC Using the Exchange System Manager Snap-In 463
Resolving Destination Bridgehead Server Addresses for RGCs 465
Configuring a TCP/IP-Based X.400 Connector between Routing Groups 466
Checking SMTP Queues Using the Queue Viewer Utility in System Manager 468
Deleting and Freezing Messages in SMTP Queues Using System Manager 469
Managing SMTP Queue Growth Automatically in System Manager 470
Enabling and Using the Message Tracking Feature in Exchange 2000 472
Enabling Protocol Logging for the SMTP Virtual Server in System Manager 475
Enabling Diagnostic Logging for an Exchange 2000 Server in System Manager 478

Chapter 12
Client Installation 481

In Depth 482

Exchange 2000 Protocols 482
The Internet Protocols 482
The Messaging Application Programming
Interface Protocol 492

Implementing Exchange Server Clients 493
The Microsoft Exchange Client 493
Outlook Clients 494
Upgrading to Outlook 2000 503
Configuring Internet Clients 504

Immediate Solutions 506

Installing Exchange Server and the Outlook Client on the Same Machine 506
Forcing Users to Select a Profile Using the Outlook Client 507
Configuring Profiles for Outlook Clients 508
Adding a Personal Folder Store within the Outlook Client 509
Creating an Offline Folder File within Outlook 2000 510
Configuring Offline Folder Settings in Outlook 2000 510
Configuring a Connection State as Offline in Outlook 2000 510
Making the Offline Address Book Available to Offline Users 511
Configuring Remote Mail in Outlook 2000 512
Enabling the Out Of Office Assistant 513
Creating a New Rule in Outlook 2000 515
Configuring a SMTP Virtual Server 516
Configuring and Controlling Access to a POP3 Virtual Server 518

Part IV Managing and Optimizing Exchange 2000

Chapter 13
System Administration 523

In Depth 524

Administrative Models 524
Administrative Groups 525
Present Administration Model 525
Routing Groups 526
Routing Administration 526
Managing Connectivity between Exchange Servers 527
Server Management 527
Aspects of Exchange Server Management 528
Managing Exchange 2000 Servers in Mixed Mode 529
Administrating Policies 529
Security and Distribution Groups 530
Managing Recipients 531
Public Folders 532
Types of Administrative Models 533
Centralized Management 533
Distributed/Decentralized Management 536
Mixed Centralized and Distributed Management 537

Knowing When to Use RGCs 539
Applying Email Related Security Procedures 540
Immediate Solutions 542
Creating System Policies 542
Displaying Administrative Groups 542
Viewing the System Policies Folder 542
Creating the Server Policy 543
Creating the Mailbox Store Policy 543
Creating the Public Store Policy 545
Creating a New Recipient Policy 547
Applying and Verifying the Policies 548
Managing Recipients 548
Creating a Mailbox-Enabled User 549
Creating a Mail-Enabled User 550
Creating a Mail-Enabled Contact 550
Creating a Mail-Enabled Group 551
Designating an Existing User as Mailbox-Enabled 551
Moving a Mailbox 552
Deleting a Mailbox 552
Managing Email Addresses 553
Adding a New Address 553
Modifying an Address for a Mailbox-Enabled User 553
Creating an Email Address for a Mail-Enabled Recipient 554
Setting the Primary Address 555
Configuring Message Settings 556
Setting Message Size Limits of Incoming Messages 556
Setting the Message Size Limits of Outgoing Messages 556
Setting Message Restrictions for Mailbox-Enabled Users 557
Delegating Sending Permissions 557
Setting Forwarding Address 558
Setting Recipient Limits 558
Configuring the Maximum Number of Recipients Sent Messages 559
Setting the Mailbox Storage Limit 559
Configuring the Deleted Item Retention Period 560
Setting Limits for Message Size 560
Setting Maximum Message Size Limit 561
Setting Message Restrictions for Mail-Enabled Recipients 561
Enabling and Disabling Exchange Features 561
Installing a SMTP Connector 562
Viewing SMTP Connector Properties Pages 563
Setting the Connection Schedule 564
Configuring the RGC Delivery Option 564

Chapter 14
Maintenance and Troubleshooting 565

In Depth 566

Establishing Goals for Maintaining Your
Exchange 2000 Organization 567
Developing Maintenance Goals for Resource Management 567
Developing Maintenance Goals for Service Levels in Your Organization 574
Control Configuration Changes 575
Tools for Maintaining and Monitoring
Exchange 2000 575
Using Server Monitors for Exchange 2000 Maintenance 577
Maintaining Message Queues 578
Maintaining and Optimizing Database Files and SGs 582
The Art of Troubleshooting 587
Troubleshooting Connectivity in Exchange 2000 588
Start of Message 590
Troubleshooting AD Issues 593

Immediate Solutions 595

Monitoring Processor Loads in Exchange 2000 595
Optimizing Memory Usage in Exchange 2000 596
Optimizing Virtual Memory Allocation for Servers with More Than 1GB of RAM 596
Configuring a Server Monitor to Track Available Virtual Memory 600
Configuring Notifications When Your Server Runs Low on Available
Virtual Memory 604
Setting Limits on the Number of SMTP Messages in Queues 605
Manipulating SMTP Queues in System Manager 607
Using a SP to Ensure Messages Queued for External Connectors and the MTA
Don't Disappear 608
Performing an Offline Defragmentation of Your Databases 609
Running **ESEUTIL** in Repair or Integrity Mode Using **/X** or **/V** 610
Checking Your Databases for Consistency 611
Enabling Circular Logging for a SG 612
Writing Transaction Log Files to a Different Directory or Drive 613

Chapter 15
Connecting to Other Messaging Systems 615

In Depth 617

Migrating Foreign Messaging Systems to Exchange 2000 618
MS Mail Connector for PC Networks 620
Exchange Lotus Notes Connector 622
Configuring Directory Synchronization 624
Configuring the Dirsync Schedule 624
cc:Mail Directory Synchronization 625

Novell GroupWise Connector 625
System Preparation 625
GroupWise Dirsync 627
Mobile Information Server (MIS) 628
Outlook Mobile Access and Outlook Mobile Manager 628

Immediate Solutions 630

Viewing Installed Connectors to Foreign Systems 630
Installing the Exchange MS Mail Connector for PC Networks 631
Verifying whether the MS Mail Connector Is Installed Properly 631
Establishing Mail Flow through a MS Mail Connector 631
Creating a PCMTA 633
Creating an Exchange 2000 Dirsync Server or Requestor 633
Creating a Schedule+ Free/Busy Connector 634
Configuring the Schedule+ Free/Busy Connector 634
Troubleshooting MS Mail Connectors 634
Troubleshooting Dirsync 635
Common Problem: Dirsync Not Working Due to Fatal 203 Rebuild Error 636
Configuring Exchange Connector for Lotus Notes 636
Creating the Connector's Notes ID 637
Installing the Notes Client 638
Configuring the Domino Server/Lotus Notes Server 638
Installing the Lotus Notes Connector 639
Configuring the Lotus Notes Connector 639
Setting Up the Connection to a Lotus Notes Server 640
Selecting and Configuring the Import Container 641
Specifying Export Containers 642
Configuring Message Routing 643
Starting the Connector Service 644
Testing the Connection between Exchange Server and Notes 644
Specifying Notes Address Books to Be Synchronized 645
Controlling the Propagation of Notes Groups to Exchange 646
Excluding Lotus Notes Groups from Propagation to Exchange 646
Manually Requesting Directory Updates 647
Installing the Lotus cc:Mail Connector 648
Configuring the Lotus cc:Mail Connector 649
Accessing the Post Office Tab 650
Accessing the Advanced Tab 650
Accessing the Address Space Tab 651
Accessing the Import Container Tab 652
Selecting and Configuring the Import Container 652

Exporting Contacts with the Export Container 654
The Delivery Restrictions Tab 654
Installing the Lotus cc:Mail Connector 654
Restricting the Delivery of Messages to cc:Mail 655
Configuring the Dirsync Schedule 655
Testing the Connection 656
Preparing the Novell GroupWise Environment 656
Creating and Configuring the API Gateway for GroupWise 4.x 657
Creating and Configuring the API Gateway for GroupWise 5.x 658
Activating DLs on GroupWise 659
Creating an External Foreign Domain in GroupWise 4.x 660
Creating an External Foreign Domain in GroupWise 5.x 660
Creating an NTGateway Group 661
Configuring the GroupWise Connector 662
Opening the Connector for Novell GroupWise Properties 662
Importing Directory Entries from GroupWise to Exchange 664

Chapter 16
Web Storage System and Dashboards 665

In Depth 666

Knowledge Management 667
Services Defined 669
Architecture Defined 671
Platform Requirements 672
The WSS 673
Resource Support 674
Event Support 675
Workflow Support 676
Web Forms 677
Portals and E-Commerce 679
Dashboards 681
Dashboard Security 682
Building Portable Web Parts 683
Dashboard Architecture 684
Building Web Parts 687

Immediate Solutions 689

Running the Proxy Configuration Utility to Support ServerXMLHTTP 689
Creating a Web Storage Instance for the Dashboard 690
Modifying Basic Dashboard Properties 691
Creating a Digital Dashboard Project 692
Adding Web Parts to a Dashboard Using Office Developer 693
Using Web Folders with a File System Dashboard 693

Setting Security for a File System Dashboard 694
Installing the File System Digital Dashboard 694
Configuring the File System Digital Dashboard 695
Creating Your First Digital Dashboard 696
Installing the Web Part Builder 696
Using the Web Part Builder to Design Web Parts 698
Adding Web Parts 698
Creating a Digital Dashboard Using Web Parts 699
Previewing and Testing Your Dashboard 699
Deploying an Exchange Server Dashboard 700
Registering a Workflow Event Sink in a Folder 700
Opening a SharePoint Portal Server for the First Time 701

Chapter 17
Outlook Forms and Exchange Workflows 703

In Depth 705

Building Collaborative Systems 706
Messaging Applications 707
Workflow Applications Architecture for Exchange Server 710
Developing Workflow Applications for Exchange Server 711
Workflow Applications 712
Workflow Events 715
Event Order 717
Workflow Engine 719
Workflow Scripting 719
Understanding the Workflow Process 720
Using the Workflow Design Surface 722
Adding and Modifying States in a Workflow 722

Immediate Solutions 723

Modifying Views via the Outlook Interface 723
Creating the Edit Compose Page View of the Outlook Form 723
Publishing the Outlook Form 724
Preparing Exchange for a Team Solution 724
Creating a Team Folder 725
Removing a Form from the Personal Forms Library 726
Creating a Workflow Process Using WDE 2000 726
Adding States to the Workflow Diagram 727
Adding Actions to States 727
Configuring Exchange 2000 for Workflow Development 728
Adding a User to the Two COM+ Roles 729
Running Workflow Applications from a Designated User's Account 730

Creating the Exchange Folder for the Project 730
Adding a Public Folder Using IE 731
Creating the Project and Workflow Process 731
Designing a Workflow Process Using WDE 2000 733
Adding a Workflow State 733
Renaming or Labeling a State or Event 734
Setting a State or Transition Caption 734
Deleting a State 735
Adding and Modifying Transitions in Workflow 735
Adding Objects Multiple Times in Sticky Mode 736
Changing the Transition Type 736
Deleting a Workflow Process for Exchange 2000 736
Enabling Script Debugging and Success Entries 737
Creating the Shared Script Procedures 737
Copying a Workflow Process for Exchange 2000 738
Activating the Workflow Process 739
Changing the Display and Printing the Workflow 739
Viewing or Printing a Workflow 740
Printing the Workflow Diagram 740
Testing Your Workflow for Exchange 2000 741

Chapter 18
Collaboration Data Objects (CDOs) and Process 743

In Depth 744

The Web Store (or Web Storage System) 744
- Outlook Web Access (OWA) Rebuilt 745
- Exchange Data Access 745

Data Source Providers 746
ActiveX Server Components 749
- Global.ASA 751
- ASP.NET 751

CDOs 753
- CDO for Windows 2000 754
- CDO for Exchange 2000 755
- The CDO Subsystems 755
- Process Flows and CDO 756

Processes and XML 757
- XSL Transformation in Access 760
- Browser Compatibility Issues 760

.NET Framework 760
- ASP.NET 763
- Moving Forward with .NET 764

Exchange 2000 and the Way of the Merchant 765

Immediate Solutions 767

Changing the Exchange Installable File System to Another Drive Letter 767
Viewing a Raw Exchange 2000 Directory 768
Installing the New MSXML Parser 769
Changing OWA Passwords Through IIS 770
Registering an Event Sink 771
Isolating a Process Application 771
Creating a Global.asa File 772
Connecting to Data Stores 773
Using Include Files to Create Connection Strings 774
Using the Open Method 775
Prompting for ODBC Connect String Arguments 775
Establishing an ADO Connection 775
Creating a Connection without a Data Source Name 776
Determining Content Type 777
Manipulating **Record** Objects 777
Adding Contact Information into Messages Using **CDOEX** 777
Using SMTP to Send Email 778
Enabling MAPI Clients Computers Through a Firewall 778
Creating an Entrance/Exit Console Script 780

Glossary 783

Index 809

Introduction

Thanks for buying *Exchange 2000 .NET Server Black Book.* This book is intended for the administrator/technician who is already familiar with design and installation issues pertaining to messaging and collaboration systems. It introduces a new orientation in Exchange Administration that parallels the .NET Framework and distributed services environment introduced with the Windows 2000 operating system. Exchange 2000, unlike its predecessors, is a robust application development and Web publishing platform. It will support the design of business solutions that apply to the classic network, inter-enterprise, and unlimited Internet e-commercial areas. We thus include immediate solutions to common client installation issues, as well as the publishing of digital dashboards, dynamic workflow applications, and business solutions using programmable collaboration data objects. This book introduces a new orientation to one of the most popular providers of robust and extensible messaging and collaboration services.

Is This Book for You?

Exchange 2000 .NET Server Black Book was written with the intermediate or advanced user in mind. Among the topics that are covered, are the following:

- Methodologies and techniques for planning and deployment of an enterprise-wide messaging and collaboration system
- Installation and maintenance of application server software
- Installation and maintenance of client software
- Migration and coexistence issues involved with outside messaging systems
- Techniques involved in troubleshooting and performance monitoring
- The role of Exchange 2000 as application development and Web-publishing platform
- The changing role of Exchange 2000 with regard to knowledge management and collaborative business solutions

How to Use This Book

Black Books traditionally provide the intermediate to experienced practitioner with summarized In Depth discussions of key technical areas in which they routinely perform daily tasks and functions. At the end of each In Depth section, the books then provide Immediate Solutions to a collection of situations, the authors believe are either most relevant or most troublesome to the reader. We wrote this book not to be read or studied in a linear fashion, but used rather as a spot reference in situations requiring specific procedural steps or topical details to help resolve some technical issue. We have laid out the chapters in this Black Book in the order of a project life cycle, with particular focus for the practiced reader in the more general areas of design planning and deployment. Similarly, we have discussed application development in the last section of the book in the broadest of terms. We do not intend to instruct the reader in how to install every server component, nor how to write Active Server Pages scripts. Instead, we provide Immediate Solutions to, what we believe are collections of "gotchas," that typically are very hard to look up in a book index or search for on the Internet. The scope of this book is admittedly ambitious. We have tried to distill essential areas into Immediate Solutions without regard, sometimes for background information. We have tried to provide specific solutions to daily problems. We did not intend to teach topics; rather we provide sufficient keywords, context, and concepts to implement the Immediate Solution. The practiced reader can then explore topics in greater detail at a more convenient time.

The *Black Book* Philosophy

Written by experienced professionals, Coriolis *Black Books* provide immediate solutions to global programming and administrative challenges, helping you complete specific tasks, especially critical ones that are not well documented in other books. The *Black Book*'s unique two-part chapter format—thorough technical overviews followed by practical immediate solutions—is structured to help you use your knowledge, solve problems, and quickly master complex technical issues to become an expert. By breaking down complex topics into easily manageable components, this format helps you quickly find what you're looking for, with the diagrams and code you need to make it happen.

In Exchange 2000 .NET Server, we propose that with the change to Windows 2000 and the shift to the .NET Framework that has been a radical but subtle change in the job description of the Exchange 2000 administrator. As evident in the change in methods used in certification examinations, Exchange 2000 competencies have drifted aware from nuts and bolts maintenance to creative application of services to specific business needs. The scope of business has similarly changed. Where legacy Exchange Administrators would deal primarily within the boundaries of a corporate messaging organization, there is a growing emphasis toward collaborative and inter-enterprise sharing of services, workflows, and knowledge resources. We have personified this shift of Exchange Administrator job description from plumber to architect. We suggest that the IT professional reading this book must adopt a more business perception of messaging and collaborative services, the Way of the Merchant rather than exclusively the Way of the Technician. We suggest that with the proliferation of distributed services, an Exchange Administrator, now more than ever, can contributed significantly to corporate profit, return on investment, and a company's competitive edge in their respective marketplace.

We welcome your feedback on this book. You can either email The Coriolis Group at **ctp@coriolis.com**, or email Phillip Schein directly at **pschein@tchouse.com**. Errata, updates, and more are available at **www.coriolis.com**.

Part I

An Introduction to Microsoft Windows 2000 Platform and Messaging Systems

Chapter 1

Messaging and Collaboration

Most of the people in this century derive their living by exchanging goods and services. Miyamoto Musashi (1584–1645) in the *Go Rin No Sho (The Book of Five Rings)* describes the "Way of the Merchant," as bringing together "ingredients" so that their value produces some profit that exceeds the total cost of ownership. This book, *Exchange 2000 .NET Server Black Book*, is about bringing together information technology that produces some profit. Our text combines the "Way of the Craftsman," with the "Way of the Merchant." "The Craftsman" of the seventeenth century can, in today's technical society, be translated as "the Technician." Unlike the "Way of the Merchant," the "Way of the Technician" is to develop skills and techniques in the use of tools, to plan and measure tasks, and finally to deliver promised work. Though "The Technician" measures success in terms of lowered costs, rather than increased profits, reducing total cost of ownership (TCO) complements increasing a return on investment (ROI). For many years, this subtle distinction has fostered the view that technical services and support is a cost rather than profit center in the financial scheme of a company. Exchange 2000 may very likely change that corporate perception. This book describes many immediate solutions that will provide companies with competitive advantages in the marketplace. The Exchange 2000 Administrator needs to consider the ways of both the Technician and Merchant in defining the scope of their job and in pursuing their professional goals.

The scalability and extensibility of Exchange 2000 accommodates the changing needs of any business concern, very often without additional overhead. Microsoft has suggested that the Microsoft Windows 2000 Certified Systems Engineer assume the role of an architect of customized business solutions, rather than a plumber; that is, a software installer who can connect pipes and tweak performance. We describe this as adopting the Way of the Merchant. This change in role also reflects the fact that both the Way of the Merchant and the Technician are merging. The success of some future deployment, system implementation, or upgrade may be measured in terms of increased return on investment (ROI) as well as a reduction in the total cost of ownership (TCO).

The ability of an Exchange 2000 Administrator to add value to business systems is rooted in the cognitive shift from processing data to managing an organization's knowledge resources. Knowledge management includes the exposure of all kinds of corporate data and information through the Web Storage System (WSS), the availability of those stores through a service provider, the manipulation of resources through HTTP-WebDAV and XML, and the extensibility of the Exchange 2000 information infrastructure. Microsoft stresses the importance of business objectives and the "Way of the Merchant" suggests that technicians contribute to the profit picture by lowering the total cost of ownership (TCO). TCO is a major method of evaluation and measurement because it quantifies corporate benefits related to a specific corporate objective. The cost of any information systems infrastructure; however, includes more than just the initial capital investment of acquiring hardware and software. Reliable global messaging and collaborative services include the initial acquisition investment, as well as variable maintenance, support, and training expenses. You will discover from experience that, over time, the capital expenditure often dwarfs the more variable operating expenses of support and training. Whether or not "the Way of the Technician" is to reduce TCO or increase ROI, controlling expenses involved in maintenance, support, and training is still a necessity and, with the .NET Framework, increasingly easier to achieve. Improvements in centralizing administration, management of group policies, and enhancements in remote monitoring and maintenance are continually simplifying the role of server administration. Improvements in the .NET development platform will simplify creation and consumption of Web Services and the design of efficient business solutions. Exchange 2000 is a significant part of this Internet-based world.

The specific functional area of administration, if well defined and thoughtfully executed, can even enhance the user experience through more accurate and rapid service and support. Exchange Administrators seek flexibility, extensibility, and scalability in the components and services they use to improve their own productivity and the productivity of the companies for whom they work. This book will describe ways to fulfill common service requests and the needs of your user population, whether you scope a workgroup, department, small or medium enterprise, or the entire Internet namespace through scalable messaging services and extensible, collaborative data objects.

NOTE: *All references to Exchange 2000 refer to the Microsoft server product Exchange 2000 Enterprise Server. References to other Exchange Server products will specifically state the product name, such as Exchange 2000 Server or Exchange 2000 Conference Server. When referring to an individual server, the lowercase* server *is used, such as "Changing Group Policy on the local Exchange 2000 Server."*

Scalable Services

The Exchange administrator wants a concise, easy-to-read reference that provides immediate solutions to daily system problems related to Exchange 2000 installation, deployment, performance, and optimization. You might think Exchange 2000 has undergone just a change in architecture rather than a change in function and scope. Isn't the suffix .NET Server in the title just another "Way of the Merchant;" a marketing term used to sell more Microsoft software and Coriolis Black Books? We think not. There has been a radical change in how Exchange 2000 is positioned in the corporate landscape. .NET isn't just a new marketing term; it describes a new gestalt or worldview of Microsoft's information technologies within the business enterprise as well. It also coincidently positions Microsoft in a strategic role as a Web services creator and consumer as well as an Application Service Provider (ASP).

.NET Initiative

Among the many Microsoft initiatives, .NET is an evolving vision of "software as a service." Microsoft is starting to integrate all its software products, beginning with Exchange and Visual Studio and eventually including all Office products, into a comprehensive framework of highly integrated, distributed services. .NET will provide a theoretically open environment within which Windows DNA (Distributed interNet Applications) can, using its quasi-biological metaphor, spawn new creations with inherited genetic components. Microsoft conceived of the .NET initiative with the proliferation and use of software components and interfaces. Visual Studio .NET clearly provides a comprehensive assortment of programming languages for the development of Web-based applications; however, does Microsoft consider Exchange a development tool?

The .NET Server suffix attached to Exchange 2000, SQL Server 2000, BizTalk 2000, and other "new breed" servers reflects a shift in emphasis from monolithic, dedicated application servers to more specialized, highly differentiated server platforms providing toolsets for the rapid development of customized application services. The key to this concept is the use of the word *platform* rather than *server*. With a change in environment, from private network to public Internet, the "Way of the Merchant" dominates the direction of information technologies. Thus, the needs of e-commercial enterprises for rapid application development based on Internet or exclusively Web services and reusable component parts are increasing in importance. Sun, another market leader, promotes a similar, though Java-based, architecture called Enterprise JavaBeans (EJB) that are executed on network clients as distributed program components.

Exchange has been described as the first .NET Server. One goal of Microsoft's software initiative is to simplify both development and deployment of Web applications and services. Even if Microsoft's initiative never achieves full fruition, Exchange 2000 remains an extensible platform for messaging and collaborative services fundamental to any e-commerce undertaking. Exchange 2000 blends transparently into the infrastructure of an enterprise while delivering both reliable and extensible levels of service appropriate to the 24×7 enterprise world of e-commerce.

The .NET framework, shown schematically in Figure 1.1, offers a unified approach for developing and deploying Web applications and services. It is a framework within which solutions are assembled or interconnected rather than a platform on which these component parts are run. This layered infrastructure rests on core network operating system (OS) services. The initiative is a necessary step in providing loosely connected distributed services in both a private namespace (such as a corporate enterprise) and a public network (such as the Internet). The framework provides a common language runtime (CLR) engine.

Unlike legacy Exchange 5.5 operating on Windows NT 4, Exchange 2000 requires that Windows 2000 have IIS 5 (Internet Information Services) properly configured and running. This dependence on IIS is another example of the partitioning of services that specifically characterize the .NET initiative and Windows 2000. Partitioning system services so that they can be distributed throughout an enterprise has been a significant architectural trend in Microsoft operating systems and other network operating systems such as Unix.

Although the details are outside the scope of this book, the .NET architecture is significant in that Exchange is the first in this family of distributed service providers. The Exchange 2000 architecture creates a central broker of information services useful in any Internet-based endeavor as well as a platform for inter-enterprise process integration. Component-based software applications have powered enterprise and commercial interests for many years. As component-based

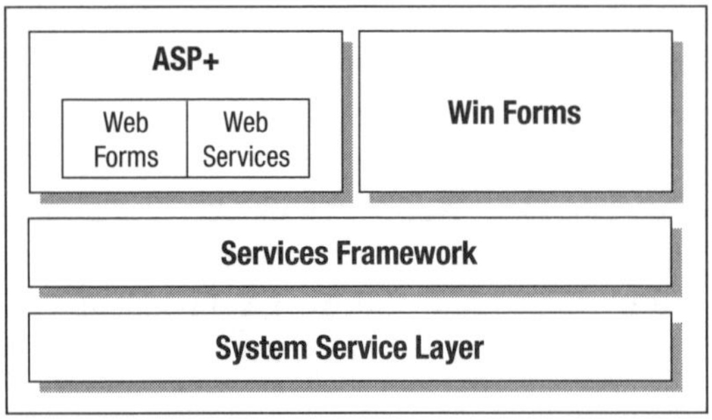

Figure 1.1 Architecture of the .NET framework.

software design increases in popularity, distribution and licensing constraints increase as well. Nevertheless, Web services are evolving into a virtual ocean filled with floating objects and functionality into which you can plug your standard browser software or share common process flows. These Web-based objects and services, although still problematic, especially in the area of security, attract attention because they clearly provide more value in scalable online services than component-based software stored on a local machine. They also offer greater efficiency through realtime sharing of common knowledge resources and collaboration across workflows.

Figure 1.2 shows a pyramid composed of the various new service providers Microsoft has released since 2000. Commerce Server 2000, providing scalable business-to-consumer (B2C) and business-to-business (B2B) sites with analytic tools, sits at the apex of this family of .NET Servers, and Exchange 2000 sits at the base. The development of Internet and Web-based services rests on messaging rather than process. Exchange 2000 provides a messaging and collaborative platform on which document and content management are built. The platform also provides an infrastructure much like Active Directory (AD) provides a namespace. Exchange's data stores now expose all kinds of knowledge resources to e-commercial activities as well as your friends and colleagues. Reliable messaging and collaboration are critical in our daily lives now because workflow can't exist without communication, and progress can't exist without collaboration.

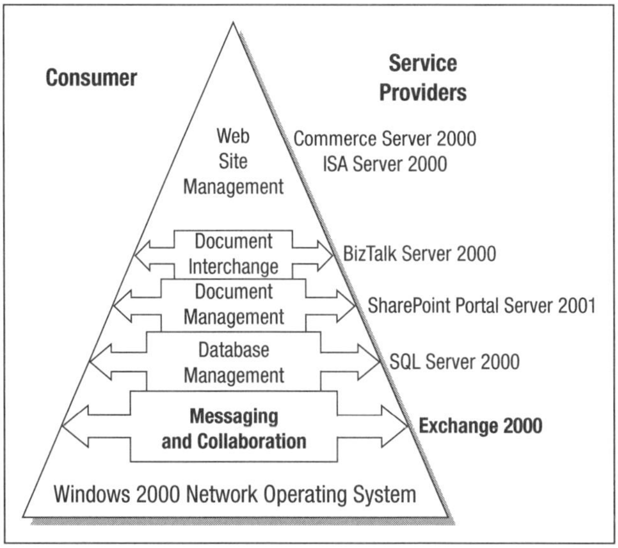

Figure 1.2 The relationship of .NET servers.

A Paradigm Shift toward Knowledge Management

The IT field has made a paradigm shift from data processing and information-sharing in the 1960s through the 1980s to a focus today on knowledge management (KM). Microsoft emphasizes the availability of information "anytime, anyplace, from any device" to those of us who perform knowledge management functions, especially in the services sector, of the world economies. The tools we use as knowledge professionals have evolved from datastores such as unstructured word processing documents and spreadsheets to digital dashboards that combine legacy unstructured documents with shared calendars, real-time scrolling marquees showing stock prices, and video conferencing in a multi-framed desktop window. Exchange 2000 can potentially provide the management of these knowledge resources on an enterprise scale; however, SharePoint 2001, another .NET server specializing in content management, is only beginning to demonstrate that potential at the department level. The key to a scalable, enterprise solution for KM is the exposure of both structured database information and unstructured data produced by Office products like Word and PowerPoint. Unstructured and semi-structured data, such as mail, calendar objects, and directory folders, do not conform to the more rigidly defined recordsets in SQL Server or databases that are compliant with ODBC (Open Database Connectivity), such as Microsoft Access.

The primary source for this exposed data is the Web Storage System or Web Store, a significant new feature in the Exchange architecture, not to mention Windows 2000. Aside from inherent multitier features, such as front-end (FE) and back-end (BE) server topology and partitioned services, Exchange 2000 has been designed to provide enhanced Web-based access, much like Outlook Web Access (OWA) first introduced in Exchange 5.x. In its current form, Exchange 2000 is an HTTP (Hypertext Transfer Protocol) server. Through services such as Internet Publishing, provided by the Web Distributed Authoring and Versioning (WebDAV) extension to HTTP 1.1, the dynamic power of scripting languages, and the now ubiquitous browser client software, Exchange 2000 efficiently meets Microsoft's goal of messaging information anytime from anyplace using any device. As other .NET servers join Exchange 2000 in providing distributed services, a more eXtensible markup language, XML, will be required to handle data content, as well as appearance, of these Web Store resources across many different software platforms.

KM requires two prerequisite technologies: a functional intranet structure that stores knowledge resources, and messaging/collaboration services. Figure 1.3 shows a block design of the idealized KM system. Exchange 2000 provides a messaging infrastructure, an accessible Web Store, Realtime Collaboration, and integration with the semi-structured data of Microsoft Office applications. The Exchange 2000 design is the first in a family of service providers that integrates deeply with Windows 2000. Exchange 2000 delivers messaging and collaboration;

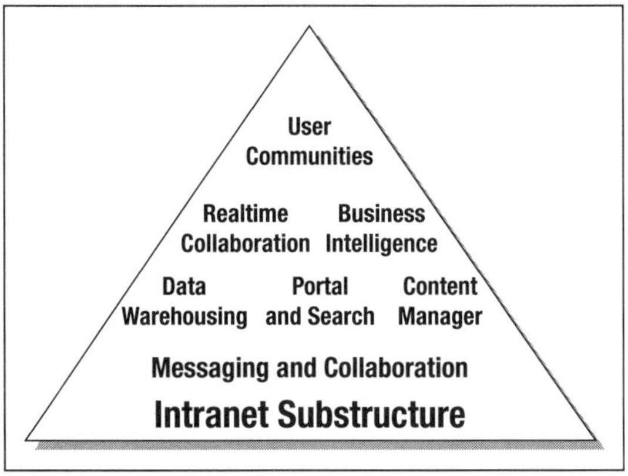

Figure 1.3 An idealized Knowledge Management system.

its partner in this relation, Windows 2000, delivers an intranet structure that includes identity, permissions, and accounting management, or what is more commonly referred to as *directory services*. The combination of both systems provides the foundation depicted in Figure 1.3 and something more for Microsoft than a marketing strategy; it is a paradigm shift away from information processing toward KM.

With the change in paradigm comes new technology initiatives such as .NET, and design changes such as the distribution of missing critical services like delegating directory services to the network operating system (NOS). .NET servers are architecturally more specialized than their earlier legacy prototypes and have shed functionality common to other service providers in the enterprise.

One such specific management functional area (SMFA), directory services, has differentiated in design and become a specialized part of the NOS called Active Directory directory services. Microsoft's shift to this new KM paradigm requires an Exchange administrator to understand the details of and rationale for architectural design changes in the enterprise, and is the new format of certification examinations. Understanding the rationale behind design and architectural changes is just as important in the listing of competencies for Exchange 2000 as understanding how to install client software.

We approach Exchange 2000 Server in this book from the more traditional perspective, through discussions of installation, deployment, client configuration, and optimization. We do add another dimension, however. Exchange 2000 .NET Server is, more than any other messaging server on the market today, a development platform within which you'll find an array of specialized interfaces and a collection of collaborative data objects (CDOs). Although not a programming text, we will discuss these objects and services as well. As administrators, the

Way of the Technician is to understand, manipulate software objects, and leverage application programming interfaces (APIs) when creating broadly applicable and profitable business solutions.

Remember the shift in paradigm to knowledge management and emerging development role of Exchange 2000 when planning and selecting messaging and collaborative services. The increasing use of scripting and markup languages helps to simplify system integration and reduce cost associated with deployment. Because most ITs use the Internet, commercial enterprises and network organizations have merged to create more robust network operating systems such as Microsoft Windows 2000. Microsoft developed Active Server technology and the Active Server Pages (ASP) scripting language to create a more scalable, extensible development platform. Software initiatives such as Web-based Enterprise Management (WBEM) based on the Common Information Model (CIM) schema standardized by the Distributed Management Task Force (DMTF) provide a standardized infrastructure that unifies cross-platform hardware and software management. WBEM supports the development of Windows Management Instrumentation (WMI), which Microsoft is using as an evolving architecture supporting remote monitoring and maintenance for its growing family of distributed application servers. Examples of WMI and centralized administrative tools include the Microsoft Management Console (MMC), Windows Scripting Host (WSH), Terminal Services Architecture (TSA), Remote Installation Services (RIS), and even Active Directory.

With improved hardware capacity and response times, an enhanced scripting language, a broader use of Application Programming Interfaces, and the capability to offload more processing to the client side of the transaction, the event architecture in Exchange 2000 has changed from a legacy client-host, component-oriented architecture to multitier, distributed systems. Web application development usually occurs in three distinct deployments of software:

- *Desktop*—This application model is the common standalone workstation. It is considered monolithic because it's totally self-contained; the three functional layers, Presentation, Application Logic, and Data Access, are all located on the same computer platform.
- *Two tier*—This is the classic client/server model in which a workstation hosts the Presentation layer, and Data Access is located on the host/server. Business or Application Logic layers can be located on the client, the host, or both machines.
- *Three tier (or multitier)*—The multitier design approach is conceptualized as three distinct service layers. In a three-tier architecture, Presentation, Business Logic, and Data Access are conceptually separated.

If you divide multitier architecture into Presentation, Business Logic, and Data Access Services layers, you see a Web- and service-oriented design. The user manipulates presentation elements to make service requests, which are handled by the Business Logic layer, typically located on the server side of the design. The Business Logic (or rules) layer provides whatever services are requested directly back to the Presentation layer, or through the redirection to another service provider. The Data Access layer provides the repository structure, which contains the knowledge resources. The fundamental layer in a multitier architecture is the Data Access layer, where resources are stored and retrieved. The sophistication of the Presentation layer in terms of specifying extensible types of objects must grow in tandem with the capacities of the Data Services layer, where these objects are stored, catalogued, and retrieved.

By assimilating IIS into its core native services, Windows 2000 significantly enhances the potential of ASP at the Presentation, Business Logic, and Data Access layers. An enterprise application written in a server-side scripting language such as ASP gains the highest levels of performance, flexibility, and control due to the proximity of the server-side scripting language to the Windows 2000 kernel and native services. Such technology, however, isn't new to Exchange Server administration and design. ASP technology has been providing OWA to Exchange data stores since version 5.5.

You also must get acquainted with the growing dominance of collaboration in the Exchange feature set, and become at least conversant in the use of scripting languages, such as Hypertext Markup Language (HTML), Extensible Hypertext Markup Language (XHTML), and Extensible Markup Language (XML). XHTML helps developers transition from the readily approachable and less demanding structure of HTML to the more rigorous, well-formed XML syntax. You must also learn to manage your systems both from the Microsoft Management Console graphical user interface, as well as through a browser client using HTML-based Windows Management Instrumentation.

The legacy server model of a monolithic software application with its own directory and security services has been replaced by a new breed of service provider that is both more specialized and differentiated in function. Multitiered enterprise applications are loosely grouped into three functional layers: a Presentation layer, typically browser-rendered HTML; a Business Logic layer, interpreting rules, procedures, and application functions with scripting languages; and a Data Access layer, providing exposure to the knowledge-based resources. Refer to Figure 1.4, which shows the three functional layers superimposed on the family of Microsoft .NET servers originally shown in Figure 1.2. When a browser client requests some service, that request process has been modeled from real-world procedures into scripts that automate the process of exchanging data. The Data Access layer prepares the data for use based on the

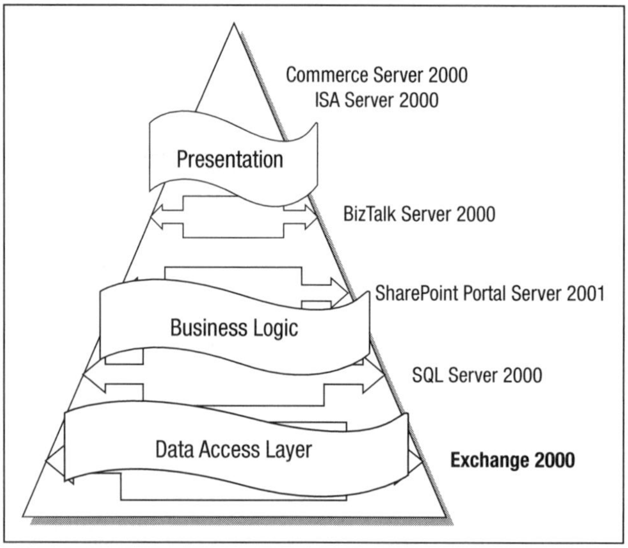

Figure 1.4 Three functional layers superimposed on the .NET Server family.

specifications of the intermediary scripting; it isn't directly accessed from the browser client.

A client/consumer must understand the structural schema or data definition of the information requested in order to access these data stores. The collection of data definitions within an XML document is provided by a centrally located schema that can be referenced by an application in receipt of the information. BizTalk 2000, another .NET server, provides a protocol-independent, open platform using XML to facilitate this loosely coupled, yet reliable exchange of business-related documents. It functions as a transport-independent messaging server and development platform that supports the creation of the XML schemas, and XSL style sheets that transform or map schemas to translate documents. Thus, the trends toward interchanging data and exposing data from a Web site are fundamental initiatives fueling e-commercial ventures, and burgeoning exchanges of information across the Internet.

The native Windows 2000 architecture, like other dominant networking cultures such as the Unix NOS, is now based on distributed network services. AD directory services provide a functional layer for the entire network enterprise. .NET application servers derive critical "life support" from the distributed "cloud" services that float in this network "atmosphere." Thus, .NET servers in an enterprise exist within a specific namespace provided by AD; different enterprises have their own namespaces much like planets follow their own orbits around the sun. Internet services provide the ether or "cyberspace" within which network enterprises exist as independent "solar systems" with their own digital namespaces.

Our virtual universe, from a "cultural" perspective of Windows 2000, rests on the physical connectivity provided by the TCP/IP (Transmission Control Protocol/ Internet Protocol) network protocol suite, or what Microsoft calls the Transport Driver Interface (TDI) layer as shown in Figure 1.5. Below the TDI layer are the Network Device Interface Specification (NDIS) and Physical layers, which are beyond the scope of this book.

Design

Features that promote extensibility in a product reduce development time. Unlike legacy Windows NT, many specific management functional areas are extensible in Windows 2000. For example, the audit/accounting and security managers—*Security Support Provider Interface (SSPI)* and *Microsoft Cryptographic API (CAPI)*—are interfaces to which future add-in "helpers" can connect and perform complementary services. In fact, the rationale behind the original design of the hardware abstraction layer (HAL) was to uncouple the hardware from the NOS kernel and micro code, making network services portable and hardware independent. Using standards-based protocols and *de facto* APIs—ODBC, ADO, and Messaging API (MAPI)—similarly increases the extensibility of the basic network structure and decreases development time and expense.

Exchange 2000 follows this same design strategy in an attempt to reduce TCO. The broadening range of clients and the Web exposure of its data stores increase Exchange's accessibility and minimize end-user training requirements. Products such as BizTalk Server 2000 foster rapid business application development through enterprise application integration (EAI) and are designed to interoperate with Exchange 2000 through standards-based protocols such as Simple Mail Transfer Protocol (SMTP), HTTP-WebDAV, LDAP, and XML. These design strategies directly address reduction in development, maintenance, and training expenses and thus improve the marketability of the .NET platform (Windows 2000, Exchange 2000, and so on), as well as reduce TCO.

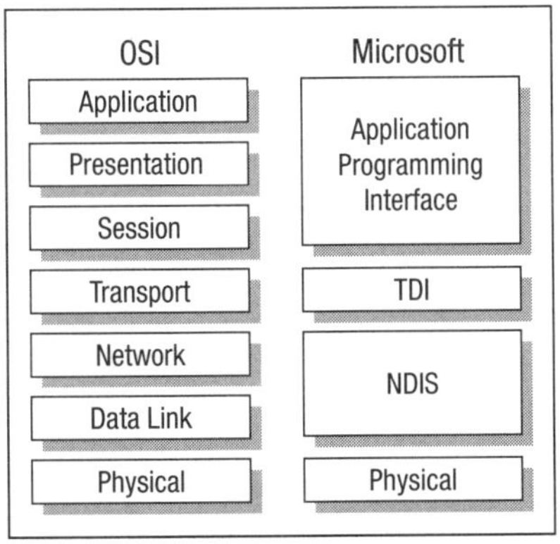

Figure 1.5 A comparison of network layer models.

Choose software companies that have the greatest market share when investing in IT solutions. You want to invest in technology produced by a company that is financially sound and a market leader. This stability often translates into longer-term support for versions of software and greater research and feature development. Companies like Microsoft and Sun aggressively pursue new technologies, as well as build extensive backward-compatibility features into their operating systems and application software.

Administration Tools: Server Access

Administrative support is simplified with well-designed instrumentation now available through customized Microsoft Management Consoles. Aside from maintenance and training expenses, support expenses increase TCO. One way to minimize this variable cost contribution is to simplify administration by centralizing management. Exchange 2000 has always provided a topological view of an organization fostering a simple, global management scheme. The Exchange topology was tightly coupled to the network infrastructure in legacy versions of the Server software and based on a nested logical structure. The functional scope of this management tool has been rooted in an all-encompassing organization within which well-connected Exchange Servers populate physically separate sites.

WARNING! When discussing servers,* well-connected *connotes one-hop connectivity across permanent network connections running at least 10MBps. This minimum connection is the most basic configuration and recommended for acceptable performance.

Legacy messaging systems are often patchwork quilts of individual Exchange Servers routing their messages through connectors that join geographically separate sites. These messaging servers provide communication and collaboration services to a single, unified namespace defined by directory services. The complexity of this network is transparent to consumers of messaging services. Given the mission-critical nature of messaging systems, users typically insist on consistent levels of service throughout the namespace, no matter what the complexity or conditions. The Exchange administrator also might have a single-seated global perspective because of job roles or out of necessity due to the installation's size!

Centralized administration of an enterprise through the familiar and extensible MMC is a major feature in Exchange 2000 design. In fact, Exchange 2000 comes with an assortment of snap-ins, including System Manager, Message Tracking Center, Public Folders, Security, and Conferencing Services. Similarly, the initiatives that surround WBEM, WMI, and the XML will continue to reduce support expenses and TCO for some time in the future.

Outlook clients interact directly with Exchange Server services. OWA clients, using any standard browser, interact with IIS Web services. The browser client communicates typically from outside the enterprise namespace by using the HTTP protocol with WebDAV extensions. When IIS receives a request to access an object in the WSS, it passes the request to the Exchange ISAPI (Internet Server API) application, which, in turn, communicates with the Data Store layer in the WSS. The WSS responds to the service request, the ISAPI layer renders it in HTML, and the browser on the client side presents it to the consumer/end user.

Front-End/Back-End Architecture

The delivery of internal network services in a front-end/back-end architecture is similar to that of multitier, or N-tier, architecture found across the Internet. Load balancing of this nature supports high traffic volume and is becoming the foundation for Web application development and e-commerce projects. In a distributed services or multitier architectural environment, one or more FE Servers broker OWA service requests by redirecting them to BE Servers that physically host the mail stores. Dedicated BE Servers form a more efficient database service layer than a single monolithic server, because their physical separation from the FE provides less work for the local system, and greater opportunity to scale the data stores more easily. Such a distributed environment is also better because it provides simpler options for scalability and the introduction of fault-tolerant architectures. In addition, distributed services help workflow through easier load balancing. Some advantages of FE/BE architecture include the following:

- *Single namespace*—The FE Servers provide a single namespace from both the client/consumer viewpoint and the perspective of the BE data layer to which service requests are directed. Best practices recommend referring to all servers that provide a common service such as mailbox storage with a single name. Scaling the Data Services layer is simplified because FE and BE equipment is separated rather than stored in a single hardware storage unit. The single namespace also provides a security advantage over a monolithic server because the mission-critical data stores are never exposed to public access.
- *Offload Secure Sockets Layer (SSL)*—Because encrypting and decrypting messages are processor-intensive operations, cryptographic services benefit from the separation of the more resource-intensive operations of storage and retrieval from FE service requests. Partitioned service layers enhance performance of the messaging platform especially when such services are performed exclusively on a FE rather than BE Server.
- *Security*—If FE Servers exposed to public access only redirect a service request, security is enhanced because knowledge resources are never directly accessed.
- *Public folder referrals*—Front-end/back-end architecture compensates for the inability of some protocols, such as Internet Message Access Protocol 4

(IMAP4), to support public folder referrals by actually retrieving the public folder information.

- *Server location*—Firewall deployment is simplified by the structural separation of services on different physical machines. When BE Servers are physically separate from FE Servers, you can configure the firewalls to pass traffic from only specific FE Servers, IP addresses to BE Servers installed behind firewalls.

Load balancing is possible in this architecture because service loads can be distributed in a nonrandom fashion, so that FE Servers redirect requests to specifically designated BE servers. If the local Exchange Server has a mailbox data store, OWA accesses the mail store directly. Alternatively, you can define a FE Server as an Exchange 2000 Server that does not host a public folder or mailbox data store, but instead functions as a proxy that forwards service requests to a remote server, which processes the request. If the local Exchange Server is a FE Server, OWA uses HTTP to proxy the service request to the appropriate BE Server. The FE server uses Lightweight Directory Access Protocol (LDAP) to query a directory services provider (in this case, AD) for the path to the BE data store that hosts the user's mailbox. HTTP/WebDAV v.1.1, Post Office Protocol 3 (POP3), and Internet Message Access Protocol 4 browser clients support FE/BE architecture.

Distributed Services

Windows 2000 distributes its functional management areas through the use of specialized application servers such as Application Server 2000 and DataCenter Server 2000, and a multi-master source of directory services provided by domain controllers. Exchange 2000 architecture is functionally divided into three SMFAs: directory services, protocol services, and storage services. While directory services are now totally controlled by the NOS, protocol services (what the MTA manages) and storage services (what the IS manages) are still handled through Exchange Server, even though the Protocol Services layer is now a functional management area of IIS 5, a part of the Windows 2000 NOS.

The interface separating Exchange storage services from protocol services is an area of shared memory called the *Exchange Interprocess Communication layer* (EXIPC, but pronounced EPOXY because it binds inetinfo.exe to store.exe). Protocol services are now managed by **inetinfo.exe**, a part of the former IIS 4 service provider now located in the NOS layer. EXIPC is a helper application that provides a queue for communication flows between Exchange and the Internet engine that is now seamlessly embedded in the NOS. The delegation of identity management to AD in the NOS repeats the pattern of differentiating functional management areas. Microsoft has categorized the Exchange 2000 feature set along three different dimensions: the messaging infrastructure, message storage, and messengers.

Physical Topology

Exchange 2000 and other .NET Servers exploit the Windows 2000 distributed services architecture by implementing partitioned services such as identity-management services on physically separate machines. Among the Exchange Server family, Exchange 2000 Server is designed for standalone SOHO business scenarios, and Exchange Enterprise Server supports enterprise environments that potentially accommodate more than a million users. This architectural scalability comes from the partition of protocol and storage services hosted in a distributed configuration on FE/BE systems. Administration of these multitier service architectures is uncoupled from the physical network topology and fault-tolerant hardware technology. The physical layer is built for the 24×7×365-day environment of the Internet and can provide five 9 reliability that translates into scheduled downtime on the order of hours within any 365-day period.

Geographically distributed organizations are also more easily maintained through centralized maintenance and support using either customized MMC or WMI using HTML. For example, three administrative views of the enterprise are provided through separate MMC snap-in tools—AD Sites and Services, AD Domains and Trusts, and AD Users and Computers—and an array of Exchange-specific snap-ins, including Exchange System Manager. The network topology is administered through routing groups. Hardware technology solutions that provide different mixes of capacity, performance, and reliability include RAID (Redundant Array of Independent Disks), NAS (Network Attached Storage), and SANs (Storage Area Network).

Alternatively, virtual server support is delivered through two-way Windows 2000 Advanced Server and four-way Windows 2000 Datacenter Server active/active clustering. *Clustering* is a Windows 2000 feature that virtualizes a server that accesses data stores physically stored on two independent machines for maximum reliability and fault tolerance. Clustering was introduced in version 5.5, but the technology was limited. In its first release, the service ran on only one node at a time in the cluster. In other words, one node was the active host; the other passively slept. If the active node failed, the passive node assumed its host role for the virtualized services. This active/passive version has been replaced by an active/active version in which the services can run on all nodes simultaneously. Current versions of Windows 2000 Advanced Server and the very expensive, high-end Windows 2000 Datacenter Server provide this active/active cluster feature with two nodes and four nodes, respectively. This technology depends on partitioned services that can be separated from one another and thus run on independent hardware platforms. Exchange Server not only partitions its SMFAs, but also the specific services within those areas.

Storage Infrastructure

The creation of dedicated service providers is a common theme through Microsoft architecture. It lowers design and implementation costs, as well as increases interoperability across different NOS "cultures" such as Microsoft, Unix, and Novell. Because the interface for the provided services is well documented, foreign systems can easily request services without excess programming overhead. Centralized directory access to a messaging infrastructure, or central repository, facilitates deployment of services by reducing redundant services and simplifying administration. Each application server doesn't have to reauthenticate network users. Specialization also enhances NOS interoperability by consolidating mission-critical services. Identity and permission management that remain in these more specialized application service providers are becoming vestigial functions left over primarily for backward compatibility.

Linking and mapping data stores across different directory services and databases are still concerns during the deployment of most systems. Solving problems of identity management includes using the various interfaces and service technologies:

- *Active Directory Services Interface (ADSI)*—This set of programming interfaces is extensible and based on the Component Object Model (COM). It provides access to proprietary directory services including legacy Windows NT 4 Security Accounts Manager (SAM), Windows 2000 AD, Novell's NetWare Directory Services, and any LDAP-based directory store.
- *Active Directory Connector (ADC) and Microsoft Directory Synchronization Services (MSDSS)*—This service layer synchronizes the data in different LDAP-compliant data stores with one another. MSDSS provides directory synchronization between Novell Directory Services (NDS) and Windows 2000 AD. It also supports legacy Microsoft Exchange versions 5 and 5.5.
- *Metadirectory technology*—This provides enterprise-wide identity management services to non-Microsoft platforms.

Legacy Exchange Server always stored details about mailboxes, distribution lists, and other messaging data in the directory store (DS). Consistent and reliable data has been very important; the DS relied on multi-master replication to ensure that all Exchange Servers in the messaging organization that provided messaging services were current and consistent. Legacy DS provided email address validation and global address list (GAL) management. Based on metadirectory technology and directory consolidation, Exchange 2000 relies heavily on AD rather than its own DS for identity management. SMFAs within one host computer or across several different servers hosting the same SMFA are totally dependent on some common specialized function that is located somewhere else in the enterprise rather than on their own internal subsystems.

AD and the Exchange DS share similar architecture. AD directory services now support far more than authentication and authorization services, as Windows NT LAN Manager (NTLM) authentication protocol did in legacy Windows NT versions. Directory integration has a tremendous impact on the design, deployment, performance, and optimization of Exchange 2000. Microsoft has collectively named these growing numbers of common enterprise services the *digital nervous system*. AD and DS provide an extensible API layer and storage engine, as is expected of any repository-based technology. The DS supports MAPI and standards-based LDAP, which are software layers on top of the Extensible Storage Engine (ESE). Microsoft stated that the repository engine in Microsoft Repository runs on top of both SQL Server 7 and the Microsoft JET database systems. The storage engine is based on a transactional logging model. A queue directory holds messages in various stages of routing until they are either written to a private or public database or sent to another server. This "holding" store is typically optimized for performance rather than capacity or reliability.

Exchange 2000 stores data in the following kinds of files:

- *Rich-text files*—MAPI data files that contain message headers, message text, and standard attachments use the .rtf file extension.
- *Native streaming files*—Multipurpose Internet Mail Extensions (MIME) data files, using the streaming or .stm file extension, contain multimedia content as MIME streams.
- *Sequential transaction files*—Log files that are especially optimized for reliability because they play a critical role in any disaster-recovery scenario.

Two data stores, each with its own EDB and STM data files, are automatically created upon installation of Exchange: a mailbox store (private) and a public folder store (public). These "storage" stores are optimized for capacity and reliability. When a message is delivered, it is written to a transaction log file, which is always 5MB in size. The database layers of both AD and DS handle self-contained, independent transactions, often described as *atomic transactions*. A *transaction* is a self-contained, independent set of changes to an object that includes creations, deletions, and updates.

The Database Layer

The *Database layer* writes transactions to the current transaction log file and memory-resident cache. Because transactions are logged in sequence, disk operations that support this logging process are sequential in nature. After the transaction is finished and when the operating system allows, the storage engine commits the transaction to the database store and advances a checkpoint to the beginning of the next uncommitted transaction.

This method of storage is efficient because messages are written to the log file first and in sequential order; the more time-intensive and random search-and-write operation to the specific data files located in the data stores is performed in an asynchronous and independent manner. Both Exchange and AD use this storage system technology in the same way. The checkpoint always marks the most recent successfully committed database transaction and plays a critical role in file integrity and disaster recovery. The mechanism for handling either Exchange users or Windows 2000 named principals is thus almost the same. Both use NTFS (NT File System) Access Control Lists (ACLs) that control access at both the container (folder) and object (file) levels. Exchange 2000 includes ADC, which provides bidirectional replication between legacy Exchange and AD data stores.

Multiple Databases

Each version of Exchange Server relied on larger message databases as the functional scope of the provided services expanded. Exchange 2000, designed for enterprise or e-commerce on the Internet, theoretically supports up to 90 databases in 15 separate storage groups (SGs) but has been reduced to 24 databases (4 storage groups) in current versions. The unlimited database size introduced in version 5.5 has been carried over into Exchange 2000. The hosting of massive data stores (more than 100GB per database) is balanced by the capability to separate those data stores into smaller physical databases. This partitioning provides the scalability of spanning large data stores over several physical devices, as well as more practical administration of, for example, backups of more manageably sized physical drives.

Classic backup and restoration strategies can now realistically handle these new storage scenarios in small business operations. The importance of these strategies in an environment that demands "five-to-nine" or 99.999% reliability is significant, although secondary, to newer technologies such as NAS and SAN that work transparently below the Open Systems Interconnection (OSI) Application layer and the end user's levels of perception. The strategies used to provide enterprise solutions differ in terms of capacity, performance, and reliability. A single storage solution for all types of data has never been the most efficient business solution. Balance among the data type, file size, scalability, and manageability of data stores is also affected by corporate IT objectives and the perceived value of the data handled. Although log files and data files in general require different deployment to optimize their use as resources, such as in the uses of different RAID configurations, the most significant selection criterion for any one storage strategy is still determined by the corporate perceptions of these data stores in terms of asset value and risk tolerance.

Distributed Configuration

Partitioning SMFAs, such as protocol services, storage services, and directory services, provides more than design efficiency. Similar to a multitier architectural model, by separating presentation services from business logic and data storage, you can deploy a FE server farm responsible for collecting incoming Exchange 2000 service requests. This bank of FE servers provides a unified namespace that can be used in an e-commercial enterprise, for example. This FE bank of servers "presents" a scalable unified namespace to the user population or target consumer market, and an easily configurable point of access into their mail system that relays requests to the appropriate private store host. FE servers also provide inherent network efficiencies, such as load balancing, which are achieved through the Windows 2000 Network Load Balancing (NLB) service, or the manipulation of Internet Protocol (IP) addresses. This latter option, referred to as a DNS (Domain Name System) round-robin configuration, means that incoming requests for service are balanced across a group of up to 32 servers acting as physically independent request queues.

This FE server role, easily configured on a server's property sheet, provides scalable access and high levels of performance necessary to support the management of an enterprise. When you enable this FE server feature, service requests are automatically relayed to the BE database storage services located on a different host server. It is important to remember that front end/back-end technology provides load balancing but does not provide any fault-tolerance measures.

Clustering

As mentioned earlier, clustering is a technology that scales a single service on multiple host servers. The virtualization of services is not associated with any specific hardware platform but does have its own name associated with an IP network address (from its current host) published by the cluster service. The cluster manages resource groups that are formed by virtual services. A resource group is owned by one node at a time and moves as a unit. A node, hosting a resource group, knows where to move the resource group in case of failure. The cluster service moves the resource group and reassigns the IP address to correspond to the new hosting node.

The cluster is assigned a single IP address to which all service requests are addressed. Within the cluster, all nodes belong to the same subnet so that the cluster's primary IP address is within a common broadcast domain and thus can be redirected to the resource group on whichever host it currently resides. This technology leverages the use of multiple databases in separate storage groups to support a failover event, when one node in a two-node cluster fails and the resource group is automatically moved to the other node, for example.

Cluster technology delivers five-to-nine reliability service levels to mission-critical operations with little impact on variable expenses for maintenance, support, or training.

Web Storage System

The *Web Storage System* is the cornerstone on which Exchange 2000 and Windows 2000 have come to depend. The Web Store Schema defines the formats of the objects that are stored in the Web Store and integrates a wide, extensible range of knowledge sources into a central repository. Exchange 2000 provides an interface to its contents through intranet clients such as Outlook, and Internet clients such as standard browsers and OWA.

You request services from Exchange or directly from the Web Store. These extensible service providers can define a set of properties for a specific item and then control how it is used. The *content class* property defines intention or purpose. The Web Store is significant because its design provides access to every item within its namespace in a systematic and human-readable way through a Uniform Resource Locator (URL). The Web Store provides an addressable namespace that contains all collaborative objects. Consumers directly access folders or collaborative objects such as calendars by appending a named directory or object to the end of the URL used to access their mailbox. Named URLs also allow users to perform operations on these messaging and collaborative objects through explicit URL addressing. The Web Store is a scalable infrastructure that can store all kinds of information, including messaging, collaborative information, file systems, and Web-related data. Corporate knowledge resources are consolidated and centralized in one repository that provides the following services:

- *File system services*—Both structured data from databases and unstructured data, such as streaming data from the Web and archives of Office products, are accommodated in both hierarchical and heterogeneous collections.
- *Database services*—A data query language must be capable of both complex searches within structured databases as well as searches performed within a file system on a Windows platform. Support services must accommodate an extensible assortment of data types and include a process for viewing data that is consistent and accurate.
- *Collaboration services*—Support services must extend beyond simple messaging to the collecting contacts, calendaring objects, and collaborating audio and video information in realtime.

Both file systems and database services require an extensible and flexible way to identify and manage content. Creation, manipulation, and deletion of isolated data, or larger knowledge objects such as group calendars and task lists, might be requested on demand and without previous preparation or planning. Although you don't have to define a property as a file system or database object before you use the Web Store, you can ensure that it is retrieved from the data store rapidly when a search query is executed by defining its nature or content. All three services mentioned above must be able to support such spontaneous activity.

The Web Store is designed to remove barriers that obstruct the sharing of heterogeneous data by combining the features of these three service areas as they relate to Exchange 2000 and other Microsoft server products, as well as Office 2000 products. Microsoft views the Web Store as an enterprise-based application service that provides ubiquitous client access, improved productivity, and a lower TCO.

The Web Store is the focus for many of the technologies discussed in this chapter because it actually contains both structured and unstructured data. The Web Store now has the potential of providing a central repository for messages, attachments, collaborative objects (such as calendars and task lists), and the heaps of data stored in formats such as Excel XLS, Word DOC, PowerPoint PPT, and Access MDB. To accommodate the greater number of categories, you need to extend the transport protocol to move these objects between the service provider and the consumer requesting the service. This extension must provide support for a variety of document formats, such as rich HTML and other Web-based scripting languages, Win32 file structures, streaming file formats, offline folder objects, and native collaborative objects. Database management plays a major role in the extension of these services.

Rich HTML Support

Beginning with Internet Explorer version 4 (IE4), Dynamic HTML (DHTML) support of scripting and robust Document Object Models (DOMs) has added richness to the standards-based HTML and the rendering of Web documents. A *DOM* is a standardized API that provides programmatic control over a document's content, structure, formats, and processes. The Web Store leverages these native features in the more current versions of the browser client. Legacy browser versions 3.x are also supported with functionality provided by increased server-side support.

Scripting Support

Web-based applications are collections of distributed components and online services. Like component-based software, distributed applications require rich methods and properties to manage the many transactions and service requests passed to other service providers across the stateless environment of the Internet. Solution providers must adjust their methods of delivery as they transition from the client-side richness of DHTML to deficiencies inherent in the simple scripting of HTML/XML pages passed through a Web server. The statelessness of HTTP is necessarily encountered when object changes are passed from one Win32 component applications to another.

The advantages of migrating component-based application software across operating platforms, however, do not outweigh the expense involved in scaling services or extending functionality. Applications using distributed services are alternatively easier to scale and deploy than their component-based counterparts. The Web Store supports the development of Web-based applications by hosting technologies referred to as Application Service Providers. Scripting support of this technology, however, is not sufficient to deliver the quality of productivity tools available when you use Win32 component architecture. The Web Store supports the same database interfaces that Microsoft ASP scripts use to deliver the common database-intense software application. The Web Store's OLE DB 2.5 provider is a complex foundation upon which ADO, a subset of the OLE DB interface, runs. Thus, database services—including data query and data manipulation of language components, as well as transaction support—are available. The Web Store also includes full-text content indexing.

Microsoft Win32 Support

The Web Store must support extensible Web-based data types as well as legacy Win16 file types and document models typically found in the network-based Win32 interface. The Web Store leverages resources in existing file systems by supporting an interface that virtualizes the 32-bit Network Basic Input/Output System, or NetBIOS (Win32), share name. You can use folder-based resources in the Web Store environment, providing access to unstructured data that until now was inaccessible to Web-based manipulations. The end user accustomed to sharing folders won't notice any difference between handling data through his browser client across the Internet and handling data with Windows Explorer in a LAN environment, which is especially significant in terms of TCO. No end user support or software configuration is necessary when you access these resources.

Another important characteristic of the Web Store is its capability to provide property promotion, especially when dealing with Office file types stored in the Win32 file system. The Web Store provides consistent views of the information independent of the client used to access that information, which again minimizes the need for end user training. Properties from documents are automatically promoted and populate all record fields used in the viewing interface. The Outlook Inbox displays all file types as common entities in a unified view of information that is consistent across multiple clients. This universal Inbox integrates information, eliminates concurrent access to multiple applications, and enhances productivity by providing a customizable view of data that can be replicated on demand.

Streaming Store

The Web Store, like Exchange 2000, can natively accommodate very large message units with attachments. An important storage feature is the file-streaming interfaces that provide the retrieval access. When so many storage types are involved, it is especially important to ensure that the intended meaning of data is retained. To maintain the quality of information, the Web Store minimizes the number of file type conversions; streaming data is natively stored in the Web Store.

Offline Folders

The Web Store integrates online/offline data stores to provide support to a user population that is more often remote than on site. Synchronizing online folders and documents with offline stores, beginning with Briefcase in Windows 95, has become a necessity among users who tend to find themselves accessing network resources from portable platforms. The shift toward Web-based access has freed users from the relatively synchronous connections required by a corporate workstation. With the proper training on the front-end, users can more effectively utilize Exchange 2000 in managing folders while online. With offline folders available in Windows 2000, the Web Store synchronizes the folder contents regardless of how the data is accessed. This replication model provides support without an increase in TCO because it is transparent to the end user and therefore requires no additional training.

Native Collaboration Objects

The Web Store allows you to integrate automatically what might be more appropriately termed knowledge objects with collaborative functions such as messaging, contacts, calendaring, and workflow. Thus, a financial report in the form of an Excel workbook can be scheduled for review on a specific view. This integrative process is achieved through an object model that leverages on-demand and programmatic access to data objects. A knowledge object is not the same as a data object; a *knowledge object* is truly an entity that the consumer or end user manipulates independent of the Web Store or Exchange.

Integrating and customizing knowledge objects such as calendars or task lists into a customizable framework such as a digital dashboard to add value is an example of the difference between data processing and KM. Data access is standardized using well-known APIs such as ADO and OLE DB, so development time is minimized. In addition, popular authoring systems such as Microsoft FrontPage further expand access to the collaborative resources that the collaborative platform provides.

Database Management

The Web Store must perform very fast searches and lookups to deliver database services. The native database manages index documents for common key fields as well as attachments. The Web Store offers transaction logging at the database level and uses write-ahead transaction logs such as Exchange 2000 to ensure data integrity through redundancy. Data replication is supported at the folder level so that replicas of data can exist on multiple servers in the Exchange organization. Folder replica management also balances application loads, especially when you are dealing with data that is frequently accessed.

Using multiple databases is another way to improve reliability. The Web Store also supports Windows 2000 active/active clustering at the system level. Web Store services on one machine can assume control over data managed by the Web Store services on another machine if hardware malfunctions. Active/active clustering minimizes downtime and, when actually implemented, is totally transparent to the consumer/end user.

OWA Architecture

OWA, when it first shipped with Exchange 5, used ASP technology to render the contents of a user's mailbox in HTML. Users were able to log in from Internet sites using a standard browser to read their mail. OWA provided an access method that has always accommodated Web-based, roving users since any browser client and simplified configuration provided universal access to messaging and collaborative services. Today, the digital dashboard provides a richer API and greater exposure of stored objects through OWA. It provides a ready-made framework within which knowledge workers can customize their selection of displayed data and services. In addition, Web services provided especially by IE5 with its HTML and XML enhancements expose more than just mailboxes.

In general, OWA provides many functional benefits, including support for the following:

- *Light messaging*—OWA provides an alternative to the full Outlook 2000 client through the well-known and readily accessible standard browser client. Especially over public networks and where control over configuration is not practical, this form of access to messaging services provides a practical solution to communication needs.
- *Roving users*—With OWA, you minimize the need to configure a client, and you don't need MAPI profiles to configure the appropriate workspace for a workstation. Therefore, you can administer remote or roving users using more general system policies and standard profiles than you can with network users.
- *Kiosk and other public information sources*—This new source of information and services provides public access to mailboxes and other Web-based information with little maintenance or overhead. Kiosks are typically installed in public areas such as shopping malls, much like public telephones. Using

touch screen technology, these units are self-contained and typically enclosed in some protective structure that provides physical security to the console and CPU.

- *Migrations and rapid deployment*—OWA provides continuity of services during interim periods of migration and loss of services during maintenance periods or deployment.

OWA Administration

You should administer and manage OWA by using Microsoft's IIS snap-in, the MMC. If you open the MMC and expand the containers pertaining to IIS, you will see three virtual roots created during installation. The Exchange virtual root (**http://*server*/exchange**) points to a mailbox folder (MBX) that, for example, resides on some mailbox server in your domain. The OWA Server is installed by default during the Exchange 2000 installation. The Exchange virtual root (**http://*server*/exadmin**) and the public virtual root (**http://*server*/public**) are both added directly to the IIS directory tree structure and point back to the actual Exchange directories in the MBX folder. In addition, other virtual servers, each with separate configurations—including bound IP addresses, port numbers, and authentication—can be created on the same physical server. Virtual instances are useful in a variety of special situations that require support from multiple domains, such as different DNS configurations requiring reverse lookup or the need to communicate to separate domains with different authentication schemes.

OWA Deployment

You must consider several important factors when deploying OWA. In addition to determining baseline service levels, you need to actively monitor your servers using performance-monitoring tools in the Performance MMC snap-in, for example. Establish performance baselines for essential components such as memory, disk, network, and processor. OWA's design has changed considerably. Exchange 5.x OWA uses ASPs to communicate with the messaging platform through both CDOs and MAPI. This affects performance; for example, it limits the number of concurrent users using OWA. In Exchange 2000, however, OWA does not use MAPI or ASP technology. Instead, Exchange OWA is a part of the Web Store. It uses only IIS for protocol services. Thus, the architecture and the servicing of requests are different. In Exchange 2000 Server, performance bottlenecks usually originate from poorly maintained physical components and resources, such as insufficient memory or hard drive storage space, rather than from badly scripted Web pages.

Another important consideration is IIS authentication methods used to properly configure OWA. You need to know which ports are being used to access Internet email (usually TCP port 80). You also need to consider the impact of access in relation to using firewalls, proxy servers, or secure channels such as SSL, which uses port 443 for communication, and *Kerberos authentication* (a security protocol used by Windows 2000 Server). Finally, you must have a basic understanding of the Internet protocols that OWA uses.

Service Requests through OWA

By default, all users can access OWA, without special configuration, by typing the server's URL, which specifies the server name and the username. When this request for service is made from within the boundaries of an enterprise, hostname and username are sufficient. From outside the boundaries of an enterprise, it is necessary to use a fully qualified domain name such as ***hostname.domainname.tld*** (where .tld is the top level domain, such as .com or .edu), the name of the virtual mail directory, and the name of the user mailbox. Thus, by default, OWA does not present users with the typical SAS (Secure Attention Sequence) before access to Exchange services unless the provided security credentials fail some security criterion.

The URL passes security credentials to the Web Server. You perform these steps at the client using browser software by logging onto an OWA Server using a URL address such as **http://*servername*/exchange/*userid*** from an intranet through an HTML form. When that same user accesses the same server from a public network such as the Internet, she uses **http://*hostname.domain.tldmail-directory*/*userid***. The Web Server authenticates the user and passes the username information to AD directory services, which resolves the username to some mailbox location and redirects the service request. The location of the mailbox is returned to the Web Server, which is then used to access the data stores. OWA returns an HTML page to the user's client browser, through which the user can access her mailbox and other messaging services.

Requesting and Delivering Services

OWA in Exchange 2000 no longer uses MAPI to access the mailbox store or ASP technology for client access, but instead depends on HTTP and the WebDAV extensions. The OWA interface functions as a brokering service for all messaging traffic directed toward messaging and CDO. When the OWA client requests services, IIS acts as a proxy for the messaging traffic between the Web client and Exchange Server. IIS acts as a broker by accepting the client requests that use the WebDAV extensions to HTTP. IIS passes the requests to the OWA ISAPI layer, which either directly accesses a Database layer or proxies the request to a remote server that provides this service. ISAPI, the API for IIS, then locates the requested object's URL and redirects the client to a script that provides the logic to respond to the service request associated with a target object.

The request and delivery of services begins when a user enters a URL such as **http://servername/exchange/mailbox** in a browser Address box. The Web Server authenticates the user and determines the user's Windows 2000 account by displaying a pop-up SAS dialog box that requests the username, password, and domain, just like when a user attempts to access network resources on a local workstation.

The location of the mailbox is determined from a query to AD. OWA services return an HTML page composed of a navigational bar and mailbox contents similar in appearance to the multidocument interface (MDI) used by Outlook to display a user mailbox and its contents.

When an end user accessed OWA from a legacy Exchange Server, OWA used a separate logon page to authenticate users rather than a SAS pop-up dialog box (as described previously). Other distinctions between legacy OWA and Exchange 2000 OWA are that legacy Exchange used cookies to monitor the client session and provided a logout button that terminated the session. Exchange 2000 OWA does not provide a logout button; instead, when ending a session, the user must close all browser windows and thus all running OWA instances.

Displaying Objects

Exchange 2000 OWA displays objects through a standard browser. A consumer/end user requests an email message or another collaborative object. The Exchange ISAPI layer in IIS 5 receives the service request. The Web Storage Service determines the type of object, the specific item, and whether the user is authorized to access it. If the authenticated consumer has authorization, the object is returned to the ISAPI application. Exchange ISAPI determines the appropriate form for this object type from form definitions in the Forms Registry. If a form definition isn't found, a default form stored in wmtemplates.dll provides the services. If the browser language isn't English, other template libraries are accessed in \Exchsrvr\Res\Directory. After the form is selected, the ISAPI Application layer parses the form and makes service calls to the WSS to complete the form with the appropriate data objects. Exchange ISAPI renders the form in the appropriate HTML or XML scripting code and returns the form to the browser. The browser renders the scripting code and displays the information in an HTML document.

It is significant that, in this process flow, OWA renders a markup language appropriate for the client browser. For example, depending on the version of the browser, HTML or a combination of HTML and XML, scripting is returned to the browser client for display. Non-Microsoft browsers receive HTML code that conforms to the older HTML 3.2 standard, whereas IE 5 and more recent versions receive DHTML code that performs more complex operations within the browser DOM.

OWA Protocol Support

The major Internet protocols used with OWA include POP3, IMAP4, SMTP, and NNTP (Network News Transfer Protocol). SMTP is, in fact, the *de facto* standard server-side mail protocol on the Internet. The most common—but unfortunately weakest—client protocol in terms of features is POP3. Both SMTP and POP3 offer the broadest accessibility to messaging systems.

POP3

The *POP3 protocol* allows any computer to access a server that is holding mail for that computer. The computer itself cannot manipulate that data; it can merely download the mail from the server. After it's downloaded, the server tries to delete any copy of that mail from its memory unless you have physically configured your client to keep a copy of that mail on the server. POP3 is small, fast, and designed for simple mail retrieval. If you want to send mail, you need the SMTP protocol or a connection to a remote mail server.

Many people don't realize that POP3 has a client side and a server side. The server starts the POP3 process by listening on port 110. If you, as a client, want to use this service, you need to establish a connection with your server, which then sends you an opening message. Any POP3 commands sent between you and the server are not case sensitive.

The three basic states for a POP3 session are the following:

- *Authorization*—When a server connection is opened, the POP3 server sends you a greeting; the client must authenticate itself to the POP3 server.
- *Transaction*—The session enters this state after authorization when the server exchanges mail with the client. The client's mailbox is "locked," so messages are not modified or deleted until the transaction is updated.
- *Update*—During this phase, the client issues a **quit** command, and the POP3 server releases all resources allocated to the client. The server sends a final "goodbye" message, deletes all messages, and terminates the TCP connection to the client.

IMAP4

The *IMAP4 protocol* is actually an enhancement or improvement to POP3. Recall that after a message is downloaded from a server, it is deleted from that server. IMAP4 was developed to allow users to leave their mail on a server and to allow remote access to mail messages. It extends the POP3 protocol to allow online and offline storage and retrieval of mail. IMAP4 also allows users to manage their own mail configurations and to share mailboxes. You can manipulate mail on the server instead of just downloading a copy of it. Clients use TCP port 143 to connect to a server running IMAP. You can configure the IMAP4 server to show public folders to all clients. Best practices recommend fast message retrieval, in which messages are retrieved without prior knowledge of their exact sizes.

SMTP

SMTP originated from File Transfer Protocol (FTP) and is the native transport protocol used for Exchange Server. When you install Windows 2000, a "base SMTP" service is installed as part of IIS 5. The essence of SMTP is that you can pass information between two computers and create message headers that automatically specify all sources and destinations involved. The SMTP standard is documented in RFC 822. Each SMTP command is sent one command at a time in American Standard Code for Information Interchange (ASCII) form as a 7-bit character set. One reply is sent for every command sent. SMTP is a simple transfer specification; it does not support multiple commands sent from one host to another simultaneously, nor does it support the use of an eighth bit in its packet stream. UUEncode (Unix-to-Unix Encode), a Unix copy utility that is used to transmit data among various domains, extends the functionality of SMTP. This copy tool converts a file containing eight bits of data into a file containing seven bits of data. A recipient who receives UUEncoded mail via SMTP has to use UUDecode (Unix-to-Unix Decode) to convert this message back to an 8-bit standard.

SMTP is known as an *open message transfer system*, which means that any computer running the SMTP service can accept connections from any other computer running the SMTP service. Certain message transfer systems, such as the X.400 messaging protocol, are closed. Exchange 2000 Server enjoys greater interoperability with many more email systems than Exchange Server 5.5 ever did because of the functionality of SMTP.

MIME

MIME is another standard with which you might be familiar. It allows you to send different types of messages across different mail servers. This standard has extended the functionality of SMTP by allowing the simpler SMTP to carry binary information in the form of an attachment along with the mail message. Thus, several files of varying content can be wrapped up into one single message. The body of each message specifies a "content type" that tells you what kind of file you are dealing with. For example, you will see some messages with the label "image/jpeg." This means the file probably has a .jpg extension and can be opened with Microsoft Paint or some similar graphics package. You can make the associations between the file types and the programs that open them by using either the Exchange System Manager or Windows Explorer (choose Tools|Folder Options|File Types).

NNTP

NNTP allows you to distribute, retrieve, and post news articles on the Internet. You have to subscribe to a newsgroup to retrieve content from that newsgroup. The nice thing about subscribing is that you don't have to retrieve every single item contained within the newsgroup. Without NNTP, users have to resort to the older methods of distributing or retrieving news items: Internet mailing lists and Usenet.

Exchange Server uses NNTP to create asynchronous group discussions arranged in a hierarchical structure. This functionality was provided in legacy Exchange 5.5 through the Internet News Service. In fact, you can configure your Exchange Server to talk to external NNTP servers so that certain Usenet groups are made available to users inside your LAN. Exchange Server also allows you to create multiple NNTP servers inside your organization so users can connect to a collection of servers. This is known as a master-subordinate layout and provides fault tolerance if a main news server goes offline for any reason. As previously mentioned, an NNTP server normally communicates over TCP port 119; secure channels use the SSL protocol over TCP port 563.

Extensibility

Exchange 2000 is the most fundamental layer providing the foundation for both messaging and collaboration among all the other .NET server systems. Its role, although not often mentioned in the e-commerce context of SQL Server 2000 and BizTalk 2000, arises out of the significant architectural changes related to data integration. The most significant innovation is in the introduction of the Web Storage System, which provides a single repository for access to multiple types of semi-structured information, such as messaging and calendar objects, and its use of XML. The Web Store combines the functionality of a file system, the Web, and a collaboration server through a single, URL-addressable location for storing, accessing, and managing information, in addition to building and running applications.

Extensions to the HTTP protocol have broadened the capability of Web-based client access to data stores that until now were only accessible from within a network namespace. A wide range of scripting languages, programming interfaces, and component objects provide the extensibility and flexibility necessary to fully exploit this system. Thus, Exchange 2000 complements the more traditional data services, such as SQL Server, by increasing the depth of potential data retrieval performed by authorized users through a browser client and programmable interfaces. Microsoft has provided Universal Data Access Architecture, as shown in Figure 1.6, which provides many of the components Exchange exposes. Exchange 2000 provides many exposed objects, collectively referred to as CDOs, which access the many knowledge resources found in the Web Store.

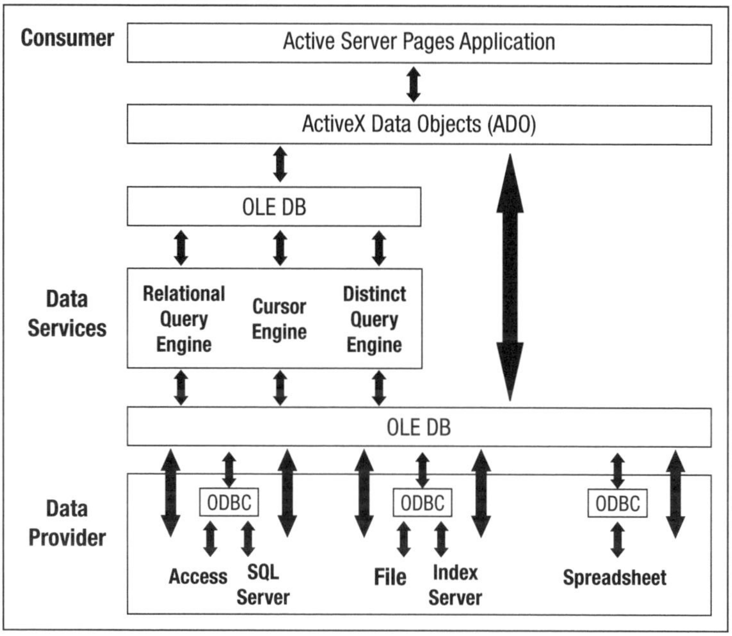

Figure 1.6 The Microsoft Universal Data Access Architecture.

Web Services

The Web Store provides a repository for managing all forms of knowledge resources, including email messages, calendar objects, and Web documents. It integrates a variety of services into a single structure to simplify search, retrieval, and sharing information with one another. This feature in the Exchange 2000 architecture will significantly lower TCO. The Web Store supports many protocols, including HTTP, WebDAV, and XML. Every object in the Web Store has a URL associated with it. If you create a folder called Secret Documents, you can, in a networked environment, create a network share to this folder from your workstation. An OWA client across the Internet can also access this folder because of the Web Store.

Basic HTTP has been extended to accommodate a broader range of data types and service operations. WebDAV (RFC 3023, 2518) is an extension to HTTP 1.1 that transforms the entire Web Store into a collaborative medium. Since 1999, WebDAV has provided HTTP with an increased feature set for providing services. It has a set of headers and methods that extend HTTP to provide capabilities for overwrite protection, properties, and namespace management. Sometimes referred to as DAV, WebDAV is a protocol for manipulating the contents of a document management system via the Web. It allows a network protocol to create interoperable and collaborative applications. Microsoft has defined a *Web service* in technical literature as an application delivered as a service that is integrated with other Web-based services using Internet standards. Thus, DAV and the Web Store are the foundation for many Web services, because they provide access to resources using standard URL addressing.

WebDAV enables collaborative publishing to Microsoft Web servers across the Internet, supports Web folders in Office 2000, and provides an interface that allows access to the hierarchical database found in the Web Store. WebDAV allows Web-based applications with APIs using HTTP requests to manipulate data objects like their networked application counterparts.

Realtime Collaborative Services (RTC)

Exchange 5.5 allowed users to work with Outlook 98 forms for collaborative purposes. These forms were designed using the Outlook email client. It is helpful to review a little of what these forms did so you can better understand how collaboration has been enhanced in Exchange Server. The management of information extends beyond rapid data access and a controlled or automated workflow. Realtime Collaboration has extended beyond novelty features to long-distance training and support, and remote monitoring and maintenance. RTC provided important communication services through cost effective methods. Entire companies can collectively manage data through Chat Service and Instant Messaging (IM) Service. Although both data and video conferencing also run on Exchange 2000, conferencing is an add-on product, which is outside the scope of this book.

A form represented a method of posting and gathering information using email and was a great replacement for regular types of paperwork. An example of a form developed with Outlook was a Help Desk Trouble Ticket. Using Exchange Server 5.5, you could develop different types of forms for collaboration, including report forms for sending reports to users and request forms such as a purchase requisition form. Other types of forms included survey forms, organization forms, and personal forms. When forms were used to communicate information to a group of people, they became known as *collaboration tools*. Microsoft itself used the term collaboration development to describe the task of designing forms.

Outlook forms were one example of a product that supported true collaboration, but collaboration among a group of coworkers extends beyond simple forms. Many organizations now desire more realtime interaction, or what's known as synchronous communication. You could use Microsoft's NetMeeting for this purpose, or you could use asynchronous communication for group collaboration in the form of email messages being sent among the groups. Synchronous technologies such as Exchange Chat Service and IM help companies lower TCO because these special forms of synchronous communication reduce overhead caused by traditional paper trails and telecommunication costs. Realtime collaboration also helps reduce travel costs and product development cycles.

Microsoft Exchange Chat Service

Microsoft has designed several different collaboration services to fit different commercial scenarios. The Microsoft Chat Service is based on *Internet Relay Chat (IRC)*, an extremely reliable Internet communication protocol. Chat Service, for example, provides users with one-to-many or many-to-many group communication methods in realtime using the same network protocol used for Internet discussion groups. The chat feature, added to the existing Exchange messaging infrastructure, provides a virtual meeting place for scheduled or on-demand meetings among your colleagues or with your distant clients. Using this type of technology also depends on the deployed hardware, but it typically supports thousands of concurrent users in one chat room on any given Chat Server. For many years, IRC has reliably supported thousands of concurrent users around the world. IM is best for one-to-one communication, and, like IRC, uses the same ubiquitous and relatively inexpensive IP-based network connections.

IRC supports realtime dialogue between two or more people. It is based on the concept of a *channel*, a virtual (online) communication space shared by many people, more commonly referred to as a *chat room*. Upon joining a chat room, you share information with other chat room members for the purpose of discussion and collaboration. IRC is in widespread use on the Internet today. In fact, Microsoft has extended this protocol as extended IRC (IRCX) with new commands for management purposes. IRC is based on RFC 1459. Users connect to a chat server using TCP port 6667 or 7000. Port 6667 is usually the first port number assigned to the first chat community you establish by default, although you can use any port that is not in use by another service.

Using the Exchange Conferencing Server for Collaboration

Conferencing Server is another special add-on tool that complements the Exchange 2000 messaging infrastructure. This product is similar to NetMeeting, except that Conferencing Server offers server-side capabilities. Conferencing Server is not a replacement for the NetMeeting package; it adds the capability of multiparty videoconferences through integration with Microsoft Outlook and access to online meetings with videoconferencing, application sharing, and text chat. You can use Outlook directory lists when you schedule a meeting. Conferencing Server uses some NetMeeting features such as a common whiteboard, application sharing, and file transfer, and provides solutions related to multiparty videoconferencing, conference scheduling, and bandwidth management. Online meetings are delivered through a standards-based browser client. A live video view of each participant depends on the client interface. The type of meeting, ranging from Public to Public Password to Private, depends on the level of security you provide. A Public meeting allows authenticated users access to your meeting. Public with Password and Private, alternatively, restrict participants to any user with the appropriate password or specific users allowed to participate in the conference.

Online meetings consume two network resources: network bandwidth and a Multipoint Control Unit (MCU). The Exchange T.120 MCU service runs as a Conferencing Server component and is used to interconnect participants of a data conference. This service is installed on Conferencing Server during installation. The Exchange H.323 Videoconferencing Bridge runs as a component of the T.120 MCU. A network can support multiple MCUs, each with separate configurations.

As already mentioned, with the addition of the video component, multiparty videoconferencing allows you to see all conference participants at the same time. The Exchange T.120 MCU service consumes a large percentage of available network bandwidth. Users who participate in multipoint videoconferencing must use the Windows 2000 product on their desktop. The number of users you can see at one time in your browser windows is limited by the physical constraints of both the hardware platform on which the software runs and the network connection. A host operator can impose a limit on the total bandwidth consumed by any single online meeting. Conference Server manages bandwidth consumption by using multicast protocols, which reduce the amount of network traffic generated by these multiparty videoconferencing products. Multicast protocols are broadcast across your network simultaneously to all group members. Thus, many users benefit from one data stream, rather than the same data stream repeating to multiple users.

Instant Messaging

Chat Service provides a many-to-many or one-to-many synchronous or realtime communication channel (sometimes called an RTC service) for text-based group discussions. Exchange 2000 Server comes equipped with another RTC component, Microsoft Exchange Instant Messaging. This service offers similar synchronous service but is exclusively for one-to-one communication among users. IM transfers text among users in realtime. Aside from the realtime communication, IM differs from email in storage methods; IM messages are not automatically written to a storage medium, and email messages are saved in a private Message Store (MS). Message exchanges during an IM session cannot be recovered once the session is terminated. IM is similar to the legacy **net send** feature except that the messaging is bidirectional. IM provides a more immediate communication channel than the telephone or email. Telephone costs, especially involving remote locations, are either reduced or totally eliminated. IM exchanges are much faster than phone calls because IM runs as a background process, allowing you to work on other projects while communication channels are fully operational. IM can transfer limited size attachments just like email.

IM Components

IM, integrated through Exchange 2000 with Windows 2000, uses a scalable Microsoft architecture that provides security and privacy. An IM client, called a *watcher*, receives presence information about other users while they are online. A watcher can send messages to an IM inbox in any domain that will accept it. Compatible with most firewall technologies, it uses Rendezvous Protocol (RVP), which operates with HTTP 1.1, and LDAP 3. RVP, based on the concept of presence, is an extension of the WebDAV protocol, which is an extension of HTTP 1.1. RVP allows notifications both within and across different Exchange organizations.

IM uses a client/server model; however, although an IM client talks directly to an IM host server, an IM server does not communicate directly with other IM servers. The IM home server maintains presence information for all its assigned subscribers. It also notifies a subscriber of changes in status. Any message sent to a subscriber first passes through the subscriber's home server. Home servers "see" their users as the IM client and function as an inbox for them. RVP sends all information through HTTP, and, by default, port 80. This feature allows presence information and instant messages to be transferred among different domains or across, for example, public networks. RVP, like HTTP, is an asynchronous protocol and therefore requires less bandwidth than other protocols. When environments are subject to exceptionally heavy message usage, best practices recommend locating IM servers in close proximity to their subscribers.

IM and DNS

Every client that sends a message needs to do a DNS service record lookup for the domain that holds the IM server. This lookup requires a DNS record called the service location (SRV) record. DNS uses a SRV record to locate a service such as LDAP or FTP on a network. The record maps the fully qualified domain name (FQDN) of a computer to the service and TCP port through which the service is provided. The domain that holds the IM server can be either a local domain or a remote domain, and it must support the SRV record type. The SRV record lookup returns the host name of the IM server responsible for a domain. If no SRV records are available, the DNS service retrieves an address record (called an *A record*) for that IM server. The SRV record makes it possible for a user's email address and IM address to be the same. Without it, the user's email address would contain the IM domain that typically begins with the "im" host prefix. The process for configuring your DNS server to accept IM is not difficult and includes the following steps:

1. *Create a DNS record.* You need an A record in the DNS database for every IM server you will use.

2. *Configure a routing server.* Clients connect to an IM home server and request a service. If the connected server is not the user's home server, it is acting as a routing server that will proxy or redirect service requests via HTTP. Best practices recommend that your routing servers have a host name of "im". A routing server thus has an FQDN of **im.mydomain.com**.
3. *Create a SRV resource record.* This record is for the RVP, which maps directly to the routing server. When an IM client logs on, it queries DNS for the SRV resource record. If the record exists, the IM client contacts the server, which refers the client to its home server. A SRV record is used so that users' email addresses are equivalent to their IM addresses.

Creating a canonical name (or CNAME) record to provide an alias name is not as effective as using IM. CNAME records are used for aliases in single-server environments, where one machine hosts multiple services such as HTTP, POP, and DNS. IM specifically provides a simple, low-bandwidth communication solution with little ongoing administrative overhead, and therefore low TCO. For example, IM users do not automatically authenticate themselves before sending an IM message. RVP, in fact, does not require a user to authenticate to his IM home server. The NTLM security access protocol or the digest authentication method provides any necessary authentication. NTLM is referred to as the Windows Integrated Authentication method or WIA Challenge/Response. The digest authentication method verifies that both parties are sharing a symmetric key (in other words, a type of *secret* or password) without communicating it publicly between them. IM uses the WIA method by default. The Kerberos authentication method, the default Windows 2000 authentication protocol, is not used.

Part II

Planning for Exchange 2000 Implementation

Chapter 2

Understanding Messaging Systems

The first chapter showed how the messaging concept has evolved from simple premises to complex schemes for many organizations in the past few years. No longer is email the sole provider of basic corporate communication. Today, sophisticated messaging systems have emerged that promise to connect multiple and diverse communication networks. Since Microsoft released their first electronic messaging product, MS Mail for PC Networks, in 1991, there has been an emphasis on developing more complete solutions, which allows for information interchange between enterprises. To understand a complete messaging system, you must examine its features and components and understand the interaction between them. You then will have a greater understanding of the underlying client/server architecture of most messaging systems in existence today.

The Primary Functions of Exchange 2000 Server

Most major corporate expenditures are justified in terms of solving mission-critical issues, or in terms of becoming a company that ventures into leading-edge technology. In other words, either a problem exists that requires immediate and forceful resolution, or your organization has no longer maintained a competitive advantage from being current with technological advances. Because this book focuses on creating and implementing an optimal and complete messaging solution for an enterprise, you can make two assumptions at this point:

- You have already decided that Microsoft Exchange 2000 Server is the appropriate "answer" to the "What messaging system will help maintain connectivity to diverse networks while allowing us to centrally manage and administer our large user population base?" question.
- You chose Microsoft Exchange 2000 Server for the ultimate solution because it has demonstrated more technological ingenuity and foresight than most other solutions on the market (for instance, Lotus Notes, Lotus Domino, or Qmail).

This chapter reveals how Exchange 2000 becomes the first choice for many organizations due to its architectural model for message distribution and retrieval and its advanced features that conform to the model of today's cutting-edge technology.

What Exchange Server Can Do for You

This chapter explains exactly what Exchange 2000 does and how these functions can benefit any organization that deploys it. Again, the primary concept to keep in mind can be stated this way: If you could design a messaging system that does as much as or more than Exchange 2000, how would you do it? Does Exchange 2000 represent the "pinnacle" in messaging services, and if so, what does Exchange contain that other systems do not? Finally, do most messaging servers mirror Exchange 2000, or does the Microsoft design of Exchange 2000 present new concepts and precedents, which can never be imitated? By doing this kind of analysis, you will not only understand and appreciate the genius behind Exchange 2000 but you will also understand and appreciate the genius behind messaging systems in general.

Exchange 2000: An Overview

Before you begin to look at standards, interfaces, and components, you have to understand the genesis of an idea. Exchange 2000 is a messaging server first. However, defining "messaging server" introduces elements of a client/server architecture that are not immediately evident. Basically, a *messaging server* is a "middleware" program, which handles strings of text, or graphics that are sent for use by other programs. These other programs use an application programing interface known as a Messaging Application Programming Interface, or MAPI-compliant client. Messaging servers are important because they prioritize and queue messages from clients as needed, so individual clients do not have to perform this task. Therein lies the beauty of client/server architecture—the server does most of the processing.

NOTE: *In the past, most messaging systems were called point-to-point or subscribe/publish messaging systems. Modern terminology dictates the terms* client/server *or* shared-file *messaging systems to describe the former terms.*

Messaging, in a broad sense, is the creation and exchange of data, including text, images, or voice, over some communications network. Exchange 2000 was designed to handle this function of messaging in an elegant and efficient manner. In fact, Exchange 2000 allows programs to share common message-handling code and communicate across various programming environments as long as compatible protocols are being used. Most messaging servers consist of components that manage objects contained within them. In other words, these messaging servers are object-oriented systems containing such objects as users, groups, servers, public folders, and address books. Exchange 2000 arranges these objects in a logical and structured manner so that every object belongs to some class, and that class belongs to another logical group of objects called a container, which itself belongs to a higher-order container. The grouping of objects is both structured and hierarchical. To better understand messaging systems, let's look at how an "ideal" system is supposed to behave and then compare the behavior of Exchange 2000 to determine whether it meets all the stated criteria.

The Ideal Messaging Server

What should the "ideal" messaging server contain to provide basic messaging functionality? Remember, we're not discussing advanced functionality; we're only concerned with what makes a messaging system tick.

Most messaging systems rely on a transport engine or a routing engine for speed and reliability. Of course, most companies are concerned with *scalability issues*, as well as data redundancy and integrity issues. Although every system has inherent scalability limits, most companies adhere to the mistaken belief that scalability should not be limited but should be in a "readily expandable" state, as justified by the high purchase price they have committed. Yet scalability and cost are two unrelated issues. No matter what price is paid for a system, both hardware and software will dictate upper boundaries for most applications, including Exchange 2000. In any case, scalability is foremost with many organizations because users are constantly being added and technology is constantly being upgraded.

The routing engine or architecture that is used should be able to track any changes in links between servers and communicate these changes to all servers affected. Common and available protocols should be used so the messaging transport language can be understood at all times. Protocols should be picked that meet all types of bandwidth requirements, be they permanent high-speed links or low-speed network connections occurring across a 56Kbps WAN dial-up connection.

The components that make up the underlying architecture should be easy to identify and subject to deterministic troubleshooting in cases of component failure or corruption. The corrective action to take when troubleshooting these components should be well documented and relatively easy to implement. Secondary corrective procedures should be applied if these primary measures fail for any reason. Components should be designed so that they are not all required to run on the same machine. In fact, fault tolerance and load balancing should be paramount in case certain components stop functioning.

The ideal system contains storage locations for mailboxes or other public information that are easily accessible if users need to retrieve mail. These storage locations also are designed with disaster recovery in mind so that minimal disruption occurs to end users in case of disaster. The modern day concerns of redundancy, fault tolerance, and high availability will naturally take center stage when designing a proper disaster recovery plan for any organization. Storage locations also facilitate groups of users working together using collaborative type applications and workflow processes. The "ideal system" should include built-in tools that monitor and help extend the useful life of the system through automatic maintenance procedures.

Every organization makes a distinction between preventive maintenance and reactive maintenance. Active and regular monitoring of a system's services is the best type of preventive maintenance you can perform for any messaging system. Any monitoring that you *don't* perform on your system becomes a problem, not an optimization. Conversely, every optimization procedure you perform becomes one less problem that you have to solve. Finally, regular system maintenance procedures provide administrators with the basis to configure levels of security and protection from Internet threats and other disruptions of service, including data interception and denial-of-service attacks. Assuring a secure messaging system becomes an ongoing daily task for many network administrators, because new and stronger types of Internet security threats appear now on a daily basis.

We can summarize our thoughts and give you an idea of what components should be included with an ideal messaging server using the following list:

- A reliable and efficient message transport architecture and protocol
- An efficient message routing management scheme
- A strong transport and routing engine
- Predictable storage locations for internal components
- A dedicated server architecture for running specific tasks
- Accessible mailbox information using standard browser interfaces
- Dependence on a centralized directory for enhanced administration
- Provision for fault tolerance and load balancing features
- Workflow and workgroup management via enhanced application development
- Implementation of workflow security
- Mechanism for disaster recovery procedures
- Procedures for monitoring and maintaining internal components
- Implementation of ongoing security measures to prevent interception of data

How Exchange 2000 Meets the Criteria

Now that you know what is required for an effective messaging solution, it's time to determine how Exchange 2000 can meet or exceed those requirements found in the ideal situation. You will then begin to understand how Exchange 2000 will not only meet your current messaging needs but also all future messaging needs.

Essential Components Needed for Message Flows

How does Exchange 2000 handle basic message flows? Exchange 2000 has an enhanced message routing architecture that uses components known as routing group masters. These "master servers" help distribute any changes made to routing tables to any server in the same routing group. The Exchange messaging transport architecture uses an Internet standard protocol known as Simple Mail Transfer Protocol (SMTP) for native message transport. It can also use the X.400 protocol for connectivity to foreign mail systems. Both the SMTP protocol and the Active Directory (AD) directory service of Windows 2000 Server help make Exchange 2000 very scalable in design. Previous versions of Exchange depended on the Message Transfer Agent (MTA), which was built on the industry-standard X.400 protocol. Exchange 2000 incorporates a somewhat modified MTA, but only to connect to legacy Exchange Servers using Remote Procedure Calls (RPC).

The server architecture consists of various processes that manage the communication protocols needed for successful messaging. The Internet Information Server (IIS) process of Windows 2000 Server, a process known also as **inetinfo.exe**, now hosts all necessary protocols such as Post Office Protocol version 3 (POP3) or the Internet Message Access Protocol version 4 (IMAP4). This design allows Exchange administrators to assign specific tasks to specific servers. Placing processes and protocols on separate servers helps reduce client network traffic and also provides faster recovery of data items. The Web Storage System (WSS) feature of Exchange 2000 separates it from other messaging systems. The WSS is discussed separately because of its tremendous importance to the current version of Exchange.

The Web Storage System

The new WSS enables you to build document-management applications and workflow applications. Developers can now store collaboration information or Microsoft Office documents in the Web Store. Think of this new feature as an updated Exchange 5.5 Server database that has been designed for document management and collaboration applications. The WSS has great potential because it uses Internet-related capabilities, including a file type for streaming video and media, multiple databases per server, and support for Windows 2000 security mechanisms such as authentication and Access Control Lists (ACL). The WSS appears very similar to a "traditional" file system such as FAT16 or NTFS (NT File System). Items are stored within this system inside folders. *Schemas*, or rules, outline an object's definition, such that every item in Exchange 2000 now has a set of attributes or properties. The schema helps define an item's properties and its content type.

Developers use the WSS to develop Web applications by creating custom Web Forms and having a MAPI-based client such as Microsoft Outlook 2000 bring it up without any user intervention. Developers also develop Web applications by creating an Active Server Pages (ASP) application and using ActiveX Data Objects (ADOs) to access the store. Although forms created with the WSS were designed for RAD (rapid application development), you might experience problems using them in very high performance enterprise applications.

The WSS provides this storage technology not only for Exchange 2000, but also for Microsoft's SharePoint Portal Server (formerly known as Tahoe). Both products now store collaborative information such as a Word document. The WSS can also respond to a simple SQL query using the ADO interface, or the HTTP 1.1 WebDAV protocol (Web Distributed Authoring and Versioning protocol, an extension to the HTTP 1.1 protocol). Developers can now build form-based applications that can be registered in the WSS's Forms Registry using Extensible Markup Language (XML) code.

The WSS also enables a company to use WebFolders, which provide a way to access Internet-based files from a standard Windows Explorer interface. WebFolders are usually implemented using the WebDAV protocol and specification, because it allows basic file procedures such as copying or moving files across the Internet using HTTP. In short, the WSS combines the best elements of the Internet with a file system and a collaboration platform into one single tool. It even uses features found in previous versions of Exchange, such as single-instance message storage and online maintenance and recovery. Finally, the WSS supports built-in content indexing by using the Microsoft Search Service, which indexes Office documents and HTML files, among other things, so users can access files easily.

Other Components Included in Exchange 2000

The WSS was originally designed to host all Internet protocols such as HTTP-WebDAV or SMTP. However, these protocols have been placed into the IIS process known as **Iinetinfo.exe** in order to help increase the flexibility of Exchange 2000; however, these protocols still have to communicate with the WSS. Microsoft has included an extra queuing layer known simply as *EPOXY*, or more formally as the Exchange Interprocess Communication layer (ExIPC). The ExIPC com-munication layer helps the **Inetinfo.exe** process exchange data rapidly with the Web Storage System. ExIPC is a high-performance utility that uses shared memory to communicate between the various processes.

Another change involving these protocols involves how they are now managed. Previous versions of Exchange used the Internet Services Manager tool to manage both protocols and virtual servers. Current versions of Exchange Server use the new Exchange System Manager snap-in tool to manage these same protocols and virtual servers. Any changes to the configuration of these protocols are saved to the Windows 2000 Active Directory directory service and replicated to a secondary directory known as the IIS *metabase*. Both Windows 2000 and Exchange 2000 benefit directly from these protocols. In fact, Windows 2000 installs a basic version of the SMTP and NNTP (Network News Transfer Protocol) as part of its default installation. Windows 2000 actually uses SMTP and NNTP for directory replication purposes. Exchange 2000 enhances or extends the basic functionality of these protocol stacks by supplying additional commands and components so that full-blown messaging functionality can be observed within the organization. For the first time, Microsoft has enabled support for multiple databases within multiple storage groups (SGs) on a single server.

NOTE: A storage group *is an* instance *of the Microsoft Extensible Storage Engine concept used in Exchange 5.5. You can have up to five databases per SG, and up to four SGs per server.*

The rules for database storage have changed. Exchange 2000 uses a database to host mailbox stores or public folder stores, which means you can increase the number of connections made to your Exchange 2000 at any time. You can also plan your storage needs by separating different types of data for each database or assigning different databases to different divisions within your enterprise. Every database in the WSS can now support three separate types of files: log files, streaming media files (STM files), and database files (EDB files). STM files now hold the native MIME (Multipurpose Internet Mail Extensions) content of a message that is received over the Internet. Each .STM file uses 4KB pages and can defragment files online.

Exchange 2000 places critical components used for primary message flows within predictable and stable locations in the Windows 2000 operating system environment. For example, the **Inetinfo.exe** process that hosts all protocols used by Exchange 2000 is always found in the *\Winnt\System32\Inetserv* directory path. The Information Store process (or **Store.exe**) is always found in the *\Exchsrvr\Bin* directory path. It manages the storage of data and holds all message contents in a content store (.stm file) and a property store (.edb file). Although these default directory paths can be changed, it is best to leave them at their default values.

OWA (Outlook Web Access) enables non-MAPI clients to access mailbox information and public folder information. A client accesses information using HTTP, and the IIS server uses WSS to provide ultimate access to the user's mailbox. The user interfaces with a Web service using a standard browser, and the browser in turn communicates with the server using an extension of the HTTP 1.1 WebDAV protocol.

NOTE: *The WebDAV standard was developed by the Internet Engineering Task Force (IETF) and provides a protocol for WSS. For more information regarding this standard, please visit the Web site for the IETF at **www.ietf.org**.*

OWA contributes to the scalability and efficiency of Exchange 2000 by supporting the following features:

- Allows gradual migration to Exchange 2000 by providing interim support for clients who need to access legacy Exchange Servers using a standard Internet browser.
- Provides easy administration because clients are not using the "bloated" version of Outlook 2000. In some cases, Outlook 2000 cannot be used, or presents unique network problems because of increased network traffic or insufficient network bandwidth being made available. OWA does not require high bandwidth connections to the back-end server that is hosting the users' mailboxes.
- Supports users who travel and have to log on from different parts of the network on a frequent basis. Instead of configuring special access for multiple users, they can benefit from the ease and flexibility of OWA for message retrieval.

Exchange 2000 benefits from a tight integration with the AD directory service of Windows 2000 Server. The management of directory objects is more centralized by using integrated management tools, and greater access is provided to directory information by using the Lightweight Directory Access Protocol (LDAP). LDAP is a directory service protocol used to gain access to information repositories based on the X.500 international directory service-naming standard, and can be used to query AD for object information. Exchange 2000 can access this service in multiple ways using multiple clients. Always remember that a MAPI-based client such as the Outlook 2000 client enjoys the fastest and most organized access to AD. However, Exchange 2000 needs access to AD to store configuration information and to perform quicker searches by taking advantage of the Directory Service Access Cache feature. This feature allows Exchange 2000 to cache all AD directory lookups without querying a global catalog server. It also enhances network performance by conserving processing power on your Global Catalog servers. The default cache holds up to 4MB of entries for a five minute time period. You can adjust this setting using the Windows 2000 Registry.

TIP: *Increasing the Time-to-Live settings for cache entries definitely improves network response times. Configuring excessive cache times, however, may consume vital resources such as system memory in the long run.*

The ideal messaging server supports enhanced application development. Exchange 2000 streamlines the workflow process so users interact more efficiently. Workflow is an application that is modeled or represented as a *business process*. Your users can also collaborate on various tasks or publish information to a company-sponsored intranet. Developers can now comfortably build collaboration applications using a multitude of protocols and APIs. An example of these applications includes the tracking of an expense report for a member of a sales team. The API components used to develop applications allow developers to reuse original programming code and include ADOs, Collaboration Data Objects (CDOs), and the OLE DB API (Object Linking and Embedding for Databases API). Exchange 2000 contains an important tool called the Workflow Designer, which can increase security for developers who are given excessive permissions when compiling code on the server. Workflow security is also an important issue because some developers include scripts or COM (Component Object Model) objects that can negatively affect your Exchange Server. Exchange 2000 provides Workflow components, which uses workflow "security modes." For example, Restricted Mode limits the capability to compile certain objects. The following list describes some of the tools included with Exchange 2000 that are used in the development of applications:

- *The WSS Schema Designer*—Use this to modify the schema for folders.
- *The WSS Application Deployment Wizard*—Use this to deploy applications on another server.
- *The WSS System Viewer*—Use this to display the contents of folders within the WSS.

TIP: *For information on any of the above Application Development Tools, please visit the Microsoft Web site at* ***www.microsoft.com/exchange****.*

Exchange 2000 makes it easy to back up and restore multiple mailbox stores as a group or individually. Recall that one storage group can contain up to five separate mailbox stores or public folder stores. You can also have up to four SGs per server. Exchange 2000 also uses the concept of circular logging to reduce overall disk storage requirements. Transaction logs (one per SG) are overwritten after transactions have been committed to the databases. This process should be used with noncritical information and must be manually enabled. A form of recovery used by Exchange 2000 is active/active clustering. Exchange clustering is a form of High Availability (HA), which is used by many organizations for messaging services.

How does Exchange's monitoring and maintenance functionality compare with the ideal system? Exchange 2000 now provides a suite of tools to optimize the overall health of your servers:

- Exchange 2000 Monitoring and Status tool
- Diagnostic logging
- Queue Viewer
- Performance logs and alerts
- Event Viewer
- Task Manager
- Network Monitor

Some of the tools in this list pertain only to Exchange 2000 and some pertain only to Windows 2000. We go into more detail regarding these tools in Chapter 14. Be careful when using these tools in a mixed-mode environment consisting of both Exchange 2000 servers and Exchange 5.5 servers. Exchange 5.5 servers have their own set of monitoring tools that cannot be used to monitor an Exchange 2000 Server.

The Monitoring and Status tool can now be used to set up email alerts when a certain threshold has been reached on one of your Exchange 2000 servers. For certain services, Exchange 2000 automatically logs a "critical state" if that service stops running (for instance, the WSS). Diagnostic logging can monitor protocol connectors or other connectors used by Exchange 2000. A Protocol Logging tool is used to obtain information about SMTP and NNTP. Event Viewer can be used to display information about applications or even the directory service running on a domain controller. Queue Viewer can monitor both X.400 queues and SMTP queues. The Windows 2000 Monitoring tools include Performance Console, System Monitor, Task Manager, and Network Monitor. Network Monitor is especially useful when observing network traffic patterns or monitoring activity such as total bytes transmitted per second and total datagrams received per second.

Security in Exchange 2000 has been bolstered not only with Exchange-specific features but also with Windows 2000 features. On the Windows 2000 side, AD has replaced the previous services of the Security Accounts Manager (SAM) database of Windows NT 4 Server. AD brings strong security features to the table because it is part of an integral subsystem of Windows 2000, which concerns itself with security for the operating system. Both Windows 2000 and Exchange 2000 allow levels of access control to be set on various objects, thereby increasing security. This new access control model is entirely different compared to the access control methods that were used in Exchange 5.5. The new model, in other words, allows even more access control than before. Exchange 5.5 only allowed access control on a container level (for example, on Organizational Units); however, Exchange 2000 allows access control limits to be set at multiple levels, including container or even object property levels.

Messaging systems need to be closely monitored for security breaches and Exchange 2000 has filled this requirement by enabling security auditing. Security logs are generated that allow you to view the security events that occurred. Examining the security log within Windows Server is important because it can help you determine whether there have been an increasing number of failed logon attempts in the past. Security auditing in Exchange 2000 is disabled by default. To activate it, use the Group Policy Microsoft Management Console (MMC), GPEDIT, MSC, or the Local Computer Policy snap-in. Security auditing in Exchange 2000 enables you to track not only logon attempts, but also changes made to configuration files.

Advanced Security Features of Exchange 2000

Exchange 5.5 had many security features that were integrated with the Windows NT 4 Server operating system. These features included the capability to create special administrative groups to monitor various configuration elements within the server, as well as advanced security features such as message encryption and public key technology. Finally, Exchange 5.5 instituted the Key Management Service (KM Service), which included the Windows NT Key Manager Service, the KM Security DLL (Dynamic Link Library), and the KM database. Recall that the Key Manager Service allowed a machine to function as a Certificate Authority (CA) for an organization. The CA created or assigned public and private keys and maintained a Certification Revocation List in the Exchange directory. The KM Security DLL supported secure communication between a client and a server, and the KM database managed all security information for the entire company.

Exchange 2000 improves upon this advanced security model by not only including encryption and PKI (public key infrastructure) technology, but also introducing Kerberos authentication as a preferred security mechanism. *Kerberos* is actually a security protocol found inside Windows 2000 Server and provides extremely secure communication between a domain and its inhabitants. The system issues a "ticket" so that a user can access network resources. These tickets provide encrypted information that confirms a user's identity to the server and an encrypted password, which is the only information that is requested for network access. Exchange 2000 is currently treated as a special network service as far as Kerberos is concerned, because it is so tightly integrated with Windows 2000 Server. If a user needed to access an Exchange Server, she would ask for an Exchange Server service ticket from the Key Distribution Center (KDC). This service ticket is needed to authenticate to the Exchange Server.

The new KM Service of Exchange 2000 uses Windows 2000 Certificate Services and multiple technologies and security mechanisms. KM Services allows you to benefit from secure messaging services via the following features:

- Encryption
- Ciphers
- Certificate Services

Encryption involves scrambling a message so that it becomes ciphered, or unreadable. *Keys* are exchanged between a sender and a recipient of the message. In essence, messages are encrypted by a sender who possesses a key, and decrypted by a recipient who possesses a matching key. The goal is to transform "cipher text" into readable text. A *cipher* is nothing more than a mathematical function used to encrypt data. For now, just note that Exchange 2000 can use four types of ciphers: symmetric ciphers, asymmetric ciphers, block ciphers, and stream ciphers. As far as Certificate Services are concerned, Exchange 2000 uses ciphers to produce X.509 certificates that are used to digitally sign and encrypt email messages.

Let's stop here to digest what has been covered. The goal was to determine whether Exchange 2000 could be compared to an "ideal messaging system" as described earlier in this chapter. The information in the preceding paragraphs showed that Exchange 2000 is comparable to the ideal messaging system. We aren't attempting to show what Microsoft "left out" (if anything); we are showing what Microsoft included or will include, if future needs warrant it. You have to understand Exchange 2000 from an architectural point of view to understand messaging systems in general. From here on, Exchange 2000 represents our overall concept of what a messaging system should be.

The remainder of this chapter looks at a few more components of Exchange 2000 from a client-side perspective. It's important to understand what the user community is looking for in a messaging system. You'll see the top five improvements Microsoft has made to this messaging platform, and learn about the deployment scenarios that enable Exchange 2000 to satisfy almost any messaging need.

Advantages of Exchange 2000

On the road to understanding messaging system behavior, we are particularly concerned with the messaging dynamics of Exchange 2000. It has evolved greatly in architectural terms from the days of the legacy Exchange 5.5 platform. The main features of interest found in Exchange 2000 are the following:

- *Design flexibility and scalability*—If you think back to Exchange 5.5, remember that the servers were organized logically and physically into sites. A good thing, because you could manage a group of servers as one single unit and replicate information between servers in the same site. But what if your site grew on a consistent basis? Your site might span one or more, less than ideal WAN links that definitely will slow down your replication traffic or messaging traffic. With Exchange 2000, clients can be placed into administrative groups without worrying about being hampered by slow-speed network connections. Directory replication is no longer constrained by site boundaries; rather it is managed by a more powerful operating system, Windows 2000. Do not confuse site boundaries applied to Windows 2000 with site boundaries applied to Exchange 5.5. Windows 2000 organizes sites according to collections of IP ranges, while Exchange 5.5 uses the site concept to describe a simple collection of Exchange Servers communicating through high-bandwidth connections. Servers within an Exchange 2000 administrative group can be organized into even more distinct routing groups. Administrative group layouts, however, are now different than routing group layouts. Administrative group layouts handle administrative and management topology, whereas routing group layouts handle discrete message flows.

- *Some clients will prefer Exchange 2000 because it is easier to access Directory information*—The "directory" that clients accessed in Exchange 5.5 is now part of the Windows 2000 structure. Windows 2000 installed Global Catalog (GC) servers, which are the first domain controllers installed in a domain. If a client is using Outlook 2000 or Outlook 98 with Service Pack 2 (SP2), directory services can now be accessed via the GC Server directly. Other clients might have to perform two queries and be directed to a Global Catalog server, but the concept of a GC makes it easier to manage information for every single object in the Windows 2000 forest. Administrators can make sure that the attributes of the objects that are being used in both Exchange 5.5 and Exchange 2000 can be found directly in the new GC Servers of Windows 2000.

WARNING! The Enterprise version of Exchange 5.5 included a connector for the Professional Office System (PROFS) or OfficeVision. However, this connector is not supported in Exchange 2000. You can use this connector if you operate in a mixed-mode environment, but not if you operate in a native-mode environment.

Clients will appreciate being able to connect to other types of foreign mail systems in Exchange 2000, just as they did in Exchange 5.5. Certain caveats apply, however, such as the following:

- *Exchange 2000 now supports multiple databases per server*—Multiple databases imply that one or more databases can be backed up while the server is still running. Even though you can back up one database within a SG, it makes sense to back up the entire SG because each SG now has one set of transaction logs available to all databases within it. Of course, the restore process also shares these benefits. You can restore one database while the other databases are still being used. Disruption to clients is minimal at best, and clients do not have to wait for data to be restored in the event that this data is lost.

- *Exchange 2000 can host almost an "unlimited" number of users*—Recall that Exchange 5.5 was limited in the number of users because it was also limited in the number and size of its private Information Store. However, Exchange 2000 can scale to massive proportions, because the old single Private Information Store can now become multiple mailbox or public folder stores. Users' mailboxes do not have to be moved or migrated in case an organization suddenly experiences a massive influx in its user population.
- *Exchange 2000 can use SGs for different purposes so that information can be segregated more efficiently*—Users can enjoy separate and unique repositories of data so that information can be more organized and retrievable. Information within a public folder store can now be "mapped" by a user so that retrieval of information is always consistent and predictable.

NOTE: *Be careful when configuring multiple public folder databases, because only one public folder store within all SGs can hold the All Public Folders tree. This default public folder tree is accessible by any MAPI-compliant client such as Outlook.*

- *Exchange 2000 now offers enhanced access to data using standard Internet browsers*—Even Web site designers can now place Exchange-related elements directly into their Web pages. If a user, Jsmith, wanted access to his calendar on a server named Orion, he would simply type the following into his browser:

```
http://Orion/Jsmith/calendar
```

- *Exchange 2000 enables clients to use Internet Explorer 5 (IE 5) to support advanced functionality for OWA*—These advanced features include drag-and-drop and new context menus. Browsers other than IE 5 might not offer equivalent functionality.
- *Exchange 2000 now indexes all content in a mailbox store or public folder store, including messages, contacts, tasks, and calendar information*—Users can find information quickly and easily. All user queries run much faster than in legacy versions of Exchange.
- *Exchange 2000 enables clients to enjoy realtime communication that complements, but doesn't replace, their email experiences*—Chat Services, Instant Messaging (IM) Services, and Conferencing Services are all performed directly from a messaging client. Of these new services, Chat and IM seem to hold the most promise for end users. Witness the growth of the IM market in recent years. In fact, since 2000 the IETF stepped up efforts to develop a

standard protocol for IM. Currently, America Online has been one of the first to use this new technology, and former attempts by Tribal Voice and iCast to stop this monopolistic behavior have proved futile. Companies need interoperability between different IM systems so they can easily roll out large-scale applications. The protocol that promises the most inter-operability is the IETF's Instant Messaging and Presence Protocol (IMPP). IMPP attempts to define a standard of detecting online presence information so users can communicate with other users regardless of physical location. The key to designing an IM standard is the security and authentication component, rather than the interoperability issues. Organizations are concerned about releasing confidential directory information to outside parties through the use of IM. This technology is even being considered for online customer-service applications so customers can contact companies in realtime, rather than waiting on hold via the telephone.

- *Exchange 2000 provides the consolidation of services when using groupware that clients want*—In fact, a new concept called "universal inbox" or "unified inbox" is driving the messaging marketplace today. This concept enables a user to retrieve all forms of electronic communication from one access point; the forms of communication include email, voice mail, faxes, workflow, and document management. Through the use of a "universal inbox," a user can access her messages from anywhere, theoretically increasing her productivity quotient. Most major groupware vendors, including Microsoft, Novell, and Lotus Corp., currently offer groupware-enabled messaging plat-forms, and they all offer some form of unified-messaging support. Some of these products even integrate with third-party unified messaging products, such as Lucent Technologies' Octel Voice Messenger. Not all email providers can or want to offer such support for unified messaging; they would rather concentrate on core messaging services.

The Case for Exchange 2000

The next few pages present almost a summary view of Exchange 2000 with an eye toward upcoming chapters. In Chapter 1, you learned essential concepts related to collaboration, including the use of the OWA client. This chapter has given you a bird's-eye view of messaging systems behavior using Exchange 2000 as a primary example. You have been introduced to certain components of Exchange, and you have been told how some of these components communicate to produce message flow. You are beginning to see the power and the potential of what one messaging server can do, given optimal design scenarios. We don't want to get to the details yet, because that would detract from the appreciation of the interrelationships occurring in the background. Chapter 11 will show you how to perform important procedures, such as configuring a Routing Group connector, or tracking messages using the Message Tracking Center.

At this point in the chapter, we want to present some recommendations and best practices as you prepare to use this product. You'll learn about planning issues and design constraints so you'll be prepared fully for what lies ahead. If you start thinking like a system architect, you will be better prepared to handle whatever catastrophe might befall you in the normal course of Exchange administration. You should use this material in conjunction with future chapters because one chapter always complements another. The immediate solutions in the following chapters will be easier to comprehend because the background presented here is complete.

Cautious Optimism

We would classify Exchange 2000 as the pinnacle of Microsoft's attempt to dominate the messaging and collaborative platform market, but that would be premature. When Microsoft first launched Exchange, it fell short in several strategic areas, including some core architectural areas. Exchange Server 4 had a storage limitation of 16GB, and it lacked Internet access tools such as NNTP for newsgroups and POP3 for mail retrieval! Microsoft decided to add Internet functionality only in Exchange Server 5 (which shipped in March of 1997). This product added a whole new suite of Internet functionality, including the POP3 protocol for incoming mail and the NNTP protocol. It also offered unlimited storage capabilities. Exchange 5.5 was released in November 1997—eight months later—because many users wanted advanced messaging beyond simple "point-to-point" email services. Exchange 5.5 offered an even more enhanced set of Internet tools, including the LDAP and the OWA client. This product, however, was not bug free. Many users complained about the Information Store "hanging" for unknown reasons. In response to these allegations, Microsoft released Service Packs to address common themes such as calendaring and interoperability.

NOTE: *SP3 is the latest SP for Exchange 5.5. Always check the Microsoft Web site at* ***www.microsoft.com/exchange*** *for the latest Service Packs or hotfixes.*

Exchange 2000 can compete with other messaging products on all levels, but does have limitations and weaknesses. For example, Sendmail, another messaging competitor that claims to be the *de facto* standard Internet Mail Server, provides higher levels of POP3 and SMTP-based security than Exchange 2000. Microsoft knows it has to offer services not provided by any of its competitors. Microsoft is doing this through product strategies, product strengths, and product challenges.

Product Strategies for Exchange 2000

Microsoft is currently using a three-pronged strategy for Exchange 2000. First, Microsoft is presenting Exchange 2000 as a "turnkey" messaging solution based on a new Web Store architectural component. The Web Store combines the concept of a file system with the versatility of Internet access protocols and Web-accessible data into one single component or infrastructure, which makes all objects within the repository immediately accessible. Second, Microsoft is concentrating on large-scale enterprise messaging solutions, such as Application Service Providers (ASPs). This is one reason Microsoft introduced enhanced Web functionality and clustering capabilities into Exchange 2000. A third objective focuses on the industry standard concept of Total Cost of Ownership (TCO). A vendor's major claim to predominance rests on the fact that its product offers a company the lowest TCO. Surprisingly, Microsoft has offered a lower TCO for Exchange 2000 than the competitors have offered for their products. As an example, Microsoft can offer an Exchange 2000 Enterprise Server License for almost $1,000. Companies needing additional Client Access Licenses (CALs) can purchase them for approximately $29 per seat. This is much lower than the price offered by Novell Groupwise ($99 per client seat), or Lotus Notes R5 ($45 per client seat). Companies actually save money by purchasing a Microsoft mail client such as Outlook 2000 because it has already been bundled into the Office 2000 suite of productivity tools. The strategy seems to be working because Exchange 5.5 has led the messaging market for the past two years compared to Lotus Notes Domino.

NOTE: *For more information on these statistics and the Electronic Mail and Messaging System (EMMS) Newsletter, please visit* ***www.biz-lib.com/ZBREMM.html****.*

Exchange 2000 Product Strengths

The primary strength of Exchange 2000 is its integration with Windows 2000 Server AD service. No other messaging system has such a relationship with AD. Even Novell's offering of GroupWise (current version 5.5) does not have the same level of integration with its own Directory service, Novell Directory Services (NDS). AD offers administrators complete and centralized control over every object that is created. For instance, if an administrator creates a Group object, then Exchange 2000 can use this for distribution list purposes. Any AD user account used in Exchange 2000 is either mail-enabled or mailbox-enabled. You need to understand the differences inherent in these terms for future chapters.

A *mail-enabled* item in AD has at least one email address defined for it; for example, a contact object is sometimes equated with a custom recipient in Exchange 5.5. After an object has been enabled, it can participate in routing activities. A *mailbox-enabled* object, on the other hand, has at least one Exchange mailbox associated with it; for example, you can designate a public folder with an email address of **finance@somewhere.com**. If anything is mailed to this specific address, it is put into the appropriate object container.

***NOTE:** In Exchange 2000, only user objects possess mailboxes. Users therefore, can be mailbox-enabled; however, a user can also be mail-enabled. This concept can be confusing because contacts, for instance, can only be mail-enabled, not mailbox-enabled. Remember it like this: To be mailbox-enabled, you have to be able to log on to Windows 2000 as a security principal (an object with logon capabilities). Security principals can be either mail-enabled or mailbox-enabled. Because a custom recipient or contact is not a security principal, they can never be mailbox-enabled, only mail-enabled.*

Recall from Exchange 5.5 that custom recipients refer to a mail location address outside the confines of your normal Exchange 5.5 organization. In Exchange 2000, custom recipients are handed a new tool called the Active Directory Connector (ADC), which helps transfer custom recipients to AD, where they will develop into "contacts." Remember from the previous note that contacts are only mail-enabled objects because they possess at least one email address.

***TIP:** Creating a contact does not mean you have to immediately associate an email address with it. You can always add email addresses to contacts at a later point in time.*

***NOTE:** The ADC is primarily used more for "synchronization" than "migration." This distinction is blurred because the ADC is always discussed in migration strategies. Simply put, the task of the ADC is to replicate directory information between an Exchange 5.5 directory and an Exchange 2000 AD structure.*

Other objects that require some planning include distribution lists, recipient containers, and address book views. Distribution lists are now incorporated into Windows 2000 security groups and will be discussed in Chapter 5. Exchange 2000 no longer supports recipient containers, they are now included in AD Organizational Unit containers—that is, Exchange 2000 no longer supports recipient containers within the management tools of Exchange 2000. Address book views have become known as *address lists* inside Exchange 2000. Recall that Exchange 5 first introduced this concept of address book views, which allowed an administrator to display various views to Outlook clients. If you had multiple organizations configured on one Exchange 5.5 server, for instance, you could prevent users in one company from displaying the address book of the other organization. Address book views were not very scalable for large enterprises, so Exchange 2000 increased the functionality by giving users more control over how these lists can be created and managed, and how these lists appear to end users. It is best to recreate any address book views that are not migrated to Exchange 2000.

Another product strength for Exchange 2000 lies in the multiple database architecture, previously discussed. Multiple database architecture allows expansion of one logical database across multiple and separate physical drives. This act improves server performance and uses the concept of load balancing and fault tolerance. In previous versions, if one database failed, the entire server would fall prey to dysfunction. If a database fails, the server continues to function. Many people are still disappointed with this feature, however, because recovery is not always successful, and results in slight disruptions in service. However, given all present flaws in the database structure (which are still not corrected following application of SP3), even the competitors are not able to design a database as flexible and scalable as Exchange 2000.

The final product feature to mention here is the new Distributed Configuration Architecture (DCA). We will describe DCA in-depth when discussing front-end/back-end (FE/BE) architectures in Chapter 9 and Chapter 12. This type of design allows you to decouple protocols and services from a single-server scenario to a multiple-server configuration, thereby increasing scalability and performance. If you combine the potential of DCA with the scalability that comes with a multiple-database configuration on one server, you have the potential to host literally dozens of mailbox stores or public folder stores for an extremely large number of users—often estimated in the tens of millions!

The FE/BE Concept

You'll learn much more on FE/BE architectures when we discuss client configurations in Chapter 12, but it's important to visualize the direction that Microsoft is taking with this type of scenario. Imagine a company that produces cars. The company has 3,000 users distributed among various retail outlets and regular corporate users distributed between New York, Georgia, and California. One major WAN link connects the offices in New York, Georgia, and California, but no wide-area link exists to the retail outlets. Various high-speed links also exist between New York, Georgia, and California, but they are not all of equal bandwidth.

Now consider the implications if this company decides to upgrade to Exchange 2000. Should they include Exchange Servers in every retail outlet as well as New York, Georgia, and California? If retail outlets enjoy the same high-speed WAN links as the other offices, then access to a mailbox on Exchange 2000 is not an issue. But for those clients who are using dial-up connections or something similar, the concept of a FE/BE architecture becomes quite appealing.

A FE server does not host or store any user configuration information or mailboxes. It forwards all client access requests to a BE server, which holds user mailboxes or public folder stores. Clients connect to the FE server using OWA or another Internet access protocol. The FE server queries AD to find out which BE server contains the user's respective mailbox information. This separation of duties helps promote load balancing and also increases security for the company, because the FE servers can be placed in a DMZ (Demilitarized Zone), or in front of a firewall. The BE servers can be placed behind a firewall for additional protection. Only offices that connect directly to the Internet require a FE server. Future chapters discuss more detailed configuration issues for FE/BE scenarios.

Microsoft Exchange 2000 Product Challenges

Many bugs have been reported in the initial releases of Exchange 2000. A challenge discovered by beta testers. Microsoft, like many other companies, often considers shipment deadlines more important in some cases than perfect products. Microsoft has actually missed shipment deadlines during initial releases of previous products or SPs. At last count, Microsoft was trying to repair inconsistencies in the Web Store, the Database Architecture, and the DCA. Microsoft also has to convince its established user base to upgrade to Exchange 2000. Some companies are so comfortable with Exchange 5.5 that an immediate upgrade isn't "feasible" or "timely," or even cost-effective. In this case, competitive upgrade pricing or offers for free or discounted training to a company's user base might prove worthwhile.

A major challenge for Microsoft is the pursuit of the ISP market. Most ISPs use some form of Internet Mail Server (such as Sendmail or Sendmail Pro) as their messaging backbone. Microsoft can dominate this market by being extremely competitive with respect to pricing, and can gain competitive advantages because of the enormous user population inherent over the Internet. Exchange 2000 already has an advantage over most messaging systems because of the inclusion of Conferencing Services—both Data Conferencing and Video Conferencing. Most ISPs purchase third-party products to meet this functionality (for instance, Microsoft NetMeeting). Perhaps Microsoft can consider designing a totally revamped version of Exchange 2000 just for ISPs.

Some Final Thoughts

Exchange 2000 has proven itself to be a feature-laden, reliable messaging server. Reviews will nevertheless differ depending on which side of the fence you are standing on. From a vendor point of view, you want increased training and very competitive price points. From a typical user point of view, however, you need time to evaluate the full set of product features. Smaller companies will fail to join the "upgrade bandwagon" as fast as larger organizations or ISPs. The benefits to be realized from upgrading have to far outweigh the costs to upgrade.

You will see in the next chapter how best to plan for a deployment using Exchange 2000. We will be taking a phased approach by using a model used by the Microsoft Solutions Framework Infrastructure Deployment Process (MSF IDP). We offer some best practice guidelines and design rules, which you should follow throughout the rest of this book. Some processes might change, but it's always helpful to have a blueprint or general checklist in place. The following items are not presented in any order but should apply to most situations involving an upgrade or migration to Exchange 2000.

Windows 2000 Guidelines and Planning Points

Because you will administer Exchange 2000 using management tools that come prebundled with Windows 2000 Server or Windows 2000 Advanced Server, it's helpful to know how to access these tools.

The Microsoft Management Console

The MMC is a framework in which you can create administrative tools to manage various services. It provides a common interface for all administrative tools used within Windows 2000 and Exchange 2000. Applications called *snap-ins* are written so that administrators can "plug" them into custom consoles they have created. Exchange 2000 registers any snap-ins in the Windows 2000 Registry. By default, you are given access to the following snap-ins when administering Exchange 2000:

- *Active Directory Users and Computers*—A tool used for recipient creation and management.
- *Exchange Conferencing Services*—A tool used to configure resources such as scheduling meeting rooms or online video conferences.
- *Exchange Folders*—A tool used to configure configurations for public folders.
- *Exchange System Manager*—A tool used to configure your Exchange 2000 organization. This replaces the Exchange Administrator tool used for Exchange 5.5.

The Windows 2000 Topology

Every Exchange 2000 design has to conform to some predetermined Windows 2000 topology or layout. In other words, messages flow through a planned architecture consisting of the following objects:

- *Sites*—A collection of IP address ranges.
- *Domains*—A collection of computers that share one directory database and one collection of Organizational Units.
- *Organizational Units*—A method of delegating administrative authority over the items in a domain. You can move objects between Organizational Units.
- *Directory Objects*—A set of attributes representing a distinct item in a domain, such as a user, computer, or group.

Any Exchange 2000 design plan incorporates administrative models based on the elements in the previous list. An administrative model used to manage recipients can be described as either centralized or delegated. The differences are subtle. *Centralized administration* involves grouping users into Organizational Units and applying Group Policies to the objects. One account has management rights to all Organizational Units. A *decentralized or delegated administration* implies that management rights to specific Organizational Units will be assigned to certain groups.

Exchange 2000 Components

Always remember the multitude of components that are working together to make messaging possible in Exchange 2000. Some components are considered essential and some are considered nonessential as listed here:

- *Information Store*—Also known as **Store.exe**, it can be found in the default directory of *\Exchsrvr\Bin*. It splits all user information into a private mailbox store or a public folder store. These stores can reside in one SG, or in different SGs. In fact, up to five databases can reside in one SG, with up to four SGs being contained on one single server.
- *SMTP*—The native transport protocol used by servers within the same routing group to transfer messages between themselves. SMTP works equally well over high-speed and low-speed connections. SMTP is hosted by the IIS in Windows 2000.
- *SGs*—The unit of organization for the Information Store, a SG is a set of databases that share one common transaction log file. Up to four SGs can exist on a single Exchange 2000 server.
- *System Attendant*—A Windows 2000 Service known as **Mad.exe** that performs maintenance routines for Exchange 2000 and monitors the server's running services and connectors. It is found within the *\Exchsrvr\Bin* directory.

NOTE: *The System Attendant service is needed by other services such as the Information Store. If you shut down the System Attendant service, other services such as the SMTP service will continue to function.*

- *Inetinfo.exe process*—The Inetinfo.exe process hosts the IIS process and also hosts all Internet related protocols such as SMTP and HTTP. This structure allows you to develop Exchange subsystems based on the concept of a "virtual server." The **Inetinfo.exe** process communicates with the WSS through the ExIPC queuing layer.
- *MTA*—The former routing engine for Exchange 5.5, it is now used to route messages using the X.400 protocol to foreign messaging systems. The MTA reserves its own message queues independent of the **Store.exe** process in the *\Exchsrvr\Mtadata* directory path.
- *KM Service*—The KM Service component is used for advanced security in Exchange 2000 and provides encryption and digital signatures. It works with Microsoft's Certificate Server to issue X.509 certificates and encryption keys to users desiring advanced security in their communications.

Component Communication in Exchange 2000

Table 2.1 provides a brief overview of intercomponent communication, which results in message flow within Exchange 2000.

Table 2.1 Intercomponent Communications within Exchange 2000.

Component	Communicates With	Reason
Information Store	AD	Retrieve configuration information
Information Store	MAPI clients	Email notification
Information Store	MTA	Deliver mail to foreign messaging system
System Attendant	AD	Build routing tables
System Attendant	Information Store	Store messages regarding server monitoring
System Attendant	IIS processes	Update the IIS metabase (configuration database)
SMTP service	AD	Expand distribution groups

Using this information, the following list describes a typical messaging scenario to show how a message gets delivered. Details on this process are given in upcoming chapters. Just remember that all messaging systems depend on an underlying transport mechanism and routing engine. For Exchange 2000, this is the SMTP service, which contains an advanced queuing engine. A typical message flow scenario occurs like this:

1. A SMTP system or client connects to another SMTP service and tries to send a message.
2. The SMTP service creates files for every incoming message in the \Exchsrvr\Mailroot directory path. It then confirms receipt of each message and notifies the advanced queuing engine that it's ready for the next step.
3. The advanced queuing engine directs these messages to the Categorizer component, which classifies all recipients. The Categorizer puts all messages into a special precategorizer queue.

NOTE: *If a message needs to be sent to multiple recipients, the Categorizer classifies each intended recipient and creates multiple copies of the message to be sent when ready. The Categorizer can also expand distribution groups and check whether restrictions have been placed on the sender or the recipient of a message. The official name of the Categorizer is PHATCAT.DLL, found in the \Exchsrvr\Bin directory path.*

4. The Categorizer then processes all messages and puts them in appropriate delivery queues for either local delivery or remote delivery. If local delivery, the Information Store holds on to the message before delivering it to the end user. If remote, the SMTP service is responsible for the message at this time.
5. Messages placed in a special destination-domain queue are given to the routing engine, which notifies the SMTP service where to transfer the message. The SMTP service then delivers the message.

6. For local messages, an Information Store driver is used to notify the Information Store about the local delivery queue.

Getting Ready for Deployment

Understanding messaging system architecture does not guarantee that you will correctly design your own Exchange 2000 environment. You must go through a period of strict deployment consideration and planning; otherwise, your well-intentioned messaging infrastructure will not function as desired. Here are some general questions to consider.

- *What kind of management structure do you want in place?*—Do you want centralized or decentralized administration of your servers? Also, do you have adequate in-house support resources available to properly maintain your servers? Taking advantage of directory services within Windows 2000 Server gives you the chance to employ centralized administration.
- *What permissions do you have?*—If you want to install Exchange 2000, you must belong to certain groups from the outset, otherwise installation will surely fail. Assigning proper permissions makes it easy to manage the installation of subsequent Exchange Servers within your organization.
- *What is the topology of your network?*—Remember that Exchange 2000 will be looking for the physical and logical layout of your organization. You will be defining a namespace, an administrative group(s), and a routing group(s). The *namespace* represents your top-level domain name (such as **Microsoft.com**). This is also referred to as your *forest*. Your *administrative groups* define the topology or layout of your company and also the groups of users who can be assigned administrative roles for servers in different parts of the organization. A *routing group* is a physical representation of message flow across a network. Your routing groups can span multiple administrative groups.
- *Will you operate in mixed mode or native mode?*—In simple terms, will your organization consist entirely of Exchange 2000 Servers or a mixture of Exchange 5.5 and Exchange 2000 Servers? This decision becomes important for interoperability reasons. Also, a decision to operate in native mode only is irreversible and permanent.
- *Will you use a front-end/back-end architecture?*—This design is useful if Internet clients (such as OWA or POP3) want to access a remote Exchange 2000 Server using a standard Web browser, and you want to dedicate a special server that will only handle all incoming connections and will redirect these connections to a back-end server that does all the processing. Remember that your primary goal is to introduce load balancing and fault tolerance. Your related goal is to heighten security by placing a firewall or packet-filtering router between the front-end server and the back-end server.

Chapter 3

The Envisioning Stage

If you need an immediate solution to:	*See page:*
Outlining Project Management Steps	88
Performing a Business-Impact Analysis	88
Performing a Risk-Assessment Analysis	89
Evaluating the Cost/Benefit of SLAs	90
Maintaining Recovery Capabilities	90
Designing a Pilot Study	91
Conducting a Gap Analysis	91
Building a Contingency Plan	92
Building a Help Desk Workflow Protocol	93
Constructing a Disaster-Recovery Plan	93
Assessing the Environment	94
Planning Steps Prior to Deployment	94
Planning Public Folders	95
Calculating Hardware Storage Space	95

In Depth

The *envisioning stage* combines the Ways of both Merchant and Technician in defining a business initiative based on needs and current resources. The Exchange Administrator must assess user needs in the context of both current resources and the objectives of corporate management and must "fill the gap" through deployment of the various Exchange Server features and services. Tools and procedures that help chart the progress of the project are critical in achieving success. *Contingency management* is the Way of the Technician; the availability of promised service levels the requirements of the Merchant. The envisioning stage provides the opportunity for the Technician to plan, measure, and deliver these services.

Exchange 2000 Server is both more specialized in function and streamlined in architectural design than previous versions of any application server in the Microsoft family. These functional and structural changes include the following:

- Delivery of enhanced client-side functionality and an emphasis on knowledge management (KM) features rather than communication and control
- An uncoupling of function from structure that changes the way messaging and collaborative services are provided to the user population
- Internal partitioning of protocol, storage, and directory services
- Changes in protocols from Messaging Application Programming Interface (MAPI) and X.400 to the more common Simple Mail Transfer Protocol (SMTP), as well as use of a new, enterprise-wide routing engine

These changes affect how you need to plan and implement Exchange 2000 in an enterprise. Although you still face many similar physical requirements in the server deployment across an organization, you now manage a collection of distributed messaging and collaborative services providing access to knowledge resources. The role as administrator now encompasses areas involved in shaping those distributed services to improve the productivity of your user population.

Exchange 2000 features that must be carefully considered and incorporated into a long-term deployment strategy include the following:

- Long-term impact on TCO (total cost of ownership) with respect to greater platform scalability and easier centralized management
- Enhanced reliability through greater fault-tolerant design
- More extensible workflow services

These specific functional areas of concern impact both server-side and client-side services and infrastructure. Server-side features are totally transparent to the end user. Alternatively, Realtime Collaboration (RTC), Outlook Web Access (OWA) functionality, and the flexibility of Outlook Express will have immediate effects on end-user productivity and support. These factors outweigh initial costs in the deployment, configuration, and support of specialized client-side software.

A Vision Statement

Any business initiative begins with a vision. A vision/scope document identifies a problem and a proposed solution in clear, precise terms. When you describe the proposed solution, you need to define the scope within which your solution will be evaluated. Developing any sort of business initiative involving Information Technology (IT) is not a trivial undertaking even in the comfortable confines of a Small Office/Home Office (SOHO) environment. When you envision a project that leverages the power of Exchange 2000, you must begin not with technology but with the knowledge resources you plan to store within it. Your vision statement outlines plans for mapping your particular business process to an information or knowledge management system.

Corporate Objectives

The interests of decision-making management have the greatest influence on the project planning and deployment processes. Nevertheless, you must carefully research the more mundane needs of users from various segments of your user population. Their work habits and attitude have just as great an influence on the "corporate" culture and the success of an enterprise-wide deployment project as top-level management objectives and goals. A good deployment plan includes "marketing" a few favorite aspects of the new system. Involving representative portions of the user population early in the process will help foster a more receptive "corporate attitude" toward the project and help identify popular system features. You must remember that any change in workflows—an integral part of most deployment plans—no matter how beneficial, will upset people as well as disrupt jobs and procedures in the short term. Though not commonly solicited in a corporate setting, generating goodwill from your users by allowing them to participate in the project helps build a positive "corporate" perception that can keep a project moving forward even in the worst possible scenarios. Count on at least one of your "worst possible scenarios" happening especially over a long-term project.

Divide corporate objectives into three areas:

- *Organizational*—This area covers the policies and standards that achieve corporate objectives, the mission, and the legal and financial aspects of running a corporation or business concern. Corporate objectives come from top-level management or decision-making bodies within an organization.

- *User*—This area includes workflows and daily tasks performed by your workforce. These task lists are often parts of the broader deployment plan and are interdependent; they might require carefully planned execution sequences.
- *Administrative or support*—Planners, who, prior to the deployment project, are responsible for daily support and maintenance, and usually build technical solutions that more readily conform to existing configuration and support requirements. Their solutions tend to be more practical and effective because they will inherit these systems after solutions are brought online.

You must systematically communicate with as many separate groups of users as possible when collecting a comprehensive list of user requirements. In an effort to achieve corporate readiness, you need to understand the "who" before you can understand the "what, when, and how." Your deployment plan begins with the structure of your organization and its corporate objectives. It is also essential for the planning and deployment team to consider technical needs involved in supporting and maintaining any proposed business solution on a regular basis after the installation is completed. The design team also must solicit information as well as support from the various segments of your user population during installation and upon completion of the project. You define management roles according to six scopes responsible for corporate readiness:

- Assessment management pertaining to the identification and prioritization of needs as outlined in the enterprise architecture plan needs to be followed.
- Organizational management ensures that plans reach fruition.
- Education and development management develop support materials that will assist in user training.
- Business management monitors budgetary issues and resource allocation.
- Analysis management supplies various forms of data that pertain to performance benchmarks and project milestones.
- Sponsorship provides the project leaders with credibility and critical support to facilitate decision-making.

Your deployment team planners are expected to devise technical solutions that satisfy these user requirements and leverage new Exchange features such as the use of a person's online presence when using Instant Messaging (IM).

The Problem Statement

A *vision statement* begins with the identification within an enterprise of some business process you want to make more efficient through the combination of software and hardware infrastructure that supports the business model. A vision statement identifies one or more applied processes within your business model that can be automated into a more efficient workflow. You can identify the process flows you want to automate from a variety of perspectives, including the following:

- Functional business model
- Technological architecture
- Data architecture
- Application architecture
- Procedural workflow

The Proposed Solution

After you state the problem, you can propose the solution. Some essential objectives in the deployment of an Exchange organization include the following:

- Provides a single scalable, extensible mail environment that eliminates multiple host-based systems and interoperates with all desktop applications
- Supports seamless directory integration with Single Sign-On (SSO)
- Reduces support and administration, which increases system usability, improves communications and workflow, increases employee productivity, and improves reliability of both local and remote messaging services
- Offers a developmental platform for collaborative business solutions

The Risk Analysis

The problem statement is followed by a proposed solution that carefully details implementation and risk analysis. *Risk* is the probability of suffering some loss in the form of diminished services, quality, reputation, or financial resources. Effective risk management takes into account the business environment within which the project will operate. Many subtle factors such as corporate culture, political pressure, financial concerns, and competitive pressure can put even the simplest project at risk. It is important to realize that an assessment of these organizational influences will affect each project in a different way. You must perform a separate risk analysis for each new project proposal as well as for the same project run at different times. Good risk management also assesses the operating environment continuously to proactively measure any changes to risk.

Strategies to reduce risk include applying resources needed to reduce the risk or the developing workaround solutions to avoid the risk. Changing hardware configurations and modifying system features sometimes reduce risk probabilities. Sometimes, the most prudent strategy is to outsource the responsibility of design, development, or implementation to more experienced personnel or an application service provider.

The Project Scope

Planning is critical to any business initiative. Whereas the project vision statement outlines future goals, the implementation plan and risk analysis require detailed information about how the goal will be achieved. You must define what you want when you are planning. You then can determine what you have, define a way to get where you want to go, and determine the effectiveness of what you have accomplished. By defining what you want, you need to identify all present capabilities (processes, practices, and business principles) and competencies (knowledge, skills, and abilities). These assessments provide a baseline of the current position of your organization. You then need to assess what gaps exist between this current position and some future state in which business goals, processes, and resources are strategically aligned.

A prioritized list of the gaps between current state and future objectives, called a *gap analysis*, prioritizes "shortcomings" or deficiencies that need to be corrected. A change plan, which includes overall strategies and detailed action plans, is completed when all action plans have been implemented and reviewed. The evaluation phase in the life cycle is reached when deployment has transitioned to regular operations.

Planning Guidelines

Following the envisioning stage of a project, you must formulate a plan. The planning process needs to be carried out in a systematic fashion to ensure that all aspects of the plan as it relates to people, property, and process are completed.

Using a Process Model

Microsoft has proposed a series of three frameworks that describe best practices in the preparation of both personnel and business processes in the adoption of new IT. These detailed guiding principles provide structure and models to describe how people, property, and processes can synergistically interact during the deployment of hardware and software business solutions. Each Enterprise Services (ES) framework targets a different aspect of the IT life cycle. The *Microsoft Solutions Framework (MSF)* supports solution design, development, and deployment from a project and team perspective. The *Microsoft Operations Framework (MOF)* supports the maintenance and management of the deployed solution. MOF is a collection of best practices that provides guidance for achieving mission-critical production, system reliability, availability, supportability, and manageability in an IT environment. The *Microsoft Readiness Framework (MRF)* is a collection of best practices that helps assess an organization's readiness to adopt that business solution. Figure 3.1 shows how the MRF phases ensure corporate readiness prior to the implementation of some business initiative.

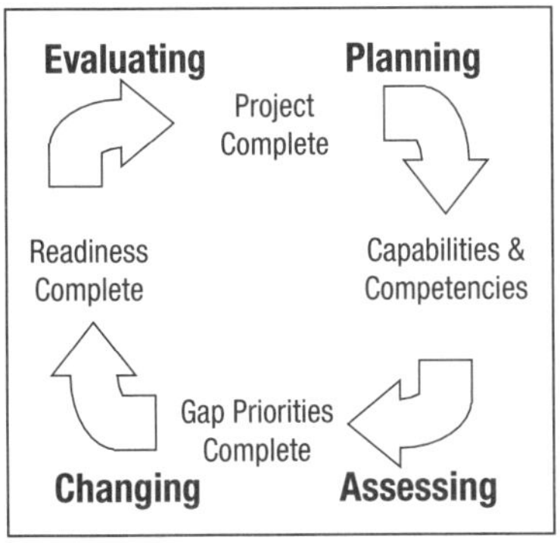

Figure 3.1 The four phases of the MRF.

The first step in developing and deploying some business solution is what MRF calls the *envisioning phase*. The frameworks provide best practices through the entire implementation process, from envisioning a business initiative, through deployment, to daily maintenance and support for its ongoing operations. A critical, but often overlooked, part of any successful deployment plan is in the management of the human side of the business initiative. Planning a deployment project begins not with a particular technology, but with an appraisal of all the projects and business solutions needed to close the gap between the current state of an organization's IT and the perceived required future state that will satisfy all corporate objectives. The deployment project fundamentally deals with people. Critical risk areas that are associated with project failures include problems with sponsorship, corporate culture, behavioral resistance, the human capacity to change, and the vehicle through which the change is implemented. A thorough appraisal of business objectives is typically outlined in an enterprise architecture plan. The human factors are often overlooked, but will have a significant impact on the project's success. The envisioning phase is critical in identifying and bringing together people, process, and property into a synergistic strategic alliance.

From the enterprise architecture plan, we suggest you compile a list of prioritized projects. Consider these projects in terms of interdependencies and financial, operational, and technological impact on the ongoing business concerns. When you envision some business initiative, it is prudent to confirm that your particular project is perceived as high enough on a prioritized list of projects to garner support to carry you through the final implementation and deployment phase. All large-scale corporate projects involving the deployment of any form of business solutions will invariably have political overtones. It is imperative that you begin to build a public relations program for your project early in its life cycle to protect the project and your professional career. Also compile a list of stakeholders or specific individuals that are significantly affected by your proposed business initiative. Identifying a sustaining list of sponsors who can legitimize, sanction, or to help strategically position your project is highly recommended when planning your project. It is important to build a strategic alignment between sponsors of business objectives and your IT solution during the envisioning phase. This alignment should be based on the convergence or overlapping of goals between key dimensions in commerce; business strategies or goals, your proposed application architecture, knowledge resources that include both people and data, and finally, technology architecture that provides the platform for the development, deployment, and operation of the applications.

An Operational Framework

An *Exchange platform* provides fundamental services to any enterprise. No functional difference exists between the levels of reliability and availability critical in the business-to-business (B2B) and business-to-consumer (B2C) world. Those levels expected by the user population of a corporate enterprise. These service demands are categorized as IT service solutions and service management. Service solutions are the functional capabilities provided by the Exchange services. From the perspective of Windows 2000 and .NET services, these service solutions include the following:

- Application hosting
- E-commercial projects
- Messaging
- Knowledge management

As more applications are distributed across a variety of hosts inside and outside the enterprise, envisioning the deployment of any IT project using an operational framework will increase the probability of a successful implementation. IT services management is more concerned with the maintenance, support, and training TCO components. These functions include the following:

- Help Desk or Ongoing Technical Support
- Problem management
- Contingency planning

An operational framework fosters a well-defined service management strategy that provides consistent policies, procedures, standards, and best practices applicable to the entire life cycle of service solutions.

Contingency Management

Contingency management is part of the support phase in which the IT services are successfully running. It focuses on business service reliability, which affects a customer base or user population. When envisioning the distribution of messaging and collaborative services, you must also consider service provisioning, service level management, and the cost of "doing business." Accounting processes are strongly emphasized. The goals for contingency management are defined in terms of the recoverability of services within some projected timeframe defined explicitly or implicitly by a service level agreement (SLA). These minimum requirements depend on the organizational structure, the enterprise topology, the corporate culture, and the strategic direction of business and technological goals as described in the corporate mission statement.

TIP: *A service level agreement defines the service relationship between service provider and consumer both in the outsourcing of IT operation as well as within a corporate structure. It lists the provider's obligations and establishes the scope of services, including performance levels. The SLA contains a statement of purpose, service description, duration of service, installation timetable, and, where appropriate, termination conditions, warranties, indemnities, and limitations of liability. Depending on the nature of the SLA, metrics defining performance such as service availability, mean time to restoration, latency, and technical support response time are ways to determine compliance with the agreement.*

Because the business process is continually changing, contingency management similarly optimizes its plan by identifying current and future risks and proactively planning disaster recovery procedures. The Central Computer and Telecommunications Agency (CCTA) in its IT Information Library (ITIL) provides a comprehensive outline of recommended practices. Microsoft extends the ITIL documentation specifically in the areas of distributed IT environments, application hosting, mobile device computing, and Web-based applications involving e-commerce and transactional systems. All these areas significantly impact the design and management of Exchange 2000 in a .NET environment.

Contingency planning includes identifying any threats to service. Using risk-management principles, countermeasures can be formulated to eliminate vulnerabilities or limit risk. *CERT*, a registered service mark of Carnegie Mellon University, grew out of the computer emergency response team formed when the Defense Advanced Research Projects Agency (DARPA) provided detailed guidelines that address a wide range of these and more security-related issues. It is critical for you to formulate and regularly test all contingency procedures before vulnerabilities are exploited. In addition to reviews, reformulations, and rehearsals of these contingency plans, it's important to train both support personnel and the user population. Contingency management delivers a significant and practical benefit by providing the following:

- Credibility in support of SLAs that impact long-term growth and expansion goals
- Closer relations between service-provider and "client" in terms of structuring solutions according to current client requirements
- More receptive, tolerant corporate culture to future changes in technology

Contingency management is closely integrated with the other Enterprise System frameworks. Change and configuration management are dependent on both system monitoring/measurement and administration. Support teams monitor system events defined as failures of service (incidents) that, in turn, might lead to the triggering of some contingency action plan. The careful selection and distribution of customized instrumentation through; for example, of a MMC (Microsoft Management Console) saved console file (having the extension MSC) is critical in the support of this operational phase. You can create and easily distribute customized tools that are appropriately scoped for a particular support task. Thus, local administrators only see local machines and locally provided services.

A major objective is to maintain continuity of service while simultaneously correcting the failures. Carefully consider the metrics used prior to, during, and following resolution of a service incident because the remaining parts of the organizational system need to continue providing agreed levels of service. Monitoring tools must be carefully selected to provide definitive information without excessive operating system (OS) overhead. Within the MOF, an optimization phase is responsible for managing capacity and availability. Capacity management is concerned with the minimum resource requirements of any single or combination of contingency plans in the event of a service incident. Alternatively, availability planning is concerned with the resources requirements for maintaining typical baseline services through all phases of the disaster predicated on the SLAs. The size of the gap between these two management areas is part of the risk assessment determined by top management and corporate objectives.

TIP: *A redundant array of independent disks (RAID) is a technology used in the reliable storage and retrieval of data. Through the use of multiple disks, input/output (I/O) operations can be overlapped, for fault tolerance, and synchronized, for improved performance, yet appear, to any supporting operating system, as a single logical drive. The use of multiple disks increases mean time between failures (MTBF). Techniques include stripping (RAID 0), where storage areas across physical disks are interleaved and addressed in a sequential order; mirroring (RAID 1, 0+1), where resources are duplicated, and stripping with parity (RAID 5), where both the efficiencies of interleaving and fault tolerance are provided.*

Contingency Countermeasures

You can reduce the risk of a service failure in various ways, including the following:

- Regularly scheduled maintenance and proper prevention methods
- Regular testing and drills in all contingency procedures
- Fault-tolerant hardware component designs such as RAID configurations, alternate power supplies, and redundant hardware components

- Dual service datacenters, dual service access, redundant equipment, load balancing, and round-robin configurations
- Antivirus software and an aggressive policy that maintains the latest virus detection and Trojan prevention updates and procedures

The estimated likelihood that a service failure will occur is an important determination in the prioritization and breadth of a contingency action plan. Risk assessment determines not only if knowledge assets are vulnerable but also the level of threat involved in the exploitation of that vulnerability. The third dimension of importance is the level of impact. Countermeasures must be designed and implemented to manage all three dimensions.

Service Management

The second basic operational concept is service management and the delivery and support of the IT services. With design changes in Exchange 2000 as compared to legacy versions, the potential range of services is greatly enlarged. Service management is closely interrelated to customer-relationship management, which is just as important in a corporation as it is in the retail and e-commercial worlds. Service management is more closely related to the delivery of established levels of service rather than managing a more variable customer base. Performance requirements within an enterprise, for example, are more predictable, which allows you to focus on operational and tactical issues of deployment and implementation. Service management often defines the SLA and thus is the basis for contingency management.

Customer Relationship Management (CRM) is another term used to define many of these methodologies, software, and Web-based systems that organize and support user populations in an enterprise environment. CRM consists of the identification and targeting of key segments in an end-user population that require specialized support, optimized support services systems, and the building of effective consumer-provider relations. Such relations help maintain service level agreements and end-user satisfaction.

Change Management

The capability for businesses to adapt to changes in the marketplace is critical to remain competitive. The corporate technological infrastructure must accommodate similar changes in workflow and business needs. Managing these changes is an important aspect in the reliability and availability of services. A change control process provides a logical framework that clearly identifies how and when some event occurs within the enterprise. Procedural guidelines are critical from a security perspective in identifying legitimate system changes from unauthorized ones brought about by rogue agents. Such a procedural system monitoring changes would allow legitimate system modifications without triggering an alarm and forcing expensive and wasteful risk-assessment analyses. System changes that occur in a controlled environment often are synchronized to occur with the performance of scheduled maintenance procedures. Deploying totally new systems (green-field deployment) as opposed to modifying or upgrading legacy systems is an extreme case of changes with this specific management area and is not common in most corporate settings. You must carefully plan what changes will be implemented or services deployed in regards to maintenance, downtime, and the availability of additional resources in the context of these legacy systems. Best practices in this management area include the following:

- Whenever possible, perform a pilot study prior to deployment and laboratory tests of all upgrades, service packs, and new business systems prior to implementation.
- Test the capacity and availability of the fallback/contingency plan associated with the implementation or deployment project prior to launching the project. A fallback plan must provide a clear back out from the implementation or deployment and a return to full service levels in the event the project fails to achieve its intended objectives.
- Formalize an approval process that provides both reviews and requests for changes. Archive the documentation, which includes project definitions, implementation or deployment objectives, and metrics used for implementation or deployment, risk assessment, and the contingency plan. Risk assessment should cover both the implementation or deployment project and the proposed fallback/contingency plan.
- Perform rolling upgrades and phased deployments rather than doing them all at once.
- Perform upgrades or deployments within one geographical area or site at a time rather than across multiple sites all at once.
- Whenever possible, maintain a separate fallback site as part of a contingency plan.

Ongoing Technical Support Solutions

A critical key to the success of any IT project is end-user support, whether in the form of a Help Desk or integrated into customer relations' management solutions. During the envisioning of a project, you need to plan support and maintenance. The wise general counts the number of troops, the amount of resources, and the methods of communication before going to war. Especially during the deployment of some business initiatives, whether procedural or technical, even a trivial incident has the potential of escalating into a service issue that can create negative publicity and undermine user confidence, or seriously disrupt the delivery of service. Multiple escalation paths are important especially after the implementation or deployment is complete. Turnaround time on technical issues, inquiries, and requests for service is an important metric that should be monitored carefully. If possible, baselines for support and maintenance prior to initiation of the project will provide information about the technical readiness of the user population.

Communication protocols need to filter Help Desk calls into attention categories:

- *Problems*—This call is a situation involving a service failure.
- *Requests*—This call is for an action to be taken to assist in the use of services.
- *Inquiry*—This call is a call topic not filtered as a problem or request.

The communication protocol defines a series of procedures or actions that are triggered by the categorization of a service call. The categories or levels of severity triggering a support response or event should be carefully established within the guidelines of the SLAs, and prioritized to escalate the processing of situations that cause disruption to or threaten the service.

Problem Management

Problem management is positioned outside service management because it is concerned with reducing business losses and ensuring end-user confidence in the reliability and availability of services as defined in the SLA. The service objectives of this management area are to reduce business losses by reducing the impact or recurrence of service disruption. Strong end-user confidence and efficient problem resolution, which reduce service costs, enhance return on an investment in a business initiative or IT project. Problem management provides a standardized methodology that is triggered by causing or threatening to cause some disruption in service. This methodology is designed to minimize the problem's impact as quickly as possible through any means available, including circumvention. Upon successfully completing this action and restoring the service, the accumulated information about the problem is used to eliminate all possibilities of its future occurrence and works particularly well with customer relations management (CRM) solutions.

Problem management provides both problem registration and tracking. Various roles, depending on the organizational structure of the corporation, from technical specialist to customer liaison, are typically empowered to focus on rapid diagnosis and resolution depending on the severity of the service incident. In fact, the severity level not only determines the roles assigned, but also the resolution timeline, escalation path, and end-user response commitment. The severity level drives the incident to some conclusion.

Only after the incident is either resolved or eliminated does the methodology change from a reactive to a proactive mode. All information that was accumulated during the lifetime of the incident is analyzed to help support personnel avoid future occurrences. Proactive activities include the following:

- Systematic analysis to determine root causes
- *Ad hoc* trend analysis of problems
- Service-impact predictions based on problem registration profiles
- Support group performance statistics
- Cost estimates on problem-resolution methodologies

Problem management is part of the delivery of services that any technology-based business initiative provides to its client population. Because the primary performance metric is time to resolution, problem-management staff requires both appropriate tools and sufficient training to handle the scale and complexity of any envisioned business initiative. Problem-management team members must be competent in management, business processes, IT systems, and tools that support assigned projects. Their mastery of these resources will directly impact TCO.

Needs Assessment

Project planning requires methodologies that are systematic and easy to replicate. Because many business initiatives are difficult or impossible to change after installation, a thorough assessment of needs, resources, and administrative infrastructure prevents costly and wasteful mistakes. Even the most complicated systems can be broken down into manageable units with specific milestones to chart progress and evaluate actual versus expected performance. Best practices suggest using a milestone-driven project-management method for department-level or enterprise-scaled deployment of a business solution. You should take advantage of this approach when you must evaluate ongoing progress and take compensatory or corrective action when necessary. Although lab-messaging systems are valuable prototyping tools, performing a pilot study before an enterprise-wide rollout provides benchmarks and raises service issues that are critical in completion of your deployment plan far in advance of the final cutover. Measurement of your progress in the deployment of your project comes from the choices of instrumentation you select or design during the planning stage. Everything from a punch list to sophisticated system-performance monitoring has the potential of providing benchmark, milestone, and quality assurance information. A pilot study provides an opportunity to test your plans before it's too late.

Define Consumer Needs

You must first identify corporate and user needs before formulating an effective deployment strategy within the context of the network operating system (NOS) architecture, Exchange Server features, and management instrumentation. A variety of areas require detailed study, specifically in the deployment of a messaging-and-collaborative platform such as Exchange 2000.

Messaging

Compile information regarding how the population uses basic messaging services. This information should include details about volume estimates, usage frequencies, and message flows inside and outside the enterprise. Where appropriate, divide the organization into intranet, Internet, and extranet (if necessary). Determine the volume of messaging within and across these three logical boundaries, including statistics regarding attachments. Create a low, average, and heavy user profile with characteristic workloads covering different periods of time during the day, week, and month. Create an inventory of any custom applications that are associated with or complementary to the messaging platform such as, for example, virus and Trojan scanning software as well as current virus signature databases. Microsoft Outlook provides complementary services such as scheduling and contact management that generate additional network volume. If you are upgrading an existing system, thoroughly test these applications with the new version of software prior to deployment. Test the copies of all local data stores to confirm that backup copies can be restored. Determine the location of the primary storage site for all messaging. Collect security information that includes access rights, the use of encryption and digital signing, the levels of encryption, and the storage location of security credentials.

Other Exchange Services

Determine the need for remote access, video/audio conferencing, instant messaging (IM), or Chat Services within the organization. In view of additional storage overhead that some of these services may require, it may be more cost-effective to outsource these services to a third party, such as MSN, especially for IM. Remote access often requires the exposure of public and private folders from outside the enterprise across potentially unsecured communication channels. Remote access covers direct dial-up and Internet-based access to your network. Create a separate plan that describes the special needs of these remote users, including security requirements, placement of dedicated RAS (Remote Access Services) servers, virtual private networks (VPN), and an analysis of traffic patterns.

Other Online Services

Determine the use of all online services such as simple mail, Web-based services, Network News Transfer Protocol (NNTP) services, File Transfer Protocol (FTP) services, list servers (ListServ), Internet Relay Chat (IRC) services, and so on. It is important that you understand the security ramifications of using any of these services. FTP, and especially IRC, within a corporate setting expose an enterprise to increasingly sophisticated forms of threats like Distributed Denial (or Degradation) of Service (DoS) attacks, and penetration by remotely controlled software agents (referred to as zombies) used by crackers to compromise computer systems. Create an inventory of applications used to communicate online. If possible, standardize your user population on the most current stable version of one browser client, and eliminate the need for third-party, Web-based application software. Collect security information that includes access rights, use of encryption and digital signing, levels of encryption, and storage locations of security credentials.

Public Folders

If *public folders* will be used as a form of group discussion, compile information regarding demographics, usage rates, the kinds of published material, and the frequency with which that material will be accessible or change over time. Create a low, average, and heavy user profile with characteristic folder usage (posting) covering different periods of time during the day, week, and month. This profile should include security access to top-level folders and subfolders, and whether or not these individuals can create folders. Determine whether public folders are accessible from outside the enterprise through, for example, Internet newsgroups.

Assessing Current Resources and Infrastructure

Server sizing is a fundamental part of the design and planning process. You must consider scalability along both a horizontal and vertical dimension. *Horizontal scalability* deals with adding additional servers to deliver the same set of services, load balancing, and hardware solutions, such as clustering. *Vertical scalability* is concerned with configuring a single machine to deliver several different messaging and collaboration components for a broader range of services. Microsoft Windows clustering and performance optimization through load balancing and front-end/back-end (FE/BE) servers can dramatically affect a messaging system's performance and scalability. As with previous discussions of sizing and deployment of domain controllers (DCs), fault-tolerance issues are also important considerations in your final plans for deployment.

Define Physical Structure

Build a geographic profile of your organization. If appropriate, begin with countries and map the location of each site. Depending on the size of your organization, you might consider using software products that include geographical information to save time. These products typically accommodate inventory information that can be compiled into a database format for generating management reports. Investing in well-designed planning tools at this early stage of the project can save significant time and money later. Best practices also recommend investing in project-management software, even for the simplest of deployments for similar reasons.

Define Your Network Topology

Create a topological map that specifically details the network infrastructure of your enterprise. With respect to the geographical distribution of hardware, compile information about wide area network (WAN) links between various sites that includes bandwidth statistics down to the network segment level. *Available bandwidth* is defined as the amount of bandwidth not consumed during average network activity. Best practices recommend the regular collection of baseline information to determine the most current estimates of this average activity. Although the frequency of peak values is important information, it doesn't represent average network bandwidth consumption. Nevertheless, carefully document the frequency and characteristics of these peak values as a valuable benchmark and for future analysis:

- Compile information regarding network segment size in terms of number of servers, hubs, and physical boundaries. Include information about the physical security and physical infrastructure. Determine the types of media access. Inventory information about hubs and switches should include current usage and maximum capacity as well as on-site replacement hardware.
- Compile statistics regarding the segment bandwidth, including current usage levels; maximum levels; and the occurrence of daily, weekly, or monthly peaks.
- Create a specification that details how the segment is connected to other segments. Compile similar bandwidth information across these connections.

It is imperative that you clearly define site boundaries, site connections, and server deployment. Compile contact information of all key personnel at the site and include it with the analysis. Where possible, collect IP (Internet Protocol) address and subnet information as well as the location of DNS (Domain Name System) and DHCP (Dynamic Host Configuration Protocol) servers and proxies.

When defining your network and deploying new technologies, your plan can include the consolidation or optimization of a variety of areas, including the following:

- Routing group definitions
- Number and placement of servers
- Message routing
- Directory replication
- Public folder access and replication

Defining Your Software Environment

When planning server deployment, you should carefully consider both server names and function. Create an inventory of all application-server software, including license and version information. Determine the number of users accessing each of these servers by application. Create a profile of low, average, and heavy user that details frequency and length of access, the operating systems and software on the client machines, security levels, and the kinds of tasks the user performs.

Defining the Enterprise Model

When assessing current resources, you need to document the Windows 2000 networking model. Compile logical information regarding the number of domains and their relationships to one another. Your Exchange organization relies on the efficient operation of this logical layer. Compile information that includes the following:

- Server names, specific naming conventions, and key administrative personnel
- Categorized domains by function, organizational role, or user characteristics
- Statistics about user accounts, special resources, and geographical boundaries
- Information about trust relationships, including estimations of traffic volume

Defining Administrative Needs

Changes in the Windows 2000 architecture have merged many administrative roles. Because Exchange 2000 makes extensive use of Active Directory (AD) directory services, in small organizations the same person typically administers both the messaging and network systems. When planning administrative needs, consider the following specific functional management areas:

- *User management*—The same GUI interface manages both user and mailbox administration.
- *Routing*—The administrative model separates routing from administrative topologies. Group policies used for permission management can be applied to administrative groups independent from the routing groups that determine message flow. This management area includes the definition and administration of both administrative and routing groups, connectors, and permission management.
- *Public folders*—This area is important from a collaborative perspective and has grown more complex when compared to legacy versions of Exchange. Public folders can be managed from a central role or be delegated to a user with specific responsibility for a public folder tree.
- *Collaboration*—Best practices recommend designating a separate administrative group to manage the technical areas of RTC services, which include Chat Services, conferencing, and IM.

Planning Deployment

The compilation of user needs, current resources, and administrative needs completes the first step in the planning of a deployment project. Because Exchange organizations are best considered from an enterprise perspective, you should develop your implementation from the top conceptual levels of your organization down to the specific hardware platform that will support the messaging and collaborative functions.

Design an Organizational Plan

Organizational planning involves determining the number and boundaries of both administrative and routing groups. After they are defined, you need to determine the messaging links that connect them. Following the planning of these groups and the determination of appropriate connectors, you can proceed to plan public folders, and the placement of *gateways*, a server that is configured with a connector to some foreign mail system. When you install the first Exchange Server on a production platform, make certain your organization name is appropriate within the context of your corporate objectives and organization. SMTP uses the organization and routing group names to construct email addresses for the Internet. Changing an organization name after installation is not a recommended practice.

Naming conventions and addressing is a major consideration when you establish objects in your organization. These names are the addresses used by external messaging systems to send messages to your user population. Exchange 2000 maintains a separate address space for each type of messaging system to which it has a connection.

Design the Hardware Infrastructure

Following the logical planning of the organization and the determination of its routing structure, you need to plan the deployment of your hardware. Just as you can optimize a Windows NT or Windows 2000 Server configuration to handle the characteristic workload of a DC, Exchange Servers need to support characteristic application workloads and unique server-to-server interactions. Exchange 2000 organizations must support both horizontal and vertical scalability. Any single Server in a messaging system might need to work with other servers supporting similar functions to balance service loads. This is horizontal scalability. It must also vertically support other functional components, such as the Web Storage System (WSS), mail connectors, and the Message Transfer Agent (MTA) if it functions as the only Exchange Server in its own site.

Planning Server Deployment

The Exchange 2000 platform is actually comprised of many server types that can perform specific management functions in isolation or in association with other servers online in the same network subnet or physically contiguous site. Depending on the size of your messaging and collaboration system and your budget, you might independently deploy many different types of servers to maximize performance, including the following:

- *Mailbox servers*—These servers are dedicated message stores that hold and provide access to messaging data through a variety of protocols, such as MAPI, HTTP (Hypertext Transfer Protocol), IMAP4 (Internet Message Access Protocol 4), or POP3 (Post Office Protocol 3).
- *Public folder servers*—These servers provide public Information Stores to clients using the MAPI, HTTP, HTTPDAV (HTTP Distributed Authoring and Versioning), WebDAV (Web Distributed Authoring and Versioning), or IMAP4 protocols.
- *Connector servers*—These servers specifically perform a mail transfer function that runs one or more specialized connector types, such as X.400, SMTP, Lotus Notes, or Novell GroupWise. You typically install these connectors to support existing foreign or legacy systems so that, where necessary, the servers can run as a dedicated service.
- *FE servers*—These servers optimize performance and simplify administration by providing centralized access to all clients. Service requests are consolidated and redirected to BE servers, where data stores are handled as a dedicated service. Partitioning services provides greater opportunity to optimize the host machine's functions.
- *SAN (Storage Area Network)*—Though not a server, a SAN is another technology that plays a server-side role in fault-tolerant data storage supporting disk mirroring, data migration, and data sharing. This special-purpose subnetwork provides a high-speed connection between various data storage devices and any data server supporting large user populations. It can be included either within the intranet or remotely in some distant location, for additional security and contingency planning. Often, remote sites are used exclusively for backup and archival storage. If located outside a network, connections to the SAN will most likely use wide area carrier technologies, such as Asynchronous Transfer Mode (ATM) or Synchronous Optical Network (SONET).
- RTC servers are made up of the following:
  - *Data conferencing servers*—Exchange Data Conferencing Service (DCS), running on these dedicated machines, delivers online text-based conference, chat, and application and file sharing services.
  - *Video conferencing servers*—Exchange Video Conferencing Service (VCS), along with DCS, are conference technologies. VCS allows users to manage multiuser video and audio conferencing services.

- *IM Servers*—These servers run the IM Service as either a home server that hosts users or an IM router that manages routing requests.
- *IRC Servers*—These dedicated servers run the Chat or IRC Service.

To optimize the performance of any of these servers, deploy servers so that each messaging and collaboration component service operates on its own dedicated platform wherever possible. Distributing services simplifies software configuration and interoperability issues. Dedicating one server to one Exchange 2000 Service component simplifies support and maintenance as well as improves stability, reliability, and horizontal scalability. For optimal AD performance, operate physically separate, dedicated DCs and GC (Global Catalog) Servers. Because Outlook clients and Exchange 2000 Server components depend on access to the GC, we strongly discourage installing Exchange Server servers that provide DC services. Corporate objectives and financial resources, however, should always temper such recommendations.

Configuration Options: Clusters

Windows 2000 provides both a scalable and reliable OS platform for mission-critical services such as application, storage, printing, directory, and security. Messaging and collaboration, although architecturally separate from the NOS, have also become fundamental services that drive mission-critical operations. Messaging-system failures quickly impact the user population, immediately disrupt workflows, and generate lost revenue. SLAs now even minimize scheduled downtime for maintenance. When e-commerce systems exposed to public networks are involved, any downtime is unacceptable.

Concepts of fault tolerance have been replaced by five 9 or 99.99999 percent reliability in system accessibility and uptime performance. Hardware solutions, such as clustering, achieve these levels of service by eliminating single points of hardware failure by grouping independent servers. Clustering Services is a technology that increases system availability by reducing the chance that any single system component can halt system services. Windows 2000 cluster connects two or more server platforms together in a physical resource group; this managed group supports one Virtual Server. Windows 2000 Advanced Server supports two-node active/active clustering, where each node shares part of the processing at all times. Through redundancy, a server cluster supports a common disk subsystem that behaves like a single, network-addressable virtual computer. The Virtual Server's configuration reflects each of the individual servers in the cluster. At any one instant, one server in the cluster is the active node while the other nodes passively stand by for service. From an end-user perspective, the virtual server, hosting (for example) mailboxes, is accessible at all times. Because the disk subsystem is common to all clustered servers, the location of the active node among the clustered machines at any given time is irrelevant to delivery of services. Clustering Services, which runs only on Advanced Server and Datacenter Server, controls all cluster activity. The current version of Windows 2000 Advanced Server runs two nodes. Exchange Server can use the active/active implementation of clustering. Not all the components are currently supported in a clustered environment.

Configuration Options: Client Access

An advantage of using Exchange 2000 is that it's accessible from a wide range of client software. Microsoft maintained backward compatibility with previous versions of Exchange, so deploying an Exchange 2000 Server does not necessarily require simultaneously upgrading client software or retraining the user population on software. Client accessibility contributes greatly to lowering TCO when you are planning to deploy an Exchange 2000 system. Thus, all client software that accesses Exchange messaging services is compatible with Exchange 2000.

Outlook 2000, of course, takes full advantage of the design changes in Exchange 2000. For example, Outlook 2000 is currently the only client that can access the GC directly; legacy Outlook clients access Exchange Server, which relays address list information. Furthermore, Outlook 2000 is more functionally integrated with Office 2000 and AD directory services than with the monolithic structure of legacy versions of Exchange. It thus provides more collaborative support through extensibility of customized digital dashboards, filtered offline synchronized data storage, and personal management features than either legacy Office or Exchange versions.

Exchange 2000 has significantly enhanced the OWA client feature as well. You access data resources in almost the same way as in other Office products when you view data stores through Internet Explorer (IE) 5, except that you are on the Internet and using a browser client. Microsoft has designed OWA so that browser access and features such as drag-and-drop object manipulation, toolbar operations, menus, and rich-text Hypertext Markup Language (HTML) editing function exactly the way they do in a local Office application. Thus, deployment plans are simplified because the user population more than likely already uses client software such as Outlook or IE. The most important information you need to collect concerns the version of client software and any special client configuration necessary to access specialized services.

Determining Pilot Study Objectives

Within the context of project management, a pilot study represents the most important piece of management instrumentation. Exchange 2000 is a multifaceted, development platform that messaging and collaborative business solutions are based on. Choices of featured services, their proper configuration in an existing network capacity, and their collective synergism in provided solutions to corporate objectives will determine the overall TCO. In a carefully scaled model, a well-designed pilot study can confirm the following:

- Whether your choices of services are optimally mixed to support your targeted user population
- Whether your systems provide acceptable risk-tolerance levels
- The degree of interoperation and dependencies
- Operational overhead

The cost-benefit analysis of running a pilot study must be thoughtfully conducted and not arbitrarily dismissed due to preconceived notions or perceived budgetary constraints.

The Microsoft BackOffice Resource Kit contains another valuable tool called Load Simulator (**Loadsim.exe**). This utility simulates the load placed on a server by specified numbers of users sending and receiving characteristic workloads over extended periods of time. Use the profiles you compiled during your initial analysis of your users' needs to make the best use of this tool.

The *envisioning phase* charts the scope of the business initiative in terms of differences between the current state of people, process, and property within the enterprise and where corporate objectives require the enterprise to be. We propose planning guidelines using a variety of models that provide assessment and contingency management tools to bridge the gap and achieve the objectives. At the conclusion of this phase, the Technician can now follow the choreographed steps in delivering the promises of the corporate goals.

Immediate Solutions

Outlining Project Management Steps

Corporate strategy involves establishing corporate objectives and determining user needs. Project management proceeds in a series of defined steps, which include the following:

- *Design/development life cycles*—Includes a functional design phase, an architectural design phase, an implementation phase, a pilot study (if possible), and cutover
- *Design issues*—Includes source/revision controls, coding standards, and naming conventions
- *Test assessment/quality control*—Includes metrics that define and monitor service level agreements
- *Security issues*—Includes database-level security, hardware volatility, concurrent access, user authorization, and security goals

Performing a Business-Impact Analysis

The objective of a business-impact analysis is to quantitatively assess the initial loss in business opportunity, profit, goodwill, or service revenue resulting from a service incident. This analysis also must estimate the speed of escalation of these business losses over a protracted period of time. The business-impact analysis needs to identify the following:

- Critical-mission business processes as defined in either SLAs or internal workflows and procedures
- Categories of corporate damage or loss, including lost income, damaged goodwill and confidence, reimbursement costs, and loss of any competitive advantage within the enterprise or from a public perspective
- Ramifications of the loss in service, such as the different levels of the damage accumulated over time, how the damage escalates within and across systems, and what areas suffer indirect damage over a protracted service failure

Performing a Risk-Assessment Analysis

Information collected by assessing risk provides the basis for the systematic formulation of contingency strategies that optimize risk reduction with the recovery or continuity of services. The contingency plan is a compromise between the amount of investment required to implement the plan and the perceived impact a disaster would have on the corporation. These estimates, however, are subject to constant change and revision. It's important that some systematic method of assessment be performed on a regular basis to ensure that the cost/benefit analysis is valid with respect to provided business services and SLAs. Perform this analysis as follows:

1. Identify all process and/or service components that support mission-critical processes. These processes are defined in operational terms; their interruption would impact some agreed-upon level of service.
2. Estimate the levels of vulnerability at which these identified areas are exposed.
3. Estimate the threat these exposed vulnerabilities present to the identified service if they were compromised or exploited in any way.

NOTE: *An operational definition of* threat *is the perceived likelihood that a service failure will occur.* Vulnerability *is the extent of sustainable damage to the organization if the threat was carried out. Threats are not necessarily defined as malicious; the innocent or careless exposure of confidential information can have major implications on goodwill and corporate morale as well as the perception of a coherent, enforceable corporate security policy. The combination of opportunity, motivation, and knowledge will determine the vulnerability.*

---

4. Estimate and prioritize levels of risk using both quantitative and qualitative data. Often, a subjective assessment is all that's available. When faced with such qualitative data, simplify the categories of your metrics, such as low, medium, and high. A sample assessment of high probability of occurrence might be based on the subjective determination that a service represents a high threat level and is highly vulnerable. These determinations would support the conclusion that a service failure is highly probable.
5. Compile these prioritized services into a risk-measurement table that identifies in a structured and reasonably consistent manner the greatest vulnerabilities in your organization. From this list, suitable countermeasures for the most likely occurrences can be implemented.

Evaluating the Cost/Benefit of SLAs

Determining cost estimates in the maintenance and recovery of service levels during and after a service failure helps determine the compromise between levels of service and levels of reliability and availability. These analyses are best performed in the context of real business scenarios, such as committing a business transaction, or the inability to engage a service related to messaging and collaboration over an extended period of time. The cost/benefit ratio provides a quantitative measure of how critical the reliability/availability of some services are in relation to others. By creating a ranking of associated elements, the impact of varied failures in service can be prioritized in terms of risk and recovery. Metrics that provide the cost-benefit information are the following:

- Cost estimates involved in maintaining contingency action plans over time to provide minimum service levels
- Cost estimates involved in recovery following a service incident with projections of escalation as the service failure continues over extended periods of time
- Cost estimates of the time required for returning to normal service levels as a function of the length and severity of the service incident

Maintaining Recovery Capabilities

To maintain recovery capabilities, perform the following steps:

1. Maintain a rigorous review process of all configuration and logical changes in business workflows on a regular basis by support personnel and representatives of top management.
2. Administer a training program that relates to contingency management for both support staff and end-user personnel.
3. Include the individual participation in all contingency management programs as part of every job description.
4. Conduct regular testing of all contingency and disaster-recovery plans.

Designing a Pilot Study

Given the scope of the potential financial impact an Exchange system deployment can have on enterprise KM, pilot tests should be performed on carefully chosen test architectures that accurately model functional and topological features of the production platform. Server-side functionality includes the following:

- Storage technologies
- Front-end/back end and virtual servers
- Active Directory Connector (ADC)
- Clustering Services
- Outlook Web Access services
- Collaboration Data Objects (CDO) extensibility

Client-side functionality includes the following:

- Data and video conferencing
- Instant Messaging services
- Outlook Web Access services

Conducting a Gap Analysis

The goal of the gap analysis is to determine the difference or gap between where corporate objectives expect capabilities and competencies to be and where they are at the current time. Current levels, revealed through assessment results, are compared to future state metrics established during the planning stage of a project. After the gap is revealed, priorities are established to close the gap. The gap analysis reveals the following:

- Deficiencies in capabilities and competencies between current and future states
- A ranking of the gaps to determine the most effective change planning
- An assessment of project risks if gaps are not closed

The gap analysis provides a compare-and-contrast structure, which organizes the material to make it easier to interpret.

Building a Contingency Plan

A contingency plan should clearly describe the service involved and risks to that service. It should also include some statement explaining the justification for this particular contingency action plan and what conditions trigger its implementation. These facts help members of the deployment team assess whether any unplanned actions subsequently taken are appropriate with respect to the original intentions that the contingency plan is based on. It is important to define the conditions and the point in time when the contingency plan goes into effect. Similarly, the goal of the plan must be described, as well as a metric indicating when that goal is reached. You need to consider metrics that indicate a change in the status of the service incident that might warrant a reassessment of risk and possible changes in the contingency plan. When constructing a contingency plan, your objective is to recover full service levels at possibly an alternative location using replaceable parts with current application software and data. The plan must describe all aspects of the alternative service, including alternative service disruption, restoration of service at the alternative site, and return of service to the original site. This plan needs to include the following:

1. Obtain an estimate of the time needed to restore service from the business-impact analysis. Restoration of service is defined by SLAs. Plans to restore an Exchange 2000 Server should be measure in hours rather than days.
2. Select a suitable alternative location that is separate from the platform on which the original service failure occurred to minimize risk of additional losses. The location of alternative sites might require a minimum distance of separation from other sites.
3. Incorporate a timeline and dependency diagram, such as a Gantt chart, that specifies scope, resources, and milestones. This diagram should contain all complementary services associated with the SLA. When testing these plans, all services should be tested together to maximize the simulation of an actual service failure.

NOTE: *A Gantt chart is a project management tool that uses a horizontal bar chart to graphically display task-related information, typically on a timeline, in the context of a common project or business objective. The horizontal axis usually represents the duration of the project, the vertical axis, a list of tasks (or project scope), and the length of any single horizontal bar, the estimated time some specific task requires in relation to the entire scope of the project.*

4. Ensure that all key personnel have the correct version of this plan and that all aspects of its implementation are understood. Maintain a current distribution list (DL) of this plan, including primary and secondary means of communication so that every member of the DL can contact all the other members of the list.

Building a Help Desk Workflow Protocol

Communication protocols based on the categorization of calls to a Help Desk should be created within the context of a SLA. Events are escalated from support personnel to incident manager to contingency manager. Multiple escalation paths should be established and prioritized to minimize turnaround time on both service support and noncritical inquiry issues. When a call is categorized, the following action plan can be used:

1. Log a call to the Help Desk as a service problem.
2. Based on the categorization, identify the service problem.
3. Support personnel attempt to isolate the identified problem.
4. Depending on the SLA, and based on the number of attempts and the time expended in isolating the problem, assess the problem regarding risk and impact on service. Assign a severity level.
5. Depending on the severity level, collect additional information based on the nature of the problem. From this information, redirect the problem to a specialist or individual empowered to diagnose and resolve or eliminate the problem. Within a problem management workflow, a problem will eventually reach a status of circumvented, resolved, or closed.
6. Retain the log that has tracked the problem for problem-analysis activities.

Constructing a Disaster-Recovery Plan

You should always include members of your technical support team in the planning stages so that any proposed solutions are conceived in a strategic framework compatible with the levels of ongoing support and maintenance. Similarly, when you are planning to deploy a messaging system, you must formulate contingency plans for a critical system failure that occurs either during installation or during daily ongoing operations. In most deployment scenarios, some form of messaging system is already in operation. Migrating recipients to Exchange 2000, even when performed in stages, rarely runs to completion without an unforeseen event disrupting an aspect of service.

The deployment team must carefully consider various disaster scenarios and contingency plans because any migration plan should be conceptualized as a cutover from one system to another, not a less obtrusive redirection of workflows. When you are formulating these contingency plans, it's vital that you estimate realistic downtime. When you are dealing with a mission-critical system, such as a messaging platform, business decisions are based on quantifiable amounts of lost revenue due to disrupted services. You choose alternative plans during a disaster based on these projected recovery times. Rehearsing even parts of a disaster-recovery plan provides more reliable downtime and recovery estimates than listing them as possibilities on a piece of paper. The accuracy of these estimates are critical when you are choosing a proper course of action and want to minimize the loss due to a critical system failure.

Assessing the Environment

Designing an enterprise begins fundamentally with defining the namespace through AD directory services. New Windows 2000 administrative features, such as Organizational Units (OUs), have significantly altered the messaging infrastructure's flexibility as well as the role of trust relationships and replication. Assess the messaging infrastructure in several phases as follows:

***NOTE:** An Organizational Unit is the smallest Active Directory container object that will organize users, groups, and machines primarily to facilitate the delegation of administrative permissions. You can nest OUs in other Organizational Units.*

1. Define required functionality and design goals.
2. Analyze nontechnical needs that complement functional requirements.
3. Compile a detailed implementation plan that achieves the stated goals.
4. Compose a procedural list of necessary preparatory steps prior to implementation.

Planning Steps Prior to Deployment

Key issues that need to be systematically addressed prior to deployment include the following:

- *Formal action plan*—Create a formal, well-documented, and perhaps even partially tested disaster plan designed especially for this deployment project.
- *Chain of command*—Assign key personnel responsible for deciding when contingency plans need to be executed and in what order they need to be performed.
- *Ancillary support procedures*—Confirm that all backup and support systems have been tested before actual deployment.

Planning Public Folders

Exchange 2000 public folders serve as platforms for discussion groups, custom applications, and public document collections. You can configure multiple public folder trees that each contain any number of public subfolders. Folders in the root level of a public folder are referred to as *top-level folders*. When a user creates a top-level folder, it is placed on the owner's home server. *Lower-level folders* are placed on the same server as the folder in which they are created. The contents of a public folder can be stored on a single server or replicated to other servers in the routing group and organization. When planning public folders, perform the following steps:

- Determine the organization of the public folders in terms of the number of public folder trees. Based on the organizational needs and administrative resources, individual departments in an organization can manage their own trees. Alternatively, an organization can have a single tree beneath which all department folders can be placed.
- Determine whether to distribute public folders on multiple servers throughout your routing group or a centrally located server.
- You need to decide based on use, organization structure, or security objectives whether it is appropriate to dedicate a specific server to exclusively support public folders by having them only contain public folder stores. Alternatively, a server can contain both private and public stores.
- Compile statistics regarding the use of public folders for collaborative purposes, application distribution, or other specific and perhaps local departmental purposes.

Calculating Hardware Storage Space

Consider the following factors when planning disk space:

- Windows 2000 Advanced Server requires about 750MB, depending on the options installed.
- The standard Exchange 2000 Server installation requires 200MB.
- You need to add the number of user mailboxes and public folders. Calculate the amount of additional space each of these objects will consume based on your compiled planning information.
- Transaction logs are 5MB each but should always be written to separate hard drives.
- You must plan for additional services including Microsoft SQL Server and Exchange extensions for virus protection.

Chapter 4

Planning the Implementation

If you need an immediate solution to:	*See page:*
Identifying Pre-installation Tasks	125
Determining the Scope of AD Groups	125
Planning a DNS Namespace	126
Planning Naming Contexts	127
Managing the Configuration Container	128
Planning Recipient Management	128
Configuring Recipient Settings	129
Removing Recipient Policy	129
Defining a New Recipient Policy	130
Determining the Scope of Groups	131
Creating Security and Distribution Groups	131
Performing a Foreign Mail System Audit	132

In Depth

Essential functional and structural changes in Exchange 2000 Server that affect your deployment plan include the following:

- Enhanced client-side functionality emphasizing knowledge management (KM) features rather than communication and control
- The separation of the services layer from underlying network structure
- The partitioning and distribution of protocol, storage, and directory services
- The use of Application Programming Interfaces (APIs) such as ActiveX Data Objects (ADOs) and Collaboration Data Objects (CDOs); protocols such as Hypertext Transfer Protocol (HTTP) and Simple Mail Transfer Protocol (SMTP); and standard software interfaces such as a Web browser

These changes affect how you position Exchange 2000 in an enterprise. You still must face many of the same physical requirements in the server deployment across an organization as you were with legacy products. You now, however, can manage a more flexible, scalable, and extensible collection of distributed messaging and collaborative service layers providing access to knowledge resources. Your administrative role now encompasses areas more commonly considered project management and application testing for shaping those distributed services into customized solutions that improve productivity to the user population.

As mentioned in Chapter 3, you can use the Microsoft Readiness Framework (MRF) to help assess your organization's readiness to adopt your business solution. The first step in formulating the deployment plan is the envisioning phase. After envisioning a business initiative, you use a phased approach to design the business solution, deploy the business solution, manage personnel, and measure progress.

A Project Management Methodology

Having identified corporate and user needs, we suggest using a milestone-driven, project management methodology when deploying a business solution for a department or enterprise. It is important to evaluate progress in order to apply compensatory or corrective action when necessary. A pilot study prior to an enterprise-wide rollout provides critical information before you begin your deployment plan. Measure progress with everything from a punch list to system-performance monitoring. A pilot study provides both the opportunity to test your plans as well as refine estimates of task duration and feasibility before it's too late.

We chose a project management approach because we need to formalize a way to manage resources and track progress. The management methodology should be based on milestones to clearly mark the inception and completion of tasks, and should be driven by risk, so that the most critical, high-risk tasks are performed first. This way, you complete tasks that might have exposed the project to failure before wasting additional resources and time. Alternatively, you give yourself more time to correct or modify a project plan to work through fatal flaws in the design.

Make your timeline and cost estimates from the bottom up; in other words, the person projecting these variables is the person responsible for delivering products or services. Bottom-up estimations produce more accurate scheduling and resource commitment information because they are derived from the most accurate sources of "real-world" information.

Finally, you need to instill a zero-defect mentality in your project team with the goal to reach some point of closure as often as possible. This translates into independent, testable tasks leading to specific milestones rather than parallel deployment streams that only synchronize periodically at each milestone. In terms of hardware or software deployment, using quantitative benchmarks to provide smoke tests—especially as an end-of-day procedure—offers quality assurance and helps maintain production schedules. A pilot study also provides valuable information for designing the smoke tests that lead to project milestones.

Planning Objectives

Your deployment plan begins with corporate objectives and the structure of your organization. *Organizational readiness* refers to the condition in which an enterprise is prepared not just for a successful deployment of technology, but for full adoption and realization of all the features that technology has been envisioned to provide to the user population. It also includes both hardware and software aspects in the growing collateral use of technology with respect to the proposed solution. Readiness must include people, process, and property. Although it might be perceived as additional overhead during its initial installation, the deployment of, for example, Terminal Services will reduce long-term support and maintenance costs. You need to address these and other support and maintenance issues with your various support teams and deployment group during the design phase of an enterprise service-providing platform deployment.

Although maintenance and support are key considerations when formulating a deployment plan, other important issues include the capacity and growth of the underlying business concern, user population, and the network infrastructure, sometimes referred to as the *physical plant* or datacenter. Although difficult to anticipate, new and changing technology could also impact the delivery of mission-critical services to your enterprise. In view of the initial capital investment in most hardware and software enterprise systems, Information Technology (IT) is usually the most resistant to changes in equipment versions, revisions in software, and manufacturers prior to the realization of some return on investment (ROI). The need to achieve a ROI, especially from an accounting perspective, often works against the introduction of new, more effective technologies and the retirement of legacy IT systems. It is thus likely you will encounter legacy messaging platforms like Exchange 5.5 somewhere in your organization or over the short term among clients. These systems continue to deliver reliable mission-critical services.

The human and financial pain that was involved in the installation of legacy systems often discourages migration to more modern systems, especially with the profound design changes in Windows 2000 and its .NET Servers. In fact, embedded legacy systems will most likely support capacity and growth for some time to come. Similarly, consolidating foreign systems under a common directory system or migrating foreign systems to Exchange 2000 also complicates installation and must be considered a part of many typical installations. You must carefully balance corporate objectives and the "promise" of new technologies with the need for reliability, stability, and well-practiced support and maintenance methodologies gained from working with "known" evils and network system eccentricities.

The deployment project should be perceived as a process of transforming a currently disjointed state—in which the dimensions of process, property, and people do not fully or efficiently achieve corporate objectives—into a future state of readiness. All three dimensions would at that point be aligned and synergistically interact for the maximum advantage. Before formulating a deployment design, you should thoroughly educate your staff. You should ensure that your deployment team has some formal training in Windows 2000, Exchange 2000, and any associated .NET application Servers before formalizing any plans. The staff must also be familiar with the way your organization has implemented Windows 2000, including the following:

- DNS (Domain Name System) organization
- Deployment of domain controllers (DCs) and Global Catalog Servers (GCs)
- Deployment of Operation Master (Flexible Single Master Operations, FSMO) servers
- Active Directory (AD) replication topology
- Replication between AD and Exchange Directory Services

- Software applications used in your organization
- Upgrade procedures from Windows NT 4 to Windows 2000

Your deployment project must provide a structured, yet flexible, approach to specific organization changes caused by improved messaging and collaborative services. You are installing more than a "mail system." Exchange 2000 topology varies, of course, depending on corporate objectives and the current configuration of the network infrastructure (such as the distribution of GC Servers, proximity of DCs to an installed Exchange Server, and so on). Furthermore, rarely will you start from scratch in what is called a "green-field" deployment scenario; most projects involve a combination of Exchange 2000 and legacy Microsoft servers, as well as possible interaction with foreign messaging systems such as Novell GroupWise and Lotus Notes. Here again, the enlistment of users from all levels of IT involvement, as well as support from stakeholders and sponsorship from management, must be systematically nurtured through all phases of the project's life cycle.

Perceived Benefits

A successful deployment strategy of any application service depends on the design of an enterprise's underlying network structure, specifically the infrastructure below the API. Application services also depend on directory and other core services provided by the network operating system (NOS). The design of Microsoft .NET Servers has so thoroughly integrated application services with these core services that a carefully balanced synergy among all three components—Exchange 2000, Windows 2000, and AD—is critical. You need to identify critical dependencies in your enterprise to build an effective plan that provides a benchmark you can measure your progress against. These API-related dependencies often functionally overlap. Although functional relationships do not necessarily reflect physical deployment in a Windows 2000 enterprise, a site topology alternatively delineates how areas interconnect. The infrastructure forms the plumbing through which all system traffic flows. Unlike legacy systems, Exchange 2000 administration cuts vertically through these functional layers rather than horizontally on top of or below a distributed services layer in the API. The effectiveness of a messaging and collaborative system lies in this synergy between Microsoft's Application Programming Interface and Transport Driver Interface (TDI). This is seen, for example, in a security implemented as Internet Protocol Security (or IPSec), as well as with the underlying Windows 2000 native domains, their controllers, and hierarchical positioning within an enterprise.

One expects to simplify the infrastructure when moving to Windows 2000 by eliminating resource domains, reducing master account domains, and the need for DCs. Further reduction in hardware inventory is possible with the migration of servers to more reliable, fault-tolerant Windows 2000 clusters. Uncoupling functional needs from physical topology supports a more flexible organizational infrastructure and simplifies any immediate or long-term changes, such as mergers or acquisitions, with minimal need for physical design changes. The maintenance and support costs for servers are dramatically reduced. Windows 2000 management instrumentation such as the snap-in architecture of the Microsoft Management Console (MMC) is specifically designed for enterprise-wide support. Exchange 2000 and the other .NET servers leverage all these NOS features. The greatest impact to Total Cost of Ownership (TCO) is in the delivery of more robust and stable services to the user population.

Determining Pilot Study Objectives

In project management, a pilot study is the most important instrument for evaluating the three components mentioned previously—Exchange 2000, Windows 2000, and AD—for your deployment plan. Exchange 2000 is a multifaceted, development platform that messaging and collaborative business solutions are based on. Choices of featured services, their proper configuration in an existing network capacity, and their collective synergism in provided solutions to corporate objectives determine the overall TCO. Remember, in a carefully scaled model, a well-designed pilot study can confirm the following:

- Whether your choices of services are optimally mixed to support your targeted user population
- Whether your systems provide acceptable risk-tolerance levels
- The degree of interoperation and dependencies
- Operational overhead

The cost/benefit analysis of running a pilot study must be thoughtfully conducted and not arbitrarily dismissed due to preconceived notions or perceived budgetary constraints.

Carefully consider the long-term impact on TCO of most Exchange 2000 features and issues of reliability through greater fault-tolerant design and extensible workflows. Specific functional areas within Exchange impact both server-side and client-side services and infrastructure. Remember that server-side features are totally transparent to the end user. Given the scope of potential financial impact an Exchange 2000 system deployment can have on enterprise KM, you should always recommend pilot tests to evaluate how your project plans will affect the production platform. A realistic pilot study entails more than just building a "lab" to familiarize yourself and your deployment team with the various features of Exchange 2000. In fact, a significant amount of preparation and effort should be invested in a pilot study. It should be perceived as a rehearsal for the actual deployment and provide a real-world test of specifications, methodology, and envisioned benefits to the corporation. The pilot study should incorporate representative versions of hardware; a "simulation" of the network and routing topology; legacy and foreign systems if appropriate; and representative samplings of data, software applications, and desktop environments that will be encountered during the actual deployment phase. You need to test both server-side and client-side functionality. A common approach is to shadow the old system during a final testing phase with the new system running as a parallel installation alongside the legacy system. Isolated architectural features that need to be tested for server-side functionality include the following:

- Storage technologies
- Front end/back end (FE/BE) and virtual servers
- Active Directory Connector (ADC)
- Windows 2000 Clustering
- OWA (Outlook Web Access) and the Web Store
- CDO extensibility

Client-side functionality involves a different set of features, including data and video conferencing, Instant Messaging (IM) service and OWA support, as well as a different set of support, maintenance tools, and deployment plans.

Implementing the Plan

You assess a messaging infrastructure by identifying required functionality, determining nontechnical needs, and constructing a detailed action plan that will achieve the stated goals. The second phase of the Microsoft Enterprise Services Framework begins the actual planning of the project, starting with definitions and the determination of project scope. The various steps involve the following:

- Defining a namespace by establishing naming conventions and organizational structures
- Charting the organizational topology that best supports administrative areas with common permissions and access needs
- Drawing the actual network topology
- Creating the first domain in the enterprise
- Building trees and trusts when deploying additional domains

Windows 2000, especially in the separation of function from structure, is different from the legacy Windows NT 4 operating system (OS). In a monolithic service environment such as Exchange 5.5 and SQL Server 7, instrumentation was predictable and easy to standardize. Windows 2000 uses extensible tools such as the MMC to accommodate a broader, more eclectic suite of tools. As an Exchange

2000 administrator, you can use either the Exchange System Manager MMC snap-in or fashion your own management console to personalize administrative choices. Make certain you have properly designed tools before you begin a deployment project. The following management areas need to be monitored:

- *Directory services*—The AD-related MMC snap-ins—AD Users and Computers, AD Domains and Trusts, and AD Sites and Services—are critical tools that monitor AD directory services, including recipient management, organizational design, Group Policy, replication, and synchronization among stores that provide the directory services. Recipient management includes creating user, contact, and group accounts as well as mailboxes, address lists, and special features such as IM.
- *Transportation/protocol services*—Tools such as Internet Services Manager, the DNS console, and Exchange System Manager support network management. Functional areas include designing and deploying transport, communication, and name-resolution services such as Windows 2000 Dynamic Domain Name System (Dynamic DNS), Dynamic Host Configuration Protocol (DHCP), and Windows Internet Name Service (WINS) for backward compatibility to legacy systems. The designing and managing connectors and routing groups are also critical functions.
- *Storage services*—Exchange System Manager helps manage data stores including both Windows NT File System (NTFS) and Web Store architectures. Fault-tolerant services must protect the integrity of the data and transaction logs, provide disaster-recovery solutions, and include reliable backup and restore strategies.
- *Administrative services*—This huge management area is divided between system management—services supporting the messaging and collaborative platform—and server management—the integrative management of storage groups (SGs) and databases, public folders, connectors, administrative groups, and routing groups. Separating the two areas helps delegate roles and responsibilities. Administrative tools such as Event Viewer, Computer Management and Performance assist in monitoring both process and performance as well as creating and reviewing system service logs. Integrating Exchange 2000 with other services such as Internet Information Server (IIS) is also important, especially since these services provide auditing capabilities through logging features.

Windows 2000 separates functional areas—a physical, server side and a more functional, user management side. Windows 2000 leverages the extensible framework of the MMC graphical user interface (GUI) to administer these various specific functional management areas.

Basic Management Tools

Exchange 2000 can be easily divided into server-management and user-management areas. Server management is implemented through the MMC snap-in System Manager. You handle users, and other recipients such as contacts and groups, by directly manipulating the AD through the AD Users and Computers console. Exchange 2000 automatically installs the System Manager and AD Users and Computers MSC console files only on DCs; their inclusion in the Exchange 2000 installation ensures that an administrator will have access to the AD from any Windows server platform. Other AD-management tools to consider include the following:

- *NTDSUTIL*—This utility performs maintenance by managing the operations master roles (formerly FSMO roles) within a forest; it acts directly on the AD data store ntds.dit. Use this tool to manage Lightweight Directory Access Protocol (LDAP) policies that control how the protocol delivers its directory services within the enterprise. You can configure the memory page size and control the number of entries returned upon submission of an LDAP query. Set this **maxpagesize** property through the **NTDSUTIL** interface.
- *ADSI Edit*—This utility performs low-level AD object manipulation and is similar to the low-level AD editor, LDP.
- *NTBACKUP*—This utility works both locally and online as a backup to create copies of AD and other data stores.
- *ESENTUTIL*—This utility performs low-level operations, such as compression and minor repairs, on Extensible Storage Engine (ESE) data stores, including the AD and the Exchange Information Store.
- *LDIFDE*—This utility, driven with text-based scripts, is an LDAP bulk import/export utility. It can analyze and export information about AD entries to an output text file in LDAP Data Interchange Format (LDIF). This utility processes updates that extend the AD schema to accommodate new and enhanced object attribution when the first Exchange 2000 Server is installed in the forest.

These and other utilities are standard OS tools located in the System32 subdirectory under ***<systemroot>***. ADSI Edit and LDIFDE are part of the Windows 2000 Server Resource Kit and specifically installed in a user-defined directory.

Physical Structure

Exchange 2000 servers must support characteristic application workloads and unique server-to-server interactions and they must be optimized just like a Windows NT or Windows 2000 server configuration to handle the workload. Exchange 2000 organizations must support both horizontal and vertical scalability. Any single server in a messaging system might need to provide horizontal scalability to work with other servers supporting similar functions to balance service loads. The server must also vertically support specific functional management areas, such as the Web Storage System (WSS), mail connectors, and the Message Transfer Agent (MTA) if it functions as the only Exchange 2000 Server in its own site.

Best practices recommend the operation of each messaging and collaboration component service on its own dedicated platform wherever possible. Distributing services simplifies software configuration and interoperability issues. Dedicating one server to one Exchange 2000 service component simplifies support and maintenance as well as improves stability, reliability, and horizontal scalability. Use dedicated DCs and GC Servers for optimal AD performance. The installation of Exchange 2000 servers on the same platform that provides DC services is not recommended because Outlook clients and Exchange 2000 Server components depend on access to the GC at all times. Corporate objectives and financial resources, however, should always determine design selections and decisions.

Application Server Software

Carefully select both the version of Exchange Server software and the hardware platform on which it will be installed. The determination of a hardware platform for the Exchange 2000 Server should be based on the number and class of CPU processor, RAM, disk controllers, number and size of disks, RAID (Redundant Array of Independent Disks) configuration, and backup devices. The location of mission-critical files, such as the sequential transaction logs as compared to randomly accessed message stores, will influence your choice of RAID configurations.

Whether installing a new application server or upgrading from a legacy Exchange Server, hardware standards have significantly changed to accommodate the greater capacity and breadth of the Exchange 2000 feature set. The following are the minimum requirements:

- *Processor*—Any Pentium III available today can handle several hundred users with varying workload characteristics. When possible, select machines with dual processors because Exchange 2000 runs as a multithreaded process that can take advantage of additional CPUs.
- *Memory*—A recommended minimum memory configuration for any Windows 2000 machine should be 256MB. When possible, get as much memory as the budget allows. When running Exchange 2000, dedicate the physical machine for only Exchange-based applications.
- *Hard drive configuration*—Whenever possible, consider hardware RAID and network storage solutions (or storage area networks for large scale operations) when deploying Exchange 2000; disable write-back caching to reduce the risk of corrupted Exchange 2000 databases. Best practices recommend using SCSI (Small Computer System Interface) drives for speed and for security.

If a server fails during a write process with caching enabled, the data stored in the cache is lost. Use separate disks for Exchange 2000 transaction logs; placing them on a single disk can reduce the life span of the disk.

- *Tape drive*—Best practices recommend using SCSI digital linear tape (DLT) drives that can perform backups faster, hold more information than those with competing technologies, and have a longer life cycle.
- *Network interface card (NIC)*—The NIC, running at no less than 100MBps, should be on a separate PCI (Peripheral Component Interconnect) slot rather than integrated on the system board. You avoid replacing the entire motherboard if the NIC fails. Alternatively, dual NIC cards provide either load balancing or failover capability.

After you have determined the appropriate hardware, you must choose the appropriate version of Exchange 2000. Although this book makes all references to Exchange 2000 Enterprise Server, which includes all connectors, support for clustering, message store partitioning, IM service, and connectivity to the exceedingly more expensive Windows 2000 Datacenter Server, two other versions of the application server software also are available:

- *Exchange 2000 Server*—This version meets the needs of most installations and includes both SMTP and X.400 connectors. It is limited to a single 16GB message database. This version also includes IM service.
- *Exchange 2000 Conference Server*—This application server supports online conferencing capabilities.

You will upgrade legacy systems more often than deploy entirely new messaging platforms. It is important to remember that though Exchange 2000 is directly dependent on Windows 2000, it can be deployed in a mixed operating system environment as long as the Active Directory and DNS namespace are running in a reliable manner. You need to carefully document the configuration specifications for the various server platforms in your organization. These platforms include dedicated mailbox and public folder servers, FE/BE servers, and messaging bridgeheads. Determine the location of these hardware platforms in relation to firewalls installed throughout your enterprise. In large installations, this information would typically be determined through coordination with a network or WAN manager. You need to secure licenses for both server and client access. Every network client needs a Client Access License (CAL) to connect to any version of Exchange Server.

Network Infrastructure

Determining network traffic patterns, public folder data usage, and net available bandwidth throughout your enterprise is typically collected during the design stage. After factoring expected growth over three to five years into these statistics, you must determine how Exchange-related services, such as public folder replication and messaging traffic over a 24-hour period, impact network use rates. You must also consider the effect complementary applications have on network capacity. You need to anticipate how collaborative tools will be used throughout your enterprise after they are made available to your user population. Make certain your team has reviewed all relevant documentation related to your organization's use of the TCP/IP (Transmission Control Protocol/Internet Protocol) infrastructure, as well as DNS, DHCP and RAS (Remote Access Services). You also must factor WINS traffic into your statistics in mixed-mode environments.

Connectivity issues, especially when dealing with foreign mail systems, must be carefully researched prior to deployment. Issues of interoperability extend beyond server and client software to the nature of the information that is exchanged. You should also research the use of other forms of messaging such as the Network News Transfer Protocol (NNTP), fax, General Packet Radio Services (GPRS), and voice mail. Compile an inventory of third-party products, hardware, and services such as fax services; virus and network intrusion hardware/software; document-management systems; online, nearline, and offline backup systems; monitoring and performance tools; and systems that support information security. Knowledge resources stored in foreign mail–directory services must be migrated to Exchange 2000 or interoperated in a synchronized enterprise environment.

NOTE: *Data storage can be divided into categories that describe access times and the density of the data store. Online typically connotes stores that are directly connected to a system and provide the fastest access times. This category includes traditional hard disks and other high-cost media with rapid access times. Nearline storage, such as traditional magnetic tape, is less costly and has slower access speeds. It is also typically connected in some way to a network. Offline storage is not connected directly to a system. Microsoft typically refers to online storage as local storage and nearline storage as remote storage.*

Directory Service Components

AD defines the universe of named objects, or *namespace*, and manages identity and permissions within the enterprise. Identity and permission management are two specific management functional areas (SMFAs) that shape the logical structure or namespace of the enterprise. Exchange 2000 or any other application service provider within the enterprise calls upon these two areas to deliver their own service support. Directory services have three basic components:

- *Naming contexts*—These logical constructs define information boundaries or namespaces within a specific database structure.
- *GC Servers*—These specialized DCs are the local source for directory database information. This information is provided through stored copies or replicas of the domain-naming context for each local domain and the surrounding domains; together, they form a forest with a common schema-naming context.

- *Groups*—These administrative units correspond to legacy distributed lists (DLs) but with an added property scope. Administrative groups define either AD security or distribution groups; their scope can include domain local, global, or universal areas of control.

These three components enable an organization's messaging and collaborative platform to function effectively. They must be properly configured to accommodate your corporate objectives, user requirements, and administrative constraints.

AD Logical Structure

AD is a distributed service that scales from a single domain functioning as a classic, legacy domain model to thousands of servers that provide support for a namespace that includes millions of named objects. The logical structure that provides this scalability is based on a new multi-master domain model and a hierarchical namespace. Both concepts have been fundamental designs of the Exchange organizational view from its earliest version. The design concepts and the logical structure they provide have differentiated into an SMFA that has seeped down to lower levels in the NOS itself. The separation of directory services at the application level and their consolidation at the NOS level are typical of other .NET Servers such as SQL 2000. When you consider that both Exchange 2000 and SQL 2000 use AD, advantages to the .NET Server platforms begin the partitioning of services. A single directory design is one example of simplified administration and a single replication mechanism. Partitioning of services within the Windows 2000 enterprise leads to Web-based distributed services and advantages in the use of standardized scripting languages like Extensible Markup Language (XML) handling content between service layers in a platform-independent way. Because XML is an intrinsic part of the .NET Server design, programmatic access to distributed services in Exchange 2000 as well as other .NET Servers is now a growing part of the administrative responsibilities in providing business solutions.

Defining a Namespace

A *namespace* is a logical boundary that defines a collection of uniquely named objects. The capacity of an AD namespace is well beyond a million objects. The collections of named objects are constrained only by their naming convention needed to uniquely identify one member item from another.

This universe of named objects, sometimes called *nodes*, has been catalogued using the DNS, which maps or resolves a unique 32-bit node IP (Internet Protocol) address to a literal character string known as a *Uniform Resource Locator (URL)*. The URL syntax is divided into three components separated by dots or periods. The last component identifies class membership in a vertical tree or hierarchical structure, organized around a set of top-level domains (TLDs) such as .com, .edu,

.org, .net, and .mil. The other two components are the hostname and the registered domain name associated with a TLD class such as **mysite.com**. The first URL component designates the host machine in that specific domain, as in **mymachine.mysite.com**. .tld is used to replace the .com, .net, or .edu in this book as a placeholder for one of these well-known TLD branches. A *fully qualified domain name (FQDN)* is composed of a label or hostname associated with a domain name that carries its .tld tag, as in **www.mydomain.com**. Although DNS with its Unix background is the most common namespace in view of its Internet role, it provides only one service: name resolution of IP node addresses to URLs. Because Microsoft, in designing an enterprise structure, required a more comprehensive management of objects than DNS provides, it adopted AD directory services to manage object identities within a Windows 2000 enterprise.

AD directory services provide identity management to all distributed services in a Windows 2000 enterprise. It uses IP to communicate, so it relies on DNS to resolve AD object names to IP node addresses. AD is a fundamental part of every service layer in the NOS. Through synergy with this centralized directory service, core services, such as Kerberos security, and applied services, such as Exchange 2000 and SQL Server 2000, provide distributed services to a namespace that can literally extend around the earth.

The enterprise, organized into logical subunits of forests, trees, and domains, is composed of AD named objects. A branch of a tree is formed when two domains are linked using two-way, transitive trusts. This is structurally similar to the logical connections found in the legacy Windows NT 4 model. A *forest* is a collection of these domains that share a common object schema, configuration, and GC. Named objects within domains are resolved to, and identified by, unique IP node addresses. All AD objects in the forest use a DNS-style naming convention as well as an AD identifier. The AD name is compatible with NetBIOS (Network Basic Input/Output System), which remains one of the oldest parts of the Windows 2000 NOS. For example, a named object in a domain in New York State provides messaging services. Its NetBIOS name is NYCE2K23, which might translate to Exchange 2000 Server #23 in New York City. The DNS name is **e2k23.ny.mycompany.tld**, which translates to the e2k host in the New York domain of **mycompany**.

Organizational Topology

You need to carefully consider the NetBIOS names of servers. Any naming scheme that clearly distinguishes Exchange 2000 from legacy Exchange 5.5 might be useful in planning future design and deployment. Exchange 5.5 Servers can be mixed with Exchange 2000 Servers and will likely continue to deliver reliable service to an organization for many years to come. Use friendly NetBIOS names that help identify these legacy servers. However, if an essential corporate objective is secure installations, avoid any reference to messaging and collaboration services because an Exchange 2000 Server is a strategic target for network attacks.

Unlike historic workgroups in which broadcasting a name often yielded a response from a host machine, enterprise networks (because of their scale) will fail without name resolution because a consumer will not be able to locate a service provider. When planning a namespace, create a design that efficiently resolves names. Plan your DNS and AD namespace so that naming conventions coexist without conflict and easily scale as the namespaces increase in size and forests grow. Because of the growth of networks on the Internet, specific DNS namespaces often exist through formal Internet registration procedures. You must design your enterprise AD as a separate namespace or subdomain under an existing TLD. Research naming conventions carefully to avoid your selected DNS namespace conflicting with currently registered Internet naming schemes.

TIP: *There are a variety of Internet registrars designated by the Internet Corporate for Assigned Names and Numbers (ICANN), formerly Internet Assigned Numbers Authority (IANA), that provide access to registration information. Programs such as* ***whois*** *and* ***betterwhois*** *(at* ***Betterwhois.com****) help search the registration databases of all accredited registrars in a single search. References within these databases are linked to detailed reports about each registered domain.*

Best practices suggest planning a namespace that systematically builds a layered structure distinguishing external from internal names. Both DNS and AD must coexist within this logical space to avoid naming conflicts, but you keep them separated for security reasons. Information is made available to public access through a variety of domain registration services and external DNS. Secure your internal network namespaces through internal DNS name servers isolated from outside the enterprise and public review.

Domain Topology

AD directory services add several significant features to the DNS originally formulated in the 1970s. Similarly, Microsoft has also extended the features of several field-tested technologies such as public key infrastructure (PKI) and Kerberos authentication protocol in Windows 2000 long available in the Unix environment. PKI enhancements include, for example, support for Transport Layer Security (TLS) and smart cards. The Kerberos feature set now includes auditing, public-key encryption in the authentication process, and permission management at the resource level.

Microsoft has similarly extended the DNS. AD namespace defines the identity of objects through stored security credentials rather than just resolving hostnames to IP addresses. An object's identity includes attributes that empower that object and, when combined with permission management, give it power to function within the enterprise. Identity management depends upon the efficient replication of this directory information across the enterprise. Microsoft considers *Single Sign-On (SSO)* an essential network feature; no matter where a named principal logs on to the network, its identity is authenticated and authorization validated. This accessibility is a major Windows 2000 theme; no matter how an enterprise and domain structure might change, named objects need the capability to use network resources and request services within a scope of authorization.

The domain is the most basic administrative unit in Windows 2000 and Windows NT 4. The *domain* is a collection of resources, managed as an administrative unit, that shares a common identity and access management policy. Its autonomous character and structure in Windows NT 4 has changed in Windows 2000 to better support AD directory services and the scalability of an enterprise compared with a domain. A single domain is a logical unit that can span many physical nodes. AD uses a multi-master controller model rather than the single-master model found in Windows NT 4. Instead of a central or primary directory service provider, all Windows 2000 DCs are equal in functional scope and authority. Any single controller can accept changes to the directory store (DS), propagate those changes, and thus equally share authentication responsibilities and database maintenance. Each controller contains a replica of the domain-naming context to which it belongs as well as a replica of the configuration and schema-naming context for its own forest. Use the AD Installation Wizard (**dcpromo.exe**) to promote any member server to the role of DC. After the wizard creates this controller, a DNS query determines the local configuration for name resolution. If queries are unsuccessful, the wizard configures the local computer to function as a DNS root server.

A Windows NT or Windows 2000 server configuration can be optimized to handle any one of three different workloads: a network file and print server, a dedicated application server, or a DC. These settings include change in cache sizes, buffer space allocation, configuration refreshes, and response latencies across a myriad of SMFAs. A Windows 2000 DC must have a basic server configuration to support directory services and the associated workload characterization. A domain is defined by the physical presence of at least one controller that holds a complete replica of its domain-naming context or directory database. A complete replica of the configuration and schema naming contexts for the forest the domain is located in also defines it. **Dcpromo.exe**, as mentioned earlier, promotes and demotes member servers to or from this functional role.

The First Domain

The first domain running AD establishes the root server of a forest, just as creating the first DC in an installation defines a domain. The forest name is based on the DNS name of this first domain. When you define this first domain, consider two important factors:

- The first domain can never be removed from the forest it defines.
- The hierarchical structure of a domain tree and root server in a forest precludes the possibility of representing other domains above the first domain in a domain tree.

The first domain is the TLD; all subsequent additions to that domain tree are below this top level. A common design strategy is to create a TLD placeholder that exclusively contains only DC machine accounts. This TLD name is registered on the Internet and is freely published. You then create child domains beneath it or separate internal domains that form other domain trees. A placeholder domain provides a unified hierarchical forest structure within which internal domains can be independently brought online without fear of complicating an enterprise design.

Fault tolerance and network load considerations determine sizing additional DCs. A standard design includes at least two DCs for each domain due to the dependence of distributed services such as messaging and collaboration on the Windows 2000 AD architecture. If the domain spans multiple sites, consider the capacity of the wide area network connection to provide failover support. Determine DC deployment from both site topology and baseline information that portrays daily levels of client workload, such as creating new accounts, changing passwords, and monitoring periods of peak authentication activity. DCs within a site share a characteristic "domain controller" workload rather than service loads for application servers or file/print servers.

Adding a Windows 2000 DC to an existing legacy Windows NT 4 domain creates a mixed-mode environment. An AD domain in mixed mode is restricted by the legacy limitations of the Windows NT 4 directory database, which handles up to 40,000 objects. The first Windows 2000 DC assumes the role of primary DC in this single-master state. There is a one-time election, in which all DCs upgrade to Windows 2000, to change to native mode. Irreversible configuration changes that provide scalability needed in an enterprise namespace occur when systems convert to native mode. Windows NT 4 clients access all these changes in the NOS without modification. Best practices recommend that all NOSs operate in native mode to simplify the Exchange 2000 installation process.

Trees and Trust Relationships

Domains in Windows 2000 form special parent-child hierarchical domain trees. The first domain spawns child domains, which thereafter share their DNS name and create a contiguous namespace. **Mycompany.com** as the first domain in a tree has, for example, child domains that all share the same DNS root name. **Child1.mycompany.com** can, in turn, extend the domain tree in a systematic function by spawning the domain **grandchild101.child1.mycompany.com**. Domains within a common forest with different domain names are by definition in different domain trees.

AD simplifies security administration across domains in the same contiguous namespace by unifying the authentication process and eliminating administrative overhead found in the legacy complete trust and master domain models. If a named principal is authenticated in one domain during an SSO, trust relationships between that trusted domain and other trusting domains support the recognition of this authentication without the need for additional validation. Permission management remains a function of individual object-level access control entries (ACEs).

The nature of these trust relationships has changed in Windows 2000 Native mode from early legacy versions; each child domain automatically has a two-way transitive trust relationship established with its parent domain or other domain trees in the forest. A transitive trust is automatically applied through the Kerberos security protocol to all domains. If a named principal is authenticated in a parent domain, access to resources in any child or grandparent domain is automatically made possible without additional administrative overhead. In addition, shortcut trust relationships reduce the number of nodes through which a DC in one domain tree, for example, needs to communicate with a DC in another domain tree. Transitive trusts, in general, unify all domains in an AD forest whether they are children trusting parents or tree-root domains trusting other noncontiguous tree-root domains under the same forest root domain.

No easy way exists to break trusts between domains in the same forest. When designing an AD enterprise, carefully consider granting rights to user accounts and groups within a forest to change that forest. The Exchange Administrators Group is trusted across the forest and is a high-profile target for a security attack through, for example, impersonation. If transitive trust relationships are not acceptable for geographic or political reasons, you should separate business entities into separate forests. You can always create explicit one-way trust relationships among domains in separate forests that provide limited access to resources in specific domains.

AD Logical Components

AD is organized into logical units that enable objects to be partitioned into manageable administrative units by creating a naming context. A specially designated DC, called the GC Server, catalogs and publishes these various contexts throughout the forest. Logical groupings of recipient objects also help organize and facilitate the delivery of directory services for permission management and message distribution.

GC Server

In addition to domain, configuration, and schema data categories, specially designated DCs share a select set of object attributes. This partial listing of object attributes includes the most frequently used search information to facilitate AD querying. A GC of named principals and their select attributes is stored strategically throughout the enterprise so you can efficiently locate an object from anywhere in the entire forest. This availability is critical to AD operations; for example, in a native-mode domain, logons require the lookup of a user principal name (UPN) to process a logon request. A local DC sends a query to a GC Server to determine group membership of a named principal. The local DC must know everything about a user's group memberships to properly manage the permissions of its own resources. Without access to all of a user's security credentials through this lookup service, most logon requests are denied.

Deployment of GC Servers is significantly affected by AD usage, failover, and load distribution. Outlook 2000 directly queries the GC Server for addressing information by searching the GAL. Other clients use Exchange 2000 as a proxy to the GC Server. You need to monitor AD usage after adding an Exchange 2000 Server, because it expands the schema and might significantly increase network consumption. If services are distributed across several servers, you can use Network Monitor to view objects such as LDAP traffic passing between the Exchange 2000 Server and the GC Server. These requests for address book searches and message routing are balanced across the closest GC Servers. Depending on the Exchange 2000 Server configuration, a variety of factors affect storage sizing, including the following:

- The hardware power of your servers
- The number of users
- The volume of messaging
- The kinds of messaging and collaboration objects exchanged among recipients

A domain with Exchange 2000 attributes requires a specialized server that provides *Recipient Update Service (RUS)*. RUS generates the email proxy addresses specified in the recipient policies for each user on the mail system. Carefully plan which controller will host RUS and how often RUS will run in the domain. If your users do not use proxy addresses, best practices recommend that you set the RUS schedule to Never Run. Alternatively, when you make frequent changes (such as during a migration), you should run RUS more often (or as needed) shortly after any updates have been applied to the AD.

Exchange 2000 Servers typically request two AD services: address book searches and configuration data searches. Address book searches are performed on the closest available GC Server. An Exchange 2000 Server establishes several LDAP connections to both DCs and nearby GC Servers. Routing and configuration data is obtainable from any DC within the local domain because the Configuration container naming context is replicated to all DCs in the forest. A recommended practice is to place a GC Server near Exchange 2000 Servers, especially in the same site. The Exchange 2000 Server prefers to use the same DC to service these requests rather than poll different controllers.

Administrative Roles

Installing Exchange 2000 extends the structure of objects in native-mode AD to accommodate the additional properties and methods necessary to function in a messaging and collaboration environment. This close integration of Exchange 2000 with the NOS directory services affects how you manage accounts in the messaging organization because administrative roles and boundaries in Exchange 2000 are a function of native-mode Windows 2000. Best practices suggest using AD Users and Computers to administer all aspects of servicing your user population even in a mixed-mode environment that is still running legacy Exchange Servers. Use both nested OUs and properly scoped AD groups (discussed in the next section, "AD Groups") to simplify administrative tasks. If your organization has many domain trees that form a forest, introducing the physical placement of GC Servers as well as the hierarchical design of data stores and domain controllers can have subtle but significant effects on the successful and rapid exchange of messages across the enterprise.

Providing access to objects and resources in the form of permissions and granting rights to principals impact the administrative role. Recipient managers can function in a dual capacity as system administrator (SA) and Exchange 2000 administrator, or just as the manager of Exchange 2000 objects. Similarly, their responsibilities can extend to the physical side of the installation. These administrators must have appropriate permissions to various aspects of not just the Exchange 2000 Server but also the AD so that valid AD principals can access their mailbox stores to retrieve messages. Assign Exchange 2000 administrators to security groups that have adequate permissions to access both AD and Exchange 2000. Best practices suggest assigning permissions to security groups and not to individuals so that you can change group memberships quickly and efficiently without introducing possible permission conflicts or errors associated with the broader group designations themselves. Each principal assigned to a group receives the rights and permissions of that group; although individuals often change, group categories are typically a persistent part of the organizational structure.

AD Groups

AD contains two types of groups for organization purposes: security groups and distribution groups. Security groups can be mail enabled, and can act as the equivalent of a legacy Exchange 5.x DL if you assign a SMTP. Group membership can include assigned permissions to public folders. Distribution groups provide similar advantages for mass distribution of information through bulk message exchanges and can function as universal groups even in a mixed-mode domain in which legacy Windows NT 4 limitations are imposed on Windows 2000 servers. Unlike security groups, however, distribution groups cannot be assigned network resource permissions nor permissions to public folders. AD groups, formerly legacy

Exchange 5.x DLs, are discussed later in the Immediate Solutions section "Determining the Scope of AD Groups."

Group scoping is flexible because membership is stored in the GC Server and replicated throughout the forest. Replication between GC Servers, however, increases and impacts network use across the entire enterprise. Best practices suggest that changes to universal groups occur as infrequently as possible. If you modify domain local and global groups, replication and its associated impact on available bandwidth are confined within the boundaries of the domain. The compromise here is that group membership is not published in the GC and hence is not visible to users in other domains. For example, Outlook users can view the group membership of domain local or global groups within their own domain only.

Consider several factors when you are determining group scopes. For example, universal groups are necessary in enterprises with multiple domains. In a single-domain enterprise, a universal group isn't necessary because all domain objects are local. If network connectivity exists among domains, static universal groups provide greater functionality than global groups. If connectivity is poor or membership is especially dynamic, domain scoping is more efficient than scopes that extend across the enterprise. Finally, if messaging originates from outside the domain, universal scoping again provides greater efficiency than global groups. The type and scope of groups depend on your corporate objectives and the needs of your user population.

Policies

Policies are a major theme in the administration of a Windows 2000 enterprise. It was essential that Microsoft provide an administrative tool that delivered centralized, simplified administration, and granular control of all AD objects without increasing TCO in view of the scalability of the network architecture. Group Policy is a key component in the implementation of Windows 2000 security services. System and recipient policies play similar roles in an Exchange 2000 organization.

Policy is the collection of configuration settings globally applied across a namespace of objects, and is the primary method used in an enterprise environment to control NOS and application services. Best practices recommend that you systematically configure the largest administrative unit possible in NOS or application services. You can override global configurations at the object level. There are two policy categories: system polices, which are applied to server objects, and recipient policies, which affect the AD objects. Remember at the policy level, especially in a native-mode Windows 2000 and Exchange 2000 environment, one subtle change can replicate through an entire forest and dramatically affect service performance.

Default Recipient Policies

Default recipient policies differ in implementation depending on whether an Exchange 2000 organization is in a mixed-mode or native-mode environment. In a legacy Exchange 5.5 site, only one default policy can be compatible with legacy site addressing schemes and mailboxes physically located on site servers. In a native Exchange environment, default policy automatically generates, for example, SMTP or X.400 address proxies for all recipients with the domain name. By modifying this policy, which applies to all mail-enabled recipient objects, you can update attributes, such as email addressing, throughout the entire organization. You can delete or modify alternative address proxies at the object level. You can create additional recipient policies, and through filtering, apply settings to specific object types and individual objects that match a parameter value. Additional policies can either overwrite or be appended to attribute settings as primary values.

Determining a primary policy is based on priority in an environment with multiple policies; default recipient policy has the lowest priority and is applied only in the absence of other policies that affect an object. If a recipient object is affected by two or more policies, the highest prioritized policy applies. If you need to create or modify a recipient policy, you can force the changes to be applied immediately rather than wait for RUS to update all valid objects. A new policy is typically applied to all subsequently created objects. When creating such a custom policy in an established organization, remember to manually apply changes to existing objects and select that option to apply the change to existing users when the policy is created.

Exchange 2000 Structure

Server sizing is a fundamental part of the design and planning process. Consider scalability along both a horizontal and vertical dimension. *Horizontal scalability* deals with adding additional servers to deliver the same set of application services, load balancing, and hardware solutions, such as clustering. *Vertical scalability* refers to how you configure a single machine to deliver several different messaging and collaboration components for a broader range of services. Windows clustering and performance optimization through load balancing and FE/BE servers can dramatically affect a messaging system's performance and scalability. Fault-tolerance issues are also important considerations in your final plans for sizing and deployment of DCs.

Recipient Management

When planning to deploy a messaging and collaboration system, focus on organization, then users, and then support and maintenance. Organizational planning within the Exchange 2000 namespace involves defining users, resources, and even names of departments with standardized naming conventions, and arranging recipients in groups. It is important to focus on naming standards, their inherent structure, and their organization within the enterprise. You can organize recipients either functionally or physically in administrative and routing groups, respectively. As suggested in the planning stages of the AD structure, recipient management within your Exchange 2000 organization will be simplified if you systematically deploy recipient objects in two separate stages. Best practices first define naming standards for users, groups, and contacts. This step is followed by the design and deployment of public folders.

Naming Standards

Exchange systems can grow to hundreds of thousands of users. Although you can use nested groups, it is important to require unique names for objects—users, resources, and servers—especially when you are administering enterprise messaging systems. Exchange 2000 is a fundamental part of the NOS and is directly affected by any addition or migration of a foreign system to the enterprise. An Exchange administrator needs to review any recipient-related change to an enterprise for possible duplication or conflict in named objects when dealing with multiple messaging platforms. Areas of possible conflict include the following:

- *Organization names*—Though it's possible to create multiple organizations in a single enterprise, these names usually reflect the identity of the corporate entity they service. Such names can have a maximum length of 64 characters, but a best practice is to limit their length because users often manually enter them as a part of an email or messaging address.
- *Routing group names*—Naming conventions for these groups typically reflect distinct physical boundaries based on WAN links (such as geographical regions and network subnets) or functional workflows (such as departments and corporate divisions). Just like organization names, they have a maximum length of 64 characters, but you should limit their length because manual entry of the name might be required occasionally.
- *Server names*—You should establish naming conventions for servers before installing any NOS. These object names are fundamental to the installation process. In a Windows NOS, the server name for an application server is the same as its NetBIOS name registered with NOS system services. NetBIOS server names are restricted to a maximum of 15 characters and often cannot be changed after the installation process.
- *Recipient names*—Exchange 2000 categorizes recipients as users, contacts, groups, and public folders. A display name can have as many as 256 characters, although using this maximum length is discouraged. Using the common length restriction among legacy systems—8 characters—is considered a best practice among Exchange administrators.

It is also important to consider how the naming convention you choose will affect the addresses that outside messaging systems use to communicate with your recipients. Foreign systems, by definition, do not necessarily use similar addressing conventions. Exchange 2000 can resolve inbound messages from foreign messaging systems within separate address spaces designated for each system; foreign addressing schemes are translated and processed for delivery to Exchange recipients.

Thus, in association with good system administration, you must thoughtfully establish and carefully maintain naming conventions for primary objects. Standards for distribution groups and connectors, as well as users and contacts, are also important considerations in distributed administration models that include multiple administrators in different regions.

Public Folders

You configure public folders in Exchange 2000 as multiple trees, each of which contains any number of hierarchically arranged public folders. Users with the appropriate security context create top-level or root folders of each tree on their own home servers. Lower-level, child folders are located on the same server as the folder in which they were created. You can store folder contents on a single server or replicate them to other servers in the routing group and organization. Thus, designing public folders is associated with planning routing groups. When considering public folder storage and replication, you need to determine the following:

- *The number of public folder trees*—Determine whether trees are centrally managed as an enterprise-wide tree or independently managed in a decentralized fashion by, for example, separate departments or corporate divisions.
- *Patterns of replication*—Determine whether stores remain on a single server or are replicated to other servers in the routing group or to remote routing groups.
- *Resource allocation*—Determine whether a server will be dedicated to the distribution of public folders or both public and private message stores will be available.
- *Permission management*—Determine whether these public folders are accessible to all principals in the enterprise or to specific groups that require additional security overhead, and whether access extends to the creation of top-level public folder trees.

Like naming conventions for other Exchange 2000 recipient objects, public folders can also have names up to 256 characters long. As mentioned previously, excessively long names are discouraged because of the occasional need for manual entry. It is important to consider that client software you use to display public folders typically truncates long names within the allocated space of their windowed interfaces. Put the most distinguishing characteristics of the information at the beginning of the name rather than at the end. For example, in some situations, 99 Financials Marketing is a better name than Marketing Financials 99 when other calendar or fiscal years are published in the same folder tree. Shorter, more succinct names make it easier for end users to view these important shared resources.

Hierarchies

The public folder hierarchy organizes information so that it's easy for users to locate, and easy for support and maintenance personnel to administer. Carefully plan and define the structure of public folder trees to make delegating administrative tasks easier. Consider the following issues when using public folders as a primary vehicle for mass distribution of information:

- *Target audience*—Identify the target user population for this information. Determine the distribution of the audience within and across sites in your enterprise.
- *Service level*—Determine the access frequency of this information.
- *Management*—Determine the security needs required for access, such as Read Only, Read/Write, and Create/Read/Write.
- *Support and maintenance*—Determine the support and maintenance needs of the public folder tree. This can be safely delegated to an interested and reliable party with a vested interest in the information, or should the trees be centrally administered?

After you have considered levels of security access, you can easily add permissions and maintain folders delegated to end users or a group administrator if you carefully plan from the beginning.

Public Folder Affinities

Public folders distribute information with little ongoing maintenance. Replication of folder information, although relatively automatic, does incur operational costs due to network bandwidth consumption. Consider reducing bandwidth consumption, for example, by segregating remote users who preferentially access the public folder trees on a dedicated server specially located to optimize the distribution of information to the greatest number of users. Unlike Exchange 5.5, public folder affinities in Exchange 2000 are transitive. If an affinity exists between Site A and Site B, and between Site B and Site C, there will also be an affinity between Site A and Site C. Thus, if one routing group is connected to another, all servers will receive public folder referrals. You can configure routing group connectors, alternatively, to deny public folder referrals. Determine possible alternative public folder servers based on the routing cost to reach any one server across routing groups.

Public Folder Replication

Public folders are special messaging objects because they can synchronize their contents across data stores located throughout an organization. Public folder replication involves the contents of the public folder trees and is based on user utilization of that data store and available bandwidth among folder trees. The penalty of replication within, and especially across, sites can be excessive. Conserve network bandwidth by using public folder affinities rather than relying on the expensive process of creating replicas of data stores across physically separated public folder trees. You must carefully plan the effect an Exchange 2000 deployment might have on user access to public folders within an enterprise. Upgrading to Exchange 2000 will not upgrade public folder affinities. Public folder affinity applies to all connectors, including the following:

- *Routing Group Connector*—Connecting two routing groups
- *SMTP Connector*—Connecting to two organizations, or an organization to a third-party messaging system
- *X.400 Connector*—Connecting to two organizations, or an organization to a third-party legacy messaging system

Conversely, you can optimize high use of data stores by distributing copies throughout an organization. A punch list of planning issues involved in public folder replication should include the following:

- *Use of replication*—Determine whether replication optimizes or wastes resource use and network bandwidth.
- *Folder content*—Determine which data stores need to be replicated.
- *Distribution of users*—Determine distances between sites and the user population at these remote sites.

You need to regularly review all public folder sites. Examine which replicas are copied, how often they are replicated, changes in a site's effective bandwidth, and changing user needs. Best practices limit the amount of public folder replication because of its affect on network bandwidth use.

Foreign Mail Systems

You need to identify any foreign mail systems associated with your organization. Exchange 2000 provides software interfaces or connectors to a wide variety of systems, including legacy Microsoft (MS) Mail, Lotus Notes, Novell GroupWise, and IBM SNADS and PROFS. Use SMTP connectors to connect to Internet mail systems such as Netscape and OpenMail. Alternatively, X.400 connectors usually connect to legacy proprietary systems that typically predate Internet-based systems. During your planning stage, statistics should have been collected that provide information about users on each foreign system as well as the amount of information that flows between the two systems. When you design your connector architecture, determine the workload characteristics, including the composition of the mail in terms of package sizes and message flow patterns with the foreign user population.

RTC Services

Several issues regarding service offerings, capacity planning, and support need to be incorporated into the Exchange 2000 design to accommodate the Microsoft Exchange Conference Server (ECS) messaging and collaborative tools. ECS components, installed as either a department server or an enterprise-wide platform, include the following:

- Data Conferencing Services (DCS)
- Audio and Video Conferencing Services (VCS)
- Schedule management via Conference Management Services (CMS)

IM features include both Chat Service and IM. Of all these RTC Services, ECS has the heaviest impact on network bandwidth. In fact, ECS is actually deployed with Windows 2000 sites rather than with the deployment of Exchange Servers. Exchange 2000 is used to store and manage the schedules and reservations for the conferencing resources rather than actually to support the multimedia services. Relevant issues in planning ECS and IM deployment include the following:

- Determine whether both Chat and IM are provided to the desktop.
- Determine IM and Chat access outside the intranet to either the Internet, extranet, or both.
- Determine the size of the participating user population for the RTC services.
- Compile specifications regarding connections using telephony, network resources, and server resources for IM and Chat Service.
- Design ECS and IM topology especially in view of network use.
- Determine locations for the installation of server software, potential FE/BE configurations, and additional support services.

A tremendous number of hardware and software issues exist with RTC. It is important that you carefully consider and justify the inclusion of these services in your enterprise design in view of their potential security issues and support requirements. Because ECS is an additional service layer, it is outside the scope of this book.

***NOTE:** You may find the following two books helpful references: The* Visual Studio.NET Black Book, *written by Julian Templeman and published by The Coriolis Group, covers .NET architecture, libraries, and services, and how to use them from the programming languages supported by VS.NET. It also covers the new Web and database access technologies in WinForms, ADO+, ASP+, with emphasis on XML, including the SOAP protocol. In addition,* Designing Visual Basic.NET Applications, *written by David Vitter and also published by The Coriolis Group, provides a desktop reference that helps the Visual Basic developer get up to speed on .NET, while avoiding topics experienced developers are already familiar with. It encompasses all language enhancements to Visual Basic, and explains the .NET framework concepts and real-world examples of their use. It includes object models for developing ADO.NET, ASP.NET, SOAP, and XML.*

In summary, planning an implementation requires the prioritization of many steps that mostly involve the definition of namespaces and scopes of authority. An enterprise namespace can be categorized as collections of various objects with common attributes such as permissions. Organizational and domain topologies are now more easily mapped to real-world schemes due to the architecture of both Exchange 2000 and Windows 2000. After a first domain is created, trees and trust relationships must be carefully established to build a stable foundation on which Exchange 2000 services will be installed. Both horizontal and vertical scalability affect the deployment of hardware and services across the enterprise as well as within a single server respectively. Issues such as clustering and performance optimization through load balancing dramatically affect the ability to deliver reliable levels of service for 24 hours over any one seven-day period. Issues of process and property must be aligned with the administration of people through recipient management services. Finally, collaborative objects like Public Folders must be carefully deployed to serve the largest portion of a user population in the most efficient manner.

Immediate Solutions

Identifying Pre-installation Tasks

When finalizing your plans for deployment, make sure all the following have been accomplished:

- All network documentation is current.
- All system backups are current and tested.
- Ownership of all knowledge resources has been verified.
- All network-related information, such as IP addressing and subnet masks, has been documented. Where possible, configuration parameters have been transferred to DHCP profiles.
- When possible, hardware components, such as NICs, and software components, such as browser clients, have been updated to current versions and standardized on manufactured products of market leaders.
- A security audit has been performed to verify the use of properly authenticated user groups. Roaming user profiles have also been reviewed for temporary or miscellaneous data. Use Security Configuration Manager to apply appropriate security policies to both servers and workstations.
- All current service packs have been installed on both system and application server platforms. All workstation OSs have been standardized.
- Using user profiles to standardize all workstations with a preconfigured desktop has been considered.

Determining the Scope of AD Groups

AD groups are equivalent to legacy Exchange 5.x DLs. Each has a scope attribute that determines membership and use within the organization. Depending on whether a domain is mixed mode or native mode, you can restrict a group scope to a local domain, a global group between domains, or a universal group that extends across a forest. Group scoping is flexible because membership is stored in the GC Server and replicated throughout the forest. However, this flexibility comes with a cost because replication between GC Servers impacts network use across the entire enterprise. Changes to universal groups occur as infrequently as possible. If you modify domain local and global groups, replication and its associated impact on available bandwidth are confined within the boundaries of the domain. The compromise here is that group membership is not published in the GC and hence is not visible to users in other domains. For example, Outlook users can view group membership of domain local or global groups within their own domain only. When working with groups, you need to consider the following:

- *Naming conventions*—Mail-enabled groups should use a naming convention compatible with Windows 2000 naming standards.
- *Ownership*—Group ownership is typically assigned to the creator of the group.
- *Size*—Microsoft suggests nesting groups that contain more than 500 objects while keeping total group membership to fewer than 5,000 named objects.

NOTE: *There are several IP address ranges as specified in RFC 1918 that have been designated exclusively for private use. IP addresses within these private address spaces will only be unique within an enterprise; they cannot be used on a public network like the Internet. The address ranges, allocated by Internet Corporation for Assigned Names and Numbers (ICANN), for private rather than public networks, are as follows:*

10.0.0.0	-	*10.255.255.255 (10/8 prefix)*
172.16.0.0	-	*172.31.255.255 (172.16/12 prefix)*
192.168.0.0	-	*192.168.255.255 (192.168/16 prefix)*

Planning a DNS Namespace

A fundamental guideline to follow when you are planning a namespace is to build a layered structure systematically that distinguishes external names from internal names. Both DNS and AD must coexist within this logical space to avoid naming conflicts, but you must also keep them separate for security reasons. External DNS namespaces are typically in the public record; internal namespaces can be secured through internal DNS name servers isolated from outside the enterprise through a form of firewall technology. It is particularly important to register the TLD, use different internal and external namespaces, create AD child domains subordinate to parent domains in the DNS namespace, and partition the internal and external namespaces on physically separate servers. Thus, you need to do the following:

- Register your domain to avoid current or future design conflicts.
- Use different internal (private) and external (public) namespaces for both security and a more flexible design. You can, for example, create a private subdomain structure independent of a previously registered public domain namespace. After you create subdomains, partition your hierarchical name-space beneath these subdomains to support your design needs; better reflect functional, geopolitical, legal, or business concerns; and simplify administration.
- Deploy public and private IP address ranges on physically separate network nodes or servers. External servers are exposed to public networks such as the Internet and must be secured from all forms of attack. By separating external from internal namespaces on physically separate machines, you build "air gaps" that isolate and help secure your private network.
- Centralize DNS name resolution of external servers on a "bastion" server. Have all other internal DNS servers forward requests to it. This configuration simplifies the installation of firewall technologies.
- If you use public and private IP address ranges, avoid overlapping internal and external namespaces anywhere in your enterprise.
- Create AD child domains immediately subordinate to their parents in the DNS namespace. Construct your domain tree just as you would build a folder structure on a file server. Based on design objectives, create child domains under appropriate parents, such as **child2.child1.parent.mycomp.tld**.

NOTE: *Firewall technologies include many hardware and software tools as well as specific network topologies. Among these specialized network schemes, a bastion host is a specially designated computer that is configured so that it is the only directly accessed enterprise address from a public network. It is designed to screen the flow of IP packets passing between the internal enterprise and an external public network.*

Planning Naming Contexts

A *naming context* is a partitioned section of the AD hierarchy with specific properties that are distinguishable from those of other directory sections. These defined subspaces are categorized by domain, configuration, or schema data. They form information units that are replicated among DCs. A specially designated GC Server holds a fourth category of information: a limited set of attributes of every object in every domain in the forest. Multidomain forests have a common configuration and schema but unique domain data. Naming contexts include the following:

- *Domain*—This subspace is the collection of all AD objects (such as users, contacts, and groups) in a domain that is replicated to every other DC inside, but not outside, the domain.
- *Configuration*—This information subspace contains, for example, information about the physical network. It is replicated to every domain in the forest in the Configuration container in the AD. Data in this partition of the AD is critical for creating replication connections with correct and consistent configurations among DCs in the forest.
- *Schema*—This subspace provides the information used to define data, including the object classes and attributes that collectively make up the AD. Object classes are the kinds of named principals that populate an enterprise and must be consistent across all domains through representations in every DC in the forest.

Managing the Configuration Container

The Configuration container in the AD contains replication topology and related metadata for the entire enterprise and stores configuration information for service-providing servers such as Exchange 2000 as well. Exchange 2000 consolidates data about recipient objects, configuration, schema, and the GAL as object attributes in the AD.

- The majority of the data is stored in the configuration-naming replicated to every DC in the forest.
- The configuration of distributed services is replicated along with other AD data among all domains in the forest. When the first Exchange 2000 Server is installed in the forest, AD schemas are further extended to accommodate messaging and collaboration system data. This extension of the schema can include modifying existing attributes as well as adding new attributes. LDIF files are imported as part of this installation process.

Planning Recipient Management

You need to focus on organization, then users, and then support and maintenance when planning to deploy a messaging and collaboration system. Organize the Exchange namespace by defining users, resources, and even names of departments with standardized naming conventions and arranging recipients in groups.

Organize recipients functionally in terms of routing groups or physically in terms of administrative groups. Just as we suggested in the planning stages of the AD structure, recipient management within your Exchange organization will be simplified if you systematically deploy recipient objects in three separate stages.

- Define naming standards for users, groups, and contacts.
- Design the folder hierarchy with particular attention to naming standards, inherent structure, and organization within the enterprise.
- Deploy the public folders.

Configuring Recipient Settings

Configure the global recipient settings through System Manager. Override system-wide settings by reconfiguring specific options in the specific Properties sheets at the object level. You need to configure the following settings:

- *Email addresses*—Proxy addresses are defined through recipient policies and constructed by RUS for recipients to receive mail. By default, proxy addresses consist of one SMTP and one X.400 address. The address, marked in bold, is the primary messaging path that appears in the From field of all outgoing messages. You cannot delete a primary address.
- *Content format*—The SMTP format is configured at the organization-wide level of a messaging system in Internet Message formats, located in the Global Settings node of System Manager. Configure different formats for specific domains. Consider changing the order of the display name from its default pattern of ***<first name> <last name>*** using Active Directory Services Interface (ADSI) Edit. Another consideration is changing the email SMTP format of ***alias@mycompany.com*** to an organization-level recipient policy that uses %g (first name),%s (last name), and %i (middle initial) for an email address.
- *Delivery restrictions and options*—Delivery settings define outgoing and incoming message size limitations and universal or restricted access of users to each other. Block incoming messages from external sources in Message Delivery under Global Settings in System Manager. You can also delegate authority to send messages on behalf of a recipient and to automatically forward mail to another recipient in the organization.
- *Storage limits*—Set storage quotas on data stores that will trigger warning messages or block the composition or receipt of messages. *Nondelivery reports (NDRs)* are directed to sender, recipient owner, or both. The administrator can set data store limits and then override these levels for special recipient objects.

- *Protocol settings*—Enable or specially configure various recipient protocols such as HTTP, Internet Mail Access Protocol 4 (IMAP4), and Post Office Protocol 3 (POP3).
- *Published information*—Determine levels of visibility of various recipients in the GAL. You can hide recipients so that the general user population won't know the identity or property of that object. Best practices recommend hiding the list of group members so that any one user in the group cannot view the membership when mail is distributed. Members of the Exchange Administrators accounts and Exchange Server accounts do, however, have access to these hidden objects.

Removing Recipient Policy

On a global level, there are three ways to remove policies or proxy addressing schemes in an existing organization so they are no longer applied to recipients:

- *Proxy is disabled*—Clear the Option box on an existing proxy object. New objects under this particular policy will not receive this proxy address.
- *Proxy is removed*—Deleting the proxy prevents new objects from receiving the addressing scheme, although existing objects will still have the proxy address. You cannot delete an object's primary addressing scheme.
- *Policy is removed*—Deleting a policy object prevents new objects from receiving the addressing scheme but has no effect on existing records. You might need to apply a new policy to each orphaned object manually. This is not recommended because any one policy can have more widespread effects on a domain or organization than you might have anticipated.

You can also modify the specific attributes in existing objects manually to remove a policy.

Defining a New Recipient Policy

Define a new policy by identifying the object to which the policy will apply. Best practices recommend testing queries using the **find** command. This common menu-driven tool is actually an LDAP query interface that creates a filter based on AD attributes according to Request for Comments (RFC) 2254. For example, you can create a policy that generates email addresses for users, groups, and other mail-enabled recipient objects, such as contacts, based on specific filter rules. Using the **find** command helps you troubleshoot the range of objects to which a recipient policy will be applied. After the LDAP query is created, it's displayed in the General tab of the specific recipient policy. Use this policy to modify an SMTP addressing scheme so that messages using different addressing schemes (such as **sales.mysite.com** and **mysite.com**) will be directed to the same mailbox-enabled recipient. Similarly, you can modify the object-addressing scheme so that, for example, it appears as ***<first name>.<last name>*@support.mysite.com** by providing a template such as **%g.%s@support.mysite.com**. You can make these changes in the Email Address tab on a recipient object's Properties sheet.

Determining the Scope of Groups

Administrative groups are collections of recipient objects that share common sets of permissions. These permissions apply to ranges of other Exchange objects in the AD namespace. You need to determine the scope of authority among three administrative groups as follows:

- Universal groups are necessary in enterprises with multiple domains. In a single-domain enterprise, a universal group is not necessary because all domain objects are local. If network connectivity exists among domains, static universal groups provide greater functionality than global groups.
- If connectivity is poor or membership is especially dynamic, domain scoping is more efficient than scopes that extend across the enterprise.
- If messaging originates from outside the domain, universal scoping again provides greater efficiency than global groups. The type and scope of groups depend on your corporate objectives and the needs of your user population.

Creating Security and Distribution Groups

Once an administrative group is created, you can now add members to the group, add this group to another group, assign a manager as a point of contact, set message size restrictions, and limit the users who can send messages to the group.

1. Start Active Directory Users and Computers.
2. Right-click the container in which you want to place the group.
3. Select New and then Group from the Context menu.

4. In the Group Name text box, type the name of the group you want to create. Notice that the first 20 letters are used to create the pre-Windows 2000 group name. This is initially an empty container under the Administrative Groups node. You will add servers and other resources like system policies into it.
5. Select the appropriate group scope from the option box on the left side.
6. Select the appropriate group type from the option box on the right side.
7. Click the Next button. If extensions are installed properly, you can determine whether the group should have an email address, Exchange alias, and administrative group.
8. Click the Next button, and then click Finish to create the group.

Performing a Foreign Mail System Audit

You need to document the kind of message transfer, the topology, and the capacity of foreign mail systems. A physical audit of these foreign systems should include the following:

- Physical resources
- Network connectivity and protocols
- Geographic distribution of servers
- Proximity to mail servers

The audit should include information about the host OS, and both the structural and functional architecture of the foreign mail systems. Determine how users exchange messages among themselves and through the connector with your local messaging system. Construct bridgeheads to control message flow from both a maintenance and security perspective even though they might not have been essential before you established connectivity. Best practices recommend not running connectors, for example, on mailbox-hosting servers.

Chapter 5

Planning Recipient Objects

If you need an immediate solution to:	*See page:*
Creating a Mailbox-Enabled Recipient Object	150
Adding Mailbox Information to Existing Users	151
Creating a Mail-Enabled User Recipient Object	153
Mail-Enabling a Security or Distribution Group	156
Planning Recipient Access to Exchange 2000 Using Only a MAPI-Based Client	157
Mail-Enabling Groups in a Multidomain Environment	160
Optimizing Replication Traffic for Mail-Enabled Groups	160
Planning a Postmaster Mailbox	161
Planning Dedicated Mailboxes with Disabled User Accounts	161
Determining the Number of Mailboxes You Can Add to a Single Exchange 2000 Server	162
Setting Storage Limits for Recipient Objects	163
Using Recipient Policies for Recipient Objects	165
Updating Recipient Objects Using the Recipient Update Service	167
Implementing Administrative Groups and Assigning Permissions to Them	168
Administrative Groups You Created Are Not Visible in System Manager	170

In Depth

Planning recipients for a new Exchange 2000 Server installation involves many steps that are part of an overall design scheme. You must tie together many elements from Windows 2000 and Exchange 2000 so that users can receive messages or work with information in public folders. The concept of a "user" has changed dramatically compared to previous versions of Exchange Server. This chapter covers the definitions you need to know and the interrelationships that exist between Windows 2000 and Exchange 2000 so that recipient management won't seem as complicated at first glance.

New Concepts in Exchange 2000

A user is not simply a user anymore in Exchange 2000. It is important to start with concepts that were used in Exchange 5.5 and build a new conceptualization of recipient in Exchange 2000. In Exchange 5.5, a *recipient* was any object that could receive a message. These recipients included:

- *Mailboxes*—Mail was delivered to this location on the Exchange Server. Every user created in Exchange 5.5 could have multiple mailboxes but only one primary Windows account associated with it. For example, a user named "Jdoe" would have one primary account created for him in the Windows NT User Manager for Domain tool, but could be associated to two different mailboxes in the Exchange Administrator program (one for personal email and another for a Help Desk function). Exchange 2000 associates a mailbox directly to a Windows 2000 account, prohibiting multiple mailboxes per user.
- *Distribution lists*—A logical grouping of users created for the purpose of mass mailings. One message could be sent to a list of 500 users, for example, instead of sending 500 individual messages to 500 separate users. Distribution lists took advantage of an Exchange Server feature known as *single instance storage*, in which only one copy of a message was involved. This process conserved bandwidth and data transfer between mailboxes. Exchange 2000 still uses this concept of distribution, however it does so in the context of a group object known as a universal distribution group for all mixed mode Windows 2000 domains (or universal security group if the Windows 2000 domain it is located in runs in native mode).

- *Public folders*—A storage location or repository for information that could be shared among other recipients. Public folders were used to share applications and other types of information that could be easily accessed by multiple users at the same time. Multiple public folders could be created and information was replicated or copied between them. A public folder tree is a hierarchical grouping of folders that exist in a component known as an Information Store. Exchange 5.5 Server was limited to one single public folder tree called Public Folders, while Exchange 2000 could host multiple public folder trees.
- *Custom recipients*—This group of user's was treated differently than other types of recipients. This object referred to an external address, or address that existed outside the Exchange 5.5 organization. Exchange 2000 defines these objects as "mail-enabled" objects.

These objects were created in the Exchange Administrator system utility. This administrative tool showed a Recipient container that displayed all recipients on your servers. Although Exchange Administrator displayed every server in your site, each mailbox could only exist on a single server. In these containers, you could arrange your organization in a hierarchical manner and put different groups or divisions within their own containers.

For example, if your company was named BookCover Inc. and you had users in two different divisions, Accounting and Sales, you could create two subcontainers underneath the Recipient container and manage mailboxes within these containers as separate units. You could even assign different administrators to manage each container separately.

NOTE: *You had to be careful when working with Exchange Administrator because lower-level containers could inherit configurations from containers located above them, unless you provided different arrangements. Even if you created different Recipient containers, you could be caught with excessive permissions assigned to that container as a result of permissions inherited from a container directly above it!*

To create a new container within another container in Exchange 5.5, you had to follow these steps:

1. Select Start|Programs|Microsoft Exchange.
2. Select the Exchange Administrator program.
3. Click your Site container or Recipient container.
4. Select File|New Other|Recipient container.
5. Type in a new name for your new container.

When planning permissions for your containers, you had to assign permissions at three distinct levels in Exchange Administrator: the Organization level (the top level), the Site level or container, and the Configuration container within the Site level. Your recipient information could be found within the Site level, which then contained a Servers container.

One more important concept must be discussed before we move to Exchange 2000. All the objects discussed so far were stored in a central directory known as the Exchange directory service database (DS). This server created and managed all objects within the organization, which made it possible to easily find resources so they could be managed at some time. All objects in the DS possessed *attributes* or properties as well as permissions. A user object such as "Fred Smith" would have associated attributes such as First Name, Last Name, and Email Address. The DS was considered a crucial component because every server contained a single directory service database. Each DS replicated its information to all other directory stores in the same site. It was also possible, however, to engage in directory replication between sites and between foreign messaging systems such as X.400. We will refer to this concept when comparing the new directory structure of Windows 2000 Server, because it plays an important role in managing recipient objects for Exchange 2000. This directory integration with Windows 2000 makes management of Exchange 2000 simple and efficient as the Active Directory structure is much more scalable compared to the directory structure found within earlier versions of Exchange Server, or even earlier versions of Windows NT 4. Microsoft has provided consolidation of services and processes in Exchange 2000, which enhances the administrative experience while simultaneously affecting TCO. Administrators can now benefit from the implementation of administrative groups and organizational units when managing recipients, which was not possible with earlier versions of Exchange. More information concerning these new features is discussed in Chapters 9 and 13.

Directory Objects in Exchange 2000

Knowing how Exchange 5.5 defined recipient objects helps you understand recipients in Exchange 2000, but it doesn't provide a complete picture of the new models involved. We need to define some new concepts and terms before actually laying out the new model for recipient management in Exchange 2000.

The New Recipient Containers

The Recipient containers in Exchange 5.5's Exchange Administrator program have been replaced with new structures called *Organizational Units (OUs)*. The major difference between Exchange 5.5 and Exchange 2000 is not the tools but rather the underlying operating systems used to administer these systems. Because of the design structure of Windows 2000 Server, Exchange 2000 bases all its components on AD, rather than the old DS database used in Exchange 5.5. The Windows 2000 AD structure helps you design a custom-built, object-based directory structure. This means your organization can be further broken down into *logical structures* and *physical structures*.

A logical structure can help you find a resource by name instead of actual physical location. So objects are now organized into groups of objects called classes. An OU is an example of a class of objects. As stated previously, OUs replaced the traditional Recipient containers found within Exchange 5.5. An OU is a container object that organizes objects within a larger *domain structure*. OUs contain objects such as users, groups, and computers. An OU can even contain other OUs, creating its own hierarchy of objects.

Mailbox-Enabled Objects

You now have to make a distinction between a "mail-enabled" object and a "mailbox-enabled object in Exchange 2000. A *mailbox-enabled object* is the ideal type of recipient object because it can possess multiple Exchange mailboxes. A mailbox-enabled object has direct rights within Windows 2000 Server because it can log on to a Windows 2000 domain and is known as a Windows 2000 *security principal*.

All objects you create are potential recipient objects in the AD structure of Windows 2000 and Exchange 2000. A *potential recipient* becomes an *actual recipient* when you add email information to it. Recall that the four types of recipient objects in Exchange 5.5 were mailboxes, distribution lists, public folders, and custom recipients. The main types of recipient objects in Exchange 2000 include the following:

- User accounts
- Group accounts
- Contacts
- Public folders

You can add email address information to user accounts, group accounts, and contacts. Public folders present a different story and are discussed in future chapters. Public folders actually are found in hidden containers called Microsoft Exchange System Objects, and they do not automatically possess email addresses. Even if you assign an email address to a public folder, these addresses will not be seen in the Global Address List (GAL) by default.

Careful consideration has to be given when creating mailbox-enabled recipients (see "Creatiing a Mailbox-Enabled Recipient Object" for further details later in this chapter). You will find that user account objects are typically mailbox-enabled. Group accounts are nothing more than collections of user accounts; contacts do not possess the same attributes as user objects and are therefore not capable of becoming mailbox-enabled. However, contacts can be mail-enabled as shown in the following section, "Mail-Enabled Objects." As noted earlier, public folders normally are not given email addresses.

Planning mailbox-enabled objects involves several additional concepts, including assigning permissions to user accounts and defining storage limits for users. Ideally, you want to add mailbox information to certain user accounts when you first create them, but you also want to delete mailboxes when these accounts are taken away from AD. The user accounts that you work with are now separated from the actual mailboxes associated with them. The user accounts are found in AD (a part of Windows 2000 Server), but the mailbox structures are found within the Information Store service of Exchange 2000. So there is some planning involved when mapping user accounts to mailboxes in Exchange 2000. The administrative burden, however, is less compared to Exchange 5.5 because there is no longer a separate Directory structure to maintain. Recipients can be easily organized into container objects in AD without disturbing mailbox properties in Exchange 2000.

Another topic to consider is updating recipient information for mailbox-enabled objects. For instance, when you create a new mailbox-enabled object (such as a new user who has just joined your company), you might experience a small delay before these new addresses are displayed in the GAL. You must plan the configuration of the new *Recipient Update Service (RUS)* in Exchange 2000. RUS is part of the internal *System Attendant* component. The RUS can also update address lists found within the AD structure of Windows 2000 Server.

WARNING! The RUS is applied at the domain-level, so you might need to configure one Update Service (US) for each domain in your Windows 2000 forest that will hold any type of recipient object (users, computers, groups, and so on). If a mailbox-enabled object, such as a user, exists in a domain that does **not** ***have RUS configured, that object might not have an email address associated with it.***

Mail-Enabled Objects

A *mail-enabled object* in AD is any object possessing at least one email address. How does this differ from a mailbox-enabled object in AD? For one thing, a mail-enabled object is not a security principal and cannot logon to a Windows 2000 domain. Can a user be mailbox-enabled *and* mail-enabled at the same time if it's already a security principal that can logon to a Windows 2000 domain? The answer is yes.

A mailbox-enabled user not only has one or more Exchange mailboxes, but also at least one defined email address associated with it. Therefore, a user can be both mailbox-enabled and mail-enabled at the same time. However, some objects cannot have mailboxes associated with them because they cannot log on to a Windows 2000 domain. Therefore, they can possess only an email address, and are considered to be mail-enabled rather than mailbox-enabled. A contact is an example of an object that is considered to be mail-enabled only in Exchange 2000.

Contacts are objects with addresses or locations that exist outside your normal Exchange 2000 organization (foreign mail addresses that you need to maintain contact with only occasionally). If you move a custom recipient from an Exchange 5.5 organization into an Exchange 2000 organization, it becomes a new type of recipient object called a *contact*. You can immediately assign a newly created contact or email address in AD or do it later. The act of assigning a contact an email address means that it is mail-enabled, not mailbox-enabled. Understanding this difference is vital to successfully administering an Exchange 2000 Server.

Planning for mail-enabled objects involves knowing which user objects, group objects, or contacts will be assigned email addresses, as opposed to being assigned a "mailbox." It also means preparing to coexist with foreign messaging solutions such as Lotus Notes or Novell GroupWise. In this case, any user in your domain is assigned an email address to work with the foreign messaging system's mailbox structure. Your users are then considered mail-enabled rather than mailbox-enabled users. Confusion arises when you try to mix the concept of mail-enabled users with mail-enabled contacts. Remember that contacts do not exist within your organization. It is impossible to mail-enable a contact, which is linked to a user that exists within your organization.

NOTE: *A handy rule to keep in mind regarding email addressing is that any given email address cannot be linked to more than one recipient object type. For example, if* **Bob@BookCover.com** *refers to a mail-enabled contact existing outside your organization, the user object Bob cannot be a* mailbox-enabled user *or even a* mail-enabled user *within your organization, because Bob is considered a* contact *only in this situation.*

Assigning email addresses to groups involves additional planning because Windows 2000 now includes different types of groups for different purposes. You have to distinguish between *security groups* and *distribution groups*. Sometimes you will create groups strictly for security so you can assign permissions, and other times you use groups for purposes not related to security, such as sending email messages to distribution lists. Security groups and distribution groups represent *group types* within Windows 2000. These group types determine *how* you use a group.

NOTE: *You are not allowed to use distribution groups to assign permissions in any case.*

Also, groups now fall under three different scopes, including domain local, global, or universal. Table 5.1 lists the features for each type of group scope.

Table 5.1 List of group scopes and their differences.

Name of Group	Membership	Access to Resources
Domain local	Members from any domain, including trusted domains	Can access resources located in the same domain where you created the group
Global	Only members from the domain where you created the group	Can gain access to any resource in any other domain beside the domain that created the group
Universal security	Can add members from any domain	Can assign permission for access to resources located in any domain*

**A universal security group is only possible if your Windows 2000 organization is in native mode. Such a group cannot exist within a mixed-mode organization. If your organization remains in mixed mode, you can only create a universal distribution group, not a universal security group.*

Not all objects need to be mailbox-enabled to enjoy the full functionality of Exchange 2000. For instance, a mail-enabled object can still participate in Instant Messaging (IM), although it's not attached to a particular mailbox. You can plan the following features with a mail-enabled object:

- SMTP (Simple Mail Transfer Protocol) or X.400 addressing schemes
- Simple display names (or have their account names hidden from any address lists)
- Participation in Realtime Collaboration (RTC), such as IM or Chat Services
- The size of any incoming messages

***NOTE:** You are not concerned with outgoing messages because a mail-enabled object can only receive messages; it cannot send messages like a mailbox-enabled object can.*

Certain features, such as IM, apply only to mail-enabled *users*, not mail-enabled *groups* or mail-enabled *contacts*. The configuration settings for these types of mail-enabled objects will also be similar. Knowing these configuration settings helps you plan additional components. For example, if you mail enable a group, you have to provide the name of an *expansion server*, which will expand the distribution lists.

We have emphasized the concept of mail-enabled objects because they are often confused with their "cousins," mailbox-enabled objects. We have discussed these differences and provided examples, hence the concept of simultaneously being both mailbox-enabled and mail-enabled is difficult to visualize.

In addition, Microsoft says you should always mail-enable your universal security groups. Doing this depends on whether or not you have one domain or multiple domains configured for operation.

If all your users reside in a single domain (and a single forest), membership in all domain local groups, global groups, and universal groups can be the same. All users can exist in all three groups. With multiple domains, however, group membership is very different depending on the type of group you create. For example, a global group cannot contain members from any domain other than the domain in which you created the global group. This happens regardless of whether your organization is in a mixed-mode or native-mode operation. A universal security group, on the other hand—operating in Native mode—is not restricted in membership or access to resources. More importantly, all membership lists in a universal group (both security and distribution types) are automatically replicated to the *Global Catalog (GC)* server in a domain, so any Exchange client has access to this information in the entire Windows 2000 forest. The SMTP service is optimized to work with universal, security, or distribution groups.

WARNING! Although membership information in a universal group is replicated to a GC Server, this can be disastrous for very large universal security or universal distribution groups. Frequent changes in group membership can cause excessive replication traffic because the entire group list is replicated every time.

Administrative Groups

Planning for recipient objects involves an understanding of the logical architecture of administrative groups in Exchange 2000. Previous versions of Exchange Server used the concept of *sites* to describe a collection of Exchange Servers that could replicate their directory information using permanent high-speed, high-bandwidth connections via Remote Procedure Calls (RPCs). Recipients created in one site could communicate with recipients in a remote site, and Site Connectors connected one site to another.

Exchange 2000 logically group servers into administrative groups, which are totally independent of the physical structure of a network. You can group servers for administrative reasons and to assign permissions to various groups. You can also use the Exchange Administration Delegation Wizard to assign permissions to administrative groups for servers, policies, and even public folder stores.

Routing Groups

Though recipient objects normally communicate with each other on the same server, exchanges can occur between servers in the same administrative group, and between servers in different administrative groups. Communication even occurs among servers between different domains and different forests. For these reasons, you need to carefully plan the existence of a new routing structure called a *routing group (RG)*. RGs are collections of servers that all share one permanent, high-speed connection between them. These collections of servers all communicate using the SMTP protocol, which is the new native transport for Exchange

2000. Multiple RGs rely on connectors for message delivery between the recipient objects.

All servers are automatically added to the *first routing group*. You can, however, manage a server in a single RG that spans multiple administrative groups. Multiple RGs can assist in controlling access to public folder stores or even in reducing overall client network traffic. Multiple RG containers can reside within an Administrative Group container. If your organization is placed in Native mode, it's possible to assign a server to a RG without paying attention to which administrative group it belongs to.

Offline Address Books and Lists

The Exchange 5.5 Administrator program showed a System Folder container under the Organization Name/Folders/System Folder hierarchy that contained a list of recipients to which remote users could address a message. A remote user would download an offline address book and use it to send email messages to any recipient object in the Exchange 5.5 organization.

Exchange 2000 will not upgrade an Exchange 5.5 Server containing an offline address book if other Exchange 5.5 Servers are in the same administrative group. An offline address book is specific to an organization in Exchange 2000, as compared to being site-specific in Exchange 5.5. You cannot synchronize an offline address book between Exchange 5.5 and Exchange 2000. Exchange 2000 will generate an offline address book from AD, while a mailbox residing on an Exchange 5.5 Server uses offline address books generated by the Exchange 5.5 directory.

Storage Groups

A new boundary has been created in Exchange 2000—called *storage groups (SGs)*—that defines the limits for both mailbox stores and public folder stores. Each Exchange 2000 Server is capable of hosting four SGs. SGs hold databases or stores. Each database can hold mailbox information or public folder information, but not both at the same time. One SG is capable of holding up to five separate databases or stores. This flexibility means that recipient objects can reside on different databases within multiple SGs on a single server.

SGs aid in the development and configuration of dedicated servers for Exchange 2000. All users can exist on one server while all public folders can exist on another. This is ideal because the replication of the public folders will not interfere with email message flows. More importantly, high priority users can be placed within their own mailbox store while lower-priority users can share a separate mailbox store. Having separate mailbox stores within one SG means that recovery of one database will not interrupt the normal functions of any other database within the SG. All backup and restore operations are done in parallel while the system is still online. This type of activity could not be performed using Exchange 5.5.

It is important to realize that every SG shares only one set of transaction logs. Exchange 5.5 used a file called edb.log for logging current transactions before committing them to the appropriate database on the local hard drive (either the \Mdbdatadirectory for the Information Store or the \Dsadata directory for the DS). Transaction log files were always 5MB in size, and continue to be that way in Exchange 2000. Although it's easy to mount and unmount individual database stores or backup individual stores, the normal procedure includes the entire SG and its corresponding transaction log file in a single backup.

NOTE: *When planning multiple databases or multiple SGs, install the transaction logs and the physical databases onto separate physical drives to boost your server performance and help avoid corruption when backing up or restoring files. Monitor these database files because they become fragmented over time, which could slow down your server. The Information Store will defragment databases automatically—a process known as* online defragmentation*—but this will not reduce the size of the databases. You can use the Exchange 2000 tool* ***Eseutil.exe*** *to reduce the size of database files.* ***Eseutil*** *is a low-level database utility that lets you perform* offline defragmentation *(meaning all services are stopped) and allows for database consistency and failure correction at the level of the Extensible Storage Engine within Exchange 2000.*

Organizational Units

Proper creation and management of recipient objects in Exchange 2000 mean employing OUs to hold these objects. Recipient objects need to follow some type of administrative model. No matter which model you select, it will depend on the proper design of OUs. If the highest unit of organization is a domain, the next level of organization is the OU. By grouping recipients into an OU, you can delegate permissions and authority to restricted personnel over the items contained within the OU. You also can easily move recipient objects from one OU to another; trying to do this between different domains involves a bit more effort.

If you tried to create more than one Recipient container in Exchange 5.5, it was difficult to move a recipient object between different containers. However, moving a recipient object from one OU to another OU is a relatively easy task that does not even involve moving the object's mailbox. Remember that both AD *and* the Information Store are at work here, so performing an action on one component does not necessarily affect the other component. Also, an OU differs from a legacy Recipient container in one other important respect. An OU won't be present in the Outlook Address Book, while users were always able to view Recipient containers in their Exchange 5.5 Address Books.

NOTE: *Even if you ultimately plan to move recipient objects between* domains, *the object's mailbox that resides in the Information Store won't be affected. However, you must use more complicated tools to do this, such as the AD Migration Tool.*

Every organization goes through physical and administrative changes of some kind, resulting in recipients being moved or deleted from their current configuration. Objects such as mailboxes are easily moved in the following situations:

- You can move a mailbox between different mailbox stores in the same SG on the same Exchange 2000 Server.
- You can move a mailbox between servers that exist in the same administrative group.
- You can move a mailbox between servers that exist in different administrative groups if Exchange 2000 is operating in a native-mode environment.

The last two conditions in the previous list will prevail even if the corresponding user object has not been touched in any way in AD.

WARNING! Although you can move* mailboxes *between servers or other mailbox stores, you* cannot *move* entire servers *between different administrative groups! This rule must be followed at all times.

Global Catalog Server

Planning for recipient objects involves an understanding of AD directory services in Windows 2000 Server and how it relates to the use of a GC Server. The GC Server is usually the first domain controller server installed in a Windows 2000 domain (or domain tree) in your Windows 2000 forest. The GC is responsible for actually producing the GAL in Exchange 2000. If you are a client using Outlook 2000 and you are seeking address information, you automatically query a GC for this information. If you are using another client (such as Outlook Express), your request is still routed indirectly to the GC Server in your domain.

GC Servers are associated with the overall design of your Windows 2000 environment. For example, all domains in your organization should be contained within one forest. If you design your Exchange 2000 organization improperly, you could end up spanning more than one forest, which is not permitted. If you end up with multiple forests, you must create multiple Exchange 2000 organizations.

GC Servers allow users to perform relatively fast searches for directory information, so it's important to have the proper number of GC Servers and to place them within a reasonable distance of the users. Microsoft provides the following recommendations:

- Place at least one GC Server for every Windows 2000 site that you have. A Windows 2000 site is a logical structure configured for a range of distinct IP addresses (for example, a range of 192.168.10.1–192.168.12.1 is considered one site). Multiple sites can exist within one domain.
- Because a GC holds a replica of certain attributes from certain objects found within AD, make sure the attributes that are most important to your organization are replicated over to the GC Server.

Administrative Models for Recipient Objects

The best plan for managing recipient objects is to select an appropriate management model in advance. Exchange 2000 designers usually choose from a *centralized model*¸ a distributed *model*, or some combination of these two models applied to legacy systems such as Exchange 5.5 and Windows NT 4 Server (see Figures 5.1 through 5.3).

Centralized Model

The *centralized model* involves the use of OUs and grouping recipient objects into multiple OUs so that effective group policies and system policies can be applied as needed. A system policy allows one group of settings to be applied universally to one group of servers. These policies are usually applied at the server level, the mailbox level, or the public folder level. A centralized management model usually has one centralized group that has administrative rights on all OUs within an administrative group.

NOTE: *When working with the centralized model, be sure to create your administrative groups before you add new servers to your organization, otherwise all servers are put into the default first administrative group. After you place a server into an administrative group, it cannot be moved.*

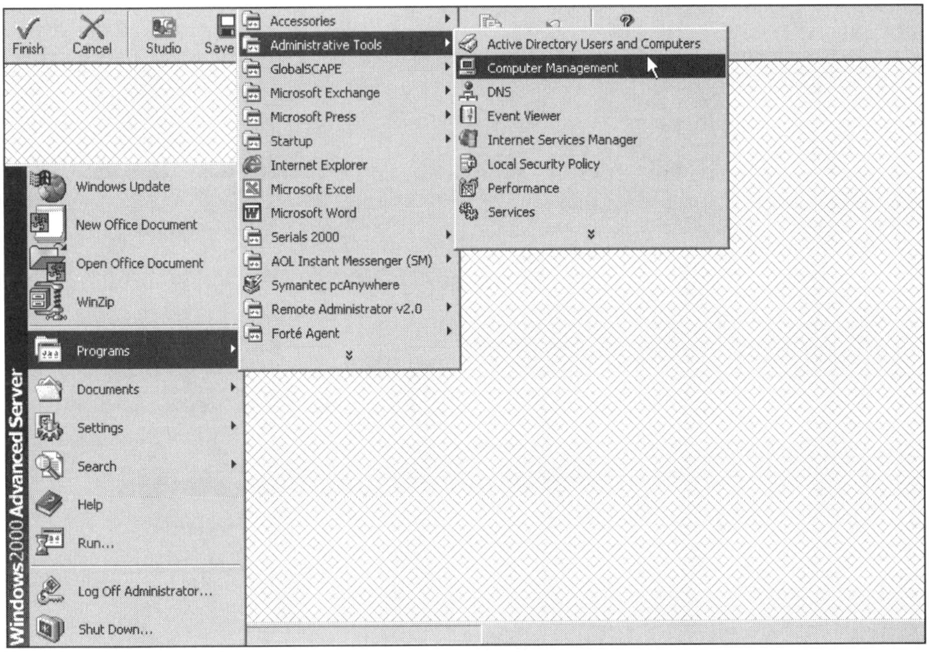

Figure 5.1 The centralized administrative model.

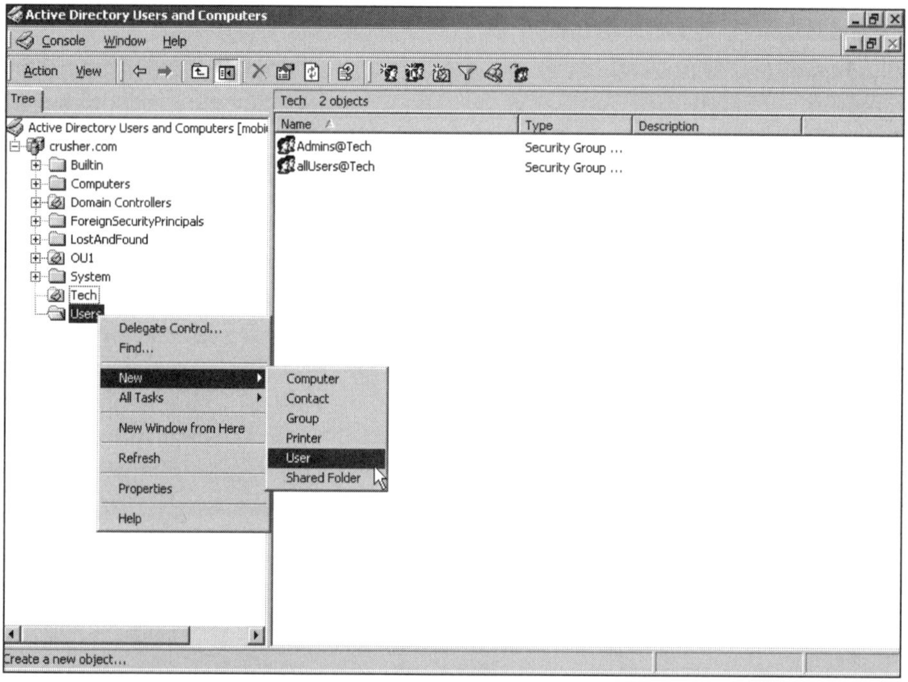

Figure 5.2 The distributed administrative model.

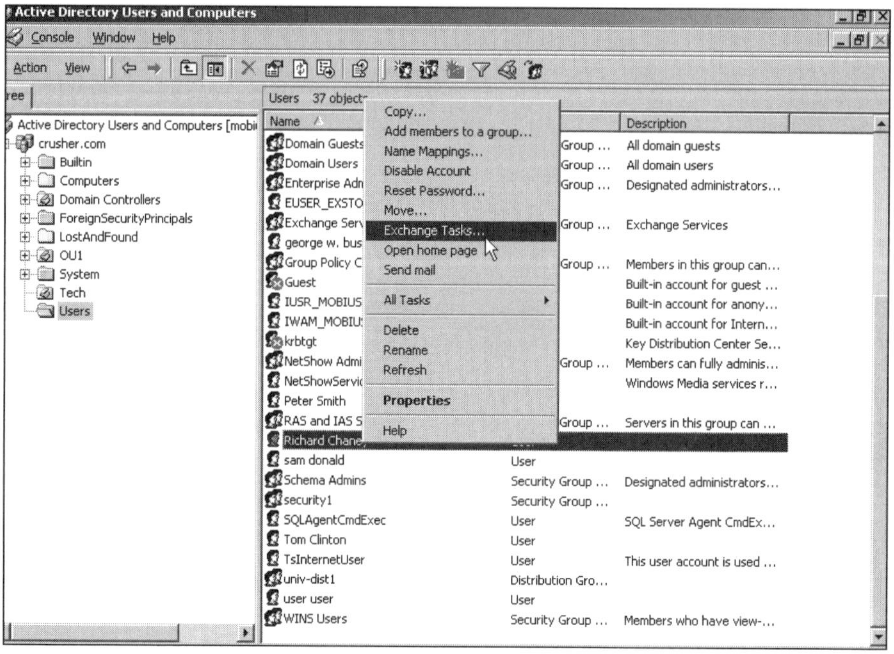

Figure 5.3 The mixed administrative model.

Distributed Model

The *distributed model* divides your servers into respective administrative groups as before, but different administrators control different administrative groups, and each administrative group is now grouped according to geographic location or function (such as Sales or North America). Every distinct administrative group divides servers further into multiple RGs.

Legacy Recipients in Exchange 2000

Many organizations continue to run Exchange 5.5 Servers in their Exchange 2000 organizations for several reasons:

- The legacy servers have connectors to foreign messaging systems, such as the PROFS/OfficeVision connector or the SNADS (Systems Network Architecture Distribution System) connector used to connect to IBM systems. These systems are still in use but unsupported by Exchange 2000.

NOTE: *Exchange 5.5 users are familier with the SNADS connector used to establish connectivity with legacy IBM mainframe messaging systems.*

- Multiple users are using the Exchange 5.5 Server and the change would be too dramatic to move all users at once to Exchange 2000.
- The legacy servers are running custom public folder applications that run perfectly on Windows NT 4 Server and there is no need to port them over to a new Exchange 2000 computer that is running Windows 2000 Server.

No matter what the reasons, recipient objects will be residing on legacy Exchange Servers that must be able to communicate with recipient objects on your Exchange 2000 Servers. We don't want to discuss formal migration or upgrade strategies at this point, but we do want to mention the Active Directory Connector (ADC) tool that helps replicate and synchronize directory information from Exchange 5.5 with directory information in Exchange 2000.

The Importance of ADC for Recipient Management

In any coexistence scenario between Exchange 5.5 and Exchange 2000, you will find a need for ADC. As stated previously, ADC replicates information in AD with information in the Exchange 5.5 directory and vice versa (see Figure 5.4). You will use this tool to plan an upgrade of an existing Exchange 5.5 Server to Exchange 2000. This plan might also involve upgrading Windows NT 4 machines to Windows 2000 Server machines.

The essential point to remember is that you will be using the ADC to replicate recipient properties from an Exchange 5.5 directory. To make this happen, you

Figure 5.4 The function of the Active Directory Connector.

need to plan on creating *connection agreements*. These agreements specify where you will be replicating *from* as well as where you will be replicating *to*. You will also specify the object classes and the replication schedule. Proper planning is necessary because you can define more than one connection agreement for one ADC, which means that you can synchronize and replicate multiple Exchange 5.5 sites with the AD database.

NOTE: *ADC comes in two versions, one for Windows 2000 and one for Exchange 2000. The difference between these two versions is somewhat subtle; the Windows 2000 version of ADC specializes in replicating objects, such as users, to AD. The Exchange 2000 version specializes in replicating configuration information, such as connector information.*

If you are planning to design a Mixed-mode environment, the ADC is required because every Exchange 5.5 mailbox will need to be associated with a Windows 2000 mailbox-enabled user or group (a security principal). The only time you do *not* need this tool is when all Exchange 5.5 Servers have been formally upgraded to Exchange 2000.

Planning to Use the ADC

Consider the following items when planning to use the ADC to migrate recipient information between an Exchange 5.5 site and the AD used by Exchange 2000:

- The ADC should be installed on member servers, not domain controllers, because replication consumes a lot of processing power and time, especially if more than one connection agreement is employed.
- Your connection agreements ideally should be directed toward a GC Server in a Windows 2000 domain because all servers in the Windows 2000 forest are configured to query the GC for domain information.

- Although it's *not* a good idea to plan multiple instances of the ADC on one server, it *is* a good idea to plan multiple servers, each running one instance of the ADC. In other words, your goal is not simply "fault tolerance" of one ADC in case the other ADCs go down. Your goal instead is to reduce the time taken to replicate recipient objects between two different directories, especially when you can configure different objects to be replicated across different connection agreements.
- Try to put any server running an ADC on the same subnet as the server containing the Exchange 5.5 directory to minimize replication traffic that might tie up low-bandwidth connections that arise when the servers are *not* located in the same subnet.
- You will experience problems if you try to use the ADC with an existing Exchange 5.5 site containing mailboxes that are associated only with a Windows NT 4 Server domain. Recall that Exchange 5.5 associated each mailbox with a primary Windows NT 4 account. If no Windows 2000 account exists for this Exchange 5.5 mailbox, the ADC creates a mail-enabled user account in AD that is disabled by default. The only way to remove these disabled accounts is by using the Active Directory Account Cleanup Wizard, or ADClean.exe, found in the \%systemroot%\Exchsrvr\bin directory on your local hard drive by default.
- Plan on mirroring your container structure and OU structure between the Exchange 5.5 site and the Exchange 2000 organization. For example, if you created four separate containers in Exchange 5.5 that need to be replicated to four different domains or OUs in Exchange 2000, plan on creating four different connection agreements from the ADC Server to the Exchange 5.5 site. Doing this maintains the organization of information both before and after the replication process.

Immediate Solutions

Creating a Mailbox-Enabled Recipient Object

Remember that only user accounts can become mailbox-enabled recipients in Exchange 2000. You cannot create a mailbox-enabled contact, for example. To create these recipients, perform the following steps:

1. Open Active Directory Users And Computers by choosing Start|Programs|Administrative Tools (see Figure 5.5).
2. Right-click the container that you will place the new recipient in, for example, Users. Select New|User.
3. Fill in the First Name, Last Name, and Full Name (if desired), along with the naming convention you want to use in your organization for the user logon name (for example, First Initial Last Name). Then click Next (see Figure 5.6).
4. Type and confirm your password, and then select any checkbox that applies to this recipient object. Click Next.

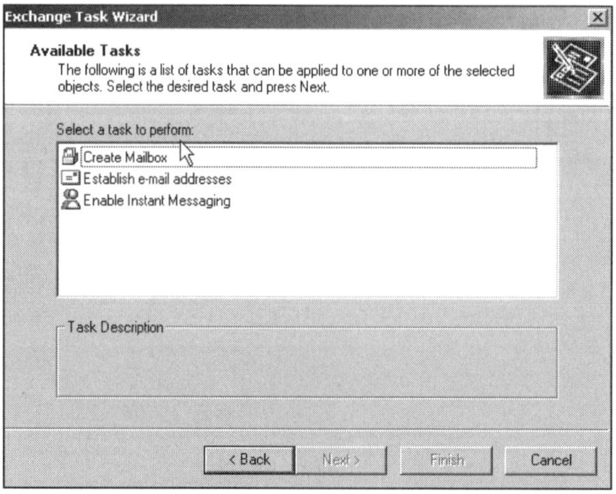

Figure 5.5 The Active Directory Users And Computers snap-in.

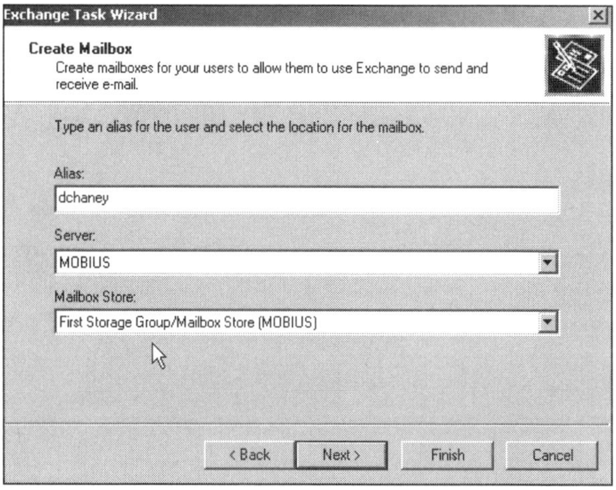

Figure 5.6 Creating a New User in Active Directory Users And Computers.

5. Select the Create An Exchange Mailbox checkbox, verify the Alias name, along with the Server name and the Mailbox Store, and then click Next.

NOTE: *The default SG named First Storage Group will contain your new recipient object unless you have explicitly defined other SGs on this server. Remember that each server can only contain up to four distinct SGs.*

---

6. Review the information that appears in the next dialog box. When you are satisfied with this information, click Finish; otherwise, click Back and change the incorrect information.

NOTE: *The moment you click Finish, your recipient object is ready to participate in all messaging-related activity.*

Adding Mailbox Information to Existing Users

To mailbox-enable a user that already exists in AD (and is already displayed in the Details pane on the right-hand side in Active Directory Users And Computers), perform the following steps:

1. Right-click the desired recipient object and select Exchange Tasks from the menu that appears.
2. Click Next on the Exchange Task Wizard screen that appears.
3. Select the Create Mailbox option on the Available Tasks screen, and then click Next (see Figure 5.7).

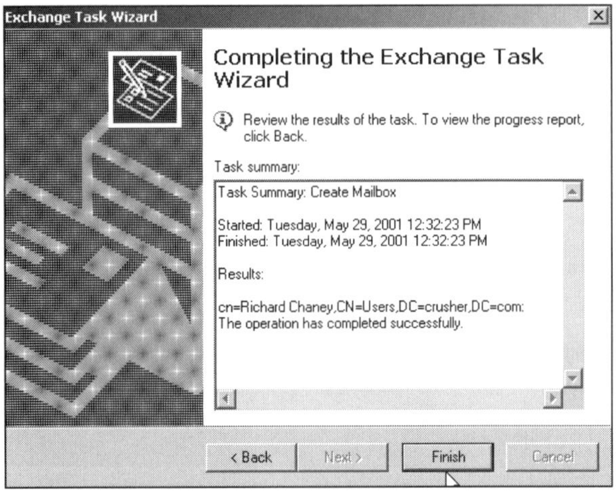

Figure 5.7 Creating a new mailbox for a recipient.

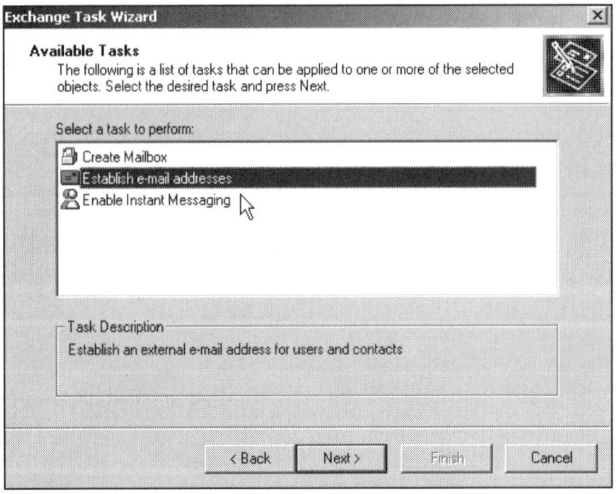

Figure 5.8 Selecting a mailbox location for a new recipient.

4. On the Create Mailbox screen, type an alias for the user, select the location for the mailbox, and click Next (see Figure 5.8).
5. Review the results of the task on the Completing The Exchange Task Wizard screen and click Finish if you're satisfied with the results or Back to change your information (see Figure 5.9).

Related solutions:	Found on page:
Planning Recipient Management	128
Configuring Recipient Settings	129

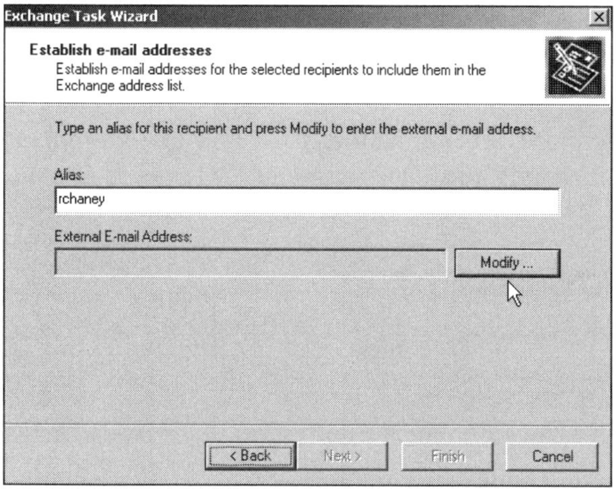

Figure 5.9 The final screen for the Exchange Task Wizard.

Creating a Mail-Enabled User Recipient Object

Remember, not all users are *mailbox-enabled*. If you want a user recipient object to become *mail-enabled*, you only want an email address to be associated with this object, not a mailbox. To accomplish this result, perform the following steps:

1. Click Start|Programs|Administrative Tools|Active Directory Users And Computers.
2. When the console opens, select the container in which you want to place the new mail-enabled object (for example, Users).
3. Right-click the container you selected, and choose New|User.
4. Fill in all relevant account information (First Name, Last Name, Full Name, and user logon name), and click Next.
5. Type in a password, confirm the password, and select the appropriate checkboxes below the password boxes. Click Next.
6. Deselect (uncheck) the Create An Exchange Mailbox checkbox. You will notice that the areas describing the alias of the recipient and the location of the mailbox are now dimmed. Click Next.
7. Verify the full name and the user logon name of your new recipient object, and click Finish.
8. Right-click the new recipient object appearing in the Details pane of Active Directory Users And Computers, and select Exchange Tasks on the pop-up menu.

9. Click Next on the Exchange Task Wizard screen, and then select Establish Email Addresses on the Available Tasks screen that appears (see Figure 5.10). Click Next when ready.
10. Type an alias for this recipient, and click Modify to enter an external email address on the Establish Email Addresses screen that appears (see Figure 5.11).

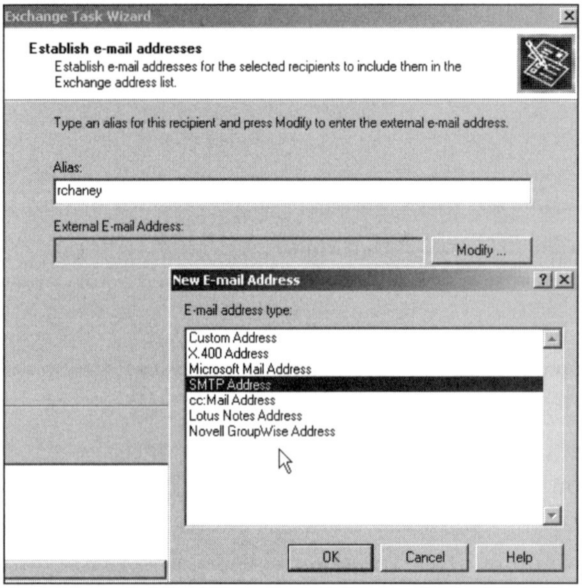

Figure 5.10 Establishing an email address for a mail-enabled recipient object.

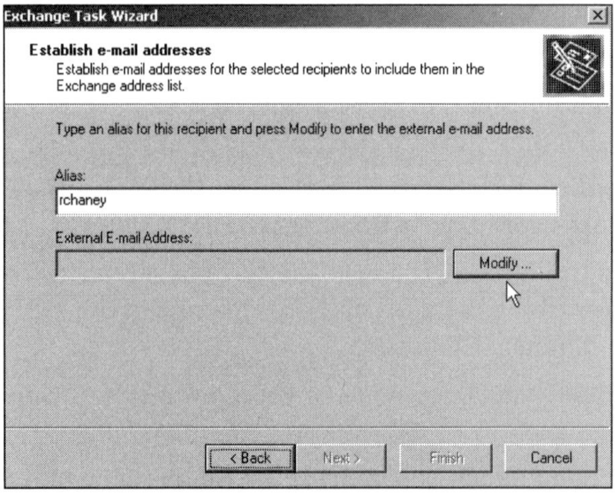

Figure 5.11 Choosing an alternate email address scheme for your new recipient.

11. In the New Email Address dialog box that appears, select an alternate email addressing scheme (such as SMTP Address) and click OK (see Figure 5.12).
12. Type a new address in the Internet Address Properties box that appears and click OK.
13. Notice that your new address appears in the External Email Address box. If all looks good, click Next (see Figure 5.13).

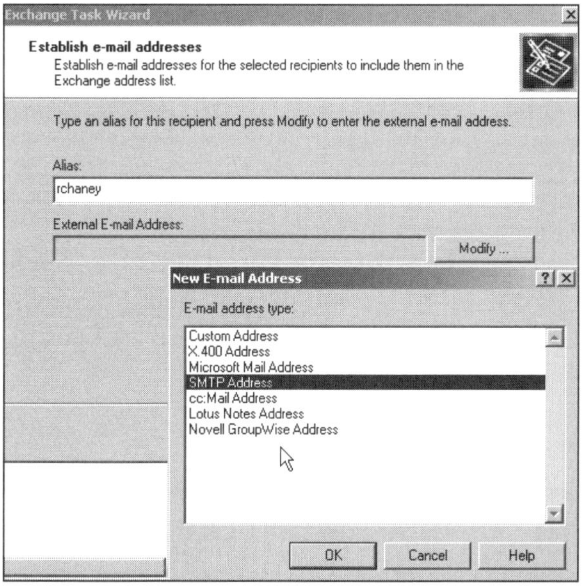

Figure 5.12 Selecting an alternate email naming convention for a new recipient object.

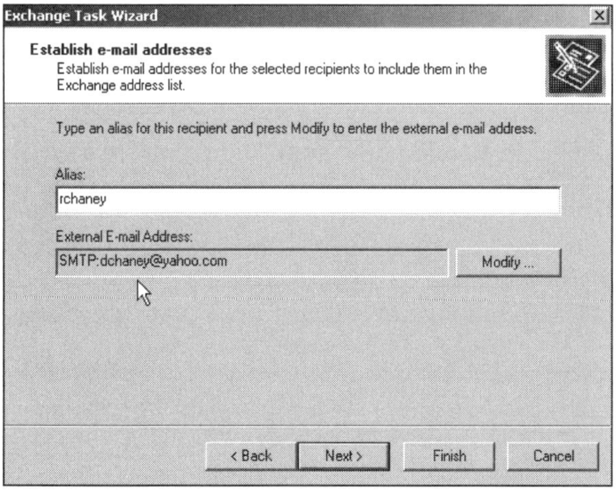

Figure 5.13 Verifying your new external email address for your recipient object.

5. Planning Recipient Objects

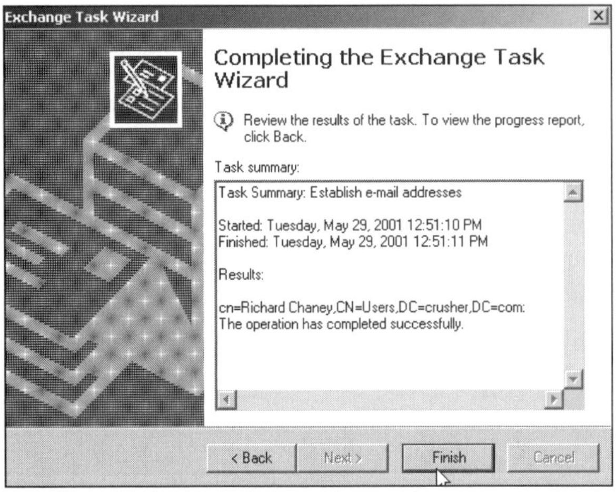

Figure 5.14 The Completing The Exchange Task Wizard dialog box.

14. Look at the final information in the Completing The Exchange Task Wizard box and click Finish if you're satisfied with it. Otherwise, click Back to correct any information entered prior to this screen (see Figure 5.14).

Mail-Enabling a Security or Distribution Group

The steps to perform here are similar to those of creating a mail-enabled user in the previous section except for some minor modifications:

1. Right-click your desired group in Active Directory Users And Computers (for example, the Domain Guests listed in the Details pane), and select Exchange Tasks.
2. Click Next on the Welcome To The Exchange Task Wizard screen.
3. Select Establish An Email Address and click Next.
4. Select an alias on the Establish An Email Address screen.

NOTE: *Remember that Microsoft recommends mail-enabling universal groups as compared to global groups or domain local groups because universal groups replicate information about their members to a GC Server, which is then made available to every server in the forest.*

Planning Recipient Access to Exchange 2000 Using Only a MAPI-Based Client

If you want to allow users to access their mailboxes using a MAPI (Messaging Application Programming Interface) client such as Outlook 2000, without being able to use other Internet-based clients such as Outlook Express, perform the following steps:

1. Select a user that you want to enable MAPI-based access for in Active Directory Users And Computers.
2. Double-click the user and open his Properties pages. Notice the content on the following tabs: (Figure 5.15 shows all tabs for a user's Properties pages) Exchange General, Email Addresses, Exchange Features, and Exchange Advanced (see Figures 5.15 through 5.17).
3. Select the Exchange Advanced tab, and click Protocol Settings. The Protocols dialog box appears (see Figure 5.18).
4. Select the HTTP protocol, and click the Settings button. The HTTP Protocol Details box appears. Uncheck the Enable For Mailbox checkbox and click OK (see Figure 5.19).

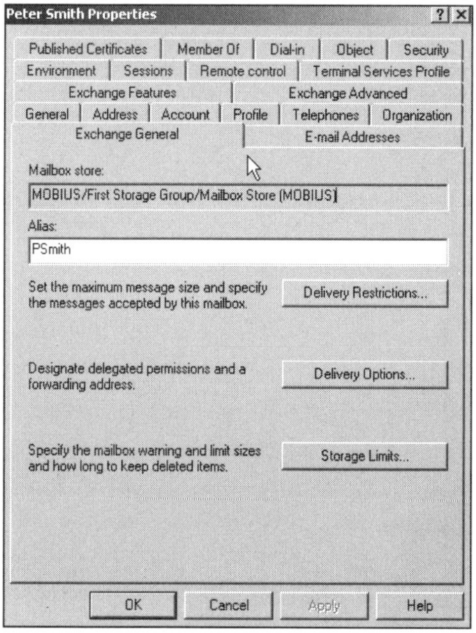

Figure 5.15 The Properties pages for a user account showing four Exchange-related tabs.

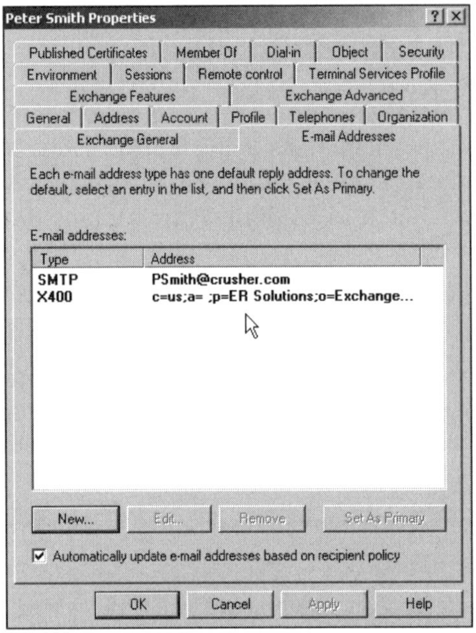

Figure 5.16 The Email Addresses tab of a recipient's Properties pages.

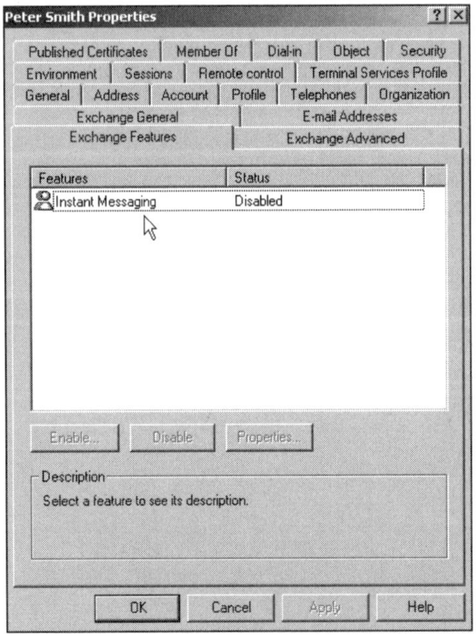

Figure 5.17 The Exchange Features tab of a recipient's Properties pages.

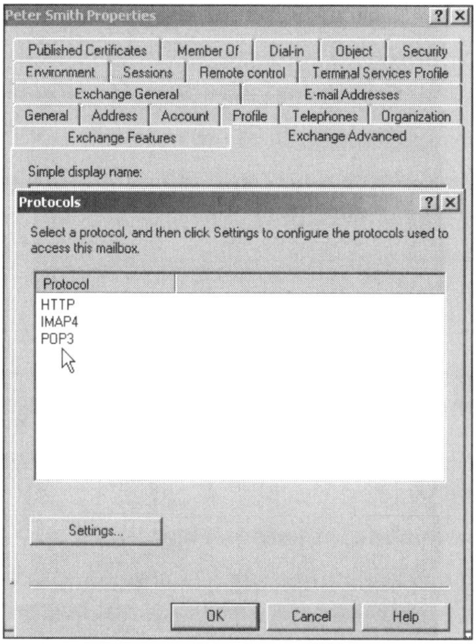

Figure 5.18 The Protocols dialog box from the Exchange Advanced tab.

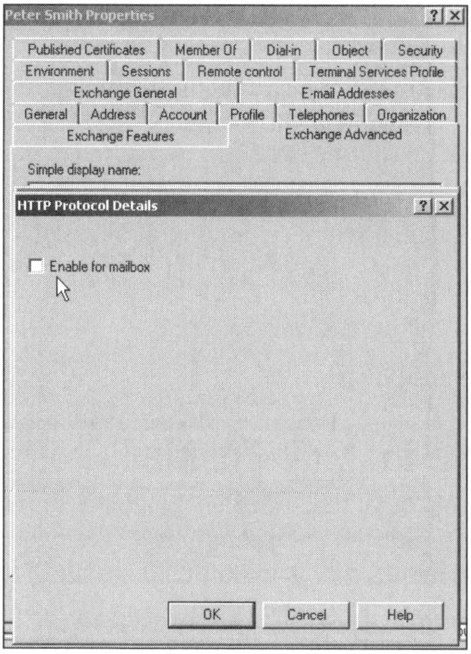

Figure 5.19 Deselecting the HTTP protocol for your mailbox.

5. Repeat the steps for IMAP4 (Internet Message Access Protocol 4) and POP3 (Post Office Protocol 3) that appear in the Protocols box, and click the OK button twice to return to the Active Directory Users And Computers console screen.

If performed correctly, the user selected in the previous set of steps cannot access her mailbox using an Internet-based client. She can only access this information using a MAPI-based client such as Outlook 2000.

Mail-Enabling Groups in a Multidomain Environment

You should mail-enable universal groups as opposed to domain local groups or global groups for the following reasons:

- Global groups cannot contain recipients from other domains.
- Local groups *can* contain recipients from other domains, but can only assign permissions to resources contained in *that domain.*
- Group memberships of global groups or domain local groups are not replicated to GC Servers, which provide easy access to domain information in a Windows 2000 forest. However, universal groups (both security and distribution types) *do* replicate this information to a GC Server.
- It's easier for the native SMTP transport protocol to expand the membership list of a universal group, compared to a global group or domain local group. This makes it easy to determine optimal routing for messages for each member of the group.
- Specifying a *group owner* for mail-enabled groups enables you to assign management responsibilities for the group to specific people so they can track the behavior of individual group members.

Optimizing Replication Traffic for Mail-Enabled Groups

It isn't a good idea to create excessively large mail-enabled groups or universal groups, because information is being replicated consistently to GC Servers in a Windows 2000 forest. Microsoft recommends that you limit the number of users in a mail-enabled group to approximately 5,000 to restrict the effect of unwanted or excessive replication traffic in your network.

You could devise a *nested group* if you ever need to include more than 5,000 users in one mail-enabled group. Let's say you create a group of 20,000 users. The optimal solution is to create 5 groups of 4,000 users or even 10 groups of 2,000 users and "nest" these groups. If you now add a user to this "subgroup" structure, only this new data will be replicated instead of the entire membership list.

NOTE: *Using mail-enabled global groups instead of mail-enabled universal groups results in less replication traffic; however, you will not be able to add users from other domains.*

Planning a Postmaster Mailbox

The SMTP service uses a postmaster address for certain administrative tasks within Exchange 2000. For example, the postmaster can deliver a nondelivery report (NDR) when messages cannot be delivered due to nonexisting or incorrect recipient addresses. A sender can respond to the postmaster address, such as **postmaster@crusher.com** for assistance.

Consider the following points when you want to create a "postmaster" account:

- You have to mailbox-enable the local administrator account and give it the postmaster address for the SMTP service (by double-clicking the Administrator account in Active Directory Users And Computers, then clicking the E-mail Addresses tab, highlighting the SMTP type and clicking New|SMTP Address, and then typing in the address of **postmaster@domain.com**.
- Use your own login account as the postmaster address.
- Create a special account with this address, but grant yourself Full Mailbox Access to this account using the Mailbox Rights button on the Exchange Advanced tab in the Properties page for each user.

Planning Dedicated Mailboxes with Disabled User Accounts

Sometimes you want to create a disabled user account using the Active Directory Users And Computers snap-in tool because you don't want to use the Administrator mailbox for personal email, or for collecting important system messages. Even though you could use your own personal account, it's always a good idea to keep things separate. Create a dedicated disabled user account for specific email messages that you anticipate (such as company announcements or for distribution-list purposes) and mailbox-enable them (see the earlier section, "Creating a Mailbox-Enabled Recipient Object").

If you do this, you will need access to this custom mailbox-enabled object. In other words, you need to assign yourself Full Mailbox Access or Read As permissions to this mailbox. Your goal is not to log on to this account but simply to open it and read the contents inside. You can even send on behalf of this account by clicking the Delivery Options in the Exchange General tab of the mailbox Properties pages (see Figure 5.20). Click Add to add your account to this mailbox.

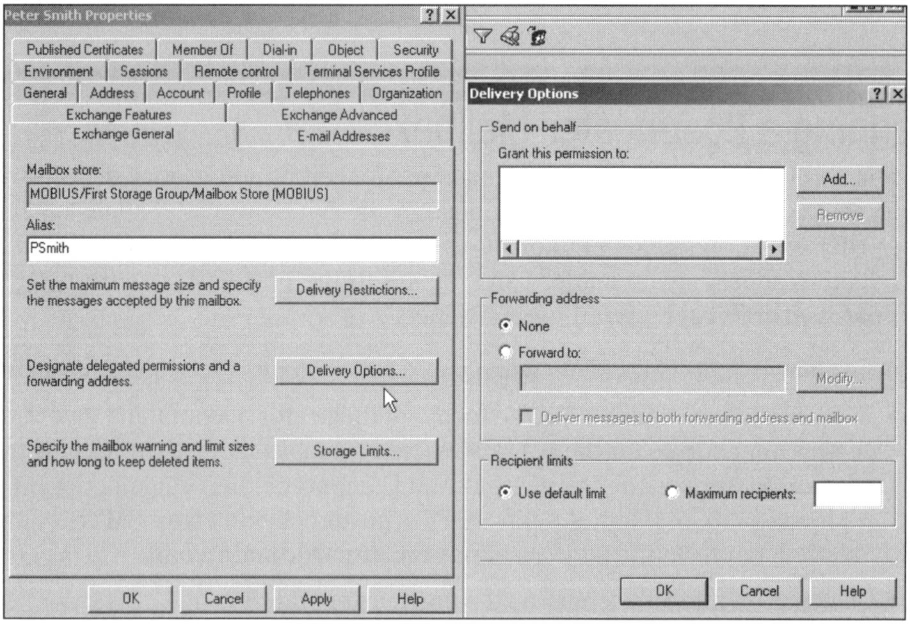

Figure 5.20 Configuring delivery options for a mailbox-enabled recipient object.

Determining the Number of Mailboxes You Can Add to a Single Exchange 2000 Server

A recent study by eTesting Labs (a technology testing service of Ziff Davis Media) found that, given large numbers of simulated users, Exchange 2000 showed significant scalability increases compared to Exchange 5.5. The scalability of Exchange 2000 using the Windows 2000 Advanced Server operating system was compared to that of Exchange 5.5 using Windows NT 4 Enterprise Edition. The Ziff Davis Email Server Test Tool (ZDESTT) simulated real-world conditions for large populations of POP3 and SMTP users. The results can be found on the **www.microsoft.com/exchange/techinfo/planning/2000/E2KvsE55.asp** Web site.

The results generated by ZDESTT show how productive and responsive each server was during the measurement phases of the test. The following are some significant findings based on server response time, messages received, and messages sent:

- Exchange 2000 was found capable of delivering mail to a potentially larger user population than Exchange 5.5. Scalability between the two versions of Exchange was compared on a four-way SMP (Symmetric Multiprocessing) server, and Exchange 2000 processed messaging traffic for almost 80,000 simulated users, whereas the limit for Exchange 5.5 was almost 50,000 simulated users before reaching total capacity levels.
- Exchange 2000 *even outperformed* Exchange 5.5 by more than 20 percent in terms of server response time. Stated another way, Exchange 2000 produces lower server response times (by at least 20 percent) compared with Exchange 5.5 at all server levels capable of being tested.

No magic formula—despite all the rigorous testing mentioned previously—will help you gauge *exactly* how many users will fit onto a single Exchange 2000 Server; it all depends on the available hard drive space found on your server. You can use tools such as the Mailbox Statistics Tool on the BackOffice Resource Kit to generate information about mail-usage patterns within your organization. Putting many users on one server to save hardware costs will ultimately degrade server performance due to increased server response times for your current user population.

NOTE: *Another metric or measure that will help you plan for an appropriate number of users per server is Total Messages Sent Per Second, which can be measured using the Windows 2000 System Monitor snap-in.*

Setting Storage Limits for Recipient Objects

Apply *storage limits* to users who regularly exceed usage thresholds for your messaging environment. These limits warn users when their mailboxes have exceeded a predefined maximum value and prevent users from sending or receiving new messages (and their related attachments). You can define these settings using system policies or you can define them for individual mailboxes using the System Manager snap-in.

To use the System Manager snap-in:

1. Select Start|Programs|Microsoft Exchange|System Manager.
2. Expand the node for your server under the Administrative Group. Locate your SG, right-click your Mailbox Store, and select Properties.

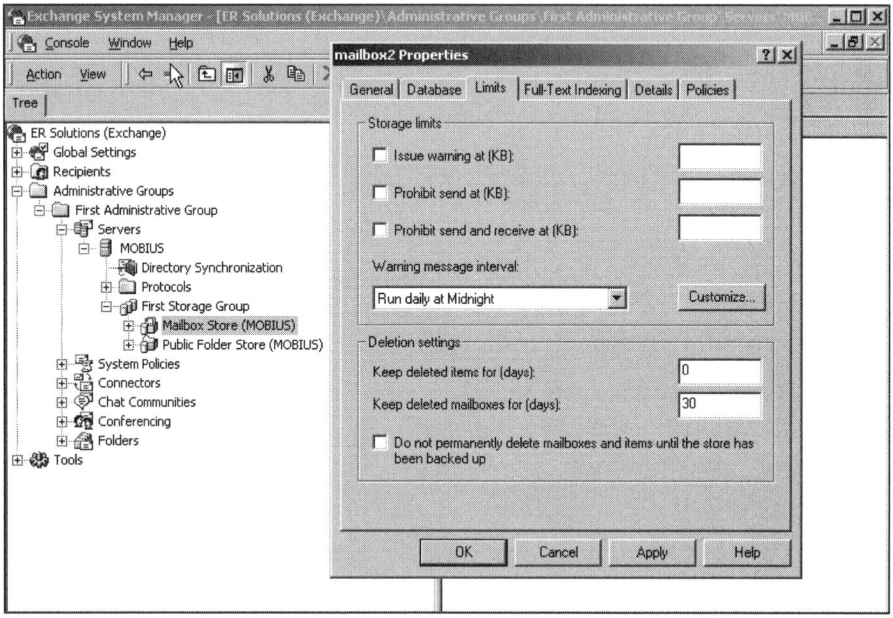

Figure 5.21 The default values on the Limits tab.

3. Click the Limits tab and notice the default values (see Figure 5.21).
4. Select the Issue Warning At (KB) checkbox and type in "5000".
5. Select the Prohibit Send AT (KB) checkbox and type "10000".
6. Notice the Warning Message Interval causes a warning message to be generated at midnight by default for users who exceed their mailbox quota.
7. Type "5" in the Keep Deleted Items For (Days) text box.
8. Notice the default value of 30 in the Keep Deleted Mailboxes For (Days) text box. You can keep this default value or change it to a value that is appropriate for your organization. (We suggest keeping the default value for now).
9. Check the Do Not Permanently Delete Mailboxes And Items Until The Store Has Been Backed Up checkbox, and then click OK.

Using Recipient Policies for Recipient Objects

Exchange 2000 uses default policies to determine how email addresses will appear for recipient objects that you mail-enable or mailbox-enable using Active Directory Users And Computers. For instance, a new user automatically receives an email address in the following form:

userlogon@domain

You can change this default behavior by adjusting the Default Policy or by creating a new Recipient Policy that has a higher priority than the Default Policy.

To plan to adjust Default Policy settings, consider the following points:

- Use the System Manager snap-in to configure Default Policy settings.
- The Default Policy is normally found in the Recipient container and is labeled Recipient Policies.
- Double-clicking Recipient Policies shows all policies created including the Default Policy, which has the lowest priority by default.

To change the properties of the Default Policy:

1. Right-click the Default Policy appearing in the Recipient container and select Properties.
2. Notice the Filter Rules on the General tab (**mailnickname = ***) (see Figure 5.22).
3. Click the E-mail Addresses tab and highlight the line for the SMTP entry. Click the Edit button to change the rules for future SMTP address generations (see Figure 5.23).
4. Type in a placeholder in the Address field that corresponds to the new rule you want to implement; for example, if all email addresses will correspond to **lastname@domain**, type in "%s@domain" to signify this. The list of placeholders you can use is given in Table 5.2.
5. After changing the Address field, click OK to verify your new rule is displayed, and then click OK again. You are prompted to update existing recipients, but the update might not happen immediately.

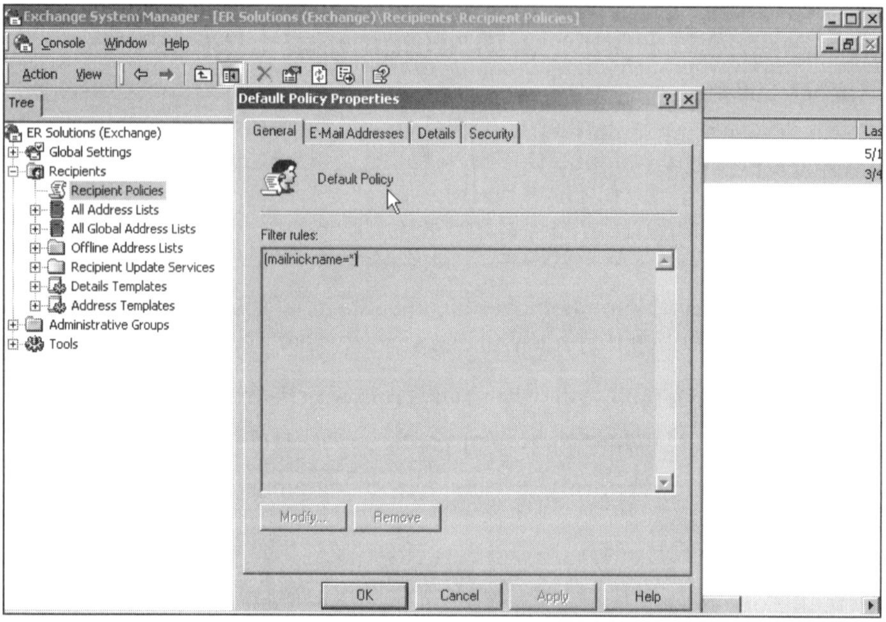

Figure 5.22 The Filter Rules for the Default Recipient Policy.

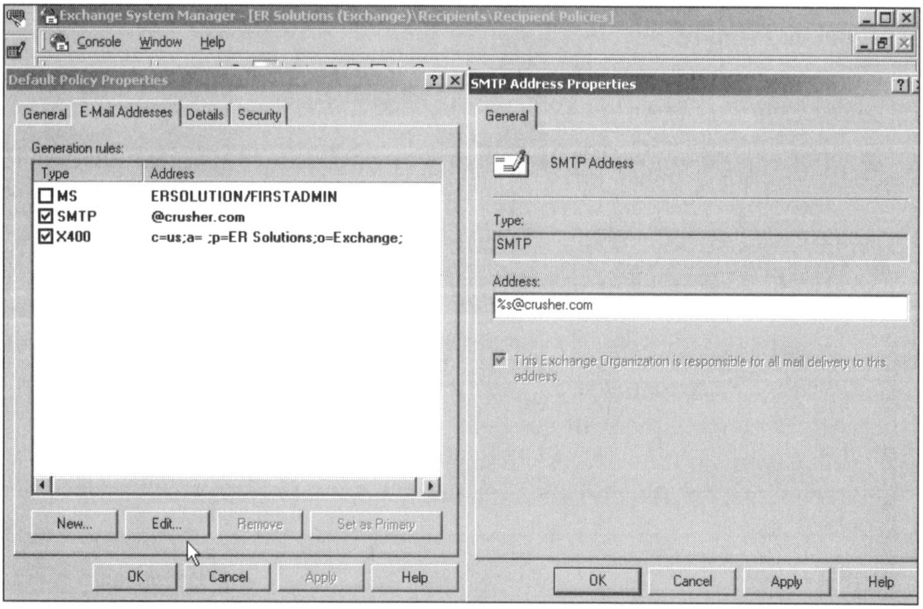

Figure 5.23 Changing the SMTP email address generation rule.

Table 5.2 Placeholder attributes you can use to change default SMTP behavior.

Placeholder Value	Description
%s	Will display the last name of all users in email addresses for current or future recipient objects
%d	Will display the display name in email addresses for current or future recipient objects
%I	Displays initials in email addresses for current or future recipient objects
%g	Displays the given name (first name) in email addresses for current or future recipient objects
%m	Displays the alias in email addresses for current or future recipient objects

Updating Recipient Objects Using the Recipient Update Service

You will notice a delay in displaying new addresses in the GAL whenever you create a new mail-enabled or mailbox-enabled object in the Active Directory Users and Computers snap-in. Any domain containing users configured with Exchange-specific information needs at least one server that runs the Recipient Update Service. This service, a part of the System Attendant component of Exchange 2000, allows proxy email addresses to be generated for every user. Microsoft recommends configuring a separate domain controller or global catalog server for the Recipient Update Service in each domain. You can schedule how often you want to run this service.

To update Address information within a domain:

1. Open the Exchange System Manager snap-in and expand the Recipients container by clicking the "+" next to it.
2. Select Recipient Update Services (notice the two service objects in the right-hand pane of the console window).
3. Right-click the first service object (which represents the naming context for your domain) and choose Update Now to immediately update your recipient addresses after a new user is added or a recipient policy has been changed.

To configure a schedule for your RUS:

1. Right-click either service object appearing in the right-hand pane and select Properties.

NOTE: *The first service object is for updating data in the naming context of your domain; the second service object is for updating information on an enterprise level (for the naming context of the entire Active Directory structure).*

2. When the Properties dialog box opens, click on the Update Interval list box on the bottom of the General tab and select the time interval you want this service to run in. Note that by default, the RUS will Always Run. Keep the default option here and click OK.

Implementing Administrative Groups and Assigning Permissions to Them

You can group servers using two types of objects: administrative groups or routing groups. Administrative groups are designed based on the organizational structure of your enterprise, not your physical structure. The sole purpose of administrative groups is permission management, such that an administrator with appropriate rights to an administrative group can configure all objects within that group. This is done via the Exchange Administration Delegation Wizard tool. You can place all servers into the default First Administrative Group or you can place them into decentralized administrative structures that conform to geographical locations or divisions within your firm.

To create an administrative group within System Manager:

1. Open the Exchange System Manager and expand your Organization object.
2. Right-click the Administrative Groups folder and select New, and then Administrative Group.

NOTE: *Administrative Groups are not displayed by default, so if you do not see this Administrative Groups folder initially, then right-click your Organization object in System Manager and select Properties, and then check the box Display Administrative Groups on the General Tab and click OK.*

3. In the General tab of the Properties dialog box that appears, type the name of your new Administrative Group (for example, type the name AG#2, then click OK. Now expand the "+" next to the Administrative Groups folder and verify that your new administrative group appears in the hierarchy.

NOTE: *A name is the only property required of new administrative groups. The name can be up to 64 characters in length, so be as descriptive as possible. If you use duplicate names for administrative groups, you will receive a message box stating that this name already exists and that you should enter a unique directory name for this object.*

4. You can add a server to this new administrative group only during initial installation of Exchange 2000 on that server. You are not permitted to move a server to a different administrative group once you have placed it inside another administrative group. If System Manager only displays the First Administrative Group, then any new installations of Exchange 2000 will be automatically placed inside this group by default.

To assign permissions to this new administrative group using the Exchange Administration Delegation Wizard tool:

1. Right-click your new administrative group created in Steps 1 through 3 above and select the option Delegate Control. The Welcome To The Exchange Administration Delegation Wizard box appears. Click Next.
2. In the Users Or Groups box that appears, select a user or group that you would like to assign permissions for this administrative group. Click the Add button to make your selection (notice the Administrator account appears by default in the Users And Groups section).
3. In the Delegate Control box, under Groups (Recommended) Or User, click the Browse button to bring up the Select Users, Computers, Or Groups dialog box. Select a user or group that you would like to assign permissions to and click OK.
4. You will be returned to the Delegate Control box. Click the Role text box to select one of four Exchange 2000 Server permission-based roles:
   - *Exchange Administrator*—Users or groups can fully administer Exchange 2000 system information without modifying permissions or controlling access.
   - *Exchange Full Administrator*—Users or groups can fully administer Exchange 2000 system information and modify permissions as well.
   - *Exchange View Only Administrator*—Users or groups can only view Exchange 2000 configuration information without being able to change permissions or control access.

NOTE: *You may see a role called Mailbox Manager, however, according to article ID Q273367 in the Microsoft Knowledge Base (**http://support.microsoft.com/support/kb/articles/Q273/3/67.asp**), this role no longer applies to Exchange 2000 Server. The Online Help documentation regarding this role has been corrected, according to Microsoft.*

Select an appropriate role (for example, Exchange Administrator), and click OK. Then click Next and Finish to return to the System Manager console screen.

Administrative Groups You Created Are Not Visible in System Manager

To view administrative groups that you create in System Manager:

1. Open the System Manager MMC snap-in and right-click your Organization object. Select Properties to open the Organization Properties dialog box.
2. Check the boxes labeled Display Administrative Groups and Display Routing Groups (if desired), and then click OK.
3. Click OK when you see the message box prompting you to start a new instance of the Exchange System Manager snap-in. Close this instance of the System Manager snap-in console.
4. Open another instance of System Manager and expand your Organization object to expose the Adminstrative Groups container. Verify that the First Administrative Group node appears inside this container. All subsequent administrative groups you create will now appear inside the Administrative Groups container.

Chapter 6

Planning Site Topology

If you need an immediate solution to:	*See page:*
Planning an OU Structure	191
Accessing Knowledge Resources Using a Browser	191
Considering AD Group Types	192
Determining AD Group Scopes	192
Creating Groups in Mixed Mode	194
Creating Mail-Enabled Groups	194
Planning AD Security Groups	195
Planning AD Distribution Groups	195
Planning Site Boundaries	195
Determining the Number of GC Servers	196
Estimating GC Database Sizing	196
Determining GC Server Sizing	198
Planning GC Server Placement	198
Selecting Attributes to Replicate to the GC	199
Planning Routing Strategies	199
Planning System Message Flows between Sites	200
Planning How Sites Are Linked	201
Testing whether ESMTP Is Enabled	201
Enabling ESMTP Support	202
Requesting **ETRN/TURN** from a Different Server	202

In Depth

Windows 2000 sites are designed around the location of domain controllers (DCs) for both client access and replication. Exchange 2000 Server uses routing groups to organize Exchange 2000 servers to manage message routing and scheduling. This routing function is the same function performed by legacy Exchange 5.5 Server sites. Message-routing information, which includes routing group and bridgehead lists, is maintained in the configuration-naming context of Active Directory (AD). Exchange 2000 servers contact DCs to retrieve this information.

By uncoupling the logical from the physical structure, you can organize network resources more closely to actual business workflows, yet configure and manage your network traffic according to the more rigid structure of the underlying physical topology. The infrastructure of the physical topology is comprised of DCs and physical sites that determine how replication and logon traffic flow between network nodes. No necessary correlation exists between the Windows 2000 domain structure and the physical infrastructure, nor between sites and domain namespaces.

You need to carefully consider your Windows domain model because of the following:

- After the domain structure is deployed, it's difficult to change.
- Boundaries and sizing characteristics are dependent upon the domain structure.
- Administration and management of recipients are dependent on the domain structure.
- The domain structure affects the deployment of new business initiatives and technology. Best practices recommend the migration of systems and personnel in a multiphased approach when an organization is built across multiple sites. Having multiple sites within a single domain simplifies the management of such an organization.

Enterprise Organization

AD divides objects in an enterprise into a collection of logical containers. Most objects are in domains but can be further divided into Organizational Units (OUs) within those domains. The domain defines a security and replication context; an OU within a domain defines locations of objects for easier administration and management. For example, application of Group Policy is simplified. When planning OUs, consider the following within an enterprise:

- OUs can be nested and, thus, can support the construction of hierarchical trees using child OUs.
- OUs support the delegation of control and management. The combination of a hierarchical, nested OU structure with Access Control Lists (ACLs) provides an excellent context within which to decentralize administration of huge collections of objects in an enterprise.
- OUs are not security principals nor can they be part of a security group but are subject to Group Policy.
- OUs are transparent to the user population and do not constrain the way an end user will navigate through or locate resources within their administrative scope.

You create an OU structure based on the corporate or department needs to organize the functional topology of an enterprise or domain. Thus, the organizational structure may differ when nesting OUs to support a local administrative role as compared to arranging objects to facilitate the application of a Group Policy. Best practices recommend creating OUs to support the management and administration of objects before considering any other action. After you have logically arranged objects in your enterprise into manageable units, you can plan the physical infrastructure.

Remember that the Installation Setup Wizard checks the versions of all Exchange Servers within a site. It also confirms installed components, language, and server type. If you are upgrading from legacy versions of the Exchange software, you must plan additional time for each gigabyte of directory data that needs to be converted to the new schema. Best practices suggest approximately 30 minutes for the conversion of 1GB to the new format. Based on site surveys performed during the envisioning phase, upgrade issues would have typically been addressed by this phase. Best practices recommend that you first upgrade all legacy servers to, at least, Exchange 5.5, though Exchange 2000 is, of course, preferable. Consider issues related to managing recipients when establishing these boundaries as well.

We also recommend that you designate an administrative role for handling all security-related tasks. This person or team (depending on the size of your organization) would be responsible primarily for maintaining an updated security policy. The scope of this role includes aggressive maintenance of the most current software patches, virus signature dictionaries, security alerts, as well as continual end-user education compatible with your company's corporate culture. Performance issues and security access will be vulnerable during deployment and will most likely need careful review following any changes in site boundaries. After sites are defined, it's difficult to alter their boundaries or rearrange objects because organizational names cannot be changed unless Exchange Server 2000 is reinstalled.

NOTE: *Numerous patches are periodically recommended for Exchange 2000 to make it more secure and address ongoing security problems. Microsoft dedicates a portion of TechNet specifically to security issues at* ***www.microsoft.com/technet/security****.*

Creating a Physical Structure

A site topology defines a physical network in a forest in terms of available bandwidth and network reliability. Clients and servers route queries and replication data within this topology. When you create a topology, list all physical subnets, media types, network speeds, and connections between networks. Sites, site links, and subnets are stored in the configuration container of the AD. A change to the site topology causes replication to every DC in the forest.

The following concepts are important when designing your site topology:

- Assign a name to every site created for each local area network (LAN) or set of LANs connected by a reliable, high-speed backbone.
- Create a site for each location that does not have reliable connectivity and, for example, can only be reached by SMTP (Simple Mail Transfer Protocol) mail.
- Determine the location of DCs and merge sites so that traffic is routed efficiently. No traffic can be routed without a DC within the site.
- Balance the use of bandwidth across networks when determining site boundaries because clients communicate with DCs in the same site. If an entire network has fast, reliable connectivity, consider it a single site to simplify administration. Conversely, networks connected by overused links are best put in separate sites. Replications between the two sites can be scheduled during times of lower use to prevent competition for available bandwidth.
- Remember that a client on a subnet not defined in AD is not part of a site and thus randomly selects from all DCs in a given domain. This can occur when a new subnet has just been added to a network and replication across the enterprise has not yet occurred.

Network Structure

Windows 2000 sites provide a physical network structure. Unlike a legacy Exchange 5.5 site that was both an administrative and message-routing unit, the Exchange 2000 site does not necessarily correspond to either the AD namespace or an administrative unit. The site, in a Windows enterprise, is a localized collection of Internet Protocol (IP) subnets. All computers in the same site typically share a high-speed connection with one another on a LAN. Exchange 2000 sites do not necessarily share the same part of the AD namespace and thus replicate the domain-naming context within a domain through synchronous Remote Procedure Calls (RPCs). Multiple sites can exist within a single domain and a single site can span multiple domains. The site defines zones within which this synchronous replication occurs and in which users can connect to a DC.

Protocols

Microsoft has rebuilt message routing on the Exchange 2000 platform by doubling the speed of the Exchange 5.5 Internet Mail Service (IMS). The platform has moved from remote procedure calls to a Simple Mail Transfer Protocol or SMTP-centric message model. Exchange 2000 has shifted away from internal directory services to standards-based LDAP (Lightweight Directory Access Protocol) and DNS (Domain Name Service), long available with Unix implementations. The role of the MTA (Message Transfer Agent) has decreased in significance as an SMTP-based transport core assumes greater responsibility for moving messages across network connections. How messaging routes are determined has also changed. Message flows, determined by the Gateway Routing Table (GWART) in Exchange 5.5, have been replaced by a dynamic routing algorithm in Exchange 2000 that uses updated data about the state of network links throughout the messaging organization.

RPC and SMTP

The legacy Exchange Server was efficient, but based on a proprietary design that used Messaging Application Programming Interface (MAPI) and RPCs over what was, by necessity, a collection of servers that communicated across LAN links. The success of RPCs rested on a tight network mesh that supported the overhead traffic the RPCs generated in acknowledgements. Although a high-capacity bandwidth greater than 64Kbps existed, the legacy RPC-based site connector was the connectivity method of choice. As service loads have increased, SMTP performance provides a more reliable alternative. The bandwidth problems and loose connectivity between systems have forced messaging systems away from RPC and toward more efficient messaging protocols, such as SMTP, because they provide higher bandwidth or better quality connections.

X.400 and SMTP

SMTP, originally defined in RFC 821 in 1982, is the primary messaging protocol for Windows 2000 and Exchange 2000 and the de facto messaging protocol on the Internet as well. When Exchange Server 4 was originally released in 1992, however, SMTP was not the messaging protocol of choice. The original version did not accommodate binary attachments, the nontext extensions to any mission-critical operation. X.400 was championed as a well-defined messaging specification by members of the networking industry, especially in Europe.

NOTE: *Early designs of Exchange Server MTA were based on X.400 specifications by default and used RPCs to transmit information. Microsoft took the original MTA code acquired from an outside company and reworked the engine based on this X.400 model. The legacy X.400 addresses are still an intimate part of the software and necessary to route messages to Exchange 5.5 mailboxes.*

The Exchange MTA structure enabled the robust speed with which messages were routed through servers to mailbox destinations. Messages have been quickly accepted from **STORE.EXE**, addresses have been routed, and the messages sent to their destinations in a highly efficient fashion. The X.400 connector remains better integrated into the MTA than other connectors; it uses less bandwidth overhead when messages are sent between locations. However, this efficiency in design actually limits X.400 outside the defined boundaries of the Windows NT 4 domain model. Legacy Exchange 5.5 was a closed backbone message transfer system due to efficient, explicitly defined X.400-based connections. In an enterprise environment or on the Internet, explicit connections are problematic because one server typically doesn't know where to route messages in advance of their receipt.

A SMTP Server, in comparison, uses TCP/IP port 25 and functions as its own MTA by routing messages based on information supplied through outside directory services such as DNS. The expansion in scope of delivery and the need for greater network efficiency caused the change from RPC to SMTP and the deployment of more Exchange 2000 Servers. The role of the MTA has been relegated to a support position for legacy X.400 systems. For now, the MTA is still responsible for RPC-based communications among Exchange 5.5 Servers in Mixed-mode organizations and also supports legacy workflow connections fashioned from the Exchange Development Kit (EDK) and add-on components such as fax connectors.

MIME and S/MIME

The basis of support in X.400 rested in its comprehensive and well-defined specifications. Compared to X.400, the original version of SMTP was a limited protocol that would transfer only 7-bit ASCII (American Standard Code for Information Interchange) text from server to server. Unfortunately, systems needed greater flexibility than just the transfer of text-based documents. A new protocol, Multipurpose Internet Mail Extensions (MIME), supported additional binary extensions or attachments to this simple transfer protocol. MIME (RFC 1341 and 1342) did not replace SMTP; instead, MIME extended SMTP's functionality and gave SMTP the flexibility to eventually dominate all other messaging protocols such as X.400.

MIME defines different parts of the message—header, body, and attachment—and includes various header fields to specify content. These MIME-encoded messages use a Base64 encoding scheme, which translates the binary data of an attachment into a form that is transferable as a simpler 7-bit transmission. The original specification has been modified to handle secure transmissions of data.

Secure MIME (S/MIME) manages security using encrypted messages that can be reliably transmitted between SMTP connectors. The encryption process, supported since Exchange 5.5, requires keys to both encode and decode the messages.

ESMTP (Extended SMTP) Features

In 1995, the command structure of SMTP was extended to accommodate greater interaction between servers. In addition to handling more complex forms of data through MIME and S/MIME, SMTP expanded its functionality with new commands features in *Extended SMTP (ESMTP)* as defined in RFC 1869. In fact, these extensions were formalized with an Internet-governing body, the Internet Assigned Number Authority (IANA), to ensure that a target- or receiver-SMTP Server could communicate the extended support features it supported to some source or sender-SMTP Server. The capability of servers to communicate their protocol feature sets to other servers facilitates future extensions to SMTP or any other messaging protocol.

Exchange 2000 includes these ESMTP-enhanced features to provide support for the changes in, for example, the routing algorithm:

- *Pipelining*—This feature (RFC 2197) allows servers to issue instructions without suffering delays due to slow command acknowledgements present in the original SMTP specification (RFC 821). Network overhead in the form of excess data transmission is reduced and increased speeds in command transmission improve client/server communications.
- *8-bit clean*—This feature complies with the Transmission Control Protocol (TCP) 8-bit per byte transmission channel and the 8-bit MIME specification (RFC 1652) so that protocol packets are exchanged across servers without translation or conversion.
- *Delivery Status Notification (DSN)*—This feature provides notification when messages are successfully delivered as defined in RFC 1891, 1892, and 1894. This feature standardizes the forms of notification received through different interfaces such as Outlook Express and Outlook 2000. Notifications received by the Outlook 2000 interface come from a system administrator (SA) rather than Post Office postmaster and provide an opportunity to resend the message.
- *Binary Data Transfer (BDAT) or chunking*—This feature, which is a part of chunking large encoded attachments commonly used in messaging systems, replaces older specifications as the method of transferring information. BDAT passes an argument that specifies the length of the data stream in octets so that the receiver of the message knows when the transmission is complete. BDAT is the default mode when directing outbound messages and is always used between Exchange 2000 Servers. This chunking of data provided by ESMTP is a significant improvement over X.400 transmissions that use both acknowledgments and other control features.

Basic Windows 2000 SMTP also supports the extended feature set. Some of the enhanced features that are available in both Windows 2000 and Exchange 2000 are as follows:

- **VRFY** *and* **EXPN** *(RFC 821)*—**VRFY** is defined in RFC 821 and confirms the deliverability of messages to a local recipient. **EXPN**, also defined in RFC 821, expands distributed lists (DLs) into their separate listings of recipients.
- **ETRN**—Defined in RFC 1985, this feature extends the **TURN** command used to reverse sender and receiver roles. The **TURN** command enables a client to download a message without any validation of the sender. **ETRN** provides a client an alternative way to request a download for a specific message queue. The host of the message queue can determine whether or not to honor the request.

Other commands include **SIZE** (RFC 1870), which provides both a measurement of message size and a server's maximum size limit; **TLS** (RFC 2487), which provides Transport Layer Security for secure transmissions; and **AUTH** (RFC 2554), which provides for negotiations over authentication methods between client and server. Use the Telnet service to query a SMTP Server on port 25 with the **EHLO** command to request a list of keywords from a SMTP Server's feature list.

The most significant difference between legacy Exchange 5.5 SMTP features as provided by the IMS Connector with those now available in Exchange 2000 is how SMTP is deployed. Table 6.1 lists these major differences. The Exchange 2000 platform and Windows 2000 use SMTP for fundamental messaging services rather than as a separate software layer in the form of a connector. Both the network operating system (NOS) and Exchange 2000 depend on SMTP for server-to-server communications.

Table 6.1 Comparison of SMTP services in Exchange 5.5 and Exchange 2000.

Exchange 5.5 IMS	Exchange 2000 SMTP Service
Service provided as separate software layer, IMS Connector	Service provided as layer in both NOS and Exchange
Partial support for ESMTP	Full support for ESMTP
Single SMTP connection	Multiple SMTP connections as Virtual Servers
Single SMTP namespace	Each SMTP Virtual Server supports a separate namespace
Connector dependent on DNS	Virtual servers use either AD via Routing Group Connector or DNS for SMTP Connector
Single set of configurations	Each Virtual Server has a separate set of configurations
No specific features for event handling	Special event handlers through event sinks

Virtual Servers

Legacy 5.5 and Exchange 2000 differ in the support of SMTP Virtual Servers. You can create multiple SMTP Virtual Servers on the same physical server that can provide separately configured services to different messaging systems. Virtual servers on the same physical server must belong to the same routing group. In most cases, however, you don't need more than one routing group. Multiple Virtual Servers will not improve messaging system throughput because the Virtual Server is multithreaded. *Multithreading* means the server process runs different subfunctions simultaneously and thus can optimize delivery of the protocol services. You can also configure a Virtual Server to have different domain names. Multiple Virtual Servers can accommodate different user groups with specific authentication requirements.

In the legacy product, the protocol is bound to a specific port and remains associated with it as a single instance or process. For example, TCP port 25 is the only network port that will handle SMTP traffic in an Exchange 5.5 Server. Alternatively, Exchange 2000 defines a Virtual Server as a socket made up of a combination of both protocol and port. If the SMTP protocol is configured or bound to a range of IP addresses, the Virtual Server is able to process messages directed to any of those ports. The default configuration, however, is to have a SMTP Virtual Server listen for incoming messages on port 25. Each Virtual Server has its own IP address configuration. Thus, each Exchange 2000 Server has at least one Virtual Server with a defined namespace that runs on port 25 and listens to all addresses. This SMTP Virtual Server is the foundation for both the SMTP and Routing Group Connector.

Exchange Components

Windows 2000 installs a SMTP service that supports the ESMTP command set. This is installed as a part of the now integrated Internet Information Services (IIS) version 5. It forms the communication foundation for the NOS. The installation of Exchange 2000 upgrades this base SMTP service layer. The .NET Server installation adds additional functionality through commands like **X-LINK2STATE** that support the link state routing algorithm (LSA) and other components such as the advanced queuing engine (AQ), the message categorization agent, and the Exchange Installable File System (ExIFS) store driver. These components are all part of the Exchange Transport Core as described in the following section.

Transport Core

The *Transport Core*, the center of message routing in Exchange 2000, is composed of four major components:

- *AQ*—This component handles inbound and outbound messages and supports the grouping of messages according to the final destination in *domain-level queues*. Messages can be grouped according to the next drop point (or *hop*) they will travel through on their way to some final destination. This grouping, called a *link queue*, also generates delivery service notifications.

- *Categorizer*—The Categorizer reads message headers and analyzes properties to correctly process messages. A limited version of this component is built into Windows 2000 for the expansion of mail-enabled security and distribution groups. Exchange 2000 has additional features, such as the monitoring or management of mailbox quotas, mailbox restrictions, connector restrictions, and mailbox storage locations.
- *Exchange store driver*—This driver interface separates the AQ component from the NTFS (NT File System). Windows 2000 ships with a basic store driver that processes inbound SMTP messages. The Exchange version includes Exchange Installable File System support that provides AQ with direct access to messages in **STORE.EXE**.
- *Routing Engine (RE)*—This component replaces the legacy Relative ID (RID) master and GWART used to determine routing paths in a legacy Exchange 5.5 organization. The RE adjusts message routing based on updated reports on the state of the network. The route of any one message is based on size, sender, and message priority in combination with assigned costs of links and the current state of those links. Exchange 2000 uses a link state routing algorithm, a commonly used method to determine the shortest distance between two points, to provide the link state updates between SMTP Servers. The LSA protocol, a modified version of Dijkstra's algorithm, has been proposed as a formal RFC to the IETF (Internet Engineering Task Force).

Component Communication

Message flow within Exchange 2000 Server relies on various forms of intercomponent communication. Table 6.2 summarizes these interactions.

Table 6.2 Intercomponent communications within Exchange 2000.

Component	Communicates With	Reason
Information Store	AD	Retrieves configuration information
Information Store	MAPI clients	Provides email notification
Information Store	MTA	Delivers mail to foreign messaging system
System Attendant	AD	Builds routing tables
System Attendant	Information Store	Stores messages regarding server monitoring
System Attendant	IIS process	Updates the IIS metabase (configuration database)
SMTP service	AD	Expands distribution groups

All messaging systems depend on an underlying transport mechanism and routing engine. For Exchange 2000, this is the SMTP service, which contains an advanced queuing engine. A typical message flow scenario is as follows:

1. A SMTP system or client connects to another SMTP service and tries to send a message.
2. The SMTP service creates files for every incoming message in the \Exchsrvr\ Mailroot directory path. It then confirms receipt of each message and notifies the advanced queuing engine that it's ready for the next step.
3. The advanced queuing engine directs these messages to the Categorizer, which classifies all recipients. The Categorizer puts all messages into a special *precategorizer queue.*
4. The Categorizer processes all messages and puts them in appropriate delivery queues for either local delivery or remote delivery. If local delivery, the Information Store holds the message before delivering it to the end user; otherwise, the SMTP service is responsible for it at this time.
5. Messages placed in a special *destination-domain queue* are given to the RE, which notifies the SMTP service where to transfer the message. The SMTP service then delivers the message.
6. For local messages, an Information Store driver notifies the Information Store about the local delivery queue.

NOTE: *If a message needs to be sent to multiple recipients, the Categorizer classifies each intended recipient and creates multiple copies of the message to be sent when ready. The Categorizer can also expand distribution groups and check whether restrictions have been placed on the sender or the recipient of a message. The official name of the Categorizer is PHATCAT.DLL, which is located in the \Exchsrvr\Bin directory path.*

Accessing Messages and Other Objects

When a user clicks a message in an open mailbox, the IIS request processor calls the Exchange HTTP Internet Server Application Programming Interface (ISAPI) application, which parses the request. This action determines the following:

- Specific action to be performed, such as opening a folder, reading or creating a message, and so on.
- Specific browser (navigation object) information, such as browser type, version, rendering information, and so on.

The server, upon determining whether user permissions in the ACL support the action, collects information about the target object state (read, unread), object type (message, folder, calendar, and so on), and item type (specific message, appointment, and so on) to perform the requested service. The Exchange HTTP

ISAPI extension matches the object attribute to some corresponding form definition. A default form, such as the one typically used to read an email item, is used if no form definition exists for a particular object attribute. The Exchange HTTP ISAPI extension then parses the form and queries the Web Storage System (WSS) to bind the data. Exchange HTTP ISAPI renders the data received in HTML or XML depending on the browser type and version. The user views the marked-up information through the client browser interface.

CDO (Collaborative Data Objects)

Collaborative Data Objects version 2 (CDO 2) for Windows NT Server (also known as *CDONTS* or *CDOSYS.DLL*) is part of IIS within the Windows 2000 platform. It is a basic server-to-server messaging system without support for recipient objects or mailboxes. Although common in all Windows 2000 software products, the Professional version of Windows 2000 has many features disabled. This relationship of CDO with IIS in the NOS explains why the Exchange 2000 System Attendant must synchronize the AD with the IIS metabase on a regular basis. Exchange 2000 configuration information is stored in the AD, and its protocol services are provided by IIS in the NOS. The IIS metabase needs regular updating of changes in configuration located in the AD. The Exchange 2000 installation upgrades CDONTS 2 to CDO for Exchange 3 (CDOEX) and provides the base SMTP with additional functionality. The significant difference between CDO 2 and CDOEX is that the latter includes management of mailboxes. The upgrade of base SMTP services rather than replacement when Exchange is installed means that the NOS and Exchange depend on the SMTP service layer but through different—although complementary—mechanisms. Remember this fact if you ever have to reinstall system software. Much like the application of old service packages on legacy operating systems (OSs), the reinstallation of the base Windows 2000 SMTP service layer and, for example CDO 2, requires a reinstallation of dependent application software such as Exchange Server and its upgraded CDOEX.

WebDAV and HTML

Web Distributed Authoring and Versioning (WebDAV) extends the HTTP 1.1 protocol (RFC 2518) to provide the collaborative interaction with CDOs and other data stored in the WSS. A browser client supporting HTML 3.2 can access these stores through OWA (Outlook Web Access). The browser caches the user interface (UI) elements and reformats the UI through client-side data binding on demand without requesting additional service support.

How Components Work Together

Messages enter the Transport Core and are placed in the inbound queue. Messages from other Exchange Servers travel on SMTP services and are processed through the ExIFS, often as NTFS files. Exchange 5.5 messages are transferred by the MTA through RPCs. MAPI messages originating from mailboxes are processed through the store. Internet-based clients using Internet Message Access Protocol (IMAP4) or Post Office Protocol (POP3) pass messages via SMTP through IIS and then through ExIFS into streaming files. HTTP clients use a direct connection to the store via ExIFS to generate WebDAV messages. The Queuing Engine then uses the Message Categorization component to process these inbound messages, checking for various properties such as mailbox quotas and routing permissions. Distributions lists (DLs) are also expanded here.

After they are processed, messages are placed in the categorized message queue while the Transport Core process checks for triggered routing events such as filtering words. The body and any mail attachments are scanned and, if necessary, returned to the sender. A query against the Domain Mapping and Configuration Table tells the Transport Core process to route the message for local delivery or to a SMTP Virtual Server. Messages intended for local delivery are first placed in a local delivery queue. From there, they are passed either to the Exchange store driver or to the MTA. Messages allocated for SMTP Virtual Servers are redirected to destination queues that handle different domains. The Connector Manager handles SMTP server links from these destination queues. If a hub server is unavailable, the Connector Manager reroutes the message. All outbound mail, dispatched using SMTP, is handled by two different queues. Messages are either stored in link queues and maintained for routes mapped on a hop-by-hop basis or are stored in domain queues and generated and maintained on a per-need basis.

This specific queuing by destination is a departure from the legacy Internet Mail Service Connector, in which all messages were held in a single outbound queue. Specific queuing also doesn't allow the delivery to any one domain to block delivery to all other destinations. Multiple available routes between routing groups are an important enhancement for reliable delivery. The new RE attempts to find alternative paths among the other available routes, which further reduces the possibility of downtime.

Processing Incoming Messages

A major design achievement is the growing number of ways messages can arrive into an Exchange 2000 Server. In summary, however, they all come together at the message Categorizer in the Transport Core. The most common way messages arrive is probably across TCP port 25 from other SMTP Servers acting as clients. This port is monitored by IIS, and, when the new message arrives, SMTP generates a process thread to handle it. At some point, a protocol event might fire even before the message is fully received to confirm its acceptability or reject it before the message transaction is complete. A store driver event is fired when the transaction is complete. The Windows NTFS store driver is used here rather than ExIFS to increase overall consistency within the system because the Exchange executable files are located on the same drive as the mail-drop directory. If the drive fails, the Exchange Server fails as well as delivery of mail to the mail-drop directory. Messages are redirected or returned rather than partially processed. Furthermore, directing messages into an NTFS folder rather than the store uncouples the initial receipt of the mail from message processing and delivery.

The new message is placed in an **onSubmission** queue, which also fires an event. If an error in delivery of the package is detected at this point, a notification of non-delivery message can be sent back to the sender or the message can be redirected to the badmail directory. In fact, if any error occurs while the incoming SMTP message is being processed, the message is removed from the queue and placed in the badmail directory. Messages destined for local delivery are inserted into the store. Outgoing messages are handled the same way, except that IIS-provided protocol services reads them out from the store via ExIFS.

MAPI Messages

MAPI clients do not use IIS to connect to the store. After a message is accepted through, for example, the MTA, the store notifies the Transport Core store driver that the message is waiting in a special SendQ folder. The Transport Core store driver processes the content of the message and submits it to AQ. MAPI messages sent between Exchange 2000 Servers using SMTP are translated into *Transport Neutral Encapsulated Format (TNEF)*, which can rapidly be returned to MAPI properties and content. Messages are formed from RFC 822–compliant headers and an application-specific body. Because Exchange 2000 Servers use SMTP, the TNEF needs to be converted to MIME before it is transported across a network, unless transported as binary content. Messages directed outside an organization can thus end up 25–30 percent larger. This is a general criticism of SMTP as compared to X.400. However, even though the X.400 protocol adds less overhead to packets than SMTP, the actual method of SMTP communication is simpler, which compensates for the complicated data conversions.

Just like the legacy Exchange 5.5 process, X.400 messages in Exchange 2000 are handled by the MTA. After a message is accepted, the MTA places it in an MTA-Out folder located within the store. The Transport Core store driver moves it eventually to the AQ and the precategorizer queue. Foreign connectors maintain their own MTA-Out folder. After the incoming message is accepted, it is processed the same way as X.400 messages.

Categorization

The AQ component processes all inbound messages and places them in the precategorizer queue. The Categorizer then performs several tests on each message, including the following:

- *Address resolution*—The sender and receiver addresses are applied to AD stores for name resolution. A determination is made of restrictions, such as a recipient mailbox quota or other limitations, on either sender or receiver, upon resolution of the receiver address. If the recipient is a DL, the list is expanded. If the receiver cannot be resolved, the recipient is marked as unknown.

- *Message format*—The message format and properties are checked to ensure that the message can be rendered properly.
- *Request for multiple copies*—Some messages require special handling because different recipients require different versions of the same message, such as when one receiver in a list of recipients can be found but another is not listed in an address book. One recipient might have a local mailbox, while another, in the same organization, must receive the message through delivery across other MTAs in the organization.

After categorization is complete, messages are directed to a prerouting queue that determines how to redirect the messages for the final phase of routing through this particular Exchange Server.

Outbound Mail

Recipients with mailboxes are identified in the AD of an Exchange 2000 Server. If an attribute in the recipient's AD entry includes the distinguished name of the mailbox store, the message for the recipient is delivered where the path points. Thus, an examination of a routing table on a neighboring server immediately determines whether a mailbox destination exists on that contiguously linked server, or in other words, within one "hop." This kind of information is stored in a next-hop identifier. A mailbox stored on the same server is made locally; the message is placed on the local delivery queue. Actual messages that are stored in queues remain in the store or NTFS directory until they are transmitted, typically in a subdirectory named queue under mailroot. Messages delivered to other Exchange 2000 Servers in the same routing group or over a routing group connector are placed in an appropriate outbound queue—either link or domain—until actually dispatched.

Planning Routing Groups

Routing groups are similar to the legacy Exchange 5.5 concept of site. Within a *site*, peer machines link to each other across high-speed connections forming a topological mesh across which messages are transferred with significant delay. These messages are transferred via SMTP except when legacy servers are also part of the routing group in a mixed-mode configuration. As explained previously, when legacy servers are part of an Exchange organization, the MTA transfers messages using the older RPC protocol.

Creating a Routing Group

A routing group is simply an administrative container. Unlike Exchange 5.5 sites, this administrative unit can be created in advance of a server joining the group in both native and mixed modes. A routing group provides an organization structure separate from the actual deployment of physical servers. To create a new routing group in the Routing Groups container, right-click the node icon and select New in the context menu. The routing group is another container within the Configuration container for the organization of various Exchange objects. Following the creation of a group, you can add servers by, for example, clicking and dragging the icon in System Manager to the Members folder in the new routing group.

Although routing groups, in general, are simpler to use than the legacy site concept, restrictions must be observed when assigning servers. For example, if a server is a bridgehead for a connector, its position within the organization is fixed; you cannot move this machine to a different routing group. Connectors and routing groups provide an organizational structure to a routing table; major changes in their relationship to other servers within this structure can have disastrous effects. To move such a server, you must first delete connectors, which releases the candidate machine from any relationship with other machines in the organization.

The Role of the Routing Group Master

The first server (or person for that matter) that creates some kind of administrative unit in Windows 2000 tends to inherit some special roles with respect to that unit. In the most fundamental way, the first person who installs the OS is the administrator or super user. Similarly, the first server in each routing group is defined as the *Routing Group Master (RGM)*. The first server assumes this role by default but it can be changed by an administrator. The most important task the RGM performs is maintaining the Link State Table (LST). This important information is automatically shared between all servers in a routing group. Updates of links between servers are relayed to the RGM, which broadcasts information to all members of the routing group. Each member of the group keeps its own copy of this LST in memory. The RGM acts as a contact point for the entire group.

To change the RGM role, follow these steps:

1. Open the System Manager.
2. Under the Member node in the routing group of choice, select the specific server you want to assign this role to.
3. Then, select the Set As Master feature in that server's context menu.

If, for whatever reason, a RGM is unavailable, all routing is performed based on the more recent copy of the LST replicated to all the members of the routing group.

Routing Information in the AD and DNS

The RE needs to know the IP address of a mail server to route mail. The advantage of SMTP is that it relies on the mail exchange (MX) DNS record in the DNS server to locate mail servers for handling domain mail traffic. If MX records are unavailable, a mail server uses an address (A) DNS record, which specifies a host address, to locate mail servers in the domain. The AD also can look up a mail server if it's located inside an organization. The AD can provide the RE with the target mail server's Globally Unique Identifier (GUID), which is a 128-bit number assigned to every object in the AD. The RE can determine a host name by using the GUID. The host name is resolved to an IP address, which is similar to using an MX record. Given the importance of mail service, these redundant methods of identifying and routing messages add a layer of fault tolerance to the process of locating a mail server in case routing information is incorrect or missing.

Message Routing and Group Expansion

Message routing information, which includes routing groups and bridgeheads, is held in the configuration-naming context of the AD. Exchange 2000 determines routing information by contacting its local DC and retrieving this information. The SMTP Virtual Server expands messages to the universal group by using information SMTP receives from the Global Catalog (GC) Server. Best practices recommend that only local GC Servers should expand local and global group address lists. Every Exchange Server attempts to use a local GC Server but can request GCs from any domain in a local site. You can ensure that address lists are expanded correctly by locating expansion servers in a Windows 2000 site that contains only GCs for the domain that both the expansion server and groups reside in. Site placement and routing groups depend upon the following:

- Permanent and reliable network connectivity exists between all servers.
- Sufficient bandwidth exists to support queries between servers.
- Low communication latency exists within sites, as well as low bandwidth use across sites. The location of DCs has a significant impact on the availability of directory services within your enterprise.

Link State Routing

The major difference between legacy Exchange 5.5 and Exchange 2000 is that the legacy version used the GWART to manage routes messages can take to reach some final destination. The GWART did not track moment-by-moment changes in these routes, however it recorded cumulative costs and next-hop information. In fact, Exchange 2000 sends updated routing information between servers in two ways:

- *Between routing groups*—A LST is passed between bridgehead servers to the RGM. SMTP over TCP port 25 is used instead of the LSA protocol over port

691 if either the routing group connector or the SMTP Connector is used. The **EHLO** command is sent as soon as a connection is started to confirm that the server is using ESMTP.

- *Within a routing group*—LST sends updates between bridgehead servers using the routing server across the assigned TCP port 691. The information is passed using the proprietary Microsoft protocol, LSA. Based on these updates, the RGM broadcasts changes to all the servers in the routing group.

The LSA protocol greatly improves on the more static mapping used in the legacy product. As mentioned previously, LSA operates over TCP port 691 within the routing group. The RGM is the primary beneficiary of this information and, as mentioned in the earlier "The Role of the Routing Group Master," acts as a central administrative focus for the group. Alternatively, bridgehead servers exchange the information over TCP port 25.

The LSA protocol forms the foundation for the Open Shortest Path First (OSPF) protocol used by routers today. LSA propagates the routing conditions very close to realtime. Networks that combine this information and build collaborative tables for routing are called *directory-enabled networks*, which have the following characteristics:

- Exchange Servers make the best routing decisions because they determine the route before the message is directed downstream.
- Message loss is eliminated because alternative route information is propagated to each server.
- Message looping is eliminated.

The link state information is especially important when an organization has multiple routing groups with multiple paths between groups. The RGM maintains the link state information and shares it with other RGMs in other routing groups. The link state information only includes information in a binary form; that is, whether the link is up or down. This information is held in memory rather than written to disk. If the RGM fails or needs to reboot, this information must be replicated from other RGMs in the organization. Routing information, connector information, and costs are actually stored in the AD naming partition. As mentioned previously in the "Routing Information in the AD and DNS" section, the link state protocol references each connector by its GUID.

Finally, if a RGM goes offline, a new master isn't automatically determined through some election or promotion process. A new RGM must be manually configured to refresh the link state information each server in the group is referencing.

Site Links

Site links model the amount of available bandwidth between two connected sites. Any two networks connected by a link slower than LAN speed, typically 10MBps, are considered connected by a site link. Consider any fast connection that is near capacity as having a low effective bandwidth and, thus, a site link. These site links have four parameters of interest:

- *Cost*—The cost value of a site link helps determine when to use a link for replication.
- *Replication schedule*—A link has an indicated time of day scheduled for the replication of data to other DCs.
- *Replication interval*—The time interval indicates how often systems poll remote DCs for replication changes.
- *Transport*—The kind of transport used to replicate system data.

Arrange the site links to reflect the connectivity of your physical infrastructure. Site links are transitive. Thus, if site A is connected to site B, and site B is connected to site C, the knowledge consistency checker will assume that DC "A" can communicate with DC "C". If you need a distinct network connection between site A and site C, create a specific link between them as well. A backbone connecting many sites is considered a single link rather than a series of separate connections. Best practices recommend reducing the number of links wherever possible, especially between sites with common characteristics. You should maintain the following information on each site:

- Link speed and current levels of use
- Nature of the link, such as pay-by-usage
- History of link in terms of reliability and availability

Exchange 2000 maintains accurate information about link states by replicating configuration information along with link state information under the control of the AD. If a domain is unreachable, the SMTP service registers a warning in the system event log. While link queues are transient and only appear when in use, the *Messages waiting directory lookup* queue and the *Messages waiting to be routed* queue are visible. When messages are found in the first queue, the Categorizer has not yet processed them. Messages in the second queue, however, might indicate that the Categorizer cannot retrieve routing information from the routing tables in memory. In addition to confirming that a GC Server is available to the Exchange Server, review the application event log to confirm that the system is running properly.

Summary

This chapter has covered some of the topics involved in planning both the site topology and the foundation for the functional organization of an Exchange system. AD provides new ways of mapping real-world scopes of authority and responsibility to logical structures in the Windows 2000 enterprise through, for example, organizational units. Exchange 2000 leverages these logical structures with administrative and distribution groups. These two AD group types help to categorize recipients and simplify management. This chapter discusses some of the physical issues involved in site topology such as the various protocols that support both messaging and collaborative services. Both SMTP and HTTP have been enhanced to provide larger feature sets and greater functionality. The Exchange core components are briefly discussed in relation to the functioning within an individual site. Link State Routing is described as the method Exchange 2000 uses to move messages across sites. Planning these routing strategies and support the flow of messages between sites is dependent not just on connectivity issues but the support of directory services provided by GC Servers and AD. These topics are the physical basis upon which the functional organization of an Exchange system is based.

Immediate Solutions

Planning an OU Structure

When you create an OU structure, consider the following issues:

- Create OUs to facilitate administrative functions.
- Build the OU structure in a nested configuration to hide objects.
- Design your OUs to transparently arrange objects to make assigning Group Policy easier.
- Carefully consider the ramifications of changing OUs to support future changes to an enterprise after deployment.

Accessing Knowledge Resources Using a Browser

If you are not authenticated, you will be prompted for a logon ID, password, and domain when attempting to access resources using a browser. If you access an OWA server that does not contain your mailbox, the server redirects the session to the appropriate mail server.

- To open a mailbox, type "*http://servername/exchange/userid/*" or "*http://servername/exchange*".
- To open the top-level public folder, type "*http://servername/public*".
- To open your calendar, type "*http://servername/exchange/userid/calendar*".

Close all instances of the browser to exit the OWA session and clear any authentications remaining in the browser cache.

Considering AD Group Types

An *AD group* is the equivalent of a legacy Exchange 5.5 DL. The two AD group categories—security group and distribution group—differ in terms of their scope. The scope of the group determines membership and access to network resources. The three group scopes are domain local, global, and universal, with the domain mode imposing the greatest limits on choice of group type and scope. Both groups can be mail-enabled and used as DLs. Consider the following when using these groups:

- *Group name*—Use Windows 2000 naming standards when creating these mail-enabled groups.
- *Group ownership*—Assign ownership of a group to the user requesting the group to simplify administration and reduce overhead.
- *Group size*—Group membership should not exceed 5,000. Best practices recommend nesting membership in groups of about 500 members.

Determining AD Group Scopes

Universal groups provide the greatest flexibility compared to global and domain local scopes. Universal group membership is stored in the GC Server, however, and when changed, is replicated between all other GC Servers in the enterprise. Best practices recommend that universal groups typically remain static. Alternatively, domain local and global groups are best where membership does periodically change because replication data is confined within the domain. Because this information is not included in the GC, these membership lists are not visible to users in other domains. Consider the following attributes for the domain local scope:

- Domain local accounts in native mode contain user accounts, global groups, and universal groups from any domain in the forest in addition to domain local groups from the same domain. In mixed mode, the domain local accounts contain just user accounts and global groups from any domain.
- You grant permissions to domain local groups only for objects within the existing domain. You cannot grant permissions to network resources or public folders in other domains.
- Domain local groups can be converted to universal groups in native mode as long as they do not contain other domain local groups.
- The GC lists group objects but not memberships. Outlook users in other domains cannot view the full membership because it is not listed in the GC.

- Group membership must be retrieved on demand if expansion takes place in a remote domain.

Consider the following attributes for the global scope:

- Groups with global scopes contain user accounts from the same domain and global groups from the same domain when in native mode. In mixed mode, however, groups cannot contain user accounts from the same domain.
- You can grant global group permissions for all domains in the forest regardless of their location.
- You can convert groups with global scopes to a universal group in native mode as long as they do not belong to any other global group.
- Groups with global scopes can only contain recipient objects from the same domain.
- Group objects are listed in the GC, but the group membership is not. Thus, Outlook users in other domains cannot view the full membership.
- Group membership must be retrieved on demand if expansion takes place in a remote domain.

Consider the following attributes for the universal scope:

- Groups with universal scope contain user accounts, global groups, and universal groups from any domain in the forest when the domain is in native mode.
- Although universal security groups are used only in native-mode domains, universal distribution groups can be used in mixed-mode and native-mode domains.
- You can grant permissions to universal groups for all domains in the forest regardless of their location.
- Groups with universal scope cannot be converted to any other kind of scope.
- Because membership is listed in the GC, Outlook users in any domain can view full membership of the group. Membership does not have to be retrieved from a remote DC. Similarly, membership modifications are replicated across all GC Servers in the forest.

Best practices recommend limiting membership of universal groups to groups only, rather than individual accounts, to minimize any changes in the listings and subsequent generation of network traffic due to replication. When creating universal groups, consider the following:

- Determine whether single or multiple domains should be in the enterprise. Universal groups are not needed in single domains because all objects are local.

- Use universal groups for multiple domains in which the groups are fairly static. Remember that users might not have access to all object attributes from other domains in the universal group.
- Determine the nature of the network connectivity possible between the domains.
- If direct connectivity is possible, use the universal scope if the group is relatively static and needs to include users from other domains. Otherwise, use local domain and global scope, especially if membership changes often and users need complete access to all attributes of the group members.
- Determine the frequency of change in the group membership list. Frequent changes increase replication in universal groups; therefore, dynamic lists are best for domain local or global groups.
- Determine whether the source of email to the group is from inside or outside the local domain. If the email is local, use local domain or global scope because the user population typically uses a common DC. If the email is from outside a domain, you need to publish the list using universal groups.

NOTE: *Remember that groups are also used for determining public folder access. The store no longer needs to expand a group when a user accesses a public folder as it did in legacy versions of Exchange. Public folder ACLs are based on AD attributes. The group membership is included in the user's access token and presented to the Exchange Server upon connecting to the resource.*

Creating Groups in Mixed Mode

When an administrator creates a new group in mixed mode, it is configured by default as a security group with universal scope. In mixed-mode domains, you cannot change the scope of a group after it is created. Thus, creating a group with the appropriate group type for both distribution and public folder access needs to be carefully considered before its implementation. Group scope, size, and membership, especially in a mixed-mode environment, significantly affect the choice of group type.

Creating Mail-Enabled Groups

When creating mail-enabled groups, keep the following guidelines in mind:

- It is best to use security groups as the primary group type, but only mail-enable them when necessary.

- Distribution groups are best for lists that include nontrusted recipients.
- Use groups with a universal scope when membership lists tend to be static and need to be published. In mixed mode, you can only use DLs. You can manage these distribution groups with regard to group accessibility by specific domain or by all users.
- Remember that group types are particularly important with respect to Outlook users across the forest because only universal membership lists are published.

Planning AD Security Groups

Characteristics of security groups include the following:

- Members are mail-enabled with a SMTP address, which acts as an equivalent to a DL. This grouping consolidates the number of groups and simplifies AD maintenance because security groups have the same functionality as DLs.
- This group can be used to assign public folder permissions in Exchange 2000.
- This group can be used to assign network permissions.
- A major disadvantage to security groups is that membership grants permissions that might not be appropriate for all members.

Planning AD Distribution Groups

Characteristics of distribution groups include the following:

- Distribution groups provide bulk-mailing capability.
- Membership has the same characteristics as universal scoping, except that distribution groups can be used in mixed-mode environments.
- Distribution groups cannot support permission assignments to network resources or public folders in Exchange 2000.

Planning Site Boundaries

Determining the number of sites affects the arrangement of site boundaries. The following guidelines help determine boundaries:

- Differences in bandwidth capacity and availability between WAN (wide area network) and LAN connections.

- Types of network infrastructure, including network links.
- Number of users, cumulative usage profiles, and the resultant LAN segment workload characterization and traffic patterns.
- Corporate and administrative policies and procedures applied to specific sections of the user population in specific areas of the corporation. These areas can be either logical, such as a department, or geographical, based on the location of the site.

Determining the Number of GC Servers

In the Windows 2000 environment, users access directory service information from the GC. A GC Server is a specially designated Windows 2000 DC. All DCs expose port 389 and contain an updatable copy of the directory and configuration partitions of the domain. Servers that are also schema masters contain an updatable version of the schema partition as well. A GC Server also exposes port 3286 with objects from every partition but only a subset of object attributes in the GC's own domain. Although the GC Server exposes partition objects on ports 389 and 3286, only a partial set of attributes are visible on 3286. The entire object is exposed on 389 of the DC for the domain that contains the object. MAPI properties appear only on GCs and are available to Outlook users in other domains.

Even though Exchange 2000 balances the load of service requests distributed to available GC Servers, consider the number of clients requesting support from these specially designated servers. Best practices recommend deployment of at least two GC Servers per Windows 2000 site. If the site spans multiple domains, configure a GC Server for each domain that the Exchange 2000 Server and clients are located on. The number of GC Servers depends on the physical capacity of each server, the number of users, message volume, and any other factors that impact the processor load. Monitor Exchange 2000 demands on the GC Server carefully and add servers to gain optimal performance.

Estimating GC Database Sizing

Primary factors that affect size and performance of the GC Server include the following:

- Database size on the DCs
- Database size on the GC Server
- Bandwidth requirements for replication

You can download the Active Directory Sizer tool to estimate database size on DCs from the Microsoft Web site at **www.microsoft.com**. Table 6.3 helps estimate the database size of the GC Server. The total number of needed kilobytes is a good estimation of the total database space required for the GC Servers from all domains in your enterprise forest.

Table 6.3 Database sizing of the GC.

Object Type	Number of Objects	KB per Object	Class Total in KB
AD initial database	1	12,000	12,000
User with mandatory attributes	Number of users in population	4.366	Total users×4.366KB
Additional attributes	Users with additional attributes	0.100	Number of attributesxusers×0.100KB
Contact	Number of contacts	1.678	Number of contacts×1.678
Group	Groups in forest (including mail-enabled or security)	2.097	Number of groups×2.097KB
Group membership (small group)	Members in small groups (20 members)	0.200	Number of small groups×0.200KB
Group membership (medium group)	Members in medium groups (100 members)	0.100	Number of small groups×0.100KB
Group membership (large group)	Members in large groups (more than 200 members)	0.070	Number of small groups×0.070KB
OU	OUs in forest	1.992	Number of OUs×1.992KB
Certificate	Certificates in AD	2.181	Number of certificates×2.181
Computer	Machine accounts in forest	4.086	Number of machine accounts×4.086KB
Volume	Volumes registered in AD	1.573	Number of volumes×1.573KB
Printer	Printers in forest	2.412	Number of printers×2.412KB
Binary Large Objects (BLOB) (typically image or sound)	Number of BLOBs	File size+25 bytes	Total BLOB file sizes+(Number of BLOBs×0.025)

Determining GC Server Sizing

A GC Server can support a large number of users depending on workload characterizations and other available GC Server services provided to the forest. You should anticipate initially providing services in a remote office to 25 to 30 users within a single site. High-end GC services are a function of the following variables:

- Number of users
- Application performance accessing the GC
- Workload characterization including queries per second and types of queries
- Network availability
- User expectations

Planning GC Server Placement

Best practices recommend providing at least one GC Server for each Windows 2000 site. Your objective in planning this placement is to provide adequate levels of service for directory queries as defined by some minimum latency meeting the needs and expectations of your user population. Microsoft recommends that you should have one GC Server for every four Exchange Mailbox Servers within a datacenter or concentrated location of Exchange Servers. Table 6.4 summarizes these estimates assuming that each server is at least a 500MHz Pentium III processor with 512MB RAM. It is strongly recommended that you test any configuration of hardware prior to deployment.

Table 6.4 Planning the placement of GC Servers.

Environment	User Number	GC Number	GC Placement
Branch office users	1 to 25	1	Local with at least 25
Small office	26 to 250	2 for load balancing	Local
Regional Office	251 to 5,000	2 for fault tolerance, and 1 additional as needed	Local
Main Office	5,001 to 10,000	2 for fault tolerance, and 1 additional as needed	Local

Selecting Attributes to Replicate to the GC

When selecting attributes that populate the GC, you must consider the impact additional overhead would have on the replication traffic. If you have slow network links, best practices recommend using some survey technique to determine which directory attributes your end users actually use. In mixed-mode environments, you need to determine whether any custom CDOs or Active Directory Services Interface (ADSI) applications require specific legacy Exchange 5.5 attributes. The installation of Exchange 2000 extends AD schema and tags many attributes for GC replication. You must determine whether all relevant attributes are tagged as well, but understand that each additional attribute causes additional replication traffic.

Microsoft argues, however, that total replication traffic caused by legacy Exchange 5.5 is far greater than traffic generated by AD, based on the following assumptions:

- Each legacy server must contain a full copy of the Exchange organization, whereas AD only replicates data to DCs and GC Servers.
- Changes to a legacy Exchange 5.5 object cause it to replicate again to all other servers in the organization. AD uses a per-property replication method that replicates only small changes at a time.
- The legacy Exchange directory replicates data in addition to the data that legacy Windows NT 4 replicated to DCs. AD consolidates this information and thereby decreases total traffic by a significant percentage.

Planning Routing Strategies

When planning a route, you must choose the appropriate connector. Routing within a site is a point-to-point procedure. Routing outside a site alternatively requires both planning and configuration and involves the use of various connector types. Choose routing strategies that provide optimal point-to-point traffic flow. Policy and deployment of resources, such as public folders, can affect this optimization just as significantly as the choice of connector. Factors to consider include the following:

- *Traffic volume*—Traffic consists of both number and size of messages passed between sites. Consider maximum message sizes of enclosures and attachments.
- *Directory replication between sites*—The replication of information concerning recipient objects, such as users, mailboxes, DLs, and public folders, especially outside a site to some foreign mail system, must be carefully

monitored. Schedule such message flows during nonpeak periods whenever possible. Carefully monitor the scoping of AD groups to minimize replication traffic. In fact, replication messages can be limited in terms of size to reduce traffic bottlenecks due to gateway delays.

- *Public folder replication*—Public folders send replica changes to all other folders in an Exchange organization. Schedule such exchanges during non-peak hours. Limit the replication message size wherever possible. Consider using public folder affinity parameters rather than replicating the folder itself. The affinity parameter redirects users from one folder to another, much like shortcuts, and an object alias points to a single source location. Use of this public folder feature reduces replication traffic, redundant storage, and replication latencies.

Planning System Message Flows between Sites

A Windows 2000 site is typically a collection of one or more IP subnets. The site infrastructure is built on top of the physical network. As new sites are created, DCs connect to other DCs and exchange system messages like a domain replica. Plan for this replication to proceed across site links that are the functional equivalent to the *Directory Replication Connector (DRC)* used to connect two legacy Exchange 5.5 Servers together. Site links are explicit point-to-point connectors that rely on a bridgehead server on each side of the link to handle the replication traffic and represent the underlying Windows 2000 infrastructure. Although intra-site replication is automatic, you must plan site links before inter-site replication will proceed.

When planning traffic flows between sites, plan the flow of replication data carefully. You need to consider two factors: the physical link characteristics and the importance of the replicated data. Given the cost of the link, you must control how often the connection will occur as well as the duration of the link to exchange data. Table 6.5 summarizes characteristics of these system message flows within and between sites.

Remember that this replication traffic can be passed either synchronously or asynchronously between sites. *Synchronous replication* passes messages directly to the bridgehead server at the target site. *Asynchronous replication* over slower, less-reliable connections uses a version of SMTP called Inter-Site Messaging SMTP (ISM-SMTP) that uses CDOs to create and send messages digitally signed by the sending DC. The receiving DC can verify that the data belongs to a known replication partner using this asymmetric encryption method furnished through the Windows 2000 public-key infrastructure.

Table 6.5 Characteristics of replication traffic within and between sites.

Category	Intra-Site	Inter-Site
Transport protocol	RPC	RPC or SMTP
Topology	Ring	Spanning tree
Replication timing	Automatically every 300 seconds by default	Scheduled on demand
Replication model	Notify (pull)	Store and Forward (push)
Compression	None	Full when over 50KB

Planning How Sites Are Linked

Site configuration determines how the sites are linked to each other and where these connections are placed. Message flows affecting an entire organization will be slowed if bandwidth across connections is not sufficient to handle the volume of data. When planning site linkages, the amount of bandwidth determines the connection speeds, as well as the quality of service. Bandwidth considerations have a significant impact on site boundaries and the placement of DCs on the local side of slow enterprise links.

Testing whether ESMTP Is Enabled

Create a Telnet session to determine whether ESMTP is supported. If you don't get an ESMTP list of keywords when you type "EHLO", you can conclude that this server is running the basic SMTP protocol rather than the Extended SMTP protocol. To create the Telnet session, you perform the following steps:

1. Choose Start|Run, type "CMD", and press the Enter key.
2. At the command prompt, type "TELNET SS1 25".
3. The server responds with a text line that reads READY and the system date.
4. At the command prompt, type "EHLO" and wait for a response. If the server supports the **EHLO** command, it returns a list of keywords.
5. At the command prompt, type "EHLO". The server SS1 returns a list of key words.

Enabling ESMTP Support

Assuming that you have enabled ESMTP, repeat the Telnet session mentioned on the previous page and the ESMTP test to confirm that the extended features are enabled. Next, you can configure remote triggering of mail delivery by following these steps:

1. Start System Manager.
2. In Connectors, right-click the specific SMTP Connector and select Properties.
3. Click the Advanced tab.
4. To disable ESMTP, clear the top Send **EHLO** Instead of **EHLO** option box.
5. Click OK.

Requesting **ETRN/TURN** from a Different Server

Once you've confirmed that the server is using ESMTP, follow these steps to configure a feature that allows the triggered delivery of queued messages:

1. Start System Manager.
2. In Connectors, right-click the specific SMTP connector and select Properties.
3. Click the Advanced tab.
4. To configure remote triggered message delivery, select the Request **ETRN/TURN** When Sending Messages option in the middle of the Property sheet.
5. Click OK.

NOTE: *The* ***ETRN*** *feature (RFC1985) is an extension of SMTP and the* ***TURN*** *command that addressed the problem of remotely starting a mail queue to process distant messages.Because there was no verification of the remote host name, the* ***TURN*** *command could be used by a rogue mail system to control mail flow.* ***ETRN*** *reverses the sender/receiver roles and requests a remote server ("receiver-SMTP") to create a new SMTP session and "send" its queued messages to the local machine.*

Chapter 7

Planning Services

If you need an immediate solution to:	*See page:*
Connecting to an Exchange Server for Services	235
Creating a MMC	236
Creating an Emergency Repair Disk (ERD)	237
Modifying the MMC **RestrictAuthorMode** Registry Key	239
Modifying the MMC **RestrictToPermittedSnapins** Registry Key	240
Installing and Managing Certificate Services	240
Installing a CA	241
Installing KM Services	242
Granting Manage Permissions to KM Services	244
Enrolling Users in KM Services	244
Creating a Chat Community	245
Creating a Chat Channel	246
Creating a Restricted Chat List	247
Disabling without Removing a Chat Community	249
Removing a Chat Community	249
Troubleshooting IM	249
Creating a New Chat Community	250
Installing an IM Service	251
Changing the Password Policy for an IM Server	251
Limiting the Number of IM Connections	252
Providing IM Service Access	252
Configuring IM Channel Defaults and Language Options	253
Creating a Chat User Class	253
Creating a User Ban from an IRC Channel	254
Enrolling Users Using AD Rather Than KM Services	255

In Depth

Enrolling Users via AD Instead of KM Services

In a corporate setting, planning messaging and collaborative services involves straightforward delivery of mail, distribution lists, public folders, and the data objects we typically associate with personal information management tools such as Outlook. In a customer relationship management paradigm or commercial setting, clients or the generic customers has a different constellation of needs and desires. A customer will typically progress through a series of stages in their relationship with some service or product provider. This customer life cycle has been described as five distinct phases: reach, acquisition, conversion, retention, and loyalty. After a customer's attention is won, a provider must educate the potential consumer, and convert them to use the provided services. After the initial use, a consumer must be persuaded to consume further products and services and finally introduce others to consuming the same service. Studies suggest that the retention phase is cyclical and must be repeated through reacquaintance with the product or services. For this reason, the simple transaction paradigm of e-commerce has transitioned into a more service oriented business environment.

The Way of the Technician especially in a .NET world will be defined more by business objectives and service level agreements than by legacy concepts of mail and network connectivity issues. A service level agreement (SLA) is a contractual understanding between service provider and consumer that specifies, in measurable terms, what services will be delivered, the breadth of those services, and the quality of service. Providing messaging and collaborative services requires tools to manage an enterprise-wide user population, metrics to measure performance, and administrative models to facilitate the delivery of highly reliable services at those promised service levels. Many administrators might find themselves overtime, providing application services beyond their own enterprise to the Internet at large. The core business mission of these Application Service Providers (ASPs) is in the reliable delivery of these SLAs. This is the personification of how the Ways of Merchant and Technician will merge.

Exchange 2000 Server architecture differs from legacy versions in the way it was designed to handle real-world issues such as scalability and an extensible organizational design. There is an advantage to having flexible, organizational groupings of people uncoupled from the physical infrastructure because an administrator can shape a messaging system to accommodate any business need or changing corporate objectives in spite of the limitations inherent in underlying physical hardware. This administrative flexibility has an immediate and dramatic impact on the return on investment (ROI) by providing a competitive advantage in the marketplace and on the Total Cost of Ownership (TCO) by lowering costs of deployment and training because the business logic of the workflow remains unchanged. The components that work together to provide both messaging and collaborative services to the Windows 2000 enterprise include the following:

- *Information Store*—**STORE.EXE** is found in the default directory of \Exchsrvr\Bin, where it divides user information into a private mailbox store or a public folder store. These stores can reside in a single storage group (SG) with up to five databases or across different SGs with up to four SGs being contained on one single server.
- *SGs*—The organizational unit for the Information Store, it is a set of databases that shares one common transaction log file. Up to four SGs can exist on a single Exchange 2000 server.
- *System Attendant*—**MAD.EXE**, found within the \Exchsrvr\Bin directory, performs maintenance routines for Exchange 2000 and monitors the server's running services and connectors. **MAD.EXE** is needed by other services such as **STORE.EXE**. If you shut down the System Attendant service, however, other services such as the SMTP service still continue to function.
- *Inetinfo.exe process*—**INETINFO.EXE** hosts the Internet Information Service (IIS 5) process and all Internet-related protocols, such as SMTP (Simple Mail Transfer Protocol) and HTTP (Hypertext Transfer Protocol). It manages the protocol layer and provides Exchange subsystems based on the concept of a "Virtual Server." **INETINFO.EXE** communicates with the Web Storage System (WSS) through a queuing layer known as the Exchange Interprocess Communication Layer (ExIPC).
- *Message Transfer Agent (MTA)*—This legacy routing engine is now used to route X.400 protocol messages to foreign messaging systems. The MTA reserves its own message queues independent of the **STORE.EXE** process in the \Exchsrvr\Mtadata directory path.
- *Key Management Service (KM Service)*—This component, working with Microsoft's Certificate Server, uses X.509 digital certificates and encryption keys for users desiring advanced security in their communications.

.NET servers, as a group, share a close integration with the Windows 2000 operating system. Many services, such as Exchange's legacy internal directory service, are redundant in the Windows 2000 environment. .NET Servers, such as Exchange 2000, now defer directory service requests to the Windows 2000 Active Directory (AD) and the Global Catalog (GC). Legacy Exchange was managed as a namespace separated from the Windows NT 4 operating system (OS); Exchange 2000, and many of the tools that manage it, are a seamless part of the Windows 2000 network operating system (NOS). In the real world, you probably will need to understand and manage an Exchange organization within this new *gestalt* or worldview, as well as deal with the structural eccentricities of older legacy services.

A shift of emphasis has occurred in both planning and deploying distributed services such as the Exchange messaging system, especially in view of the uncoupling of the messaging function from the networking infrastructure. Messaging-related object attributes are now a more fundamental part of the enterprise fabric as compared to that of version 5.5, where the administrator modified messaging-related objects in the Exchange directory services area running on top of Windows NT directory services. In Windows 2000, recipients are managed through AD at the level of the NOS rather than legacy Exchange directory services. The roles of administering network and messaging systems have become far more codependent. From an Exchange 2000 administrative perspective, you shape messaging and collaborative solutions not on a separate horizontal layer above the OS, but vertically down through the messaging layer to the NOS directory object itself.

Another significant dimension in administrative services relates to the nature of the services provided to the user population. In terms of the Microsoft Enterprise Services Framework, a closer relationship now exists between solution-providing services and service-management services than in past versions of the software. *Microsoft Solutions Framework (MSF)* helps you focus on planning, building, and deploying messaging, collaboration, and knowledge management solutions. *Microsoft Operations Framework (MOF)* addresses the ongoing operational aspects of the provided solution. Most employers expect an Exchange 2000 administrator to perform both the solutions and operations function at high levels of reliability.

A corporate information officer or board of directors measures the success of an Exchange 2000 implementation in terms of TCO and ROI rather than network use or bandwidth consumption. These particular metrics of success aren't new to even legacy Exchange 5.5 administrators. However, the way you apply them in the context of an enterprise by using MSF and MOF gives them far greater focus and precision than they had in Windows NT 4 domain models. Accountants and investment analysts can now assign real variable cost value to operational definitions such as service level agreements, problem management, and Help Desk professionals. The dimensional aspects and performance measures of an Exchange administrator, especially in a Windows 2000 enterprise system, have changed in subtle, although significant, ways.

Microsoft Frameworks and TCO

MOF emphasizes two separate, but related functional areas: service solutions and service management. After a system is deployed, the "other side" of the IT job description deals with administering this newly installed "solution," called a *production platform*. Service-management issues in Exchange 2000 are enhanced scalability, reliability, and capacity. Performance-related measures ensure that the solution delivers promised features at agreed service levels. The factors that affect performance are woven into the fabric of a solution not just during the planning stages of the messaging solution, but also from the start of the design of the Windows 2000 enterprise itself.

To help design and deploy an Exchange 2000 organization, messaging solutions have been partitioned or separated into specific management functional areas (SMFAs): protocol services, directory services, and storage services. This division of functional roles offers greater flexibility and scalability than the legacy monolithic design structure, and is a characteristic of a distributed services environment. The potential of this greater flexibility, however, can be realized only when the system design is well conceived and properly deployed. MOF processes that provide business-specific service solutions will lower TCO in-house, though significantly more in an outsource scenario, when MSF methodologies have been implemented.

Related solution:	Found on page:
Planning Steps Prior to Deployment	94

Administrative Tools

In all the planning steps for deployment just mentioned, you must assess the needs of the people in your target user population and the processes in your target installation, as well as determine how these needs will be managed in an enterprise. Unlike legacy messaging platforms that were relatively separate from the administration of the underlying NOS, Exchange 2000 makes extensive use of Windows 2000 directory services. Tools necessary to manage these integrated administrative needs support SMFAs involved in the following:

- *User management/directory services*—This management interface, providing different views of AD and other network-related resources, must support an administrative topology that handles permission management and administrative system policies.
- *Server/network/routing management*—Functionally separate from the administrative topology, network components and routing groups, in particular,

need to be similarly viewed and managed. They are, however, clearly separate administartive entities dealing respectively with infrastructure and connectivity issues between groups and with foreign mail systems.

- *Storage services/public folder management*—You need to manage various aspects of storage services in the form of SGs and multiple databases. Similarly, the management of public folders, which can now form potentially complex, hierarchical trees, has been segregated and spun off as a possible separate, specialized area of administration.
- *Collaborative services management*—The addition of Realtime Collaboration (RTC), such as Chat Service, data- and videoconferencing, presence management, and Instant Messaging (IM), requires specialized areas of administrative management to support an already wide array of Exchange services.

The Interplay of Roles

You can manage each one of the management areas listed in the previous section either from a single seat or as a separate branch of one messaging service that extends across an entire enterprise. The *Microsoft Management Console (MMC)* is an example of Windows Management Instrumentation (WMI) you use to provide the extensible features and the scalable platforms across an entire enterprise forest. Notice the list of snap-ins that significantly extend the usability of this interface. This single-tool framework can support the addition of any number of specific snap-in tool components, as shown in Figure 7.1, that extend functionality

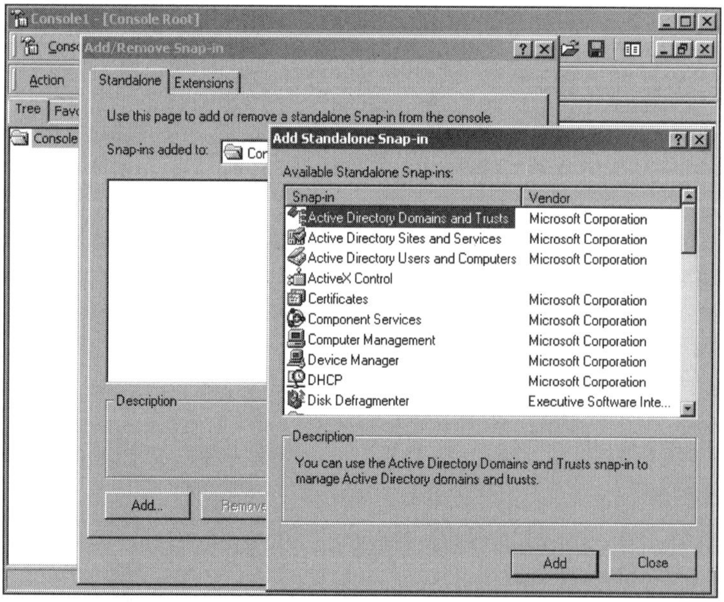

Figure 7.1 MMC showing the list of available snap-ins.

as well as the scope of control. One console can be used as either a single-seat global administration or a modular, customized toolset for managing SMFAs within the range of messaging and collaborative services or any other distributed service.

Careful scoping of these SMFAs in terms of people, processes, and the underlying network infrastructure contributes to how well the instrumentation achieves its design objectives. Deployment plan effectiveness is a function of how well management has defined scope, time constraints, and resources. One particularly useful trick to deploying any system is to rehearse what you need to do, where you need to go, and what resources you need to accomplish the project *before* you actually start the project. Because every messaging system has unique characteristics based on specific corporate objectives, good instrumentation and effective methodologies will rarely come from prebuilt or shrink-wrapped sources. Effective procedures and measuring tools typically come after systems are deployed and have stabilized. The recursive nature needing good tools to measure the performance of newly deployed systems is usually solved by staff that has already experienced the life cycle of a deployment plan, and the daily needs of a user population. Thus, you oftentimes have to first deploy a system to know how to deploy a system. This concept reinforces the earlier mentioned interplay between MSF and MOF. The key to successfully reducing TCO is to have operations people intimately involved and fully vested in developing proposed solutions.

MMC

As a part of the WMI initiative, the MMC framework was first introduced with IIS 4 on Windows NT 4. MMC is a fundamental part of Windows 2000 both in its ubiquitous nature within the NOS and in the theory on which Windows 2000 rests. MMC is nothing more than a featureless Windows Explorer-type interface that provides absolute extensibility and scalability. Its component windows are divided into two separate sections or panes: a scope pane on the left side and a details pane on the right. The MMC supports two types of snap-in components:

- *Standalone snap-in tools*—This instrumentation functions alone without additional support.
- *Extension snap-in tools*—This instrumentation augments the functionality of a parent snap-in tool and depends on it.

This Component Object Model (COM)-based frame, like Windows 2000 itself, was designed to accommodate third-party applications developed by independent software vendors (ISVs). COM+, an extension to the COM model, represents a strategic approach to developing business solutions through a building block approach combining operating system services with an object-oriented programming architecture. ISVs are thus encouraged to use COM+ within a MMC design framework to assemble their own specialized combinations of network tools and utilities. Because MMC is a multidocument interface (MDI), the MMC implicitly enforces a design standard for all future Windows-based snap-in tools. This standard, reflecting the association of the WMI initiative with the Web-Based Enterprise Management (WBEM) initiative, uses the Common Information Model (CIM) standard to simplify managed components in an enterprise environment. All .NET servers and other Windows-based applications share well-known user features such as hierarchical displays and drag-and-drop capabilities. Standardizing this interface minimizes end-user training and thus reduces TCO. The MMC can accommodate as many or as few snap-ins as are necessary to complete some predefined task. Toolmakers (known as authors) secure the frame to prevent future unauthorized modifications. This locking feature implicitly controls feature availability and access by local administrators or end users. The most significant aspect from an administrative perspective, however, is that the frame or console is a self-contained MSC (Management Saved Console) object file. Administrators/authors can thus delegate administrative responsibilities and email a saved console file for use in some remote part of the organization. The MMC runs on Windows NT 4, Windows 2000, and Windows 9x OSs without additional assembly, and epitomizes the network philosophy of Windows 2000: extensibility, scalability, modularity, and portability.

MMC Construction and Operation

Prebuilt Exchange management consoles are available on the Microsoft Exchange menu below the Programs menu. *Management consoles*, in general, have a user mode with three varying levels of access: full access, limited access multiple windows, and limited access single window. Alternatively, you can launch consoles in author/creator mode when you create or modify a specific console frame. These two general modes—user and author—parallel how toolbars work in any Windows-based Office application when you use the Customize feature found under View|Toolbars. If you choose to build your own console and want to include directory services, you can use several snap-in tools related to the functioning of directory services and the AD:

- *AD Sites and Services*—This snap-in specifically manages sites, subnets, forests, and DCs, the delegation of authority, and directory replication schedules. It conceptualizes your administrative workspace in terms of uniform, distributed enterprise-wide Windows 2000 services.
- *AD Domains and Trusts*—This snap-in tool manages trust relationships between domains within a Windows 2000 forest and across forests, non-Windows Kerberized realms, and legacy Windows NT 4 domains. It provides a Windows 2000 workspace that accommodates older legacy domain models and non-Microsoft systems.

- *AD Users and Computers*—This tool manages daily administrative tasks that relate to domain controllers (DCs), including identity and permission management of users, computers, groups, organizational units (OUs), printers, and shared folders within an enterprise workspace.
- *Other specialized snap-in tools*—You can add more tools such as Active Directory Services Interface (ADSI) Edit, a powerful low-level editor that allows expert users to view, modify, create, and delete any object in the AD, and ADC (Active Directory Connector) Management, which handles connections to legacy Exchange 5.5 sites.

The AD Sites and Services snap-in supports a Group Policy extension. Right-click on the specific site in the MMC console and select the Group Policy tab. The AD Users and Computers tool also includes Group Policy extensions on the server and Remote Control (Remote Access Services, or RAS), Dial-in, and Terminal Services Profiles extensions at the user account level. The Terminal Services extension, which appears as an additional tab in each user account property sheet, allows you, for example, to control Terminal Services features for each user from a central interface through setting TS user profiles, enabling logons, connecting devices, and so on. MMC snap-ins, whether standalone or extension, conform to the MDI specification. Administrators can use either user profiles or Group Policy settings to preserve the integrity of a MMC and prevent intentional or accidental changes to snap-ins. Windows 2000 automatically installs some management consoles; for example, all three directory services consoles—AD Users and Computers, AD Sites and Services, and AD Domains and Trusts—are installed on a DC in native mode.

Exchange 2000 Tools

Microsoft Exchange provides both reactive and proactive tools. *Reactive tools* evaluate and manage problems after they have occurred. *Proactive tools* forecast potential problems. Some tools are actually triggered by performance irregularities. These more sophisticated tools execute a wide variety of responses from simple notification of an administrator to scripted corrective actions. Three key tools are the following:

- *Exchange Monitoring and Status Tool*—Located under Tools in the Exchange System Manager, this tool replaces the Server Monitor and Link Monitor tools in legacy Exchange versions. Instead of registering information above some static threshold set by an administrator, it provides information related to the continued growth of queues. All servers and connectors are listed in the Status container. Baselines in the Default Exchange Services node are monitored. Some services included in this container are the Information Stores, MTA

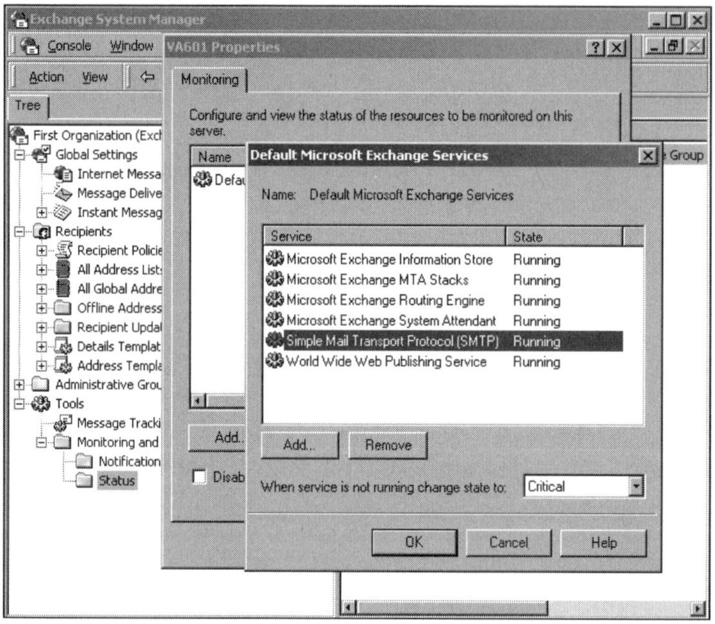

Figure 7.2 The listing of available services running on an Exchange Server.

stacks, Routing Engine (RE), protocol services, and Web Publishing Service. The Properties sheet for Email notification is shown in Figure 7.2. You can add other services to this container.

- *Queue Viewer*—This tool, used to view the state of all message queues, is useful in troubleshooting problems after they have been identified in the Monitoring and Status tool. Diagnostic events pertaining to message flow issues are reported in Event Viewer logs. The functionality of the Viewer in displaying, for example, details about messages, varies depends upon the protocol you select. The context menu for a SMTP queue is shown in Figure 7.3.
- *Message Tracking Center*—This tool tracks one or more messages from a sender to recipients through the Exchange system. Messages routed through a designated server are added to message tracking logs. You have records describing sender, receiver, and, optionally, even the subject line of the message. An example of message history associated with a single message found through a simple scan based on a sender's identity is shown in Figure 7.4.

These tools provide, in addition to message-tracking logs, corroboration of reports about the user population. Collect baseline data on a routine and proactive basis to help you forecast a problem before it escalates to a level that impacts the messaging system's overall performance. Monitor the frequency of occurrence

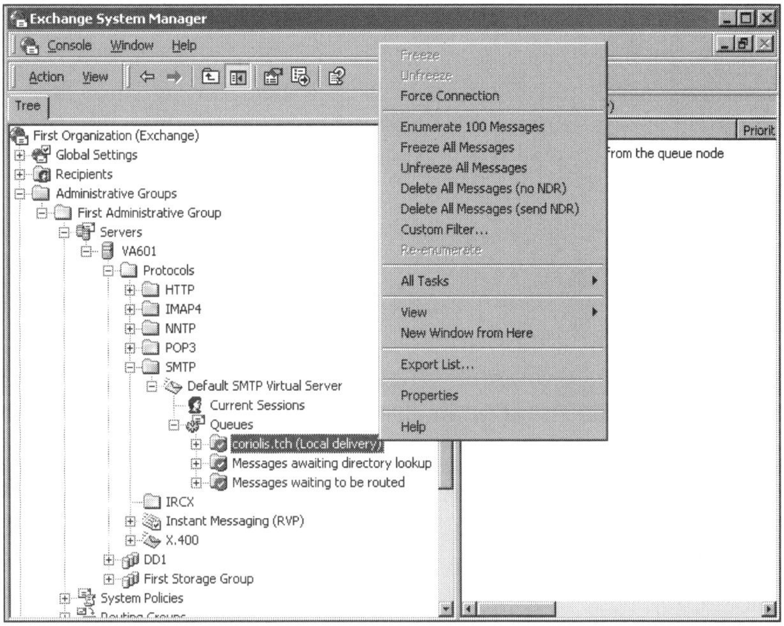

Figure 7.3 Context menu of a SMTP queue.

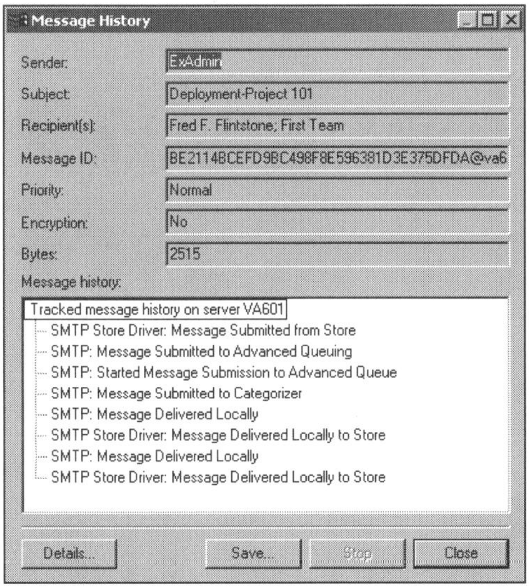

Figure 7.4 Message history generated after enabling message tracking.

and size of attachments sent within your user population. Seek alternative methods of distribution like public folders or even FTP as ways to maintain productivity while controlling bandwidth utilization.

Windows 2000 Tools

We distinguish between reactive and proactive tools that monitor the operating system layer, which is the foundation on which Exchange services run. These tools are common across all application software, and provide a well-known interface that evaluates the nature of an irregular event or problem. Well-known examples are the following:

- *Performance Monitor*—System Monitor, available when you select Performance in the Administrative Tools folder, charts ongoing activity in realtime or through redirection to a log file for future analysis. Alerts triggered by selected conditions such as MTA Work Queue Length are useful when monitoring the MTA's dynamic state. Analyzing server activity can help you predict the impending failure of some component and the changing trends in system capacity.
- *Event Viewer*—Applications that run on the Windows NT and Windows 2000 platforms log error messages and warnings to the event log. You can view and filter generated messages through Event Viewer in the MMC. This one tool is fundamental to the NOS and is probably the most important piece of instrumentation in your administrator's toolkit. For example, you can use performance monitors to trigger error messages logged by date and time. Use the Filter tab on the Log Property sheet to identify an error source, category, user, computer, user, and so on.

You should consider filtered scans of the Event Viewer, third-party add-on products that support more refined event tracking, and a handful of favorite corroborative tools as a part of your daily procedure; in fact, a review of Event Viewer should be one of the first activities every morning. Collect data for baseline purposes on a regular basis. Collect additional samples, when necessary, as a daily maintenance task. Remember that any accumulated data is useless unless carefully and thoughtfully analyzed, not just collected. You can forecast serious problems by noticing subtle changes in a baseline or seemingly innocuous warning messages from some application. It is also important to listen to end users and systematically cross-check user complaints with data collected from your instrumentation.

Recipient Management

Business solutions are the glue that Microsoft expects you to provide when connecting corporate needs and objects with information technology. TCO and ROI measure this productivity. Now more than ever, you can shape Exchange 2000 to your organization's needs. You should propose solutions using MSF to provide ongoing maintenance and support. Exchange 2000 has changed how basic recipient objects are viewed because it no longer "owns" these objects; the NOS and AD do. Thus, depending on the size of a corporation, your role as an Exchange

Administrator overlaps network and system administration as well. In small corporations, these three job roles are combined into one. In larger enterprises, you need to work closely with other technical support teams. Your effectiveness in managing a messaging environment depends on how well you organize the objects within it. Because these objects are actually part of AD, the key to your organizational abilities lies in how well you understand the way AD manages the enterprise namespace.

Domain Structure

One of the primary responsibilities of an Exchange Administrator is to ensure that the messaging and collaborative platform is accessible to users at all times. We suggest you use learn how to use complementary systems, services, and methodologies that reliably provide this accessibility. Both the identity and permission management functions in Windows 2000 have been delegated to system related services. Don't forget that many troubleshooting tips begin with these related service layers. For example, AD provides a named object within its directory database that has attributes that can be Exchange specific. The old legacy Exchange Directory Services mailbox and distribution list (DL) objects, which were separate from the named principal account in the DC's directory database, have been replaced by AD mail-enabled user and group objects, respectively. In the past, the Windows NT 4 primary DC authenticated a user, or named principal account. The user also had an assigned mailbox in the Exchange directory store. Windows 2000 consolidates identity management; the same named principal or user has extensible attributes that support Exchange services. Pay particular attention to the design of the domain model and how it affects the Exchange organization. You can mail-enable identity management, centralized in AD, by adding appropriate object attributes to the AD schema and assigning meaningful values to them. Any Windows 2000 named object or principal, with its collection of relevant attributes, is still known by DCs in Windows 2000 just like in the legacy Windows NT 4 domain model; however, now all DCs share equal information and equal power and responsibility in general within the native Windows 2000 enterprise.

Single-Master Domain Model

The single-master primary DC model of Windows NT 4 has grown into a more robust, fault-tolerant, and scalable multi-master model in Windows 2000. All DCs within this larger enterprise domain namespace know each individually named object and its attributes. Legacy domains in comparison needed to form trust relationships in Windows NT 4. You need a more flexible administrative category, such as an OU, as an Administrative container to compensate for this larger namespace and potentially greater number of objects. OUs, or OUs within an OU, provide more flexible boundaries than the more formal, traditional domain boundaries within which to apply permissions.

OUs

You manage permissions within the boundaries of a domain or one or more of the flexible OUs within it. Legacy permission management works at two levels; it uses global and local groups to simplify the assignment of permissions to individual users. Microsoft suggests you assign users to global groups first, and then assign those global groups to local groups in resource domains with access to those specific local resources. Groups as Organizational containers are more stable objects than individual users in the namespace. We suggest you control the inheritance of local resource permissions by moving users in and out of global groups located in some master domains. In Windows 2000, OUs similarly help to organize named objects across more inclusive namespaces like domains. As in the legacy scenario with global group usage, we recommend delegating control through OUs because of their flexibility. Because function and structure are separated in Windows 2000, mailbox-enabled recipient objects and their Exchange Server mailboxes do not have to be a part of the same OU or domain. Thus, an administrator can design and delegate control over a messaging system in a manner that more readily reflects that specific corporation's organizational structure.

Administrative Models

Even legacy versions of Exchange have followed the more intuitive model you now see in Windows 2000 native-mode enterprises. In its most fundamental sense, an "exchange" of messages occurs within the boundaries of some namespace or organization. This logical boundary defines recipients; those outside this defined namespace are foreign. Two different models—a centralized administrative structure and a delegated administrative structure—describe methods of managing Exchange 2000 recipients; a third model—the messaging group administration of Exchange attributes—is appropriate in a mixed-mode Exchange 2000 architecture that supports the older Windows NT 4 domain structure and legacy Exchange 5.5.

Centralized Administration

Just as it is simpler to use global groupings to administer users in a Windows NT 4 domain model, an Exchange Administrator can group all recipient objects in one centralized OU. Centralizing objects in one container simplifies permission management by applying Group Policy, a fundamental management strategy Microsoft expounds upon in Windows 2000 design. For example, child groups inherit the policies and permission of the container group. Management is not only simplified within one centralized container of recipients, but the administrator group who manages this container is also clearly defined as compared to the legacy concept of administering recipient objects distributed across several sites.

Delegated Administration

Delegated administration decentralizes the management responsibilities among separate groups of administrators and recipients. The focus on one centralized container shifts to a collection of separate containers, each possibly distinguished by any number of geopolitical or functional differences. Such a structure actually can simplify the administration of some organizations, especially those broken up into heterogeneous units. The structure still provides the native-mode substrate for an Exchange 2000 deployment.

Specialized Tools for Recipient Management

You need various MMC toolsets to manage any Exchange organization. Best practices recommend installing Windows 2000 Administrative Tools to run Windows 2000 serves remotely on. You can install the necessary administration tools by launching adminpak.msi, located in the I386 folder on the Windows 2000 Server Installation CD-ROM. You can remotely manage Exchange 2000 using Windows Professional clients by selecting Exchange 2000 System Management Tools in the Exchange 2000 Setup Wizard. You can also install these tools using the Software Installation node of the Group Policy snap-in on a server running Windows 2000. You can publish programs in AD, as well as assign an application to a specific computer. Use Add/Remove programs, located in Control Panel, to install the tools.

Terminal Services

Another solution is to install Windows 2000 Terminal Services on any server that is running in remote administration mode. You should now consider this tool to be an important part of your administrator's toolkit. Install Windows 2000 Terminal Services on Exchange Servers that operate in remote administration mode for access through a console session across a local area network (LAN) or dial-up connection. If the user has the appropriate permissions, Terminal Services in Windows 2000 Server automatically provides two user licenses for remote monitoring services, and the following advantages:

- Remote control of all server-provided services over network or dial-up connections
- Access from any workstation that supports the Terminal Services client

We recommend that you install Windows 2000 Terminal Services on all servers that operate in remote administration mode. Any workstation running Windows 2000 Professional should have both Windows 2000 Administration Tools and Exchange 2000 System Management Tools installed. By adding the Windows 2000 Terminal Services client to the set of management tools, an administrator can control any server from anywhere without loading a single client application, rather than, for example, using Exchange System Manager, or prebuilt MMCs on remote workstations.

TIP: *Carefully deploy MMCs that have specialized administrative tools especially on highly portable laptops or notebooks. With improvements in the capacity and speed of hardware, these highly portable units represent significant security targets because they are typically configured with snap-ins designed to administer application and system services.*

Logical Organization

Combine these administrative tools with careful organization of recipients within your organization. OUs, unlike legacy Recipient containers in Exchange 5.5, impose structure but do not affect object naming in the Outlook Address Book. Similarly, the logical nature of the OU, as opposed to the nature of legacy Recipient containers, does not impact the movement of mailboxes, as it formerly did between containers. The OU provides a logical structure that makes administering objects simpler and applying Group Policy easier to control. Exchange 2000 enables you to organize your namespace according to your business workflow without placing artificial constraints on address-book views or changes in mailbox locations.

Permission Management

Permission management in Windows 2000 extends across two dimensions:

- Vertically through access scoping of the account operator, administrator, and domain administrators group
- Horizontally through inheritance or overriding permissions in the object hierarchy

Full control over AD objects now includes mailbox location and other messaging-related information. Using AD Users and Computers, like creating a published NetBIOS (Network Basic Input/Output System) file share, restricts the access of a local administrator to create mailbox-enabled users or move mailbox containers unless the appropriate permissions, such as Mailbox Manager rights, have been assigned. Restrict the use of a command-line utility because, in the appropriate security context—such as AD Administration Tool (**ldp.exe**)—these utilities can subvert security restrictions controlling access to the AD. Use the AD Delegation Wizard to grant permissions to any AD group, including the built-in account operators group; use the Exchange Administration Delegation Wizard to grant those special Mailbox Manager rights. The more centralized the model, the more simplified the organization. Best practices recommend combining both user account management and mail-related administration roles into one central administrative group.

AD Delegation of Control Wizard

Another tool that helps in administrative tasks is the AD Delegation of Control Wizard, which grants a wide range of access rights to both domains and OUs.

This wizard allows you to assign specific read/write properties to many levels of object classes. Given the level of control made accessible by a host of tools and wizards, you should make delegating authority and assigning permissions as simple as possible over the broadest and most flexible of objects, for example, OUs. Be sure you don't specify different, and possibly conflicting, permissions among different objects at different class levels.

Exchange Administration Delegation Wizard

The *Exchange Administration Delegation Wizard* is similar to the AD Directory Delegation of Control Wizard in that it helps you delegate responsibility for managing messaging configuration objects in AD. You can use the tool to assign one of three roles to a group or individual; these roles are similar to those used in Exchange 5.5:

- *Exchange Administrator (View Only)*—All Exchange object configurations are read-only.
- *Exchange Administrator*—All Exchange object configurations are read/write.
- *Exchange Full Administrator*—All Exchange object configurations are read/write and change permissions.

Assign these delegated roles to various groups that administer the Exchange organization. Actual rights and permissions are assigned to groups rather than individuals, just as in the legacy Windows NT 4 domain model. Assign individuals to these groups, and thus, simplify the assignment of administrative rights.

In the Windows 2000 distributed services environment, permission settings of different objects with different scopes can cause unpredictable and often undesirable changes in an entire class of objects in an enterprise hierarchy. These effects also can be difficult to troubleshoot and correct. This wizard manages the administrative group and the right to create mailboxes. You should use this administrative group in the same way global groups are used in legacy Windows NT 4 systems; users are added to or removed from this group that are delegated with the responsibility of managing the Exchange organization.

Policies

Exchange 2000 recipient policies are another form of scoping access like legacy Exchange 5.5 site addressing. A *policy* is a collection of settings applied to one or more objects found in the same class. You can control objects in the same class with a single set of configurations or policies. Exchange 2000 supports two kinds of policies, system policies and recipient policies.

System Policies

System policies are server-side collections of configurations that include the Mailbox Store, the Public Folder Store, and the server engine itself. After you configure an attribute through a policy change, the only way to change it is to modify and reapply the policy or to delete the policy object itself.

Recipient Policies

Recipient policies are user-side objects that relate to users, contacts, and groups. Exchange 2000 supports a single recipient-policy class that controls email address generation, similar to but more flexible than the legacy Exchange 5.5 counterpart. During installation, the "default policy" is placed in the Recipient Policies container under the Recipients node in the organizational tree. Recipient policies are not immediately applied, but instead are associated with a collection of objects forming a Lightweight Directory Access Protocol (LDAP) query recordset from a built address list. The System Attendant applies the recordset of LDAP specifications approximately every 10 minutes. Filter rules are applied to multiple address lists created to implement policies. For example, different SMTP addresses could use recipient policies to control the conditions under which one address or another is used. The recipient policies update the recordset stored in the domain-naming context in the AD, which are then replicated throughout the forest. Thus, Exchange 2000 uses policy-driven settings to cause a specific output of data, which is important, especially in the management of distributed services.

Server Management

The separation of function from structure enables the administrator to mold the Exchange organization to meet corporate objectives and the user population without the constraints imposed by a physical network. A second dichotomy, the separation of clients from server-side management, has a similar impact on how a system is used because, generally speaking, the client never has access to server-side features. An Exchange Administrator can totally automate installation and restrict the range of features to minimize the need for user intervention, maintenance, or training. Server-side management centralizes control of the messaging platform and significantly reduces TCO. Microsoft categorizes server-side management for .NET servers into three SMFAs of control and management:

- *Exchange 2000*—The specific, service-providing application
- *AD*—The directory services provider
- *Windows 2000*—The system services platform

Service-providing platforms such as Exchange 2000 and SQL 2000 have delegated internal directory services to the NOS. Unlike Exchange 5.5 running on Windows

NT 4, operating environment design and the performance of AD directory services affect how Exchange 2000 will run. Vertical management of all three layers rather than partitioning of Exchange administration from the OS exposes the Exchange Administrative role to potentially more involvement in corporate strategic planning. Joint administration of the NOS and Exchange was less likely in legacy Windows NT 4, because the messaging and OS services were horizontally arranged and functionally separate. Especially in a .NET distributed services environment, messaging and collaborative solutions will very likely extend beyond the boundaries of the enterprise. The sharing of the same or parallel workflow processes across, for example, trading partners is now a growing consideration in maintaining competitive leads in an industry. Vertical management can simplify decision-making and increase the speed of application/solution development life cycles. When migrating from an older messaging platform like Exchange 5.5, prepare yourself to address Exchange's *gestalt* change from horizontal to vertical management, and AD directory services. Exchange 2000 will most likely be the first enterprise-wide system an organization deploys; merging administrative areas of responsibility in the technical services area can profoundly improve support services and the organization's ongoing operation. Your ability to deliver solutions within a wider scope of authority and control will depend on how well you have mastered the development side of the Exchange platform concerned with dynamic processes such as workflows and scripting languages including ASP and XML.

Related solutions:	Found on page:
Designing a Workflow Process Using WDE 2000	732

Administrative Models

Just as with recipient management, three administrative models are used to manage server-side services:

- *Centralized management*—Centralized management is typically the simplest model to create and manage services and thus results in a lower TCO.
- *Distributed management*—Especially in organizations that are divided into geopolitical groupings, distributed management might correspond more closely to the actual corporate arrangement.
- *Mixed management*—In native mode, Exchange 2000 provides far more flexibility in design than legacy versions of the messaging product. Best practices suggest using different administrative groups to control message routing and recipients, as well as apply different policy levels to the server, user, or both.

In a mixed-management model, it's important for you to manage large-scale deployments both horizontally and vertically, depending on corporate needs and the specific circumstances of any particular group of Exchange Servers and DCs.

Centralized Management

A *centralized management model* divides Exchange Servers into one or more administrative groups. You cannot move servers among these groups after you have assigned them. In addition to these administrative groups, you can assign one or more routing groups to handle message transfer. A centralized model is most appropriate for small- to medium-sized organizations with a central technical support group. Microsoft recommends that you leverage both AD and Exchange 2000 scalability by minimizing the number of organizational layers. Exchange System Manager, by default, does not even suggest the existence of administrative groups. The system has been designed with the implicit assumption that you won't need or use separate administrative groupings. As you install servers, they are all added to a common group unless you create a new administrative grouping. To do this, you must first display this object in the console tree by selecting the General tab on the organization's Properties sheet. The Display Routing Groups and Display Administrative Groups enable you to display one or both of the groups in the console tree. These options are available in all three management models.

You must display an administrative group before you can add new servers to it. If you subsequently clear these group display options, the group divisions will be lost and all servers will be grouped back into the same Servers node in the Exchange System Manager console tree. If you re-enable the display of the Administrative Group node, servers are not restored to prior settings.

Distributed Management

Exchange Servers are assigned to administrative groups based on the corporation's needs in the distributed-management model. Typically, you'll find large installations with patches of legacy hardware and software. You have flexibility with a distributed management model to assign responsibilities and personnel to specific groups that are based on the existing corporate topology. Remember that when Exchange 2000 interfaces with legacy Exchange 5.5 systems, flexibility is lost as groups reassume the more rigid constraints of the legacy version. In other words, an Exchange 2000 administrative group behaves like a legacy Exchange 5.5 site when the two messaging systems coexist in one organization.

Mixed Management

The capability to mix different groups and manage routing in specific areas is based on the flexibility of Exchange 2000. The *mixed-management model* requires that the messaging organization be composed exclusively of Exchange 2000 Servers. Mixed management does not work in a heterogeneous installation that mixes Exchange 2000 with legacy systems. Exchange 2000 provides the advantages of administrative groups, routing groups, and permission management of both server features and recipients.

Tools That Support Server Management

Administrative and technical support is predicated on both good organization and the proper tools. You can conceptualize the messaging and collaborative service platform as a collection of Exchange Servers that together form a specialized layer of software resting on top of the NOS and AD directory services. Distinguishing features found in organizing the Windows 2000 enterprise are just as relevant when you are dealing with Exchange 2000. The integration of messaging platform with the NOS, especially in the areas of server management, requires a thorough understanding of both the NOS and directory services design before you assume responsibility for designing, deploying, or managing an Exchange system.

Logical Grouping

The flexibility of Exchange 2000, combined with new Windows 2000 features such as OUs, provides many ways to organize people, processes, and property. Structural solutions such as creating resource domains in legacy systems have been replaced by logical groups that can more accurately reflect a corporate workflow.

OUs

OUs are the best way to scope permissions and rights. Creating domains instead of OUs for managing the delegation of rights and responsibilities is not recommended because it wastes resources such as a DC, unnecessarily increases network use because of support traffic, and needlessly complicates organizational structure. Creating an OU, alternatively, provides vertical resource management that extends from the messaging platform down through the directory services layer into the NOS. Vertical management should include an Exchange Administrator's ability to start or stop services and install software within an OU. Such specific vertical control over system services is difficult to provide in legacy systems such as Exchange 5.5.

Administrative Groups

Exchange Servers differ in terms of system policies, groups, public folders, or IRC (Internet Relay Chat) communities. You can manage these SMFAs by assigning a collection of machines to an administrative group. Membership in an administrative group does not preclude membership in a routing group in some other administrative group. Remember, however, that after membership is assigned, you cannot move a server to another group. The Exchange Tasks Wizard will move mailbox data stores between servers. You can uncouple the administrative groups from routing groups in native mode to gain further flexibility. In mixed mode, however, many features drift back to their more limited legacy characteristics.

Routing Groups

You can create one or more routing groups that handle message transfer within administrative groups and help support differences in the quality of network connectivity within an OU. In native mode, you can assign servers to any routing group regardless of their administrative group membership. These groupings provide support for underlying infrastructure in which the following is true:

- Servers are running different versions of Exchange software or have different connectivity characteristics.
- A single routing group consolidates servers in different administrative groups to simplify management and control.

Using routing groups can provide an organized, unified view of connectivity separate from a more complex, but functional, arrangement of people and processes.

System Policies and Groups

One of the advantages of administrative groups to provide a clearer view of topology, membership, and relations among various components. Another benefit is that you can apply system policies easily and systematically. Policies are configuration settings applied to a specific grouping of system objects. Create policies in one administrative group and apply them in other groups, thereby simplifying administration and consistency when applying server settings. In a distributed management model, you can easily administer organization-wide standards, such as mailbox size and message retention times, through a common set of system policies located in an administrative group.

Other Administrative Areas

Managing recipients and servers is just one aspect of administering an Exchange system. In Exchange 5.5, you organized users by *mail DLs* to simplify the simultaneous delivery of mail to many people; in Exchange 2000, you change an attribute in an AD group object to receive that mail. What was an Exchange 5.5 mailbox is now an enabled user in Exchange 2000. The legacy custom recipient similarly has become a mail-enabled user. Attributes associated with these objects are changed to produce a desired feature. Because these features are merely enabling some object attribute, changes such as a new phone number or mail address are performed through any DC. Such record modifications in legacy systems would have required access to a specific directory in a specific Exchange Server. These changes would have been far more complicated to perform as compared to Exchange 2000 and its enterprise-wide accessibility to users and the features they need to perform their work. Administration is simpler than in legacy Exchange, because certain concepts, such as user, have been consolidated in the more logical directory services of the NOS. From a similar administrative perspective, sharing information through public folders has always been part of the Exchange Server feature set, and a powerful collaborative vehicle among groups. Of the four basic types of recipients—user, group, contact, and public folder—the administrative features of public folders have also been simplified.

Security and Distribution Groups

Groups in any NOS reduce administrative effort and enhance the management of users through consolidated changes. Two basic groups in Windows 2000 serve this function: security groups and distribution groups. *Security groups* are collections of security principals or named users within AD that simplify the assignment of special permissions to network resources. *Distribution groups* replace legacy DLs in Exchange 5.5. You use distribution groups exclusively for mailing lists, but they are also appropriate for nontrusted recipients. You can also use the universal group in native-mode Windows 2000 for viewing list membership; mixed mode requires DLs.

Public Folders

You might need to design public folder hierarchies to provide common access throughout the enterprise. AD directory services simplify the permission management of these messaging objects. Unlike legacy Exchange versions that control permissions to mailbox containers and users through internal directory services, Exchange 2000 provides access control in a unified manner through AD and the OS. In legacy Exchange, you granted access to a public folder at the object level of the mailbox or user; you controlled mailbox access through the user account in the directory database located in the DC. The unification of objects within the AD namespace has not only simplified the security model, but has also allowed an increase in the granularity or specificity of permission management at the object level. In Exchange 2000, you can grant access to public folders and all other messaging objects directly to the user and group object in AD. In a heterogeneous or mixed installation in which Exchange 2000 coexists with legacy Exchange, group types involved in permission management are very important. ADC synchronizes legacy DLs with AD universal distribution groups, but does not provide access control for Exchange 2000 public folders. You can convert universal distribution groups to universal security groups when you upgrade or replicate public folders from legacy Exchange to Exchange 2000, or when you use Outlook clients to assign access rights to public folders.

Public Folder Affinity

Public folder hierarchies can be an important addition to the feature list of a messaging and collaborative platform. The folders can also be part of an Intranet distribution system. These containers provide a highly visible central data store that is accessible across the enterprise. You can replicate a data store in one public folder to all the other folders throughout the enterprise. When users access a folder not located on their local server, the server can provide the Outlook client with a sorted list of servers that have replicas of the original stored material. Public folders replicate by default across all available connectors. Exchange 2000 can determine the location of the closest replica with information available through routing groups. In legacy Exchange public folder referrals, called *public folder affinity*, the server used these lists for routing to determine the order in which requests were referred to these remote servers. Unlike in Exchange 5.5, affinities in Exchange 2000 are transitive; in other words, an affinity between a routing referral on server A and server B, and between server B and server C, provides a referral path from server A to server C. Thus, if all server locations are connected, all servers receive public folder request referrals by default.

RTC

Exchange 5.5 allowed users to work with Outlook 98 forms for collaborative purposes. These forms were designed to reflect a workflow using the Outlook email client. A form represented a method of posting and gathering information using email as a vehicle, rather than static paperwork. A Help Desk trouble ticket is an example of a form developed with Outlook. Using Exchange 5.5, you could develop different types of forms for collaboration, including Report Forms for sending reports to users and Request Forms for creating a purchase-requisition form. When forms were used to communicate information to a group of people, they became known as *collaboration tools*. Microsoft itself used the term "collaboration development" to describe the task of designing forms.

Collaboration Technologies and Concepts

Outlook forms were one example of a product that supported collaborative work, but group collaboration extends beyond simple forms. Organizations require more realtime or synchronous communication interaction. Alternatively, asynchronous communication can be used for group collaboration in the form of email messages being sent between the groups.

Microsoft Exchange Chat Service

Chat Services provide group communication in realtime, much like the more static role of users in a threaded discussion group on the Internet, and especially in the following scenarios:

- Open forums or discussion groups
- Semistructured meetings
- Standards-based client

To use this technology, determine the number of supported users. You can typically support thousands of concurrent users in one chat room on any given Chat server. Best practices suggest numbers ranging from 1 user to almost 20,000 users on one server. The Chat Service is based on the well-known and field-tested *IRC protocol*. This standard (RFC 2899, 1459, 1060) supports realtime dialogue between two or more people. IRC uses channels, more commonly known as chat rooms. Microsoft has decided to extend this protocol in the form of IRCX *(extended IRC)*. This "extension set" enhances the IRC protocol by adding commands for management purposes. Users connect to a Chat server using TCP (Transmission Control Protocol) ports 6667 or 7000. Port 6667 is the first port number that will be assigned to the first chat community established. You also can use any port that is not already being used for other services.

NOTE: *Depending on the needs of your company, the size and expertise of your technical support staff, and your security policy, Chat Services, especially exposed on the Internet, are high-risk service areas. Outside the need to providing customer service support or other specific e-services to your user population, the poorly planned installation of Chat Services tends to be an unproductive use of bandwidth.*

People meet on designated channels for group discussions and determine whether they will use a dynamic channel or a registered channel. A *dynamic channel* is a temporary channel created using special commands, such as IRC **join**. A dynamic channel has a channel host or operator—typically the first to enter the channel—who manages the channel or chat room. A channel host can be one or more persons.

The other type of channel is the *registered channel*, which is created by a system administrator (SA) and is permanent. Registered channels start when someone joins a chat room, or automatically when the Chat Service starts on the server. You see all the channels from your browser client as long as they are not hidden using the IRC **list** command. An operator can also be assigned to control registered channels.

Administrative Controls for Chat Services

You need to control certain features of your Chat Server. Configure your chat rooms to be either secure or open to cloning. Also, determine who can and cannot connect to your chat community. A *secure channel* or chat room means that access has been restricted in some way. Restrict access if you are using some form of authentication, or you want to control who can talk in a chat room at any given time. You can allow only a certain group of users to access a channel using the security that is built into AD. Alternatively, you can design a chat room that can be cloned to create a copy of itself when a certain member limit has been reached. Only registered, permanent channels can clone themselves; all settings are copied over to the duplicate channel.

Employ user classes and user bans to allow access to chat rooms. A user class can be created outside the confines of AD. Assign users to classes, which have specific permissions. Class membership is based on the following:

- User domain name and IP (Internet Protocol) address
- Network login method
- Login time

Use class membership to restrict users from joining other dynamic channels and to prevent someone from becoming a channel owner or operator.

Creating a Chat Community

Chat communities are associated with Exchange administrative groups. When you install the Chat Service the first time, a chat community is created in the first administrative group. This special chat community, called *Default-Chat-Community*, can be renamed according to organizational naming conventions and needs.

You can choose speaking restrictions based on the size of your channel, as shown in Figure 7.5, under the user class Properties sheet. For smaller channels, speaking restrictions under the Modes tab of the channel's Properties sheet provides a Moderated Mode box to keep users from posting unauthorized messages. On the same Modes panel, as shown in Figure 7.6, select Auditorium for larger channels so that users cannot send messages to each other, but speakers can both see and send messages to all channel participants. Limit channel access to users who are invited or users who have been fully authenticated according to a predefined authentication scheme.

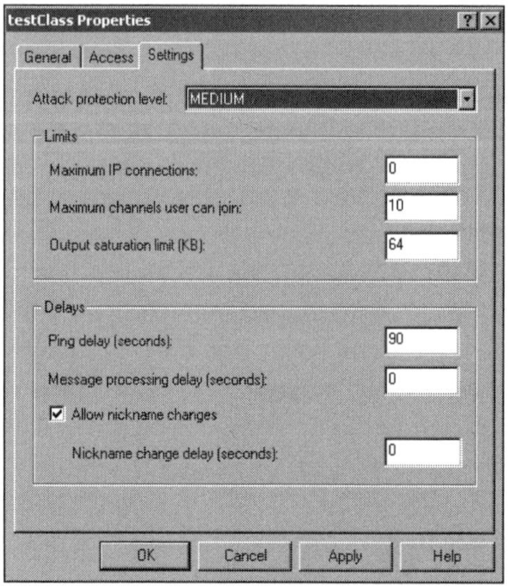

Figure 7.5 Size limitations restrictions.

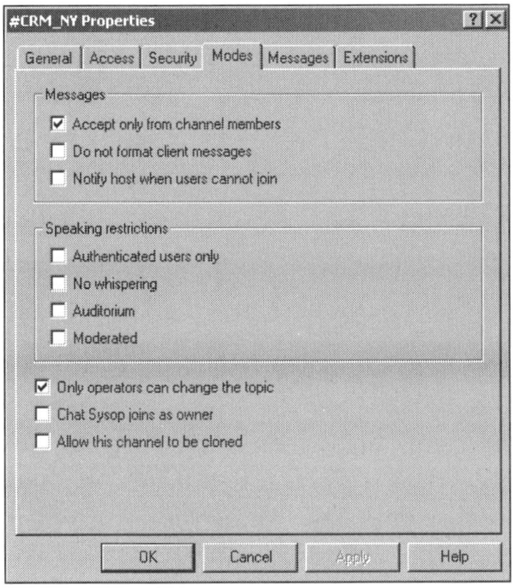

Figure 7.6 Speaking restrictions such as Moderated and Auditorium.

Chat Clients

The Chat Server runs on Exchange 2000. Previous versions of Exchange used a client called Microsoft Chat 2. Because Exchange 2000 does not support Chat 2, you need to install the Chat 2.1 client available online or on the Exchange 5.5 SP3 CD. Upon first installing the Chat client, you can access two separate Properties sheets: the Connect tab and the Personal Info tab. The Connect tab prompts you for the server and community to which you want to connect. The Personal Info tab allows you to update or modify your personal information such as real name, nickname, and email address.

The Chat client can be customized by choosing View|Options from the Chat client. You can create a personal configuration using these six property sheets: Character, Background, Automation, Personal Info, Settings, and Comics View. You can choose the communications you see (for example, whispers or invitations), the character you want to represent you in the room (using the Character tab), and the automatic greeting that is displayed whenever you are the host of the room.

Installing IM

The requirements for an IM Server include Exchange 2000 Server running on Windows 2000 Server or Advanced Server, and IIS 5. The Windows 2000 machine can be configured as either a DC or a Member Server. Domain authentication is not required. IM uses two Virtual Server components in most cases: a home server and a routing server. Users send and receive IMs through the home server. A routing server redirects messages to a home server. The home server is also responsible for communicating "presence information." The only time you don't need a routing server is in a single-server type environment. Best practices recommend installing routing servers as a function of growth in the user population rather than home servers. For every two home servers, install at least one routing server. Make certain all servers have appropriate group permissions in AD. To create and manage the IM settings in the System Manager snap-in, you have to belong to the Exchange Admins global group.

Managing IM Servers

Administrative functions regarding IM Servers involve moving IM data files to alternate locations on your IM Server, or removing an IM Server altogether.

You can physically remove the IM Virtual Server from the Exchange System Manager snap-in to the Microsoft MMC by right-clicking the IM Virtual Server and selecting Delete. You will have to specify where you want your IM users moved. Keep in mind that you are either removing your IM Virtual Server or you're removing the IM Service entirely. To remove the IM Service entirely, you have to use Add/Remove Programs in Control Panel.

If you just want to take your IM Server offline for some reason, you have to first stop the corresponding Virtual Server that has been defined in the Internet Service Manager snap-in when you installed IIS 5. You right-click your virtual IIS site and select Stop. At this point, all IM Services on your Web site stop and users can't send messages. Selecting Start on the same shortcut menu restarts your Virtual Server.

If you create more than one home server, best practices recommend at least one routing server. You need an IIS Web site to host a Routing Server. Keep in mind the following points:

- Using the Instant Messaging Virtual Server Wizard, specify the DNS (Domain Name System) domain name. Identify your IM Routing Server with the naming convention of ***server_name.domain_name.com***.
- Accept all other defaults in the wizard.
- Configure your DNS for the appropriate resource records for your IM Routing Server. Every IM Routing Server has to have one "A" (address) record in DNS.

By default, IM uses the *Windows Integrated Authentication (WIA)* method rather than the Digest Authentication method. The WIA method does not require *users* to enter additional usernames or passwords to send IMs. Use the Digest method if you use a Proxy Server, or if you run a non-Windows IM client. The *Digest Authentication* method requires IM to retrieve unencrypted passwords from AD. You must change the password policy on your DC so that passwords are stored in an encrypted format.

Besides deleting IM Servers and taking them offline, you might also want to move some of your data files to other locations on your server. Use Exchange System Manager to locate the RVP (Rendezvous Protocol) Instant Messaging container in Protocols. Right-click this container and change the location for your data and log files on the General tab of the Properties sheet.

IM and Clients

The primary client used for IM is the MSN Messenger client software, which is included with Exchange 2000. This product is free, so no licensing issues are involved with its use. There are also freeware and vendor-neutral IM products available on the Internet. After the client is installed, configure special options by choosing Tools|Options. You can choose from several Property sheets including the following:

- *General*—Customize visual prompts that notify users when an IM has arrived. You can allow users to change their display names when they are dealing with a remote domain.
- *Privacy*—Display results of any actions you might have taken with AD or the MSN Messenger client. If you know someone has subscribed to your presence information, you can block that user from subscribing. You can also block that user from sending you messages. You cannot block a user from Email Services or Chat Services; only IM services.
- *Exchange*—Configure the IM user logon name and select which service the MSN Messenger client will connect to using either the Microsoft Exchange Instant Messaging service or the MSN Messenger Service, which requires Internet access.
- *Accounts*—Configure MSN Messenger Service account information.
- *Connection*—Configure proxy services for users who dial into your network. The IM client automatically looks for the Internet Explorer profile. Remote, dial-up users must be redirected to the appropriate file location via proxy to obtain this profile.

Sometimes, you will experience problems with proxy servers because IM uses the Internet Explorer profile to log on initially. This profile relies on the Windows NT LAN Manager (NTLM) for authentication and sometimes has difficulty passing through proxy servers. Determine whether a user's browser is configured to use the address of a proxy server.

KM Service in Exchange 2000

Exchange Server supports advanced security features using a variety of clients, ranging from Windows 3.x-based clients to Macintosh clients. Advanced security includes the signing and sealing of messages generated by a client such as Outlook.

Message signing allows a user to place a digital signature on a message so a recipient can verify that the message originated from that user. *Message sealing* encrypts a message with its related attachments so that it can only be unsealed using a correct "key." Exchange 2000 leverages the built-in security of Windows 2000 Server, but it also provides advanced security in the form of the optional KM Service component. This service works in conjunction with AD services to manage encryption keys used in encrypting email messages and integrates well with Microsoft Certificate Services. Windows 2000 supports public-key infrastructure (PKI) to ensure security for messaging. Consider incorporating Certificate Services and PKI to design and maintain public-key security systems.

Exchange Server uses two types of keys for encryption, symmetric, or *shared keys*, and asymmetric or complementary keys. *Symmetric keys* are identical; both the sender of a message and the recipient of a message use the same key to encrypt and decrypt data. *Asymmetric keys* complement one another, but are not identical; one key encrypts the data, while the complement key decrypts the data. Public keys are made accessible to the public through some centralized locations, such as public folders or AD. With key pairs, either the public or the private key can encrypt data, as well as decrypt data. Both Windows 2000 and Exchange 2000 use public keys to encrypt data, and private keys to decrypt data.

Exchange Server uses the KM Service, which works with Windows 2000 Certificate Services, to provide a centralized PKI. The Windows 2000 PKI consists of Certificate Services, digital certificates, Cryptographic service providers (CSPs), and certificate stores for storing certificates. Installing Certificate Services allows you to own your own Certificate Authority (CA), which issues and manages digital certificates on your behalf. AD maintains information for your CA such as user accounts and group memberships. Security credentials are passed between communicating parties when the CA issues a digital certificate to verify a user's identity. You trust a digital certificate if you trust the CA that issued the digital certificate. CAs create keys and issue digital certificates according to guidelines of the international X.509 standard. The X.509 standard normally describes different levels of authentication, including simple authentication, which uses a password as the only verification of identity. Other types of strong authentication require public-key technology. For two users to communicate using strong authentication, they have to use the same encryption algorithms during the authentication process.

KM Services and Certificate Services

The KM Service works with Certificate Services and installs its own CSP, which stores a user's private keys that only the KM Service server can access. Certificate Services generate a user's certificate based on requests from the KM Service. The KM Service also uses the concept of a trusted third party (TTP), in which

Certificate Services can also generate a user's certificate based on a request from a TTP server who is acting on behalf of a KM Service server. The CA certificate is a part of all the clients who enroll through a KM Service and a CA, so all clients can trust each other's certificates because the same CA has issued them all.

The most vital function KM Services perform, however, is server-side key recovery. Messaging security, including generating the keys, storing the keys, and encrypting and decrypting messages, are actually client-side operations. Outlook 97 clients (and earlier versions of Outlook) store all user keys and certificates in an encrypted file that uses an .EPF file extension. Outlook 98 stores this same information in the *IE protected store*. Outlook 2000 stores all this information in the local machine *Registry*.

The KM Service uses AD to store trust lists, revocation lists, and even the user certificates. The KM Service communicates with Certificate Services through the Policy module of the CA. The Policy module inside the CA defines user certificates and templates used by the KM Service. The KM Service has its own encrypted database for storing user key pairs. You can't view this database because it is strongly encrypted. Use the Exchange System Manager snap-in to administer KM Services. Because of integration between KM Services and AD, you can see a Security tab on the Property sheet of every user account, after installing Certificate Services and the KM Services add-on component for Exchange Server. Some organizations already have KM Services running using an older version of Exchange Server, such as version 5.5. Best practices recommend upgrading these servers to Exchange 2000 KM Services. Any key stored within the database is encrypted using a *master encryption key*. This key maintains the security of the information within the database. When you initially installed the KM Services server, you created a password that was used by the KM Server to start the KM Services and access the Key Manager database.

Policy-Based Management

Planning for remote access to services is a significant part of your project design. Managing this access typically involves administering a majority of your user population and many systems-related issues. Policy management, using standards-based protocols such as LDAP and Remote Access Dial-Up User Service (RADIUS), promotes more efficient management and simplified administration and support. These protocols simplify administration of multivendor platforms and centralize management tasks. When planning the delivery of requested services, consider well-known Application Programming Interfaces (APIs) and standard-based protocols supporting user authentication and authorization across any network access device. Windows 2000 includes RADIUS services in its Internet Authentication Service (IAS).

Outsourcing Collaborative Services

Even simple RTC solutions can become tedious from a management perspective. You may want to consider outsourcing these intranet services. Although appearing to function as a private site, you outsource the full intranet operation, which includes sharing calendars, messaging, scheduling, and sharing documents. Consider these reasons for outsourcing an intranet for collaborative purposes:

- No expensive technology investment is involved.
- Secure access is available from anywhere.
- Collaboration services are almost immediate because outsourced solutions are easy to install.
- Upgrading storage capacity for additional Web pages or documents is not necessary.

Services and the software interfaces created by companies providing this type of service are simple to use and typically have Web-based rather than GUI administrative interfaces.

Immediate Solutions

Connecting to an Exchange Server for Services

Exchange clients need ways to connect to both the network and the specific server to request services. The following factors need to be considered:

- Number of remote clients versus networked clients
- Frequency and length of sessions
- Nature and volume of data exchanged including policies regarding, for example, the size of attachments
- Sophistication of user population regarding application needs
- Available connection speeds
- Usage of resources by collaborative services like Chat and IM

Storage considerations must be carefully planned to determine whether data is stored on the server or locally using personal storage files (PST). Also consider the amount of traffic caused by newsgroups, synchronized files located on both platforms, and client security connections to a key management server. Standardization of client is an especially important issue. The following two lists show the advantages and disadvantages to running Exchange client from a network.

Advantages:

- Easier control over software upgrades and policy on the client side
- More rapid and controlled deployment on the client side
- Reduced need for client-side disk space
- Better control, guaranteed compliance, and reduced support issues involving backup and virus control

Disadvantages:

- Additional TCO on the server side, such as hardware capacity, network traffic, administrative installation issues, and support
- Slower response times

- Installation issues regarding offline access to data and services
- Additional hardware and software support for user-related maintenance

Creating a MMC

To create a new console frame, sometimes called a *console root container*, explicitly in author mode, type the following command-line information in the Run dialog box:

```
mmc path/filename.msc /a
```

Where *path/filename.msc* is the proposed location and console file name, and **/a** explicitly confirms author mode (in which, as stated previously, modifications are allowed from the console). Add snap-in components through the Add/Remove Snap-in feature selection on the Console menu (or by using the keyboard equivalent, Ctrl+M).

The primary concerns when creating and distributing consoles are simplicity and security. Your first objective is to create custom MMC snap-in tools using the MMC. You need to then apply various restrictions (such as restricting author mode and using various snap-ins) to those snap-ins. Finally, you can delegate various administrative tasks to different people by controlling the range of control through the distribution of various administrative tool sets. In order to create a MMC file, perform the following steps:

1. Run **mmc.exe** at the command line.
2. Click Console|Add/Remove Snap-in.
3. Select Add to display the available snap-ins.
4. Select the Computer Management snap-in in the Add Standalone Snap-in dialog box as shown in Figure 7.7, and click the Add button.
5. Upon completing your selection, click the Close button.
6. Click OK.
7. Select Console|Options.
8. Select the Console tab and choose Author Mode in the Console Mode box.
9. Click Console|Save As and specify a file name that will be saved with an .msc extension.

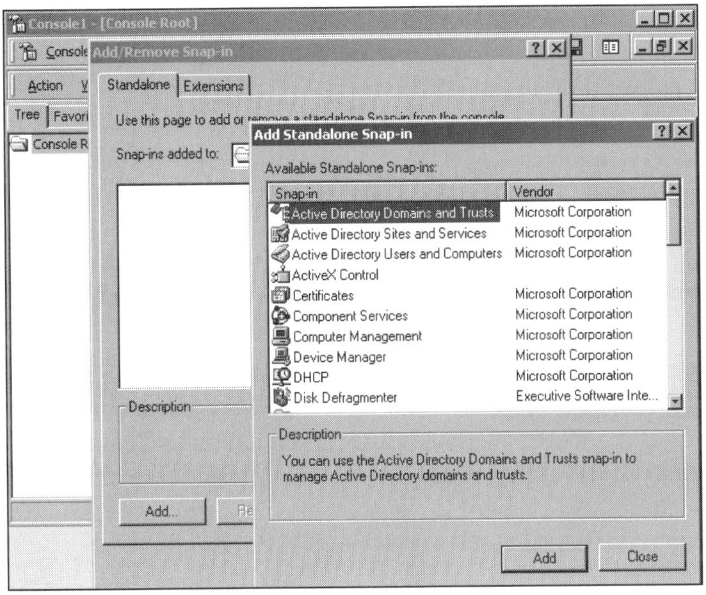

Figure 7.7 Adding a Standalone Snap-in.

Creating an Emergency Repair Disk (ERD)

Use the Backup system utility to create an Emergency Repair Disk to recover your system in the event of a hard drive failure. Repairs are limited to basic system files, the partition boot sector, and startup environmental information. The ERD does not recover registry files, data or programs, nor a substitute for regularly backing up your local machine. In order to recover corrupted system files, the repair process searches for information in a folder located under *systemroot\repair*. When you select the option Also Back Up The Registry To The Repair Directory on the Backup utility screen, you are refreshing these files. Do not change or move the contents of this folder.

1. From System Tools|Accessories under Programs, select Backup.
2. Click the Emergency Repair Disk button on the Backup And Recovery Tools dialog box.
3. Enable the option box that will backup the registry and, per the instructions in the dialog box, insert a blank, formatted diskette in the A: drive. A dialogue box will indicate whether or not the system data is successfully copied to the diskette.

4. If you want, when you click to confirm the successfully saved data, the Backup interface will appear to begin a backup of selected files. Alternatively, cancel out of the utility screen.

NOTE: *In order to replace registry files, you need to use the Recovery Console, a command-line interface that is useful in repairing damage to the hard drive and file system. There are two ways an administrator can launch the recovery console: from the Setup disks or from an installed version on your computer. To run the Recovery Console, you must restart your computer and boot the Recovery Console option from the list of available operating system options listed by the boot manager. Start the Recovery Console from \i386 directory on the CDROM logical drive and type* ***Winnt32.exe /cmdcons****.*

You can make specific setting selections and save the MMC file for distribution. You also can restrict MMC features through Group Policy by choosing Administrative Templates|Windows Components|Microsoft Management Console. You can also do this at the Registry level. For example, you can restrict users from opening the MMC in author mode, from opening console files in author mode, and from opening any console files that open in author mode by default.

WARNING! Use Registry Editor at your own risk. Incorrect entries in the Registry can cause damage to your system configuration that might require you to reinstall your OS. Create an Emergency Rescue Disk before you attempt this lab exercise.

You must first create the following key in the Registry:

```
HKEY_CURRENT_USER\Software\Policies\Microsoft\MMC
```

Populate this Registry key with various string names and values to create the appropriate conditions. Before you can set string values in the Registry, you must create the **MMC** subkey under **Microsoft** key:

1. Run **REGEDIT** at the command line.
2. Expand **HKEY_CURRENT_USER**, **Software**, **Policies**, **and Microsoft**.
3. Right-click the Microsoft key name and select New.
4. Select Key, type "MMC" in the text box, and press Enter. You will see the **MMC** key shown in the Registry path. For the rest of the lab exercises in this chapter, you'll place all the strings and their values in this key.

Modifying the MMC **RestrictAuthorMode** Registry Key

To prevent users from opening the MMC in author mode, or using any console files that open in author mode by default, modify the **RestrictAuthorMode** Registry key of the MMC console by using the Registry:

1. Right-click the **MMC** key and select New.
2. Select DWORD Value and type "RestrictAuthorMode" in the open text box. Press the Enter key to confirm the string name. Notice the string is still selected.
3. Press the Enter key a second time and enter "1" to enable the feature. The Base section of the dialog box should indicate that you have entered a hexadecimal value.

NOTE: *Hexadecimal values, using either a 0x prefix or h suffix, use base-16 and thus consist of 16 symbols, 0 thru 9, and A thru F. Base-16 simplifies the eight binary digit (bit) byte as two consecutive symbols. To convert a hexadecimal digit to binary, translate each of the two symbols to a four bit binary equivalent. Thus, the hexadecimal FA would translate to 1111 1010 in binary. Registry entries sometimes use hexadecimal values.*

This **RestrictAuthorMode** Registry key stores the Restrict The User From Entering Author Mode Group Policy setting as "1" for enabled or "0" for disabled. If it's set to Not Configured, Group Policy deletes the entry from the Registry. If it isn't configured or you delete the entry yourself, the system behaves as though the value is "0". The **RestrictAuthorMode** Registry key prevents users from opening the MMC in author mode or opening any console file that opens by default in author mode. This key value restricts the user workstation from possible alteration of any console file. When this key is disabled or not configured, users can open the MMC in author mode and create their own consoles. The users can, however, open MMC user mode console files such as those on the Administrative Tools menu. To disable this **RestrictAuthorMode** feature, return to the string value and either double-click it or right-click it and select Modify. Replace the hexadecimal "1" with a "0" and press Enter. To remove this feature, right-click the string value and select Delete.

Modifying the MMC **RestrictToPermittedSnapins** Registry Key

To modify the **RestrictToPermittedSnapins** Registry key of the MMC console by using the Registry, follow these steps:

1. Right-click the **MMC** key and select New.
2. Select DWORD Value and type "RestrictToPermittedSnapins" in the open text box. Press the Enter key to confirm the string name. Notice the string is still selected.
3. Press the Enter key a second time and enter "1" to enable the feature. The Base section of the dialog box should indicate that you have entered a hexadecimal value.

The **RestrictToPermittedSnapins** Registry key stores the setting of Restrict Users To The Explicitly Permitted List Of Snap-Ins Group Policy. If you disable this key with "0" or set the key to Not Configured, all snap-ins are permitted, except those explicitly prohibited. Snap-ins are explicitly prohibited when the **Restrict_Run** value in the Snap-ins Class ID subkey is disabled. A value of "1" prohibits users from running any snap-ins except those that are explicitly permitted for use. This value is best to use when most or all snap-ins are prohibited. Disabling this key (the default value) enables users to run snap-ins unless they are specifically prohibited from doing so.

To disable this **RestrictToPermittedSnapins** Registry key feature, return to the string value and either double-click it or right-click it and select Modify. Replace the hexadecimal "1" with a "0" and press Enter. To remove this feature, right-click the string value and select Delete. You can now choose to specify the access level to any specific console file when a MMC snap-in is added through Group Polices or through modifying the Registry of a machine to restrict the modification, running, or extension of any console by adding snap-ins.

Installing and Managing Certificate Services

A CA issues certificates and enables secure exchanges of information. The CA's private key signs the certificate. This digital certificate is then used to verify a subscribing client's signature. Both clients and CAs maintain a list of "trusted certificates." The CA also publishes a *certificate revocation list (CRL)*. This list shows all certificates that are invalid and therefore no longer trusted. Digital certificates also expire after a random time period has elapsed. Certificate Services

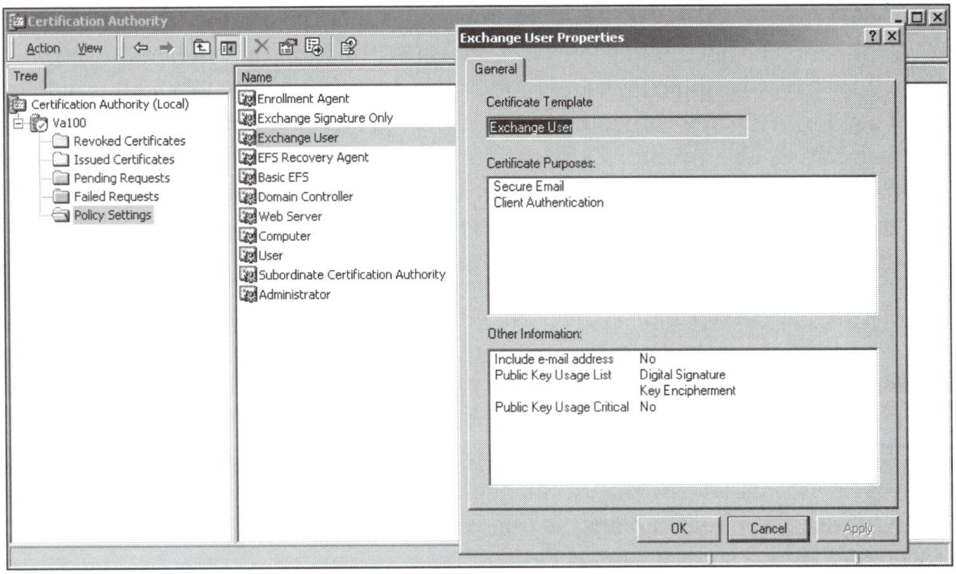

Figure 7.8 Certificate Authority showing Exchange policies.

can be installed any time by using Add/Remove Programs in the Control Panel, as well as during the initial installation of Windows 2000. Remember that after Certificate Services are installed, you cannot rename or move the hosting server from your current domain. An example of Exchange User policies is shown in Figure 7.8.

Installing a CA

You can choose from four types of CAs:

- Enterprise root CA
- Enterprise subordinate CA
- Standalone root CA
- Standalone subordinate CA

Enterprise root CA, the default selection, is the most trusted CA in an enterprise and it should be installed before you install any other CA. It also requires AD. Configure options for public and private keys when you install Certificate Services, which includes choosing the CSP to be used to generate your public and private keys, and a hash algorithm. The default algorithm, SHA-1 (Secure Hash Algorithm-1), produces a 160-bit hash value and is similar to Message Digest 5.

SHA-1 provides the strongest cryptographic security among the hash algorithms available. The default key length shown is 512 or 1,024 bits, depending on whether a Base Cryptographic Provider or Enhanced Cryptographic Provider is being used. The longer the key value, the longer the life of a private key. Certificate Services installation also prompts for the name of your CA. Windows 2000 uses this CA name to identify all CAs and requires each CA name to be unique. The root CA certificate has a default lifetime of two years. When you're finished installing Certificate Services, stop and restart the IIS.

Certificate Services also affect Web enrollment and viewing certificate information. By default, installing Certificate Services also installs the Web enrollment support service on the same machine, although you can decide to install this *Web enrollment form* on another Windows 2000 machine. When a user accesses this Web enrollment form using ***http://server_name/certsrv***, selecting Retrieve The CA Certificate Or Certificate Revocation List retrieves the CA's certificate or the current CRL. Users can access this Web page to obtain a new user certificate.

Installing KM Services

Exchange 2000 KM Service is compatible with KM servers running Exchange 5.5, even with SP1 (Service Pack 1) running. We recommend you run the latest SP for Exchange, which is SP3. To successfully install KM Services, regardless of which version you are using, you have to follow a prescribed sequence of steps:

1. Install Windows 2000 Certificate Services.
2. Install Exchange Certificate Templates.
3. Install Exchange 2000 KM Services.
4. Decide where you will put the startup password for KM Services.
5. Grant Manage permissions to KM Services.
6. Request a certificate from the CA.

If you look at the previous list, you notice that we have already discussed step 1, installing the Windows 2000 Certificate Services. Step 2 comes into play because you need at least one Enterprise CA that can issue special types of certificates before KM Services can be successfully installed.

To create an Enterprise CA, open the Certification Authority snap-in and select your Policy folder. Right-click and select New|Certificate To Issue, which offers a choice of Exchange Certificate Templates to install. Exchange 2000 uses three templates to issue certificates to users:

- *The Enrollment Agent (Computer) certificate*—This allows KM Services to issue certificates on behalf of Exchange Advanced Security users.
- *The Exchange User certificate*—This certificate is used to encrypt mail and digital signatures.
- *The Exchange Signature Only certificate*—This certificate is used for digital signatures only.

You can start the Exchange 2000 Installation Wizard from the CD-ROM to install KM Services. Remember that Exchange defaults to a Typical installation mode. You can select the KM Services component from the Component Selection screen if you change this to Custom installation mode. Select Install Next To Key Management Service, and click Next. Select Install The System Management Tools Along With Your Key Management Server. Choosing a Custom installation ignores the System Management Tools, which you'll need for your KM Services.

When prompted for the administrative group to install KM Services in, remember that you can have only one instance of KM Services per administrative group. Carefully consider the startup password as well. You can either type this password manually every time you open your KM Services management console, or store this password on a floppy disk. Unauthorized access to this password will provide complete access and control to your KM Services database. The kmserver.pwd file stores this password. After securing your secret password, the KM Services installation is finished.

The default KM Services password is *password*. Always consider changing this. If you add additional administrators later, they will be given their own administrative passwords, which they can change at any time.

To change an administrative password, follow these steps:

1. Click the Advanced Security container in Exchange System Manager.
2. Right-click the Key Manager object in the Detail pane and choose Properties.
3. Select the Administrators tab, and click Change Password after selecting the administrator whose password you want changed. Any KM Services password must contain six characters at a minimum.

The Passwords tab of the Key Manager Properties sheet is used to configure multiple password policies. All KM Services server operations need only one administrator password; however, you can configure certain functions to require authentication from multiple administrators. If you have three different administrators, you can require different passwords.

Granting Manage Permissions to KM Services

Add the KM Services computer account to every Certificate Services server that issues certificates to KM Services. The KM Services server must have Manage permissions on the Certificate Services server. Open the CA snap-in and right-click your CA. Choose Properties and find the Security tab. Then click Add and select the computer name for every KM Services server in your company.

While on the Security tab, make certain the Allow column for Manage Permissions is checked. Your Permissions box should show three permissions—Manage, Enroll, and Read. Each permission can be assigned an Allowed or Denied value. To start the KM Services service, use the Exchange System Manager snap-in. When you open the snap-in after installing the KM Services Server, you will notice a new container called Advanced Security. This container appears in the administrative group into which you installed KM Services. Highlight this container and you will notice two objects in the right pane: **Encryption Configuration** and **Key Manager**. Right-click the **Key Manager** object in the right pane and select the Start option. Then, enter the KM Services password. The KM Services password can be entered either in the pop-up dialog box, or from the floppy disk that contains the kmserver.pwd file previously created. Use the **Key Manager** object to add additional KM Services administrators.

The person who installs KM Services is allowed to administer KM Services. Best practices recommend allowing other administrators to administer this service. Right-click the **Key Manager** object and select Properties. Upon gaining access, you will see four tabs: General, Administrators, Passwords, and Enrollment. Select the Administrators tab, click Add, and select one or more users who are allowed to administer your KM Services Server.

Enrolling Users in KM Services

KM Services uses AD to enroll users. It request certificates for users from Certificate Services. These certificates are used to create *two key pairs* for every user—not two keys, but two key *pairs*. One pair is for digital signatures and is created on the client. This key pair is private and is stored on the client's machine. The other pair is for encryption, and is created on the server—the KM Services Server. The process for enrolling a user is as follows:

1. Launch the Exchange System Manager snap-in.
2. Click the Advanced Security container and right-click the **Key Manager** object in the right-hand pane.

3. Select the Enroll Users option. If you want individual users, select Display An Alphabetic List Of User Names from the Global Address Book, and click OK.
4. Select the users you want to enroll through KM Services. Clients receive a "token" or notification via email advising them of their advanced security temporary key. They are instructed to open their email clients (usually Outlook 98 or Outlook 2000), choose Options|Security, and select Get A Digital ID. Security is then set up for them on the Exchange Server.

If you want to enroll a group of users, select the second radio button: Display Mailbox Stores, Exchange Servers, And Administrative Groups Of Eligible Users. When you see the containers of users, select the containers that hold users you want to enroll. Each user receives an email confirming enrollment.

Creating a Chat Community

Chat Services are playing a growing role in providing synchronous and relatively inexpensive support to users in many organizations. Though seen, in some corporate environments, as unproductive use of bandwidth, synchronous forms of collaborative communication in, for example, the context of customer relations is far superior to asynchronous email and expensive telephone alternatives. To create a chat community, perform the following:

1. Launch Exchange System Manager.
2. Right-click Chat Communities, choose New|Chat Community, and make configuration entries in the following Property sheets.

- *General*—Name your new community and give it a descriptive title. Community names must be a maximum of 200 bytes, begin with one or two characters identifying IRC or IRCX channel type, cannot contain any spaces, and must end with a letter. The title is limited to 63 characters. Set Connection Limits so that Maximum Anonymous Connections is less than the Maximum Total Connections (both default to 10,000). Specify whether you want client DNS names resolved by choosing either Disable, Attempt, or Require.
- *Channels*—Select channel defaults such as the default language for your chat room. Configure users who create dynamic channels to become the host for that channel and enable dynamic channels for your community. Configure the maximum number of users allowed on any dynamic channel in your community between 0 and 99,999, where a 0 value means you are allowing unlimited membership. Check Chat Sysop Joins As Owner to grant owner status to chat users with sysop permissions when they join a dynamic channel. A registered channel is not affected by this option.

- *Messages*—Specify a message of the day (MOTD) or any message you want displayed to users who use the IRC **admin** command.
- *Authentication*—Set authentication properties for your chat communities.

***NOTE:** A registered channel is created by an Exchange Administrator as a permanent communication resource for a chat community. The channel name is the only parameter that is required during setup. A dynamic channel alternatively can be created by any user logged in to a chat client. Administrators can manage dynamic channel creation through configuration of the Property sheet of the specific chat community in which dynamic channels are an issue.*

To create a chat community, you have to connect this community to your Chat server. Launch Exchange System Manager, and locate the server object that is hosting your chat community. Under this object, locate the IRCX container. Right-click this container and select Properties. To add a new community, click Add on the General page and select the name of your desired chat community. Every community you add has to be identified by a unique IP address.

Creating a Chat Channel

Every chat community needs at least one channel to support chat dialogues. To create any type of channel, perform the following:

1. Right-click the Channels container under your chat community.
2. Select New|Channel and complete the configuration using the various property sheets.
3. The New Properties sheet has six different tabs: General, Access, Security, Modes, Messages, and Extensions. Use the General tab to name your channel. A channel name can contain up to 200 characters. Every channel name must begin with a valid prefix, such as #, &, or %#. This prefix identifies the type of channel in use. For example, a pound sign (#) or ampersand (&) identifies an IRC channel. Any prefix containing two characters (for example, %#) denotes an extended channel using the IRCX protocol. Select the Create This Channel When The Service Starts checkbox on the General tab so your channel is always available when the Chat Service is running.
4. The Access tab of the Channels Property sheet allows you to configure channel modes that control the channel's visibility to a user. These visibility settings include the following:
   - *Secret*—Users who are not members of the channel cannot locate this channel using queries.

- *Public*—Nonmembers can obtain all information except text messages about a channel from any chat client using the IRC **list** command.
- *Hidden*—Equivalent to a public channel except that it can't be found using the IRC **list** command. You can display all the properties of this channel only if you know the exact name of the channel.
- *Private*—Nonmembers can obtain only the name, number of members, and Platform for Internet Content Selection (PICS) rating of this channel mode from a chat client by using the IRC **list** command. The PICS rating is provided by organizations like Recreational Software Advisory Council (RSAC) that evaluate the nature of content based on language, nudity, sex, and violence.

You can configure additional modes for your channel on the Modes tab of the Channel Properties sheet. Configure host notification when a user is not able to join and also allow channels to be cloned and moderated. When you check Allow This Channel To Be Cloned, you are allowing all registered channels to duplicate themselves when your member limit is reached. The limit for all systems is 99 clones, and each clone is a new channel.

Creating a Restricted Chat List

Use the Extensions tab to configure filters on your channel if you want to block any kind of objectionable language. Some chat communities filter sensitive communications, such as invitations, on both registered and dynamic channels. To use this feature effectively, create a list of restricted words. If a message contains a filtered word, the entire message is blocked. The user who initially sent the offensive message is notified. To create your restricted list, perform the following:

1. Launch the Exchange System snap-in and open the Protocols folder beneath your server object.
2. Right-click the specific IRCX folder and choose Properties.
3. Choose the chat community you want to filter and click the Properties button on the IRCX Properties dialog box.
4. Select Extensions beneath the IP address as shown in Figure 7.9.
5. Click the Add button and confirm the addition of an extension such as Profanity Filter (Pfilter) or Transcription Extension (Tscript).

***TIP:** You must shut down and then restart the IRCX Service after adding these extensions in order to configure the filters.*

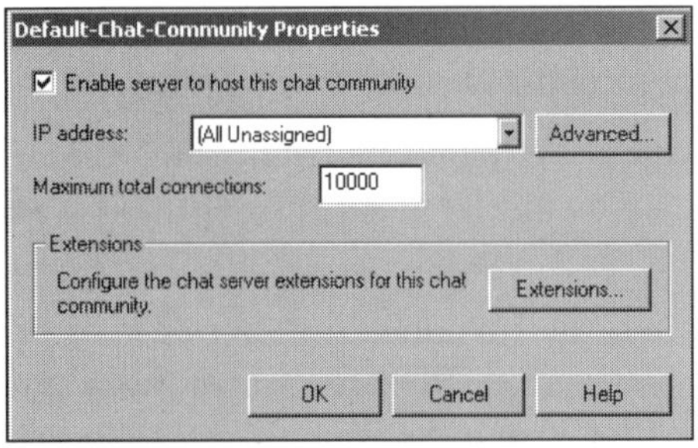

Figure 7.9 The Default-Chat-Community Properties sheet showing chat server extensions.

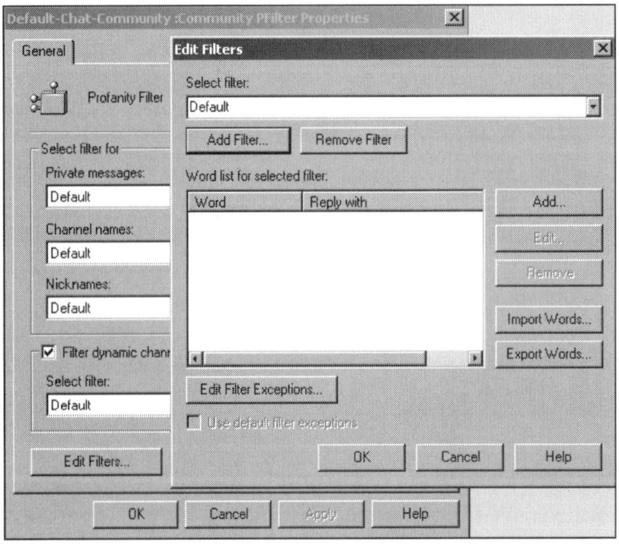

Figure 7.10 The Edit Filters for a default Profanity Filter.

6. You can edit the Profanity Filter extension under the Properties screen as shown in Figure 7.10. Filters can be applied on many different levels. You can set multiple filters for different groups. Each filter has a different word list. If you want to apply a different word list to different messages, you need to create a new filter. The order in which the extensions are listed will determine which extension receives notification that an event has occurred in a community first. A higher prioritized extension can block notification to a lower prioritized extension.

Disabling without Removing a Chat Community

To disable a chat community without removing it, access the appropriate Chat Community Property sheet. On the General tab, clear the Accept New Connections checkbox to disable the chat community. If you recheck this box, you will re-enable the chat community service. You do not have to restart your Chat Service if you check or uncheck this box.

Removing a Chat Community

You can remove a chat community in three ways; only the last method retains configuration information:

- In Exchange System Manager, select Properties for the IRCX container and display communities associated with a given server. Select a community, and right-click Remove; the community is disassociated from the Chat Server.
- Delete it from the chat community's container in the Exchange System Manager snap-in tool.
- Clear the Enable Server To Host This Chat Community checkbox in the Property sheet for the chat community to remove a chat community, but keep the association with the server. Use this alternative method to maintain configuration information for later use.

Troubleshooting IM

Many issues arise with IM. A list of common problems and suggested solutions is shown in Table 7.1.

Table 7.1 Common problems and solutions for the IM client.

Problem with IM Client	Suggested Solution
User closes client and loses messages	No solution here; the Messenger client retains messages as long as the dialog box is open. Messages are only held in memory, not on disk.
User wants to print her conversation	Move the conversation into a text editor and print.
User needs to communicate with four people	IM allows only one-to-one conversations. Multiple conversations require opening multiple IM dialog boxes on the user's desktop.

(continued)

Table 7.1 Common problems and solutions for the IM client *(continued)*.

Problem with IM Client	Suggested Solution
User cannot log onto IM	(1) Exclude the domain name of the IM routing and home servers in Internet Explorer properties. (2) Confirm a SRV (service location record) resource in DNS, and that the client is logging into the same domain within which the IM routing server resides. (3) Confirm the user has MSN Messenger version 2.1 or newer. Earlier versions might not work properly with the IM features of Exchange 2000. (4) Confirm the user has entered a valid password; blank passwords are not accepted.
The IM Client disappears from a user's screen	Restart Web Service or the IM server's Web site; have users log into IM.
Users can send messages but not receive messages	Restart Web Service on the IM routing server.

Creating a New Chat Community

To create additional chat communities under different administrative groups in your Windows 2000 system, follow these steps:

1. Right-click Chat Communities in the Exchange System Manager.
2. Select New|Chat Community.
3. On the General tab, name your new community "Production". (The name cannot contain spaces.)
4. Type in the title of your community—keep it under 63 characters.
5. Keep the default connection limits, but always remember the Maximum Anonymous Connections should be less than your Maximum Total Connections.
6. In the Resolve Client DNS name section, choose Attempt. This directs the server to try hostname-to-IP resolution.

Installing an IM Service

Installing the IM Service usually consists of four or five steps, depending on what method of authentication you use. Follow these steps to install an IM Service:

1. Create the Home Server—launch Exchange System and find the server object that will be your "home server."
2. Right-click the RVP container under the Protocols container.
3. Choose New|Instant Messaging Virtual Server and start the Instant Messaging Virtual Server Wizard. Keep in mind the following points:
    - When entering a display name, specify either a home server or a routing server.
    - Associate a Web site with any IM Server. You need one Web site for every IM home server you create.
    - Check your Web site and verify that you have a virtual directory called *Instmsg*. All messages are routed through this directory.
    - Enable the server to host user accounts using the Instant Messaging Virtual Server Wizard. Any server that hosts user accounts is a home server or else it is a routing server.

Changing the Password Policy for an IM Server

To change the Password Policy for an IM server, perform the following:

1. Right-click your domain OU, choose Properties, open the Group Policy tab, and select Default Domain Policy.
2. At the command line, type "GPEDIT.MSC".
3. Open Computer Configuration in the Group Policy MMC, then Windows Settings, and then Security Settings.
4. Open Account Policies, and then select Password Policy. Double-click Store Password Using Reversible Encryption For All Users In The Domain.
5. Select the Define This Policy Setting checkbox, and select the Enable radio button. Click OK.

Limiting the Number of IM Connections

When an IM Server becomes saturated with messages, you can limit the number of users who can concurrently connect to the IM Server as follows:

1. Launch Internet Services Manager MMC from the Administrative Tools menu.
2. Right-click your Web Site container under the host object and select Properties.
3. Display the Web Site tab on the Property sheet, and click Limited To in the Connections panel area. Enter the maximum number of simultaneous connections, and then click OK.
4. On the same tab, click Enable Logging to track user activity on your IM server. Note the Active log format that appears by default (W3C Extended Log File Format). You can change the log format if you desire.

Providing IM Service Access

To provide access to IM, perform the following:

1. Assign users to your IM home server on the user's Property sheet in the Active Directory Users And Computers MMC.
2. After locating a user, right-click the user account, and choose Exchange Tasks from the pop-up menu.
3. The Exchange Tasks Wizard allows you to select the IM home server for the user.
4. Enable IM for multiple users (or all users in your domain) by selecting all users in Active Directory Users And Computers, right-clicking the group selection, and then choosing the Exchange Task Wizard. This operation can only be done one time.
5. Distribute the IM Client to your users. The IM Client that comes with Exchange 2000 is the MSN Messenger. Locate this client software on the Exchange 2000 Server CD in the following path:**|Instmsg|I386\Client\Usa\Mmssetup.exe**. Install this to a network share for installation on work-stations.

Keep the Property sheet from this exercise open; it will be used in the next section.

Configuring IM Channel Defaults and Language Options

To configure unlimited membership in this channel, and to allow dynamic channels with no more than 1,000 users, perform the following:

1. In the Properties sheet from the previous exercise, click the Channels tab.
2. Notice the default number of users allowed on this channel (25). Change this number to 0 to signify unlimited membership in your channel or chat room.
3. Check the Allow An Owner Or Host For Channel So Any User Who Creates A Dynamic Channel Can Become The Channel Owner box.
4. Now check the Allow Dynamic Channels box, and type "1000" in the Number Of Users Allowed In Channel box.
5. Finally, check the Chat Sysop Joins As Owner To Grant Owner Status To Chat Users With Sysop Permissions when they join a dynamic channel. Notice that registered channels will not be affected by this setting.

Creating a Chat User Class

To create a chat user class, perform the following:

1. Locate and right-click the Classes folder under your chat community in the Exchange System MMC snap-in.
2. Select New|Class.
3. On the General tab, enter a class name, and then configure a Member Scope. The Member Scope can be configured either by using an identity mask, or by using an IP address with a subnet mask. Identity masks can use wildcard characters such as an asterisk (*) or question mark (?). Each identity mask uses three distinct fields: a nickname, a username, and a domain name or IP address.

   For example,

   Nickname: Poweruser *User Name:* * *Domain or IP address:* *

   means that this user class will contain all users with the nickname "Poweruser" from anywhere.

In addition to the General tab, the Access and Settings tabs also affect a user class. The Access tab defines your class based on a user's logon state and what users are not permitted to do. Check the Hide Class Members' IP Addresses And

DNS Names box to prevent disclosing security information. The Settings tab is to set attack-protection levels to protect your Chat Server. Choose any four levels ranging from none to high. An attack-protection level corresponds to a delay time, in seconds.

The Settings tab also has values regarding Limits and Delays. The Limits settings are as follows:

- *Maximum IP Connections*—This determines the number of connections per IP address for this user class with the exception of the channel operator.
- *Maximum Channels User Can Join*—This determines the number of simultaneous channels or chat rooms a user can join, and is based on a user's nickname.
- *Output Saturation Limit*—This number, in kilobytes, shows the amount of data your Chat Server will buffer or queue for a client before the connection is terminated.

The Delay settings are the following:

- *Ping Delay*—The number of seconds used to ping an active client to determine its presence on the remote side of an active connection. A client responds to a PING message with a PONG message in return. The timeout value for this delay ranges between 15 seconds and approximately 3,600 seconds.
- *Message Processing Delay*—The number of seconds the server waits before processing the next message from any client. The default value is 0 seconds with a maximum of 10 seconds.
- *Nickname Change Delay*—This setting determines the frequency in seconds in which a user can change his nickname.

Creating a User Ban from an IRC Channel

Another important parameter is a user ban that restricts individual users from accessing a specific chat community. Any attempts at accessing a banned chat room result in strict denial. You can ban chat communities by either their domain name or their IP address. This community-specific rule implies that users banned from one chat room might be able to access other chat rooms. The procedure for banning users is similar to creating user classes:

1. Launch the Exchange System snap-in.
2. Locate and right-click the Ban container within your chat community.
3. Choose New|Ban. Only one tab appears—the General tab. You can ban users based on their nickname, username, domain name, or IP address.

Enrolling Users Using AD Rather Than KM Services

Configure users to receive certificates in Advanced Security through Active Directory instead of through KM Services. Use AD to recover a lost key or revoke a user's key. Alternatively, you can use Advanced Security in AD because of the additional detail given for each user, such as current security status, current KM Services server, and even when certificates were activated. You may have to enter your KM Services service password when completing these steps. You can enroll a user, recover a user's key pairs, or revoke a user's certificates. Enrolling users via Active Directory is different from using the Exchange System Manager snap-in as follows:

1. Highlight an OU from within Active Directory Users And Computers.
2. Right-click a specific user account in the Details pane and choose Properties.
3. Go to the Exchange Features tab and find the Features column.
4. Click Email Security, and then click Properties to display the corresponding property sheet.
5. Configure properties according to your needs.

Part III

Installing and Configuring Exchange 2000

Chapter 8

Security, Disaster, and Recovery

If you need an immediate solution to:	*See page:*
Protecting Your Mission-Critical Mailbox Stores	288
Deleting a Mailbox in Exchange 2000	288
Configuring a Deleted Items Retention Period	290
Configuring a Deleted Mailbox Retention Period	290
Reconnecting a Deleted Mailbox to a New User Object	292
Recovering a Mailbox from a Backup	293
Changing the Legacy Distinguished Name for a Recovery Server	296
Creating a SMTP Virtual Server	297
Configuring Authentication for SMTP Virtual Servers	300
Restricting Connections via IP Address or Domain for SMTP Virtual Servers	301
Creating a GPO for a Domain	304
Installing the Security Analysis and Configuration Snap-In	306
Planning an Optimal RAID Configuration	308
Disabling EFS for All Users in a Domain	309
Running **ISINTEG** and **ESEUTIL** to Check Your Databases for Inconsistencies	310
Troubleshooting the Inability to Apply Security Permissions Because of Missing Security Tab	314

In Depth

This chapter provides key information concerning the implementation of security within Exchange 2000 Server. It relates this information to the broad concepts of disaster and recovery. No single book exists that can adequately cover these topics in the breadth or depth that is required. Therefore, our intention is to provide you with sufficient detail that allows you to manage many complex disaster scenarios, while providing a framework for applying this information to future scenarios, which happen when you least expect them.

Why Security Is Important

Every Exchange administrator should understand the options available for bolstering the security of messaging infrastructures. The "normal" enterprise usually employs a variety of hardware platforms and operating systems (OSs), which can be problematic when attempting to guarantee the security and integrity of the data within the enterprise. This means you can impose different levels of security while still ensuring that different systems "talk" to each other. Throughout this book, we have emphasized the integration between the Windows 2000 Server OS and the software that runs Exchange 2000. We suggest that security with Exchange 2000 is a result of the security features present within Windows 2000 Server and Windows 2000 Advanced Server.

Given this integration, you have to understand the enhancements and improvements that Exchange 2000 adds to your security infrastructure, in and of itself. For example, with Exchange 2000, you can now create and configure a *protocol Virtual Server* for different sets of users within your organization. Internet users can use a Simple Mail Transfer Protocol (SMTP) Virtual Server different from the one used for an internal local area network (LAN), with different authentication schemes and security settings. One Virtual Server can even put restrictions on hosts that relay mail (a concern for administrators who want to block spam from infecting their mail systems), or control the number and type of incoming connections to an Exchange Server. Implementing adequate security measures in your organization not only protects your network from prying eyes, but also helps you in the long run by preparing you for disaster recovery and planning.

Security Measures Protect Your Network

Though it is obvious, you know that security measures protect your network; you must determine *how* effective security plans can protect both your internal network *and* your external network. The modern trend for networks is remote access using "secure" or "encrypted" channels of communication between a *public network* (such as the Internet) and a *private network* (or internal LAN).

The components used to protect an internal network are different than those used to protect an external network. Active Directory (AD) plays a big role in providing security inside a LAN. AD provides the directory infrastructure used by Exchange 2000, and provides an environment in which you can create a Public Key Infrastructure (PKI) using the Windows 2000 Certificate Services. Windows 2000 now provides some worthwhile security utilities, which helps administrators centralize their security implementations. For example, you can create a *Group Policy Object* (GPO) on a local computer or domain controller (DC) that applies certain configurations on a site, domain, or Organizational Unit (OU) level. You can edit a GPO using the Microsoft Management Console (MMC) window, as long as you have Administrator rights to the system.

Using Group Polices to enhance security, you can effectively restrict your users because you can dictate how objects will "behave." For instance, you can dictate how users will see their Start menus or how they will access certain files or folders. You should never use Group Policies in a vacuum; they should always be used in conjunction with other Windows 2000 features, such as NTFS (NT File System) rights and permissions, roaming and mandatory profiles, and auditing of user rights. The proper use of Group Policies can prevent users from installing destructive software packages or obtaining access to restricted corporate data.

Even though an administrator does not have to know the exact architecture of a GPO, it is helpful to keep some important points in mind when configuring these objects using the MMC consoles:

- All GPOs store their information in a folder known as the Group Policy Template (GPT).
- Multiple GPOs can be applied to one site, or even one domain. Conversely, multiple OUs can be associated with the same GPO.
- If a GPO is relatively small, it is found within a Group Policy Container (GPC). If a GPO is relatively large (configuration data includes many options and is applied to a large organizational structure), it is stored in a GPT. A GPT changes its data more frequently than a GPC.
- By default, three GPOs are in every Windows 2000 system: *Local Computer*, *Default Domain*, and *Default Domain Controller Policies*.

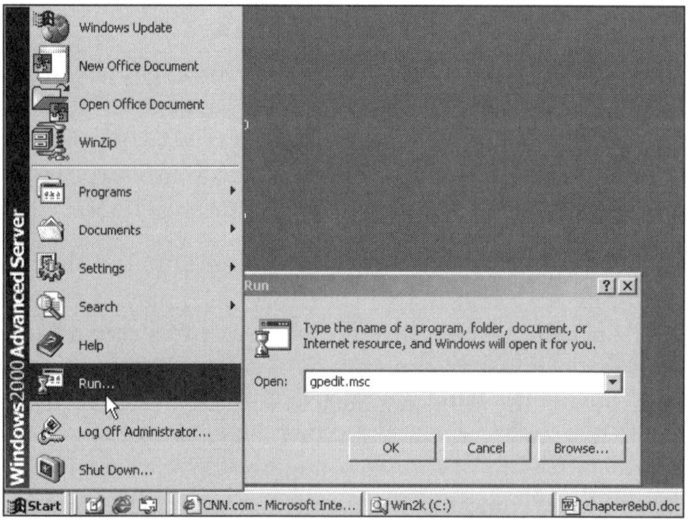

Figure 8.1 Opening up Local Computer Policy with gpedit.msc in the Run dialog box.

NOTE: *You can call up the Local Computer GPO by selecting Start|Run, typing "gpedit.msc", and then clicking OK. The Group Policy console opens by default, showing Local Computer policy settings (see Figure 8.1).*

As you can see in Figure 8.2, Group Policies allow you to configure both Computer Configurations and User Configurations. For each category, you can define Software Settings, Windows Settings, and Administrative Templates. You will be most concerned with the Windows Settings folder in the Computer Configuration container because it contains settings for *Account Policies* (for example, Password policies and Account Lockout policies) and *Local Policies* (for example, Audit policies and User Rights Assignments).

Local GPOs exist by default on every Windows 2000 computer, but only security settings are configured. You can find this local GPO in the Winnt\System32\GroupPolicy folder.

NOTE: *The Administrators group will have Full Control rights to this GPO. A system group, known as* Authenticated Users, *will possess three different permissions to this object: Read and Execute, Read, and List Folder Contents. It is important to always know who has default permissions to an object so you don't inadvertently add the wrong user to one of these groups and grant them inappropriate access levels.*

The difference between a GPC and a GPT is subtle, yet important to understanding how best to apply security settings to your Windows 2000 Server, and ultimately your Exchange 2000 Server. A GPC holds property information for a GPO, and includes additional *containers* for computer Group Policies or user Group Policies. The container indicates whether your GPO is enabled or not. On the other

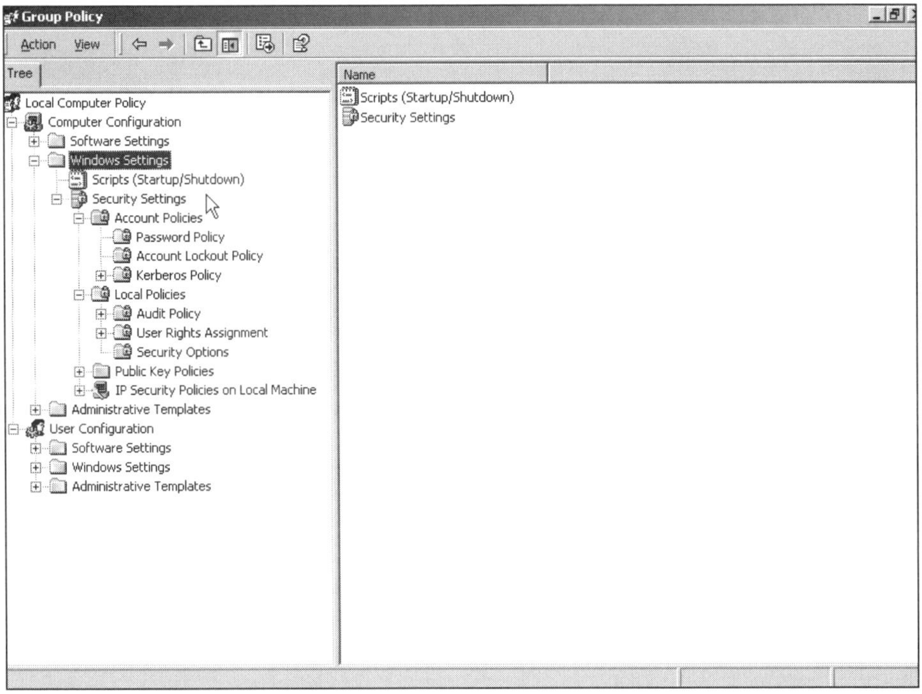

Figure 8.2 The Group Policy console containing Computer Configurations and User Configurations.

hand, a GPT (found within *Winnt\SYSVOL\sysvol\[domain]\Policies* of a DC) is a folder containing security settings for administrative templates, script files, and software settings. See the Immediate Solution "Creating a GPO for a Domain" to see how Group Policies are created and administered.

Although we've mentioned on internal security measures using GPOs, we can't leave out external security measures because Microsoft designed Exchange 2000 to be fully integrated with the Internet. Security plays an important role in optimizing the use of built-in protocols such as SMTP or NNTP (Network News Transfer Protocol). It also plays a role in using services such as NetMeeting or Instant Messaging (IM). Exchange 2000 was designed to be used in a front-end/back-end (FE/BE) type architecture, in which external users would access a front-end Exchange 2000 Server that would proxy or redirect all user requests to a back-end Exchange 2000 Server hosting users' mailboxes. For this type of scenario to work, you need strong authentication or encryption schemes in place to protect sensitive internal data from public access. Firewalls and proxy servers are used in these cases to protect an internal network from an external network. It is important to know which ports are being used and which are better left closed. Table 8.1 lists some of the more common ports and protocols used by Exchange 2000.

Table 8.1 Ports and protocols used by Exchange 2000.

Port	Service/Protocol
20	FTP-Data
21	FTP (File Transfer Protocol)
23	Telnet Services
25	SMTP
53	DNS (Domain Name System) Service used for name resolution
67	Bootstrap Protocol Server/DHCP (Dynamic Host Configuration Protocol) Lease
68	Bootstrap Protocol Client/DHCP Lease
69	TFTP (Trivial File Transfer Protocol)
80	HTTP (Hypertext Transfer Protocol) World Wide Web
88	Kerberos
107	Remote Telnet Service
110	POP3 (Post Office Protocol version 3)
113	Auth Identification Protocol
119	NNTP
135	RPCs (Remote Procedure Calls) and DHCP Manager
143	IMAP4 (Internet Message Access Protocol version 4)
158	PC Mail Server
161	SNMP (Simple Network Management Protocol)
162	SNMP-Trap
194	IRC (Internet Relay Chat) Protocol
389	LDAP (Lightweight Directory Access Protocol)
443	HTTP-Secure
464	Kerberos version 5 kpasswd
500	Internet Key Exchange
531	Conference services-Chat
636	LDAP over TLS (Transport Layer Security) or SSL (Secure Sockets Layer)
749	Kerberos administration
1732	PPTP (Point-to-Point Tunneling Protocol) for VPNs (virtual private networks)

Because mobile users are becoming more prevalent, you need to secure access to internal data from external users on more stringent levels than you might have in the past. You can use the Routing and Remote Access Service (RRAS) within Windows 2000 to offer these users strict control of internal networks. RRAS is automatically installed in Windows 2000 in a *disabled state* and allows any computer to become a VPN server that supports the PPTP or the Layer 2 Tunneling protocol over IPSec (Internet Protocol Security), a Layer 3 Tunneling protocol. A VPN server extends your private network across a public network by encapsulating and encrypting the communication that is being transported.

NOTE: *A* tunnel *is nothing more than communication that has been* encapsulated *with additional header information. A tunnel can be either voluntary or compulsory, depending on whether the client workstation can act as a tunnel client and whether the appropriate tunneling protocol is installed on its computer.*

If you are using the previously mentioned technologies to secure and protect your network, the proper authentication scheme that you use also becomes very important. For example, you have to decide whether Basic Authentication will serve your needs (in which case you'll use the Password Authentication Protocol [PAP]), or whether the Challenge Handshake Authentication Protocol (CHAP) will serve your needs. *CHAP* is an authentication protocol used by some clients for remote access purposes. Authentication and encryption go hand in hand, so you have to choose the proper form of encryption, such as 128-bit Data Encryption Standard (DES) or 128-bit Message Digest 5 authentication (MD5). The preceding information should demonstrate how security measures can help protect your network. They can also be used to prevent disasters.

Other security tools are used to secure messages in Exchange 2000, including the Key Management Service (KM Service) and the Encryption File System (EFS). You also can assign predefined permissions and roles to users or groups of users who become responsible for different tasks. The most important tools are covered in the following sections.

The KM Service

The *KM Service* helps create a PKI in your Exchange 2000 enterprise and integrates with the Windows 2000 Certificate Service. You install the KM Service on one server *per administrative group*. This KM Server can ultimately be responsible for numerous other administrative groups or even your entire company. Every KM server contains the KM Service and a storage database; however, the KM Service actually processes client security requests. KM Service "talks" directly to the Information Store Service and forwards requests for certificates from users directly to the Windows 2000 Certificate Service. The KM Service database contains advanced security configuration for all Exchange Server users and can be found in the *\Exchsrvr\KMSData* directory on the KM Server.

NOTE: *Only one KM Service storage database exists per administrative group.*

The Microsoft Certificate Service is integrated with AD and Exchange 2000 PKI, as well as Internet Explorer and the EFS. Exchange 2000 uses certificates for data encryption and digital signatures. You can establish a root Certificate Authority (CA) within your enterprise, or you can allow Certificate Services to be subordinate to a third-party CA, such as Verisign. KM Service produces X.509 version 3 user certificates used by both Exchange and the Outlook client for digital signatures. You have to install and enable a special policy known as the Enroll Agent (Computer) policy for your CA before installing the KM Service. KM Service administrators can use various encryption algorithms and hash functions when starting this service. Every user receives two sets of certificates—one for *encryption* and one for *digital signing*.

NOTE: *The act of encrypting a message is also known as* sealing *a message. Sealing and signing are two different processes and one does not necessarily invoke the other.*

A user's *private key* is stored in an EPF file in Outlook 97, or in the Registry in Outlook 2000. A user's *public key* is stored in AD. Users can even be moved from one KM Server to another KM Server without decrypting existing messages or devising other complicated schemes. Most security services, including the KM Service, apply some form of messaging security to various layers of the TCP/IP (Transmission Control Protocol/Internet Protocol) protocol stack. The KM Server provides security to the application layer of the messaging infrastructure.

IPSec

IPSec provides security to Layer 3 of the IP networking model, a layer that concerns itself with message routing and transportation. It uses the Diffie-Hellman algorithm for key exchange between users and can automatically create new keys for users. The default authentication method used for IPSec is the Kerberos v5 authentication scheme. You set IPSec policies using the GPO MMC snap-in on a site, domain, or OU basis in AD. IPSec provides security on a much different level than a KM Server and often is used in environments employing VPNs. IPSec can only guarantee that a sending computer and a receiving computer have security mechanisms in place when sending and receiving communications; it cannot guarantee that messages are secure when traversing the medium between the computers.

TIP: *A router or switch that lies in between a sending computer and receiving computer forwards all IP packets to their correct destinations. If you use a firewall between computers, make sure you have IP forwarding enabled so packets reach their intended destination.*

EFS

EFS is a Windows 2000 feature that allows a user to encrypt his data on any volume that supports NTFS. It uses certificates issued by a CA supporting the X.509 v3 standard. A unique feature of EFS is that if no root or subordinate CA is available to issue certificates, EFS generates its own certificates (self-signed) for all users. When users encrypt a file or folder, EFS automatically puts a *recovery policy* into place. This ensures that users can decrypt their files or folders using a recovery agent if they lose their encryption certificates or private keys. The following points summarize the essential features and benefits of using EFS in Windows 2000 (to supplement security in Exchange 2000):

- If an encrypted file leaves the hard drive, it's no longer encrypted.
- If a user sends a file as an attachment, the file is no longer encrypted.
- If a user runs an application that has to retrieve a file from the hard drive, the file is decrypted.
- EFS is used solely to encrypt data on a hard disk. To encrypt data traversing a network, use technologies such as IPSec or SSL to encrypt this type of data.
- It's possible to prevent all users from encrypting any data on their computers by modifying a GPO on a domainwide basis or on a local basis. See the Immediate Solutions section for "Disabling EFS for All Users in a Domain."

Security Measures Help Prevent Disasters

Disasters are hardly "planned for." Rather, they just happen and are, out of necessity, resolved. These sections consider how proper security measures can help you avoid disasters in the first place.

You need to establish some sort of "baseline security" within your organization. This baseline or threshold represents security settings and conditions that should not be exceeded. For example, Windows 2000 now allows you to configure security settings and perform regular analyses of your system to make sure all configurations remain the same over time. Because Microsoft knows that most networks and most OS configurations are changing all the time, it provided the Security Analysis and Configuration snap-in tool, which gives you time to review all security settings dynamically. The tool reviews or analyzes your system settings and makes recommendations to your system as needed. You then can adjust your current security policy on a small or large scale.

NOTE: *See the Immediate Solutions section for "Installing the Security Analysis and Configuration Snap-In" for more details on this valuable tool.*

The Security Analysis and Configuration tool can be used proactively to prevent disasters resulting from something minor such as improper access rights, to something major, such as someone trying to shut down your server. The only problem with this tool is that you can only audit a local system to determine whether it complies with a predefined security template. You cannot apply this on a domain-wide level yet. It is better to use GPOs as discussed in the beginning of this chapter for that purpose.

Can effective security measures help an *organization* proactively prevent a "disaster"? It depends. Many disasters are caused by computer unauthorized destructive agents. Viruses or worms can wreak havoc on large computer systems and usually there hasn't been enough time to come up with an antivirus solution. Educating your workforce on how to recognize and combat viruses using proper antivirus solutions (such as McAfee's antivirus package or Symantec's Norton AntiVirus 2000) can prevent disaster in these cases. Many corporations ideally should employ centralized security measures such that antivirus solutions are maintained on a server and distributed to clients on a regular basis. Administrators would be responsible to maintain updated virus definition files on both the server and the client, and care would also be taken to include defenses against hidden and destructive Trojan code that is easily downloaded via software applications from the Internet. The version of client software that is being deployed will determine the seriousness of the threat brought about by malicious software. For instance, the Outlook 97 client cannot render HTML documents as well as Outlook 98 or Outlook 2000. See the sidebar "Outlook and HTML" for further details on this.

Outlook and HTML

Outlook integrates HTML in many ways, including Custom Folder Home pages and HTML mail messages. This is why HTML plays an important role for developers who create Outlook-based solutions. You must install the Internet Explorer (IE) browser with Outlook even if you are using another default browser because all Microsoft Office applications use IE to render HTML in certain parts of these applications. The Outlook client does not contain any code designed to render HTML; rather, it will use either the "full version" of the IE browser to display HTML or it will use the "core" part of the browser to render HTML. The full version means that the *general* Internet security settings of IE will apply. The "core" version will bypass the typical security settings of IE so HTML pages will be rendered more quickly. In certain cases, however, you may not be able to render HTML code for tables or frames using the "core" version of IE.

You can also send HTML text as the body of an email message, but you will need the full version of IE to render this HTML correctly. You should use the Preview feature of Outlook to view HTML messages because this feature is designed to render less active content that could prove malicious. More active HTML content would be rendered if you were to open the same HTML message in a separate window.

The less "programmable" a client is, the lower the risk of disaster it introduces into your environment. Users should understand that plain text messages or RTF (Rich Text Format) messages are usually safe to open using the Outlook client. However, if users open a HTML message, they increase the risk of introducing disaster because these messages contain scripts (or executables) and ActiveX controls disguised as innocent programs containing harmful virus code.

ActiveX controls have not declined in importance; rather they are still as persistent as ever. These controls pose a high threat to the security of an internal network, especially if you run multiple services on one computer (for example, you run Exchange 2000 on the same machine as your Web server or DNS server). ActiveX controls are usually embedded within a normal Web page, so a determined software programmer can actually write a custom control that can cause disastrous results for a network. Your goal as an administrator is to not allow such controls to exert any type of control over your system. Custom controls include ActiveX controls and VBScript controls, however code written using the Java specification is not included because Java, by design, operates in a secure address space and will not directly access your system hardware as the other controls are apt to do.

TIP: *You should research the topic of a* security zone *within IE. This allows you to assign levels of trust to any code that you download from different* zones. *The zones include Local Intranet, Trusted Sites, Internet, or Restricted Sites. You can configure security for zones within IE by selecting Tools|Internet Options|Security. For additional details, see the Microsoft Web site at* ***http://support.microsoft.com/support/kb/articles/Q174/3/60.asp****.*

To help deal with virus control and overall security implementation, many administrators today employ some form of *content-management software*. Many viruses or worms bypass traditional email virus scanning programs, which only scan *attachments*. These viruses actually contain active content in the message body itself and are capable of damaging an organization extensively. The practice of content management includes filtering for destructive code as well as regulating every type of email arriving into your enterprise. Content management helps you avoid receiving Unsolicited Commercial Email (UCE)—more commonly known as *spam*—and assists your organization in screening offensive content that might prove damaging to users inside your network.

Running Exchange 2000 and Internet Information Server (IIS) can prove disastrous as recent press articles have pointed to many security flaws within Microsoft's Internet server software (see **http://news.cnet.com/news/0-1003-202-5946732.html** for further details concerning this latest security threat). This particular flaw allows hackers to gain control of a company's Web server and affects both IIS 4 and Windows 2000 IIS 5. The software runs an additional security check every time a user requests a URL (Uniform Resource Locator) address. An experienced hacker could use this additional check as a means of breaking into a system and wreaking havoc.

NOTE: *This latest flaw was advertised in May of 2001; Microsoft has since released a patch that addresses this vulnerability. It was found that hackers were not given administrative control to the system from this vulnerability. In any case, you should take every security vulnerability seriously, and download the latest patches or hot fixes that exist for them.*

Administrators have to continually ask what is the worst that could happen in terms of a disaster, and determine how they can best prepare for it. Most organizations are aware of denial-of-service (DoS) attacks, which occur when extreme server overhead is created so that legitimate requests for service are denied because not enough resources are available. A denial of service attack can result from UCE being sent through your Exchange Server—a condition known as spamming—or by a *buffer overrun*, in which software code is executed as an infinite loop in a protected memory address. These types of security threats are more common because it's sometimes easier to disrupt or destroy a network than it is to gain access to it. An Exchange 2000 Server can be quickly brought down because someone has consumed all the bandwidth available to that particular server. Either that person has a higher connection speed than the connection speed of your network, or that person has enlisted the assistance of multiple sites so that your network connection is flooded with useless packets.

TIP: *Be careful when working with ICMP (Internet Control Message Protocol) used to "ping" a remote system to test for network connectivity. This protocol is easily abused and is used most often to consume necessary bandwidth on remote networks. It is hard to trace the source of an ICMP attack in some cases because the sender spoofs or hides his true identity and makes it seem as though he is on your local network.*

Malicious users of software called *bacteria* can consume *system resources* as well as *network resources* to bring permanent destruction to your environment. Administrators should become familiar with the most common types of DoS attacks so they can best protect their Exchange 2000 organizations from ultimate disaster. Table 8.2 lists the most common types of attacks and how you can circumvent their disastrous outcomes.

TIP: *Many good books are available on Internet security that discuss these and other types of attacks perpetrated on modern ultrasensitive networks. One of the best discourses you can use to update your knowledge of network security is* Hacking Exposed: Network Security Secrets & Solutions, 2nd Edition, *by Joel Scambray, Stuart McClure, and George Kurtz (McGraw-Hill, 2001, ISBN 8325403473).*

Table 8.2 DoS attacks and effective countermeasures to protect your organization.

Common Name	Description	Action to Take
Smurf Attack	Hacker sends directed broadcast requests to a target network that responds to each of these requests.	Disable directed broadcasts at all border routers in your network.
SYN Flood Attack	Hackers abuse the mechanism whereby potential connection requests are sent between systems in the form of SYN data packets so all available system resources are consumed in setting up this connection.	Adjust parameters for the size of your *connection queue* or your *connection establishment timeout period*. You also can purchase a reliable *intrusion detection system* to combat a potential SYN Flood Attack.
Spool Leak in Windows 2000	Hackers connect to a share known as SPOOLSS and consume all memory resident in a target server.	Remove SPOOLSS from the Registry of the target system.
Stacheldraht Attack	Hackers disable intrusion detection systems to allow damaging DoS attacks.	Apply the appropriate patches to your OS kernel and do not allow any ICMP traffic into your network from the outside world.

Although some attacks are obvious, others are more arcane and less open to scrutiny. For example, Exchange 2000 had an account vulnerability that was only recently exposed. During the installation of Exchange 2000, a user account called EUSR_EXSTOREEVENT is created by default and assigned a password. If you installed Exchange 2000 on a member server, this special account would inherit whatever permissions a normal local user had on that server. However, if you installed Exchange 2000 on a DC, this special account suddenly possessed Domain User rights. If hackers broke into this server, they would be able to introduce disaster on a domainwide level. A successful exploit of this system would grant access to whatever files the special account had permissions to, including write permissions or execute permissions. This scenario would invariably lead to total disaster because a malevolent user could install a malicious executable or obtain higher privileges to cause further destruction.

NOTE: *For further information on this vulnerability, please visit* **www.securityfocus.com** *and click on the Vulnerabilities link.*

Although it's hard to determine the best course of action to take when planning for security in your enterprise, a recommended course of action is to place all Exchange Servers within a demilitarized zone (DMZ), which acts as a "buffer" between your internal network and a very public Internet (see Figure 8.3).

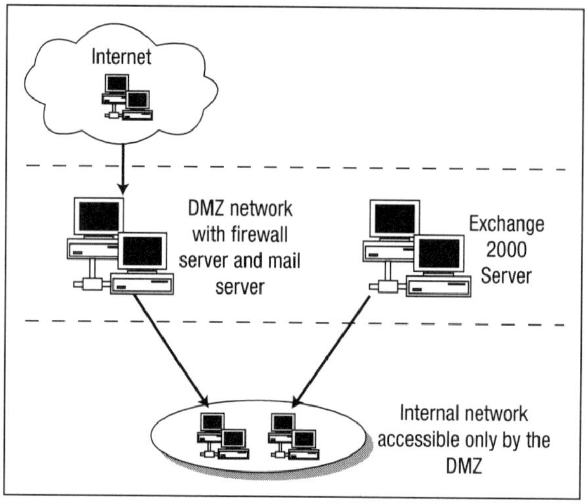

Figure 8.3 A DMZ network protecting an internal LAN from Internet connections.

You then gradually add layers of defense around both sides of this zone. Many administrators place their Exchange Servers and DNS servers inside a DMZ, although this does not guarantee that you are fully protected from attack. A DMZ is neither part of your internal network nor directly part of the Internet; it lies between an Internet access router and a *bastion host* (the only computer on a network that is directly addressable by a public network). You can sometimes create a DMZ by creating Access Control Lists (ACLs) on an access router within your network. Doing so minimizes the exposure of hosts on your external LAN because only recognized services on these hosts are accessible by hosts on the Internet. Many commercial firewalls—such as Checkpoint's Firewall-1 product—create a third network interface off a bastion host and call this the DMZ. In any case, your network is neither inside nor outside, but in between.

Remember these tips concerning bastion hosts and DMZs:

- Ideally, a bastion host should sit inside a DMZ and act as a *relay* or *gateway* for your Exchange Server.
- You can use an SMTP proxy that sits inside a DMZ and relays mail from the Internet directly to the Exchange Server. You should consider employing a machine that does nothing but route SMTP traffic without hosting mailbox stores or public folder data.
- Consider using two network interface cards in every Exchange Server machine that sits inside your DMZ. This ensures that one network card will communicate with your private internal network and service all user requests, while the other network card communicates with the public external network and passes mail to and from the Internet.

***NOTE:** Make sure you disable routing between the network cards, otherwise data packets will continue to traverse your network, despite the fact that you have enabled packet filtering on your routers. Also, be sure to disable any unnecessary services that may be running and bound to your external network card.*

For instance, the following services and ports may need to be disabled:

- *Port 137*—NetBIOS Name Service used for pass-through validation and network browsing
- *Port 139*—TCP port used for NetBIOS Session services such as file sharing, printing, logon, Windows NT 4 trusts and directory replication, and DNS administration
- *Port 389*—TCP port used for LDAP communications
- *Port 119*—TCP port used for the NNTP service
- *Port 135*—TCP port used for client/server communication and Remote Procedure Calls
- *Port 2980*—TCP/UDP port used for Instant Messaging services

Disaster recovery in Exchange 2000 differs in several ways from disaster recovery in Exchange 5.5. Most notable is the fact that you no longer have to back up a "directory" as you did in Exchange 5.5. The directory that stores Exchange 2000 information is now part of the Windows 2000 OS, so you must restore AD before you can restore Exchange 2000. Another difference is that Exchange 2000 depends on the IIS 5 component of Windows 2000 for access to all Internet protocols such as SMTP or NNTP. Because IIS keeps a separate configuration database known as the *metabase*, you must back this up on a regular basis as well.

You also will be concerned with disaster planning and recovery when you upgrade or migrate Exchange 5.5 Servers to Exchange 2000 Servers. When you try to upgrade a legacy server to Exchange 2000 and it fails, you must consider one of the following three alternatives:

- Recover the server that is not the *first* Exchange 2000 Server in your organization.
- Recover the *first server* you tried to upgrade in an Exchange 5.5 site and then upgrade it to Exchange 2000.
- Recover the *first server* you tried to upgrade in an Exchange 5.5 site, but *do not upgrade* to Exchange 2000 (that is, *restore* it to Exchange 5.5).

Not every company shares a similar disaster recovery plan, but the key is to execute and implement whatever plan is in place. Knowing where such a plan is kept or if a plan has been fully tested can mean the difference between "disaster" and "recovery." A crucial component of any disaster recovery plan is effective backups. You must have an effective backup schedule in place and these backups must be both operational and validated at all times. The importance of backups is discussed in the sections that follow.

The Ultimate Disaster Recovery Plan?

There is no such thing as an ultimate disaster recovery plan. You can come close to such a plan, however, by considering certain facts. To fully recover from a disaster, you must restore both Windows 2000 Server and Exchange 2000 Server. The complication with this is that you now have to deal with multiple storage groups (SGs) per server and multiple databases per SG. The other complicating fact is that no two Exchange Servers are alike. They were not alike in Exchange 5.5, and they are definitely not alike in Exchange 2000. The restoration of a KM server cannot be compared to the restoration of a FE server that resides behind a packet-filtering router acting as a firewall. And, restoring an Exchange 2000 Cluster Server is not the same as restoring an Exchange 2000 Member Server. The *role* of a server now plays an important part in determining the ease of restoring that server.

TIP: *Microsoft has made disaster recovery* somewhat *easier in Exchange 2000 by including a new Setup option called* ***/DisasterRecovery****. This means you can run Setup in* Disaster Recovery mode *to completely rebuild your server if it goes down for any reason.*

To restore *most* Exchange 2000 installations, make sure you have the following items in your possession:

- The original Windows 2000 Installation CD and the Exchange 2000 Installation CD including the Windows 2000 Server Service Pack CD or disk.
- Any tape backups made of all data on the original Exchange 2000 computer, including backups of all system configurations and the Web Storage System (WSS).
- Any documentation that records your original server configurations, including network diagrams that show the physical and logical structures of your organization.

The recovery steps will differ depending on whether your Exchange Server is functioning as a *member server* or a *DC*. If it's functioning as a DC, you should obtain a recent *system state backup* of your Windows 2000 configuration. This information isn't normally found in a regular *file system backup*. A system state backup also includes critical data such as the Registry. To restore AD on a DC in your domain, you must back up AD as part of your system state backup.

WARNING! Make sure you do not delete the* server object *within AD if your Exchange 2000 Server ever becomes damaged. Some people have accidentally deleted this object using the System Manager tool, for example. The server object may be deleted only* after *the original server has been restored.

The Underlying Technology

What makes disaster recovery and planning possible in Exchange 2000? You should understand the underlying database technology to appreciate the planning process. Microsoft based the Exchange 2000 architecture on a database technology called the Extensible Storage Engine (ESE). The ESE is actually a part of the WSS, which integrates the Information Store component of Exchange 2000 with protocols such as Extensible Markup Language (XML) and Distributed Authoring and Versioning (DAV—an extension of the HTTP 1.1 protocol). Even Outlook Web Access (OWA) is now based on this new database technology. The WSS allows users to access mailbox or public folder resources using standard URL names and standard Web browsers. You can also access data using the Windows Explorer interface and treat Exchange 2000 as you would any other file server on your network.

A single ESE database can store large amounts of information (up to 16TB [terabytes] of information, with 1TB equal to 1,000GB [gigabytes] of information). Every Exchange 2000 Server is composed of *databases* and *SGs*. The following rules are always maintained:

- You can create multiple databases within a single SG (up to five is permitted; more than five requires a separate SG).
- You can restore databases within a SG on an individual basis or as one group.
- All databases within a single SG share only one set of transaction log files.
- Each SG is one part of the ESE architecture.
- Each single database consists of an EDB file for messaging data, and a STM file for native Internet content and streaming media files. EDB files store messages as RTF files.
- The EDB files and STM files always work in tandem and are both constructed as 4KB pages.
- Databases also consist of SRS files and KMS files. The former allows compatibility with Exchange 5.5 Servers by mimicking an Exchange 5.5 directory, while the latter helps provide security and encryption for data within the Exchange 2000 server.
- All databases have a unique identifier known as a Globally Unique Identifier (GUID). One GUID is assigned to an individual database and another GUID is assigned to AD. If these GUIDs do not match for any reason, that specific database will not mount.

- Mailboxes within a database have a GUID separate from the GUID assigned to its database. A matching GUID is assigned to the user account in AD that owns this mailbox. This concept is important for recovery planning because a user can always be *reconnected* to a mailbox with a matching GUID.
- Any changes to a database are stored in transaction log files, which are used to restore any *committed transactions* that you might lose if you suffer some type of power failure or other type of data loss. These log files should always total 5MB; otherwise, they could be corrupt.
- Log files and database files (the EDB and STM files) should always be kept on separate physical hard disk drives as a recommended best practice to promote optimal functioning of your server.
- Each SG can reserve special log files called Res1.log and Res2.log to reserve extra disk space in the event that space is not available to that SG. You should treat these files as normal transaction log files.

Two additional important concepts need to be defined before revealing a formal backup-and-restore process for Exchange 2000. A *checkpoint file* is used to indicate that transactions have been successfully saved to your server's hard disk subsystem. You will notice an edb.chk file is kept for each SG on your server. These files point to all transactions that have been successfully committed to your database files. *Circular logging* is used to overwrite transaction log files *after* they have been committed to a database. Circular logging is *disabled by default*. Some important points regarding circular logging include the following:

- Circular logging helps to reduce your overall storage requirements because some transactions are overwritten after being committed to a database.
- Use circular logging with data that is not important; critical data should not be overwritten arbitrarily.
- If circular logging is enabled when you are restoring data, you can only capture data up to the moment of your last full backup. This moment differs from the exact time that your server went offline, so you are at risk of losing transactions that were not committed into your database.

A Note on Exchange 2000 Clusters

You cannot discuss disaster recovery without bringing up the cluster. A *cluster* is a group of multiple (two or more) computers that you manage as a virtual single system. In other words, they are connected to a shared storage system, they are managed as a single system, and they provide high availability for most enterprises, as well as high scalability options in terms of adding hardware in the future. The relevance to disaster planning is highlighted by the fact that clusters tolerate most component failures rather easily and allow new hardware to be added without disrupting the normal workflows of your enterprise. In other words, the process is completely transparent to your end users.

Exchange 2000 now supports *active/active clustering*, so that more than one instance of a component can run in the cluster. For example, you can have multiple instances of the WSS in one cluster. Each node can support 4 SGs with up to 12 SGs being held in reserve for restore purposes. A cluster is made up of multiple *nodes*, and each node has the same type of processor and the same amount of RAM (Random Access Memory). A cluster contains an Exchange *Virtual Server* that runs on one node in the cluster. You can run more than one Virtual Server on any given node simultaneously, which provides high availability for Exchange 2000. The Cluster Service continually monitors these Virtual Servers; when one node fails, the Cluster Service can move all affected Virtual Servers to a fully functioning node in the cluster. The Cluster Service can provide fault tolerance as well through the use of failover and failback procedures, so that resource groups can be easily moved between nodes in the cluster if one node fails for any reason. Exchange 2000 clusters use management tools such as the Resource Manager and the Failover Manager to move resource groups from nodes that have failed to nodes that are fully functioning. When the original node recovers, you can configure the Failover Manager to "fail back" a resource group to the node that is recovered.

Some components, such as the MTA (Message Transfer Agent) component, cannot exist in more than one instance in a cluster. The MTA can only be found in one Exchange 2000 Virtual Server. Another example of a single-instance cluster component is the Chat Service. All other Exchange 2000 components, including the System Attendant, the POP3 protocol, and the IMAP4 protocol, are capable of running multiple Virtual Servers per node for any given cluster arrangement.

NOTE: *As of this writing, Windows 2000 offers 2-way clustering and 8-way Symmetric Multiprocessing (SMP) (or 2-node active/active clustering) with its Advanced Server edition. If you use the Datacenter Edition, you will reap the benefits of 4-way active/active clustering with 16-way SMP (or 32-way SMP using OEM enhancements).*

Backup-and-Restore Strategies

It is important to design a backup-and-restore strategy for your specific organization. This plan needs to be written down formally, and placed in a location where it can be easily accessed when needed. Also, the plan should be subject to regular revision and review because the hardware and software needs of any organization are constantly subject to change. Part of this design process includes determining your optimal server configuration so that your Exchange design uses the concept of fault tolerance to its best advantage. A good goal is to use different storage areas for different uses, for example a RAID-5 or a RAID-1 configuration. The proper use of RAID (Redundant Array of Independent Disks) technology helps ensure both high performance and high availability of your Exchange Server (sometimes at high cost as well).

NOTE: *RAID is a system that protects data and provides immediate access to this data in situations involving disk failure. This definition also includes the ability to reconstruct disk contents and data to alternate disk subsystems or physical drives.*

RAID and Dynamic Disks in Windows 2000 Server

Remember that Windows 2000 Server only provides a software implementation of this fault-tolerance technology. The storage types used by Windows 2000 Server or Advanced Server are totally distinct from a hardware-level disk array setup. If you actually try to implement a hardware-level RAID within Windows 2000 Server, you will see *unallocated space* when using the Disk Management MMC utility. Understanding these fault-tolerant configurations means understanding the types of disks used in Windows 2000.

Windows 2000 supports only two types of storage mechanisms: basic storage and dynamic storage. This means that every single physical disk inside your Exchange 2000 server must be either a basic disk or a dynamic disk (assuming you are using Windows 2000 Server or Advanced Server as the underlying OS). It is impossible to use both of these storage types on one physical disk unless you implement multiple disks (as in a RAID configuration). A basic disk simply involves dividing a physical disk into partitions, either primary or extended, and it can even support software RAID configurations created in Windows NT 4. A dynamic disk is only supported by Windows 2000 and is divided into *volumes*, not partitions. This is an important difference to comprehend. A dynamic disk contains one of the following configurations:

- *A Simple Volume*—This contains space from one single disk, but the drawback is no fault tolerance. You can extend a simple volume by combining up to 32 areas of free space on a *single disk*. Because no fault tolerance is provided here, this is not recommended for mailbox stores or public folder stores in Exchange 2000.
- *A Spanned Volume*—This contains space from *multiple disks* (up to 32 different disks at one time). The drawback here is that Windows 2000 has to completely fill one disk before writing data to another physical disk. No fault tolerance is provided here, and if one disk in the volume fails, all data in the volume is lost.
- *A Mirrored Volume*—This is nothing more than two copies of one *simple volume*, with each being contained on a *separate physical disk*. These RAID-1 configurations provide fault tolerance in the event of a catastrophe and are recommended for Exchange 2000 data.

- *A Striped Volume*—This contains free space from more than one physical disk and combines everything into one *logical volume*. You can use up to 32 physical disks in one striped volume. Data is written to all physical disks simultaneously, but if any disk in the volume fails, the entire volume is lost. Fault tolerance is not present in this system.
- *A RAID-5 Volume*—This is a fault-tolerant version of a striped volume. A parity-information *stripe* is written to each partition or segment in the volume set. This stripe is used to recover or reconstruct data if any physical disk in the volume fails. Three physical hard disks are required for this scenario.

WARNING! As of this writing, dynamic volumes were not supported on any type of portable computer, such as laptops. Also, you cannot create any fault-tolerant configuration—RAID-1 or RAID-5—on computers that run Windows 2000 Professional Edition.

NOTE: *The advantage to using dynamic disks is that you can resize them without having to restart Windows 2000 Server or Advanced Server.*

See Table 8.3 for a summary of information concerning these dynamic volumes.

Table 8.3 Dynamic volume do's and don'ts.

Dynamic Volume Name	Hardware Needed	Issues to Watch For
Simple Volume	One physical dynamic disk	Extending a simple volume actually *increases* the total points of failure for your disk subsystem; no fault tolerance.
Spanned Volume	At least two physical dynamic disks; can include up to 32 physical dynamic disks	Cannot be part of a mirror volume or striped volume. No fault tolerance here, and areas included in the spanned volume do not have to be of equal size. Volumes formatted with FAT16 or FAT32 cannot be extended. It is not possible to extend a spanned volume containing the system or the boot partitions.
Striped Volume	At least two physical dynamic disks; can include up to 32 physical dynamic disks	Offers the best performance because data is written across all physical dynamic disks in 64KB increments. Data is added to all disks at the same speed. A Striped volume without parity (RAID-0) offers no fault tolerance, whereas a striped volume with parity (RAID-5) offers fault tolerance. You cannot extend a striped volume, and you cannot mirror a striped volume.

Different RAID technologies have different levels of functionality. For instance, RAID-1 offers high availability at a relatively high cost. Both RAID-1 and RAID-5 offer Extended Data Availability and Protection services to physical disk subsystems. However, RAID-1 requires almost 100 percent redundancy (redundant data in the form of an exact copy) while requiring 50 percent of total disk capacity. The advantage to RAID-1 is that read performance is enhanced at the expense of write performance. RAID-5, although known as parity RAID or stripe with parity, is not the only configuration offering parity services. In fact, RAID-3 through RAID-6 offer redundancy in the form of parity. All cases of parity RAID suffer some type of system degradation as data is being written to the disks in the array; however, users typically don't concern themselves with this minor interruption. The following points summarize important RAID concerns:

- RAID-0+1 is now the "preferred configuration" for most Exchange Server implementations involving mailbox stores or public folder stores. It offers faster read and write performance compared to other RAID implementations.
- RAID-2 can require the use of nonstandard disk drives and is not used on a widespread basis.
- A RAID-3 configuration allows disk drives to operate in parallel for some applications that require high transfer rates or bandwidth.
- RAID-4, RAID-5, and RAID-6 parity configurations are best suited for applications supporting high transaction rates or input/output requests that involve small amounts of data for each input/output task. Although RAID-3 through RAID-5 provide extended data protection when one disk system fails, RAID-6 provides this protection even when two disks fail simultaneously (or a second disk fails while you are reconstructing a primary disk).

TIP: *For more information regarding various RAID configurations and other references to this valuable technology, please consult the Web site* ***www.raid-advisory.com****.*

Planning the locations for your mailbox stores and public folder stores is important when designing security solutions for your Exchange 2000 Server. You should use SGs and dynamic volumes in conjunction with each other so that fault tolerance is optimized. For example, mailbox stores should be placed in one SG defined by a RAID-5 volume, whereas public folders can be placed in a separate SG using similar redundant technology. Certain files, such as transaction log files, can be placed in one RAID volume that might span multiple SGs. Because a RAID configuration uses multiple physical hard drives, it's possible to include multiple SGs in your configuration.

One final thought concerning RAID technology is that administrators often select RAID-5 arrays based solely on cost. However, RAID-5 technology often reduces disk performance, so it's better to consider a mirrored stripe technology such as RAID-0+1 for performance reasons. In fact, some administrators in the field claim those RAID-5 arrays are not recommended on large drive arrays (for example, drives exceeding 18GB). For transaction logs, consider RAID-1 technology due to higher performance factors and greater reliability as compared to RAID-5. To maximize the use of RAID-1 even further, consider using disk controller caches instead of disk drive caches. Any cache used in Exchange 2000 should ideally be *write-back cache*, not *read-ahead cache*. The difference is that most disk operations in Exchange 2000 are not sequential, so most disk controllers are incapable of using the next available disk block.

NOTE: *A read-ahead cache is used for sequential page reads and occurs when data in a current read request is on a page on the hard disk adjacent to the data page of a previous read request. It increases the speed of sequential reads for data stored on the Exchange Server. It also increases throughput on the server by sending a few large packets instead of many small packets through the server. A write-back cache, on the other hand, implies that all write operations to data in the L1 cache of the server are not copied to main memory (system RAM) until it is absolutely needed by the system. Although it reduces the number of write operations to main memory, it introduces the risk that data will be lost if the server becomes unavailable for some reason.*

Backup Planning

Backing up Exchange 2000 is somewhat different than backing up other types of information you might encounter because so many different elements are involved. For instance, you are backing up more than just files, you are also working with *data stores* and *data structures*. Also, whatever backup strategy you decide on ultimately affects your restore strategy. Calculating how long it takes to back up your disk means calculating how long it takes to restore this information. You need enough hard drive space to restore all your databases and all your transaction log files. Consider the following points when planning your backups of Exchange 2000:

- You have to choose an appropriate backup application. You can use the Windows Backup utility provided with Windows 2000 Server, or you can use a third-party application such as UltraBac (visit **www.ultrabac.com** for further details on this product).
- You can perform either an online backup or an offline backup. Online backups are preferable because databases can continue to run while data is being backed up. Partial backups also can be performed so that only transaction logs are backed up and not the mailbox stores or public folder stores.
- The four types of online backups are: Full—or normal—backups, incremental backups, differential backups, and copy backups (see Table 8.4 for a comparison of these backup types).

Table 8.4 A comparison of backup types in Exchange 2000.

Backup Type	What Is Being Backed Up
Full	All databases and all transaction log files*
Incremental	Only the transaction log files
Differential	Only the transaction log files
Copy	All databases and all transaction log files

**NOTE: The transaction logs are purged only when a Full backup or Incremental backup is being performed. They are* not *purged for Differential backups or Copy backups.*

A Full backup generates a *patch file* for every database in your backup; however, Differential or Incremental backups do not. Patch files allow you to back up an Exchange database without interrupting service for your users. Transactions written to a database file (such as an EDB file or STM file) that has already been backed up are recorded in a patch file (PAT file). After the patch file is created, a new Edb.log file is generated and the Windows 2000 Backup program (assuming this is being used) starts to copy about 64KB of data. Any new transactions are saved as normal and all patch files are deleted when the backup finishes.

Backing up individual databases in a SG is easy for two reasons. First, the backup process itself runs on SGs; second, SGs represent an instance of the ESE and the Backup Application Programming Interface (BAPI). All backups run sequentially against all databases in a SG. This also means that you can back up different SGs in *parallel* because every SG runs independently of every other SG (remember that each SG is *one separate instance* of the ESE database architecture).

TIP: *Both databases and SGs in Exchange 2000 can be backed up in parallel, without affecting the operation of other databases or SGs.*

When you back up a database, you are actually backing up two distinct files, an EDB file for headers and message text, and a STM file for native Internet content. These files are always backed up together. All transaction log files or patch files have *checksums*, which will be validated during your backup. After a Full backup, all transaction log files are deleted along with any transactions committed to your databases that have been backed up as well. In any case, a database has to be online for it to be backed up. If you dismount a database, it will not be backed up.

WARNING! When circular logging is* enabled, *any information in a STM file will* not *be recorded in the transaction log files. However, information in an EDB file will be recorded in the log files. Remember this fact if you suddenly* disable *circular logging and plan to restore these log files!

The backup process is much faster in Exchange 2000 compared to previous versions of Exchange Server. Microsoft has posted rates of up to 70GB per hour on backup (and up to 40GB per hour on restore). Backing up to a tape device is preferable to backing up to a disk drive because disk drives are not considered efficient *streaming devices* like tape devices. Using compression on a digital linear tape (DLT) device can help increase backup speeds; in fact, multiple tape devices can be used in parallel for this function. A normal backup process should not coincide with normal system maintenance routines. For example, if you begin to back up a certain SG while you are simultaneously trying to perform maintenance on a database in that SG (such as defragmentation), the system maintenance procedure will never happen.

Knowing exactly what to back up is also very important. The following represents a list of important data that needs to be included in every backup:

- Configuration data for Exchange 2000 including AD information and the Windows Registry. (*User data* is not included in this category.)
- System drives such as the local root drive C: and the Exchange root drive M: that contain all Windows 2000 or Exchange 2000 files.
- User data including mailbox stores, public folder stores, and transaction logs. Data in this category does not include configuration data from the first bulleted item in this list.
- Any other *nonchanging data* including service packs, hot fixes, application software, or scripts.
- All other *dynamic* or *changing data* including WSS databases, KM Service databases, or system state information such as the IIS metabase.

System state data is important because it's found on both Windows 2000 Professional and Windows 2000 Server editions. Examples of system state data include boot files, the Registry, AD (if on a DC), and the Sysvol shared folder (also if on a DC). Understand that AD is not a direct component of Exchange 2000, but it is still relied upon, as is the IIS 5 component. If you perform a backup of system state data, you are automatically backing up AD. You should back up AD and all Exchange 2000 databases at the same time to help retain configuration information on all DCs and Global Catalog (GC) Servers in your Windows 2000 forest.

Before using the actual backup utility, NTBackup.exe, make sure you belong to the built-in local groups of Backup Operators and Server Operators. You can use the Backup Wizard to back up your data or you can back up data manually. It doesn't matter whether your Exchange Server is online or offline. The only difference between an online backup and an offline backup is that the latter can only be a Full backup type because you are shutting down your databases. All databases have to be dismounted to complete an offline backup.

NOTE: *Online backups require that the System Attendant be running on your server along with the Information Store services. Offline backups require that all Exchange 2000 services be stopped before the backup is started.*

The Backup utility allows you to verify data after a backup procedure is completed, but this isn't recommended. Windows 2000 includes Cyclical Redundancy Checksums (CRCs) as part of the backup and needs to verify all checksums as part of the restore process.

NOTE: *Microsoft always recommends that you download the latest service pack or hotfix before running the Windows 2000 Backup program for Exchange 2000. A description of the latest Service Packs (SPs) and hotfixes are found in Table 8.5.*

Table 8.5 Hotfixes and SPs as of May 2001.

Name of Product	Release Date	Problem Addressed
Exchange 2000 post-RTM Hotfix roll-up	April 3, 2001	All the latest updates for Exchange 2000 (see **http://support.microsoft.com/support/kb/articles/Q291/2/22.asp** for details). Microsoft will probably update this roll-up with even more fixes. If you downloaded this prior to April 3, 2001, Microsoft recommends that you download this again.
Windows 2000 SP2	May 14, 2001	Contains fixes for Exchange 2000 as well as plenty of fixes to the core OS, IIS 5, and AD services. For optimum stability, Microsoft recommends upgrading all Exchange 2000 Servers, Exchange 2000 Conferencing Servers, and all DCs to SP2.
Windows 2000 SP1	August 15, 2000	The minimum fix needed on any computer running Windows 2000 Server and Exchange 2000. Microsoft strongly recommends you install SP1 on all DCs, GC Servers, AD Connector Servers, and Exchange 2000 Conferencing Servers. You should also apply the Windows 2000 post-SP1 roll-up (described at **http://support.microsoft.com/support/kb/articles/Q271/9/76.asp**) to all your AD servers.
Windows 2000 post-SP1 roll-up	September 7, 2000	Used in conjunction with the Windows 2000 SP1 download on all Exchange 2000 Servers, GC servers, DCs, AD Connector servers, and Exchange 2000 Conferencing Servers. This roll-up hotfix addresses such issues as LDAP performance degradation and problems with issuance of non-delivery reports (NDRs). This roll-up, like most other roll-ups, is constantly being updated with new hotfixes. Microsoft strongly recommends reapplying this hotfix if it was applied prior to September 7, 2000.

Restore Planning

Before restoring a database or SG, it must be dismounted so that users cannot access it. You can use either the Restore Wizard or the Restore tab inside the Backup utility. The restore procedure depends on the backup types selected. For instance, if a Full backup was performed, one tape is used for the restore process. If a Full backup is used in combination with an Incremental backup, multiple tapes are used for the restore process resulting in longer restore times. The best compromise is to use a Full backup scheme in combination with a Differential backup because only two tapes are required—the tape containing the Full backup and the tape containing the last Differential backup before you experienced disaster.

The server role is also important for recovery purposes. If you plan to restore files to a member server running Exchange 2000 in a domain, you must verify (using System Manager) that a server object exists for your Exchange 2000 Server in AD. AD always has to be restored before Exchange 2000 if the previous condition does not exist. Regardless of whether you are using member servers or DCs, you must decide on the *type* of data being restored. For instance, you can restore the following categories of information:

- An online or offline backup
- Transaction log files
- A single mailbox or database store
- An entire Exchange 2000 Server

Keep in mind that system state data, such as that found in AD or the Sysvol shared folder, is not restored on DCs. Rather, it is replicated to your DC after it has been restarted. This helps prevent important DC information from being overwritten. You do not have to restore data to production servers. In fact, you can restore WSS data to a server other than the server used to back it up. You can also restore a single mailbox for a user if that user's mailbox retention time has expired (for example, after 30 days). To do this, make sure the following is true:

- The server you are restoring to exists in a separate forest than the one containing your production server.
- The database or SG you want to restore will have the same display name as that found on your original production server.
- Your organization name and administrative group names are equivalent.

The restore process has actually changed more than the backup process has, compared to previous versions of Exchange 2000. The current version of Exchange Server requires that the WSS is running and that all databases that need to be restored are physically dismounted. You can restore more than one database from a single SG in one restore operation. In this case, you must provide a path for temporary disk space. A good estimate for this temporary space is to combine all transaction log files and patch files that are being restored and add approximately 10MB. The backup process works with the restore process to make all databases consistent by using an instance of the ESE to perform a recovery. Database files are almost never consistent because of changes being made to memory. Procedures such as defragmenting databases or performing a soft recovery help make databases more consistent.

NOTE: *Defragmenting a database eliminates unused storage and can be classified as either online defragmenting or offline defragmenting. The former type will not decrease the size of your database and is performed automatically by default. The latter creates a new database and needs plenty of available disk space equal to the size of the database created. In a soft recovery, the ESE replays all transactions from a checkpoint file before starting the database.*

The main points to remember for a restore job in Exchange 2000 are as follows:

- Exchange 2000 uses a Restore Application Programming Interface (RAPI) to write EDB files, transaction log files, and patch files to the same locations they were found in when they were backed up.
- The restore process communicates with the Information Store component, not the System Attendant. For this reason, you have to ensure that the Information Store Service is running before attempting a restore.
- The restore process creates a file called restore.env that contains information specifying what happens during a hard recovery; that is, the locations of the original files and the locations of the restored files. After files have been restored, the ESE applies all patch files and replays all transaction logs.
- All EDB and STM files are restored to their original locations, but all patch files and log files are placed into an alternate and temporary directory that you specify when configuring the restore job.

Using ESEUTIL and ISINTEG for Database Consistency

At certain times, you will find that your database files are not consistent. In times of extreme disaster, you might experience high database or log file corruption (for example, your hard drive containing all mailbox stores is nonfunctioning). Exchange 2000 provides two valuable tools to help bring your databases back to a consistent state: **ESEUTIL** and **ISINTEG**.

ESEUTIL

If your database files are inconsistent, it's a good idea to treat all database folders as though they were one complete file. You can use **ESEUTIL** (a database compaction tool found in \%systemroot%\Exchsrvr\bin) to extract header information from a database file or a transaction log file for the purposes of viewing diagnostic information and to assist you in repairing your databases. The information in the header section of the file might provide clues as to why the database is corrupt or why it cannot be mounted. You view output lines such as **DBSignature** or **State** to see if your databases have been shut down properly. A good rule to remember is that if you restore a database from an *online* backup, it will be *inconsistent.* If you restore a database from an *offline* backup, it will be *consistent.* **ESEUTIL** can be used with a variety of switches or options (see Table 8.6).

ISINTEG

ISINTEG *(Information Store Integrity Checker)* is a battery of tests that also check your database for inconsistencies. The key to using this tool is to dismount the database that you want to run **ISINTEG** against. You do not need to run every test available with **ISINTEG**, so you should decide which tests suit your immediate needs. **ISINTEG** only works if your SGs contain five or fewer databases because it has to create a temporary database to run successfully. If you have more than five databases in a single SG, you have to dismount all databases in your SG so **ISINTEG** can create the temporary *reference database.*

Table 8.6 ESEUTIL and some of its options.

Switch Used	Description
ESEUTIL /ml	Used to extract transaction log file header information to determine why transaction logs cannot be replayed into your database.
ESEUTIL /p	Used to examine your database tables and restore your original database.
ESEUTIL /g	Used to check database integrity, this read-only tool won't make any changes to your database.
ESEUTIL /R/I	Used to initiate and maintain a *soft recovery* (the R option) and ignore any missing databases (for instance, if a database was located on a hard drive that completely fails).

Immediate Solutions

Protecting Your Mission-Critical Mailbox Stores

Providing protection for mission-critical mailboxes in your organization means separating those mailboxes into their own database within a SG. Because Exchange 2000 allows you to back up databases in parallel, you can restore only the database containing those mailboxes. Restoring a database is easier than restoring a single mailbox.

Another method of protecting mission-critical mailboxes is to use the **EXMERGE** (Exchange Mailbox Merge) tool, available on the Exchange 2000 CD. The **EXMERGE.EXE** program allows you to extract data from mailboxes on your Exchange Server computer and merge this data into the same mailboxes on another computer running Exchange 2000. You can back up mailboxes for individual users by copying data from a source server into a personal folder or PST file, and then merging the data in the .PST file into mailboxes on a destination Exchange Server. **EXMERGE.EXE** can be run in One Step mode or Two Step mode:

- *One Step mode*—The program copies data from a source mailbox to a PST file, and then merges the data in the PST file into the same mailbox on a destination server. The mailbox on your destination server will have the same mailbox name as the mailbox on your source server.
- *Two Step mode*—You have the option of either copying data to a PST file *or* merging data from PST files into a server.

EXMERGE.EXE can also be used to rename default folders in a destination public folder store.

Deleting a Mailbox in Exchange 2000

This process is covered here because you might have to delete a corrupt mailbox or delete mailboxes for people who have left your organization. In many cases, mailboxes and user accounts are merely disabled for some time after someone leaves an organization, but leaving empty mailboxes and user accounts for too long a time period contributes to excessive system maintenance overhead and administrative bookkeeping. Therefore, to delete a mailbox in Exchange 2000, follow these steps:

1. Click Start|Programs|Administrative Tools|Active Directory Users And Computers.
2. Right-click the user whose mailbox you want to delete and select Exchange Tasks. Click Next when you see the Welcome page of the Exchange Task Wizard (see Figure 8.4).
3. Select the Delete Mailbox option and click Next (see Figure 8.5).
4. Click Next one more time, and then click Finish to flag the mailbox for deletion. The mailbox is deleted at the end of your preconfigured mailbox retention period unless you personally recover it (see the upcoming Immediate Solution "Configuring a Deleted Mailbox Retention Period").

TIP: *You might still have to go back to System Manager to fully delete your mailbox if it still appears there. Right-click the desired mailbox and select Run Cleanup Agent so that your selected mailbox becomes a* deleted mailbox.

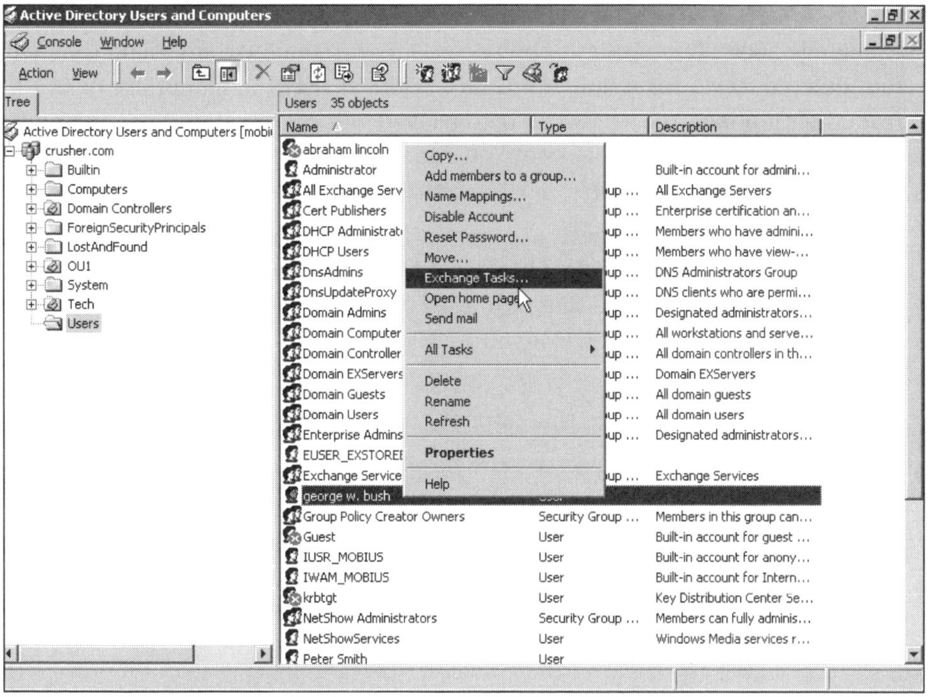

Figure 8.4 The Exchange Tasks selection for a user object.

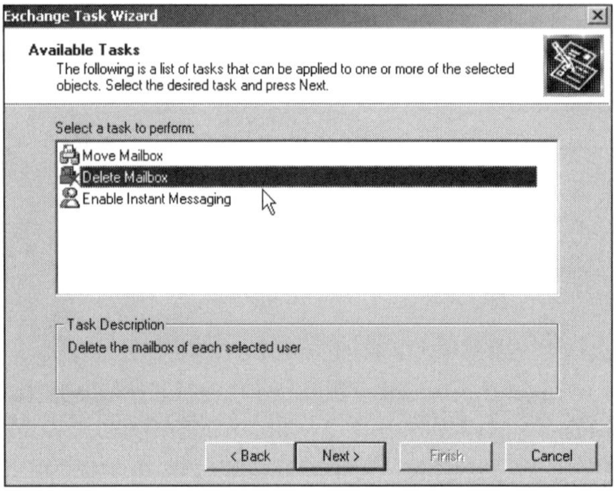

Figure 8.5 Choosing to delete a mailbox using the Exchange Task Wizard.

Configuring a Deleted Items Retention Period

Exchange 2000 gives you the ability to configure mailbox stores so they will retain deleted items for a specific time period. If users accidentally delete items from their inboxes, the items can be retrieved without great difficulty and without having to perform a Full backup. You can tell Exchange 2000 how many days to retain mail that users delete; you configure this at the mailbox store object level. To do this, follow these steps:

1. Open System Manager by choosing Start|Programs|Microsoft Exchange and find the mailbox store that you want to configure a deleted-item retention period for.
2. Right-click the mailbox store you are interested in and select Properties from the context menu that appears.
3. Find the Limits tab and type the number of days you want Exchange 2000 to retain deleted items in the Keep Deleted Items For (Days) setting. The default setting is 0 days (see Figure 8.6).

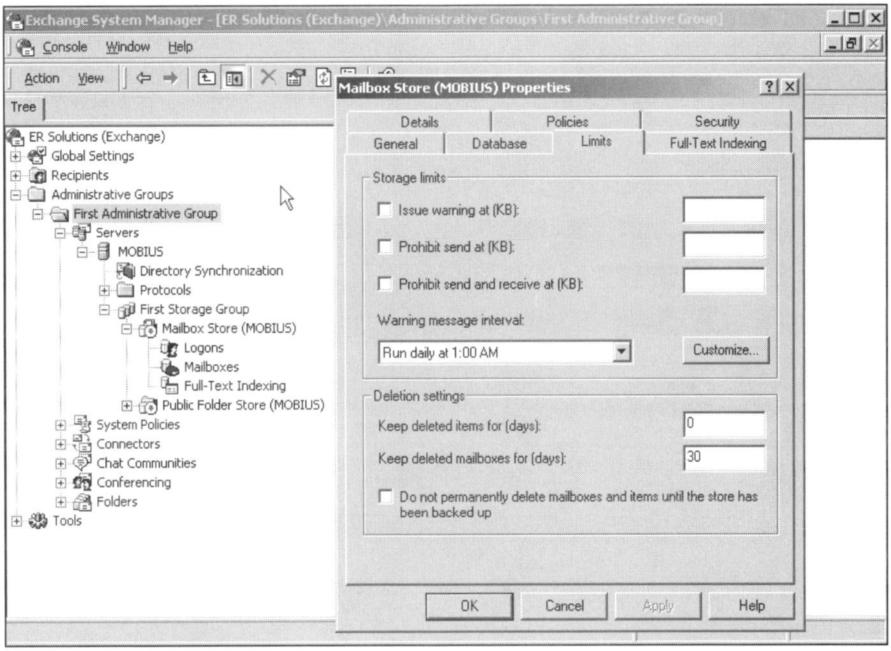

Figure 8.6 Configuring deleted items retention in System Manager.

Configuring a Deleted Mailbox Retention Period

Using System Manager, you can configure the number of days that a mailbox remains disconnected if you delete that mailbox. The default number of days that a mailbox is disconnected after deletion is 30 days, but you can always reconnect it during this time. To configure an alternate time period:

1. Select Start|Programs|Microsoft Exchange|System Manager.
2. Find the mailbox store object you want to configure and right-click it.
3. Select Properties from the context menu that appears.
4. In the Mailbox Store Properties dialog box, select the Limits tab (see Figure 8.7).
5. Enter the setting that is applicable to your situation in the Keep Deleted Mailboxes For (Days) text box or retain the default period of 30 days, and then click OK when finished.

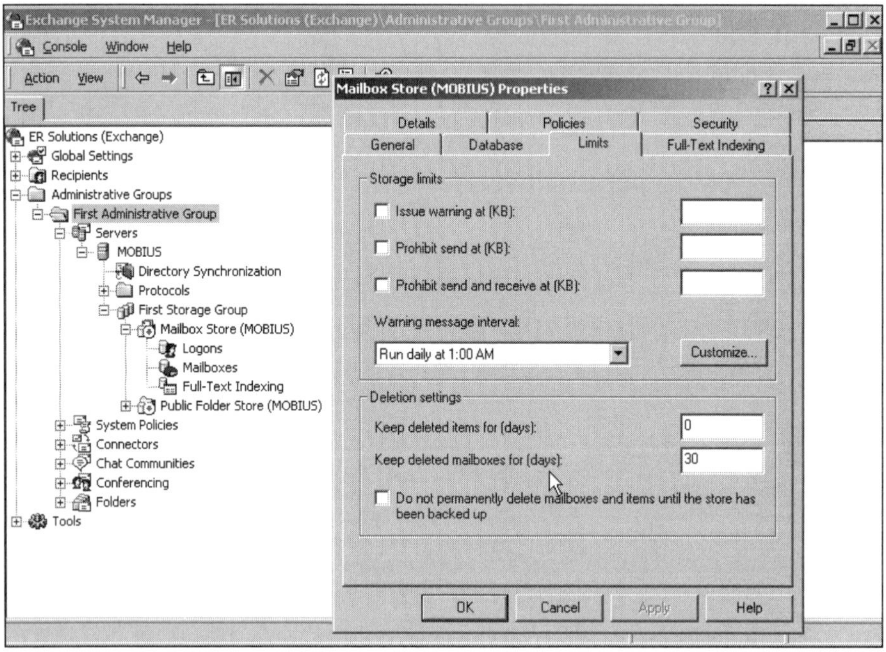

Figure 8.7 Changing the mailbox retention period on the Limits tab.

Reconnecting a Deleted Mailbox to a New User Object

If you delete a user who is mailbox-enabled in Active Directory Users and Computers, but you have not deleted the actual mailbox in Exchange System Manager, you can *reconnect* a new user to the existing mailbox by using the following procedures:

1. Create a new user in Active Directory Users And Computers (select Start|Programs|Administrative Tools|Active Directory Users And Computers).

2. When creating the user in Step 1, don't check the Create An Exchange Mailbox option. You want to create a user without a corresponding mailbox.

3. Open System Manager by choosing Start|Programs|Microsoft Exchange. Find the mailbox store where the original user's mailbox was located.

4. After you locate the mailbox—you will notice a red "X" next to it—right-click it and select the Reconnect option. When the New User For This Mailbox box appears, select the *new user you just created* in Active Directory Users and Computers. Click OK.

Recovering a Mailbox from a Backup

Recovering mailboxes in Exchange 2000 is similar to the procedures employed with Exchange 5.5. In theory, it's much better to restore an entire database from backup to an *offline recovery server* because it allows you to reconnect one single mailbox to a user account. This is because the WSS component of Exchange 2000 performs more optimally if you work with a large subset of database files instead of working with individual mailboxes.

Using an offline recovery server means having an additional server that uses the same names for the Information Stores and databases. The actual restoration takes place on the recovery server so that the desired mailbox can be extracted to the original server. This means that both Exchange 2000 and AD must reside on your recovery server. However, you do not want this recovery server to be part of your original Windows 2000 forest, so it's important to install AD services as part of a new forest structure. The version of Exchange 2000 running on your recovery server must match the version of Exchange 2000 running on your original server with respect to organizational name, administrative group name, SG name, Mailbox Store name, Public Folder Store name, and **LegacyExchangeDN** attribute names for certain system objects.

The **LegacyExchangeDN** is an attribute of the site in which you want to recover a mailbox and is adopted by almost all Exchange 2000 objects, including mail-enabled and mailbox-enabled users. For example, if you are running Exchange 2000 in an organization named BookCover with one administrative group (the **First Administrative Group**), and you have a mailbox user named jsmith in the Recipients container, your **LegacyExchangeDN** value for this user would be:

```
/O=BookCover/OU=First Administrative Group/CN=Recipients/CN=jsmith
```

WARNING! Be careful when you rename administrative groups because the OU portion of the LegacyExchangeDN name will not be updated.

You can determine the exact name of the **LegacyExchangeDN** attribute by using tools such as the ADSI Edit utility found in the \Support\Tools directory of the Windows 2000 installation CD-ROM, or the Windows 2000 LDAP viewer known as LDP.EXE. These tools allow you to view all properties of your administrative group object. If you don't have access to these tools, you can use the LDIFDE utility (LDAP Data Interchange Format Directory Exchange) tool from a command prompt to display your administrative group onscreen. Using LDIFDE means you need the DNS name of your root domain in your Windows 2000 forest, your Exchange 2000 organization name, and your administrative group name.

NOTE: *The LDAP Data Interchange Format (LDIF) is a feature of the LDAP protocol. LDIF is a standard file format used to manipulate data inside an LDAP-compliant database, such as Windows 2000 AD services or Novell's Directory Services (NDS) database. LDIFDE allows you to use this LDIF file format to access AD, which is LDAP-compliant.*

Follow these steps to recover a database store (and ultimately a mailbox) from a backup:

1. Install Windows 2000 Server or Advanced Server on your alternate recovery server, and then use **dcpromo.exe** (the Active Directory Installation Wizard). You have to create a brand-new forest for your recovery server. You also have to configure the DNS on this server.
2. Install Exchange 2000 on your recovery server using the same organizational name as you did in your original Windows 2000 forest (remember that you will have two distinct Windows 2000 forests at this time).
3. Create a new SG on the recovery server (using System Manager) that has the same name as the SG on your original server from which you backed up your mailbox store. You only create this SG if you are using anything *other than* the first SG (which appears by default).
4. Now create mailbox stores in this SG that match your original mailbox stores. After doing this, you can *dismount* the database that you want to restore.
5. Open System Manager on the server that you are restoring the database to and right-click this database to select the Properties option. Check the This Database Can Be Overwritten By A Restore box on the Database tab (see Figure 8.8).
6. Now use the Windows 2000 Backup program to restore the database containing the mailbox that you want to recover. Make sure you choose the Last Backup Set checkbox on the Restore tab, otherwise you might have to use the **ESEUTIL** repair utility with the **/CC** switch to verify the restored files before the database store can actually start (see Figure 8.9).
7. Now, start the database that you just restored from tape and use System Manager to run the Cleanup Agent. Right-click the Mailbox container in your SG and click Run Cleanup Agent. A red "X" appears on any mailbox that is not linked to an AD account.
8. Use Active Directory Users And Computers to create user objects that are not mailbox-enabled for every mailbox you want to recover from backup. To do this, you have to clear the Create An Exchange Mailbox box when creating a new user. You want to reconnect these user accounts to the mailboxes that you previously restored from backup on your recovery server.

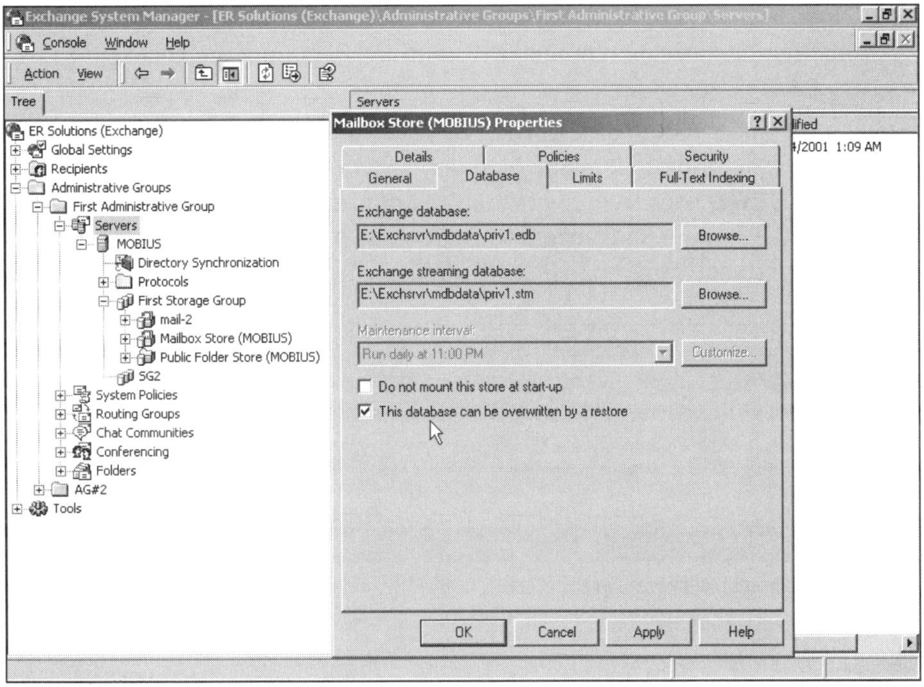

Figure 8.8 The option to overwrite a database with a restore.

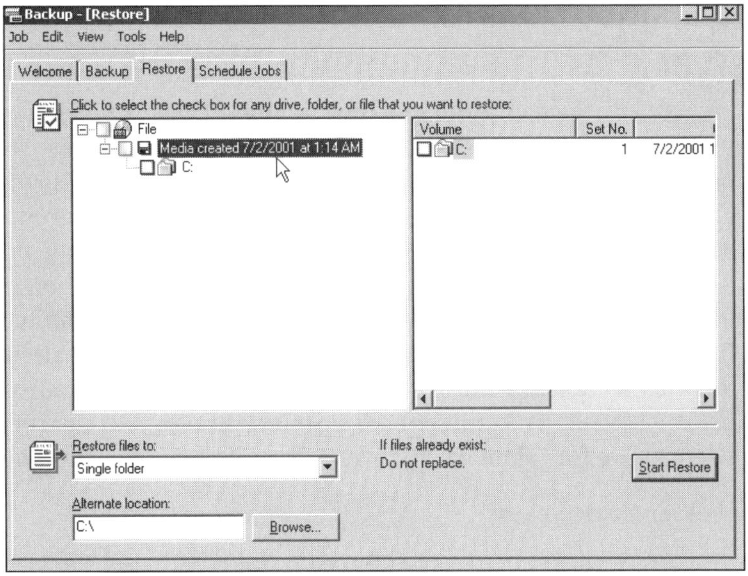

Figure 8.9 Selecting the last backup set in the **NTBackup** program.

9. Now, you can manually link a mailbox to a user using the procedures outlined in the previous Immediate Solution "Reconnecting a Deleted Mailbox to a New User Object."
10. Using a utility such as **EXMERGE.EXE**, you can now transfer the contents of your mailbox from your recovery server to your original server. **EXMERGE** tries to convert mailbox contents on the recovery server into PST files, and then transfers these to your original server after converting them into native Exchange 2000 mailbox formats.

NOTE: *Using* ***EXMERGE.EXE*** *on an Exchange 2000 Server will not work correctly unless you use an account that possesses Receive As and Send As permissions to the mailboxes on which* ***EXMERGE*** *is importing messages. By default, even an administrator will not have these rights (see* ***http://support.microsoft.com/support/kb/articles/Q273/6/42.asp*** *for further details regarding* ***EXMERGE.EXE****).*

Related solutions:	Found on page:
Adding Mailbox Information to Existing Users	151
Creating a Mail-Enabled User Recipient Object	153

Changing the Legacy Distinguished Name for a Recovery Server

Two instances require you to change the **LegacyExchangeDN** attribute name on a recovery server used to recover deleted mailboxes. The first instance occurs when the mailbox you want to recover is located on a server that was upgraded from Exchange 5.5. The second instance occurs if your administrative group has a name other than the First Administrative Group. After installing Exchange 2000 on a recovery server that is separate from your original server, you should not restore your databases until you have manually changed the **LegacyExchangeDN** values, or you have upgraded from Exchange 5.5 to make sure that you are using proper values for this attribute. Another alternative is to use a method called *Two-Server Recovery* (visit **www.microsoft.com/exchange** and search the Microsoft Knowledgebase for "Mailbox Recovery" for details on this method).

To perform a Two-Server Recovery:

1. Determine the name of the **LegacyExchangeDN** attribute for whatever administrative group that you want to recover your mailboxes. Establish the hardware that will be used for the first recovery server and the second recovery server.

2. Install Windows 2000 Server on the first recovery server, and then promote this to a DC by choosing Start|Run and typing "DCPROMO" to start the Active Directory Installation Wizard. You must create a new forest for this recovery server. When finished, you can install Exchange 2000 on this recovery server and use the same organization name that was used on your original server.
3. While still using the first recovery server, create a new second administrative group that has the same name as the administrative group that you will be restoring.
4. Choose your second recovery server and install the Windows 2000 OS without using **DCPROMO**. When finished, install Exchange 2000 into the second administrative group.
5. Follow all procedures in the previous Immediate Solution "Recovering a Mailbox from a Backup."

Creating a SMTP Virtual Server

For security reasons, you might want to create a new Virtual Server for your Internet protocols separate from the default Virtual Servers that will be created for the HTTP, IMAP4, NNTP, POP3, and SMTP protocols. A user outside your network can access your internal network by accessing a custom SMTP Virtual Server instead of the default SMTP Virtual Server. This enhances security on your internal network.

To create a new Virtual Server:

1. Click Start|Programs|Microsoft Exchange|System Manager.
2. When the System Manager console appears, open your Administrative Group(s), and all your Server containers to expose the Protocols container. Under each Internet protocol, you will find a default Virtual Server, with the exception of the HTTP protocol.
3. Right-click the SMTP protocol folder, select New, and then select New SMTP Virtual Server (see Figure 8.10).
4. In the New SMTP Virtual Server Wizard box that appears, enter the name for your new Virtual Server, and click Next. Then assign your Virtual Server a new IP address. If you want to use all available IP addresses, specify (All Unassigned) under the IP Address box (see Figure 8.11).
5. Click Finish when you're done. Check System Manager to see whether it has added your new SMTP Virtual Server (under the SMTP folder in the Protocols container).

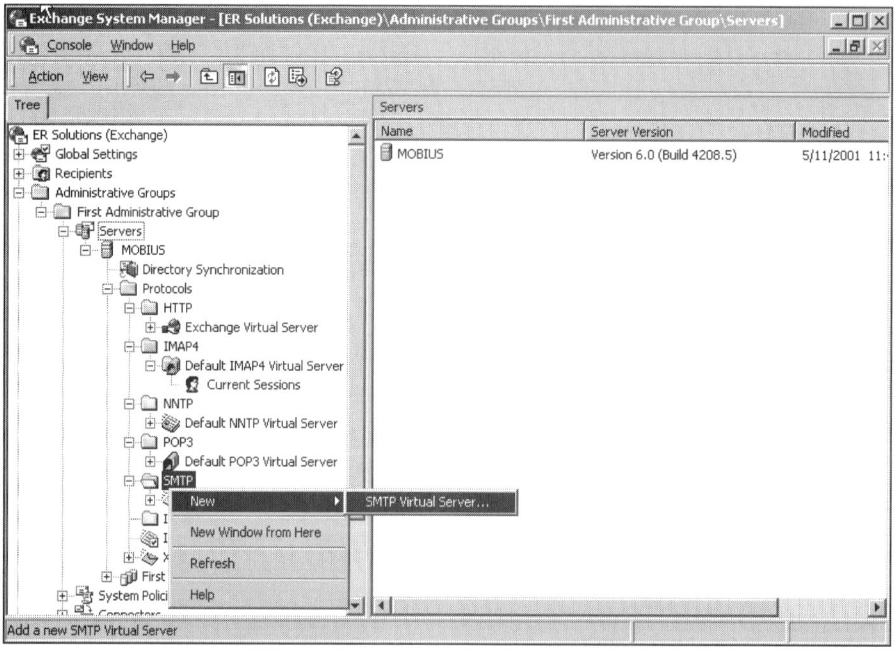

Figure 8.10 Creating a new SMTP Virtual Server in System Manager.

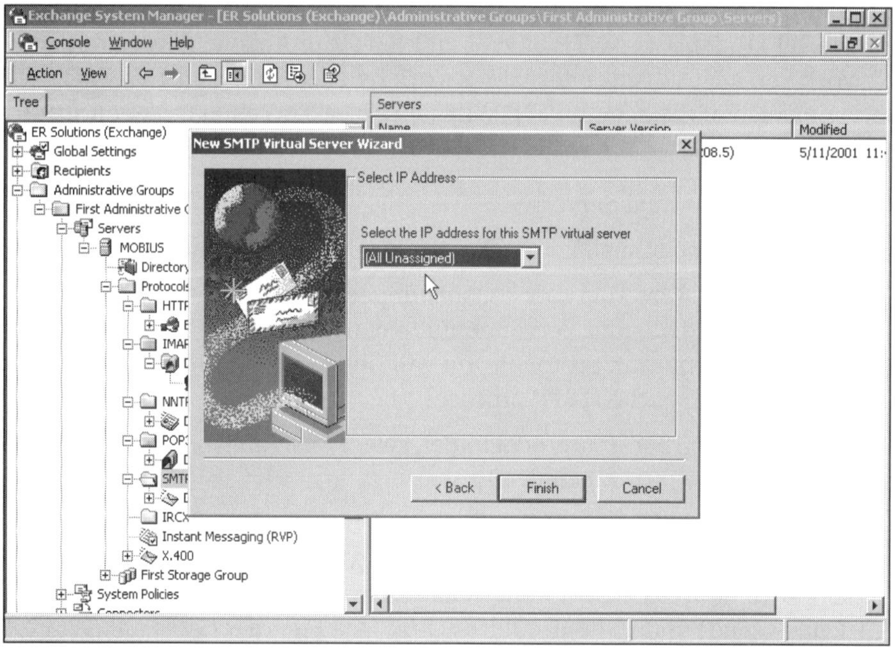

Figure 8.11 Choosing (All Unassigned) for your Virtual Server's IP address.

TIP: *You have to assign each Virtual Server either separate IP addresses or separate port numbers. If you try to assign the same IP address and port number settings to two different Virtual Servers, even if for the same protocol such as SMTP, you will see a warning displayed as shown in Figure 8.12. Also, System Manager will show the new Virtual Server with a yellow question mark next to it as shown in Figure 8.13. You have to edit the properties of this Virtual Server before being able to accept connections through it. To edit a Virtual Server, right-click the Virtual Server in System Manager, choose Properties, and then change the IP address or port number on the General tab (you might have to click the Advanced button to change the IP address or port number).*

Related solution:	*Found on page:*
Configuring and Controlling Access to a POP3 Virtual Server	518

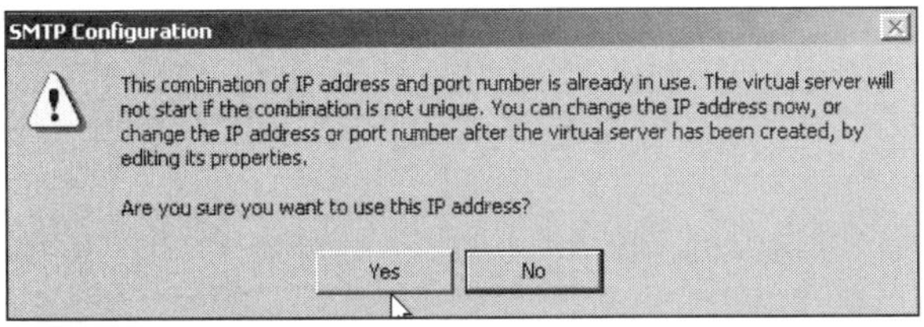

Figure 8.12 The warning message displayed when two protocol Virtual Servers contain the same IP address and port numbers.

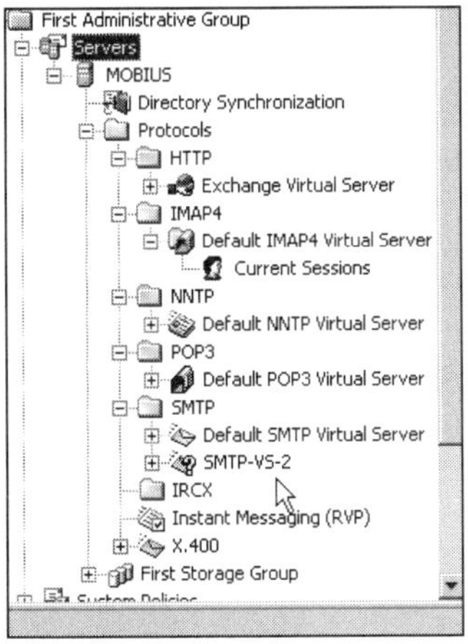

Figure 8.13 System Manager displaying a question mark when two protocol Virtual Servers contain similar IP configurations.

Configuring Authentication for SMTP Virtual Servers

In some cases, users might need to log on to your private network from external public channels such as the Internet to access their mailbox information or public folder information. To enhance security for your enterprise and to avoid potentially damaging situations in which external users can compromise or destroy your sensitive data, enable different forms of authentication on all your protocol Virtual Servers using the Exchange 2000 System Manager snap-in tool. To configure authentication for a Virtual Server in System Manager:

1. Open up the Exchange System Manager Snap-In from the Programs menu.
2. Navigate through your Administrative Groups and Server containers and right-click the specific protocol Virtual Server that you want to configure security on in the Protocols folder (for example, the SMTP default Virtual Server or a custom Virtual Server that you have created). Select the Properties option.
3. Click the Access tab, and then click the Authentication button found in the Access Control section (see Figure 8.14).
4. For the SMTP default Virtual Server, you will see a screen similar to the one shown in Figure 8.14. Notice the different forms of authentication provided here, and notice that Basic Authentication is not enabled by default for the default SMTP Virtual Server.

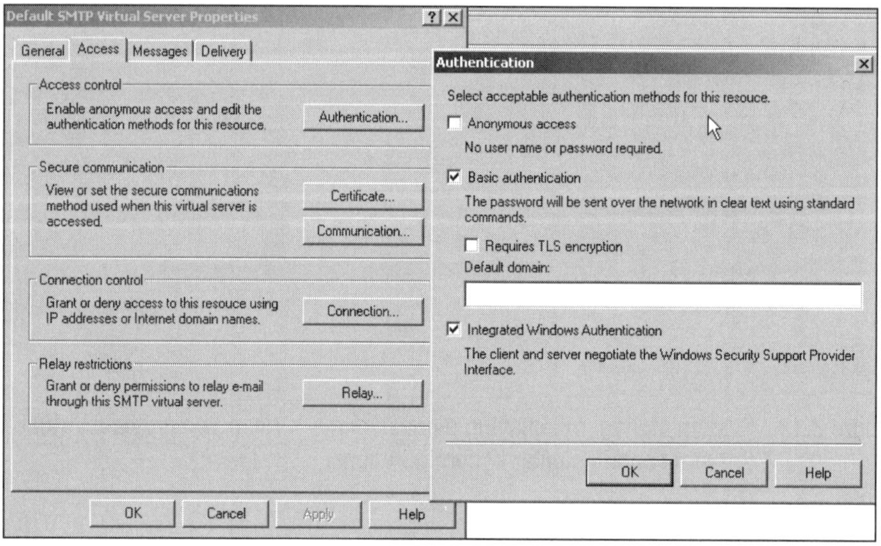

Figure 8.14 The authentication options for the default SMTP Virtual Server.

NOTE: *Some authentication methods do not apply to certain protocols. For instance, Anonymous Access will not apply to the POP3 protocol because it would open the door to potential abuse with respect to individual mailboxes or public folder resources.*

Each type of authentication is described here:

- *Basic Authentication*—Clients do not have to encrypt their usernames or passwords. Rather, they transmit all information in clear text to an Exchange Server. Do not use this method if users need to access their mailboxes over the Internet.
- *Anonymous Access*—This is used to access public folders over HTTP or NNTP. No user account information is needed to access resources. This must be enabled for each protocol within System Manager.
- *Integrated Windows Authentication*—This was formerly the Windows NT Challenge/Response Authentication method and is more secure than Basic or Anonymous Authentication. This method combines the strengths of Challenge/Response with the new Kerberos version 5 authentication protocol, which uses AD to store security information for users.
- *Digest Authentication*—This is used to support IM users who want to connect to an IM Server located in your network using the public Internet. This method transmits a user's password in encrypted form to a home server. You have to enable Reversible Password Encryption using a GPO for Windows 2000 to support this form of authentication.

NOTE: *Digest Authentication does not appear in the Authentication dialog box in System Manager, but in the Web site container containing the* **InstMsg** *virtual directory in the Internet Services Manager snap-in found in the Administrative Tools menu (Start|Programs|Administrative Tools).*

Restricting Connections via IP Address or Domain for SMTP Virtual Servers

Exchange 2000 permits restricting access to Virtual Servers either by IP address or by domain name. You can actually identify which IP address or domain name is trying to establish contact with your protocol Virtual Servers configured using the Exchange System Manager tool. This action helps you thwart many Internet attacks because you can exercise granular control by preventing certain computers, subnets, or domains from accessing your internal network. There are two settings to choose from, either All Except The List Below or Only The List Below:

- All computers can access a Virtual Server *except* for those specified in a list.
- Only computers specified in a list can access the protocol Virtual Server.

You can establish connection control on any protocol Virtual Server that is created on your Exchange 2000 server except for the HTTP Protocol Virtual Server.

NOTE: *The HTTP protocol is also subject to other exclusions that do not apply to the other protocol Virtual Servers. For example, no Secure Communication button appears on the Access tab for the HTTP Virtual Server to enable SSL-based encryption between a server and a client. Also, the HTTP Virtual Server doesn't have a Connection Control button on the Access tab like the other Virtual Servers. You configure many properties for the HTTP Virtual Server using the Internet Services Manager snap-in found under Start|Programs|Administrative Tools.*

To configure connection controls, perform the following steps:

1. Choose Start|Programs|Microsoft Exchange|System Manager.
2. Navigate to the protocol Virtual Server you want to configure, for example, the SMTP Virtual Server under the Protocols container (found in the Administrative Group|Servers container for your organization). Right-click the appropriate Virtual Server and click Properties.
3. Choose the Access tab, and then click the Connection button in the Connection Control section (see Figure 8.15).

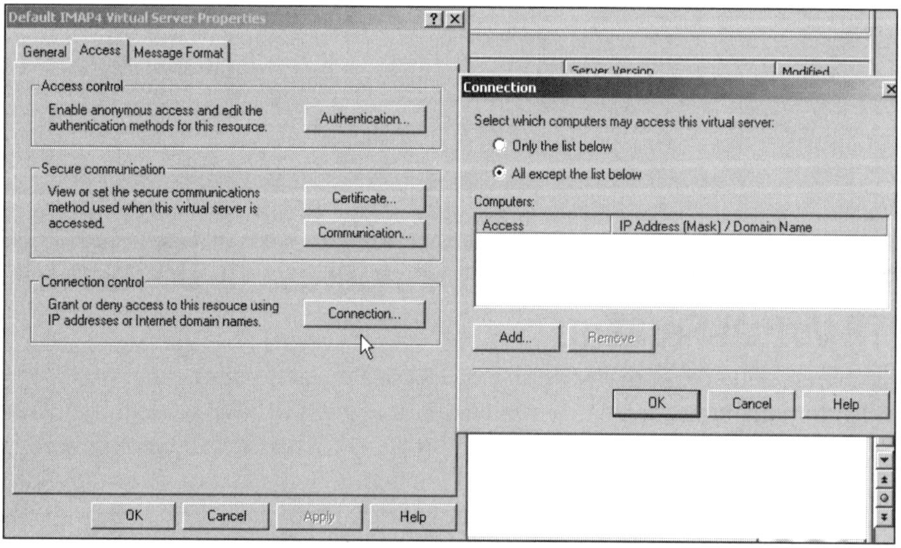

Figure 8.15 Establishing connection controls for a protocol Virtual Server in System Manager.

4. Decide whether to allow a group of computers to access this Virtual Server (Only The List Below option), or whether to allow all computers access to this Virtual Server except for a group of computers (All Except The List Below option). You can choose based on IP address or domain name. Click the Add button to open the Computer dialog box.
5. Choose among Single Computer, Group Of Computers, or Domain (see Figure 8.16). If selecting a Single Computer, enter an IP address; if selecting a group of computers, enter a valid subnet address and a subnet mask; if selecting a domain, enter a Fully Qualified Domain Name (FQDN) such as sales.books.org.
6. Click OK three times to close all the property dialog boxes and return to the System Manager console window.

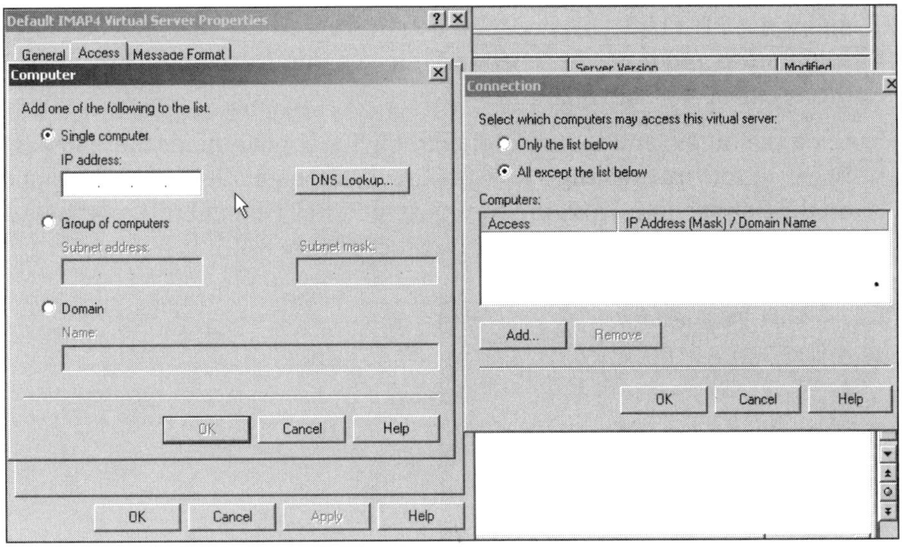

Figure 8.16 Choosing to allow or restrict access to a virtual server by computer or by domain.

Creating a GPO for a Domain

You can create GPOs at the site level, the domain level, or the OU level. Use the Active Directory Users and Computers snap-in to create a GPO for a domain or an OU. Use the Active Directory Sites and Services snap-in to create a GPO for a site.

To create a GPO at the domain level for your Exchange 2000 organization:

1. Log on to your domain with Administrative privileges.
2. Select Start|Programs|Administrative Tools|Active Directory Users And Computers Snap-In.
3. Right-click your domain in the console that appears and select Properties.
4. Choose the Group Policy tab and notice the Default Domain Policy listed under the GPO Links section. You do not want to use this now, so click the Add button and the Add A Group Policy Object Link dialog box appears (see Figures 8.17 and 8.18).
5. Click the All tab and the two default policies appear under the Name field. Because you are creating a new policy, click the middle button that appears on the toolbar, known as the New Group Policy Object button in the Add A Group Policy Object Link dialog box (see Figure 8.19).

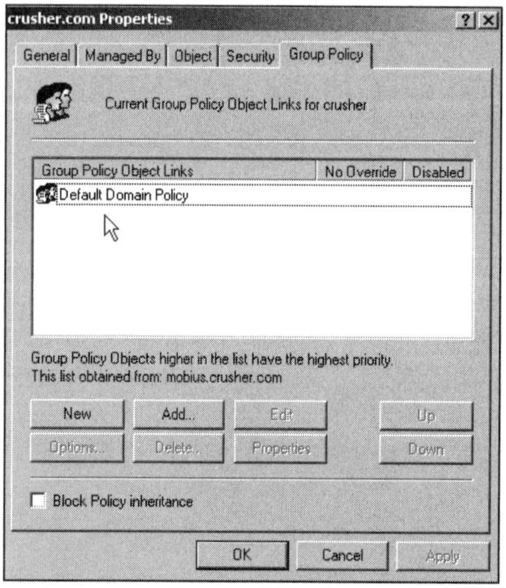

Figure 8.17 The Group Policy tab showing the Default Domain Policy listed.

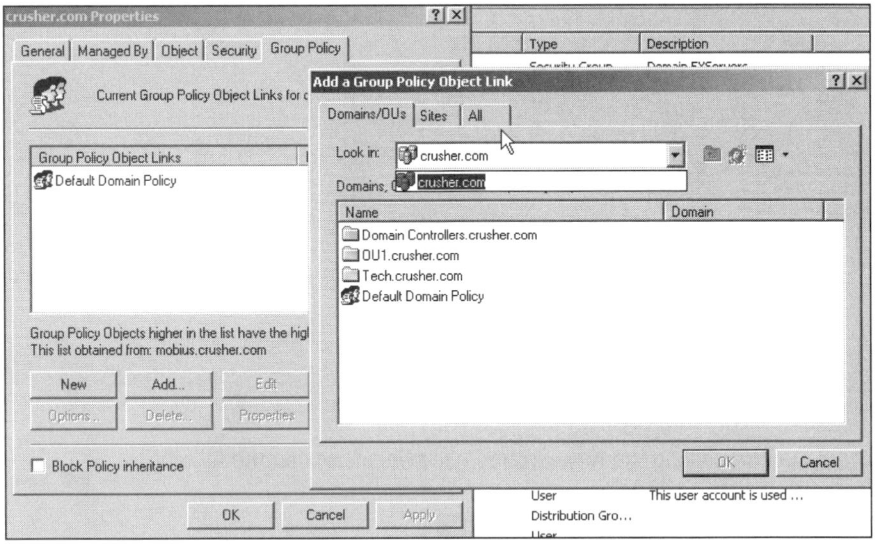

Figure 8.18 Adding a new GPO link.

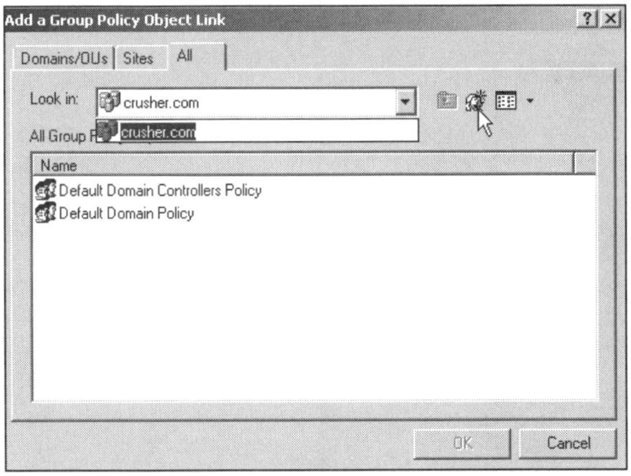

Figure 8.19 Clicking the New Group Policy Object toolbar button on the All tab creates a new Group Policy Object link.

6. After clicking the New Group Policy Object button, you will see New Group Policy Object in the Name field (see Figure 8.20). You can rename this object and click OK. The new GPO appears under the Default Domain Policy on the Group Policy tab of your domain's Properties sheet (see Figure 8.21). Click Close to return to the Active Directory Users and Computers interface.

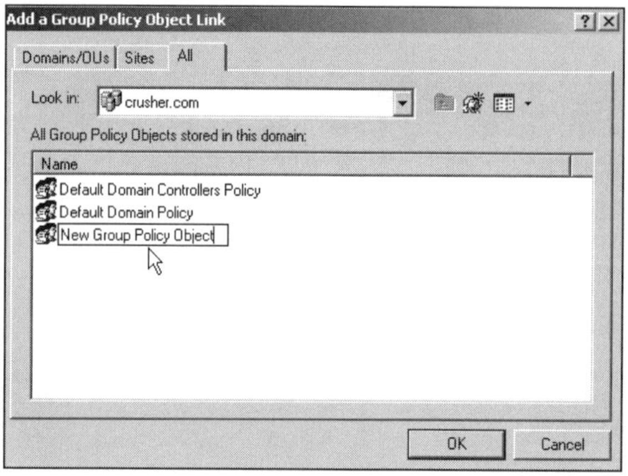

Figure 8.20 Displaying the New Group Policy Object box on the All tab.

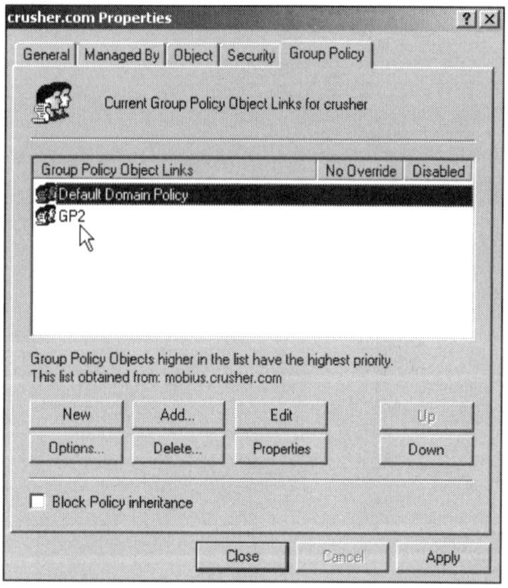

Figure 8.21 Displaying the new GPO renamed on the Group Policy tab for the domain.

Installing the Security Analysis and Configuration Snap-In

The *Security Analysis and Configuration Snap-in* lets administrators configure local system security. You import security templates and apply these templates to a GPO for a local computer system. The goal is to configure your system's security with security levels found inside the templates.

You need to install a standalone snap-in as follows:

1. Choose Start|Run; then type "mmc" in the Open text box. Make sure you are logged in as Administrator on your local system.
2. A blank MMC console named Console1 appears on your screen (see Figure 8.22). Choose Console|Add/Remove Snap-In.
3. In the Add/Remove Snap-In dialog box that appears, click the Add button on the Standalone tab (see Figure 8.23).

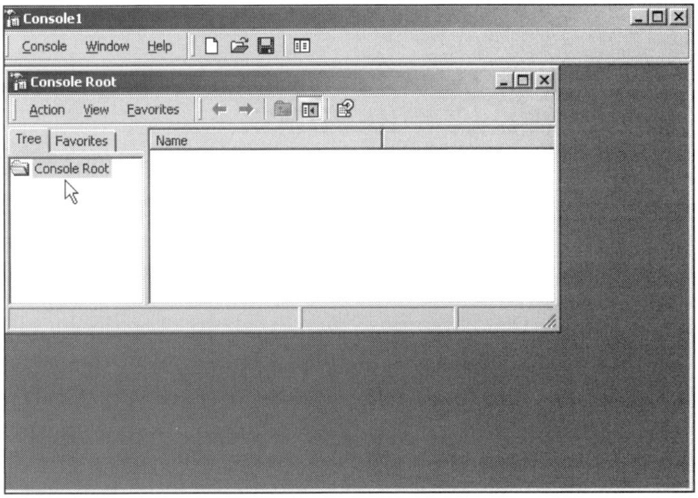

Figure 8.22 The blank Console1 MMC console.

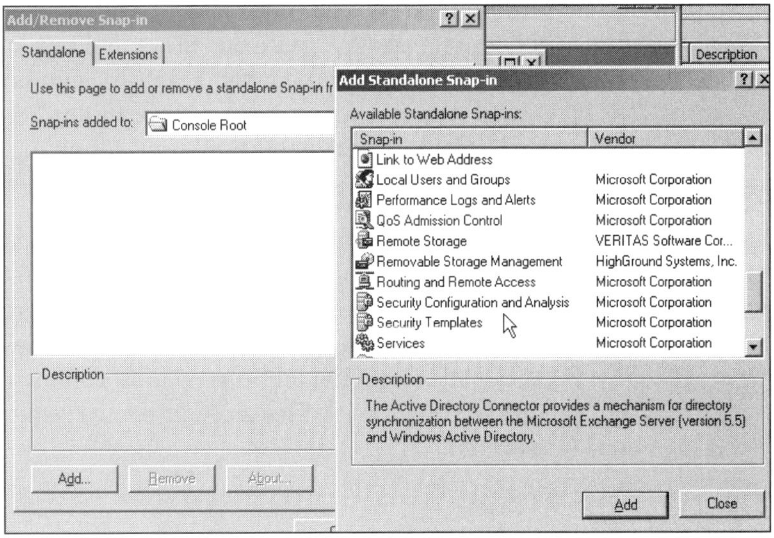

Figure 8.23 Adding a snap-in on the Standalone tab.

4. In the Add Standalone Snap-In window, scroll down with your mouse and choose the Security Configuration And Analysis Snap-In. Click Add, and then click Close to view your snap-in added to the Add/Remove Snap-In dialog box.
5. Finally, click OK to return to the Console1 interface screen. Save this custom MMC by clicking on Console|Save and typing a file name that is appropriate for this console (for example, security-config). Then, click Save to finish this procedure.

Planning an Optimal RAID Configuration

Every SG you configure requires its own directory path for transaction logs; this directory path should be different than the directory path used to store the database files. Microsoft always recommends separating transaction log files from database files to improve disaster-recovery efforts in the event of system failure.

Some administrators attempt to place database files for each SG on distinct RAID-1 or RAID-5 volumes (mirrored volumes or striped volumes). But this is not an absolute necessity. Instead of implementing software or hardware RAID solutions for database files, it might be best to place these files on separate physical disk structures, so that if one disk set becomes corrupt for any reason, then only those databases can be moved to other physical disk structures without affecting the other databases that might be running.

If you have two different SGs configured on one physical server that contains multiple physical hard drives, it might be best to create one SG of mailbox stores that spans all physical hard drives, and also create a second SG of mailbox or public folder stores that spans the same physical hard drives. In any case, a different RAID structure or volume would be created for all transaction log files belonging to both SGs.

This last scenario still creates a single point of failure for all transaction log files, so it is recommended that you keep transaction logs on separate disk subsystems so that only certain SGs would be affected in the event of disaster. Microsoft actually recommends separating transaction log disks for every SG you have to enhance system reliability. Putting transaction log files on separate volumes also can increase performance because transaction log files are written in a sequential manner, whereas database files are not.

Most mailbox stores benefit from RAID-5 (striped with parity) or RAID-0+1 (a mirrored stripe set). If you compare the two, you will discover the following:

- A RAID-5 array costs less than a RAID-0+1 array depending on how many drives make up the array.
- A RAID-0+1 array benefits from fast disk reads and fast disk writes.
- It takes more time to rebuild a RAID-5 array than to rebuild a RAID-0+1 array.
- RAID-5 arrays are useful in the event of a *single* disk failure. If a second disk were to fail while you were rebuilding the first disk, you would have to restore the entire volume from tape backup. RAID-5 does not enjoy the benefits of RAID-6, which can handle this scenario easily.

Microsoft recommends using RAID-1 for volumes containing transaction log files due to performance and reliability factors. When selecting different RAID configurations, you must always balance performance and availability factors with cost factors. A RAID-1 implementation affords more availability compared to RAID-5, or even a RAID-0+1 solution. The latter is considered more for performance reasons than anything else.

Disabling EFS for All Users in a Domain

The EFS permits users in a domain to encrypt data on local hard drives, which take advantage of NTFS 5. This occurs as a result of certificates being issued that conform to the X.509 standard (this implies a CA is available to issue certificates). In certain cases, the EFS can issue its own certificates.

The only way to turn EFS off is to configure a data-recovery policy and set its value to Empty. In every case, you need to set some type of data recovery policy to use EFS. The two values to configure for a data recovery policy are Empty and No Policy. If you set a policy to No Policy, you are allowing a default local computer policy to take the place of whatever data-recovery policy you have configured.

If you want to prevent all users from encrypting any data on their local machines, you have to change the settings for a GPO that has been applied to the domain level. You have to modify the Default Domain Policy GPO found on the Group Policy tab of a domain's property page for a local domain. Perform the following steps:

1. Open Active Directory Users And Computers from the Start menu.
2. Right-click the node for your domain and select Properties from the context menu.

3. Select the Group Policy tab and click the Default Domain Policy object that appears in the window. Then click the Edit button that appears below this window. The Group Policy Editor snap-in appears (see Figure 8.24).
4. In the Group Policy Object console that appears, search the Computer Configuration container and open Windows Settings, and then Security Settings until you are able to see the folder for Public Key Policies.
5. Click the "+" next to Public Key Policies and highlight the first folder underneath labeled Encrypted Data Recovery Agents. If you see any certificates listed in the righthand pane, delete them by right-clicking them and selecting Delete (see Figure 8.25).
6. Now right-click the Encrypted Data Recovery Agents folder and select Delete Policy; then, choose Yes.
7. Finally, right-click the Encrypted Data Recovery Agents folder again and select Initialize Empty Policy.

Now all users affected by this policy setting cannot encrypt files or folders on their local hard drives. If they attempt to do so, they are notified that no encryption recovery policy is configured for their local system.

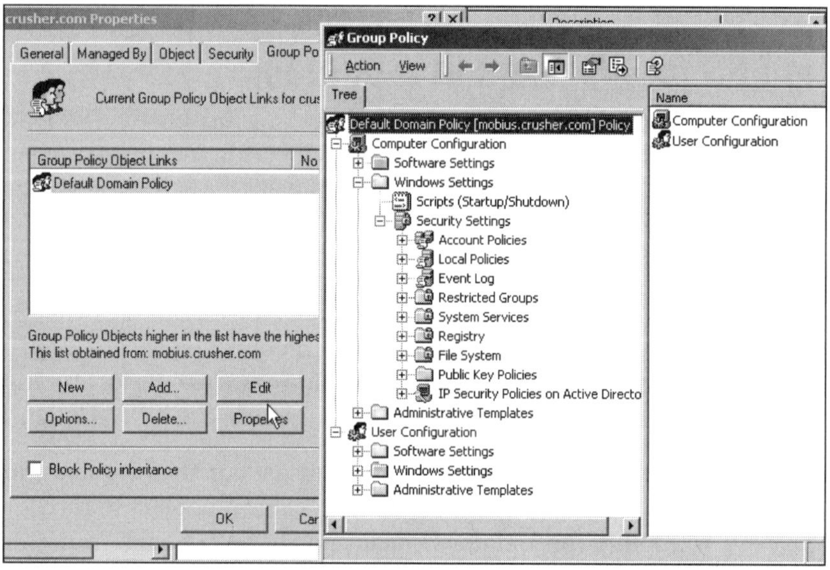

Figure 8.24 Opening the Default Domain Policy for your local domain from Active Directory Users and Computers.

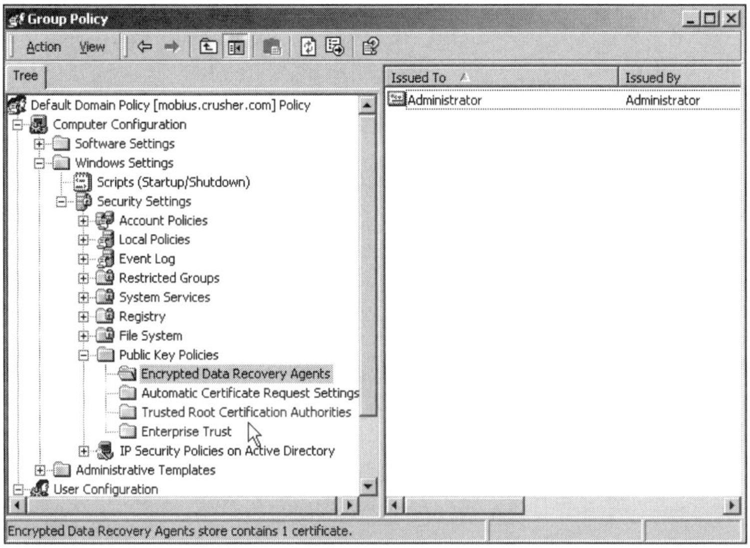

Figure 8.25 Selecting the Encrypted Data Recovery Agents folder under Public Key Policies.

Running ISINTEG and ESEUTIL to Check Your Databases for Inconsistencies

Both **ISINTEG** and **ESEUTIL** can be used to troubleshoot problems with your databases. Both utilities are found in your default installation directory for Exchange 2000, which is normally \Exchsrvr\Bin.

ESEUTIL exists because regular online defragmentation of databases by the Information Store service does nothing to reduce the physical size of the databases. You want to reduce your databases to recover free space that is not being used. Check your Application event logs in Event Viewer for some indication of available free space within your databases after regular defragmentation cycles. **ESEUTIL** can actually help compact your databases and is considered a "low-level" tool that should not be used as part of your regular system maintenance routines. Because you run this tool from a command prompt, typing "ESEUTIL" by itself shows you all the valid options you can use (see Figure 8.26).

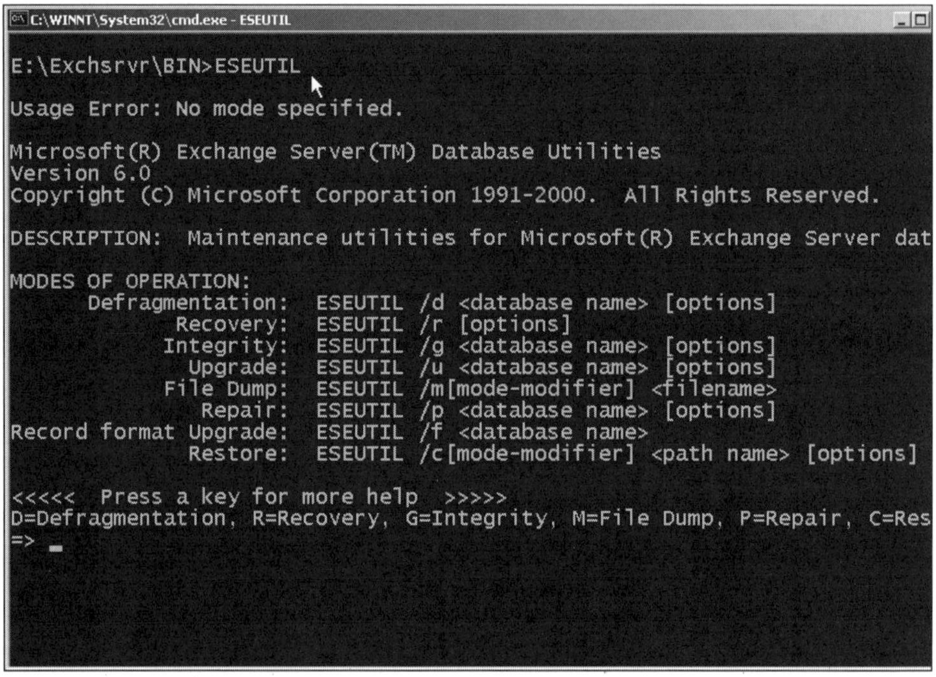

Figure 8.26 The options available for the **ESEUTIL** utility.

You cannot compact a database while its store is still mounted. **ESEUTIL** performs database defragmentation while the Information Store service is stopped. The primary uses for **ESEUTIL** are the following:

- *Defragmentation*—Using the **/d** switch, you can throw away unused pages in your databases and recover any empty space that becomes available for other data.
- *Repair*—Using the **/p** switch, you can try to restore any broken links in your database. If your database suffers any form of physical corruption, certain pages are taken away and the rest of the database is reformed. This means, however, that you might have to delete all current transaction log files because some of the database page numbers are no longer there.
- *Integrity*—Using the **/g** switch, you can check the integrity of your databases; however, this option does not make any changes to your database.

ESEUTIL can repair corrupted database pages and their tables of data, but data that cannot be fixed is purged. You can fix corrupted databases using **ESEUTIL /p** from a command line. The **ESEUTIL** compaction tool returns your databases to a consistent state; however, **ESEUTIL** works *below* the Information Store level. You need to check your databases at the Information Store level, and that's where **ISINTEG** comes into play.

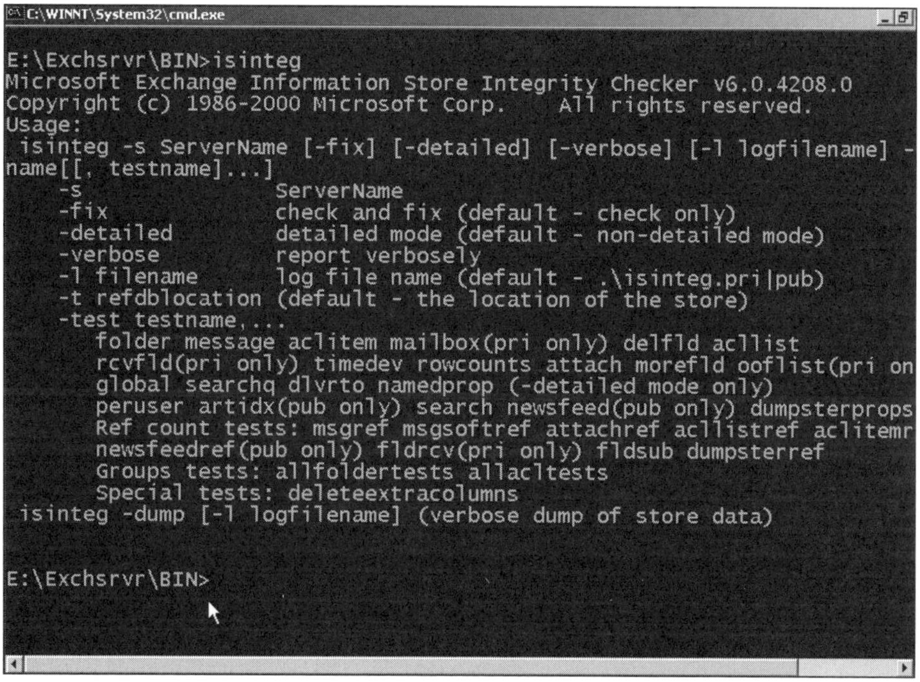

Figure 8.27 A list of options used with **ISINTEG** from a command prompt.

ISINTEG fixes database errors if you use the **–fix** option at a command prompt. See Figure 8.27 for a list of options you can use from a command prompt. Remember that **ISINTEG** will fail if your SG has more than five databases because it needs to create a temporary database to run successfully. The proper syntax to run **ISINTEG** takes the following form:

```
ISINTEG -s Mobius -fix -l ISINTEG.PRI -t c:\exchange
```

In this syntax, **–s** refers to a server named **Mobius**, **-fix** instructs **ISINTEG** to fix any problems that it detects, and **–l** specifies an output log file name. You should know that fix mode is not the default mode for this utility. The default behavior is to report problems without fixing them (known as check-only mode). Using the **–t** switch specifies the location of a temporary reference database, which is constructed from the original database being examined. The reference database is removed immediately after **ISINTEG** has terminated operations.

Troubleshooting the Inability to Apply Security Permissions Because of Missing Security Tab

The System Manager Console snap-in allows you to configure security on most objects. If you right-click an object and select the Security tab, you can choose granular levels of permission or configure no access to various objects. However, this tab is only displayed for the following objects by default:

- Global Address Lists (GALs)
- Mailbox Stores
- Public Folder Stores
- The top-level public folder hierarchy

If you want to enable this tab for all objects, you must configure a Registry setting by performing the following steps:

1. Select Start|Run; then type "Regedt32" in the Open box.
2. Locate the following Registry key:

```
HKEY_CURRENT_USER \ SOFTWARE \ MICROSOFT \ EXCHANGE \ ExAdmin
```

3. Choose Edit|Add Value; then type the following values:

```
Value Name: ShowSecurityPage
Data Type: REG_DWORD
Value: 1
```

4. Close the Registry Editor—your changes will take place immediately.

Chapter 9

Exchange Server Issues

If you need an immediate solution to:	*See page:*
Configuring Message Formats for the POP3 Virtual Server	346
Configuring Overriding Message Formats for Individual Users	348
Configuring MIME Formats for the Default Internet Message Format	350
Using the Rules Wizard in Outlook 2000 for Content Management	351
Using the Junk and Adult Content Filters with the Outlook Client	356
Finding Appropriate Content-Management Software	357
Dealing with Mail Abuse Prevention on Exchange 2000	358
Working with the Email Security Update in Outlook 2000	360
Connecting Exchange 2000 to the Internet Using a Static IP Address	362
Setting TCP/IP Port Numbers for Firewalls in Mixed-Mode Exchange Environments	364
Using the Delegation of Control Wizard to Assign Permissions	365
Restricting Access to Public Folders in the Outlook 2000 Client	367
Converting Universal Distribution Groups to Universal Security Groups to Secure Access to Public Folders	369
Installing the ADC with a Connection Agreement in a Mixed-Mode Exchange Server Environment	370

In Depth

Previous chapters looked at some server design issues concerning the implementation of various server components such as mailbox stores and storage groups (SG). These chapters introduced general messaging features to help you understand the structure of Exchange 2000 Server, and covered topics related to recovery of Exchange 2000 under various disaster scenarios. You have learned about the efficiencies of the new Exchange 2000 architecture and which services to choose for different environments.

This chapter will complement previous chapters that have introduced server design issues concerning the implementation of various server components such as mailbox stores and storage groups. It concentrates on message routing and system administration. Consider this chapter a synthesis of sorts—one that bridges past and future chapters while tying loose ends together. You can categorize most Exchange 2000 server deployments according to the following generic types of activities:

- *Security*—Those activities involving the enhancement or deployment of security tools specifically designed for Exchange 2000, including content management, intrusion detection, email virus detection and management, and regulation of Unsolicited Commercial Email (UCE), more commonly known as "spam." This chapter covers MIME (Multipurpose Internet Mail Extensions) and S/MIME (Secure MIME) in detail, as well as planning for email content management and virus management.
- *Network*—Those activities involving the configuration and management of the DNS service as it relates to Exchange 2000 as well as issues related to the integration of Exchange 2000 with the TCP/IP model of network communications. This chapter takes an in-depth look at the integration of DNS with Exchange 2000 and TCP/IP ports important to Exchange 2000.
- *Recipient*—Activities related to the general configuration and management of recipient items such as mailbox stores, SGs, and public folder stores. Also, activities relating to the implementation of these objects for access control purposes and permission management. The implementation of SGs and administrative groups are discussed, including how you can best manage the administrative delegation process in your enterprise.

- *Migration*—Activities related to upgrading or migrating previous versions of Exchange 5.5 Server, or activities related to maintaining coexistence between Exchange 2000 and previous versions of Exchange Server. The focus revolves around public folder interoperability between Exchange 5.5 and Exchange 2000, including the proper use of the Active Directory Connector (ADC).

This chapter covers relevant and practical topics that you are sure to benefit from in your own messaging environments.

Server Issues Related to Security

Security ranks among the top concerns for email administrators in general, and Exchange Server is not immune to this in any way. Like other email systems, Exchange Servers have to be protected from multiple threats, including malicious ActiveX controls or harmful viruses. You should consider both hardware-related and software-related steps when fortifying your Exchange 2000 Servers. These steps include the following:

- Using hardware firewalls to block out unwanted Internet traffic that might contain destructive email viruses or other unwanted code.
- Using encryption and authentication for external Internet clients that are trying to access an Exchange Server in your internal network. Technologies here include S/MIME and Secure Sockets Layer (SSL) encryption.
- Installing content-management software on your Exchange Server(s) to filter out unwanted attachments or message texts containing harmful VBScript code or ActiveX controls.
- Installing antivirus software on all Exchange Servers to catch or quarantine viruses emanating from external servers that carry destructive payloads.
- Deploying an Intrusion Detection System (IDS) to monitor potential denial-of-service (DoS) attacks. These attacks are sometimes initiated by a malicious computer virus or application containing a Trojan horse.

NOTE: *A computer virus is a program often hidden within another program that replicates itself or files in order to perform malicious actions, such as erasing a computer's hard drive. A Trojan horse, on the other hand, is a nonreplicating malicious program that does something harmful that the developer intended, but that most users would not approve of if they were aware of it. In some cases, a virus can be a specific type of Trojan horse, because it is able to spread to other programs (that is, it turns them into Trojans too).*

Previous chapters offered suggestions for increasing security, ranging from the use of "strong passwords" or complex passwords consisting of a mixture of letters and digits to the use of Windows 2000 authentication methods, including Digest Authentication, which enables the use of password "hashes" or encrypted password digests. However, passwords are not a complete security solution. Administrators know that additional security measures are needed to fully protect their resources and that these additional measures are a combination of hardware and software tools that are specifically designed for such purposes.

We touched briefly on the use of firewalls and DoS attacks in previous chapters, so this chapter concentrates on investigating some of the other topics listed previously, including a look at the MIME protocol and the use of content-management software for Exchange 2000 deployments.

Using Message-Based Security

Email traffic is normally secured using *session-based security* or *message-based security*. The first method employs such technologies as SSL encryption to build secure messaging tunnels or channels between a mail server such as Exchange 2000 and a client such as Outlook 2000. Both authentication and encryption are used in the message-delivery process. Message-based security, on the other hand, is more concerned with securing the message body text, not just the pipe or channel that the message is traveling in. A Public Key Infrastructure (PKI) deploys both session-based and messaged-based security. A PKI is a combination of many elements, including Certificate Authorities (CAs) and other authorities that help authenticate users involved in the exchange of data. A PKI uses such technologies as digital signatures and message sealing to ward off potential threats to message security.

It's easy to confuse various technologies when discussing advanced security issues for Exchange 2000. For example, SSL and S/MIME are usually grouped together in the same context, yet they are each used for somewhat different purposes. SSL is used for encrypted communications especially between front-end (FE) servers and remote Internet clients who are accessing mailboxes hosted on protected back-end (BE) servers. S/MIME is an Internet standard protocol that allows you to exchange signed messages with any email client that supports this protocol, such as Outlook Express. S/MIME is a secure way of sending email by using the RSA (Rivest-Shamir-Adleman) encryption system. RSA is included in most Web browsers supplied by Microsoft and Netscape (although it only provides basic security compared to other forms of security such as Triple Data Encryption Standard [3DES] supporting 168-bit encryption with Secure Hash Algorithm or SHA-1 message authentication). S/MIME has been proposed as a standard to the Internet Engineering Task Force (IETF), along with a competing protocol known as Pretty Good Privacy/Multipurpose Internet Mail Extensions (PGP/MIME). A basic understanding of MIME will help you appreciate message-based security using S/MIME.

The MIME protocol is described in the IETF RFC 1521 and defines how electronic messages are organized. It differs from S/MIME in that S/MIME defines how encryption information and digital certificates can be part of an email message body.

NOTE: *S/MIME actually follows the syntax of the Public-Key Cryptography Standard format #7.*

MIME is an extension of the SMTP (Simple Mail Transfer Protocol) Internet protocol. MIME allows you to use SMTP to exchange various data files, such as audio files or video files, over the Internet. The objective of MIME was to extend the basic SMTP protocol so that an email client could handle multiple data types besides simple ASCII text. Exchange Servers usually insert a MIME header at the beginning of any data transmission over the Internet. Email clients such as Outlook 2000 use this MIME header to select appropriate applications for whatever type of data is being represented in the header. For instance, the client might need to download a special type of application, such as an MP3 player, if that type of data is found in the header and the client or browser doesn't already have this functionality built in. Any new MIME data types that appear from time to time usually are registered with the Private Internet Corporation for Assigned Names and Numbers (ICANN) (previously by the Internet Assigned Numbers Authority (IANA)).

NOTE: *For further details regarding the MIME specification, you can review RFC 1521 and RFC 1522, which modify the original specifications for the SMTP protocol, found in RFC 821 on the IETF Web site at* ***www.ietf.org/rfc.html***.

In earlier versions of Exchange Server, all MIME messages were converted to a MAPI (Messaging Application Programming Interface) format right away. MAPI formats were not the only form that email messages could take because it depended on where the message was being sent. Possible formats for email messages included the following:

- *EDB*—The file type used to represent Exchange 5.5's Information Store databases.
- *MAPI*—A standard that defined program interfaces and properties used to represent an email message. A MAPI message cannot be represented as a native MIME message at the same time.
- *MIME*—A standard used for representing an email message's header, body, or attachments.
- *MTA*—The Message Transfer Agent in Exchange 5.5 used to route messages between servers. Exchange 2000 now uses the SMTP protocol for this purpose, while using the MTA to connect to legacy Exchange 5.5 Servers.
- *NNTP*—Network News Transfer Protocol Internet standard used for retrieving messages in newsgroups.

- *POP3*—Post Office Protocol 3 Internet standard used only for the retrieval of messages.
- *SMTP*—An Internet standard used for sending email messages.

After a message was converted to a MAPI format, the original MIME representation was forever gone. However, if a POP3 client later requested this message, Exchange Server would convert it back to a MIME format depending on how the server was configured. Exchange 2000 has changed this process somewhat, because it can store native MIME messages without having to convert to MAPI or back to MIME. This is because all MIME messages retrieved using the SMTP, NNTP, or HTTP protocols are automatically stored in a file containing the .stm extension. This file is actually a database that holds the MIME content for all users' messages (including mailbox store data and public folder store data).

NOTE: *Native MIME content is popular because users see exactly the message that has been sent to them without worrying about losing any data due to conversion errors.*

Remember that every mailbox consists of a EDB file and a STM file. When the Exchange 2000 SMTP service receives a message, it stores the MIME content in the STM file. It then reads all message headers and stores fields such as From and Subject as *MAPI* properties in the EDB file (the EDB file contains a Messages table to hold this information). The EDB file has a pointer to the STM file, so all components know where to retrieve native MIME content for the user.

Because we are focusing on MIME versus MAPI here, consider a few scenarios in which messages might or might not be converted to native MIME (the ideal situation). Outlook users should know that Outlook creates messages as a set of MAPI properties, and Exchange converts this set to MIME depending on the destination for that message. Even Outlook Web Access (OWA) 2000 is incapable of creating or retrieving email messages in native MIME format. This is true whether your intended recipient is remote or situated on the same server as the sender of the message. If both sender and recipient are situated in the same mailbox store (and hence, the same SG), all messages are delivered to the recipient as a set of MAPI properties, not native MIME.

NOTE: *It's interesting to note that messages destined for other servers in Exchange 5.5 were sent as a set of MAPI properties using the MTA. If the message was destined for SMTP recipients external to the organization, the Internet Mail Connector (IMC) converted this message to MIME.*

You can request MIME messages using the NNTP, HTTP, or POP3/IMAP4 protocols. If using NNTP, all MAPI messages are converted to MIME format automatically (MIME messages are sent without conversion). Using HTTP, any MAPI messages are converted to MIME format, and MIME messages are streamed to Web browsers without any conversion overhead involved. Finally, with POP3 or IMAP4, a lot depends on the server settings you have chosen. You can check the settings configured for your POP3 or IMAP4 Virtual Servers using the System Manager snap-in tool (see Figure 9.1). You can determine whether the client is going to receive plain text message bodies, HTML message bodies, or a combination of the two.

Microsoft has introduced a new message format unique to Exchange 2000 called the Transport Neutral Encapsulation Format (TNEF). TNEF provides one way of expressing rich-text data in Outlook 2000 messages in a MIME format. This format is a binary attachment on a message and only MAPI clients such as Outlook 2000 or earlier versions know how to decode this format. When messages are sometimes sent between servers in different organizations, it's hard to guarantee the integrity of Outlook rich-text data, and some data such as OLE objects will not be expressed in standard MIME format. This is where the TNEF format can help. You can configure the Internet Message Format in System Manager to determine whether outgoing messages will be converted to MIME, UUEncode (Unix-to-Unix Encode), or TNEF formats. Just remember that this configuration applies only to MAPI-style messages because a native MIME message is never converted using these options.

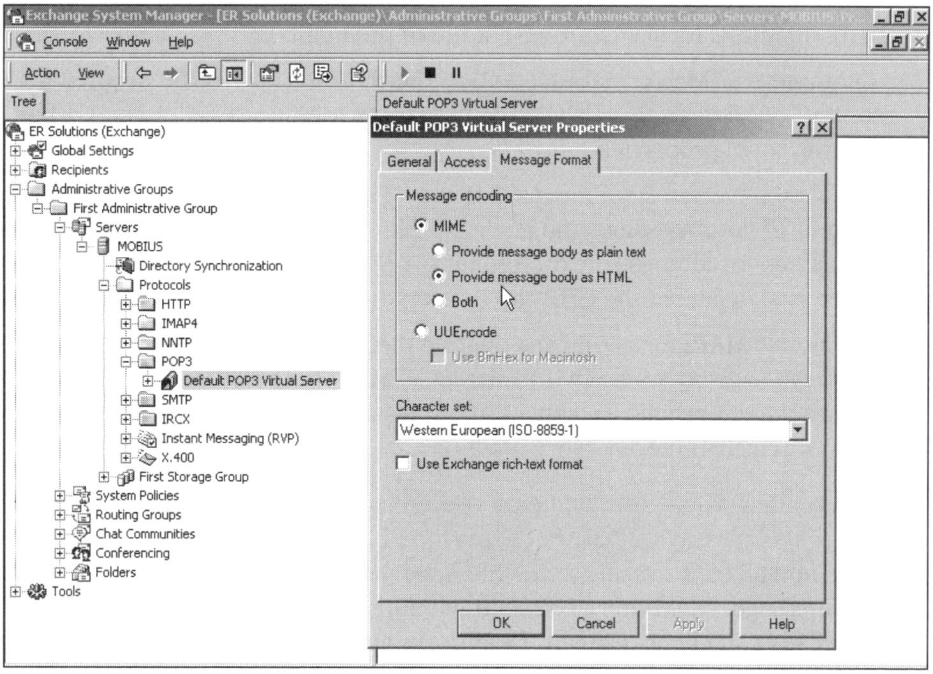

Figure 9.1 The Message Format tab for the POP3 Virtual Server in System Manager.

NOTE: *Because Exchange 2000 uses the SMTP protocol to communicate between servers, all MAPI messages are first converted to TNEF format before being sent to another server. If you send a TNEF-formatted message using protocols such as HTTP, NNTP, or SMTP, it is stored as a MAPI-based message in the EDB file of the message store database and not the STM portion of the database.*

When using the OWA 2000, know that it will not retrieve or create any native MIME content. OWA allows a browser such as IE 5 to request messages from any Exchange 2000 server and the server converts these email messages into Web pages for display within your browser. The end result for OWA is a MAPI-based message, not MIME. It is important to know the types of formats that Exchange 2000 uses to store messages in its databases. At any given time, a message exists in three basic formats: MIME, MIME converted, or MAPI. So, remember the following principles concerning these formats:

- If a MAPI client requests a MIME message, Exchange 2000 converts this message to a MIME-converted state and creates an entry in the EDB database attachment table. The original MIME content is left in the STM file of the mailbox store.
- Because every mailbox has both an EDB file and an STM file, it's important to know that the properties for the message body in the EDB file don't hold the actual message. The EDB files reference the location of the original message body (in MIME format) in the STM file of the mailbox.
- A complete MIME format means that the STM file stores the original MIME content of all messages. The EDB file stores message headers and other informational properties.
- A MIME-converted state means that the STM file contains the original MIME content of your message and the EDB file stores all message headers. The properties for all message attachments are stored in the attachments table, which is also part of the EDB file of every mailbox.
- A complete MAPI format means that the message body and all other properties of the message are found in the messages table of the EDB file for the mailbox. All attachment properties and data for messages are stored in the attachments table of the EDB file for every mailbox.

Understanding these formats helps you understand what happens when clients modify email messages. If MAPI clients modify an email message, it stays in MAPI format, and all data relating to the message is taken away from the STM file. The entire message—the body and its attachments—is saved in MAPI format in the mailbox store. If clients use MIME-conforming protocols to modify an email message, the message stays in MIME format. Always be aware of situations in which you can't access native MIME content. For instance, some administrators use the Move Mailbox tool (found in Exchange 5.5) to move users between servers. In this case, all messages are in a MIME format, but any message that happens to fall across an X.400 connector is converted to a MAPI-based format. To summarize, Exchange 2000 handles MIME messages in a much different way than previous versions of Exchange Server. There are fewer conversions to MAPI formats and more message integrity for your users.

If the MIME format dictates how messages are organized, then S/MIME dictates how encryption information and digital certificates can be included as part of all message bodies. Establishing an S/MIME design means establishing a PKI, which is an overall system using digital certificates and CAs to authenticate all users participating in electronic communications such as email. You use the Windows 2000 Certificate Services to establish your PKI, and the Exchange 2000 Key Management Service (KM Service) to deploy S/MIME using the Outlook 2000 client. The Outlook client is responsible for encrypting (or sealing) and signing all messages.

Digital certificates are objects containing two important pieces of information: a public key and a subject (or owner) of the certificate. A CA tries to verify the relationship between a public key and the organization that owns the related private key. The Windows 2000 PKI uses certificates that conform to the industry standard X.509 version 3 standard; however, other forms of certificates exist (most notably, those that conform to the Pretty Good Privacy standard). The CA is a trusted organization that issues certificates to other organizations based on established criteria called *policies* that are published in a *certification practice statements* document. The main types of CAs used in a PKI design (and ultimately a S/MIME design) include the following:

- *Root CA*—Equivalent to a self-signed CA, in which the public key in a certificate is also the key used to verify the certificate. The issuer of the certificate is equal to the subject or owner of the certificate. All root CAs are unconditionally trusted by clients and all self-signed CAs are automatically root CAs.
- *Subordinate CA*—A situation in which the public key in the certificate is different from the key used to verify the certificate.

Content Management

Email management is becoming increasingly important because the number of viruses appearing in email bodies and attachments is growing at an almost exponential rate. We will first discuss the importance of establishing an active content-management scheme, and then we show you how to proactively defend against malicious viruses that are wreaking havoc with modern messaging systems.

Content management of email does more than help you contain the spread of malicious viruses. Software designed for content-management purposes filters any type of malicious words or code appearing in an email body or attachment.

Administrators design filters so that certain words are intercepted in email messages. These words range from mildly annoying to blatantly offensive. You can use content-management software to filter out mail classified as spam or UCE, so that users are not bombarded with trivial or useless email advertisements. You can also use content-management software to filter out words associated with Web sites that are intended for mature audiences (or sites containing pornographic material). A third use of this type of software involves screening outbound mail so that sensitive information is not propagated involuntarily to the outside world.

NOTE: *Many organizations now adopt specific corporate policies that mandate the type and form of information that can be sent to external parties. All employees implicitly abide by these policies when they first agree to work for the organization and sign employee contracts.*

Content management can be deployed either on SMTP gateways in your company, or directly on your Exchange 5.5 or Exchange 2000 Servers. You can also use content management on your email clients. Most products are designed to implement content management on SMTP gateways that connect directly to an Exchange 2000 Server; however, more and more vendors are designing content-management software to run directly on an Exchange 2000 Server.

NOTE: *We've used MailSweeper from Baltimore Technologies as a content manager with great success. This product can be employed on most SMTP Servers that connect to an Exchange 2000 Server via a SMTP Connector. Other similar products worth checking include Mail Essentials for Exchange Server by GFI (**www.gfi.com/me/mailessentials.htm**) and Trend Micro's InterScan VirusWall (**www.antivirus.com/products/isem**).*

If the cost for content-management software becomes prohibitive, you can always use the built-in content-management feature found within the Outlook 2000 client (also known as the Rules Wizard or Inbox Assistant). Outlook also provides Junk Email and Adult Content filters that identify messages based on keywords you select (these filters are less than 100 percent accurate in detection, which makes a commercial content-management package more desirable for some organizations). Even though Outlook allows you to color code offensive material arriving from external sources, you have to implement this one time for each client. This requirement isn't favorable for large client installations.

NOTE: *Inbox rules established with the Rules Wizard are never as flexible as commercial content-management software that is server-based. Rules that are based on the Outlook client are only valid if the Outlook client is actually running on a user's machine. Also, any rules that monitor email content will not be able to move messages to a personal store folder or PST file, which are stored locally on clients' machines. Finally, these rules will not work with the OWA client because you can't configure rules using OWA.*

The Immediate Solutions section "Finding Appropriate Content-Management Software" at the end of this chapter contains important information regarding the selection of content-management software that provides certain minimum features. These features are often present in content-management software but not always present in virus-scanning software. For that reason, you should not always trust your virus-scanning software to perform content-management duties (even though some virus-scanning software now contains content-management plug-ins). For example, virus-scanning software normally doesn't scan information that is encrypted in any form (such as password-protected ZIP files). However, a good content-management program can actually use filters so that these types of files are set aside or "quarantined" for further analysis or action.

TIP: *If you see excessive Unsolicited Commercial Email on your server as a result of using content-management software, you can assume that your Exchange 2000 Server is being used as an "open-relay" server or "spam server." An external user is probably using your mail server to route his mail, including mail classified as UCE. In a worst-case scenario, your servers are also being used to perpetrate DoS attacks on external servers as well.*

Virus Management

Viruses carried by messaging systems during 1999 cost most businesses nearly $8 billion of lost revenue. They also incurred expenses in dealing with eradication of this malicious code. Most virus-protection programs focus on the client side of the organization; however, more and more organizations are now "scanning the horizon" for enterprise-wide, server-based products because an increasing number of viruses are now being spread via LAN/WAN (local area network/wide area network) connections and direct server connections. You should deploy virus-scanning software at various entry points in your organization, just as you should with content-management software.

Regardless of where you deploy this software, you should be familiar with the concepts of virus scanning, including the virus search engine and the virus signature file. The search engine searches all memory looking for actual viruses, while the signature file tries to generate descriptions of virus patterns directly to the search engine. Most antiviral programs use the search engine to find viruses that match the signature file pattern (however, most virus-scanning software cannot prevent the spread of Trojan horse programs, and you may require additional software in order to track and prevent these types of programs). The problem facing most email administrators today is with viruses replicating and propagating at such a fast rate, clients do not have time to update their signature file patterns. That is why some products are now incorporating dedicated "live update" servers so that virus signature files can be updated almost continuously at the push of a button across hundreds of desktops simultaneously.

Microsoft introduced a new virus-scanning Application Programming Interface with Exchange 5.5 using Service Pack 3 (SP3). This API was built specifically with the Exchange architecture in mind and considers such Exchange-specific features as single-instance storage of messages within the Information Store.

NOTE: *This API is used within Exchange 5.5 only if you have SP3 installed; it's also used within Exchange 2000. You should be using SP2 for Windows 2000 Server because Exchange 2000 is so dependent on Windows 2000 Server.*

The scanning API allows Exchange developers to create custom programs that detect or quarantine any destructive messages residing on an Exchange 2000 server. This is represented as a Dynamic Link Library (DLL), which is accessed by the Web Storage System (WSS). So, in essence, the virus-scanning interface works because Exchange 2000 loads a DLL in memory as long as the Information Store (or Web Store) is running. If you implement a virus-scanning DLL on every Exchange 2000 server you own, you definitely will notice downturns in performance because the DLL has to scan every message attachment that enters the WSS. Attachments are stored within an attachment table and single-instance storage within the database is preserved because anyone needing to retrieve the attachment can use a reference pointer to locate the original attachment.

Many third-party vendors have not fully developed a virus-scanning solution that can be directly implemented on an Exchange 2000 Server that is compatible with the virus-scanning API present in Exchange 2000. For this reason, it is best to implement virus-scanning solutions at all SMTP proxies or gateways, or even on all clients themselves. You can't log information regarding messages that contain viruses in Exchange 2000, and, unfortunately, any message that you encrypt cannot be scanned with the virus-scanning API unless you decrypt the message and its attachments.

NOTE: *It is better to run virus-scanning software or Trojan horse–prevention software directly on your servers and not individual workstations, because network traffic will be minimized if the scanning process runs on the server. Also, any infected attachments that are sent to multiple email addresses generate only a single virus alert instead of multiple virus alerts (which occurs if infected emails are able to reach users' desktops).*

You should make sure that users in your organization are educated about how viruses start and how they are propagated using common email clients such as Outlook 2000 or Outlook Express. Not every virus can or will spread as email attachments because some of them are written in a scripting language such as JavaScript or VBScript. Educate your users about the differences between a virus and a worm. The latter is any program that propagates itself over regular network connections automatically (without direct user intervention). On the other hand, a Trojan horse requires some kind of intervention, such as users clicking on an

EXE file, to start malicious applications within their networked environment. Most viruses in existence today are either worms or Trojan horses (and ironically, many virus-scanning programs are not designed to scan thoroughly for these Trojan horses. A Trojan horse program could contain a destructive worm that runs automatically to infect vulnerable computer systems without any user intervention).

TIP: *To gain a better understanding of these various types of viruses, consult any antivirus vendor's Web site, such as* ***www.mcafee.com*** *or* ***www.symantec.com****. For security information that is time-sensitive and considered critical, check out* ***www.symantec.com/avcenter/security/****.*

Scanning for viruses on the client side is the most common counterattack attempted by many Exchange administrators. Many client-side virus-scanning software products try to check all files for known virus signatures as these files are being written to a hard disk. You want to use email clients that have security features built-in, such as Outlook 2000. If you use Outlook 2000 Service Release 1 (SR-1), you can tell Outlook to automatically store certain attachment files on the hard disk before they are opened by the user. No matter which client you use, make sure you always update your virus-scanning software (for instance, Symantec uses the LiveUpdate feature to do this automatically for users with an Internet connection available).

Because virus attacks were becoming so prevalent, Microsoft released an Attachment Security Patch for Outlook 97, 98, and 2000 in 1999 that required users to save certain attachments to disk before opening or running them. In June of 2000, Microsoft released the Outlook Email Security Update, which not only blocked users' access to malicious file types, it also displayed warning boxes when that malicious code tried to access information in Outlook. The Outlook Email Security Update provides the following security precautions:

- *Increased default security settings*—The default Internet Security Zone setting is increased from a setting of "Internet" to "Restricted Sites." Active scripting within a restricted site is disabled by default.
- *Object Model guard*—Prompts a user with a warning dialog box if any external program tries to access their Outlook Address book.
- *Email attachment security*—Prevents users from accessing certain file types if these files are sent as email attachments. These files include executable files and .vbs files (representing VBScript files).

NOTE: *Using the Outlook Email Security Update will cause performance degradations within the Outlook client because it is providing a higher level of security. It should be noted, however, that this update was not created to address specific vulnerabilities within the Outlook client itself.*

Remember that Outlook security depends on the version being used and the updates that you apply. For instance, Outlook 2000 is more susceptible to virus threats because it is more programmable than earlier versions of Outlook. Outlook 97 cannot even render simple HTML commands, so the risk of "infection" from a virus is lower than the risk presented to Outlook 2000.Plain text emails and Rich Text Format (RTF) emails are always safe to view; it's only their attachments that are presenting the real threat for your network. HTML messages pose an extremely high risk of infection from a virus unless you configure your Security Zones properly in your browser. They are capable of carrying harmful scripts or ActiveX controls that are viruses in disguise, and ActiveX controls will run unless you manually disable them in your browser settings.

NOTE: *Two actions you can perform to protect your systems include disabling the default action for VBScript files (appearing as .vbs files) and disabling Windows Scripting Host, which can serve as an open invitation to .vbs worms. For detailed information regarding these actions, please visit* ***www.zdnet.com/zdhelp/stories/main/0,5594,2568111,00.html****.*

Server Issues Related to DNS and TCP/IP

When monitoring and troubleshooting Exchange 2000, it helps to understand the interrelationships and dependencies between Exchange Server and the DNS service found within Windows 2000 Server. Ultimately, both DNS and Exchange Server are benefiting from services provided by the TCP/IP protocol stack. You cannot install Exchange 2000 without Active Directory (AD), and AD will not function properly without DNS. However, there are other reasons that Exchange 2000 is so dependent on this naming service. Exchange Server uses the DNS service to query Global Catalog (GC) Servers in a Windows 2000 forest, and it also uses DNS to find addresses of other foreign messaging servers. DNS is needed anytime Exchange needs to send a message. Other scenarios in which DNS is needed include message routing, FE/BE communications, and Instant Messaging (IM).

DNS Used for AD Queries

All objects in your messaging environment are ultimately stored in the AD database of Windows 2000 Server. This includes all your mailbox servers, public folders, users, and connectors. Exchange Server accesses this information on an ongoing basis by using the DNS service to search for specific resource records (SRV records), and by querying for servers that host LDAP (Lightweight Directory Access Protocol). Most GC Servers are used to host both SRV records and the LDAP protocol. You are not required to use a GC Server to host LDAP; however, Exchange will be looking for this type of server, so many administrators combine all these functions on one dedicated GC Server. The GC Server keeps a record of properties and information relevant to your AD structure, including site names and domain names. When Exchange 2000 seeks SRV records on a DNS Server, it knows that all SRV records will contain the FQDN (fully qualified domain name) of a domain controller (DC) that is acting as a GC Server. A query for the name of a GC Server also provides its IP address.

NOTE: *Most DNS queries normally are cached in memory on the Exchange Server, so subsequent queries to a DNS server won't take as long as the initial query. This time period is known as the Time To Live (TTL) period and specifies how long a response to a DNS query will remain valid.*

DNS Used for FE/BE Configuration

You can deploy a FE/BE configuration if you have many users who are accessing a mailbox or public folder server over the Internet through a firewall or Proxy Server. This FE/BE configuration uses DNS to query AD for a server that contains the recipient's mailbox or public folder. Suppose you have one FE Server that receives a message over the Internet from one of your employees who is working at home and using a dial-up connection to connect to your network. The FE Server attempts to locate the corresponding BE Server that holds the user's mailbox so it can pass this message along. It does this by querying AD and performing a DNS lookup for the LDAP Server (which is most likely a GC Server, as stated before). The FE Server queries DNS for the name and IP address of the BE Server, or it uses a messaging bridgehead server to relay this message to the appropriate mailbox. FE Servers not only pass messages from the Internet, they also retrieve messages directly from a BE Server. This happens every time a user on the Internet is accessing information already stored in her mailbox server's Information Store using Internet protocols such as HTTP, POP3, or IMAP4. The FE Server queries AD for the name of the BE Server, and then queries DNS for the IP address of the BE Server. If a successful match is found, direct communication is established between the FE Server and the BE Server as long as the client connection remains open.

Integrating AD Service with Existing DNS Servers

In some cases, you will be concerned with integrating AD services with an existing Windows NT DNS Server, or with a non-Windows DNS Server. Whatever the case might be, the DNS Server has to support AD and its associated SRV records. It's also a good idea to plan for the dynamic update feature of Windows 2000 DNS. Introducing AD services into existing DNS infrastructures means introducing a new AD namespace. Either this new namespace joins your existing DNS namespace or it replaces your existing namespace. Much depends on whether your existing DNS hierarchy is configured on a machine running Windows NT 4 DNS or a machine running some other version of the DNS software.

NOTE: *An example of a non-Microsoft DNS configuration is Checkpoint Software's METAIP 4.1 DHCP/DNS package, which integrates the DHCP (Dynamic Host Configuration Protocol) and DNS services on a single machine, while also providing capacities for RADIUS (Remote Access Dial-Up User Service) authentication and LDAP searches.*

If you are currently using a Windows NT 4 DNS implementation, you should upgrade your network to the Windows 2000 implementation of DNS. However, if you are using a non-Microsoft version of DNS (which is based on the Berkeley BIND 8.x software upon which DNS is modeled), you have to determine whether this can be upgraded to the Windows 2000 DNS implementation that supports SRV records and dynamic updates. If it cannot be upgraded, your only course of action might be to add another DNS Server that supports SRV resource records and dynamic updates, and then delegate certain DNS zones to this new server.

NOTE: *SRV records in DNS refer to resource records that specify the location of a server for a specific protocol and domain. This type of DNS record allows an administrator to use several servers for one single domain so they can move services from one host to another host with little administrative effort. They can also designate one host as a primary server for a given service (such as FTP) and other servers in the domain to function as backup servers for this service. SRV records help alleviate the condition of having to know the exact address of a server in order to contact it.*

When working with non-Microsoft DNS Servers (such as Unix Servers), slowly introduce Windows 2000 DNS servers as secondary servers so you can perform a zone transfer from a master server to a secondary server. The zone transfer process should complete without destroying or corrupting any associated resource records. After zone transfers are completed, the secondary DNS zones can be upgraded to an AD integrated zone, so that the original master DNS Servers can be safely removed from your network. When selecting or configuring zones, remember three basic types of zones are available:

- *Standard primary zone*—The master copy of a new zone stored in a standard text file. You can manage a primary zone on the same machine in which you created this zone.
- *Standard secondary zone*—A replica or copy of an existing zone, these are read-only and stored in standard text files. You cannot configure a secondary zone without configuring a primary zone first. When creating a secondary zone, you have to specify a *master server* capable of transferring zone information to a DNS server containing a standard secondary zone. Secondary zones help provide fault tolerance for primary zones.
- *AD-integrated zone*—A master copy of a new zone, this uses AD services to replicate zone files. You won't find standard zone transfers with this type of zone; rather, zone files are replicated in conjunction with AD database replication.

When deploying Exchange 2000 in a new AD or Windows 2000 DNS environment, your goal should be to design an efficient topology for replication while minimizing the overall replication traffic that results. You can do this by properly configuring your domain and site topology so that every AD domain has one DNS zone associated with it. These zones are usually placed on a Windows 2000 DNS Server running on DCs or GC Servers in that particular domain. All zones should be AD-integrated (as described in the last bullet of the previous list). Also, your DNS Servers should be planned with fault tolerance in mind by using at least two DCs in every domain (or at least one DC in every Windows 2000 site).

Exchange 2000 and TCP/IP

You know that all underlying services used by Exchange 2000 depend on the operation of the TCP/IP protocol stack. Even the SMTP native transport protocol is a member of this protocol stack, as are NNTP and HTTP. You can troubleshoot basis connectivity to other hosts by using the PING tool from a command prompt with a known IP address, as the following example shows:

```
c:/>PING 10.2.24.128
```

Both Exchange 5.5 and Exchange 2000 use various TCP and UDP ports (see Table 9.1).

Table 9.1 Ports used by Exchange 5.5 and Exchange 2000.

Port Number	Name of Service or Protocol Using this Port
25	SMTP service
53	DNS service
80	HTTP protocol
102	X.400 service
135	RPC (Remote Procedure Call) service
143	IMAP4 service
110	POP3 service
119	NNTP service
389	LDAP protocol
443	HTTP with SSL
465	SMTP with SSL
563	NNTP with SSL
993	IMAP4 with SSL
995	POP3 with SSL
6667	IRC (Internet Relay Chat) protocol

Knowing which ports are used by a particular service or protocol can greatly aid in troubleshooting certain services that are not working properly because two services could be in contention for the same port number, or could be using a port number that is reserved for another well-known service (the sidebar below introduces the concept of certain well-known port numbers being used specifically by Trojan horse programs such as Deep Throat and Happy99).

Port Numbers Used by Well-Known Trojan Horses

Trojan horse programs are capable of using any TCP or UDP port on most computer systems, but some of them are directed at well-known TCP/UDP ports, for example port 31337 or port 12345. Sometimes you will find probes directed against TCP/UDP ports that are not usually used. This can be an indication of a malicious user trying to connect to a Trojan horse inside your network. Table 9.2 lists some default ports used by some well-known Trojan horse programs as of the early part of 2001 (this list is by no means exhaustive; please visit **www.sans.org** for more information on port numbers used by Trojan horse programs).

Table 9.2 Port numbers used by some Trojan horse programs.

Trojan Horse Program	TCP Port Used
Death	port 2
Senna Spy FTP Server	port 20
Blade Runner	port 21
Fire HacKer	port 23
Happy99, Antigen	port 25
Deep Throat	port 41
DMSetup	port 59
Firehotcker	port 79
CGI Backdoor, RingZero	port 80
Hidden Port	port 99
ProMail Trojan	port 110
Happy99	port 119
NetTaxi	port 142
Infector	port 146
Backage	port 334
TCP Wrappers Trojan	port 421
RPC Backdoor	port 514
Net Administrator, Phase Zero	port 555

(continued)

Table 9.2 Port numbers used by some Trojan horse programs *(continued).*

Trojan Horse Program	TCP Port Used
Secret Service	port 605
Attack FTP, Cain & Abel	port 666
AimSPY	port 777
Dark Shadow	port 911
Doly Trojan	ports 1010, 1011, 1012, 1015, 1016
WinHole	ports 1080, 1081, 1082, 1083
Remote Administration Tool (RAT)_	ports 1095, 1097, 1098, 1099
BackDoor-G, SubSeven	port 1243
VooDoo Doll	port 1245
Matrix	port 1269
Millennium Worm	port 1338

For example, the POP3 protocol combined with SSL uses port 995, but so does the IRC protocol with SSL. It is possible to change port numbers if conflicts ever arise, or if you want a select group of users to make connections using certain protocols, such as X.400. You might even be configuring a firewall that is refusing to accept a port number that Exchange Server uses by default (see the Immediate Solutions "Setting TCP/IP Port Numbers for Firewalls in Mixed-Mode Exchange Environments" for an example of this). Table 9.3 shows TCP/IP ports that are specific only to Exchange 2000 and Windows 2000.

Table 9.3 Ports specific to Exchange 2000 and Windows 2000 Server.

Port Number	Service or Protocol Using this Port
80	IM service opening a session using RVP (Rendezvous Protocol)
88	The Kerberos authentication protocol
379	Site Replication service using the LDAP protocol
522	User Locater service for Microsoft NetMeeting
691	Link State Information update service
995	POP3 or IRC protocol over SSL
1720	Videoconferencing service
1731	Audioconferencing service
3268	LDAP lookups on GC Servers
3269	LDAP lookups on GC Server with SSL enabled

Server Issues Related to Delegation of Rights

This section covers three topics related to delegating control of your Exchange 2000 Server to certain individuals within your organization. It also deals with protecting your Exchange environment by allowing users limited access to information stored on your server.

It All Began with the Design of AD

Any Exchange 2000 deployment begins with proper AD planning and design. You have become familiar with creating domains, sites, and organizational units (OUs). You recall the difference between a physical AD object and a logical AD object where a domain represents the former object, whereas an OU represents the latter type of object. You designed your organization with an emphasis of "location over group;" by using a more *geopolitical* design structure. Creating domains matched to locations helped you created OUs within these domains. You then configured the Delegation of Control Wizard to assign permissions to these OU objects to certain users or groups. The AD infrastructure has taken shape. The AD design phase incorporated the following salient points:

- Created global security groups within your OUs to make assigning permissions an easy task, so users can be easily added or removed.
- Located all servers that communicate with each other in the same Windows 2000 site because all these servers expect fast high-bandwidth connections between themselves, and replication traffic is minimized.
- Included at least two GC Servers for every AD site you have to facilitate the logon process and also provide some measure of fault tolerance.
- Always preferred an OU hierarchy to a domain hierarchy because it's easier to move users or groups between different OUs than it is to move the same objects between different domains. It's also easier to apply administrative permissions to an OU than to a domain.

Then Came Exchange System Management

After all the AD elements were in place, the next logical phase of the Exchange 2000 deployment centered around creating and implementing administrative groups and storage groups to further delegate rights to your Exchange 2000 Server. The AD schema was updated by running the setup program with the **/ForestPrep** switch, which created all Exchange Server groups and also the Organization object in the AD naming context. Installing Exchange 2000 created a default administrative group called First Administrative Group, which was not visible until you enabled it in the properties of your organizational object in the System Manager snap-in. The sites found in Exchange 5.5 no longer function as administrative boundaries for Exchange 2000 organizations because administrative groups into which servers are placed have replaced them. System management now involves creating an OU, creating a group within the OU, placing certain accounts you want to manage within this group, and applying the group to an administrative group. After the administrative groups were in place, you could then give control to various administrators in your organization by using the Delegation of Control Wizard for each administrative group in System Manager. You assigned one of four administrative roles to each administrative group:

- *Exchange View Only Administrator*—Allows users to view configuration information but does not allow them to make any changes.
- *Exchange Administrator*—Allows users to fully administer the Exchange Server without being able to modify permissions.
- *Exchange Full Administrator*—Allows users to fully administer the Exchange Server and also modify permissions. This allows users to control access to Exchange 2000.

Delegating Control

Recall that the Delegation of Control Wizard controls access to Exchange without giving anyone local administrative access or rights to modify the local Registry. If users need such rights, they must become members of the local administrators group for the machines they want to manage. Delegating control to a user or group means that those users or groups do not necessarily have to belong to global security groups such as Domain Admins or Enterprise Admins. Be careful at what level you delegate permissions, however, because using the Delegation of Control Wizard at the Organization level means that users will have certain administrative rights throughout your entire organizational structure.

TIP: *Besides the three roles listed previously, you can also assign a* mailbox manager *role to users or groups so that they can mailbox-enable other users or groups. However, anyone possessing this role must also become a member of the Account Operators local security group.*

You also defined access limits and policies on SGs configured on each server. SGs allowed you to run multiple private and public databases on each server, with each server containing no more than four such SGs, and each SG containing no more than five databases each. Every Exchange 2000 Server ran only one instance of the Store.exe service or process in which these SGs could function. Each SG was a single instance of the Extensible Storage Engine (ESE) database structure, which ran all databases in that SG. Also, every SG was associated with only one set of transaction log files, regardless of the number of databases in that SG. Ultimately, each SG held a different class of users or groups and each was configured with various recipient or server policies. Policies covered such things as allowable message size, allowable mailbox size, or deleted-item retention periods for mailbox data. A goal in this phase of server management was to group all users by type within SGs to preserve the Exchange feature of single-instance storage, so that each Information Store retained only one physical copy of every message while recipients maintained pointers to that message.

Even More Granular Control for Exchange 2000

It is possible to define controls to AD elements and Exchange 2000 objects such as SGs and OUs. You can define even more granular levels of access control by restricting how certain users can view information within your organization. Specifically, you can manage Global Address List (GAL) views and public folder views.

Exchange 2000 uses an access control model similar to that used by Windows 2000 Server. Windows 2000 Server allows you to control access to most objects in your network by assigning *security descriptors* to objects in AD. This descriptor lists all users who have access to an object as well as the permissions assigned to those users. Exchange 2000 uses a different access control model than that employed in Exchange 5.5 and bases this control on various levels, including the container, item, or property level of an object. The main difference between access control in Exchange 5.5 and Exchange 2000 is that the latter uses a more direct relationship between a user account stored in AD and the mailbox for that account stored on the Exchange Server.

The reason you want to define these controls for your GAL is because it contains a view of all mail-enabled objects in your enterprise by default, and you might not want all users to benefit from viewing this information. The GAL actually allows users to query AD using LDAP on TCP port 389 and combines information stored on all GC Servers in your Windows 2000 forest. Creating some type of partitions within your GAL might help users confine themselves to a restricted portion so they are not overwhelmed with information when performing a search for a user or group. This means you can create multiple GALs, each containing separate access control rules for different classes of users.

Filtering GAL views usually reduces administrative headaches; however, it could cause one potential problem. Suppose that Bob and Sue are internal users for the same email organization but they appear in different administrative groups or OUs. You now filter the GAL so each user sees a different view of the GAL in his Outlook client. If Bob tries to send Sue an email message using only her name, Outlook rejects this message if Sue does not appear in Bob's GAL. Bob can work around this issue by using Sue's SMTP proxy address instead of just her name.

Public folders also create a problem for many administrators because they serve as "dumping grounds" for data that is not relevant or not designed for those public folders. Users see them as "storage objects" for unused email or documents. You should design a public folder hierarchy consisting of parent folders and associated child folders. For example, you could create a parent folder called Sales with child folders broken down geopolitically by locations such as North, South, East, or West. Exchange 2000 provides multiple ways of configuring access to public folders by viewing the properties of each public folder appearing in System Manager. Example configurations include hiding a public folder from all address lists or making this folder invisible to users who should not have rights to access it.

Server Issues Related to Migration from Exchange 5.5 Server

The migration issues covered here include public folder interoperability between Exchange 2000 and Exchange 5.5, and planning and configuring the ADC in Exchange 2000. Both issues involve objects known as *connection agreements* and both issues involve mixed-mode Exchange Server organizations.

A mixed-mode organization involves any combination of Exchange 2000 and Exchange 5.5. When you decide to upgrade or migrate your organization to Exchange 2000, you have to migrate all Exchange 5.5 directory information to the Windows 2000 AD database. Migrating information is desirable to manually replicating or recreating important user and contact information maintained on legacy Exchange 5.5 Servers. To aid in this migratory process, Microsoft has provided the ADC service tool, which runs on all Windows 2000 servers and allows for synchronization and replication of information between the Exchange 5.5 and Windows 2000 directories. We first discuss the implications of implementing the ADC, and then incorporate our findings into public folder interoperability between Exchange 5.5 and Exchange 2000.

The ADC comes in two versions: a Windows 2000 version and an Exchange 2000 version. The Windows 2000 ADC allows for replication of object information between Exchange 5.5 and the Windows 2000 AD, while also permitting the Windows 2000 administrator to perform administration on the Exchange 5.5 directory. The Exchange 2000 ADC replicates the same directory information as the Windows 2000 ADC, but it also permits replication of configuration data between Exchange 5.5 and Exchange 2000.

TIP: *Just because two versions of the ADC exist doesn't mean you have to install both versions simultaneously. In fact, installing the Exchange 2000 ADC overwrites the Windows 2000 ADC if it's already present.*

You can configure replication between the directories by using a connection agreement. Replicating information helps users query the AD for objects that are found in their GALs. The GAL in Exchange 5.5 does not use AD because users query the Directory database existing on the Exchange 5.5 Servers. Remember that the basic function of AD is to replace the original DIR.EDB directory database file on all Exchange 5.5 servers. ADC can manage one or more connection agreements simultaneously, and multiple connection agreements can be configured even if you only have one Exchange 5.5 site. Ideally, multiple connection agreements should communicate with multiple Exchange 5.5 sites.

NOTE: *An Exchange 5.5 "site" is somewhat different than a Windows 2000 "site." The former is a physical boundary formed by a group of Exchange 5.5 Servers all communicating via permanent high-bandwidth connections. The latter refers to a range of IP subnets consisting of servers that communicate using high-bandwidth connections. However, Exchange 5.5 maintained separate directory stores on each server while Windows 2000 integrates all objects in one central AD directory.*

All connection agreements contain information, such as the target servers being used, the objects being replicated, and a replication schedule. It's important to define the direction of replication because you can replicate either *from* the Exchange 5.5 directory or *to* the Exchange 5.5 directory. However, Exchange 5.5 proved a bit inflexible in that it only used one container to store most of its recipient data—this was usually the Recipients container found in the Exchange 5.5 Administrator utility. Exchange 2000 allows for the creation of multiple containers stored in AD, namely OU containers. These concepts affect your connection agreement design and you are not forced to replicate objects into only one container. It is possible to synchronize multiple Exchange 5.5 Recipient containers into one AD container, or conversely, multiple AD containers into one Exchange 5.5 Recipient container.

Connection agreements are defined as either one way or two way. A one-way agreement means you are replicating information from Exchange 5.5 to AD or vice versa. A two-way agreement includes both ways between Exchange 5.5 and AD. Most of the time you will select a one-way connection agreement so every time you make modifications to your Exchange 5.5 directory, AD is automatically updated. Only one connection agreement is needed to replicate an entire Exchange 5.5 organization to AD, but you should consider multiple connection agreements only because replication can take a long time, especially in large Exchange 5.5 sites. Using multiple connection agreements to replicate groups of objects at a time is more efficient and reduces replication traffic, especially if you schedule replication for off-peak times. Deploying connection agreements means deciding where you want to administer most of your directory objects. If you want to administer all objects directly from AD, you can use the Windows 2000 Active Directory Users and Computers snap-in. However, you must make sure that your connection agreements are configured as one way and that each connection agreement has write permissions to each Exchange 5.5 directory. In this scenario, any new objects created in AD can be automatically written and replicated to each Exchange 5.5 directory. On the other hand, if you want to use the legacy Exchange 5.5 Administrator program to manage objects such as users or groups, your connection agreements will be configured as *one way from Exchange* and the connection agreement will not have write permissions to the Exchange 5.5 directory.

The most flexible arrangement is to create separate subcontainers under your Recipients container in Exchange 5.5 for users, groups, or distribution lists (DLs), and replicate each subcontainer to an associated AD container using a separate connection agreement. This type of design allows you to create new accounts in both Windows 2000 and Exchange 5.5, especially when using two-way connection agreements. A two-way connection agreement gives one directory write permissions to the other directory. The salient points regarding connection agreements are as follows:

- If you have only one Exchange 5.5 site, configure a one-way connection agreement to preserve this same configuration in AD.
- Anyone possessing Enterprise Admin or Schema Admin rights can install a connection agreement by pointing one end to the Exchange 5.5 directory store (DS) and the other end to the Windows 2000 AD service.
- You have to use the Exchange 2000 ADC when deploying Exchange 2000 because it extends the functionality of the "basic" Windows 2000 ADC that ships with the Windows 2000 Server setup program. The Windows 2000 ADC replicates recipient information, whereas the Exchange 2000 ADC replicates configuration information as well.
- Exchange 2000 can deliver messages natively to Exchange 5.5 Servers using RPCs (not the SMTP protocol) because it stores information about the Exchange 5.5 configuration using special connection agreements known as Configuration Connection Agreements (or ConfigCA).

NOTE: *The ConfigCA replicates information between the Configuration container of Exchange 5.5 and the configuration-naming context found within AD.*

- A ConfigCA is automatically created every time you upgrade an Exchange 5.5 Server to Exchange 2000, or when you install Exchange 2000 into an Exchange 5.5 site. Only the Exchange 2000 ADC creates this ConfigCA, not the Windows 2000 ADC.
- Decide if you are going to use AD or Exchange 5.5 to manage all objects. Even though AD can manage all objects, sometimes you'll want to use a

mixed-management model. However, using both the Exchange 5.5 Administrator tool and the AD Users and Computers tool to modify the same object attributes results in modification conflicts or errors. Whoever modified the object last prevails.

- The two major types of connection agreements that are viewable using the AD Connector Management snap-in are user connection agreements and configuration connection agreements. User connection agreements replicate recipient objects and their data, whereas configuration connection agreements replicate configuration information specific to Exchange 2000.

The ADC is an important component to understand because it can be used to replicate and synchronize mailboxes, public folders, and other important system data. *When* you replicate something, however, is more important than *what* you replicate. The ADC can be configured to replicate objects as frequently as every five seconds, which definitely impacts your server or network performance with increased CPU loads and packet traffic. The ADC uses the LDAP protocol to access the different directories involved; these constant LDAP queries might cause severe performance degradations in large networks.

TIP: *Even though Microsoft strongly suggests not modifying the Registry for any purpose, you* can *use the Registry to successfully modify this default synchronization time interval of "every 5 seconds." Open the Registry editor and add a DWORD value called* ***Synch Sleep Delay*** *to the following key:* ***HKEY_LOCAL_MACHINE\SYSTEM\CurrentControlSet\Services\MSADC\Parameters****. Set the value of this DWORD to something higher than 5 (for example 600 seconds or 10 minutes) so Exchange 2000 will wait longer between replication intervals.*

You might wonder whether it's possible to control the mapping of individual object attributes because the main purpose of the ADC is to synchronize object attributes between the Exchange 5.5 directory and the AD directory. *Attributes* include such things as addresses, names, or telephone numbers for various objects, such as users. Microsoft offers a snap-in for the ADC called the Active Directory Connector Manager, which presents a predefined selection of attributes that you can include in your synchronization schedule. Such attributes as names and addresses are synchronized automatically to AD when you establish your connection agreements between a container in Exchange 5.5 and a target container in AD (such as an OU). If you want to change this default list of attributes to include custom attributes, you have to modify your default ADC policy by using the Active Directory Connector Management snap-in tool. Modifying your default policy means including attributes not synchronized by default, or preventing synchronization of attributes that will not be needed in AD if those attributes are being replicated from alternative sources or directories (such as names of custom recipients that will not be mailbox-enabled in Windows 2000). Figure 9.2 shows the attributes you can select when synchronizing from Exchange 5.5 to AD by using the From Exchange tab of the AD Connector Management Properties pages.

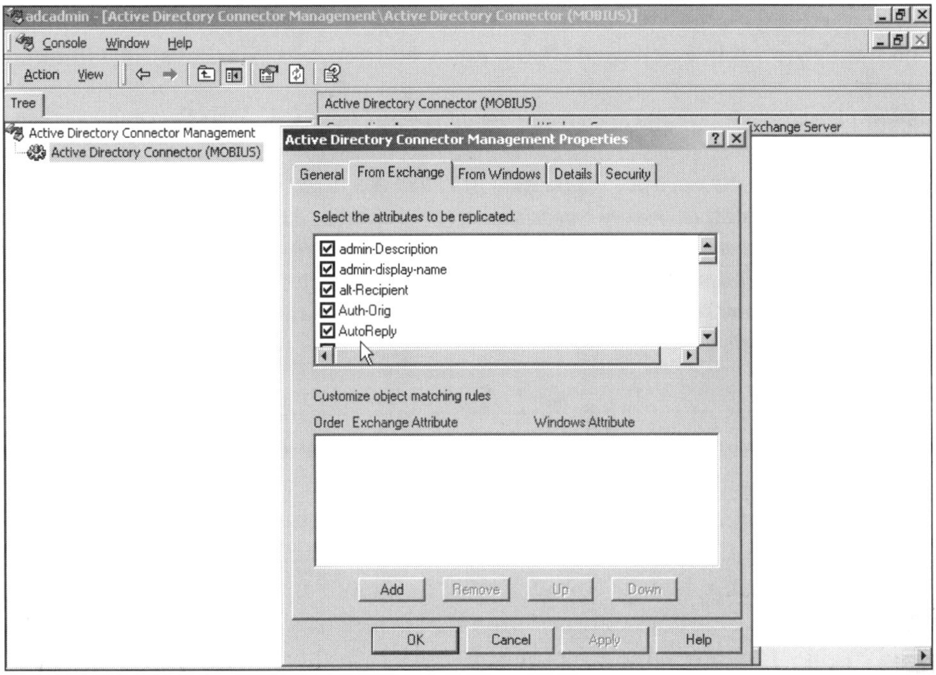

Figure 9.2 Selecting attributes on the From Exchange tab of the Active Directory Connector Management snap-in.

You define all attribute-mapping conventions on the Default ADC Policy; the ADC enforces these conventions for every connection agreement associated with it. The important point to remember is that you can set individual mapping rules for every connection agreement you configure. When you first install the ADC, multiple attribute-mapping tables are populated from certain text files that appear on the Exchange 2000 installation CD. These files are known as local.map and remote.map and are found in the *ADC\i386* directory of the CD. These files contain mapping rules that populate various attributes or characteristics of the Default ADC Policy. For example, the local.map files affect the **msExchServer2SchemaMap** attribute of the Default ADC Policy, which defines attribute-mapping rules from Exchange 5.5 to AD. You normally shouldn't interfere with attribute-mapping conventions associated with the Default ADC Policy because all object attributes in Exchange Server 5.5 have automatic associated counterparts in AD. Installing the ADC defines default mappings between the two directory services.

Finally, consider the interoperability of public folders between Exchange 5.5 and Exchange 2000. A small but subtle link connects the function of the ADC with the concept of assigning permissions to public folders in Exchange 2000. To understand this link, you have to appreciate the changes in access control required by

Exchange 2000. Native Windows 2000 domains will properly support public folder administration in Exchange 2000 compared to mixed Windows 2000 domains.

WARNING! We strongly urge you to consider the differences between a mixed environment and a native environment as it applies to both Exchange 2000 and Windows 2000 Server. A mixed Windows 2000 domain implies the existence of pre–Windows 2000 DCs in the same domain or forest. A mixed Exchange 2000 organization implies a coexistence with Exchange 5.5 Servers. A native Windows 2000 domain implies the complete absence of any Windows NT 4 or earlier DCs, whereas a native Exchange 2000 organization implies the complete absence of any Exchange 5.5 Servers. Notice that you can run a mixed Exchange scenario in a native Windows design, or you can run a native Exchange scenario in a mixed Windows design.

Administration of public folders has changed somewhat from Exchange 5.5. Any mixed Exchange scenario involves replicating and migrating public folders to Exchange 2000. The discussion of connection agreements in the previous paragraph can be extended to public folders because the ADC provides a special connection agreement for public folders (remember that other connection agreements include user connection agreements and configuration connection agreements). This connection agreement is responsible for synchronizing email addresses for Exchange 5.5 public folders into the AD, which allows mailbox-enabled Exchange 2000 users to send email messages to these public folders (as was possible in Exchange 5.5). Problems can arise when replicating public folders between Exchange 5.5 and Exchange 2000 if these objects are serving as recipients for Exchange 5.5 DLs. If you configure a user connection agreement to synchronize an Exchange 5.5 DL into AD, you will discover that AD has created a special type of group object called a universal distribution group. The problem with a universal distribution group is that you cannot include a public folder's email address unless it's specifically defined in AD and user connection agreements are unable to define a public folder's email address. Hence the need for a separate public folder connection agreement.

NOTE: *The original design for connection agreements included the capability for all user connection agreements to automatically replicate public-folder email addresses; however, this design requirement was removed at the last minute, leading to the development of the public-folder connection agreement.*

Public-folder connection agreements synchronize mail addresses of all Exchange 5.5 public folders to AD or the mail addresses of Exchange 2000 public folders to the Exchange 5.5 directory. They also help you administer Exchange 5.5 public folders using the System Manager MMC snap-in, or Exchange 2000 public folders using the Exchange 5.5 Administrator program. All public folders have email addresses associated with them by default in Exchange 5.5, and all public folder directory entries are also hidden from the GAL by default. You should understand all default behaviors for public folders when working in a mixed Exchange 2000 environment. Microsoft has made the configuration of public-folder connection agreements much easier than that needed for user connection agreements. All public-folder connection agreements are automatically configured as two-way connection agreements by default.

Public folder permissions are handled differently in Exchange 2000 than in Exchange 5.5. The latter used Access Control Lists (ACLs) to manage access to public folders. This ACL was not considered a distinct property of the public folder. Exchange 2000, on the other hand, considers this ACL as a direct property of the public folder. This property is held in the public folder store and contains security identifiers of all users or groups who have rights to the public folder. Exchange 5.5 used the **Distinguished Name** property of an object to identify all users who had permissions to a public folder configured with an ACL. Exchange 2000, meanwhile, uses the security identifier of an object stored in AD to identify these users, so any ACL data is converted when a public folder is replicated from Exchange 5.5 to an Exchange 2000 public folder store database.

The link between the ADC and public folder replication from Exchange 5.5 to Exchange 2000 becomes important because DLs were used in a public-folder's ACL. In other words, a DL controlled access to public folders. As stated before, this does not mean that you can replicate an Exchange 5.5 DL to AD because Exchange 2000 now uses certain group types to control access to public folders.

Why Group Types Are Confusing in Windows 2000 Server

Certain objects in Exchange 5.5 become other objects when replicated to Exchange 2000. For example, a recipient object in Exchange 5.5 can become either a mail-enabled object or a mailbox-enabled object in AD, depending on whether the new object will merely possess an email address or actually be associated with a mailbox in AD. A custom recipient in Exchange 5.5 always becomes a *mail-enabled* object, not a *mailbox-enabled* object, in AD. However, a DL in Exchange 5.5 becomes a mail-enabled *group object* in AD. Different types of group objects can be defined, either according to group *types* or group *scopes.*

The two categories of group *type* include the following:

- *Security groups*—Used to assign permissions to resources in a Windows 2000 forest structure.
- *Distribution groups*—Used for functions not related to security. A distribution group would be used to send email messages to a group of users all at once. They can never be used to assign permissions to resources.

The three categories of group *scope* include the following:

- *Domain local groups*—Used to assign permissions to resources. You can include members from any domain in your forest, but they can gain access only to resources that are located in the domain where this group was created.

- *Global groups*—Used to organize users with similar access needs. You can include members only from the domain where you created this group, but they can access resources in any domain in your forest.
- *Universal groups*—Used to assign permissions to resources in multiple domains. You can include members from any domain and they can access resources located in any domain in your forest. They are further broken down as follows:
  - *Universal security groups*—Available only when you run Windows 2000 in native mode.
  - *Universal distribution groups*—Available in both Native-mode and mixed-mode Windows 2000 environments, but used mainly in mixed-mode operations for the purpose of sending email messages to multiple users at the same time.

Group types determine *how* groups are used, whereas group scopes determine *where in the network* groups are used. You can convert all your domain local and global groups to universal groups, but only if Windows 2000 is operating in native mode (your domain local or global groups also cannot contain other groups of the same scope if this conversion is to take place). Microsoft recommends the following group strategy to reduce the number of permission assignments you have to make in your organization:

1. Assign users with common needs to a new or existing global group.
2. Create domain local groups for any resources you want shared, such as network printers or files.
3. Add global groups to domain local groups associated with certain resources they need access to.
4. Assign relevant resource permissions to this domain local group from Step 3.

It might seem easier to place users directly into a domain local group and assign this group permission to resources; however, this strategy won't allow them to use resources outside of their local domain. Only members of global groups and universal security groups can access resources in any domain.

NOTE: *Placing users directly in universal groups and assigning permissions directly to them is not always practical either, because you require a native-mode Windows 2000 forest in this scenario and you might want the functionality of a mixed Windows 2000 forest if earlier Windows NT 4 Servers are still present.*

Exchange 2000 has replaced Exchange 5.5 DLs with mail-enabled universal distribution groups. A universal security group can also be mail-enabled and replace this DL, but this can *only* happen if you are administering a native-mode Windows 2000 forest (see the previous sidebar, "Why Group Types Are Confusing in Windows 2000 Server"). For all mixed-mode Windows 2000 forests, you will be working with universal distribution groups, not universal security groups. Distribution groups are used more frequently in these cases because you avoid the possibility of mistakenly granting access to important resources (as automatically happens with security groups). In any case, the ADC synchronizes all Exchange 5.5 DLs into universal distribution groups in AD, and these universal distribution groups cannot control access to public folders in Exchange 2000.

Windows 2000 Server only allows security principals to control access to synchronized objects and universal distribution groups are not considered security principals (universal security groups are security principals because they can log on to a domain). In some cases, a universal distribution group can be converted to a universal security group if public folders are upgraded to Exchange 2000, or when the Outlook client is used to assign permissions to public folders in Exchange 2000. Because universal security groups can enforce access to public folders, it's best to make sure that all your Windows 2000 domains are in Native mode when replicating Exchange 5.5 DLs to AD. If you are setting up user connection agreements to replicate a DL, the ADC tries to alert you if your Windows 2000 domain is not presently in native mode.

Related solutions:	Found on page:
Planning Public Folders	95
Determining the Scope of Groups	131
Creating Security and Distribution Groups	131
Mail-Enabling a Security or Distribution Group	156
Determining AD Group Scopes	192
Planning AD Security Groups	195

Immediate Solutions

Configuring Message Formats for the POP3 Virtual Server

You will configure everything for the POP3 virtual server using the Exchange 2000 System Manager snap-in as follows:

1. Open the System Manager snap-in by selecting Start|Programs|Microsoft Exchange|System Manager.
2. Click the "+" next to the Administrative Groups folder, and then click the "+" next to the First Administrative Group container.
3. Expand the Servers container, the Server logical object, and the Protocols subcontainer inside the same way.
4. Expand the POP3 folder inside the Protocols container to reveal the Default POP3 Virtual Server object. Right-click this object and select the Properties option.
5. Your screen automatically displays the General tab of the Default POP3 Virtual Server Properties dialog box. Click the Message Format tab as shown in Figure 9.3.
6. Notice the default MIME encoding scheme of Provide Message Body As HTML. Click the Use Exchange Rich-Text Format checkbox (as shown by the cursor in Figure 9.4) and notice what happens to your default MIME settings. Click OK to return to the System Manager interface.

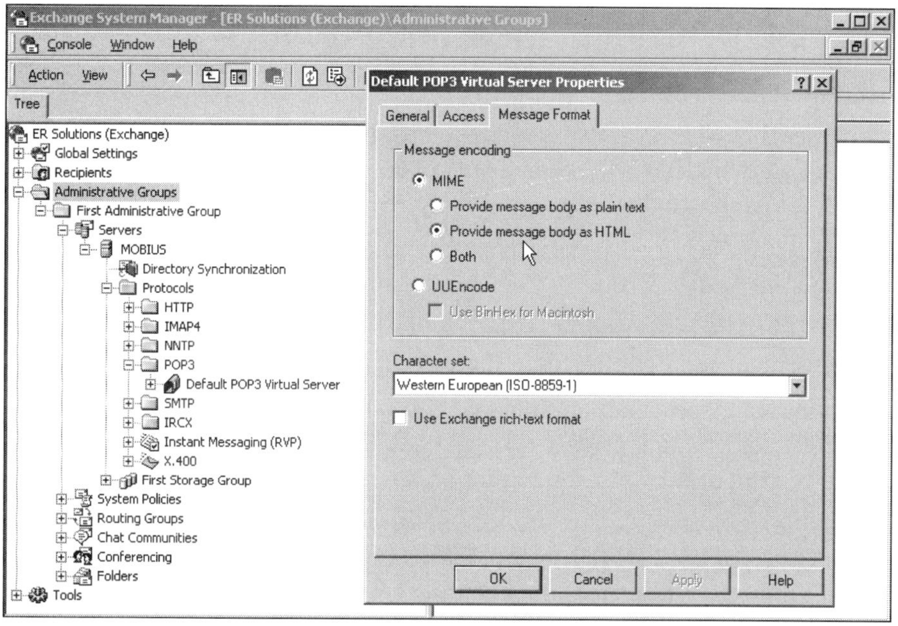

Figure 9.3 The Message Format tab of the Default POP3 Virtual Server Properties dialog box.

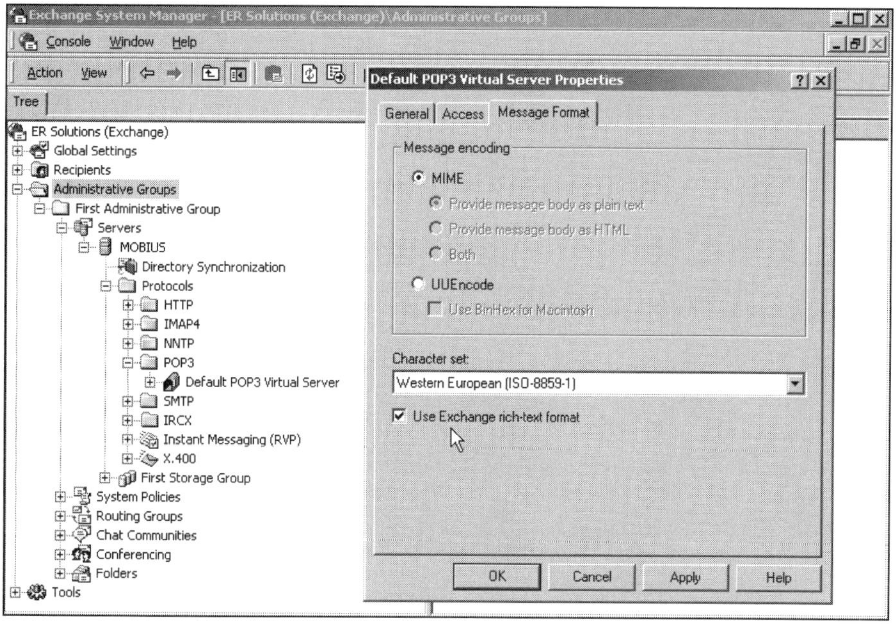

Figure 9.4 The Message Format tab showing the setting for Exchange Rich-Text Format.

Configuring Overriding Message Formats for Individual Users

Remember that whenever users request messages using POP3 or IMAP4, you can configure whether they will receive only plain-text message bodies or HTML message bodies (or both). You can also specify whether you want to override settings for individual users by performing the following steps:

1. Open the Active Directory Users and Computers MMC snap-in.
2. Click the Users container. Then, right-click this container and select View|Advanced Features (see Figure 9.5).
3. Double-click any user and select the Exchange Advanced tab in the user Properties box that appears. Then, click the Protocol Settings button near the bottom of this tab (see Figure 9.6).
4. Double-click the POP3 protocol that appears in the Protocols dialog box and wait for the POP3 Protocol Details box to appear (see Figure 9.7). In the Protocol Details box, uncheck the Use Protocol Defaults box, and then configure the options you desire for this user. Finally, click OK to return to the Protocols dialog box.

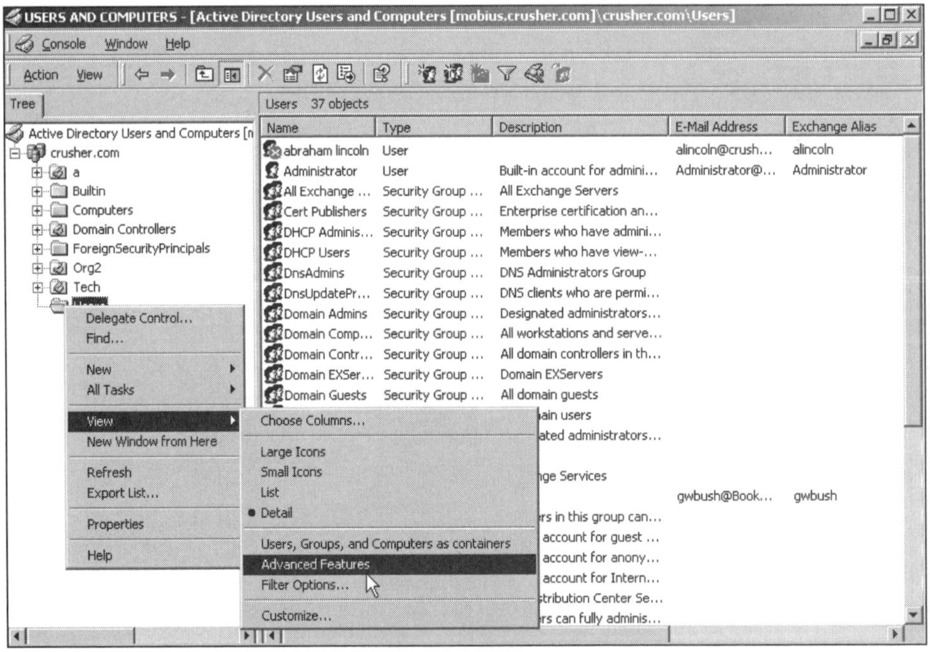

Figure 9.5 Enabling Advanced Features for the Users container in AD Users And Computers.

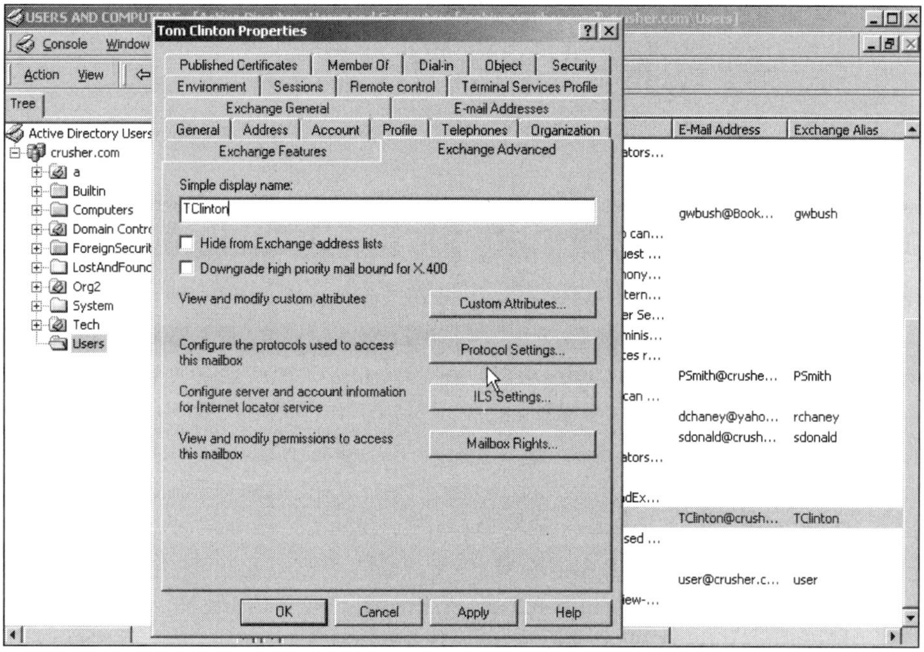

Figure 9.6 Configuring Protocol Settings on the Exchange Advanced tab for a user in AD Users And Computers.

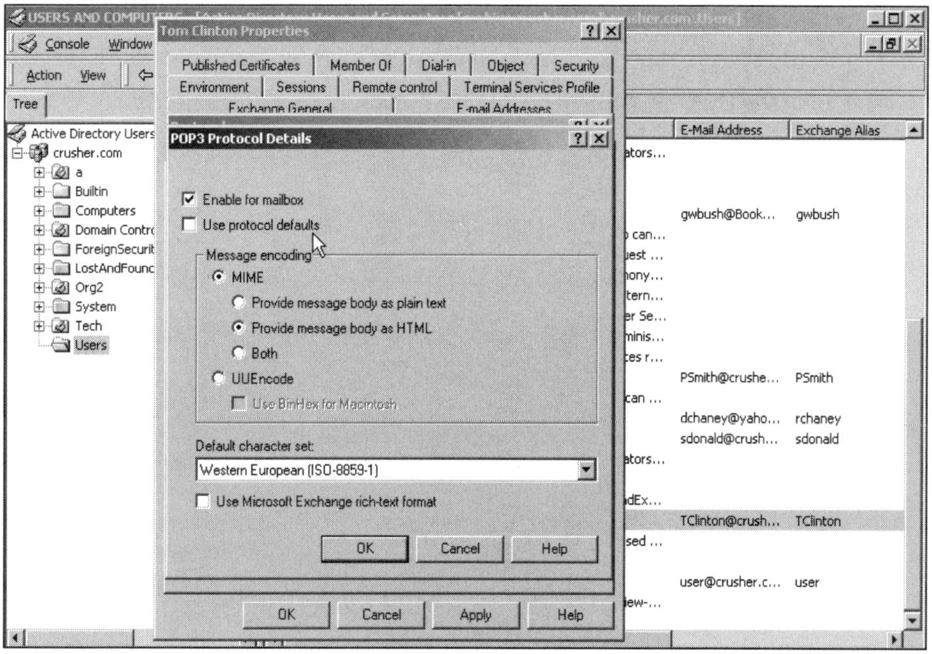

Figure 9.7 The POP3 Protocol Details dialog box.

5. Click OK to return to the user's Properties pages, and then click OK to return to the AD Users And Computers interface. Click the "X" in the upper-right corner to close the AD Users And Computers interface screen.

Configuring MIME Formats for the Default Internet Message Format

To configure MIME formats for the Internet Message Format object appearing in the Global Settings container under the Organizational object in Exchange System Manager, do the following:

1. Open the Exchange System Manager snap-in and click the "+" next to the Global Settings container. You will see the Internet Message Formats leaf object inside.
2. Click this object and notice the appearance of the Default format in the Details pane on the right-hand side (with a domain of "*" listed next to it). Right-click this object and select Properties.
3. On the Default Properties screen that appears, click the Message Format tab and notice the default MIME encoding of Provide Message Body As Plain Text. Choose the radio button labeled Provide Message Body As HTML, check the Apply Content Settings To Non-MAPI Clients box, and then click OK to return to the Exchange System Manager interface (see Figure 9.8).
4. Close the System Manager interface by choosing Console|Exit.

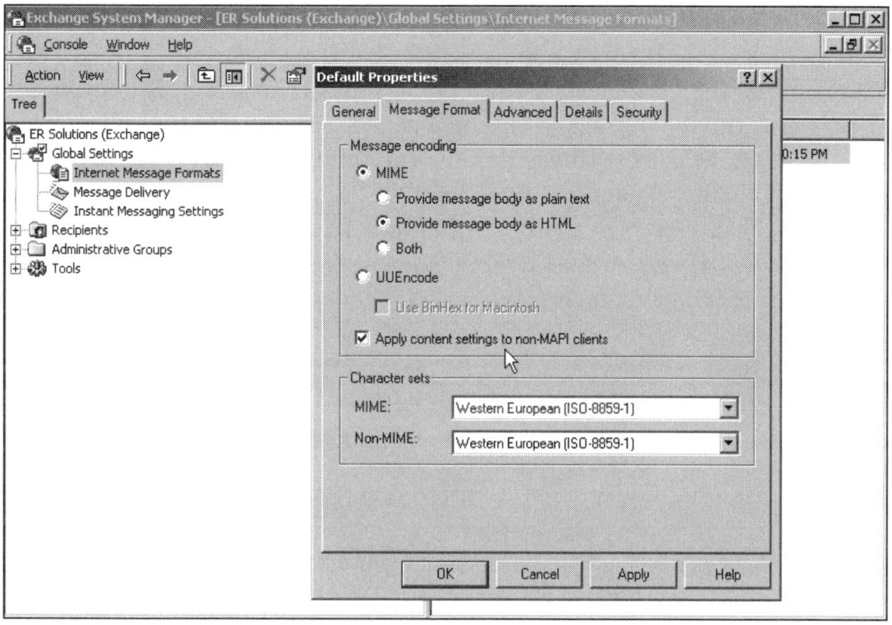

Figure 9.8 Choosing MIME settings for the Default Internet Message Format in System Manager.

Using the Rules Wizard in Outlook 2000 for Content Management

A desired feature in all email applications is the capability to process both incoming and outgoing messages effectively. Outlook provides this functionality using the Rules Wizard, which can help you define instructions so that certain actions are performed on both incoming and outgoing email messages. You can use the Rules Wizard to assign categories to incoming or outgoing messages based on content, or even set notifications to alert you when important messages arrive in your Inbox folder. You can even flag email messages that are being sent by certain users.

TIP: *Users can use the Inbox Assistant in Outlook 97 and Outlook 98 to emulate the functionality of the Rules Wizard. The Rules Wizard is installed automatically when using the Outlook 98 and Outlook 2000 clients, but it has to be installed manually when using the Outlook 97 client.*

The Rules Wizard can work with the Inbox Assistant used in the Outlook Express client to filter and sort email messages that do not meet certain criteria. The main difference between the Rules Wizard and the Inbox Assistant is that the former can process both incoming and outgoing messages, whereas the latter processes only incoming messages. However, only the Inbox Assistant can forward email messages with all message headers intact. When you first start the Rules Wizard in Outlook 2000, you might be prompted to convert all existing Inbox Assistant Rules to Rules Wizard rules. Clicking Yes to this prompt and then clicking OK converts all existing Inbox Assistant rules (except rules containing custom form conditions).

NOTE: *If you are using a version of Exchange Server prior to Exchange 5.5, certain server issues might arise when converting these Inbox Assistant Rules because the Rules Wizard in Outlook 2000 keeps all old Inbox Assistant rules when converting in addition to the newly converted rules. The total combination of all these rules might consume precious hard drive space on your server.*

To use the Rules Wizard, perform the following steps in your Outlook 2000 client:

1. In your Outlook Inbox, choose Tools|Rules Wizard. The Rules Wizard dialog box appears. Click the New button and select the type of Rule you want to create.
2. Click the Assign Categories Based On Content rule and notice the Rule description that appears in the large text box (see Figure 9.9).
3. Click the Next button to select a condition you want to check. Notice that the With Specific Words in the Subject Or Body checkbox is already checked (you can uncheck this if you want). Leave this box checked and notice the building of the Rule description in the box underneath. Click the Specific Words link to specify words or phrases to search for in the subject or body of all email messages.
4. Type "Free Junk Mail" in the Add New text box and click Add to add this to the Search List text box (see Figure 9.10). Then click OK to return to the Rule Description box.
5. Notice that your words have been added to the Rule Description box at the bottom of the screen. Now click the Category link and type the name of a Category you want to monitor, such as Junk. If everything looks satisfactory in the Rule Description box, click Next.

NOTE: *When you are adding multiple words or phrases in Step 4, you are prompted that these rules won't work correctly in Outlook versions prior to the one you are using (we are using Outlook 2000 in this example). If this is acceptable, click Yes; otherwise, click No when asked if you want to create this rule.*

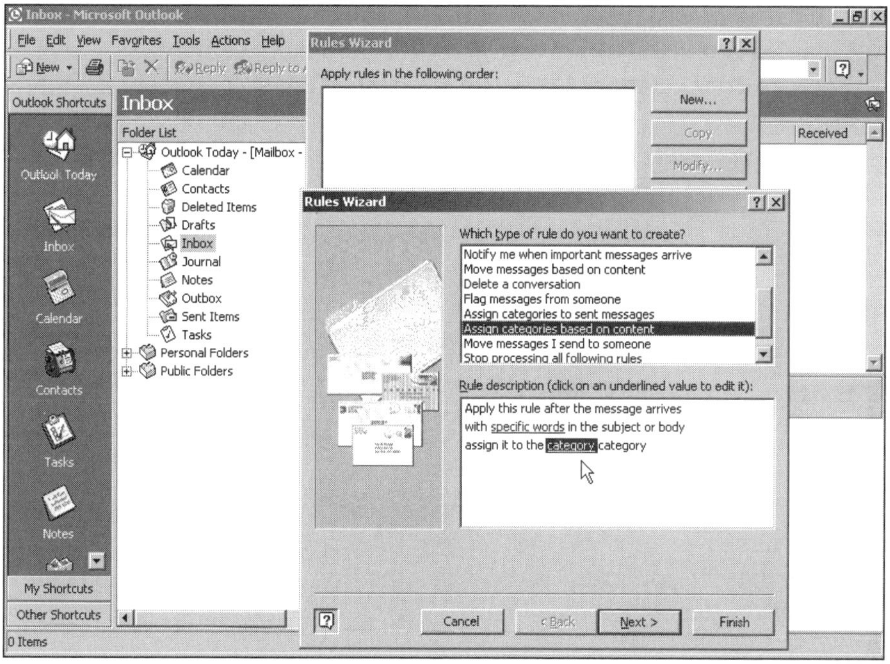

Figure 9.9 The Rules Wizard with the Assign Categories Based On Content rule selected.

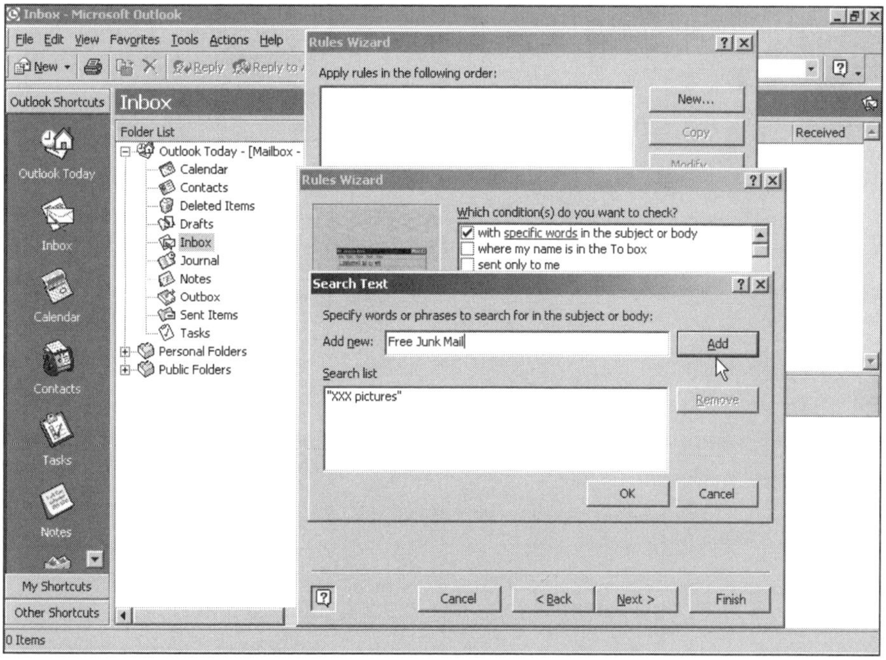

Figure 9.10 The Search Text dialog box showing which words or phrases will be used as filters.

6. In the next box of the Rules Wizard, select a checkbox to answer the prompt What Do You Want To Do With The Message? Select either the Assign It To The Category category or the Delete It And Check It checkbox, and then click Next.
7. Ignore the next box stating Add Any Exceptions (If Necessary), and click Next.
8. Specify a name for this rule in the next box by typing the words "Junk Mail" in the text box. Check Run This Rule Now On Messages Already In "Inbox" and notice that the Turn On This Rule checkbox has already been checked (see Figure 9.11). Click Finish when you are done creating this rule.
9. If you get a message stating This Rule Is A Client-Only Rule, And Will Process Only When Outlook Is Running (see Figure 9.12), click OK to return to the Rules Wizard dialog box.
10. In the Rules Wizard box that appears, notice the options that you can configure at this time: You can create a new rule, or copy, modify, rename, and delete the rule you just created. Click the Run Now button to open the Run Rules Now dialog box (see Figure 9.13).

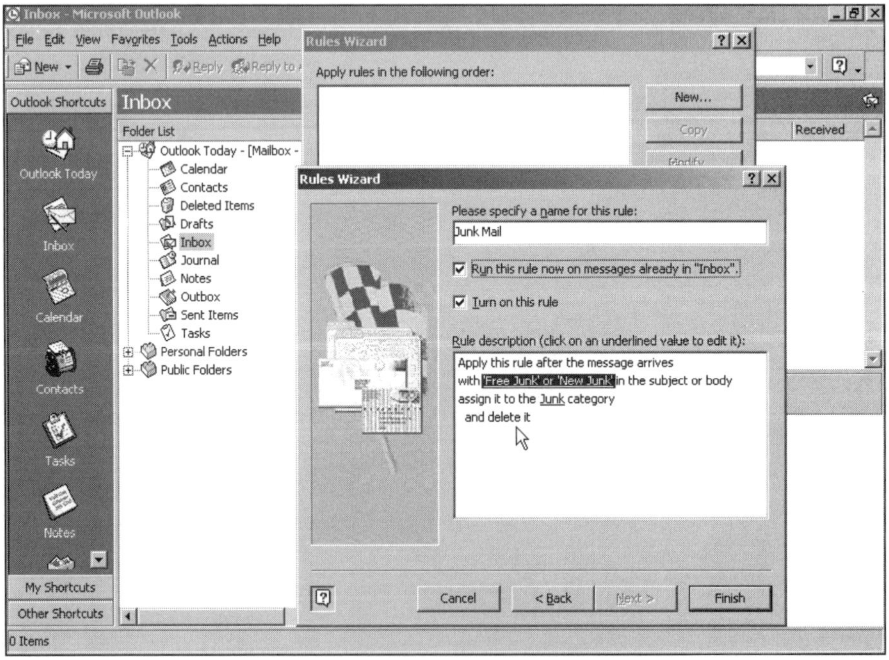

Figure 9.11 Specifying a name for your new rule and turning on the rule.

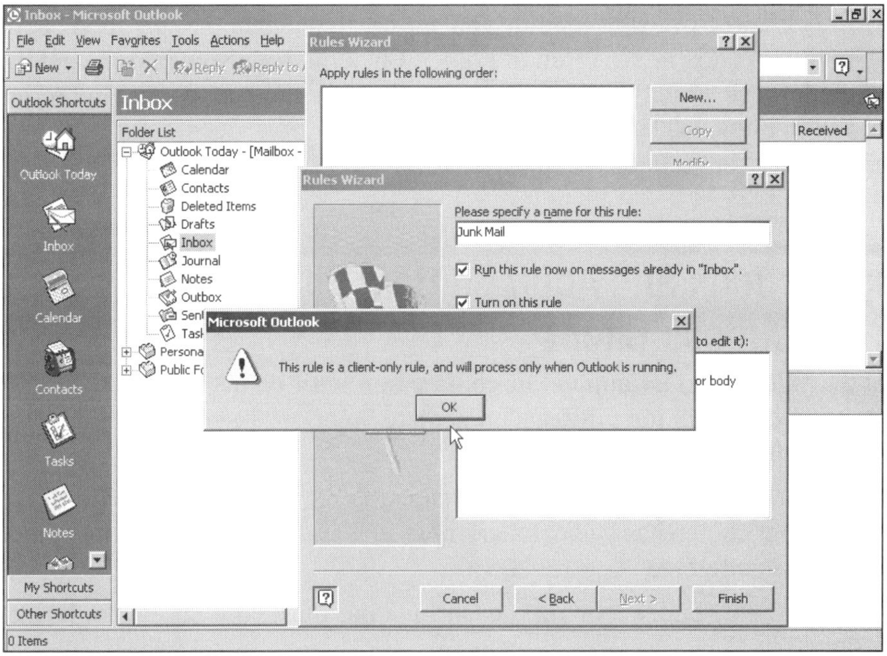

Figure 9.12 Dialog box showing the status of your new rule.

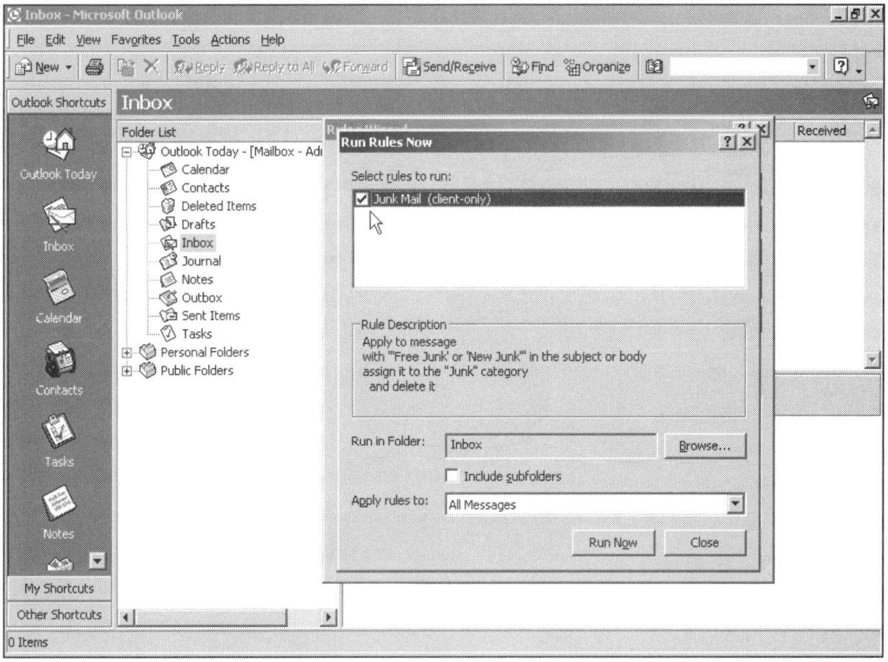

Figure 9.13 The Run Rules Now dialog box.

11. Check the box next to the rule you just created and make sure Inbox appears in the text box next to Run In Folder. Click the Run Now button, and then click Close. Finally, click OK to close the Rules Wizard button and return to the Outlook 2000 interface.

Using the Junk and Adult Content Filters with the Outlook Client

Content filters can be applied in conjunction with or in addition to the Rules Wizard discussed in the previous Immediate Solution. To enable these filters using the Outlook 2000 client:

1. Open the Outlook 2000 client and click the View menu. Make sure the Outlook bar choice has a checkmark next to it and then return to the opening Outlook interface.
2. Click the Organize icon on the Outlook bar until your screen looks like Figure 9.14.
3. In the upper-right corner of your screen, click the Junk EMail link in the Ways To Organize Inbox section. Your screen will appear as in Figure 9.15.

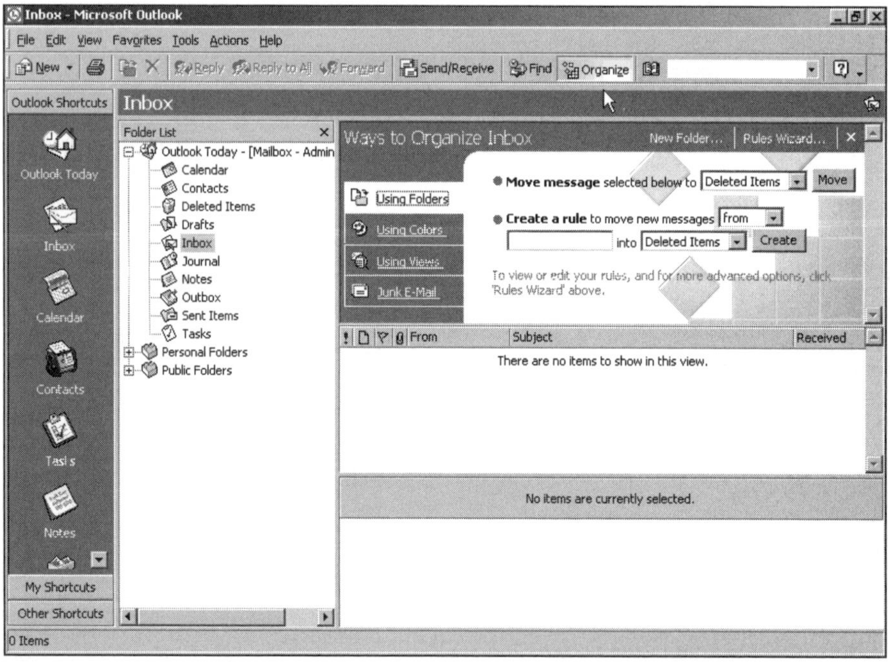

Figure 9.14 The Outlook screen after clicking the Organize icon on the Outlook bar.

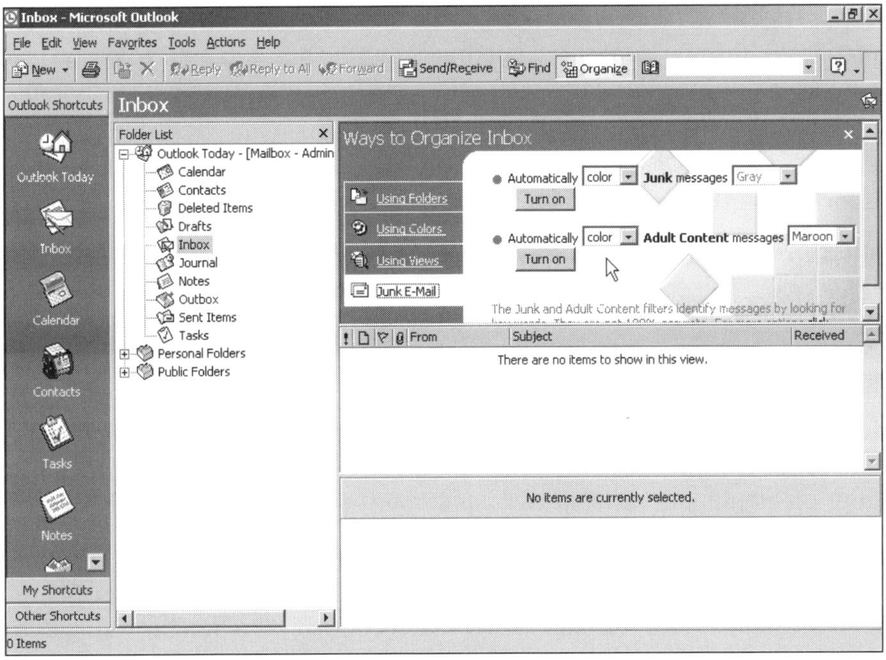

Figure 9.15 The Junk Email options in Outlook 2000.

4. Make sure the first row in this section reads Automatically Color Junk Messages, select the color Red, and then click Turn On. Make sure the second row in this section reads Automatically Color Adult Content Messages, select the color Purple, and then click Turn On.
5. Click the Organize icon on the Outlook bar to turn this display off.

Finding Appropriate Content-Management Software

When selecting an appropriate content-management software package for your company, you should make sure that it contains certain minimum features. The software chosen should be used for much more than simple mail blocking. It should also intelligently route mail within your organization. Also, this software can be installed on multiple entry points in your firm, including SMTP gateways and email clients. Make sure your software does the following:

- *Checks for HTML scripts, executables, and .vbs files*—It should scan for all types of active content including executable files, ActiveX files, and files with VBScript extensions (.vbs) in all incoming messages. Scripts are usually blamed for perpetrating harmful viruses within an organization. Some, but not all, antivirus products are capable of scanning for such active content.

- *Supports foreign languages*—A good content-management product can recognize harmful content in languages other than English. Your software package should understand character sets for foreign languages commonly found on the Web, such as French or German.
- *Protects encrypted communications*—Many antivirus packages cannot scan information that is encrypted, but most content-management packages can now block or quarantine encrypted messages and their attachments.
- *Integrates with Windows 2000*—Your package must be able to support all features of AD and Windows 2000. It should be managed and monitored using custom MMC consoles, if possible, or it should be integrated into existing Exchange 2000 or Windows 2000 MMC snap-ins.
- *Uses lexical analysis*—Good content-management software checks all content for both message bodies and message attachments. It also allows you to filter on combinations of words using *Boolean logic*.

An excellent site on the Web that gives examples of content-management products for Exchange 2000 can be found at **www.slipstick.com/addins**. Search for "Content Control" or "Automatic Message Processing" when browsing this site. Many of the products act as plug-ins or add-ins to your Exchange 2000 server, whereas other products operate only on email clients or SMTP gateways. Also, many content-management tools work in conjunction with virus-scanning products and offer other ancillary functions such as message archiving.

Dealing with Mail Abuse Prevention on Exchange 2000

Some users can wreak havoc on unsuspecting Exchange 2000 organizations by using the organization's mail server for relay purposes. They send unsolicited commercial bulk email (UCE or UBE, respectively), also called spam with the organization's domain listed as a return address. Because your domain name is being used for this purpose, your Exchange Server is the subject of bad publicity or even attack by users who perceive your organization as the source of all such spam. Also, your Exchange 2000 Server will be host to all nondelivery reports (NDRs) generated from messages that do not reach their intended destination.

Exchange 2000 cannot distinguish between email sent to "legitimate" users and email sent to "nonlegitimate" users in your organization. It is also hard to filter out all SMTP mail that does not belong to your organization. Organizations such as MAPS (Mail Abuse Prevention System LLC) actively campaign to prevent email systems from abuse by spammers.

NOTE: *See the Web site* ***http://maps.vix.com*** *for more details regarding the MAPS not-for-profit organization that helps track third-party mail relay abuse.*

Your goal is to prevent your server from being used as an "open third-party mail relay." This happens when your Exchange 2000 Server processes mail messages and neither the sender nor the recipient of this message is hosted on your local server. In some cases, using a server for third-party mail relay can actually help in troubleshooting efforts (for example, to test for mail connectivity between multiple systems in a single network).

Spammers use third-party mail relays to propagate junk email across the Internet. This means that multiple Exchange Servers can become victim to such plans. You want to stop all instances of mail relay abuse because it can cause severe damage to your mail systems by consuming unnecessary bandwidth or processing power. Worst of all, your organization can be *blacklisted* on the "MAPS Realtime Blackhole List," a list of ISPs (Internet Service Providers) who are partial to propagators of spam. This list is in realtime, so an ISP is placed here as soon as spam is received. You can visit this list at **http://maps.vix.com**. You can also visit the Anti-Spam Project at **www.bitgate.com/spam**, which contains a list of domains that send out junk email as well as a mail filter program called BlackMail, which you can install to filter incoming mail based on certain criteria.

Microsoft addressed the issue of mail servers relaying spam as far back as August 1999, when it released an Exchange 5.5 post-SP2 hotfix, which addressed a specific mail-relaying vulnerability and closed a security gap that allowed the Internet Mail Service (IMS) to relay encapsulated SMTP messages. Most antispam measures should conform to RFC 2505, or Anti-Spam Recommendations for SMTP MTAs. This RFC identified problems associated with spam and specified the functions that should be carried out by the SMTP MTA to reduce the effects of spam.

If your organization is added to the MAPS "quarantine list" of servers that are vulnerable to open relay abuse by external parties, your internal users won't be able to send outgoing email, even to addresses that worked in the past. You can check the resources listed on the MAPS site at **www.mailabuse.org**. You can also contact the MAPS Relay Spam Stopper (RSS) service to request that your server be removed from the quarantine list. If MAPS tests your server and finds that all relaying capabilities have been disabled, it will honor your request and remove your server from this list.

Working with the Email Security Update in Outlook 2000

The Outlook client can be made secure against potentially destructive worms and viruses, but a lot depends on the version of Outlook being used and the security updates that you apply to it. Viruses affect three different areas in Outlook:

- *The Preview Pane*—Turning off this pane will not prevent viruses from attacking your system. All ActiveX controls run automatically within this pane. The Outlook 2000 Preview Pane is a lot safer than the Outlook 98 Preview Pane because all active content (including ActiveX controls and Active Scripting) is disabled, regardless of Security Zones settings.
- *Opened messages*—These are always safe to open, whether they are in plain-text form or RTF form. Opening HTML messages might present a bit of a problem because they contain Active Scripting code or ActiveX controls that might contain viruses.
- *Attachments*—These are the message components you should be most concerned with. Attachments cannot be opened without some type of user involvement or intervention. Office 2000 SR-1 prompts you with a dialog box if you try to open any executable files in Outlook. Almost 20 file types or extensions are constantly being monitored, including the .vbs, .bat, and .zip extensions.

Because of destructive viruses, such as the ILOVEYOU.VBS worm, Microsoft released the Outlook Email Security Update for Outlook 98 and Outlook 2000 that addressed many relevant security concerns. It contained the following components:

- A component that prevents users from opening or saving any file extensions that can potentially execute dangerous or malicious code. You can give trusted users permission to access some attachment types or permissions to use the OWA client; however, users not created on Exchange Server cannot access these attachments in any way within the Outlook client.
- A component that configures Security Zones within Outlook and also stops certain scripts in Outlook forms from executing unless you publish these forms to a forms library.
- A component called the Outlook Object Model Guard that provides code to block access to the Outlook Address Book.

NOTE: *Microsoft also released an Attachment Security patch prior to releasing the Email Security Update. This former patch prevented users from opening attachments in Outlook, but the Outlook version of this patch was taken off the market because it was being built into the SR-1 version of Office 2000. However, the Outlook 98 version of the Attachment Security patch is still available and is still effective in preventing users from opening attachments.*

The Email Security Patch provides an attachment warning message that runs for all attachments with executable file name extensions. It will not detect or clean viruses from infected attachments; if you save a file that has a virus and then run this file from your disk, your system will be infected with a virus. This update will not affect native Office files with .doc, .xls, and .ppt extensions. Files containing the .shs extension (scrap object files) or .vbs extension (script files) are also not affected by this update.

The Security Update defines certain levels of attachments based on file extensions. For example, Level 1 attachments are considered an "unsafe" category of attachments and represent all file extensions with script or code associated with it. This means you *cannot access the attachment* if the security patch is installed. Some of the file types considered unsafe are shown in Table 9.4.

Level 2 file attachments are not considered "unsafe" like Level 1 attachments; however, they still require a high level of security configuration. When you receive a Level 2 attachment, you are prompted to save this attachment to disk and you can't open or view the attachment within the message itself. This update only

Table 9.4 File extensions considered unsafe in Outlook 2000.

File Extension Name	File Extension Type
.adp	Access 2000 Project
.bas	Visual Basic Class Module
.cmd	Windows NT/2000 command script
.com	MS-DOS executable program
.exe	Any executable program
.hlp	Any Help file
.js	Any JavaScript file
.lnk	Any shortcut file
.mdb	Any Access 97/2000 program
.msi	Windows Installer package
.mst	Microsoft Visual Test source file
.pif	Microsoft Program Information file (shortcut to MS-DOS program)
.scr	Any screen saver file
.url	Any Internet shortcut
.vbs	Any VBScript file or program
.wsh	Any Windows Scripting Host file

works if you have installed the Outlook 2000 SR-1 on your system. Also, this update is considered an integral component of the Outlook client. In other words, if you want to uninstall the update only, you have to completely uninstall the software package that Outlook is a part of, namely the Office 2000 suite (or Office 97 suite).

Some final issues regarding the Outlook Email Security Update include the following:

- You have to create a folder in Outlook under All Public Folders and name it Outlook Security Settings. It must be a top-level folder in the root of All Public Folders. Outlook examines all forms put in this folder to determine security settings for every user.
- If you forward any message with an "unsafe" (Level 1) attachment, the attachment won't be included with the message. You can use this feature to your advantage if you want to remove an "unsafe" attachment from an email message that you receive. Forwarding the message to yourself leaves the attachment behind because all forwarded messages do not contain the attachment.
- If you install a standalone version of the Outlook 2000 client on a machine and try to upgrade this computer to the full version of Office 2000 SR-1, the Outlook Email Security Update install fails. The update fails because you did not first run the Office 2000 SR-1 Update to force Outlook to be upgraded to SR-1 status. After running the Office 2000 SR-1 Update, you can successfully install the Outlook Email Security Update patch.
- If you try to apply this security update to an Outlook 98 client while also trying to upgrade the client to Outlook 2000, the security update is not updated to the 2000 version. You must manually install the Outlook Email Security Update to Outlook 2000.

Connecting Exchange 2000 to the Internet Using a Static IP Address

You can set up an Exchange 2000 server using a static IP address given to you by your ISP. You do not need to register any DNS names for this IP address; however, registering a DNS name and configuring appropriate mail exchange (MX) records in the DNS database means that you can use "friendly" DNS names instead of "unfriendly" IP addresses (see the sidebar "Configuring DNS for Email" below). To register a domain name, visit **www.networksolutions.com** or **www.register.com**.

Configuring DNS for Email

The following example illustrates how a DNS server functions with respect to email in general, and MX records in particular. Suppose you are configuring a mail server named Orion (running Exchange 2000 Server) for a company known as CaramelTreat. The company runs a DNS server on a Windows 2000 Server computer called Phantom. An external user, Tarek, wants to send two email messages to your company CEO, whose address is **Camille@CaramelTreat.com** (Camille has been configured as a mailbox-enabled recipient object on this mail server). How do these email messages find your email server, Orion, so that they can be delivered to **Camille@CaramelTreat.com**?

The answer to this question can be determined once you understand the structure of the Internet. The Internet contains top-level root servers that know the location of every DNS server with domain information for the *.com domain (meaning every domain name that ends with the suffix .com). The mail server on Tarek's computer (the external user sending the messages) will query this backbone root server for information regarding the domain **CaramelTreat.com**. The root server will respond that this domain is handled by a DNS server that is located on **Phantom.CaramelTreat.com**.

After the DNS server for **CaramelTreat.com** is found, Tarek's computer will query the DNS server on **Phantom.CaramelTreat.com** for information regarding the domain **CaramelTreat.com**. The DNS nameserver installed on Phantom will check its resource records and send a response to Tarek's computer in the external domain. The information sent in this response will include both MX records and A records, and will indicate that all mail intended for **CaramelTreat.com** should be directed to **Orion.CaramelTreat.com**. The TCP/IP address for **Orion.CaramelTreat.com** will also be provided at this time. Using this TCP/IP address, Tarek can direct his email messages to **Orion.CaramelTreat.com**, which then forwards the message to **Camille@CaramelTreat.com**.

MX records are required within the DNS database if you expect to receive email directly from the Internet because they tell other email servers on the Internet how to route their mail. MX records convert domains that do not point to any specific host into a Fully Qualified Domain Name. They also route messages from one host to another host running a mail server (like Exchange 2000).

The following line illustrates how CaramelTreat would set up a MX record (along with its associated A resource record that resolves the name of its mail server to an IP address) in the DNS database on the computer named Phantom. The first line is the MX record entry and the second line represents the entry for the "A" resource record that identifies the IP address for the mail server, Orion (whose IP address is given as 192.168.10.5):

```
CaramelTreat.com           IN     MX      10
Orion.CaramelTreat.com
Orion.CaramelTreat.com     IN     192.168.10.5
```

__TIP:__ A good reference site on the Internet containing information on MX records can be found at __http://supportnet.merit.edu/m-spectop/t-dns/mx.html__. Or you can read RFC 974 to understand how Internet mail systems route their messages based on information contained in DNS systems as described in RFC 882 and RFC 883. RFC 974 can be found at __www.faqs.org/rfcs/rfc974.html__.

Setting TCP/IP Port Numbers for Firewalls in Mixed-Mode Exchange Environments

When configuring Internet firewalls or routers, you might want to configure your Exchange 5.5 Information Store and directory services to use predefined TCP port numbers. Some firewalls might have trouble accepting TCP port numbers needed by Exchange Server for RPC communications. You should add port number 135 to your firewall configuration or access list and configure Exchange to use ports that the firewall allows.

You can configure the RPC port for the Exchange 5.5 Information Store by using the Registry Editor (either regedit or regedt32.exe). To change the RPC port for the directory service in Exchange 5.5:

1. Start the Registry Editor by clicking Start|Run; then type "regedt32.exe" in the Open box.
2. Navigate to the H**key_Local_Machine\System\CurrentControlSet\Services\MSExchangeDS\Parameters** subkey and click Edit|Add Value on the menu bar as shown in Figure 9.16.

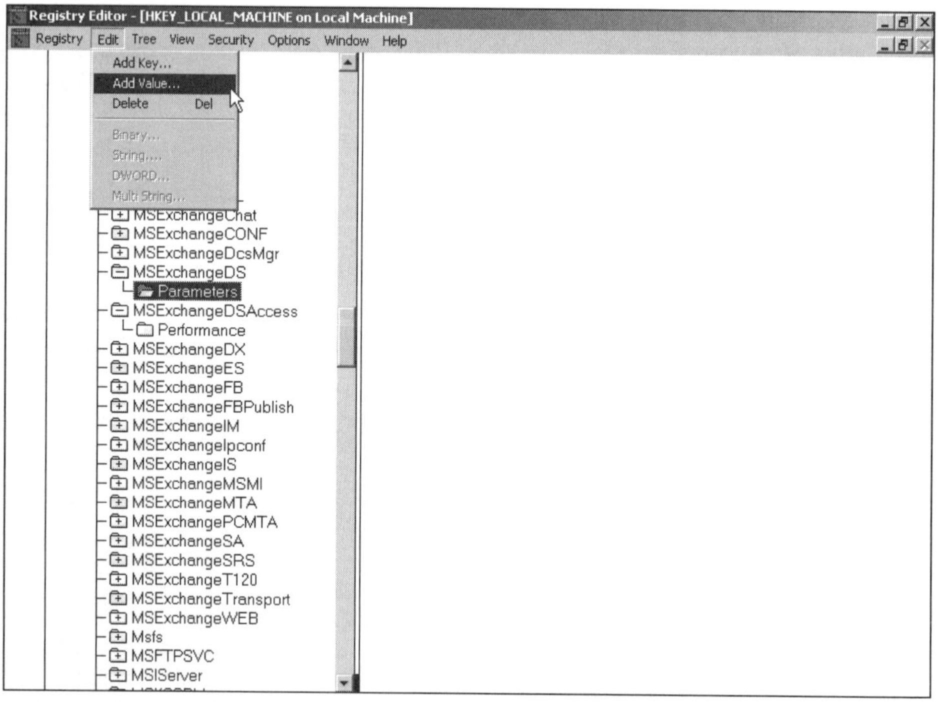

Figure 9.16 Adding a new value to an existing Registry Key.

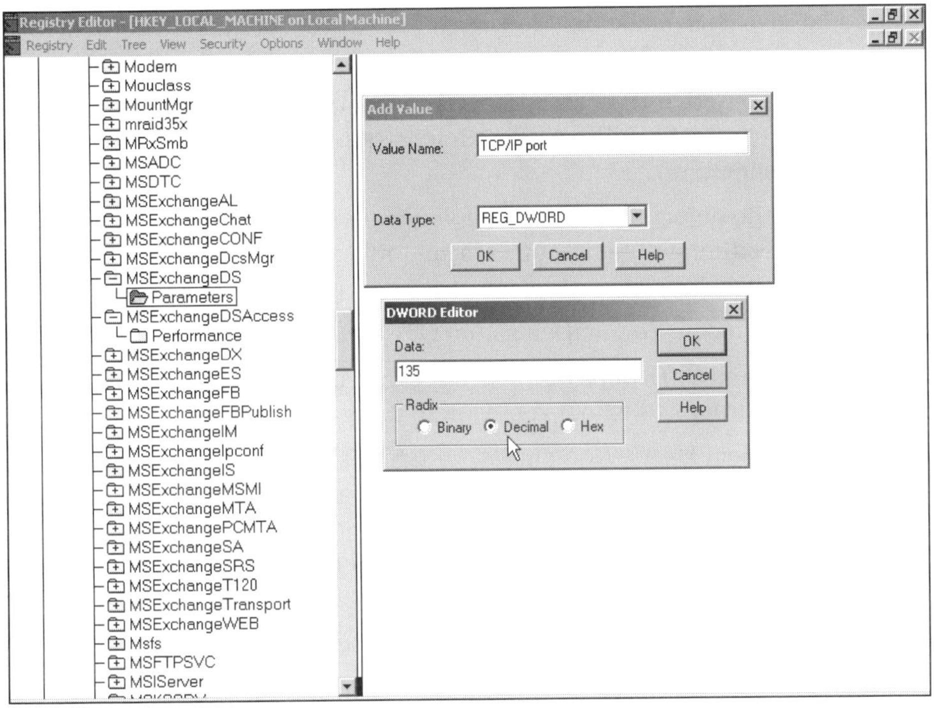

Figure 9.17 The Add Value dialog box and DWORD Editor dialog box for your new Registry value.

3. In the Add Value dialog box that appears, type the Registry value **TCP/IP port** as a **DWORD** value and click OK. You then specify a port number (such as 135) in the DWORD Editor dialog box that appears while selecting the radio button for Decimal when typing your value (refer to Figure 9.17 for an example of this).
4. When finished, close the Registry Editor by choosing Registry|Exit.

Using the Delegation of Control Wizard to Assign Permissions

You can delegate control of objects in Windows 2000 to certain individuals so they can perform administrative tasks on these objects. You use the Delegation of Control Wizard to delegate control of various objects in both Windows 2000 and Exchange 2000 by assigning permissions to objects. Use this wizard to assign permissions to users or groups so they can create objects in an OU, or to assign permissions to users so they can modify permissions for object attributes (for instance, giving users the right to change passwords for other users in an OU). To do so, perform the following:

1. Open the Active Directory Users And Computers snap-in from the Start menu (choose Start|Programs|Administrative Tools|Active Directory Users And Computers).
2. Select the object in the tree that you want to delegate control to (you can choose either a domain object, a site object, or an OU object). Right-click your domain object and choose Delegate Control.
3. In the Welcome To The Delegation Of Control Wizard, click Next.
4. In the Users Or Groups box that appears, click the Add button to select the users or groups to whom you want to delegate control.
5. In the Select Users, Computers, Or Groups dialog box that appears next, click the user or group that you want to delegate control to (use the Ctrl key to select multiple users or groups), and then click the Add button in the middle of the box. Finally, click the OK button to return to the Users Or Groups screen.
6. Click Next to view the Tasks To Delegate screen as shown in Figure 9.18.

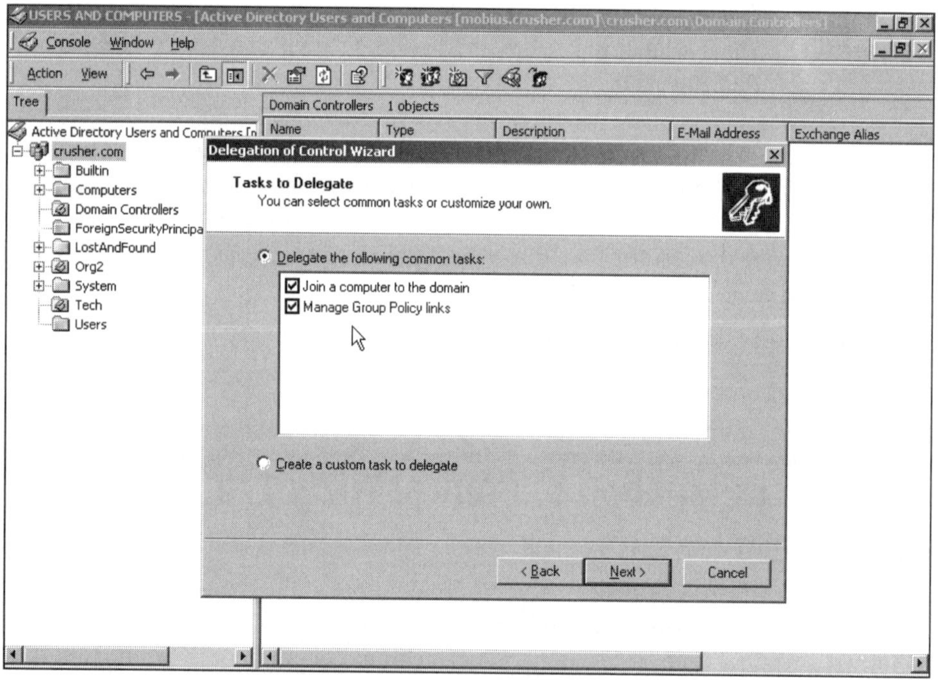

Figure 9.18 The Tasks To Delegate screen in the Delegation Of Control Wizard.

7. Under Delegate The Following Common Tasks radio button, check the two boxes labeled Join A Computer To The Domain and Manage Group Policy Links. Click Next.
8. In the Completing The Delegation Of Control Wizard box, review all the information that is presented in summary form, and then click Finish to close the Delegation Of Control Wizard. You are returned to the Active Directory Users And Computers interface.

The same steps you performed in the previous list can be performed in the Exchange System Manager snap-in to assign administrative roles to users or groups for administrative groups. You can delegate control to users without making them members of higher groups such as the Domain Admins global security group. You can delegate permissions at the organizational level or the administrative group level. The following permissions can be given using this wizard:

- *Exchange Administrator*—The user or group can fully administer Exchange 2000 system information, but cannot control access to the organization or modify permissions to other objects.
- *Exchange Full Administrator*—The user or group can fully administer Exchange 2000 system information and modify permissions.
- *Exchange View Only Administrator*—The user or group can view Exchange configuration information.
- *Mailbox Manager*—The user or group can mailbox-enable other users, groups, or contacts, but you need to add them to appropriate Windows 2000 security groups such as Account Operators as well. This option appears when configuring permissions on the administrative group level only.

Restricting Access to Public Folders in the Outlook 2000 Client

Public folders can be created using either the Exchange System Manager snap-in or the Outlook client. In either case, the properties of the public folder can be configured to limit or restrict access to certain users or groups for administrative delegation purposes. To delegate permissions to a public folder using the Outlook 2000 client:

1. Open your Microsoft Outlook 2000 client and expand the Public Folders container in the Folders list. Right-click All Public Folders and select the New Folder option.

2. In the Create New Folder box, type the name "Public2" for your new public folder, select Mail Items in the Folder Contains text box, and then click the All Public Folders in the hierarchy shown underneath. Finally, click OK.
3. When prompted to create a shortcut for this public folder in your Outlook bar, click No.
4. Now right-click your new public folder in the All Public Folders path and select Properties. Click the Permissions tab and view the default properties as shown in Figure 9.19.
5. Highlight the Administrator account in the Name list and then click the Roles list box to view the potential roles that can be assigned to users or groups for this public folder:
   - *Owner*—Grants all permissions to this folder so users can read, create, modify, or delete all items in the folder.
   - *Publishing Editor*—Gives users permission to create, modify, read, or delete all items in this folder, and also create subfolders if necessary.
   - *Editor*—Gives permission to read, create, modify, and delete all items in this folder.

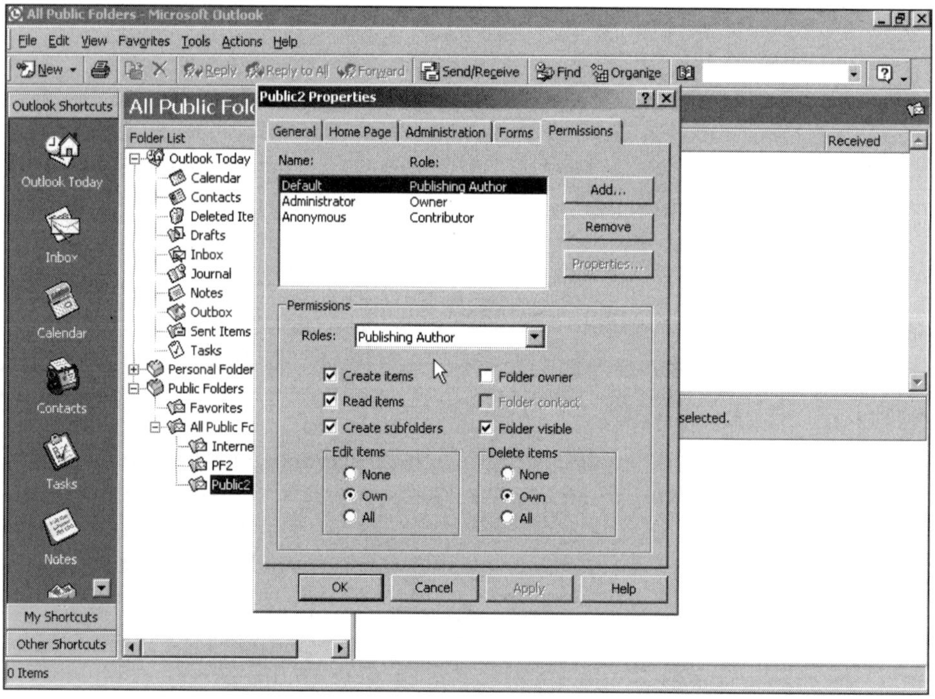

Figure 9.19 The Permissions tab for your new public folder in Outlook 2000.

- *Publishing Author*—Gives users permission to read and create items in this folder, or modify and delete items that they have created.
- *Author*—Gives permission to read and create items in this folder as well as to modify or delete items that users have created.
- *Nonediting Author*—Gives permission to read and create items in this folder.
- *Reviewer*—Gives read-only permission to this public folder.
- *Contributor*—Gives permission to create items in this public folder without being able to view the contents of this folder.
- *None*—Gives no permission whatsoever to this public folder.

6. Select the Publishing Editor role and notice the checkboxes that are now checked for this role. Also notice that this user can now edit all items and delete all items. Note also that you can make the folder "invisible" to this user by unchecking the Folder Visible box.
7. Click the OK button to return to the Outlook 2000 interface.

Converting Universal Distribution Groups to Universal Security Groups to Secure Access to Public Folders

In Exchange 5.5, a DL was used to control access to public folders. In Windows 2000, the AD universal distribution group has replaced the Exchange 5.5 DL. The ADC converts Exchange 5.5 DLs into universal distribution groups. Even though a universal distribution group can help expand email addresses much like its DL counterpart, a universal distribution group does not qualify as a security principal within Windows 2000, so you cannot use this to enforce permissions on public folders. You need to create universal security groups to secure access to public folders in Exchange 2000.

A universal distribution group can be converted into a universal security group for security purposes only if your Windows 2000 domain operates in a native-mode capacity. There are conditions under which universal distribution groups can be converted into universal security groups for public folder access:

- If you replicate an Exchange 5.5 public folder to an Exchange 2000 Server and use a universal distribution group in the ACL of the public folder, the ADC temporarily creates a universal distribution group in Windows 2000 before converting this to a universal security group.

- If you upgrade an Exchange 5.5 public folder store and use a universal distribution group in the ACL for this object, the Exchange 2000 public folder store converts all universal distribution groups created by the ADC into respective universal security groups.
- If you add a universal distribution group to an ACL on a public folder in Exchange 2000, the public folder store converts this universal distribution group to a universal security group.

Please note that if a universal distribution group is not converted to a universal security group (because the conversion process fails for some reason), the Exchange 2000 public folder store tries to convert again the next time a user accesses this folder. This can happen if the universal distribution group is in a mixed-mode Windows 2000 domain. You will run into problems if Exchange 2000 has already converted a universal distribution group to a universal security group and you manually convert this universal security group *back to* a universal distribution group. These problems arise because subsequent user access to this public folder will not convert the universal distribution group back to a universal security group, unless you physically have changed permissions that belong to the universal distribution group.

WARNING! The public folder store won't convert any universal distribution groups that you have added as members of an existing universal security group.

Installing the ADC with a Connection Agreement in a Mixed-Mode Exchange Server Environment

A crucial step in a migration to Exchange 2000 is the consolidation of two different entities—an Exchange 5.5 mailbox and its primary Windows NT 4 account—into one Windows 2000 mail-enabled or mailbox-enabled user. Before you deploy your first Exchange 2000 Server, you must populate your Windows 2000 AD with user objects from Exchange 5.5. This is because Exchange 2000 won't have direct access to the Exchange 5.5 directory database. Both the Exchange 5.5 directory and the Windows 2000 AD must remain synchronized with each other for the migration to be successful.

To maintain this synchronization, you need to deploy and configure the Exchange 2000 ADC. The ADC will continue to be used until the last Exchange 5.5 Server has been upgraded to Exchange 2000. At that point, your Exchange 2000 organization is said to be in native mode.

To install the Exchange 2000 ADC, make sure you meet the following requirements:

- You are installing the ADC on hardware that is running both Windows 2000 Server as a member server and Exchange 2000. You have also installed SP-1 for Windows 2000 Server.
- The Windows 2000 account used to install the ADC is not an Exchange 5.5 Service account, and this account is logged into the same domain as the Exchange Server.
- The account used to install the ADC has Exchange 2000 Enterprise Admins rights to the member server and also Domain Admins rights to every domain that the ADC will connect to. This account also needs Server Operator rights to the Exchange 5.5 Server.
- You are deploying all necessary Windows 2000 or DNS services that are needed for ADC implementation, including the dynamic update feature of DNS.
- The target endpoint of the ADC includes an Exchange 5.5 computer running SP-3 or later.

To install and configure the ADC, perform the following steps:

1. Place your Exchange 2000 CD in your CD-ROM tray and click Start|Run. In the Open text box, type the path to the ADC executable located on the CD-ROM (use the *drive letter* for your particular CD-ROM). Type the following:

```
drive letter:\ADC\I386\SETUP.EXE
```

2. Click OK to continue.
3. When you see the Welcome screen for the Active Directory Connector Setup Wizard, click Next. Then on the Component Selection screen, select both the Microsoft Active Directory Connector Service Component and the Microsoft Active Directory Connector Management Components, and click Next (see Figure 9.20).
4. Accept the default folder location of C:\Program Files\MSADC on the Install Location screen and click Next.
5. On the Service Account screen, specify the username and password under which the ADC service will run and click Next.
6. A progress meter on the next screen shows the ADC being installed. This is evidence that the Windows 2000 schema is being updated. After this part of the wizard completes, you will see the Completing The Active Directory Connector Installation Wizard screen. Click Finish.
7. Now open the ADC tool by selecting Start|Programs|Microsoft Exchange|Active Directory Connector. The Active Directory Connector Management console now opens.

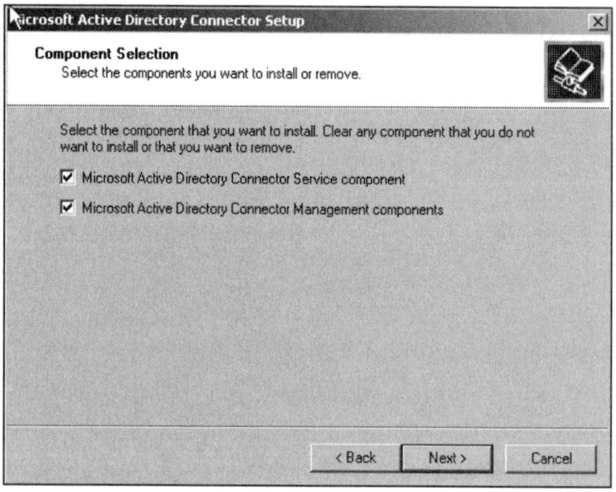

Figure 9.20 The Component Selection screen of the Active Directory Connector Setup Wizard.

8. Right-click the ADC in the left-hand pane of this console, select New, and then select Connection Agreement. The Properties screen appears.
9. Type the name "CA-1" in the Name box on the General tab, and then click the Two-way radio button in the Replication Direction section on the same tab (see Figure 9.21). The two-way radio button produces a new message box asking you to supply a Windows 2000 account that has permissions to write to the Exchange 5.5 directory. Click OK.
10. Select the Connections tab and verify that your server is listed under the Windows Server Information box, and the Authentication being used is Windows Challenge/Response.
11. Under Connect As, click Modify. You will see the Connect As (Windows Server) dialog box. Type "Administrator" and your administrator password in the box underneath. Then click OK.
12. Now in the Exchange Server information part of the Connections tab, type the name of your Exchange 5.5 Server and change the port number to "390" (not 389).
13. Under Connect As, click Modify again and type "Administrator" and the relevant password in the Connect As (Exchange Server) dialog box. Click OK.
14. Click the Schedule tab and select the Always radio button for your replication schedule. Also check the Replicate The Entire Directory The Next Time The Agreement Is Run checkbox.

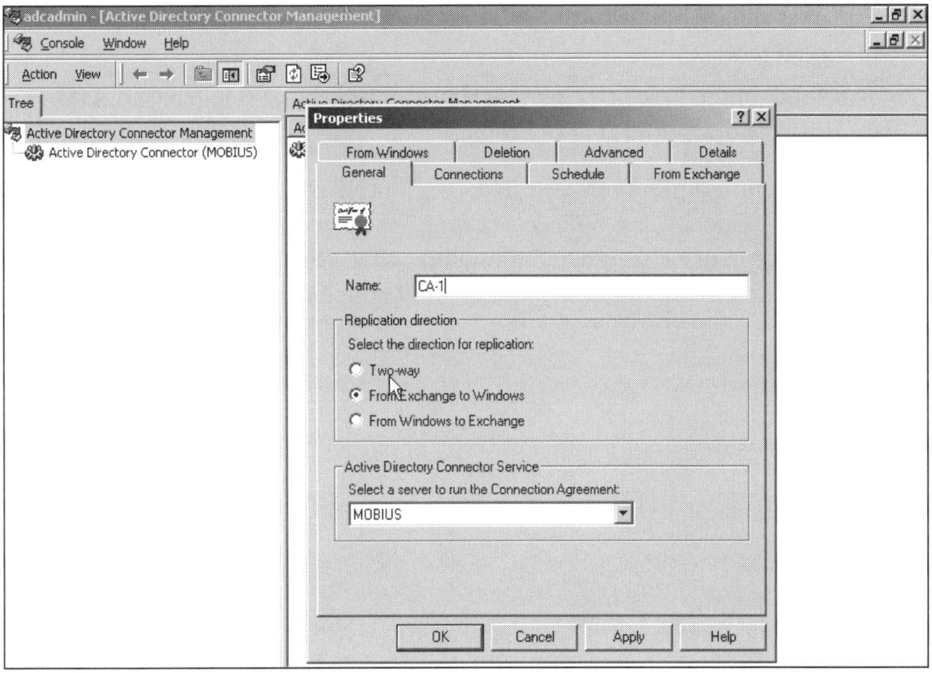

Figure 9.21 The Properties screen for a new connection agreement for the ADC.

The final steps for installing and configuring the ADC involve choosing containers that will be the source and destination for replication of objects. Begin this task on the From Exchange tab:

1. On the From Exchange tab, click Add to select a Recipient container from which to take object updates. When you see Choose A Container, navigate to your Exchange 5.5 server and select the Recipients Container. Click OK.
2. For the Default Destination, click Modify, and then select the Users Container in the Choose A Container dialog box. Now switch to the From Windows tab.
3. Click Add to select an OU container to take updates from. When you see the Choose A Container dialog box, select the Users OU, and then click OK.
4. For the Default Destination on this tab, click Modify, and then select the Recipients container in the Choose A Container dialog box. Click OK. Also, check the box on the bottom labeled Replicate Secured Active Directory Objects To The Exchange Directory and click OK one final time.

At this point the ADC is installed and configured. You might see dialog boxes confirming the following points (agree to all of them by clicking OK):

- The first dialog box informs you that this is the first intra-organizational connection agreement.

- The next dialog box informs you that your Windows 2000 domain is operating in mixed mode.
- The final dialog box informs you that Exchange 2000 has created universal security groups with the ADC.

The connection agreement you just configured will now replicate user objects between the Exchange 5.5 directory and AD by creating disabled Windows 2000 accounts for every Exchange 5.5 mailbox that does not have an associated AD object. You can close the ADC Management console (or adcadmin.exe) when you are done.

Chapter 10

Installing Core Components

If you need an immediate solution to:	*See page:*
Installing Exchange 2000 Components	392
Installing Exchange 2000 in a Forest without Earlier Versions of Exchange	393
Installing Exchange 2000 in a Forest with Earlier Versions of Exchange	394
Installing Additional Exchange 2000 Servers	396
Installing Exchange 2000 on Windows 2000 Member Servers	397
Installing Exchange 2000 on Clustered Servers	397
Installing Exchange 2000 Unattended	397
Transferring the Schema Master	398
Transferring the Schema Master Role When the Schema Master Fails	398
Setting Schema Write Operations in the Registry	400
Configuring the Exchange 2000 System Attendant	402
Configuring the Information Store	404
Setting Mailbox Properties	406
Creating a New Public Folder Tree	409
Adding a Public Folder Store	410
Setting Public Folder Store Properties	410
Changing Public Folder Home Servers	412
Replicating Public Folders	413
Scheduling Replication for All Folders in a Database	413
Scheduling Replication for a Singl1e Folder	414
Installing IM Service	414
Configuring IM	415
Enabling a User for IM	416
Installing the MSN Messenger Service Client	417

(continued)

If you need an immediate solution to:	See page:
Configuring Exchange 2000 Chat Service	417
Creating a Chat Community for Selected Administrative Groups	418
Connecting a Chat Community to a Server	419
Removing a Chat Community from the Server	420
Disabling a Chat Community Temporarily	420
Deleting a Chat Community from the Server	421
Creating Channels	421
Configuring an Internet Connection	422
Creating Additional SMTP Virtual Servers	422
Creating a SMTP Connector	423
Configuring a NNTP Connection	423
Configuring a NNTP Virtual Server	424
Creating Newsgroups	425
Configuring Message Tracking	426
Adding a Configuration Item Using MMC	426
Configuring a Console Taskpad	427
Determining Workload Using Load Simulator	428
Benchmarking Using LoadSim	429
Creating the LoadSim Topology	430

In Depth

Because Exchange 2000 is a product that encompasses new technologies, we first have to understand its new concepts and enhancements over legacy systems before we can use it as a business tool.

Storage Groups (SGs)

The *storage group* is one of the many new enhancements in Exchange 2000 Server. Inclusion of this technology is a great relief for administrators who have been limited to using single huge information store databases older versions of Exchange.

A *SG* is a logical grouping of information store databases. In Exchange 2000 terminology, these databases are called *data stores*, which are either *mailbox stores* or *public folder stores*, with each data store containing the corresponding data type. You can have up to 5 databases per SG, and up to 4 SGs per server. Exchange 2000 can hold up to 20 data stores. All data stores in a single SG share a common set of transaction logs.

Although Exchange 2000 can hold this large number of SGs and data stores, you must be cautious when implementing multiple SGs, because server performance can be greatly compromised. Make sure the transaction logs for multiple partitions—preferably on separate disks—because these logs demand heavy input/output (I/O) operations. To optimize the performance of Exchange 2000, you can use controller-based RAID technologies. When possible, store the Exchange storage group databases, log files, and indexes on their own RAID volumes. You can use RAID-1 for the transaction logs and systems files while it is recommended to have the SGs stored in a RAID-5 volume. This configuration will tremendously increase the performance of your Exchange Server.

In Exchange 5.5, and the earlier versions, maintaining an EDB (Exchange database) file that grew unexpectedly (or expectedly) was a nightmare because of the time consumed backing up and restoring the system. It was often necessary to free up some disk space or add physical disks to accommodate the expanding EDBs. Configuring Exchange 2000 to use multiple SGs is an answer to the need for segregating the EDBs by allocating, for example, a SG per department, per location, per position, and so on. Each SG functions independently. One SG can be unavailable (dismounted), while the others are running (mounted). Backup and restore procedures are a lot more flexible because they can be done on a per SG basis.

Internet Connectivity

SMTP (Simple Mail Transfer Protocol) is an industry standard for Internet email delivery and the native mail transport for Exchange 2000. To install Exchange 2000, the Internet Information Services (IIS)—SMTP and NNTP (Network News Transfer Protocol)—must be installed as well. Prior to the Exchange 2000 installation, the SMTP service in IIS acts as the SMTP provider. The Mailroot directory is located on the INETPUB\Mailroot. The Exchange 2000 installation modifies this, and a *default SMTP server* is created upon installation. The default Mailroot directory is relocated to root:\EXCHSRVR\Mailroot. Each SMTP Virtual Server has its own folder within EXCHSRVR\Mailroot. The default SMTP server has a folder named VS 1, which contains Pickup, Queue, and Badmail subdirectories. These subdirectories serve as temporary storage for messages that are currently processed (Pickup), those waiting to be delivered (Queue), or messages that cannot be delivered at all (Badmail).

External mail or Internet mail is crucial to an organization. An organization wants to extend the internal messaging system so that it can connect to the outside world. Some of the key points to remember when configuring Exchange 2000 for Internet connectivity are explained in the following sections.

Additional SMTP Virtual Servers

Normally, additional SMTP Servers aren't necessary unless Exchange 2000 will be hosting multiple domains. In a single-domain environment, the default SMTP Virtual Server typically could do the job and serve the purpose. The default SMTP Virtual Server is responsible for all the mail routing for both local mail and mail bound for remote delivery. To configure Internet connectivity, you provide two Network Interface Cards (NICs); one NIC is bound to the internal IP (Internet Protocol) address, and the other NIC is bound to the external (fully qualified) IP address. The default SMTP Virtual Server should be associated with the internal IP address. You must create an additional SMTP Virtual Server and associate the external IP address.

Mail Gateway

The next step after configuring the SMTP Virtual Server is to decide which among the existing Exchange 2000 Servers will act as the mail gateway. A mail gateway is a computer that stands between the internal network and the external network. All Internet emails, both incoming and outgoing, pass through the mail gateway. Setting a mail gateway is a common and an effective way to regulate external and internal mail flow within the organization. Note, however, that your mail gateway should only be configured to receive mails from the internal network to be relayed to the external network and to receive Internet mails bounded for your domain.

Never configure your mail gateways to allow relaying mail from one external host to another in the Internet.

SMTP Connector

A *SMTP Connector* can be used to connect computers running Exchange 2000 Server; computers running earlier versions of Exchange; other SMTP-compatible messaging systems, such as the Unix sendmail daemon; or SMTP hosts on the Internet.

The SMTP Connector is the best choice for connecting Exchange Server to foreign systems that support SMTP. This is also the easiest and simplest connector to configure when you want messaging systems such as Lotus Notes, cc:Mail, Unix-based or Linux-based mail systems and other legacy systems to communicate with the Exchange Server. You use the SMTP connector also to connect two Exchange organizations.

The SMTP Connector has to be associated with the SMTP Virtual Server that is bound to the external IP. For Internet communication, the SMTP Connector in Exchange 2000 works the same as the Internet Mail Service (IMS) worked in Exchange 5.5. Note, however, that SMTP Connectors also can be used as messaging connectors within native-mode or mixed-mode Exchange 2000 topologies. Although a Routing Group Connector (RGC) is preferred, a SMTP Connector can also be used to connect routing groups.

Domain Name System (DNS) Configuration

The first thing an organization should do to connect its SMTP server to the Internet is set the *fully qualified domain name (FQDN)*. The intended domain name has to be registered and propagated over the Internet. Two DNS records have to be created as well: the *address (A) record* and the *mail exchange (MX) record*. The A record maps a given FQDN to its IP address. The MX record is set up to associate an email domain with the FQDN of one or more SMTP Virtual Servers that serve that domain. An A record is used for general purposes (such as HTTP), whereas the MX record is used solely for SMTP. A sample DNS zone file with an A record and an MX record:

```
@                        IN  SOA london.toyzone.com.  cherryb.toyzone.com. (
    6            ; serial number
    900          ; refresh
    600          ; retry
    86400        ; expire
    3600       ) ; minimum TTL
;  Zone NS records
```

```
@                         NS london.toyzone.com.
;  Zone records
london                    A          192.168.2.133
@                         MX 10      london.toyzone.com.
```

Active Directory

The Active Directory implementation requires proper planning. The reason why many companies have not migrated yet, or have taken some time before migrating to Windows 2000, is because they are carefully designing the structure of their ADs. Before deploying Exchange 2000, a well-planned and executed AD should already exist. The success of the Exchange 2000 implementation depends on the AD structure. Unlike the earlier versions of Exchange, Exchange 2000 no longer maintains its own directory. The Exchange 2000 directory is tightly integrated in the AD. Maintaining a single repository for objects yields the following benefits:

- *Centralized administration*—Administration can be done using a common administration tool in a single window.
- *Centralized object management*—This simplifies the administration of Windows 2000 and Exchange 2000 because administrators locate and manage objects in a single location.
- *Simplified security management*—The Exchange 2000 Information Store uses native Windows 2000 Discretionary Access Control Lists (DACL) for setting permissions on public folders and other Exchange 2000 objects.
- *DL sharing*—Both Windows 2000 and Exchange 2000 can use the mail-enabled security groups for mass mailing as well as assigning permissions.
- *Easier access to directory information*—Lightweight Directory Access Protocol (LDAP) is the favored protocol for accessing directory information.
- *Global address lists (GALs)*—The global address book that is accessed by the clients is provided by the AD.

In a Windows 2000 forest in which Exchange 2000 Servers are installed in multiple domains, at least one server in each domain must be configured as a Global Catalog (GC) Server. The number and placement of domain controllers (DCs) and GCs depend on your network and messaging system topology.

Set Up Forests

Exchange 2000 relies heavily on the AD directory service, so it is important to determine whether all Windows 2000 domains are part of the same forest. An Exchange 2000 organization cannot span multiple Windows 2000 forests. If multiple forests exist, the only possible solution for an enterprise messaging system is to use multiple Exchange 2000 organizations.

Exchange 2000 needs to extend the AD to accomodate the larger set of objects and properties supporting messaging and collaboration. Before installing Exchange 2000, ensure that the administrative account used for the installation is a member of the Schema Admins, Enterprise Admins, and local server administrators group. If the designated administrative account cannot be assigned to these groups, you must have a user account with the appropriate security access to run the **/ForestPrep** utility on your behalf. **/ForestPrep** is a command-line switch of the Exchange 2000 **setup.exe**. Its syntax is the following:

```
SETUP.EXE/FORESTPREP
```

/ForestPrep should be run once per forest. **/ForestPrep** accomplishes different tasks depending on whether you are installing Exchange 2000 into an Exchange 5.5 organization or you are creating a new Exchange organization.

/ForestPrep for New Exchange 2000 Organizations

Running **/ForestPrep** in a new Exchange 2000 organization makes the following changes to the organization:

- Extends the AD schema to include Exchange-specific information. This affects the entire forest and it might take a considerable amount of time to replicate changes to every domain and DC.
- Prompts for and creates the Exchange organization name and object in AD. When Exchange is installed and **/DomainPrep** runs in each domain where Exchange is to be installed, Setup queries AD for configuration information. This simplifies deployment of Exchange throughout the forest.
- Assigns Exchange Full Administrator permissions for the account that you specify. This account is authorized to install Exchange throughout the forest. After the first installation of Exchange 2000, you can use this account to run the Exchange Administration Delegation Wizard, which configures Exchange-specific roles for administrators throughout the forest.

If you run **/ForestPrep** in a forest without earlier versions of Exchange Server, perform the following:

1. Check all Windows 2000 dependencies; namely, that there is a GC in the domain where Exchange 2000 should be installed, the DNS Server is properly in place, and Windows 2000 SP1 is applied. You must review connectivity; for example, confirm the quality of connections between the DC, GC, DNS server, and the machine where **/ForestPrep** is run should be connected. Confirm that permissions are properly assigned to the account initiating the **/ForestPrep** command, and lastly prepare the media where the installation files will be taken.

2. If you are running **/ForestPrep** from an Exchange 2000 CD, insert the CD; if you are running it over the network, map the network drive or connect to the network share.
3. Choose Start|Run, and type "Source :\setup\i386\setup /Forestprep", or from the command prompt type "F:\setup\i386\setup /Forestprep", where F is your CD-ROM drive or the drive letter assigned to the mapped network share (see Figure 10.1).
4. The Exchange 2000 Installation Wizard appears. On the Welcome screen, click Next.
5. Read End User License Agreement (EULA) and click I Agree if you accept the terms, and then click Next.
6. On the Product Identification page, enter the 25-digit product identification number found on the back of your Exchange 2000 Server CD case. Click Next.
7. On the Component Selection page, verify that the action next to Exchange 2000 Server is **/ForestPrep**, and then click Next (see Figure 10.2).
8. On the Installation Type screen, click Create An Exchange 2000 Organization.
9. On the Organization Name screen, type the name of your new organization.

WARNING! The name you choose for your Exchange organization cannot be changed without reinstalling the system.

10. On the Exchange 2000 Administrator Account screen, type the name of the user or group that is responsible for installing Exchange. The account that

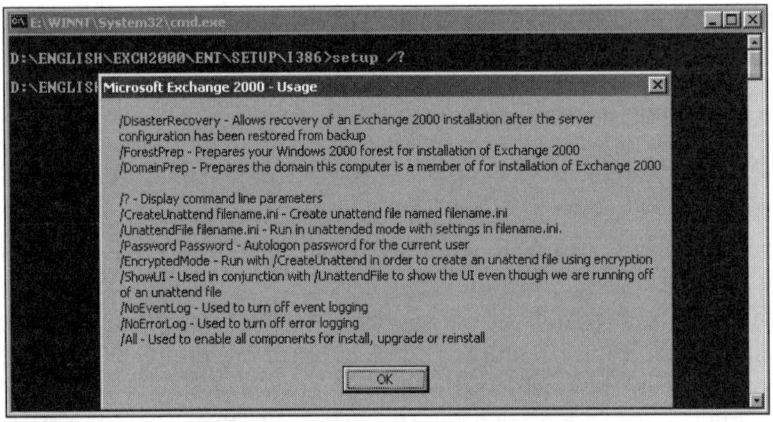

Figure 10.1 Using the command line to run **/ForestPrep**.

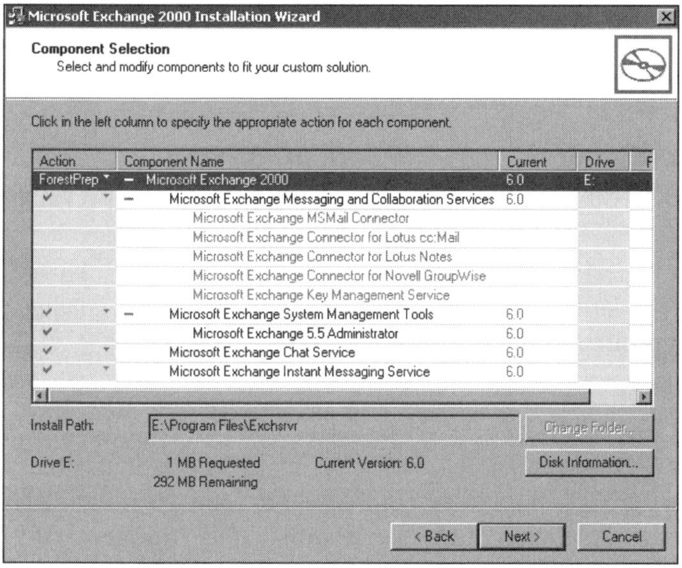

Figure 10.2 **/ForestPrep** Component Selection screen.

you specify will also have permission to create all types of Exchange administrator accounts in the Exchange Administration Delegation Wizard. Click Next (see Figure 10.3).

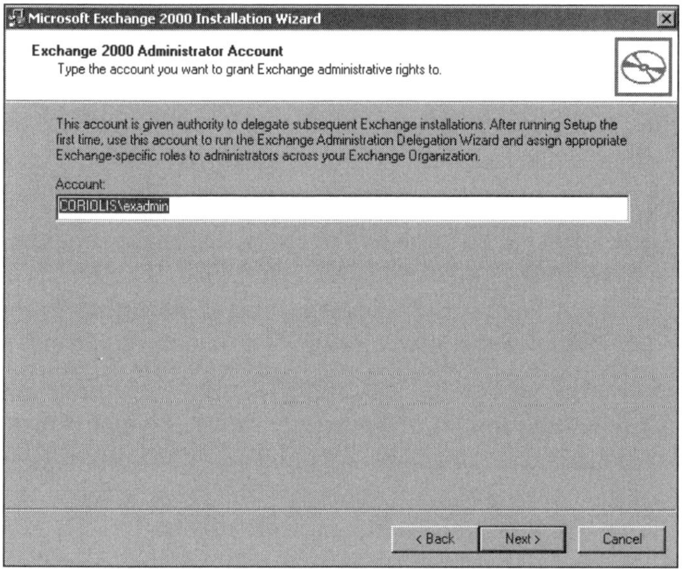

Figure 10.3 Exchange 2000 Administrator Account screen.

11. **/ForestPrep** begins and then a prompt asks you to verify the schema update. Click OK.
12. On the Completion screen, click Finish.

/ForestPrep for Existing Exchange 2000 Organizations

If you are running **/ForestPrep** in a forest that is running an earlier version of Exchange, running **/ForestPrep**:

- Extends the AD schema to include Exchange-specific information. This affects the entire forest, and depending on the size of AD, it might take a considerable amount of time to replicate changes throughout the forest.
- Creates the Exchange Organization object in the AD schema based on configuration information from your Exchange 5.5 organization.
- Assigns Exchange Full Administrator permissions for the account that you specify. This account has the authority to install Exchange throughout the forest. After the first installation of Exchange, you can use this account to run the Exchange Administration Delegation Wizard, which configures Exchange-specific roles for administrators throughout the forest. You might want to consider granting existing Exchange 5.5 administrators these permissions.

To run **/ForestPrep** in a forest with earlier versions of Exchange Server, perform the following:

1. Check all dependencies: Ensure that there is a GC in the domain where Exchange 2000 should be installed, the DNS Server is properly in place, and Windows 2000 SP1 is applied. Review connectivity. The DC, GC, DNS Server, and the machine where **/ForestPrep** is run should be connected. See to it that permissions are properly assigned to the account initiating the **/ForestPrep**, and lastly prepare the media where the installation files will be taken.
2. The **/ForestPrep** utility is called upon by the Exchange Setup program. To run **/ForestPrep** from an Exchange 2000 CD, insert the CD in the CD bay. If you are running it over the network, connect to the Exchange 2000 shared folder or map a drive letter to the shared folder.
3. Choose Start|Run, and type "Source :\setup\i386\setup /Forestprep". The Exchange 2000 Installation Wizard appears. Another way to start the **/ForestPrep** is to go to the command prompt and type "F:\setup\i386\setup /Forestprep" from the command line (where F is the drive letter of the CD-ROM or the drive letter assigned to the network share).
4. On the Welcome screen, click Next.
5. Read the EULA, and click I Agree if you accept the terms, and then, click Next.

6. On the Product Identification page, enter the 25-digit product identification. Click Next.
7. On the Component Selection page, verify that **/ForestPrep** is selected next to MS Exchange 2000. Click Next.
8. On the Installation Type page, select Join An Existing Exchange 5.5 Organization.
9. On the Select A Server From An Exchange 5.5 Organization screen, type the computer name of an Exchange Server that resides in an existing Exchange 5.5 site. The server that you specify must be running Exchange 5.5 SP3 (see Figure 10.4).
10. On the Exchange 2000 Administrator Account screen, enter the name of the user or group that will be responsible for installing Exchange. This user or group will be able to create Exchange administrator accounts throughout the forest by using the Exchange Administrator Delegation Wizard.
11. On the Service Account page, type the account name and password for the existing Exchange 5.5 service account, and click Next.
12. **/ForestPrep** begins; the Component Progress box appears after approximately 30 seconds and prompts you for verification to update the schema. Click OK.
13. On the Completion page, click Finish.

Make sure the server on which **/ForestPrep** is running (or intended to run) is connected to the schema master of the Windows 2000 domain. When joining an

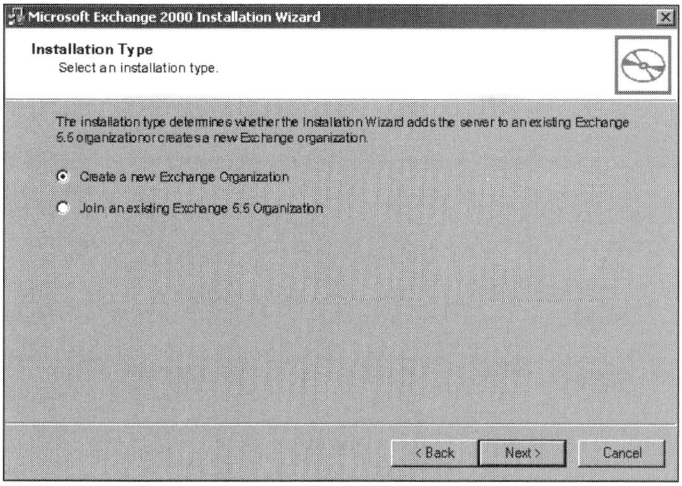

Figure 10.4 Select an Exchange 5.5. Server screen.

existing Exchange 5.5 SP3 organization, run **/ForestPrep** from an account that also has at least View Only Administrator permissions on the Exchange 5.5 SP3 Site container and Configuration container. **/ForestPrep** asks for the account with Exchange Full Administrator permissions. The person or group responsible for installing Exchange uses this account to perform subsequent Exchange 2000 installations. Remember, however, when the schema has been updated by the **/ForestPrep**, it can never be rolled back. This is because **/ForestPrep** has already extended the schema of the AD to make it Exchange-aware. Extending the AD schema means that hundreds of new attributes are introduced to the AD. Because all those attributes are stored in the AD, they will stay there for as long as your AD will be in existence.

Set Up Domains

Domains must be prepared before building an Exchange environment. You prepare a domain for Exchange 2000 by using the command line syntax:

```
SETUP.EXE switch /DOMAINPREP
```

/DomainPrep is run once per domain to create the container for the public folder proxy object and to set permissions within the domain. You do not need to run **/DomainPrep** in a domain until you are ready to install Exchange 2000.

/DomainPrep Uses

/DomainPrep is a tool that you use to prepare the forest without performing an Exchange installation. **/DomainPrep** must be run in each domain that contains recipient objects, such as users, mailboxes, and DLs.

Running **/DomainPrep** performs the following actions:

- Creates the global security group, Exchange Domain Servers (formerly known as Domain EXServers).
- Creates the domain local security group, Exchange Enterprise Servers (formerly known as All Exchange Servers).
- Adds the Exchange Domain Servers group to the Exchange Enterprise Servers group.
- Creates the container for the public folder proxy object.
- Grants appropriate permissions for Exchange 2000 administrators and Exchange Servers.

NOTE: *The first Exchange 2000 Server installed in the domain becomes the* Recipient Update Service (RUS) *by default. The RUS updates the recipient objects within a domain with specific types of information.*

Account permissions needed to run **/DomainPrep** include the following:

- Use an account that is a member of the Domain Admins security group for the domain.
- Use an account that has local administrative permissions on the computer from which you are running **/DomainPrep**.
- Exchange 2000 and Exchange 5.5 administrative permissions are not required to run **/DomainPrep**.

/DomainPrep in a Domain

After running **/ForestPrep**, run **/DomainPrep** in each domain that you want to install Exchange 2000 in, including the domain in which you ran **/ForestPrep**.

The procedure for running **/DomainPrep** is the same whether or not your AD forest includes earlier versions of Exchange 2000 or if you are running the first instance of Exchange 2000.

To run **/DomainPrep** in a domain, perform the following:

NOTE: *If you are running **/DomainPrep** in the same domain where you ran **/ForestPrep**, skip Steps 4 and 5.*

1. If you are running **/DomainPrep** from an Exchange 2000 CD, insert the CD: if you are running it over the network; map the network drive or connect to the network share. You can run **/DomainPrep** on any computer running Windows 2000 Server in the domain.

NOTE: *After running **/ForestPrep**, make certain ALL changes have replicated in a domain before running **/DomainPrep** in that domain.*

2. Choose Start|Run, and type "E:\setup\i386\setup /Domainprep" or from the command prompt type in: "E:\setup\i386\setup /Domainprep", where drive E is the location of the Exchange 2000 installation files. The Exchange 2000 Installation Wizard appears after the command is initiated.
3. On the Welcome page, click Next.
4. Read the EULA and click I Agree if you accept the terms, and then click Next.
5. On the Product Identification page, enter the 25-digit CD key that is written on the product CD case. Click Next.

6. As with the Setup **/ForestPrep** process, you will see the Component Selection screen. You will not be able to change anything except the folder where Exchange will be installed. You should be able to use the default folder. Click Next to accept the default installation path and continue, or click Change Folder to choose another path (see Figure 10.5).
7. On the Recipient Update Server screen, type the name of the computer that will be your Exchange RUS for this domain. This computer must not be installed yet, but a computer account must exist in the Active Directory Users and Computers snap-in. When you install the first instance of Exchange in this domain, it must use the computer account that you enter in this step. Click Next.
8. On the Completion page, click Finish.

Set Up Mailboxes

Unlike the previous versions of Exchange, mailboxes in Exchange 2000 are not treated as individual objects; instead, they are an attribute of an AD object. Objects in the AD can be mail-enabled or mailbox-enabled. Accounts are administered using the Active Directory Users and Computers snap-in. When Exchange 2000 is installed, the property pages of each AD object are extended, including a number of Exchange-related tabs. AD objects and mailbox-enabled AD objects (user accounts, security groups, public folders) are created using the same

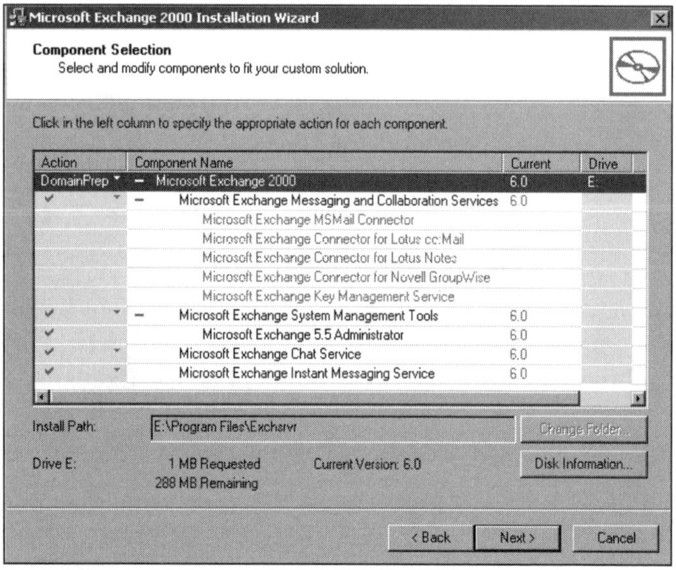

Figure 10.5 Component Selection screen.

Active Directory Users and Computers snap-in. Exchange 2000 mailboxes are created in different ways. Mailboxes can be created as an upgrade initiative or as a new installation of Exchange 2000.

Create a Mailbox Through an Exchange 5.5 Upgrade

You can create mailboxes two ways when upgrading previous versions of Exchange Server:

- *In-place upgrade*—For an in-place upgrade of previous versions of Exchange Server, all the Exchange mailboxes are converted to mailbox-enabled AD objects. Exchange Custom Recipients are converted to mail-enabled contacts. DLs are converted to mailbox-enabled security groups (for native-mode Windows 2000 domains).
- *Move-mailbox method*—In a move-mailbox method, all the Exchange 5.5 mailboxes are re-homed to Exchange 2000, thus making each corresponding primary account residing in the AD mailbox-enabled.

Create a Mailbox on a Fresh Installation of Exchange 2000

Creating a mailbox means making the AD object mailbox-enabled. A mailbox-enabled account is an AD object that has an Exchange mailbox associated with it. A user has to be mailbox-enabled so that he can be given mail storage in the information store. To mailbox-enable an existing AD user, follow these steps:

1. Open Active Directory Users And Computers. Expand the Windows 2000 root domain by clicking the + sign.
2. Locate the Organizational Unit (OU) containing the account you want to enable for Exchange 2000. By default, all created AD users are grouped in the User OU.
3. Right-click the user and choose Exchange Task to open the Exchange Task Wizard.
4. From the list of Available Tasks, select Create Mailbox to create a mailbox for the selected user. Click Next.
5. On the Create Mailbox page, type the alias, choose the server, and choose the Mailbox Store. The server is the Exchange 2000 home server of the user and the Mailbox Store is the SG and data store where the user belongs. Click Next.

The Progress Report appears displaying the task status. Then, the Task Summary page appears to allow you to review the whole process.

Install Exchange 2000

Before jumping into the installation proper, make certain all the hardware, software, file system, and account dependencies are met. Exchange 2000 runs only on top of Windows 2000 servers, which must be AD members as well. The NNTP component of IIS 5 also must be installed. For Exchange 2000 joining an existing Exchange 5.5 (or earlier) site, the Active Directory Connector (ADC) also must be configured. If a failed installation of Exchange 2000 has taken place, make sure the MDBDATA folder (exchsrvr\mdbdata) is empty.

Install Exchange 2000 in an NTFS (Windows NT File System) partition. Because the installation process is memory intensive, the page file must be set to twice the amount of the physical memory. If the machine has over 1GB of RAM, reconfigure the page file by adding the **/3GB** parameter to the startup line of the boot.ini file. The following explains how to install Exchange 2000 for the first time. If an earlier version of Exchange is running, the procedures vary slightly.

Components for Exchange 2000

Exchange 2000 installs many components, each of which provides a different functionality. Table 10.1 lists the Exchange 2000 components and their functions.

Table 10.1 Exchange 2000 components.

Component	Function
Exchange 2000	Components required for every Exchange Server. This installs the core components of Exchange 2000.
Exchange MSMail Connector	Provides connectivity and coexistence with MSMail post offices.
Exchange Connector for cc:Mail	Provides connectivity and coexistence with cc:Mail post offices.
Exchange Connector for Lotus Notes	Provides connectivity and coexistence with Lotus Notes Domino 4.x and later.
Exchange Connector for Novell GroupWise	Provides connectivity and coexistence with Novell GroupWise.
Exchange Messaging and Collaboration Services	Basic messaging components (required to install Instant Messaging [IM] Service or Chat Service). This contains all the available connectors.
Exchange Key Management Service (KM Service)	Exchange-specific security enhancements for Windows 2000 Server Certificate Services.
Exchange System Management Tools	Tools, including System Manager, for managing Exchange 2000 components, and Exchange 5.5 Administrator Program to administer Exchange 5.5 Servers.
Exchange Chat Service	Components necessary for hosting chat communities.
Exchange Instant Messaging Services	Components necessary for IM.
Exchange Conferencing Server	Components necessary for online conferencing.

Notice that Exchange 2000 Conferencing Server (ECS) is not in the list of components during Exchange installation. In fact, Microsoft Conference Server is another product that must be installed separately. ECS is not included in the Exchange 2000 Server (Standard or Enterprise) packaging.

Exchange System Management Tools

The following are some of the more important Exchange system management tools:

- *System Manager*—System Manager is a Microsoft Management Console (MMC) file that provides a graphical two-pane view of Exchange objects with a console tree and a details pane. You can right-click objects to see their context menus and use drag-and-drop to move objects.
- *Microsoft Exchange 5.5 Administrator Program*—This tool allows the administration of earlier versions of Exchange Servers.

Realtime Collaboration (RTC)

If you plan to deploy realtime collaboration within the organization, it is best to include the Exchange collaboration components during installation. If you have not decided if instant collaborations can help increase the productivity of users, you can, however, install them on a later date by rerunning the Exchange 2000 setup program.

The following are some RTC elements:

- *Instant Messaging*—IM allows users to see presence information (such as online, offline, out-of-the-office, busy) for other users and provides the ability to send instantaneous communications. For example, members of a team that are collaborating with one another might need the convenience of information delivered instantaneously.
- *Chat Service*—Exchange 2000 Chat Service provides a multiuser chat system in which people convene for conversations on channels (more commonly known as chat rooms).
- *Conferencing Server*—Allows users to host virtual meetings and conferences using audio, video, shared whiteboard, direct file transfer, and chat.

Immediate Solutions

Installing Exchange 2000 Components

You can select the type of installation, as well as the components to include for Exchange 2000. To install Exchange 2000 components after running **/ForestPrep** and **/DomainPrep**, log on to the Windows 2000 Server with an account that is a member of both the Domain Admins security and local administrators group. If you install before running **/ForestPrep** and **/DomainPrep**, log on with an account that has membership to the Enterprise Admins, Schema Admins, Domain Admins, and local administrators group.

To start the Exchange 2000 Installation Wizard, follow these steps:

1. Log on to the Windows 2000 Server on which you want to install Exchange. Insert the Exchange 2000 CD. On the Microsoft Exchange Server 2000 screen, click Setup, and then click Exchange Server Setup. If installing over the network, connect to the Exchange 2000 installation shared directory. Double-click **setup.exe**.
2. On the Welcome screen, click Next.
3. Read the EULA and click I Agree if you accept the terms, and then click Next.
4. On the Product Identification screen, enter the 25-digit CD key located on a sticker on the back of the product CD, and then click Next.
5. On the Component Selection page, click the node in the Action column that corresponds with the component you want to install. Click Install.

Figure 10.6 shows the Component Selection screen in Exchange Setup.

6. To change the drive location of the installation, select Microsoft Exchange, and then click Change Folder. Select or create a folder that will contain the Exchange installation files.
7. Read the Per Seat licensing agreement. To continue, click I Agree, and then click Next.
8. Succeeding steps differ depending if you're installing Exchange 2000 in a new Exchange organization, or if you are joining an existing Exchange organization. Procedures in any of these options are outlined in the next pages.

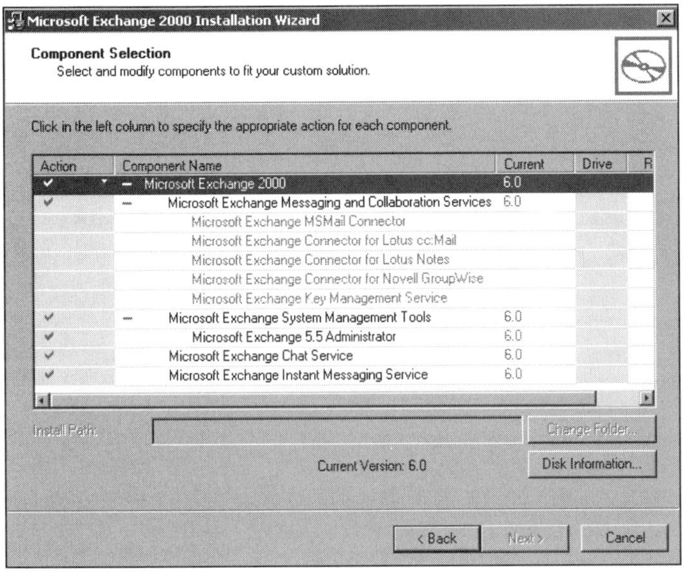

Figure 10.6 Exchange 2000 Installation Wizard Component Selection screen.

Installing Exchange 2000 in a Forest without Earlier Versions of Exchange

To install your initial version of Exchange 2000, make certain you have completed the following prerequisites:

- You deployed Windows 2000 and DNS according to the Windows 2000 documentation.
- You ran **/ForestPrep** and **/DomainPrep**.
- You are installing Exchange on the same computer that you specified as the Address List Server when you ran **/DomainPrep**.
- If you are upgrading from Exchange 5.5, you installed ADC and ran the connection agreements accordingly.

After the prerequisites are met, follow these steps to install Exchange 2000 in a forest with no earlier version of Exchange:

1. Start the Installation Wizard and select the components you want to install.
2. Read the Per Seat licensing agreement. To continue, click I Agree, and then click Next.
3. On the Installation Summary page, verify your information, and then click Next.

4. On the Licensing Agreement page, click I Agree and then click Next. If you do not select this option, the installation will stop.
5. On the Completion page, click Finish.

Installing Exchange 2000 in a Forest with Earlier Versions of Exchange

To install Exchange 2000 in a forest with earlier versions of Exchange, perform the following:

NOTE: *When you install Exchange 2000, the account you use must have Exchange Full Administrator rights for Exchange 2000 and Exchange 5.5. Thus, before you install Exchange 2000, make sure you grant the appropriate account Service Account Admin rights on the Site and Configuration objects across your Exchange 5.5 organization.*

1. Start the Installation Wizard and select the components you want to install.
2. Read the Per Seat licensing agreement. To continue, click I Agree, and then click Next.
3. From the Installation Summary page, verify that you have chosen the Exchange components you want to include in the installation, and then click Next.
4. On the Licensing Agreement page, click I Agree to accept the licensing agreement.
5. On the Select A Server In An Exchange 5.5 Organization page, type the name of a server in the site you wish to join and then click Next (see Figure 10.7).

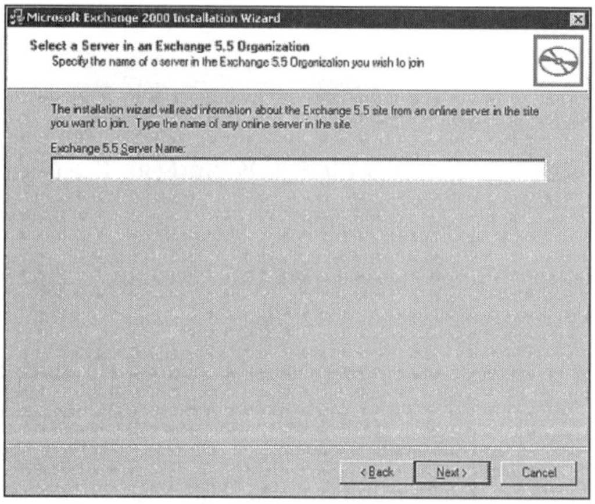

Figure 10.7 Select Exchange 5.5 Server screen.

After setup has determined that it has enough information about your Exchange 5.5 organization and your logon account to perform the installation, it prompts you for the Exchange 5.5 Service Account password to ensure that you are a current Exchange 5.5 administrator. Type the password and then click Next (see Figure 10.8).

6. On the Administrative Groups page, select the administrative group that corresponds to the Exchange 5.5 site name where the computer that you specified in **/ForestPrep** resides, and then click Next.
7. On the Routing Groups page, select the routing group that corresponds to the Exchange 5.5 site name where the computer that you specified in **/ForestPrep** resides, and then click Next.
8. On the Completion page, click Finish.

Subsequent installations of Exchange 2000 require a different procedure that allows you to select administrative groups and routing groups. By default, in organizations where no previous versions of Exchange exist, Exchange Setup creates the first administrative group and first routing group. These are not displayed in System Manager unless specifically enabled. To view the administrative group and routing group, follow these steps:

1. Open the System Manager.
2. Right-click Exchange 2000 Organization, and choose Properties.
3. On the General tab of the Organization Properties page, enable Display Routing Groups and Display Administrative Groups (see Figure 10.9).

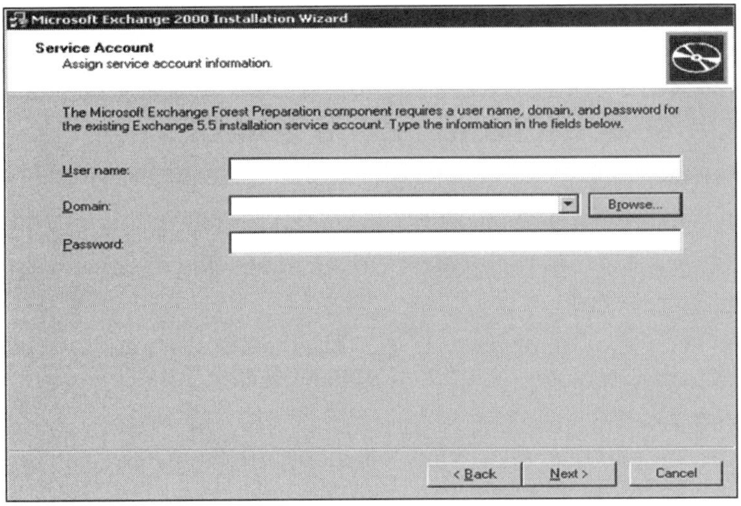

Figure 10.8 Exchange 5.5 Service Account screen.

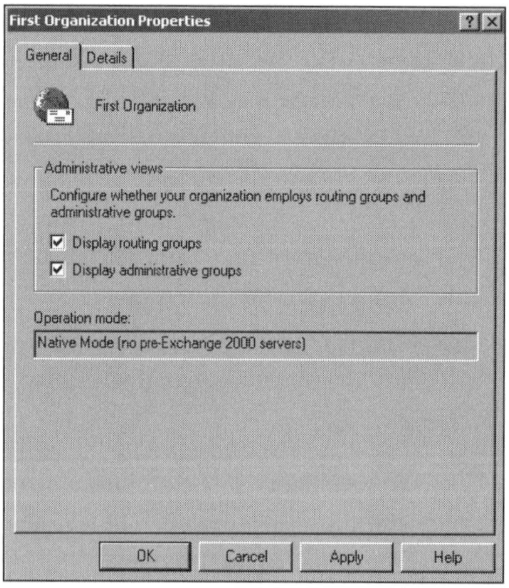

Figure 10.9 Displaying the Organization Properties page in the System Manager.

When you make both administrative groups and routing groups visible, you can add new administrative groups and routing groups to fit your deployment strategy. After you create an administrative group or routing group in System Manager, you can select them during setup when you install additional servers. If you are not using multiple administrative groups and routing groups in your organization, select the default groups, First Administrative Group and First Routing Group, during setup.

Installing Additional Exchange 2000 Servers

To install additional instances of Exchange 2000, perform the following:

1. Start the Installation Wizard and select the components you want to install.
2. Read the Per Seat licensing agreement. To continue, click I Agree, and then click Next.
3. On the Administrative Groups page, select the administrative group in which you want to install Exchange, and then click Next.
4. On the Routing Groups page, select the routing group in which you want to install Exchange, and then click Next.
5. On the Installation Summary page, verify your information, and then click Next.
6. On the Completion page, click Finish.

Installing Exchange 2000 on Windows 2000 Member Servers

Exchange 2000 can be installed on a Windows 2000 Member server. No special installation procedures are required except for an additional setting on the TCP/IP (Transmission Control Protocol/Internet Protocol) configuration. When installing in a Windows 2000 server, make sure the Append Parent Suffixes Of The Primary DNS Suffix checkbox is selected on the DNS Properties page.

Installing Exchange 2000 Server on Clustered Servers

Installing Exchange Servers in a clustered environment is a lengthy procedure. Exchange 2000 supports active/active clustering. With active/active clustering, multiple instances of a component, such as Exchange, can run simultaneously in a cluster. For guidelines on clustering Exchange 2000, refer to article Q263272 in Microsoft's Knowledge Base.

Installing Exchange 2000 Unattended

You can perform an unattended install of Exchange 2000 by using a predefined initialization file. To prepare for an unattended setup, run Exchange 2000 setup program from the command prompt with the appropriate switches. To view all the available setup switches with their descriptions, type "Source:\setup\i386\setup.exe/?" at the command prompt. The switches used for unattended installations are: **/CreateUnattend**, **/UnattendFile**, and **/EncryptedMode**.

To perform an encrypted unattended installation of Exchange 2000, perform the following:

1. Create an encrypted initialization file (*.ini) that stores all the responses to the setup question. To create the encrypted initialization file, run the following: setup.exe /CreateUnattend filename.ini /encryptedmode.
2. After creating the answer file, run Exchange Setup with the command-line switch, **UnattendFile**. From the command prompt, type: "setup.exe/UnattendFile filename.ini /encryptedmode".

Transferring the Schema Master

Schema Master is one of the five AD flexible single master operation (FSMO) roles. Schema Master is a forest-wide role, which means only one schema master can exist throughout the entire forest. The Schema Master DC controls all updates and modifications to the schema. To update the schema of a forest, you must have access to the Schema Master.

To determine the Schema FSMO Holder in a forest, perform the following:

1. Choose Start|Run, type "mmc", and click OK.
2. Select Console|Add/Remove Snap-In|Add, and double-click Active Directory Schema. Click Close, and then click OK.
3. Right-click Active Directory Schema in the top-left pane, and then click Operations Masters to view the server holding the Schema Master role.

NOTE: *For the Active Directory Schema snap-in to be available, you have to register the Schmmgmt.dll file. To do this, choose Start|Run, and type "regsvr32 WINNT\SYSTEM32\schmmgmt.dll". Click OK. Wait for a message that states the registration was successful.*

Transferring the Schema Master Role When the Schema Master Fails

Temporary loss of the schema operations master is not visible to either network users or network administrators, unless, for example, an administrator tries to modify the schema or install an application that modifies the schema during installation. The Schema Master role can be transferred to any Windows 2000 DC. If for any reason, the current Schema Master has to be replaced, a proper procedure to transfer the FSMO role has to be followed. To transfer the Schema Master role:

1. Open Active Directory Schema.
2. In the console tree, right-click Active Directory Schema and then click Change Domain Controller.
3. Click Any DC to let AD select the new schema operations master. Or, click Specify Name, and type the name of the new Schema Master computer (see Figure 10.10).
4. In the console tree, right-click Active Directory Schema, and then click Operations Master (see Figure 10.11).
5. Click Change.

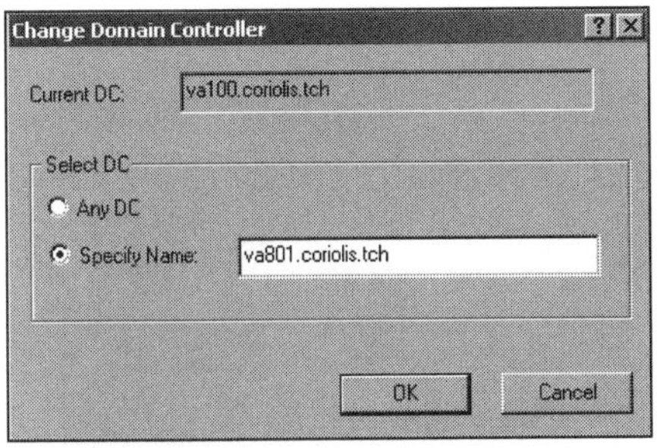

Figure 10.10 Change DC dialog box.

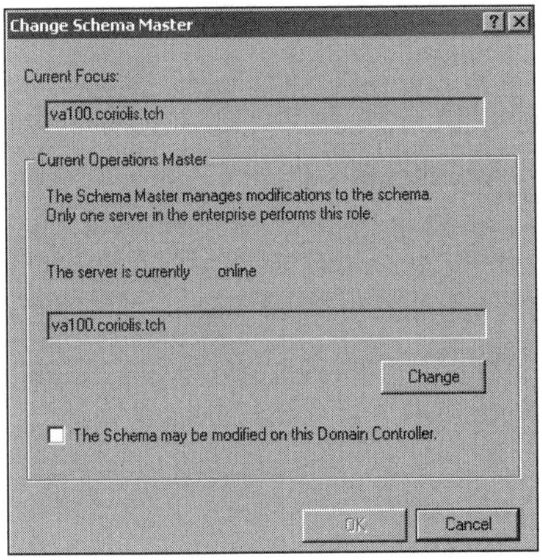

Figure 10.11 Changing the Schema Master role.

If the Schema Master has been unavailable for an unacceptable length of time, you can seize the role from the standby operations master. However, seizing this role is a drastic step taken only when the failure of the Schema Master is permanent.

WARNING! A DC whose Schema Master role has been seized must never be brought back online. It is recommended that you remove the server with the existing FMSO on the network before seizing the FSMO role.

To seize the Schema Master role, perform the following:

1. Click Start|Run, and then type "cmd".
2. At the command prompt, type "ntdsutil".
3. At the **ntdsutil** prompt, type "roles".
4. At the fsmo maintenance prompt, type "connections".

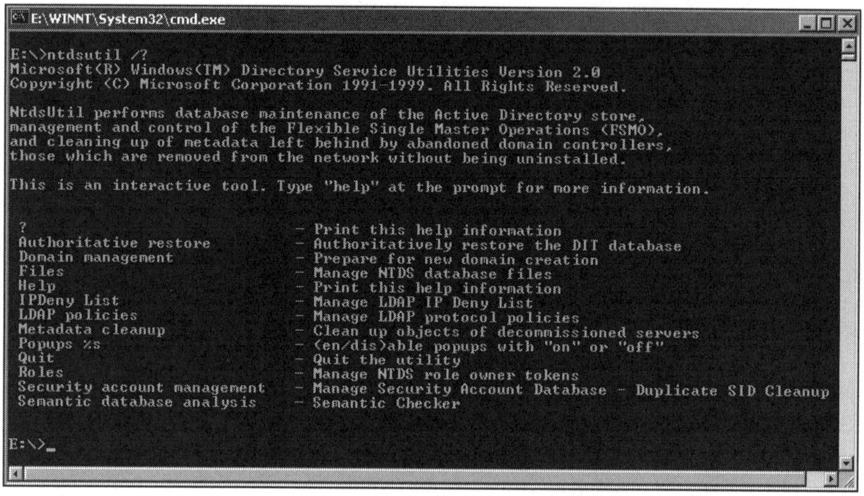

Figure 10.12 Transferring Schema Master using ntdsutil.

5. At the server connections prompt, type "connect to server", followed by the fully qualified domain name.
6. At the server connections prompt, type "quit".
7. At the fsmo maintenance prompt, type "seize schema master" (see Figure 10.12).
8. At the fsmo maintenance prompt, type "quit".
9. At the **ntdsutil** prompt, type "quit".

Setting Schema Write Operations in the Registry

A user account requires write access to the schema, enabled by the **Schema Update Allowed Registry** key to extend or modify the AD schema. The schema updates can only be enabled on the DC that holds the Schema Master role. Schema updates can be enabled by means of the Schema Management Console or by editing the Registry.

WARNING! Using Registry Editor incorrectly can cause serious problems that might require you to reinstall the OS. You should update your Emergency Repair Disk (ERD) before continuing with any procedure of this nature.

To enable schema updates using the Schema Management Console, follow these steps:

1. Open Active Directory Schema.
2. Click Active Directory Schema so that the Classes and Attributes sections are displayed on the right-hand side.
3. Right-click Active Directory Schema and click Operations Master.
4. Select the Schema May Be Modified On This Domain Controller checkbox. Click OK, and then exit the console.

The schema can now be updated on the DC that holds the schema operations master role. It is not recommended to enable schema updates by directly editing the **Schema Update Allowed** Registry key. Schema updates should be enabled through the console method, whenever possible. If for some reason the console method cannot be used, the following Registry key can be edited directly:

```
HKEY_LOCAL_MACHINE\SYSTEM\CurrentControlSet\Services\NTDS\Parameters
```

To directly edit this Registry key, follow these steps:

1. Select Start|Run, and type "regedit". Then press Enter.
2. Locate the following Registry key:

   ```
   HKEY_LOCAL_MACHINE\SYSTEM\CurrentControlSet\Services\NTDS\Parameters
   ```

3. Choose Edit|New, and then click **DWORD** value.
4. Enter the value data when the following Registry value is displayed:

   ```
   Value Name: Schema Update Allowed
   Data Type: REG_DWORD
   Base: Binary
   Value Data: Type 1 (to enable this feature) or Type 0 (zero) to
     disable it.
   ```

5. Close the Registry Editor.

The schema can now be updated on the DC that holds the schema operations master role.

NOTE: *Enabling the Schema May Be Modified On This Domain Controller checkbox in the console adds the* ***Schema Update Allowed*** *Registry value if it isn't present. When the Schema May Be Modified On This Domain Controller checkbox is cleared, the* ***Schema Update Allowed*** *Registry value is set to 0, but it does not delete the value.*

Configuring the Exchange 2000 System Attendant

The System Attendant is one of the core Exchange 2000 services that perform functions usually related to directory information such as generation of address lists, offline address books, and directory lookup facilities. Some System Attendant functions are configurable via the System Manager Server component. To configure the server, set the following properties:

1. Right-click the server, and then choose Properties.
2. Click the General tab.
3. To log all messages to the message-tracking log file, click Enable Message Tracking. You can view the messages with the Message Tracking Center.
4. To log message subjects to the message-tracking log file, click Enable Subject Logging And Display. You can view the messages with the Message Tracking Center (see Figure 10.13).
5. To automatically remove log files, click Remove Log Files. This is enabled by default and set to seven days.
6. To make the server a front-end server, click This Is A Front-End Server.
7. Exchange automatically provides the name of the domain controller where it retrieves configuration information. You can view the Windows 2000 Domain Controller (from which services running on this server retrieve their configuration information) in Domain Controller Used By Services On This Server text box.

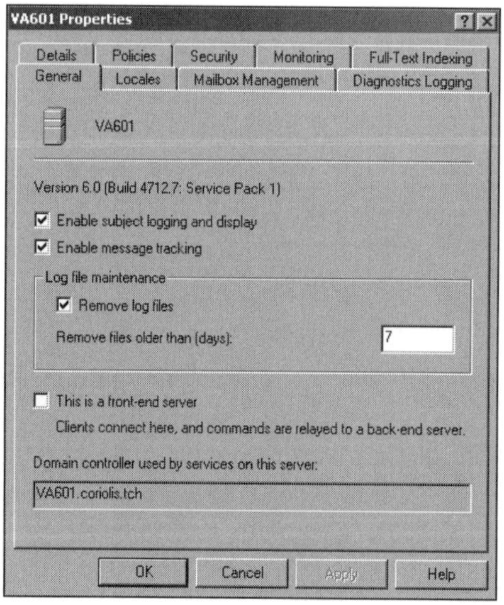

Figure 10.13 Server Properties General tab.

You set locales to determine how date, currency, and time values are displayed, and control international settings such as sorting order. Add locales if there are clients connecting to the Exchange 2000 Server using languages other than the default setting (U.S. English). Configuring multiple locales can affect the performance of the Exchange 2000 Server. Locales may decrease server performance because the directory database must use processing power and memory to maintain extra indexes for each client language. If your foreign language clients do not connect to the Exchange Server often, it may not be a good idea to maintain multiple locales. Ideally, there should only be one locale configured. To add server locales, perform the following:

1. Right-click the server, and then click Properties.
2. Click the Locales tab.
3. Click Add to display Add Locale.
4. Click the locale you want to add, and then click OK.

To remove server locales, perform the following:

1. Right-click the server and then click Properties.
2. Click the Locales tab.
3. Click the locale you want to remove, and then click OK.

To set Diagnostic Logging properties, perform the following:

1. Right-click the server, and then click Properties.
2. Click the Diagnostics Logging tab.
3. To see the current logging levels for a particular service, click a service in the Services list. The available services are X.400 Protocol, System Attendant, Site Replication Service, Transport, and Post Office Protocol version 3 (POP3).
4. To see the logging level for a service category, click a category.
5. To change the logging level for a service category, click a logging level. The levels are as follows:
    - *None*—Only critical events, error events, and events with a logging level of 0 are logged. This is the default level.
    - *Minimum*—Events with a logging level of 1 or lower are logged.
    - *Medium*—Events with a logging level of 3 or lower are logged.
    - *Maximum*—Events with a logging level of 5 or lower are logged.

Set Full-Text Indexing properties by performing the following:

1. Right-click the server, and then click Properties.

2. Click the Full-Text Indexing tab.
3. Select one of the four available usage levels: Minimum, Low, High, or Maximum.

To set Monitoring properties, perform the following:

1. Right-click the server, and then click Properties.
2. Click the Monitoring tab.
3. To monitor a new server resource, click Add.
4. Select one of the following resources, and then click OK.
   - Available Virtual Memory
   - CPU Usage
   - Free Disk Space
   - SMTP Queue Growth
   - Windows 2000 Service
   - X.400 Queue Growth
5. To disable Monitoring, click Disable All Monitoring Of This Server.

Configuring the Information Store

Exchange 2000 Enterprise's support for multiple mailbox stores and public folder stores—instead of a single private Information Store and public Information Store, as in earlier versions of Exchange—allows you to design your storage so that individual databases are smaller. This storage design will support faster backup and restore and increased flexibility in managing disaster recovery efforts. The default SG created upon installation of Exchange 2000 is the First SG; the first data stores within it are the Mailbox Store and Public Store. These could be used to store mailboxes and public folders respectively. The Mailbox Store is comprised of two databases, the standard private information store (PRIV) and the streaming database file (STM). Consequently, the public folder store also is composed of the public information store database (PUB) and the streaming database file (STM). The Information Stores can be administered using the Exchange System Manager.

To add a SG, perform the following:

1. Choose Start|Programs|Microsoft Exchange|System Manager.
2. Open the Servers container in the console tree.

3. Right-click the server to which you want to add a SG, point to New, and then click SG.
4. On the General tab, set the following properties:
   - To name the SG, use the Name Textbox.
   - To change the name and location of the transaction logs, use Transaction Log Location. To move the logs, use System Manager on the server on which the logs reside.
   - To change the name and location of the system path, use System Path Location. This is where temporary (tmp.edb) and recovered (edb.chk) files are stored.
   - To clear each 4KB page of data from the drive at deletion, click Zero Out Deleted Database Pages. This is a security measure because enabling this checkbox will clear deleted data from the drive. Though providing security, this option does have an impact on the performance of the server.
   - To reuse the same log file instead of creating a new one when the 5MB limit is reached, click Enable Circular Logging.

NOTE: *Enabling Circular Logging prevents you from performing differential or incremental backups. Reserve this option for NNTP SGs that do not require log files.*

Figure 10.14 below shows the SG General tab.

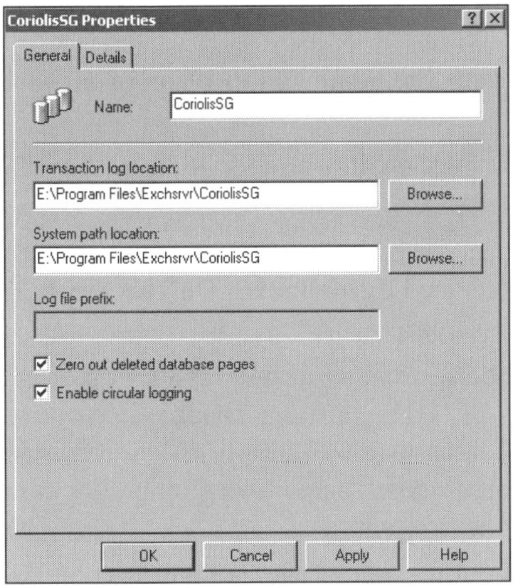

Figure 10.14 Storage Group Properties sheet.

To add a mailbox store, perform the following:

1. Choose Start|Programs|Microsoft Exchange|System Manager.
2. Open the Servers container in the console tree.
3. Click the server to which you want to add the mailbox store.
4. Right-click the SG container to which you want to add the mailbox store, point to New, and then click Mailbox Store.
5. On the General tab, set the following properties:
   - In Name text box, type a name for the mailbox store.
   - To change the name and location of the default public store, use Default Public Store.

Setting Mailbox Properties

To set the mailbox properties, follow these steps:

1. Choose Start|Programs|Microsoft Exchange|System Manager.
2. Navigate to the mailbox store in the console tree.
3. Right-click the mailbox store, and then click Properties. The Properties page contains seven tabs.
4. On the General tab, set the following properties:
   - Type a new name in Name Textbox.
   - Use Default Public Store to change the name and location of the default public store.
   - Use Offline Address List to change the name and location of the offline address list.
   - To archive messages sent or received by mailboxes on this store, click Archive All Messages Sent Or Received By Mailboxes On This Store. Then click Browse, and select or name an archive.
   - If your clients support Secure/Multipurpose Internet Mail Extensions (S/MIME), click Clients Support S/MIME Signatures. Disable this option to convert messages with S/MIME signatures to Multipurpose Internet Mail Extensions (MIME) unsigned messages. This allows clients that cannot interpret MIME to view signed messages.
   - To convert scalable fonts to fixed fonts, click Display Plain Text Messages In A Fixed-Sized Font.

5. On the Database tab, set the following properties:
   - To change the name and location of the Rich Text Format (RTF) file, use the Exchange Database Textbox. Use System Manager on the server on which the databases reside to move the databases.
   - To change the name and location of the MIME format file, use the Exchange Streaming Database Textbox. Use System Manager on the server on which the databases reside to move the databases.
   - To build a custom schedule graphically, click a value in the Maintenance Interval drop-down list or click Customize to make your own database maintenance schedule.
   - To prevent the automatic mounting of the store, click Don't Mount This Store At Start-Up checkbox.
   - To allow database overwrites, click This Database Can Be Overwritten By A Restore checkbox.

Figure 10.15 shows the Database Properties page.

6. On the Limits tab, set the following properties:
   - To set a retention period for deleted items, provide a value in the Keep Deleted Items For (Days) textbox.
   - To set a retention period for deleted mailboxes, provide a value in the Keep Deleted Mailboxes For (Days) Textbox.

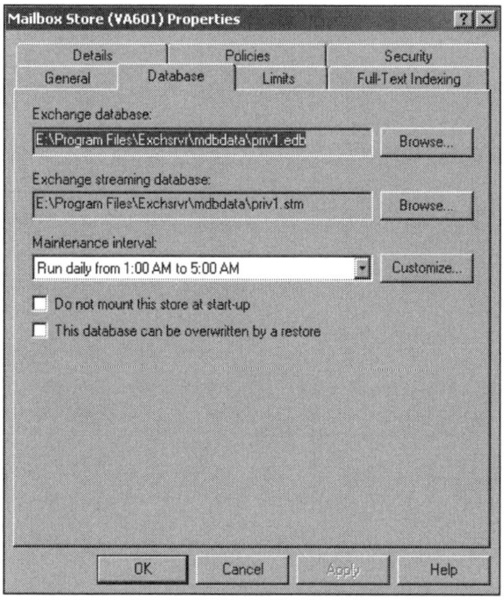

Figure 10.15 A Mailbox Store Properties sheet.

- To preserve items until backup, click Do Not Permanently Delete Mailboxes And Items Until The Store Has Been Backed Up checkbox.
- To send a warning when the storage used reaches a specific size, click Issue Warning At (KB) checkbox and provide a value in the textbox.
- To stop sending items when the storage used reaches a specific size, click Prohibit Send At (KB) checkbox and provide a value in the textbox.

NOTE: *This option is not used when messages are sent by POP3 or Internet Message Access Protocol version 4 (IMAP4) clients because those protocols do not support this functionality.*

- To stop sending and receiving items when the storage used reaches a specific size, click Prohibit Send And Receive At (KB) checkbox and provide a value in the textbox.
- To build a custom schedule graphically, click a value in Warning Message Interval drop-down list or click Customize.

Figure 10.16 shows the Mailbox Store Limits tab.

7. On the Details tab, select Administrative Note to add additional information.
8. On the Security tab, set permissions for the mailbox store for users and groups by clicking a user or group, and then clicking Allow or Deny to grant or deny permission.

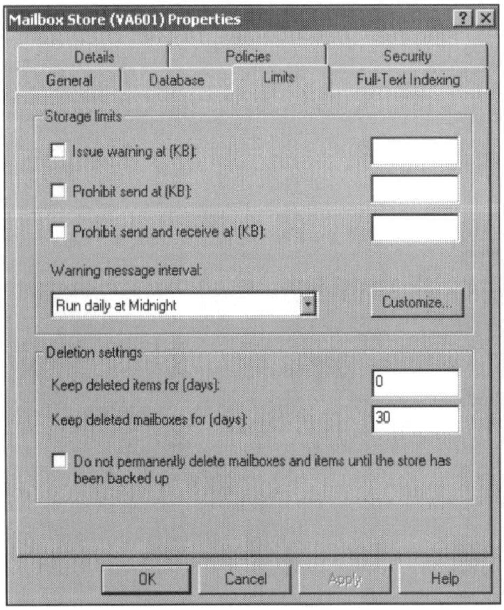

Figure 10.16 The Limits tab on a Mailbox Store Properties sheet.

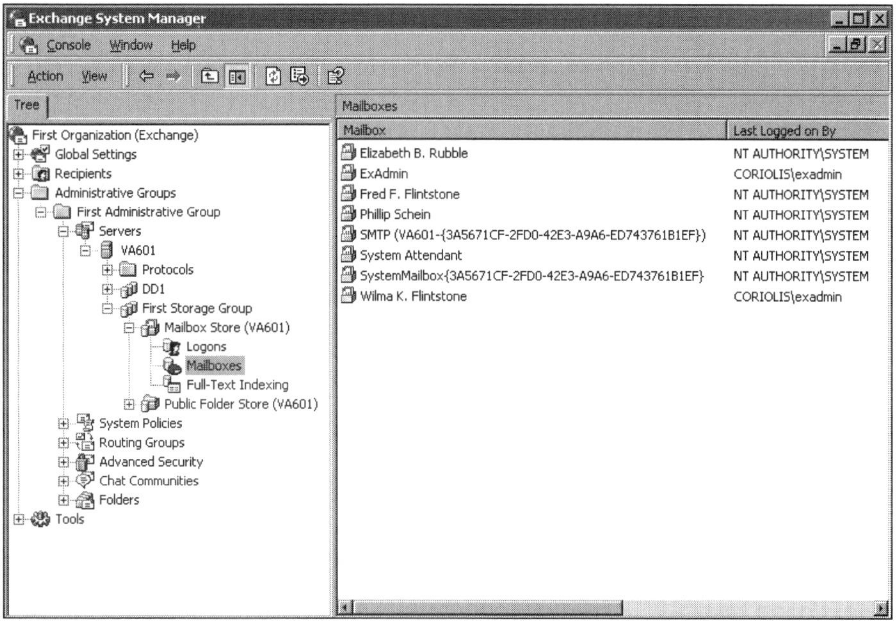

Figure 10.17 A Listing of Mailbox Stores from System Manager.

NOTE: *Permissions inherited from the parent object (the SG) are indicated by shaded checkboxes. Scroll to the bottom of the Permissions list to see the extended permissions specific to Exchange.*

You also can view logon and mailbox information, apply policies to the mailbox store, and run full-text indexing on the mailbox store. These actions can be performed in the System shown in Figure 10.17.

Creating a New Public Folder Tree

A public folder store cannot be created without first creating a public folder hierarchy in which to store it. The default public folder tree is the only MAPI-accessible public folder tree. Additional public folder trees are only accessible by applications and Web browsers. The default public folder tree is associated with the default public folder store.

To create a new public folder tree, perform the following:

1. Choose Start|Programs|Microsoft Exchange|System Manager.
2. Expand the Administrative Groups, and go to the group you want to work with.

3. Right-click Folders, point to New, and then click Public Folder Tree.
4. Type a name for the new public folder tree in the Name box.

Adding a Public Folder Store

The only other property required when adding a public folder store is the public folder name. To add a public folder store perform the following:

1. Choose Start|Programs|Microsoft Exchange|System Manager.
2. Open the Servers container in the console tree.
3. Click the server to which you want to add the public folder store.
4. Right-click the SG container to which you want to add the public store, point to New, and then click Public Store.
5. On the General tab, set the following properties:
   - Type a name for the public folder store in the Name box.
   - To select the name and location of the public store hierarchy to associate with the new public folder store, click Associated Public Store Tree.

The public folder store properties can be changed using the System Manager.

Setting Public Folder Store Properties

To set public folder store properties, perform the following:

1. Choose Start|Programs|Microsoft Exchange|System Manager.
2. Navigate to the Public Folder Store in the console tree, right-click the Public Folder Store, and then click Properties. The property page contains eight tabs.
3. On the General tab, set the following properties:
   - Type a new name in the Name Textbox.
   - To change the name and location of the associated public folder tree, use Associated Public Folder Tree.
   - If your clients support S/MIME, click the Clients Support S/MIME Signatures checkbox. Disable this to convert messages with S/MIME signatures to MIME unsigned messages. This allows clients that cannot interpret MIME to view signed messages.

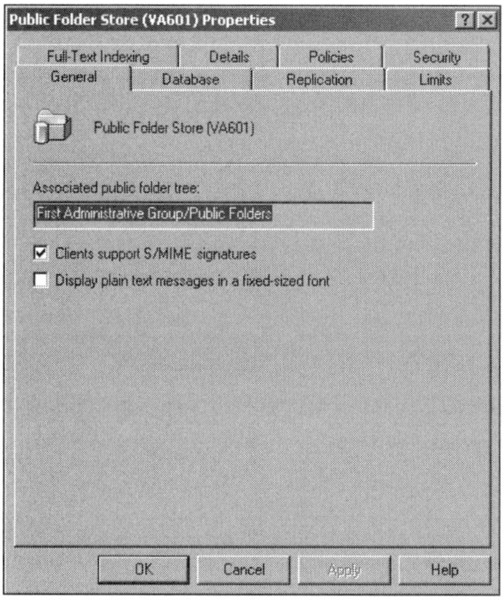

Figure 10.18 The General tab from Public Folder Store Property sheet.

- To convert scalable fonts to fixed fonts, click the checkbox Convert Inbound Internet Messages To Fixed Font.

Figure 10.18 shows the General tab/Public Folder Storage Properties page.

4. On the Database tab, set the following properties:
   - To change the name and location of the RTF file, click Exchange Database. Use System Manager on the server on which the databases reside to move the databases.
   - To change the name and location of the MIME format file, click Exchange Streaming Database. Use System Manager on the server on which the databases reside to move the databases.
   - To build a custom schedule graphically, choose a value in the Maintenance Interval drop-down list or click Customize.
   - To prevent automatic mounting of the store, click Don't Mount This Store At Start-Up.
   - To allow database overwrites, click This Database Can Be Overwritten By A Restore.
5. On the Limits tab, set the following properties:
   - To set a retention period for deleted items, click Keep Deleted Items For (Days).
   - To preserve items until backup, click Don't Permanently Delete Items Until The Store Has Been Backed Up.

- To send a warning when the storage used reaches the value specified, click Issue Warning At (KB).
- To stop sending and receiving mail when the storage used reaches a specific size, click Prohibit Send And Receive At (KB).
- To build a custom schedule graphically, click a value in Send Over-Limit Messages or click Customize.
- To set an age limit for folders, click Age Limit For All Folders In This Store (Days) and type a value.

6. On the Details tab, use Administrative Note to add information.
7. On the Security tab, set permissions for the public folder store for users and groups by clicking a user or group, and then clicking Allow or Deny to grant or deny permission.

NOTE: *Permissions inherited from the parent object (the SG) are indicated by shaded checkboxes. Scroll to the bottom of the Permissions list to see the extended permissions specific to Exchange.*

You also can view logon information, public folder instances, and Replication Status from the public folder store. You also can define indexing and policies.

Changing Public Folder Home Servers

You can move and copy objects from one administrative group to another as long as it's done from within the same container. You can move a public folder from the original home server to change its home server. To move the public folder, perform the following:

1. Choose Start|Programs|Microsoft Exchange|System Manager.
2. Expand the Administrative Groups.
3. Go to the Administrative group on which the original public folder tree resides.
4. Expand Folders, right-click the Public Folder Tree that has to be moved, and select Cut from the menu.
5. Go to the Administrative group to which you intend to transfer the public folder tree.
6. Right-click Folders and select Paste. (Alternatively, you also can drag-and-drop the public folder.)

Replicating Public Folders

To replicate a public folder to another server, ensure that a storage location has been created on the destination server. Replicating public folders provides fault tolerance and load balancing. An effective public-folder strategy includes identifying the public folders to be replicated and the corresponding Exchange 2000 Servers or corresponding Public Folder Stores that will contain the replica. To configure Exchange to replicate public folders, perform the following:

1. Choose Start|Programs|Microsoft Exchange|System Manager.
2. If administrative groups are displayed, expand Administrative Groups, and then expand the group you want to work with.
3. In the console tree, expand Folders, and then expand the folder hierarchy for the Public Folder Store.
4. Right-click a public folder you want to replicate, and then click Properties.
5. Click the Replication tab, and click Add in the Replicate Content To These Public Stores section.

To remove a replica of the public folder, on the Replication tab, select the server on which you do not want to maintain a copy of the folder, and then click Remove.

Carefully configure how often the replicas of public folders are replicated. Careless setting of the replication schedule can unneccessarily increase the network bandwidth. Best practices recommend public folder replication should be scheduled during low network use.

Scheduling Replication for All Folders in a Database

If all public folders are used with the same frequency, create one replication schedule for all folders. After you set the schedule on the database in the public store, all folders set to Default Schedule replicate according to the database's schedule. All folders use the schedule set on the database by default. To schedule replication for all folders, follow these steps:

1. Choose Start|Programs|Microsoft Exchange|System Manager.
2. If administrative groups are displayed, expand Administrative Groups, and then expand the group you want to work with.
3. In the console tree, expand Folders, and then expand the folder hierarchy for the Public Folder Store.
4. Right-click a public folder you want to replicate, and then click Properties.
5. Click the Replication tab.

6. Choose a replication schedule or create a new schedule in the Public Folder Replication Interval drop-down list. To create a new schedule, click Customize. In the Schedule window, click Selected Times. Click the time on the grid to specify when replication of this folder will take place. Click OK to save your settings.

Scheduling Replication for a Single Folder

You can schedule a single folder to replicate as often as necessary to ensure that all replicas remain current. A schedule set for a specific folder overrides the schedule set for the parent folder and the database.

To schedule replication for a single folder, perform the following:

1. Choose Start|Programs|Microsoft Exchange|System Manager.
2. If administrative groups are displayed, expand Administrative Groups, and then expand the group you want to work with.
3. In the console tree, expand Folders, and then expand the folder hierarchy for the Public Folder Store.
4. Right-click a public folder and then click Properties.
5. On the Replication tab, click Customize to create a new schedule.
6. Click Selected Times.
7. Set the Detail View to display time in blocks of 1 hour or 15 minutes.
8. For each day of the week, click the block of time on the grid when you want replication to take place.

Installing IM Service

IM Service provides a means of communication between individuals that is immediate, interactive, and private. IM uses the RVP (Rendezvous Protocol), which is an extended subset of HTTP. Each transaction in HTTP includes a message and response code pair. Thus, there is always a response to an IM, and the connection exists until that response code returns. There are two types of IM servers: IM home server and IM router.

- *IM Home Servers*—These servers host IM user accounts and communicate directly with clients to deliver IMs and presence information.

- *IM routers*—These machines, which receive incoming messages, locate the recipient's home server and then transmit messages to the home server for further action. IM routers do not host users, but instead refer messages to other servers on the network.

If IM is not included in the Exchange 2000 installation, install the service using the Add/Remove Programs in Control Panel:

1. Choose Start|Settings|Control Panel.
2. Click Add/Remove Programs, and then click Add New Programs.
3. Browse to the Exchange 2000 Setup.exe file.
4. Click the Exchange 2000 Instant Messaging Service from the menu selection.

NOTE: *IM Service could also be installed on Exchange 5.5 SP3 Servers.*

Configuring IM

To configure IM, you need to create a Virtual Server. If you create an Exchange 2000 IM Virtual Server, Windows 2000 users can communicate with other users in realtime using the MSN Messenger Service client program. To create a Virtual Server, perform the following:

1. Click Start|Programs|Microsoft Exchange|Exchange System Manager.
2. Click to expand the Administrative Groups container, and then click to expand the first administrative group.
3. Click your server and then click Protocols.
4. Right-click Instant Messaging (RVP), and then click New.
5. Click Instant Messaging Virtual Server.
6. The Instant Messaging Installation Wizard, which helps you create the IM Service Virtual Server, is displayed. In the Welcome dialog box, click Next.
7. In the Display Name dialog box, type the display name of your Virtual Server.
8. In the IIS Server dialog box, click the Web site that you want to use in the list.
9. The FQDN of your IM Virtual Server is automatically displayed in the Domain Name dialog box. This information is gathered from the host header data that is associated with the Web site you selected in Step 8.

10. In the Host Server dialog box, select the Allow This Server To Host User Accounts checkbox. This means the server is responsible for hosting users; otherwise, the server becomes an IM router that directs incoming IM traffic to the appropriate destination.

Create and configure a DNS service location (SRV) record:

1. Start the DNS.
2. Click the zone you want.
3. Right-click that zone, point to Other New Records|Service Location|Create Record.
4. In the Service box, type "_rvp".
5. In the Protocol box, type "_tcp".
6. In the Priority box, type "0".
7. In the Weight box, type "0".
8. In the Port Number box, type "80".
9. In the Host Offering This Service box, type the FQDN of the server.

NOTE: *The FQDN is the same as the FQDN that was displayed when you created the IM Virtual Server.*

Enabling a User for IM

To enable a user for IM, perform the following:

1. Click Start|Programs|Microsoft Exchange|Active Directory Users And Computers.
2. In the console tree, double-click the domain, and then click Users.
3. Right-click the name of a user, click Exchange Tasks, and then click Next in the Welcome dialog box.
4. Click Enable Instant Messaging and then click Next.
5. Next to Instant Messaging Home Server, click Browse. In Select Instant Messaging Server in the Server Name column, click the IM Virtual Server that you created in Step 1, and then click OK.
6. When the server is displayed in the dialog box, click Next.
7. Click Finish.

NOTE: *Repeat the preceding steps as needed for any additional users that want to use the service.*

Installing the MSN Messenger Service Client

You can use a computer running Windows 2000 Server, Windows 2000 Professional, Windows NT Server 4, Windows NT Workstation 4, or Windows 9x to connect and communicate with an IM server. Winsock 2 must be installed on Windows 95–based computers to use IM. To install the MSN Messenger Service client, follow these steps:

1. Insert the Exchange Server CD.
2. Click Start|Run.
3. Click Browse, locate *drive letter*:\instmsg\i386\client\usa\mmsetup.exe (where *drive letter* is the letter of your CD-ROM drive), and then click OK.
4. Read the end user license, and then click Yes. The MSN Messenger Service client is installed.
5. In the Welcome To MSN Messenger Service dialog box, click Next.
6. In the Provide Microsoft Exchange Instant Messaging Information dialog box, type the email address of the IM user that you want to configure in the following format: "*alias@domain_name*.com", where *alias* is the Exchange 2000 alias and *domain_name* is the name of the domain.
7. In the Get A Free Passport dialog box, either import an MSN passport or use Exchange IM only, as applicable.
8. Click Finish.

After you install the MSN Messenger Service client, the client can log on to the IM server and communicate with other IM clients. The IM client relies on Internet Explorer (IE) for the connectivity settings. If a period (.) is in the user's IM logon domain (for example, **someone@.microsoft.com**), IM determines that the destination is "external." If IE has a Proxy Server defined for connectivity, this request is passed to the proxy server for a connection. To prevent the Proxy Server from mistakenly passing the IM request to the external network, enable the Bypass Proxy Server For Local Address option and include the IM domain name (or IP address) on the exclusion list.

Configuring Exchange 2000 Chat Service

In order to deploy Chat Service, perform the following steps:

1. Plan chat communities, including required network and server resources.
2. Establish a naming convention for your chat communities and channels (chat rooms).

3. Install Chat Service.
4. Configure the chat community on the server.
5. Create registered channels and, if necessary, user bans and classes.
6. Grant administrative permissions. Give administrative access (Sysop and Administrator) to selected members of your organization.
7. Make chat client software available to users.

If Chat Service is not included in the Exchange 2000 installation, install the service using Add/Remove Programs in Control Panel. The Chat Service installation requires Exchange 2000 Enterprise edition. To install the Exchange Chat Service, perform these steps:

1. Choose Start|Settings|Control Panel.
2. Click Add/Remove Programs, and then click Add New Programs.
3. Browse to the Exchange 2000 Setup.exe file.
4. Click the Exchange 2000 Chat Service from the menu selection.

You can use System Manager to create and configure chat communities and channels, set channel topics and properties, and set access restrictions for each chat community.

Creating a Chat Community for Selected Administrative Groups

A default chat network is automatically created for the first administrative group when you connect Chat Service. You can use the default community and modify it to meet your needs or you can create a new community.

In the console tree, right-click Chat Communities, click New, and then click Chat Community. On the following property tabs, modify the properties for the chat community:

- *General*—Make top-level settings for the community, including the following:
  - *Name*—Choose a name for the chat community that is unique in the domain and that reflects the owner, users, or purpose of the community. The name must not contain any blank spaces or end in a number.
  - *Connection Limits*—The number you type in Maximum Total Connections should be your estimate of the maximum number of users who might connect to the chat community at any given time. The number you type

in Maximum Anonymous Connections should be less than the number in Maximum Total Connections.

- *Accept New Connections*—Select this checkbox to allow connections to a chat community.

- *Channels*—Configure Channel Defaults and Dynamic Channels for a chat community.
- *Messages*—Type in the Message Of The Day (MOTD) or the Message For ADMIN.

NOTE: *Message for ADMIN is available to users issuing the* ***ADMIN*** *command from a chat client and should display information about the server.*

- *Security*—Configure security permissions for the chat community.
- *Authentication*—Configure the authentication methods for the chat community.

When you confirm your selection, the new chat community appears in the console tree. To give your chat users access to the chat community you created, connect the chat community to a server.

Connecting a Chat Community to a Server

To connect a chat community to a server, perform the following:

1. Choose Start|Programs|Microsoft Exchange|System Manager.
2. Right-click IRCX, and then click Properties.
3. On the General tab, click Add.
4. In the Add Community list, select the name of the chat community you want to add to this server.
5. Click Enable Server To Host This Chat Community.
6. In the IP Address drop-down list, select All Unassigned if the community needs just one IP address. This allows the server to automatically pick the correct IP address, and the default port 6667 is used or the displayed numerical value if you want a specific IP address.

NOTE: *Steps 7 through 9 are unnecessary if the IP address you chose in Step 6 and the default port 6667 are acceptable. If you don't use the Advanced button, the port for the chat community is set to the default.*

---

7. To set the port for the chat community, click Advanced. To edit the settings for the community's IP address, click Edit. To add an additional IP address for the community, click Add. In the Edit Identity dialog box, specify a port number in the TCP Port Textbox.

NOTE: *The TCP Port setting box accepts any port number from 1 to 65,535. Microsoft Chat 2.5 supports ports numbered from 6,000 to 7,000. Other chat clients support other port numbers.*

8. From the Advanced dialog box, verify that the IP address and TCP port you configured for the community are listed, and then click OK.
9. On the Chat Community tab, type the number of allowable client connections for the chat community on this server in the Maximum Total Connections box.

NOTE: *The number allowed in Maximum Total Connections ranges from 0 to 99,999. You also can set Maximum Total Connections for a chat community on the community's General tab. If the Maximum Total Connections value set on the Chat Community tab differs from the Maximum Total Connections value set on the General tab, the lesser value is used.*

Removing a Chat Community from the Server

To remove a chat community from a server, disconnect all current users, and prevent a chat community from accepting new connections:

1. Choose Start|Programs|Microsoft Exchange|System Manager.
2. Right-click IRCX and then click Properties.
3. In the Chat Communities list on the General tab, click the name of the chat community you want to remove from this server.
4. Click Remove.

Disabling a Chat Community Temporarily

To remove a chat community from a server, but retain the community and its configurations so you can re-enable them at a future time:

1. Choose Start|Programs|Microsoft Exchange|System Manager.
2. Right-click IRCX, and then click Properties.

3. In the Chat Communities list on the General tab, click the name of the chat community you want to remove from this server.
4. Click Properties.
5. Clear the Enable Server To Host This Chat Community checkbox.

Deleting a Chat Community from the Server

To delete a chat community from the server, perform the following:

1. In the console tree, right-click Chat Communities, and then click Delete.
2. When you are prompted to verify that you want to delete the following chat community, click Yes.

Creating Channels

You can create one or more registered channels in a chat community. You create a registered channel with a predefined configuration, an established topic, or a limited number of users. You also can configure registered channels to start automatically each time Chat Service starts. You can create moderated and auditorium channels when necessary for chat events by using the Channel Modes tab. Sample scenarios when to use moderated and auditorium channels:

- You can use moderated channels for small chat events such as meetings or training. A chat user can't post messages to a moderated channel, but the user can see messages that the speakers post; however, a speaker who moderates a channel can grant speaking permission to specific users.
- You can use auditorium channels for large chat events such as celebrity chats. Again, a chat user can't post messages to an auditorium channel, but the user can see messages that the speakers post. Only the speakers, as channel hosts, are notified when event participants join or leave an auditorium channel.

When exposing the Chat Services to the external network, ensure that all proper security measures have been implemented for user access.

Configuring an Internet Connection

As soon as there is an MX record already defined in your External DNS server (please refer to the earlier section "Configuring the DNS Server Records") and your Exchange Server has already been configured to connect to the Internet, incoming and outgoing Internet mail can freely flow. The Windows 2000 SMTP service can do the job of transferring Internet mails. However, best practices recommend that you use an Exchange SMTP Connector for more administrative control.

Creating Additional SMTP Virtual Servers

A default SMTP Virtual Server is created when you install Exchange Server. You can use this default VS to handle both SMTP connections for internal as well as external mails. Normally, multiple SMTP Virtual Servers are not necessary unless your Exchange Server is hosting several domains. But in cases where the Exchange Server is directly connected to the Internet, it is advisable to configure two SMTP Virtual Servers, the default VS for internal SMTP mail routing and the additional SMTP VS for Internet mail routing. For dual NIC Exchange Server, the default SMTP Virtual Server should be associated with the internal IP address. You must create an additional SMTP Virtual Server and associate the external IP address.

To create an additional SMTP Virtual Server:

1. On the Start menu, point to Programs, point to Microsoft Exchange, and then click System Manager.
2. Navigate to the SMTP.
3. Right-click SMTP, point to New, then click SMTP Virtual Server.
4. Complete the New SMTP Virtual Server Wizard. When you select an IP address, remember that the IP address/TCP port combination must be unique on every SMTP Virtual Server. The recommended TCP port is 25, the SMTP standard TCP port. More than one Virtual Server can use the same TCP port, provided they are configured with different IP addresses.

Creating a SMTP Connector

You use a SMTP Connector to transfer mails between Exchange Servers and other SMTP-based messaging systems such as the Internet. To control the flow of emails, a SMTP Connector might be configured. You can associate the additional SMTP VS that you created for your Internet connection to this SMTP Connector.

To create a SMTP Connector, perform the following:

1. Click Start, point to Programs, point to Microsoft Exchange and System Manager.
2. Navigate to Connectors.
3. Right-click Connectors, select New, and then select SMTP Connector.
4. On the General tab, type the name of the connector. The name is usually the name of the routing group to which you are connecting.
5. On the General tab, select Use DNS to route to each address space on this connector, which specifies the address to use in mail exchange records, or select Forward All Mail Through This Connector To Following Smart Host, and then type the name or IP address of the server through which you would like to route messages for this remote domain. This value overrides the smart host setting on the Delivery tab of the SMTP Virtual Server Properties page.
6. On the General tab, under Local Bridgeheads, click Add, and then select a local bridgehead server from the list.
7. On the Address Space tab, click Add. Select an address type, and then type all necessary information in Properties, including cost.

Configuring a NNTP Connection

The *NNTP service* is an optional Windows 2000 component that is designed to support a standalone newsgroup server, making it easy to create group discussions. Exchange 2000 enables Outlook users to participate in online discussions over the Internet using NNTP newsgroups. Exchange also enables users running client applications that support NNTP to access newsgroup public folders available on Exchange Servers. Users can read and post messages and documents to NNTP newsgroups, which are represented in Exchange as public folders. To enable Exchange 2000 NNTP service, you need to configure the NNTP Virtual Server first.

Configuring a NNTP Virtual Server

A NNTP Virtual Server is automatically created when you install an Exchange 2000 Server. Most configuration options are assigned default values when a new NNTP Virtual Server is created. These options can be configured to control how the newsgroup server functions. Complete these tasks to configure a NNTP Virtual Server:

- Assign an IP address, TCP port, and SSL (Secure Sockets Layer) port.
- Set connection limits.
- Set posting limits.
- Control access to the server.

To assign an IP address, TCP port, and SSL port, follow these steps:

1. Choose Start|Programs|Microsoft Exchange|System Manager.
2. Right-click a Virtual Server in the console tree, and then click Properties.
3. On the General tab, select (All Unassigned) or choose a specific IP address from the list of available network cards in the IP Address drop-down list.
4. To configure the TCP or SSL port, click Advanced.
5. On the Advanced tab, click Add.
6. Type a TCP port number, and then type an SSL port number.

The default Virtual Server is created with an IP address of (All Unassigned). The server running the NNTP Virtual Server allows the NNTP service to receive incoming connections on TCP port 119, and SSL port 563. For instant operation, use the default IP address, TCP port, and SSL port; or, assign a different IP address from any available network card. However, if you are creating multiple NNTP Virtual Servers, you must create a unique combination of IP address, TCP port, and SSL port for each server. To make use of SSL, there has to be a certificate server running.

To set the connection limits, follow these steps:

1. Right-click a Virtual Server in the console tree, and then click Properties.
2. On the General tab, click Limit Connections To, and then type an integer between 1 and 999,999,999.
3. In Connection Time-Out, type the number of minutes that elapse before idle connections are disconnected.

To set the posting limit, follow these steps:

1. Right-click a Virtual Server in the console tree, and then click Properties.
2. Click the Settings tab.

3. Select the Allow Client Posting checkbox to allow clients to post articles to newsgroups on this NNTP Virtual Server. To limit the size of a single article that a user can post, click Limit Post Size (KB), and specify the file size. The default is 1,000KB. To limit the amount of data that a user can post to a newsgroup during a single connection, click Limit Connection Size (MB), and modify the file size. The default is 20MB.
4. Select the Allow Feed Posting checkbox to allow clients to post articles to newsfeeds on the NNTP Virtual Server. To limit the size of a single article a user can post to a newsfeed, click Limit Post Size (KB), and change the default limit size of 1,500KB. To limit the amount of data that a user can post to a newsfeed during a single connection, click Limit Connection Size, and modify the default limit of 40MB.

Access to the NNTP server can be controlled in many ways. The users can connect anonymously or supply valid Windows 2000 account names and passwords. If users connect over a public network, you can encrypt that connection using SSL so that other users cannot intercept articles that are sent and received. You can also explicitly grant or deny access based on the IP address of the client. To restrict access to administrative tasks on the NNTP Server, you can list only the accounts that are authorized to modify server settings.

Creating Newsgroups

You can use the New Newsgroup Wizard to create a newsgroup. When a new newsgroup is created, the NNTP service creates the directory for the newsgroup automatically. If you want a moderator to review new articles before they are posted, you can create a moderated newsgroup. To create a newsgroup, follow these steps:

1. Navigate the NNTP Virtual Server.
2. In the console tree, right-click Newsgroups, point to New, and then click Newsgroup. The New Newsgroup Wizard appears.
3. On the New Newsgroup Welcome screen, type the name of the newsgroup in the space provided. Click Next.
4. Type a description for the newsgroup you want to create. Provide also a Pretty Name. The Pretty Name refers to the alias of the newsgroup that will be displayed on the client. Create New Newsgroup Wizard.
5. Click Finish. This will create a new newsgroup.

Configuring Message Tracking

In Exchange 5.5, message tracking can be enabled at various levels of operation. In Exchange 2000, message tracking is on or off for the entire server. Message tracking is used for troubleshooting purposes such as identifying the number of hops the messages pass, tracing failing connectors, and verifying message delivery. All messages that are routed through a server are added to the message logs and information about the sender, the message, and the recipient are recorded. To enable message tracking:

1. Choose Start|Programs|Microsoft Exchange|System Manager.
2. In the console tree, double-click Server, right-click a server, and then click Properties.
3. To log information about the sender, the time the message was sent or received, the message size and priority, and the message recipients, select the Enable Message Tracking checkbox on the General tab.
4. To record the subject of any message sent to, from, or through the server, select the Enable Subject Logging And Display checkbox.

Adding a Configuration Item Using MMC

To facilitate and ease the administrative task, you can create a customized MMC containing all the administration tools—called snap-ins—you use most frequently. To add items to the console tree, you can use the Add/Remove Snap-In command on the Console menu of the main MMC toolbar. Save the console on the desktop or create a shortcut to the console on the desktop for faster access. To create a customized console:

1. Choose Start|Run; then type "MMC".
2. Choose Console|Add/Remove Snap-In.
3. In the Add/Remove Snap-In, click Add.
4. All the available standalone snap-ins appear. Add the appropriate snap-in.
5. Save the console.

Configuring a Console Taskpad

To create a Taskpad view for a console, the console must contain at least one snap-in. You can create a Taskpad using the New Taskpad View Wizard. After completing the New Taskpad View Wizard, use the New Task Wizard to add tasks to the Taskpad view. Tasks can include menu commands for the items in the console, as well as commands that are run from a command prompt. To create a Taskpad view in a saved MMC console, perform the following:

1. Open a saved console in author mode by right-clicking the MSC file, and then clicking Author (alternatively, you can click Start|Run, type "mmc path\filename.msc /a", and then click OK.
2. In the console tree, click a snap-in item.
3. Choose Action|New Taskpad View. The New Taskpad View Wizard appears.
4. On the New Taskpad View Wizard Welcome screen, click Next to proceed.
5. On the Taskpad Display screen, select the style you want for the details pane and for the task descriptions. Click Next (see Figure 10.19).
6. Select the items you want to be included in the Taskpad View. Click Next (see Figure 10.20).
7. Assign a Name and Description for the Taskpad View. Click Next.
8. If you want to create tasks immediately after you create the Taskpad view, select the Start New Task Wizard checkbox in the final screen of the wizard.

NOTE: *You also can create a Taskpad view in a new console, but you must first add a snap-in to the console.*

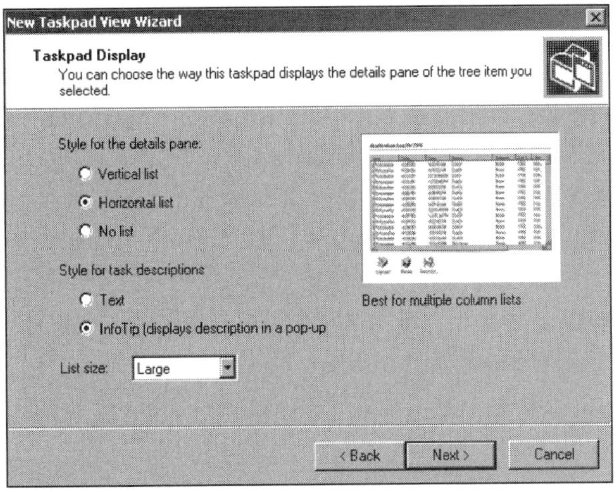

Figure 10.19 The Taskpad Display screen.

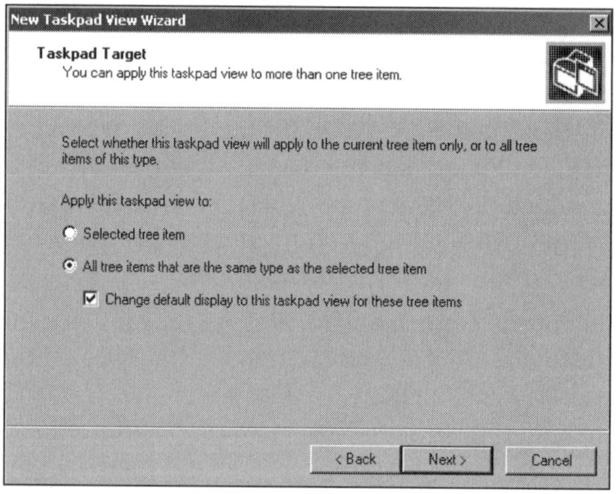

Figure 10.20 Taskpad Target screen.

Determining Workload Using Load Simulator

Load Simulator (LoadSim) can be used to test how the messaging server performs under different message loads. Specific workloads in LoadSim can be defined to test servers in a controlled manner. This enables the accurate study of server behavior under specific conditions. Information gathered by LoadSim is used to help determine the optimum number of users for each server, locate performance bottlenecks, and evaluate server hardware performance. LoadSim is one of the Exchange 2000 tools included in the Exchange 2000 Resource Kit (you also can download it from the Microsoft site).

To install LoadSim, follow these steps:

1. Install from the Exchange 2000 Resource Kit CD or extract the downloaded LoadSim package.
2. Install LoadSim System Monitor counters by opening a command prompt window on the LoadSim client computer.
3. Type "lsperf.reg" to create the necessary Registry key for LoadSim System Monitor objects.
4. When prompted, type "lodctr lsperf.ini" to load the new counters.
5. Move Lsperf.dll into either the default Winnt directory or the Windows installation directory you specify (which must be in the path).
6. Start System Monitor. Verify that the System Monitor objects LoadSim Global and LoadSim Action are present when running System Monitor.

NOTE: *Windows 2000* ***unlodctr*** *and* ***lodctr*** *commands do not return any status to the command prompt window, but will cause an entry in Event Viewer. Unloading and loading the counters should generate information-level messages, for example:*

When doing unlodctr:

Event Type:	*Information*
Event Source:	*LoadPerf*
Description:	*Performance counters for the LoadSim service were removed successfully. The Record Data contains the new values of the system Last Counter and Last Help registry entries.*

When doing lodctr:

Event Type:	*Information*
Event Source:	*LoadPerf*
Description:	*Performance counters for the LoadSim service were loaded successfully. The Record Data contains the new index values assigned to this service.*

Benchmarking Using LoadSim

To use LoadSim, set up the topology by performing the following:

1. Open the LoadSim program.
2. Select Configuration|Topology Properties.
3. Enter the number of users for each mailbox store by clicking the User Count Number in the right column. This number should be a fourth of the total number of users.

You need to set test properties to specify the range of clients to run on a given client computer and the length of time for a given test (eight hours for the users-per-server tests).

1. Open the LoadSim program.
2. Select Configuration|Test Properties.
3. To add a client computer, click Add, and then fill in the Client Machine, First User, and Number Of Users fields appropriately.
4. To save the configured topology, select File|Save As.

Creating the LoadSim Topology

To create the defined topology, choose Run|Create Topology. This step creates the users and DLs for the test. You only have to do this once; that is, you don't have to do it on every client computer. Wait for the RUS to finish updating the necessary attributes for the users before running tests. One way to determine whether this service is still running is to look at the percent of CPU being used by the Local Security Authentication Server (**LSASS.Exe**). After the recipient updates are finished, this service should not be using a significant percentage of CPU. The users are created in the AD directory service under the LoadSim Users folder. To initialize the test, select Run|Initialize Test. When the LoadSim warning message appears, click Yes. To run the test, select Run|Run Simulation on each client computer in your test. The test runs for the duration specified in the test properties. You can stop all client activity immediately at any time by selecting Run|Stop Now.

NOTE: *After the test runs, rename the Lsperf.log and LoadSim.out files so they are not overwritten on the next run. Also, check the LoadSim.out file for error messages. Depending on the type and number of errors that occurred, the entire test might be invalid.*

After the initial test, it's likely that subsequent tests will be performed using different client numbers and characteristics. Doing so will give a better idea about the capabilities of the server.

Chapter 11

Developing a Routing Strategy

If you need an immediate solution to:	See page:
Understanding Message Routing in Exchange 5.5	455
Planning Single Routing Groups in Your Organization	455
Planning Multiple Routing Groups in Your Organization	456
Deploying Public Folder Replicas in Remote Routing Groups	457
Designing Routing Group Strategies Based on Administrative Models	458
Selecting the RGM within a Routing Group	459
Creating a New Routing Group Using System Manager	461
Moving Servers between Routing Groups Using System Manager	462
Using Link State Routing with All Connectors in Exchange 2000	463
Resolving Target Bridgehead Addresses Using the SMTP Connector	463
Creating an RGC Using the Exchange System Manager Snap-In	463
Resolving Destination Bridgehead Server Addresses for RGCs	465
Configuring a TCP/IP-Based X.400 Connector between Routing Groups	466
Checking SMTP Queues Using the Queue Viewer Utility in System Manager	468
Deleting and Freezing Messages in SMTP Queues Using System Manager	469
Managing SMTP Queue Growth Automatically in System Manager	470
Enabling and Using the Message Tracking Feature in Exchange 2000	472
Enabling Protocol Logging for the SMTP Virtual Server in System Manager	475
Enabling Diagnostic Logging for an Exchange 2000 Server in System Manager	478

In Depth

Designing an appropriate messaging topology can be a challenge if your organizational structure is complex or poorly designed. You want to deploy a topology that is able to meet all current and future capacities. You'll definitely want to take advantage of routing features—such as routing groups—in Exchange 2000 Server. These new features also can be integrated with legacy Exchange 5.5 Server sites, so routing is covered in this chapter as it applies to both versions of Exchange Server. First, you'll learn about the components needed for message transport and mail flow in Exchange 2000.

Transport Components in Exchange 2000

The key components needed for message processing include queuing modules, queuing layers, file systems, and connectors. When designing a routing-group scenario or strategy for your company, you have to consider all network links between your various office locations. Most companies enjoy permanent or semi-permanent, high-bandwidth connections between divisions or between branch offices, but your total available bandwidth is always affected by other traffic that might not be readily apparent when analyzing your messaging traffic. You should always monitor the users on your network who consume the largest amount of bandwidth and tailor your messaging topology around this.

NOTE: *Some organizations use bandwidth allocation software, such as Checkpoint Software's Floodgate-1, so that users do not arbitrarily consume bandwidth when using the Internet for personal reasons. Other organizations may simply restrict users to specific applications or Internet sites in order to preserve whatever bandwidth is possible based on the underlying telecommunication infrastucture (for example, T-1 versus T-3 lines).*

Classifying users according to usage frequency, average message sizes, and recurring destination addresses is oftentimes useful. Knowing the average size of messages that travel across your network will help you determine baselines of performance against which you can monitor activity. If you want to optimize routing or transport functions in Exchange 2000, you have to become familiar with all necessary transport components.

Exchange 2000 now extends the basic functionality of SMTP (Simple Mail Transfer Protocol) that is part of the Windows 2000 Server default installation process. The *advanced queuing engine* or module (AQ) queues messages for every destination. AQ maintains all inbound and outbound message queues as the central component for all message processing and delivery in Exchange 2000. AQ is represented by the Phatq.dll DLL file (Dynamic Link Library), which is found in the *\Exchsrvr\Bin* directory. A *Routing Engine (RE)* is a different service within Exchange 2000 that provides routing information to the AQ engine. It also contributes link-state routing to the AQ structure by providing next-hop routing information to the AQ modules.

NOTE: *The RE uses a modification of the Open Shortest Path First (OSPF) algorithm or the Dijkstra's Single Source Shortest Path algorithm, which can find the shortest path from a source computer to a destination computer.*

A *dynamic distribution list* (DL) component represents a collection of mail-enabled or mailbox-enabled recipients to whom you can send email messages by submitting a LDAP (Lightweight Directory Access Protocol) query. You do not have to physically create or manage lists containing these users. No physical interface or screen is available for defining a dynamic DL in Exchange, so you have to use interfaces such as ADSI (Active Directory Services Interface) in Windows 2000.

NOTE: *The ADSI tool provides a single set of interfaces that can be called in scripts using the Windows Script Host or other scripting languages such as VBScript (although caution must be exercised with such scripts as they can contain harmful or malicious code that may damage a computer system by, for example, destroying file allocation tables). You can, for example, use ADSI to script the creation of user accounts within the AD.*

Both Exchange 2000 and Windows 2000 now integrate functions within the Exchange transport mechanism through Windows Internet Information Services (IIS 5). Previously, all routing components were hosted directly on the Exchange 5.5 Server, but the current version of Exchange is designed so that Internet protocols run as part of the IIS process. This allows you to configure dedicated Exchange Servers to manage specific tasks such as processing client requests over the Internet. The IIS process, or **Inetinfo.exe**, hosts such protocols as SMTP, POP3 (Post Office Protocol 3), IMAP4 (Internet Message Access Protocol 4), NNTP (Network News Transfer Protocol), and the HTTP DAV (Distributed Authoring and Versioning) extension to HTTP 1.1. The IIS Admin service manages all these processes so that if you pause or stop the IIS Admin service, you effectively pause or stop all Exchange 2000 services hosted by the IIS process. Although services are uncoupled from the Web Storage System (WSS), the protocols themselves must still communicate with this storage system. A special layer called *ExIPC (Exchange Interprocess Communication)* makes this communication possible between the IIS process and the WSS ExIPC. This queuing layer allows IIS and the **Store.exe** process to transfer data back and forth rapidly. The ExIPC layer can pass information at very high speeds by using the Shared Memory Circular Queue (SMQ) model. Exchange 5.5 usually integrates Internet protocols such as POP3 directly into the Information Store service, but Exchange 2000 separates these protocols from the actual database structure to ease some of the administrative burdens that are present with the old architecture.

NOTE: *ExIPC functions asynchronously using Lightweight Remote Procedure Calls (LRPCs). This means that Exchange 2000 can allocate memory immediately after a process terminates.*

All protocols used to access the WSS are administered using the Exchange 2000 System Manager snap-in, rather than the Internet Services Manager snap-in used in Windows NT 4 Server. Protocol configurations are replicated to the IIS metabase, similar to the Windows 2000 Registry database used to store system configuration. The *Installable File System (IFS)* is an interface that allows you to read or write directly to a streaming media file (STM) in the Information Store. This helps to stream files more efficiently by maintaining all Internet mail in its native MIME (Multipurpose Internet Mail Extensions) format. The *Link State Algorithm (LSA)*—based on the OSPF protocol—is used to propagate routing information between Exchange 2000 Servers. It transfers Link State Information (LSI) between routing groups you create using a special command verb over SMTP called **X-LSA-2**. It also uses a connection to TCP (Transmission Control Protocol) port 691 in every routing group. Link State Tables (LSTs) are used to store LSI propagated by the LSA. LSTs can evaluate the most effective route for a message based on available connections and cost factors.

The *Message Categorizer* examines all messages arriving on a SMTP Server and tries to determine exactly what will happen with those messages. It acts as an addition or plug-in component for the AQ engine and performs address resolution services for every message passing through the AQ module. It can examine attributes of both senders and recipients and expand DLs. A DL can be expanded locally or be forced to expand on specific servers in your organization. Message Categorizer is represented by a DLL known as Phatcat.dll and is found in the *\Exchsrvr\Bin* directory. This component can communicate with the DSAccess service in Windows 2000 so clients can directly access information in AD on Global Catalog (GC) Servers using TCP port number 3268. The *Message Transfer Agent (MTA)* is still an important part of Exchange 2000, and has been updated for the current release of Exchange. The MTA makes calls to the Exchange 2000 RE instead of relying on the outdated GWART (Gateway Address Routing Table) technology used in Exchange 5.5 for route selection. GWART is a less reliable mechanism because it used the distance-vector routing algorithm and next-hop routing, which is susceptible to routing loops. Exchange 2000 benefits from the LSA, which is free of any routing loops.

A *routing group* is a collection of Exchange 2000 computers that transfer data between themselves in a single hop, which eliminates the need for messaging bridgehead servers used so prevalently in Exchange 5.5. Servers in a routing group share permanent, high-bandwidth network connectivity. Routing groups also define boundaries for public folder access for MAPI (Messaging Application Programming Interface) clients such as Outlook 2000. A one-way Routing Group Connector (RGC) connects local or remote bridgehead servers and determines which servers in the routing group can communicate with one another. Servers communicate here using the native SMTP transport, but they can also use RPC communications if operating in a mixed-mode environment. AN RGC from the perspective of an Exchange 5.5 Server is equivalent to a Site Connector. Messages are routed between servers using LSI.

The SMTP protocol is an Internet standard that allows various messaging servers to transfer data between each other. It uses simple command verbs to transfer messages over TCP port 25 and processes incoming traffic from SMTP clients such as Outlook Express. Outbound SMTP traffic can be sent using connectors such as the SMTP Connector or a RGS. When you configure the SMTP service in the System Manager snap-in, the System Attendant component of Exchange 2000 stores these configuration changes in AD and applies them directly to the **Inetinfo.exe** process.

Two additional components of interest are the *Information Store* and the *store driver*. The Information Store manages the storage of data in the form of email messages and documents such as spreadsheets and databases. All message contents are stored in a native STM file; an EDB (Exchange database) file inside the store holds all header information for your messages. The store driver is responsible for many different functions including delivering inbound messages from the AQ module to the Information Store for local delivery, submitting messages to AQ for categorization and outbound delivery, and delivering messages from the AQ engine to other messaging gateways. Two DLLs make up the store driver, one that runs within the IIS process and another that executes within the Information Store itself. These two DLLs communicate with each other using the ExIPC queuing layer, the shared-memory queuing system.

NOTE: *ExIPC uses the SMQ algorithm to shuttle data between different components. SMQ represents a shared memory circular queue, which is an algorithm or process describing how to use shared memory for various components within Exchange 2000.*

Each store driver resides on different sides of the ExIPC layer. The driver on the Store side is named *Exsmtp.dll* and can be found in the *\Exchsrvr\Bin* directory on the local Exchange Server hard drive. The second DLL—Drviis.dll—exists on the Inetinfo.exe side and is also found in the *\Exchsrvr\Bin* directory. Most components of Exchange 2000 are physically present inside the *\Exchsrvr\Bin* directory.

It is also important to understand the phases of developing a routing strategy within your organization. Phase 1 includes analyzing your existing messaging too_logy and administrative structure and planning for future growth. Phase 2 includes planning and developing routing groups and routing group boundaries. Phase 3 includes planning and developing message flow strategies—such as a hub and spoke topology—and then connecting your routing group structure using RGCs.

Phase 1—Your Current Environment

Your current environment might consist of a centralized regional office with many branch offices scattered across the globe requiring hundreds of Exchange 2000 servers, or it might consist of a single office that requires only one dedicated Exchange 2000 server running all Windows 2000 services on a single machine. You must consider many issues when planning to deploy Exchange 2000, especially regarding message routing in a Windows 2000 environment. You have to consider the design and organization of Windows 2000 IP subnets, AD, DNS (Domain Name System) servers, domain controllers (DCs), and Global Catalog Servers. The Windows 2000 site architecture affects your Exchange 2000 deployment because, for one thing, the Global Address List (GAL) used by all clients now exists within the AD database of Windows 2000. Recall that a Windows 2000 site is really a collection of IP subnets that are "well-connected" to each other; in other words, they share permanent, high-speed connectivity between themselves. A properly designed site topology can control AD replication across any slow WAN (wide area network) links in your organization and help locate DCs needed by users for logon and authentication purposes. All Exchange 2000 clients use Windows 2000 sites to locate DCs so they can access their individual mailbox stores.

Phase 1 includes analyzing your current environment to see how current systems manage message flow within your organization. It also entails analyzing the future needs of your company to determine the possible impact on existing bandwidth or utilization if your company should grow beyond projected levels. This analysis is needed in Phase 2, so you can determine the number of routing groups that you will need for maximum efficiencies. If your company is undergoing rapid change and an expansion in capacity or personnel is imminent, you might decide to open up new locations in geographically dispersed regions. This decision affects your planned administrative structure so it's important to think about these things early on. These factors have more of an impact on legacy Exchange 5.5 administrators, because they have to get used to new administrative designs within Exchange 2000. When administrators deployed Exchange 5.5 in remote offices, they had to consider which *site* to place their Exchange 5.5 Servers in. Then they had to select an appropriate *connector* that would connect different sites. Exchange 2000 no longer uses sites; you now have to plan administrative groups and routing groups to define both the logical and physical boundaries of your organization. Administrative groups organize servers according to your administrative structure, whereas routing groups map out your physical network structure. Notice in Figure 11.1 that routing groups are integrated within administrative groups.

This breakdown is important because you must assign routing groups to specific administrative groups. Doing so allows you to assign administrators to specific routing groups based on the administrative structure of your company. You also can decide which servers to place in each routing group and move them to other routing groups at any time. When considering your existing environment, pay careful attention to existing routing boundaries and network connections. If you are expecting a substantial increase in client populations or messaging traffic levels, these boundaries or connections might have to be upgraded. This could mean additional financial outlays for software and hardware.

Phase 2—Planning Routing Groups

This phase incorporates two important categories: coexisting with Exchange 5.5 and planning the number of routing groups. You have to consider coexistence issues with Exchange 5.5 because many companies are faced with migrating existing sites into the routing-group architecture of Exchange 2000. Very few companies operate in a pure Exchange 2000 native-mode environment, unless

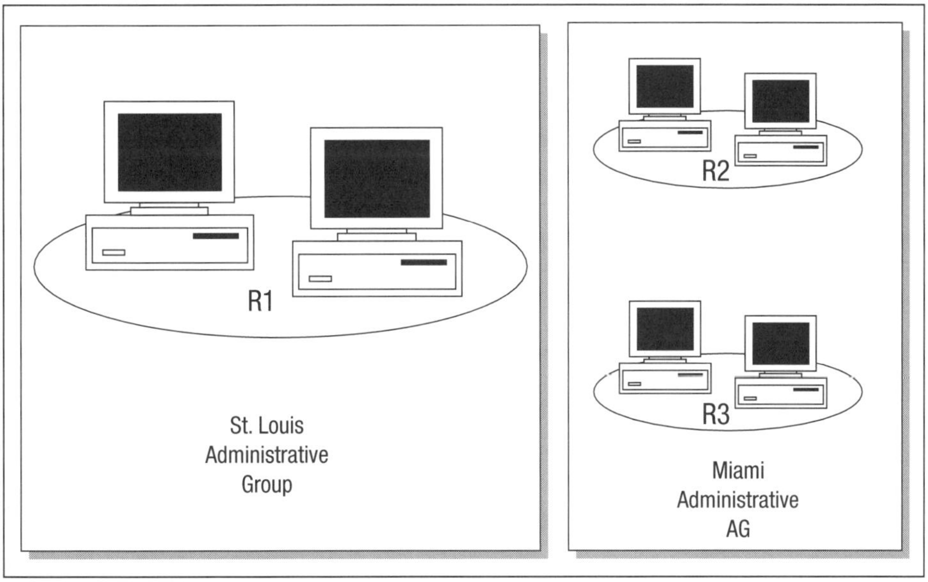

Figure 11.1 Planning routing groups within administrative groups.

they are migrating from other third-party foreign messaging systems such as Lotus Notes or Microsoft Mail for PC Networks. The other category includes planning the number of routing groups needed by considering existing network links and connections and using this information to help develop appropriate routing boundaries.

Exchange 5.5 Routing and Coexisting with Exchange 2000

Exchange 5.5 used the concept of sites to place servers with high-speed reliable connections between them in one logical group. Message routing MTAs, which were through MTAs was based on the X.400 standard for transporting email. Every server in a site transferred messages to other servers using Remote Procedure Calls and Site Connectors were used to connect one site to another. You also could use the X.400 Connector or the Internet Mail Connector (IMC).

We recommend you know how to handle routing in mixed environments because it is common to migrate messaging systems from Exchange 5.5 to Exchange 2000. Migrating to Exchange 2000 does not mean that you have to eliminate or decommission all your Exchange 5.5 Servers. You can install Exchange 2000 within existing Exchange 5.5 sites as long as one computer in the site is running Exchange 5.5 with Service Pack 3 (SP3). Notice that all computers in the site are not bound by this requirement. The existence of Exchange 2000 in an Exchange 5.5 site automatically creates one administrative group and one routing group in the AD structure of Windows 2000 (because Exchange 2000 can only run on a Windows 2000 system even when coexisting with an Exchange 5.5 Server). This administrative group and routing group have the same name as the Exchange 5.5 site.

Exchange 5.5 depended on the creation of a GWART to disseminate connector information between servers and calculate routing costs between servers and sites. GWART is considered an unreliable mechanism because it uses a distance-vector algorithm, which is susceptible to internal routing loops. Exchange 2000 uses a LSA instead of a distance-vector algorithm, and depends on a Routing Group Master (RGM) in each routing group you create that updates and maintains the LST of all routing groups in your organization. The RGM is capable of generating a GWART in AD; however, a different service—Site Replication Service—is responsible for replicating the GWART to any Exchange 5.5 directories residing in nearby or adjacent sites. Though Exchange 2000 ignores the GWART, Exchange 5.5 still uses it to inform other Exchange 5.5 Servers regarding the status of message routes to an Exchange 2000 Server located in the same site.

You can install multiple Exchange 2000 Servers in a single Exchange 5.5 site, but they will communicate with one another using the native SMTP protocol. An Exchange 2000 Server will know when it's communicating with another Exchange

2000 Server and when it's communicating directly with an Exchange 5.5 Server. In the former case, SMTP is used; in the latter case, RPC is used. If you are using bridgehead servers within your Exchange 5.5 site, you can update these to Exchange 2000 for message-routing purposes. These bridgehead servers will now use SMTP for native communications instead of RPC.

Developing Routing Groups and Routing Boundaries

Best practices recommend grouping Exchange 2000 servers into routing groups to pass messages between servers. It is thus important to understand how a routing group will function in both mixed-mode and native-mode Exchange Server organizations. This section covers planning and creating routing groups and using the LSA to determine the route all messages take. You'll see how Exchange 2000 routes messages within a routing group as well as between different routing groups.

Messages flow through routing groups and across connectors (see "Phase 3—Message Flow in Exchange 2000 Using Connectors"). Your design should include an optimal number of routing groups to control all your message traffic and to route messages efficiently throughout your organization.

Some environments need more routing groups than others, even though best practices dictate that you operate with as few routing groups as possible to make administration easier. For example, many smaller organizations do not need more than the default First Routing Group provided by Exchange 2000 upon initial installation. There are no hard and fast rules for the number of routing groups needed by organizations so judgment and experience play an important role in this decision process. Using more routing groups than necessary makes it difficult to track servers that are moved between multiple routing and administrative groups. Factors such as the quality of links between your various offices and the reliability of your network connections can impact your decision to create additional routing groups. For example, bandwidth connections become important when Outlook clients or Outlook Web Access (OWA) clients try to access public folders on remote Exchange 2000 Servers, where clients have to log on to Windows 2000 DCs or GC Servers existing in different Windows 2000 sites. You might have to create multiple routing groups if network connections in one site are not permanent or reliable and users experience difficulty accessing important public folder information because of this. The danger in creating too many routing groups is that users are allowed to send messages of any size between any two routing groups and this can cause a negative impact on messaging traffic.

You are not required to integrate Windows 2000 sites with the development of routing groups. Sites merely assist in the placement of GC Servers, which Exchange 2000 clients need when querying AD for object information. Using multiple sites per routing group helps you distribute the workload among different GC Servers in each site. When a client in one IP subnet performs a query to a site that does not have a GC Server, Exchange 2000 queries a GC computer in a different site. A site has different requirements compared to a routing group and this affects your implementation decisions. For example, all servers within a site use RPCs for communication, whereas all servers within a native-mode routing group use SMTP for communication. Different protocols have different requirements based on bandwidth or speed (SMTP is more tolerant of low-bandwidth connections, for instance).

NOTE: *The exception to using SMTP in a routing group occurs when you introduce an Exchange 5.5 Server into this group. In that case, RPC communications are used between the Exchange 2000 Servers and the Exchange 5.5 Servers. This is an example of mixed-mode communication.*

Exchange 2000 makes it easy to add or remove routing groups using the System Manager snap-in tool. When developing your routing-group boundaries for your organization, decide whether to implement a single routing group or multiple routing groups. Also, decide on how best to implement public-folder referrals for MAPI clients, such as Outlook 2000. Routing groups are flexible because they can change with your network as it grows. Though RGs are easy to reconfigure, you must run your Exchange organization in native-mode to make changes. As stated before, the quality of your network connections is paramount in determining how many routing-group boundaries to create. If your network connections are prone to interruptions, multiple routing groups will serve you best because servers with slow network connections can be put into the same routing group, even if they belong to different IP subnets or Windows 2000 sites. Be careful when changing membership in routing groups too often because you might affect public-folder access for MAPI clients if they suddenly find themselves connecting to a server in a new routing group across unstable network links.

Public Folders and Routing Groups

An important connection exists between public folders and routing groups. Managing public folders includes creating public folder replicas and public folder referrals. Creating a public folder creates only one copy of this folder in your entire organization. This means that all public folders either exist as a single copy or as multiple copies. If a public folder exists in the form of multiple copies, it is known as a *replica*, and replicas are used for fault tolerance and load balancing. They are copied between servers and are separate instances of the parent folder they represent.

A public folder *referral* is different from a public folder replica in that it helps you route information to a specific folder. If you configure a RGC between two routing groups (see "The RGC in Exchange 2000" section later in this chapter), you can enable a public folder referral to a server in a different routing group. Exchange 2000 allows public folder referrals over connections involving Exchange 5.5 Servers. If you need to prevent users from accessing public folders or public folder replicas in remote routing groups for security purposes because these public folders, for example, contain sensitive corporate information such as budget or payroll information, you can disable public folder referrals when configuring your connectors. A "cost" factor is established between routing groups, and public folder referrals are made in accordance with these costs. Exchange 2000 directs all access across the connector configured with the lowest cost.

NOTE: *A connector cost determines which connector will be preferred when transferring messages across this connection. Exchange 2000 assigns a cost value between 1 and 100 and associates this value with an address space (for example a SMTP address space of* ***@domain.com****. Any connector associated with an address space that is configured with the lowest cost value will be tried first when message transfer is initiated. If a message cannot pass through this connector for some reason, the next available connector with a value just above the previous connector will be tried (for instance, if the first connector with a value of 1 fails for some reason, a connector with a value higher than 1, if it exists, will be tried next).*

When you design your overall routing group scenario, determine how many users need to access public folder replicas in remote routing groups across your organization.

Creating and Managing Routing Groups

If you install Exchange 2000 in an administrative group such as the default First Administrative Group or another administrative group you created, Exchange 2000 automatically creates the First Routing Group in that administrative group. Any subsequent server you install is placed into this default routing group, unless you manually create additional routing groups. Routing groups are associated with administrative groups, so if you created 10 administrative groups, you'll see 10 First Routing Groups by default. Many organizations are content using the default First Routing Group, and Microsoft recommends using the fewest number of routing groups possible. However, as your organization grows in size, it might be best to configure additional routing groups. Routing groups are created and configured using the Exchange 2000 System Manager snap-in console. Consider the following points when managing routing groups in your organization:

- An organization in Mixed mode associates all administrative groups with routing groups to emulate an Exchange 5.5 Server site.
- If your organization is running in Mixed mode, a routing group cannot be associated with more than one administrative group.

- If your mixed-mode organization contains one administrative group containing multiple routing groups inside, any Exchange 5.5 Server contained in that administrative group will not be able to recognize these routing groups. Exchange 5.5 treats this administrative group as if it were an Exchange 5.5 site.
- If you want your routing groups to span multiple administrative groups, or if you want to move routing groups between administrative groups, convert your mixed-mode organization to native-mode operation.

WARNING! Converting a mixed-mode organization to a native-mode organization is a one-time, irreversible process. Do this only if you are positively sure that interoperability with Exchange 5.5 Server is no longer a needed feature.

- All messages between servers within a routing group are sent *in a single hop* because the servers in a routing group communicate with each other using direct SMTP communication. These messages cannot be scheduled.
- Two or more servers can be put in the same routing group if direct and permanent connectivity exists between them, and if they all belong to the same Windows 2000 forest. These servers must also connect to the RGM configured within that routing group.

Phase 3—Message Flow in Exchange 2000 Using Connectors

Consider message-flow architecture after you design a routing group structure, but *before* you deploy your RGCs. Planning message flows will help you choose and configure the most appropriate connectors for your given environment because you can base this flow on your current topology. Two basic topologies should be considered when you are developing a strategy for message flows: hub-and-spoke topology and full-mesh topology.

Message Flow Topology in Exchange 2000

Messages can flow using either a *hub-and-spoke topology* or a *full-mesh topology* (see Figure 11.2 and Figure 11.3 for a description of these models).

The first case involves a central office—the hub—that manages message flow to remote branch offices—the spokes. This topology is ideal for organizations that want to manage all routing functionality from one central location. The central office manages most mailbox servers in a *hub routing group* as well as critical public folder servers. A bridgehead server can be created in the hub routing group to communicate directly with a spoke routing group. Spoke routing groups contain local mailbox servers for only that group or branch office as well as a *connector server* to communicate directly with the hub routing group.

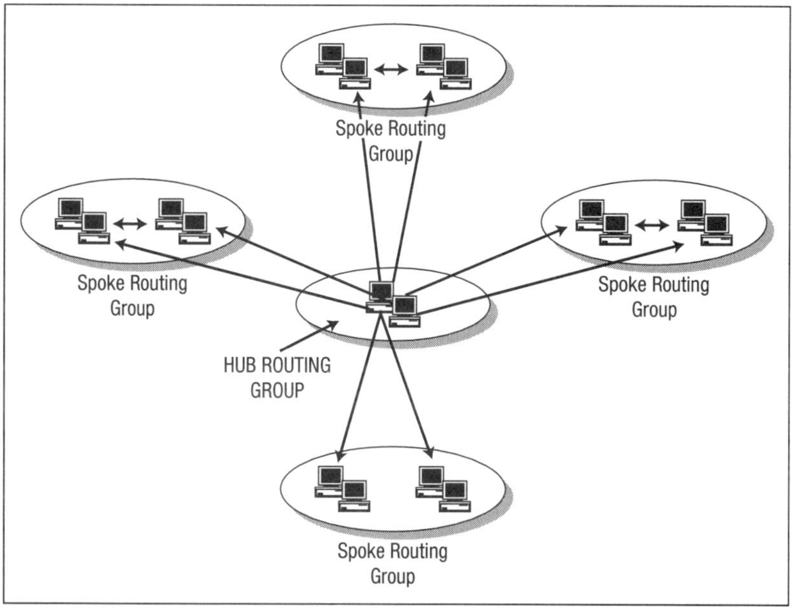

Figure 11.2 A hub-and-spoke routing topology.

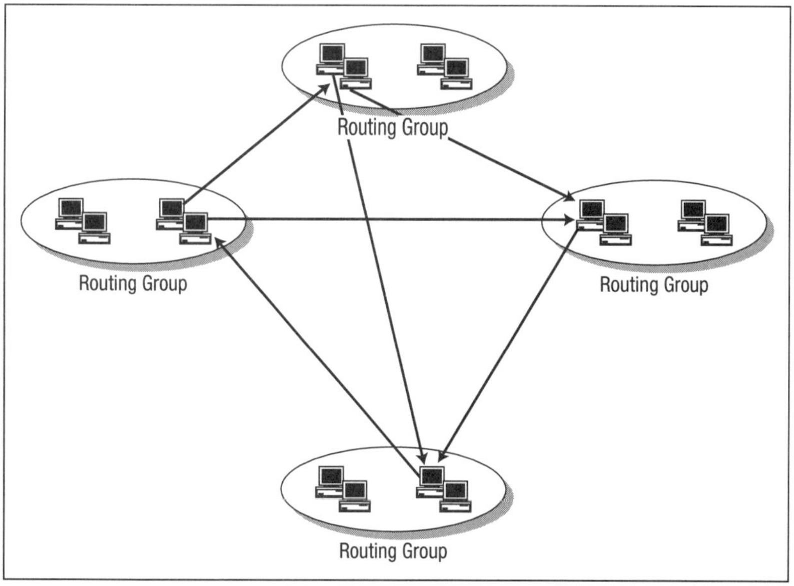

Figure 11.3 A full-mesh routing topology.

NOTE: *You don't need a* dedicated *connector bridgehead server in many cases. Some small environments deploy all services on a single Exchange 2000 Server, including connectors, mailboxes, and public folder stores. We recommend separating these services to avoid single points of failure for all services.*

The opposite of a hub-and-spoke topology is a full-mesh topology, with every routing group connecting to every other routing group in the organization. Only smaller organizations truly benefit from this type of design because larger organizations see too large of an increase in network traffic and congestion resulting from this type of design. One advantage of a full-mesh design is that most messaging traffic is defined over a single hop between routing groups. Additionally, if a connection between two routing groups is down, alternate routes are already configured and ready to use. The goal of fault tolerance is easily achieved using this design as long as permanent, high-bandwidth connections are available between every single routing group in the organization.

Message Flow Architecture in Exchange 2000

Many components in both Windows 2000 Server and Exchange 2000 help promote message flow. Remember our earlier discussion of the Information Store, the ExIPC layer, and the IIS process known as **Inetinfo.exe**? Messages flow in many directions in Exchange 2000. They can flow from one user to another user located on the same server; they can flow to users located on different servers; they can flow to foreign recipients hosted on external messaging systems such as X.400 Servers; or they can flow into an Exchange 2000 Server from an external SMTP gateway.

It is also important to distinguish a Windows 2000 Message Flow from an Exchange 2000 Message Flow. The former represents a very basic flow of SMTP data emanating from within Windows 2000 Server through **Inetinfo.exe** on port 25. The messages can travel through the IIS layer, which then hands them off to the AQ engine and the Message Categorizer for name resolution. The messages are then passed to a routing and queuing component and delivered through an outgoing SMTP message. For Exchange 2000, messages can arrive inbound through the SMTP service, the Information Store, a MTA connector or an X.400 connector. The upcoming example shows an inbound message from SMTP that is heading straight for the local Information Store (the first flow scenario just presented).

The following describes the process of receiving an inbound message:

1. The message arrives via port 25 through the IIS layer. As soon as it meets the SMTP protocol in this layer, an IMAIL *message structure* is created. This structure is nothing more than a message header plus a pointer. The header contains information about the recipient and the sender. The pointer is added to give the location of the message on the hard drive of the local system.
2. The physical message is streamed on the hard drive in a STM file. The IMAIL structure travels to the AQ engine, where it is processed into a queue called the *PreCategorizer* or PreCat queue.

3. The Categorizer component then resolves the sender and recipient information and expands any DLs that are present. It checks all the mail attributes, applies all the message formats, and divides the messages into two identical messages, each with different message formats.

***NOTE:** The process just described normally occurs when a message is addressed to different recipients including Rich-Text recipients and MIME recipients. A bifurcated message is divided into identical IMAIL message objects, one for each recipient.*

---

4. After the message has been bifurcated, each message object is marked as either *local* or *gateway*. The Categorizer now attempts to contact the AD using port number 3268 (reserved for the GC Server), and then transfer the message back to the AQ engine.
5. The AQ selects the proper queue for this message. The first queue chosen is the prerouting queue using Reapi.dll. AQ uses this DLL to communicate with the RE, which provides AQ with next-hop information. AQ can queue this message in multiple locations, including a remote SMTP queue or the local delivery queue. For inbound SMTP messages, it selects the local delivery queue.
6. The store driver on the IIS side picks up this message from the queue, processes it, and gives it to the store driver on the EXSMTP or Information Store side. It is finally delivered to the local recipient in the store.

Implementing Messaging Connectors

Now that you have designed your routing group structure and considered the implications of message flows within your organization, you are ready to deploy your RGCs. These objects connect two or more routing groups together and assist in message delivery along predefined paths. Each connector has a *cost* assigned to it so that Exchange 2000 automatically routes message packets along the connector with the lowest cost value. The next step is to connect routing groups and plan your connector costs.

Exchange 2000 provides two major types of connectors for joining multiple routing groups together in a single communication link. The first type includes both RGCs and SMTP connectors. Both types bypass the MTA component of Exchange and use SMTP directly. Many people think only the SMTP connector uses SMTP, but this is not the case. A RGC "knows" to use SMTP by checking the version of the target server configured at one of its end points. If the server at one end of your connection is running Exchange 2000, SMTP is automatically used. On the other hand, if the target server at this end is running Exchange 5.5 or earlier versions of Exchange, all messages are automatically sent to the MTA component of Exchange, which treats the RGC as if it were an additional Site Connector in the Exchange 5.5 environment. In that case, all messages are delivered using RPC connections, not SMTP connections.

The other major type of connector includes X.400 Connectors, which automatically use the MTA component of Exchange instead of SMTP to deliver messages. You must note that not all Exchange 5.5 Connectors have been migrated to Exchange 2000, and some connectors are not capable of coexistence with Exchange 2000 either. Table 11.1 shows which Exchange 5.5 Connectors are still compatible with Exchange 2000.

NOTE: *The SNADS Connector allowed Exchange 5.5 Servers to connect to the IBM SNA Distribution Messaging System, whereas PROFS represented the Professional Office System messaging environment hosted by IBM servers.*

The SMTP Connector in Exchange 2000

Deploying messaging connectors involves understanding which connector can best be used in a given situation. The SMTP Connector is used mainly to connect to the Internet and is compared to the IMS used in Exchange 5.5. This connector is appropriate in the following situations:

- You want to enable the use of triggered message delivery using the command verbs **TURN** or **ETRN** between two servers.
- You want to exercise control over SMTP-level parameters such as authentication parameters.

Table 11.1 Exchange 5.5 connectors still compatible with Exchange 2000.

Connector Name	Status in Exchange 2000
Site Connector	Replaced by the RGC, which can use either SMTP connections to an Exchange 2000 Server or RPC connections to an Exchange 5.5 Server
X.400 Connector	Exists as a component of the MTA and only uses RPC connections
Internet Mail Service (IMS)	Replaced by the SMTP connector in Exchange 2000
Microsoft Mail	Still exists in Exchange 2000
SNADS (Systems Network Architecture Distribution System)	No longer supported in Exchange 2000
PROFS (Professional Office System)	No longer supported in Exchange 2000

SMTP Message Delivery

TURN and **ETRN** are extensions to the SMTP service defined in Request For Comments (RFC) 1985 of the Internet Engineering Task Force, or IETF (see **www.ietf.org** for further information regarding RFC 1985). These extensions to the SMTP protocol allow SMTP clients and servers to interact so the server can start processing its queues. These extensions are normally used for mail hosts possessing temporary or transient connections to an Internet service provider (ISP).

The normal **TURN** command verb used by the SMTP protocol attempted to address the problem of processing mail queues on remote computers. This command introduced security holes because a remote computer's hostname wasn't verified; malicious users could use the **TURN** command verb to download mail to other unknown sites. **ETRN**, or Extended **TURN**, was introduced to compensate for this security hole. **ETRN** was officially known as the *Remote Queue Processing Declaration service extension* to the SMTP protocol and allowed mail clients to request that a mail server start the processing of its mail queues for messages waiting at the server for that client. If necessary, the server would start new SMTP sessions so that it could send clients their messages and avoid the security loophole of sending messages randomly to any client that requested it. The server responds to **ETRN** commands initiated by the client.

On receipt of the extended **TURN** command from a client, the server host inspects the node name specified in the command and decides whether it should honor this request. If the request is not honored, the server returns appropriate error codes to the client. If the request is honored, the server forces its **retry queues** to send messages to the client in the remote site using a brand-new SMTP connection. This connection does not have to take place within a defined time period. **ETRN** has an advantage in that it does not expose any security threats to the SMTP protocol itself; it lessens the time period that clients have to wait before their messages are retried on the server.

NOTE: *RGCs are incapable of using* ***TURN*** *or* ***ETRN*** *command verbs, so if you want to download queued server messages from a remote host using these commands, you are expected to use only the SMTP Connector for your routing groups.*

- You want to use Secure Socket Layer (SSL) connections between routing groups instead of using SSL connections on your SMTP Virtual Servers config-ured in Exchange System Manager. Defining SSL on your SMTP Virtual Server means deploying this technology on a server-wide basis, and sometimes you want to enable this for *specific* connections.
- You want to enable SMTP communications between one Exchange 2000 routing group and one Exchange 5.5 site. You have to use the SMTP Connector in this case because the RGC cannot connect an Exchange 2000 routing group to an Exchange 5.5 site using SMTP; rather, it uses RPC connections. If the target server at the end of your connector is running Exchange 5.5, you have to configure the IMS as well.

SMTP Connectors can be used to identify local bridgehead servers in your routing group and use these local bridgehead servers to deliver messages between routing groups. Unfortunately, you can't define remote bridgehead servers when configuring the SMTP Connector. This connector uses Transport Layer Security (TLS), which overrides any security settings you define on the SMTP Virtual Server level. TLS transfers messages over an encrypted SMTP Connector.

The RGC in Exchange 2000

The RGC is used for most routing group scenarios. It's chosen more frequently over the SMTP Connector or the X.400 Connector because it provides the easiest method to connect two different routing groups. The RGC is equivalent to the Site Connector used in Exchange 5.5 and can be configured in Exchange 2000 for scheduled message transfers. However, you cannot use this connector if you are trying to connect routing groups located in separate Exchange organizations. Other restrictions that prevent you from using the RGC include the following:

- Configuring SSL connections at the connector level, not the SMTP Virtual Server level in System Manager, requires separate SMTP connectors.
- Using SMTP command verbs such as **TURN** and **ETRN** requires the SMTP connector.
- Connecting routing groups that are based on the X.25 network standard can only be connected using an X.400 Connector.

NOTE: *The X.25 protocol is a network protocol that allows computers on different public networks to communicate through intermediary computers at the network layer level. Protocols used in X.25 communication are often found in the data-link and physical layers of the OSI (Open Systems Interconnection) reference model, an industry standard model of the International Standards Organization (ISO).*

This connector has no default configuration because the protocol used depends on the bridgehead servers being deployed between any two routing groups. If all target bridgehead servers run Exchange 2000, the SMTP protocol is used to transfer messages between routing groups. If even one target bridgehead server is running Exchange 5.5, the RPC protocol, along with the MTA component of Exchange 5.5, is used to transfer messages between routing groups.

TIP: *When you want to deploy only the SMTP protocol to transfer messages between routing groups containing Exchange 5.5 Servers, you must use the Exchange SMTP Connector for all Exchange 2000 Servers and the IMC for all Exchange 5.5 Servers to connect affected routing groups. The presence of any RGCs causes Exchange 2000 to use RPCs instead of SMTP between your groups.*

RGCs provide the advantage of configuring multiple bridgehead servers on either end of your connector. Connectors are configured using the Exchange System

Manager snap-in. Using multiple bridgehead servers allows you to control which server can send or receive messages, and if one bridgehead server is unavailable, Exchange 2000 can choose another bridgehead server within a routing group to transfer messages. Exchange 2000 can also use load balancing to distribute message loads across different bridgehead servers in a routing group. You can even configure a bridgehead server to host multiple SMTP Virtual Servers using System Manager with each Virtual Server containing a different IP address and port number combination. In this case, each SMTP Virtual Server can become a separate bridgehead server and be used for fault tolerance or load balancing within routing groups.

Best practices recommend configuring restrictions on message types for RGCs so that only messages with specific message types or content are delivered. You can also define a schedule for message delivery for all RGCs and apply this schedule to messages exceeding a certain size. For example, you can specify that all messages over 2MB be delivered after 11:00 P.M. so the message delivery doesn't have such a negative impact on your network performance as it would during the day when all users are present. The only thing you can't configure for connectors is security because messages transferred between routing groups using the RGC can't be encrypted in any form.

NOTE: *You could configure Transport Layer Security on all SMTP Virtual Servers to encrypt messages, but this means that all bridgehead servers defined by a SMTP connector use the same TLS protocol for both inbound and out-bound security. You also have to install security certificates in this situation using the Windows 2000 Certificate Service component.*

The X.400 Connector in Exchange 2000

The X.400 Connector represents a *foreign messaging component* of Exchange 2000 because Exchange uses SMTP as a primary message transport. You can use the X.400 Connector to connect two routing groups if you are connecting across an X.25 type network, or if your network contains users who regularly send messages that are relatively large in size or have large attachments associated with them. Although the RGC can be appropriate for large messages as well, the X.400 Connector is more efficient in terms of messaging overhead created after establishing a message transfer session.

An X.400 Connector also can establish a route between a routing group in your organization and a foreign X.400 system. In any case, use the X.400 Connector when you have slow network connection between routing groups. You must configure one connector in each routing group, creating a two-way connection. However, this configuration won't create a fault-tolerant scenario by itself. You have to create multiple connectors for fault-tolerance purposes because one connector cannot support more than one bridgehead server. You might be tempted to use pure SMTP communications when sending large messages between two groups, but always remember that X.400 performs better when compared to SMTP, even when sending large messages or message attachments between different hosts, although initially it creates more messaging overhead.

In environments containing Exchange 5.5 Servers, all X.400 Connectors are also configured directly from one bridgehead server to a remote bridgehead server. If you try to upgrade an Exchange 5.5 Server with an X.400 Connector to Exchange 2000, the Setup Wizard determines whether the remote MTAs for this X.400 connector are on a server running Exchange 2000. If they are, all X.400 Connectors existing in the Exchange 5.5 environment are upgraded to Exchange 2000 SMTP Connectors, not RGCs. Every X.400 Connector is associated with either an X.25 transport stack or a TCP/IP transport stack. This means that the MTA service used in Exchange 2000 can use either TCP/IP or X.25 for communication with remote hosts. You have to add an MTA transport stack before you configure an X.400 Connector. Use a TCP/IP transport stack to establish X.400 connections over the Internet, and an X.25 transport stack to communicate with remote X.400 hosts over a packet-switched-type network. The good news for X.400 connections is that they are always secure because any X.400 MTA that tries to contact another MTA has to identify itself by including a name and password for both the local MTA and the remote MTA. If any of this information does not agree with the information for the remote X.400 system, messages are not transferred using theX.400 Connector.

Optimizing and Troubleshooting Message Routing in Exchange 2000

Recall that Exchange 2000 uses all features of the SMTP transport for all communications, and thus removes some of the issues associated with other transport mechanisms such as RPC or X.400. For instance, RPC communications suffer under low-bandwidth conditions due to its synchronous characteristics and requirements. Routing groups are the basic constructs of messaging flow in Exchange 2000 and they group servers that are connected over permanent network links. Routing groups allow you to exert some control over message flows and also troubleshoot message transfer between server groups. When planning routing groups, remember that SMTP does not expect constant high-bandwidth connection between servers because it is more efficient over low-bandwidth connections. You should plan servers in a group so that they all have *reliable* connections between them, rather than *high-bandwidth* connections between them.

We recommend the following points regarding message routing and transport in Exchange 2000:

- Plan multiple routing groups if network connectivity is unreliable, or you want to control message paths in your organization (for instance, you want to use multiple-hop routing if your servers are placed in separate locations). Multiple routing groups are also used when you want to schedule message delivery between locations.
- If you regularly monitor your messaging traffic and see which servers communicate with each other, you can decide which servers can be best placed in the same routing group. However, placing too many servers in one routing group based solely on this messaging traffic can cause unnecessary performance drains on network resources.
- Optimizing your routing groups can enhance public folder access for your users, because public folder referrals follow a hierarchy in which referrals are made first to servers within the same routing group before being made to servers in a remote routing group via connectors.
- The RGC can be configured using multiple bridgeheads on either end of the connector so you can control the servers that send and receive messages between your routing groups. You can configure SMTP authentication between bridgehead servers, however, message encryption is disabled by design.

***NOTE:** You can implement alternate encryption schemes such as the IPSec (Internet Protocol Security) protocol, a developing security standard that implements security at the network or packet-processing layer of network communications. It can be used to design virtual private networks (VPNs), or in remote access situations for users who use dial-up connections to access private networks.*

- SMTP Connectors are used when a Remote Server Connector is in the form of an IMC from previous versions of Exchange Server, and also when servers communicate with each other using the **TURN** or **ETRN** command verbs associated with the SMTP protocol. You can also deploy this connector when it's necessary to define TLS security for all communications.
- Every SMTP connector can specify many bridgehead servers within each routing group you configure. Any message from a bridgehead server sent to a destination remote routing group is delivered directly by querying a DNS server for mx (Mail Exchange) resource records.

***TIP:** You also can send messages using the SMTP Connector to a* smart host, *which is an intermediary host using DNS to resolve a destination machine's IP address. The smart host is responsible for sending a message to a target host machine and is used to relay messages between servers over the Internet. Often, remote servers on the Internet are not always available for immediate communication.*

- Exchange 2000 determines the best route for a message to take based on the connectors configured between routing groups. The status of every connector is stored in a LST. A LSA updates this LST whenever a change occurs. A link only has two states—either it is UP, or it is DOWN. Messages are routed if connectors are in an UP state.
- Exchange 2000 uses cost factors when selecting connectors to use for message transfers. These costs are cumulative, so if you deploy two connectors, each with a cost of 10 (not a dollar cost but a numerical value based on preferences), and the message has to travel through both connectors to reach its destination, the cumulative cost is set to 20. However, Exchange always picks the route with the lowest cumulative cost, a process known as *least cost routing*. Cost values range from 1 to 100, and they can never be assigned a value of 0. Do not use costs unless you are using more than one route to a destination.
- You can add additional bridgehead servers to existing connectors to provide fault tolerance to your messaging topology. If a connector you are using will not support additional bridgehead servers, you can always add additional connectors and attach those connectors to multiple bridgehead servers in a remote routing group.

Troubleshooting Tools Used in Exchange 2000

Exchange 2000 provides logging, reporting, and tracing tools to troubleshoot routing and transport problems. If you are confronted with problems related to message routing in your organization, you can view the status of your message queues using the Exchange System Manager snap-in. You can also use the feature in Exchange 2000 known as the Message Tracking Center. When users complain that messages are not being delivered because they are sitting in a queue, or messages are being returned undeliverable, these methods can provide some assistance and resolution. The Que Viewer is located underneath the SMTP Virtual Server object in the System Manager snap-in and contains the following message queues:

- remote delivery queues
- local delivery queues
- messages waiting for directory lookup
- messages waiting to be routed to a queue

Messages awaiting directory lookup include messages currently in the Categorizer or PreCategorizer queue, whereas the local delivery queue is the queue to the Store Driver. Messages waiting to be routed are messages in a postCat queue waiting for the RE to apply its logic. You can freeze messages in the various queues or you can return messages back to the person who initiated them. You should check your message queues frequently before an excessive number of queued messages cause performance problems in your network.

The message tracking feature of Exchange 2000 can trace the paths of all sent messages. All messages that are routed through the transport engine of an Exchange 2000 Server are added to *tracking logs*, but only if you enable message tracking (it is disabled by default when you first install Exchange 2000). Using message tracking, you can find specific messages in a message queue or you can verify that messages have been delivered. Exchange 2000 generates a daily log file that contains running histories of every message transferred into your company.

***NOTE:** You also can use message tracking to track public folder postings because these postings are similar to email messages.*

The Message Tracking Center can search through message tracking logs, which are found in the \Exchsrvr*servername*.log directory on your Exchange 2000 Server. The logs are named by date of creation, for instance 19990823.LOG refers to a log file created on August 23, 1999 (the format is always *yyyymmdd*.LOG). These files use standard tab-delimited text and can be viewed using any standard text editor such as Notepad. If you aren't careful, these log files will consume a lot of valuable disk space, so delete some log files after a certain time period (for example, every seven days). Also, for message tracking to function properly, log files are normally shared on every Exchange 2000 Server in your company as *servername*.LOG and should be readily accessible by all users.

Two other tools used to troubleshoot message routing in Exchange 2000 include protocol logging and diagnostic logging. *Protocol logging* allows you to track commands received by protocol Virtual Servers in Exchange System Manager. You can troubleshoot problems for the HTTP, SMTP, or NNTP Protocol Virtual Servers, but this process is very CPU and memory intensive and could degrade server performance if enabled for all Protocol Virtual Servers you configure in System Manager. Protocol logging allows you to track such items as the following:

- Connection date and time for various email clients
- IP addresses of clients who are sending messages
- The server name and IP address of the server on which any log entries are being generated
- The number of message bytes sent and received by the server

You can view the actual protocol log files in the \%*systemroot*%\System32\LogFiles directory on your Exchange 2000 Server to determine whether your users are able to connect to certain Virtual Servers or whether they are able to send or receive data. These log files also tell you how long it takes to establish connections with users, and provide information about any server errors that might be hindering proper message flow in your organization. Protocol logging is enabled on each Virtual Server individually. For example, HTTP Virtual Servers are used to track protocol logging for both the HTTP protocol and the OWA client. SMTP Virtual Servers are used to track protocol logging for SMTP mail transport, and NNTP Virtual Servers track protocol logging for NNTP newsgroups.

Diagnostic logging is similar to protocol logging in that it helps you find performance problems for certain Exchange 2000 services; however, a diagnostic log isn't written to a separate log file as protocol logs are. Diagnostic logs are written to logs in the Windows 2000 Event Viewer tool instead. Use these types of logs to monitor your Exchange 2000 Connectors. When a connector sends a message, diagnostic logs check the logging level of the message with the logging level you configured when you enabled diagnostic logging for a particular server.

TIP: *Both protocol logging and diagnostic logging are resource intensive, so use them sparingly if possible!*

Most Exchange 2000 Services record events in the Event Viewer diagnostic tool found within Windows 2000 Server. You can configure four distinct logging levels for these services:

- *None*—This is the default logging level at which Exchange Server records only *significant* events, which are written to the application, system, or security event logs within Event Viewer. Only error messages are logged.
- *Minimum*—Logs with summary entries are written only in Event Viewer. One entry is written in Event Viewer for every task that is performed. This type of logging won't help you troubleshoot a problem completely. Both warning messages and error messages are logged.
- *Medium*—This level writes both summary and detail entries in Event Viewer and can be used to help identify the source of a problem. The log files record only the major tasks performed by each service within Exchange Server. Informational messages, warning messages, and error messages are logged.
- *Maximum*—Logging includes complete details of all actions performed by a given Exchange 2000 Service. At this level, server performance is subject to degradation if you allow the log files to grow unchecked. All types of messages are logged, including detailed information, informational mes-sages, warning messages, and error messages.

Immediate Solutions

Understanding Message Routing in Exchange 5.5

When a user is trying to send a message using Exchange 5.5, the following process takes place:

1. The Information Store puts the message in the appropriate mailbox if it determines that the destination address or recipient is located on the same server as the source address or sender.
2. If the recipient is not local to this Exchange Server, the MTA initiates a transfer to the MTA residing on the destination server using RPCs between the two machines.
3. The action in Step 2 occurs only if the destination machine is in the same Exchange 5.5 site as the sender's machine. If these two machines exist in different sites, the MTA routes this message using a predefined connector (either the Site Connector, the X.400 Connector, or an IMC Connector). The message is routed regardless of whether it's being sent to an adjacent site or a site that resides outside the boundaries of your Exchange 5.5 organization.

Planning Single Routing Groups in Your Organization

You can simplify your administrative burden by using single routing group designs in your organization instead of multiple routing groups. Your servers can belong to multiple Windows 2000 sites because routing groups can span multiple sites, and each site can contain its own GC Server for authentication purposes (or a combination of a DC and a GC Server).

Apply the following recommendations if you plan to deploy a single routing group in your organization:

- Every server that will be running Exchange 2000 must belong to a single Windows 2000 forest and a single Exchange 2000 organization. A routing group cannot span multiple forests or multiple organizations.

- Within a routing group, all servers use SMTP to communicate with each other and the network connections between all Exchange Servers in the routing group must be well defined and permanent.
- Within your routing group, all Exchange 2000 Servers must be able to communicate with the RGM, which is responsible for updating the LSTs. You can specify which machine will serve this function, but normally the first Exchange 2000 server you install in a routing group becomes the RGM. If the RGM becomes unavailable for any reason, the other Exchange 2000 Servers in the routing group will be unable to make efficient routing choices and LSI will not be correctly forwarded between the servers. You might want to consider redundancy and fault-tolerance for any server currently acting as your RGM.

Planning Multiple Routing Groups in Your Organization

Best practices recommend using single routing groups to reduce administrative overhead and simplify management. We recommend you use multiple routing groups, however, under the following conditions:

- Your users require dial-up connections between multiple servers in your company. In this case, you need more than one routing group with multiple GC Servers for fault tolerance.
- Your network performance decreases when messaging traffic levels increases at peak times of the day. You can schedule message delivery for off-peak times if you create more than one routing group and place a connector between the groups.
- Your current network connections between remote offices are slow or unreliable, and you don't want to place all users into one routing group. You can distribute the client load across multiple routing groups containing different Windows 2000 sites.
- You are trying to control message traffic between branch office locations and you notice that client application performance has been degrading because all users in your organization are connecting to a single mailbox server in your central office. You can implement different routing groups for each branch office, with each routing group containing different ranges of IP subnets for different locations.

NOTE: *Multiple routing groups require more time to manage and they require the implementation of connectors between groups. This introduces more overhead on your messaging infrastruc-ture. Data packets crossing more points on your network when traveling from a source computer to a destination computer also leads to more server overhead because more processing power is needed to maintain and update LSI between all routing groups.*

Related solution:	Found on page:
Performing a Foreign Mail System Audit	132

Deploying Public Folder Replicas in Remote Routing Groups

Public folder referrals allow you to provide your users with general access to various public folders if their local public folder server is not available. Sometimes, users access a public folder server that does not contain an instance or replica of the public folder that was requested. Figure 11.4 shows how public folder referrals take place.

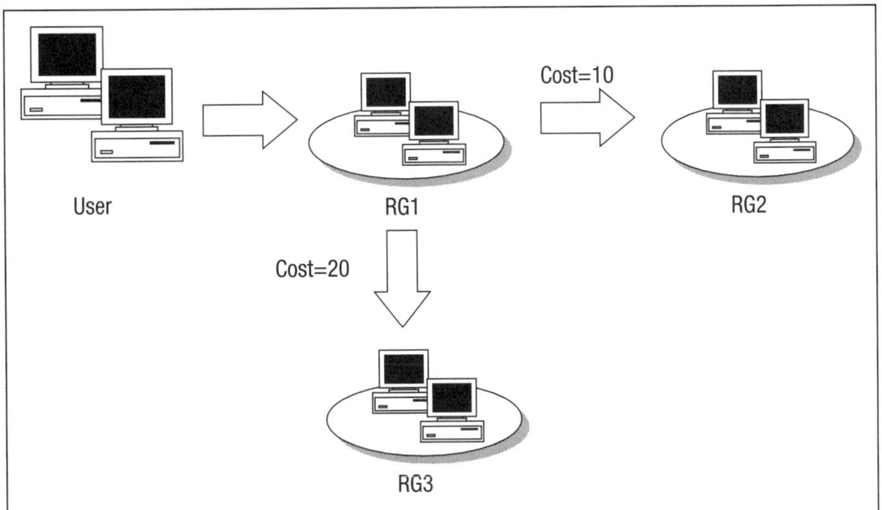

Figure 11.4 The public folder referral process.

When users try to view the contents of a public folder, the Information Store service (**Store.exe**) obtains the most recent replica folder list and finds all locations where replicas of this folder exist. If the replica of this folder resides on a local public folder server that the user is connecting to, that user can view the contents as long as they have permission. If this replica resides on another server *in the same routing group* (RG1 in Figure 11.4), the user is referred to the server on which the replica is located.

If, however, no public folder server exists in RG1 that contains the content this user wants, Exchange 2000 refers this request to other routing groups that might contain this specific public folder (RG2 and RG3). The Information Store sorts its "replica list" according to connector cost and selects the routing group at the end of a connector having the lowest total cost (RG2). In any case, you can disable public folder referrals across a RGC, even if that connector has a lower total cost compared to other connectors that are being deployed.

You should store public folders that are frequently accessed on servers that appear in the *same routing group* as mailbox servers. If this is not possible, configure public folder referrals based on connector costs that are totally under your control. You can assign costs based on the location of specific servers in your network. You also can disable public folder referrals to prevent MAPI clients—such as Outlook 2000 users—from obtaining access to certain public folders that might contain private or sensitive information.

NOTE: *Even though Figure 11.4 shows names such as RG1 and RG2, these names should never be used in real practice. A routing group name can support up to 64 characters, so you should use creative and descriptive names for all your routing groups (for example, St. Louis-Routing group). You are* not *allowed to use the following characters for routing group names: # * ; , " / \ < > +.*

Designing Routing Group Strategies Based on Administrative Models

You can administer Exchange 2000 using a centralized administrative model or a distributed administrative model. The first scenario involves administration from one location, whereas the second involves administration from multiple remote locations. You can even combine these two administrative models if needed.

If you select a centralized administrative model, all administrative and routing groups are managed from a central location. Each branch office should have permanent and high-bandwidth connections to the central office for maximum results. All your mailbox servers should be placed in the central office so they can exist in a *central hub routing group*. All servers in the routing group also share high-speed and high-bandwidth connectivity as well. You might want to place public folder servers in this routing group, too. If you need to create additional routing groups, place a server in this group dedicated to hosting a RGC. This server then acts in the capacity of a Bridgehead Connector Server.

Sometimes a centralized model uses a front-end/back-end (FE/BE) configuration so that branch offices connect to the central office over the Internet to retrieve their mail. You could place FE or BE Servers in a separate routing group in the central office to provide redundancy for primary routing groups that serve MAPI clients from other locations. MAPI clients cannot use a FE/BE scenario, so this routing group should be reserved for clients who use Internet protocols to retrieve mail or public folder information, such as IMAP4, POP3, or HTTP. Because the FE Servers will be resolving queries for remote clients, they should be configured as GC Servers to decrease logon and authentication times.

If you are using a distributed administrative model in your organization, consider how your branch offices connect to your central office, because all administrative groups and routing groups are now being managed from your branch office locations. Network links and connections are important here because additional routing groups should be created for connections between offices that are unreliable or subject to frequent interruptions in service. Each distributed routing group can contain a mixture of both mailbox servers and public folder servers. If all branch offices are connected to your central office with high-speed or high-bandwidth connections, you can use a combination of a centralized model with a distributed administrative model in your organization. In this case, one central hub routing group can be created in your central headquarters containing all mailbox servers that are accessed by users. All other routing groups (for connector servers or public folder servers) can be created in the branch offices that will administer these groups from their locations. If branch offices deploy their own routing groups, they have to ensure that all servers in their routing groups have high-speed permanent connections between them.

Selecting the RGM within a Routing Group

Every routing group has a RGM that maintains LSI for the routing group. The RGM uses TCP port 691 to propagate changes to its LST to the other servers within the group. Exchange 2000 configures the first server that you add to a routing group as the RGM and displays this in the System Manager snap-in. You can set any subsequent server that you add to this group to become the new RGM.

To display the current RGM or select a new RGM, perform the following:

1. Open the System Manager by selecting Start|Programs|Microsoft Exchange| System Manager.
2. When the console opens, expand your Organization object by double-clicking it, and then expand your Administrative Groups by clicking the "+" next to it.
3. Expand the First Administrative Group and then the Routing Groups container in the same way.
4. Expand the First Routing Group node, and then click the Members folder underneath it. The Details pane on the right-hand side shows all servers in this routing group (see Figure 11.5).
5. Right-click the first server displayed in the right-hand pane and make sure the Set As Master option has a check mark next to it (see Figure 11.6). If another server is displayed in this pane, right-click it and select Set As Master to make this your new RGM.
6. Close the Exchange System Manager snap-in console.

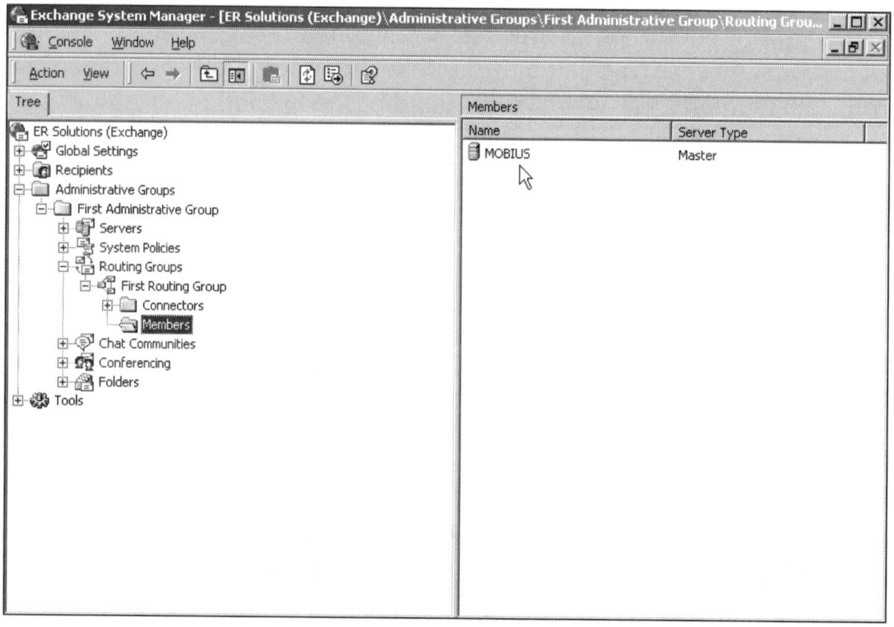

Figure 11.5 Displaying the RGM in System Manager.

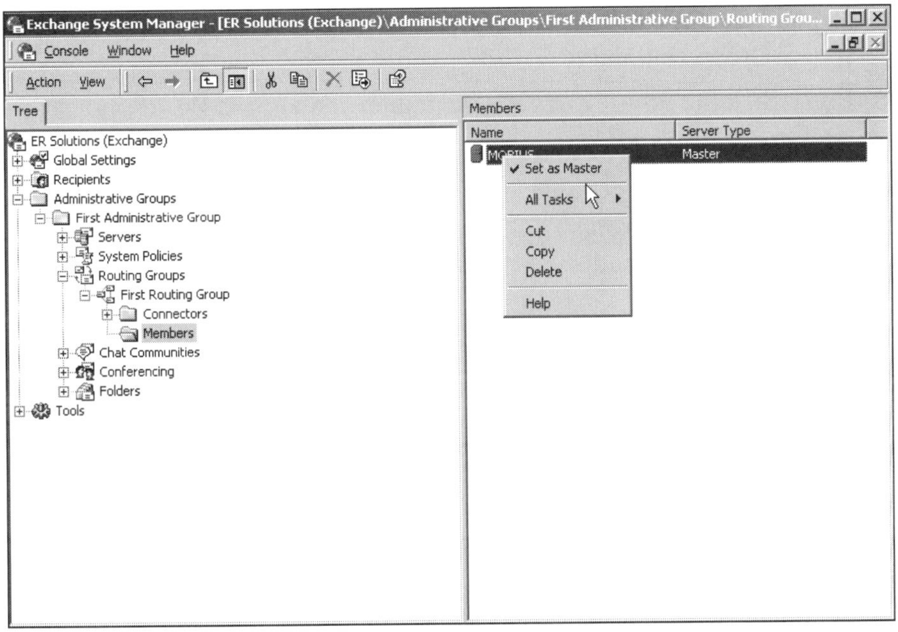

Figure 11.6 Displaying the option to select the RGM in System Manager.

You select a new RGM if your first RGM fails for any reason. You must do this in a timely fashion, or any new LSI won't be transferred to other servers. The exception to this rule occurs within routing groups. When a RGM is not available within a routing group, messages can still be transferred between servers *in that routing group only*. Even if the servers notice they don't possess the most current link state updates, the server with the most recent information updates the other servers in that group.

NOTE: *If a local bridgehead server in a routing group receives link state updates from a remote bridgehead server in a different routing group, the local bridgehead server updates all its LSTs and tries to continue informing the RGM that this information is now available. This process continues until the RGM is fully functional again within that routing group.*

Creating a New Routing Group Using System Manager

If an organization contains one DC and three member servers, you should create routing groups on the DC so users can easily query AD on the DC. To do this, perform the following:

1. Open the System Manager console and expand your Organization object.

2. Expand the Administrative Groups container, and then the First Administrative Group container.
3. Right-click the Routing Groups container, and choose New|Routing Group.
4. Type "RG2" in the Name box, and then click OK.
5. Expand the Routing Groups container in System Manager and verify that your new routing group—RG2—is there. If it isn't, right-click the Routing Groups container and select Refresh, or press the F5 key to refresh the window.

Moving Servers between Routing Groups Using System Manager

You can easily move servers between two different routing groups using the System Manager snap-in. To do this, perform the following:

1. Open the System Manager console and expand the Administrative Groups container.
2. Expand the First Administrative Group container, and then expand the Routing Groups container. Make sure that multiple routing groups exist in this container.

NOTE: *You can always create additional routing groups by following the previous Immediate Solution "Creating a New Routing Group Using System Manager."*

3. Click the Members folder for the First Routing Group and see any servers located in the right-hand Details pane of the console.
4. Click one server listed in this Details pane and drag it into the Members folder of the Second Routing Group in the Routing Groups container. Right-click the Routing Groups container and select Refresh.
5. Verify that the Members folder of the Second Routing Group now contains the server that was formerly in the Members folder of the First Routing Group.
6. Close the System Manager console when you are finished.

Using Link State Routing with All Connectors in Exchange 2000

Link state routing does not work with all connectors in Exchange 2000. It performs properly with all native Exchange 2000 Connectors, such as the RGC, the SMTP Connector, and the RPC Connector because they are "link state aware." Even X.400 Connectors can detect the status of network links as being available or unavailable. Other connectors—including the IMS connector used in Exchange 5.5, the cc:Mail Connector, the MS Mail Connector, and the Lotus Notes Connector—are, however, unable to detect link status information. These connectors always show link status as being *available* or "up." Even when there are problems with LSTs, these connectors show an *available* status. LST algorithms detect only connectors native to Exchange 2000.

Resolving Target Bridgehead Addresses Using the SMTP Connector

Whenever you try to connect routing groups using the SMTP connector, the connector resolves the destination computer's IP address using DNS for MX resource records. This means you cannot choose specific target or destination bridgehead servers, because the SMTP Connector always tries to resolve IP addresses of the destination computers. If no corresponding MX records exist for these target servers, the machine trying to send messages tries to resolve the *hostname* of the destination target server by querying the DNS server for host (or "A") resource records, not MX records. Using multiple target destination servers with the SMTP connector means you have to configure one MX resource record for each individual target bridgehead server.

Creating an RGC Using the Exchange System Manager Snap-In

To create a new RGC in the System Manager snap-in MMC, you must first create two routing groups in your organization. To do this in System Manager, perform the following:

1. Open the System Manager console and expand the Administrative Groups folder and the First Administrative Group.

2. Right-click the Routing Groups container, and select New|Routing Group.
3. When the dialog box appears, type "RG2" in the Name box and click OK.
4. Verify that both routing groups appear under the Routing Groups container in System Manager.

If you already have multiple routing groups configured, you can proceed to the next sequence of steps to create a new RGC in System Manager. You must have at least one server in each routing group that you create. You can check this by clicking the Members folder under each routing group and noting the servers that appear in the Details pane of the console. The following steps assume you have just opened the System Manager console:

1. Open the Exchange System Manager MMC.
2. Expand your Organization container and Administrative container.
3. Expand the First Administrative Group, and then the Routing Groups container.
4. Expand the First Routing Group container to expose the Connectors and Members folders.

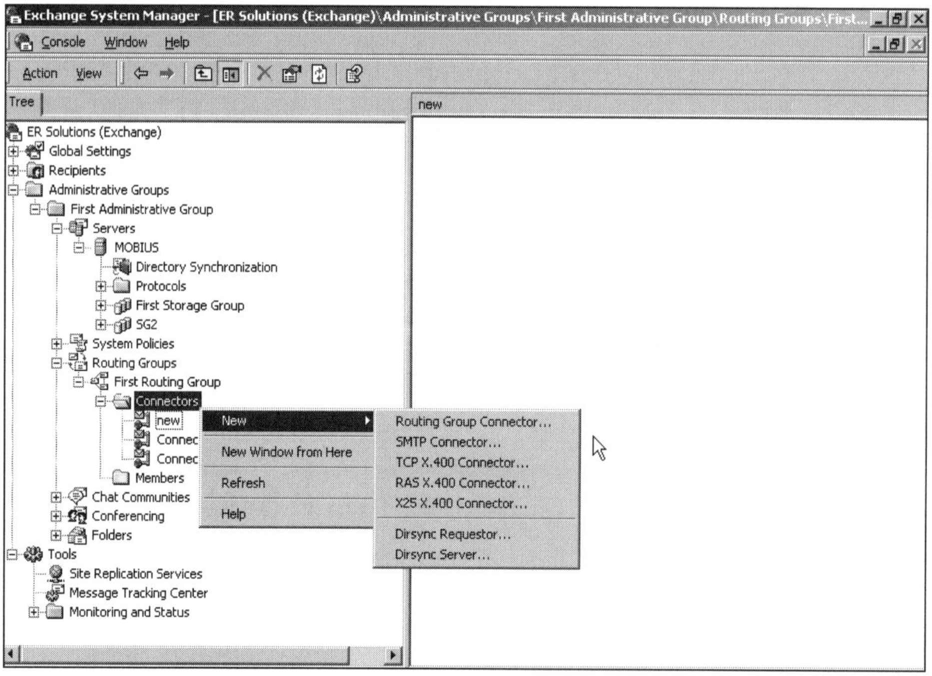

Figure 11.7 Creating a new routing group in System Manager.

5. Right-click the Connectors folder, and select New|Routing Group Connector as shown in Figure 11.7.
6. When the Properties dialog box appears, click the General tab and type "Connector To RG2". The Connects This Routing Group With text box should display RG2 (First Administrative Group).
7. Click the Remote Bridgehead tab, and then click Add. When you see the Add Bridgehead message box, select the server that exists in the RG2 routing group, and then click OK.
8. Now select the Delivery Options tab and verify that the option for Always Run is displayed in the Connection Time list box. Then click OK.
9. If you receive a prompt asking you to create a RGC in RG2, click No. After completing these steps, allow some time for AD replication to take place.
10. Close System Manager when you are done.

Resolving Destination Bridgehead Server Addresses for RGCs

If you have a local bridgehead server in one routing group trying to deliver a message to a remote target bridgehead server in a remote routing group across a RGC, the following occurs:

1. You cannot select a target bridgehead server for messages delivery, so the local bridgehead server selects a target bridgehead server at random.
2. The local bridgehead server resolves the target bridgehead server on the other end of the RGC by querying the local DNS Server for any MX resource records associated with the target bridgehead server. If no MX records exist for this target server, the local bridgehead queries AD for the fully qualified domain name of the target bridgehead server.
3. If name resolution is successful, the local bridgehead server queries DNS for the IP address of this name. If name resolution is not successful, the local bridgehead can use other name resolution methods such as WINS (Windows Internet Naming Service) resolution to resolve the IP address of the target bridgehead server.

Configuring a TCP/IP-Based X.400 Connector between Routing Groups

When configuring a TCP/IP based X.400 connector between two routing groups using the System Manager snap-in MMC, you first have to create a new TCP/IP X.400 Service Transport Stack in System Manager. To do this, perform the following:

1. Open the System Manager snap-in console and expand your Organization object, your Administrative Groups container, and your First Administrative Group object.
2. Expand the Server container, and then your *Server* object.
3. Expand the Protocols folder, and then right-click the X.400 Container. Select New|TCP/IP X.400 Service Transport Stack as shown in Figure 11.8.
4. In the Properties dialog box that appears, accept all default settings and click OK. Then right-click the X.400 container, select Properties, and make sure your Local X.400 Name agrees with the name of your server.
5. Click the Modify button and delete all asterisks appearing under Password and Confirm Password (you can change this later, and you do not want any

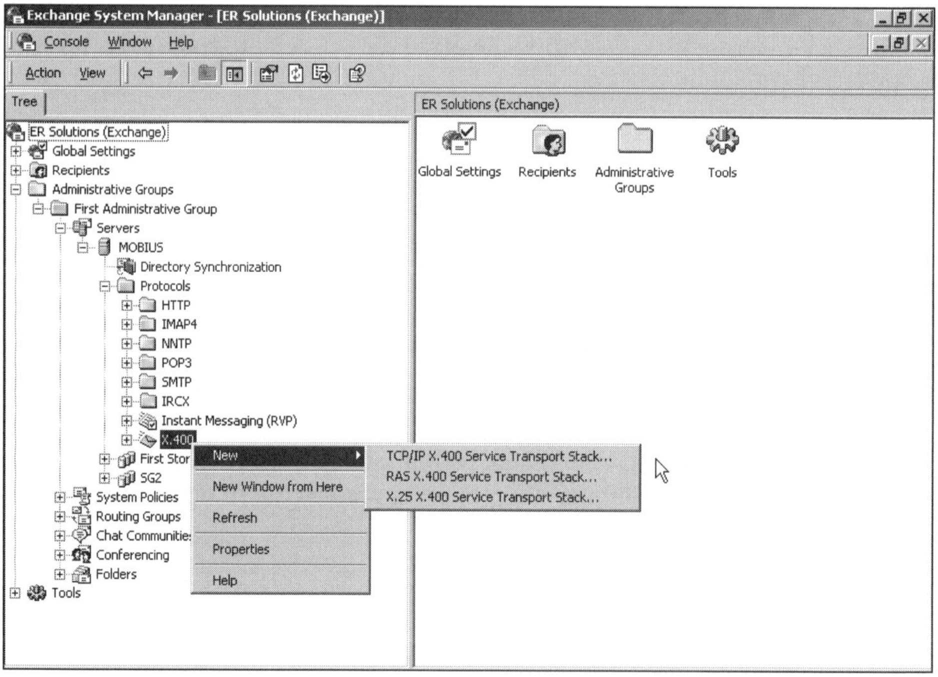

Figure 11.8 Creating a new TCP/IP X.400 Service Transport Stack in System Manager.

leftover characters appearing here that might interfere with operation of your connector when you are done). Then, click OK twice to close these boxes.

6. Now expand your Routing Groups container and First Routing Group. Right-click the Connectors folder that appears underneath, and then select New|TCP X.400 Connector. Select a server in another routing group to which you want to establish a connection.
7. In the Name box, type "X.400 to *[name of server in second routing group]*". Then under Remote X.400 Name, click Modify to open the Remote Connection Credentials box.
8. Type the name of your remote routing group server in the Remote X.400 Name box as shown in Figure 11.9.
9. Clear all entries under Password and Confirm Password, and then click OK. Click the Schedule tab and verify that the Schedule is set to Always.
10. Click the Stack tab, select the Remote Host Name option, and type the name of your second routing group server under Name. Then, click the Connected Routing Groups tab, and click Add.
11. When the Properties box appears, verify that First Administrative Group/ *Second Routing Group* (whatever you configured for this) is selected, and then click OK. Now click the Advanced tab and check to see whether the Allow Exchange Contents checkbox is selected.

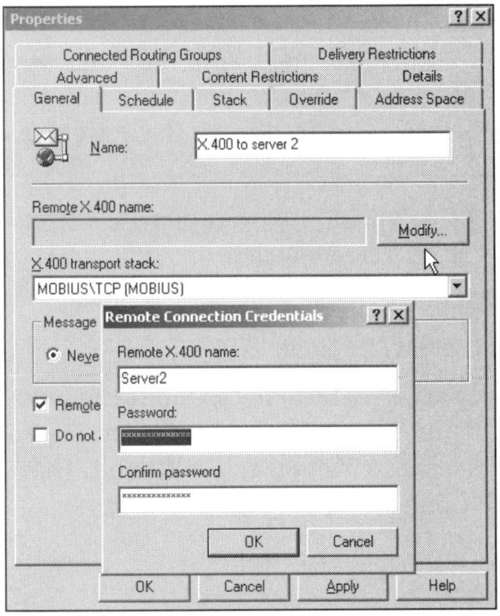

Figure 11.9 Typing the name of a remote routing group server in the Remote Connection Credentials.

12. Click OK. You see a dialog box telling you that you have to configure both sides of this connection. Click OK. You have now configured one end of your X.400 connector. Repeat the steps on the server in the second routing group, making sure to list the name of the first routing group's server for the Remote X.400 Name, and also making sure to clear any password entries that might exist (you can create new case-sensitive passwords for your X.400 connector at any time).

Checking SMTP Queues Using the Queue Viewer Utility in System Manager

Every SMTP Virtual Server you create displays a Queues container showing you messages in the connector queue. Queues take two forms: *system queues* and *connector queues*. System queues include three types of distinct queues:

- Local delivery queues
- Messages awaiting directory lookup
- Messages waiting to be routed

Even though these three system queues are always displayed, connector queues are only displayed when messages are physically present. You can test the configuration of a new connector—such as a RGC—by sending messages to remote recipients, and then viewing the system and connector queues in System Manager. To fully examine any SMTP message queues, make sure the Windows 2000 SMTP service has been started, and that you have RPC connections between the System Manager interface and the SMTP service. To display the system queues using System Manager, perform the following:

1. Expand the Organization object, the Administrative Groups object, and the First Administrative Group object in System Manager.
2. Expand the Servers container, and then expand *your_server* object.
3. Expand the Protocols folder and the SMTP folder.
4. Expand the Default SMTP Virtual Server, and then expand the Queues container. You will notice three distinct queues: Local Delivery, Messages Awaiting Directory Lookup, and Messages Waiting To Be Routed. These are your system queues for the SMTP Connector (see Figure 11.10).

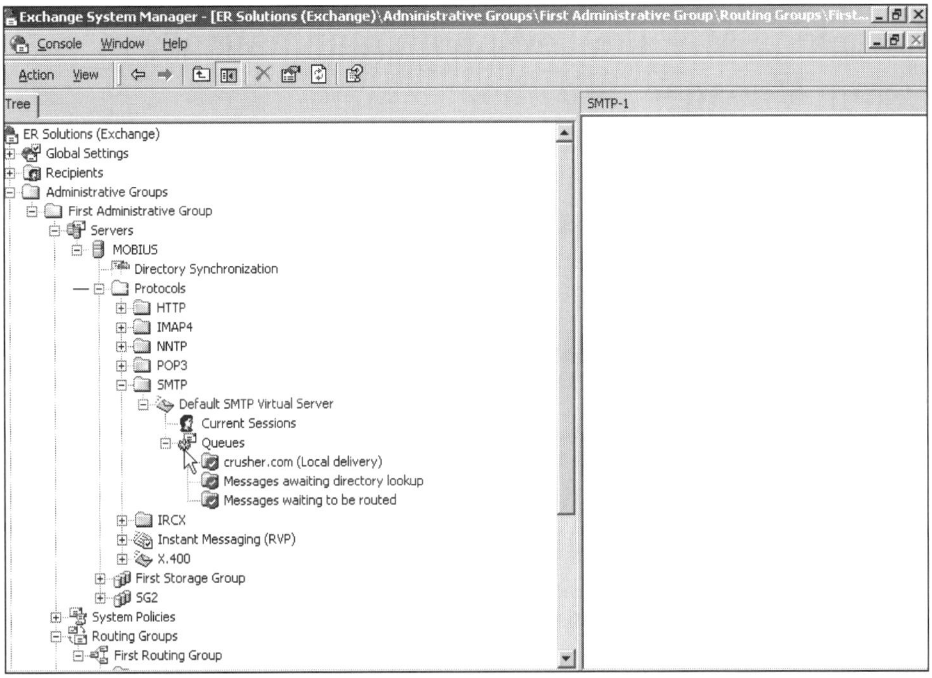

Figure 11.10 Viewing the system queues in Exchange System Manager.

Deleting and Freezing Messages in SMTP Queues Using System Manager

The previous Immediate Solution discussed how to view messages in SMTP system queues using Exchange System Manager. Using this same Queue Viewer tool, you can delete or freeze messages if you think they are blocking a queue. Right-click the message and choose the Delete (Send NDR) option or the Delete (No NDR) option, depending on whether you want to inform the sender about this message deletion. If you like, you can delete the entire queue, and not just one individual message. To do this, right-click the queue you want to work with in System Manager (see previous Immediate Solution for the steps involved in this process), and choose the Delete All Messages (Send NDR) or Delete All Messages (No NDR) option.

Freezing a message does not delete it; rather, the message remains frozen until you unfreeze it. This can give you time to troubleshoot a problem message or attachment if it is too large, or if it contains unknown MIME content. Right-clicking a SMTP queue in System Manager also gives you the option to Freeze or Unfreeze All Messages with or without the NDR option.

Managing SMTP Queue Growth Automatically in System Manager

To manage SMTP queue growth automatically using the System Manager snap-in, perform the following steps:

1. Make sure your System Manager snap-in is open.
2. Expand your Administrative Groups folder, and then your First Administrative Group container.
3. Expand your Servers container, right-click your *Server* object, and choose the Properties option.
4. In the Properties dialog box, click the Monitoring tab, and then click the Add button as shown in Figure 11.11.
5. In the Add Resource box that appears, select the SMTP Queue Growth option in the list, and click OK (see Figure 11.12).
6. In the SMTP Queue Thresholds box that appears (see Figure 11.13), select time intervals for both Warning State and Critical State so that Exchange 2000 can notify you when your queue grows continuously for these specified intervals. Click OK when you are finished doing this.
7. Notice the SMTP Queues growth period has been added to the Name section of the Monitoring tab with the Warning State and Critical State you configured. If you want to remove this service in the future, click the Remove

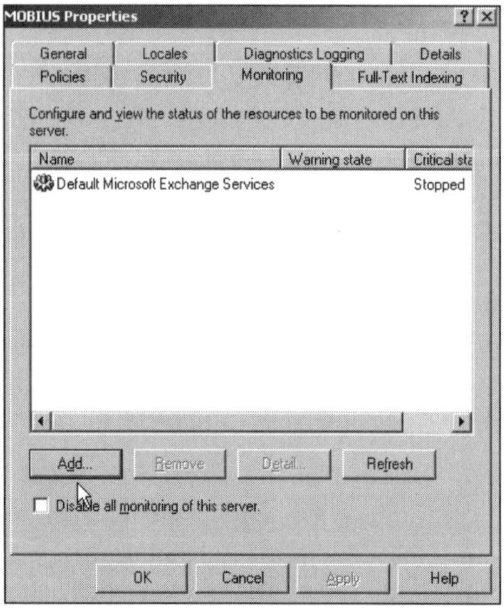

Figure 11.11 The Monitoring tab in the Server Properties dialog box.

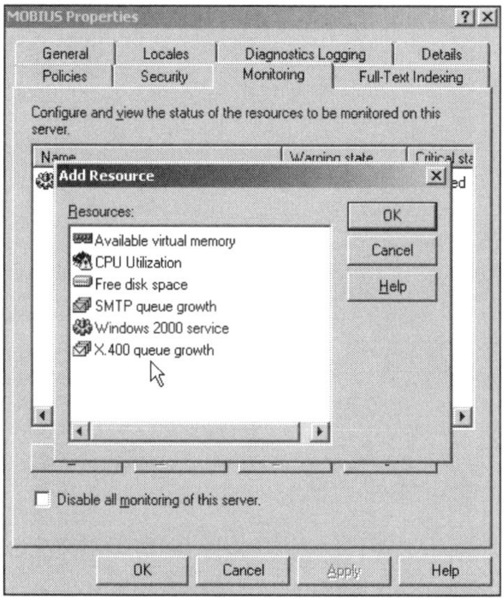

Figure 11.12 Adding the SMTP Queue Growth resource to monitor.

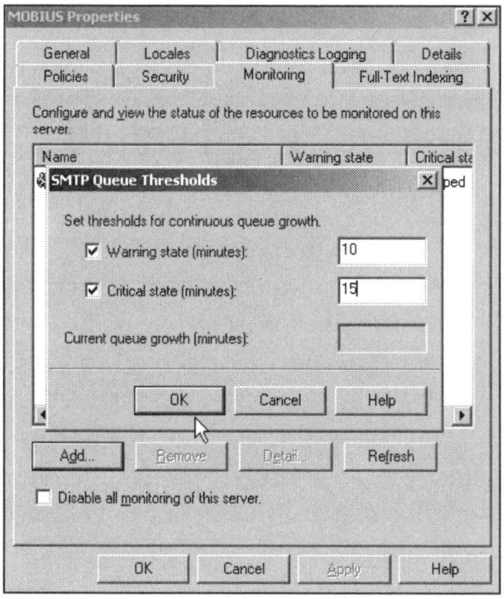

Figure 11.13 Configuring the Warning State and Critical State for notification purposes.

button. If you want to change the Warning State or Critical State time periods, click the Detail button. When you are done viewing this box, click OK to return to the System Manager interface (see Figure 11.14).

NOTE: *Your Critical State time period must exceed your Warning State time period, otherwise Exchange displays a message box asking you to make this condition true.*

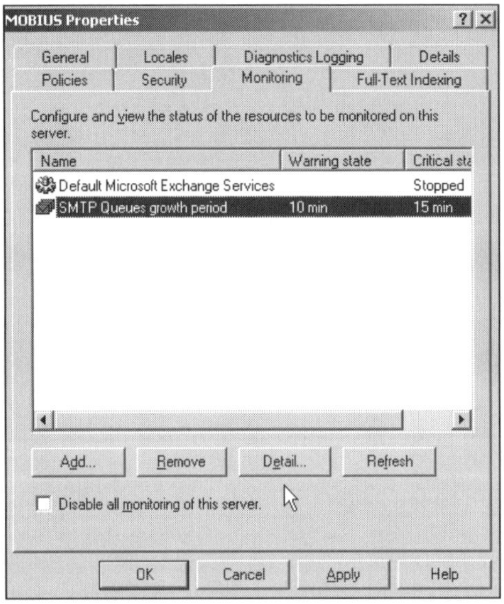

Figure 11.14 The new service added to the Monitoring tab in System Manager.

Enabling and Using the Message Tracking Feature in Exchange 2000

The Message Tracking Center is a standalone snap-in that is integrated with Exchange System Manager (located under Tools in System Manager and also can be installed as an *extension snap-in*). This tool reads information from network shares located on all Exchange 2000 Servers that are involved in the message-transfer process. You have to specify what server you want to start with when you first open this utility in System Manager. First, you have to make sure that message tracking is enabled for a particular server (you also can enable message tracking on a global basis by creating a server policy for this in one of your administrative groups in the System Policies container).

To enable message tracking for a single server in System Manager:

1. Open System Manager by choosing Start|Programs|Microsoft Exchange|System Manager.
2. Expand your Organization object, then the Administrative Group container, and then the First Administrative Group folder.
3. Expand Servers, right-click your *Servername* object, and choose Properties. When the *Servername* Properties dialog box opens to the General tab (by

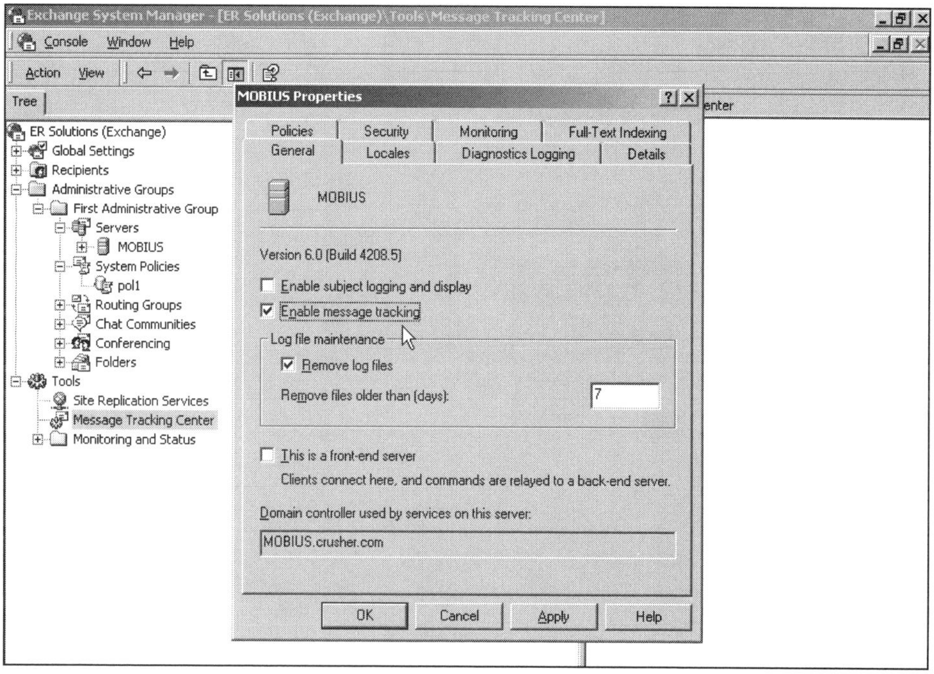

Figure 11.15 Enabling message tracking in System Manager.

default), check the Enable Message Tracking box in the top section (see Figure 11.15).

4. Open your Outlook 2000 client and send a message to someone inside your organization. Make sure you keep the System Manager snap-in open as well.
5. When the message has been sent, expand the Tools container in System Manager.
6. Right-click Message Tracking Center and select the Track Message option (see Figure 11.16).
7. When the Message Tracking Center box opens, you will notice three tabs, General, Date & Time, and Advanced. The General tab is used to select the server that is involved in the message transfer. Next to the Server(s) text box, click the Browse button and select the server you want to work with. Click Add, and then click OK to return to the Message Tracking Center box.
8. When you are ready to find a message, click Find Now, and select the message you want to track. You might see a message stating that certain log files cannot be found. Click OK to receive a list of the most recent message log (it might not be completely updated yet if you just enabled message tracking in the earlier Steps 1 through 3). Figure 11.17 displays the Message Tracking Center dialog box.

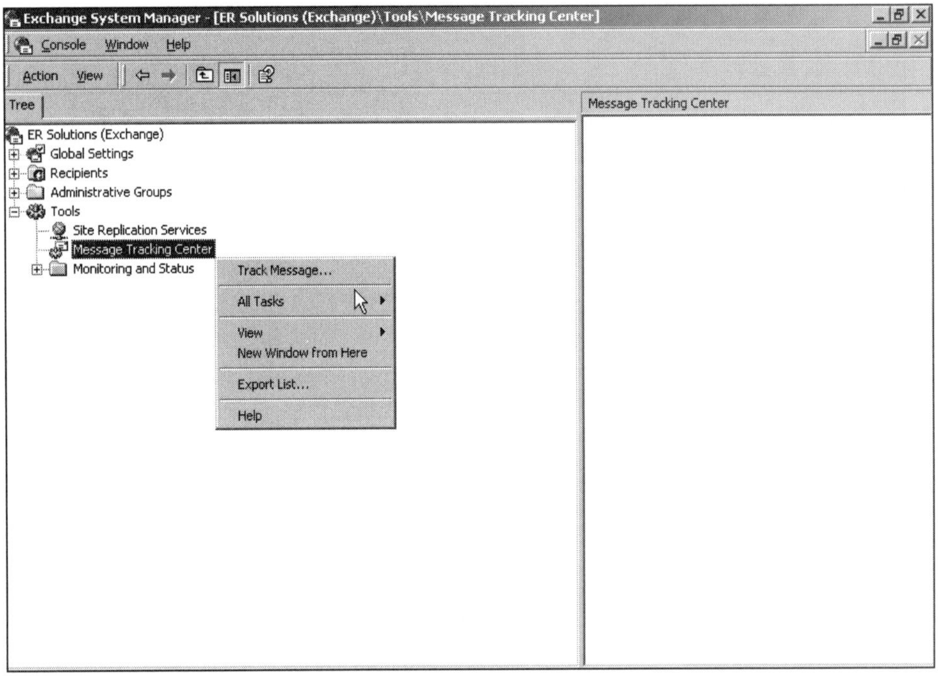

Figure 11.16 Selecting the Message Tracking Center in System Manager Tools.

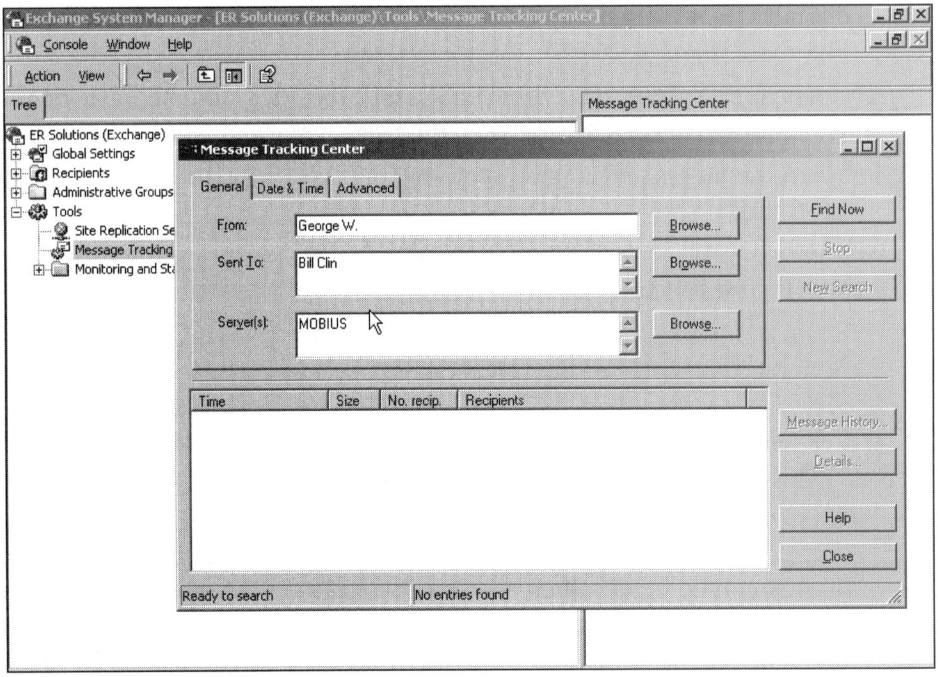

Figure 11.17 The Message Tracking Center dialog box in System Manager.

Enabling Protocol Logging for the SMTP Virtual Server in System Manager

You can enable protocol logging for individual protocol Virtual Servers in the Exchange System Manager snap-in tool. Complete the following steps:

1. Open System Manager by choosing Start|Programs|Microsoft Exchange| System Manager.
2. Expand all Administrative Groups and Servers objects in System Manager. Continue doing this until the Protocols container becomes visible. Expand the Protocols container and the SMTP folder under it.
3. Right-click the Default SMTP Virtual Server object in the SMTP folder and choose Properties. The Default SMTP Virtual Server Properties dialog box appears showing four tabs: General, Access, Messages, and Delivery.
4. In the General tab, check the Enable Logging box (see Figure 11.18).
5. Use the Active Log Format list box to select a log format. Your choices include the following log formats (see Figure 11.19):
   - *Microsoft IIS Log File Format*—Logs are written in ASCII file format and fields are tabulator-delimited, in which each entry is written to a new line.

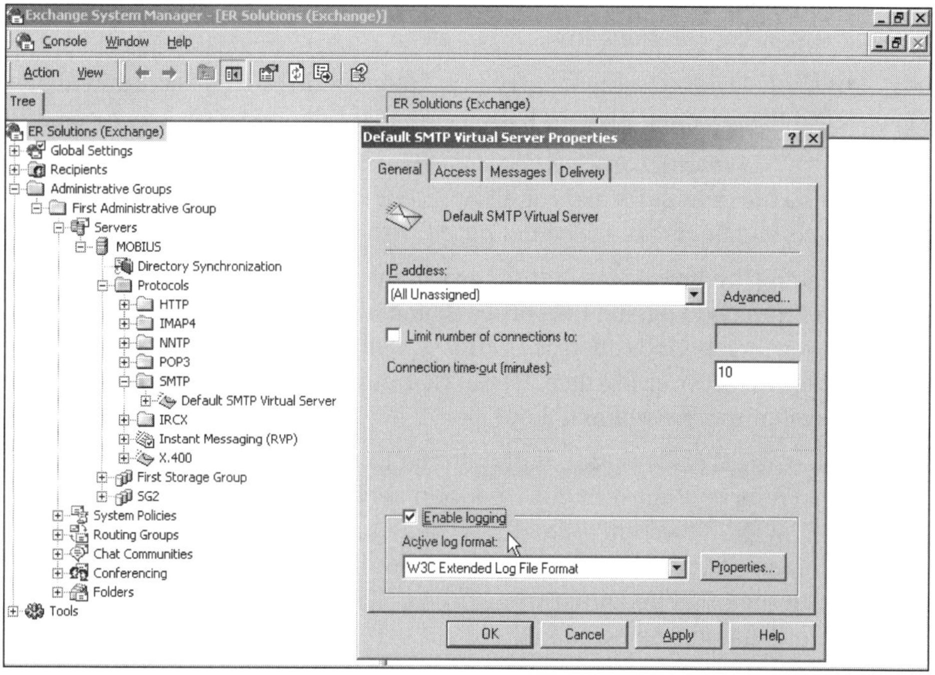

Figure 11.18 Enabling protocol logging in System Manager for the SMTP Virtual Server.

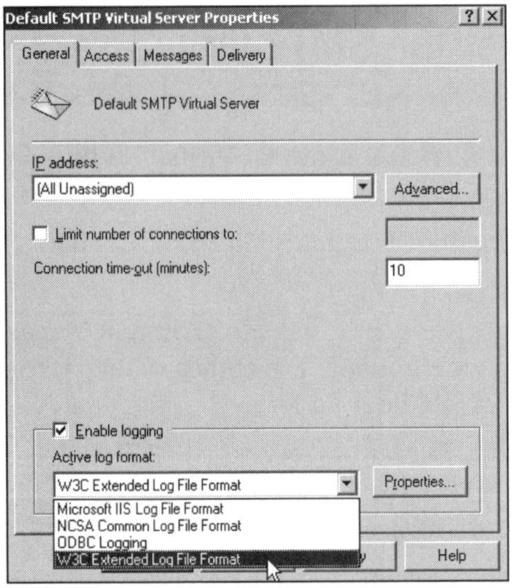

Figure 11.19 The log file formats available in the Default SMTP Virtual Server Properties dialog box.

- *NCSA Common Log File Format*—Log files are written according to specification developed by the National Center for Supercomputing Applications (NCSA). All fields are space-delimited with every entry appearing on a new line.
- *ODBC Logging*—Each entry in a field is written as a record in an Open Database Connectivity (ODBC) compliant database such as Access 2000.
- *W3C Extended Log File Format*—This is the preferred log file format and also the default format for all protocol logs. All logs are written in ASCII text and fields are space-delimited with each entry written to a new line.

Clicking the Properties button next to the Active Log Format text box opens the Extended Logging Properties dialog box shown in Figure 11.20. You can set log time periods such as Hourly or Daily and you can also select the main folder for all your log files. Recall that the default directory for log files is \%systemroot%\System32\LogFiles.

6. Select the Weekly option button in the Extended Logging Properties dialog box (refer to Figure 11.20), and then accept the default log file directory of C:\WINNT\System32\LogFiles (depending on where you installed your Exchange 2000 Server, of course). Note the Log File Name directly underneath the Log File Directory text box. This name depends on the log file format that you selected in Step 5.

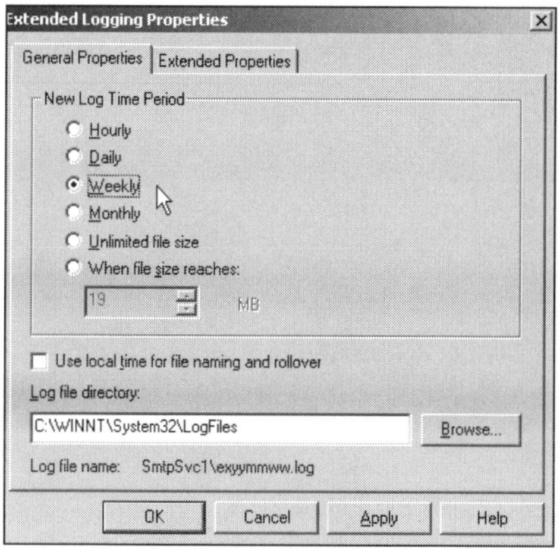

Figure 11.20 Configuring the New Log Time Period and the Log File Directory in System Manager.

NOTE: *The Log File Name determines the* subdirectory *under the LogFiles directory used to hold log files. When configuring the SMTP Virtual Server—as you did for this Immediate Solution—with weekly log files, all log files are placed in the following directory path:*

```
C:\Winnt\System32\LogFiles\SmtpSvc1\EX010634.LOG
```

where the name of the log file follows the convention: EXYYMMWW.LOG and:

EX="Exchange"
YY=the last two digits of the current year
MM=the current month in digits
WW=the current week in digits

```
.LOG = the file extension for the log file
```

---

7. Click the Extended Properties tab and select the additional fields you want recorded in the logs (see Figure 11.21). Note that the logging options you see on this tab do not add additional services to be logged.
8. Click OK twice to return to the Exchange System Manager console.

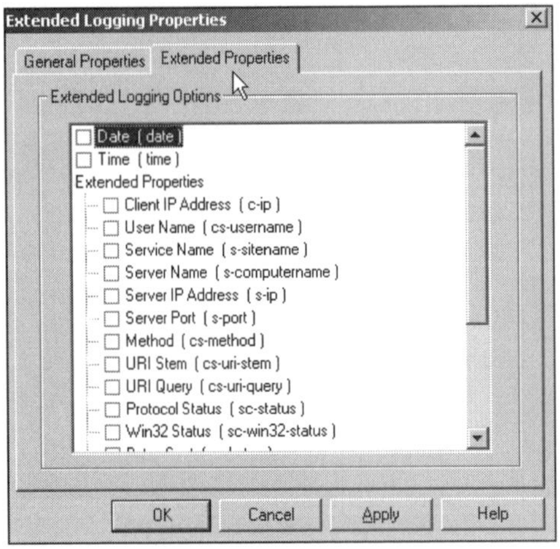

Figure 11.21 The Extended Properties tab of the Default SMTP Virtual Server.

Enabling Diagnostic Logging for an Exchange 2000 Server in System Manager

Diagnostic logging helps you detect performance problems related to Exchange 2000 services. All log entries are written to the Windows 2000 Event Viewer application, system, or security log. To configure diagnostic logging for your server using Exchange System Manager, perform the following steps:

NOTE: *Diagnostic logging has to be configured for each server separately throughout your organization. The default diagnostic logging level is* ***None****.*

1. Open System Manager by choosing Start|Programs|Microsoft Exchange|System Manager.
2. Expand all Organization objects and Administrative Group objects that appear in System Manager, including the First Administrative Group folder under the Administrative Groups container.
3. Expand the Servers container and right-click your server object that appears under it. Select the Properties option and view the General tab.
4. On the General tab, check the Enable Subject Logging And Display box (see Figure 11.22). Notice the Log File Maintenance default time period of 7 Days (you can increase or decrease this value by typing in a new value).

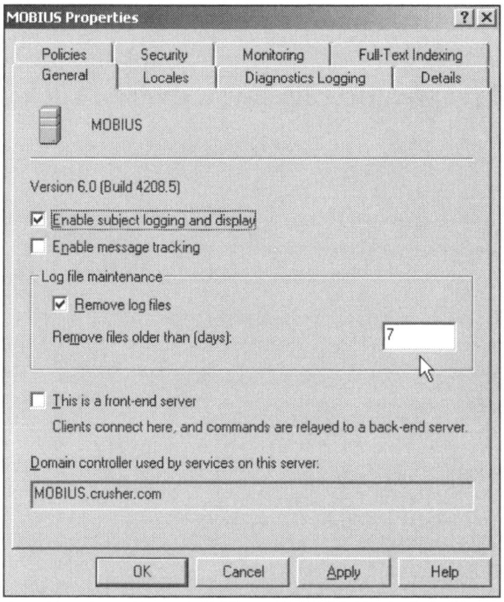

Figure 11.22 Enabling subject logging and display for your server object in System Manager.

5. Click the Diagnostics Logging tab and select a service that you want to track. Click POP3Svc, under the Services column, and notice the Category list on the right-hand side (see Figure 11.23).

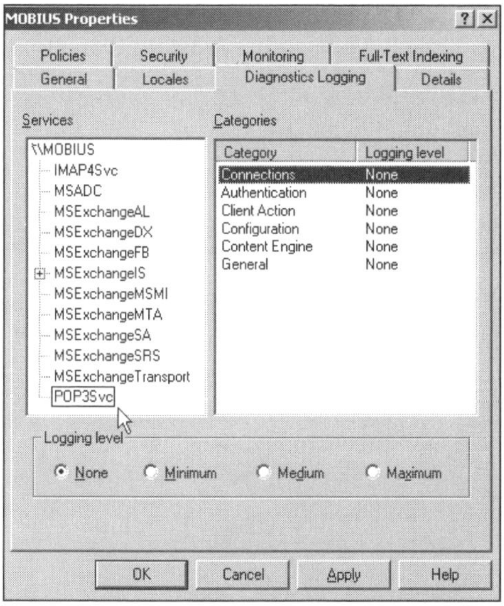

Figure 11.23 The Diagnostics Logging tab for your Server object in System Manager.

6. Notice that all logging levels are set to None by default. Try to change the logging level for the Connections Category on the right-hand side to Minimum. Logging begins immediately at whatever level you specify. Click OK when you are finished.

Chapter 12

Client Installation

If you need an immediate solution to:	See page:
Installing Exchange Server and the Outlook Client on the Same Machine	506
Forcing Users to Select a Profile Using the Outlook Client	507
Configuring Profiles for Outlook Clients	508
Adding a Personal Folder Store within the Outlook Client	509
Creating an Offline Folder File within Outlook 2000	510
Configuring Offline Folder Settings in Outlook 2000	510
Configuring a Connection State as Offline in Outlook 2000	510
Making the Offline Address Book Available to Offline Users	511
Configuring Remote Mail in Outlook 2000	512
Enabling the Out of Office Assistant	513
Creating a New Rule in Outlook 2000	515
Configuring a SMTP Virtual Server	516
Configuring and Controlling Access to a POP3 Virtual Server	518

In Depth

Administrators who plan any installation of Exchange 2000 for their companies must include decisions regarding both client and server software in their planning process. Before your deployment is complete, you should standardize on one or two particular Exchange clients (and their related protocols or services) you will be implementing and managing. Simplifying the range of software affects TCO by reducing both support and training expense. Selecting a "client" also involves selecting various Internet access protocols (such as HTTP [Hypertext Transfer Protocol] or SMTP [Simple Mail Transfer Protocol]) as well as a proper authentication method so that clients have the convenience of accessing resources in a secure fashion from anywhere, at any time, with any device. The use of various protocols is facilitated through the creation and management of *Virtual Servers*. These Virtual Servers can help make certain protocols available to a select group of users. This chapter compares differences between the various Exchange clients that are currently available. Exchange 2000 supports most existing messaging technologies and provides endless collaboration possibilities.

Exchange 2000 Protocols

Exchange 2000 has many options for client access methods. You have to evaluate the functionality gained by each method, the requirements of your organization, and the limitations of the access method that you choose before making a final decision. Choosing the most efficient Exchange client for your organization will benefit all employees and employers. Choosing a proper access method depends on understanding the various client access protocols that are available. The types of protocols supported by Exchange 2000 can be categorized into two groups: Internet protocols and Messaging Application Programming Interface (MAPI) protocol.

The Internet Protocols

An Internet protocol represents standards that are designed to allow different computers to talk to each other using a defined digital structure to which data packets can adhere to. Internet protocols allow multiple machines to exchange huge quantities of information and data over the Internet regardless of the network operating system (NOS) or hardware being used. Exchange 2000 supports many Internet protocols, including POP3 (Post Office Protocol 3), IMAP4 (Internet Message Access Protocol 4), HTTP, SMTP, LDAP (Lightweight Directory Access

Protocol), and NNTP (Network News Transfer Protocol). Each of these protocols is defined and described in the following sections.

Post Office Protocol Version 3

POP3 is known as a "retrieval" protocol because it is used to retrieve mail messages from a POP Server and is designed primarily for viewing email messages offline. All email messages received by a POP Server are delivered to a server mailbox; messages reside there until an individual with a POP3-compliant client retrieves them. POP3, shown in Figure 12.1, enables clients to read mail messages and download email attachments from a mail server. This specific protocol is consequently recommended for clients who cannot maintain continuous connections to a mail server or store messages offline.

POP3 clients use TCP (Transmission Control Protocol) port 110 to download email from a POP3 server. The POP3 protocol provides no mechanism for sending mail to another host; it is a mailbox protocol. Because a POP3 client downloads the entire message, a user might have to wait for large messages (or messages with large attachments) to be delivered. Users cannot preview messages using POP3. Although they can check email in their inboxes using POP3, users cannot access any other folders on the server that runs Exchange 2000.

Because the POP3 client typically deletes all server-side copies of user email messages, the protocol will minimize storage requirements on a mail server. Many email client applications thus allow a user to place persistent flags on messages to leave a copy of the message on the POP3 Server because of this feature. A POP3 message, however, can only be manipulated locally, so copy changes to messages are not seen if the user downloads a new copy of this message from other POP3 clients. Consider using the POP3 Protocol in the following situations:

- A client cannot maintain a connection to the server (as in a dial-up environment).

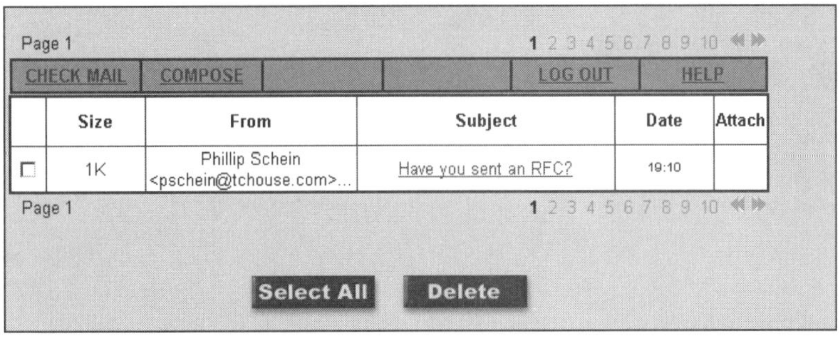

Figure 12.1 An example of a Web-based commercial POP mail reader.

- Storage on the POP3 Server must be kept to a minimum.
- Support for multiple operating systems (OSs) and client email programs is required.

TIP: *Because POP3 is a messaging protocol designed for message retrieval only, it must be capable of working with a protocol that can send messages as well (for example, SMTP).*

The Internet Message Access Protocol Version 4

If users need access to folders other than their inboxes, or server-side message storage is necessary, consider using a protocol other than POP3. Using the IMAP4 messaging protocol can alleviate some of the restrictions found with the POP3 protocol because IMAP4 is well suited for environments in which downloading all email to one specific computer is impractical. An example of an IMAP4 mail client is shown in Figure 12.2. In simplest terms, a POP Server provides basic "store-and-forward" services; IMAP delivers remote file server functionality. Unlike the POP3 protocol, the IMAP4 protocol allows users to access public folders or multiple email folders. It also allows them to search through a mailbox and maintain read/unread message flags.

IMAP4 allows users to download an entire message or even portions of a message (such as attachments). It permits users to access and manipulate messages in a remote Information Store as if these messages were local (without requiring an email client to download the files first). IMAP4 is a read-only messaging protocol and—like POP3—relies on SMTP to send messages. Because IMAP4 clients can read more than just their Inbox folders, this protocol can be used to manage multiple mailboxes as well as shared mailboxes. Recall that POP3 is inappropriate for accessing shared mailboxes because all messages are downloaded to a local computer and manipulated only through a local file system.

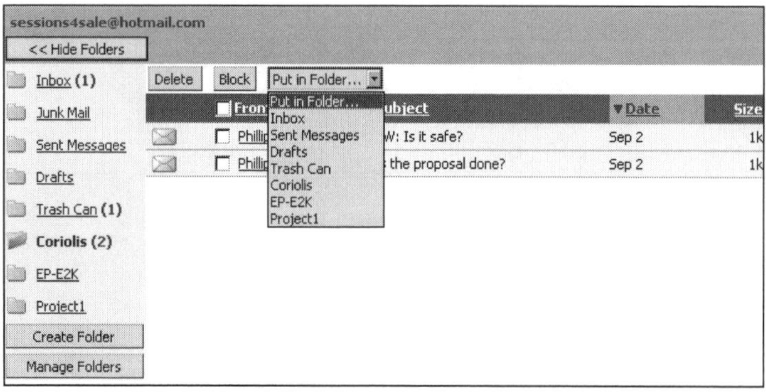

Figure 12.2 An example of a Web-based commercial IMAP4 mail client.

All IMAP4 clients connect to an IMAP4 Mail Server through TCP port 143 (or SSL port 993 for secure communications). Upon successful authentication, this protocol retrieves a list of folders for the user (including the Inbox folder, the Sent Items folder, and the Exchange Public Folders folder). These folders are viewed online so users do not have to download the entire contents of their mailboxes to their local machines just to read mail. The IMAP4 protocol provides full access to all messaging folders residing on the IMAP4 Server.

NOTE: *When an IMAP4 client browses a folder and requests a list of messages within the folder, the client only downloads the headers to these messages, not the entire message. This feature helps save time and disk space, especially when users receive a large number of messages, or messages with large attachments. However, these messages also can be downloaded to a local Information Store for offline viewing.*

Consider using IMAP4 in the following situations:

- Users need to access their mail from more than one computer. IMAP4 offers functionality for roaming users so they can read email from any IMAP4 client on the network.
- Users need to access multiple folders (or all folders on an IMAP4 Server).
- Users need to access multiple mailboxes or shared mailboxes from a single computer.
- Users need to sort through and manage email without having to download it to their computers first.
- Users have more persistent connections to their email server.

NOTE: *More information on IMAP (RFC2060) can be located at* ***www.imap.org****.*

The Hypertext Transfer Protocol

HTTP is the underlying protocol used by the Web. It is a client/server protocol used over the Internet to send and receive HTML documents. Exchange 2000 supports this protocol when providing the Outlook Web Access (OWA) client to users. All HTTP-based clients access a server running Exchange 2000 through the OWA client using TCP port 80 (or SSL port 443 for secure communications). The OWA client is optimized for Internet Explorer (IE) 5, but also supports other browsers and earlier versions of IE. OWA also can be used with browsers that support HTML 3.2 and the European Computer Manufacturer Association (ECMA) compliant JavaScript scripting language. The current version 1.1 of this protocol has been extended with a new protocol called WebDAV (Web Distributed Authoring and Versioning).

***NOTE:** To access a mailbox using OWA from an internal network, a user would type **http://servername/exchange/aliasname** from the address bar of her browser. With WebDAV, this user can access other folders besides the mailbox using standard URL (Uniform Resource Locator) notation. For example, to access a user's calendar, she would type **http://servername/exchange/yourname/calendar**.*

Exchange 2000 natively supports HTTP 1.1, an Internet standard Request for Comments (RFC 2616) that provides access for Web browsers and other services. Exchange also supports the WebDAV extension to HTTP 1.1, which can be found in RFC 2518 and allows clients to perform file-system operations on a remote server, including file publishing. WebDAV transmits data in Extensible Markup Language (XML) format. Using WebDAV, a developer can create custom workflow and collaboration applications.

With the IIS 5 (Internet Information Server 5) implementation of WebDAV, you can allow remote authors to move, search, edit, or delete files and directories on your server. This protocol is configured using the Web server permission settings. WebDAV addresses issues such as file access permissions, offline editing, file integrity, and conflict resolution when competing changes are made to a document. You can use WebDAV to create anything you store in a file. WebDAV includes these features:

- *Overwrite protection (file locking)*—WebDAV allows users to write, edit, and save shared documents without overwriting another person's work, regardless of which software program or Internet service is used.
- *Namespace management*—This allows users to manage Internet files and directories; for example, users can move and copy files using a familiar paradigm. The process is similar to the way users manage word-processing files and directories on a local computer.
- *Property (metadata) access*—The WebDAV properties feature is an efficient means of storing and retrieving metadata. Metadata is information about a Web document—such as the author's name, the copyright, the publication date, and keywords—that Internet search engines use to find and retrieve relevant documents.
- *Client-side rendering*—WebDAV uses XML to transfer the data from the server to the client, allowing it to move the task of HTML rendering from the server to the client. This essentially distributes the processing and, as a result, increases the capacity of the server.
- *Backward compatibility*—Exchange supports standard HTTP methods (**GET**, **POST**, **PUT**, **DELETE**, **OPTIONS**) and adds new methods for WebDAV-specific functionality. Because WebDAV is an extension of HTTP, existing methods are not changed.

NOTE: *More information on WebDAV (RFC 2518) can be located at* ***www.webdav.org***.

HTTP allows users to access the Information Store on a machine running Exchange 2000 and use this as a central repository for email and Office documents. With Office 2000 applications, users can open and save documents in the Information Store. The Office 2000 Web Folders feature provides a solution for shared document access and collaborative authoring on your intranet or over the Internet.

Consider using HTTP in the following situations:

- You want to give users access to the Information Store on your Exchange 2000 server using a simple URL address (such as **http://*company.com*/Inbox**).
- You want to allow Internet client access to your public-folder hierarchy. Configure the system to point to a *virtual root* defined for your HTTP Virtual Server managed by the IIS Admin MMC (Microsoft Management Console) snap-in.
- You want your users to collaborate on documents over the Internet by publishing a WebDAV directory on your HTTP Web Server. WebDAV also can provide resource locking so other users cannot modify a document at the same time that you are modifying it on the server.

The Simple Mail Transfer Protocol

SMTP is the native mail submission and transport protocol for Exchange 2000 used to deliver email from any SMTP-based messaging system. This robust protocol is designed to overcome unreliable network connections. Clients establish SMTP connections using TCP port number 25 for submission of messages, and servers use SMTP to route messages or to replicate information between servers. SMTP is based on RFC 821 and 822 and is installed as a default protocol (or transport stack) when you first install Windows 2000 Server. Exchange 2000 enhances this protocol by adding components such as a Routing Engine (RE) and advanced message queuing (AQ) capabilities. Exchange 2000 also allows you to view queues associated with a SMTP Virtual Server.

As a messaging protocol, SMTP has gained wide acceptance through its implementation as an Internet standard. It is supported by most messaging systems currently deployed. Both the POP3 and IMAP4 Protocols rely on SMTP for message delivery. Because Exchange 2000 is a native SMTP messaging system, no message translation is required to submit mail from a SMTP client such as Outlook Express. All clients send a series of command verbs to the server—such as **HELO** or **EHLO**—and the server replies to each command with a response—such as **250-OK**. Typical SMTP commands notify the server of the sender's domain and hostname, the sender's email address, and the identity of one or more recipients of the message. A server can reject a message based on information contained within these commands.

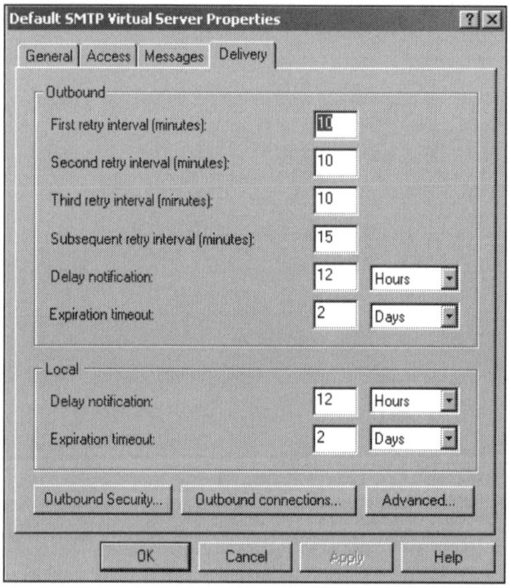

Figure 12.3 SMTP delivery settings configured in the Protocol Properties sheet.

SMTP is based on specifications in RFC 821 and 822. This protocol is installed by default as an IIS transport stack when you install Windows 2000 Server. An example of delivery settings is shown in Figure 12.3. Also, Windows 2000 includes a basic message categorizing utility, which is deactivated by default. Exchange 2000 activates and extends this utility by adding it to the queuing engine. This provides advanced address resolution. After installing Exchange 2000, you can set remote domain settings directly on the SMTP connector, rather than the IIS Virtual Server. These enhancements give greater control over your messaging system at every transport stage.

Lightweight Directory Access Protocol

LDAP is a directory service implementation that allows access to user information using the X.500 directory standard. It is a communication protocol designed for use on TCP networks. LDAP defines how a directory client can access a directory server and how the client can perform directory operations and share directory data. Exchange 2000 supports LDAP versions 2 and 3 through Active Directory (AD), whereas Exchange 5.5 supports LDAP 3.

NOTE: *Exchange 5 supported LDAP 2 only, a read-only version of LDAP that allows directory database browsing only.*

LDAP is designed to be an efficient method for accessing directory services without the complexity of other directory service protocols. LDAP defines operations that can be performed to query and modify information in a directory using TCP port 389. You can use this protocol to find or enumerate directory objects and also to query or administer AD. Although it's not a strict messaging protocol—such as POP3 or IMAP4—LDAP is often used in conjunction with these protocols to connect to an Exchange 2000 directory and perform address lookups. In reality, LDAP is used to connect to the Windows 2000 AD service (because Exchange 2000 doesn't have its own directory). LDAP-based searches are based on syntax shown in Figure 12.4, which is found by clicking Properties on the General tab on any specific address list in Exchange System Manager. The preview of this LDAP query is shown in Figure 12.5.

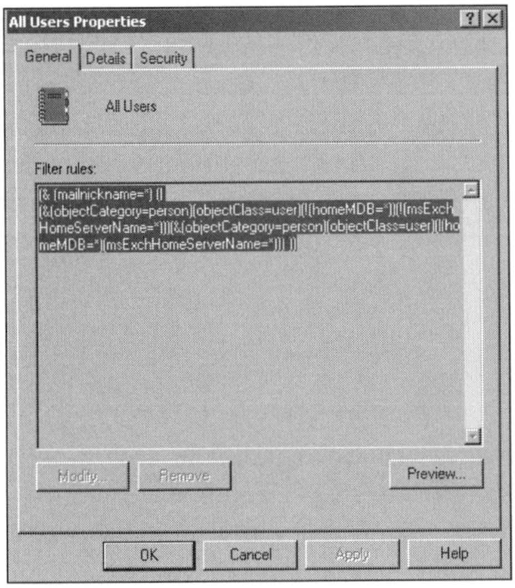

Figure 12.4 An example of a LDAP query.

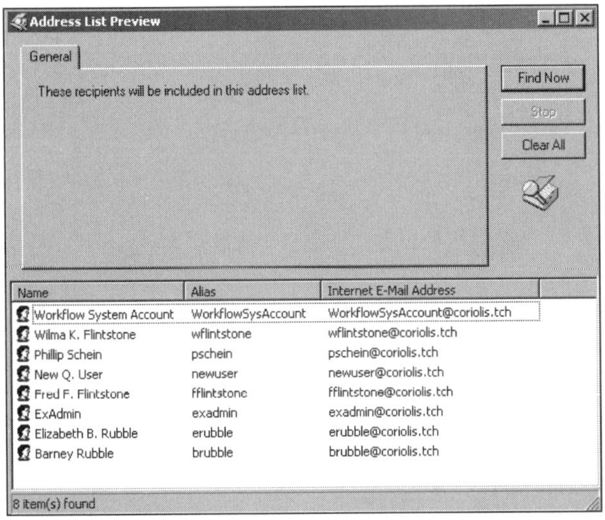

Figure 12.5 The preview listing of data resulting from the LDAP query.

Network News Transport Protocol (NNTP)

NNTP allows users who run NNTP-capable applications to read or post messages to a Usenet Client Installation newsgroup (a worldwide discussion system that consists of newsgroups classified by subject matter; some email clients—such as Outlook Express—which contain a built-in newsgroup reader so users can post articles or messages to these newsgroups). Exchange 2000 extends the basic functionality of this protocol by allowing an Exchange Server to host various news feeds or downloads in public folders. Any protocol that can access a public folder also can access a newsgroup hosted in that public folder.

NNTP can distribute network news messages to NNTP Servers and NNTP clients (also known as news readers) over any TCP/IP (Transmission Control Protocol/Internet Protocol)-based network (such as the Internet). Figure 12.6 shows a NNTP Properties sheet. The protocol defines a set of client and server commands that provides for the distribution, inquiry, and retrieval of news articles by using a reliable stream-based transmission of news on the Internet. Exchange 2000 supports NNTP through server connections or feeds, and through client connections. Outlook users can participate in online discussions over the Internet, and client applications that support this protocol can access newsgroup public folders on computers that run Exchange 2000.

Exchange 2000 uses NNTP to gain access to private or public newsgroups; it can also send and receive newsgroup messages to external Usenet hosts that Exchange 2000 is configured to communicate with. When a client connects to a NNTP Virtual Server and requests a list of available newsgroups, the NNTP service

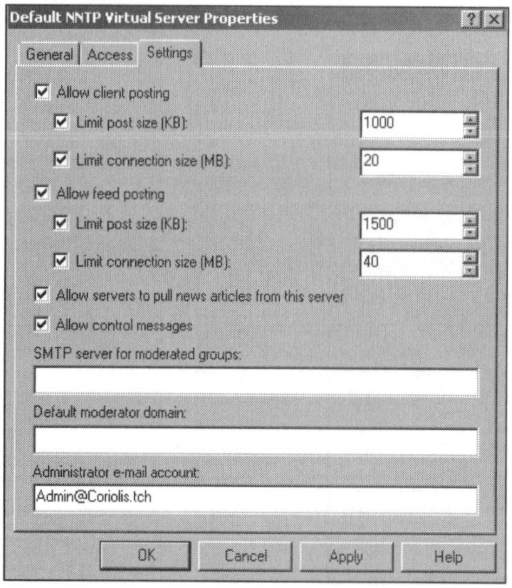

Figure 12.6 A NNTP Properties sheet.

receives the connection request and verifies that this client is authorized to access the newsgroup(s). If the client authenticates properly, the NNTP service sends the client a list of all available newsgroups using TCP port 119 (or TCP port 563 if SSL encryption is being used).

All these protocols communicate with the Web Storage System (WSS) component of Exchange 2000 and run as part of the IIS process, **Inetinfo.exe**, found within Windows 2000 Server. **Inetinfo.exe** communicates directly with the WSS so that all email clients can have immediate access to the Information Store service, **Store.exe**. WSS is a large hierarchical database capable of storing documents and email messages. You can access WSS using a Component Object Model (COM)–compliant programming language such as Visual Basic (VB), and for example, Collaboration Data Objects (CDO). WSS is significant because it is a hierarchy of folders that is readily accessible using standard URLs. It allows users to manipulate data using the WebDAV protocol so they can add or modify items in the Information Store.

Exchange 2000 is fully integrated with the Internet because of the protocol management now provided by Windows 2000 through Internet Information Server (IIS). IIS5 provides for all the protocols used by Exchange Server. The integration between IIS and Exchange is made possible through the Exchange 2000 Installable File System (ExIFS). ExIFS allows network redirectors found within the Windows 2000 NOS to share folders so users can map drive letters to any public folder or mailbox. This means an application such as Word can manipulate information within the native content portion of the Information Store.

NOTE: *Recall that each database file is composed of two distinct files: a native content file (STM file), and a property file (EDB file). ExIFS allows applications to read or write data directly to the native content STM file of a message database.*

No special software is needed to make use of the ExIFS other than a network redirector. Every Exchange 2000 installation displays a default share labeled **BackOfficeStorage**. This share is assigned a drive letter of M: and provides access into the Information Store. If viewing this share using Windows Explorer, you will see two folders directly underneath the drive letter: one labeled MBX, and one labeled Public Folders. The MBX folder serves as the root folder for all mailboxes on your Exchange Server, whereas Public Folders performs the same function for all public folders on your server. The ExIFS driver of Exchange 2000 also allows you to view message streams when opening messages using a standard text editor such as Notepad.

Another significant ExIFS feature regarding ExIFS is that you can store Web pages inside a public folder and launch them using HTTP. Developers can use this feature to create collaborative applications and store them inside virtual directories in the WSS. Placing information directly within the WSS means that applications can be managed using the Exchange System Manager interface. WSS can take advantage of Windows 2000 security features; it also supports transaction logging.

The facts presented in the last few paragraphs emphasize the tremendous amount of planning and foresight that Microsoft has built into Exchange 2000. The integration of so many components—including the WSS, the ExIFS, and IIS—implies that most application services can be integrated and managed from one central location so users can find and share information with each other. Collaborative applications can be directly installed into a public-folder hierarchy for easy replication to other servers in your organization. Disaster recovery procedures and maintenance procedures can be centralized because everything can be placed onto one central server.

The Messaging Application Programming Interface Protocol

The *MAPI protocol* provides a feature-rich set of functionality for accessing an Exchange 2000 Server. MAPI is a *de facto* Windows OS standard and key industry standard API for messaging and workflow applications. It allows Windows-based applications to interact with many different messaging services using a single interface. The MAPI architecture defines the way in which MAPI applications and messaging clients interact with various messaging service providers. Permanent RPC (Remote Procedure Call) connectivity is required between a MAPI-based client and an Exchange 2000 Server. MAPI clients generally assume persistent network connections, such as that found in traditional LANs.

TIP: *If you support the more bandwidth intensive MAPI clients over slower WAN links—such as ISDN (Integrated Services Digital Network) or 56Kbps links—make certain to carefully monitor how much bandwidth is by each additional MAPI client using the system resources.*

MAPI clients include all Outlook clients as well as older Exchange clients (used in Exchange 5.5 and earlier versions of Exchange Server). MAPI clients are more complicated in structure than other Exchange Server clients because they interface directly with the Exchange Server rather than, for example, through an Internet connection. The clients require more server-specific settings and thus, some technical skills for deployment. In addition to accessing typical messaging objects like mailbox folders and public folders, MAPI clients can also access electronic forms, Calendar, Journal, and even Contacts components. The Outlook messaging and collaboration MAPI client provides access to the Global Address

List (GAL), views, and rules. Outlook supports server-side rules, allowing a server running Exchange 2000 to sort and categorize messages even when the client is not connected.

The extra functionality that MAPI clients provide comes with a price, however. In addition to the increased hardware and software requirements on the client side, MAPI clients place an increased load on the server, reducing the number of clients that a server can support. In addition, MAPI clients typically require more network bandwidth than clients using HTTP, POP3, or IMAP4.

Implementing Exchange Server Clients

Through the past couple of years, Exchange Server has gone through several improvements. These improvements were called product upgrades and appeared either as Service Packs (SPs) or totally new product versions. Each Exchange Server product yielded more advanced features in addition to existing features. Several access methods also have been developed to extend its usefulness. The first version of Exchange Server (Exchange Server 4) supported only MAPI-based clients. The single client access method in Exchange 4 was limiting because it didn't embrace other Internet-based clients. Compatibility with industry standard Internet protocols was first introduced in Exchange Server 5. The support for more popular Internet protocols paved the way for additional methods of client access to a machine running Exchange Server. The following sections discuss the different clients and introduce configuration concepts that are applicable to these clients, as well as methods of upgrading a legacy client to a more modern implementation—for example, Outlook 2000 or Outlook XP.

The Microsoft Exchange Client

The Microsoft Exchange Client (Exchng32.exe) shipped with Exchange Server versions 4 through 5. It employed Exchange Server as its primary service provider and offered a user interface that provided a method for browsing and manipulating a component known as the *universal Inbox*. This Inbox contained all information in a user's mailbox and was displayed in a window consisting of two *panes*, a hierarchy table in the left pane, and a folder contents list in the right pane. The Exchange Client offered users an opportunity to request different views of this window, as well as the chance to send and create messages. Although limited in capability, the Exchange Client was designed for flexibility and extensibility, and it allowed developers to build systems that more accurately reflected the needs of users. The Exchange Client was MAPI-based and supported protocols such as SMTP, POP3, and NNTP in addition to other third-party POP3 messaging systems.

NOTE: *Exchange 5.5 Server supports the Exchange Client, but it is not included with this version of Exchange Server.*

Unfortunately, Microsoft has not provided an upgrade strategy for Exchange Clients, assuming that people would most likely use Outlook as part of Microsoft Office. If Exchange Client users want to move to a client such as Outlook 2000, they have to make sure their hardware system can support this upgrade. It is most likely Outlook would not be installed without other Microsoft products. Nevertheless, an Outlook deployment should not be considered on less than Pentium II class workstations with a minimum of 32MB of RAM. These memory requirements should be increased to 64MB when other components of Microsoft Office are included in the installation. If the current messaging system can support the extra processing power needed by Outlook 2000, the upgrade from the user perspective will be successful. Both the Exchange Client and the Outlook 2000 client are MAPI compliant, so Outlook 2000 can completely replace the Exchange Client. After installing Outlook 2000 on a machine that used to run the Exchange Client, users can continue working with email messages in Outlook in the same manner that they worked with email messages using the View option in Exchange Client. Outlook 2000 uses the same profile used by the Exchange Client, and it also uses all Exchange Client extensions and custom forms.

Outlook Clients

All *Outlook clients* are MAPI-based messaging clients. The Outlook client is fully optimized for Exchange Server 5 and later. It was first introduced as a component of Office 97 and shipped with Exchange Server 5. Outlook is a full featured, 32-bit client that provides users with the ability to organize and manage multiple functions from their desktops. Outlook is designed for use with all Internet protocols—including SMTP, POP3, and IMAP4—and works with Exchange Server or any other standards-based communication system supporting MAPI, including voice mail. The Outlook client currently has several distinguishable versions:

- *Outlook 97*—This client combines email, calendar, and scheduling features with contact, task management, journaling, and custom forms–based applications in a single interface.
- *Outlook 98*—This client also includes complete and native support for major Internet mail, news, and directory standards such as IMAP4, LDAP, HTML, NNTP, MIME (Multipurpose Internet Mail Extensions), and S/MIME (Secure/MIME). It also supports the Internet calendar and contact standards of vCard, vCalendar, and iCalendar Free/Busy lookup.
- *Outlook 2000*—This client is the premier messaging client for Exchange 2000, providing the most complete client support. In addition, it uses the MAPI interface, which includes support for native Internet features such as HTML email, and iCalendar. Outlook 2000 offers LDAP compatibility, server synchronization, and offline support. You should use Outlook 2000 in Corporate/Work-group mode (also known as MAPI mode) to take advantage of all scheduling and collaboration features offered by Exchange 2000. Outlook

2000 integrates Office applications with email and workgroup software. It provides support for collaboration applications so that you can develop and deploy workgroup applications based on Office. It also provides full messaging and group scheduling functionality as well as management of contacts, tasks, and views.

- *Outlook 2002*—This client is a component of the newly released Office XP version of the Office suite. It is a rich messaging client that provides new features—such as Internet and Exchange accounts—in one profile and in one mode. It also provides Hotmail support and Instant Messaging (IM) support in one package. Using this client helps application developers because it enables complete access to data by other Office applications. With its object library, you can enable access by other applications to Outlook email, appointments, tasks, and journal items. The Outlook object library allows programmatic access to Office command menus and the Office Assistant. The object library supports separation of the user interface and data, and the root Application object enables you to create new mail messages with a single line of code.
- *OWA*—This client provides secure access to emails, personal calendars, and group scheduling on any Exchange Server computer. It can be used to retrieve data stored on Exchange 2000 from any Unix, Macintosh, or Windows-based computer. In addition, it provides Web-based access to public folders and address books. This client was first introduced in Exchange Server 5. Although OWA 2000 appears similar to the regular Outlook client, it is not intended to be a complete replacement of the Outlook client. OWA lacks the robustness of the standard Outlook client and is intended for large-scale organizations comprised of heterogeneous OSs such as Windows and Unix systems. It is best used by roaming users or by small-to-medium-sized companies that cannot provide computer terminals for every employee. OWA is probably the easiest client to deploy because it uses the IE browser, which is found in most Windows OSs, including Windows 95. OWA is perfect for organizations desiring a light messaging solution that is both user-friendly and browser-centric.
- *Outlook Express*—This client is included as an email companion client to IE 4 and 5. It is a cost effective Exchange Server access method because it's free. Outlook Express is easy to use and has lower hardware requirements than Outlook. Outlook Express allows users the freedom to send and receive email from anywhere that is convenient, making it well suited for home use and occasional email users. Keep in mind that Outlook Express does not offer the full range of collaborative and scheduling features that Outlook 2000 does. Outlook Express supports email in S/MIME and HTML format. Other Internet protocols supported by Outlook Express are POP3, IMAP4, SMTP, NNTP, and LDAP. Outlook Express does not need permanent connectivity. When used as an IMAP4 client, it can handle users roaming between computers. Users view messages from anywhere in the network. Because it supports LDAP, Outlook Express can run searches directly against a Global Catalog (GC) Server.

Features Found in Outlook but Not OWA

The Outlook 2000/9x client offers some features not present in the OWA client, including the following:

- Offline folder use
- Task configuration and Journal configuration
- Outlook rules
- Copying between public and private folders
- Telephony options and user-defined fields when accessing contacts
- Mail features, including the spellchecker and expiration options
- Reminders
- The ability to type and edit directly in the Calendar view

When configuring any MAPI-based Exchange Server client, you must configure a user profile. A *user profile* is a group of settings that defines how Outlook is set up for a particular user. An Outlook profile (or Exchange profile) basically summarizes the Exchange information services that the user intends to access. Figure 12.7 shows data file settings. When creating Outlook profiles, consider which messaging services will be installed, where new email will be delivered by default (for example, a local Information Store), and which address book to show by default. You can create an Outlook profile using Control Panel on a Windows 2000 machine.

Outlook Client Configuration Issues—General Configuration

You can configure Outlook 2000 in many ways. Users can set their own preferences and choose how they want to manage their desktop information. Some organizations prefer to customize the Outlook client for their users and implement only the features they feel are suited for the needs of the organization. Many

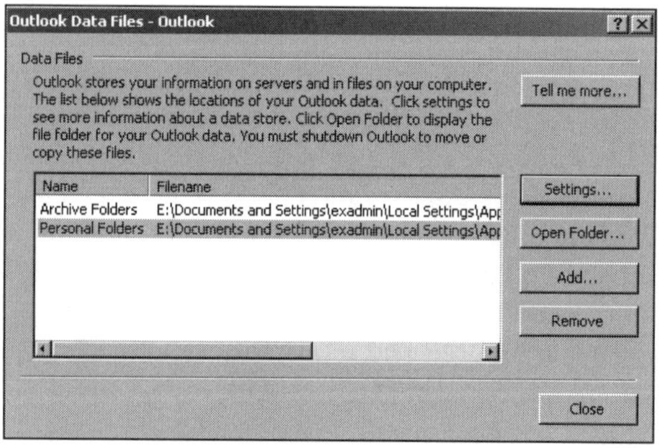

Figure 12.7 Setting data files in Outlook.

administrators and Help Desk personnel want all Outlook clients to have uniform configurations to make troubleshooting problems easier.

The heart of all Outlook configurations is found on the Tools menu. The Tools menu contains the Options item, which helps you set all Outlook client configurations. The Options dialog box that appears when you choose Tools|Options consists of seven distinct tabs:

- *Preferences*—Use this tab to configure how Outlook handles Email, Calendar, Tasks, Contacts, Journals, and Notes. You can tell Outlook to request read receipts for all outgoing messages. You also can add holidays to your Calendar and change the appearance of tasks, contacts, and journals.
- *Mail Services*—The startup settings are configured here. You can tell Outlook whether to use a particular profile when starting or, in cases where there are multiple profiles, you can tell Outlook to prompt you for a profile to be used. You also set your Mail Options, which allow you to choose the default mail service to check emails from. The mail service providers listed are taken from the list of information services defined in Tools|Services. Finally, you can enable or disable offline access here; if offline access is enabled, synchronization methods and offline folder settings will be enabled as well.
- *Mail Format*—Change the default settings on how Outlook sends email in this area. You can change the format for all outgoing mails and choose your email editor. You also can define what fonts to use or whether to affix an email signature.
- *Spelling*—This tab allows configuration of the Spell Checker, where you can add or remove words from an installed dictionary.
- *Security*—Configure advanced security options here so that your emails are not tampered with in any way. Security providers chosen here include the Key Management Service (KM Service), if implemented in your organization, or other third-party security providers, such as Verisign. You also can import or export a digital certificate from any Certificate Authority (CA).
- *Other*—You configure other advanced options such as modifying how Outlook uses custom forms, reminder options, and advanced task options here. You can also configure the appearance and behavior of the Preview pane or set the schedule for the Auto Archive feature of Outlook 2000 so files that are not frequently used will be archived.
- *Delegates*—This tab has settings that will provide other users access to your mailbox so they can compose and send emails on your behalf. Providing delegate access can be useful if the user has no means to access his mailbox but he wants to be notified if something critical happens. More likely, this configuration will be set for assistants so they have permission to compose messages or reply to messages concerning meeting requests for their superiors.

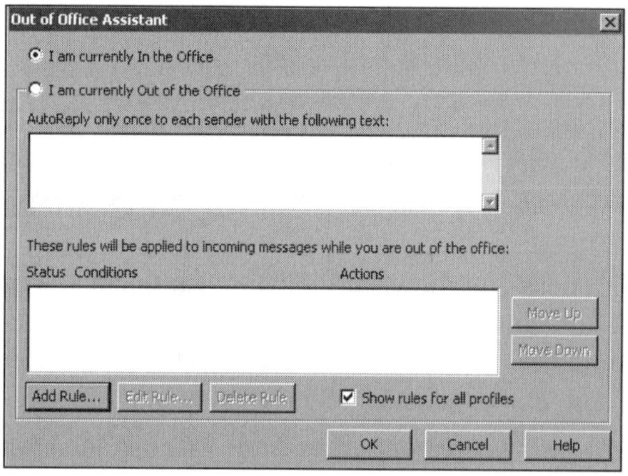

Figure 12.8 The Out Of Office Assistant tab off the Tools menu in Outlook 2002.

An option that is worth configuring on the Tools menu relates to rules applied to email messages. You can set rules on Outlook to respond to incoming messages by using the Out Of Office Assistant shown in Figure 12.8. This wizard defines a rule that sends an automatic reply to all incoming emails informing the sender of your temporary unavailability. The Out Of Office Assistant is available only if you configure a Corporate/Workgroup installation of Outlook 2000. See the Immediate Solution "Enabling the Out Of Office Assistant" for details on configuring this wizard.

You can run the Outlook Rules Wizard to define instructions for performing actions on incoming and outgoing mail messages. The Outlook Rules Wizard is a messaging manager for Outlook 2000 and uses a systematic process to guide you through the rule creation process. Use the Rules Wizard to perform the following tasks:

- Assign categories to incoming or outgoing messages based on message content.
- Set notifications such as message boxes or sounds—when important messages arrive.
- Move messages to a folder based on who sent the message.
- Delete all messages in a conversation.
- Delay delivery of messages by a specified amount of time.

All rules are either server-based or client-based. Server-based rules run even if the Outlook client is not running. On the other hand, client-based rules involve client activity—such as moving messages to personal folders—and can be performed only if the Outlook client is running.

NOTE: *If you upgraded from a previous version of the Outlook client that used an Inbox Assistant, Outlook 2000 gives you an option to convert rules from the Inbox Assistant to the Rules Wizard.*

Outlook Client Configuration Issues—Personal Folder Stores

When configuring MAPI clients—such as Outlook 2000 or Outlook 9x—you have to understand special configuration issues, such as profiles and personal folder stores. Every user that accesses an Exchange Server needs a profile specific to that user. Outlook has a default configuration using one profile per user logon. When the Outlook client is started, it uses the default profile as specified in the original configuration (see the Immediate Solution "Configuring Profiles for Outlook Clients"). Multiple profiles can exist on one computer. This occurs if several users are sharing the same computer. When multiple profiles are configured on a single computer, each user should use the profile that belongs to him. Failing to choose the right profile might produce error messages in using the Outlook client. You also can force a message to appear that prompts the user to choose an appropriate profile from a drop-down list (see the Immediate Solution "Forcing Users to Select a Profile Using the Outlook Client").

Profiles have to be created manually. To automate profile generation for Outlook 2000, you can use the Office Custom Installation Wizard. Outlook 98 uses the Outlook 98 Deployment Kit (ODK) to automate the deployment of the Outlook 98 client. Using the Office Custom Installation Wizard or the ODK provides an option to automate the creation of every user's profile. It is automatic because a profile for an individual user is created the first time a user double-clicks the Outlook client. The profile generated is based on the user's logon credentials. If automating profiles using the ODK, make sure your organization has implemented a good naming convention. Outlook 97 and the Exchange clients use a utility called **Profgen.exe** to automate the process of creating profiles for users. This utility is located under Admin Tools in the Exchange 2000 Resource Kit as shown in Figure 12.9.

Besides profiles, you should become familiar with creating personal folder stores for all Outlook clients. Personal folders store mail messages on local hard drives or other servers. You can add a main Personal Folder service to a user's profile and give it a file name. All personal folders have a .pst extension. Exchange Server supports personal folders as an added service. You can add multiple personal folder stores to your profile and each PST file can hold up to 2GB of information. Each PST file can contain folders, messages, forms, and files. You typically work with a personal folder file as you would with any other file. This means you can save, copy, or move a PST file to other locations, including hard drives, floppy disks, or other file servers. You also can designate a personal

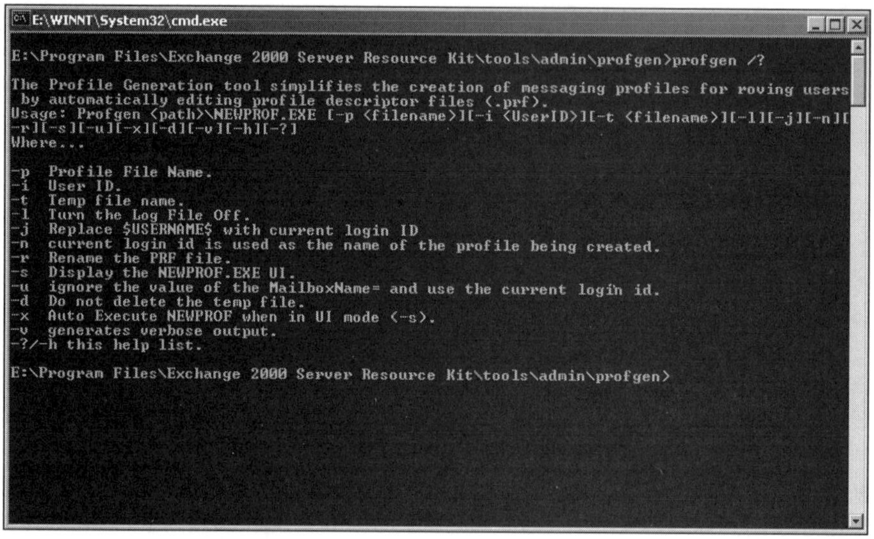

Figure 12.9 The **Profgen.exe** usage screen.

folder file as a delivery location for all incoming messages. Remember to create personal folder stores (PST files) in the following situations:

- To back up folders and messages
- To copy or move messages and folders to a notebook computer so they will be available when you work away from the office
- When you want to archive old email messages
- When you want to prevent unauthorized access to messages (all PST files can be password protected if they contain confidential information)

Outlook Client Configuration Issues—Offline Folder Stores

Offline Folder Storage files (also known as OST files) are files that contain replicas of a user's Exchange Server–based private and public folders as well as custom forms. An offline folder is stored on the local hard disk with an .ost extension and makes your mailbox available for use while working offline (or if you lose connection to your Exchange 2000 Server). An OST file is scheduled to synchronize from time to time with the server-based mailbox and is specific to a particular mailbox; it cannot be accessed by other users of the Exchange 2000 Server.

When working offline, you must work with the contents of the offline folder in the same manner that you work with any other folders on the server. For example, you can change and move items in your offline Inbox, send messages placed in your offline Outbox, and read your offline public folders. You will continue to receive new messages in your mailbox; however, you will not be aware of these changes on the server until you reconnect to the network containing your Exchange 2000 Server.

When deploying systems that have a significant percentage of roaming users, you need to consider both online and offline storage. It is important to clarify whether corporate users can store proprietary information on local machines that are mobile and potentially unsecured. Similarly, if proprietary information is stored offline, the responsibilities of backup and maintenance must be similarly clarified. This is especially important if this information is critical to operations or confidential in nature. The ability to easily synchronize online with offline data not only fosters good backup practices, it limits losses due to carelessness, accidents, or malfunction. When these users need to update the contents of their offline folders, they synchronize the folder with the server and continue to work offline. The **Synchronize** command connects to the Exchange 2000 Server using a dial-up networking connection (a DUN connection), that copies any changes made to the folder, and then disconnect the DUN session. Any item that is deleted from either the offline folder or the corresponding server folder will be deleted from both sources after synchronization is complete.

When composing email messages offline, you need the services of the GAL. The GAL is used to locate user email addresses. Because you are working offline, you need to have an offline version of the GAL. This offline version is known as the *offline address book*. You have to configure an offline address book server, which is organization specific in Exchange 2000 (in Exchange 5.5 it was site specific). Exchange 2000 generates all offline address books from AD.

TIP: *Initially, the Offline folders feature only creates local replicas of the default Outlook folders such as the Inbox, Calendar, Contacts, Drafts, Journals, Notes, Outbox, Sent Items, Tasks, and Deleted Items. All user-defined folders have to be configured manually to make them available offline.*

Outlook Client Configuration Issues—Roaming User Support

A roaming user is defined as a user who needs to access her mailbox from different workstations anytime, from anywhere, with any device. Roaming users are individuals who do not necessarily access one specific computer. They need access to their messaging accounts regardless of their physical location on the network. Supporting users who move from computer to computer has always been a challenge for messaging administrators. This issue is typically addressed through the use of system policies and server-based profiles that are centralized; sometimes these accounts can require additional administration to keep performance high and system overhead low. For example, if there is extensive use of Desktop resources as a long-term storage area, a user profile can grow to several megabytes in size and slow the logon process. Using Windows 2000, however, on both the client and server can solve issues surrounding roaming user support with minimal administrative effort.

NOTE: *Windows NT administrators can support roaming users on Windows 95 and Windows NT computers if MAPI profiles are stored on a domain controller (DC) in a user's home domain so users can access them from anywhere in the organization. If your roaming users will use computers in other domains, you must permit the roaming users to log on to multiple domains, and those domains must trust the user's home domain.*

Table 12.1 describes roaming user support for Windows 2000, Windows NT, Windows 9x, Windows 3.x, and MS-DOS.

TIP: *If it's impractical to implement Group Policies or System Policies, you can implement OWA. OWA is an attractive solution if there is no client to install other than a browser and no MAPI profile to consider.*

You might want to use Outlook in many situations; for example, when you don't have access to a network, when you are traveling with a laptop, or when you are working at a remote site. Working offline and Remote Mail are available in most situations. If users need dial-up connections to connect to their Exchange Server, the best strategy is to have these users combine offline folders and Remote Mail. This method reduces network use and limits the connection time and cost particularly for the Exchange Server that has to be called via long distance telephone. By connecting offline to Outlook 2000, you can compose new mail messages and read and respond to mail. When you are finished making changes, you can use the Remote Mail feature to connect to your Exchange Server and send the mail you wrote while offline. Remote Mail enables you to connect remotely to your messaging service. You can use it with Internet Mail, MS Mail, Exchange Server, and some online services.

Table 12.1 Roaming user support for various versions of the Windows OS.

Operating System	Description
Windows 2000, Windows NT, Windows 9x	To store messaging profiles on a network file server, create and configure user profiles with User Profile Editor and User Manager for Domains. Users must have rights on Windows NT computers and access to appropriate domains.
Windows 3.x	Clients can be installed on a network file server by storing messaging profiles in the user's home directory or network file server. Clients also can be installed locally. In Win.ini under the [**MAPI**] section, add "ProfileDirectory16=*path to profile*".
MS-DOS	Store messaging profiles in the user's home directory on the network file server. Clients also can be installed on a network file server.

NOTE: *The purpose for Remote Mail is to transfer mail only; it does not transfer calendar appointments, contacts, or any other Outlook information. If you want to transfer this type of information, you must use offline folders and synchronize with the Exchange Server.*

Upgrading to Outlook 2000

Outlook 2000 has many desirable features that your organization can take advantage of. If you want to move to Outlook 2000 but are uncertain concerning the existing Outlook 9x or Exchange client configuration, don't worry because nothing will happen to your existing user profiles. These profiles are retained, including original OST files, delivery options, and rules.

NOTE: *Any OST file from Outlook prior to version 8.0.3 are not compatible with Outlook 2000. In this case, any OST files have to be recreated.*

Upgrading Outlook 9x to Outlook 2000

Outlook 2000 is compatible with all earlier versions of Outlook and the Exchange clients, which simplify both deployment and migration. Mixing different Microsoft messaging clients means that your functionality will not be compromised even when deploying sections of your user population in, for example, a staged rollout. Outlook 2000, however, carries with it additional overhead due to the greater integration of Office 2000 products. Although you can replace legacy clients with just Outlook 2000, the more expensive issue of Office 2000 to truly leverage the Outlook feature set is more problematic. The decision to upgrade to Outlook 2000 is best determined using TCO as a benchmark where enhanced productivity due to application integration is measured against hardware costs as well as the expenses of training and support. Though not often fully exploited, the Outlook application provides many extensible features that can be programmed using VBScript, Visual Basic for Applications, and Collaboration Data Objects.

TIP: *A well-known online source for technical information and programming tips for both Outlook and Exchange is* ***www.slipstick.com****.*

Your major upgrade tasks include selecting an upgrade strategy and solving any problems related to distribution and deployment. You should decide the following issues:

- Which installation option to undertake: Internet Mail Only or Corporate/Workgroup?
- Which default calendar to use: the existing calendar or the Outlook 2000 Calendar?

- Which browser to use: Microsoft recommends upgrading your current browser to IE 5 for the advanced features it supports (XML support, Java and ActiveX support, among other things).

Before performing the upgrade, make sure your users clean up existing email folders and delete any unnecessary email messages or personal folders. Users should also create backup copies of existing email folders so data is not permanently lost during the upgrade process. Finally, you should back up all private and public Information Stores on all Exchange Servers.

You either can plan a one-time upgrade to Outlook 2000 and upgrade all existing Outlook versions at one time, or perform a gradual upgrade to Outlook 2000. This latter option is best for environments in which users need to continuously exchange email messages and scheduling data with users of other Microsoft email and calendar applications. Outlook 2000, like other Office 2000 applications, will migrate user settings stored in the Registry. If a MAPI profile already exists on a user's computer, Outlook 2000 will continue to use this profile.

Upgrading an Exchange Client to Outlook 2000

No direct upgrade strategy exists for Exchange clients. If an Exchange client user wants to move to Outlook 2000, make sure the hardware system is ready for this. If it meets all system requirements, you can move to Outlook 2000. Because both the Exchange Client and the Outlook 2000 clients are MAPI compliant, the Outlook 2000 client can completely replace the Exchange Client. If the Exchange Client user wants Outlook 2000, Outlook 2000 must be installed following normal Outlook installation procedures. After Outlook 2000 is installed, you can continue working with email messages in the same way that you worked with email messages using the Exchange Client. Outlook 2000 uses the same profile and other configuration information.

Configuring Internet Clients

You must create a mailbox-enabled user in AD before a POP3 or IMAP4 client can connect to a server. The POP3/IMAP4 client must also be configured with account information that is needed to allow the client to connect to a POP3 or IMAP4 Virtual Server. Creating mailbox-enabled users requires you to specify information such as account name and user principal name (similar to an email address of ***user@company*.com**). After you create a place to store a user's messages (by specifying a Storage Group [SG] location and mailbox server location), you need to direct the client to an appropriate server and configure account information so the user can log on.

NOTE: *If you have multiple users in one AD domain that share a common username, a user only can be authenticated if they log on with a unique username. Users have to log on to the IMAP4 server using the format of* domain\username*—for example, Coriolis\Gregb—or use a user principal name (UPN). To use a UPN, the user can log on using his email address—for example,* ***gregb@coriolis.tch****. Make sure that all IMAP4 users have a UPN.*

Configuring Protocol Virtual Servers

Exchange 2000 supports SMTP, HTTP, and NNTP as well as IMAP 4 and POP3. Each protocol has an associated Virtual Server with a defined set of IP addresses and configuration properties. In Exchange 2000, Internet protocol support has been removed from the Information Store; protocols are now managed by the IIS. You configure independent instances of each protocol by creating Virtual Servers. A *Virtual Server* is a collection of services that appear as a logical server to clients. The server includes all resources needed to run a particular application, including a network name resource and an IP address resource. Although Internet protocols are enabled for all resources and recipients by default, you can restrict the use of one or more protocols for a specific user or specific Virtual Server. Default Virtual Servers for each mentioned protocol are installed in a typical Exchange 2000 installation. You can modify these default configurations or you can add another instance of a Virtual Server depending on the needs of the organization.

A Virtual Server accepts an unlimited number of inbound connections, which are limited only by the resources of the computer on which the Virtual Server runs. The IP address and corresponding TCP port designation must be unique on each Virtual Server. Different Virtual Servers can provide services through the same TCP port as long as their IP addresses are unique. To prevent a computer from being overloaded, best practices recommend limiting the number of connections that a Virtual Server accepts. You can limit the length of time idle connections remain logged onto a server and enable a filter that will restrict access by specific email addresses. Carefully monitor traffic when granting or denying access to entire domains. Determination of an email's source domain requires a reverse DNS lookup on each connection. These reverse lookups consume increasing amounts of bandwidth in direct relation to the number of incoming messages. The reverse lookups can severely affect server performance.

TIP: *By default, Exchange 2000 does not limit the number of incoming connections and disconnects idle sessions after 10 minutes.*

Immediate Solutions

Installing Exchange Server and the Outlook Client on the Same Machine

According to Microsoft, installing Exchange 2000 and the Outlook client (versions 2000 or higher) on the same physical server is considered an unsupported configuration. You might want to install both applications on one machine to demonstrate the functionality present in both programs, but doing so results in a probable loss of functionality in either one of these applications. This is because Exchange 2000 and the Outlook client each install different versions of the MAPI subsystem, and these two versions conflict with each other if installed on the same system.

Exchange 2000 normally installs its version of the MAPI subsystem in the \%systemroot%\system32 directory on the local hard drive. Although the Outlook MAPI subsystem can be found in the \Program Files\Common Files\System\Mapi\1033\NT folder, it still installs a separate but smaller version of the MAPI subsystem—known as a "stub" version of MAPI—in the same directory as Exchange 2000: \%systemroot%\system32. The consequence of this action is that all MAPI function calls are routed to the Outlook application. Both Exchange 2000 and Outlook 2000 (or higher version) rely on the MAPI dynamic link library file, Mapi32.dll. However, if you install the Outlook client at the same time the Exchange 2000 server is functioning, the Exchange Mapi32.dll file continues to function without being replaced by the Outlook version of Mapi32.dll. The negative result is two different versions of MAPI on your system. You can try to stop all relevant Exchange services (such as the Information Store, the RE, and the System Attendant) before you install the Outlook client, but this might force Exchange to use the MAPI associated with Outlook, not the MAPI associated with Exchange 2000, when you restart your services. This is not a supported configuration as the Exchange 2000 MAPI interface supports higher levels of functionality for features such as SGs and back-end (BE) server configurations. Microsoft recommends placing Exchange 2000 and the Outlook 2000 or higher client on separate physical servers for optimum results.

Forcing Users to Select a Profile Using the Outlook Client

You should configure the Outlook client so that users can select an appropriate client profile from a drop-down list. This ensures that users will be using the correct profile when multiple users all use the same machine to access email on an Exchange 2000 computer. To set this option in Outlook 2000, perform the following:

1. Open the Outlook Client by selecting Start|Programs|Microsoft Outlook.
2. Click Tools|Options to open the Options dialog box (it opens to the Preferences tab by default).
3. Click the Mail Services tab and select the Prompt For A Profile To Be Used under the Startup Settings section (Always Use This Profile is selected by default) as shown in Figure 12.10.
4. Click OK to close the Options dialog box and return to the Outlook client window. A user will be presented with a drop-down box as shown in Figure 12.11.

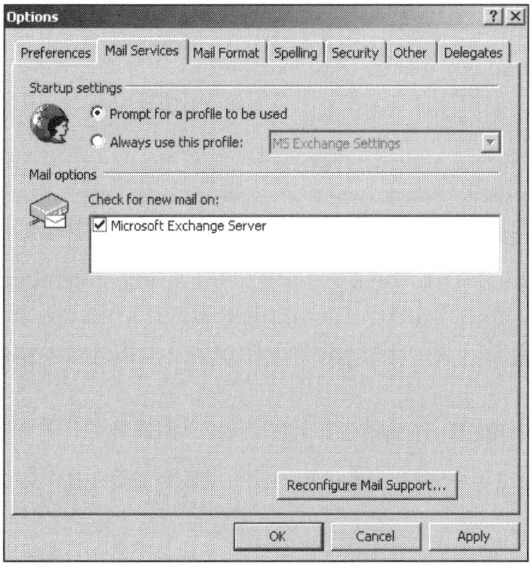

Figure 12.10 Configuring a profile to be chosen at startup.

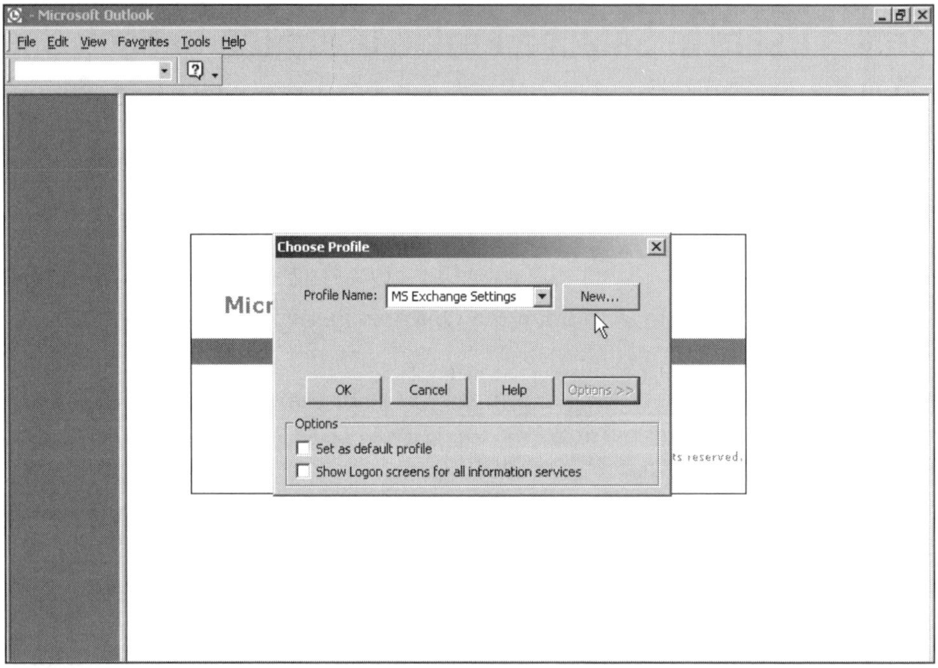

Figure 12.11 The initial profile selection box for the Outlook client.

Configuring Profiles for Outlook Clients

To configure a new profile for a user with the Outlook 2000 client, perform the following steps (this solution assumes that you have performed all steps in the previous Immediate Solution "Forcing Users to Select a Profile Using the Outlook Client"):

1. Choose Start|Programs|Microsoft Outlook.
2. When the Choose Profile dialog box appears, click the New button.
3. In the Microsoft Outlook Setup Wizard dialog box, click the Use The Following Information Services button and check the box next to Microsoft Exchange Server. Click Next.
4. In the next Microsoft Outlook Setup Wizard dialog box that appears, type a name for this profile (for example, type the name "Profile1"). Click Next to continue.

5. In the Microsoft Exchange Server dialog box that appears next, type the name of your Exchange Server and verify the mailbox that you will be using (the Administrator mailbox appears by default). Click Next to continue.
6. The final dialog box informs you that You're Now Ready To Use Microsoft Outlook With The Following Information Services. Click Finish to close this wizard.
7. In the Choose Profile box that appears, select your new profile (Profile1 in this example) and click OK. Your new profile appears in the Outlook window.

Adding a Personal Folder Store within the Outlook Client

You can add a personal folder store to Outlook 2000 in several ways. To do this using the Outlook 2000 client itself:

1. Open Outlook by choosing Start|Programs|Microsoft Outlook.
2. Select Tools|Services.
3. Click Add on the Services tab of the Services dialog box to open the Add Service To Profile dialog box. From the list of additional information services, choose the Personal Folders option and click OK.
4. In the Create/Open Personal Folders File dialog box, choose a new file name for your PST file and a location on your hard drive where this file will be saved. The default location for this file is C:\Documents and Settings\Administrator\Local Settings\Application Data\Microsoft\Outlook. Click Open when you have entered a name and location for this file.
5. In the Create Microsoft Personal Folders dialog box, you can name your personal folders, select an Encryption Setting (either No Encryption, Compressible Encryption, or Best Encryption), and choose a password to protect your new PST file. The default encryption scheme is Compressible Encryption, and no password is selected by default. Click OK when satisfied with all your selections.
6. The Personal Folders service is added to the Services tab of the Services dialog box. Click OK to close the Services dialog box and return to the Outlook 2000 client window.

Creating an Offline Folder File within Outlook 2000

To create an offline folder file within Outlook 2000, perform the following (assume that you have already selected a profile if you have multiple profiles configured on this machine):

1. Open Outlook by choosing Start|Programs|Microsoft Outlook.
2. Select Tools|Services.
3. Highlight Microsoft Exchange Server on the Services tab, and then click the Properties button.
4. On the Microsoft Exchange Server dialog box that appears, click the Advanced tab.
5. Click the Offline Folder File Settings and type the path to the file that you want to use as the offline folder file. If the message stating the *path/ .filename*.ost Could Not Be Found. Would You Like To Create It? appears, click OK.
6. Click OK twice to close all dialog boxes.

Configuring Offline Folder Settings in Outlook 2000

You can choose which folders you want to be available offline in Outlook 2000 by performing the following steps:

1. Choose Start|Programs|Microsoft Outlook.
2. Choose Tools|Options. Select the Mail Services tab and then click the Offline Folder Settings button. Select the folders you want to be available offline.

Configuring a Connection State as Offline in Outlook 2000

Before you work with offline folders as shown in Figure 12.12, you need to configure Outlook 2000 to specify whether you want the client to automatically detect the connection state or manually control the connection state. To configure the connection state in Outlook 2000, perform the following:

1. Choose Start|Programs|Microsoft Outlook.
2. Choose Tools|Services.

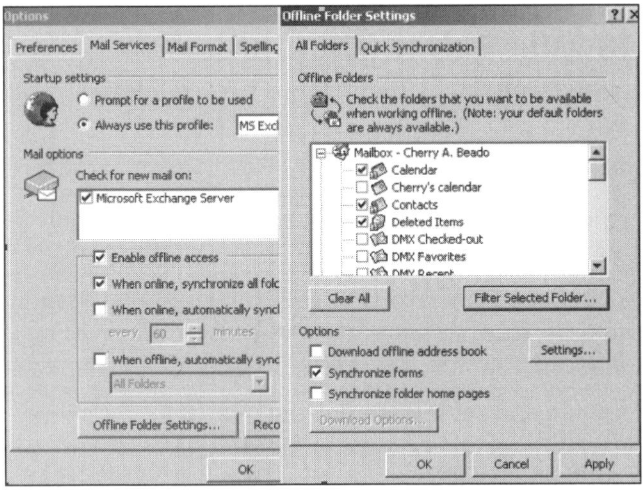

Figure 12.12 Offline Folder Settings in Outlook 2000.

3. Select Microsoft Exchange Server on the Services tab and then click the Properties button.
4. On the General tab, choose the Manually Control Connection State button and then choose Work Offline And Use Dial-Up Networking As Your Default Connection State.

Making the Offline Address Book Available to Offline Users

You must synchronize and download the address book before logging off Exchange 2000 if you want to make the offline address book available to offline users for the first time. Doing this ensures that all offline folders are updated. To download the offline address book to an offline address book server:

1. Choose Start|Programs|Microsoft Outlook.
2. Click Tools|Options. When the Options dialog box opens, click the Mail Services tab.
3. On the Mail Services tab, click the Offline Folder Settings button. It opens the All Folders tab by default.
4. On the All Folders tab, check the Download Offline Address Book box in the Options section. Then, click OK to close this dialog box. Click OK once more to close all dialog boxes.

Configuring Remote Mail in Outlook 2000

To configure and work with the Remote Mail feature in Outlook 2000, perform these steps:

1. Start the Outlook client.
2. Choose Tools|Services. Click Microsoft Exchange Server, and then click the Properties button.
3. On the General tab, click the Manually Control Connection State radio button, and then click the Work Offline And Use Dial-Up Networking checkbox.
4. Click the Remote Mail tab and set the options that you want for connection management and remote transfer as shown in Figure 12.13.

To work with the Remote Mail service in Outlook 2000:

1. Open Outlook 2000 using the offline folder file (OST).
2. Compose and send an email message. This puts the message in your Outbox, where it remains until you make a remote connection.
3. Choose Tools|Remote Mail|Connect to open the Remote Connection Wizard.
4. Under Connect To Which Information Service(s), click to select the services you want, and then click Next. The information services in your profile determine what is available in this list.
5. Under While Connected, click to select either the Retrieve And Send All New Mail checkbox, or the Retrieve New Message Headers Only checkbox. If you choose Retrieve And Send All New Mail, you are done. If you choose Retrieve New Message Headers Only, continue with Step 6.

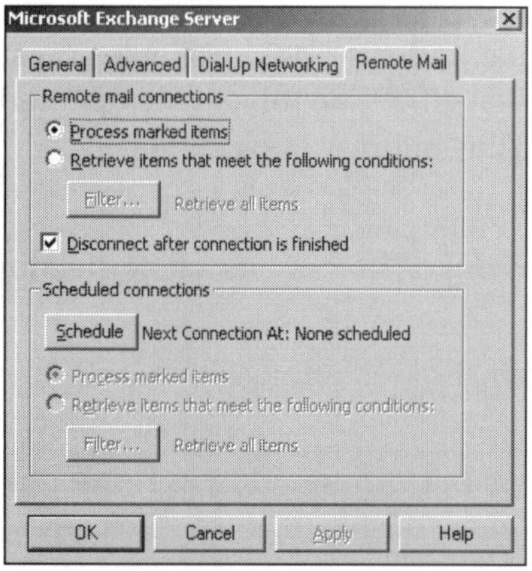

Figure 12.13 The Remote Mail tab for the Microsoft Exchange Server Properties dialog box.

6. If you chose to retrieve only headers, click Tools|Remote Mail, and click Mark To Retrieve or Mark To Retrieve A Copy to mark the messages you want to retrieve.
7. Choose Tools|Remote Mail|Connect.
8. Run the Remote Connection Wizard again to retrieve the marked messages.

Enabling the Out Of Office Assistant

To enable the Out Of Office Assistant in Outlook 2000, perform the following steps:

1. Open the Outlook 2000 client.
2. Select Tools|Out Of Office Assistant.
3. In the Out Of Office Assistant dialog box, click the I Am Currently Out Of The Office radio button located near the top of the dialog box.
4. In the text box marked AutoReply Only Once To Each Sender With The Following Text, type the message that you want to send while you are out of the office, as shown in Figure 12.14, and also referred to in Figure 12.10.

To create a rule for the Out Of Office Assistant:

1. Choose Tools|Out Of Office Assistant.
2. In the Out Of Office Assistant dialog box, click the Add Rule button on the bottom of this dialog box.

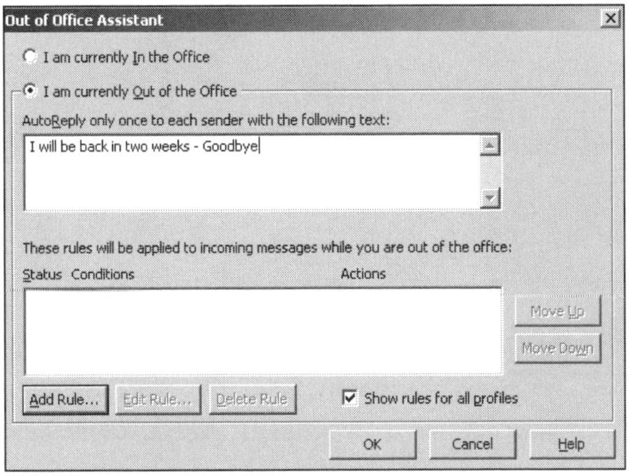

Figure 12.14 Creating an Out Of Office Assistant message.

3. In the Edit Rule dialog box, specify message criteria in the When A Message Arrives That Meets The Following Conditions section of this dialog box. Criteria include messages sent from a particular person, or words found within the message body itself.
4. Click the checkbox marked Do Not Process Subsequent Rules in the middle of this dialog box to specify that this rule must be the last one applied as shown in Figure 12.15.
5. Click the Advanced button on the far right side of the Edit Rule dialog box to select more options for your rule, and then click OK. Figure 12.16 shows certain options selected on the Advanced tab.

To disable a rule in Outlook 2000:

1. Select Tools|Out Of Office Assistant.
2. In the These Rules Will Be Applied To Incoming Messages While You Are Out Of The Office section, clear the checkbox that appears next to the rule in this bottom window. If the rule is no longer needed, delete this rule by clicking the Delete Rule button.

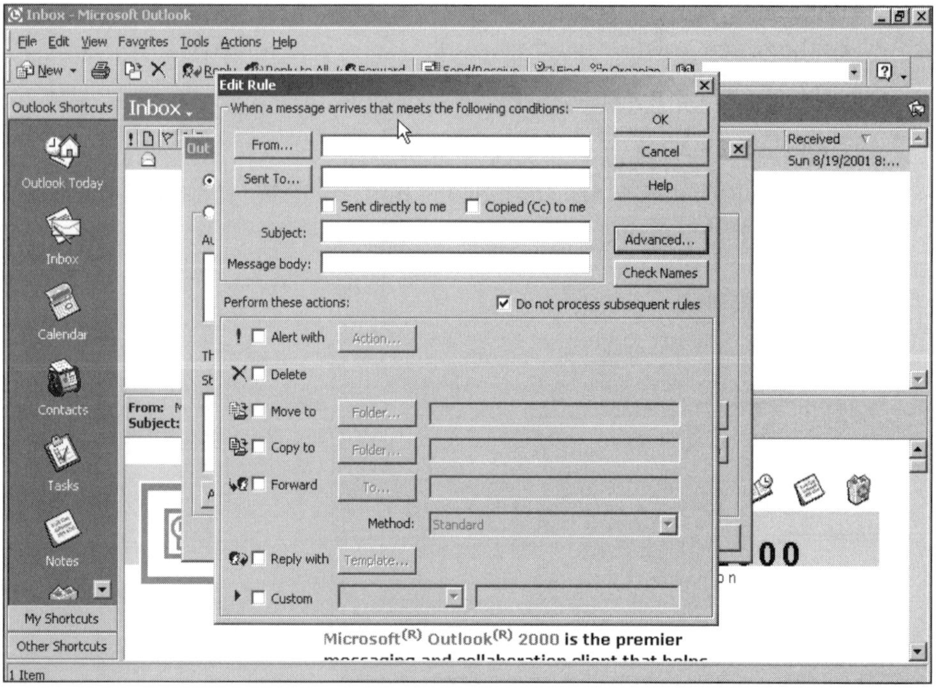

Figure 12.15 The Edit Rule dialog box.

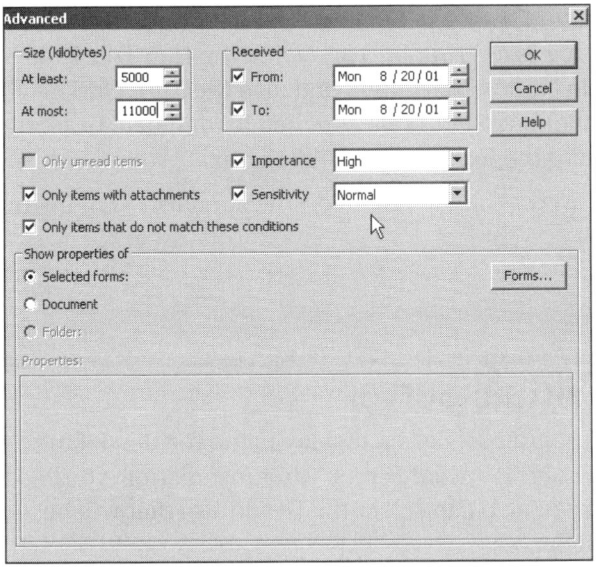

Figure 12.16 The Advanced options of the Edit Rule dialog box.

Creating a New Rule in Outlook 2000

Rules can be created from scratch, or you can modify an existing rule. You also can base rules on messages sent and received. To create a new rule for incoming messages in Outlook 2000, perform the following steps:

1. Open the Outlook 2000 client.
2. Click Tools|Rules Wizard.
3. In the Rules Wizard dialog box, click the New button.
4. In the next Rules Wizard dialog box, highlight Check Messages When They Arrive in the Which Type Of Rule Do You Want To Create? section. Then, click Next.
5. In the Which Condition(s) Do You Want To Check? section of the third dialog box, click the checkbox marked Where My Name Is In The Cc box and click Next.
6. In the next dialog box, under What Do You Want To Do With The Message?, click the checkbox marked Delete It. Click Next.
7. In the next dialog box, leave all boxes unchecked under the Add Any Exceptions (If Necessary) section. Click Next.

8. In the next dialog box, under Please Specify A Name For This Rule, type "Rule1" (or any name that is appropriate) and click the Run This Rule Now On Messages Already In "Inbox" checkbox and also the Turn On This Rule checkbox (this last checkbox should be checked by default). Click the Finish button to return to the Rules Wizard dialog box.
9. Click OK on the Rules Wizard dialog box that now appears to complete the Rules Wizard process.

Configuring a SMTP Virtual Server

The Exchange 2000 setup program assigns a display name for the default SMTP Virtual Server called Default SMTP Virtual Server. After installation, you can keep this name or change it, and you also can select the IP address that will be associated with this SMTP Virtual Server.

NOTE: *When changing a SMTP Virtual Server configuration, you might want to pause or stop and restart the SMTP service first. Pausing a Virtual Server prevents new client connections but enables Exchange to continue processing existing client connections and delivering queued messages. Any time you make changes to a Virtual Server, you might need to allow a few minutes for your changes to take effect.*

To configure a SMTP Virtual Server:

1. Click Start|Programs|Microsoft Exchange|System Manager.
2. Expand the Organization object, then the Administrative Groups folder, then the First Administrative Groups folder, and then the Servers container to expose your *Server* object.
3. Click the + next to your Server object, and then expand the Protocols folder by clicking the + next to it.
4. Expand the SMTP folder, and then highlight the Default SMTP Virtual Server folder. Right-click this Virtual Server, click Rename, and then type a new name (for example, "Virtual2").
5. Right-click this Virtual Server again, and choose Properties. On the General tab of the Properties dialog box that opens, use the IP Address drop-down

menu to select an IP address for this Virtual Server. The SMTP Virtual Server can respond to connection requests for all IP addresses configured on this computer.

6. To identify the TCP port associated with each IP address configured for the Virtual Server, click the Advanced button to open the Advanced property dialog box. Click the Add or Edit button to add or edit a TCP port for this Virtual Server. Port 25 is the SMTP standard TCP port and is recommended. More than one Virtual Server can use port 25, if they are associated with different IP addresses. The IP address/TCP port combinations must be unique on all Virtual Servers for clients to connect successfully. Figure 12.17 shows both property pages used in Steps 5 and 6.

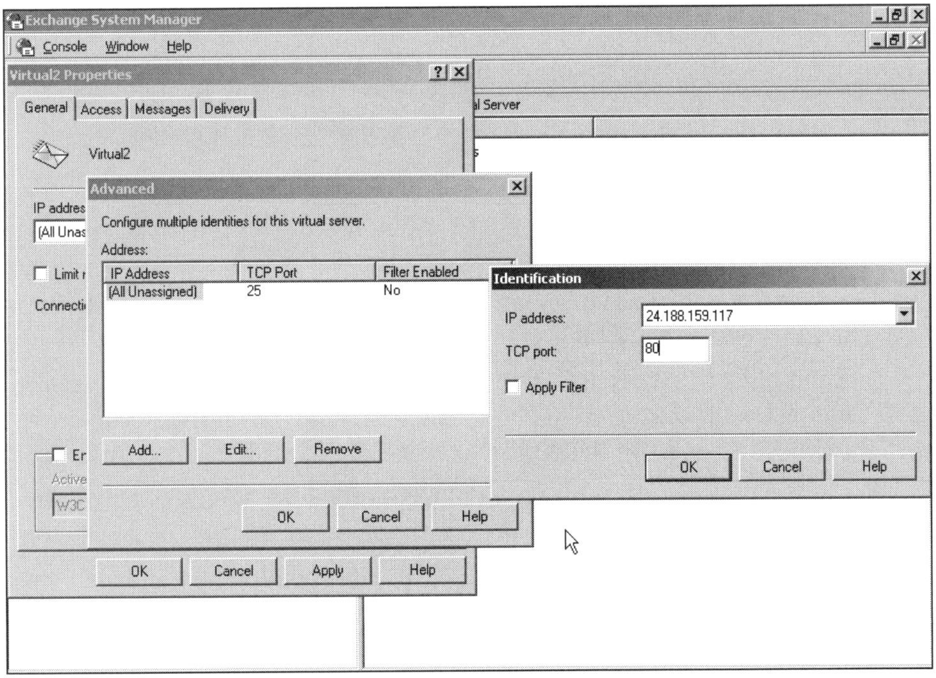

Figure 12.17 The SMTP Virtual Server Property page and Advanced Property page.

Configuring and Controlling Access to a POP3 Virtual Server

A default POP3 Virtual Server is provided with Exchange 2000. You can edit the default Virtual Server and create additional Virtual Servers on a single computer to handle multiple local mail domains and provide administration for several messaging scenarios. The number of POP3 Virtual Servers is limited only by the resources of the Exchange 2000 Server. The default Virtual Server is created with an IP address of (All Unassigned). The POP3 service is identified on the network with the Exchange Server's IP address. This allows incoming connections on TCP port 100, and uses a SSL port of 995. If creating multiple POP3 Virtual Servers, you must create a unique combination of IP addresses, TCP ports, and SSL ports for each server.

To assign an IP address, TCP port, and SSL port, perform the following:

1. Choose Start|Programs|Microsoft Exchange|System Manager.
2. Expand the Organization object, and the Administrative Groups object.
3. Expand the First Administrative Groups object, and then expand the Servers object.
4. Expand your *Serverobject*, and then the Protocols folder. Finally, expand the POP3 folder and the Default POP3 Virtual Server.
5. Right-click this Virtual Server and click Properties. When the Properties dialog box opens, select (All Unassigned) in the IP Address drop-down box or choose a specific IP address from the list of available network cards.
6. Click the Advanced button on the General tab to open the Advanced Property dialog box. Click the Add button on the bottom of this dialog box.
7. Select a new IP address on the Identification dialog box and also type a new port number and SSL port number (if needed). Then, click OK three times to return to the Exchange System Manager snap-in console.

Access to the POP3 Virtual Server can be controlled by setting the authentication method, enabling SSL, or granting access to only a specified IP address, subnet, or domain. To control access to the POP3 Virtual Server in Exchange System Manager:

1. Open System Manager and navigate to the POP3 Virtual Server as you did in Steps 1 through 5 in the previous set of steps.
2. Right-click the POP3 Virtual Server and then click Properties. Click the Access tab, and then click the Connection button in the Access Control section. The Authentication dialog box now appears on your screen as shown in Figure 12.18.

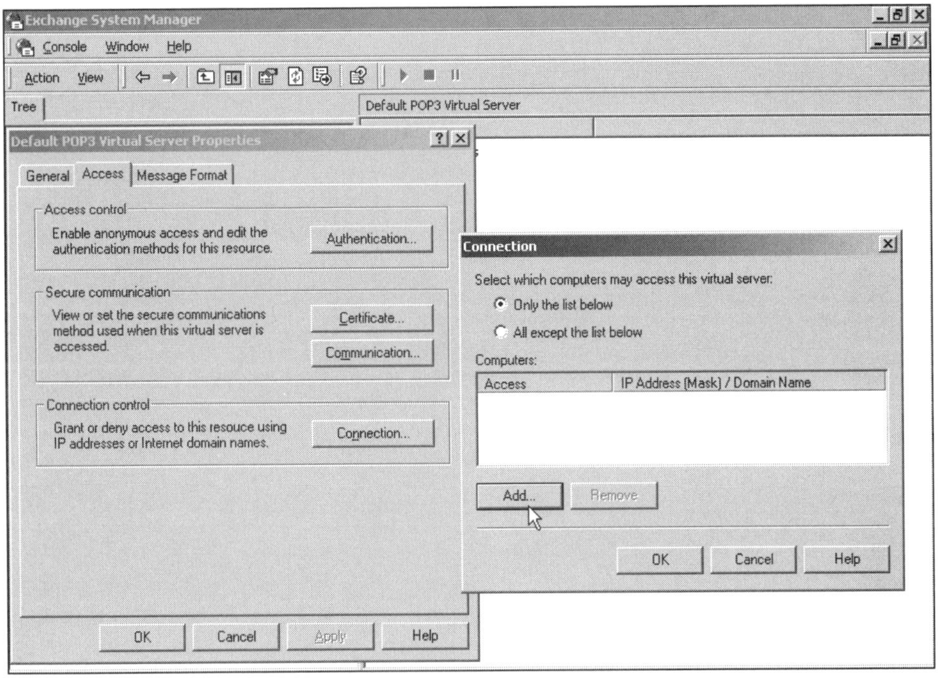

Figure 12.18 Connections for the POP3 Virtual Server.

3. In the Connection window, click Only The List Below, and then click the Add button.
4. In the Computers window, type the IP address of "192.168.2.133", and then click OK twice to return to the Default POP3 Virtual Server Properties dialog box.

NOTE: *Alternatively, you can select a group of computers and specify its subnet address and subnet mask, or specify a domain name, such as* ***www.coriolis.com****.*

To set a connection limit for your POP3 Virtual Server:

1. Open the General tab of the POP3 Virtual Server's Properties sheet (it should still be open from the previous exercises). Check the Limit Number Of Connections To box, and then specify an integer value such as "10" (you can specify any value between 1 and 999999999).
2. Type a value for your Connection Time-Out in minutes (note the default value of 10 minutes). This time represents the number of minutes before idle connections are disconnected.

Part IV

Managing and Optimizing Exchange 2000

Chapter 13

System Administration

If you need an immediate solution to:	See page:
Creating System Policies	542
Managing Recipients	548
Moving a Mailbox	552
Deleting a Mailbox	552
Managing Email Addresses	553
Creating an Email Address for a Mail-Enabled Recipient	554
Setting the Primary Address	555
Delegating Sending Permissions	557
Setting Forwarding Address	558
Setting Recipient Limits	558
Configuring the Maximum Number of Recipients Sent Messages	559
Setting the Mailbox Storage Limit	559
Configuring the Deleted Item Retention Period	560
Setting Limits for Message Size	560
Setting Maximum Message Size Limit	561
Setting Message Restrictions for Mail-Enabled Recipients	561
Enabling and Disabling Exchange Features	561
Knowing When to Use RGCs	561
Installing a SMTP Connector	562
Viewing SMTP Connector Properties Pages	563
Setting the Connection Schedule	564
Configuring the RGC Delivery Option	564

In Depth

Administrative Models

Earlier versions of Exchange defined administrative and routing boundaries by the physical configuration of the site. Legacy Exchange defined *sites* based on message routing, and administrative models based on connectivity between Exchange Servers. The site also defined the permission context within which objects worked. Connectivity and administration are no longer bound to each other in an Exchange 2000 Server organization. Instead, physical network topology determines message routing, and the corporate demands of an organization's structure determine the administrative model. Any Exchange 2000 administrative model is tightly integrated with Active Directory (AD) and its replication structure. Efficient Exchange 2000 deployment requires careful and thorough planning because even though routing groups are still constrained by the permanency of high-bandwidth connections, administrative groups are logical and conform to any organizational criteria. Administrative models define boundaries within which administration tasks and responsibilities are applied. Different administrative models are implemented by different organizations. Factors that contribute to a corporate decision regarding which specific administrative model to apply depend on the size of the organization. Size is determined by the number of accounts or mailboxes, the geographic locations of the offices, network connectivity between these locations, and the IT (Information Technology) staff responsible for managing the whole Exchange 2000 organization.

The architecture of organizations and sites has also changed in Exchange 2000. The organization no longer uses an independent directory that resides on every Exchange Server. Rather, the AD is fully integrated and bounded within the Windows 2000 forest in which it resides. Exchange 5.5 sites are assimilated into this structure as administrative groups and routing groups. Exchange 2000 uses administrative and routing groups to separate the logical and physical organization of your company. Administrative groups organize servers according to the administrative structure of a corporation; routing groups map the physical topology. No administrative correlation exists between administrative groups and routing groups. Therefore, the assignment of Exchange 2000 mailboxes, server configurations, and routing architecture is scalable and flexible.

Administrative Groups

Administrative groups are collections of Exchange 2000 Servers that share a common administrative model; they are collections of AD objects that share common permissions. Administrative groups define the administrative topology of the organization in terms—such as locations, departments, or divisions—rather than the network connectivity. Administrative groups are particularly useful in large companies with a number of departments or divisions and many Exchange Servers. Best practices recommend that small- to medium-sized enterprises (SMEs) or companies typically don't need more than one administrative group. Exchange 2000 support for administrative groups is disabled by default upon installation for this reason.

Administrative groups are organization-specific, and thus, function differently depending on the Exchange 2000 environment. Unfortunately, in Exchange 2000 mixed mode, you cannot use the full capabilities and functionalities of an administrative group. An administrative group can contain any of the following AD objects: recipient policies, routing groups, public folder trees, servers, conferencing services, and chat communities. All Exchange 2000 Servers or routing groups administered by the same group of administrators can be placed in the same administrative group. Exchange 2000 Servers can't be moved from one administrative group to another, so plan server assignments carefully.

Present Administration Model

Several layers and administrative roles have been associated with administering the Exchange 2000 Servers. Most of these tasks incorporate administration of the AD as well as Exchange 2000. When upgrading from an earlier version of Exchange Server, it's important to consider the administration model previously implemented. The Exchange 2000 administration model that you want to implement can be based on the current Exchange 5.x model, or you can totally reconstruct the administrative model to cater to or be patterned after the AD model already in place. Before choosing the Exchange 2000 administrative model for your organization, identify how the following tasks are accomplished and who is responsible for each task:

- Administration of the messaging backbone
- Exchange Server maintenance and configuration
- AD/Exchange recipient management
- Collaborative platform administration

Routing Groups

Routing groups define the physical network topology of the Exchange Servers. Routing groups are collections of Exchange Servers that have full-time, reliable connections. Messages sent between any two servers within a routing group go directly from source to destination. Exchange Servers that are members of a routing group are required to be connected by fast, permanent, and reliable links. In a native Exchange 2000 environment, servers in a routing group communicate via SMTP (Simple Mail Transfer Protocol), the native transport protocol of Exchange 2000. In a mixed environment containing earlier versions of Exchange Server, Exchange 2000 and the earlier versions communicate using a MTA (Message Transfer Agent) over RPCs (Remote Procedure Calls). Routing groups have no real functional significance until you switch your organization to native mode. In an environment where Exchange 2000 and legacy versions coexist, routing groups and administrative groups are identical. Routing groups are optional and are not visible in System Manager unless they are enabled. All Exchange 2000 Servers placed in routing groups must be in the same Windows 2000 forest. You can, however, locate Exchange 2000 Servers from multiple Windows 2000 domains in a single routing group.

Routing Administration

Exchange 2000 is designed for SMEs with flat hierarchical organizational designs that scale to large complex enterprise organizations. A deployment ranges from a single Exchange Server in a single Windows 2000 domain to multiple Exchange Servers spanning many Windows 2000 domains in a single forest. Administering Exchange 2000 Server in a single routing group is relatively simple. Difficulties in management arise when multiple routing groups are involved in the organization. In a single routing group environment, Exchange Servers communicate directly among themselves. In Exchange 2000 native mode, servers within the same routing group use SMTP as the native transport protocol because transfers of information between servers are fast and reliable. When Exchange 2000 and Exchange 5.5 coexist in a routing group, message and information flow between them through RPCs.

Remember that routing group configuration is necessary only when you are connecting two or more routing groups or installing connectors to foreign messaging systems in your Exchange installation. You must upgrade all server software prior to fully deploying your Exchange 2000 organization. You also must decide which connector will best serve routing-group communications. The primary types of Exchange 2000 Routing Connectors are the RGC, SMTP Connector, and X.400 Connector. Exchange 2000 also supports these other types of connectors: Lotus

Notes Connector, Lotus cc:Mail Connector, MS Mail Connector, and Novell GroupWise Connector. These connectors provide extensible message routing and coexistence between popular non-Microsoft messaging platforms and Exchange 2000 organizations.

Managing Connectivity between Exchange Servers

If all your Exchange Servers are connected via high-bandwidth, reliable connections, you don't need to perform any special routing configuration or management. Routing configuration and management are necessary only when you connect two or more routing groups that have low-bandwidth, unreliable, or intermittent connections. For example, your company has a presence in two different locations, one in New York and another in Phoenix. You need two separate routing groups, one for each city, to minimize operating costs. Creating only a single routing group for these two cities is expensive because with only one routing group, the two cities must have reliable, permanent connectivity. Install a connector between the two routing groups, and optionally, set up a schedule or limits for transmitting mail. In general, when your organization has a full mesh, well-connected network, you don't need multiple routing groups. However, your corporate design might require multiple routing groups for administrative purposes—such as controlling public-folder referrals and connector scope—or to manage message tracking and flow between two locations.

Server Management

Managing the servers running Exchange might include managing permissions, message routings, protocols, Exchange system policies, storage groups (SGs), and databases. Managing Exchange Servers also includes server maintenance on a daily or a periodic basis. Server monitoring is also an important administrative task. Servers are managed using the MMC (Microsoft Management Console) snap-ins: the Exchange System Manager and Computer Management. The Exchange System Manager is a preconfigured management console that includes several smaller snap-ins used to fully manage and administer the Exchange Server's components. You use the Exchange System Manager to manage all aspects of your Exchange Server organization. Three management areas must be considered:

- *Exchange 2000*—Administration and operation of Exchange Servers using Exchange System Manager in MMC
- *Windows 2000*—Operating system (OS) configuration and management of the servers Exchange runs on
- *AD*—Management and operation of the domain controllers (DCs) that provide AD services

Aspects of Exchange Server Management

Maintaining the Exchange databases is probably the most important aspect of server management. Exchange databases must be backed up regularly to help prevent irrecoverable data loss. The team member(s) responsible for database maintenance should be clearly defined to make sure this task is accomplished. Although many organizations use automated backup systems, these administrators are responsible for ensuring that the backups take place and that a policy for testing those backups and for performing trial restores is in place. Because Exchange 2000 uses SGs, it's possible to make different team members responsible for different sets of databases. This might be necessary if your security model restricts access to certain mailboxes or public folders. For example, a subset of administrators might have access to the mailboxes of the sales team or the marketing department.

Protocol management is another important concern. The team members given permission to access these settings can view and flush message queues, change message sizes, and restrict protocol availability—such as restricting the users who are permitted to access Exchange through a Web browser. Team members who are given the permission to modify Exchange System Policy are responsible for managing logging, message tracking, database maintenance, mailbox and database limits, and indexing. System policies have a significant impact on the operation and maintenance of the servers running Exchange, so access should only be granted to those who are knowledgeable in all aspects of Exchange 2000.

Managing an Exchange Server organization can be a broad responsibility. Best practices recommend that you designate different administrators to perform specific tasks. Learn to delegate the routine, everyday tasks. The overall administrator of the Exchange Servers can do a more crucial job and can get away from the daily, routine maintenance tasks. Designating different administrators for different tasks also makes it easier to audit and pinpoint anyone who has been negligent. Learn to use the various Windows 2000 administration tools for managing Exchange Servers, such as the following:

- *Active Directory Users and Computer*—This tool is used to manage, create, modify, and delete recipients as well as enable or disable Exchange features. This tool is also used to configure user-specific Exchange-related attributes.
- *Computer Management*—This tool includes an Exchange Server container in its Services and Applications container. The Exchange container included in Computer Management is the equivalent of a server container in System Manager. It enables you to manage all facets of your server within a single snap-in. Unlike System Manager, you can use the Computer Management snap-in only to manage the server to which it is directed. You can use this snap-in to remotely manage the services of another Exchange Server.

- *Event Viewer*—This tool is used to view all error messages and warnings encountered by the Windows 2000 Server. All messages related to all applications running on the Windows 2000 machine are written in the application log.
- *System Monitor/Performance*—This tool provides performance monitoring through charting the activity of the server, capturing realtime activity. You also have the option to save the captured performance and view it later.

Managing Exchange 2000 Servers in Mixed Mode

Special considerations exist when Exchange 2000 operates in mixed mode with Exchange 5.5. Exchange Server administration must be performed separately. You manage all Exchange 5.5 servers from the existing Exchange 5.5 administrator program, and you manage all Exchange 2000 Servers from the Exchange 2000 System Manager. Problems might occur if you attempt to manage Exchange 5.5 from Exchange 2000 System Manager or if you attempt to manage Exchange 2000 from the Exchange 5.5 administrator program because Exchange 5.5 does not recognize AD. If your system does not have a Site Replication Service, the Exchange 2000 Server does not recognize the Exchange 5.5 directory. If you attempt, for example, to access Exchange 5.5 mailboxes from Active Directory Users and Computers, the tool doesn't resolve the mailboxes the way that the Exchange 5.5 administrative tool does. You are unable to move mailboxes that exist on Exchange 2000 Servers by using the Exchange 5.5 administrative tool.

Administrating Policies

The new policy feature in Exchange 2000 provides you with great flexibility to administer large numbers of Exchange objects. This powerful policy model for administration enables administrators to change administrative options across a set of objects (for example, user mailboxes, servers, and public folders). Administrators define system policy across hundreds of objects and, once implemented, can change configuration options or enforce particular settings across these multiple objects in a single operation. Administrators can also define recipient policies across hundreds of thousands of users, groups, and contacts in Windows 2000 AD using a powerful LDAP (Lightweight Directory Access Protocol) query interface in a single operation. The two types of policies are called system and recipient.

System Policies

You create *system policies* and apply them to a server, a mailbox store, or a public store. Often, system policies are referred to as server-based policies because they are applied to Exchange 2000 Server components and they affect the Exchange configurations. System policies use an apply-time implementation to effect configuration changes. An *apply-time* implementation means that the administrator creates a policy, defines the settings that policy implements, associates that policy with one or more objects of the same class, and then applies the policy. Objects that have an applied policy list the applicable policies and disable the settings that the policy overrides. This enables administrators to prevent further changes. Exchange supports three classes of system policies: mailbox store, public folder store, and server policies.

Recipient Policies

Recipient policies are applied to mail-enabled Exchange objects—that is, any AD object with at least one email address—primarily to generate email addresses. Recipient policies are used on objects typically thought of as user-side objects—users, groups, and contacts. Exchange includes a default recipient policy. The default single recipient policy is used to automatically generate email addresses for mail-enabled Exchange objects such as users, groups, contacts, public folders, stores, and system attendants. Recipient policies use a background-apply implementation to effect configuration changes. In a background-apply, an administrator creates a policy, defines the settings that policy implements, and associates that policy with one or more objects using the Exchange LDAP query engine. The policy is applied later based on the schedule of the Address List Service running under System Attendant. Multiple recipient policies can be implemented within an organization. If your organization is hosting several email address types, you can create a recipient policy that handles each address. Adding them to the policy and applying it to the recipient can generate SMTP, X.400, Lotus cc:Mail, Lotus Notes, or MS Mail addresses. These policies appear in MMC as Recipient Policies of the Recipients item.

The first recipient policy in an organization is configured as the default policy for all objects. In addition to address generation, you can create policies that filter specific AD object types, distinguishing, for example, User from Group or Contacts. You can apply recipient policies to specific Organizational Units (OUs), such as a Marketing, Accounting, or Sales department. Finally, you can set policies based on locations. Remember, although several policies can be assigned to an object, only one policy is applied to that specific object at any given time. Application of this single policy is determined by the Exchange Server and based on the priority of an object's assigned policies. The default policy is applied when no other policy is assigned to an object.

Security and Distribution Groups

AD maintains two group categories: the security groups and the distribution groups. Security groups are security principals within AD that are often used to group users or computers to reduce the points of administration and provide permissions to network resources. Distribution groups are similar to the distribution lists (DLs) in previous versions of Exchange. Distribution groups cannot be used

Table 13.1 Security groups.

Advantages	Disadvantages
Can be mail-enabled by assigning a SMTP address so the group can act as a DL equivalent.	Accidentally placing users in the group can give users unauthorized access to network resources.
Can be used for assigning permissions to public folders in Exchange 2000.	N/A
Useful if you also want to assign network permissions for the members in this group.	N/A
Lowers the number of groups in AD and the messaging system, as well as the maintenance they require.	N/A

Table 13.2 Distribution groups.

Advantages	Disadvantages
Can be used for bulk mailing.	Cannot be assigned as permissions to network resources.
Membership's only purpose is to send messages to its membership.	Cannot be assigned as permissions to public folders.
Can be used for universal groups, even in a Mixed-mode domain.	N/A

to grant access rights to resources. Tables 13.1 and 13.2 list the advantages and disadvantages of the two groups.

Managing Recipients

In previous versions of Exchange Server, recipients (mailboxes, custom recipients, DLs, public folders, agents) are, in themselves, objects that reside on the Exchange directory database. Each Exchange Server directory is being maintained by an Exchange core component called the *directory service.*

In Exchange 2000, a mailbox is not an object by itself, but rather, a mailbox is only an attribute of an AD object. An object in the AD that can take advantage of Exchange functionality is called a *recipient.* A recipient is an AD object that is mail-enabled or mailbox-enabled, or an object that can receive email. Recipients in AD are the users, contacts, groups, or public folders. Among these, only the user object is capable of being mail-enabled or mailbox-enabled; all the rest are mail-enabled. A mail-enabled recipient is an object in the AD that has at least one email address defined. A mail-enabled recipient has an associated email address, but does not have an associated Exchange mailbox. A mail-enabled AD object is like a custom recipient in early Exchange Server versions. A mailbox-enabled AD object refers to users that can both send and receive emails because mailbox-enabled objects are associated with Exchange mailboxes.

Exchange 5.5 objects are referred to differently when migrated to Exchange 2000. An AD mailbox-enabled user was formerly known as an Exchange 5.5 mailbox. A custom recipient is now known as an AD mail-enabled contact (or mail-enabled user). An Exchange 5.5 DL is known as an AD mail-enabled group and a public folder is an AD public folder. Recipient management in Exchange 2000 involves manipulating the object attributes of the windows AD directory service. When an AD user is mail-enabled or mailbox-enabled, Exchange-specific attributes are included. Additional Exchange-related tabs also are visible on the Property pages of the AD object.

Public Folders

Public folders replace the online bulletin board system (BBS) in which organization-wide information, announcements, and advertisements are placed. With Exchange 2000's built-in support for streaming files, information with Internet contents can also be posted on the public folders. Data such as employee vacation and expense report forms that were previously distributed through a department or company intranet can be managed through public folders. Individual or group access to folders is controlled by setting permissions and optimized by replicating folders to other servers in your organization. Public folders are replicated for load balancing as well as fault tolerance. Exchange 2000 public folders contain the following new innovative features that make the Exchange Server a complete collaboration server:

- *Multiple store support*—The public-folder hierarchy can be configured into smaller logical units to reflect departments in an organization. In addition to the default public-folder hierarchy, you can create other top-level folder hierarchies. Each folder hierarchy is represented by its own database in the Information Store. Multiple stores increase scalability by allowing you to segment the folder data and distribute it across servers in your organization.
- *Web exposure*—Each public folder has a HTML page associated with it. When a folder is created, Exchange automatically creates a default HTML page. You can replace the automatically generated Web page with a custom page or you can change the URL (Uniform Resource Locator) to point to another Web site. In addition to the folder container, a dynamically generated URL exposes all contents within a folder.
- *Replication*—A public folder can be configured to have copies on multiple servers. Replicas are useful for distributing the user load on servers, distributing public folders across geographical areas, and backing up public-folder data. Configure replication schedules based on how often data in the public

folder changes and set this schedule for all public folders or for a specific public folder.

- *Affinity*—When a client must use an alternate server to access public folder content, Exchange uses a routing group that is configured to refer the client to another server. This allows the client to access content when a specific server is not known, and eliminates the need for a cost-based referral list. Because routing groups are intended to serve as collections of well-connected servers, the connections between all servers in a routing group are likely to be of the same bandwidth.
- *Multiple public folder trees*—Exchange 2000 now supports multiple public folder trees. The support for multiple public folder trees allows the Exchange Server to be more productive. An additional public folder tree is created to store specialized applications that have to be deployed within the organization. Be careful when you are implementing multiple public folder trees because only the default public folder tree is accessible using MAPI (Messaging Application Programming Interface) and IMAP (Internet Message Access Protocol). Succeeding public folder trees are not accessible through IMAP-based and MAPI-based clients; the public folder trees are accessed using other methods—such as NNTP (Network News Transfer Protocol)—via any Windows application, or using WebDAV (Web Distributed Authoring and Versioning).

Types of Administrative Models

The *administrative model* addresses corporate or business needs and satisfies process-related requirements. You can delegate management to multiple groups. When deciding which administrative model to use, remember that a centralized model is the simplest to create and manage. Exchange 2000, however, has the flexibility to support any administrative model that is dictated by your organization's structure. The three main administrative models for managing Exchange 2000 messaging system are the following:

- Centralized management
- Distributed management
- Mixed management

Centralized Management

Centralized management is the simplest of all administration models and is characterized by a single point of administration regardless of the number of administrative groups and routing groups in the organization. For distributed networks, the centralized administrative approach works best when each location is connected to the central location with high network reliability and availability, but this is not a requirement. In a centralized management model, Exchange Servers are divided into several administrative groups. Several routing groups might be used to control message transfer as well. Remember that servers cannot be moved between administrative groups after they are placed within a group. This model is most appropriate for SMEs that have a single IT group, or in large organizations with a centralized IT authority. The centralized model is also used in any company with few geographic locations. These organizations often rely on a single administrative team for all their network services.

Because administrative groups are disabled by default when Exchange 2000 is first installed, administrative groups are not displayed. However, any server that exists in the organization before displaying administrative groups belongs to the first administrative group. If you add servers to your organization before creating the administrative groups, the new servers all belong to the first administrative group. If you want to add new servers to a new administrative group, you must first manually display administrative groups. You must then create the new administrative groups before installing Exchange 2000 on the new servers. After servers are placed in an administrative group, they cannot be moved. If you do not want all servers to belong to the same administrative group, install Exchange 2000 on one server, create your administrative groups, and then install Exchange 2000 on the remaining servers and place them in the appropriate administrative groups.

To view the administrative group, open the Exchange System Manager, right-click the Organization node (Organization name), and choose Properties. On the General tab of the Administrative View property page, click the Display Administrative Groups option. This Properties sheet is shown in Figure 13.1.

NOTE: *After you have defined the administrative groups, if you clear the Display Administrative Groups option, all servers are grouped into the same Servers node in Exchange System Manager and all group division is lost. If you then choose to display administrative groups again, all servers now belong to the first administrative group and are not restored to any prior group configuration. If your Exchange 2000 organization coexists with an Exchange 5.5 organization, administrative groups are always enabled.*

Implementing Routing Groups in a Centralized Model

Best practices recommend limiting the number of routing groups in any organization. For a distributed network with centralized administration, it's best to keep all mailbox servers in the main location or in a central hub routing group. Keep in mind that each server must maintain high network availability among all other servers in the same routing group. Place collaboration or application servers such as dedicated public folder servers, in addition to mailbox-only servers, in this same routing group hub. If you cannot place all mailbox servers in this hub routing

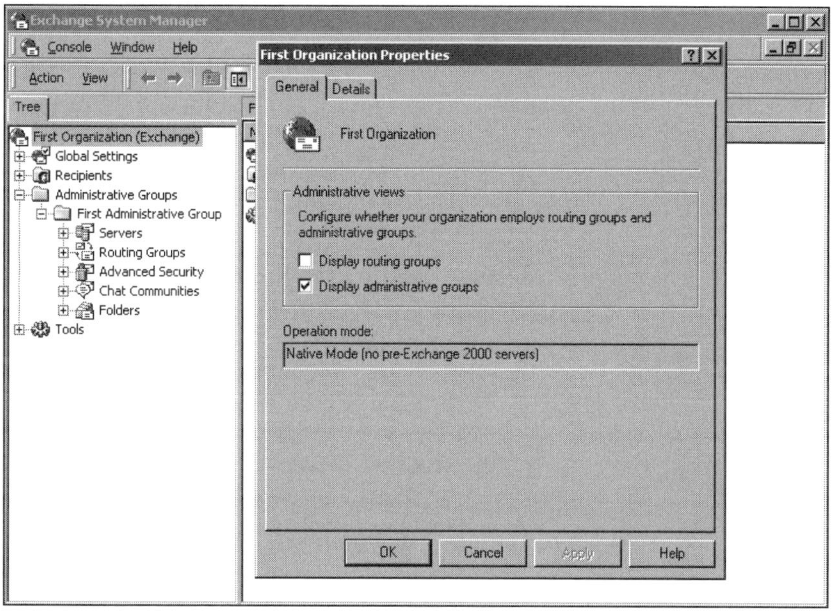

Figure 13.1 The General tab of an Organization's Properties sheet.

group and you must create other routing groups, designate one or two dedicated connector servers in the hub routing group as bridgehead connector servers that connect all other branch office routing groups.

Implementing Administrative Groups in a Centralized Model

Because the routing group design is uncoupled from your administrative group design, simplify your administrative group architecture whenever possible to facilitate centralized administration. Placing all your Exchange 2000 servers in one administrative group is a good design strategy because that one administrative group can contain several routing groups. This administrative group shares its administrative security context with all the routing groups within its boundaries. Servers or routing groups that you want administered by the same group of administrators can be placed in the same administrative group.

AD Account Management and Exchange 2000 Centralized Model

Centralized administration of all Windows 2000 accounts and Exchange 2000 mailboxes requires creating a simple organizational hierarchy using as few OUs as possible. Avoid nesting the accounts and mailboxes within OUs several layers deep in the AD hierarchy. This configuration simplifies account and mailbox administration because the accounts are managed in fewer locations. Consider placing all your Windows 2000 accounts and Exchange 2000 mailboxes in one or two high-level OUs.

Distributed/Decentralized Management

A number of administrators are responsible for managing the company's network resources in the distributed management model. Divide your administrative personnel by location, division, or business unit. A central group typically manages standards and guidelines, but not daily administration. At least one administrative group exists for each region or division in this model. In Exchange 2000 mixed environments and legacy Exchange, administrative groups and routing groups are automatically arranged in this way. Existing Exchange sites are mapped on a one-to-one basis to administrative groups and routing groups when you upgrade to Exchange 2000.

Implementing the distributed administrative model is similar to implementing earlier Exchange sites. The administrative responsibilities of these Exchange sites can be distributed among several people or departments. This model is best suited for organizations requiring different administrators and different levels of administrative access. Organizations made up of independently operating branch offices often use this management model.

Multiple administrative groups are created in a distributed model. As stated previously, these administrative groups often contain several routing groups. Each administrative group has its own administrator. Each administrator for an administrative group is responsible for all Exchange Servers belonging to that specific administrative group. Administrative tasks typically include managing recipients, policy and address lists, servers, routing, public folders, and collaboration services. The distributed management model distributes control over management of the Exchange organization to company regions or divisions. The distributed administrative approach is most appropriate where each branch office or division is administered separately or operated in a relatively independent fashion.

Implementing Routing Groups in a Distributed Model

When using distributed administration with Exchange 2000, create routing groups based on the topology of remote locations. The network reliability between these locations is the fundamental criterion upon which your design is based; when the link between offices is not reliable, create a separate routing group. Depending on the total number of routing groups, each distributed routing group probably contains mailbox-only servers. It might also contain servers dedicated to RGCs. In addition, locate collaboration or application servers—such as dedicated public folder servers—in the distributed routing group. Remember, when multiple routing groups are implemented, additional administrative overhead is added to the organizational structure. Routing groups communicate through the RGC. If multiple routing groups are created, corresponding RGCs also must be built in to support connectivity.

NOTE: When designing RGCs, you should always configure at least two paths to every other routing group to provide redundant routing paths in case a network link is not available or a bridgehead server goes offline. Providing multiple routes for the routing groups also ensures message flow and delivery.

Implementing Administrative Groups in a Distributed Model

In a distributed administrative model, you can define an administrative group that matches the structure of your organization. You can have an administrative group for each of your branch offices or divisions. At least one Exchange 2000 Server should be placed in each administrative group, based on your regional or branch administration model and the size of your recipient object pool.

AD Account Management and Exchange 2000 Distributed Model

As previously mentioned, moving servers between administrative groups is not a simple matter; plan carefully before assigning servers to administrative groups. To distribute the administration of Windows 2000 accounts and Exchange 2000 mailboxes, place recipient objects in division-based or branch-based OUs. Distributing AD accounts to the appropriate OUs provides a more precise set of Group Policy and directory permissions based on the needs of the particular divisions or branch offices.

Mixed Centralized and Distributed Management

The mixed administrative approach works best when each remote office is connected to a central office with a highly reliable network connection. Define each administrative role in your organization carefully to determine proper assignment of server components to central or remote locations. This model uses a hybrid implementation of both the centralized and the distributed models. Organizations use this model to decentralize administration of some resources while centralizing the management of other resources. A company might centralize the management of mission-critical or global support services while it decentralizes routine or geographically localized tasks such as adding, deleting, and managing user accounts. This model is best suited for large organizations that have clearly defined IT job descriptions and responsibilities. This is a complex model to implement; perform careful analyses of the messaging system and current messaging infrastructure before deployment. Security and administrative boundaries must be determined prior to deploying this mixed administration model.

Administrative groups play an important role in a mixed administrative model. Specialized administrative groups are usually created to support specific functional management areas. If, for example, you want to restrict a local administrator's ability to create and maintain policies, you can create an administrative group for policies. You also can assign permissions to restrict the list of people who can create policies. You can use specialized administrative groups to separate the administrative responsibilities for different geographical locations or assign an administrative group that defines central organization responsibilities. It is thus easier to administer an Exchange 2000 organization because you can create administrative groups to manage message routing, and you can create other administrative groups to apply server policies or to grant user rights for particular servers.

Implementing Routing Groups in a Mixed Model

You can choose several routing group approaches in a mixed administration model. These approaches are based on the logical assumption that you have distributed offices across geographical locations. You might also adopt the same approaches even if your Exchange 2000 routing groups are within the same network if appropriate to your business requirements. One approach is to assign as many mailbox servers as possible to the central office, and then place all mailbox servers in a central hub routing group. Create the remaining branch office routing groups so that each branch can maintain its own messaging infrastructure. When using this approach, keep in mind that each server must maintain high network availability between all other servers in the same routing group. Another approach to consider is placing collaboration or application servers—such as dedicated public folder servers—in your hub routing group in addition to mailbox-only servers. If you cannot place all mailbox servers into the hub routing group and must create other routing groups due to bandwidth considerations, assign one or two dedicated connector servers to act as bridgeheads to all other branch office routing groups. If your messaging or networking backbone support team is centrally located, you can also use a mixed approach that assigns all routing groups to a central location.

Implementing Administrative Groups in a Mixed Model

With a mixed administrative model, you can adopt a variety of administrative approaches depending on the needs of your company. Simplify your administrative group architecture to facilitate administration. Placing all Exchange 2000 Servers in one administrative group provides support for the consolidation of multiple routing groups and helps simplify permission management and security. After you create and assign permissions for an administrative group, for example, new objects added to the container inherit the permissions you set for the group. This feature significantly reduces labor costs if you have one administrator who manages multiple servers in multiple locations. If you have five Exchange Servers, it's easier to define a set of permissions for one administrative group that contains the five servers than to define the same set of permissions separately for each server. Because routing groups define only the physical topology, using one administrative group simplifies the management process.

NOTE: *You can't move servers between administrative groups, so plan carefully before assigning servers to administrative groups. Moving servers between routing groups, however, is easy.*

AD Account Management and Exchange 2000 Mixed Model

In centralized and distributed administrative models, Windows 2000 account administration and Exchange 2000 mailbox administration are either centralized or distributed. Your choice is determined by the placement of your Exchange 2000 mailboxes and Windows 2000 accounts in the structure of your AD OUs. You should locate all your accounts and mailboxes in one or more high-level OUs, or in several OUs based on branch office or division. Mixing distributed and centralized management is the most common scenario in organizations with multiple divisions or offices dispersed geographically. In this environment, use special administrative groups for one or both of the following:

- *Centralized routing management*—Because of the importance and complexity of routing topology, you can restrict routing management to a special group of professionals, who usually belong to the central group of administrators. This is typical when the central group is responsible for the messaging backbone and regional administrators are responsible for day-to-day administration of servers and other services. Centralizing the routing management is essential so that routing topologies can be properly controlled and monitored.
- *Centralized policy management*—A central group of administrators is responsible for the policies that enforce standard configuration across the organization to avoid the creation of overlapping or conflicting policies. For example, the regional administrators are responsible for day-to-day management and monitoring of servers, but they are restricted to creating policies. A variation on this scenario is to have the central group define some organization-wide policies, and have the regional administrators control the remaining policies.

Knowing When to Use RGCs

RGCs are SMTP-based Connectors that function similarly to a legacy Exchange Site Connector. If the RGC is used to connect to an Exchange 5.5 Server, it automatically routes the message to the Exchange 5.5 Server's MTA and uses RPC to transfer messages. The RGC, like the Exchange 5.5 Site Connector, enables single or multiple servers in a routing group to act as routing servers. These routing servers are called *bridgehead servers*. Bridgehead servers facilitate communication outside the routing group. You can create single or multiple local (source) bridgehead servers, or you can specify that no local bridgehead server exists and every server in the local routing group can make connections through the RGC. This allows each server in the routing group to act as a bridgehead server. If you want all mail to flow through one computer for the purpose of tracking messages or archiving, a single bridgehead server is appropriate. Multiple bridgehead servers provide load balancing or fault tolerance in the event of a bridgehead server failure.

Applying Email Related Security Procedures

Exchange 2000 uses a virus scanning API similar to the one in Exchange 5.5. In addition, however, Exchange 2000 must scan native Multipurpose Internet Mail Extensions (MIME) content. The main goal of Exchange 2000 is to make sure that the virus scanning API is backward compatible. With changes in Exchange 2000 architecture, some new features can be added to the API to provide access to message properties and improve logging features. For maximum protection and the prevention of a system security breach, train your user population to minimize their exposure to viruses with the following practices:

- Never open email attachments from unknown sources. Establish procedures and protocols that provide anti-Trojan solutions. Teach your users to be extremely cautious and suspicious of any attachments. When in doubt over the danger of a critical message attachment, develop standard quarantine procedures that can be easily followed so that neither business workflow nor network security is compromised. Depending on the corporate social culture, you or members of your department might randomly send attachments to users that simulate this possible attack modality. Remind your users to always be cautious.
- Train users to log off their email accounts, or any other secured logon, when they finish a work session. Instruct “road warriors” who are more likely to logon from a public terminal about clearing Send To files and browser history lists as well as temporary file directories before terminating a session.
- Do not respond to unsolicited commercial or bulk email (UCE or UBE), chain letters, or any form of digital exchanges commonly known as spam. Consider investing in third-party anti-spam packages that will eliminate the need for users to delete UCE and decrease wasted storage capacity on Exchange Servers. Tell your users that when they respond to unsolicited email, they are confirming an active email address. This form of social engineering opens your organization to different forms of attack from both internal and external intruders. Ask your users to forward all suspicious or unsolicited digital exchanges to those responsible for Exchange administration so that appropriate actions can be implemented such as filtering or blocking transmissions from “problem” IP domains and addresses.

- Use common sense and never make casual assumptions. Teach users not to respond to requests for any company or personal information, such as the name or email address of their superiors or more obviously, their passwords, even if the request appears to come from a reputable source inside or outside your organization. In a customer service situation, insist that a representative from your organization or your superior will contact some unknown party. Avoid wherever possible releasing information that might help structure or direct a security attack within your organization.

Immediate Solutions

Creating System Policies

The server policy allows you to enable logging, message tracking, and log file maintenance on multiple servers in your administrative group. The mailbox store policy applies administrative tasks—such as storage limits, indexing updates, maintenance intervals, and mappings—to public stores, and offline address lists to multiple mailbox stores. Use public store policies to apply administrative tasks—such as maintenance, replication intervals, storage limits, and index updates—to multiple public stores. Before creating server, mailbox, or public folder policies, you must follow the steps in the following section.

Displaying Administrative Groups

To display administrative groups, perform the following:

1. Click Start|Programs|Microsoft Exchange|Exchange System Manager.
2. Right-click the organization and then click Properties. On the General tab, select Display Administrative Groups. Exit and restart Exchange System Manager.

Viewing the System Policies Folder

To view the System Policies folder, perform the following:

1. Click Start|Programs|Microsoft Exchange|Exchange System Manager.
2. Click the plus (+) sign to expand the Administrative Groups container and then click + to expand the First Administrative Group (or the name of the administrative group where you want the server policy applied).
3. If no System Policies folder appears on the contents pane, create one. To create a System Policies folder, right-click the administrative group name, and choose New|System Policy Container.

NOTE: *Only one System Policy container is created per administrative group.*

Creating the Server Policy

To create the server policy, perform the following:

1. Click Start|Programs|Microsoft Exchange|Exchange System Manager.
2. Expand the Administrative Groups container and then expand the First Administrative Group (or the name of the administrative group where you want the server policy applied).
3. Right-click the System Policies folder and choose New|Server Policy.
4. In New Policy, check the boxes of the tabs you want to use in the policy. In this case, only the General box is available.
5. Type a name for the policy on the General tab of the Properties window.
6. On the Details tab, use Administrative Note to add additional information about the policy.
7. On the General (Policy) tab, set the following options:
    - Click Enable Subject Logging And Display to log all message subject fields.
    - Click Enable Message Tracking to log all mail activity performed by all Exchange components.
    - Click Remove Log Files to remove all log files older than the value set in Remove Files That Are Older Than (Days).

Creating the Mailbox Store Policy

Perform the following steps to create the mailbox store policy:

1. Click Start|Programs|Microsoft Exchange|Exchange System Manager.
2. Expand the Administrative Groups container, and then expand the First Administrative Group (or the name of the administrative group where you want the server policy applied).
3. Right-click the System Policies folder and choose New|Mailbox Store Policy.
4. In New Policy, check the boxes of the tabs you want to use in the policy.
5. On the General tab of the Properties window, type the mailbox store policy name.
6. On the Details tab, use Administrative Note to add additional information.
7. On the General (Policy) tab shown in Figure 13.2, set the following options:
    - Use Default Public Store to set the default public store.
    - Use Offline Address List to set an offline address list.

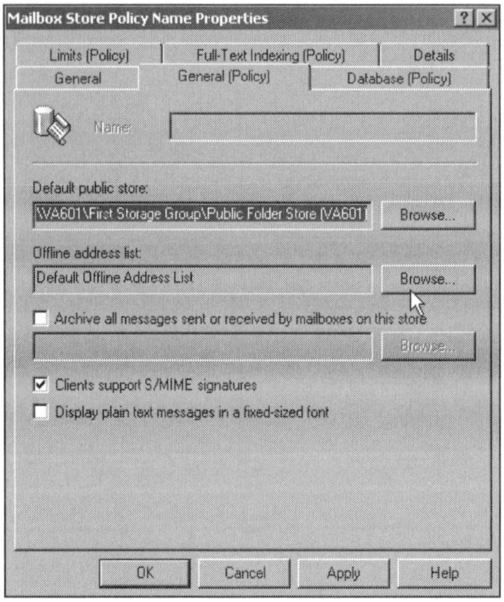

Figure 13.2 The General (Policy) tab of a Mailbox Store Policy Name Properties sheet.

- Click Clients Support S/MIME Signatures if your mail clients are using the Secure/Multipurpose Internet Mail Extensions (S/MIME) standard.
- Click Display Plain Text Messages In A Fixed-Size Font to display variable-width message fonts in a fixed font.

8. On the Database (Policy) tab, select a value in Maintenance Interval or click Customize to build a custom schedule graphically.
9. On the Limits (Policy) tab, set the following options as shown in Figure 13.3:
   - Click Issue Warning At (KB) to issue a warning when the storage space used reaches the size you specify.
   - Click Prohibit Send At (KB) to stop sending items when the storage space used reaches the size you specify.
   - Click Prohibit Send And Receive At (KB) to stop sending and receiving items when the storage space used reaches the size you specify.
   - Select a value in Warning Message Interval, or click Customize to build a custom schedule graphically.
   - Use Keep Deleted Items For (Days) to set the maximum number of days to keep deleted items in the store.
   - Use Keep Deleted Mailboxes For (Days) to set the maximum number of days to keep deleted mailboxes in the store.

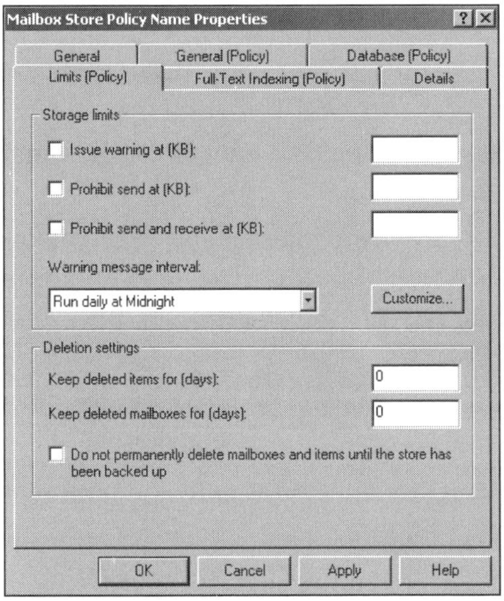

Figure 13.3 The Limits (Policy) tab of a Mailbox Store Policy Name Properties sheet.

- Click Do Not Permanently Delete Mailboxes And Items Until The Store Has Been Backed Up to preserve mailboxes and items until the store is backed up.

10. On the Full-Text Indexing (Policy) tab, set the following options:
    - Select a value in Update Interval or click Customize to build a custom schedule graphically.
    - Select a value in Rebuild Interval, or click Customize to build a custom schedule graphically.

Creating the Public Store Policy

To create the public store policy, perform the following:

1. Click Start|Programs|Microsoft Exchange|Exchange System Manager.
2. Expand the Administrative Groups container and then expand the First Administrative Group (or the name of the administrative group where you want the server policy applied).
3. Right-click the System Policies folder and choose New|Public Store Policy.
4. In New Policy, check the boxes of the tabs you want to use in the policy.
5. In the Properties window, on the General tab, type the public store policy name.
6. On the Details tab, use Administrative Note to add additional information.

7. On the General (Policy) tab, set the following options:
   - Click Clients Support S/MIME Signatures if your mail clients are using the S/MIME standard.
   - Click Display Plain Text Messages In A Fixed-Size Font to display variable-width message fonts in a fixed font.
8. On the Database (Policy) tab, select a value in Maintenance Interval, or click Customize to build a custom schedule graphically.
9. On the Replication (Policy) tab, set the following options as shown in Figure 13.4:
   - Select a value in Replication Interval, or click Customize to build a custom schedule graphically.
   - Type a value in Replication Interval For Always (Minutes) to limit replication frequency.
   - Under Limits, type a value in Replication Interval For Always (Minutes) to limit the replication interval, and then type a value in Replication Message Size Limit (KB) to limit the messages replicated.
10. On the Limits (Policy) tab, set the following options:
    - Click Issue Warning At (KB) to send a warning when the storage space used reaches the size you specify.
    - Click Prohibit Post At (KB) to prohibit messages over the size you specify from posting.

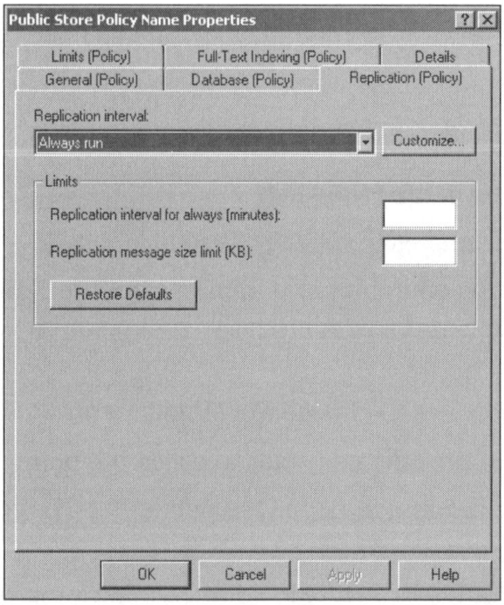

Figure 13.4 The Replication Property sheet of a public store policy.

- Click Maximum Item Size (KB) to set a maximum limit for items in the policy.
- Select a value in Warning Message Interval, or click Customize to build a custom schedule graphically.
- Use Keep Deleted Items For (Days) to set in the maximum number of days items can remain in the store.
- Click Do Not Permanently Delete Items Until The Store Has Been Backed Up to preserve items until the store is backed up.
- Click Age Limit For All Folders In This Store (Days) and type a value.

11. On the Full-Text Indexing (Policy) tab, set the following options:
    - Select a value in Update Interval, or click Customize to build a custom schedule graphically.
    - Select a value in Rebuild Interval, or click Customize to build a custom schedule graphically.

Creating a New Recipient Policy

To create a new recipient policy, perform the following:

1. Click Start|Programs|Microsoft Exchange|Exchange System Manager.
2. Expand the Recipients item, right-click Recipient Policies, and choose New|Recipient Policy.

NOTE: *A default policy already exists because it is created by default.*

3. On the General tab, use Name to name the policy.
4. Click Modify to access Find Exchange Recipients and build the LDAP query to select the set of recipients to which your policy applies. Use the General tab to build a simple query. Use the Storage tab to select the set of mailboxes you want to include in your query. Use the Advanced tab to build an advanced query using field-level attributes of the recipients and search conditions.
5. Back on the General tab, use Filter Rules to see the LDAP query filter created in the Find Exchange Recipients window.
6. On the Email Address tab, set the following options:
    - Use Generation Rules to view the current rules of how email addresses are generated for the recipients selected by the LDAP query. Any recipient under this policy automatically has the addresses in this list. Use New to create a new rule and Edit to change an existing rule.

- Use Set As Primary to designate one address as the primary when you have two or more email addresses of the same address type.

7. On the Details tab, use Administrative Note to add additional information.

Applying and Verifying the Policies

After the policies have been created, you need to apply them to the servers and stores they were created for. To apply these policies, you have to add Exchange objects to them. Verify also that these policies have been properly applied to the corresponding Exchange objects.

To apply server policies, perform the following:

1. Right-click the policy that you want to apply, and then click Add Store or Add Server (depending on the type of policy you are applying).
2. In the top pane, click the server or store name, and then click Add.
3. Click OK to save the settings.

To verify an applied policy, perform the following:

1. Right-click either the server or store that you have applied a policy to, and then choose Properties.
2. Click the Policies tab. You see which policies have been applied to this object and which policy options are enabled.

Under certain circumstances, two policies are applied to a single Exchange object. If this happens, a message prompt appears telling you that a policy has already been applied to that specific object. You are then given the option to override the old policy with the one you are currently applying or keep the old policy and disregard the new policy that you are about to apply to the object.

Managing Recipients

Managing the recipients includes creating, modifying, and deleting the following: recipients, email addresses, message settings, and other related properties. The task of managing recipients in Exchange 5.5 and Exchange 2000 is the same, except that Exchange 2000 does not have a separate administrative tool to carry out the task. In Exchange 5.5, administration of the recipients as well as configurations of an Exchange Server is concentrated on the Exchange Administration Program. In Exchange 2000, no separate mailbox administration tool exists; instead, you administer mailboxes, groups, contacts, and public folders using the

Active Directory Users and Computers. To administer all aspects of Exchange 2000 configurations, you make use of the Exchange System Manager.

Creating a Mailbox-Enabled User

If you have the permission on the AD, you can create a mailbox-enabled user readily upon the creation of the Windows 2000 user object. A mailbox-enabled user has one or more mailboxes associated with it.

1. Click Start|Programs|Administrative Tools|Active Directory Users And Computers.
2. In the console tree, navigate to the node that will contain the new mailbox-enabled user, right-click the node, and choose New|User.
3. In the New Object-User dialog box, type the user's information in First Name, Initials, Last Name, and User Logon Name. Then click Next.
4. In the Password box, type a password for the new user. Confirm the new password by retyping the password in Confirm Password. Select the password options that apply, and then click Next.
5. Verify that the Create An Exchange Mailbox checkbox is selected. Verify that the information in Alias and in the Server and Mailbox Store drop-down lists is correct as shown in Figure 13.5, and then click Next.
6. In the final view of the New Object-User dialog box, verify that the information displayed is correct, and then click Finish. If the information is not correct, click Back to correct the information.

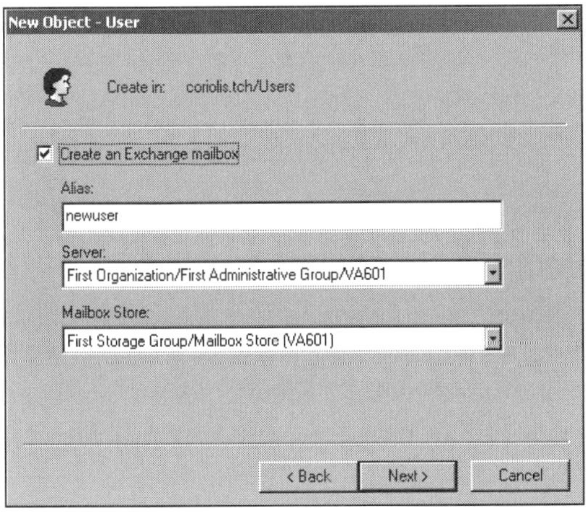

Fig 13.5 Mailbox information when creating a mailbox-enabled user.

Creating a Mail-Enabled User

A mail-enabled user has an associated email address but no associated mailbox. Mail-enabled users appear on the address lists and email messages can be sent to them; however, messages are not saved on an Exchange Server.

1. Click Start|Programs|Administrative Tools|Active Directory Users And Computers.
2. In the console tree, navigate to the node that will contain the new mailbox-enabled user, right-click the node, and choose New|User.
3. In the New Object-User dialog box, type the user's information in First Name, Initials, Last Name, and User Logon Name; then click Next.
4. In Password, type a password for the new user. Confirm the new password by retyping the password in Confirm Password. Select the password options that apply, and then click Next.
5. Click to clear the Create An Exchange Mailbox checkbox. The alias, server, and mailbox store selections will be dimmed. Click Next, verify the information for the new user, and then click Finish.
6. In the Details pane, right-click this new user, and then click Exchange Tasks. In the Exchange Task Wizard, click Next, select Establish Email Addresses, and then click Next.
7. In Alias, verify the alias, and then click Modify.
8. In the New Email Address dialog box, select an email address type, and then click OK.
9. In the Email Type Properties dialog box, type the email address information in Email Address for the type you selected in the previous step. Click Apply, and then click OK.
10. In the Exchange Task Wizard, verify the email address in External Email Address, and then click Next.

Creating a Mail-Enabled Contact

You can create a Windows 2000 contact and consequently mail-enable it. A mail-enabled contact is like a custom recipient in Exchange 5.5. It is an object in the AD that points to another object in another directory. Email addresses associated with a mail-enabled contact can be SMTP, Lotus Notes, Lotus cc:Mail, MS Mail, or X.400.

1. Click Start|Programs|Administrative Tools|Active Directory Users And Computers.
2. In the console tree, navigate to the node that will contain the new mail-enabled contact, right-click the node, and choose New|Contact.

3. In the New Object-Contact dialog box, type the contact's information in First Name, Initials, Last Name, and Display Name; then click Next.
4. Verify that the Create An Exchange Email Address checkbox is selected, and that the alias is correct. Then click Modify.
5. In the New Email Address dialog box, select an email address type, and then click OK.
6. In Properties of the selected email address type, type the email address information on the General tab for the email address type you selected in the New Email Address dialog box. Click Apply, and then click OK.
7. Click Next, and then verify that the information for the new contact is correct.

Creating a Mail-Enabled Group

You can create a Windows 2000 group and designate it as mail-enabled. A mail-enabled group facilitates sending mail to a group of people, which is primarily used for mass mailings.

1. Click Start|Programs|Administrative Tools|Active Directory Users And Computers.
2. In the console tree, navigate to the node that will contain the new mail-enabled group, right-click the node, and choose New|Group.
3. In the New Object-Group dialog box, type the Group Name, and then select Group Scope and Group Type. Then click Next.
4. Verify that the Create An Exchange Email Address checkbox is selected and that the alias is correct.
5. Click Next, and then verify that the information for the new group is correct.

Designating an Existing User as Mailbox-Enabled

You can designate the existing Windows 2000 users as mailbox-enabled if the AD is in place before you install the Exchange 2000 Servers.

1. Click Start|Programs|Administrative Tools|Active Directory Users And Computers.
2. In the console tree, double-click Users, or double-click the node that contains the recipient information you are modifying.
3. In the Details pane, right-click the user you want to modify, and then click Exchange Tasks.
4. In the Exchange Task Wizard, click Next, select Create Mailbox, and then click Next again.
5. Verify that the information in Alias and in the Server and Mailbox Store drop-down lists is correct, and then click Next.

Moving a Mailbox

If multiple Exchange 2000 Servers exist or multiple mailbox stores exist on an Exchange 2000 Server SG, you can move the mailboxes from one Exchange 2000 Server to another or from one mailbox store to another. Moving a mailbox is helpful if you need to do maintenance on the server or dismount a mailbox store but you don't want a particular mailbox to be affected. Moving mailboxes is also beneficial if you need to offload a certain Exchange Server.

1. Click Start|Programs|Administrative Tools|Active Directory Users And Computers.
2. In the console tree, double-click Users, or double-click the node that contains the recipient information you are modifying.
3. In the Details pane, right-click the user, and then click Exchange Tasks.
4. In the Exchange Task Wizard, click Next, select Move Mailbox, and then click Next again. The current location of the user's mailbox is displayed.
5. To specify the new destination for the mailbox, select a server in the Server drop-down list. Then select a mailbox store from the Mailbox Store drop-down list and click Next.
6. In the final screen of the Exchange Task Wizard, verify that the information is correct, and then click Finish. If the information is not correct, click Back to correct the information.

Deleting a Mailbox

Removing a mailbox from a user account is a common administrative procedure. If not enforced, the password to that box represents a serious security gap. Removal of such a user object, however, can cause other administrative problems due in part to the deletion of ownership access to specific user resources. Both steps should be carefully documented in some standardized listing of procedures. The removal of the box from the account also deletes any email addresses associated with the account. The action will mark the primary box for deletion. Normally, the actual object is removed after the system retention period has expired. You remove a mailbox as follows:

1. Right-click the specific user in Active Directory Users And Computers.
2. Launch the Exchange Wizard under Exchange Tasks.
3. Select Delete Mailbox under Available Tasks.
4. Confirm the action by clicking Finish.

Managing Email Addresses

Part of recipient management is making sure that an individual recipient has the correct email address associated with it. You can manage email addresses manually or automatically. To manually manage email addresses, you use the Email Address tab on the property pages of each recipient to view, add, modify, or remove email addresses. If you want to automate the creation of email addresses, you must create a policy that defines how email addresses are generated for your recipients; you can create a recipient policy in System Manager. Managing email addresses involves creating new addresses, modifying addresses, removing addresses, and setting the primary address of a recipient.

Adding a New Address

You can add a new email address for a mailbox-enabled user or mail-enabled recipient. You also must define the address type for the address you are creating.

1. Click Start|Programs|Administrative Tools|Active Directory Users And Computers.
2. In the console tree, double-click Users, or double-click the node that contains the recipient information you are modifying.
3. In the Details pane, double-click the recipient for whom you are adding an address.
4. In the Email Addresses tab, click New.
5. In the New Email Address dialog box, select the type of address you want to add, and then click OK.
6. In the Address Properties dialog box, type the email address information for the address type you selected, and then click Apply.
7. If multiple addresses exist for an address type, the primary address appears in bold. To change the primary address, select the address you want to use for the primary address, and then click Set As Primary.

NOTE: *By default, if a newly created email address is the only one of its type, it is the primary address and appears in bold.*

Modifying an Address for a Mailbox-Enabled User

When a mailbox-enabled user in your company transfers to another department or to another OU, you might need to modify the email address. Modifying email addresses is essential for volatile organizations in which people are constantly reshuffled.

1. Click Start|Programs|Administrative Tools|Active Directory Users And Computers.

2. In the console tree, double-click Users, or double-click the node that contains the recipient information you are modifying.
3. In the Details pane, double-click the mailbox-enabled user you are modifying.
4. On the Email Addresses tab, double-click the address you want to modify.
5. In the Address Properties dialog box, modify the email address information that appears for the address you selected in the previous step, and then click Apply.

Creating an Email Address for a Mail-Enabled Recipient

You can create a new email address for mail-enabled users, contacts, and groups. Email addresses identify recipients to the gateways and connectors that connect Exchange with other messaging systems. Creating a new email address (of a different email address type) for a mail-enabled recipient enables the recipient to communicate with users on messaging systems indicated by the email address type, such as Lotus cc:Mail and GroupWise.

1. Click Start|Programs|Administrative Tools|Active Directory Users And Computers.
2. In the console tree, double-click Users, or double-click the node that contains the recipient information you are modifying.
3. In the Details pane, double-click the mailbox-enabled recipient you are modifying.
4. On the Exchange General tab, click Modify.
5. In the Email Address dialog box, select Create New Email Address, and then click OK.
6. In the New Email Address dialog box, select the type of address you want to add, and then click OK.
7. On the General tab, in Email Address, type the email address, and then click Apply.

To modify an address for a mail-enabled recipient, select Modify Existing Email Address in the Email Address dialog box. If a recipient no longer needs an address of a certain address type, you can remove it. To remove an address, double-click the recipient you are modifying. In the Email Address dialog box, select the address you want to remove, and then click Remove.

Setting the Primary Address

The primary address is the first address created for each address type. The primary address is the email address that appears on the From field of the email client whenever a mailbox-enabled user sends email. For mail-enabled recipients, the primary address appears on its property pages on the Exchange General tab. If a newly created email address is the only one of its type, it is the primary address, by default. If multiple addresses exist for an address type, you can designate one address to be the primary address. You only can select a primary address if more than one email address exists for an address type. For example, when a user has two associated SMTP addresses, you have to designate one SMTP address to be the primary address. This address serves as the reply address for the user. If a user has only one SMTP address associated with his account, you need not specify the primary address because it is set by default.

1. Click Start|Programs|Administrative Tools|Active Directory Users And Computers.
2. In the console tree, double-click Users, or double-click the node that contains the recipient information you are modifying.
3. In the Details pane, double-click the recipient you want to modify.
4. In the New Email Address dialog box, select the address you want to be the primary address, and then click Set As Primary. The new primary address appears in bold, as shown in Figure 13.6.

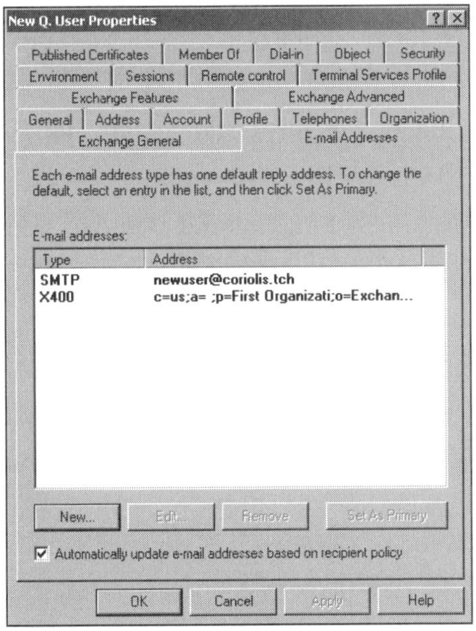

Figure 13.6 Primary email address information.

Configuring Message Settings

Best practices recommend implementing rules describing how Exchange users will use the service. You must also implement a measure that ensures your Exchange Server databases are healthy. Exchange Server has an unlimited store capability, but this should not be an excuse for an administrator to be lenient about the storage capacity of each Exchange user. Known issues pertain to Exchange databases. Although Exchange 2000 can store so many SGs or mailbox and public folder stores, you must make sure your Exchange databases are manageable. A huge Exchange database is difficult to manage, back up, and support in terms of disaster recovery. Message settings should be configured for each recipient. For the mailbox-enabled user, you need to configure the message settings that limit the storage size, message size, and recipients, such as deleted items retention period, message restrictions, privilege delegation, and forwarding addresses. Message size and message restrictions should be configured for a mail-enabled recipient.

Setting Message Size Limits of Incoming Messages

You can set the size limit for an incoming or outgoing message by either using default limits or selecting the maximum size of the incoming message in kilobytes. Because maximum message size limits are set on the mailbox-enabled user's Properties dialog box, you can set different maximum size limits for different users.

1. Click Start|Programs|Administrative Tools|Active Directory Users And Computers.
2. In the console tree, double-click Users, or double-click the node that contains the recipient information you are modifying.
3. In the Details pane, double-click the mailbox-enabled user you are modifying.
4. On the Exchange General tab, click Delivery Restrictions.
5. In the Delivery Restrictions dialog box, select Maximum KB under Incoming Message Size, and then type the maximum incoming message size in kilobytes.

Setting the Message Size Limits of Outgoing Messages

To set the message size limits of outgoing messages, perform the following:

1. Click Start|Programs|Administrative Tools|Active Directory Users And Computers.
2. In the console tree, double-click Users, or double-click the node that contains the recipient information you are modifying.
3. In the Details pane, double-click the mailbox-enabled user you are modifying.

4. On the Exchange General tab, click Delivery Restrictions.
5. In the Delivery Restrictions dialog box, select Maximum KB under Outgoing Message Size, and then type the maximum outgoing message size limit in kilobytes.

Setting Message Restrictions for Mailbox-Enabled Users

By default, mailbox-enabled users can accept messages from everyone in an Exchange organization. You can set restrictions so that messages can be accepted only from a specific list of recipients; or you can allow messages to be accepted from everyone except a specific list of recipients.

1. Click Start|Programs|Administrative Tools|Active Directory Users And Computers.
2. In the console tree, double-click Users, or double-click the node that contains the recipient information you are modifying.
3. On the Exchange General tab, click Delivery Restrictions.
4. In the Delivery Restrictions dialog box, do one of the following:
   - Select From Everyone under Message Restrictions to accept all messages from everyone in the organization.
   - Select Only From under Message Restrictions, and then click Add to accept only messages coming from particular users.
   - Select From Everyone Except under Message Restrictions and then click Add to accept all messages from everyone in the organization except from particular persons or groups.

Delegating Sending Permissions

Delegating another user is granting that user permission to a particular mailbox. Delegated privileges are granted to users who should be sending on behalf of the person who gave the delegate access. The usual scenario for this is between the boss and the secretary. The boss gives the secretary delegate permission so the secretary can reply to important emails while the boss is not available. To delegate sending permissions, perform the following:

1. Click Start|Programs|Administrative Tools|Active Directory Users And Computers.
2. In the console tree, double-click Users, or double-click the node that contains the recipient information you are modifying.

3. In the Details pane, double-click the recipient whose sending privileges you want to delegate.
4. On the Exchange General tab, click Delivery Options.
5. In the Delivery Options dialog box, click Add.
6. In the Select Recipient dialog box, under Name, select the recipient you want to send email on behalf of the mailbox-enabled user, and then click Add. Repeat this step for each recipient.

Setting Forwarding Address

You can set a forwarding address for a mailbox-enabled user. A forwarding address is configured if you want to have duplicate copies of an email. You use this if you maintain several email accounts or if you want another user to receive all your incoming messages. Forwarding address is set too if you will be away from the office and you can't access the corporate mail. Forwarded messages can be delivered to both the forwarding address and the user's mailbox.

1. Click Start|Programs|Administrative Tools|Active Directory Users And Computers.
2. In the console tree, double-click Users, or double-click the node that contains the recipient information you are modifying.
3. In the Details pane, double-click the recipient you want to modify.
4. On the Exchange General tab, click Delivery Options.
5. In the Delivery Options dialog box, click Forward To under Forwarding Address, and then click Modify.
6. In the Select Recipient dialog box, select a recipient under Name, and then click OK.
7. (Optional) To have forwarded messages delivered to both the forwarding address and the user's mailbox, select the Deliver Messages To Both Forwarding Address And Mailbox checkbox.

Setting Recipient Limits

The number of recipients a mailbox-enabled user can send messages to is limited. You can set the maximum number of recipients to the default recipient limit under Global Settings in System Manager, or you can specify the maximum number of recipients the mailbox-enabled user can send messages to.

Configuring the Maximum Number of Recipients Sent Messages

To configure the maximum number of recipients to which a mailbox-enabled user can send messages, perform the following:

1. Click Start|Programs|Administrative Tools|Active Directory Users And Computers.
2. In the console tree, double-click Users, or double-click the node that contains the recipient information you are modifying.
3. In the Details pane, double-click the mailbox-enabled recipient you are modifying.
4. On the Exchange General tab, click Delivery Options.
5. In the Delivery Options dialog box, click Maximum Recipients under Recipient Limits, and then type a number.

Setting the Mailbox Storage Limit

Storage limit defines the maximum mailbox storage for each mailbox-enabled user, and how you want the system to act in response to mailboxes that exceed the limits. A mailbox-enabled user that exceeds the mailbox limit is first warned or can be prohibited to send and receive emails.

1. Click Start|Programs|Administrative Tools|Active Directory Users And Computers.
2. In the console tree, double-click Users, or double-click the node that contains the recipient information you are modifying.
3. In the Details pane, double-click the mailbox-enabled user you want to set storage limits for.
4. On the Exchange General tab, click Storage Limits.
5. In the Storage Limits dialog box, click to clear the Use Mailbox Store Defaults checkbox under Storage Limits.
6. To specify the maximum amount of space that a mailbox can occupy before a warning message is sent to the user, select the Issue Warning At (KB) checkbox, and then type the storage limit in the text box.

NOTE: *The value you specify for Issue Warning At (KB) should be less than the value you specify for Prohibit Send At (KB). The value you specify for Prohibit Send And Receive At (KB) should be greater than the value you specify for Prohibit Send At (KB).*

---

7. To specify the maximum amount of space that a mailbox can occupy before the user is prohibited from sending more messages, select the Prohibit Send At (KB) checkbox, and then type the storage limit in the text box.
8. To specify the maximum amount of space that a mailbox can occupy before the user is prohibited from sending or receiving more messages, select the Prohibit Send And Receive At (KB) checkbox, and then type the storage limit in the text box.

Configuring the Deleted Item Retention Period

If mailbox-enabled users do not permanently delete a deleted item, it is stored on the server for a certain number of days before Exchange permanently deletes it. You can set the length of the deleted item retention period by either using the mailbox store defaults or selecting the number of days a deleted item is kept before it is permanently deleted.

1. Click Start|Programs|Administrative Tools|Active Directory Users And Computers.
2. In the console tree, double-click Users, or double-click the node that contains the recipient information you are modifying.
3. In the Details pane, double-click the recipient you are modifying.
4. On the Exchange General tab, click Storage Limits.
5. In the Storage Limits dialog box, click to clear the Use Mailbox Store Defaults checkbox, and then type a value in Keep Deleted Items For (Days).
6. To prevent deleted items from being permanently deleted before they are backed up, select the Do Not Permanently Delete Items Until The Store Has Been Backed Up checkbox.

Setting Limits for Message Size

A mail-enabled recipient is allowed to send messages of any size. Message limits are configured on the recipient's Properties dialog box, so to set the message size of No Limit to a particular mail-enabled recipient, it has to be done individually. To set unlimited message size, perform the following:

1. Click Start|Programs|Administrative ToolsActive Directory Users And Computers.

2. In the console tree, double-click Users, or double-click the node that contains the recipient information you are modifying.
3. In the Details pane, double-click the recipient you went to set an unlimited message size for.
4. On the Exchange General tab, select No Limit under Message Size.

Setting Maximum Message Size Limit

You can set the maximum message size limit for a mail-enabled recipient. Because message limits are set in the mail-enabled recipient's Properties dialog box, you can set maximum size limits on an individual basis. Message size restrictions reduce the amount of disk space required to store messages.

1. On the Exchange General tab, select Maximum (KB) under Message Size.
2. Type the maximum message size allowed for messages in kilobytes.

Setting Message Restrictions for Mail-Enabled Recipients

By default, mail-enabled objects accept messages from everyone in an Exchange organization. You can set restrictions so that messages can be accepted only from a specific list of recipients, or you can allow messages to be accepted from everyone except a specific list of recipients. Configuring message restrictions on mail-enabled recipients is the same as configuring the message restrictions on a mailbox-enabled user.

Enabling and Disabling Exchange Features

If additional features or services are added on the Exchange Server, you can enable these new features on each user. If you want to discontinue a particular feature for a specific user, you also can disable it. You can enable and disable a user from using Exchange functionality in several ways. One way is to use the Exchange Feature tab on the Properties pages of the user. You also can use the Exchange task on the list of tasks available when you right-click the username from Active Directory Users And Computers. You can circumvent these manual steps by creating a policy for each on the settings you want to implement. You can create a recipient policy to define the email address and to set the primary email address. You can create a mailbox store policy to define the mailbox storage limit and the deleted items retention period.

Installing a SMTP Connector

The Exchange 2000 SMTP Connector is comparable to the Internet Mail Service (IMS) in earlier versions. In fact, in systems upgraded from Exchange 5.5, IMS is turned into a SMTP connector, and IMS address spaces are added to a single SMTP connector. Although it's possible that not all information will transfer over, the Exchange upgrade log provides details on any such "lost" information. To reach other messaging systems, SMTP connector relies on DNS (Domain Name System) Mail Exchanger (MX) Record, or a smart host for message transmission.

1. Click Start|Programs|Administrative Tools|Exchange System Manager.
2. Navigate to Connectors node.
3. Right-click Connectors, and choose New|SMTP Connector.
4. On the General tab, type the name of the connector (usually the name of the routing group to which you are connecting).
5. Select Use DNS To Route To Each Address Space On This Connector, which specifies the address to use in MX Records, or select Forward All Mail Through This Connector To Following Smart Host. Then, type the name or IP address of the server through which you want to route messages for this remote domain. This value overrides the smart host setting on the Delivery tab of the SMTP Virtual Server properties.
6. On the General tab, click Add under Local Bridgeheads, and then select a local bridgehead server from the list.
7. On the Address Space tab, click Add. Select an address type, and then type all necessary information in Properties, including cost.

***NOTE:** Alternatively, you can click New on the Connected Routing Groups tab. On the General tab, in Organization, type the name of the organization that contains the routing group to which you want to connect. Then type the name of the routing group to which you want to connect. The organization must exist on an Exchange Server so that the naming conventions are known. On the Routing Address tab, type the email domain name of the organization to which you want to connect and then type a cost between 1 and 100.*

After installing the SMTP Connector, some post-configuration tasks have to be completed. These tasks include the configuration of the delivery options, outbound security, and Advanced options. Configure or view these parameters in the Properties pages of the SMTP Connector.

Viewing SMTP Connector Properties Pages

To view the SMTP Connector Properties pages, perform the following:

1. Click Start|Programs|Administrative Tools| Exchange System Manager.
2. Navigate to Connectors node.
3. Right-click an SMTP Connector, and then click Properties.
4. To configure the settings for the delivery options, outbound security, and the Advanced options, select their corresponding tabs shown in Figure 13.7.

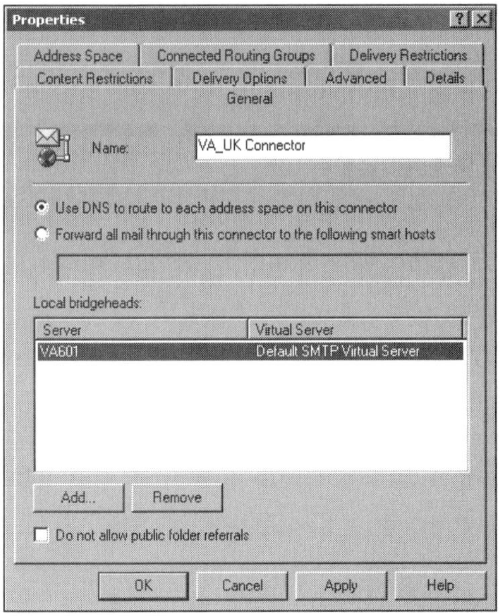

Figure 13.7 Configuration information on the SMTP Connector Properties page.

Setting the Connection Schedule

To set the Connection Schedule, perform the following:

1. Click Start|Programs|Administrative Tools|Exchange System Manager.
2. Navigate to Connectors node.
3. Right-click a Connector, and then click Properties.
4. Click the Schedule tab, and then click Never, Always, Selected Times, or Remote Initiated to specify this connector's availability.
5. To specify times when the X.400 Connector initiates a connection, click the Selected Times option, and then highlight the appropriate times on the timetable grid. You can highlight areas on the timetable grid by holding down the left mouse button, and dragging the mouse over the areas of the table you want to highlight. Shaded areas represent selected time periods. Within a highlighted area, you can clear certain times by holding down the left mouse button and dragging the mouse again. To change the level of detail of the grid, select 1 Hour or 15 Minutes in the Detail view.

Configuring the RGC Delivery Option

To configure the RGC Delivery Option, perform the following:

1. Click Start|Programs|Administrative Tools|Exchange System Manager.
2. Navigate to Connectors node.
3. Right-click a Routing Group SMTP Connector, click Properties, and then click the Delivery Options tab.
4. To specify times when messages are sent through the connector, select one of the standard values in the Connection Time drop-down list. The default is Always Run.

NOTE: *Alternatively, you can click Customize, and select the appropriate connection times on the timetable grid. To change the level of detail on the grid, in Detail View, select 1 Hour or 15 Minutes.*

5. To specify delivery times based on message size, select Use Different Delivery Times For Oversize Messages. In If Oversize Messages Are Greater Than (KB), type the size, in kilobytes, of messages you want to designate as oversized. Under Connection Time, specify times when oversized messages are sent, as described in the previous step.

Chapter 14

Maintenance and Troubleshooting

If you need an immediate solution to:	*See page:*
Monitoring Processor Loads in Exchange 2000	595
Optimizing Memory Usage in Exchange 2000	596
Optimizing Virtual Memory Allocation for Servers with More Than 1GB of RAM	596
Configuring a Server Monitor to Track Available Virtual Memory	600
Configuring Notifications When Your Server Runs Low on Available Virtual Memory	604
Setting Limits on the Number of SMTP Messages in Queues	605
Manipulating SMTP Queues in System Manager	607
Using a SP to Ensure Messages Queued for External Connectors and the MTA Don't Disappear	608
Performing an Offline Defragmentation of Your Databases	609
Running **ESEUTIL** in Repair or Integrity Mode Using **/X** or **/V**	610
Checking Your Databases for Consistency	611
Enabling Circular Logging for a SG	612
Writing Transaction Log Files to a Different Directory or Drive	613

In Depth

Monitoring a complex system such as Exchange 2000 Server on a regular basis is a necessary component of preventive maintenance for a server. The monitoring process yields valuable information and data, which is used to diagnose problems that might be recurring in your organization. This same process also can be used to project future capacity and resource planning for your organization. If, for example, your current server is not configured with proper amounts of memory, message queues can grow to unacceptable levels. Many organizations provide some guarantee of service with respect to message delivery for the users within that organization. Users are promised various levels of service that are defined in a written agreement known as a Service Level Agreement (SLA). The purpose of the SLA is to set expected levels of performance for various departments and users inside the organization. Because different users and departments will have different needs regarding email delivery and performance, the SLA has to be specific regarding the action the company will take if these service levels do not meet the stated customer requirements. If a company wants to maintain these levels of service for their users, they must adhere to a well-defined maintenance schedule for mission-critical servers (such as Exchange 2000) that provide business-critical services for the entire organization.

NOTE: *If expected levels of performance cannot be met for a given user or department, the company should consider providing some type of service "credit" to that user or department. For instance, if a department is being charged for usage of an organizational email system (based on the number of messages sent or received per day), then this department will be credited for an amount equal to the number of messages not received because of poor server performance or message queues that are constantly backed up.*

No system is perfect, however. Regardless of how much performance-tuning measures you perform on your servers, you will encounter errors that are immune to short-term quick fixes. These types of problems might require more intensive disaster recovery procedures (some of which were covered in Chapter 8). As system administrator, you are responsible for ensuring that your Exchange 2000 Servers run at optimal performance levels given the tools that Microsoft provides.

Establishing Goals for Maintaining Your Exchange 2000 Organization

Designing maintenance goals requires a concerted effort of everyone who will maintain your Exchange 2000 Servers. The objective in maintaining a system is to prevent failure of this system, so maintaining an Exchange 2000 system involves corollary actions of tuning and optimizing system parameters to minimize the overall risk of disaster. Unlike Exchange 5.5, Exchange 2000 does not provide a single tool or utility that optimizes system performance. Exchange 5.5 provided administrators with the Performance Optimizer tool (also known as **Perfwiz.exe**). This tool allowed administrators to specify a desired configuration using a graphical user interface (GUI) tool that was enabled at the end of a typical installation of Exchange 5.5. Exchange 2000 does not provide this tool because Microsoft wanted a system capable of higher levels of self-tuning and optimization compared to earlier versions of Exchange Server. Because Exchange 2000 offers more dynamic system changes than Exchange 5.5, administrators can spend less time performing manual optimizing or configuration.

Exchange 2000 is not, however, a completely independent system because it can still be vulnerable to disaster if left unattended. Administrators still have opportunities to tweak system parameters and enhance system performance. The challenge that administrators face is selecting the appropriate set of parameters to manage or tune. Tuning or optimizing system parameters does not always lead to enhanced performance. For example, you could make a change to the Registry within Windows 2000 in an effort to optimize settings for the Message Transfer Agent (MTA), but an incorrect setting suddenly can increase message latency over your unreliable wide area network (WAN) links for one of your remote offices. Planning and documenting all configuration changes can help avert problems down the road.

Your maintenance goals should be categorized according to common activities. For instance, you should list the objects or resources that you are trying to maintain on a regular daily, weekly, monthly, or even yearly basis. Most resources include hardware, such as servers, and software including clients. Best practices recommend setting maintenance goals for all resources upon which you depend to provide messaging and collaborative services.

Developing Maintenance Goals for Resource Management

Most organizations are concerned with managing three separate types of objects: the servers that host Exchange 2000, the clients that connect to these servers, and the network topology that allows mail to flow between servers inside the or outside your organization. Establishing plans to monitor and maintain these resources helps you plan for and prevent a majority of issues that could arise at any time. These issues can disrupt normal messaging operations at best, or cause complete system failure at worst.

The difficulty level of monitoring or maintaining server resources depends on the server and storage hardware choices you've made in your organization. It also depends on the level of usage that is expected for these resources. Heavily used resources demand more frequent levels of monitoring than resources that are less frequently used. Different organizations have different Exchange 2000 configurations requiring different levels of monitoring or maintenance. For instance, Exchange 2000 can be configured with varying numbers of storage groups (SGs) or databases. Every organization also experiences varying levels of server load in terms of the number of users who access the server either inside or outside the organization. In all these cases, you are monitoring the collective performance of one primary resource, your Exchange 2000 Server(s).

Monitoring client resources and the network topology are closely associated because you must not only maintain software clients connected to your Exchange 2000 Server, but also the server software and routing topology used to deliver messages to these clients. If, for example, your users are trying unsuccessfully to access Outlook Web Access (OWA), you are better equipped to solve this issue by determining whether its primarily a server-related issue, a client-related issue, or a topology-related issue. After you find the source of the problem, you can monitor the issue to determine whether longer-term issues are involved. For example, in the previous scenario, a problem with the Internet Information Server (IIS) in Windows 2000 caused the default Web site to stop functioning properly, which caused problems with Internet mail clients and OWA. Monitoring this might demonstrate that the IIS service was accidentally disabled, or that the IIS Service itself is unstable within Windows 2000 and should be corrected with the latest hotfix or Service Pack (SP) (easily downloaded from **www.microsoft.com**).

TIP: *Microsoft always recommends downloading and installing the latest Service Pack or hotfix from their Web site (which you can find by typing "http://www.microsoft.com/downloads/search.asp)". Service Packs and hotfixes exist for both Windows 2000 and Exchange 2000 and should be installed separately. In other words, do not assume that a service pack for Windows 2000 will resolve all issues occurring with Exchange 2000 Server, or vice versa.*

Features That Need Tuning

Exchange 2000 provides certain features that are easily optimized through a regular maintenance and tuning routine. Some of these features include hard disks, memory, the MTA, the Information Store database, and the Simple Mail Transfer Protocol (SMTP) Service. (Far more features exist than we could cite on this page.) Tuning certain parameters, such as memory, can help you achieve your maintenance goals because not all parameters are dynamically tuned by the server. Exchange 2000 can tune (or optimize) some system parameters dynamically, such as the network interface subsystem in your server—but other parameters—such as the memory subsystem—need manual adjustments.

NOTE: *Memory might need manual adjustment because Exchange 2000 uses all physical memory available by default. If you plan to use other software applications on your Exchange 2000 Server, you have to allocate memory for these applications and restrict the amount of memory used by Exchange 2000.*

To determine the parameters or features that require manual adjustment, you have to collect and analyze server data through monitoring tools such as the Windows 2000 Performance Logs and Alerts snap-in, or the Windows 2000 System Monitor snap-in. Both these tools taken together comprise the Windows 2000 Performance Console accessed through the Start|Programs|Administrative Tools menu. Using tools such as System Monitor allows you to measure important object counters relating to server memory or server hard disks over time. These measurements give you some idea of the underlying characteristics of Exchange 2000. Figures 14.1 and 14.2 illustrate how these snap-ins appear on a typical Exchange 2000 Server.

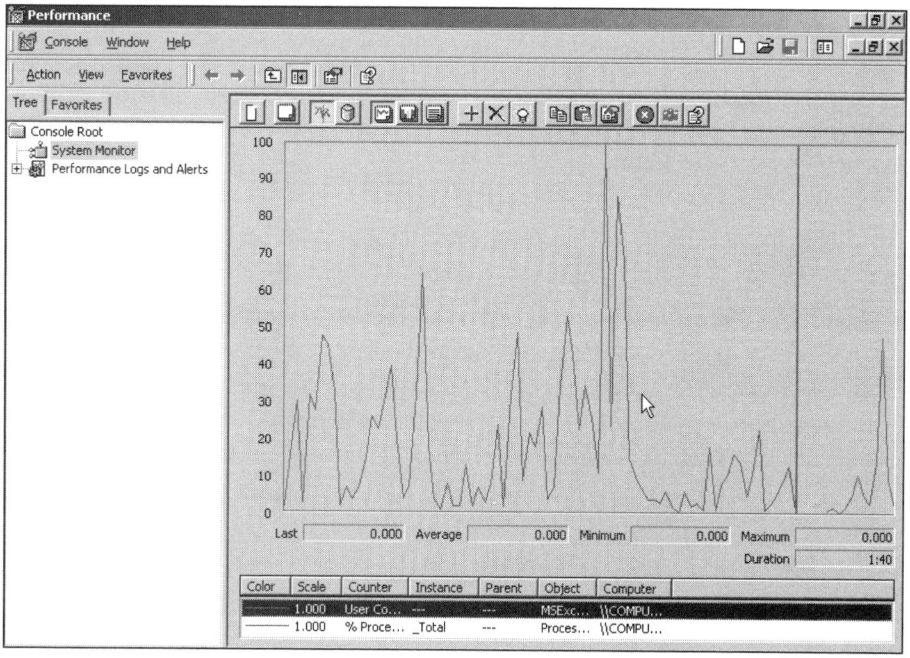

Figure 14.1 The System Monitor snap-in showing a chart of realtime activity for a system.

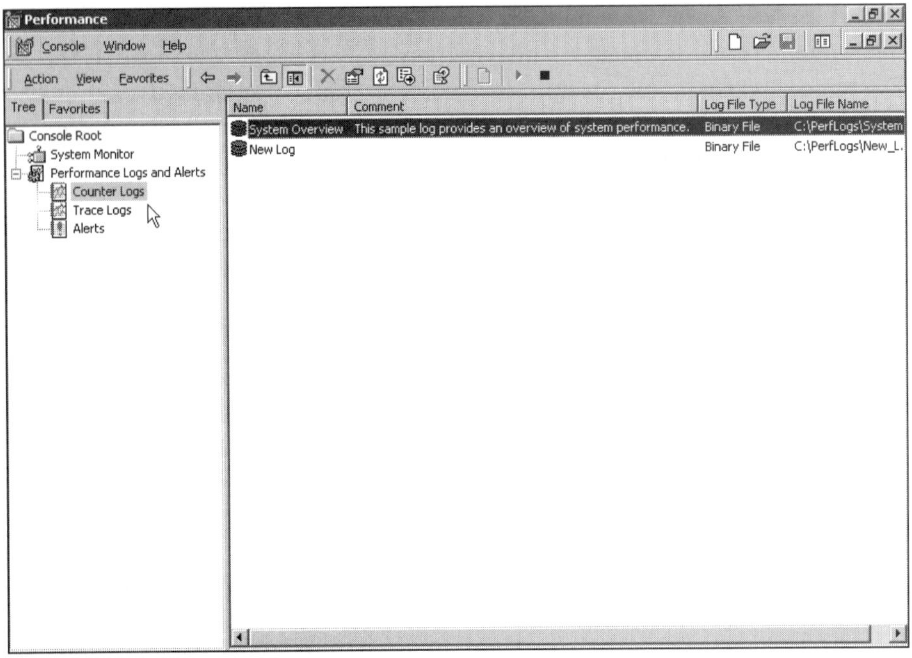

Figure 14.2 The Performance Logs and Alerts snap-in found in the Performance console in Windows 2000.

NOTE: *Only the System Monitor snap-in provides realtime measurements of various objects such as the processor or hard disk in your Exchange 2000 computer. The Performance Logs and Alerts snap-in is used to generate data in counter logs or trace logs, which can be analyzed at some future point in time using a tool such as System Monitor (or even Microsoft Excel or Microsoft Access).*

Resource management within your organization can be broken down into various categories. Examples of these categories include the following:

- *Hardware configuration*—Your overall hardware configuration includes such subsystems as the server processor, server memory, server disk subsystem, and network interface. Each of these various components can be maintained and monitored by tuning or optimizing parameters associated with these components using various Windows 2000 utilities such as the Registry Editor or the Active Directory Services Interface Edit utility (also known as ADSI Edit).

NOTE: *You should also be aware of defragmentation that normally occurs with most hard drive configurations. When users receive many files on one physical disk, these files can sometimes be written in a fragmented fashion to noncontiguous locations on the drive, making it harder to efficiently access these files when needed. Exchange 2000 can perform both online and offline defragmentation of the Information Store files that contain important messages for end users, and most administrators configure defragmentation to occur on a regular basis (for example, every Friday night) to optimize message access for users.*

- *MTA*—This component plays a prominent role in mixed-mode organizations that use a combination of Exchange 5.5 and Exchange 2000 Servers. The MTA is used for most intrasite communications between the servers. The MTA is also heavily used for intersite communications if you use Site Connectors or X.400 Connectors to communicate with external messaging hosts. Finally, the MTA can be tuned for optimal performance when connecting to foreign systems such as Lotus cc:Mail systems or Novell GroupWise systems.
- *SMTP protocol configuration*—The SMTP protocol is the native transport protocol used by Exchange 2000 and is receptive to manual optimization efforts because Exchange 2000 does not dynamically optimize it internally. The SMTP protocol exists in a basic form within Windows 2000 Server and is given extra functionality within Exchange 2000 (in terms of being more robust); however, certain manual adjustments—such as changing directory location for SMTP files—show a positive performance gain.
- *Web Storage System (WSS) and database configuration*—Exchange 2000 attempts to optimize the Information Store performance, you can make manual adjustments while monitoring the service to realize even greater efficiencies of scale in special situations. These components require some type of online maintenance so that the Information Store is kept in an optimal state without fragmentation or corruption.
- *The Windows 2000 Active Directory (AD)*—Any configuration changes here have a direct impact on certain Exchange 2000 components—such as the Active Directory Connector (ADC). Even though the ADC normally doesn't require much manual tuning, you can effect changes in the ADC's replication cycle by adjusting Registry entries in the Windows 2000 Registry Editor (**regedit.exe**).

WARNING! The Registry is one of the most useful tools in Windows 2000, but should be handled with extreme care. Back up your current Registry database by exporting it to some external file before making any type of configuration change inside the Registry. Only edit the Registry when you have no other alternative that will help you achieve your configuration objectives!

- *OWA configuration*—This client-side parameter can be tuned for multiple configuration items, including content expiration. Maintaining optimal client-side configurations means that network traffic and server resources also can be optimized as a result. For example, increasing the time period in which clients request information from a server optimizes and reduces network traffic when clients access their email using the OWA client.

The example detailed in the following paragraph shows how server resources can be maintained and monitored within an actual Exchange 2000 organization, especially in configurations involving Symmetric Multiprocessing (SMP) Servers, or servers that contain an extraordinary amount of physical RAM (say, over 1GB of RAM). These latter configurations benefit from established maintenance routines to optimize performance.

Suppose you are managing an Exchange 2000 organization consisting of 5,000 users. You want to allow users to perform fast searches for object information using their Outlook 2000 clients. You also want them to take advantage of advanced communication features offered through the Exchange 2000 Conferencing Server (an additional product you can purchase separately from the Exchange 2000 Server or Enterprise Server editions of Exchange). What activities can you perform to both optimize and maintain the performance of these services?

NOTE: *The goals of optimization and maintenance are not mutually exclusive. Monitoring and maintaining a service usually result in optimization of this service, especially if you begin to notice bottlenecks in your systems. Simply watching how a system behaves without performing proper corrective procedures on this system might lead to substandard or unacceptable levels of performance and, in extreme cases, system failure resulting from data corruption.*

If you configure the full-text indexing feature of Exchange 2000, users can search through extremely large amounts of Information Stored in Exchange 2000 and retrieve information they want within a matter of seconds (this also depends on the hardware configuration being used). Full-text indexing works in conjunction with the Microsoft Search service and can place an enormous load on the server's CPU. Therefore, you should consider upgrading the server processor or adding multiple processors to distribute the server workload for full-text indexing. A slow processor takes time to build index catalogs and users will complain that they cannot perform efficient searches for data, even data that has been recently added to the Global Catalog (GC). This is one example of server tuning and optimization inspired by monitoring current conditions relating to a particular feature within Exchange 2000.

Table 14.1 summarizes some of the hardware resources you can monitor to determine whether optimal levels are being used. The resources are considered objects if you are using the System Monitor utility, and Table 14.1 shows relevant counters and thresholds for some important hardware resources used by Exchange 2000 and Windows 2000 Server.

Table 14.1 Resource monitoring in Exchange 2000.

Monitored Resource Object	Counters Associated with the Object	Description of Counter	Appropriate Counter Threshold to Monitor
Memory	Pages/Sec	Total activity occurring when applications reference data not located in physical memory	A value consistently over "10" could indicate a performance bottleneck.

continued

Table 14.1 Resource monitoring in Exchange 2000 *(continued).*

Monitored Resource Object	Counters Associated with the Object	Description of Counter	Appropriate Counter Threshold to Monitor
Memory	Available Bytes	Amount of physical memory still available to the system	If the server is running 256MB or less of physical RAM, at least 4MB of RAM always should be available to the system.
Process	Virtual Bytes	The amount of virtual memory available to each process in your system	Should not approach 2GB of virtual memory on Windows NT 4 or 3GB of virtual memory on Windows NT 4 Enterprise Edition.
LogicalDisk	Average Disk Queue Length	The average queue length during a monitoring period	Should not exceed two spindles for normal operations.
Processor	% Processor Time	The time the processor is running active threads	If consistently over 75 percent, the server could be overloaded.
Redirector	Bytes Total/sec	The total bytes sent per second and received by the network redirector service on your network	Should be monitored for constant increases but no defined threshold as for other parameters described here.
MSExchangeMTA	Work Queue Length	The queue length for the entire MTA covering both inbound and outbound messages for the Information Store	If greater than zero for sustained periods of time, it might indicate problems with connectors or remote MTA service.
MSExchange Private + Public	Average Time for Local Delivery	The average time taken for the last 10 messages for local delivery within the Information Store	This should never remain at a *non-zero* value for more than a few seconds, otherwise it could indicate backlogs in the local delivery queue of the **Store.exe** process.

Developing Maintenance Goals for Service Levels in Your Organization

Defining service levels within your organization ensures that all users can benefit from reliable and efficient messaging flows. By defining certain levels of service, you can better focus your performance measurement routine and monitor those processes or services that directly impact your agreed-upon service levels. Service levels help you project the future need for technical support resources in an effective manner when problems surface later on. To provide these future levels of service, you need to establish current baselines of performance. These baselines form a foundation against which you can compare future levels of messaging activity. If users are constantly exceeding baseline thresholds that you set (for example, the number of messages being sent during an eight-hour period is greater than the number you originally anticipated with your baseline), steps can be taken to enhance server resources to support the new projected levels of messaging that users need.

When establishing baselines, you should track basic messaging functionality such as:

- *The times that the messaging server will be available*—Not all systems are up 24 hours a day, seven days a week, for example, unless you are an application hosting organization or application service provider (ASP) that promises this type of messaging functionality for your clients.
- *The average time you expect for messages to be delivered*—You can determine this in a test environment by sending a variety of message sizes and attachment sizes to determine the length of time it takes for these messages to be sent.
- *The average time taken to read a message*—This helps determine how long messages will sit in the Information Store, which could possibly tie up system resources such as hard disk space. You could use this information to help configure deleted-item retention periods, for example.

You also have to define certain assumptions about your environment before attempting to establish a baseline. For example, what maximum mailbox size are you willing to give your users? What is the average message size being sent within your organization? If you cannot plan these items in advance, it will be difficult to configure optimal messaging settings in the future. The usage levels you set up in advance impact service delivery levels expected by your users. These usage levels must be monitored on a regular basis so changes can be easily detected. For instance, if you notice average message sizes increasing on a regular basis, you can take proactive steps—such as increasing mailbox quotas to accommodate this increase—or you can adopt countermeasures—such as decreasing quotas to prevent users from storing such large messages or attachments.

Control Configuration Changes

When you first install Exchange 2000, many default configurations are put into place. For example, Exchange 2000 automatically creates a SG for all users called First Storage Group. If you only used these default settings in your organization, your administrative duties would certainly be simplified. You would not benefit from the full functionality of Exchange 2000. For example, a single SG isn't accessible while it is being backed up.

Based on the premise that you will configure advanced settings that enhance these default configurations of Exchange 2000, you must document all configuration changes to your original system and also prevent unauthorized users from arbitrarily changing your configuration settings. All such changes should be authorized and written in a Change Log, which is kept under strict administrative overview. This Change Log should contain columns for the following:

- *Activity performed*—To document the exact configuration setting that is being undertaken and the purpose of this setting (how it helps or the impact it will have).
- *Responsible party*—To indicate who was authorized to make this change (or who was asked to make this change).
- *Change date*—To indicate the exact day and time for error-tracking purposes. If serious errors occur due to a specific configuration change, you can determine whether the impact of this change has had time to affect multiple components of your system.

Controlling configuration changes is highly recommended to effectively monitor and maintain your server and client resources. Configuration management is a good way to focus on problem avoidance in your organization.

Tools for Maintaining and Monitoring Exchange 2000

The previous section encouraged you to adopt a proactive approach in establishing performance baselines within your organization. You will use a variety of tools to do this, so it's helpful to know which tools are useful for monitoring the services that Exchange 2000 depends on. Such tools include the following:

- *Event Viewer*—Found in the Administrative Tools section of the Programs menu (Start|Programs|Administrative Tools|Event Viewer), this tool is available as a standalone snap-in, or as part of the Microsoft Management Console (MMC). It is used to evaluate error and warning information returned by services that are not functioning correctly. Exchange 2000 usually records service or application errors in the Application Event Log.

TIP: Check these logs at least once a day because Exchange 2000 and Windows 2000 constantly update them with system-specific information. If any of the logs becomes full, you are presented with a message box informing you to either save or clear your Event Viewer logs.

- *Active Directory Users and Computers*—Found inside Start|Programs|Administrative Tools or Start|Programs|Microsoft Exchange, this tool allows you to view Exchange 2000 attributes of all mail-enabled or mailbox-enabled objects that you create. Every mail-enabled object or mailbox-enabled object has four Exchange-related tabs in its Properties settings: Exchange General, Exchange Advanced, Email Addresses, and Exchange Features. Only mailbox-enabled users have more settings that can be configured on the Exchange General and Exchange Advanced tabs.
- *Exchange System Manager*—A departure from the Exchange 5.5 Administrator utility, this management interface is found by clicking Start|Programs|Microsoft Exchange|System Manager. This MMC snap-in is used to manage various Exchange 2000 objects, including administrative groups, routing groups, system policies, and recipient policies. The following sections describe additional functionality of the System Manager snap-in.

Many tools are provided by both Windows 2000 and Exchange 2000 from your maintenance arsenal, some provided by Windows 2000 and some provided by Exchange 2000. Windows 2000 provides the Event Viewer snap-in, the Active Directory Users and Computers snap-in, the Task Manager utility, and the Performance Console. Exchange 2000 provides the System Manager snap-in, the Active Directory Users and Computers snap-in (to store Exchange 2000 attributes not found within the Windows 2000 version), and the Migration Wizard by default. If you install or deploy the ADC (a tool that synchronizes an Exchange 5.5 directory database with the AD database in Windows 2000 during a migration to Exchange 2000), you will notice new tools within the System Manager program group—such as the Active Directory Connector Management console, and the Active Directory Account Cleanup Wizard.

NOTE: The Active Directory Account Cleanup Wizard is used to merge duplicate accounts created during an upgrade to Exchange 2000 from Exchange 5.5.

All the tools just mentioned are used in some capacity to manage critical system resources. The tools provided by Windows 2000 or Exchange 2000 can be used to set specific server monitors and server notifications to alert you when critical services have stopped functioning. An ongoing system maintenance schedule can help address slow server response times or delays in message deliveries to your users. This section covers three important topics related to maintaining critical Exchange 2000 Services:

- Configuring server monitors and link monitors.
- Maintaining SMTP queues.
- Performing database optimization on SGs and message databases.

Using Server Monitors for Exchange 2000 Maintenance

You can view the status of all the Exchange 2000 servers in your organization using the Exchange System Manager snap-in. You can enable server monitors to show the system resource usage, such as CPU use or the amount of free disk space in your server. Notifications can be configured to alert you via email when problems arise.

Exchange 2000 polls or queries all servers located in your organization and displays their statuses in the right-hand pane of the System Manager snap-in. A server is Available (all services are running properly), Critical (it's available, but one or more services have stopped functioning for some reason), or Unreachable (a server is physically down or disconnected from the network).

NOTE: *If you see a red "X" next to a server or connector in System Manager, that server or connector is in a critical state or it is unreachable. If you see a yellow "!" next to these objects, a server monitor you have configured has reached a warning threshold.*

You configure monitors to check the condition of resources on your Exchange 2000 Server. A default monitor known as the Default Microsoft Exchange Service is created when you first install Exchange 2000 in your organization. This default monitor specifically checks the progress of these conditions:

- *Available virtual memory*—A low setting here could degrade your server performance. Maintaining or optimizing this setting involves adding more RAM if usage levels increase or message sizes increase. You might configure all services to stop if available virtual memory ever dips below 5 percent of total available memory.
- *CPU use*—A high setting could cause other applications to hang. You don't want CPU use to approach 100 percent usage levels, so you might want to configure a warning level of 95 percent use and 100 percent only for critical levels of use.
- *Free disk space*—You want to maintain sufficient space on your hard drives for messaging databases and transaction logs. If disk space becomes unavailable, critical Exchange 2000 Services might not function at all. For example, you can configure your system to notify you with a warning if disk space falls below 75MB, and alert you if disk space falls below 20MB. You even can specify that multiple hard drives be monitored.

- *Windows 2000 Services*—You can add most Windows 2000 Services and even some Exchange 2000 Services into one *service group*. When one or more services within this group stops functioning, System Manager indicates a warning or critical state for this monitor. It is possible to create multiple monitors for multiple groups of services and give each monitor a different name.
- *X.400 queue growth*—You want to maintain the growth in the number of messages in your queues. You might want to consider setting a warning monitor if your queues are growing or expanding for more than 5 minutes. If queue growth occurs for longer periods of time, say over 10–15 minutes, you can configure a critical threshold alert to take place.

Each monitor you configure specifies either a warning state or a critical state, or both. A warning condition indicates a threshold that has been reached in the use of some resource. You should resolve any warning conditions as soon as you see them. A critical condition is less tolerant of the passage of time between initial onset and resolution. If a resource reaches a critical state, server performance will be negatively impacted if the issue isn't given immediate attention. You can specify custom warning or critical states as long as you specify higher thresholds for critical conditions than for warning conditions.

Monitors and Notifications

As you already know, a server monitor indicates either a red "X" or a yellow "!" in the Status folder listed in the Tools|Monitoring And Status container in System Manager (see Figure 14.3 for a view of the Status folder in System Manager).

We recommend that you check this container regularly to see the current status of your system. Exchange 2000 also notifies you via email or script when your server has reached warning or critical thresholds. These modifications might make sense if you are frequently away from your server location. It might be best to configure a script that automatically shuts down all services and restarts your server if you are not able to manually shut down your server (if you are away from the office or servicing a remote location when these problems occur, for example).

Maintaining Message Queues

Many tools are available for use within Exchange 2000 that allow you to monitor transport components and transport issues related to basic messaging flows in your organization. Such tools include Diagnostic Logging, Protocol Logging, and the Queue Viewer. This section discusses issues related to message queues, including X.400 and SMTP queues. The Queue Viewer utility helps maintain all messaging queues and is available for SMTP Virtual Servers and MTA-X.400 Connectors.

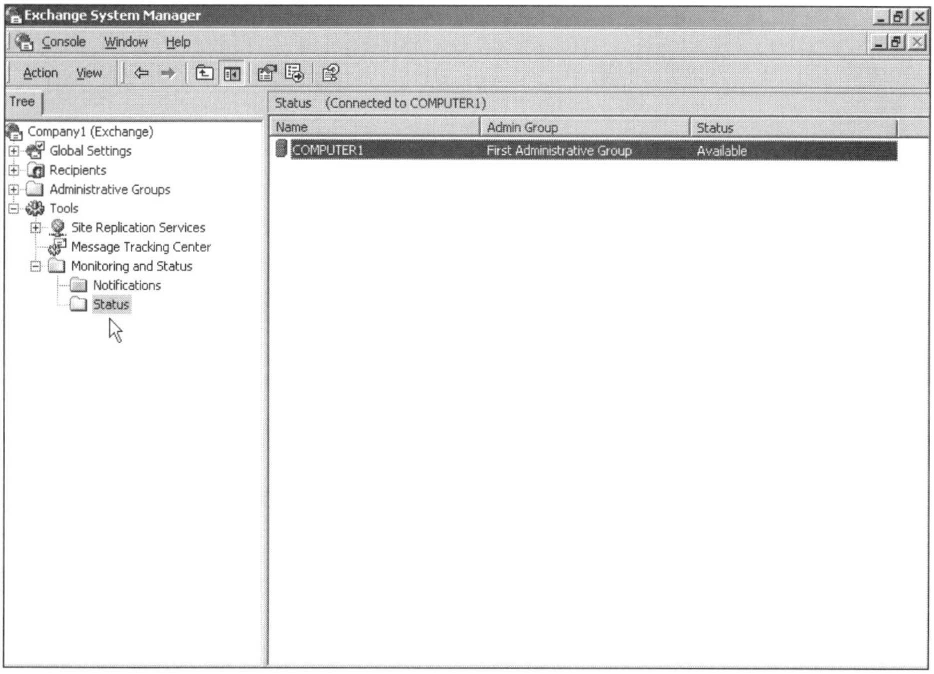

Figure 14.3 The Status folder in System Manager.

Using the Exchange System Manager snap-in, you can access the Queue Viewer utility in a number of ways. After you have opened your organization object (by clicking the "+" next to this icon), you can expand your Administrative Groups folder, and then the First Administrative Group folder (or whichever administrative group you have configured for your organization). Then choose one of the following paths to view the appropriate message queue in System Manager. To view a message queue, locate the Servers container in System Manager, expand this to show your individual *servername*, then expand the Protocols Container. A message queue is found inside the SMTP Container and also the X.400 Container, as shown in Figures 14.4 and 14.5.

NOTE: *If using the SMTP Container to locate the message queue, you must first open the Default SMTP Virtual Server that appears directly under the SMTP Container in System Manager, as Figure 14.4 displays. The X.400 Container displays a Queues subfolder directly underneath without displaying any type of Virtual Server.*

A message queue can also be seen in the Routing Groups container in System Manager by expanding the Routing Groups Container under the First Administrative Group folder, then expanding the First Routing Group folder and the Connectors folder. The Connectors folder will contain all third-party or custom

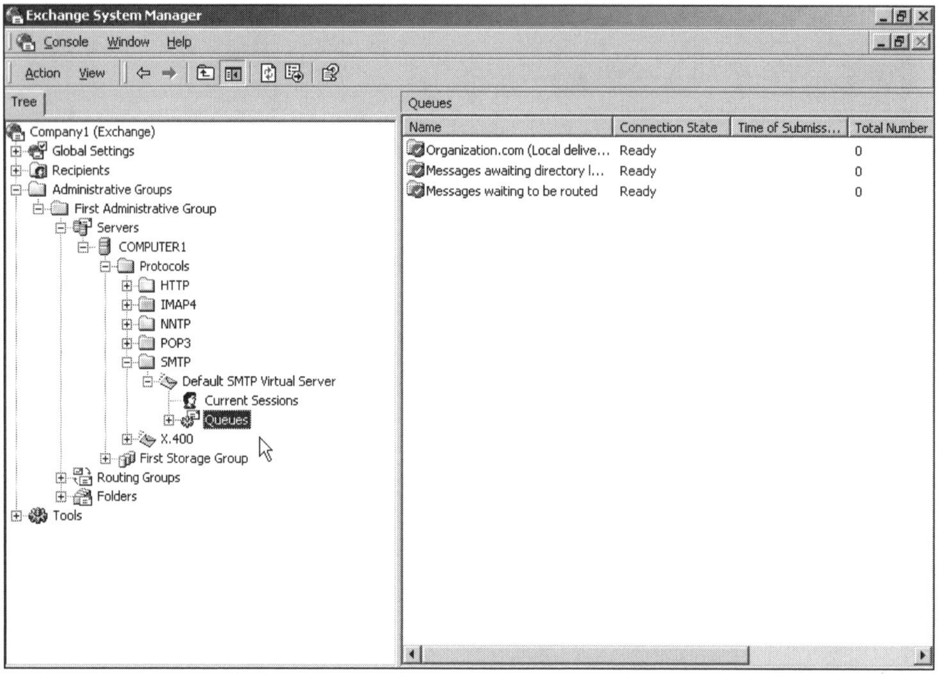

Figure 14.4 The path to the SMTP message queue as seen in System Manager.

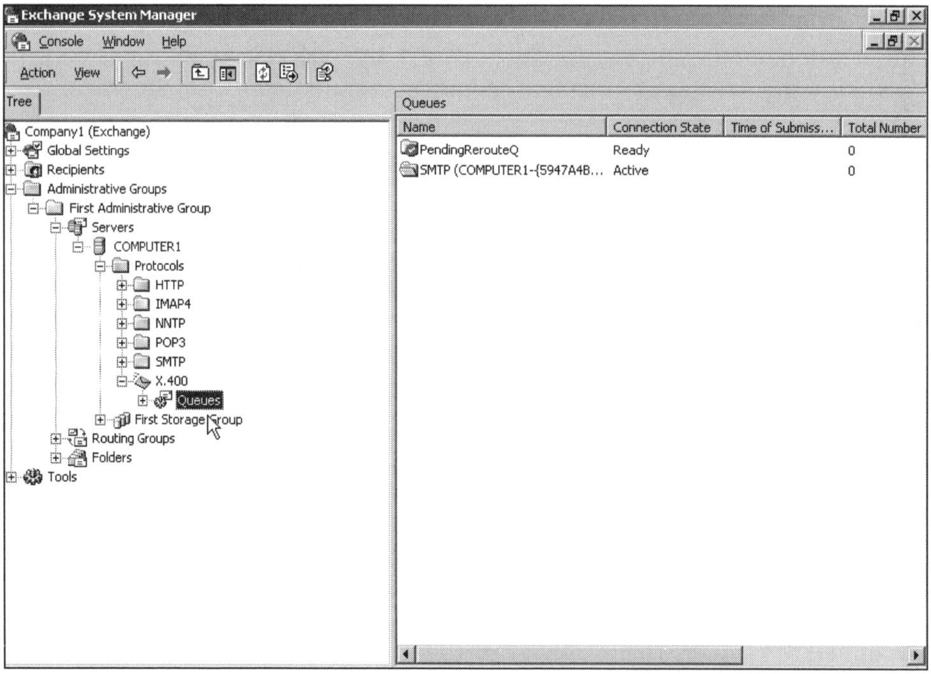

Figure 14.5 The path to the X.400 message queue as seen in System Manager.

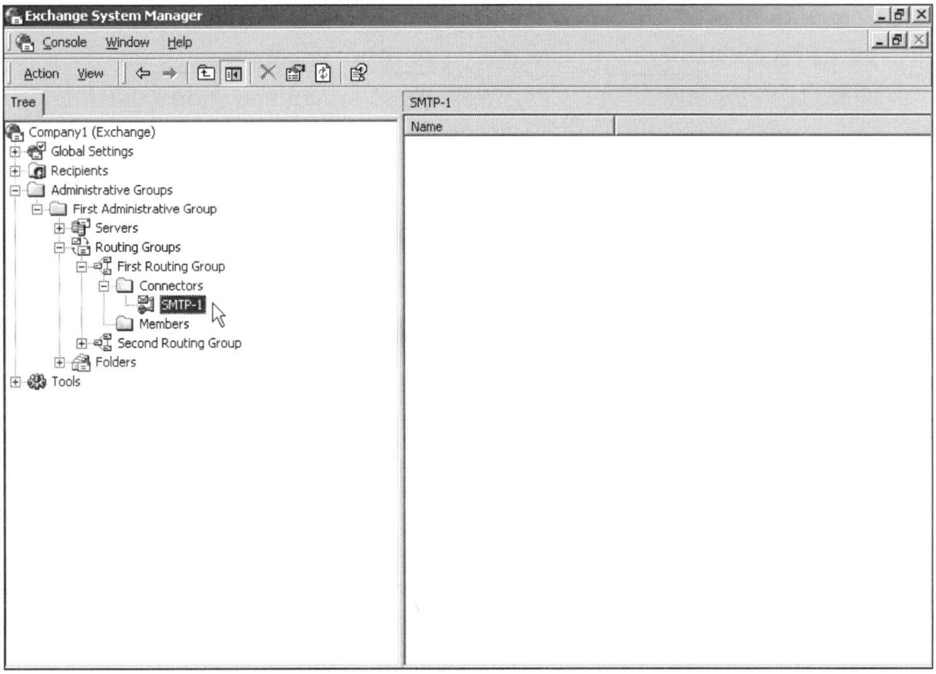

Figure 14.6 **The path to a message queue for a connector found in the Routing Groups Container in System Manager.**

connectors you have configured (such as the Routing Group Connector or the SMTP Connector), and these connectors all have queue folders directly inside them (Figure 14.6 shows a SMTP Connector without a Queue folder in a case in which no messages have been sent).

The first method locates all SMTP queues, the second method locates all X.400 queues, and the third method locates all MAPI (Messaging Application Programming Interface) system queues associated with third-party connectors, such as MS Exchange Connector for Lotus Notes. Whichever method you use, the Queue Viewer displays common information for all queues in System Manager in column form. This information includes the following:

- *Connection State*—This column indicates whether a queue is functioning properly or not. Current connection states include Active (messages are being routed correctly), Frozen (messages are being received into the queue, but not routed or delivered), Ready (the queue is waiting to receive messages and deliver them), Retry (the queue has tried to route messages but has failed for some reason), and Scheduled (the queue waits for some scheduled time to route or deliver messages).

- *Total Number Of Messages*—A large number in this column could point to a potential connection problem within your organization.
- *Time of Submission Of Oldest Message*—This column shows the time that the oldest message in the queue was sent by a client. If this number increases to many days, it could imply that a connector has failed or a network connection is malfunctioning somewhere.
- *Total Message Size In KB*—This column represents the total size of all messages in the queue, measured in kilobytes.
- *Time Of Next Connection Retry*—This column indicates the time that another connection will be made if a queue is in a retry state.

To examine any SMTP-based queue, you need to make sure the SMTP service is started within Windows 2000 Server. Some connectivity also must exist between the Exchange System Manager interface and the SMTP service for you to view the contents of the SMTP queue. Certain queues always are displayed in System Manager, including the queues for local delivery and the queue for messages waiting for directory lookup. Queues for connectors, such as the Routing Group Connector (RGC), are displayed when actual messages are present. X.400 queues are monitored if you have configured any X.400 connectors to remote routing groups. The contents of all X.400 queues are displayed in System Manager only if the Exchange 2000 MTA Stacks service is running in the background. See the Immediate Solutions "Manipulating SMTP Queues in System Manager" for details on specific actions you can perform on all SMTP queues, including the local delivery queue, the messages awaiting directory lookup queue, and the messages waiting to be routed queue.

Maintaining and Optimizing Database Files and SGs

When monitoring your database files or SGs on all your Exchange 2000 servers, you must ensure that you have adequate disk space for all files, including native content files and transaction log files. Many administrators do not plan a regular defragmentation schedule for their server database files, which can seriously impact and downgrade server performance and messaging reliability. Disk defragmentation should be performed on a regular and consistent basis so that message retrieval is not hindered or prevented. Exchange 2000 attempts online defragmentation while all services are still running, however, it may be best to perform offline defragmentation using such tools as **eseutil.exe**. Managing and maintaining these key server components helps ensure messaging consistency and integrity and helps you plan for future growth. The following paragraphs concentrate on performance and scalability characteristics of online maintenance for Exchange 2000 database files, such as disk optimization, multiple SG planning, and online defragmentation of the Information Store.

Optimizing Through Defragmentation

Your initial designs of Exchange 2000 should incorporate considerations of disk capacity, especially concerning the Information Store. The size of this repository and all the databases that come with it will grow in proportion to your user population. As the number of users increases in your organization, so will the frequency and size of messages that these users send to each other. The Information Store has to scale to accommodate the growth that you will be expecting in mailboxes, public folders, connectors, and users. Your goal here is to allocate and control the amount of disk space that can be consumed by these resources by placing appropriate quotas on mailbox or message size. More efficient methods of managing disk space include using multiple SGs within a server, or configuring dedicated hardware for mailbox stores and public folder stores.

These optimization techniques should match your current budgetary and personnel constraints. Sometimes its not possible to deploy a dedicated service configuration in which one computer devotes itself entirely to hosting mailbox stores while another machine devotes itself entirely to public folder stores. Even smaller organizations can benefit from optimization procedures that are relatively easy to implement. By creating additional SGs within your server, you are expanding the amount of information that can flow throughout your organization. You need to develop Exchange 2000 implementations that take full advantage of the scalable architecture that Exchange 2000 is built upon. This architecture allows you to distribute users across multiple databases in one SG (up to five mailbox or public folder stores if running the Enterprise Edition of Exchange 2000), or across multiple SGs in one server (up to four different SGs if running the Enterprise Edition of Exchange 2000).

Unfortunately, when you are planning or configuring multiple databases or SGs, Exchange 2000 doesn't provide a method of determining exactly how much free space exists in a database at any given point in time. Administrators realize that files and databases become fragmented over time because of the dynamic addition of many messages and other types of information that occur within a normal messaging enterprise. If you perform some type of online defragmentation of the databases within the Information Store, you can see how much free space is available in your databases because an event is logged in the system event logs after every online defragmentation of a database. The format of this message looks something like this:

```
Event:  1221
Source: MSExchangeIS Private
Type:   Information
Category: General
Description:  The database has nnn megabytes of free space after online_
defragmentation has terminated
```

The **Eseutil.exe** utility is used to defragment the Information Store in Exchange 2000. In Exchange 5.5, **Eseutil.exe** was used to defragment not only the Information Store, but also the directory database (dir.edb). This utility examines all your database tables and records within those tables. You can find this tool in the *%systemroot%*\Exchsrvr\Bin folder on the local hard drive of your Exchange 2000 computer. It can be run against one database at a time from a command prompt (accessed through Start|Programs|Accessories|Command Prompt). When **Eseutil** defragments a database, it compacts the database to a smaller size, reduces unused storage space, and copies all database records to a new database. After defragmentation is complete, the original database is deleted and the new database is given the name of the original database.

TIP: *Before running* ***Eseutil.exe*** *on your database(s), open the Exchange System Manager snap-in, right-click the Information Store you want defragmented, and click the option to Dismount Store. Then, the defragmentation process can complete normally. If a store is not dismounted when running* ***Eseutil.exe****, you receive an error message stating that the database is in an inconsistent state.*

If you run **Eseutil.exe** from a command prompt, make sure you change to the Exchsrvr\Bin directory where this tool is located, and then type "eseutil /d" along with other switches or options that are used with this tool (see Table 14.2 for a list of switches you can use with **Eseutil.exe**). If you wanted to defragment a mailbox store database called **StoreOne.edb**, you would use the following syntax:

```
C:\exchsrvr\bin > eseutil /d c:\exchsrvr\mdbdata\StoreOne.edb [options]
```

When you defragment a mailbox store database, make sure you have sufficient free disk space. The usual amount of free disk space needed for defragmentation of a database is 110 percent of the total size of the database being defragmented.

Table 14.2 Switches used with the Eseutil utility.

Switch or Option	Purpose
/b [database]	Makes a backup copy of your database using the name specified.
/t [database]	Sets a temporary database name (the default name used is Tempdfrg.edb).
/s [file]	Used to set a streaming file name.
/f [file]	Used to set a temporary streaming file name (the default streaming file is Tempdfrg.stm).
/p	Used to preserve your temporary database. Using this option means that your original database file will be preserved in an uncompacted state and any temporary databases created will hold the defragmented version of the database.
/l	Tells **Eseutil.exe** not to defragment your streaming files.

Therefore, for a database that is approximately 100MBs, you would need approximately 110MB of free disk space for defragmentation purposes.

An interesting situation occurs with respect to defragmentation if you have recently removed a large number of database objects from your server. For example, if you have recently performed an online defragmentation (see the previous paragraph concerning the **Eseutil** utility), and also moved a large group of recipient objects to another Exchange 2000 Server in your organization, you might have to perform an offline defragmentation to make sure the database is in a consistent state. A few organizations have noticed this effect at various times and Microsoft recommends that these companies perform offline defragmentations of their databases if they have attempted to move objects to different servers. The objects are not limited to recipients, however. For instance, if you have recently changed your disk quotas for messages that can be sent, you should perform this offline defragmentation to ensure that your databases are consistent.

Online Maintenance of the Information Store

Performing online defragmentation of all database files is only one aspect of online maintenance of the Information Store. The Information Store actually requires that regular online maintenance procedures be run against every messaging database, or MDB, file that exists. Each MDB file in the Information Store runs online maintenance routines between 1:00 A.M. and 5:00 A.M. by default. These routines are needed to keep the store.exe process in a healthy state and include the following activities:

- *AD lookups*—This routing involves checking for deleted mailboxes in AD, and is done for each user in the database file. This ensures that the Information Store synchronizes with all changes made to the AD database. A large number of users in your organization will require many AD searches for these users using the Lightweight Directory Access Protocol (LDAP). An excessive number of LDAP queries might cause some performance degradation on your AD servers.
- *Online defragmentation*—This process is similar to the defragmentation that occurs with **Eseutil**, except that databases are not compacted and unused storage space is sometimes wasted. It's best to run offline defragmentation using **eseutil /d** even though the Information Store performs normal online defragmentation by default. Online defragmentations can be very disk intensive and have a negative impact on the server that is undergoing this type of online maintenance procedure. This means that users might notice the server as being "slow" if multiple database files are undergoing online maintenance simultaneously.

- *Deletion of messages or mailboxes*—Online maintenance also includes regular deletion of messages or mailboxes that have exceeded the time limits set by your retention periods. To find the current retention period settings for both email messages and mailboxes in System Manager, right-click the mailbox store you are working with and check the current settings on the Limits tab. If, for example, the current setting for deleted mailbox retention is 30 days, any online maintenance routine will permanently delete all mailboxes in the system that remain after 30 days. This process is known as *hard deletion* and could result in performance hits to your server if a large number of messages or mailboxes need to be permanently removed from your system.

Performing online backups while online defragmentation is taking place introduces additional problems. Any backup of an Exchange 2000 SG stops all online defragmentation of any database inside that SG. Suppose you have three databases in a single SG and one is running online maintenance procedures. If you run an online backup on any of these databases, the online defragmentation that is currently taking place halts. You must make sure that you run backups for all databases within a SG after online maintenance has been run against this SG, otherwise the databases might always be in a state of fragmentation.

Maintaining Your Databases Through Circular Logging

A final point to consider in your maintenance efforts involves the concept of transaction logs and circular logging used by Exchange 2000. Circular logging is disabled by default in Exchange 2000 (although it was enabled by default in previous versions of Exchange, including Exchange 5.5). Exchange writes every transaction to a transaction log; these logs are committed to all databases that exist in a single SG. The circular logging option limits the amount of disk space used by these transaction logs.

All current transaction log files are maintained in the Edb.log file found in the Exchsrvr\Mdbdata directory. When this log file reaches 5MB, Exchange creates a temporary log file named Edbtmp.log that accepts all new transactions while the original Edb.log file is renamed to Edb00001.log. As soon as the Edb.log changes its name, the Edbtmp.log file changes its name also (and becomes the new Edb.log file). This process repeats itself every time the Edb.log file reaches 5MB. The danger here is that log files are increasing in number and occupying valuable disk space as more and more transactions take place in your system.

If you disable circular logging, your system creates log files until you perform a backup. In this case, the only way to remove this growing list of log files is to back up your Exchange Server. Increasing log files can cause the Information Store to run out of operating space eventually. To prevent this from happening, make sure that log files are written to a different drive or partition or perform a backup of your Information Store. You also can manually delete transaction log files from their location in the Exchsrvr\Mdbdata directory. You might not be able to perform these types of backups, however, because the transaction logs you deleted are used for incremental or differential backups, to perform these types of backups if you manually delete transaction logs. Normal full backups can be performed, however, if you delete these transaction logs.

The Art of Troubleshooting

Troubleshooting is both an art and a science, especially when maintaining and optimizing a server running Exchange 2000. You can use numerous guidelines to correct problems as they arise and the challenge lies in selecting the proper tool for the proper situation or problem that you are suddenly facing. This section covers common troubleshooting scenarios, especially as they relate to connectivity issues for Exchange 2000. We conclude with specific troubleshooting scenarios that are encountered by practicing Exchange administrators so you can gain insight into the art and science of troubleshooting.

First, realize that troubleshooting does not always imply disaster recovery. Troubleshooting involves both small-scale and large-scale issues when Exchange 2000 is involved. A small-scale problem involves a user who cannot access his email because he forgot the password. A large-scale problem occurs if, for example, one of your WAN links becomes inactive and you don't know the exact cause of this breakdown. Sometimes problems occur with remote SMTP hosts that you are trying to communicate with and you must wait for the other side to correct a problem. In all these cases, it might be helpful to devise a flowchart or written action log describing steps to take when specific problems occur. For example, if users complain that they suddenly cannot connect to a remote host to obtain network resources, most administrators are taught to follow a simple but effective plan of action to resolve this issue:

1. First, check the local machine to test for general connectivity. You can make sure the Network Interface Card (NIC) is fully seated and in its slot on the motherboard properly. You can also make sure that this card is showing a solid green light (since most NICs register a green light in the back of the computer when connected). Test that all network cables are properly connected and not frayed or bent (which could affect responsiveness if these wire were bent somewhere). If the hardware doesn't seem to be the focus of the problem, proceed to Step 2.
2. Step 2 involves using the ping utility on this machine to verify that TCP/IP (Transmission Control Protocol/Internet Protocol) has been properly installed. You typically test the local loopback by pinging reserved IP address 127.0.0.1 to determine whether the TCP/IP protocol stack is properly configured and bound to the network adapter in the local machine. If this step is successful, proceed to Step 3.

3. Step 3 involves pinging another computer on the same subnet as the user's machine using the syntax ping IP address of a remote computer. If the user receives a reply from another user's computer on the same subnet, proceed to Step 4.
4. Step 4 involves pinging the default gateway used by all computers on a given subnet. The gateway provides access to remote networks and acts as a bridge or tunnel for all data packets coming from one network and going to a remote network. If the default gateway can be contacted, proceed to Step 5.
5. Step 5 involves pinging a computer on the remote subnet that the target or destination computer is located on. If communication can be made with the default gateway, but not to hosts beyond the gateway, you can assume that a configuration setting is incorrect on the remote subnet, instead of looking for problems on the local subnet.

This type of analysis helps avoid random guesswork when trying to solve most types of network-related problems. You should develop a similar plan of attack to address specific Exchange 2000 issues such as message-routing client connectivity.

NOTE: *Many sources may introduce errors in your environment. For example, you may have a faulty switch or a loose or faulty cable to a local router or switch in your wiring closet that is suddenly loose and is causing connectivity issues. Your system may be trying to use an IP address that another system is currently using. This also causes one system to lose connectivity. Maintaining written system procedures may help to alleviate problems in these types of situations.*

Troubleshooting Connectivity in Exchange 2000

As stated in "Developing Maintenance Goals for Resource Management" earlier in this chapter, most organizations are concerned with managing three types of resources: servers, clients, and "mail flow" between servers. Connectivity issues usually involve some combination of these three resources. The server is involved because it contains the Routing Engine (RE) component of Exchange 2000, which maintains Link State Information (LSI) and message-routing information. Clients usually provide issues of their own, including improper configurations with client software or incorrect setup of client profiles. Troubleshooting messaging flows between servers and clients often involves using advanced troubleshooting tools provided by Exchange 2000 such as **Winroute.exe** or **RPCPing**, which are discussed later in this chapter.

When troubleshooting intermittent mail delivery or message-flow issues, consider that all message flows occurring outside your routing groups occur using one of two protocols: the SMTP protocol or the X.400 protocol. Message flows also depend on services such as the SMTP service and the MTA stack service. You should configure any monitoring tools to issue warnings or alerts on the status of SMTP and X.400 queue growth in this case. What would you do to resolve the issue presented in the following sidebar?

Troubleshooting Mail Delivery Issues in a Mixed-Mode Setting

Suppose you run a mixed-mode Exchange 2000/Exchange 5.5 organization consisting of recipient objects on both Exchange 2000 and Exchange 5.5. You have implemented the Internet Mail Connector (IMC) on your Exchange 5.5 Server named Orion. Some Exchange 5.5 users complain that they cannot send mail to other users in the organization. Exchange 2000 users complain that they cannot receive Internet mail, even though all Exchange 5.5 users can. As time goes on, more Exchange 2000 users complain that they cannot send mail to Exchange 5.5 users or to Internet recipients.

You notice some messages being queued on the IMC, but a flow of messages still is taking place. You check the MTA queue on the Exchange 2000 Server and notice messages stacking up rapidly. How can you rectify this situation?

Check the MTA stacks in Exchange 2000 because this provides connectivity between Exchange 5.5 and Exchange 2000. If the MTA stack service has stopped for some reason, mail won't flow between the two systems. Problems with the MTA stack service could cause mail to continue queuing on any Exchange 5.5 bridgehead server. Mail will also queue in the X.400 or MTA queues in Exchange 2000 while waiting to communicate with any Exchange 5.5 bridgehead servers. Stopping and restarting the process that controls the MTA stack service usually solves this problem, but if it doesn't, you might have to consult with Microsoft Product Support Services. They might recommend a SP or hotfix that addresses any issues with the MTA stack service.

The sidebar example illustrates a connectivity issue related to a component located directly inside Exchange 2000—the MTA stack service. Applying a hotfix (or restarting the service) is all that is needed to troubleshoot this type of error. However, not all connectivity problems are that direct. For example, consider what happens when you attempt to send messages using a standard Outlook 2000 client and you receive error messages regarding these attempts. What would be a logical starting place to troubleshoot this type of error? Problems such as this are not immediately resolved and require an understanding of the steps taken by a message as it leaves one server and proceeds to another destination server. For example, consider a user on Server X sending a message to a user on Server Y. If the user on Server X is repeatedly receiving errors when sending a message to Server Y, you need to understand the path that this message is trying to take to troubleshoot the delivery process.

Start of Message

The message path can be summarized as follows (explanations of possible troubleshooting steps are provided to illustrate the concepts that are discussed in this section):

1. Message is entered on Server X and presented to the *store driver* on Server X as it tries to move from the client's Outbox to the client's Sent box on the client's Outlook 2000 computer.
   - **Troubleshooting Tip:** Make sure the message actually resides in the Sent box on the client's machine.
2. The message on Server X is presented to the advanced queuing engine in Exchange 2000.
   - **Troubleshooting Tip:** Check to see whether the SMTP service is fully functioning; if it isn't, the message might not make it to the advanced queuing (AQ) engine component of Exchange 2000.
3. The message on Server X is now presented to the Categorizer component of Exchange 2000.
   - **Troubleshooting Tip:** Check the SMTP queues or the X.400 queues in System Manager to determine whether messages are building up in the queue. You also can check queues for third-party connectors you might have configured, such as the Lotus Notes Connector or the Microsoft Mail for PC (Networks) Connector.
4. The SMTP service on Server X now tries to transfer this message to Server Y.
   - **Troubleshooting Tip:** Make sure the SMTP service is still running. If problems occur at this state, you might be experiencing general issues with your domain controllers (DCs) or GC Servers. You can also check the Messages Awaiting Directory Lookup queue in System Manager to check for queues that are backed up.
5. The SMTP service continues transferring this message over TCP port 25 and sends this message to the store driver on Server Y.
   - **Troubleshooting Tip:** Problems in this area again indicate that the SMTP service might not be functioning, so check the status of the SMTP service using the Services snap-in or the Performance Console.
6. If the message makes it to Server Y, it is presented to the AQ engine and the Categorizer component of Exchange 2000 running on Server Y.
   - **Troubleshooting Tip:** Check the SMTP service to make sure it is running (unless you've already done this in previous steps). Also, check your SMTP queues in Exchange System Manager for backlogs.

7. The message is being presented for local delivery via the WSS and IIS, and then is presented to the Information Store for final receipt.
   - **Troubleshooting Tip:** If problems occur at this point, you can check to see whether the WSS is running. If it gets past the WSS and IIS, there is a good chance that delivery to the final recipient will be successful.

As you can tell from this scenario, many "points of failure" can arise when a simple message is being relayed from one server to another server, even if both servers are in the same routing segment or Windows 2000 domain. Understanding the message flow process can help you troubleshoot many common messaging issues.

NOTE: *Sometimes you encounter SMTP errors that are related to authentication and not routing. For example, if users have difficulty sending emails to Exchange 2000 because they receive the error "Client must be authenticated", it means the server they are connecting to does not allow anonymous SMTP connections and they have to authenticate. You either can configure users for SMTP authentication, or change settings on the server so it will allow anonymous connections.*

Most connectivity issues relate to clients that cannot access services on Exchange 2000 either because a dependent Windows 2000 service is not functioning, or because of general network-related issues. An example of this includes having users who want to access Exchange 2000 using the OWA client. Imagine that you have just installed Exchange 2000 in your network and everything appears to be working at first. Users can access mail using a MAPI client—such as Outlook 2000—but they are suddenly having problems accessing mail using their OWA client. What should you check first? The WSS of Exchange 2000 and the IIS of Windows 2000 should be checked because they allow Exchange Server resources to become available via the Hypertext Transfer Protocol (HTTP), a protocol used by all OWA clients. Therefore, you should check the configuration of IIS using the Windows 2000 Administrative tool known as the Internet Services Manager (ISM). If any problems occur with the default Web site within ISM, clients will experience problems with their OWA clients.

Usually connectivity issues for MAPI clients (such as Outlook 2000) are more problematic than connectivity issues for non-MAPI clients (such as OWA or Outlook Express users). MAPI clients often use protocols carrying higher overhead compared to protocols used by non-MAPI clients (for example, the Remote Procedure Call [RPC] protocol, which has more overhead than the Post Office Protocol version 3 [POP3]). Also, MAPI clients often use a variety of name-resolution procedures compared to their non-MAPI counterparts, and this introduces more layers of complexity into a messaging network as well. Suppose that users complain they cannot connect to Exchange 2000 using their Outlook 2000 client, but they can connect using their OWA client. If your network consists of multiple DHCP (Dynamic Host Configuration Protocol), DNS (Domain Name System), and WINS

(Windows Internet Name Service) servers, you need to check all possible failure points, including the databases present on all servers as well as all DHCP scopes and DNS zones that have been configured. Successful resolution of these types of problems is inversely proportional to the complexity of the network configuration. The more complex your network is in terms of services and servers used, the harder it is to solve problems that arise. Organizations that only manage a single DNS Server, for instance, find it easier to manage connectivity issues than organizations that manage multiple DNS Servers in conjunction with multiple routers and multiple DHCP Servers.

Using the Proper Troubleshooting Tools

The previous section alluded to situations involving connectivity issues. Administrators often use various tools to troubleshoot these problems. This section lists two important tools used to troubleshoot connectivity issues in Exchange 2000: **RPCPing** and **Regtrace**. **RPCPing** is used to troubleshoot MTA connections, and only applies to an Exchange 2000 Server that wants to connect to an earlier version of Exchange (such as Exchange 5 or 5.5). **Regtrace** is used by Microsoft Product Support Services to troubleshoot most transport and routing problems.

RPCPing is found in the Support\RPCPING directory on the Exchange installation CD-ROM. As stated in the previous paragraph, this tool is used to test connectivity between an Exchange 2000 computer and an Exchange 5.5 or Exchange 5 computer. It cannot test communication between Exchange 2000 Servers. You can use this tool to test communication between a "calling server" and an "answering server." The calling server initiates all communications while the answering server receives the call. The utility consists of two files: **Rpings.exe** and **Rpingc32.exe**. Both files are executed on the calling server and the answering server and tests RPC communication in both directions. If **RPCPing** is successful when pinging the remote server in both directions, your Exchange 2000 network is properly configured. If **RPCPing** does not ping the remote server in either direction, you can assume that your network is not correctly configured. RPC communications in Exchange usually involve reliable connections between servers, and these connections are made using network components such as TCP/IP, hostname resolution services (such as DNS or host files), firewalls, and routers that might exist between servers.

WinRoute.exe is another good tool to use for troubleshooting purposes. **WinRoute.exe** is found in the Microsoft Exchange 2000 Server Resource Kit CD (and also in the Support\Utils\i386 directory of the Exchange 2000 installation CD). This tool can connect to a Link State Port (LSP) on any server that runs Exchange 2000 and extract LSI for your entire Exchange 2000 organization.

NOTE: *LSI is usually obtained over TCP port 691 on a server running Exchange 2000. Make sure no other application or service is using this port number.*

WinRoute matches the Globally Unique Identifier (GUID) of all connectors or bridgehead servers to objects stored in AD; it then displays LSI in an easy-to-read format. You can copy the WinRoute.exe file from the Exchange 2000 Server Resource Kit CD directly into your Exchsrvr\bin directory on your local hard drive.

TIP: *If you copy* ***WinRoute*** *into the Exchsrvr\bin directory, you must make sure that three other Dynamic Link Library (DLL) files are also present in the Exchsrvr\bin directory: Dsaccess.dll, Pttrace.dll, and Exchmem.dll.*

Use **WinRoute** to view information concerning routing groups, including an attribute that shows the current sequence number of your routing groups. If one routing group shows a version number of zero, LSI from the Routing Group Master (RGM) in that routing group has not been received. You can save information displayed in **WinRoute** using the .rte file extension and open this saved file remotely using **WinRoute** on another machine. To use **WinRoute**, make sure the Exchange RE service, the SMTP service, and the MSExchangeMTA service (or the Microsoft Exchange MTA stack service) have all been started.

Troubleshooting AD Issues

AD is well integrated with Exchange 2000. Problems with AD components such as GC Servers or DCs can affect services and components within Exchange 2000. You should document your AD design, which should solidify the design of your Windows 2000 sites as well as the placement of your DCs and GC Server. Exchange 2000 has to query a GC Server if it needs information on any AD object (such as a user or a group object). Most problems concerning AD can be solved by ensuring that Exchange 2000 is able to contact GC Servers and DCs (a DC can be configured to be a GC Server, but a GC Server *must* be a DC by design!) Exchange 2000 queries a DNS Server for service location records (or SRV records) when searching for GC Servers and DCs, so you want to make sure that your DNS Servers are functioning properly when managing an Exchange 2000 Server.

Exchange 2000 needs fast and reliable access to a GC Server. Without this fast and reliable access, Exchange 2000 will forget information about its own configuration. In this case, all message stores within this server can be taken offline until a GC Server can be successfully contacted. You will know you have a problem because all your mailbox stores might go offline at the same time, and you might not be able to manually remount them. This will impact all MAPI-based clients—such as Outlook 2000 users—but it will have very little impact on non-MAPI clients—such as OWA clients. MAPI clients need to be authenticated directly to a GC Server, although not all OWA clients need this authentication service at all times (remember that OWA clients can sometimes browse public folders without authenticating to their mailboxes).

Problems with AD can also cause issues with other Exchange 2000 components. For example, the System Attendant component of Exchange 2000 might not start successfully if it cannot locate a DC. The System Attendant component is responsible for referring or proxying all client requests (including "down-level" client requests such as Outlook 97 or Outlook 98 clients) to AD. If no DC is available to proxy these requests, the service might not start. Also, any incoming message queues can indicate they are full, but the messages inside them will not be delivered if an AD GC Server is not available to perform LDAP queries on behalf of a SMTP Virtual Server. Microsoft recommends having multiple GC Servers in a Windows 2000 forest because the Exchange 2000 Categorizer service uses the LDAP protocol to perform AD lookups so that all incoming SMTP messages can be delivered to their intended location.

Immediate Solutions

Monitoring Processor Loads in Exchange 2000

Exchange 2000 is more processor intensive than Exchange 5.5. The services within Exchange 5.5 did not consume much processor power; however, certain services in Exchange 2000 place a relatively large load on server CPU cycles. These services are as follows:

- *Conferencing services*—The Exchange 2000 Conferencing Server is composed of three subservices: the Conference Management Service, which manages virtual meeting rooms; the Multipoint Control Unit (MCU), which provides a data conferencing facility; and the H.323 bridge service, which allows unicast clients to stream audio and video data packets to an Exchange Server and bring this into a group conference. Of these three subservices, the H.323 bridge service is the most processor intensive. You might want to implement any service requiring the H.323 protocol on a dedicated and more powerful server.
- *Front-end (FE) Exchange 2000 Servers*—These servers are very processor intensive because they perform many services for non-MAPI Internet clients who need access to a back-end (BE) Exchange 2000 Server. These services include protocol translation, AD lookups, data-encryption processing, and network load balancing. You can optimize this configuration by using multiprocessor machines (processor optimization yields higher performance gains compared to memory or disk optimization in this scenario).
- *Full-text indexing*—This feature allows clients to search for information in a rapid manner, including information found within message attachments (a feature that does not exist by default in Exchange 2000). In performing these searches, an index catalog containing frequently searched items is built and refreshed on a regular basis (indexes are normally updated daily at 10:00 P.M. by default in System Manager, but you can change this if you want). Full-text indexing works with the Microsoft Search service and can consume over 50 percent of CPU cycles while searching the catalog. You might want to use multiple processors or faster processors to optimize this search process, otherwise users might not be able to search for recent items because the catalog is not being updated fast enough.

Optimizing Memory Usage in Exchange 2000

If you do not physically optimize memory in Exchange 2000, it tries to use all available memory by default. This presents problems if you try to run other memory-intensive applications on the same server that is running Exchange 2000.

NOTE: *The Information Store can be blamed for this memory consumption because it tries to cache all information it uses in a special storage area in Exchange 2000 known as the Dynamic Buffer Allocation (DBA). If no other applications are competing for this memory, the DBA allocates almost all available memory to itself (it is a self-regulating allocation mechanism within Exchange 2000).*

To optimize the amount of memory, plan to distribute users across multiple SGs and multiple databases within each SG. Usually the first database that you create in a SG tries to absorb the largest amount of virtual memory in the system. However, memory consumption decreases as you add additional stores within this existing SG. Therefore, when faced with the decision to either create additional stores within a SG, or create a new SG, you should opt to completely fill one SG before creating a new SG. This action results in less memory being consumed and less hard disk overhead. The disadvantage of running multiple databases in one SG is that if one database in this group goes offline for some reason, the other databases in this group might go offline for a few seconds and then try to reconnect to the Store.exe service. You also are limited to backing up one database at a time within a single SG.

Optimizing Virtual Memory Allocation for Servers with More Than 1GB of RAM

All Exchange 2000 Servers containing more than 1GB of RAM need adjustments concerning the allocation of virtual memory internally. By default, all Windows 2000 Advanced Server computers reserve 2GB of virtual address space within the Windows 2000 kernel component, and all user-mode processes are allowed to use 2GB of virtual memory space. The actual working set of any process is less than that address space that has been allocated for this process. If you manage any Exchange 2000 Server running on Windows 2000 Advanced Server and containing more than 1GB of physical memory, you must modify the configuration of Windows 2000 so that 3GB of virtual memory becomes available for all user-mode applications (for example, the Information Store process).

WARNING! You should monitor the Information Store so that it does not run out of virtual memory space; otherwise, you will be forced to restart the Information Store service and disrupt all messaging services for your users. You can monitor virtual address consumption by using the System Monitor utility and selecting the Process: Virtual Bytes counter for all instances of the Store.exe process running on your system.

To make this memory available, you have to modify the Boot.ini hidden system file found in the root directory of your system (usually the active system partition known as C:\). To modify this file:

1. Open Windows Explorer by choosing Start|Programs|Accessories|Windows Explorer.
2. When the Explorer window opens, choose Tools|Folder Options to open the Folder Options dialog box.
3. Click the View tab and uncheck the Hide Protected Operating System Files (Recommended) checkbox in the Advanced Settings section. Click the OK button (see Figure 14.7).
4. You will see a message asking whether you want to enable these files (which are marked System and Hidden in Explorer). Click Yes, and then click OK to close the Folder Options dialog box (see Figure 14.8).
5. Click the View menu on top of your screen, and then click the option to Refresh. This refreshes the display on your screen and makes all OS files visible in the right-hand pane view of Explorer.

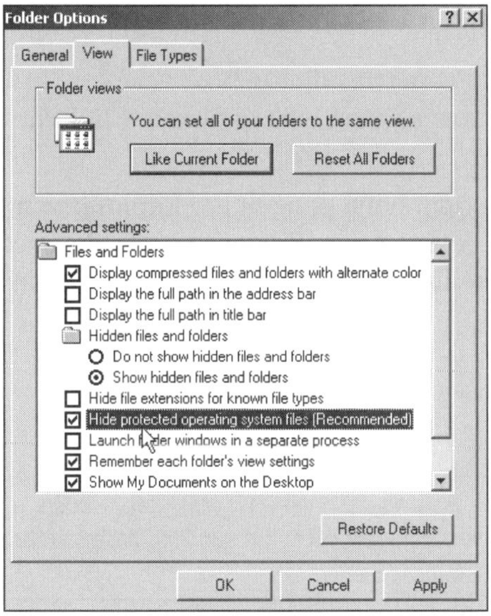

Figure 14.7 Checking Folder Options to display protected operating system (OS) files in Explorer.

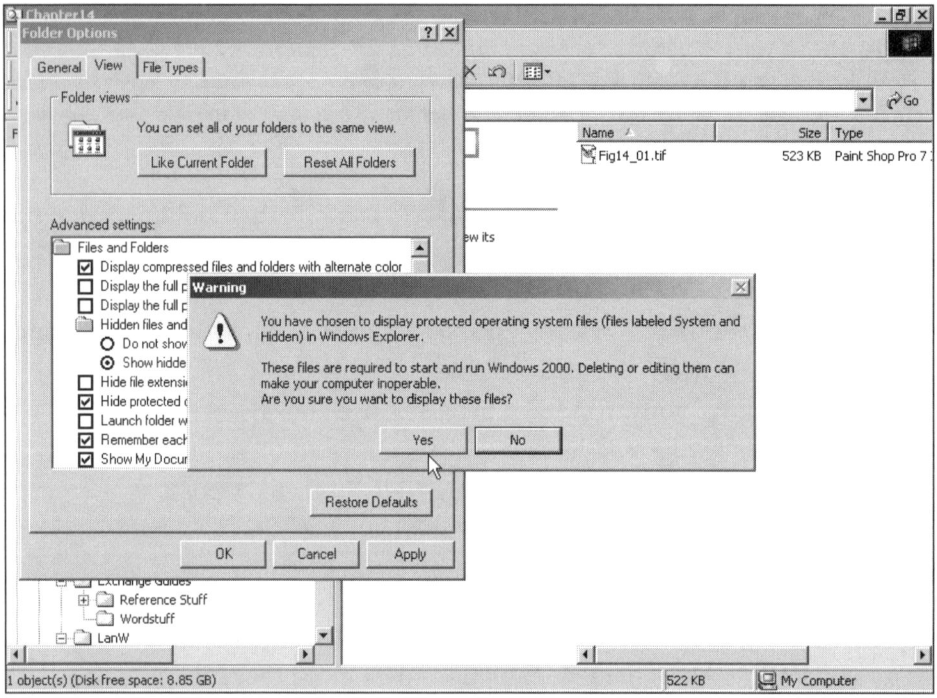

Figure 14.8 The Warning box to display protected OS files.

6. Click the (C:) folder in the left-hand pane of Explorer and locate the Boot.ini system file that is now displayed in the right-hand pane of Explorer. Right-click this file and select Properties.
7. On the General tab of the Boot.ini Properties dialog box, verify that the Read-Only checkbox in the Attributes section isn't checked. Click the OK button to close this dialog box.
8. Double-click the Boot.ini file in the right-hand pane of the Explorer window to open the contents of this file in Notepad (see Figure 14.9). In the section called Operating Systems, locate the line containing the following code:

```
multi(0)disk(0)rdisk(0)partition(1)_
\WINNT="Microsoft Windows 2000 Advanced Server" /fastdetect
```

NOTE: *You might have multiple lines that seem to have the same lines of code; however, the numbers for* ***disk ( )***, ***rdisk ( )***, *and* ***partition ( )*** *might differ depending on how your system is configured. If this is the case, change the line of code containing* ***partition (1)***. *Remember that the setting you are about to type applies to Windows 2000 Advanced Server, so the line should specify* ***\WINNT="Microsoft Windows 2000 Advanced Server"***.

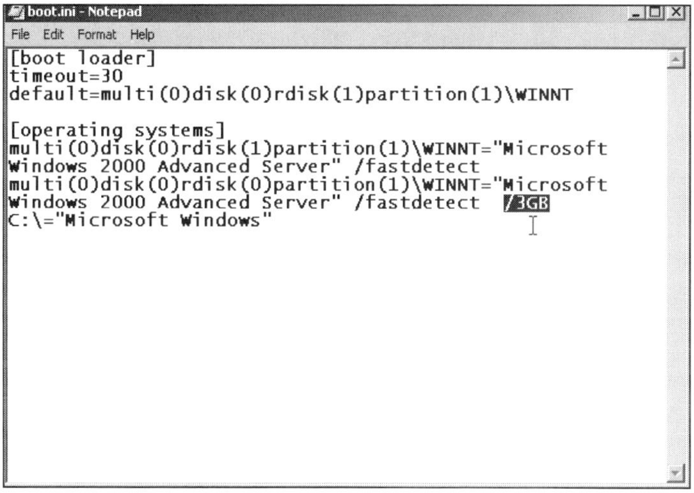

Figure 14.9 The Boot.ini system file found in the root directory of C:.

9. Add the following option to the end of this line of code, after the **/fastdetect** option:

```
/ 3GB
```

   Your new line will now appear as:

```
multi(0)disk(0)rdisk(0)partition(1)_
\WINNT="Microsoft Windows 2000 Advanced Server" /fastdetect /3GB
```

10. Click File|Save. Then, click File|Exit to close the Boot.ini–Notepad dialog box.
11. Now undo the option to display protected OS files by clicking the Tools|Folder Options. When the Folder Options dialog box opens, click the View tab and recheck the Hide Protected Operating System Files (Recommended) box so these files (including C:\boot.ini) are no longer visible within Windows Explorer. Click the OK button when you are finished.

NOTE: *When the Folder Options box closes, the protected OS files again are hidden without any further action on your part. You don't need to refresh the views within Explorer by choosing View|Refresh (although you can refresh your views at any time).*

Configuring a Server Monitor to Track Available Virtual Memory

You can configure server monitors using the Exchange System Manager snap-in. Server monitors can be enabled, disabled, or removed from your servers at any time. To configure a server monitor, perform the following:

1. Open the System Manager snap-in by clicking Start|Programs|Microsoft Exchange|System Manager.
2. When the System Manager console opens, expand the top Organization object (if necessary) by clicking the "+" next to this object one time.
3. Double-click the Tools container to reveal the subcontainers inside (it's the last item appearing in the folder hierarchy in System Manager). Click the "+" appearing next to the Monitoring And Status folder.
4. Click the Status folder and view all objects appearing in the right-hand pane of the System Manager window (the Details pane as it is known). Notice that this pane reveals the status of all servers and connectors within your organization (see Figure 14.10).

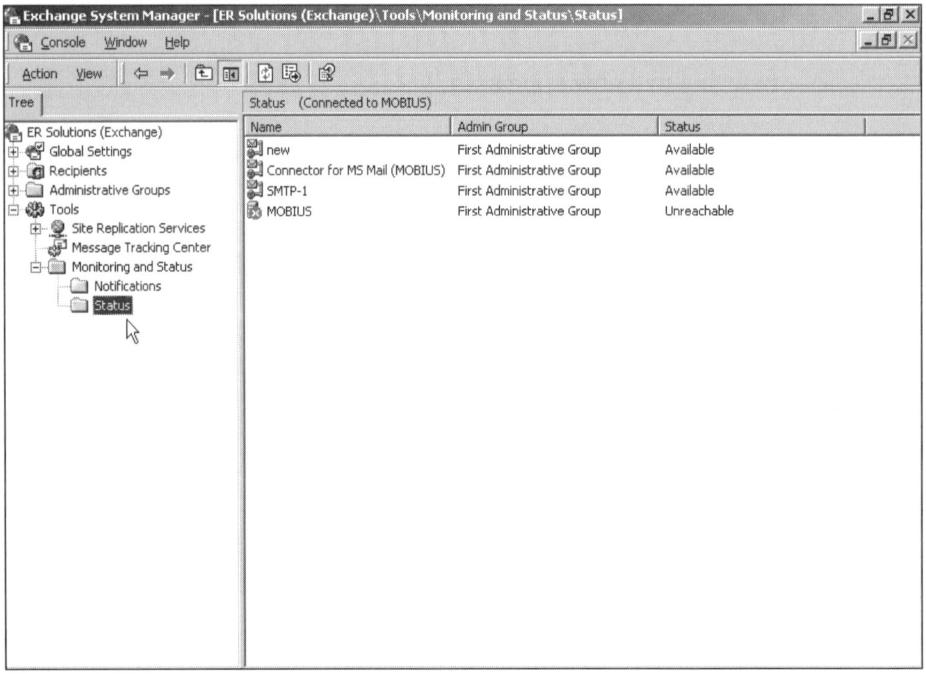

Figure 14.10 The Status folder within System Manager showing all servers and connectors.

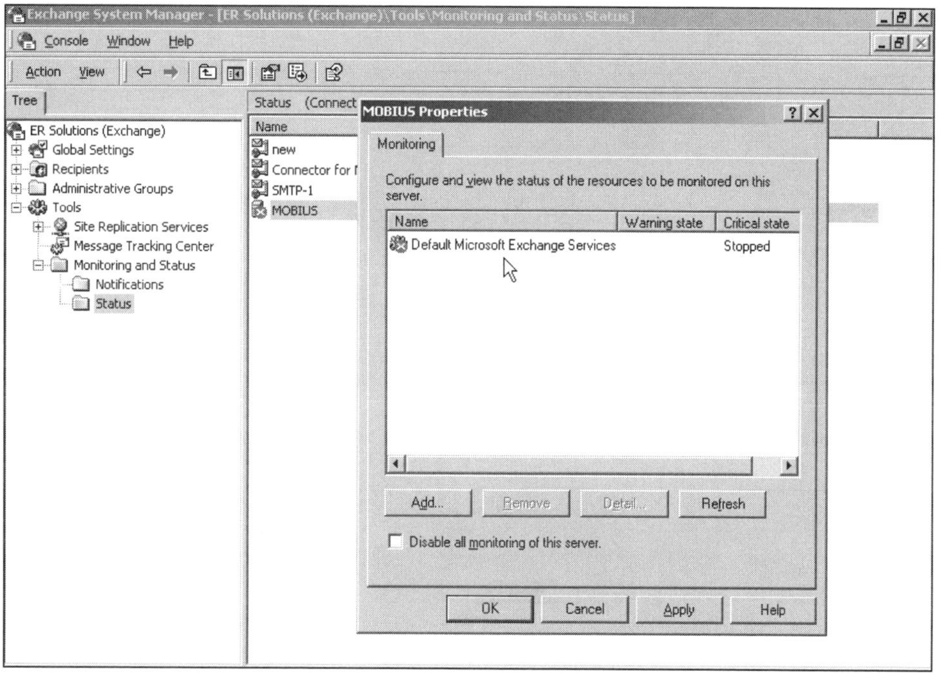

Figure 14.11 The Monitoring tab of your server's Properties dialog box.

5. Double-click the server in the Details pane of System Manager to bring up the server Properties dialog box. Notice the Default Microsoft Exchange Services shown under the Name column on the Monitoring tab (see Figure 14.11).
6. Click the Add button at the bottom of the Monitoring tab to introduce the Add Resource dialog box shown in Figure 14.12.
7. Click Available Virtual Memory, and then click the OK button to display the Virtual Memory Thresholds dialog box. Under Set The Period Of Time That Virtual Memory Must Fall Below A Threshold To Change The State, type "5" (this specifies that virtual memory must fall below your warning or critical thresholds for at least 5 minutes before a new state will be displayed in System Manager).
8. Under Set Minimum Available Virtual Memory Thresholds, check the Warning State (Percent) box and set it to 10. Notice that 5 percent is the default threshold value for virtual memory warning states.
9. Check the Critical State (Percent) box and verify that it reads 5 percent (the default setting). You want the critical state threshold to be lower than the warning state threshold because you want to be warned first when virtual memory is approaching unsafe levels (as defined by your specific

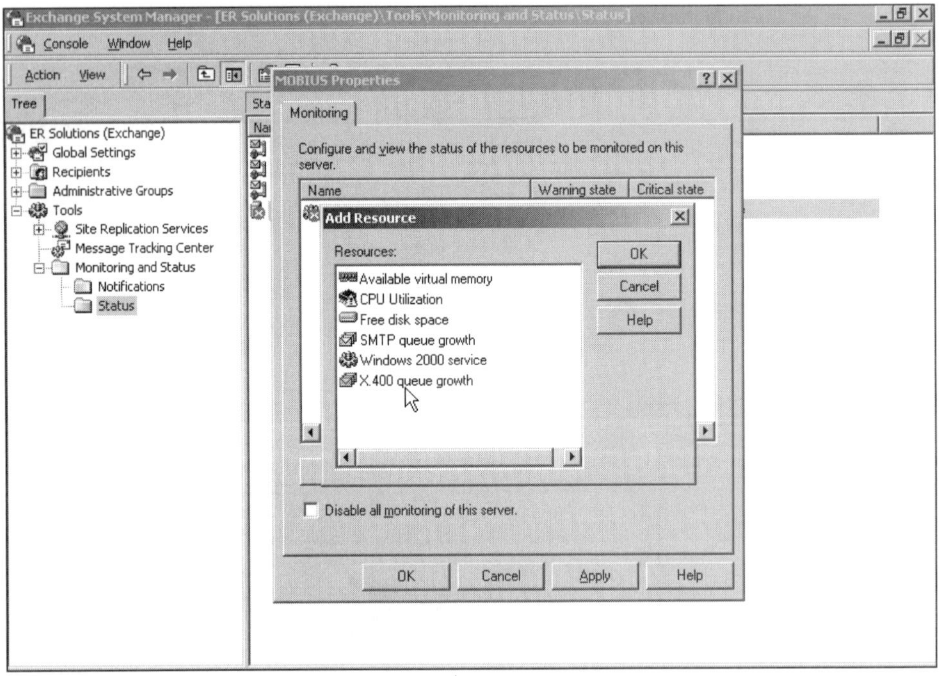

Figure 14.12 The Add Resource dialog box for a server monitor.

hardware and software configurations). See Figure 14.13 for a sample of these settings.

10. Click the OK button and your new virtual memory threshold appears on the Monitoring tab of your server's Properties sheet indicating a warning state of 10 percent and a critical state of 5 percent.
11. Highlight the new virtual memory threshold on the Monitoring tab and click the Details button on the bottom of this tab. A box at the bottom of the Virtual Memory Thresholds dialog box indicates the Current Available Virtual Memory (Percent). Click OK to close this dialog box and OK once again to close your server's Properties sheet. (Figure 14.14 shows the current available virtual memory after the virtual memory monitor has been configured.)

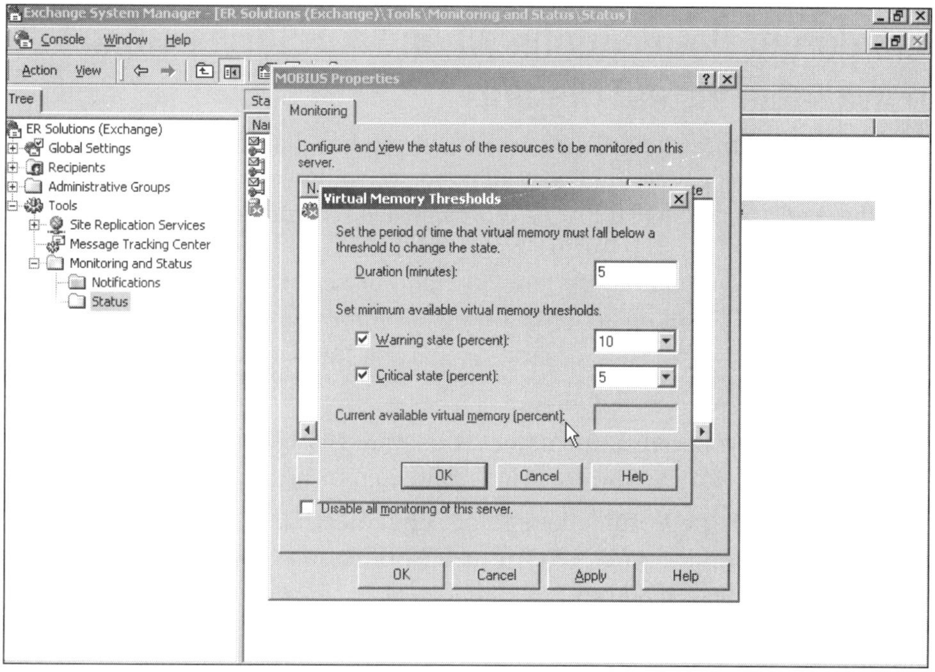

Figure 14.13 The Virtual Memory Thresholds dialog box.

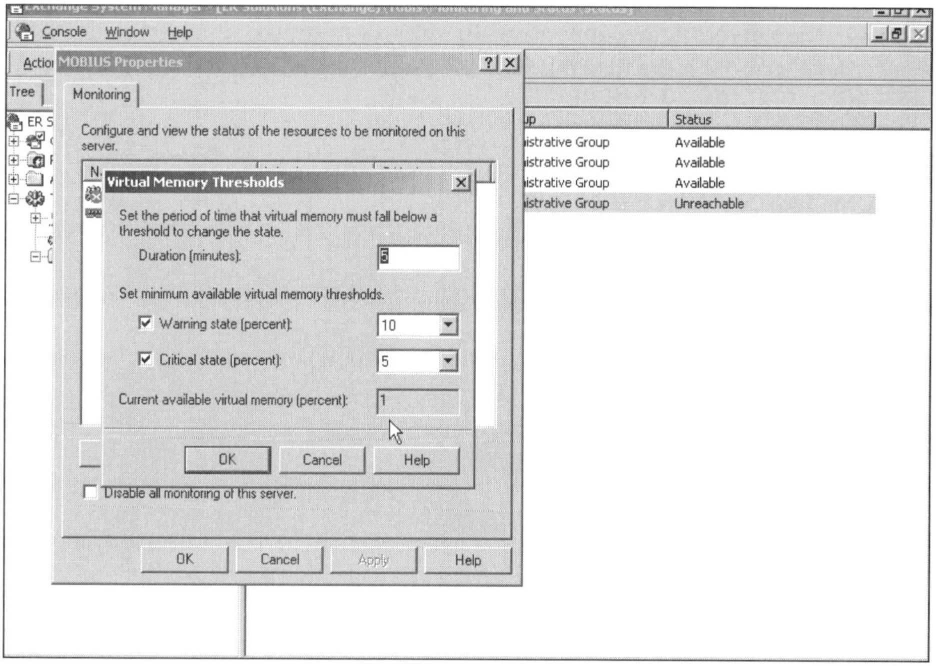

Figure 14.14 The current available virtual memory displayed in the new virtual memory threshold monitor.

Configuring Notifications When Your Server Runs Low on Available Virtual Memory

The previous Immediate Solution showed you how to configure a server monitor that measures the amount of virtual memory available and indicates whether virtual memory has reached low or critical levels. This Immediate Solution extends this procedure one step further by allowing you to set up a notification scheme, so that the server can notify you via email or script if such critical levels have been reached. To set up an email notification for the virtual memory monitor:

1. Open up System Manager by selecting Start|Programs|Microsoft Exchange|System Manager.
2. Expand the organization object (the topmost object displayed in System Manager). Expand the Tools icon, and then the Monitoring And Status folder.
3. Right-click the Notifications folder underneath the Monitoring And Status folder, and then choose New|Email Notification. The Properties dialog box opens to the E-mail tab.
4. In the Monitoring Server text box, click the Select button to bring up the Select Exchange Server dialog box from which you can choose your Exchange Server. Select the appropriate server, and then click OK to return to the Properties dialog box.
5. In the Servers And Connectors To Monitor text box, choose the default This Server or click the down arrow to reveal the choices shown in Figure 14.15.

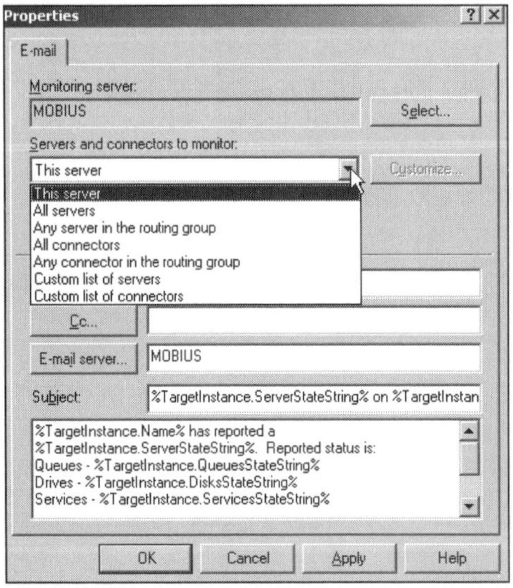

Figure 14.15 Choosing the server or connector to monitor in System Manager.

6. In the Notify When Monitored Items Are In text box, choose either Critical or Warning state (this example uses a critical state).
7. Click the To box to bring up the Select Recipient dialog box. Choose a user object that will receive notification when your system enters a critical state. Then, click OK.
8. Enter a name in the C: box if you want to copy this notification to an alternate person other than the person listed in the To: box. If you do not want to alert a second person or group, leave this field blank (as shown earlier in Figure 14.14).
9. In the Email Server text box, make sure your current server is listed, or click the Email Server button to select the appropriate server from the Select Exchange Server dialog box, and then click OK.
10. In the Subject text box, you might see a string that resembles the following:

    ```
    %TargetInstance.ServerStateString% on %TargetInstance.Name%
    ```

    Do not change this code because Exchange uses these environment variables to customize the resource being monitored and the server it is being monitored on in the Subject field of the email message.
11. Notice the environment variables listed in the text box directly under the Subject box. Exchange 2000 customizes this information depending on how you set up the server monitor previously. You don't need to modify or add to this code. Click OK to close this Properties sheet.

Setting Limits on the Number of SMTP Messages in Queues

You can use the Windows 2000 Registry Editor (**regedit.exe**) to limit the number of SMTP messages available to be queued on any SMTP Server, including Exchange 2000. If you set a limit for 100 messages in the queue, for example, no messages over 100 will be accepted by the SMTP service.

WARNING! Remember that the improper use of the Registry Editor (regedit.exe) can seriously affect the operation of your server. Microsoft will not always support operations that arbitrarily involve Registry modifications. You should always back up your Registry before making any changes to it.

To limit the number of SMTP messages that can be queued at one time:

1. Click Start|Run, type "Regedit" in the Open box, and click OK.

2. Expand the following Registry keys:

```
HKEY_LOCAL_MACHINE\SOFTWARE\MICROSOFT\EXCHANGE
```

3. Right-click the Exchange key and select New Key.
4. Type "MailMsg" exactly as shown here.
5. Right-click this new key, and then select New|DWORD Value as shown in Figure 14.16.
6. Type "MaxMessageObjects" as the name of this new value, and then press Enter. Next, right-click this new value in the right-hand pane and choose the Modify option.
7. Now set a value for the maximum number of messages that you want in your message queues at any one time. Click the Decimal radio button and enter your number. By default, 100,000 messages are in the SMTP queue at any one time.

NOTE: *The key value* ***MaxMessageObjects*** *indicates the maximum number of messages allocated by your Exchange 2000 system at any one time. If more than this number arrive in the SMTP queue, those messages will be rejected.*

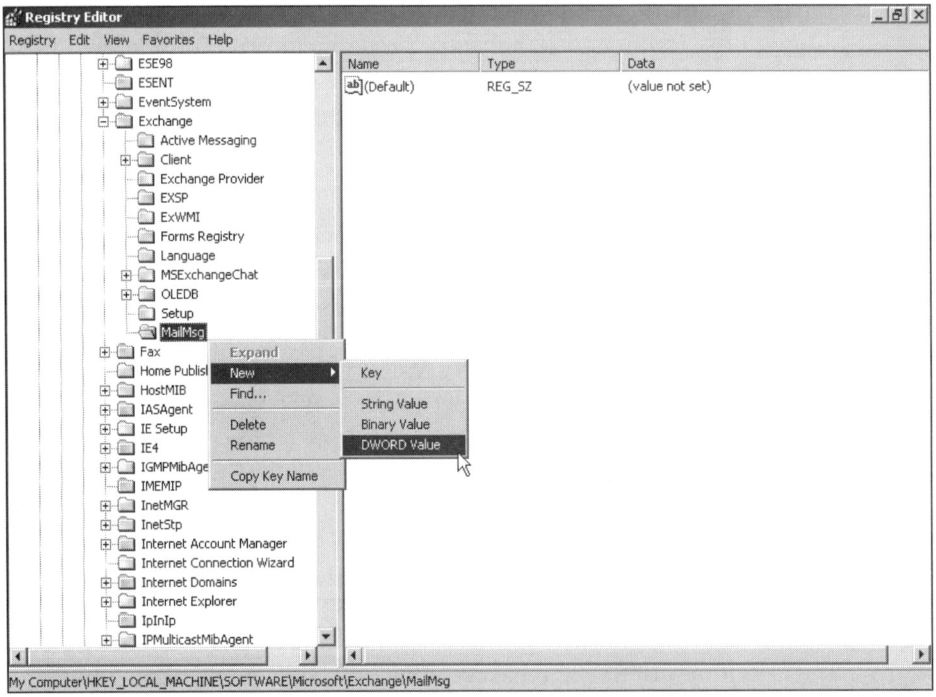

Figure 14.16 Creating a new DWORD value for the new MailMsg key in the Registry Editor.

Manipulating SMTP Queues in System Manager

You can perform certain actions on all SMTP queues found within the Exchange System Manager snap-in console. To see which actions can be performed, follow these steps:

1. Open System Manager by clicking Start|Programs|Microsoft Exchange|System Manager.
2. When the System Manager console opens, expand the organization object (if not already expanded). Then expand the Administrative Groups folder and the First Administrative Group folder inside.
3. Expand the Servers container and your *Server* object.
4. Expand the Protocols folder, and then the SMTP folder contained within the Protocols folder to reveal the object labeled Default SMTP Virtual Server. Expand the Default SMTP Virtual Server container to reveal the Queues container directly underneath.
5. Click the Queues container to reveal three separate queues in the right-hand side of the System Manager console window. Right-click the first queue labeled domain.com (Local Delivery) and choose the All Tasks menu option to view the options available to you (see Figure 14.17). These options are as follows:
   - *Force Connection*—Used to force a queue to change states, for example to change a queue's state to Active from Retry.
   - *Enumerate 100 Messages*—Used to display individual messages in the queue. If chosen, you can enumerate 100 messages at a time for this queue. Selecting this option a second time enumerates additional messages, or you can select the option to Re-enumerate after you have already chosen the Enumerate 100 Messages option to refresh the current list.
   - *Freeze All Messages/Unfreeze All Messages*—Used for troubleshooting purposes if one of your WAN links goes down and you do not want non-delivery reports (NDRs) to be generated while you are fixing your links. Freezing all messages allows new messages to enter the queue without being able to leave this queue. Unfreezing all messages re-enables all messages to leave the queue.
   - *Deleting All Messages (No NDR)/Delete All Messages (Send NDR)*—The first option deletes all messages in the queue after they have been enumerated and displayed, but does not send NDRs to the originator of these messages. The second option deletes all messages in the queue and sends NDRs to the originators of these messages. If you are trying to limit the amount of traffic on your network, choose the first option.

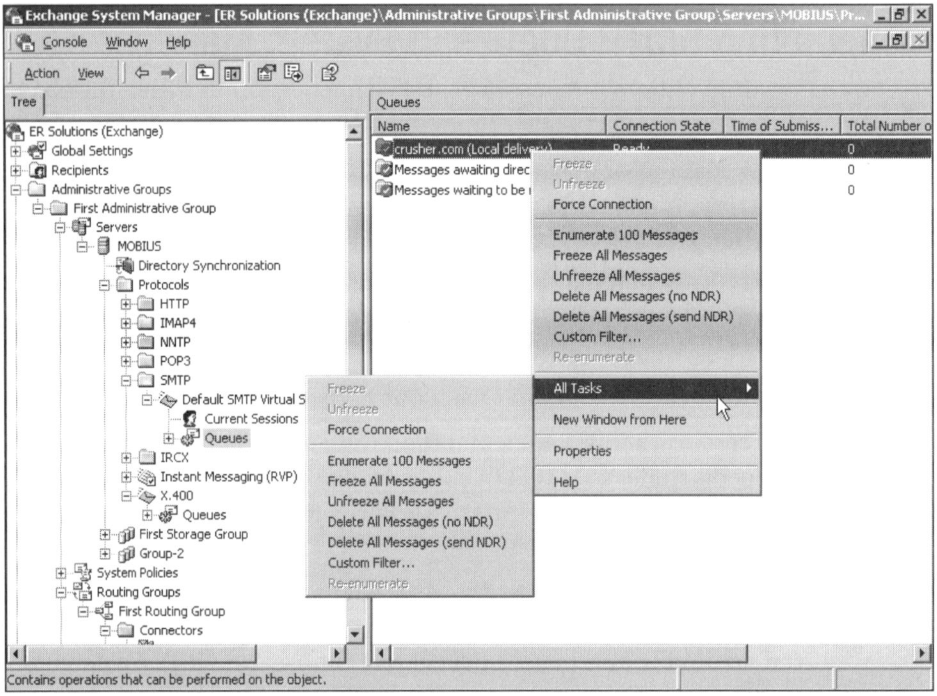

Figure 14.17 The All Tasks option for the local delivery SMTP queue in System Manager.

Using a SP to Ensure Messages Queued for External Connectors and the MTA Don't Disappear

Administrators who rename an Exchange 2000 RGC and restart the Exchange 2000 RE service and the MSExchangeMTA service while messages are queued for an external connector (such as the Exchange Connector for Lotus Notes) might notice that the queued messages never make it to their final destination. These messages might even disappear altogether from the message queues (the same behavior could occur when renaming an administrative group in the System Manager snap-in).

Downloading and applying the latest SP for Exchange 2000 (SP1 as of July 30, 2001) usually resolves this unusual behavior (you should verify that SP1 contains the latest version of the **Emsmta.exe** file, which is version 6.0.4720.1).

Performing an Offline Defragmentation of Your Databases

To perform an offline defragmentation of your database after moving a large number of users to another server, or even after receiving a large number of messages and deleting these same messages from the Information Store, do the following:

1. Click Start|Programs|Administrative Tools|Services.
2. Double-click the Microsoft Exchange Information Store service to open the Microsoft Exchange Information Store Properties (Local Computer) dialog box as shown in Figure 14.18.
3. Click the Stop button on the General tab of the Properties dialog box shown. The Service Status now shows Stopped. Click the OK button to close this dialog box.

***NOTE:** Stopping the Information Store service also stops other services that are dependent on the Information Store service, such as the Event service, the IMAP4 service, the POP3 service, and the SchedulePlus Free-Busy Connector.*

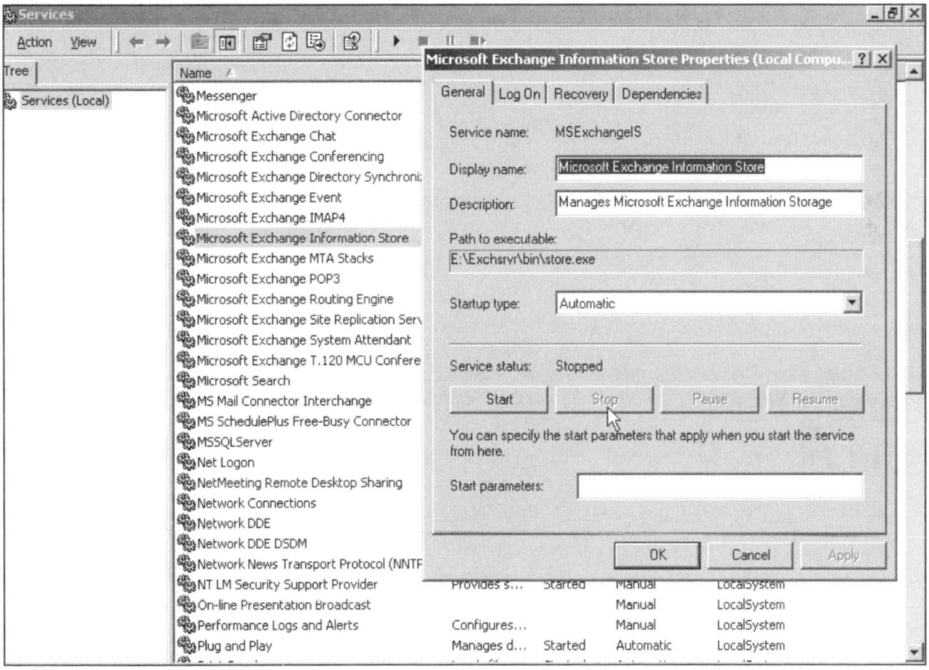

Figure 14.18 The Information Store Properties dialog box in the Services snap-in.

4. Now defragment your public and private Information Stores by using the **Eseutil** utility from a command prompt. Using **Eseutil** in Exchange 2000 means that you have to specify the directory path to the database that you are defragmenting (for example, if you want to defragment the private Information Store streaming content file, specify the path on your hard drive for the priv1.stm file normally found in the Exchsrvr folder on your local hard drive). The syntax for the **Eseutil** command is as follows:

```
eseutil /d e:\path\filename.[.edb | .stm ]
```

5. When **Eseutil** has completed its task, restart the Information Store service by clicking Start|Programs|Administrative Tools|Services, selecting the Microsoft Exchange Information Store service in the Services dialog box that opens, right-clicking this service, and choosing the Start option.
6. Start other services that are dependent on the Information Store service if they have not already been started (refer to the NOTE to this Immediate Solution listed previously). When all relevant services have restarted, back up all Information Store databases online (a backup is always recommended after defragmentation to take a "snapshot" of your new database for future recovery if needed. An online backup occurs while all services are running).

*TIP: If you receive errors that your database is in an inconsistent state when running **eseutil /d**, your database might still be mounted. Right-click this database in the System Manager snap-in and choose All Tasks|Dismount Store to put your database in a consistent state. If you run an offline defragmentation on a database in which other databases are mounted or running, you might have to dismount all the databases located in the same SG for offline defragmentation to be successful.*

Running **ESEUTIL** in Repair or Integrity Mode Using **/X** or **/V**

Earlier versions of Exchange Server (5.5 and earlier) used the **/V** switch for **Eseutil** to specify verbose mode and **/X** to display more detailed error messages. The current version of **Eseutil** used in Exchange 2000 no longer uses these switches or options.

When running **Eseutil.exe** in Repair mode (using **/P**) or Integrity mode (using **/G**) in Exchange 2000, the **/V** switch and **/X** switch are automatically incorporated into the **Eseutil** utility and are used as default options. If you attempt to specifically use these options from a command prompt, Exchange presents a message notifying you that these switches are invalid options.

If you want to see any verbose output produced by the **Eseutil** utility, search for a file called *databasename*.Integ.raw. **Eseutil** adds new output to this file every time you defragment a database. For example, running **Eseutil** on a mailbox store named StoreOne.edb appends output to a file called StoreOne.Integ.raw in the Exchsrvr\bin directory on the local hard drive of the Exchange 2000 computer.

Checking Your Databases for Consistency

A database within the Information Store is considered consistent only after it has been formally dismounted and shut down. At all other times, it is considered in an inconsistent state, even during normal operations. If you terminate the Information Store service for any reason during normal operations, Exchange 2000 detects an error condition when the service is restarted, and it tries recovery procedures by either backing out or committing needed transactions to the database to restore integrity to this database.

You can check a database for consistency and integrity by using the following command from a command prompt. Make sure you execute this from the Exchsrvr\bin directory on your local hard drive (on the drive partition where Exchange 2000 is installed):

```
eseutil /mh <database path and name> | more
```

For example, Figure 14.19 shows this command being run for the following mailbox store: E:\Exchsrvr\Mdbdata\mail-2.edb. The overall syntax for this command would then become:

```
E:\Exchsrvr\bin> eseutil /mh E:\Exchsrvr\Mdbdata\mail-2.edb | more
```

The State line in the output from this command shows either **Consistent** or **Inconsistent** (see Figure 14.19).

You should not try to move a database that is marked **Inconsistent** (as displayed when running **eseutil /mh**). Because all log files contain the path of a database in its header information, you might have problems playing log files into this database to make it consistent if the database is not where the path specifies it should be in the header information.

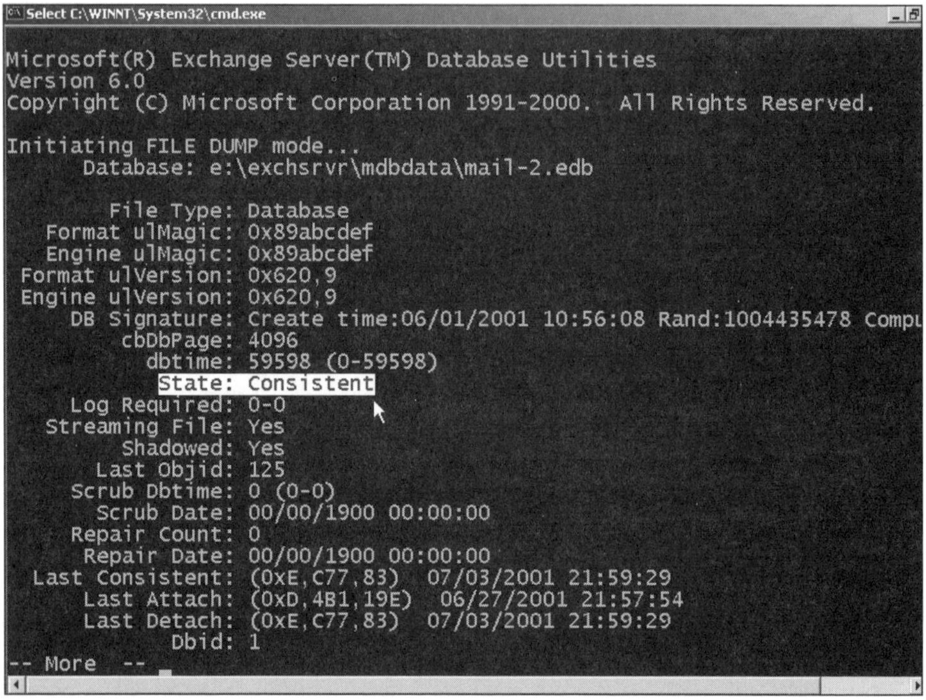

```
Select C:\WINNT\System32\cmd.exe

Microsoft(R) Exchange Server(TM) Database Utilities
Version 6.0
Copyright (C) Microsoft Corporation 1991-2000.  All Rights Reserved.

Initiating FILE DUMP mode...
      Database: e:\exchsrvr\mdbdata\mail-2.edb

        File Type: Database
     Format ulMagic: 0x89abcdef
     Engine ulMagic: 0x89abcdef
   Format ulVersion: 0x620,9
   Engine ulVersion: 0x620,9
       DB Signature: Create time:06/01/2001 10:56:08 Rand:1004435478 Compu
          cbDbPage: 4096
            dbtime: 59598 (0-59598)
             State: Consistent
      Log Required: 0-0
    Streaming File: Yes
          Shadowed: Yes
        Last Objid: 125
      Scrub Dbtime: 0 (0-0)
        Scrub Date: 00/00/1900 00:00:00
      Repair Count: 0
       Repair Date: 00/00/1900 00:00:00
   Last Consistent: (0xE,C77,83)  07/03/2001 21:59:29
       Last Attach: (0xD,4B1,19E)  06/27/2001 21:57:54
       Last Detach: (0xE,C77,83)  07/03/2001 21:59:29
              Dbid: 1
-- More  --
```

Figure 14.19 Output displayed by typing **eseutil /mh** from a command prompt.

Enabling Circular Logging for a SG

Circular logging is turned off by default for Exchange 2000. To enable this feature at the SG level using the Exchange System Manager snap-in, perform the following steps:

1. Open System Manager by clicking Start|Programs|Microsoft Exchange| System Manager.
2. When the System Manager console opens up on your screen, expand the organization object (if not already expanded). Then expand the Administrative Groups folder and the First Administrative Group folder inside.
3. Expand the Servers container and your *Server* object.
4. Right-click the First Storage Group object that appears inside your *Server* container and choose the Properties menu option. The First Storage Group Properties dialog box opens to the General tab by default (see Figure 14.20).
5. Check the Enable Circular Logging checkbox on the General tab to turn on this feature. Then, click the OK button to close the First Storage Group Properties dialog box and return to the System Manager snap-in window.

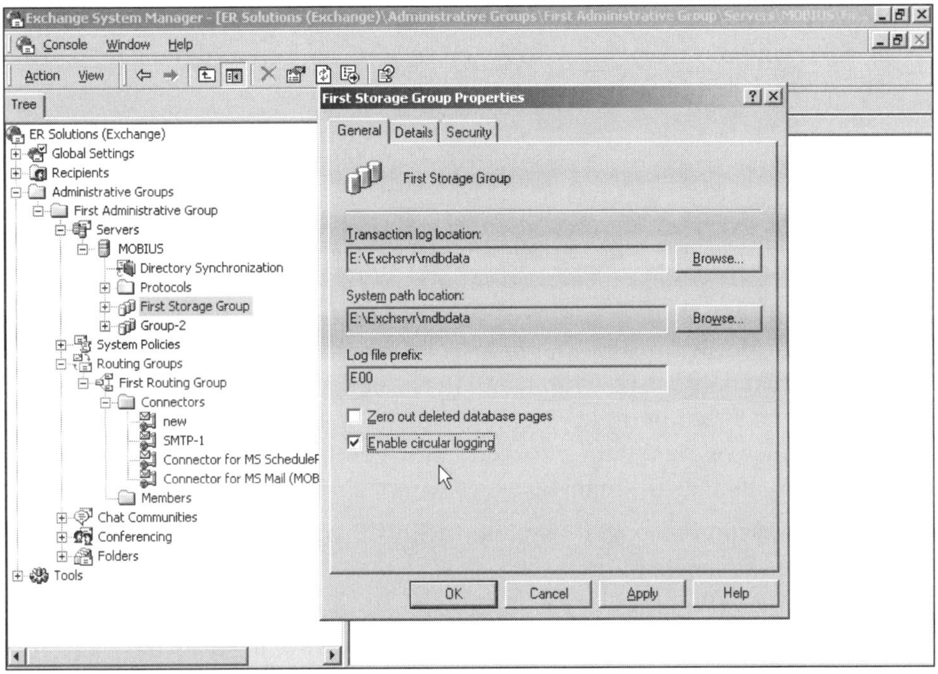

Figure 14.20 The General tab of the First Storage Group Properties dialog box.

Writing Transaction Log Files to a Different Directory or Drive

By default, Exchange 2000 places all database file and transaction log files into the same common directory path. For example, if you install Exchange 2000 on the local C: drive of your Windows 2000 Server or Advanced Server computer, the default mailbox store created in the default First Storage Group will contain files in the following directory path:

```
C:\Exchsrvr\Mdbdata\priv1.edb
C:\Exchsrvr\Mdbdata\priv1.stm
```

All default public store files found in the default First Storage Group are placed into the following directory:

```
C:\Exchsrvr\Mdbdata\pub1.edb
C:\Exchsrvr\Mdbdata\pub1.stm
```

Also, all transaction log files for the default First Storage Group are placed into the following directory location (each related file is approximately 5,120KB or 5MB in size):

```
C:\Exchsrvr\Mdbdata\E00.log (the main transaction log file)
C:\Exchsrvr\Mdbdata\E00.chk (the checkpoint file)
C:\Exchsrvr\Mdbdata\res1.log (a reserved transaction log file)
C:\Exchsrvr\Mdbdata\res2.log (a secondary reserved transaction log file)
```

You should change the location of your transaction log files so they are located on separate physical drives. This helps increase the performance of your Exchange Server so that data can be written into these log files on a continuous basis without affecting the speed of input or output operations into your permanent database files (the files marked pub1.edb, pub1.stm, priv1.edb, and priv1.stm). To do this using the Exchange System Manager snap-in:

1. Open System Manager by clicking Start|Programs|Microsoft Exchange|System Manager.
2. When the System Manager console opens, expand the organization object (if not already expanded). Then, expand the Administrative Groups folder and the First Administrative Group folder inside.
3. Expand the Servers container and your *Server* object.
4. Right-click the First Storage Group object that appears inside your *Server* container and choose the Properties menu option. The First Storage Group Properties dialog box opens to the General tab by default.
5. Click the Browse button next to the Transaction Log Location text box to open the Transaction Log dialog box. Select the new drive that will contain the transaction log files, and then click OK to return to the First Storage Group Properties dialog box.
6. Verify the change in the Transaction Log Location text box. Click OK to return to the Exchange System Manager console window.

Chapter 15

Connecting to Other Messaging Systems

If you need an immediate solution to:	See page:
Viewing Installed Connectors to Foreign Systems	630
Installing the Exchange MS Mail Connector for PC Networks	631
Verifying whether the MS Mail Connector Is Installed Properly	631
Establishing Mail Flow through a MS Mail Connector	631
Creating a PCMTA	633
Creating an Exchange 2000 Dirsync Server or Requestor	633
Creating a Schedule+ Free/Busy Connector	634
Configuring the Schedule+ Free/Busy Connector	634
Troubleshooting MS Mail Connectors	634
Troubleshooting Dirsync	635
Configuring Exchange Connector for Lotus Notes	536
Creating the Connector's Notes ID	637
Installing the Notes Client	638
Configuring the Domino Server/Lotus Notes Server	638
Installing the Lotus Notes Connector	639
Configuring the Lotus Notes Connector	639
Setting Up the Connection to a Lotus Notes Server	640
Selecting and Configuring the Import Container	641
Specifying Export Containers	642
Configuring Message Routing	643
Starting the Connector Service	644
Testing the Connection between Exchange Server and Notes	644
Specifying Notes Address Books to Be Synchronized	645
Controlling the Propagation of Notes Groups to Exchange	646

(continued)

If you need an immediate solution to:	See page:
Excluding Lotus Notes Groups from Propagation to Exchange	646
Manually Requesting Directory Updates	647
Installing the Lotus cc:Mail Connector	648
Configuring the Lotus cc:Mail Connector	649
Accessing the Post Office Tab	650
Accessing the Advanced Tab	650
Accessing the Address Space Tab	651
Accessing the Import Container Tab	652
Selecting and Configuring the Import Container	652
Exporting Contacts with the Export Container	654
Installing the Lotus cc:Mail Connector	654
Restricting the Delivery of Messages to cc:Mail	655
Configuring the Dirsync Schedule	655
Testing the Connection	656
Preparing the Novell GroupWise Environment	656
Creating and Configuring the API Gateway for GroupWise 4.*x*	657
Creating and Configuring the API Gateway for GroupWise 5.*x*	658
Activating DLs on GroupWise	659
Creating an External Foreign Domain in GroupWise 4.*x*	660
Creating an External Foreign Domain in GroupWise 5.*x*	660
Creating an NTGateway Group	661
Configuring the GroupWise Connector	662
Opening the Connector for Novell GroupWise Properties	662
Importing Directory Entries from GroupWise to Exchange	664

In Depth

Foreign systems refer to messaging systems other than Exchange Server. These foreign messaging systems include the following:

- Microsoft Mail (for PC Networks and for AppleTalk Networks)
- Systems Network Architecture Distribution System (SNADS)
- Lotus cc:Mail
- Lotus Notes
- Novell GroupWise
- IBM Professional Office System (PROFS)
- Digital Equipment Company (DEC) ALL-IN-ONE
- Verimation MEMO (now known as NetSys)
- Collabra Share

The earliest versions of these messaging systems were available long before the first version of Exchange Server was released.

In a large organization that implements heterogeneous email systems oftentimes due to mergers and reorganizations in corporate structure, an environment must be provided in which these different email systems can interoperate. Coexistence in this context means making these different email systems work together to allow seamless communication among their users. Maintaining messaging interoperability between Exchange and another messaging system is one of the primary goals of any coexistence strategy.

Although Exchange 5.5 supports all the previously mentioned foreign systems, Exchange 2000 only provides connectors for MS Mail for PC Networks, Lotus cc:Mail, Lotus Notes, and Novell GroupWise. These are shown in Figure 15.1. When upgrading Exchange 5.5 with these connectors in place, the connectors are upgraded to their Exchange 2000 versions as well. If a connector is configured in Exchange 5.5 that Exchange 2000 doesn't support—such as SNADS, PROFS, ALL-IN-ONE, MS Mail for AppleTalk Networks, and more—it isn't upgraded and the setup program stops with an error. If you have services that the Exchange 2000 connectors will not support, maintain these services on an Exchange 5.5 Server.

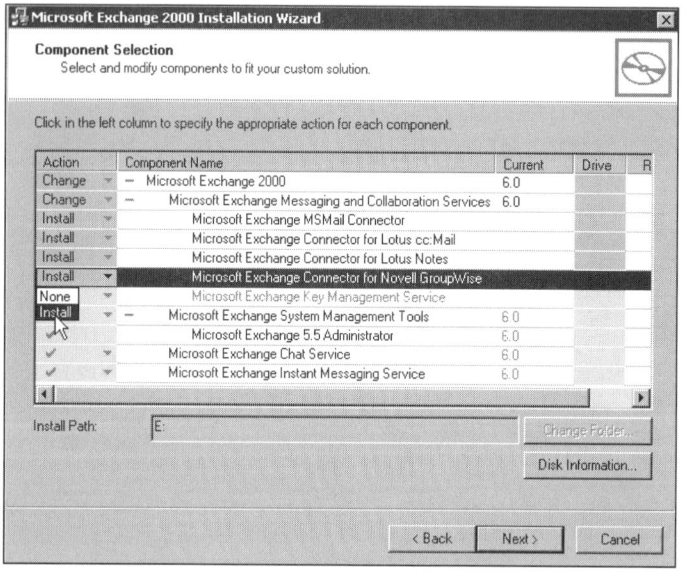

Figure 15.1 The installation of various connectors.

Exchange 2000 supports only the following connectors or import formats:

- *Exchange Lotus Notes Connector*—Provides connectivity and directory synchronization (Dirsync) with Lotus Notes environments. Enables send and receive meeting notifications from Notes.
- *Exchange MS Mail Connector*—Enables connectivity to MS Mail Servers for messaging. Dirsync is through the MS Mail Dirsync protocols. In addition, meeting requests and free/busy information can be synchronized with the Schedule+ Free/Busy Connector.
- *Exchange Lotus cc:Mail Connector*—Provides connectivity to cc:Mail networks with built-in Dirsync between cc:Mail and Active Directory (AD).
- *Exchange Novell GroupWise Connector*—Provides connectivity and Dirsync between GroupWise and AD. It supports calendaring functionality, such as meeting requests.
- *The MS Schedule+ Free/Busy Connector*—Enables Exchange 2000 to share Schedule+ free/busy information with MS Mail for PC Networks post offices.

Migrating Foreign Messaging Systems to Exchange 2000

Migration is the process of moving your existing messaging system to Exchange 2000. Migration involves exporting a copy of your existing mailboxes, messages, and other data, and then importing that information into Exchange.

Exchange 2000 provides a set of migration tools that can help you migrate your non-Exchange Server messaging system. These tools allow you to migrate users, messages, calendar information, and custom applications from your existing messaging system. You can use the tools to prevent system downtime, minimize the impact on users, and prevent data loss. The first tool is the Exchange Migration Wizard.

The Exchange Migration Wizard allows you to migrate information from the following foreign messaging systems:

- MS Mail for PC Networks 3.*x*
- Lotus cc:Mail database versions DB6 and DB8
- Lotus Notes 3.*x*, 4, 4.1, and Lotus Domino Server 4.5, 4.6, and 5
- Novell GroupWise 4.*x* and 5.*x*
- Collabra Share 1.*x* and 2.*x*
- Any LDAP-compliant (Lightweight Directory Access Protocol) Internet directory service

Any IMAP4 (Internet Message Access Protocol)-Based System

To migrate from a foreign system that is not on the list, you use one of the source extractors provided in the Migrate folder on the Exchange CD. Additional standalone extractors are provided for MS Mail for AppleTalk Networks, IBM PROFS, NetSys (formerly Verimation MEMO), and DEC ALL-IN-ONE host systems. These extractors let you extract directory information and mail data. The source extractors are not integrated into the Migration Wizard, but after extraction, you can use the wizard to import the extracted files.

This chapter concentrates on the different connectors supported by Exchange 2000 and describes what they can and can't do and how to make them work. Before you begin thinking about configuring the connector to enable Exchange 2000 to communicate with another messaging system, you have to fully understand how it will affect your entire Exchange organization. You must determine what messaging coexistence will do to your AD. If you are going to implement directory synchronization (which is more likely to happen) between the Exchange 2000 and the foreign system, how will the AD be affected?

Remember that Exchange 2000, unlike Exchange 5.5, does not have its own directory service anymore. AD provides directory service for Exchange 2000. When configuring directory synchronization, make sure that all directory information from the foreign messaging system is created in the AD properly. In previous versions of Exchange, recipients from other messaging systems were stored as custom recipients. In AD, users from foreign systems can be created either as contacts or as users. You then have to be careful when configuring Dirsync because you might inadvertently compromise your AD design. All these connectors are managed using the System Manager.

MS Mail Connector for PC Networks

MS Mail Connector transfers information between Exchange and MS Mail for PC Networks 3.*x*. Each server can run one instance of MS Mail Connector, servicing one or more connections to MS Mail post offices and Gateways using a LAN (local area network), X.25, or asynchronous connections. The MS Mail Connector provides seamless messaging connectivity to MS Mail for PC Networks. The MS Mail Connector for PC Networks is comprised of these components:

- *MS Mail Connector MTA (Message Transfer Agent)*—Similar to the MS Mail 3.*x* MTA, this routes mail between a MS Mail post office, the connector post office, a MS Mail Gateway, and the computer running Exchange Server.
- *MS Mail Connector Post Office*—This is the data file structure used to store messages in transit between users of Exchange, MS Mail 3.x, and Gateways.
- *MS Mail Connector Interchange*—This transfers and translates messages between the connector post office and the Exchange Server.

These components allow Exchange users to send and receive messages and files, and to exchange directories, meeting requests, and free/busy information with users on other systems. After the connector is in place and Dirsync has taken place, these components allow Exchange administrators to use the Migration Wizard to migrate MS Mail users easily. If you plan your Exchange Server to coexist with an MS Mail post office, you need to prepare for the tasks that coexistence entails. Before you connect to Exchange and synchronize directories, you should do the following first:

- Document the current MS Mail routing topology, Dirsync configuration, and each post office's current user population.
- Evaluate whether any routing changes are required to improve coexistence with Exchange Server.
- Have all users clear their MS Mail inboxes and reorganize their other mail folders to help ensure a smooth migration. Aside from ensuring a better migration, forcing users to periodically reorganize their email folder trees is a good preventive maintenance practice.
- Repair any existing problems with the MS Mail post office data, message delivery, or directory systems.

Completing these tasks will save you time and effort during the actual coexistence and migration phases.

MS Schedule+ Free/Busy Connector

Installing the MS Mail Connector also installs the Schedule+ Free/Busy Connector. The *Schedule+ Free/Busy Connector* allows users from Exchange Servers and MS Mail post offices to exchange free/busy information. The free and busy information refers to the times when the user is either available or unavailable for meetings. The connector processes a users' free and busy information from MS Mail (PC) post offices and updates the information in the Schedule+ Free/Busy system folder (public folder). The connector then sends updated free/busy information from Exchange Server to the MS Mail (PC) post offices. The Schedule+ Free/Busy Connector supports the exchange of free/busy information between MS Mail (PC) users and Exchange Server users on the following:

- Outlook for 32-bit platforms
- Outlook Calendar for 16-bit platforms
- Schedule+ 7
- Schedule+ 1

To configure the MS Schedule+ Free/Busy Connector, you need to understand the following objects and features:

- *Administrator's Mailbox*—This account is responsible for receiving all NDRs (nondelivery reports) generated from the failure to transmit free/busy updates.
- *Schedule+ Group*—A distribution group (distribution list [DL] in Exchange 5.5) that contains MS Mail (PC) post offices that share free/busy information with the Exchange Server site. The list should contain all AdminSch accounts.
- *Update Frequency*—You specify how often the Schedule+ Free/Busy Connector sends free/busy information to MS Mail (PC) post offices in the Schedule+ Group.
- *Full Export*—Use this option to direct the Schedule+ Free/Busy Connector to export free/busy information for all Schedule+ users. A full export is necessary when new members have been added to the Schedule+ DL.

NOTE: *If you want to limit the sending of the free/busy updates exclusively to a particular administrative group, enable the Send Updates To This Administrative Group Only checkbox. This is essential if you have multiple Exchange administrative groups that use multiple Schedule+ Free/Busy Connectors and you want to provide a one-to-one ratio between an individual Exchange administrative group and a particular MS Mail post office.*

MS Mail Dirsync

Exchange uses *Dirsync* to share address information with other messaging systems. Dirsync is the process of exchanging address information between your organization and any system that uses the MS Mail Dirsync protocol. You must run the MS Mail Dispatch program on a LAN to service MS Mail directory requestors. The Dispatch program launches programs necessary to carry out Dirsync requests on the network. Without Dispatch, automatic Dirsync won't run on MS Mail post offices. Before setting up Dirsync, verify that the Exchange and MS Mail systems you want to include are installed and running correctly. Verify that you can transfer messages between systems. Without mail flow, Dirsync won't work. MS Mail Connector must be installed on the Exchange Server you plan to use as either a Dirsync requestor or Dirsync Server. The Dirsync portion of MS Mail is accomplished via a Dirsync Server and Dirsync requestor as described here:

- A Dirsync Server sends updates to all other post offices. There is one Dirsync Server per MS Mail network.
- A requestor solely sends updates to the server, and receives updates from the server. A requestor exists on each post office in the MS Mail network, including the Dirsync Server.

NOTE: *The Dirsync Server is also a requestor.*

Exchange Lotus Notes Connector

The *Exchange Lotus Notes Connector* can connect Exchange with Notes servers. The connector has built-in messaging, Dirsync, and meeting request capabilities. In addition to allowing message exchange between the two systems, the connector provides:

- Synchronization of directory information between Exchange (AD) and Lotus Notes Name and Address Book (called in Notes release 5, Domino).
- Exchange of Rich Text Format (RTF) messages between Exchange and Notes users.
- Exchange of file objects—such as video, graphics, word processing documents, and spreadsheets—between the two systems, with file name, icon, and launch capability preserved.
- Exchange of calendar and schedule information, including the capability to schedule single and recurring meetings between users on each system.
- Support for Object Linking and Embedding (OLE) attachments.
- Support for Notes Document Links (doclinks). A *doclink* is a link embedded in a Notes document, which a user clicks to jump to a location in the same document, or to another document, folder, or database.
- Conversion of mail objects, such as attachments and Notes doclinks.

The Notes Connector runs as a Windows 2000 service on a single Exchange Server. The General tab for the Lotus Notes Properties sheet is shown in Figure 15.2. It

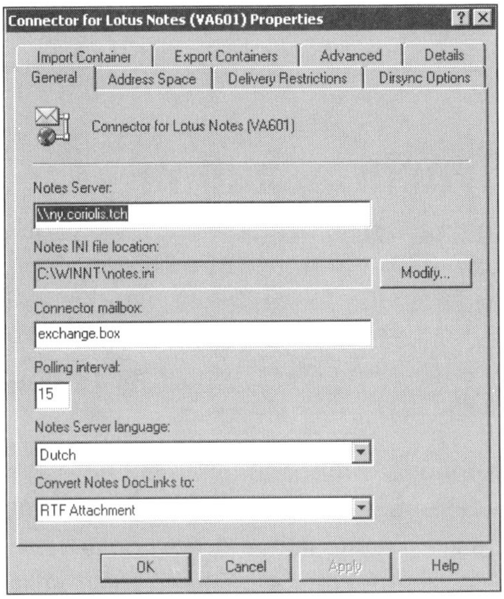

Figure 15.2 An example of a Lotus Notes Connector General Properties sheet.

uses a Lotus Notes 4.*x* or 5.*x* client on the Exchange Server to establish a network connection to a Lotus Notes/Domino Server. The Exchange Server on which the connector is installed and the Notes Server with which the connector communicates directly are called bridgehead servers. The connector also can connect downstream Exchange organizations with Notes domains. You configure and manage the connector using the System Manager snap-in. You can manage the connector from the server running the connector, or from a remote Windows 2000 Server or Windows 2000 Professional computer.

Lotus Notes Connector requires the same software as Exchange 2000. In addition, the connector requires the following software:

- Lotus Notes client 4.*x* or—if you want to use release 5.*x*—Lotus Domino Administrator. Lotus Domino Administrator includes the Notes client and enables you to perform administrative tasks on a Lotus Notes/Domino Server.
- A network connection to a Lotus Notes 3.*x* or 4.*x* Server, or a Lotus Notes/Domino 4.5.*x* or 5.*x* Server.

NOTE: *While the connector is running, do not run the Notes client or other OLE-enabled application software on the same computer as the connector. Such applications can interfere with the processing of OLE objects by the connector. Optimization of Exchange performance typically involves a trade-off between serving the needs of local users and processing message and Dirsync traffic through the connector. For best performance, install the connector on an Exchange Server other than the one that hosts user mailboxes.*

After the Notes client software has been obtained and the LAN connection to the Lotus Domino 4.*x* or 5.*x* has already been configured, you're ready to install and configure the connector.

Configuring Directory Synchronization

The Lotus Notes Connector supports bidirectional Dirsync with full-load or delta options. This means you can perform a full load or reload of the Properties page by reusing delta options; that is, instead of pulling an entire directory from your Exchange or Notes site you can request updates from either system. The default configuration in the current connector release provides the most commonly used attributes, though more might be added in subsequent releases.

The current connector release also supports multiple Notes containers, name books, and address books. In many Notes configurations, particularly those involving complex directory scenarios, users keep name and address books separate. You can allow for this with the help of the connector's extensive customization capabilities, which provide granular control of the books' presentation.

The connector also supports Notes groups and Exchange DLs, and includes some filtering capabilities. For example, you can exclude selected Notes groups, prohibit moving selected groups into Exchange DLs, and determine which custom recipients are to be included in these lists.

Configuring the Dirsync Schedule

The frequency with which Exchange sends directory updates to and receives directory updates from the connected Lotus Notes/Domino Server can be customized. If you prefer to synchronize directory information manually, you can choose not to turn off the Dirsync schedule. How often you decide to run Dirsync is influenced by the following:

- The frequency with which additions or changes are made to directories
- The estimated number of additions or changes in a given period of time
- Peak message traffic times

The more changes to the directory, the longer synchronization takes. Remember that Dirsync does not only affect the performance of the Exchange Servers, but it also slows down message throughput and consumes significant network bandwidth as well. Make sure you configure the Dirsync schedule to run during off-peak hours.

cc:Mail Directory Synchronization

Automatic Directory Exchange (ADE) is the synchronization mechanism in Lotus cc:Mail. Successful ADE updates must occur on a daily basis throughout the Lotus cc:Mail messaging system. All post offices must contain an accurate and up-to-date Lotus cc:Mail directory. When you install a post office in Lotus cc:Mail, decide whether ADE resides on the post office or not. ADE allows Dirsync between one Lotus cc:Mail post office and another.

The current design of the Lotus cc:Mail installation determines the coexistence phase and the position of the connectors. Most large installations follow a hub and spoke design with central hubs and post offices connected to the hubs. It is possible for the mail post offices to have two or three post offices connected in turn, creating longer spokes. The logical mail flow between these post offices might not be as expected because point-to-point connections can be created between any of the connected post offices.

Often, the Lotus cc:Mail administrator amends the Dirsync process and creates a mail-synchronization procedure that takes into account worldwide time zones and updates at less busy times. Only one connector has both message and Dirsync enabled.

Novell GroupWise Connector

The *Exchange Connector for Novell GroupWise* supports message transfer, Dirsync, and calendar requests between Exchange 2000 and Novell GroupWise users. Exchange Connector for Novell GroupWise performs bidirectional interchanges of major message types between Exchange 2000 and GroupWise. A GroupWise connector connects an Exchange organization to a single GroupWise post office; however, through this single connection, multiple downstream GroupWise post offices can be connected to Exchange.

When you deploy Exchange Connector for Novell GroupWise, the two systems coexist. This coexistence might be temporary, only as a path for migration; for example, the systems might need to coexist only while you migrate users from your existing messaging system to Exchange 2000. Other cases might require long-term coexistence; for example, the messaging system of a department that is not moving to Exchange 2000 might require a permanent connection. You configure the GroupWise connector using the System Manager snap-in.

System Preparation

Before you install the connector, you need to determine whether both the Exchange 2000 Server and the GroupWise Server can properly communicate.

Software requirements for running the Novell GroupWise Connector are listed as follows:

- *On the Windows Network*—Gateway and Client Services for NetWare, or the Novell NetWare Client 32 (to enable mapping to a NetWare Server). If you use Gateway and Client Services for NetWare and have trouble logging on, try configuring the service in Windows Control Panel to use Preferred Server rather than Default Tree and Context options to connect to NetWare.
- *On Novell GroupWise*—Connector for Novell GroupWise supports Dirsync and messaging for GroupWise 4.1 or later running on NetWare Server 3.*x* or 4.*x*.

NOTE: *The connector must have access to an API (Application Programming Interface) Gateway dedicated to it.*

The following are required on the Novell NetWare Server that hosts the GroupWise recipients:

- Novell NetWare 3.*x* or later
- GroupWise 4.1 API Gateway NetWare Loadable Module (NLM) (GW41API.exe)
- Novell NetWare Administrator
- Novell GroupWise 4.1 or later
- GroupWise Patch 2 for API NLM/OS2 (GW41API2.exe)

Exchange Server GroupWise Address Generation

When the GroupWise Connector is installed, it creates a GWISE address type for all the objects in AD. The default GWISE email address generated is in the format: **Exchange.First Administrative Group.%m**. The **%m** stands for aliasname. For example if the aliasname is **cherryb**, the GWISE address for this account is **Exchange. First Administrative Group.cherryb**. You can customize how Exchange Server generates the address by modifying the Recipient Policy. Other name format specifiers are indicated in Table 15.1.

Table 15.1 Recipient Policy name format specifiers.

Format Specifier	Name Component
%g	First name
%i	Initial
%s	Last name (surname)
%d	Display name
%m	Alias
%#specifier	The number of characters for the username. For example, the format specifier **%3s** for the last name Beado generates "BEA."

GroupWise Dirsync

Dirsync consists of two separate processes: exporting user data from Exchange to GroupWise and importing user data from GroupWise to Exchange. When you synchronize a schedule, one process follows the other. Note that in Novell GroupWise, each individual directory update is transmitted in a separate mail message, so Dirsync can take a long time. The update schedule option is shown in Figure 15.3. You also can export directory entries from Exchange to GroupWise. Exporting actually consists of two cycles. In the first cycle, the GroupWise Connector polls the GroupWise directory to take a snapshot of current GroupWise users before it begins the cycle of exporting directory entries. In the second cycle, directory entries are exported.

Synchronizing Groups

The connector for Novell GroupWise supports propagation of the names of groups to Exchange and GroupWise. The connector does not synchronize the memberships of the groups. The target system (either Exchange or GroupWise) must expand the group for message delivery to the membership of the list. In Exchange, GroupWise groups (DLs in GroupWise 5.*x*) appear as contacts. In GroupWise, Exchange groups appear as foreign users.

Synchronizing Resources

GroupWise has a directory object class called Resource, which is used for conference rooms, equipment, and other shared resources. In Exchange, GroupWise resources appear as contacts.

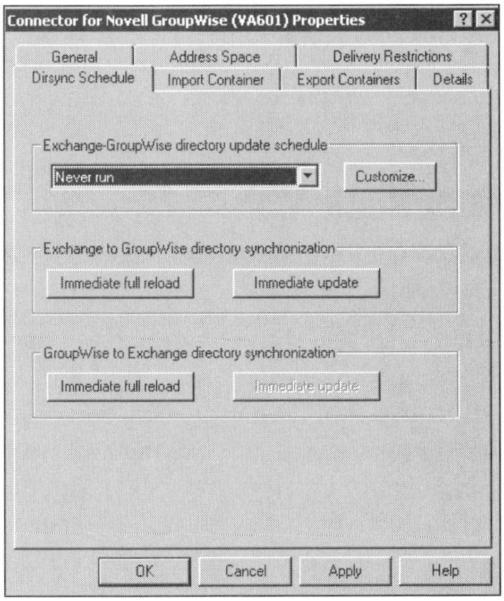

Figure 15.3 The Dirsync Schedule tab on the Novell GroupWise Connector Properties sheet.

NOTE: *Use the Dirsync Schedule tab to schedule synchronization of the GroupWise directory and the Exchange directories.*

Mobile Information Server (MIS)

With the popularity of telecommuting and wireless communications, Microsoft has released the *Mobile Information Server (MIS)* as a part of the .NET initiative. It has two editions: Enterprise Edition and Carrier Edition. MIS is a new product line from Microsoft that aims to be a reliable and scalable mobile applications server. MIS basically extends .NET applications, enterprise data, and intranet content to the mobile user. MIS Enterprise Edition includes Outlook Mobile Access, which allows users of the latest generation of mobile phones to browse their email, calendar, contacts, and tasks stored in Exchange Server in realtime. In addition, Outlook Mobile Access gives users more control over their communications by enabling them to specify how and when to be notified of high-priority items on their mobile devices.

As a mobile applications server, MIS Enterprise Edition provides a corporate mobile firewall, enabling IT administrators to set up and manage security for users who need mobile access to other intranet sites or line-of-business .NET applications within the enterprise. In addition, MIS serves as the mobile notification router for .NET applications, allowing them to send notifications to devices on mobile networks around the world.

MIS Carrier Edition will give mobile network operators a carrier-class server product that interfaces with their existing mobile data infrastructure to provide subscribers with greater security and performance for notifications originating from MIS Enterprise Edition. MIS integrates tightly with the .NET Enterprise Servers and Windows 2000 Server operating system to extend applications to multiple mobile devices.

Outlook Mobile Access and Outlook Mobile Manager

MIS ships with Outlook Mobile Access and Outlook Mobile Manager. These are two of the first applications that work with MIS:

- *Outlook Mobile Access* enables realtime access to Exchange Server-based Personal Information Manager (PIM) applications—such as email inbox, calendaring, contacts, and tasks—all from a mobile phone. Outlook Mobile Access is the mobile portal experience for browsing and receiving notifications from Outlook email, calendar, tasks, and contacts. It allows you to quickly extend the reach and utility of Exchange 2000. With secure, realtime access to live Outlook-based information, it's easy for users to control the communication and information sent through their mobile phones.

- *Outlook Mobile Manager* is a desktop computer application that extends the power, reach, and functionality of the Outlook messaging and collaboration client to a wide variety of mobile devices. Mobile Manager enables millions of Exchange users worldwide to take greater control of their mobile communications by allowing them to intelligently filter and prioritize email notifications. Outlook Mobile Manager determines when to send calendar entries, contacts, and tasks to mobile devices. Outlook Mobile Manager is available as a free Internet download from the Outlook Mobile Manager site at **www.microsoft.com/mobile**.

Exchange 2000 must be able to communicate with other messaging systems. Exchange 2000 provides built-in ways for these different messaging systems to communicate. By using different Exchange Connector Components to exchange data with other messaging systems, you provide a way for different messaging platforms to coexist. As an administrator, you can manage hybrid systems and still make the most of your current capital investments. The basis for a compromise of services across hybrid platforms lies in a simple strategy of first providing coexistence between the messaging platforms before you can migrate one system to another. Mobile Information Services integrates with Exchange 2000 to an entirely new dimension: devices. It provides anytime, anywhere access to emails, calendars, tasks, and other items that are essential to busy individuals.

Immediate Solutions

Viewing Installed Connectors to Foreign Systems

To view all installed connectors in Exchange 2000, perform the following:

1. Choose Start|Programs|Microsoft Exchange|System Manager.
2. Navigate to the Connectors container under the Administrative Groups or Routing Groups container. All the installed connectors are displayed as shown in Figure 15.4.

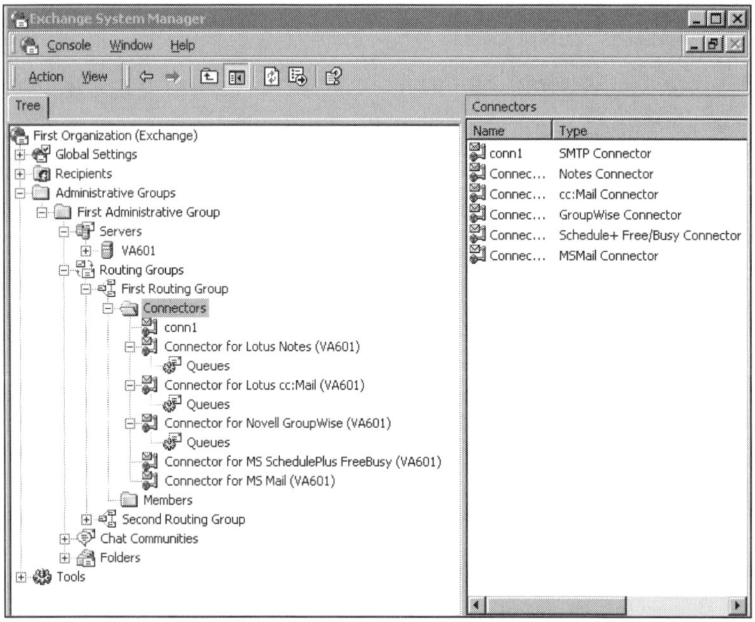

Figure 15.4 Exchange System Manager with connectors.

Installing the Exchange MS Mail Connector for PC Networks

After all the necessary preinstallation tasks have been settled, you are now ready to install the connector. To install the Exchange Connector for MS Mail, follow these steps:

1. Run Exchange 2000 Setup.
2. Click Change under Microsoft Exchange 2000.
3. Click Install under Microsoft Exchange MSMAIL Connector.
4. Complete the setup.

Verifying whether the MS Mail Connector Is Installed Properly

Following the logging of a service call, one of the first checklist items in any troubleshooting procedure is to confirm that services are running. When dealing with outside messaging platforms, always confirm proper running of the associated connector before performing any other diagnostic tests.

1. Choose Start|Programs|Microsoft Exchange|System Manager.
2. Navigate to the Recipient Policies node.
3. In the Details pane, right-click the appropriate Recipient Policy, and then click Properties.
4. On the Email Addresses tab, verify that MS is among the listed email address types. Selecting the MS checkbox updates the Recipient Policy, which includes the displayed MS Mail address.

Establishing Mail Flow through a MS Mail Connector

After you have installed the Exchange MS Mail Connector, perform the following steps to establish mail flow on the Exchange 2000 side. MS Mail Connector configurations are done on the Properties pages of the connector. The Properties

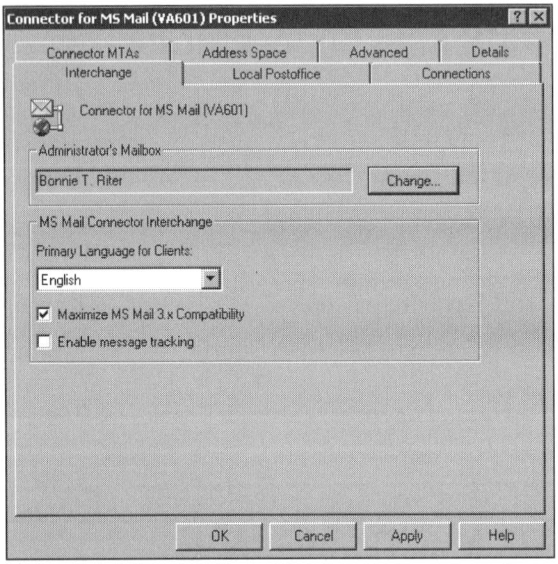

Figure 15.5 MS Mail Connector.

pages are viewed via the Exchange System Manager shown in Figure 15.5. Follow these steps:

1. Choose Start|Programs|Microsoft Exchange|System Manager.
2. Navigate to the Connectors container under the Administrative Groups or Routing Groups container.
3. Open the Connector for MS Mail Properties.
4. On the Interchange tab, select a user for the Administrator's Mailbox.
5. On the Connections tab, create a post office definition from the following four choices: LAN, Async, X.25, and Indirect. If you select LAN, you need the full Universal Naming Convention (UNC) path and logon credential information to the MS Mail post office. If you select Async, you need information for the MSMAIL Network, MSMAIL post office, Sign-on id, Password, and Telephone Number fields. If you select X.25, you need information for the MSMAIL Network, MSMAIL post office, Sign-on id, Password, and X.121 Address fields. The Indirect option is not available until you define at least one direct route.

Creating a PCMTA

Mail can be transferred between Exchange 2000 and MS Mail only with the aid of the MS Mail (PC) MTA (PCMTA). You must create and start this service for mail to flow. Use the following steps to create and configure the PCMTA:

1. Choose Start|Programs|Microsoft Exchange|System Manager.
2. Navigate to the Connectors container under the Administrative Groups or Routing Groups container.
3. Open the properties for Connector for MS Mail.
4. Click the Connector MTA tab.
5. Click New, and then create your MTA service.
6. On the Connector MTA tab, under Post Offices Serviced, click List, and then add the post office you want this MTA to send mail to and receive mail from.

Creating an Exchange 2000 Dirsync Server or Requestor

When the MS Mail Connector is selected from setup, the MS Mail Connector and the Free/Busy Schedule Connector install by default. Because the Dirsync service appears at setup, configure only the connectors. The following steps will configure the Dirsync service.

1. Choose Start|Programs|Microsoft Exchange|System Manager.
2. Navigate to the Connectors container under the Administrative Groups or Routing Groups container.
3. Right-click Connectors, point to New, and then click Dirsync Requestor or Dirsync Server. You must configure the connectors in the following order:
   - *MS Mail Connector*—Sends mail between Exchange and MS Mail.
   - *Dirsync Requestor or Server*—Populates the user list with the other system's mail addresses.
   - *Free/Busy Connector*—Free and Busy schedules appear in meeting requests.

The Dirsync service populates the mail addresses and allows for easier selection of the relevant email addresses from either system. The Dirsync service can be a requestor or a server. Your current MS Mail configuration determines the required type of service.

Creating a Schedule+ Free/Busy Connector

Setting up the Schedule+ Free/Busy Connector to transfer schedule information between Microsoft Exchange Server recipients and MS Mail (PC) recipients requires the following:

- Installing the MS Mail Connector.
- Creating an AdminSch account on all post offices participating in schedule sharing.
- Installing the Schedule+ program files on a MS Mail (PC) Post Office Server.
- Installing the Schedule+ Administrator program.
- Configuring the **Schdist.exe** program.
- Configuring the Schedule+ Free/Busy Connector.

Configuring the Schedule+ Free/Busy Connector

To configure a Schedule+ Free/Busy Connector, use the Exchange System Manager snap-in:

1. Choose Start|Programs|Microsoft Exchange|System Manager.
2. Navigate to the Connectors container under the Administrative Groups or Routing Groups container.
3. Right-click Connector for MS Schedule+ FreeBusy to bring up the Connector for MS Schedule+ Free/Busy Properties.

Troubleshooting MS Mail Connectors

If you suspect that something is wrong with your configuration, the best way to troubleshoot is to test the MS Mail Connector and verify that it can transport messages from MS Mail post office to Exchange Server and vice versa. The following lists the most common MS Mail Connector issues, causes, and resolutions.

If you cannot receive mail from a MS Mail post office, the MS Mail Connector interchange service may not be running: check the Event Viewer. The following message in Event Viewer indicates that the connector post office has corrupt or missing files: "MS Mail Connector Interchange has failed to start the mailer component." Return code from mailer is 0x2, and the return code Win32 is 0x3. Check that the MS Mail Connector Interchange Service Account has access to the MS

Mail Connector Post Office Share. Alternatively, the connector post office might have received a corrupt message. If you suspect post office is corrupt, check the /KEY, /MBG, and /P1 directories and validate the following:

- The subdirectories listed previously exist on the system.
- The files in these subdirectories are valid.
- All files with a .key extension are 560 bytes.
- All files with an .mbg extension are 116 bytes.

If you think the connector post office received a corrupt message, take the following steps:

1. View the messages in the Exchange MTA queue for the connector interchange.
2. Return the oldest message and restart the service.
3. Continue returning the oldest message and restarting the service after each return.
4. When you find the corrupt message, talk with the sender to determine what was wrong with the message.

Another problem might be that the MS Mail Connector MTA service is not running. Check the event log. If the connector must be reinstalled, the log will tell you to do so. You could have received a corrupt message in the ingoing or outgoing queue. Check the MTA queues on the Connector MTAs tab of the MS Mail Properties dialog box.

If the MS Mail post office has not been configured to recognize Exchange, verify that the connector interchange is running. Check the Event Viewer. If a connector has failed or needs reinstallation, an event will indicate the situation, verify that the connector MTA is running. After you configure the connector, you must confirm that each connected MS Mail post office recognizes the other connector post office on. Check the MTA queues from the Connector MTAs tab in MS Mail Properties.

Troubleshooting Dirsync

In an environment with one MS Mail server, it can coexist with the Exchange Server acting as a Dirsync Server. Plan which post offices are to be Dirsync requestors and which server is to be the Dirsync Server. In a new environment, make the Dirsync Server the Exchange Server. Remember, only one Dirsync Server exists in a MS Mail environment. This rule also applies to a company using

Exchange 2000. MS Mail uses a concept of time points—T1, T2, and T3—to define its Dirsync cycle:

- *T1*—All the requestors send their updates to the Dirsync Server.
- *T2*—All the updates process on the server. T2 indicates when all changes propagate back to the requestors.
- *T3*—Requestors receive the new updates from the Dirsync Server.

If Dirsync is not working after the T1, T2, and T3 time points, you can manually synchronize on the Dirsync Server and use the command prompt to force the updates. If the Dirsync service fails, check the configuration. Manual updates do not necessarily fix the failure. Run the DOS commands in the *MS Mail Administrator's Handbook* on the mail post office Dirsync Server, which is assigned to the M drive.

Common Problem: Dirsync Not Working Due to Fatal 203 Rebuild Error

This is usually caused by older versions of the MS Mail client locking open certain Global Address List (GAL) files on a MS Mail post office, specifically the MS Mail Windows client files MSSFS.DLL (prior to 3.2.4079), or AB.DLL (prior to 3.2.4048). Make sure you have the latest updates and versions for all clients.

Configuring Exchange Connector for Lotus Notes

Among the Exchange connectors, the connector for Lotus Notes is the most complex to configure and often the most difficult to troubleshoot. The following list summarizes the tasks you must do to configure the Lotus Notes Connector; it's important that you do the tasks in the following order:

1. Create a Lotus Notes ID for the connector on the Lotus Notes/Domino Server.
2. Install the Lotus Notes 4.52/R5 client software.
3. Configure the Lotus Notes/Domino Server to operate with the connector.
4. Set up the connector's Exchange Server components.
5. Configure the connector.
6. Start the connector service.
7. Test the connector.
8. Synchronize the directory information.

Creating the Connector's Notes ID

To transfer messages to and from Lotus Notes and to perform Dirsync, the connector requires access to several Lotus Notes databases. Complete the following procedure to create a certified Lotus Notes ID file, which the connector uses to access the Lotus Notes/Domino Server and to create a Person document in the Lotus Notes/Domino registration server's Name and Address Book. To create a user ID for the connector:

1. Start the Lotus Notes 4.*x* client or, if you are using release 5.*x*, the Lotus Domino Administrator program.
2. Choose File|Tools|Server Administration.
3. Click People, and then click Register Person.
4. Verify that you have a license for the user ID you are creating. If you meet the licensing requirements, click Yes.
5. Type the administration password for the specified certifier, and then click OK.
6. If the local server is not the registration server, click Registration Server, select the registration server, and then click OK. To select a different certifier, click Certifier ID, select the certifier, and then click Open. Type the administrator's password, and then click OK.
7. In Security Type, click North American or International.
8. In Certificate Expiration Date, type the date in *mm-dd-yy* format to change the expiration date, and then click Continue.
9. In Last Name, type a name for the connector (for example, "Connector").
10. In Minimum Password Length, click 0 and leave the Password box blank. This allows the connector to operate unattended when accessing its databases on the Lotus Notes/Domino Server.
11. In License Type, click Lotus Notes Desktop.
12. Click the Mail icon.
13. On the Mail Type menu, click None.
14. On the Home Server menu, select the Lotus Notes/Domino Server on which the connector's databases will be located.
15. Click the Other icon.
16. Verify that In Address Book is not selected. This is required because the password of this user ID file is set to blank.

17. Click In File to generate the user ID as a file. Click Set ID File and specify the file name (for example, "Exchconn.id"). The user ID file must be in a location that is accessible to the server on which the connector is installed.
18. Click Save, and then click Register.

Installing the Notes Client

Because the Notes Connector requires access to Notes client program files, you must install the Notes client on the Exchange Server on which you installed the connector. To install the Notes client program, perform the following:

1. From the Notes CD or from an installation point, double-click the Notes Install program.
2. Install the client software. If you are installing Notes client R5, select Domino Administrator. This option also installs the Notes client.
3. When configuring the client after installation, provide the connector's username or ID file for identification.
4. Note the location of the Notes.ini file (*drive*:\Lotus\Notes\ by default). You will need this information when you configure the connector.
5. Verify that the *drive*:\Lotus\Notes\ directory is added to the system path. To locate the Notes client installation, the connector searches the system path on the Exchange Server.
6. Start the Notes client and verify that you can establish a connection to the Lotus Notes/Domino Server.

Configuring the Domino Server/Lotus Notes Server

You must configure the Lotus Notes/Domino Server before configuring the connector. The Lotus Notes/Domino Server has to be readied to work with the connector. To configure the Lotus Notes/Domino Server to operate with the connector:

1. Update the Notes Person document for the connector's Notes user ID to exclude it from Dirsync.
2. Grant the Connector Depositor access to Mail.box, the Lotus Notes/Domino Server router mailbox.
3. Grant the Connector Editor access with Delete documents privileges to the Notes Name and Address Book.

4. Grant the connector Reader access to databases from which users create doclinks.
5. Identify the Exchange organization as a foreign domain to Notes.
6. Grant the connector's Notes user ID permission to perform routine database maintenance.
7. Enable the Lotus Notes/Domino Server to route Internet-bound messages through Exchange.

NOTE: *If you configure separate source and target Name and Address Books, you only need to grant the connector Reader access to the source Name and Address Book. In this case, the target Name and Address Book requires Editor access.*

Installing the Lotus Notes Connector

To install the Lotus Notes Connector, perform the following:

1. Run Exchange 2000 Setup.
2. Click Change under Microsoft Exchange 2000.
3. Click Install under Microsoft Exchange Lotus Notes Connector.
4. Complete the setup.

Configuring the Lotus Notes Connector

After installing the connector for Lotus Notes, you use the System Manager snap-in to configure the connector and enable it to communicate with Notes. Before you configure the connector, make sure a Notes user ID for the connector is on the Lotus Notes/Domino Server, the Lotus Notes 4.*x* or 5.*x* (R5) client software is on the Exchange Server on which the connector is installed, and the Lotus Notes/ Domino Server has been configured for Exchange. Almost all configuration settings for the Lotus Notes Connector are done on the Properties pages of the connector.

To configure the Lotus Notes Connector, perform the following tasks:

1. Set up the connection to the Lotus Notes/Domino Server.
2. Enable Notes proxy addresses in the appropriate Recipient Policy.
3. Specify the Import container for Notes objects.

4. Specify Export containers for Exchange addresses.
5. Configure message routing.
6. Set the Dirsync schedule.
7. Specify the Notes Address Books you want to synchronize.
8. Control the propagation of Notes groups to Exchange.
9. Synchronize the directory information. This identifies the Exchange organization as a foreign domain to Notes and exchanges directory information between the two messaging systems.
10. Test the connection between the Exchange organization and the Notes system. If your Exchange organization contains one or more downstream Exchange Servers, Lotus Notes Email Address Generator automatically replicates to these servers after you install the connector. However, if you need to connect downstream Notes domains to your Exchange organization, you must identify those domains to the connector. Choose how Notes doclinks are represented in messages sent from Notes to Exchange. Restrict the flow of messages from Exchange to Notes.
11. Start the Connector Service.

Setting Up the Connection to a Lotus Notes Server

To set up the connection to a Lotus Notes Server, perform the following:

1. Choose Start|Programs|Microsoft Exchange|System Manager.
2. Navigate to the Connectors node.
3. Right-click Connector For Lotus Notes (*server_name*), and then click Properties.
4. On the General tab, in Notes Server, type the full name of the Lotus Notes/Domino Server you want the connector to connect to. Use the *Notes server/Notes organization* convention.
5. Verify that Notes INI File Location displays the full path and file name of the Notes.ini file. If you need to designate a different location, click Modify.
6. Verify that Connector Mailbox displays the name of the connector's primary mail file, Exchange.box. If you used a different name for the connector mailbox, type the new name in the text box.
7. In Polling Interval, type a new value or accept the default of 15. The polling interval specifies how often, in seconds, the connector checks its primary mail file (Exchange.box) for messages to be delivered to Exchange recipients.

8. Verify that Notes Server Language displays the operating language of the connected Lotus Notes/Domino Server. The server language is used for messages that the connector inserts into a message (for example, an explanation of a NDR).

Selecting and Configuring the Import Container

The *Import container* stores Notes objects imported from the Lotus Notes/Domino Server to the Exchange Server. Imported Notes objects include users, groups, and resources. (A Notes *resource* is a physical item that can be reserved for a meeting, such as a conference room or an overhead projector.) Each imported object can be represented in AD as a Windows user or contact. The Import Container tab for the Lotus Notes Connector is shown in Figure 15.6. To select and configure the Import container, perform the following:

1. Choose Start|Programs|Microsoft Exchange|System Manager.
2. Navigate to the Connectors node.
3. Right-click Connector For Lotus Notes (*server_name*), and then click Properties.
4. Click the Import Container tab, and then click Modify to select the Import container.

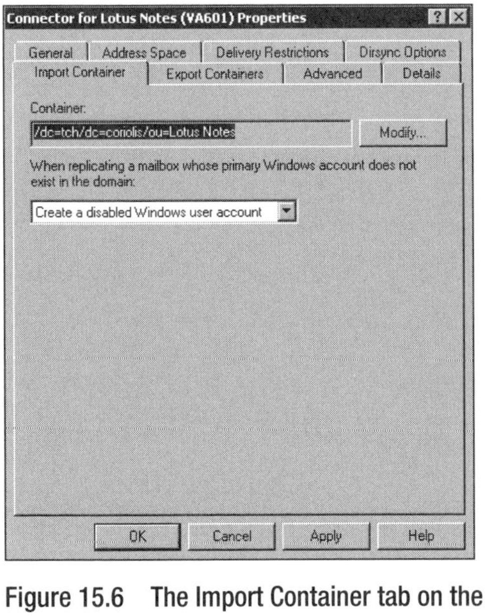

Figure 15.6 The Import Container tab on the Lotus Notes Connector.

5. In Choose A Container, open the domain node, select the container, and then click OK.
6. Select one of the following options to determine how the Dirsync process handles imported Notes objects that do not already have Windows 2000 accounts:
   - Create A Disabled Windows User Account
   - Create A New Windows User Account
   - Create A New Windows Contact

Specifying Export Containers

Export containers contain Exchange recipient addresses that you want to export to Notes Name And Address Books when you run Dirsync. Notes Email Address Generator creates a Notes address, based on the defined address rule, for each exported Exchange recipient. You can designate an existing Organizational Unit (OU) as your Export container or you can create one if necessary. The Export Containers tab on the Notes Connector Properties sheet is shown in Figure 15.7. To specify the Export containers, perform the following:

1. Choose Start|Programs|Microsoft Exchange|System Manager.
2. Navigate to the Connectors node.

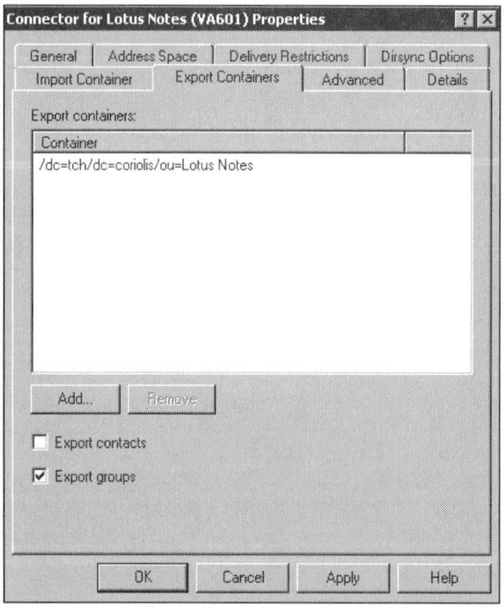

Figure 15.7 The Export Containers tab on the Lotus Notes Connector.

3. Right-click Connector For Lotus Notes (*server_name*), and then click Properties.
4. Click the Export Containers tab. To export contacts to Notes, select Export Contacts. Groups are exported by default. Export Contacts and Export Groups allow you to choose which Exchange recipients you want to make known to the Lotus Notes system.
5. Click Add to select an Export container. In Choose A Container, open the domain node, and then select the container.

NOTE: *If you need to stop the export of recipients in a container, select the container in the list of Export containers, and then click Remove. This does not remove the container from AD.*

Configuring Message Routing

Messages that pass through the Notes Connector must have the correct address space so that they can be routed to the correct destination in Notes. The address space specifies which messages bound for the Notes system are accepted and routed by the connector. To configure message routing for the connector, perform the following:

1. Choose Start|Programs|Microsoft Exchange|System Manager.
2. Navigate to the Connectors node.
3. Right-click Connector For Lotus Notes (*server_name*), and then click Properties.
4. On the Address Space tab, click Add.
5. In New Address Space, select Notes, and then click OK. Provide the following information:
   - *User Name*—This option designates who the connector accepts messages from. You can enter an asterisk (*) to allow all users in the connected Exchange organization to send messages to users on the Notes system. If you want only a specific group to use the connector, enter the display name of the group.
   - *Domain*—This option specifies the Notes domain to which the connector is connected.
   - *Cost*—This option specifies a routing metric that indicates the relative "cost" of using a particular connector to send messages. The cost determines the preferred route for a message among multiple routes.

Lower-cost routes take precedence over higher-cost routes. To balance the message load across multiple connectors, assign the same cost to each connector. The range is 0 to 100; the default is 1.

If you want to limit the connector's scope to Exchange Servers that belong to the routing group where the connector is installed, click Routing Group. Start the Connector.

Starting the Connector Service

The Notes Connector runs as a Windows 2000 service:

1. Choose Start|Programs|Administrative Tools|Services.
2. In the Details pane, right-click Microsoft Exchange Connector For Lotus Notes, and then click Start. You configure the Notes Connector service to start automatically when setting the startup type to Automatic Start The Server.

Testing the Connection between Exchange Server and Notes

After configuring the connector, you should test the connection between the two systems before allowing users to exchange messages. You first synchronize the Exchange and Notes directories, and then you check the Import container (an OU in AD) and the Notes Name and Address Book on the Lotus Notes/Domino Server. To test the connection:

1. Choose Start|Programs|Microsoft Exchange|System Manager.
2. Navigate to the Connectors node.
3. Right-click Connector For Lotus Notes (*server_name*), and then click Properties.
4. Click the Dirsync Options tab.
5. Under Exchange To Notes Dirsync, click Immediate Full Reload to populate the target Name and Address Book with Exchange addresses.
6. Under Notes To Exchange Directory Synchronization, click Immediate Full Reload to populate the Exchange Import container with Notes addresses.
7. Start AD Users and Computers by choosing Start|Programs|Administrative Tools|Active Directory Users And Computers.

8. Verify that the container you specified in the Import Container tab contains Notes users.
9. On the Lotus Notes/Domino Server, verify that the target Name and Address Book contains Exchange recipients.
10. Wait a few minutes, and then send a message from an Exchange user to a Notes user. If the mail goes through, you're halfway done.
11. Send a reply from the Notes user. If the exchange user receives the email, the Lotus Notes Connector configuration is successful.

NOTE: *Depending on the size of the directories, it might take awhile for Recipient Update Service (RUS) to populate the Exchange address lists.*

Specifying Notes Address Books to Be Synchronized

Use the Notes Address Books dialog box to specify the Notes Address Books that will participate in Dirsync with Exchange. You can specify the default Notes Name and Address Book in which Exchange AD objects are created, and the Name and Address Book from which Notes directory objects are sent to AD. The connector also can be configured so that addresses from Exchange that contain specific domain names are placed in different address books. To specify the Notes Address Books you want to synchronize, perform the following:

1. Choose Start|Programs|Microsoft Exchange|System Manager.
2. Navigate to the Connectors node.
3. Right-click Connector For Lotus Notes (*server_name*), and then click Properties.
4. Click the Dirsync Options tab, and then click Address Books Settings.
5. In Default Name And Address Book, type the name of the Notes database file you want to use as the target for Exchange updates. The default is Names.nsf. If you don't want to synchronize the Notes Address Book with the Exchange domain, leave this text box blank.
6. Under Domain-Specific Target Name And Address Books, click Add. Exchange objects that contain one of the domain names in Domain-Specific Target Name and Address Books are stored in the corresponding Notes Name and Address Book. Exchange objects that have a domain value that does not match one of the specified domain names are stored in the default target Name and Address Book.

7. In Add Address Book For A Specific Domain, type a domain name and the name of the associated Address Book in which you want to store addresses from that domain.
8. Repeat the previous two steps for each domain for which you want a separate Address Book.
9. Under Source Name And Address Books, click Add. Type the names of the Notes database files that contain objects that you want to propagate to Exchange. Separate each name with a comma. The default is Names.nsf.

NOTE: *Using the Notes Name and Address Book (Names.nsf) as a target for Exchange updates simplifies Dirsync in a Notes environment. If you do not want the connector to update Names.nsf, you can specify a different target Name and Address Book.*

Controlling the Propagation of Notes Groups to Exchange

The propagation of specific Lotus Notes groups (DLs) to Exchange can be controlled. This enables Exchange users to address messages to a group of Notes users by specifying the name of the group as a message recipient. When the Lotus Notes/Domino Server receives the message, it distributes the message to each Lotus Notes user who is a member of the group. You can prevent the propagation of Notes groups to Exchange by:

- Excluding all Lotus Notes groups from propagation in the specified source Name and Address Books
- Excluding specific groups from propagation

Excluding Lotus Notes Groups from Propagation to Exchange

To control the propagation of Lotus Notes groups to Exchange, perform the following:

1. Choose Start|Programs|Microsoft Exchange|System Manager.
2. Navigate to the Connectors node.
3. Right-click Connector For Lotus Notes (*server_name*), and then click Properties.

4. Click the Dirsync Options tab.
5. Click Address Book Settings.
6. Under Source Name And Address Books, Propagate Groups is selected by default. To prevent the propagation of all groups, clear Propagate Groups.
7. To prevent the propagation of a specific group, click Add, type the name of the group in Exclude Following Group, and then click OK.

***NOTE:** By default, the groups OtherDomainServers and LocalDomainServers are excluded because they define servers, not users.*

Manually Requesting Directory Updates

Directory information is typically synchronized according to a predefined schedule that you set. Sometimes, however, you might need to synchronize directory information before the scheduled time. The Notes Connector enables you to propagate directory updates separately in each direction: from Exchange to Notes, and from Notes to Exchange. To force Dirsync, perform the following:

1. Choose Start|Programs|Microsoft Exchange|System Manager.
2. Navigate to the Connectors node.
3. Right-click Connector For Lotus Notes (*server_name*), and then click Properties.
4. Click the Dirsync Options tab.

To synchronize directory information from Exchange to Notes, click one of the following under Exchange To Notes Dirsync:

- *Immediate Reload*—This option initiates an immediate reload of AD to the Notes directory.
- *Immediate Update*—This option initiates an immediate update (changed and new objects only) from AD to the Notes directory.

To synchronize directory information from Notes to Exchange, click one of the following under Notes To Exchange Dirsync:

- *Immediate Full Reload*—This option initiates an immediate reload of the entire Notes directory to AD.
- *Immediate Update*—This option initiates an immediate update (changed or new objects only) from the Notes directory to AD.

Installing the Lotus cc:Mail Connector

The Exchange Connector for Lotus cc:Mail supports DB8 type Lotus cc:Mail post offices. Lotus cc:Mail users join the AD as contacts, mail-enabled users, or disabled users. Dirsync is part of the connector, and only requires the latest versions of Import and Export, which are available from Lotus cc:Mail. All connector configuration is available in System Manager.

Installing is easier and more reliable if you are connecting to a Lotus cc:Mail post office running DB8. Verify that the routing Lotus cc:Mail post offices have the latest versions of Import.exe and Export.exe installed. Import.exe and Export.exe are available on the Lotus cc:Mail software disks.

Exchange uses the cc:Mail Connector and the cc:Mail Import and Export programs to communicate and exchange messages with cc:Mail messaging systems. The following components work together to transfer messages and other objects between the two systems:

- *cc:Mail Connector Service*—A Windows 2000 Server service that transfers messages between Exchange and cc:Mail. It also synchronizes selected AD users, groups, and contacts with the cc:Mail directory.
- *cc:Mail Connector Queue*—A location on the Exchange Server that holds messages in transit.
- *Lotus cc:Mail Import and Export programs*—Imports Exchange messages and directory entries to cc:Mail post offices and exports cc:Mail messages and directory entries to Exchange.
- *Configuring Lotus cc:Mail Connector*—Before installing the Lotus cc:Mail Connector, make sure that the cc:Mail post office you intend to connect to is running DB8 and that it's using the Import/Export version 8.3 or later. Earlier versions of the cc:Mail Import/Export are not compatible with Exchange 2000. Make sure you have copied the Lotus cc:Mail Import and Export programs and their resource files (for example, Impexp.ri) to a directory listed in the Windows 2000 Server system path, such as \Winnt. Or, you can copy the programs and resource files to another directory, and then add that directory to the Windows 2000 Server system **PATH** environment variable.

To install the Lotus cc:Mail Connector:

1. Run Exchange 2000 Setup.
2. Click Change under Microsoft Exchange 2000.
3. Click Install under Microsoft Exchange Lotus Notes Connector.
4. Complete the setup.

Configuring the Lotus cc:Mail Connector

After installation, you can configure the settings for the Lotus cc:Mail Connector. To configure the cc:Mail Connector, you use the System Manager snap-in. To configure the connector, you need to do the following:

1. Set up a connection to the cc:Mail post office.
2. Enable cc:Mail proxy addresses in the appropriate Recipient Policy.
3. Select and configure the Import container.
4. Specify the Export containers.
5. Configure message routing.
6. Set the Dirsync schedule.
7. Start the connector.
8. Synchronize the directory information. This identifies the Exchange organization as a post office to cc:Mail and exchanges directory information between the two messaging systems.
9. Test the connection between the two systems.

The following section lists the configuration of the Exchange Connector for Lotus cc:Mail by defining each tab on the Lotus cc:Mail Connector Properties page. These properties are available in System Manager. The Exchange Lotus cc:Mail Connector Properties pages are shown in Figure 15.8. To configure your connector, use the Post Office tab. This is where you set up the connection to the cc:Mail post office.

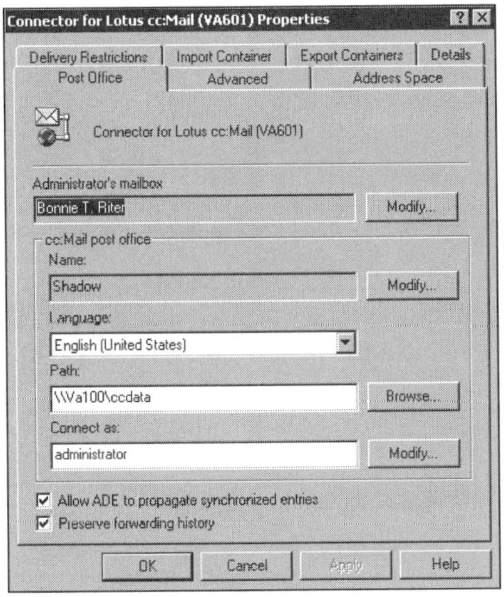

Figure 15.8 Lotus cc:Mail.

Accessing the Post Office Tab

To access the Post Office tab, perform the following:

1. Choose Start|Programs|Microsoft Exchange|System Manager.
2. Navigate to Connectors.
3. Right-click Connector For Lotus cc:Mail (*server_name*), and then click Properties.
4. On the Post Office tab, provide information for the following as needed:
    - *Administrator's Mailbox*—Enter an administrator to receive messages from the connector for delivery information, and issues that arise with the connector.
    - *cc:Mail Post Office*—Enter the name of the post office you are connecting to the connector. The post office must be a DB8 post office.
    - *Language*—Enter the primary language used by the post office.
    - *Path*—Enter the path to the post office. You can use a UNC such as "*ccmailserver**ccmdata*". If the cc:Mail post office is on Novell NetWare, you have to configure the Gateway Services for Novell NetWare (GSNW).
    - *Connect As*—Enter a Windows account with access to the shared path mentioned previously.
    - *Allow ADE To Propagate Synchronized Entries*—Select this box for updates sent from AD to Lotus cc:Mail to be propagated to other connected Lotus cc:Mail post offices with ADE.
    - *Preserve Forwarding History*—Select this box to preserve the forwarding history of messages sent from Lotus cc:Mail to Exchange. This history appears in Exchange as an attachment.

Accessing the Advanced Tab

You configure the message size restrictions for all messages that will be crossing the connector on the Advanced tab. You also set the synchronization schedule on this tab.

To access the Advanced tab, perform the following:

1. Choose Start|Programs|Microsoft Exchange|System Manager.
2. Navigate to Connectors.

3. Right-click Connector For Lotus cc:Mail (*server_name*), and then click Properties.
4. Click the Advanced tab and configure the following:
   - *Message Size*—You can restrict the size of messages that go through the connector.
   - *Exchange-Lotus cc:Mail Directory Update Schedule*—Select the time when you want to run Dirsync. This should be coordinated with the times set for the Lotus cc:Mail environment. Before synchronizing the directories, verify that all the changes in the Lotus cc:Mail environment have arrived at the Lotus cc:Mail post office where the connector runs. In addition, you need to make sure the updates inserted in the Lotus cc:Mail post office from Exchange propagate back to connected Lotus cc:Mail post offices.

Accessing the Address Space Tab

The Address Space tab determines the type of addresses for which the connector is responsible. Two fields are required for address space configuration: mailbox and post office. Most companies use wildcards for this so that the Exchange Connector for Lotus cc:Mail routes any messages—such as **at** *—to the cc:Mail Connector.

Some companies might decide to separate their traffic across many connectors. You can decide which connector is responsible for which post office by using the address space. The format is **CCMAIL:* at postoffice**.

To access the Address Space tab, perform the following:

1. Choose Start|Programs|Microsoft Exchange|System Manager.
2. Navigate to Connectors.
3. Right-click Connector For Lotus cc:Mail (*server_name*), and then click Properties.
4. Click the Address Space tab.
5. Click the Add button to add an Address Space.
6. Choose the Connector Scope. The default is Entire Organization, which makes the Address Space known throughout the entire Exchange organization. If you want the connector to be seen only by a group of Exchange Servers, set the Connector Scope to Routing Group Only.

Accessing the Import Container Tab

You specify how the Lotus cc:Mail entries are stored in AD on the Import Container tab. Plan your AD strategy before configuring this tab. You can separate each outside group by OU. For example, you could create an OU under Users for Lotus cc:Mail Users, and select that as your container for Lotus cc:Mail users.

Additionally, this tab specifies how Lotus cc:Mail users import. There are three options:

- *Contacts*—Users with email addresses that do not log on to Windows 2000, and therefore, do not have access to Windows 2000 resources
- *Mail-Enabled Users*—Users that are mail-enabled and that log on to Windows 2000 for access to Windows 2000 resources
- *Disabled Windows Account*—Notes users that might or might not log on to a Windows NT 4 domain, but are scheduled to migrate to Windows 2000 later

Decide which type of address goes into the Dirsync. You have the option of entering filters that allow only certain addresses to be propagated to Exchange:

- *Import All Directory Entries*—Select this if you do not want to filter any entries.
- *Only Import Directory Entries Of These Formats*—Select this if you want to receive only certain post offices. For example, if you only want users on PO1 and PO2 to synchronize back to Exchange, enter the following two filters: "* at PO1 and * at PO2".
- *Do Not Import Directory Entries Of These Formats*—Select this to exclude some post offices. For example, if you do not want to receive any users in the post office London, you would enter the following filter: "* at London".

Selecting and Configuring the Import Container

To select and configure the Import container, perform the following:

1. Choose Start|Programs|Microsoft Exchange|System Manager.
2. Navigate to Connectors.
3. Right-click Connector For Lotus cc:Mail (*server_name*), and then click Properties.

4. Click the Import Container tab.
5. Select the Import container and then click Modify.
6. In Choose A Container, open the domain node, select the container, and then click OK.
7. On the Import Container tab, select one of the following options to determine how the Dirsync process handles imported cc:Mail users who do not already have Windows 2000 accounts. The options are shown in Figure 15.9. You can create a new user, new contact, or a new, but disabled user.
   - Create A Disabled Windows User Account.
   - Create A New Windows User Account.
   - Create A Windows Contact.
8. To indicate the cc:Mail addresses you want to import, select one of the following options:
   - Import All Directory Entries.
   - Only Import Directory Entries Of These Formats.
   - Do Not Import Directory Entries Of These Formats.

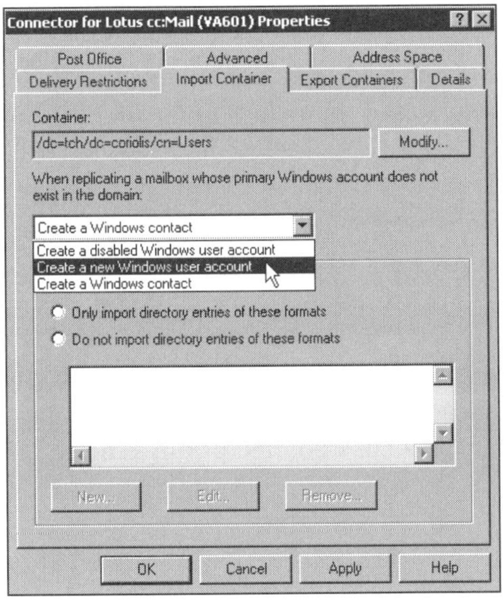

Figure 15.9 Import options for cc:Mail users.

Exporting Contacts with the Export Container

The *Export container* extracts AD objects to be transferred into Lotus cc:Mail. You can add as many containers as necessary here. Decide if you want to synchronize contacts and DLs back to Lotus cc:Mail. The following steps will export the contact list.

1. Choose Start|Programs|Microsoft Exchange|System Manager.
2. Navigate to the Connectors node.
3. Right-click Connector For Lotus cc:Mail (*server_name*), and then click Properties.
4. Click the Export Containers tab.
5. To export contacts to the cc:Mail post office, click Export Contacts. Groups are exported by default. The options here allow you to choose the Exchange recipients you want to make known to the cc:Mail system. If you want to export only users, clear Export Contacts and Export Groups.
6. To select an Export container, click Add.
7. In Choose A Container, open the domain node, and then click the container. If the domain where the connector is running is connected to a trusted domain, you can import OUs belonging to the trusted domain.
8. If you need to stop the export of recipients from a container, click the container in the list of Export containers, and then click Remove. This does not remove the container from AD.

The Delivery Restrictions Tab

This is common in all connectors and restricts which users have access to and receive messages from the connector. For example, the cc:Mail connector can accept or reject the message from any user, group, or contact in the AD who sends a message to a cc:Mail user. These restrictions apply only to the Exchange organization from within which the message is sent to connected cc:Mail systems. They do not affect incoming mail because connectors in general accept incoming messages by default.

Installing the Lotus cc:Mail Connector

After you have followed the previous steps to the letter, you can proceed with the installation of the GroupWise Connector. To install, perform the following:

1. Run Exchange 2000 Setup.
2. Click Change under Microsoft Exchange 2000.

3. Click Install under Microsoft Exchange Lotus Notes Connector.
4. Complete the setup.

Restricting the Delivery of Messages to cc:Mail

To restrict the delivery of messages to cc:Mail, perform the following:

1. Choose Start|Programs|Microsoft Exchange|System Manager.
2. Navigate to the Connectors node.
3. Right-click Connector For Lotus cc:Mail (*server_name*), and then click Properties.
4. Click the Delivery Restrictions tab.
5. To accept messages only from specific recipients, under Accept Messages From, click Add. In Select Recipient, make your selections, and then click Add.
6. To reject messages only from specific recipients, under Reject Messages From, click Add. In Select Recipient, make your selections, and then click Add.
7. Restart the cc:Mail Connector Service.

Configuring the Dirsync Schedule

You can schedule when Exchange sends address list updates to and receives address list updates from the connected cc:Mail post office. If you prefer to manually synchronize directory information, you can choose not to run Dirsync according to a schedule. To set a Dirsync schedule, perform the following:

1. Choose Start|Programs|Microsoft Exchange|System Manager.
2. Navigate to the Connectors node.
3. Right-click Connector For Lotus cc:Mail (*server_name*), and then click Properties.
4. Click the Advanced tab.
5. The default setting is Never Run. If you want to synchronize directory information, you must either set a synchronization schedule or manually synchronize the information by clicking Synchronize Now.

6. To synchronize directory information according to one of the predefined schedules (Run daily at 11:00 P.M., Run every hour, and so on), select a schedule from the drop-down menu.
7. To specify your own synchronization schedule, click Customize, and then fill in the schedule grid. After you close the Schedule, the Use Custom Schedule setting appears automatically in the Schedule list.
8. To force synchronization, click the Synchronize Now button.
9. Click OK to close the Properties pages.

Testing the Connection

After you configure the connector, you should test the connection before allowing messages to flow between the Exchange organization and the cc:Mail messaging system. This makes sure the connector is working properly and a two-way connection exists between the systems. To test the connection between Exchange and cc:Mail:

1. Choose Start|Programs|Administrative Tools|Services.
2. Verify that the cc:Mail Connector Service is running. If it isn't running, start it now.
3. Using an email client such as Outlook, send a message from an Exchange user to a cc:Mail user.
4. On the cc:Mail system, create a recipient address for the Exchange mailbox to which you are sending the message. After you create the address, the recipient appears in your cc:Mail address list.
5. You must know the mailbox name for the Exchange recipient. Use System Manager to find this information.
6. Send a message from a cc:Mail user to an Exchange user.
7. Verify that the message reached its destination.

Preparing the Novell GroupWise Environment

Before installing the GroupWise Connector, you must prepare the GroupWise environment for connecting to Exchange. Perform these tasks on the Novell NetWare Server:

1. Install GroupWise 4.1 API Gateway NLM on the GroupWise domain that you are connecting to with the GroupWise Connector. GroupWise 4.1 API

Gateway NLM is available from Novell (see **http://support.novell.com**), and installation instructions are available from the Novell Web site for NetWare 3.*x* and 4.*x*.

2. Install the GroupWise Patch 2 for API NLM/OS2 (GW41API2.exe). The patch allows GroupWise to expand messages sent to GroupWise groups from Exchange. The patch also is available at **http://support.novell.com**. The /**group** line in the NGWAPI.PRM API Gateway configuration file must be uncommented for the group expansion to work. The API Gateway must be restarted for these changes to take effect.
3. Create and configure the API Gateway for GroupWise 4.*x*/GroupWise 5.*x*.
4. Activate the DLs.
5. Start the API Gateway.
6. Create an External Foreign Domain In GroupWise for the Exchange organization served by the GroupWise Connector, and then configure the link type. Different procedures are followed for GroupWise 4.*x* and GroupWise 5.*x*.
7. Create a Windows NT Gateway Group in NetWare.

NOTE: *When all is set, install and configure the Novell GroupWise Connector. Do not proceed with the installation of the connector unless the Novell environment has been properly set up.*

Creating and Configuring the API Gateway for GroupWise 4.x

Use the GroupWise Administrator utility (Ad.exe) to create and configure GroupWise 4.1 API Gateway NLM for GroupWise 4.1 or later. Be sure to select the following parameters:

1. In the Gateway ID section of the Gateway Information Properties page, type a GroupWise name that is unique within the GroupWise domain (for example, “API”). This is the name for the API Gateway within GroupWise.
2. In Directory, type the name of the directory where API Gateway files are installed.
3. Be sure that Time Zone is set to the same time zone used by the Exchange 2000 Server that runs the GroupWise Connector.
4. In the Settings section, click Specific to open the API Gateway Configuration Properties page.

5. Change the root directory paths in the Gateway File Paths section to absolute paths, in the form *Server name/Volume:\Path*. The default paths are drive paths that are relative to the GroupWise client.
6. In the API Gateway Configuration Properties page, click Component under Addressing Format, and then click OK.
7. In the Settings section, click Time To Open Gateway Time Settings.
8. In Idle Sleep Duration, select a value of 5 seconds or less, and then click OK. (1 second is recommended.) This setting controls how often the API Gateway is checked for messages. This should be adjusted to fit your performance requirements. Selecting the lowest number possible is recommended.
9. In the Settings section, click Optional.
10. Make sure that Directory Synchronization is set to No.
11. In Directory Exchange, click Yes. In Outbound Status Level, click Full, and then click OK.

Creating and Configuring the API Gateway for GroupWise 5.*x*

Perform these steps on the NetWare Server. You need to create the Gateway in the GroupWise domain that you are connecting to with Connector for Novell GroupWise.

1. In NetWare Administrator, choose Tools|NDS Browser.
2. Select the GroupWise domain that is connecting to Exchange. Choose Object|Create.
3. Click GroupWise Gateway Internet Agent.
4. In Create GroupWise Gateway/Internet Agent, click Gateway. Be sure Internet Agent is canceled. In GroupWise versions 5 and 5.1, this Properties page is referred to as Create GroupWise Gateway.
5. Type a Gateway Name that is unique within the GroupWise domain (for example, type "API").
6. In Gateway Home Directory, type the name of the directory where Gateway files are installed.
7. Be sure that Time Zone is set to the same time zone used by the Exchange Server that runs the GroupWise Connector.
8. In Database Version, click 4.*x* (this refers to the Gateway version).

9. In Platform, click NetWare Loadable Module.
10. In Gateway Type, click API.
11. Click Define Additional Properties, and then click Create. This opens the GroupWise Gateway/Internet Agent Properties page.
12. Click Optional Gateway Settings.
13. In Directory Sync/Exchange, click Exchange. This means that GroupWise will wait until prompted to send a directory update to Exchange.
14. In Convert Status To Messages, click Yes. If you don't, Exchange will not receive status messages such as delivery receipts.
15. In Outbound Status Level, click Full.
16. Click Required Parameters.
17. Change the root directory paths in the Gateway File Paths section to absolute paths, in the form *Server name/Volume:\Path*. You can find the UNC path to the Gateway on the Information Properties page. The default paths are drive paths that are relative to the GroupWise client.
18. In Addressing Format, click Component.
19. Click Gateway Time Settings.
20. In Idle Sleep Duration, select a value of 5 seconds or less. (1 second is preferred). This reduces the time taken by free or busy queries, and Dirsync.
21. Click OK to complete the configuration.

Activating DLs on GroupWise

For Novell GroupWise to expand DLs, the GroupWise Patch 2 for API NLM/OS2 (GW41API2.exe) must be installed. To activate DLs on GroupWise:

1. Find the NGWAPI.PRM file, which was installed in the API Gateway root directory *[path to domain]\wpgate\[api directory]*.
2. Open this file with either Notepad (Windows) or Edit (NetWare).
3. Find the line that contains **;/group**.
4. Remove the preceding semicolon.
5. Save the file.
6. Restart the API Gateway.

To start the API Gateway, type "API" on the NetWare Server Console, and then confirm by pressing Enter. The API Gateway should be visible as its own screen on the NetWare Server.

Creating an External Foreign Domain in GroupWise 4.*x*

Exchange users are propagated into the external foreign domain in GroupWise. All changes made in Exchange are propagated to the designated GroupWise foreign domain. The GroupWise Connector overwrites changes made directly to users that are imported from Exchange by the GroupWise system administrator. After you create the domain, you need to select the API Gateway as the link between Exchange and GroupWise. To create an external foreign domain for the Exchange organization and configure the link table:

1. In the GroupWise 4.x Administrator (Ad.exe), choose Create|Domain.
2. Type an external domain name that matches the default Recipient Policy name in Exchange and repeat for other policies if necessary. The name is the first part of the GWISE proxy address on each Exchange organization. You can edit the name on the Email Addressing tab of Recipient Policies. The default name is Exchange.
3. In Domain Type, click Foreign, and then click OK.
4. Select the GroupWise domain that is performing Dirsync with Exchange. This is the domain that contains the API Gateway.
5. Click Action|Edit.
6. Click Message Server Configuration, and then click Network Links.
7. For the external domain created in Steps 1 through 3, click Edit Link. In Link Type, click Gateway.
8. Click the API Gateway you have configured, and then click OK.

Creating an External Foreign Domain in GroupWise 5.*x*

Exchange users are propagated into the external foreign domain in GroupWise. All changes made in Exchange are propagated to the designated GroupWise foreign domain. The GroupWise Connector overwrites changes made directly to users that are imported from Exchange by the GroupWise system administrator. After you create the domain, you need to select the API Gateway as the link between Exchange and GroupWise. To create an external foreign domain for the Exchange organization and configure the link table:

1. In NetWare Administrator, choose Tools|GroupWise View|Mail System.
2. Choose Object|Create|External Domain.

3. Type an external domain name that matches the default Recipient Policy name in Exchange and repeat for other policies if necessary. The name is the first part of the GWISE proxy address on each Exchange organization. You can edit the name in the Email Addressing tab of Recipient Policies. The default name is Exchange.
4. In Domain Type, click External Foreign.
5. In Database Version, select 4.x (to match the API Gateway).
6. Be sure that Time Zone is set to the same time zone used by the Exchange Server that runs the GroupWise Connector.
7. Click Create.
8. In NetWare Administrator, select the GroupWise domain that is performing Dirsync with Exchange. This is the domain containing the API Gateway.
9. Choose Tools|GroupWise Utilities|Link Configuration.
10. In Link Configuration Tool, click the newly created external domain.
11. Choose Edit|Link.
12. In Link Type, select Gateway.
13. In Gateway Link, select the API Gateway that connects to Exchange, and then click OK.

Creating an NTGateway Group

You need to create a group called NTGateway in the NetWare Administrator program. This is a special group whose membership has Read and Write permissions to the API Gateway directories. The router service component of Connector for Novell GroupWise uses the credentials of an NTGateway group member to access API Gateway directories. To create the group, perform the following:

1. In NetWare Administrator, choose Tools|NDS Browser. Select a tree and a context.
2. In NDS Browser, right-click the tree.
3. Click Create|Group.
4. Type "NTGATEWAY", and then click Create.
5. In NetWare Administrator, double-click the NTGateway group. In the Members tab, click Add.
6. Add a NetWare user with administrative rights to the Novell NetWare Server that is hosting GroupWise. This same user's credentials must be used on Exchange to specify the connection to GroupWise.

Configuring the GroupWise Connector

After installation, you can configure the settings for the GroupWise Connector with the System Manager snap-in. To configure the connector, you need to specify the connection to Novell GroupWise and the mail delivery options, including controls, which allow you to configure message routing. You can send mail through the connector from any domain in the organization. You can decide to restrict which Exchange recipients can send mail to GroupWise. You also can specify whether to restrict mail delivery by size or specific delivery order (for example, by specifying that messages marked with a priority are delivered first). This applies only to mail being sent to GroupWise. You also can specify Dirsync options, including the following:

- Choose Export containers. Decide whether to export contacts and groups.
- Choose an Import container. Decide which type of account to give GroupWise users in AD: security-enabled user, security-disabled user, or contact.
- Specify an import filter.
- Synchronize directories immediately or schedule Dirsync. Synchronizing directories populates each directory with users from the other system, which enables mail addressing and delivery.

Opening the Connector for Novell GroupWise Properties

The following steps configure the Exchange Connector for Novell GroupWise by examining the GroupWise properties in System Manager. The Properties pages of the Connector for Novell GroupWise are shown in Figure 15.10.

1. Choose Start|Programs|Microsoft Exchange|System Manager.
2. Navigate to the Connectors node.
3. Right-click Connector For Novell GroupWise (*server_name*), and then click Properties.
4. From the General tab, you can select from the following:
   - *API Gateway Path*—Enter the path to the Gateway.
   - *NetWare Account*—Enter a NetWare account with rights to the path specified in the API Gateway path. Make this account a member of the Novell Directory Service (NDS) group called NTGateway.

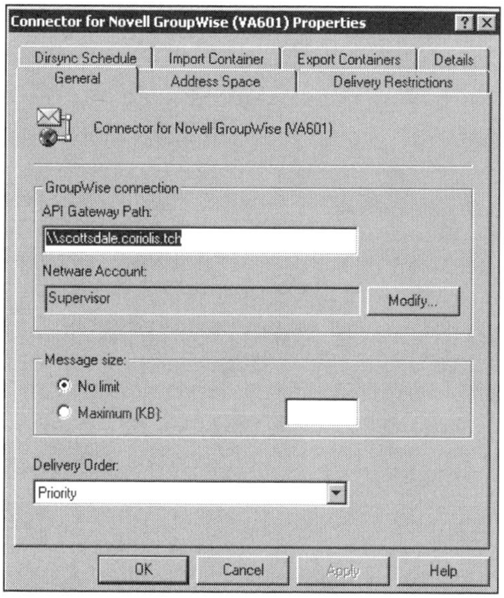

Figure 15.10 Novell GroupWise Connector.

- *Message Size*—You can restrict message sizes passing through the connector.
- *Delivery Order*—This defines the order in which mail messages arrive. The default is to deliver by priority.

5. From the Address Space tab (common to all connectors), you can set the addresses type that the connector is responsible for routing.
6. From the Delivery Restrictions tab (common to all connectors), you can restrict which users have access to and receive messages from the connector.
7. From the Dirsync Schedule tab, you can configure the details of your Dirsync.
    - *Exchange-GroupWise Directory Update Schedule*—Before connecting to the GroupWise system, define the Dirsync Schedule. For most companies, changes to the address books or AD occur once a day. Decide how often synchronizing directories will occur. Limit the number of synchronization cycles to the minimum necessary.
    - *Synchronization*—The Full Reloads and Updates Only buttons initiate your choice of full reload, or a partial update immediately. They do not change the state of subsequent Dirsync cycles. A scheduled synchronization performs a bidirectional partial update.

8. From the Import Container tab, select where the GroupWise entries reside in AD. You must plan your AD strategy before you configure this tab. Separate each outside group by OU. For example, you could create an OU under Users for Novell GroupWise and select that as your container for GroupWise users. Additionally, this tab is used to specify how GroupWise users will be imported. There are three options:
   - *Contacts*—Users that have email addresses but do not log on to the Windows 2000 system; they do not have access to Windows 2000 resources.
   - *Mail-Enabled Users*—Users that are mail-enabled and that log on to Windows 2000 to use Windows 2000 resources.
   - *Disabled Windows Account*—Notes users that might or might not log on to a Windows NT 4 domain, but are scheduled to be migrated to Windows 2000 later.

Importing Directory Entries from GroupWise to Exchange

When directory entries are imported from GroupWise to Exchange, the GroupWise Connector generates a request for a full reload, and the router puts the request in the input queue (API_IN) of the API Gateway. The API Gateway then routes the message to the GroupWise system. The GroupWise system generates a response after polling the GroupWise directory. GroupWise sends the response back to the output queue (API-OUT) of the API Gateway. The router checks the output queue of the Gateway according to determined polling intervals. After it acquires messages, it places them in the Dirsync folder. The connector will map the GroupWise attributes to Exchange attributes according to configured mapping rules. It adds GroupWise users and groups to AD as contacts, users, or security-disabled users in the Import container that you choose.

Chapter 16

Web Storage System and Dashboards

If you need an immediate solution to:	See page:
Running Proxy Configuration Utility Support Server XMLHTTP	689
Creating a Web Storage Instance for the Dashboard	690
Modifying Basic Dashboard Properties	691
Creating a Digital Dashboard Project	692
Adding Web Parts to a Dashboard Using Office Developer	693
Using Web Folders with a File System Dashboard	693
Setting Security for a File System Dashboard	694
Installing the File System Digital Dashboard	694
Configuring the File System Digital Dashboard	695
Creating Your First Digital Dashboard	696
Installing the Web Part Builder	696
Using the Web Part Builder to Design Web Parts	698
Adding Web Parts	698
Creating a Digital Dashboard Using Web Parts	699
Previewing and Testing Your Dashboard	699
Deploying an Exchange Server Dashboard	700
Registering a Workflow Event Sink in a Folder	700
Opening a SharePoint Portal Server for the First Time	701

In Depth

Exchange Server 2000 is the foundation for all .NET services because it exposes the deepest, least structured—though nonetheless significant—knowledge resources to other Web service providers. The thesis that the Way of the Technician merges with the Way of the Merchant rests on the fact that while BizTalk 2000 and SQL Server 2000 provide business-to-business (B2B) communication and enterprise application integration (EAI), e-commerce remains fundamentally based on people to people (P2P) messaging and collaboration. Exchange 2000, in combination with Web Storage System (WSS), native support for WebDAV (Web Distributed Authoring and Versioning), and XML (Extensible Markup Language), provides a development platform that can potentially remove barriers of access to data. These valuable resources have, until recently, been referred to as the *deep Web*; content inaccessible to conventional search engines. The Exchange administrator can assume a strategic role in bringing Web-related technologies in alignment with business strategy. Exchange 2000 provides an enterprise-wide portal to deep Web content that will continue to grow significantly faster than the more accessible surface Web content, which is content that holds greater ROI (return on investment) than shallow Web content when made accessible to analysis and collaborative sharing. The Exchange administrator is emphasized more as architect and solution provider rather than plumber because of the emergence of the Exchange platform and this changing technological scope coinciding with a third generation of business initiatives in commerce on the Internet (more commonly referred to as e-commerce). The "Portals and E-commerce" section, later in this chapter, discusses how Exchange provides e-commercial business solutions.

Exchange administrators must design dynamic workflows and applications based on needs and experiences of all segments of their user populations. Needs analyses should now include procurement or delivery of goods or services defined within the scope of the corporate mission statement. The final three chapters of this book focus on Exchange 2000 as a Web-services provider and, along with BizTalk 2000, a fundamental tool in strategically transforming simple commercial transactions into collaborative exchanges, value-added supply chains, and sustainable trading partnerships. This chapter focuses on the Digital Dashboard as a scalable and extensible enterprise portal structure. Chapter 17 discusses the dynamic workflows and collaborative Outlook Forms. Chapter 18 deals with more technical issues that are necessary to support a knowledge-management (KM) system.

NOTE: *As with Exchange Server, we capitalize Digital Dashboard or Dashboard when we refer to the generic object. We will refer to individual instances in lowercase, such as Digital Dashboards are installed in Public Folders; we will install a dashboard in our department public folder area.*

Knowledge Management

A more progressive e-commercial operation will focus on outward-facing, inter-enterprise process engineering that aligns corporate strategies with Web-based technologies. This is in direct contrast to the more prevalent business process reengineering based on the legacy data processing mentality of previous decades. An Exchange administrator must leverage .NET services to provide customer services such as relationship marketing and value-added networks that build online business communities. Exchange's messaging and collaborative architecture can add value to information flows via increased realtime interconnections and reduced process barriers. Microsoft expresses a similar objective in providing information without walls to knowledge workers.

The WSS features provide the KM tools that e-commercial interests demand and knowledge workers need, as Microsoft has promised, to "work without limits." The WSS combines a file system, Web publishing system, and collaboration server in one central repository. All items—including unstructured or semi-structured data such as messages, contact records, HTML files, documents, and Active Server Pages (ASPs)—are URL-addressable, which makes them accessible from remote locations using a standard browser client. The platform also supports consistent search, data categorization, and workflows that are all critical in building KM solutions. As shown in Figure 16.1, Exchange 2000 provides the requisite substrate for a generic KM solution. All the other current .NET servers—namely, a self-contained intranet technology—support all forms of messaging and collaboration (see Figure 16.2). The other KM-enabling services—such as Realtime Collaboration (RTC), Content Management, Data Analysis, and Search/Portals—are handled by Exchange Conference Server, SharePoint Portal Server, SQL Server 2000, and Commerce 2000 respectively.

Similarly, the synergy of FTP (File Transfer Protocol), IRC (Internet Relay Chat), and Usenet is more efficient than each single online service alone. The integration of these services is characteristic of peer-to-peer Internet networks such as **Hotline.com**, Gnutella protocol, and Napster. Although not perceived as a more conventional online community, the consumers of these Web services make up Internet organizations sharing collections of data on an enterprise scale. Net-based technologies are moving toward creating logical domains or realms bound together in the common sharing of collections of knowledge "nuggets." Traditionally, businesses with common or complementary venues are referred to in a similar way.

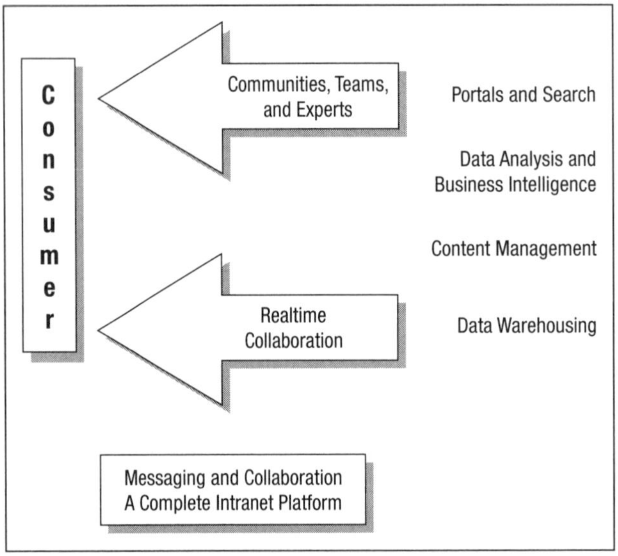

Figure 16.1 A generic KM system.

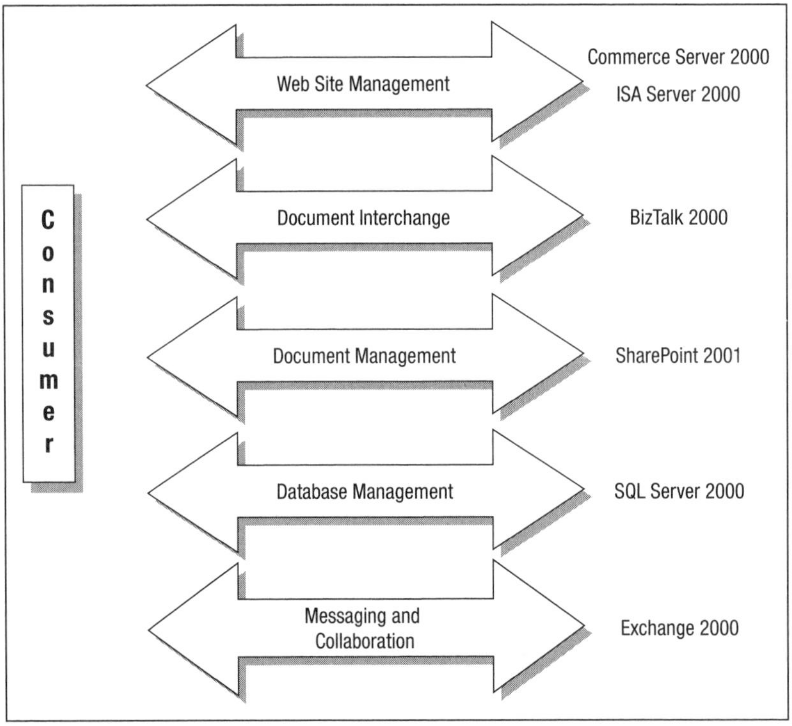

Figure 16.2 The .NET Server service architecture.

Shared data is increasingly becoming less structured and more context-dependent; its value arises out of the extent of its association with other bits of data found in a similar context. The context provides value in its associative relationship to other bits of data openly shared between community members. Synergies of organization, process, and technology emerge from a recasting of the information system rather than automation of an existing process. Again, the Exchange administrator must refocus the gestalt of a process. It is best to reengineer an entire process flow incrementally from end to end. Innovation is not just reworking current processes to run more efficiently; it is the reconceptualization of design and objectives. Business solutions based on the KM of the WSSs and Exchange 2000 platform need to be perceived in terms of strategic business issues rather than technical solutions to business problems.

Web services are assuming a greater role in both software development and e-commerce. In the .NET application architecture, an application is often both provider and consumer of multiple Web services. Web services are often part of a more general business model found with increasing frequency in descriptions of e-commercial projects and corporate mission statements. Exchange 2000, working in conjunction with other .NET Server software, provides a platform for building these core business and mission-critical applications that support the exchange of information over the Internet. To understand how Exchange 2000 contributes to .NET business solutions, you need to define Web services and a generic architecture for those Web services as they relate to Microsoft Windows DNA (Distributed interNet Applications) and .NET architectures. You'll also learn what is necessary to provide reliable support for building, deploying, or consuming Web services.

Services Defined

The early online services—such as FTP, Gopher, Hypertext Transfer Protocol (HTTP), and Telnet—could be characterized more as session-based protocols providing online services. Today, a Web service, in contrast, connotes varying layers of programmable application logic that are accessible using these same standard information protocols. In fact, just as MIME (Multipurpose Internet Mail Extensions) extended the functionality of SMTP (Simple Mail Transfer Protocol), WebDAV has expanded the capabilities of HTTP 1.1 to enable distributed Web authoring through write as well as read access, concurrency control, property configuration, namespace manipulation, and DASL (DAV Search and Locating) protocol. Web services can now leverage the communication capabilities of the Web with a component-based architecture that supports both scalable and extensible development. These services can exploit the structurally self-contained functionality of these protocol-neutral components over and over in different applications as reusable building blocks. Current component technologies are DOM (Document

Object Model)-specific protocols based on Distributed Component Object Model (DCOM), Remote Method Invocation (RMI), or Internet Inter-ORB Protocol (IIOP). Web services, using these components, instead are accessed from some provider via ubiquitous information protocols such as HTTP and XML. A Web service is requested through an interface using some message format the Web service supports. Applications that are Web-service consumers run on any platform in any programming language, if they can interpret messages delivered through their Web service interface. These elements of Web services need to be standardized:

- Methods of data representation
- Extensible message format
- Extensible service description languages
- Methods of discovery for Web-based services within a Web site
- Directory service providers across Web sites

Electronic Data Interchange (EDI), and more recently XML, have become the standard way to represent data. Web service–related specifications in the form of data dictionaries use XML for data representation and XML schemas to describe the nature or types of the data. The Simple Object Access Protocol (SOAP) similarly defines a lightweight protocol for information exchange and a set of rules for how to use XML. It defines an extensible message format and conventions for representing remote procedure calls (RPCs) using the SOAP message format and the bindings to the HTTP protocol. The current specification only defines bindings for HTTP, even though the protocol has broader applicability. SOAP is a Microsoft protocol that is likely to become the standard message format for communicating with Internet Web services. Web services need a standard way to document both messages and Web service contracts. A standard protocol or mechanism facilitates tool and software component development necessary to create and interpret those contracts.

The Web services Description Language (WSDL) is an XML-based contract language developed by Microsoft and IBM that is also gaining wide use among developer tools for creating Web services. Several contract languages have been proposed over the past years, such as Service Description Language (SDL) by Microsoft and IBM, SOAP Contract Language (SCL), and Network Accessible Services Specification Language (NASSL). Even though WSDL supercedes them all, in order to consume a Web service, it's still necessary to translate the provided contract into a legacy contract language supported by development tools. Web applications and services also need ways to discover other Web services. The Discovery Protocol (Disco) specification based on XML defines a discovery document format and a protocol for retrieving the discovery document, enabling an application to discover services at a known URL. If a URL is unknown, Universal Description, Discovery, and Integration (UDDI) specify a mechanism for Web service providers to advertise the existence of their Web services and for consumers to locate Web services of interest.

Architecture Defined

The .NET vision imagines applications constructed from multiple Web services that work together to provide data and services for the application as shown in Figure 16.3.

This diagram, as well as the definition of Web services just provided, is concerned with the external appearance of the Web services. After all, as long as a client application can create and consume the appropriate messages, it doesn't need to know anything about the internals of the Web services it uses. Developers of Web services obviously care about the internal structure as well.

Figure 16.4 shows a generic architecture for a Web service. The 3-tier architecture, shown in Figure 16.3, can be superimposed into five NOS-specific management functional areas (SMFAs); configuration, performance, fault management, security, and accounting. The data layer stores information required by the Web service. A data access layer presents a logical view of the physical data to the more process-oriented business layer. The data access layer isolates scripted business logic from the physical structure and location of the data stores and thereby ensures both security and integrity of the knowledge resource. The business logical layer can be subdivided into two parts: a business facade and the scripted logic. The business facade acts as an interface that maps the outside API (Application Programming Interface) of the Web service to the scripted logic below. Best practices recommend that all business logic is implemented only through the business

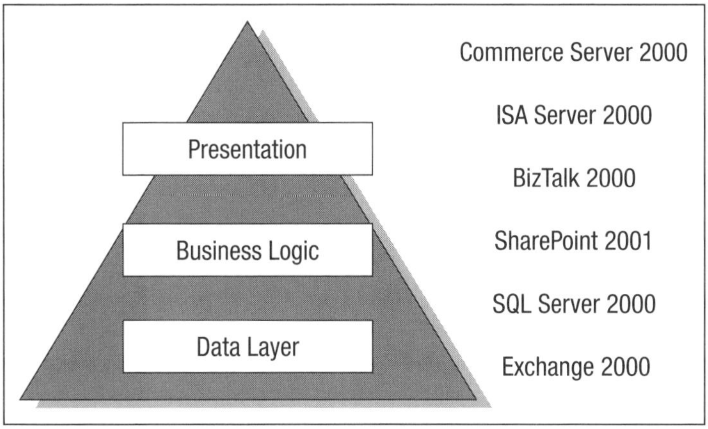

Figure 16.3 .NET applications with the three-tier architecture superimposed.

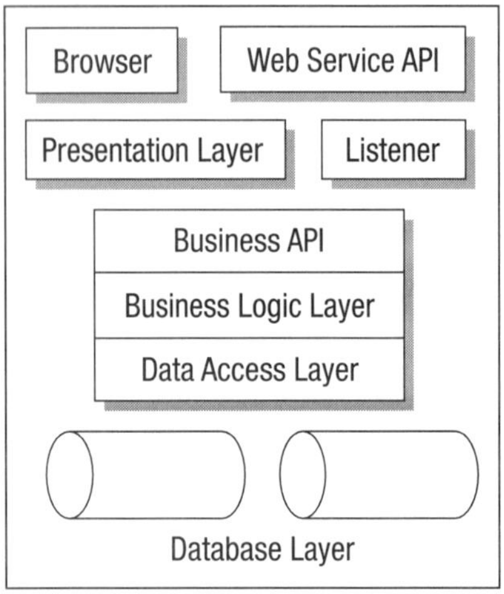

Figure 16.4 Web services architecture.

facade. Thus, both the business facade and the data access layer insulate proprietary design and information from outside manipulation. All client applications interact with the business facade through a specialized Web service listener. The listener receives incoming requests for service, parses the message, and directs the request to the appropriate object method exposed to the Internet on the business facade. The listener also packages the service response sent back to the consumer client. The listener has additional roles in negotiating service contracts and other administrative requests for the Web service. This architecture, shown schematically in Figure 16.4, mirrors the *n*-tier application architecture defined by Windows DNA.

Platform Requirements

Systems administrators for service providers won't deploy Web services unless they are relatively easy to manage. The more you can leverage your existing skills, components, applications, and data stores, the better. Much of the difficulty in implementing scalable, highly available code is connected with properly managing resources—such as processes, threads, and shared state—when multiple concurrent requests are received by a service. Middleware that manages these resources and lets you write service logic as if a single client is accessing it can greatly improve the reliability, scalability, and availability of Web services, as well as greatly simplify development of the Web service. In practical terms, the middleware provides a standard hosting environment for the implementation of Web service code and provides for critical functions, including the following:

- Listening for incoming HTTP requests.
- Performing security authentication and authorization checks.

- Dispatching authorized requests to the correct service.
- Isolating/insulating services from each other and the hosting environment. A service must have its own memory space and be prevented from blocking or interfering with the execution of other services. Any one service fault cannot cause other services or the hosting environment to fail.
- Automatic recovery from service, hosting environment, and system failures.
- Administrative support for deploying, monitoring, and controlling services.
- Resource management that includes administration of processes, threads, and shared state on behalf of each service.

Some Web services have nonstandard requirements that the standard hosting environment does not support. An environment must be flexible enough to support the easy substitution of best-of-breed feature components. APIs for constructing and parsing messages will also enhance your productivity. APIs must provide minimal support for reading and writing XML streams. As mentioned earlier, standardized APIs—such as SOAP, WSDL, and UDDI—improve productivity as well as overall reliability by eliminating the need for scripting parsing and formatting logic. APIs also reduce the need to learn detailed and often highly technical specifications. If you are implementing Web services using component technologies, productivity increases even more if the system provides services to activate objects on demand and map messages to object method calls, which essentially implements the Web service listener for you. Similarly, if you are a Web services consumer, you need tools that construct proxy objects that hide details regarding formatting and sending a service request as well as interpreting a service response.

The WSS

The *Exchange Web Storage System* is a database technology that you can use to store, share, and manage unstructured, heterogeneous data, such as email messages, Web pages, multimedia files, and Office XP documents. The WSS is organized much like a traditional file system, in a hierarchy of folders. Each folder within the WSS contains any number of items called *resources*. A resource is any Exchange item, including email messages, tasks, appointments, contact information, streaming video, or even other folders. You can access items in the WSS using many protocols and APIs, including HTTP, Microsoft ActiveX Data Objects Version 2.5 (ADO), Object Linking and Embedding for Databases (OLE DB) Version 2.5, Collaboration Data Object for Exchange 2000 (CDOEX), the Messaging API (MAPI), through the file system, and several other industry-standard wire protocols.

Related solutions:	Found on page:
Enabling MAPI Clients Computers Through a Firewall	778

WebDAV is an extension of HTTP 1.1 that adds enhanced flexibility when working with WSS resources because the protocol extension can access and manipulate resources in programmatic ways. In fact, the WSS supports server-side ASPs that use this broad access to resources to programmatically request and provide services using HTTP. Thus, WSS resources are accessed using a URL just like Web pages. Every resource in the WSS is addressable. A Request for Proposal (RFP) for a Wireless Application Protocol (WAP) Web site within a public folder, for example, can be accessed from any remote Internet location with any standard browser client from the following URL: **http://servername/public/RFP/wap0804.doc**.

Resource Support

The WSS is defined by a collection of properties describing these resources called a *schema*. The WSS default schema describes resource items, implements security, and provides the business logic. Because the schema defines an email message resource with a To:, From:, and Subject: property, you can design dynamic processes using those properties to index, sort, or query that resource. The WSS can optimize search-and-retrieval capabilities by supporting the cataloging and indexing of common schema properties. An Exchange administrator or designers can extend this schema by adding new properties that are relevant to specific situations to enhance content indexing and facilitate search functions. Depending on the needs of your user population or corporate goals, you can extend this default schema by adding or modifying resource properties and thus customize resource definitions for special programming needs.

The WSS integrates knowledge sources by providing a single repository for managing email messages, documents, Web pages, and other resources within one information domain. The WSS supports remote client access, and a wide range of APIs to facilitate programmatic access to its data stores. The WSS thus serves as a platform for unified messaging or Universal Inbox, where knowledge workers access all information: their personal information, files, calendar and contacts, and email and voice mail messages. This range of knowledge resources stored in and accessible from the Web Store is shown in Figure 16.5.

The WSS provides three areas of enterprise-based application services and resources. First, it provides addressable access to its data stores through a wide

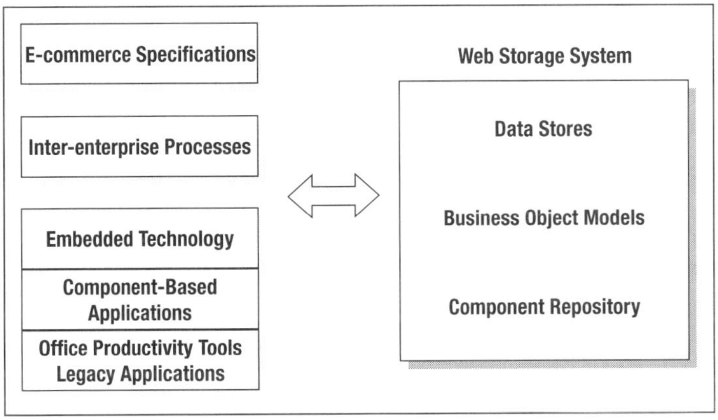

Figure 16.5 The range of WSS data access.

range of software; from MS Office applications like Word and Outlook to browsers retrieving audio and video streaming data. The WSS supports both hierarchical and heterogeneous collections of folders that accept any file type. Second, it provides database access to multiple types of information in a single repository. Information can be diverse types of data including OLE DB and ADO Recordsets, MIME messages, and XML data. The WSS also provides database services, which present a consistent view of data to end users when updated. Finally, through Exchange 2000, it provides a rich development platform that supports messaging, contacts, calendaring, and workflow, as well as RTC.

Event Support

The WSS provides resources that have properties and conditions, or states. You can programmatically arrange for scripts to perform some specific processing task when a particular resource is created, moved, modified, or deleted. These actions alter the condition, or state, of the resource. Such a change or transition in state is defined as an *event*. Events can enable or trigger applications to run your scripts. Support for event programming allows you to build application logic that runs when some action is performed on a resource. This event triggers a script that can be determined by the type of transition (state change) the resource has undergone. These events can involve clients accessing data—such as the Outlook or MAPI client, a HTTP or standard browser client, or a Win32 or MS Office application. Events can also occur at the transport protocol layer and involve SMTP, IMAP (Internet Message Access Protocol), or NNTP (Network News Transfer Protocol). Event support thus simplifies writing script because you don't necessarily have to partition your application code to provide some requested resource or service to a client; the event trigger determines which script is executed.

Legacy versions of Exchange Server used asynchronous events, which run only once after some state change has occurred. Synchronous events, on the other hand, run within the context or during the state transition. Thus, Exchange 2000 has added support for application logic that can perform some processing task before a transition is actually completed. For example, a synchronous event can trigger application code to check data integrity before an item has been committed to a storage folder or authorization of a financial transaction before it has been finalized. The significance of synchronous event support involves concurrently triggering script before some event has been concluded or terminated. This dynamic processing enhances the depth of the application logic, decision support, and sensitivity to a broader, more complex collection of resource states.

Workflow Support

WSS events trigger application logic and drive workflow applications that can, for example, track the progress of a document through some approval process. Microsoft Workflow Designer for Exchange (WDE), Office XP Developer, and CDO Workflow Objects for Exchange 2000 provide tools that define a workflow process to a folder. Use WDE or XP Developer to design workflow logic that maps the business process to actual script. Figure 16.6 shows the design surface of the Development Environment. Notice the objects depicting transitions and

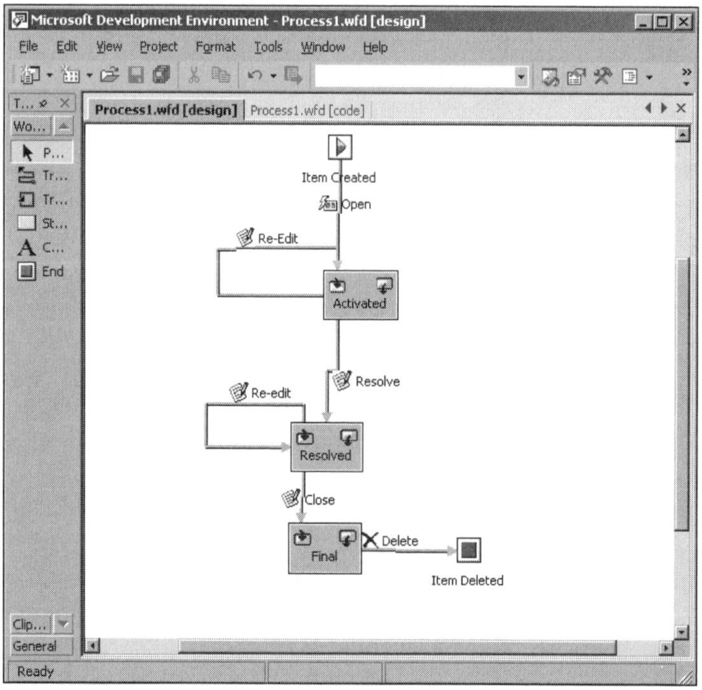

Figure 16.6 Designing a workflow from the Development Environment.

states in the Toolbar palette on the left side of the interface. As you click and drag these icons across the design surface, you actually build the process definition of the workflow. You can customize this code by accessing the code sheet below this design surface window.

WDE uses CDO Workflow Objects to create the workflow application logic. CDO Workflow Objects provide a workflow engine needed to design and implement a workflow process. This specialized API can combine with customized COM (Component Object Model) objects to model any workflow necessary to provide business solutions specified in the process definition. It is significant that, although a comprehensive programming background is necessary for advanced applications, these graphical design tools enable a competent Exchange administrator to design simple workflows and deliver effective business solutions without additional support. By abstracting detailed code into easily manipulated graphic icons, these development tools provide a simplified integrated development environment in which to assume the role of software architect. After you have designed and tested a prototypical workflow and proven the efficacy of a business solution, you should enlist the aid of more experienced programmers to build custom COM objects to optimize performance on a production platform.

Related solution:	Found on page:
Running Workflow Applications from a Designated User's Account	730

Web Forms

An important task in developing any application is designing the user interface. A poorly designed user interface can create confusion, errors, and frustration for the user. Furthermore, more data is often less information. In technical terms, the signal-to-noise ratio decreases when instrumentation contains too many channels of data; important signals are lost in the information noise! A well-designed user interface, whether it is a Web page, a Web Form, or Digital Dashboard can make the application appealing, intuitive, and extremely effective. Your user interface could be a Word document, an Outlook Form, or another presentation layer you design. These all work, because the WSS provides heterogeneous document storage. Your user interface choice is up to you, and typically, it's not related to the functionality of underlying resources and objects. Usually, the user interface is independent of the information source and runs on a client computer or in the browser. With paradigm shifts in Windows philosophy, design, and technology, the concept of enterprise and distributed services has replaced the legacy Windows NT 4 domain model and the monolithic design of application servers. Microsoft's philosophical shift in marketing strategy with the introduction of Windows 2000 and Microsoft .NET servers has shifted to extensibility, where services are differentiated into relatively independent, specialized functional areas loosely distributed throughout the organization. Web Forms simplify dynamic access to these services and WSS resources. A Web Form simplifies KM by consolidating service requests in a single front-end (FE) interface and the presentation of data based on browser client characteristics such as version and language settings. This single FE presentation layer also simplifies the display of data based on its inherent properties and characteristics. Designing this presentation layer requires authoring tools. Web Form applications use a variety of technologies, including client- and server-side scripting languages such as VBScript and ECMAScript (formerly JavaScript, now a standard promulgated by the European Computer Manufacturers Association). More frequently, XML, Extensible Stylesheet Language (XSL), and Java components are incorporated with Active Server technologies to enhance Web Form functionality.

Related solution:	Found on page:
Establishing an ADO Connection	776

Tools for the Developer

In addition to Visual Studio and FrontPage, Office XP Developer provides tools and infrastructure that facilitate building collaborative and other business-related solutions on the Office platform. You can visually design, debug, and deploy highly customized Office, workflow, and Digital Dashboard applications as well as build departmental, KM solutions without a detailed knowledge of scripting code. This is particularly important for an Exchange administrator who needs to design or communicate a collaborative solution or Exchange workflow, but doesn't necessarily need to build the coded application. Office XP Developer includes graphically based productivity tools and add-ins such as the following:

- *Code Librarian*—Leverage code with the Code Librarian that is integrated in the Microsoft Development Environment. The Code Librarian contains additional samples and code snippets of common programming tasks. Distribute your own code libraries using the read-only Code Librarian Viewer.
- *Access Runtime*—Create and deploy Access applications.
- *Visual Basic for Applications add-ins*—Make common development tasks such as error handling and source code control easier.
- *Deployment tools*—Easily deploy your applications using the Packaging Wizard.

Portals and E-Commerce

A transition has occurred from simple MAPI forms to Web Forms rendered by a standard browser client. The growing sophistication of processing capabilities provided by Exchange has also culminated in the powerful dynamic processing of workflows based on COM+ objects and CDOs. The growing emphasis on Web-based enterprise management has moved these business solutions from proprietary tools and platforms to standards-based development environments. In a similar way, the emergence of HTML documents as a de facto file format and the emphasis on collaboration in the context of KM has produced another productivity tool: the Digital Dashboard.

A *dashboard* is the presentation of a set of components or Web Parts in a consolidated HTML page that often provides a collaborative solution to some business need. The dashboard has typically been designed with a departmental scope and used primarily as a collaborative tool within an intranet. This Outlook-based application is composed of three parts: the form, the folder container (usually a public folder), and the folder design, which includes views, filters, and rules. This collection of folder home pages allows you to associate a HTML Web page with a mailbox or public folder. Well-designed Web Parts, included among these pages, are reusable components that surround Web-based content such as XML, HTML, and scripts within an XML schema. Their schema defines a collection of standard feature set of properties controlling the presentation of information within the digital dashboard framework.

Digital dashboard applications refer generically to the digital dashboard and all the other support pieces, including customization pages and custom Web Part forms that are rendered in the presentation layer. These digital dashboards relate to e-commercial Web portals just as the SharePoint Portal Server relates to Exchange 2000 and its enterprise-wide collaborative platform. In fact, the power of the Exchange 2000 development platform resides in the fact that in the .NET environment, it is now fundamentally more of a Web-publishing tool than Internet Information Services (IIS), as shown in Figure 16.7.

The first generation of e-commercial Web investment produced nothing more than electronic brochures and display catalogs. The second generation of e-commercial initiatives brought reliable and cost-effective transactions to cyberspace. Most B2B interaction is based on the exchange of information as commodities using structured messaging protocols such as EDI. Limitations in this form of transaction have evolved in part due to a legacy mentality cultivated in the data-processing era of the 1970s and 1980s. E-commerce is growing beyond just the simple procurement of goods. Although initiatives such as Open Buying on the Internet have fostered efficient commercial models, highly efficient but simple transactional exchanges are shifting to KM and collaborative commerce. Open Buying on the

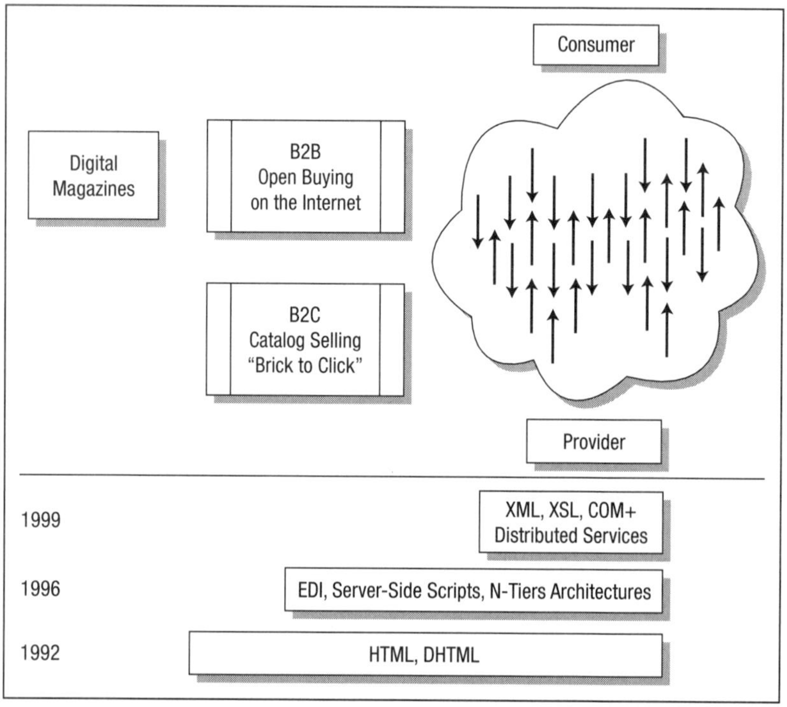

Figure 16.7 Shifts in e-commerce.

Internet is an e-commerce specification using open, nonproprietary technologies. It focuses primarily on high-volume, low-cost business-to-business transactions. Other specifications and models of value-added markets are emerging coincidentally with technological advances in e-services. The one-to-one nature of the Internet fosters more intimate and stronger business relationships between consumer and provider, and between trading partners through collaborative technologies such as Instant Messaging (IM), co-browsing, and conferencing. Exchange 2000—unlike BizTalk 2000—is designed to provide these P2P e-services. An Exchange administrator provides these services through intelligent agents and dynamic processing of data in the WSS. The third generation of e-commerce initiatives can be viewed as the creation of virtual infrastructures that transforms inward-focused, specialized business processes into outwardly directed, more readily accessible knowledge resources for collaborative sharing among customers, trade partners, suppliers, or distributors.

Interconnections in the form of associative or collaborative links make new business solutions possible. The richness of the Exchange development platform and the simplified GUI (graphical user interface)-based tools that design dynamic processes will leverage these steadily growing resources and simplify their management. It is noteworthy, especially to an Exchange administrator, that e-commerce initiatives are mission-critical processes that work with neither off-the-shelf products nor legacy network system services; they require home-grown, inter-enterprise process engineering based on an organization's people, processes, and property, which are defined as knowledge resources.

Inter-enterprise engineering is the design and deployment of business solutions based on KM technologies. With the third generation of e-commercial products, and the emphasis on collaborative networking and trading communities sharing realtime information, the development platform that provides the fundamental service of connecting people to people forms the foundation on which most business strategies rest. Departmental-level KM systems—such as SharePoint Portal Server—are information centers providing events that trigger business action plans within and across enterprises. For example, a consumer's purchase of common maintenance, repair, and operational (MRO) supplies can be triggered by inventories reaching their order points. If both consumer and provider/supplier share the same view of the inventory levels in realtime, supply/demand planning systems are optimized with little additional overhead. Digital dashboards are nothing more than extensible Outlook Forms that can be scaled in scope to accommodate Web communities spanning multiple Internet domains as well as Windows 2000 forests. With respect to Exchange 2000, the Way of the Technician must merge with the Way of the Merchant to achieve a synergy of business strategy with .NET distributed services.

Dashboards

The Internet provides information workers with easy access to large volumes of data from anywhere, at any time, and from almost any device. The resulting information overload has made access to any one specific nugget of information difficult. Information overload results in lost income, lost productivity, and lost information. A *Digital Dashboard* is a logical framework within which one can easily assemble a consolidated view of the desired information from a variety of remote sources. Dashboard applications consist of three tiers or layers. A storage layer can be maintained in the Windows 2000 file system, whereas Web Parts and dashboard folders are stored under an IIS virtual root. It is both significant and critical that all the components are kept in a WebDAV-compliant store because the Dashboard factory uses the WebDAV protocol extension to create, edit, and delete dashboard components. The Dashboard factory is copied to the hosting server during dashboard installation. Windows 2000 and Exchange 2000 both provide the native support for WebDAV. The Digital Dashboard Resource Kit installs an IIS extension to enable WebDAV access to the data store. The Dashboard Factory provides the assembly logic for a dashboard and receives client requests through WebDAV, read/write requests through XML and XSL, and control requests to assemble and transform folders containing Web Parts into a digital dashboard. The Dashboard Factory delivers the assembled Dashboard application to the presentation tier provided by client browser software.

Dashboard Security

Dashboard security is configured through the M: drive in the Windows 2000 file system, or through the Exchange System Manager. Dashboards inherit the Access Control List (ACL) of their underlying dashboard folders and Web Parts. The Dashboard factory runs under the security profile of the authenticated and authorized user. Confirm the inherited security of the parent folders of a resource if you are having difficulties with security permissions. To propagate the parent folder's permissions to a subfolder on which you are setting permissions, select the Allow Inheritable Permissions From Parent To Propagate option for the child object. Users are prevented from seeing dashboards and Web Parts by setting security on dashboard folders and Web Parts. Three user permission levels apply to dashboards and Web Parts:

- *No Access*—The dashboard or Web Parts are invisible to a user denied read and write access to file system resource items.
- *Read Only*—Users just have read access.
- *Modification*—Users can create or change file system resources.

Permission management is based on the types of dashboards that are deployed within an organization. You typically give users full control over their own personal dashboards, but restrict modification to limited properties or objects on a public, team, or corporate dashboard. The designer also has various options that can completely lock down the dashboard. Writing entries to ACLs is typically restricted to some specific administrative group. For reasons of consistency in design, end users are not typically allowed to add or remove Web Parts either; their ability to modify dashboard properties is usually limited to maintain some standard functionality. Links to the Layout and Settings pages do not appear in the user interface, thus restricting the import, deletion, or modification of components. Best practices recommend defining role-based security access to provide more consistent authorization policies and easier security administration. ACLs through specific access control entries (ACEs) can limit access to a specific subsection of Web Parts within a given dashboard. You can design a dashboard with a large number of Web Parts and allow limited customization by your user population to improve both corporate morale and usability while maintaining some degree of corporate policy. Similarly, user groups could access or see different sets of Web Parts as compared to other groups. Through various security access combinations, you can allow users to customize Web Parts without allowing users to import or delete them, or give users full control.

Security associated with a File System Digital Dashboard is managed using either the authentication method on the dashboard factory and dashboards virtual roots or folder permissions on the underlying object resources. Anonymous logins or Windows 2000 Authentication is similarly applied to the virtual roots. The File System Dashboard is installed with Windows 2000 Authentication already enabled. Best practices recommend not enabling anonymous logins because the dashboard factory ASPs will run under a process logged in as a user account—**IUSR_SERVER**—that is an untrusted account, and therefore cannot write dashboard changes back to the server. Windows 2000 Authentication provides significant control over dashboard access by controlling the ACL of the underlying folders in the Dashboards directory. IIS security allows you to manage dashboard security through Windows 2000 file-system permissions. The Dashboard factory writes any ACL modifications back to the file-system resource when either a dashboard or Web Part configuration is modified.

Building Portable Web Parts

A Web Part must be interchangeable in any digital dashboard to be reusable. Web Parts should not be dependent on other Web Parts, network connectivity, or computer configurations. To guarantee portability, best practices recommend designing Web Part architecture so that it is independent of any particular document object model of any single dashboard. Components that are associated with a specific DOM of a specific dashboard might not function properly when used in a different application context. In a similar context, component design should also be independent. Creating functionality closely bound to another Web Part in the same dashboard similarly limits the ability to exchange Web Parts and customize dashboards. Another important guideline is to simplify and standardize any communication between Web Parts. Dashboard components often communicate with other Web Parts to exchange data. Best practices recommend using the Digital Dashboard Services Component for communication between Web Parts because the discovery and notification functionality in this component helps Web Parts interact independently. The Digital Dashboard Services Component also allows you to capture Internet Explorer (IE) events without causing software issues. Finally, Web Parts need to function properly when a user goes offline. Poorly designed dashboards with data requiring an online connection will fail when offline, which renders the dashboard application relatively useless.

Outlook 2000 and properly designed dashboards allow collaborative information to be used offline to add further productivity. Best practices recommend integrating collaborative information into a digital dashboard using the ActiveX component Outlook View Control. This component, in conjunction with Exchange Server public folders, supports the creation of document libraries. Because this component is a software wrapper that encapsulates the Outlook program, the Outlook client must be running on the computer to view the dashboard containing the component.

Dashboard Architecture

The *Digital Dashboard Resource Kit 2.2* provides sample dashboards that use a three-tier architectural design based on WebDAV and XML. DRK_EX.msi, the installation wizard that installs digital dashboards, runs from an installation source, such as downloaded files or a CD. The Setup Wizard copies files to \Digital Dashboard\ and \Resources*.*, and creates a virtual root for the new data store such as **http://ServerName/vRoot**. The \Digital Dashboard\ folder contains user Dashboards, whereas \Resources is for the dashboard factory, which provides dynamic rendering of dashboards at runtime. A browser launches with the new dashboard from a virtual root location such as **http://ServerName/vRoot/Firstdashboard**. These dashboards include a WebDAV-enabled data tier, such as SQL Server, Windows 2000 file system, or Exchange 2000; a middle tier composed of a store module, and the dashboard factory running on IIS; and the dashboard that presents information to the user. The store module and the dashboard factory exchange data through the WebDAV protocol, whereas the dashboard factory uses HTTP to present data to the user. Users can further customize the presentation of information through their browser client interface.

Store Module

The *store module* handles all logic and user configuration information in the core input and output APIs for dashboards and Web Parts. The store module is actually a script file called Store.vbs in the Digital Dashboard Resource Kit. You design your own store module so that it can interpret Web Parts according to standardized specifications. Because Web Parts and dashboards are wrapped in an XML schema, they are storage-neutral and equally accessible from the Windows file system, SQL Server, or the WSS. This design flexibility provides extensible dashboards that accommodate the needs of any organization or platform. Comparisons of store modules suggest the Windows file system is easy to use and provides native WebDAV support. SQL Server, alternatively, is a scalable application server offering relational database resources and Web Part management. The Digital Dashboard Resource Kit provides IIS extensions so that a dashboard application can use SQL Server as a Web Part Storage Service. Finally, the WSS easily integrates with Office resources that were previously found exclusively in the Windows file system with Internet offline accessibility, and provides native support for both WebDAV and XML.

Dashboard Factory

The *dashboard factory* assembles the dashboard for presentation to the client based on Web Part and dashboard properties located in the store module. When servicing a user request, the dashboard factory receives XML streams from Web Parts and the dashboard, applies an XSL transformation to change the streams to HTML, and then uses IIS to manage the transmission of data to the dashboard on the client browser.

Digital Dashboard Services Component

A key ActiveX component, Digital Dashboard Services Component, is a client-side object included in every dashboard page as a hidden object. The Digital Dashboard Resource Kit includes information about this and other components. This particular component simplifies reusing and building Web Parts by providing a standard infrastructure for key services, including the following:

- *Part discovery*—This service allows components to discover other Web Parts on a dashboard.
- *Notification*—This service supports the capability of a Web Part to respond to external events occurring at the dashboard or Web Part level.
- *Session state management*—This service supports exchanges between components of information and objects within a browser session.
- *State management*—This service allows dashboards and Web Parts to maintain some persistent state and global variables between activations.
- *Item retrieval*—This service supports retrieval and maintenance of an item's state in the store module.

Other COM+ Components

Other prebuilt Web Parts or collections of COM controls are available for publishing spreadsheets, charts, and databases to the Web. The Dashboard Wizard enables you to create or import these components as well as turn them on or off after they are installed in a folder. Some of these components, shown in the catalog listing in Figure 16.8, provide offline access to data and enable the designer to programmatically build sophisticated, interactive Web-based solutions. Office Web Components, using IE 4.1 and later, include four main components:

- *DataSource Control*—This control provides the connections to data sources that support other controls.
- *Spreadsheet Component*—This component provides spreadsheet functionality. It supports most of the same formulas as the full version of Excel.
- *Microsoft PivotTable Component*—Use pivot tables to analyze OLAP data sources in multidimensional data arrays. The component supports dynamic data modeling within a digital dashboard.
- *Chart Component*—This component delivers charting functionality.

Positional settings for configuring a new Web Part also can be configured through the Dashboard Wizard. Figure 16.9 shows the easy-to-use interface.

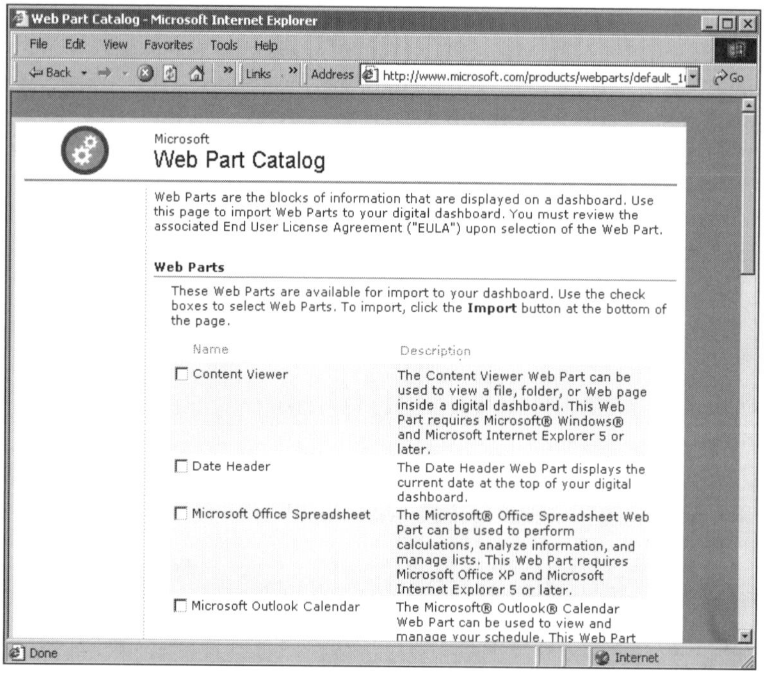

Figure 16.8 A Web Part Catalog of components available for import.

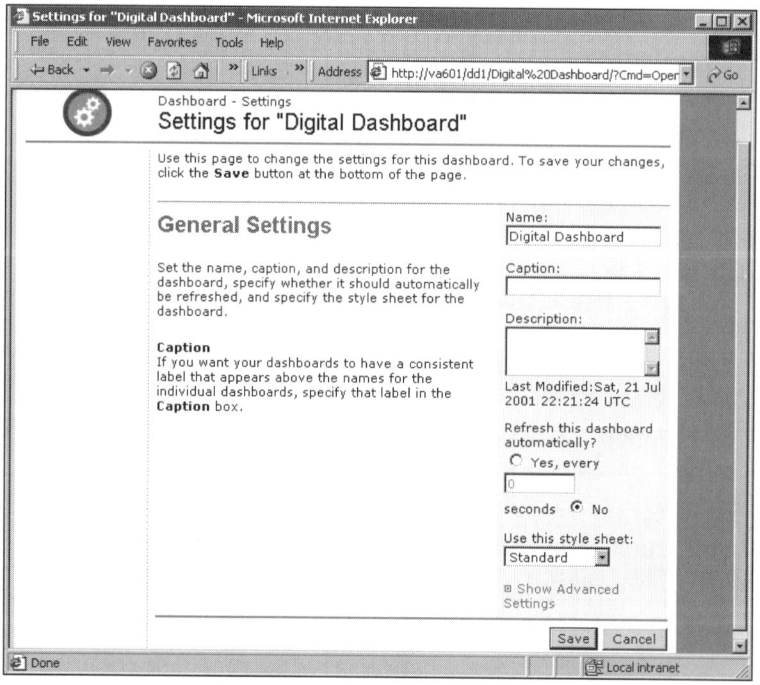

Figure 16.9 Setting a new Web Part in a digital dashboard.

Building Web Parts

You need to install the Windows 2000 file system sample digital dashboard and the Web Part Builder—an add-in to Microsoft Visual InterDev (VID) included in the Digital Dashboard Resource Kit—before building your first Web Part. The Windows 2000 File System Digital Dashboard is designed as a platform that developers can use to build and test Web Parts. Install the Windows 2000 file system sample dashboard on the NTFS (NT File System) partition of a computer running Windows 2000 and IIS 5. To install the Windows 2000 file system sample dashboard, choose Install The File System Sample Digital Dashboard from the Building Digital Dashboards page of the Digital Dashboard Resource Kit. Alternatively, you can run DDRK_FS.msi from the CD-ROM. An installation wizard guides you through the installation process. During installation, the wizard prompts you for the name of the folder or virtual root that will hold your users' digital dashboards. The default virtual root is *Dashboards*, which is the name of the virtual root containing the dashboard factory. The default virtual Web root is *Factory*.

You should build Web Parts that are both informative and customizable. A good Web Part provides targeted information designed for some specific use. Make these Web Parts both scalable and extensible. Just like designing a HTML document or Web page, the context of a dashboard includes both the look and feel of the component. Design Web Parts that are appealing to users. Your components should incorporate the contextual style of the dashboard so that the Web Part looks and behaves in a consistent manner with surrounding dashboard components. The functionality of any one Web Part should not interfere with other components on the dashboard. Isolate your Web Parts to ensure that dashboard components run without causing naming and script collisions. Always design components so that they are truly reusable. Design Web Parts so that they are self-contained; they generally should not rely on continuous network connectivity (to support offline use), or other Web Parts on the dashboard. Make certain their properties conform to the Web Part schema, and consider that Web Parts might need to function appropriately when viewed offline.

Design your dashboard to reduce information overload by delivering user information that is easy to understand and use. Consider that more information is often less information; the functionality of a dashboard is dependent just as much on the ability of your users to manipulate multiple channels of information as it is on their need to know that information. Too many channels of information at one time tend to bury important signals in too much information noise! Furthermore, the best Web Parts are both scalable and extensible. A Web Part that shows the contents of an Outlook folder must display, for example, views that are user definable via the Outlook View Control. Customizable Web Parts need to include the following:

- Ways for the user to control the presentation of information
- Locations for storing that information
- Customizable retrieval methods

Because you design Web Parts in the context of the dashboard's DOM, script collisions among Web Parts can sometimes occur. Any time you create a Web Part that contains client-side script, isolate that Web Part from the other Web Parts on the page to maintain referential integrity. Functions, objects, or variables with the same name in multiple Web Parts often can lead to runtime errors in a dashboard.

Immediate Solutions

Running the Proxy Configuration Utility to Support **ServerXMLHTTP**

You must install MSXML 3.0 on the hosting server and properly configure any proxy server prior to a dashboard installation. The **ServerXMLHTTP** object supports server-to-server HTTP connections through a new HTTP client stack; it offers a "server-safe" connection. The Proxy Configuration Utility (Proxycfg.exe) allows you to configure these **WinHTTP** proxy settings. The screenshot in Figure 16.10 shows a view of this utility when you launch it from the command line as follows:

1. Determine the proxy server name you use for Internet connectivity.
2. Type "cmd" in the Run text box from Start|Run.
3. Type "proxycfg -d" at the command line prompt, as shown in Figure 16.10, if no proxy server is accessed when connecting server to server.
4. Download the Proxy Configuration utility to your local machine.
5. Double-click the executable and choose a location in which to unzip the files.

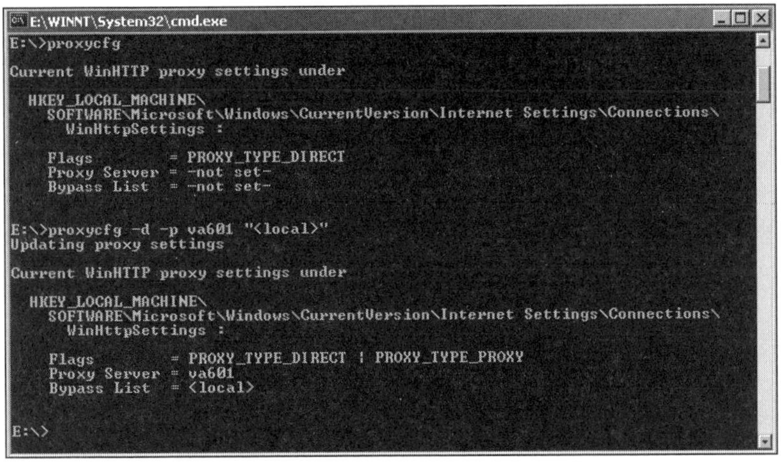

Figure 16.10 Using the Proxy Configuration utility from the command line.

6. Navigate to the folder in which the files are located using the command prompt.
7. Execute the proxycfg program with the appropriate settings. For a proxy server setting when connecting server to server, type "proxycfg -p", and add the list of proxy servers you want to use. Add optional bypass lists for servers that will not be accessed through a proxy.
8. Stop and restart IIS.

Creating a Web Storage Instance for the Dashboard

To optimize performance, allocate a standalone server for a dashboard so that a public folder system and the dashboard are not slowed down by use. Create a new folder tree, storage database, and HTTP virtual root to support your digital dashboard. To create a top-level public store, perform the following:

1. Right-click Folders in the Exchange System Manager and select New|Public Folder Tree.
2. Enter a new folder tree name in the Name field on the General tab of the Properties dialog box and click OK.
3. Right-click a specific server in the Servers tree under Servers in the Exchange System Manager.
4. Click New|Storage Group in the context menu.
5. Enter a new storage group (SG) name such as "FirstStorageGroup" in the Name field on the General tab of the Properties dialog box and click OK.
6. Right-click the newly created SG in the Exchange System Manager.
7. Click New|Public Store in the context menu.
8. In the Name field of the General tab of the Properties dialog box, type the name of your new public store, for example "FirstPublicStore".
9. Click Browse in the Name field on the General tab of the Properties dialog box.
10. Select the newly created folder tree, for example FirstFolderTree, in the Available Public Folder Trees List box in the Select A Public Folder Tree dialog box and click OK (see Figure 16.11).
11. Accept all changes by clicking OK in all the dialog boxes.
12. Open the server you just created in the Servers folder in the Exchange System Manager.

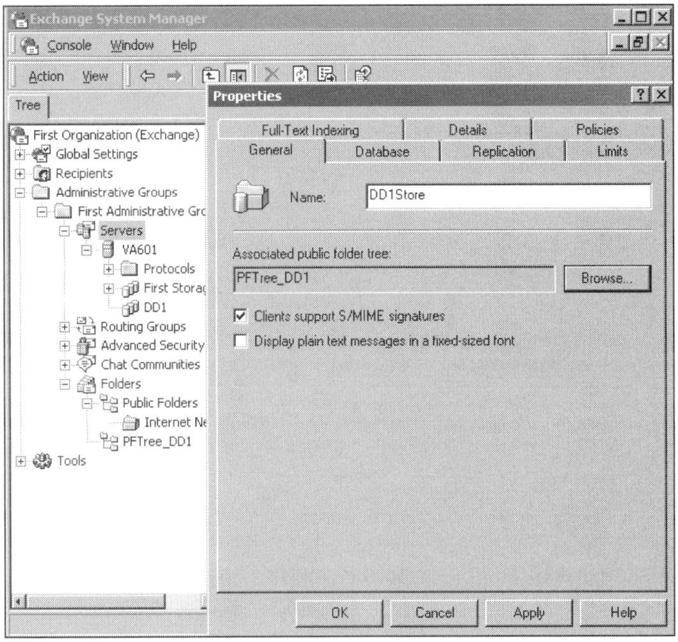

Figure 16.11 Properties sheet for a public folder store supporting a Dashboard.

13. Open Protocols, right-click HTTP, and select Create New Virtual Directory.
14. Enter a virtual root name that you will use to address the digital dashboard such as "http://ServerName/vRoot".
15. Select the Script option in the Execute Permissions Section and click the Access tab.
16. Confirm by clicking OK to complete the new store installation.

Modifying Basic Dashboard Properties

Both Dashboards and Web Parts expose standard property sets that determine dashboard appearance and behavior. The Properties window displays properties for items in the project or Web Part node. Configure these properties on a Dashboard through the Properties window using View|Properties or by pressing the F4 function key.

1. Launch Exchange System Manager from Start|Programs|Microsoft Exchange.
2. Right-click the dashboard project under the appropriate Public Folder and select Properties.

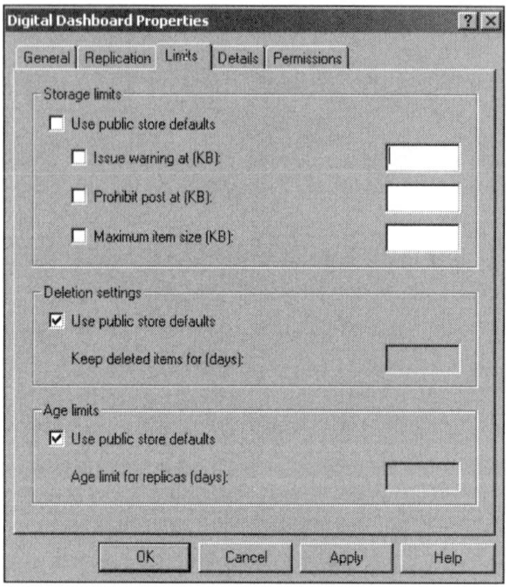

Figure 16.12 The Limits tab in a Digital Dashboard Properties sheet.

3. Select the property values such as replication interval, storage limits, deletion settings, and access permissions under the Replication, Limits, and Permissions tabs respectively. The Limits tab in the Digital Dashboard Properties window is shown in Figure 16.12.

Creating a Digital Dashboard Project

The Office XP Developer environment provides the simplest way to create a dashboard project, which consists of the project items and a HTML Web Part to the project. To create a dashboard, perform the following:

1. Select Start|Programs|Microsoft Office XP Developer|Microsoft Development Environment.
2. Click File|Project|New to display the New Project dialog box.
3. Click Office Developer Projects.
4. Click the Dashboard Project icon under Templates.
5. Type the URL to the Exchange 2000 or SharePoint Portal Server public folder location where you will create your application in the Folder Location box. The generic URL form is **http://ServerName/Public**. Alternatively, click the Browse button to specify a folder location from the Select Folder dialog box. Type the name for the folder containing the dashboard in the

Folder Name dialog box as a part of the URL, such as **http://ServerName/Public/Firstdboard** to access your dashboard project named Firstdboard.

6. Click OK to confirm.

Adding Web Parts to a Dashboard Using Office Developer

A dashboard project can consist of a variety of objects and scripting languages including JavaScript, VBScript, XML, or HTML Web Parts, and reusable components that can contain any kind of Web-based information. Web Parts use extensions such as .htm, .html, .xml, .js, .vbs, and .dwp. The Add New Item command and the Add Existing Item command are used to add parts to a dashboard project. When you add items that are already a Web Part on your local machine, property values are preserved and affect the appearance and behavior of the dashboard. Added file parts that are not Web Parts are copied into the dashboard project. To add new Web Parts to a dashboard, follow these steps:

1. Choose Start|Programs|Microsoft Office XP Developer|Microsoft Development Environment.
2. Select the specific dashboard project in Solution Explorer.
3. Select either Add New Item From Project for a new item or Add Existing Item From Project for an existing item.
4. Select the Web Part type and click Open.

Using Web Folders with a File System Dashboard

Use Windows Web folders to work with the catalog and perform basic administrative tasks after you install the File System Digital Dashboard. Double-click an item to open it in a browser window. Adding a non–Web Part item to a catalog will not automatically write those featured properties to the Web Part schema. You must create new Web Parts either through the Digital Dashboard interface or Web Part Builder. Right-click commands in the context menu provide a variety of features including rename, move, delete, and create items in the Web Part Catalog. To use Web folders, perform the following:

1. Double-click Add New Network Place From My Network Places on the desktop.
2. Type the URL, such as "http://ServerName/Dashboards", to access the folder containing Digital Dashboards.

Setting Security for a File System Dashboard

The File System Digital Dashboard stores Web Parts and Digital Dashboards in the Windows 2000 file system rather than in Exchange public folders. The dashboards containing Web Parts represent folders in the file system. These folders have WebDAV properties that identify them specifically as Web Parts and Dashboard folders. Although these folders and Web Parts appear to be normal files in the file system, they can be created only through the Dashboard or the Web Part Builder because of these special properties. After they are created, however, you can use the file system to copy, move, and delete both Dashboard folders and Web Parts as long as they remain in a root Dashboard folder. The File System Digital Dashboard consists of both a NTFS folder and an IIS virtual root to physically store Web Parts and Digital Dashboard items and properties, and an NTFS folder and IIS virtual root that stores the Web pages and other necessary components for the Dashboard factory. If the folder on which you are setting permissions is a subfolder, and you want the permissions of the parent to propagate to this folder, select the Allow Inheritable Permissions From Parent To Propagate To This Object checkbox. If you are having difficulties with security permissions, be sure to look out for security that is inherited from parent folders. You set user or group security by performing the following steps:

1. Right-click the Web Part or dashboard folder on which you want to set security in the Windows file system and select Properties from the context menu.
2. From the Security tab, either add users and groups by clicking Add and selecting the users and groups to which you want to give permissions, or remove users and groups by clicking Remove and selecting users or groups whose current access you want to remove from this folder.
3. Use Permissions to allow or deny permissions to the users and groups you've chosen by selecting the appropriate checkboxes.
4. Click Apply, and then click OK to apply the configuration changes.

Installing the File System Digital Dashboard

During installation, the names of specific locations for the dashboard components are recorded in the IIS metabase and used by the dashboard viewer and database. Best practices recommend reinstalling software to update the IIS metabase settings if either the virtual root directory names or the database name and location are modified. You will be prompted for a folder name—defaulting to Dashboards—and virtual root holding user digital dashboards. Using the specific

Web root name, you can access the default virtual root name as \Factory to access the dashboard factory files. To install the dashboard, you run DDRK_FS.msi from your software source. An installation wizard guides you through the process and copies the following files to your computer:

- *\Dashboards*—The folder that will contain users' Digital Dashboards. It is registered in IIS as a virtual folder with write and directory browsing enabled as well as script execution. The folder contains a Welcome and Administration dashboard by default.
- *\Factory**.*—The Dashboard factory is the set of files supporting dynamic rendering at runtime. These files are copied to the \inetpub\wwwroot\DDRK folder (or another folder you specify) during installation.

Configuring the File System Digital Dashboard

The Digital Dashboard is fully configured upon completion of the installation. If you encounter problems while running the software, review the error file and verify server IIS settings to ensure that the configuration is accurate and complete. Security access errors to the file system often occur during the design phase before you complete an installation. Two new IIS virtual roots, Factory and Dashboards, are created by default. Their folders are located by default at *\inetpub\wwwroot\Factory* and *\inetpub\wwwroot\Dashboards*. The dialog box showing the creation of the virtual root, Factory, is shown in Figure 16.13. Using IIS, verify that both the virtual directories have directory read, write, and listings enabled and that execute permissions are set to scripts only. In the *\inetpub\wwwroot\Factory* folder, a file named *dashboard_config.inc* should be included and configured as follows:

```
<%
Const stPortalServer = "http://server"
Const stPortalVRoot = "Dashboards"
Const stDashVRoot = "dashboards/welcome/"
%>
```

Modify the string variable **stDashVRoot** to an automatic redirection from the **http://server/factory/** to your default Digital Dashboard. The string variable **StPortalVRoot** points to the location where user dashboards are stored and is created. A second configuration file in the Dashboards folder is named **factory_config.inc**, and is used by the Web Part Builder to determine which Dashboard factory is used to process the Dashboard folders. Shown in Figure 16.13

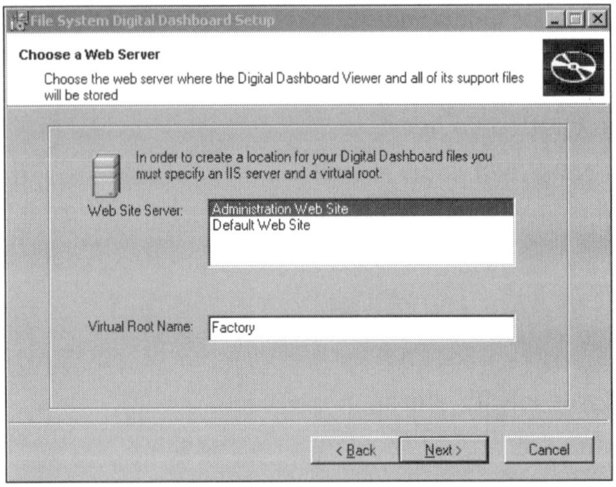

Figure 16.13 Installation of a File System Digital Dashboard.

Creating Your First Digital Dashboard

When the installation is complete, you are presented with a Welcome dashboard and Administration dashboard page that allows you to add and delete Digital Dashboards to your site after completing the installation. The default address of this dashboard is **http://server/dashboards/welcome**. Click the Add New Dashboard button and enter a dashboard name to create a dashboard. The wizard screen is shown in Figure 16.14.

Installing the Web Part Builder

The Web Part Builder requires VID running on Windows 2000. Best practices recommend closing the VID application before you begin the Web Part Builder installation. Run Setup.exe, located in the Builder directory on the Digital Dashboard Resource Kit CD, to launch an installation wizard that guides you through the installation process. After you install the Web Part Builder, connect to the dashboard site in VID by selecting File|New Project. Select Digital Dashboard as the project type. Enter the name of the server hosting the digital dashboard in the dialog box and then begin building Web Parts.

Even end users can build simple Web Parts for dashboards that display, for example, a favorite Web site or collection of Web pages. Design these components

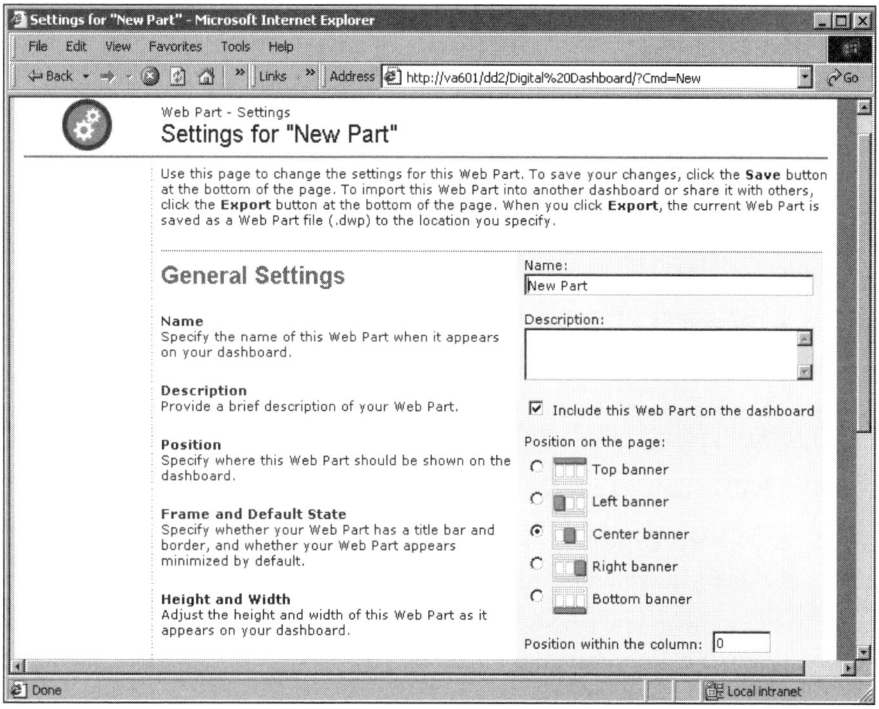

Figure 16.14 The wizard prompting for Dashboard settings.

either as an inline dashboard object or using the Web Part Builder add-in for VID. Web Parts can contain embedded content consisting of HTML, scripts, ActiveX controls, XML, or links to other Web-based content outside the dashboard. Best practices recommend using only schema properties appropriate for that Web Part. Design any one type of Web Part with an intended purpose, location, and predetermined content the Web Part will display. Creating a Web Part with static content is different from designing a component that pulls content from remote sources, such as a database or the Internet. To build a Web Part inline in the dashboard:

1. Use a browser client to access a dashboard.
2. Click Content, located in the upper-right corner of the dashboard's title bar.
3. Create a new Web Part on the Content page.
4. Define properties for the new Web Part on Properties For New Part.
5. Click OK to confirm selections and save the new Web Part.

Using the Web Part Builder to Design Web Parts

Use the Web Part Builder add-in to VID to create more complex Web Parts. You can preview your Web Part in an integrated development environment to test design and functionality. To build a Web Part using the Web Part Builder:

1. Click the Digital Dashboard drop-down list in VID or right-click the Dashboards folder in the VID Project Explorer view and select Add A Dashboard Folder.
2. Type a name and a title for the new dashboard folder.
3. Right-click your new dashboard folder and select Add Web Part.
4. Type a name, description, and content type (HTML, XML, Server-side Script) for the Web Part.
5. Select HTML in the Create Web Part dialog box.
6. Type HTML content into the Web page.
7. Select File|Save (release Working Copy if appropriate).
8. Right-click the newly created dashboard folder and select View Dashboard to preview the Web Part in the dashboard.

Adding Web Parts

To increase dashboard functionality, use the Add New Item command to include a wide variety of reusable components including JavaScript, VBScript, XML, or HTML Web Part in your dashboard project. Use the Add Existing Item command to add an existing file to the dashboard. If an added item is already a Web Part, property values are preserved and affect the appearance and behavior of the dashboard. A Web Part not previously added to the dashboard is copied into the dashboard project. Office Developer starts the registered editor for the file when you double-click the imported file. To add a new or existing Web Part to a dashboard:

1. Choose Start|Programs|Microsoft Office XP Developer|Microsoft Development Environment.
2. Select the dashboard project in the Solution Explorer.
3. Right-click the dashboard project name and select Add|New Item or Add|Existing Item in the context menu.
4. Select a part type and click Open.
5. Select the Web Part that you want to add and click OK to confirm your choices.

Creating a Digital Dashboard Using Web Parts

Creating a Digital Dashboard requires access to an Exchange 2000 server as the back end (BE) for the application and development tools—such as Office Developer—for creating the dashboard, which can reside on either a client computer with access to the server or the server itself. After it has been created, you add functionality to a dashboard with Web Parts. Office XP Developer provides a catalog of these components or you can also create your own Web Parts. Test your dashboard after adding Web Parts by viewing it in a browser. The process using Office Developer involves a series of steps, including preparing the Exchange Server, creating the dashboard project, adding components, and testing. To create a dashboard, follow these steps:

1. Choose Start|Programs|Microsoft Office XP Developer|Microsoft Development Environment.
2. Select File|New Project. The New Project dialog box appears.
3. Select Office Developer Projects. Depending on the installation, you will see three project icons under Templates: Exchange Workflow Project, SQL Server Workflow Project, and Dashboard Project. Select the Dashboard Project icon.
4. In the Location box, either enter the URL to the Exchange 2000 public folder location for your application—such as **http://*ServerName*/Public**—or click Browse to specify a folder location by using the Project Location dialog box.
5. Enter the folder name containing your application in the Folder Name dialog box as a part of the URL used to open your application—such as **http://MyServer/Public/MyApplication**—and then click OK to confirm the entries.

Previewing and Testing Your Dashboard

After creating your dashboard and adding Web Parts, you can preview and test your dashboard by viewing it in a browser.

1. Choose Start| Programs|Microsoft Office XP Developer|Microsoft Development Environment.
2. Select a dashboard project in Solution Explorer.
3. Right-click the dashboard project name and select View In Browser from the context menu.

Deploying an Exchange Server Dashboard

Exchange 2000 provides personalized, secured, shared dashboards. The Dashboard is a scalable interface for publishing Web parts and other COM+ objects. To deploy a dashboard, perform the following:

1. Choose Start|Programs|Microsoft Office XP Developer|Microsoft Development Environment.
2. Select a dashboard in the Solution Explorer from the Development Environment.
3. Click File|Save Copy As.
4. Specify the server to which you want to deploy in the Location box in File Save As.

Registering a Workflow Event Sink in a Folder

Workflow event sinks are scripts that are triggered by events or actions that affect WSS resources. Typical events in any WSS folder where it is registered include **OnSyncSave**, **OnSyncDelete**, and **OnTimer**. An event occurs when, for example, a WSS item is added or deleted from a folder. A process in the WSS looks for an event registration item in the folder when the event occurs in a folder. The registration item points to the process that handles the event. There must be some formal association or mapping that associates the workflow event sink process with the handling of **OnSyncSave**, **OnSyncDelete**, and **OnTimer** events in a specific folder. This formal association between process and event is called registering the workflow event sink in a folder. Registration of an event sink must follow specific guidelines including the following:

- Event types must be **OnSyncSave**, **OnSyncDelete**, or **OnTimer**.
- The user registering the workflow must be a member of the Can Register Workflow role assigned in the Component Services MMC (Microsoft Management Console) under Administrative Tools.
- When you create the Workflow System Account, make certain it has at least read privileges in the current folder. Events that change the folder contents require this user account to have both read and write privileges in this folder.
- You cannot set the **MatchScope** field of the registration to **Any**, nor register the event sink for a synchronous event with the **DEEP MatchScope** field if it is already registered in a parent folder or subfolder of the same folder.
- You should not set the **OnTimer** interval to be smaller than necessary, because the **OnTimer** event occurs for every workflow folder on the server.

- **DEEP MatchScope** field for **OnTimer** events is not supported in the default public folder tree. You can only have **DEEP MatchScope** field **OnTimer** events on public folder trees you have created.

Related solutions:	*Found on page:*
Running Workflow Applications from a Designated User's Account	730

Opening a SharePoint Portal Server for the First Time

Although Exchange 2000 provides portal access to the WSS on an enterprise level, SharePoint Portal Server offers similar functionality on a department level. The fundamental difference between the two servers is the dependence of Exchange 2000 on Active Directory (AD) and MAPI. Figure 16.15 shows the architecture of both servers. The shadowed components are part of Exchange 2000 and distinguish it from SharePoint Portal Server, which provides document management and collaborative services without requiring a connection to AD directory services. The procedure to add a Portal.ddp project file to the Portal folder is outlined here for comparative purposes; it places a solution file to *My Documents\Office Developer Projects\PortalX\Portal.sln.*

1. Choose Start|Microsoft Office XP Developer|Microsoft Development Environment.

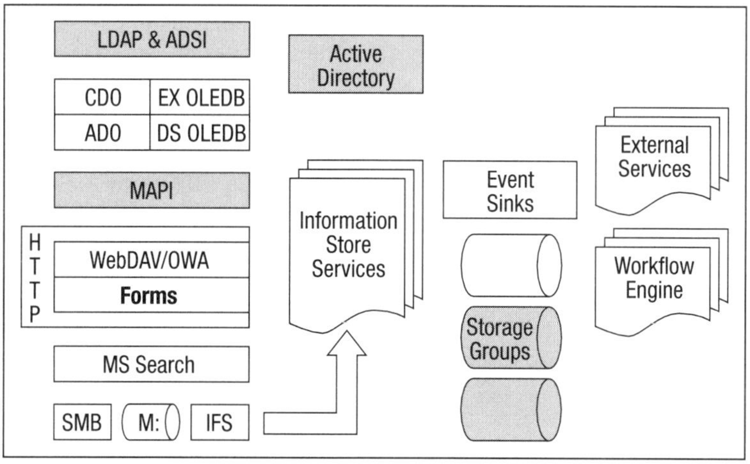

Figure 16.15 Differences between Exchange 2000 and SharePoint Portal Server.

2. Select File|Project|New.
3. Select Office Developer Projects to open the New Project dialog box. Under Templates, depending on which .NET servers are installed, you will typically see three project icons: Exchange Workflow Project, SQL Server Workflow Project, and Dashboard Project.
4. Select the Dashboard Project icon.
5. When you are prompted for a Location, enter "http://< ServerName> /<workspacename>".
6. In the Name text box, enter Portal; otherwise, you won't be able to open the SharePoint portal.
7. Click OK.

Chapter 17

Outlook Forms and Exchange Workflows

If you need an immediate solution to:	*See page:*
Modifying Views via the Outlook Interface	723
Creating the Edit Compose Page View of the Outlook Form	723
Publishing the Outlook Form	724
Preparing Exchange for a Team Solution	724
Creating a Team Folder	725
Removing a Form from the Personal Forms Library	726
Creating a Workflow Process Using WDE 2000	726
Adding States to the Workflow Diagram	727
Adding Actions to States	727
Configuring Exchange 2000 for Workflow Development	728
Adding a User to the Two COM+ Roles	729
Running Workflow Applications from a Designated User's Account	730
Creating the Exchange Folder for the Project	730
Adding a Public Folder Using IE	731
Creating the Project and Workflow Process	731
Designing a Workflow Process Using WDE 2000	733
Adding a Workflow State	733
Renaming or Labeling a State or Event	734
Setting a State or Transition Caption	734
Deleting a State	735
Adding and Modifying Transitions in Workflow	735
Adding Objects Multiple Times in Sticky Mode	736
Changing the Transition Type	736
Deleting a Workflow Process for Exchange 2000	736
Enabling Script Debugging and Success Entries	737

(continued)

If you need an immediate solution to:	See page:
Creating the Shared Script Procedures	737
Copying a Workflow Process for Exchange 2000	738
Activating the Workflow Process	739
Changing the Display and Printing the Workflow	739
Viewing or Printing a Workflow	740
Printing the Workflow Diagram	740
Testing Your Workflow for Exchange 2000	741

In Depth

Exchange 2000 Server's extensive workflow capabilities provide the dynamic processing needed for intra- and inter-enterprise process engineering, where business solutions integrate corporate team members, as well as trade partners in realtime. The capabilities of designing efficient messaging and collaborative workflows reinforce the thesis that an Exchange administrator functions as architect rather than plumber. Workflow design is fundamentally the automation of logical processes using information and business rules. This automation runs the gamut in terms of scalability: from the simplest Create-Activate-Resolve-Close scenario, to low-cost enterprise-to-enterprise processes that broaden the scope of their responsibilities to include customer relations management (CRM); maintenance, repair, and operational (MRO) supply chains; and supply/demand planning. Widening the scopes of department-level processes by collaboratively sharing or integrating workflows across enterprises introduces in the inter-enterprise process engineering we suggested in Chapter 16. An Exchange administrator can develop prototypical applications that give a company that competitive advantage in its market. This broader definition of a user population and direct contribution to a return on investment (ROI) is afforded by both the .NET distributed services architecture and the depth of the Web Store or Web Storage System (WSS).

As an Exchange administrator, you might or might not have the responsibility of choosing best-of-breed tools and clients. Nevertheless, especially in the .NET environment of distributed services, you need a client feature set that not only satisfies your end users' immediate needs, but also accommodates future changes in the environment within which the corporation functions. As you discover what Exchange 2000 now provides, you might begin to reevaluate messaging clients in terms of collaboration tools. The WSS provides a repository for managing everything from email messages and Web pages to other documents. It integrates many types of services into a single structure, so it's easy for users to find and share information with one another. Exchange 2000 has become a provider of Web resources through protocols such as HTTP 1.1 and Web Distributed Authoring and Versioning (WebDAV). Figure 17.1 shows the steps involved in accessing a message object from the Web Store using the WebDAV extension of HTTP 1.1.

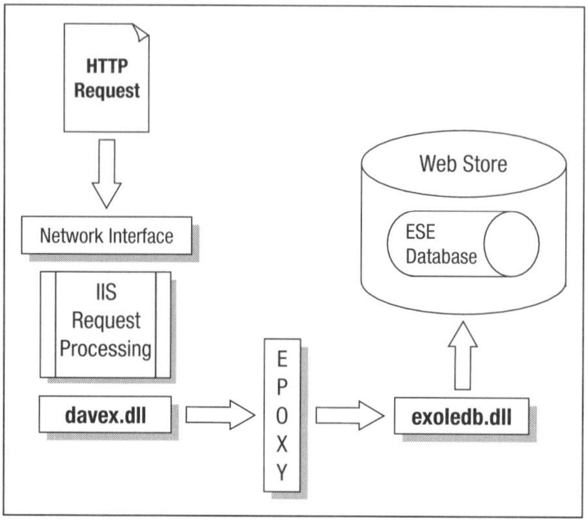

Figure 17.1 Using WebDAV to access an Exchange Inbox.

Every object in the WSS has a Uniform Resource Locator (URL) associated with it. A remote Outlook Web Access (OWA) client across the Internet can access this folder because of the WSS. It's easy to share information if you create a Web folder in advance. In fact, these folders are already built in to Office 2000. You can always create a new Web folder if you add a network place into My Network Places in Windows 2000. Even Windows 98 lets you do this if you go to My Computer|Web Folders. Clearly, Outlook is the client of choice, especially as a collaborative and messaging agent.

Building Collaborative Systems

Many networked clients access information stores across private local area networks (LANs) and wide area networks (WANs) among the many messaging clients available on the market today. Only a handful are collaborative tools. Messaging software falls into three categories: true clients, server products, and development products. Among the Microsoft applications, Outlook and Internet Explorer (IE) are true clients; the server products are obviously the Exchange platform and Internet Information Server (IIS). Other server products include SQL Server 7, Site Server 3 Commerce Edition, and .NET Servers such as SQL Server 2000, SharePoint Portal Server, and Commerce 2000. Development products in the past have come from products such as Visual Studio, which includes Visual Basic (VB) and Visual InterDev (VID). The true clients are actually collaborative applications covering a broad gamut of services, including those that handle messaging, tracking, workflow, and Realtime Collaboration (RTC).

Even though the Outlook family of clients remains central to Microsoft's desktop information management strategy, knowledge management (KM) is clearly driving integrated information environments to Web-based enterprise management protocols. KM—discussed in Chapter 16—includes RTC and close integration with both structured and unstructured data stores. In the generic KM architecture shown in Figure 17.2, you see that many key KM characteristics have been a part of Outlook Forms for many years. The highly accessible, portal-type interface characteristics of digital dashboards are nothing more than Outlook Forms rendered in a more widely accessible Web-based protocol such as HTML.

Messaging Applications

Messaging applications are the foundation services. Exchange 2000 also supports threaded discussion folders and mailbox agents. A mailbox agent, much like stored procedures in SQL Server, can programmatically process various kinds of forms available to the client. A mailing list is an example of an agent that forwards received mail to all registered users much like the ListServ program in the Unix world. An example of a mailing list agent can be found at **www.msexchange.org**.

Outlook Forms

An *Outlook Form* is an application that provides access to process workflow when you post messages, for example, to a public folder, for example. Most users have worked with the Outlook Forms design environment to create custom forms from a blank form or based on a built-in or template form. Design capabilities are further enhanced in Office XP products such as Outlook 2002. Workflow Designer for Exchange 2000 (WDE 2000) is found in the Exchange 2000 SDK (Software

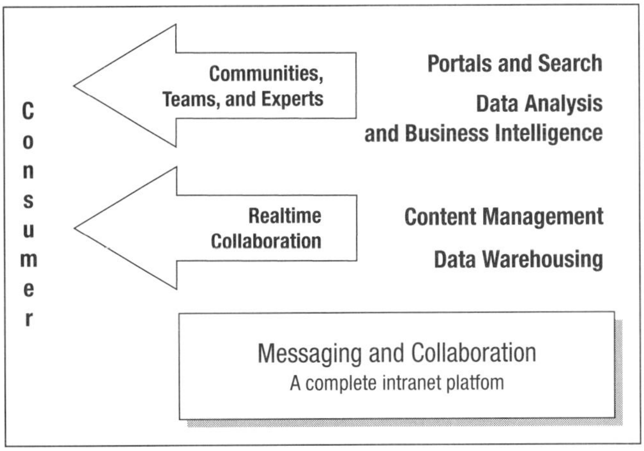

Figure 17.2 A schematic KM interface.

Developer's Kit). Microsoft Development Environment (MDE) found in the Microsoft Office XP Developer edition (MOD), provides even more capabilities in addition to the easy interface within which to generate Digital Dashboard.

You can add and remove fields, controls, options, and tabs in a form, as well as use an Office file to incorporate functionality from another Office program—such as Excel or Word—into a custom form. Forms can be saved as files for use in a forms library for reuse by other Outlook users or as a template for use in other programs. To create the user interface for a workflow, you might want to create two different views of the Post form in Outlook. For example, Edit Compose Page view is a view for data input. This view is automatically shown when you design a form. Text boxes on the form can provide values to the script used in the workflow (see Figure 17.3).

Team Folders

The *Outlook 2000 Team Folders Kit* is an example of a specialized Outlook Form that combines a Web-style HTML user interface with the collaborative features that the Outlook/Exchange interface now provides. This collaborative system includes a wizard-based installation, ActiveX controls, an Organizational Forms Library, folder documentation, customizable templates, and even an invitation form to invite prospective members to join. A specialized folder combines a Web-style user interface with the collaboration feature set provided by Exchange 2000.

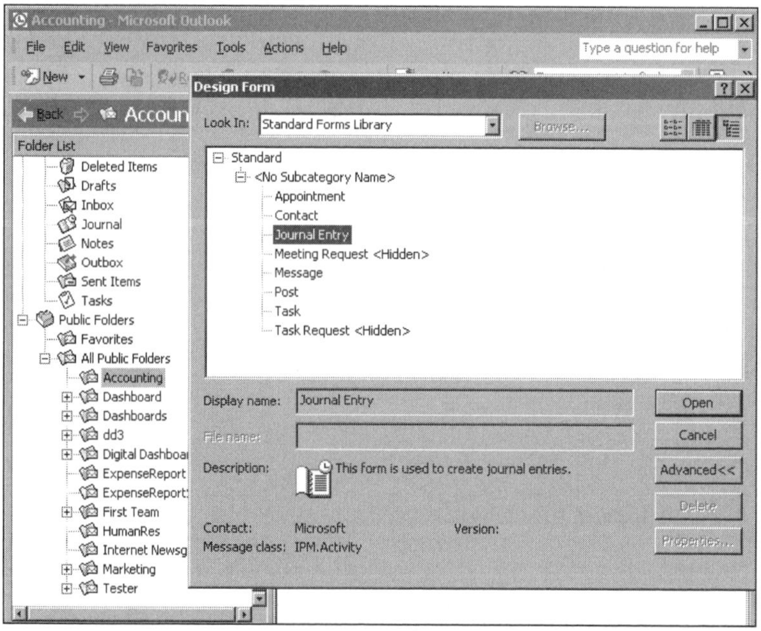

Figure 17.3 An example of designing an Outlook 2002 Journal Entry Form.

The Team Folders Wizard and the Team Folders Templates must be installed before a team folder can be created. Team Folders Wizard setup is a self-contained executable file (**Oltfwiz.exe**) run from a network share or received and applied at a distant, nonconnected location. This installation adds a Team Folder selection to the cascading menu when the user selects File|New in Outlook. The wizard provides six standard templates from which to build these folders or it can be customized. A Team Folders application can contain one or all feature modules that include threaded discussions, a document repository, a team calendar, a team task list, and a shared contacts list (see Figure 17.4).

A Team Folder template is composed of an Outlook personal folders (PST) file, one or more Web pages acting as the user interface for the team folder application, and an initialization (INI) file. The personal folders file contains one or more folders copied to the destination public folder by the Team Folders Wizard and typically has custom forms published in its form library. Forms in these libraries have predefined custom fields and views. The Team Folders Wizard uses settings in the initialization file about data and the structure of the template, the names and locations of folder home pages, and Web page configuration information to copy the contents of the personal folders file and the Web pages to their respective locations. The Team Folders Wizard is not supported in Internet-Only or PIM-Only (Personal Information Manager-Only) modes, or if you switch Outlook to Internet-Only mode after installing the Team Folders Wizard.

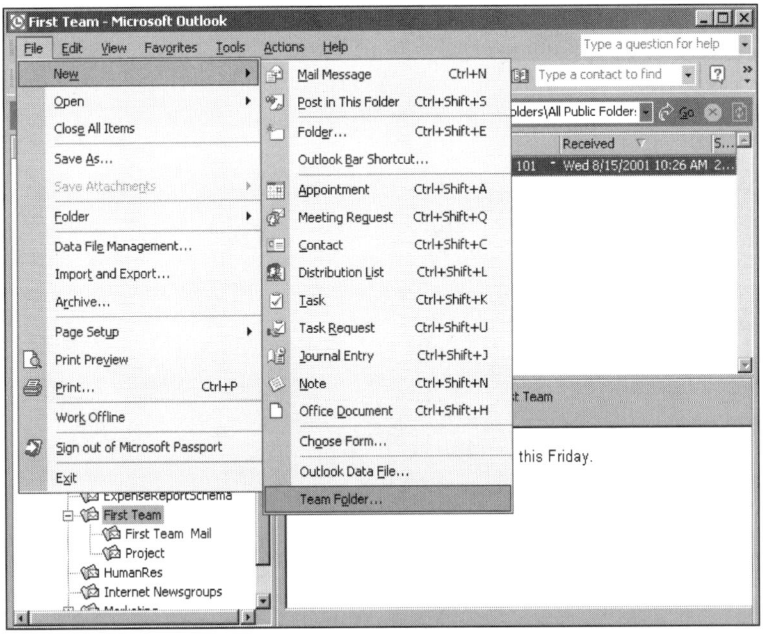

Figure 17.4 Accessing the Team Wizard from the Outlook menus.

Both an Exchange 2000 public folder and a HTTP, FTP, or file server share are required during installation to create team folder files. A Team Folder application must be created in an Exchange Server (version 5.5 or later) public folder in order to be shared. A public folder containing the Team Folder application is protected by permissions that control access to the folders. A Team Folder can be installed in a personal folders file, but you will be unable to share or administer it. The Administration page of the Team Folder Wizard, as shown in Figure 17.5, provides installation steps to complete the process. A final step sends other users an invitation message containing a button that creates a link to the Team Folder on the user's Outlook Bar.

Workflow Applications Architecture for Exchange Server

A *workflow application* consists of forms and documents that a user manipulates, and tools on the server that manage those documents according to a set of rules. The application architecture is comprised of a presentation layer and a business logic layer.

Presentation Layer

The *presentation layer* of a workflow application includes forms or documents with which the user interacts directly. This front-end (FE) layer represents the presentation logic of the application. It could be a Word document, an Outlook Form, or some other presentation layer that you design. These all work because workflows are triggered by any save or post in the workflow folder, and the WSS provides heterogeneous document storage. Whatever you use as your presentation layer is up to you, and has no relation to the functionality addressed by the CDO

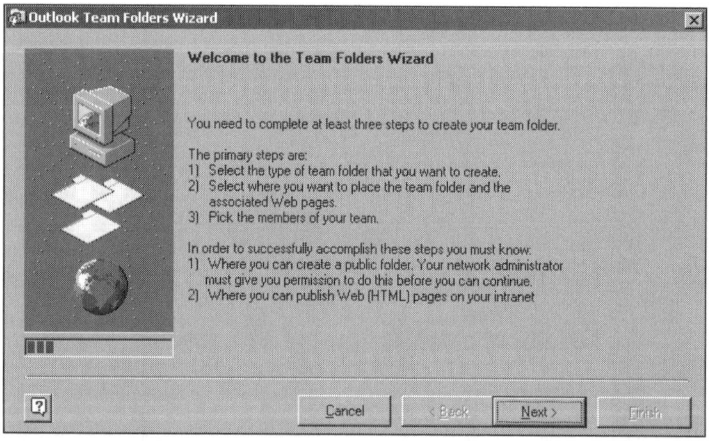

Figure 17.5 The Administration page of the Team Folders Wizard.

Workflow Objects for Exchange (CDOWF). This layer is rendered independent of CDOWF and usually runs on a client computer.

Business Logic Layer

Use CDOWF to design and run workflow applications that contain business rules controlling document approval and routing processes. Although the presentation layer usually runs on a separate client computer, the business rules run on the server hosting WSS, where the target documents are stored. Your business logic or workflow layer operates separately from the WSS process. You can create the workflow process using any language—such as VB—and create event sinks, or you can use WDE 2000 or new MOD.

Developing Workflow Applications for Exchange Server

Planning has been a consistent theme in both the creation and deployment of any successful business solution. WDE 2000 automates many activities required when creating a workflow process for both Exchange 2000 and SharePoint Portal Server. It is especially important to remember interactions between the many distributed services, related technologies, and dependencies that now populate an enterprise. Generally, the term *workflow* is used to describe applications that are modeled as business processes. These processes cut vertically through the service layers to fulfill some specific objective. These tasks involve many different services occurring either simultaneously or in sequence. When a workflow process is created, you also must consider the user interface, as well as how the users will interact with objects. Although you can implement such applications in nearly any programming language or development environment, you can simplify the task by using a workflow engine and specialized workflow modeling tools. Most elements are created outside of WDE 2000. In addition, permissions and privileges must be reviewed carefully before beginning development because workflow applications depend on user and permission management for specific permissions and rights in addition to the many layers of service.

Modeling tools make it possible for the overall design, or "flow," of a business process to be specified in a simple, high-level representation called a *process definition*. For example, assigning a trouble ticket based on an incident is created or booked in a system, but due to specific characteristics or service level agreements (SLAs), the incident might be immediately escalated to a specialist. At the same time the assignment is made, a customer representative might receive email notification indicating a service issue. Upon resolution, that same customer representative might receive another notification indicating the resolution of the issue. This entire process can be automated as a workflow application.

The developer tools allow you to modify or extend this process definition without rewriting low-level application code. To deploy a workflow process, however, you must establish the appropriate accounts, such as the workflow system account, and grant built-in permissions, such as a privileged author role. The workflow engine then executes and manages individual process instances of the workflow sequence. Use the following guidelines to help design a workflow process using the WDE 2000, or MDE in XP Developer:

1. Plan your application carefully before you start coding. When you conduct a needs analysis, identify business processes associated with the information you are tracking in your folder, for example. A process to track information might be characterized as a system concerned with assigning, analyzing, and resolving trouble tickets. Consider business objectives, the skills of your user population, and network issues.
2. Create the workflow process for your application. Identify the steps in the business process, and determine the events and conditions—such as routing and mail services—associated with each step. It is sometimes useful to first diagram the workflow using a verbal description rather than a graphic representation.
3. Add script to your application if desired to provide customized functionality. For example, write a script that has the **Delete** event trigger the sending of a database record documenting the solution to an archive file or knowledge database.
4. Create the user interface with a program that has read/write capabilities with Exchange 2000 or SharePoint Portal Server.
5. Activate your workflow process and test your application for runtime errors.
6. Ask a random sample of actual users to test your workflow application for logical errors in procedure or scope.

Workflow Applications

The term *workflow* describes applications that are modeled on business processes, such as an expense report or work schedule approval system. Typical workflow applications include the following:

- A routing/distribution list (DL) for form approval
- Document reviews
- Ticket tracking

A workflow application works with any form on any FE platform, including a standard Outlook message form. You can customize a FE with context-specific fields that are relevant to your user population and project objectives, and then access these fields through a script in your workflow. This workflow script or event sink functions as an interface between Web Storage System processes and the workflow engine, which controls the state changes to items in your workflow folder. Event sinks are registered as a Component Object Model (COM+) application package when Exchange Server is installed and after a dynamic-link library (DLL) is created that implements an Exchange 2000 Store event sink. Because workflows are triggered by saves, a prominently displayed button located on your form can be used to submit a form and trigger a workflow transition. You also can create custom views of your form for different states in your workflow.

Exchange Server and Public Folders

WDE 2000 simplifies creating and manipulating workflow processes for Exchange folders via CDOWF. *CDO* is a set of COM components that programmatically interact with scripted processes much like ActiveX Data Objects (ADO 2.5). WDE 2000 creates sets of rules—process definitions—for the selected workflow folder as you graphically design the components and make associations—event registrations—with some event occurrence detected by an event sink (by default, the CDO workflow event sink). The CDO workflow event sink, as a part of Exchange 2000, interfaces WSS processes with the workflow engine.

The graphic design orientation of WDE 2000 allows you to focus on the logic of the workflow without writing code. You can add logic that is more complex at any time through the highly extensible interface. In addition, workflow processes created using WDE 2000 use the advanced management features such as permitting ad hoc workflow processes, adding an existing workflow item, and creating an entirely new default workflow process.

A workflow process automates control of items in a folder by moving them through a series of actions and conditions you specify as states. You can add a workflow process that can affect any item in Exchange 2000 folders. In addition, you can enhance your workflow solution by scripting your own functions that run when the actions are performed. Your workflow process can, for example, track any type of item available in Outlook—such as messages, forms, or tasks—as well as any file—such as documents (DOC), spreadsheets (XLS), or text files (TXT).

The user interface for a workflow process determines how the user submits the item that moves through the process. When designing the user interface for your solution, you have a wide variety of options. You can integrate VB applications, Web pages, and any other FE that can access the Exchange folder objects.

You can create a team solution that uses a public folder, an Outlook Form, and a workflow to move an expense report through a simplified approval process. The workflow you create, for example, could use values in the form to determine how the report is sent through the various states in the process. In addition, it could use script to notify users automatically that the report has been submitted and reviewed.

Because our example is designed to highlight how to create a simple workflow process, not the user interface for the application, the user interface provided would be a simple Outlook Form. The example application created below is not designed to be a real-world solution.

During the installation of Exchange 2000, this COM+ application package is automatically registered with the host operating system (OS). The association between the folder and the event sink enables the Exchange WSS to notify the event sink when some event occurs within the designated folder. The event sink calls the workflow engine to perform these operations and thus affect a work item's *transition* or change in state. The workflow engine thus responds to system and WSS events. It executes the logical steps that define the workflow process and makes possible decision-based control and tracking. The workflow engine executes these steps based on a table of events called the *action table.* WDE 2000 builds this action table when you graphically construct a workflow diagram. Although simplified in the MDE as click-and-drag operations, creating a workflow application requires knowledge of both the CDO 1.2.1 and ADO 2.5 components for Exchange 2000.

Related solution:	Found on page:
Adding Contact Information into Messages Using **CDOEX**	777

Workflow Process

A *workflow process* is a script of tasks and events in a specific order that is executed for each event or transition of some item. In its simplest form, a workflow process automates and enforces the order of tasks. Workflow processes enforce business rules or logic that mirror an actual work application. WDE 2000 creates workflow processes specifically for Exchange folders; MOD is a more general tool that also supports Dashboard design. All items contained within a designated folder must conform to the specifications of the workflow under the programmatic control of that particular workflow process. Both MOD and WDE 2000 use a graphical user interface (GUI) to represent the workflow process as a diagram that can be edited. The conceptual model for a workflow process used in this GUI includes the following:

- *State*—This is the current condition or property values of an item in the workflow process, such as Open or Resolved.
- *Events*—Any operation that can be performed on an item—such as **Create** or **Delete**—is an event that can trigger scripted event sinks.
- *Transitions*—Some change in the state of an item. The modification of an item is an event that alters the current state and produces a state transition. Creation of a transition requires both an event and the specification of the next state.

The developer labels an empty process when a new workflow is created. Both **Create**, appearing as a starting block, and **Delete**, appearing as an ending block, are automatically added to the process. The developer can add states, events, and transitions to describe the workflow process on demand. Figure 17.6 shows a workflow process in WDE 2000; the rectangles represent Active, Resolved, and Closed states, the arrows represent transitions, and the top and bottom squares are the starting block (**Create**) and the ending block (**Delete**). The recursive loops (transition within) labeled **Edit** are events that do not cause state changes.

Workflow Events

Seven types of events are used in a workflow process. You can assign state to an **Enter**, **Exit**, and **Create** event only one time, but you can assign **Delete** (based on some specified logic), **Change**, **Expiry**, and **Receive** events as many

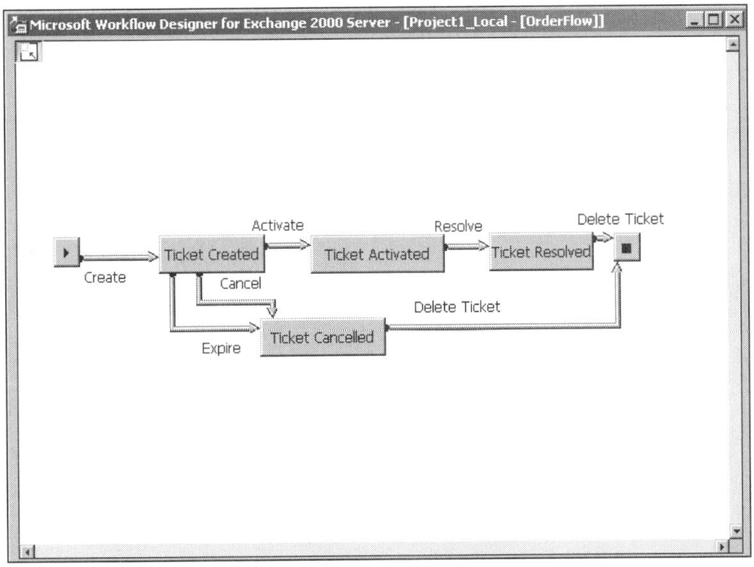

Figure 17.6 A workflow process as seen from WDE 2000.

times as required by a situation. **Change**, **Expiry**, and **Receive** events create state transitions. A single state, denoted typically as verbs, can have many transitions, denoted as adverbs; for example, from a state called **TicketCreated**, you can have different transitions to a state called **TicketCancelled**: one created with **Cancel**, and a second with **Expiry**. Workflow events are triggered by events such as the following:

- **Create**—A new item is created in the folder.
- **Enter**—A transition into a given state. The **Enter** event also starts the clock ticking for the **Expiry** action.
- **Exit**—A transition out of a given state.
- **Delete**—An item is deleted.
- **Change**—An item is changed.
- **Receive**—Mail for an item is received.
- **Expiry**—A time interval defined for the **Enter** event has elapsed. **Expiry** is a time-based event measured from the **Enter** event and the **Expiry** event in days, hours, or minutes. The minimum duration is 15 minutes.

In the following example, the transition event-type icons are displayed on the diagram using WDE 2000. Notice that between the actual creation and deletion of a ticket, this workflow identifies four transitions: **TicketCreated**, **TicketActivated**,

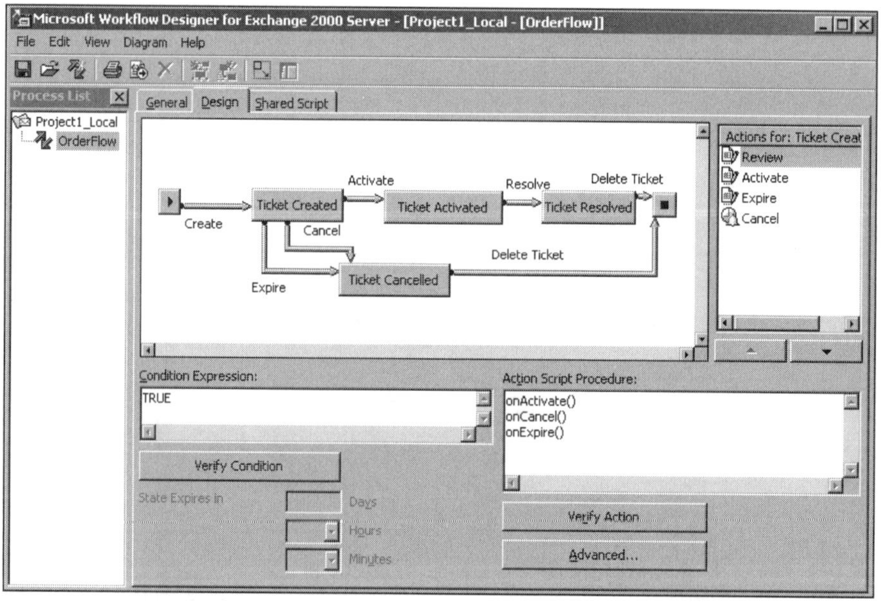

Figure 17.7 Full screen interface of a workflow diagram with transitions as seen from WDE 2000.

TicketResolved, and **TicketCancelled**. There can be many transitions, shown in Figure 17.7, from the created state. Cancellations, for example, can be based on a variety of events and business logic, such as the passive expiration of some time interval, the active cancellation by the user, a customer representative rewriting a ticket, or a supervisor performing maintenance or adjustments.

Event Order

Workflow applications are action plans that define logical steps to accomplish some business process objective. A workflow application will initiate, for example, some process upon the "event" of saving an object in a specific folder. *Trigger events* can be defined at the protocol, transport, and WSS levels. A protocol event is an action that has a relatively local scope. In comparison, transport events extend the message-processing system beyond the confines of the local machine to transport activity within the Exchange namespace. Workflow events are evaluated in a strictly defined, replicable order by the Exchange 2000 workflow engine. The workflow engine follows an action plan to identify items in a workflow-enabled folder that match some specific current state, next state, or condition. For example, a generic **Create** event is matched first to determine any new items within the domain of the workflow. If some item matches true, an associated trigger launches some piece of programmed logic to dynamically process the new item. Existing items are matched against predetermined **Change** events. Depending on the programmed transition, a scripted logical sequence performs some process related to the change in the state of that existing item, and so on. Exchange 2000 workflows work at the transport level by providing programmatic access to the SMTP (Simple Mail Transfer Protocol) and NNTP (Network News Transfer Protocol) stacks. A workflow process could attach some advertising message or service information to all outgoing email, or quarantine and scan incoming attachments. The same workflow script, called a CDO sink, could be reused in any COM-compatible language. Thus, an Exchange administrator can define a relatively simple workflow process for the mail system on top of and extending the native Windows 2000 SMTP service.

WSS Events

WSS events extend the features of the WSS by using the Object Linking and Embedding for Databases (OLE DB) Application Programming Interface (API). Events that occur within the WSS are categorized as synchronous, asynchronous, or system events. You also can control which users can register these scripted action plans—called event sinks—and what the event sinks can access through permission management provided by the OS. Registered synchronous events occur coincidental to a transition process and before a final change is committed to the store or some new state is reached. In contrast, asynchronous events, like their legacy counterparts, are notifications that a transition has occurred. You can define events as starting WSS, stopping WSS, or based on some timed interval associated with these events.

WSS events provide logical markers or hooks on which you can execute code whenever an item is saved, deleted, moved, copied, or modified. WSS events run on the server of the client that causes the event to happen. WSS events trigger application logic in MAPI (Messaging API) clients such as Outlook, a HTTP client such as IE or OWA, or a Win32 client such as any Office application. Similarly, application logic is triggered if the item is delivered using SMTP, IMAP (Internet Message Access Protocol), or NNTP. Separating the application logic from the client accessing the data is the basis for generic dynamic server page technology; you write server-side, rather than client-side, code to simplify maintenance, and the need to be rewriting the code for every client accessing the data. The application logic runs whether or not the client is connected when the item arrives in the Mailbox Store, or the client has the application installed. The WSS guarantees that asynchronous events are delivered even if the store is shut down before the event fires. When this occurs, the event fires when the store restarts WSS events supported by Exchange 2000, as shown in Table 17.1.

Synchronous Events

Application logic that processes a synchronous event can redirect a process flow, and thus modify some item before the original action concludes the ongoing transition. This dynamic control over the workflow can, for example, affect the condition of an item before it is saved to a data store, prevent the item from being saved to that store, or subsequently prevent the item from being deleted from a store. The workflow application can act to modify the item before it is perceived or accessed by the client because the application is called before the actions preformed on the item are completed. Synchronous events occur within the context of a specific, local transaction. An event is called once before, referred to as the **begin**, and after the transaction is consummated, referred to as the **commit** (or **abort**) phase. An event sink has full read/write access to the item that triggered the event during the **begin** phase. During the **commit** phase, the item is read-only. The WSS provides a synchronous **Save** and synchronous

Table 17.1 WSS events supported by Exchange 2000.

Asynchronous Events	Synchronous Events	System Events
OnSave	OnSyncSave	OnTimer
OnDelete	OnSyncDelete	MDBOnStartUp MDBOnShutDown

Delete event as shown in Table 17.1. The synchronous **Save** event occurs whenever an item is saved or delivered into the WSS.

Workflow Engine

The Exchange 2000 workflow engine provides a platform for the design of extensible and scalable workflow applications appropriate for any business scenario in almost any scripting or programming language. Best practices recommend simplifying the scripting task as much as possible by using the built-in workflow engine and specialized workflow modeling tools for .NET Servers such as Exchange 2000, SharePoint Portal Server, and SQL Server 2000 included in XP Office Developer. Leverage your knowledge as an Exchange administrator and use these design tools to create the programming specifications for business solutions in your corporation. These component-based tools allow you to easily manage the development of more complex code by more experienced programmers who will still maintain control over a working prototype. Furthermore, because the WSS provides heterogeneous document storage, the nature of the stored objects has little or no relation to the functionality addressed by CDO Workflow Objects.

The user interface of the workflow application is independent of CDO Workflow Objects and runs on a client computer. CDO Workflow Objects for Exchange provide a built-in workflow engine and an object model for programming that engine. You don't have to be encumbered by differences in Document Object Models (DOMs) or platforms. You can create a process definition or table of actions or rules that define the business process based on your perspective of the Exchange organization. The workflow engine evaluates the process definition to determine which actions it needs to run. The workflow engine then executes scripts or COM objects to execute additional business logic. Because these scripts are extensible, you can depend on others to optimize the code after the prototypical code has proven to be of business value. Furthermore, workflow event sinks simplify the integration of workflow into existing applications. Using a system integration mentality, you can manage the development of a business solution without having to build each specific part in the process.

Workflow Scripting

Built-in functionality of workflow events can be enhanced using VB Scripting Edition (VBScript). You can easily incorporate these scripts into workflow events using WDE 2000, the MDE in Office XP Developer (MOD), or the Microsoft Script Editor.

The Workflow Designer for Exchange is composed of a Process List pane and a series of tabbed options, General, Design, and Shared Script. The Process List is a tree view of various Exchange folders and workflow processes. The Workflow Process tabs provide configuration settings associated with the process flow and its associated folder. The Design tab consists of a workflow diagram area and areas for listing assigned actions and shared scripts. MOD is a more general development tool that provides more functionality. Projects currently include workflow and dashboards, but can easily be extended to accommodate other programming objects. In addition to a Solution Explorer, there is a Property window, Toolbox, and browser, all of which can be extended to accommodate future components.

Any single transition that alters the condition of some state can trigger different events. Conditional and looping statements that control the flow of your script can easily be extended with VBScript code obtainable from sources outside your own expertise. For each event in your workflow process, you can specify a conditional statement to evaluate whether a condition is True or False. Depending on the result, you can specify one or more statements that address other COM objects. For instance, if you need to validate the ability of a user to update an item, you can write a customized VBScript function that evaluates the sender property of the **WorkflowSession** object. You then can incorporate this function into your workflow script.

Understanding the Workflow Process

A *workflow process* is a series of tasks or events, the order in which they must be performed, and code that runs when they are performed. The workflow process is applied to items in the selected folder. Multiple workflow processes can be defined for a single folder. However, only one process can be designated as the default process. You can have one workflow process per item if you have set the Ad Hoc Workflow Property on the default workflow process, and have associated workflow for that item. In WDE 2000, a diagram representing the workflow process is displayed on the Workflow Designer Design Surface. Figure 17.6 shows a graphical representation of your workflow process, including the states, the transitions between the states, and the events associated with the states. MOD offers a similar display as shown in Figure 17.8.

You add additional workflow states—such as **TicketResolved** and **TicketClosed**—by dragging icons from the workflow toolbox onto the design surface. Modify the workflow process to handle multiple transitions and decision points in your process. For example, after an item is activated, you might want to cancel it rather than change it to a resolved state. If you wanted to reopen a closed item, you add an additional state—such as **ReActivate**—along with adding the appropriate events, including additional transitions—such as **Cancel** and **ReActivate**. Notice the changes in the workflow in the more familiar WDE 2000 interface.

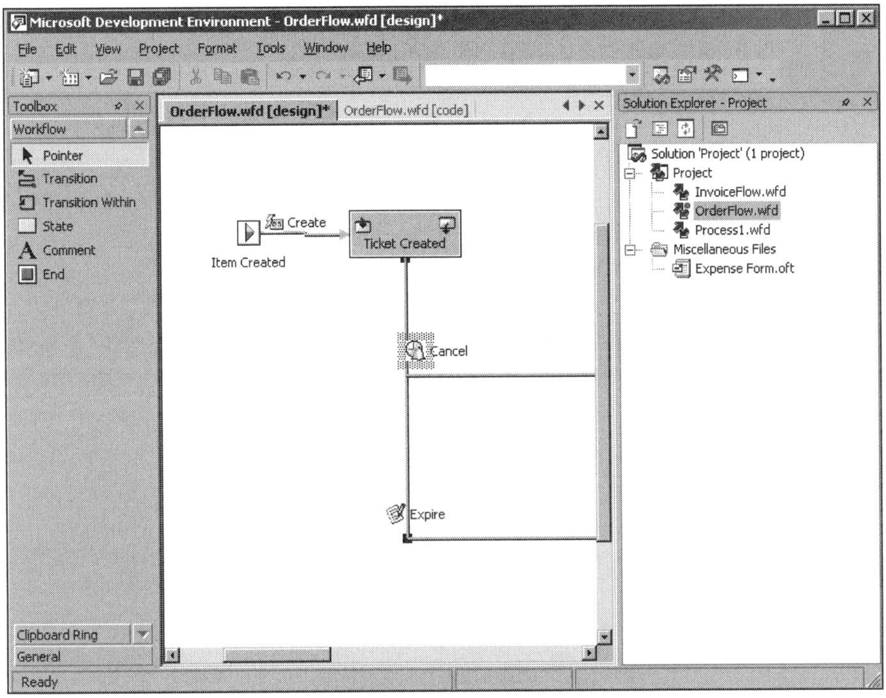

Figure 17.8 This is an example of the Office XP Developer design surface.

Workflow Components and Workflow Process

A *workflow process* is composed of workflow states, events, and (optionally) scripts. When you create a workflow state, you create a defined step or condition in the workflow process, such as **Activated**, **Resolved**, or **Closed**. Each state can have multiple events. Some events—such as **Change**, **Receive**, and **Expiry**—are used to create a transition from one state to another. Other events—including **Enter**, **Exit**, **Create**, and **Delete**—typically are used to trigger VBScript association with the workflow process. Scripts use events as triggers and add them to the Script Editor as validation functions and subprocedures. In addition, you can create common scripts that are used by multiple procedures.

In MOD, when you select the New Project|Exchange Workflow Project option from the File menu just like you would a Word document from MS Word, a new empty workflow process is created and given the default name Process1, which you can modify at a later time by choosing View|Property Pages Window. WDE 2000 provides simpler access, File|New Workflow Process. You can add objects to the workflow process including states, transitions, and events. For example, to evaluate some current item value before it is changed, you use the **Enter** event to trigger a script when a state is entered. Upon entering a **Resolved** state, information—such as the current date, current time, and Resolved By field value—is sent to the manager indicating the item is resolved.

Using the Workflow Design Surface

The *Workflow Design Surface* provides a graphical interface to design the workflow process. You can enhance or modify your workflow process using this design surface, the Workflow Developer Tools, and associated object Property sheets. Drag icons from the toolbox to the design surface to create workflow states, transitions, and comments. When you double-click a state or transition, the Script Editor is displayed with the associated event script. You also can right-click and select View Code from the context menu. The Workflow Design Surface and toolbox are used to add, modify, rename, or delete a state, as well as add or modify workflow transitions. Not all objects in the workflow diagram can have scripts associated with them.

Adding and Modifying States in a Workflow

You create an empty workflow process when you select the File|New Workflow Process in WDE 2000 or File|New|Project in MOD. You must populate this process by creating additional states, transitions, and events. In WDE 2000 either use Edit|Insert or right-click in the design window to add states to your workflow. MOD is similar to other more extensible design tools. A Toolbar area provides a variety of icons representing design tools and programming objects. You add an object like state to your workflow application by clicking and dragging any of these icons from the Design Toolbox palette in MOD to the design surface. You then must create transitions that connect your state to other items in the process and create the flow of your business rules. You enhance the workflow process by adding additional events to your states and use triggered scripts activated by these events to build various actions into your workflows. The State tool, in the Workflow toolbox, is used to place state shapes on the Workflow Design Surface. A state shape represents state operations performed by the workflow. Add a state shape by double-clicking the State tool, dragging the State Shape tool onto the design surface, or selecting an icon by single-clicking the tool and then single-clicking the design surface. A Sticky mode, enabled by holding the Ctrl key down as you click the State Shape tool, and then clicking the design surface multiple times to add states, facilitates the creation process. The Esc key will disable the Sticky mode.

Immediate Solutions

In many of these examples, we list generic portions of code to show how solutions might be built. Complete source code and accompanying documentation would be outside the scope of this book as it was originally intended; namely, as a quick reference source for generating immediate solutions to problems encountered on a regular basis by an Exchange 2000 administrator.

Modifying Views via the Outlook Interface

To modify views via the Outlook interface, perform the following:

1. Select View|Current View|Define Views.
2. Click New or Copy. If you select New, you are prompted for a view type, which can be associated with a single folder, this folder, or all folders of a specific type.
3. When you confirm by clicking OK in the Create A New View dialog box, the View Summary page appears from which you can select a customized view, which includes specific fields, customized groups, sort order, filters, and formatting.

Creating the Edit Compose Page View of the Outlook Form

You can modify the appearance of a form through a property sheet, and add predefined fields by using the Field Chooser. If the Field Chooser is not displayed, select Form|Field.

1. Open the Public folder in Outlook 2002 where you want to add the workflow.
2. Select Tools|Forms|Design A Form.
3. Select Post and then click Open in the Design Form dialog box.
4. Resize the form's message area to create space for the expense report fields.

5. Display the Toolbox from either the toolbar or Form|Control Toolbox option from the Main menubar.
6. Add the desired controls to the form by clicking and dragging icons to the design surface.
7. Right-click the specific control and select Properties to modify the control properties.

Publishing the Outlook Form

For a form to be available to a workflow process, you must have Editor, Publishing Editor, or Owner permissions to publish the form as part of a public folder. You can specify a default form for a folder. Best practices recommend publishing the form before you enable the workflow. Publishing a form to an already-enabled workflow can cause a permission error, even though you are the owner of the folder. Your form will appear when a user decides to post to that folder. To publish the form and specify it as the default form for the folder, perform the following:

1. Select Tools|Design|Publish Form As.
2. Enter a name for the form in the Publish Form As dialog box, and then click Publish. The name appears when choosing a form to post in the folder.
3. Because the form is already published, you do not have to resave your changes. Therefore, when you close the form, select No when prompted to save your changes.
4. Right-click the folder you want to add to the workflow, and choose Properties in the Folder list.
5. Select the form you created from the When Posting To This Folder dialog box and click OK.

Preparing Exchange for a Team Solution

To prepare a Team Folder Solution, you need Exchange 2000, WDE 2000 in the MDE, and the appropriate permissions on the server. Team solutions require either Windows NT 4 or Windows 2000 Server—with Exchange 2000 as the back end (BE) for development tools in Office XP Developer Edition—to create a workflow process. WDE 2000 can be run from either a client computer with access to the server or the server itself. Before you can add workflow to your folder, you should perform the following:

1. Prepare a plan for the business process that tracks an item.
2. Compile a set of items your team will measure. Create an Outlook Form that provides users with a way to input and track Exchange items. You can use a variety of data and scripting objects—such as Active Server Pages (ASP), a VB form, or Data Access Pages—as the interface for your folder and workflow in addition to Outlook Forms.
3. Select a public folder in Exchange 2000.
4. Assign workflow design permissions via Exchange 2000. When you create a folder in Outlook, you automatically are assigned owner permissions.

Creating a Team Folder

To support a Team Folder, you need the following:

- Exchange Server version 5 or later
- A file, HTTP, or FTP server that supports the creation of folders and files
- A Public Folder with owner permissions for those using the Team Folders Wizard

You can create a team folder application in an Exchange Server (version 5.5 or later) public folder. The wizard installs the Team Folder application in a public folder protected by permissions that control access to the folders. You can install a Team Folder in a personal folders file, but you will be unable to share or administer it. Users who run the Team Folders Wizard require Microsoft Outlook 2000 with Collaboration Data Objects support installed. They also need Internet Explorer 5 or greater, Web Server Extension Support for HTML Publishing and HTML Scripting Support. While the support libraries are installed with Office 2000 by default, the Windows Installer will install CDO support to Outlook 2000 when needed. Run the Team Folders Wizard and then launch Outlook. Select Team Folders from File|New.

Removing a Form from the Personal Forms Library

Best practices recommend always removing beta or release candidate versions of software prior to the installation of release to manufacture (RTM or Gold) versions. If you installed the beta version of the Team Folders Kit, including the invitation form, it's especially important to remove the invitation form from the Organization Forms Library before installing other versions.

1. Select Outlook|Tools|Options.
2. Select Other|Advanced Options.
3. Select Custom Forms|Manage Forms.
4. Select Set.
5. Select Personal Forms in the Forms Library list.
6. Select the form you want to remove and click Delete in the list below Personal Forms.

Creating a Workflow Process Using WDE 2000

You can use WDE 2000 to create a workflow process and specify the states and actions. You must add a workflow to a specific public folder, add process states that items will move or transition through, add actions that determine how the item is managed, and specify conditions for specialized handling. You can add scripting to these actions that automate the specialized handling of the items—such as sending notifications, or calling other functions you want to use—and you can create scripts and functions on the Shared Script tab for future use. After planning your workflow, create the workflow on a public folder. Because WDE 2000 works on existing folders, create the folder before designing the workflow. WDE 2000 initially generates a simple workflow with one state and **Create** and **Delete** actions between the starting and ending blocks. To add workflow to a public folder, perform the following:

1. Select Start|Program Files|Workflow Designer For Exchange.
2. Enter the appropriate Exchange Server name in the Open Folder dialog box.
3. Enter Public in the Folder box and click Browse to select a folder.
4. Click OK to confirm choices and launch the Workflow Designer.
5. Select File|New Workflow Process.
6. Enter a name for the workflow process in the New Workflow Process dialog box and click OK to confirm choices.
7. Type an appropriate name for your initial state in the Rename State dialog box and then click OK to confirm the entry.

You can make the diagram easier to read by arranging the states and actions into a more pleasing layout. To arrange the diagram, perform the following:

1. Choose Diagram|Arrange Diagram|Vertical.
2. Choose Diagram|Zoom|Zoom To Fit.

Adding States to the Workflow Diagram

You can add states to the workflow diagram representing each stage through which an item might pass during processing. In this example, the states used in the Figure Workflow diagram are **Active**, **Resolved**, and **Closed**. These states appear within the rectangle boxes in the design window. To add a workflow state to the diagram, perform the following:

1. Right-click the diagram background and select Insert State on the context menu.
2. Enter a name in the New State dialog box and click OK to confirm.
3. Right-click the **Delete** action, which is represented by the line between the **Draft** state and the endpoint, and select Remove Action in the context menu.

Adding Actions to States

Workflow actions evaluate conditions and trigger scripts that automate your workflow process. Adding actions such as **Resolve** to states or conditions such as **Open** or **Resolved** builds relationships between the states in the workflow. When you drag the icons on the design surface of WDE 2000, the graphic relationships create actual code (subroutines) that provides placeholders within which to add script for automating the workflow. To add an action to a state in the Workflow Designer:

1. Right-click the state and select Insert Action on the context menu.
2. Enter an action name (see the next procedure for details about the actions used in this walk-through) in the Action Name Text box and select an Action Type.
3. Select the state that follows the transition action in the Next State box and then click OK to add the action to the Actions list.

4. Enter the condition that must be true for the transition to occur and the script to be executed in the Condition Expression box. The condition is set to True by default. Anytime the item is read in the folder, the transition is evaluated as True, and the item moves to the next state.
5. Enter the procedure call to execute a script when the condition value is True in the Action Script Procedure box.

Configuring Exchange 2000 for Workflow Development

WDE 2000 supports three events: **onSyncSave**, **onSyncDelete**, and **onTimer**. The Web Store provides two synchronous events for scripts to use as triggers. Synchronous save is called whenever an item is delivered into a store or saved for storage. Synchronous delete is called when an item is deleted. Events like **onTimer** trigger, for example, when no user input is detected for a specified period. You enable the workflow folder through registration of the associated script—called an event sink—for the events associated with the folder and the workflow process. The user account used to run workflow applications has to be part of two COM+ roles, namely, as a Register Workflow or as Privileged Workflow Authors to configure the Exchange Server for workflow applications. Register the event sink with **DEEP** scope so that all subfolders will inherit the same workflow process. Remember to shut down the COM+ application before you add users to the COM+ roles or modify an event sink property. Any authenticated user can create a workflow design if the user has permission to register the CDO workflow event sink and has folder ownership. You can use the included designers in the built-in Privileged Workflow Authors group on each computer running Exchange 2000.

Even though Exchange 2000 setup installs workflow components by default, a workflow event sink will not have the proper security privileges unless you add a Workflow System Account to the Exchange Domain Servers Active Directory (AD) group. Use AD Users and Computers and AD Component Services. To add the Workflow System Account:

1. Select a user account. Best practices recommend using an account such as Workflow System Account with a password expiration policy that is set to Never Expire. Make sure it has an assigned Exchange mailbox.
2. Add the Workflow System Account to the AD group called **Domain ExServers** so that the CDO workflow event sink has the proper privileges for execution.

Adding a User to the Two COM+ Roles

To add a user to the two COM+ Roles, perform the following:

1. Select Start|Programs|Administrative Tools|Component Services.
2. Select the Component Services node in the Component Services dialog box and then choose Computers|My Computer.
3. Select COM+ Applications|Workflow Event Sink and then open Roles. Two workflow roles are present: Can Register Workflow and Privileged Workflow Authors.
4. Open either workflow node and right-click on the Users folder as shown in Figure 17.9.
5. Select New|User to add a user or group to the role from the Select Users Or Groups dialog box. The user account must also be a member of the Exchange Domain Servers group.
6. Select Start|Programs|Administrative Tools|Active Directory Users And Computers.
7. Right-click the username and select Properties in the Domain Users folder.
8. Select Add from the Member Of tab and add the user to the Exchange Domain Servers group.

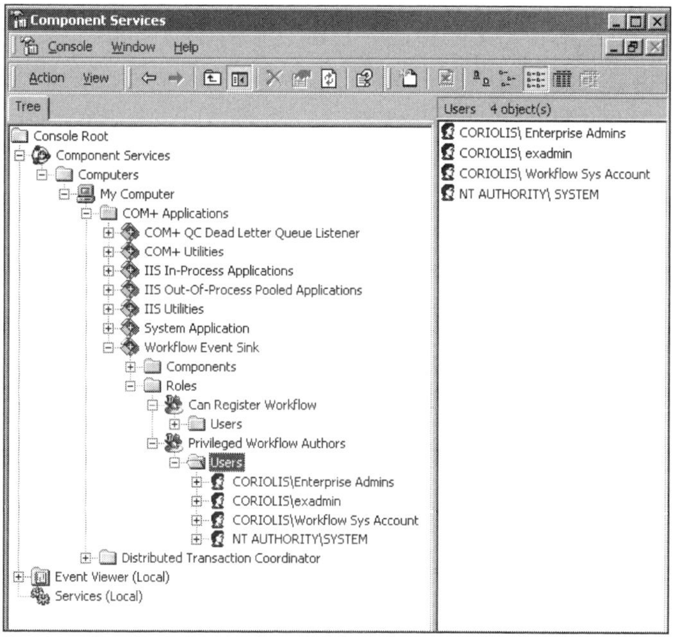

Figure 17.9 Component Services showing specialized COM+ roles.

17. Outlook Forms and Exchange Workflows

Running Workflow Applications from a Designated User's Account

To run workflow applications, you must configure the appropriate rights by designating a user's account. These safeguards insure that programmed dynamic processes are executed according to the specifications for which they were originally designed. To designate a user, perform the following:

1. Select Start|Programs|Administrative Tools|Component Services.
2. Open the Component Services node in the Component Services dialog box, and select COM+ Applications from My Computer under Computers.
3. Open COM+ Applications under My Computer and select the Workflow Event Sink node.
4. Right-click the Select Properties from the Workflow Event Sink context menu.
5. Click the Identity tab and select This User.
6. Add the user, and enter the required password. Sometimes you must shut down and restart the application for the changes to take place.

Creating the Exchange Folder for the Project

You need to create a new Exchange public folder before you can create a workflow project. For example, you could add a folder called Vacation Schedules to Public Folders in which you plan to build a form approval workflow application. To add a public folder using Outlook, perform the following:

1. Launch Outlook and select View|Folder List.
2. Select New Folder from Public Folders under the Public Folders node.
3. Enter a name for the new folder.
4. Navigate to the folder by selecting the folder you just created on the Public Folders node.

Adding a Public Folder Using IE

If it's not convenient to set up Outlook to create folders, you can also use OWA by using IE to navigate to the Exchange Server. Best practices also recommend creating a Network Place for the folder or at least for the **http://MyServer/Public location**. Double-click the My Network Places icon on the Windows 2000 desktop, double-click the Add Network Place icon, and follow the wizard.

1. In IE, type **http://*Servername*/Public** in the Address bar to display OWA. Public folders are displayed in the Folder List on the left.
2. Right-click the Public Folders node, and select New Folder. Ownership of the newly created folder is automatically assigned to the currently logged on user. Any subfolders created under an existing folder are assigned to both the logged in user and the owner of the parent folder as having owner permissions on the subfolder.

Creating the Project and Workflow Process

Creating a new workflow project adds a new solution to the folder. Workflow Designer for Exchange 2000 automatically generates a new empty workflow process, containing only starting and ending shapes. Each solution can contain multiple projects of various types, including one or more workflow projects for Exchange 2000 or SQL Server and Dashboard projects. Each Exchange Workflow Project is based on a single public folder, and might contain one or more workflow processes. Figure 17.10 shows the General tab for a process called **OrderFlow** in a public folder called Tester.

The solution file (*.sln) is stored by default. Adding a workflow to a folder requires owner permissions on the folder and membership in the Can Author Workflow role on the Exchange Server or SharePoint Portal Server on which the folder is located. Although each workflow project can contain multiple workflow processes, an Exchange folder location can contain only one Exchange Workflow Project. The following steps are performed to create that workflow project.

1. Select Start|Programs|Microsoft Development Environment In Microsoft Office XP Developer.
2. Select File|New|Project.
3. Select Office Developer Projects from the New Project dialog box.

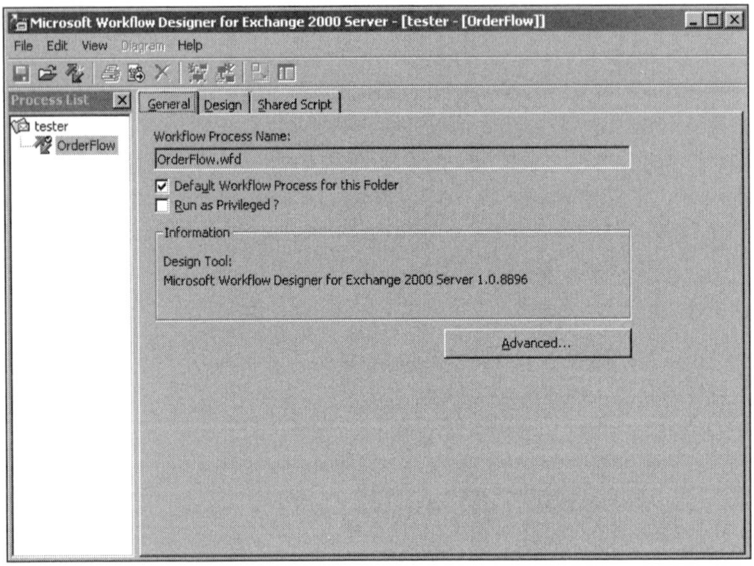

Figure 17.10 The General tab of a workflow process in WDE 2000.

4. Select the Exchange Workflow Project icon from the three project icons displayed in Templates; namely, Exchange Workflow, SQL Workflow, and Dashboard project.
5. Enter a name and a folder location for the new project in the form of a URL—such as **http://firsterver/public/myfolder**—in the New Project dialog box. The folder location defaults to the last folder opened. You cannot browse to a HTTP location unless you have created a network place.
6. Click OK to confirm your entries.
7. An empty workflow process is created, and the workflow diagram is displayed on the design surface.

Designing a Workflow Process Using WDE 2000

To design a workflow process using WDE 2000, perform the following:

1. Click and drag the State shape located in the Workflow toolbox to the design surface. You can change the caption on the state using the property sheet for the object.
2. Click the Transition shape in the Workflow toolbox, and then drag from the Item Created shape to the state you added. As you drag the cursor along

the design surface, a transition arrow appears that points from the first object to the second.

3. Add the remaining states and transitions to complete your workflow diagram. If you want to make it possible for a record to be edited without changing states, use the Transition Within shape in the Workflow toolbox, and then click the appropriate state.
4. From the code page, you can add scripts to the workflow process. WDE 2000 creates three script blocks called when an item moves from one state to the next: **previousstate_OnExit**, **OnChange**, and **nextstate_OnEnter**. For example, you might want to trigger the sending of email to the person who opened an issue when the **ResolvedState_OnEnter** script block is called.
5. Test your workflow.

Adding a Workflow State

To add one shape in the diagram window multiple times, press and hold Ctrl as you choose the shape in the toolbox. Click in the diagram to place the shape, enter a name if desired, and then click again to add another shape. Choose the Pointer in the toolbox to stop adding shapes on the design surface. Perform the following steps to add a state to your workflow application.

1. Select Start|Programs|Microsoft Development Environment In Microsoft Office XP Developer.
2. Open an existing solution, or use File|New to create a workflow project. Notice that solutions, along with any projects and existing workflow processes, are displayed in the Solution Explorer.
3. Select the appropriate workflow process from the Solution Explorer.
4. Select Open, or double-click the workflow process from the View menu. View the toolbox by selecting View|Toolbox.
5. Select the State tool, and click the design surface to create the object at the cursor location on the surface. Properties—including name and caption—can be configured for any state shape through entries in the corresponding Property Page or Properties Grid.
6. Create a new workflow transition to connect a new state with existing states.

Renaming or Labeling a State or Event

State names are comprised of letters, numbers, and underscores and must be unique. Neither spaces nor extended characters are supported. State or transition names identify a state or transition, and do not ever have to be shown or understood by the user. It is only important that the workflow author/administrator understand the meanings of the names. The names create associated event procedures, such as **State1_OnEnter**. During development, you can change the names without repercussions. When a workflow process is in production, however, changing a name can potentially change the workflow logic. Best practices recommend that if a name change is necessary on a production platform, you do not rename states without changing items to a state value represented on the diagram. To rename a state, perform the following:

1. Select the state on the Workflow Design Surface.
2. Enter a new name for the state or transition in the Properties grid. Names must consist of letters, numbers, and underscores and cannot include spaces or characters in the extended character set.

Setting a State or Transition Caption

State or transition captions also must be unique. However, both captions support extended characters, such as spaces and non-English characters. To add or modify a caption associated with some state or other object:

1. Select the state on the Workflow Design Surface.
2. Enter a new caption value directly in the state itself or in the Caption Property in the Properties grid.

Deleting a State

Remove a state in the process when you no longer need it. When you delete the state, all associated transitions, actions, and script are removed from the design surface and deleted from the workflow. Any transitions entering or leaving the state will also be deleted. To delete a state, follow these steps:

1. Make sure none of the existing items in the folder are in the state you want to delete. You must move existing items that use the state to another state. If you delete without changing existing rows to a different state, those items cannot be modified.

2. Make sure the state following the one you want to delete has another event entering it. If it doesn't, add another state or event to connect that state to the diagram.
3. Right-click the state and select Delete on the Workflow Design Surface.

Adding and Modifying Transitions in Workflow

Add transitions—such as **Change**, **Receive**, or **Expiry**—to connect one state to another state in your diagram. Workflow events can be used to trigger scripts that automate processes in your workflow applications. The Workflow Design Surface and toolbox are used to add and change transitions, rename events, and set transition captions. To add a transition:

1. Select Start|Programs|Microsoft Development Environment In Microsoft Office XP Developer.
2. Open an existing solution or use File|New to create a workflow project. The solution and any projects and existing workflow processes are displayed in the Solution Explorer.
3. Select the workflow process from the Solution Explorer.
4. Select Open from the View menu or double-click the workflow process icon within the expanded selection area.
5. Select the Transition tool and click the State shape at the start of the transition. Then, drag your cursor to the State shape at the end of the transition. The transition is created between the two State shapes. Properties—such as name, caption, and type of transition event—can be set in the Property page or Properties grid. By default, the transition is a **Change** transition type. This means a change to an item will cause the transition.
6. If you have multiple states to connect, you can turn on Sticky mode by pressing Ctrl, and then clicking the transition shape. Drag to create transitions between the states. To turn off Sticky mode, press Esc.

Adding Objects Multiple Times in Sticky Mode

To add one transition into the diagram window multiple times:

1. Press and hold the Ctrl as you select objects from the Toolbar palette.
2. Click an object in the design surface area to place the shape and enter a name if desired.

3. Click on the design surface to add as many additional shapes as needed.
4. Either choose the Pointer in the toolbox to stop adding shapes on the design surface or press the Esc key. If you drag one transition directly over another transition, it might appear that they have merged into one transition; however, both transitions still exist.

Changing the Transition Type

Transitions are created with a transition type of **Change** by default. You can modify the transition type in the Properties grid on the Property page of a selected transition. Each transition has an associated icon that visually cues to the programmed transition type. To change a transition type, perform the following:

1. Select a transition on the Workflow Design Surface.
2. Right-click the icon to display the Property page.
3. Select **Change**, **Expiry**, or **Receive** from the Type drop-down box. You also can change the type using the **Type** property in the Properties grid.

Deleting a Workflow Process for Exchange 2000

You can remove a workflow process only if you are the folder owner or have delete permissions on the folder. After you have deleted the process, you cannot undo the delete to recover it. Before deleting a workflow-enabled folder, you must deactivate workflow for the folder. The following steps will delete a workflow process.

1. Choose Start|Programs|Microsoft Development Environment In Microsoft Office XP Developer.
2. Select a folder. The folder you select is displayed with any existing workflow processes.
3. Select the workflow process in the Solution Explorer.
4. Select Edit|Delete. A dialog box displays a message confirming that you want to permanently delete the workflow. Click Yes to confirm your actions.

Enabling Script Debugging and Success Entries

To enable script debugging and success entries, perform the following:

1. Double-click a specific folder in the Workflow Designer for Exchange.
2. Select Enable Script Debugging For This Folder and Enable Success Entries For This Folder on the General tab.
3. Select File|Save All Changes.

Creating the Shared Script Procedures

You can view a common library of script routines on the Shared Script tab in WDE 2000. These scripts are triggered based on the Condition Expression value, and from the Action Script Procedure text box in the lower-right corner of the interface. The condition expression is the first script evaluated by the workflow engine in response to some triggered action, and defaults to True. You can change the Condition Expression scripting box to False, create an expression, or call a function from the Shared Script tab to perform a more complex evaluation. Action script procedures automate your workflow process.

When using a workflow script, test for both syntactical and logical errors. Confirm that all parameters and dependent functions exist in the workflow script in which they are called. If you want to send email, post a message, delete items, or add an audit entry, for example, all these activities are accomplished using action script procedures. Action script procedures are executed only when the associated condition expression returns true. User-defined fields in the Outlook Form are case sensitive. Be sure to reference them appropriately in your script. The WDE interface consists of separate panes; on the left side, you will find a tree view delineating a list of processes called the Process List. This pane is also the first set of features you see when you launch WDE 2000 as shown in Figure 17.11. Upon selecting a specific workflow, a Workflow Process pane appears with three tabs: General, Design, and Shared Script options. You can access a design surface directly or call an Action Script Procedures from a library of Shared Scripts. You insert items onto the design surface from the Edit menu.

After completing and testing the workflow design, you need to deploy the process just as you would distribute a finished application or component to other computers. You can distribute the application by copying it to other folders or servers using the Copy To menu item. These features are available from the context menu that appears when you right-click the workflow object you want to copy. To save a workflow process, it must be opened on the design surface.

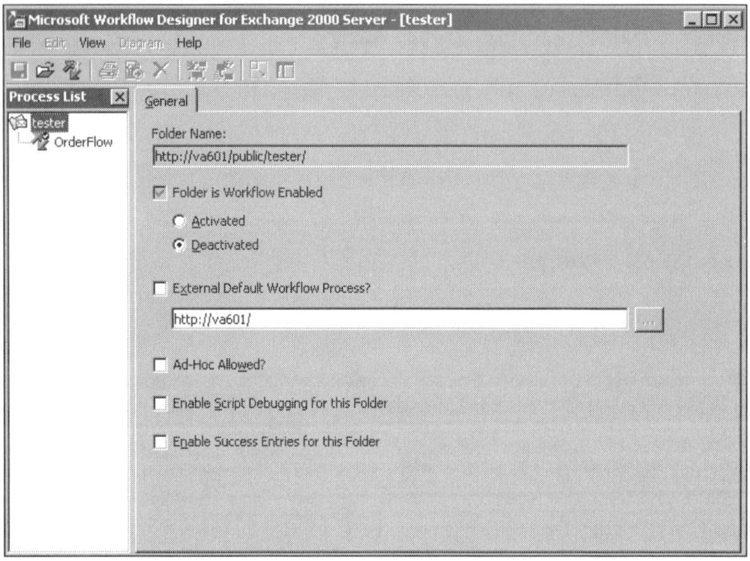

Figure 17.11 Opening selections in WDE 2000.

Copying a Workflow Process for Exchange 2000

You can copy the current folder and workflow process or modify it and copy it to another folder. Your workflow processes are saved as a Workflow Process Definition (*.wfd), or as File System Format (*.wef) file type. The Workflow Process Definition file type is the default, native format saved to the Exchange 2000 folder or SharePoint Portal Server folder. The File System Format saves the workflow process, properties, and common script out in File System (or binary) Format. This latter file type allows copies of the workflow process to be distributed more easily to those who do not have access to the same Exchange Server. To copy a workflow process, perform the following:

1. Choose Start|Programs|Microsoft Development Environment In Microsoft Office XP Developer.
2. Open an existing solution, or use File|New to create a workflow project. The solution, along with any of its projects and existing workflow processes, is displayed in the Solution Explorer.
3. Double-click a workflow process in the Solution Explorer to display the workflow design on the design surface.

4. Select File|Save Copy of <*name*>.wfd As. A dialog box displaying the current Exchange folder is shown.
5. Select a destination folder for the copy, enter a name for the copy, and then click OK to confirm your choices. You must have owner permissions and be a member of the Can Register Workflow role to save the copy to the Exchange folder.

Activating the Workflow Process

You implement completed workflows within a specific folder by activating the workflow after completing the appropriate forms. To activate the workflow on the folder, perform the following:

1. Select Default Workflow Process For This Folder and Run As Privileged on the General tab of a workflow process.
2. Select the folder you want to activate.
3. Select Advanced on the General tab.
4. Select File|Save All Changes. You must enable the success entries to use the audit trail to write entries to the Event Viewer for debugging.

Changing the Display and Printing the Workflow

Use the design surface of WDE 2000 to change how the diagram is displayed, to zoom or crop the diagram, and to print the workflow diagram. To change the diagram display or make captions easier to read, rearrange the position and orientation of the state shapes and transition lines. To rearrange states, drag each state to the desired location in the diagram. After rearranging the states, the diagram might become cluttered with overlapping lines or irregular spacing. To arrange the diagram in MOD, choose Format|Arrange Diagram, and then select Horizontal or Vertical. In both you can right-click the design surface and choose Arrange Diagram and choose either Horizontal or Vertical in the context menu. Vertical arranges the diagram from top to bottom, according to the algorithm.

Viewing or Printing a Workflow

You can view or print a workflow after you have created it on the design surface. Best practices recommend saving the application prior to printing:

1. Arrange the windowpanes to maximize the design-viewing surface. You also can alter how the diagrammed workflow is displayed by right-clicking the design surface and either changing the magnification with the zoom control, or changing the orientation by selecting either a horizontal or a vertical orientation in the Arrange Diagram cascading menu.
2. Right-click the design surface and select various features from the context menu.
3. In the Zoom dialog box, select the zoom size between 10% and 200%.
4. In the Arrange Diagram, select Horizontal or Vertical.
5. Select File|Print in the Main menubar in either WDE 2000 or MOD.

Printing the Workflow Diagram

If you want to keep a hard copy of your workflow diagram for reference, you can print it. The printer prints the entire diagram, even if you have zoomed in or cropped your view by resizing the diagram pane. Printing the workflow diagram as outlined here does not print the script.

1. Choose Start|Programs|Microsoft Development Environment In Microsoft Office XP Developer.
2. Open the workflow and select the workflow process from the Solution Explorer.
3. Choose File|Print.
4. Click Print in the Print dialog box.

Testing Your Workflow for Exchange 2000

Always test your workflow process after modifying the workflow, a script, or a user interface. Use some form of version control when you save your work prior to testing. Even without any script, the workflow states you design, along with permissible transitions and events, are enforced when you enter data into your user interface. Before you can test your workflow, you must have it enabled in the folder. The following steps begin your troubleshooting phase in the design lifecycle. Make certain you have made copies of all your work prior to testing an application, so that if you have to force a system reboot, you have backup copies of your current work. To test your workflow process, perform the following steps:

1. Use either an Outlook Form or a Web Form as a user interface to post the form to the workflow-enabled Exchange folder.
2. An email message is sent to you if you designed a workflow process to send notification mail on the **OnCreate** or **OnChange** event.
3. If workflow fails to perform as expected, return to your workflow diagram and make certain you have saved the changes to your workflow. Make certain you have created the necessary transitions and added appropriate events for your states.

Chapter 18

Collaboration Data Objects (CDOs) and Process

If you need an immediate solution to:	*See page:*
Changing the Exchange Installable File System to Another Drive Letter	767
Viewing a Raw Exchange 2000 Directory	768
Installing the New MSXML Parser	769
Changing OWA Passwords Through IIS	770
Registering an Event Sink	771
Isolating a Process Application	771
Creating a Global.asa File	772
Connecting to Data Stores	773
Using Include Files to Create Connection Strings	774
Using the **Open** Method	775
Prompting for ODBC Connect String Arguments	775
Establishing an ADO Connection	776
Creating a Connection without a Data Source Name	776
Determining Content Type	777
Manipulating **Record** Objects	777
Adding Contact Information into Messages Using **CDOEX**	777
Using SMTP to Send Email	778
Enabling MAPI Clients Computers Through a Firewall	778
Creating an Entrance/Exit Console Script	780

In Depth

Windows 2000 has introduced changes in philosophy, design, and technology. Exchange 2000 Server reflects those changes. Your role as administrator needs to reflect those changes as well. Two themes are significant. The first theme is that Exchange 2000 is designed to support standard programming interfaces—such as ADO (ActiveX Data Objects) and OLE DB (Object Linking and Embedding for Databases)—and languages—such as XML (Extensible Markup Language) and ASP (Active Server Pages)—according to Microsoft's Universal Data Access initiative. The second theme is that Exchange 2000 exposes the heretofore unstructured, yet mission-critical, information we use in our daily affairs as Web-accessible knowledge resources in a way that is universally accessible, scalable, and totally extensible. Your challenge is to use these knowledge resources like any other corporate asset to the benefit of your user population as well and in a way that contributes some competitive advantage to your organization. Engineering your internal messaging and collaborative processes implements one of the basic tenets of this book. As part of the design process, you as an administrator shape the fundamental processes that you and your team will be required to support on a daily basis.

The Web Store (or Web Storage System)

The *Web Storage System* (*WSS*) provides the environment for the storage and retrieval of knowledge resources. A schema defines these accessible resources, which include collaborative objects, files, folders, and Web sites, as a collection of properties. The schema structure—unlike the structures in relational database management systems such as SQL (Structured Query Language) Server—is managed in a more flexible way with schema-aware applications that can manipulate the resources in the various areas of the WSS.

The WSS is composed of separate schema namespaces within which objects share common properties. Though many of these messaging and collaborative objects—such as messages, contacts, appointments, documents, and folders—are prebuilt, new objects and properties can be added to the namespace at any time through the extension of the schema. Namespaces uniquely identify groups of objects with their specific properties. In fact, the concept of namespace extends beyond data objects to the system services level as well. Exchange 2000 has provided a programmatic way to even manage recipients and the servers on which messaging services are hosted. Collaborative Data Objects in Exchange 2000 have been extended over legacy CDO schemas with a specialized set of Exchange Management Objects (EMO). Thus, with CDO for EMO, an administrator can manage the structure of the information stored within the data stores.

Outlook Web Access (OWA) Rebuilt

Paralleling changes in the scalability and extensibility of access to data stores, Exchange 2000 supports a new version of Outlook Web Access. Unlike legacy versions of this service based on ASP, OWA code, paralleling the assimilation of Internet Information Server (IIS) services, is now compiled within Exchange 2000. Supporting older versions of software, HTML rendering, and data binding in many instances, are now server-side tasks. HTML documents are generated by the server, rather than as parsed scripts interpreted by the legacy IIS 4 engine. Further refinements include differently rendered versions of OWA for Internet Explorer 5 (IE5) browsers and other clients, such as legacy browsers supporting HTML 3.2 and non-Internet clients.

The distinction between IE 5 and legacy browser software is significant. When the server recognizes an IE 5 client, OWA leverages client-side XML and WebDAV (Web Distributed Authoring and Versioning) support by offloading processing overhead and pushing down XML data to the client. Using XSL (Extensible Stylesheet Language), the server delegates the responsibility for rendering the information to the client. Data management has also been refined in terms of refreshing changed data rather than entire pages. These significant improvements work transparently alongside Exchange 5.5 applications as well. Not only does Outlook 2000 still use MAPI (Messaging Application Programming Interface), but legacy versions of CDO and the Event Scripting Agent are all supported by Exchange 2000.

Exchange Data Access

Schema-aware applications are identified by their capability to use the multiple APIs, through which messaging and collaborative resources, their properties, and the namespaces in which they are stored are accessed. Outlook 2000 uses the proprietary MAPI, whereas browsers and other applications use HTTP, OLE DB, ADO. and OLE DB is a standardized API used to manipulate both structured and semi-structured data from database applications such as SQL Server and Access. ADO is an interface that simplifies the OLE DB API. Exchange 2000 supports both OLE DB 2.5 and ADO. Because of the nature of the unstructured objects with which Exchange 2000 is associated, it also provides a specialized interface for its CDOs as well. In general, although OLE DB and ADO are used to find resources within the WSS, CDO simplifies the management of the methods and properties each object possesses. Thus, best practices recommend using ADO to locate an Inbox, but CDO to read the list of recipients.

With Exchange 2000 already in the corporate network topology to manage messaging, accessing the WSS to manipulate contacts or appointments or publish them to a Web page now becomes a relatively trivial matter. In comparison, Exchange 5.5 was a standalone application that was not truly dependent on its operating system (OS) or working environment other than in terms of network connectivity. The design flexibility Exchange 2000 brings to dynamic processes automating workflows truly leverages the usefulness of the WSS as a repository for documents. Although similar in design, SharePoint Portal Server working without Active Directory (AD) at the department level, much like legacy Exchange Servers is also limited. Exchange 2000, providing enterprise-wide access to both extensible collaborative services, places administrators in a position to exercise greater control over both the usability of a corporation's data and the breadth of their own career goals.

Data Source Providers

Microsoft has proposed a programming initiative called *Universal Data Access* that consists of a collection of system-level interfaces defined by OLE DB. The stated Universal Data Access goal is to allow any software application to efficiently access and transform data across all data sources. These Universal Data Access components consist of data providers, data consumers, and service components that extend native OS functionality. Exchange 2000 was designed based on this initiative and thus offers a broad range of database features that leverage OLE DB and the application-level data access object model of ADO 2.5 (see Figures 18.1 and 18.2).

As an OLE DB provider, Exchange 2000 can offer WSS data through the API much like other data providers, such as SQL Server, Oracle, or Access. OLE DB supports navigation through WSS folder hierarchies to locate collaborative data and documents much like a database management system. Unlike those database providers, however, the contents of any one WSS folder include a wide range of CDOs. As an OLE DB provider, Exchange can accommodate the different properties assigned to each data type. Another OLE DB provider that works in association with Exchange is the Active Directory Services Interface (ADSI) that also supports AD and Internet Publishing services. Exchange as an OLE provider supports the binding of an object—such as a message, document, or folder—directly to a URL. Figure 18.3 shows the three access routes; namely, through the data access layer (CDO/ADO), WebDAV/HTTP, or the file system depicted as logical drive M:, through which you can access the WSS depicted here as Data Storage.

In fact, the interface offers several object libraries, including direct access to file system objects (FSOs), as well as databases (ADO). FSOs expose files, directories, and storage drives to programmatic manipulation. You can read and

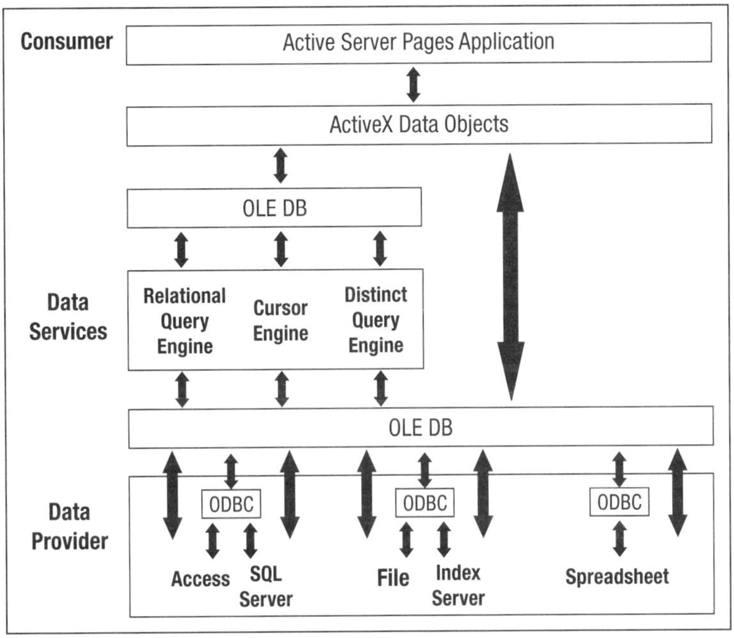

Figure 18.1 A schematic of the Universal Data Access model.

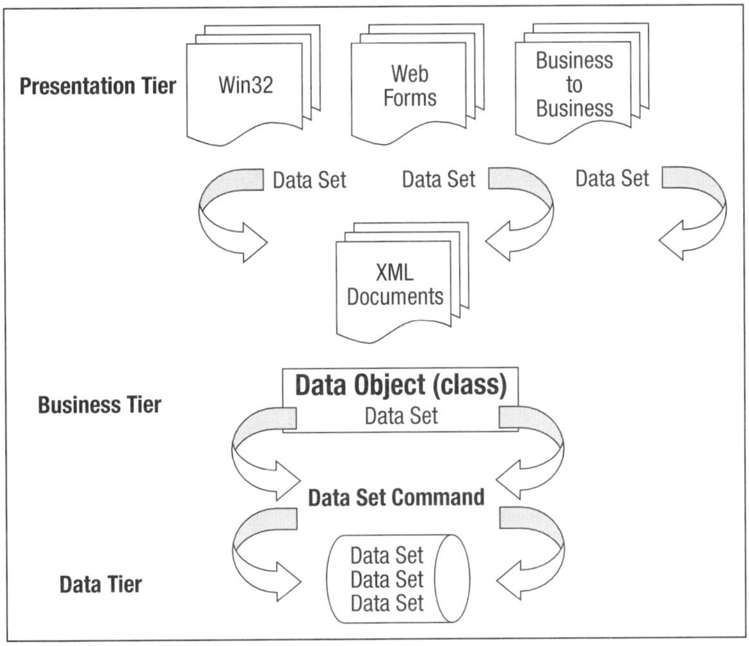

Figure 18.2 Accessing a database object using ActiveX Data Objects.

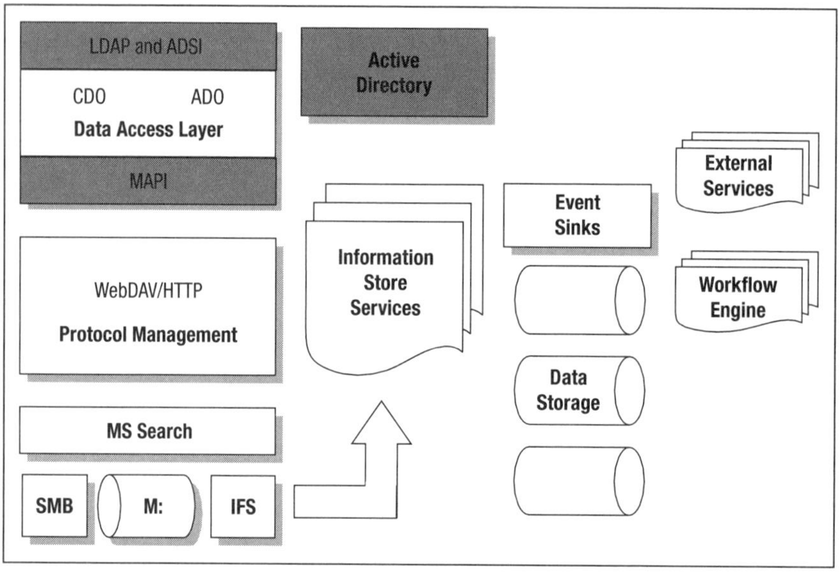

Figure 18.3 Exchange 2000 accessing WSS.

write text through the Microsoft Scripting Runtime Library using FSOs such as **FileSystemObject**, **File**, **Folder**, **Drive**, and **TextStream**. For example, the **FileSystemObject** can create directories, move files, determine whether resources exist, and so on. The ADOs provide the data access feature set. The OLE DB provider for Internet Publishing opens documents as an ADO recordset.

An ADO record object can represent a row in one of these **Recordset** objects, a single document or instance, or the folder container. Exchange 2000 can deliver the body of a MAPI message or MIME (Multipurpose Internet Mail Extensions) data from its Internet counterpart as an ADO stream object located in memory. ADO is often substituted for OLE DB because it is a simpler, high-level interface to the OLE DB data sources. It is especially popular when used in conjunction with scripting languages. ADO simplifies the number of objects and function calls necessary to access any kind of data. Exchange 2000 supports ADO 2.5 and through it can simplify the coding for URL binding, heterogeneous schemas, and hierarchical navigation necessary when accessing knowledge resources found in the WSS.

The ADO model, shown previously in Figure 18.2, has distinct components, including top-level **Connection**, **Command**, and **Recordset** objects. Similarly, a **Parameter** object is associated with **Command**; **Error** with **Connection**; and **Field** with **Recordset**. The **Property** object is associated with the three top-level components. Some of these component objects also have a dynamic character in that they consist of zero or more elements. These dynamic groups are called component collections and affect **Fields**, **Properties**, **Parameters**, and **Errors**.

- ***Connection*** *object*—This object enables you to form a logical connection with a database. You specify various criteria, including the database name, physical and logical locations, and security credentials such as username and password.
- ***Command*** *object*—This object is designed to manage or control a data source. It supports the creation and execution of commands that affect **Recordsets,** such as bulk execution operations, retrieval, and modification of data source structure.
- ***Parameter*** *object*—This dynamic object is used exclusively by the **Command** object and most frequently contains predefined statements—called stored procedures—in the SQL database. It uses the **Parameters** collection.
- ***Recordset*** *object*—You create a connection to retrieve data. The data is typically defined in records. Exchange views the collaborative items within a specific folder as a **Recordset**. This object is the collection of data as a group of records. A record object is a single instance in a **Recordset**. Data sources support different delivery mechanisms of these **Recordsets**. A *cursor*, another term for a **Recordset**, can be a static snapshot of data, or a more dynamic link directly back to the datasource. Similarly, you can manage data transition states by applying optimistic and pessimistic locking mechanisms.
- ***Field*** *object*—This dynamic object corresponds to the listing of properties associated with columns in a SQL data table. These listings are stored in the **Fields** collection.
- ***Property*** *object*—This dynamic object fills the **Properties** collection with default values from the specific data provider so that ADO can work with a variety of data stores.
- ***Error*** *object*—This dynamic object stores lists of the last ADO or OLE DB provider errors generated in response to commands. It can only be accessed from the **Connection** object.

Object models are typically hierarchical, where higher-level objects contain the lower-level objects. This relationship is significant because you typically cannot access an object at the lower level before accessing an immediate upper level. For example, you must execute the following sequence:

1. Create a **Session** object through some connection to a data provider.
2. Retrieve a **Recordset** or, for example, an **Inbox Folder** object from the **Application** object with which you have established a session.
3. Retrieve items from a collection object—such as the **Messages Collection** object—from the **Inbox Folder** object.
4. Perform some action on the item—such as a **Message** object—from the **Messages Collection** object.

Even with all these hierarchical steps, which are repeated in almost every application paradigm involving file system or data object access, there is not a large amount of overhead. The data object libraries execute these steps rapidly. In fact, many development environments—such as Front Page and Visual InterDev (VID)—automatically script either paradigm without much user intervention. Primary objects used for accessing the email system through CDO include the following:

- **Session**
- **Folder**
- **Messages Collection**
- **Message**

ADO is data-provider neutral. It accesses information in the file namespace of the WSS through a combination of URLs and a file-naming standard. Exchange uses /mbx/ as the virtual root used to access the mailbox store, whereas /public/is used to access public folders. The file name alias for the WSS—that is, *backofficestorage*—is used as follows to access the inbox for **gregb** at **www.coriolis.tch**:

```
file://./backofficestorage/www.coriolis.tch/mbx/gregb/inbox/item.txt
```

You will use this protocol and path again when accessing the WSS through the OLE DB provider (see Tables 18.1 through 18.3).

Table 18.1 Prominent namespaces used to access data programmatically.

Tag	Description
DAV	Properties specific to WebDAV and storage functions, such as **href** (a URL), **getcontentlength** (item size), and **childcount** (items in folder or collection).
urn:schemas:mailheader	These properties deal with the RFC-822 mail header, such as From:, To:, Subject:, and Date:.
urn:schemas:httpmail	Same as previous, but converted to Unicode.
http://schemas.Microsoft/exchange	Specific properties unique to Exchange Server.
urn:/schemas-microsoft-com:office:office	Specific properties unique to Office documents, including those from Word, Excel, and other software products.

Table 18.2 Item naming conventions.

Subject	Item Name
singleMessage	message.eml
single message	single%20message.eml
Single Message.doc	Single%20Message.doc

Table 18.3 URLs for common folders.

Type	URL
Inbox	**http://servername/exchange/username/inbox**
Outbox	**http://servername/exchange/username/outbox**
Calendar	**http://servername/exchange/username/calendar**
Contacts	**http://servername/exchange/username/contacts**
Deleted items	**http://servername/exchange/username/deleted%20items**
Sent items	**http://servername/exchange/username/sent%20items**

ActiveX Server Components

ASP is a collection of several tecnologies, shown in Figure 18.4, that consists of prebuilt software components, programmable interfaces, and text files containing both HTML and scripting languages, that is typically VBScript by default. Although HTML-based, these text files use a different extension: .asp. An ISAPI (Internet Server API) component exists that specifically processes these text files on the host Web server. The server parses the script, executes any instructions, and returns HTML script back to the client. Thus, any browser client can render the HTML results independent of its object model or version. An example of ASP code includes special delimiters—namely **<%** and **%>**—within which are placed instructions executed by the server. These tags and their instructions are replaced by the hyptertext markup script, some server-side stored variable, the value of some calculated expression, or constant when returned to the client. ASP can be placed anywhere in the HTML code. Thus, **<%=Now()%>** is ASP code that can be placed anywhere in the body of a HTML document; it will return the current time and date. The equal sign in the delimited expression is an abbreviation for

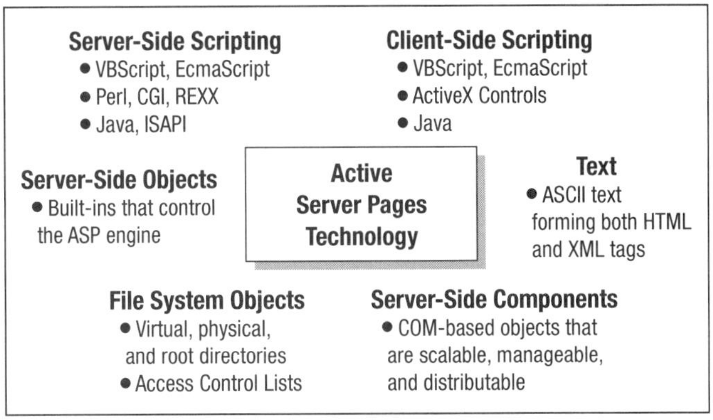

Figure 18.4 The family of ActiveX technologies.

the **write** method of the **Response** object. Five ASP objects perform assorted actions (called methods) and have various properties: **Application**, **Session**, **Server**, **Request**, and **Response**.

Global.asa

The *Global.asa file* is an optional file that provides procedure or subroutine calls to both the **Session** and **Application** objects. The **Application** object is a logical namespace within which **Session** objects exist for the time it takes them to request and receive some service from a host. An end user launches a client, which attempts to create a session within the namespace of a specific application on a server. The **Session** object provides some measure of continuity for the end user requesting services within the stateless world of HTTP. The **Application** object can store global data that can be shared by all end users accessing the **Application** services. A **Session** object holds the variable data that specifically relates to the end user who initiated a session. For example, while the **Application** object performs some specific service, the **Session** object handles specific end-user issues such as using a particular codepage, sessionID, and so on. A unique session identifier distinguishes that particular end user's session from another. Another object represents the server and provides utility methods and properties specifically dealing with the hosting system and hardware interface on which both **Application** and **Session** are run.

Within a session, an end user uses both **Request** and **Response** objects. The **Request** object allows access to provider information; the **Response** object is responsible for content returned to the client (also known as the consumer of the services).

ASP.NET

Microsoft Active Server Pages.NET (previously called ASP+) is a complete reconstruction of ASP, and is part of the .NET framework (see the schematic in Figure 18.5). It runs transparently alongside legacy ASP and on the newly released IIS5 platform, although its file extension—.aspx—clearly differentiates it from the older ASP scripting. ASP+ can access compiled code such as C++, Visual Basic, and the new C#. It's no longer necessary to register a DLL (Dynamic Link Library) with the hosting server. The .NET initiative (previously codenamed Next Generation Windows Services, or NGWS) with its base object classes and common language runtime (CLR) simplifies scripting administration, at the expense of single-version security, and stores all system configuration, syntactical structure, and definitions of concepts in XML files for greater portability. ASP.NET provides other features—such as caching and maintaining session states across servers—that promote greater performance and stability in a distributed services environment. ASP.NET is discussed further when the .NET Framework is explained.

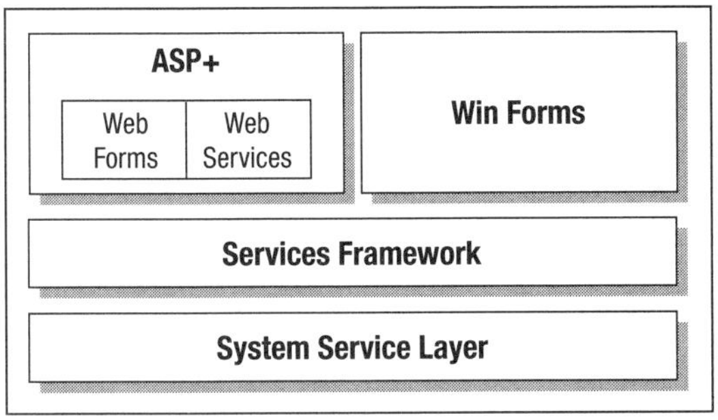

Figure 18.5 ASP.NET and the .NET Framework.

CDOs

CDOs provide a simpler and more direct way to manipulate the special objects associated with messaging and collaborative services than ADO. Previous versions of this object library relied on MAPI to access data. The collaborative data objects associated with Exchange 2000 are based alternatively on Internet-defined standards and have adopted the Universal Data Access initiative in leveraging well-known APIs such as OLE DB and ADO. OLE DB is the most complex of interfaces within the Universal Data Access framework. ADO provides a more abstracted, hence higher-level, interface than OLE DB, and thus is particularly suited for ActiveX clients such as the ActiveX Scripting Engine and ASP. Thus, programmers need to understand and manipulate ADO to access both structured and unstructured data. Collaborative Data Objects is a simpler programming interface for the manipulation of data within common Outlook objects such as messages, calendar items, and contact records. Using an API that is designed to work with these specialized data variables further simplifies the development process as it relates to messaging and collaborative workflows. Variant data types allow you to represent predefined sets of data in formats that are independent of any particular program language. Some COM (Component Object Model) objects determine their category of data from the first field they are exposed to. Similarly, a CDO library of rendering objects provides support for the presentation of data. The three current versions of CDO are as follows:

- *CDO 1.2.1*—This library of collaborative client-side objects is based on MAPI and supported by Outlook 2000.
- *CDONTS (CDOSYS.DLL, CDO 2)*—These server-side objects are included with Windows 2000 and provide support for basic SMTP (Simple Mail Transfer Protocol)-, NNTP (Network News Transfer Protocol)-, and MIME-encoded messages.
- *CDO for Exchange 2000 (CDOEX.DLL, CDO3.0)*—This server-side version is installed with the Exchange Server software and extends CDONTS. The

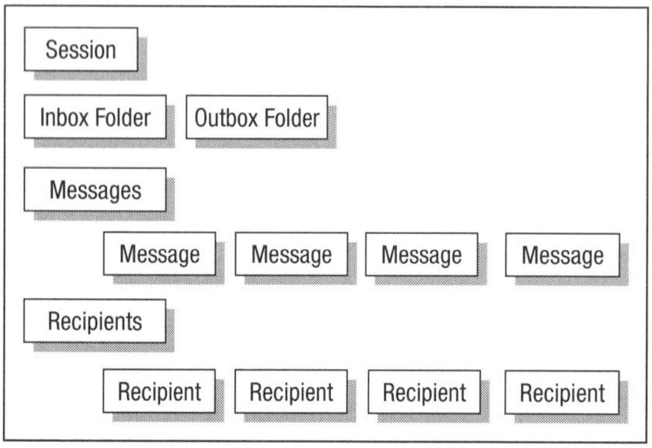

Figure 18.6 CDO Object Model.

CDOEX library is composed of subsystems that support specific collaborative objects such as messages, date and scheduling objects, contacts, and tasks as shown in Figure 18.6.

CDO for Windows 2000

CDO for Windows 2000 (CDOSYS.DLL) is sometimes referred to as CDO 2.0, and provides the object model for messaging on the Windows 2000 platform. *CDOSYS* is part of the installation that delivers the native support of both SMTP and NNTP, and the API on which Windows 2000 runs its Web-based mail applications. CDOSYS provides a new architecture over legacy versions of CDO 1.2.1, which is referred to as CDO for Windows NT Server (CDONTS) and is included in the Windows NT 4 Option Pack. Because CDOSYS isn't code-compatible with any legacy CDO libraries and MAPI, it can work alongside legacy object libraries. This transparency allows legacy Exchange 5.5 and Exchange 2000 to coexist in the same organization without translating or porting messaging applications to the more current object library. CDOSYS features include greater control over process events, which extends to workflow applications and MIME message object types.

CDOSYS differs from legacy CDO in its control over protocol events in the process flow. This control is the basis for event sinks, which are scripts or automated procedures that are triggered by changes or transitions in some state of an object. Transitional events are the foundation on which the developer can manage logical or workflow processes. CDOSYS is one distinguishing factor in moving the OS from a collection of monolithic legacy application servers to a distributed-services environment. CDOSYS, although part of Windows 2000, requires a local or remote SMTP Server for submitting messages. Like an Exchange SMTP Connector, CDOSYS is configured to direct messages to at least one other SMTP server programmatically. CDOSYS also supports the processing of incoming and outgoing mail through protocol events and their event sinks. A protocol event defined by the arrival of an inbound or departure of an outbound mail item can trigger some new, complementary process. CDOSYS, based on Internet standards, is a feature-rich API specifically created for an Internet environment and MIME/MHTML data. It integrates OLE DB/ADO features into its architecture and thus enables standardized data access. All applications built using CDOSYS are fully supported when Exchange 2000 is installed.

NOTE: *HTML (RFC 1866) uses text to mark up an ASCII script describing the layout of some browser-rendered document with referenced links to mulitmedia objects. The component objects are retrieved by the Web server and rendered by the browser software in realtime from the locations indicated by these uniform resource identifiers (URIs). When HTML is used in email, it is necessary to transfer the entire multimedia document as one message. The MIME encapsulation of this aggregate document is referred to as MIME HTML or MHTML (RFC 2557).*

CDO for Exchange 2000

CDO for Exchange 2000 (CDOEX.DLL) API is installed with Exchange 2000 on top of CDOSYS. It does not use MAPI. This object library upgrades and extends the CDO feature set found in the Windows 2000 platform; it does not replace it. CDOEX also provides critical support for the WSS, which is also part of the Exchange 2000 installation. Because CDOEX is an extension of CDOSYS, it also preserves application compatibility among Windows 2000–based scripts, Exchange 2000–based scripts, and legacy Exchange scripting.

The API library enhances both calendar and contact management, which have been major product features in Outlook and Exchange since their original release. CDOEX supports the development of Web-based applications that can manipulate collaborative objects and data in the WSS. Transport and WSS event sinks similarly provide programmatic control over the greater data access and retrieval functionality that Exchange 2000 provides.

The CDO Subsystems

CDO specifically focuses on collaborative objects working with the messaging and collaborative platform Exchange 2000 provides. It can be divided into subsystems supporting messaging, calendaring, and contacts. It also includes a set of CDOs for manipulating the built-in Exchange workflow engine (CDOWF), and a special CDOEXM specifically directed at management systems and objects. CDOs are a high-level set of COM objects that allow you to easily access the email system embedded in the Microsoft Windows product line. CDOs are generally used by client applications. For the most part, CDOs are used by clients wanting to access the email system. Service providers must be implemented using the native MAPI library. The best mechanism for introducing you to CDOs is to correlate these objects to specific elements of the Outlook client user interface. Fundamental CDOs you use in your client application include the actual session, the folder container, and the messaging objects with their recipients and other associated information. These objects exist within a structure that you access within your client program. The structure is characterized in Figure 18.6.

The upgrade path for CDO for Windows 2000 applications is transparent with application compatibility for CDOSYS scripts preserved. CDOEX includes the specialized objects found in Outlook. Thus, you can create appointments and meeting requests that support personal and group scheduling applications. Calendar protocols are standardized using Internet standards such as iCalendar. This provides full interoperability with Outlook 98 and Outlook 2000. Contact-management applications similarly use CDOs to manipulate knowledge resources in either Exchange WSS or AD. As mentioned previously, you use either OLE DB or ADO to move across and down object models, and CDOs to bind specific data after it has been located in the WSS. Besides the base objects provided in CDOEX, additional libraries shipped with Exchange 2000 include the CDO for Exchange Management libraries (CDOEXM). These objects provide an interface for managing mailboxes, system structures such as queues, and servers (see Table 18.4).

Process Flows and CDO

Messaging and collaborative systems can extend far beyond simple mail applications. For example, systems involving manufacturing control require a messaging foundation. Manufacturing-control systems typically involve several primary activities, including monitoring manufacturing hardware, evaluating the status of monitored hardware, and notifying interested engineers regarding status problems. Notification in a messaging system also has unique characteristics not found in other process flows. The capability of efficiently replicating the same message object to many recipients either on demand or based on some schedule separates

Table 18.4 CDO versioning summary.

Feature	Exchange 5.5	IIS 4	Windows 2000 Server	Exchange 2000
Active Messaging	N/A	N/A	N/A	N/A
CDO 1.2	Yes	N/A	N/A	Yes *
CDO 1.2 for Windows NT Server	Yes	Yes	Yes *	Yes *
CDO for Windows 2000 Server	N/A	N/A	Yes	N/A
CDO for Exchange 2000	N/A	N/A	N/A	Yes
CDO for Exchange Management	N/A	N/A	N/A	Yes
CDO Workflow Objects for Exchange	N/A	N/A	N/A	Yes

** Provided for backward compatibility with existing applications.*
(N/A) Not available in this specific release.

this object type and programming scenario from other kinds of scripting. For example, in Exchange 2000, recurring meetings and appointments are stored as master appointments containing the recurrence pattern and exceptions, in addition to separate instances for each occurrence of the appointment. HTTP/DAV, OLE DB, and ADO to provide user access to individual appointment occurrences with a standard database query using SQL as shown in Figure 18.7. When Exchange 2000 parses the query, a connection is opened to the master appointment and individual instances or records are created to provide an appropriate response to the client. A query is thus applied to an object representing all the recurring appointments in that month.

CDOs can work with Web-based forms to handle receipt/invoice messages involved in the completion of any kind of e-commercial transaction. Messages can be forwarded to a particular email address while keywords can redirect process flows to specific user groups or resources. A CDO script running in a transport event sink can be programmed to send alert messages from the server to an administrator mailbox to monitor the status of a server/service. Finally, corporate policy often requires that messages be tagged with disclaimers when inbound or outbound.

Processes and XML

The CDO library provides programmatic control at the collaborative object level. The API can be manipulated using either client-side or server-side scripting language. Although this interpreted scripting language based on ASCII text provides a well-known and widely accessible medium, XML provides enterprise application integration (EAI) through a universal data-transfer format across heterogeneous

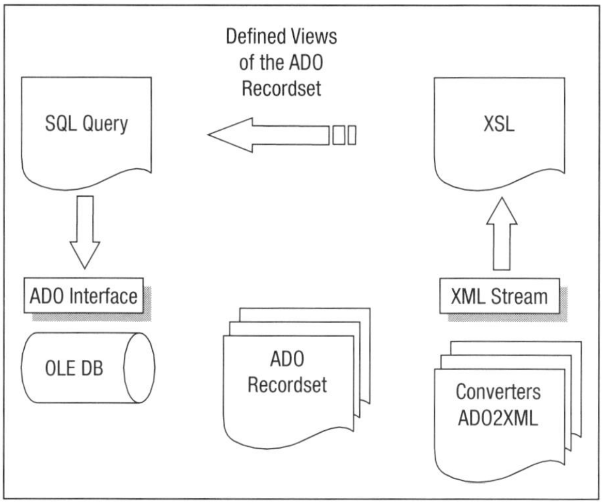

Figure 18.7 ADO supporting an Outlook service request.

information systems. Tabular, hierarchical, or semi-structured collections of data must be transferred from one platform to another in a simple yet extensible way. XML, however, only provides a data-transfer format; it doesn't participate in creating, processing, or disposing of data. The platform that performs these activities is called a *data provider*. Exchange 2000 is an OLE DB data provider.

ADO has become the Microsoft *de facto* standard for accessing these data providers when there is no direct programmatic use for logical pointers or internal system calls. It enriches access to the more architecturally complex OLE DB COM interface by simplification. The ADO **Recordset** object is the most important object here because it's the container for data requested from some source provider. The contents of this container, the **Recordset** of data, is marked up by XML, which provides a much richer set of data elements and individualized, dynamic sites and pages. It is slowly becoming the lingua franca of EAI and inter-enterprise process engineering where disparate data stores are used to support similar business workflows. Information is accessible across databases and data types *without* dependence on database engines. Common XML elements allow intelligent agents to search the Web, locate content, offload processing from the server to the client, and move between and extract information from different databases.

Consumers and providers—as objects on the same server or as economic trading partners communicating across an exchange—are exposing their internal resources and programmed operations to each other to unify application architectures and support business-to-business (B2B) services. These capabilities are now available, but at the expense of complicated code translations and multitier architecture. HTML tags refer to the instruction sets that define page layout. HTML does not provide information about what the data means in the context of the script or document called metadata. Without metadata, search engines and other data-translation techniques cannot efficiently isolate information. ADO provides direct access to the knowledge resources; XML scripting language supplies the metadata that defines how that data is structured. Like earlier attempts at Electronic Data Interchange (EDI), groups of people use similar terms and concepts to describe and organize their workflows and knowledge resources. XML uses sets of tags and declarations like HTML, but focuses on providing information about the data itself and how it relates to other data rather than formatting information on a page. Data types and acronyms—especially among members within a group or industry—are typically the same, for example, ***<First Name>***, ***<Address>***, ***<City>***, or industry-specific terms such as stock-keeping unit **<sku>** or product family **<pf>**. XML tags these data types so they are easily recognized by different proprietary software architectures.

XML thus simplifies development by delivering cross-language portability across different intranet database-driven sites. Departments across enterprises between trading partners often times have similar workflows and processes; they can now use the different translations of the same database. XML customizes the presentation of queried data in any way necessary to present the data to the end user. After the data is sent, it can be translated without having to re-access a server. You can compile information even if it exists on separate databases using similar data attributes. Hybrid XML and EDI interfaces already simplify the Internet exchanges of proprietary products and services.

XML is the foundation on which a *de facto* data description standard for groups or online communities with common workflows and data needs can be developed. XML promises standardized dialects specific to industries. By establishing a standard that characterizes data within a transaction pipeline, the markup language is evolving in a goal-directed way providing a more efficient, robust design. Rules and definitions are defined by the people who use the language. A common syntax is accomplished through a Document Type Declaration (DTD). A DTD specifies the necessary characteristics of the data elements that are being manipulated. DTDs can be made available to the public or they can exist only within one company's information domain. Moreover, DTDs are interoperable; an XML document generated under one DTD can be reformatted using another acceptable DTD.

Because XML specifies data characteristics rather than their presentation, you need style sheets to use it. Microsoft submitted XSL, an XML style sheet language to the World Wide Web Consortium (W3C). XSL adds powerful formatting capabilities to XML. Dynamic HTML (DHTML) and cascading style sheets have managed page layout since IE 4. A client browser's capability to correctly interpret these formatting instructions is very important.

Table 18.5 compares browser support for OWA for Exchange 2000. Legacy browsers enable OWA for Exchange 2000 to match Outlook more closely than OWA for earlier versions of Exchange Server. Legacy browsers minimize the use of client-side scripting and use a two-frame mode with OWA for Exchange 2000 that has a stationary navigation panel on the left side of the window. The right pane renders pages. IE 5.01 also supports Windows 2000 authentication methods such as the Kerberos protocol.

Table 18.5 Comparison of browser client software.

Feature	IE 5.01 for Windows 2000	Other
HTML text composition	Yes	No
Drag-and-drop editing	Yes	No
Preview pane	Yes	No
Tree control	Yes	No

XSL Transformation in Access

As mentioned earlier, XML acts as a data transfer protocol, while the format for rendering the data is defined separately by another language. XML must interpret information shared between two disparate data sources, and then present it so that both source and target can present it as intended. This transformation role is performed by XSL/T. A given XML document, although self-describing through its DTD, cannot contain information needed to present the content to the recipient. XSL transforms the XML document according to presentation instructions. Microsoft Access, for example, supports both transforming and presenting (or rendering) XML data. Transformation documents are thus automatically displayed by the Access import/export function as well as the Save as/Send to methods. In addition, XSL architecture allows third parties to extend the Access data and presentation transformations easily. These extensions are enabled by adding meta tags (or headers) to the XSL file and by placing the XSL document in specific locations so that administrators can manage the third party transformations. Access merges the XSL files found in areas holding program files, application data, or on a network server whenever possible.

Browser Compatibility Issues

Browsers are categorized as smart versus down-level browser clients depending on their inherent support for XML and their client-side down-level clients are legacy software. Use IE 5 or later to access OWA because the client uses DHTML in combination with XML. Legacy browsers earlier than IE 5 (IE 4 or later, or Netscape Navigator 4 or later) do not fully use OWA for Exchange 2000 capabilities because they lack the native support for these scripting languages. Browsers that are fully compliant with HTML 3.2 and the European Computer Manufacturers Association (ECMA) script standard support OWA; however, because legacy browsers are not fully compliant with the dynamic processing aspects of these languages, Microsoft recommends that you use IE 4 or later, or Netscape Navigator 4 or later.

***NOTE:** Expect to see performance problems when IE 5 is run on older computers or computers that have limited hardware resources. Consider using IE 4 for hardware platforms that lack sufficient processing power.*

.NET Framework

The .NET initiative is a distributed, Internet-based application development platform with development tools, system functional management areas, runtime services, protocol support, and application server resources. This framework is designed to enable rapid and simplified development and delivery of Web-based services with business-to-business and business-to-consumer (B2C) transactional capabilities. As collaborative services are emphasized, the specialized communication channels of person-to-person (P2P) has appeared in the emerging third wave paradigm of collaborative, inter-enterprise process integration. The .NET Framework provides a component-based environment for the development of best-of-breed cross-application, cross-enterprise, collaborative, Web automation.

Framework refers to the foundation on which a business application is built and run. Well-known or standardized frameworks provide a simplified and more consistent programming model to manipulate objects and data through. .NET Framework consists of a group of technologies that—similar to Active Server technologies shown earlier in Figure 18.5—form a consistent development foundation. Key .NET technologies include class libraries much like those object libraries discussed previously and a CLR as shown in Figure 18.8.

Windows 2000 provides the basic infrastructure required to implement Web applications and Web services. Exchange 2000 provides a Web-based storage repository, dynamic process management, and relatively easy-to-use object libraries. Windows 2000 IIS and Component Services (also known as COM+) supply protocol services and object libraries that implement all layers of a Web service:

- COM provides customized presentation, logic, and data access layers.
- ADO, OLE DB, and ODBC (Open Database Connectivity) offer data access to structured and semi-structured data stores.
- Microsoft XML Parser reads XML messages for the Web service listener.
- ASPs or ISAPI program the Web service listener.

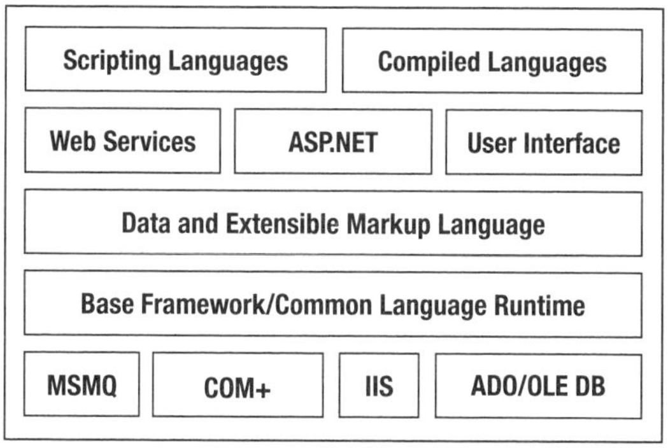

Figure 18.8 .NET Framework with .NET runtime and libraries.

A single application no longer needs to have multiple dependencies on other external components or resources, such as separate data access libraries, XML parser, and network API. Integrated functionality is now unified under the .NET Framework. Building business applications in an integrated framework maximizes ROI (return on investment) through optimized expenditures of time and resources. The environment also produces applications that can be more rapidly deployed and easily maintained than on previous development platforms. Several server products for implementing and deploying Web services are collectively known as the .NET Enterprise Servers as shown in Figure 18.9. They all have enhanced support for XML. The .NET Enterprise Servers include the following:

- *Application Center 2000*—This platform is for deploying and managing Web applications and Web services.
- *BizTalk Server 2000*—This server, specializing in business process orchestration and document interchange, contains extensive support for content and procedural protocols, namely XML and SOAP (Simple Object Access Protocol)-based messages. Both are transmitted over information protocols—such as HTTP, SSL (Secure Sockets Layer), and SMTP—expose business processes especially to EAI.
- *Commerce Server 2000*—This server service sits literally at the apex of the .NET Server model shown in Figure 18.10 providing an application platform for building e-commerce Web applications.
- *Exchange Server*—This server is the foundation platform for all messaging and collaboration application development with WSS providing hierarchical

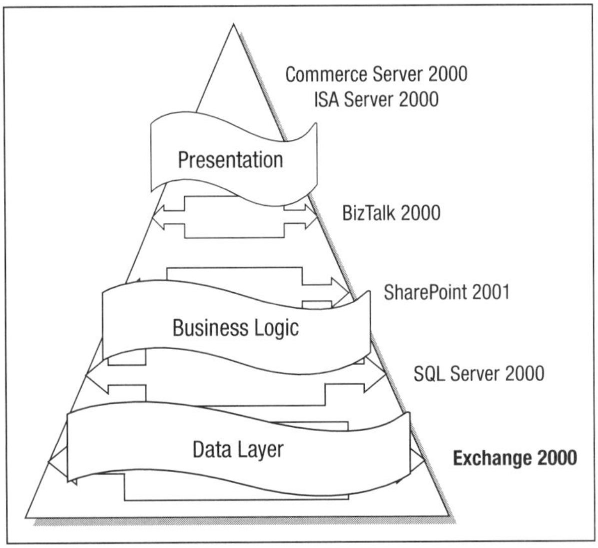

Figure 18.9 .NET Server pyramid.

data storage of heterogeneous documents and XML, a native data format for many kinds of WSS documents.

- *Host Integration Server 2000*—This server accesses mainframe applications and data stores and has evolved from Microsoft Systems Network Architecture (SNA) Server.
- *Internet Security and Acceleration Server 2000*—This server provides firewall and Web-caching services.
- *Mobile Information Server 2001*—This server provides wireless access to enterprise data.
- *SQL Server 2000*—This server is another cornerstone in the distributed services work because it provides relational data storage. SQL Server 2000, like Exchange 2000, includes extensive support for XML and significantly reduces the need for formatting logic in your applications. Direct access to SQL Server data stores and online analytical processing (OLAP) features is available using a standard browser and HTTP (see Figure 18.10).

ASP.NET

The .NET Framework includes object classes, a scripting medium, and the CLR on which the other software components rest. ASP.NET is the Internet API for the .NET Framework. As mentioned in the previous ASP discussion, ASP.NET is rebuilt rather than an enhanced version of ASP technology. ASP.NET is compiled by the CLR.

The CLR is the foundation on which .NET services run. This software layer translates application code into a common language that works with the system software layer. Like a Java Virtual Machine, a program running application code interfaces with different platforms through the same common runtime virtual

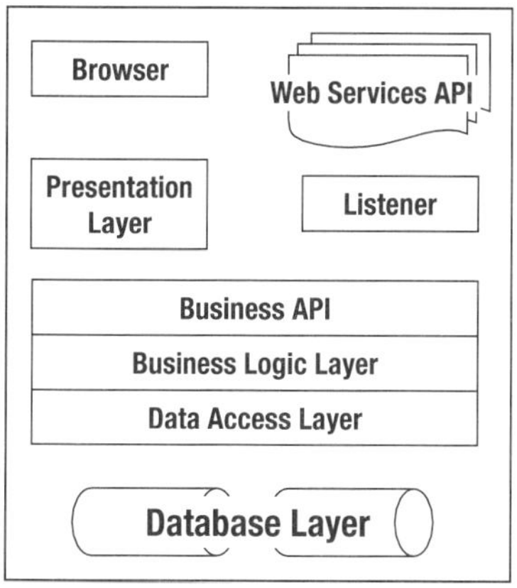

Figure 18.10 A generalized .NET Server framework.

18. Collaboration Data Objects (CDOs) and Process

machine interface. Thus, .NET services promises compatibility across languages while Java has provided it across OS platforms. The runtime language is designed to compile the scripted language, ensuring faster execution of programmed instructions than interpreted scripting after the initial compilation.

Web controls change with ASP.NET as well. ASP.NET controls can be data-bound; that is, specifically associated with data stored in a database called **Recordset**. The **Recordset** must be located on the client rather than the server, which can affect performance and network use when the server must resynchronize a dataset. Because information is stored in XML files, ASP.NET also shows the stricter syntactical rules that XML demands. Another disadvantage is that the only way Web forms gain the advantage of session-state management is to use the **POST** rather than **GET** method of passing variable information between scripts. Although more difficult to manage and write, ASP.NET represents an important broadening in the scope of Web-application frameworks. The ASP.NET Web Forms will, along with Digital Dashboard portals, provide the look and feel of the desktop to the knowledge worker. Thus, these two technologies clearly show that the promise Microsoft made of knowledge without walls accessible from any place at any time through any device is real and easily obtainable.

Related solution:	Found on page:
Establishing an ADO Connection	776

Moving Forward with .NET

Microsoft has shifted its architectural perspective from the physically limited local area network (LAN) to Web sites and application servers distributed across the entire Internet. Active Server was LAN-centric and physically-oriented as denoted in the naming of its distinguishable components; namely, Active Server, Active Client, Active Directory, and so on. .NET contrarily has no real sense of boundary or centricity; this lack of scope—like the Internet itself—is the essence of the business initiative in promising "infinite" scalability and extensibility of function. The .NET initiative includes the .NET Framework, .NET Enterprise Servers, .NET Building Block Services, .NET Orchestration, and .NET Development Tools/Environments such as Passport.NET, Windows XP, and the future spawn of Windows 2000: Blackcomb. It's hard to characterize the many core components that comprise such a grand scope. In fact, the lack of centricity best characterizes the initiative. The .NET Framework is concerned with both the creation and consumption of Web Services and making COM development more efficient and productive. The target applications are both B2B and B2C. Nevertheless, Web Services and the applications that are serviced fundamentally rest on scalable and extensible messaging and collaboration. Some of the key features of the .NET Framework for Web Services developers include the following:

- A standardized, unified CLR that manages all application dependencies written in any programming language independent of a specific programming interface.
- Interoperability with existing COM components to provide backward and forward compatibility.
- An improved application deployment model that specifies which versions of dependent DLLs to use and provides integrated services such as security.
- Subsystems such as ADO.NET, which is an enhanced ADO that provides classes to access XML documents and relational data stores. ASP.NET, another subsystem, provides a low-level programming model equivalent to ISAPI along with high-level programming models for building Web applications known as Web Forms and Web Services and supports all forms of authentication and authorization, including Microsoft Passport.NET authentication and custom cookie-based authentication for applications that use a private account database for authenticating users.
- .NET Remoting for controlling objects and requesting services across context, application domain, process, or machine boundaries. This initiative is part of inter-enterprise process engineering and will probably be the foundation on which future extensibility and collaboration of business process flows will rest.

Exchange 2000 and the Way of the Merchant

Workflow applications, collaborative services, and e-commercial transactions are part of the information technologies scene of Exchange Server. None of these processes were even associated with messaging systems when they were first introduced to the business world. However, they have all converged in a layer of networked services bundled under the product name Exchange 2000 .NET Server. An administrator of this service platform must have the technical knowledge to deploy and maintain what has become more than just store and forward mailboxes and global address lists. With the emergence of the Web Store and the extensible scripting languages that can present specialized knowledge objects like contact records and calendar appointments in a common browser window across the Internet, the scope of messaging has radically changed. We have suggested that the job description of an Exchange administrator has changed as well. If we recognize a paradigm shift from data processing through information technology to knowledge management, we must also redefine the administrative role as more architectural than technical. We have suggested that just as an architect attempts to synergize form and function, technical personnel must broaden their scope to encompass corporate costs of ownership as well as investments. The text-based peer-to-peer messaging systems of twenty years ago evolved into complex mosaics of inter-enterprise collaborative processes that can prove to be a competitive edge distinguishing one company in an entire industry. The Exchange Administrator, while typically not equipped to both configure a SMTP connector and write an Active Server Pages application, must nevertheless have enough background to suggest feasible business solutions and rudimentary designs to top management. These business solutions are best generated by the same people who will be responsible for their deployment, maintenance, and user support. Thus, the role of administrator has grown more architectural with the emergence of Exchange 2000 as a development platform. The Way of the Technician merges with that of the Merchant when an administrator proposes ways in which collaborative objects and knowledge resources can be assembled into inter-enterprise messaging and collaborative business solutions that achieve corporate missions and goals.

Immediate Solutions

In many of these examples, generic portions of code are listed to show how solutions might be built. Complete source code and accompanying documentation are outside the scope of this book as it was originally intended, namely as a quick-reference source for generating immediate solutions to problems encountered on a regular basis by an Exchange 2000 administrator. These general observations are in no way intended to be comprehensive or complete.

WARNING! Use Registry Editor at your own risk. You should back up the Registry before you edit it. If you are running Windows NT or Windows 2000, you should also update your Emergency Repair Disk (ERD).

Changing the Exchange Installable File System to Another Drive Letter

Exchange 2000 uses the Exchange Installable File System (IFS) component—drive M by default—to provide access to Information Stores as if they were file system objects. The default drive letter can be changed by making a Registry entry using the following procedure. Note that drive P is used, which will replace drive M to represent the Information Store upon a system restart.

1. Start Registry Editor (**Regedt32.exe**).
2. Locate the following key in the Registry:

```
HKEY_LOCAL_MACHINE\SYSTEM\CurrentControlSet\Services\EXIFS\Parameters
```

3. Choose Edit|Add Value, and then add the following Registry value:

```
Value Name: DriveLetter
Data Type: REG_SZ
Value: P
```

NOTE: *If the* ***DriveLetter*** *value already exists, double-click the value, and then change the drive letter.*

4. Quit Registry Editor.

Viewing a Raw Exchange 2000 Directory

An administrative view in raw mode bypassing the user interface reveals the schema and object properties without the regular safeguards of the user interface. Because Exchange 2000 writes all configuration data to the AD, ADSI Edit can show the Exchange container and type and scope of data in the AD configuration naming context as shown in Figure 18.11. Working in this mode, you need to be extremely careful about any changes you make to the current data. To view the Exchange 2000 raw directory:

1. Copy the Adsiedit.dll file from the Windows 2000 *Support\Reskit\Netmgmt\Dstool* folder to the *%SystemRoot%\System32* folder. ADSI Edit installs automatically when you install the Resource Kit.
2. Change directory to *%SystemRoot%\System32* at a command prompt and type "regsvr32 adsiedit.dll"; then, exit back to Windows.
3. Choose Start|Run, type "mmc" in the Run dialog box, and then click OK.
4. On the MMC (Microsoft Management Console) Console menu, click Add/Remove Snap-In; click Add and select ADSI Edit.
5. Click Add, click Close, and then click OK.
6. Select ADSI Edit in the MMC ADSI Edit window and click Action|Connect.
7. Click Schema from the Naming Context box.

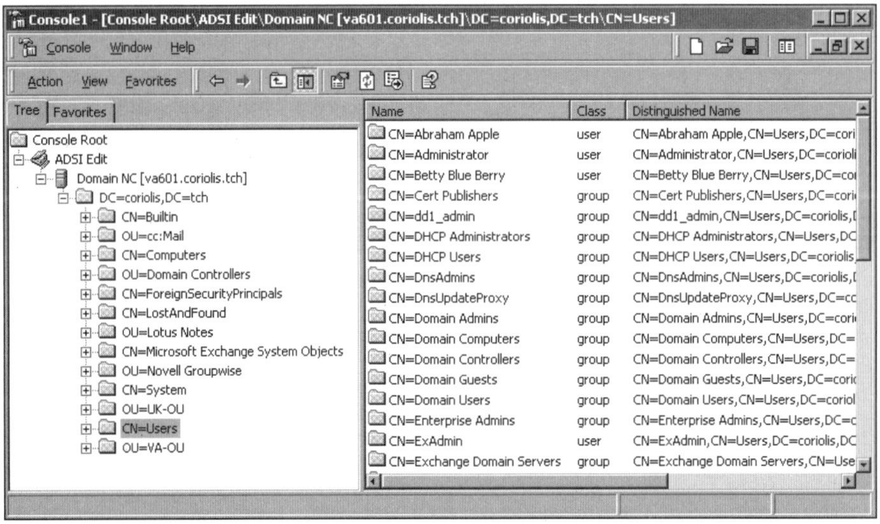

Figure 18.11 ADSI Edit MMC showing the User schema.

8. Type the fully qualified domain name (FQDN) for your target server in the Select Domain Or Server dialog box under Computer and then click OK. A **Schema** object under the **ADSI Edit** object within the ADSI Edit window should appear.
9. Expand this object, the Exchange 2000 Schema, and double-click an attribute in the right window pane to view the raw properties of an object within the schema.

Installing the New MSXML Parser

Microsoft XML Parser contains a WinInet component that provides more stable rendering for the dashboard. Before installing a dashboard, perform the following steps to get the new parser installed:

1. Install the XML Parser 3 on the machine hosting the dashboard and restart IIS.
2. Use the WinHTTP Proxy Configuration Tool to configure the proxy on the server so that users' identities pass through the server as shown in Figure 18.12. The configuration string is as follows:

```
proxycfg -d -p yourproxy "<local>"
```

NOTE: *Use a Proxy Dummy Server in the configuration even if you don't use a Proxy Server.*

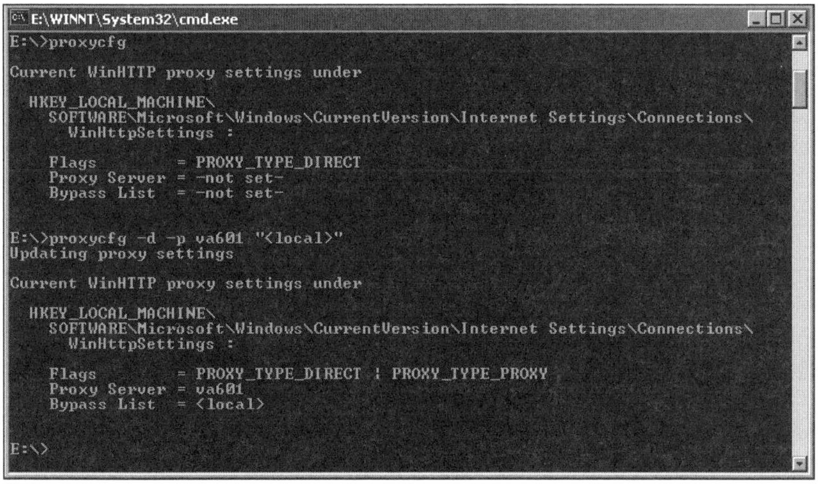

Figure 18.12 View of **PROXYCFG.**

Changing OWA Passwords Through IIS

Sometimes, it is necessary to enable users to change OWA passwords through IIS on each IIS server to which the users are redirected to minimize administrative overhead. Perform the following steps:

1. Install and configure SSL on the server.
2. Launch Internet Services Manager from Administrative Tools.
3. Right-click the default Web site and select New|Virtual Directory.
4. Type "IISADMPWD" in the Alias box in the Virtual Directory Creation Wizard and click Next.
5. Type "*local_drive*:\winnt\system32\inetsrv\iisadmpwd" in the Directory box, and then click Next.
6. Verify that Read and Run Script checkboxes are selected, click Next, and then click Finish.
7. Verify that the Iisadmpwd folder has the **Anonymous Access** authentication method enabled. Although you can select other authentication types, make certain the **Anonymous Access** authentication method is enabled.

NOTE: *The client and server will go into an endless loop if you do not enable the* ***Anonymous Access*** *option when you attempt to authenticate users with expired passwords. If a user navigates to the site and is prompted for a password, but the password has expired, the first page the user accesses redirects him to the password expiry page. The password expiry page challenges the user, but because the user is not authenticated on the first page, the second page refuses the connection because the password has expired. The user is redirected back to the initial calling page, which redirects the user back through the loop, and so on.*

8. Change the Metabase **PasswordChangeFlags** setting to zero (0) from \inetpub\adminscriptsfolder on your local machine.
9. At the command prompt, type "*cd drive:inetpub\adminscripts*".
10. Type the following at the command line: "adsutil set w3svc/passwordchangeflags 0".

NOTE: *The available options for the* ***PasswordChangeFlags*** *setting are the following:*
0 – Requires password change by SSL
1 – Allows password change by nonsecure ports
2 – Disables password changes
4 – Disables advance notification of expiration

11. Access the user mailbox using https://*server name*/exchange/*user*.

12. When you type the account information on the Aexp.htr page (or on the Aexp3.htr page, if you are accessing it from an unsecured URL), you must type "domain\username".

NOTE: *The IUSER was authenticated to the Aexp.htr page. You can't populate the Account box with the domain\username unless you hard code the domain\computer name in the Aexp.htr file (or in the Aexp3.htr file for an unsecured URL).*

Registering an Event Sink

Before using them in an application, you have to register the scripts that are triggered by events (called event sinks). Exchange Server includes an event registration script to manage this process. Alternatively, you can use Visual Basic to perform the same task as follows:

```
Dim objRec as ADODB.Record
objRec.Open newRule, asModeReadWrite, asCreateNonCollection, as
DelayFetchFields
objRec.Fields("urn:schemas:mailheader:content-class")_
="http://content-classes.Microsoft.com/exchange/storeeventregistration"
objRec.Fields("http://schemas.microsoft.com/exchange/event/methods")_
="evtOnSave"
objRec.Fields("http://schemas.microsoft.com/exchange/event/sinkclass")_
="NewSink.1"
objRec.Close.
```

Isolating a Process Application

IIS 5 runs all Web sites in the same memory space by default. The generation of a fatal error will cause instability and disruption in Web Services. Best practices recommend isolating applications so that they run in their own separate memory space. This will insure that any instability of one process will not affect the services provided by other ongoing processes running concurrently in the system.

1. Open the property window of the specific subdirectory in Internet Service Manager (ISM).
2. Click Create under Application Settings with the subdirectory as the starting point. This creates the application. You can assign it a different name in the Application Name box.
3. Select High (Isolated) in the Application Protection drop-down box as shown in Figure 18.13.

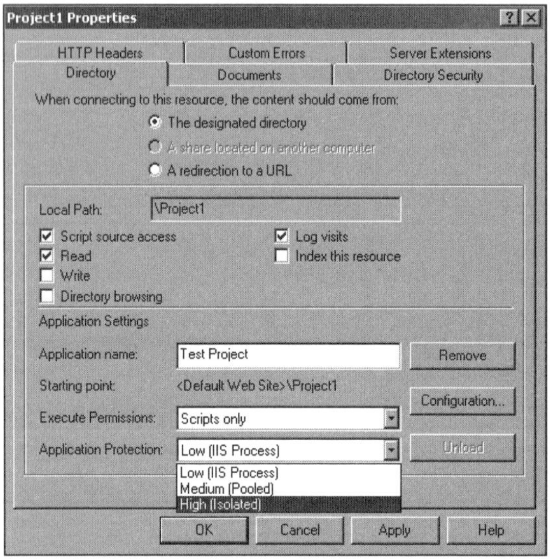

Figure 18.13 Selecting High Application Protection for a process application.

Creating a Global.asa File

The Global.asa file is stored in the same directory as an application's initial load scripts, such as index.asp, index.html, or main.html. The file contains event procedures associated with the **Session** and **Application** objects. The file also can include procedures and functions associated with these triggered events. A general Global.asa is as follows:

```
<SCRIPT  LANGUAGE=VBScript  RUNAT=server>
Sub Session_onStart
     ' Procedural statements triggered when session starts
End Sub

Sub Session_onEnd
   ' Procedural statements triggered when session ends
End Sub

Sub Application_onStart
   ' Procedural statements triggered when application starts
End Sub
```

```
Sub Application_onEnd
   ' Procedural statements triggered when application ends
End Sub
</SCRIPT>
```

***NOTE:** Use <SCRIPT> tags in the Global.asa file; do not use opening and closing <% delimiters.*

Connecting to Data Stores

To access data, you need to create a connection to the location or repository of that data. You explicitly supply information to a **Connection** object, which in turn creates the connection with the data provider for you. Two common methods to connect to a data provider are a connection string and a data source name using the ODBC interface. Direct connections are faster and easier to administer than ODBC because the former method supplies all the information when the connection string in the script is read, whereas the latter requires retrieval of details from either the local machine system Registry or separate text files. Alternatively, you can create a Data Source Name using the ODBC interface and reference the ODBC alias from within your script using the **Open** method of a connection variable **conMyData** as follows:

```
conMyData.open "DSN=myAlias"
```

Examples of connection strings you will most likely encounter include the following:

- Access using an ODBC connection without a Data Source Name:

```
Driver=(Microsoft Access Driver (*.mdb); DBQ=c:\mydatastore\database.mdb
```

- Access using a native OLE DB provider:

```
Provider=Microsoft.Jet.OLEDB.4.0: Data Source=c:\mydatastore\database.mdb
```

- SQL Server using an ODBC connection:

```
Driver={SQL SERVER}; Server=servername; Database=databasename; UID=
 username; PWD=password
```

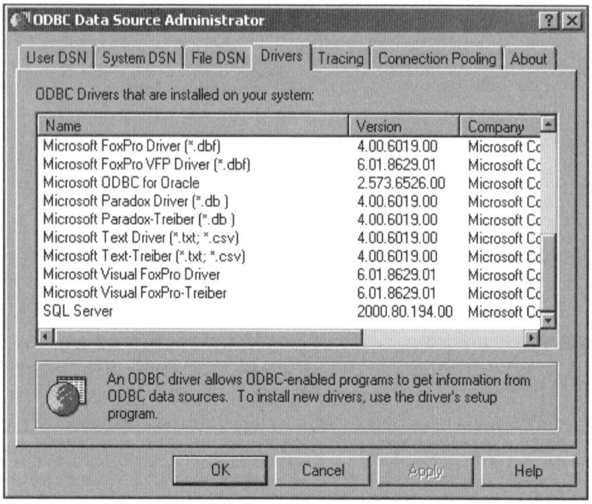

Figure 18.14 A listing of installed ODBC drivers and versions.

- SQL Server using a native OLE DB provider:

```
Provider=SQLOLEDB; Data Source=servername; Initial Catalog=databasename;
 User ID= username; Password=password
```

Driver names used in the OLE DB provider for ODBC must be copied from the list of drivers in the ODBC interface as shown in Figure 18.14. You can access this list by performing the following steps:

1. Choose Start|Settings|Control Panel.
2. Open Administrative Tools|Data Sources (ODBC).
3. Click the Drivers tab in the ODBC Data Source Administrators dialog box.
4. Use the name of the ODBC driver installed on your system.

NOTE: *Best practices suggest placing data stores in locations separate from where application scripts or Web files are stored.*

Using Include Files to Create Connection Strings

An include file is an externally located text file that is incorporated into your script at the location you indicate with an **INCLUDE** statement.

1. Create a file named, for example, connection.asp, without any headers or other details exactly as follows:

```
<%
strConn="Provider=SQLOLEDB; Data Source= MyDataStore; Initial
  Catalog=pubs;
 User ID=gregb; Password=password"
%>
```

2. When writing your application source code, insert the **INCLUDE** statement at the top:

```
<!- #INCLUDE FILE= "includeCon.asp" ->
```

Using the Open Method

To open a connection, you need to supply the appropriate information to the data provider. If you use the variable **strConn** to provide this configuration information, you can create an ADO connection using the following code in your script:

```
Set conPubs = Server.CreateObject("ADODB.Connection")
conPubs.ConnectionString = strConn
        ' Alternatively replace the above line with conPubs.Open strConn
        ' Perform procedural steps
conPubs.Close
```

Prompting for ODBC Connect String Arguments

Prompting for ODBC connect string arguments demonstrates how to use the ADO **Prompt** Property, with the ODBC OLE DB provider to display the ODBC Login dialog box and prompt for selected information.

```
Sub Prompt_ODBC_Connection()
  Dim objConn As ADODB.Connection, strConn As String
  strConn = "DRIVER={SQL Server};SERVER=(local);UID=sa;PWD=;DATABASE=pubs"
  Set objConn = New ADODB.Connection
  With objConn
  .ConnectionString = strConn
  .Provider = "msdasql"
  .Properties("Prompt") = adPromptAlways
  .Open strConn
  End With
End Sub
```

Establishing an ADO Connection

Specify a database connection string to access the data store explicitly created or built from the **Record** object. The connection for an Exchange mailbox for **gregb** on **west.coriolis.tld** would be located at **http://west.Coriolis.tld/exchange/gregb**. This string is used in the ASP script to establish the connection.

```
Set objConn = Server.CreateObject ("ADODB.Connection")
objConn.Provider = "ExOLEDB.DataSource"
objConn.Open "file://./backofficestorage/coriolis.tld/exchange/gregb"
```

You must explicitly specify the **ExOLEDB** provider before opening the connection because connection strings starting with **http://** are registered by default with the Internet Publishing provider. To avoid conflict, use the prefix **file://./backofficestorage/** to reference the mail store instead of **http://west.Coriolis.tld/exchange/gregb** to avoid conflict. Use Windows 2000 ADSI objects to avoid hard-coded references to either the Exchange Server or its domain as follows:

```
Set objInfoNT = Server.CreateObject ("WinNTSystemInfo")
Set objInfo   = Server.CreateObject ("ADSystemInfo")
varNTName     = objInfoNT.ComputerName
varDomainName = objInfo.DomainDNSName
```

Form the fully qualified domain name (FQDN) by appending the two variables: **varDomainName** and **varNTName**.

Creating a Connection without a Data Source Name

The following code sample creates a connection to a SQL Server without using a Data Source Name.

```
Dim objConn As ADODB.Connection, rsRec As ADODB.Recordset, strConn As
  String
strConn = "DRIVER={SQL Server};SERVER=(local);UID=sa;PWD=;DATABASE=pubs"

Set objConn = New ADODB.Connection
objConn.Open = strConn
objConn.Provider = "msdasql"
objConn.Open strConn

Set rsRec = New ADODB.Recordset
rsRec.ActiveConnection = Conn
```

```
rsRec.Open "Select * From Authors"
Debug.Print rsRec ("au_id")
Set rsRec = Nothing
Conn.Close
```

Determining Content Type

The **ContentType** property of the **Response** object provides the browser client with information regarding the HTTP content included in the server's response to the client request. If you don't include a **ContentType** property, the content type header defaults to **text/html**. This information is included in the HTTP header that is sent before any other output.

```
<% @LANGUAGE = VBScript %>
<%
Response.ContentType = "text/plain"
Response.Expires = 0
%>
<!- message text ->
```

Manipulating **Record** Objects

A valid connection object is used to access any data store item; you access any object as a record using a URL. If GregB has a WIP (WorkInProgress) subfolder in his Outlook Inbox, you can access that folder in ReadOnly mode as follows:

```
Set objRecord      = Server.CreateObject("ADODB.Record")
objectRecord.Open = "Inbox/WIP", oConn, adModeRead
```

Adding Contact Information into Messages Using **CDOEX**

This sample demonstrates how to add contact information into a message by using **CDOEX**. A **With** statement reduces object reference overhead.

```
Dim strServerName As String, strDomainName As String, strRecipName As
  String
Dim strURL As String, objContact As New CDO.Person
```

```
strServerName = "va601"
strDomainName = "DC=east,DC=coriolis,DC=tld"
strRecipName = "GregB"
objContact.DataSource.Open strURL
 If Err.Number = 0 Then
   Set objMessage = New CDO.Message
   With objMessage
      .Subject = "test message to contact"
      .TextBody = "This is a sample message to a contact"
      .From = "<sender alias>"
      .To = objContact.Email   'email address of found contact
      .Configuration.Fields("cdoSendUsing") = cdoSendUsingExchange
      .Configuration.Fields.Update
      .Send
   End With
End If
Set objContact = Nothing
Set objMessage = Nothing
```

Using SMTP to Send Email

Parameters include **objMessage.Send FromAddress**, **ToAddress**, **Subject**, **Body**, **Importance,** where the last parameter, **Interest Level**, is 0 for low importance, 1 for normal, and 2 for high.

```
<% LANGUAGE = VBSCRIPT %>
<%
Option Explicit
Dim objMessage
Set  obMessage =Server.CreateObject ("CDONTS.NewMail")
ObjMessage.Send "fflintstone@bedrock.com", "gregb@coriolis.com", "Urgent
  Mail",  "Have we met the deadline?", 0
Set objMessage= Nothing
%>
```


Enabling MAPI Clients Computers Through a Firewall

Exchange down level MAPI client computers can be either Exchange client computers or client computers using Outlook in Corporate or Workgroup mode in Exchange 2000 that connect to Exchange 2000 over an existing connection to the

Internet through a firewall. To enable these client computers through a firewall, add entries to the Registry to make the ports assigned to these connections static as follows:

1. Launch the Registry Editor (Regedt32.exe) by choosing Start|Run (or from the command line).
2. In the Regedit window, find the following Registry key:

```
HKEY_LOCAL_MACHINE\System\CurrentControlSet\Services\MSExchangeSA\
  Parameters
```

3. Add the following entry for the Exchange SA RFR Interface:

```
Name: TCP/IP port
Value: REG_DWORD
Data Value: Assign a Port number
```

NOTE: *Port assignments should be in the range of 1024 to 5000 decimal.*

4. Add the following entry for the Exchange Directory NSPI (Name Service Provider Interface) Proxy Interface.

```
Name: TCP/IP NSPI port
Value: REG_DWORD
Data Value: Assign a Port number
```

5. Locate and click the following Registry key:

```
HKEY_LOCAL_MACHINE\System\CurrentControlSet\Services\MSExchangeIS\
ParametersSystem
```

6. Add the following entry for the Exchange Information Store Interface:

```
Name: TCP/IP port
Type: REG_DWORD
Data Value: Assign a port number
```

7. Quit Registry Editor.
8. Restart the computer for these changes to take effect.
9. Enable port 135 and configure the other ports so that TCP (Transmission Control Protocol) connections are enabled in the packet filter (or firewall) after performing these changes to the Registry.

Creating an Entrance/Exit Console Script

You can use incoming and outgoing pop-up consoles triggered upon entering or leaving a Web site to notify site visitors of legal and corporate policy or disclaimer text. Insert **JScript** script that will open in a new console window between the opening and closing HTML **<head>** tags in your main HTML document. Use the FQDN in addressing the console page. The **_blank** attribute forces a new window object to open on top of the current window. **width** and **height** specify the size of the console that the **open** method of the window object will launch.

```
<script language="JavaScript">
<!— window.open('http://www.UseYourWebSite/
yourconsolepage.htm','_blank','width=350, height=300'));
// —>
</script>
```

A blur console pops up behind the open window from which it is called so that, when the current page is closed, your end user will see a fully loaded page. The **ECMAScript** script is as follows:

```
<script language="JavaScript">
<!— xtWindow=window.open('http://www.UseYourWebSite/
consolepage.htm','windowName';
self.focus();
if(!xtWindow.opener)xtWindow.opener=self;
// —>
</script>\
```

Place the following script within the HTML **<head>** tags in the blurred console:

```
<script language="JavaScript">
<!—
self.blur();
// —>
</script>
```

Alternatively, an **exit** console is another scripted object that is triggered by exiting a page. An **exit** is defined when a user clicks the browser Back button, clicks an external bookmark, selects a hyperlink to an outside reference, or reloads the page. The **ECMAScript** for this object is as follows:

```
<script language="JavaScript">
<!—
var exit=true
```

```
function myXitWindow()
{
if (exit)
window.open('http://www.UseYourWebSite/yourconsolepage.htm','_blank','width
=350, height=300'));
}
// ->
</script>
```

You also must add a function call to the body tag of the window that will trigger the **exit** console as follows:

```
<body bgcolor="#000000" onunLoad="myXitWindow()">
```

Include an **onClick=exit=false** attribute on hyperlink references you want users to launch *without* an **exit** console window as follows:

```
<a href="http://www.MyTradingPartner.com/" onClick="exit=false">
```

Glossary

access control entry (ACE)—A statement within an Access Control List (ACL) that contains identifying information for users and groups and specifies the type of access allowed for those objects.

Access Control List (ACL)—A security mechanism that controls access to domain objects via access control entries (ACEs). These entries specify the range of actions an authorized user can perform on some knowledge resource like a folder or file. The list is a collection of these entries. A default ACL is applied to every object you create in a directory.

active/active—See Clustering Service.

Active Directory (AD)—A fundamental structure found within the Windows 2000 operating system (OS), this hierarchically-arranged database stores and makes available object information on a network to authorized users. AD is a namespace within Windows 2000 that adds new features to the traditional Windows 2000-based directory service, including a brand new domain model. AD is a unified and distributed database of objects that uses one replication mechanism. It takes the place of the legacy Security Accounts Manager (SAM) database found inside legacy Windows NT 4 computers. Exchange 2000 uses the AD structure as a primary means of data storage.

Active Directory Connector (ADC)—A service that runs on a Windows 2000 domain controller (DC) and allows for synchronization and replication between directories, specifically between an Exchange 5.5 directory and a domain-naming partition in Windows 2000. ADC is required in a mixed-mode organization running earlier versions of Exchange Server to synchronize such information as distinguished names. Two versions of the ADC exist: a Windows 2000 ADC, which replicates objects only in an Exchange 5.5 site, and an Exchange 2000 ADC, which also replicates configuration information to AD.

Active Directory Services Interface (ADSI)—A Windows-based interface for high-level network directory services that consolidates information from various network-operating environments. It uses the features of directory services from multiple network providers to present one directory service interface so that network objects can be effectively managed. ADSI is used to update user information and browse AD across multiple operating systems (OSs).

active/passive—See Clustering Service.

Active Server Pages (ASP)—Part of Active Server technologies, these text files contain a combination of Hypertext Markup Language (HTML) and specially delimited script, typically but not exclusively written in VBScript, that provide the parsing Web server with programmed procedural instructions. The server-side code is rendered back into HTML so that any client-side browser can present the requested information to the enduser. The acronym ASP is also used for **Application Service Provider**, a company that provides access to program applications and services to individuals and businesses over the Internet.

ActiveX Data Objects (ADO)—A programming interface that provides a method of accessing BackOffice data, independent of which application the data is stored in. Developers use ADO to query and sort Exchange Server data, so they can write applications that use data found in the Web Storage System (WSS). They can also append dynamic objects to static Web pages using ADO.

administrative group—This object defines the administrative topology for a company and represents a collection of objects grouped together for management purposes. It facilitates the management of permissions and rights. In a mixed-mode environment with Exchange 5.5 Servers, the administrative group is functionally equivalent to a site. You also use administrative groups to separate the management of system policies and routing groups. You can apply system policies from any administrative group to all Exchange Servers in a domain tree.

American Standard Code for Information Interchange (ASCII)—This standardized 7-bit binary coding scheme representing 128 alphabetic, numeric, and special punctuation and diacritical markings is the most common way to represent or format text files on the Internet. IBM mainframes have typically used an 8-bit 256-character system called Extended Binary Coded Decimal Interchange Code. Windows NT and 2000, as well as other operating systems like Novell, use a newer system called Unicode Worldwide Character Standard containing more than 34 thousand coded characters.

Application—This generic term defines an addressable object in the Web Storage System (WSS) that combines documents created by end users with HTML pages, and registrations created by an application author. It will have an access control list (ACL) associated with it that defines authorized users and the range of actions they can apply to this object.

Asynchronous Transfer Mode (ATM)—This is a high-speed switching technology that passes asynchronous data in a fixed 53 byte packet called cell over some physical medium using specialized signaling hardware. ATM is the primary transmission substrate for broadband and Synchronous Optical Network (SONET) technologies.

base schema—The structural organization of item types and properties supplied by the Web Storage System (WSS) and made available to all authorized applications.

Binary Large Objects (BLOB)—This knowledge resource is an especially large file that requires specialized handling by the database management systems that store and retrieve it for processing. It is typically a multimedia image or sound file.

binding—Refers to the process of connecting information in the Web Storage System (WSS) with HTML through some formal process of registration. Data binding, for example, can take place either at the client or at the server. Clients must be using Internet Explorer version 5 or later. Binding at the server can be handled by the WSS renderer, or by an Active Server Pages (ASP) script. Similarly, an HTML tag used to display a property from the WSS is said to be "bound" to that property.

bridgehead server—A server with multiple connectors that mediates data transfers between two Exchange 5.5 sites and replicated mail and directory information between sites. Exchange 2000 uses bridgehead servers, but the Global Catalog (GC) Server now replicates directory information. You can use a bridgehead server to connect two Exchange 2000 routing groups, with one primary and one secondary bridgehead server per routing group connection.

Categorizer—A mail system plug-in component of the advanced queuing engine that checks the Active Directory for message transfer limits and other restrictions associated with some message. In a message routing scenario, this component determines where a message is to be delivered and expands distribution groups in order to deliver a single message to many recipients.

Certificate Authority (CA)—This special entity or organization is responsible for the administration and management of digital certificates and the authentication of certificate holders. The CA corroborates the security credentials of certificate holders in order to maintain secured exchanges of data between two or more parties especially across some public network.

Clustering Service—This service provides what logically appears as a single drive or storage system called a server cluster. In fact, a server cluster is composed of multiple storage devices that help maintain high levels of availability through redundancy and performance enhancements through the sharing of services called load balancing. The service is run on every physical unit or node in the cluster. An **active/active node** configuration means that all nodes concurrently run an application service; **active/passive node** configuration means that an application service runs on only one node at a time. If there is some disruption in service on that particular node there is a **failover** of services; the application is transferred from the offline node, to another node to provide what appears as continuous or **fault tolerant** service.

Collaboration Data Objects (CDOs) for System Management (previously known as Exchange Management Objects [EMO])—A library of COM objects that provide access to specific management information within Exchange 2000, including databases and storage groups (SGs).

Collaboration Data Objects (CDOs) for Windows 2000—A Simple Mail Transfer Protocol (SMTP)-based library providing a messaging feature that comes preinstalled with Windows 2000 Professional and Windows 2000 Server. It is an Application Programming Interface (API) that establishes interfaces and functions for accessing messaging data. You use CDO for applications that provide Multipurpose Internet Mail Extensions (MIME) creation and management. It also integrates with ActiveX Data Object (ADO) components to give access to both the Web Storage System (WSS) and Active Directory (AD).

Collaboration Data Objects (CDOEX) for Exchange 2000—A library of programmable Component Object Model (COM) objects that provide messaging and collaboration services without dependence on legacy MAPI. CDOEX works, for example, at the object level of message, contact, and calendar while ActiveX Data Objects (ADO) and Object Linking and Embedding for Databases (OLE DBs) perform more general data-access functions of access and retrieval.

Collaboration Data Objects 1.21 (CDO 1.21 or CDONTS, also known as active messaging and OLE [Object Linking and Embedding] messaging)—A library of programmable objects specifically related to messaging and collaboration based on the Component Object Model (COM). The library provides an interface to Messaging Application Programming Interface (MAPI) and allows you to add mail and messaging functionality to your applications. You must have MAPI installed to use this legacy version of the OLE messaging library. See CDO for Exchange 2000.

column—In the case of folder views presented as HTML tables, every row represents an item in the folder, and every column represents a property of that item.

command—Text or numbers added to a query string in the URL address of any item contained in the Web Storage System (WSS). The WSS recognizes some of these commands (for example, **new** and **contents**), while other commands are only specific to applications that you create.

Conference Management Services (CMS)—Simplifies the administration of conferencing services within Exchange 2000 by displaying one interface for meetings of various types. CMS allows administrators to regulate the number of conferences that an organization can schedule simultaneously. Users take advantage of Exchange 2000 Conferencing Server to schedule meetings using the Outlook 2000 Calendar function.

conference technology provider (CTP)—A provider of conferencing services such as realtime video and audio, it is composed of a Data Conferencing Provider and a Video Conferencing Provider. CTP integrates with Conference Management Service (CMS) and supports application sharing, chat, and multiparty video conferencing over Internet Protocol (IP) multicasts. CTP supports both T.120-compatible programs and H.323 protocol clients.

Configuration Connection Agreement—The first configuration connection agreement created by the Site Replication Service when Exchange 2000 is installed into an existing Exchange 5.5 organization. The name of this agreement takes the form of Config CA_AdministrativeGroupName_Exchange2000ServerName. The Exchange 2000 Active Directory Connector (ADC) creates it to transfer two-way configuration information between an Exchange 5.5 site and the configuration naming partition of Active Directory (AD).

connection agreement—Defines a relationship between an existing Exchange site and the Windows 2000 Active Directory (AD). You use a connection agreement in conjunction with the Active Directory Connector (ADC) to help you replicate direction information between the Exchange site and AD. A connection agreement contains such information as the name of the server being contacted for replication and the object classes being replicated. You can establish multiple connection agreements for one ADC. Two types of connection agreements exist: a user connection agreement, which replicates recipient objects and their data, and a configuration agreement, which replicates configuration information specific to Exchange Server.

contact—An object that results when you use the Active Directory Connector (ADC) to move a custom recipient, or a recipient address external to your Exchange organization, to AD. All contacts in AD are not immediately specified with an email address because you can do this later. A contact helps you reference mailboxes in a foreign messaging system and helps make common email addresses more available in the Global Access List (GAL) within Exchange 2000.

content class—Represents an item's type and helps correlate physical data with a visual form.

Data Encryption Standard (DES)—A widely used method of data encryption that uses a secret key. You can use 72 quadrillion or more possible encryption keys. For each given message, the key is chosen at random from among this enormous number of keys. Both the sender and the receiver must know and use this same private key. DES applies a 56-bit key to each 64-bit block of data. Although this is considered strong encryption, many organizations now use triple DES and apply three separate keys in succession. DES was created at IBM in 1977, and adopted by the U.S. Department of Defense (DOD). It is also specified as an American National Standards Institute (ANSI) X3.92 standard.

denial-of-service (DoS)—On the Internet, a network service can lose the ability to provide responses to legitimate requests for service when it is overloaded with large numbers of invalid requests commingled with the legitimate ones. This service request overload can be launched by a malicious party from a single or distributed number of agents (as in Distributed Denial of Service, DDoS), and force a network service to temporarily cease operations.

Digest Authentication—A security authentication method that uses the hash value or message digest of specific security credentials to validate a user's authentication. The hash value is transmitted across the network connection to prevent exposure of the security information.

Distributed Authoring and Versioning (DAV, also known as WebDAV)—See WebDAV.

DMZ (Demilitarized Zone)—This particular network topology provides protection against unauthorized access to hosting servers managing Internet traffic through the erecting of firewalls and bastion hosts. Hosting servers include devices providing HTTP, SMTP, FTP, or DNS support to public or private networks. The firewall technology includes any combination of hardware and software that prevents or deters unauthorized access from outside the zone to any mission-critical server located inside the zone. It can protect these servers from users within an enterprise just as effectively as unauthenticated agents located outside the enterprise.

Document Object Model (DOM)—This programming specification provides a basis for expressing a document in some standardized manner. The model thus ensures that some mutually agreed upon control will be applied to the representation and manipulation of data contained within the document object, independent of the language or platform on which it is represented or expressed.

domain controller (DC)—A server that manages security interactions for users and domains. It helps centralize administration because you create user accounts only once. To qualify as a DC, a computer has to be configured with Windows 2000 Server, Windows 2000 Advanced Server, or Windows 2000 Datacenter Server. All

DCs store a copy of the local domain database and replicate this information to other DCs within the same forest. The **dcpromo** utility is used to promote member servers or standalone computers to DC status.

domain mode—One of two modes of any Active Directory (AD) domain you create: mixed-mode or native-mode. By default, all domains run in mixed-mode, which emulates the conditions and limits of most Windows NT 4 networks. A mixed-mode domain can interoperate with all pre-Windows 2000 domain controllers (DCs), called down-level DCs. All clients that use the Windows NT 4 directory service authenticate to a Windows 2000 domain using mixed-mode. In contrast, native-mode prevents any support for down-level replication, forcing you to remove any DCs not running Windows 2000 Servers. No domain master exists in a native-mode domain because all DCs become peers with each other. You can change from mixed-mode to native mode at any time, but this change is not reversible.

Domain Name System (DNS)—A standardized domain naming and location service resolves user-friendly host names into Internet Protocol (IP) addresses (RFC 1035). Exchange Servers use DNS to locate other application servers. Best practices recommend locating all Exchange 2000 Servers in a DNS zone that is created on a Windows 2000 DNS Server.

domain tree—A group of multiple Windows 2000 domains that allows resource sharing between domains. Although a tree can consist of one domain, it's best to join multiple domains in a hierarchical structure by creating a large and contiguous namespace. For example, you could create a parent domain of **Toys.com** and a child domain of **South.Toys.com**. In this case, both domains belong to one domain tree and function as one unit. Each domain contains portions of the directory database that are specific to users in that domain. All domains in a tree share a common schema and a common Global Catalog (GC).

DSAccess (and DSAccess cache)—A component of Exchange 2000 providing lookup services for other Exchange 2000 components such as Simple Mail Transfer Protocol (SMTP) and the Information Store service. Allows all Exchange Services to cache or store directory lookups without querying a Global Catalog (GC) Server. This feature of Exchange helps increase the performance of servers that run the Active Directory (AD) service. All types of directory access (except for address book searches) use **DSAccess** from a Messaging Application Programming interface (MAPI) client. The default cache consists of no more than 4MB of entries cached for five minutes.

DSProxy—The Exchange 2000 Service that sends directory requests on behalf of Messaging Application Programming Interface (MAPI) clients to Active Directory (AD) through a Name Service Provider Interface (NSPI). The NSPI forwards MAPI directory system calls to a Global Catalog (GC) Server. The System Attendant uses

Domain Name System (DNS) to find the closest AD Server at startup, and then passes this name to the DSProxy process, or dsproxy.dll. **DSProxy** works using Transmission Control Protocol/Internet Protocol (TCP/IP) and Internetwork Packet Exchange (IPX), but does not work using Network Basic Input/Output System (NetBIOS).

Dynamic Buffer Allocation (DBA)—Prior to Exchange 5.5, an administrator had to manually change the allocated size of the temporary memory store (buffer storage allocation) when the server needed more memory. Beginning with Exchange 5.5 and in Exchange 2000, the database engine was designed to grow or shrink the buffer store depending on the memory requirements of Exchange Server in relation to other services, like legacy Internet Information Server 4, concurrently running in the system. On demand, Exchange flushes memory pages and releases storage space to the competing services, hence it is a dynamic allocation process. The Cache Size counter in Performance measures the amount of memory reserved for **Store.exe**.

Dynamic Host Configuration (DHCP)—This protocol (RFC 1541) manages the dynamic assignment of network configuration information like Internet Protocol (IP) addressing and other related information like common router addressing. This centralized management of network information supports dynamic readdressing, for example, of workstations so that smaller ranges of IP addresses can serve larger numbers of users who require only intermittent rather than permanent (or static) network assignments. Management is also simplified by the ability to associate a range or scope of these dynamic network assignments with some common configuration, such as a router or specific name server.

enterprise—See forest.

EPOXY—See Exchange Interprocess Communication layer (EXIPC).

event sink—A COM-compliant script that is invoked or triggered by the occurrence of some event. Event sinks provide users with, for example, a programmable "hook" at the object, file system, or protocol levels, on which to logically attach the initiation of some programmed procedure. A protocol sink, for example, extends the features of SMTP, such as rejecting mail from certain recipients. The classic event sink is the system, application, and security logs in Event Viewer.

Exchange Conference Server (ECS)—An Exchange Service that allows users to host virtual meetings by using video, audio, and Chat Services. Server-side components perform conference-management and session-coordination services, allowing users to schedule online meetings or reserve meeting rooms using the Outlook 2000 client and the T.120 protocol. ECS contains a resource reservation agent and a conference controller.

Exchange Installable File System (ExIFS)—This Exchange mail system component provides the access to the Web Storage system typically through a logical storage volume labeled by default M: in the hosting operating system.

Exchange Interprocess Communication (EXIPC) (previously known as EPOXY)—A shared area in memory to which the store.exe process and all Internet Information Server (IIS) protocols in Exchange 2000 can read and write. This layer allows information to be switched rapidly between the IIS protocols running inside the **inetinfo.exe** process and the **store.exe** process. It is best to use the EXIPC layer for small packet transfers because of the shared memory used to communicate between the two processes that are involved. Exchange 2000 also uses the Central Queue Manager (CQM) for queue cleanup if a failure in one of the two processes occurs. EXIPC consists of a protocol DLL file that implements a binding facility and a shared memory heap.

Exchange Virtual Server (EVS)—The unit of failover found in an Exchange cluster group. Exchange 2000 now supports active/active clusters, so you can manage two or more nodes as one system. If one node fails, the other nodes of the cluster take over its clients. The cluster supports one or more EVSs, and each Virtual Server runs on one of the nodes. Multiple Virtual Servers can exist on one node. See also Virtual Server.

Extensible Storage Engine (ESE), also known as JET—Also known as Joint Engine Technology (JET), the database technology on which Exchange 2000 is based. It is also part of the Web Storage System (WSS). ESE uses a B-tree structure to store its data (an inverted balanced-tree structure representing a hierarchical organization of data), and every page in the database file is a node in the B-tree structure. One ESE database can hold up to 16TB (terabytes) of information, whereas the Active Directory (AD) database, which also uses ESE technology, can hold up to 32TB of data. An ESE database can perform online defragmentation, but does not reduce the size of the database involved. The ESE DLL file (esent.dll) uses a transacted database system with log files to guarantee that all committed transactions are stable. See also Joint Engine Technology (JET).

failover event—See Clustering Service.

field—A property of an item in the Web Storage System (WSS), or an area of a form. Often used interchangeably with property.

File Transfer Protocol (FTP)—One of the original online services, this particular protocol is the most efficient way to exchange files and documents which are typically larger than messages. Best practices recommend using FTP to move objects greater then 750KB in size.

filter—An object that limits the view of a folder in the Web Storage System (WSS).

five 9—Often referred to as "five 9s," this reliability measurement, 999.99% is the desired percentage of time a system service is accessible to users. The measurement, sometimes referred to as high availability, is calculated out to 5.39 minutes of total downtime in any 365-day period.

folder—Any container that stores other objects in the Web Storage System (WSS).

forest (also known as enterprise)—A group of one or more domain trees that allows different divisions to operate independently, while at the same time, communicating with other domains. All domain trees in a forest share a common schema and procedures on how domain objects communicate with each other. All domains in the forest share the same Global Catalog (GC) and configuration information. A direct relationship exists between an Exchange 2000 organization and an Active Directory (AD) forest. The Exchange 2000 Global Access List (GAL) can display users from only one forest.

form—An HTML page displaying the properties of items in the Web Storage System (WSS). Some forms both display and update items.

form registration—An item connecting data to an HTML page in the Web Storage System (WSS). You have to specify an item type for this connection.

Form Registry—A list of form registrations, or items connecting data to HTML pages in the Web Storage System (WSS).

front end (FE) and back end (BE)—A method of separating client access from client data for non-Messaging Application Programming Interface (MAPI) clients using Exchange 2000. These include Post Office Protocol 3 (POP3) clients and clients using Outlook Web Access (OWA). An FE/BE architecture allows you to use groups of servers as protocol servers that service the Hypertext Transport Protocol (HTTP) and POP3 protocols, and allow clients to connect directly to a BE Server that hosts client mailboxes or public folders. This type of architecture allows for the use of a unified namespace and helps to isolate BE Servers from attacks. You also can use FE/BE architecture to reduce the overhead involved in Secure Sockets Layer (SSL) encryption, which is handled by all FE Servers.

fully qualified domain name (FQDN)—The fully expanded or qualified domain name includes identification of the protocol and server program to which some service request is addressed. It also includes the second-level domain name such as coriolis.tch and other naming levels, such as a specific machine or server. Thus, a fully qualified domain name would include the precise location of host server, and if necessary, socket providing services within some enterprise namespace.

Global Address List (GAL)—The logical grouping or list within an enterprise address of all the recipient objects visible in the messaging organization.

Global Catalog (GC)—A storage location for attributes of any object created in Active Directory (AD). It is the central storehouse of information regarding objects in a domain tree or forest. AD produces content for the GC through the normal replication process between the domains that are part of the master directory. You use the attributes stored in the GC in common search operations (first name, last name, and so on). Use the GC to find objects in your network without having to fully replicate all information between domain controllers (DCs).

group—A collection of user accounts that helps you centralize administration by allowing you to assign permissions to a specified group rather than individually to each user in the group. A user object can belong to multiple group objects. Windows 2000 Server uses either a security group or a distribution group. The type of group determines how you use it. The Windows 2000 operating system (OS) uses only security groups to assign permissions to resources. Applications use distribution groups for functions unrelated to security. Only programs that work with Active Directory (AD) services can successfully use distribution groups.

Group Policy—A Windows 2000 administrative feature that helps to manage network objects, such as users, and resources, such as machines, within a domain or enterprise. Group policy simplifies administration because it can be applied to entire object groupings such as a site, domain, organizational unit, or enterprise, rather than exclusively single objects.

hash function—Provides message integrity checks and digital signatures. A hash function is generally faster than an encryption or digital signature algorithm. A hash function **H** is a transformation that takes an input **m**, and returns a fixed-size string called the hash value **h**. These functions have a variety of computational uses. The inputs can be of any length, and the outputs have a fixed length. A hashing algorithm is one way, meaning you can create a hash from a document, but you cannot recreate the document from a hash. A hash is not an encryption of the document. Most importantly, it's difficult to find two documents with the same hash.

hosted organization (also known as Virtual Server, virtual machine, virtual organization)—A scenario in which multiple companies are hosted in a single Exchange 2000 environment. In this case, both Active Directory (AD) and the Web Storage System (WSS) must be partitioned correctly, so that one company's data is not accessible to other companies. All companies can be hosted in one forest within one domain, where organizational units (OUs) partition each company's users. Alternatively, each company can be hosted in a separate forest, so that each company's users can contain a distinct AD schema. Each separate company requires its own unified namespace, such as **www.baseball-for-me.com**.

HTTP-DAV—See Web Distributed Authoring and Versioning (WebDAV).

Installable File System (IFS)—See Web Storage System (WSS).

Instant Messaging (IM)—A service that allows users to see presence information (such as online, offline, or busy) for other users. Users can send instantaneous communications to each other using components found at both the client and the server. The IM Server is part of the **inetinfo.exe** process and is implemented as an Internet Server Application Programming Interface (ISAPI) extension. All IM communication uses the Rendezvous Protocol (RVP), which is a subset of Hypertext Transport Protocol (HTTP). You must use an IM client (which consists of a client user interface, the Microsoft Network provider, and support for RVP) to log on to IM servers.

Instant Messaging and Presence Protocol (IMPP)—The protocol that clients use when connecting to an Instant Messaging (IM) Server. It is more formally known as the Rendezvous Protocol (RVP) (it will become known as IMPP in a future ratified standard). All IM activity occurs over Hypertext Transport Protocol (HTTP) and port 80, so IMPP (or RVP) allows you to transmit presence information (such as online, offline, or busy) and IMs over the Internet between dissimilar networks or domains.

Internet Messaging Access Protocol version 4 (IMAP4)—A messaging protocol used to access email or bulletin board messages stored on a mail server. It is more advanced than P*ost Office Protocol* 3 (POP3) allowing email clients to access remote message stores as if they were local resources. IMAP's capability to access messages from more than one computer has become extremely important, as more companies and individuals rely on electronic messaging. IMAP also can do offline processing.

Internet Protocol Security (IPSec)—This developing standard provides security measures at the OSI network or Internet Protocol layer, where messages are exchanged as packets of data. This layer is below the OSI application, presentation, and session layers, and thus not typically accessible by a user. IPSec is especially important in securing or hardening the channel of communication through which data is transferred in a virtual private network or VPN.

Internet Relay Chat (IRC)—A TCP/IP information protocol that uses a set of rules and conventions to provide of text-based form of synchronous communication or chatting across a network channel. Popular IRC clients include mIRC and pIRCh on the Windows platform.

Intrusion Detection System (IDS)—Intrusion detection systems is designed to detect when an intruder has breached a firewall, and can include several components such as algorithms that define authorized user behavior, log-generating capabilities, and a management interface. The algorithm monitors threshold barriers; activity profiles and known attack signatures and can perform automated responses when a deviation is detected. The logs provide an activity baseline upon which to predict network attacks and develop countermeasures.

item—Any document, message, or similar knowledge resource located in the Web Storage System (WSS). These objects are URL addressable and have different properties, including a default content stream.

item type—Every item and folder in the Web Storage System (WSS) has a type stored in its content class property. It defines which properties are likely to appear on the item, as well as which HTML pages furnish the user interface. An item type is also known as its content class.

Joint Engine Technology (JET)—The underlying database technology used in Exchange 4 and 5. This technology has been replaced by the Extensible Storage Engine (ESE) structure of Exchange 5.5 and Exchange 2000. It also lies at the core of the Access database system and provides functionality and structure to other applications, including the File Replication Service and Windows Internet Naming Service (WINS).

Kerberos authentication—Developed in Unix systems, Windows 2000 uses this protocol of authenticated requests for network services. Service providers within an enterprise require a ticket distributed by a special Authentication Server to respond to any service request. Thus, a user must be authenticated in order to be given a ticket-granting ticket or session key. This session key is sent to a Ticket Granting Server, which validates the ticket and returns it to the consumer requesting the service. The consumer then sends the authorizing ticket to the service provider and receives the service. This exchange of tickets is especially suitable in environments with distributed services, such as those described in the .NET Framework.

Key Management Service (KM Service)—A specialized service designed to manage security keys for recipients requiring authenticated security credentials in an enterprise. Exchange runs an optional service that is integrated with Certificate Services and performs this function. KM Service also maintains a listing of expired or revoked keys called a key history that may be needed to decrypt old or orphaned messages.

Knowledge Management (KM)—This concept we believe represents a change or gestalt shift away from data processing to a more comprehensive approach in the organizing of knowledge that arises out of the combination of data resources, contextual associations, and people. This kind of management deals with the gathering, organizing, refining, and dissemination of information. KM involves more than just the categorization of information and its retrieval through data mining; it focuses on the relationship between the information itself, the contextual environment in which it is stored and retrieved. These activities lead to the need for the information producing what is sometimes called a knowledge map report.

Lightweight Directory Access Protocol (LDAP)—A client/server protocol used to access directory services. It was initially used as a front end (FE) to the X.500 directory service standard, but it's usually used with other types of directory servers. It does not require the upper layers of the Open Systems Interconnection (OSI) model and is a simple protocol to implement for clients accessing a directory-based operating system (OS). The LDAP model is based on information about objects in the form of attributes, which have values associated with a certain type.

Lightweight Directory Interchange Format (LDIF)—This ASCII file format is used to share data and enable synchronization between LDAP servers often called Directory System Agents that support the lookup of resources or recipients in or across enterprises.

Link State Algorithm (LSA)—Also known as a propagation protocol, this mathematical procedure or algorithm, developed Dijkstra in 1959, forms the foundation of the Open Shortest Path First (OSPF) protocol used by many routers today. Sometimes referred to as the Dijkstra Algorithm, LSA propagates the current state of the system in realtime to every server in the organization, which helps eliminate message loops or bounces between servers. This link-propagation protocol has replaced the Gateway Routing Table (GWART) used in Exchange Server 5.5. Link State Information (LSI) is usually transferred between routing groups over TCP port 691.

mail-based replication (MBR)—A method of moving directory-related information between sites in Exchange Server 5.5 organizations, by placing this information in a mail message and using the Message Transfer Agent (MTA) to deliver the data. Active Directory (AD) also uses this mechanism to replicate directory information within Exchange 2000 using Simple Mail Transfer Protocol (SMTP).

Microsoft Management Console (MMC)—This application provides a scalable and extensible framework within which Microsoft or third-party Independent Software Vendors (ISVs) can attach collections of graphical user interface (GUI) consoles or toolkits. The MMC is a standardized and easily portable container in which these administrative tools will operate in some standardized manner. It is significant that the user can combine various components in whatever combination is needed, based on function or security access of the intended user.

Message Database (MDB)—A collection of information represented by private or public stores, depending on the form of data found within the store. One Exchange Server can host up to 20 distinct messaging databases, represented by five private or public stores contained within four separate units of storage known as storage groups (SGs).

Message Database Encapsulated Format (MDBEF)—A database format implemented in Exchange Server. Exchange 2000 uses MDB files to represent database files found within storage groups (SGs). Each server can have multiple database files residing within multiple SGs.

Message Digest 5 (MD5) algorithm—Takes a message of arbitrary length and produces a 128-bit fingerprint or message digest of the input. It is not possible to produce two messages with the same message digest. The MD5 algorithm, developed by Professor Ronald Rivest of MIT, is intended for digital signature applications, in which a large file must be compressed in a secure manner before it is encrypted with a private key. MD5 is a way to verify data integrity, and is much more reliable than **checksum** or other commonly used methods.

Message Transfer Agent (MTA)—A part of Exchange Server used for addressing and transporting messages. Legacy versions of Exchange based the MTA on the X.400 standard, which supported multiple transport mechanisms, including Transmission Control Protocol/Internet Protocol (TCP/IP) and X.25. Exchange 2000 still uses an X.400-based MTA, but only to establish a route between two routing groups, or between a routing group and an external X.400 messaging system.

Messaging Application Programming Interface (MAPI)—Developed by Microsoft and other companies to allow Windows-based applications to access a variety of messaging systems, including Microsoft (MS) Mail and Novell's Message Handling System. MAPI also allows mail-aware applications to exchange both mail and data with others on a network. MAPI consists of a standard set of C functions stored in a Dynamic Link Library (DLL) file. Developers who use Active Server Pages (ASPs) access the MAPI library by using Collaborative Data Objects (CDOs). Visual Basic developers can access MAPI functions through a translation layer.

metabase—Meta means "an underlying definition or description," as well as "more comprehensive or fundamental." Thus, a metabase is a database in which Internet Information Server (IIS) stores most of the Internet site configuration information within Windows 2000. Applications can manipulate this metabase via a distributed Component Object Model (COM) interface and through an Active Directory Service Interface (ADSI) provider.

metabase update service—A service in Exchange 2000 that reads data from Active Directory (AD) and places it in the Internet Information Server (IIS) metabase. It facilitates making configuration changes to remote systems.

metadata—As mentioned in the definition of metabase, meta means "an underlying definition or description," as well as "more comprehensive or fundamental." Thus, metadata is a definition or description of data. This term describes the structure of data within a process such as the Web Storage System (WSS).

Glossary

mixed-mode site—Also known as a mixed-vintage site, a legacy Exchange 5.x site that also consists of Exchange 2000 Servers.

multidocument interface (MDI)—Microsoft Windows is actually a programming interface within which applications run in a standardized and somewhat predictable fashion. Since its inception, the interface has provided a way for a user to work in several areas of display space at the same time. Each space defines a separate document which has the capability of interacting with other open documents in the viewing area.

Multipoint Control Unit (MCU)—Also known as Multipoint Conferencing Server (MCS), the central connection for a multipoint videoconferencing session. It provides connection points to clients and manages the distribution of video and audio streams. It also provides the necessary transport services for data and application sharing.

Multipurpose Internet Mail Extensions (MIME)—Is an extension of SMTP that provided for the transfer of an attached object of different kinds of data files. The MIME extension helps the message recipient recognize and handle the data attached to the SMTP message. MIME provided extensibility to SMTP. New MIME types are standardized by being registered with ICANN, the Internet naming authority.

Name Service Provider Interface (NSPI)—A component of **DSProxy** that sends directory requests to Active Directory (AD) on behalf of Messaging Application Programming Interface (MAPI) clients. It forwards all MAPI requests to a Global Catalog (GC) Server without opening any Remote Procedure Call (RPC) packets in the process.

namespace—Usually refers to the Domain Name System (DNS) namespace established within a Windows 2000 forest. It is a distributed database organized as a hierarchical tree. Every node of the tree is referred to as a domain. A forest is usually represented by a contiguous namespace of parent and child domain hierarchies. An example of such a namespace is a parent domain of coriolis.tch and a child domain of east.coriolis.tch.

naming context—A section of Active Directory (AD) with its own properties, including replication configuration information. You use a naming context to define the boundary for information contained with the AD database. The units of replication in AD are found within the domain-naming context, the schema-naming context, and the configuration-naming context. Exchange 2000 stores most of its information in the configuration-naming context, which is replicated to every domain controller (DC) within a Windows 2000 forest.

native mode—An Exchange 2000 organization that consists exclusively of Exchange 2000 Servers and provides maximum flexibility and features. This mode of operation does not support legacy Exchange Servers. The combination of legacy servers with Exchange 2000 Servers is called a mixed mode configuration.

Network News Transfer Protocol (NNTP)—Described by Request for Comments (RFC) 997, the primary protocol that clients and servers use to manage information posted on a Usenet newsgroup. It replaced the original Unix-to-Unix-Copy Protocol (UUCP), which describes a set of Unix programs used to send files between different Unix systems or commands to be executed on other systems. A NNTP Server manages the global network of Usenet newsgroups and includes the server at your Internet service provider (ISP). A NNTP client is included as part of a standard Web browser, or you can use a separate client program called a newsreader. Most NNTP communications use TCP port 119.

nondelivery report (NDR)—This special message is notification that a message was never delivered to the intended receiver.

Object Linking and Embedding for Databases (OLE DB)—Microsoft's low-level Application Programming Interface (API) used to access a variety of data sources. OLE DB includes the Structured Query Language (SQL) capabilities of the Microsoft-sponsored Open Database Connectivity (ODBC) interface, as well as access to data other than SQL data. OLE DB uses a set of routines for reading and writing data. The "Object" in OLE DB consists of a data source object, a session object, and a command object.

one-hop connectivity—This term implies that two servers are directly connected to each other, rather than through a router-router connection. Each router-router connection requires the passing of a message from one router to its default gateway; this transfer is considered a hop. A maximum number of hops is allowed to prevent a message packet from traveling in infinite circles throughout a network.

Organizational Unit (OU)—This logical container acts as an administrative unit to organize AD objects including users, groups, machines, and other OUs. It is the smallest unit within which administrative privileges can be delegated.

Outlook Web Access (OWA)—A way of accessing email using TCP port 80 (or another port if port 80 is not available) from a standard Web browser. You install OWA when you first install Exchange 2000. It requires Internet Explorer 3 (IE3) or later, or Netscape Navigator 3, or later. These versions support HTML features such as frames and the Secure Sockets Layer (SSL). Users have access to functionality for email, calendars, group scheduling, and basic public folders. This application cannot replace the full-featured Outlook client for 16-bit Windows operating systems (OSs) or Macintosh. Two features that are *not* available when you use OWA are personal address books (which are stored locally on your workstation) and the spell checker.

policy—A group of settings applied to the same class of objects within Active Directory (AD). For example, recipient policies can control email address generation and are more flexible than the legacy site addressing features found in Exchange 5.5 sites. You can use filters to regulate which recipients the policies apply to.

Post Office Protocol version 3 (POP3)—An Internet-standard protocol for receiving email messages. It is a client-server protocol in which an Internet access provider receives and holds mail. POP3 is built into the Netscape and Internet Explorer (IE) browsers. POP3 is considered a store-and-forward service that uses a conventional TCP/IP port number of 100 to receive email. POP3 works best using one computer and offline message access, in which messages are downloaded and then deleted from the mail server. The offline mode of access that POP3 supports effectively ties the user to one computer for message storage and manipulation. POP3 is often contrasted with Internet Messaging Access Protocol 4 (IMAP4), which is more of a remote file server.

Pretty Good Privacy (PGP)—This low-cost or freeware software package was developed by Philip Zimmerman to provide private, secure email to all Internet users. It uses a variation of the public asymmetric key encryption algorithm. It is designed to integrate into most popular software packages and typically works without user intervention to decrypt messages or verify digital signatures.

property—The smallest unit of storage in the Web Storage System (WSS). It has a name, a data type, and other attributes. In the context of a form, properties are often called fields. In the context of a view, properties are often called columns.

protocol farm—A grouping of Protocol Virtual Servers that can operate together to provide one protocol service for redundancy purposes. It can even span multiple computers and serve as a primary connection point for users in an organization. Users can access information without having to know its physical location.

public folder connection agreement (PFCA)—A connection agreement that replicates public folder objects between an Exchange 5.5 directory and Active Directory (AD). Each PFCA is configured as a two-way connection agreement and replicates between the site-naming context in the Exchange 5.5 site and the appropriate System Objects container in AD.

public folder tree (also known as public folder root and top-level hierarchy [TLH])—Previous versions of Exchange Server allowed organizations to contain only one root-level public folder named All Public Folders. Exchange 2000 creates multiple root-level public folders or public folder trees that appear in addition to the All Public Folders tree. Every public folder hierarchy you configure has its own database in the Web Storage System (WSS). Multiple public stores run under one process. The default All Public Folders tree is available to all Messaging Application

Programming Interface (MAPI), Network News Transfer Protocol (NNTP), and Hypertext Transport Protocol (HTTP) clients. Other public folder trees are available only to NNTP and Web clients, not to Outlook 2000 clients.

Queuing Engine—This mail system component manages the message-delivery queues through various components like the message categorizer. For example, the engine places messages in holding queues following determination of where a message is to be delivered until an appropriate delivery route is determined. After the route is known, the engine sends the message on for delivery.

rapid application development (RAD)—This software development concept attempts to propose tools and methodologies that create software faster and of higher quality through consolidation of requirements, prototyping and testing, modulization and reuse of components, milestone-driven production schedules, and more open and candid reviewing processes.

RC2—A widespread, conventional secret-key block encryption algorithm considered as a replacement for Data Encryption Standard (DES). It is used in popular packages like Lotus Notes, Microsoft Windows, Internet Explorer, and Netscape Navigator. The input and output block sizes are each 64 bits long, and the key size is variable, ranging from 1 to 128 bytes. The current implementation of RC2 uses 8 bytes. This algorithm is easier to implement and runs almost twice as fast as the DES standard on legacy16-bit microprocessors IBM AT (Advanced Technology) hardware.

Realtime Collaboration (RTC)—This collection of services provides users with synchronous forms of communication such as Instant Messaging, online conferencing, and Chat Services. Tools like NetMeeting provide group participation, the sharing of documents, files, and applications.

Recipient Update Service (RUS)—Generates Simple Mail Transfer Protocol (SMTP) and proxy addresses for users. It checks whether any object in the forest has the same address; if it does, RUS appends a number to this duplicate address to make it unique. Every domain that contains objects with Exchange settings requires one server running RUS. It is a good idea to create separate domain controllers (DCs) dedicated to running this service.

registration—See form registration.

Remote Authentication Dial-in User Service (RADIUS)—This combination of protocol and software provide communication between remote access servers and a central authenticating server so that identity and permission of dial-up users can be efficiently managed across wide-area networks or a widely roaming user population. Centralization of policy provides more secure and easily administrated management of roaming users. The central administration of the user population also provides better accounting and auditing control.

Remote Procedure Calls (RPCs)—Also known as a function call or subroutine call, a protocol that one program uses to request a service from a program located in another computer without understanding all the network details involved. RPC uses the client/server model, where the requesting program is the client and the service-providing program is the server. RPC is a synchronous operation, meaning that the requesting program is suspended until all results from the remote procedure have been returned. This protocol covers both the Transport layer and the Application layer in the Open Systems Interconnection (OSI) model of network communications. It allows development of applications, including multiple programs distributed in a network.

Rendezvous Protocol (RVP)—The Microsoft proprietary protocol used between the Microsoft Network (MSN) Messenger service and the Instant Messaging (IM) Server that is implemented on Exchange 2000. RVP uses an extended subset of WebDAV with Extensible Markup Language (XML) that is used to send subscriptions and notifications between Instant Messaging (IM) clients and servers.

resource—An object that represents facilities in Active Directory (AD). In the context of collaboration, you use this object for data or videoconferences using components such as Instant Messaging (IM) or Chat.

resource mailbox—An object in the Windows 2000 Active Directory (AD) directory service that references a resource able to receive messages. No matter where this resource resides, it has a recipient object in AD. A resource mailbox in Exchange 2000 must exhibit a direct one-to-one correspondence with a Windows 2000 security principal.

Routing Engine (RE)—One of the three primary components of Exchange Server, the others being the Information Store service and the System Attendant. The RE service coordinates the transfer of messages between Exchange Servers. If this particular service shuts down, Exchange can no longer move messages throughout your network. It directs messages to their intended destinations and makes sure all messages arrive intact.

routing group—A group of servers that communicate with each other over a high-speed local area network (LAN) connection. Exchange 2000 uses routing groups instead of Exchange sites. Information between servers in the same routing groups flows immediately using the Simple Mail Transfer Protocol (SMTP) protocol, not a connector. A routing group helps you lay out the physical network topology of your connected servers. To be included in a routing group, all Exchange Servers must belong to the same Windows 2000 forest and have a permanent SMTP connection to one another.

Routing Group Connector (RGC)—A Simple Mail Transfer Protocol (SMTP)-based connector that is functionally equivalent to the Exchange 5.5 Site Connector. It allows servers in a routing group to act as routing servers and allows you to choose multiple servers in the routing group as bridgehead servers for either end of the connector. An RGC provides fault tolerance if one of the servers in the routing group fails for any reason. Multiple bridgeheads help you control which servers can send or receive messages between routing groups. You can use an RGC to connect to prior versions of Exchange configured with the Site Connector, which uses Remote Procedure Calls (RPCs).

Routing Group Master (RGM)—This is the specially designated Exchange 2000 Server that administers and propagates link state table (LST) information to all the participating servers in a routing group. This particular server updates the LST based on information about changes in link state detected by routing group members.

routing object—An object used to program Exchange Server's Routing Engine (RE) behavior. This object allows you to create process definitions that define the series of states to be tracked by the RE. Exchange 5.5 sometimes included routing object libraries or helper objects for creating document routing applications. These were designed for Messaging Application Programming Interface (MAPI)-based email applications. Exchange 2000 is fully compatible with routing objects and other MAPI applications. You use a routing object in applications that are modeled as business processes.

routing service—Uses a Link State Table (LST) to find the shortest path between two routing groups. Any server that cannot find a route for a message using the LST cannot attempt to deliver that message.

schema—The logical design plan that defines how attributes and methods of various objects and components are maintained by AD. When you modify the schema by using the Microsoft Management Console (MMC) or specialized software, the AD schema is extended with attributes that start with **ms-Exch**.

Secure Sockets Layer (SSL)—This protocol is the most common form of security on the Internet. It operates just below the OSI session layer and is included in most popular browser clients. Security data is passed through a specially designated TCP socket, 443. The protocol uses asymmetric encryption and digital certificates.

Security Identifier (SID)—This security object is a unique label that identifies a security principal such as a user, service, or machine that requires security credentials.

security principal—An object that can log on to a Windows 2000 domain and access some or all of that network's resources. With respect to Exchange 2000, a security principal is a mailbox-enabled user that can access network resources, as well as send and receive mail. A nonsecurity principal cannot access network resources and has email sent to an external address.

service location record (SRV record)—A resource record used by the DNS Server to specify the location of a specific service and protocol provided by a hosting server.

Simple Authentication and Security Layer (SASL)—Defined in Request for Comments (RFC) 2222, adds authentication support to connection-based protocols. To use this feature, a protocol includes a command for identifying and authenticating users to a server. A security layer is usually inserted between the protocol and the connection.

Simple Message Transfer Protocol (SMTP)—The heart of Exchange 2000 transport services, SMTP is the Internet standard for transporting messages and is based on Requests for Comments (RFCs) 821 and 822. When you install Windows 2000, a basic SMTP service is automatically installed as part of the **inetinfo.exe** process. This basic service supports many of the Extended SMTP (ESMTP) commands such as **helo**, **mail**, and **data**. Although only one SMTP service exists, you can configure multiple virtual SMTP servers on every Exchange 2000 Server in your organization. Exchange 2000 enhances the delivery functions of the SMTP service that comes preinstalled with Windows 2000.

sink—See event sink.

site—A range of Internet Protocol (IP) subnets. Active Directory (AD) uses this concept to establish boundaries for replication traffic. A site also helps clients in a remote site to locate their domain controller (DC) for validation purposes. Exchange 5.5 used this concept to describe a logical group of servers that could be referenced without consideration of their physical location.

Site Consistency Checker (SCC)—Also known as the Site Knowledge Consistency Checker (SKCC), runs within the Site Replication Service, which is responsible for replicating Exchange 5.x site and configuration information to the configuration-naming partition of Active Directory (AD). This allows an Exchange 2000 Server to be represented in the Exchange 5.5 site list so that earlier versions of Exchange Server can send messages to the Exchange 2000 Server. The SCC is an improved version of the Knowledge Consistency Checker (KCC) from Exchange 5.5 and ensures that knowledge consistency is kept for sites and administrative groups when they coexist between Exchange 5.5 and Exchange 2000.

Site Replication Service—A component that maintains two versions of the Exchange Server directory during mixed-mode operation. An instance of the Site Replication Service is installed on the first Exchange 2000 Server that is introduced into an Exchange 5.5 site and allows directory replication between the two versions of Exchange. It effectively transforms the Active Directory (AD) version of an Exchange directory into an Exchange 5.5 site and allows an Exchange 2000 Server to resemble an Exchange 5.5 Server. The Site Replication Service is displayed in the Exchange 5.5 Administrator program as the Exchange 5.5 Directory Service.

specific management functional area (SMFA)—RFC 1095 delineates terminology used to identify various structures in the OSI application layer. Using a common management information protocol, various functional areas including configuration, performance, fault management, accounting and security are defined. These specific management areas are found in all network operating systems and help categorize various components and services.

storage group (SG)—A representation of a fixed database layout within Exchange 2000. It corresponds to an instance of the Extensible Storage Engine (ESE) with its own set of transaction log files. Up to four SGs per server are supported in Exchange 2000. Each SG supports up to five databases, which can be either a mailbox store or a public folder store. All transactions for all databases in one SG are in one set of log files. You can restore a database within a SG without affecting the other databases in the same SG.

store—The name given to the storage structure on an Exchange Server. Each store is found in a storage group (SG). Two kinds of stores exist: a mailbox store for messages and a public folder store for public folder use. Each store consists of both EDB (Exchange database) and STM (streaming media) files. You cannot create a store until you have created the SG. Upon installation of Exchange 2000, you see a default SG named First Storage Group, which contains one mailbox and one public folder store.

streaming media files (STM)—This file format is transmitted across a network in a continuous or streaming fashion using data packets running typically on a fast communication technology such as broadband.

System Attendant—One of the three key services in Exchange 2000, the others being the Information Store Service and the Routing Engine (RE) Service. The System Attendant is considered the background manager for key Exchange system services because it helps maintain Link State Tables (LSTs) used for message delivery and monitors the connections between servers. It monitors many behind-the-scenes activities that are vital to an optimal configuration of Exchange Server.

T.120—This standard contains a series of protocols and services that support realtime data communications. It is a comprehensive specification that resolves complex technological issues and was established by the Telecommunications Standardization Sector of the International Telecommunications Union (ITU-T). Many major vendors, including Microsoft, MCI, and Cisco Systems, are implementing T.120-based products. For example, this protocol is used with Exchange Data Conferencing and Video Conferencing together with the Microsoft NetMeeting client. The T.120 infrastructure can work with both unicast and multicast data packets simultaneously, providing a flexible solution for a mixed multicast/unicast network.

Total Cost of Ownership (TCO)—This financially based method of measurement quantifies both direct and indirect costs of owning some form of information technology. Aside from capital investment necessary to buy assets like hardware and software, indirect costs include support and maintenance, licensing and subscriptions, and training.

Unsolicited Bulk Email (UBE) and Unsolicited Commercial Email (UCE)—More commonly referred to as spam, the receipt of junk mail or general mailings compiled from mail lists that indiscriminately target mail address for receiving messages.

user—An object that can log on to a domain and gain access to network resources, or log on to a computer and gain access to resources on that computer. Windows 2000 supports domain users, local users, and built-in user accounts. Users who can access network resources can be either mail enabled or mailbox enabled, depending on where their email is sent.

user principal name (UPN)—A friendly name for a user, used in place of a user's fully qualified distinguished name (for instance, using jsmith instead of the distinguished name CN=Jsmith, OU=Marketing, OU=East, O=Baseball, Inc, DC=Baseball, DC=com, and so on). The UPN is a combination of the username and Domain Name System (DNS) name of the domain where the user resides. For example, if Jim Smith resides in the **baseball.com** domain tree, his UPN would be **Jsmith@baseball.com**. The UPN does not depend on the distinguished name, so Jim Smith could be moved to another domain without disrupting his logon. A UPN is an attribute of a security principal object.

view—A representation or rendering of the contents of a folder in the Web Storage System (WSS) as an HTML table. Every row in the table represents an item, and every column in the table represents a specific property of the item.

virtual root—A shortcut to a physical storage location that can reside anywhere on the network. Internet Information Server (IIS) uses it to display the resources of a Web server. A virtual root allows users to connect to resources by using a user-friendly path instead of a strict and complex navigation hierarchy.

virtual server—Allows you to support users with different configuration needs, such as message formats. You create a Virtual Server for each instance of a default protocol that comes installed with Exchange 2000. For example, a default Hypertext Transport Protocol (HTTP) Protocol Server is created during installation, but you can configure multiple HTTP Virtual Servers based on this default Protocol Server, using configurations for authentication or message formats. A unique Internet Protocol (IP) port number and address specify each Virtual Server defined for each protocol. You can create a protocol Virtual Server for File Transfer Protocol (FTP), Hypertext Transfer Protocol (HTTP), Internet Message Access Protocol 4 (IMAP4), Network News Transfer Protocol (NNTP), Simple Mail Transfer Protocol (SMTP), and Post Office Protocol 3 (POP3).

Web Distributed Authoring and Versioning (WebDAV)—This standard is an extension of HTTP 1.1 and provides write support for the collaborative authoring now common within and across networks. The standard extends editing and file management features between local and remote machines. Other important collaborative features include concurrency controls, which prevent accidental overwriting of differing versions of data, namespace manipulation, search and locating features, and property setting and control features.

Web Storage System (WSS)—A technology that provides local and remote users with access to Exchange Server's file systems. It is a hierarchical database that manages documents and email messages. Every Web Store exists as a folder on the local machine so applications can store files in this store from either local or remote locations. The folder can be seen under a default M: drive that is given the share name of **BackOfficeStorage**. Any user can access any data in this store, including messages and documents, by using a Universal Naming Convention (UNC) name within a Web browser. The Web Store also includes an indexing feature that allows users to rapidly discover Web Store content. Developers can access this system using a programming language that supports the Component Object Model (COM).

Windows Internet Naming Service (WINS)—This service is part of both Microsoft NT and Windows 2000 and automatically manages the resolution of NETBIOS names to IP addresses. It complements DHCP in locating servers by name.

WSS—See Web Storage System.

X.509—A standard published by the International Telecommunications Union (ITU-T) in 1988, as part of the X.500 directory recommendations. It defines a standard certificate format. The Internet Privacy Enhanced Mail Request for Comments (RFC), published in 1993, included specifications for a public key infrastructure (PKI) based on these X.509 certificates.

Index

<% %> tags, 751

A

Access control
  Chat Service, 229–230
  digital dashboards, 682–683
  mail-enabled objects, 336
  POP3 Virtual Servers, 519
  public folders, 367, 369
  security descriptors, 336
Access rights. *See also* Permissions.
  Delegation of Control Wizard, 220–221, 334–336, 365
  Global Address List views, 336
  public folder views, 337
Access, XML transformation documents, 760
Accounts
  account vulnerability, Exchange 2000, 273
  administrative models, 535, 537, 539
  disabled user account mailboxes, 161
  mailbox-enabled objects, 138
  migrating foreign messaging systems to Exchange 2000, 618–619
Action tables, 714
Actions, adding to states, 727
Active Directory
  administrative roles, 116
  Delegation of Control Wizard, 334–336, 365
  directory service components, 108–109
  DNS queries, 328–329
  domain structure and server management, 225–226
  domains, configuring, 386–388
  enrolling users, 255
  Exchange 2000 overview, 48
  forests, configuring, 380–386
  GC Servers, 114–115
  implementation, planning, 380
  integrating DNS Service, 329–331
  mailboxes, configuring, 388–389
  message system coexistence, 619
  namespaces, 109–110, 126
  permission management, 220–221
  recipient management and domain structure, 217–218, 220
  resource management, 571
  routing information, 187
  security overview, 50–51
  structure, 109–114
  topology. *See* Active Directory topology.
  troubleshooting Active Directory components, 593–594
Active Directory Connector Manager snap-in, 340–341
Active Directory Connector tool. *See* ADC tool.
Active Directory Delegation of Control Wizard, 220–221, 334–336, 365
Active Directory Domains and Trusts snap-in, 212
Active Directory Installation Wizard, 112
Active Directory Sites and Services snap-in, 212, 213
Active Directory topology, 61
Active Directory Users and Computers snap-in
  managing Exchange 2000 Services, 213
  monitoring object attributes, 576
  server management overview, 528
Active Server Pages. *See* ASP.
Active/active clustering, 279
ActiveX components, 751, 752, 772
ActiveX controls, security issues, 271
ActiveX Data Objects. *See* ADO.
Actual recipients, 137
AD. *See* Active Directory.
ADC tool
  connection agreements, 338–340, 370
  distribution lists, 344–345
  group types and scopes, 343–344

installing, 370
legacy recipient objects, 147–148
overview, 148–149, 337–338
public folder interoperability, 341–343
replication issues, 341
synchronizing object attributes, 340–341
universal groups, 344–345
Address book views. *See* Address lists.
Address lists, 58
Address resolution, 463, 465
Address Space tab
Lotus cc:Mail Connector Properties sheet, 651
Novell GroupWise Connector Properties sheet, 663
AD-integrated zones, DNS, 330
Administering Exchange 2000 Servers. *See* Server management.
Administering recipients. *See* Managing recipients.
Administering servers. *See* Managing Exchange 2000 Servers.
Administrative groups
administrative models, 534, 535, 536, 537
administrative roles, 116, 335, 367
assigning permissions, 169
chat communities, creating, 418
creating, 168
delegating control, 335, 367
managing Exchange 2000 Servers, 225, 226
mixed centralized and distributed management, 537, 538
planning routing strategy, 437
recipient objects, 141
system administration overview, 525
viewing in System Manager, 170
Administrative models
accounts and mailboxes, 535, 537, 539
administrative groups, 534, 535, 536, 537
centralized model, 145, 218, 223, 224, 458, 533–535
delegated model, 219
distributed model, 147, 223, 224, 459, 536–537
Exchange 2000 Servers, 223–224
mixed administrative model, 223, 224, 537–539
planning routing strategy, 458
recipient management, 145–147, 218–219
routing groups, 458, 459, 534, 536, 538
selecting, 525
Administrative needs assessment, deployment planning, 82
Administrative objectives, deployment planning, 68
Administrative passwords, changing, 245
Administrative roles, 116, 335, 367
Administrative services, implementation planning, 104
Administrative tools
Delegation of Control Wizard, 220, 334–336, 365
Event Viewer, 216
Exchange 2000 tools, 213–215
Exchange Administrative Delegation Wizard, 221
Exchange Monitoring and Status Tool, 213–214
Global Address List views, 336
implementation planning, 105
maintenance tools, 575–576
Message Tracking Center, 214, 472
MMC. *See* MMC.
monitoring tools, 575–576
Performance Monitor, 216
planning Exchange 2000 Services, 209–210, 211
public folder views, 337
Queue Viewer, 214, 578–582
server monitors, 577
system administration overview, 528–529
system management tools, 391
Windows 2000 tools, 216
ADO
ADO connections, establishing, 776
Exchange 2000 support, 745–746
file and folder access, 750–751
objects and object model, 748–750
overview, 748
ADSI Edit utility, 105, 768
Adult Content filter, Outlook 2000 client, 324, 356
Advanced queuing engine
inbound message processing, 444–445
routing overview, 432–433
Transport Core components, 179–180
Advanced tab, Lotus cc:Mail Connector Properties sheet, 650–651

Affinities, public folders, 121–122, 227–228, 533
Agreements. *See* Connection agreements.
Anonymous Access Authentication method, 303
Anti-Spam Project, 359
Antiviral programs. *See* Viruses and virus control.
APIs
  ASP.NET, 763–764
  implementing Web Services, 673
  virus-scanning API, 326
Application ASP object, 752, 772
Application Center 2000, 762
Application development. *See also* Digital dashboards; Workflow applications.
  Exchange 2000 overview, 49
  Web Storage System overview, 46
AQ. *See* Advanced queuing engine.
ASP scripts
  ADO connections, establishing, 776
  connecting to data stores, 773
  connection strings, 774, 775
  contact information in messages, 777
  content type, **Response** ASP object, 777
  entrance/exit consoles, 780
  event sinks, registering, 771
  Global.asa file, creating, 772
  opening connections, 775
  sending email using SMTP, 778
ASP.NET
  API overview, 763–764
  Global.asa file, 752, 772
  overview, 751, 752
Asymmetric keys, 234
Asynchronous events, WSS, 676, 717
Asynchronous replication, 200
Attachment Security patch, 360
Attachments
  email security, 540
  Outlook security, 270, 327–328, 360
  security issues, 271
  viruses and virus control, 327–328
Attribute mapping, 340–341
Attributes, GCs, 199
Auditorium channels, Chat Service, 421
AUTH command, 178
Authentication
  external network security, 267
  File System Digital Dashboard, 683
  IM Service, 232
  Kerberos authentication, 51
  methods (list), 303
  security overview, 317
  SMTP Virtual Servers, 302
  trust relationships, 113–114
Authentication tab
  Chat Communities Properties sheet, 248
  Mailbox Store Properties sheet, 406
Author mode, MMC, restricting, 241
Author role, public folders, 369
Automatic Directory Exchange, 625

B

/b switch, **ESEUTIL** utility, 584
BackOffice Resource Kit, 87
Backup utility, 239, 285–286
Backups and restoration
  backing up databases, 284
  backing up mailbox stores, 49
  Backup utility, 285–286
  data to be backed up, 285
  database consistency, maintaining, 288–289, 313
  database stores, 296
  ESE architecture, 277–278
  mailbox stores, 290
  offline backups, 283, 285, 289
  online backups, 283, 285, 289, 586
  planning backups, 283
  planning restoration, 287
  recovering backed-up mailboxes, 295
  retention periods, 292, 293, 560
  strategies, 279–280
  system state data, 285
  types of backups, 283–284
Bacteria, denial-of-service attacks, 272
Bandwidth consumption, public folders, 121–122
Baselines, performance, 574
Basic Authentication method, 303
Basic disks, RAID configurations, 280
Bastion hosts, 274
Benchmarking, 429
Binary Data Transfer, 177
8-bit clean feature, 177
BizTalk Server 2000, 762
BlackMail, 359
Blocking language on chat lists, 249
Book of Five Rings, The, 3

Boundaries, 195
Bridgehead servers
  bridgehead addresses, resolving, 463, 465
  group expansion, 187
  optimizing routing, 452
  overview, 539–540
  RGCs, 448–449
Browsers, OWA access, 191, 759, 760
Business logic layer, workflow applications, 711
Business-impact analysis, 88. *See also* Deployment planning.

C

Caches, 283
Calendar information. *See also* Outlook and Outlook clients.
  CDO access, 757
  migrating to Exchange 2000, 618–619
CAs, 243, 268, 323
Categorizer
  inbound message processing, 183, 184–185, 445
  message flow architecture, 184–185
  routing overview, 434
  Transport Core components, 180
Cc:Mail. *See* Lotus cc:Mail Connector.
CDO 2.0, 754–755
CDO sinks, workflow scripts, 717
CDO Workflow Objects
  Workflow Designer for Exchange, 677
  workflow engine, 719
CDOEX, 755, 777
CDOs. *See also* ADO.
  CDO for Exchange 2000, 755
  CDO for Windows 2000, 754–755
  CDO versions, 756
  components overview, 182
  Exchange 2000 support, 745–746
  interoperability with Outlook, 756
  overview, 753
  process flows, 756–757
  subsystems, 755–756
CDOSYS, 754–755
Centralized administrative model
  accounts and mailboxes, 535
  administrative groups, 534, 535
  Exchange 2000 Servers, 223, 224
  overview, 533–534
  recipient management, 145, 218
  routing groups, 458, 534
Certificate Authorities, 243, 268, 323
Certificate revocation lists, 242
Certificate Services, 234–235, 242, 268
Certificates
  certificate revocation lists, 242
  KM Service overview, 234
  security overview, 268
  S/MIME format, 323
  templates, 244–245
Chain letters, 540
Change events, workflow processes, 715, 716, 717
Change Log, 575
Change management, 575
Change management, deployment planning, 75–77, 86–87
Channels, Chat Service, 229, 248, 421
Channels tab
  Chat Communities Properties sheet, 247, 248
  Mailbox Store Properties sheet, 406
Chat communities
  banning users from, 256
  channels, 229, 248, 421
  connecting to servers, 419
  creating, 230, 247, 252
  creating for administrative groups, 418
  disabling, 251, 420
  removing, 251, 421
  removing from servers, 420
  speaking restrictions, 230, 249
Chat Service. *See also* Chat communities.
  access control, 229–230
  chat user classes, 255–256
  configuring, 231, 417
  implementation planning, 123
  installing, 418
  overview, 33–34, 228–229, 391
Chat user classes, 255–256
Checkpoint files, 277–278
CHK files, 277–278
Chunking, 177
Ciphers, defined, 52
Circular logging
  backups and restoration overview, 278
  storage groups, 612
  transaction logs, 586–587, 613
Client connections to Exchange 2000 Servers, 237

CLR, 763–764
Clusters and Cluster Services, 19, 85–86, 278–279, 397
CNAME records, 36
Coexistence with foreign mail systems. *See* Messaging interoperability.
Collaboration, administrative needs assessment, 82
Collaborative application development, 49
Collaborative Data Objects. *See* CDOs.
Collaborative information, storing. *See* WSS.
Collaborative services. *See* Planning Exchange 2000 Services; RTC Services.
Collaborative systems. *See also* Digital dashboards; Workflow applications.
  CDO access, 756–757
  messaging applications, 707
  Outlook Forms, 707–708
  overview, 706–707
  Team Folders
    creating, 725
    overview, 708–710
    Team Folder Solutions, 724
    templates, 709–710
  workflow applications, 710–711
COM+. *See also* CDOs.
  components, Web Parts, 685
  MMC, 211
  roles, 729
Command ADO object, 749
Command-line utilities, security issues, 220
Commerce Server 2000, 762
Common language runtime, 763–764
Communication. *See* Chat Service; IM Service.
Compacting databases, 288–289, 313–314, 609, 610
Company information, email security, 541
Complementary keys, 234
Components, Exchange 2000. *See also Names of specific components.*
  installing, 392
  intercomponent communication, 62–63
  list of components, 62, 207, 390–391
  monitoring performance, 568–569
  routing components, 432–435
  RTC components, 391
Computer Management snap-in, 528
Conferencing Server, 33–34, 391, 595
ConfigCAs, 339
Configuration change management, 575
Configuration Connection Agreements, 339
Configuration container, 128
Configuration naming context, 128
Connection ADO object, 749, 773
Connection agreements
  attribute mapping, 340–341
  ConfigCAs, 339
  configuration connection agreements, 340
  legacy recipient objects, 147–148
  one-way agreements, 338–339
  overview, 338, 339–340, 370
  public folders, 342
  two-way agreements, 338–339
  user connection agreements, 340
Connection schedules, 564
Connection strings, 774, 775
Connections, offline, 511
Connectivity
  between Exchange Servers, 527
  implementation planning, 108
  troubleshooting, 588–593
Connector Manager snap-in, 340–341
Connector queues, displaying in Queue Viewer, 468
Connector Servers, deployment planning, 84
Connectors
  connection schedules, 564
  external connector failures, correcting, 608
  foreign mail systems. *See* Foreign mail system interoperability.
  link state routing, 463
  Lotus cc:Mail Connector, 625, 648–656
  Lotus Notes Connector, 622–624, 636–647
  messaging connectors, 445–450
  MS Mail for PC Networks Connector, 620–622, 631, 633, 634, 635
  Novell GroupWise Connector, 625–627, 656–664
  RGCs, 448–449, 539–540
  Schedule+ Free/Busy Connector, 621, 634
  SMTP Connectors
    bridgehead addresses, resolving, 463
    installing, 562
    optimizing message routing, 450–452
    planning routing strategy, 446–448
    Properties pages, 563
  X.400 Connector, 449–450, 466
Consistency, checking databases for, 611

Consoles, MMC. *See also Names of specific consoles;* Snap-ins, MMC.
  creating, 238
  customizing, 426
  distributing, 240
  overview, 212–213
  Taskpad views, 427
Consumer needs assessment, 79–80
Contacts, 139, 550
Containers
  Configuration Container, 128
  Group Policy Containers, 264–265
  Import and Export Containers, 641, 642, 652, 654, 664
  Recipient Containers. *See* OUs.
  source and destination containers for replication, 373
Content stores. *See* STM files.
Content-management software
  Inbox Assistant, Outlook 2000 client, 324, 354
  overview, 323–325
  Rules Wizard, Outlook 2000 client, 324, 351
  security overview, 317
  selecting, 357
  virus control, 271
Contingency management, 72–74, 92
Contributor role, public folders, 369
Conversations. *See* Chat Service; IM Service.
Copy backups, 283–284
Corporate objectives, deployment planning, 67–68
Corrupted databases, repairing, 314
CPUs
  monitoring usage, 577, 595
  system requirements, Exchange 2000, 106–107
Craftsman, Way of, 3
Create events, workflow processes, 715, 716, 717
Critical conditions, server monitors, 578
CRLs, 242
CRM (Customer Relationship Management), 75, 77–78
Cryptographic service providers (CSPs), 234
Custom recipients
  Exchange 5.5 recipient objects, 135
  migrating foreign messaging systems to Exchange 2000, 618–619
Customer Relationship Management, 75, 77–78

D

%d placeholder, recipient policy, 167
Dashboard factory, digital dashboards, 684–685
Dashboard Wizard, 685
Dashboards, defined, 679. *See also* Digital dashboards.
Data conferencing servers, 84
Data providers
  ADO access, 758
  connecting to data stores, 773
  OLE DB providers, 746
  opening connections, 775
Data recovery policy, 311
Data stores
  connecting to, 773, 775
  storage group overview, 377
Database layer, 17–18
Database maintenance, 288–289, 313, 528, 582–587
Database (Policy) tab
  Mailbox Store Properties sheet, 543
  Public Store Policy Properties sheet, 546
Database Properties tab, Mailbox Store Properties sheet, 407
Database storage, 47
Database stores, recovering from backups, 296
Database tab
  Mailbox Store Properties sheet, 407
  Public Folder Store Properties sheet, 411
Databases
  backups and restoration overview, 284
  checking for consistency, 611
  circular logging, 586–587, 612
  consistency, maintaining, 288–289, 313
  defragmenting, 288–289, 313–314, 583–585, 609
  ESE architecture, 277–278
  GC database sizing, 196
  maintaining and optimizing, 582–587
  memory usage optimization, 596
  multiple database architecture, 18, 58
  restoring backed up data, 287
DCA. *See* Distributed Configuration Architecture.
Dcpromo.exe, 112
DCs, 112, 113, 593. *See also* GC Servers.
Debugging, workflow scripts, 737
Decentralized administrative model. *See* Distributed administrative model.

Default recipient policies, 118, 165
Defragmenting databases
  ESEUTIL tool, 288–289, 313–314, 584–585, 609, 610
  offline defragmentation, 609
  overview, 583
Delays setting, chat user classes, 256
Delegated administrative model, 219. *See also* Distributed administrative model.
Delegates tab, Outlook Options dialog box, 498
Delegating sending permissions, 557
Delegation of Control Wizard, 220–221, 334–336, 365
Delete All Messages option, SMTP queues, 607
Delete events, workflow processes, 715, 716
Deleted mailboxes
  deleting mailboxes, 290, 552, 586
  reconnecting to new user objects, 294
  retention periods, 293
Deleting messages, 469
Delivery Restrictions tab
  Lotus cc:Mail Connector Properties sheet, 654
  Novell GroupWise Connector Properties sheet, 663
Delivery settings, 129
Delivery Status Notification, 177
Demilitarized zones, 273–274
Denial-of-service attacks, 272–273, 317. *See also* Vulnerabilities, system.
Deployment planning
  ADC tool, 147–149
  administrative needs, 82
  best practices, frameworks, 70–71
  business-impact analysis, 88
  change management, 75–77
  contingency countermeasures, 74–75
  contingency management, 72–74, 92
  corporate objectives, 67–68
  current infrastructure assessment, 80–81, 91, 94
  current network topology assessment, 81
  current software environment assessment, 82
  Customer Relationship Management, 75
  deployment team, 100
  design considerations, 64
  disaster-recovery plan, 93
  disk storage space, 95
  enterprise model assessment, 82, 94
  envisioning phase, 71–72
  gap analysis, 91
  hardware infrastructure, 83
  legacy recipients, 147–149
  messaging service needs, 79
  needs assessment, 78–82
  online service needs, 79–80
  operational framework, 72
  organizational planning, 83
  pilot studies, 86–87, 91
  planning objectives, 99–101
  planning steps, 94
  problem management, 77–78
  problem statement, 68–69
  process model, 70–72
  project management steps, 88
  project scope, 70
  proposed solution, 69
  public folder needs, 80, 95
  recovery capabilities, maintaining, 90
  remote access service needs, 79
  risk analysis, 69, 89
  RTC Services, 123–124
  server deployment, 83–85
  service level agreements. *See* SLAs.
  service management, 75
  technical support, 76–77, 93. *See also* Supporting Exchange 2000 deployment.
  vision statement, 67
Design considerations
  deployment planning, 64
  Web Parts, 683–684, 687–688
  workflow applications, 712
Destination containers for replication, 373
Development. *See* Application development.
Development tools
  WDE. *See* Workflow Designer for Exchange.
  workflow applications, 711–712
  WSS, 678
Diagnostic logging, 50, 403, 454, 478
Diagnostic Logging tab, Server Properties sheet, 403, 478
Differential backups, 283–284
Digest Authentication method, 303
Digital certificates
  certificate revocation lists, 242
  KM Service overview, 234
  security overview, 268
  S/MIME format, 323
  templates, 244–245

Digital Dashboard Resource Kit, 684
Digital Dashboard Services Component, 685
Digital dashboards
  access control, 683
  architecture, 684–686
  creating, 696, 699
  dashboard factory, 684–685
  Dashboard Wizard, 685
  Digital Dashboard Services Component, 685
  e-commerce, 679–681
  Exchange Server Dashboard, 700
  file system. *See* File System Digital Dashboard.
  modification and customization, 682
  Office XP Developer environment, 692, 693
  optimizing, 690
  overview, 679, 681–682
  previewing and testing, 699
  Properties sheets, 691
  Proxy Servers, configuring, 689
  security, 682–683
  store module, 684
  Web Parts
    adding to dashboards, 693, 698
    building inline, 697
    creating dashboards, 699
    design considerations, 683–684, 687–688
    designing, 698
    Web Part Builder, 696, 698
  Web storage instance, creating, 690
Digital signatures, 234
Directories, Exchange 2000, 768
Directory service components, 108–109
Directory services, implementation planning, 104. *See also* Active Directory.
Directory synchronization. *See also* Foreign mail system interoperability.
  Active Directory and, 619
  Lotus cc:Mail, 625
  Lotus Notes, 624
  Lotus Notes Connector, 645
  MS Mail for PC Networks, 621–622, 633
  Novell GroupWise, 627
Dirsync protocol. *See also* Directory synchronization.
  MS Mail for PC Networks Connector, 621–622, 633
  troubleshooting, 635
Dirsync Schedule tab, Novell GroupWise connector Properties sheet, 663
Disabled user account mailboxes, 161
Disaster prevention. *See also* Disaster recovery.
  risk analysis, 69, 89
  risk management, 73, 74–75, 92, 93
  security, 269–270
  viruses and virus control, 270–271
Disaster recovery. *See also* Backups and restoration; Disaster prevention.
  clusters and Cluster Services, 85–86, 278–279, 397
  disaster-recovery plan, 93
  Exchange 5.5 *vs.* Exchange 2000, 275
  messaging server overview, 44
  overview, 276
  recovery capabilities, maintaining, 90
Discovery Protocol (Disco), 670
Discussions. *See* Chat Service; IM Service.
Disk storage space, 95, 577
Distributed administrative model
  accounts and mailboxes, 537
  administrative groups, 536, 537
  managing Exchange 2000 Servers, 223, 224
  overview, 536
  recipient management, 147
  routing groups, 459, 536
Distributed Configuration Architecture, 59
Distribution groups
  converting to security groups, 369
  implementation planning, 116–117, 131
  mail-enabling, 156
  managing Exchange 2000 Services, 227
  overview, 192, 195, 343–344
  server management overview, 530–531
Distribution lists, 134. *See also* Universal distribution groups.
DMZs, 273–274
DNS Service
  Active Directory queries, 328–329
  configuring for email, 363
  FE/BE architecture, 329
  integrating Active Directory service, 329–331
  non-Microsoft DNS, 330
  routing information, 187
  SMTP Service, configuring, 379
DNS zones, 330, 331
Document Type Declarations, 759
Domain controllers, 112, 113, 593. *See also* GC Servers.
Domain local groups, 140, 192, 343–344

Domain naming context, 128
Domain topology and namespaces, 110–111
/DomainPrep utility, 386–388
Domains
  configuring, 386–388
  defined, 112
  domain controllers, 112, 113, 593
  domain structure, 217–218, 220, 225–226
  /DomainPrep utility, 386–388
  external foreign domains, GroupWise, 660
  GC Servers, 114–115
  Group Policy Objects, 306
  in mixed-mode environments, 113
  namespaces, 110, 111–112, 126
  OUs, 218, 220
  single-master domain model, 217
  top-level domains, 112–113
  trees, 113
  trust relationships, 113–114
Domains and Trusts snap-in, 212
Domino Server. *See* Lotus Notes Connector.
DoS attacks, 272–273, 317. *See also* Vulnerabilities, system.
DTDs, 759
Dynamic channels, Chat Service, 229
Dynamic disks, 280–283, 311
Dynamic distribution lists, 433

E

E-commerce
  CDO scripts, 757
  deep Web content, accessing, 666
  Digital Dashboard overview, 679
  historical perspective, 679–680
  knowledge management-based business solutions, 681
  Open Buying on the Internet initiative, 679–680
EDB files
  database storage overview, 47
  ESE architecture, 277–278
  MIME conversions, 320, 322
  storage group overview, 377
EDI, 758. *See also* XML.
Editor role, public folders, 368
EFS, 269, 311
EHLO command, 178
Electronic Data Interchange, 758. *See also* XML.
Email. *See also* Messages.
  ADO access, 750–751
  CDO access, 756–757
  content-management software, 323–325, 351, 356, 357
  DNS Service, configuring, 363
  security, 540–541
Email Address tab, Recipient Policy Properties sheet, 547
Email addresses
  adding, 553
  creating, 554
  delegating sending permissions, 557
  forwarding addresses, 558
  generated by GroupWise Connector, 626
  global recipient settings, 129
  mailbox-enabled objects, 137
  mail-enabled objects, 138–141
  modifying, 553
  primary address, setting, 555
  recipient objects, updating, 115, 167
  sharing with foreign messaging systems. *See* Directory synchronization.
Email notifications from server monitors, 578, 604
Email Security Update, Outlook, 327–328, 360
Emergency Repair Disks, 239
Encrypted unattended installation, Exchange 2000, 397
Encrypting File System, 269, 311
Encryption
  Certificate Authorities, 243, 268, 323
  digital certificates, 234, 242, 244–245, 268, 323
  digital signatures, 234
  Exchange 2000 security overview, 52
  keys, 234
  message sealing, 234
  public-key infrastructure, 234
  security overview, 317
  S/MIME format, 323
End-user objectives, deployment planning, 68
End-user support, 76–77, 93. *See also* Supporting Exchange 2000 deployment.
Enrollment Agent (Computer) certificates, 245
Enter events, workflow processes, 715, 716
Enterprise organization, site topology and, 172–174
Enterprise root CAs, 243
Enterprise subordinate CAs, 243

Entrance/exit consoles, 780
Enumerate 100 Messages option, SMTP queues, 607
Envisioning phase, deployment planning, 71–72
ERDs, 239
Error ADO object, 749
ESE, 277–278
ESENTUTIL utility, 105
ESEUTIL tool, 288–289, 313–314, 584–585, 609, 610
ESMTP
  determining support for, 201
  enabling, 202
  ETRN/TURN command verb, 178, 202, 447
  Exchange 2000 network structure, 177–178
ETesting Labs, 162
ETRN command verb, 178, 202, 447
Event sinks, WSS
  permissions, 728
  registering, 700, 771
  in workflow processes, 714, 717–718
Event Viewer, 50, 216, 454, 529, 575. *See also* Troubleshooting.
Events, workflow processes
  assigning state to, 715–716
  defined, 715
  order of evaluation, 717
  protocol events, 717
  transport events, 717
  trigger events, 717
Events, WSS
  event sinks, 700, 714, 728, 771
  overview, 675–676, 717–718
  workflow applications, 676–677
Exchange 5.5
  /ForestPrep utility, 381–384
  message routing, 438–439, 455
  recipient objects. *See* Recipient objects.
  RPCs, 175
  upgrading. *See* Upgrading to Exchange 2000.
Exchange 2000 ADC tool. *See* ADC tool.
Exchange 5.5 Administrator Program, 391
Exchange 2000 components. *See also Names of specific components.*
  installing, 392
  intercomponent communication, 62–63
  list of components, 62, 207, 390–391
  monitoring performance, 568–569
  routing components, 432–435
  RTC components, 391
Exchange 2000 Installation Wizard, 392
Exchange 2000 Server
  components. *See* Exchange 2000 components.
  features, 52–55
  installing. *See* Installing Exchange 2000.
  integration with IIS, 492
  integration with Windows 2000, 207–208, 262
  licensing costs, 57
  in .NET Framework, 762
  previous releases of Exchange 2000, 55
  product challenges, 60
  product strategies, 56–57
  product strengths, 57–59
  system requirements, 106–107
  Transport Core components, 179–182
Exchange 5.5 Server database. *See* WSS.
Exchange 2000 System Attendant. *See* System Attendant.
Exchange 2000 tools, 213–215
Exchange Administrative Delegation Wizard, 169, 221
Exchange Administrator permission, 367
Exchange Client, 494–495, 505
Exchange Full Administrator permission, 367
Exchange Interprocess Communication, 433–434
Exchange Mailbox Merge tool, 290
Exchange Migration Wizard, 619
Exchange Monitoring and Status Tool, 213–214
Exchange Server Dashboard, 700
Exchange Signature Only certificates, 245
Exchange System Manager snap-in. *See* System Manager snap-in.
Exchange User certificates, 245
Exchange View Only Administrator permission, 367
ExIFS, 492
ExIPC, 433–434
Exit events, workflow processes, 715, 716
EXMERGE, 290
EXMERGE tool, 290
Expiry events, workflow processes, 715, 716
EXPN command, 178
Export Containers tab
  Lotus cc:Mail Connector Properties sheet, 654
  Lotus Notes Connector Properties sheet, 642
Extended IRC Protocol (IRCX), 229
Extended SMTP. *See* ESMTP.
Extensible Storage Engine, 277–278
External network security, 265–267

F

/f switch, **ESEUTIL** utility, 584
Failover Manager, 279
Fault tolerance
  clusters and Cluster Services, 85–86, 278–279, 397
  dynamic disks, 280–281
  RAID configurations, 281–283, 311
  replicating public folders, 413
FE Servers, deployment planning, 84
FE/BE architecture, 13–14, 59, 265–267, 329
Field ADO object, 749
File access, ADO, 750–751
File System Digital Dashboard
  authentication, 683
  configuring, 695
  installing, 694
  security, 694
  troubleshooting security access errors, 695
  using Web folders, 693
File system objects, 746, 748
Filters
  Adult Content filter, Outlook 2000 client, 324, 356
  content-management software, 323–325, 351, 356, 357
  Global Address List views, 336
  Junk Email filter, Outlook 2000 client, 324, 356
  Profanity Filter, Chat Service, 249
  restricting language on chat lists, 249
  Unsolicited Commercial Email, 325, 358
Firewalls
  enabling MAPI clients, 778
  Mobile Information Server, 628–629
  security overview, 274, 317
  TCP/IP port numbers, 364
Folder access, ADO, 750–751
Force Connection option, SMTP queues, 607
Foreign mail system interoperability
  Active Directory and message system coexistence, 619
  connectors supported, 618
  implementation planning, 122–123, 132
  migrating foreign systems to Exchange 2000, 618–619
  Mobile Information Server, 628–629
  MS Mail for PC Networks Connector, 620–622, 631, 633, 634, 635
  overview, 617–618
  Schedule+ Free/Busy Connector, 621, 634
  upgrading to Exchange 2000, 617
  viewing installed connectors, 630
/ForestPrep utility, 381–386
Forests
  Active Directory namespaces, 110, 112–113
  configuring, 380–386
  /ForestPrep utility, 381–386
  GC Servers, 114–115
  installing Exchange 2000, 393, 394
  site topology, 174
  top-level domains, 112–113
  trees, 113
  trust relationships, 113–114
FQDNs, 110
Frameworks, 70, 761. *See also* .NET Framework.
Free disk space, monitoring, 577
Freeze All Messages option, SMTP queues, 607
Freezing messages, 469
Front-end servers
  deployment planning, 84
  monitoring CPU loads, 595
FSOs, 746, 748
Full backups, 283–284
Full-mesh topology, 442–444
Full-Text Indexing (Policy) tab
  Mailbox Store Properties sheet, 543
  Public Store Policy Properties sheet, 547
Full-text indexing service, monitoring CPU loads, 595
Full-Text Indexing tab, Sever Properties sheet, 403
Fully qualified domain names, 110

G

%g placeholder, recipient policy, 167
GAL, 336, 502
GAL views, 336
Gap analysis, deployment planning, 70, 91
GC database sizing, 196
GC Servers
  GC database sizing, 196
  GC Server sizing, 198
  implementation planning, 108, 114–115
  recipient objects and, 144
  replication traffic, 199
  server placement, 198

site topology, 196–199
troubleshooting, 593
General (Policy) tab
Mailbox Store Properties sheet, 543
Public Store Policy Properties sheet, 546
Server Policy Properties sheet, 543
General tab
Chat Community Properties sheet, 247, 418
Mailbox Store Properties sheet, 406
Novell GroupWise Connector Properties sheet, 662
Public Folder Store Properties sheet, 410
Storage Group Properties sheets, 405
Global Address List, 336, 502
Global Catalog. *See* GC Servers.
Global groups, 140, 193, 343–344
Global recipient settings, 129
Global.asa file, 752, 772
Globally Unique Identifiers, 277–278
Go Rin No Sho, 3
GPCs, 264–265
GPOs, 263–264, 306
GPTs, 264–265
Group expansion, 187
Group Policy Containers, 264–265
Group Policy Objects, 263–264, 306
Group Policy overview, 263–264
Group Policy Templates, 264–265
Group scopes
implementation planning, 117, 125, 131, 192
list of scopes, 140
overview, 192, 343–344
Group types, 192, 343–344
Groups
administrative. *See* Administrative groups.
delegating control, 335, 365
distribution. *See* Distribution groups.
global groups, 140, 193, 343–344
group scopes, 117, 125, 131, 140, 192, 343–344
group types, 192, 343–344
implementation planning overview, 108
Lotus Notes groups, propagating to Exchange, 646
mail-enabled groups, 194, 551
mail-enabled objects, 140–141
in mixed-mode environments, 194
routing. *See* Routing groups.
security. *See* Security groups.
synchronizing with Novell GroupWise systems, 627
GroupWise. *See* Novell GroupWise connector.
GUIDs, 277–278
GWART, 438

H

Hackers. *See* Vulnerabilities, system.
Hardware configuration, resource management, 570, 572
Hardware infrastructure, deployment planning, 83
Hardware requirements
disk storage space, 95
hard drives, 106–107
Hardware-level RAID, 280
Help Desk
supporting Exchange 2000 deployment, 76–77, 93
workflow protocol, 93
Hidden visibility setting, 249
Home Servers
IM Service, 231–232, 414
public folders, 412
Horizontal scalability, 80, 118
Host Integration Server 2000, 763
Hotfixes, 286, 359
HTML code, security issues, 270
HTML messages, 321, 348
HTML overview, 182
HTTP, 486–488, 506
Hub-and-spoke topology, message flow architecture, 442–444

I

Identity management, 110
IFS, 434, 492, 767
Iinetinfo.exe process, 46
IIS
IIS/Exchange 2000 security flaws, 271–272
integration with Exchange 2000, 492
interaction with Internet protocols, 492
OWA passwords, changing, 770
routing overview, 433–434
IIS Log File Format, 475
IM Service
client configuration, 233
component overview, 35, 391

configuring, 255, 415
deployment planning, 85
DNS and, 35–36
enabling users, 416
home servers, 231–232, 414
implementation planning, 123
installing, 231–232, 253, 414
language options, 255
limiting number of connections, 254
MSN Messenger Service client, 417
overview, 34–36
password policy, 253
providing access, 254
routers, 415
server management, 232–233
SRV records, 416
standards for Instant Messaging services, 54–55
troubleshooting, 251
Virtual Servers, 415

IMAP4
configuring Virtual Servers, 506
message formats, 348
overview, 485
OWA support, 28

Implementation planning
Active Directory components, 114–115
Active Directory structure, 109–114
administrative roles, 116
connectivity, 108
dependencies among components, 101
deployment team, 100
directory service components, 108–109
distribution groups, 116–117, 131, 192, 195
domain topology, 110–111
Exchange 2000 system requirements, 106–107
foreign mail systems, 122–123, 132
GC database sizing, 196
GC Server placement, 198
GC Server sizing, 198
GC Servers, 114–115
group scoping, 117, 125, 131, 192
interoperability, 108
management areas, 103–104
management tools, 105
MAPI-based access to Exchange 2000, 157
message flow, 200
namespaces, 109–113, 126
naming contexts, 108, 127
naming standards, 119–120
network infrastructure, 107–108
organizational topology, 109–110
perceived benefits of Exchange 2000, 101–102
pilot studies, 102–103
planning objectives, 99–101
policies, 117
pre-installation tasks, 125
project management approach, 98–99
public folders, 120–122
recipient management, 118–119, 128
Recipient Update Service, 115, 167
replication traffic on GC Servers, 199
RTC Services, 123–124
scalability, 118
security groups, 116–117, 131, 192, 195
server capabilities, 105–106
site boundaries, 195
upgrading legacy systems, 107
version of Exchange 2000, selecting, 107

Import Containers tab
Lotus cc:Mail Connector Properties sheet, 652
Lotus Notes Connector Properties sheet, 641
Novell GroupWise Connector Properties sheet, 664

Importing data. *See also* Foreign mail system interoperability.
migrating foreign messaging systems to Exchange 2000, 618–619
source extractors, 619

Inbound message processing, 183–184, 444–445
Inbox Assistant, Outlook 2000 client, 324, 354
Include files, connection strings, 774
Incoming messages, size limits, 556
Incremental backups, 283–284
Inetinfo.exe process, 62, 207, 433–434, 492
Information Store
configuring, 404
defragmenting, 584–585, 585
deleting messages and mailboxes, 586
Exchange 2000 overview, 62
online maintenance, 585–586
planning Exchange 2000 Services, 207
routing overview, 435

Inline Web Parts, 697
Installable File System, 434, 492, 767
Installation Wizard, 392

Installing Exchange 2000
adding Exchange 2000 Servers, 396
on clustered servers, 397
creating mailboxes, 389
with earlier versions of Exchange, 394
/ForestPrep utility, 381–384
with no earlier versions of Exchange, 393
with Outlook clients, 507
overview, 390
pre-installation tasks, 125
unattended installation, 397
on Windows 2000 member servers, 397
Installing Exchange 2000 components, 392
Instant Messaging Services. *See* IM Service.
Integrated Windows Authentication method, 303
Internal network security, 263–264
Internet clients, configuring, 505–506
Internet connectivity, 422. *See also* SMTP.
Internet Information Server. *See* IIS.
Internet Message Access Protocol Version 4. *See* IMAP4.
Internet protocols, 483. *See also Names of specific protocols.*
Internet Security and Acceleration Server 2000, 763
Interoperability
Exchange 5.5 and Exchange 2000. *See* mixed-mode environments.
foreign mail systems. *See* Messaging interoperability.
implementation planning, 108
public folders, 341–343
SMTP Connectors, 379, 422, 423
IP addresses, 301, 303, 362
IPSec, 268
IRC protocol, 229
IRC Servers, 85
ISINTEG utility, 289, 313
Isolating process applications, 771
ISPs, third-party mail relay abuse, 359

J

Junk Email filter, Outlook 2000 client, 324, 356

K

Kerberos authentication, 51
Key Management Service
Certificate Services overview, 234–235
enrolling users, 246
installing, 244
Manage permissions, 246
overview, 51–52, 62
PKI overview, 234
planning Exchange 2000 Services, 207
security overview, 267–268
Keys. *See also* Key Management Service.
PKI overview, 234
private keys, 268
public keys, 268
Registry. *See* Registry key changes.
KM. *See* Knowledge management.
KM Service. *See* Key Management Service.
KMS files, 277–278
Knowledge management. *See also* Web services.
business solutions, 681
overview, 6–11, 667
Web services overview, 669–671

L

%1 placeholder, recipient policy, 167
/l switch, **ESEUTIL** utility, 584
Language options, IM service, 255
Language, restricting on chat lists, 249
LDAP, 328–329, 489–490
LDIFDE utility, 105
Least-cost routing, 452
Legacy Exchange Servers, 175–176
Legacy recipients, 147–149
LegacyExchangeDN attribute, 295, 298
Levels of service. *See* SLAs.
Libraries, shared script procedures, 737
Licensing
connecting to Exchange Servers, 107
Exchange 2000 TCO, 57
Lightweight Directory Access Protocol, 328–329, 489–490
Limits (Policy) tab
Mailbox Store Properties sheet, 543
Public Store Policy Properties sheet, 546
Limits setting, chat user classes, 256

Limits tab, Public Folder Store Properties sheet, 411
Link State Algorithm, 188, 434, 452
Link state routing, 187–188, 463
Load balancing, 413
Load Simulator utility (**Loadsim.exe**), 87, 428, 429, 430
Locales, configuring, 403
Lodctr command, 429
Log file formats, 475
Log files and logging
  circular logging, 278, 586–587, 612, 613
  diagnostic logging, 50, 403, 454, 478
  log file formats, 475
  logging levels, Event Viewer, 454
  protocol logging, 475
  tracking logs, message tracking, 453
Logging levels, Event Viewer, 454
LogicalDisk object, monitoring, 573
Lotus cc:Mail Connector
  configuring, 649
  directory synchronization, 625, 655
  installing, 648, 654
  Properties sheet, 650–654
  restricting message delivery to cc:Mail, 655
  testing connection, 656
Lotus Notes Connector
  Address Books, specifying for synchronization, 645
  configuring, 636, 639
  connecting to Notes Server, 640
  directory synchronization, 624–625, 645, 647
  Export containers, 642
  groups, propagating to Exchange, 646
  Import containers, 641
  installing, 639
  message routing, configuring, 643
  Notes client, installing, 638
  Notes ID, creating, 637
  Notes/Domino Server, configuring, 638
  overview, 622–624
  testing connection, 644
Lower-level public folders, 95
LSA, 188, 434, 452

M

%m placeholder, recipient policy, 167
MAD.EXE. *See* System Attendant.
Mail abuse prevention, 325, 358
Mail delivery issues, troubleshooting, 589
Mail Format tab, Outlook Options dialog box, 498
Mail gateways, configuring, 378
Mail relay abuse, 359
Mail Services tab, Outlook Options dialog box, 498
Mail systems, foreign. *See* Foreign mail system interoperability.
Mailbox Manager permission, 367
Mailbox servers, deployment planning, 84
Mailbox Store, configuring, 404
Mailbox Store Limits tab, Mailbox Store Properties sheet, 408
Mailbox store policy, 543
Mailbox Store Properties sheet, 406
Mailbox stores
  backing up and restoring, 290
  storage group overview, 377
  storage locations, 282
Mailbox-enabled objects
  adding mailboxes, 151
  creating, 150
  overview, 57–58, 137–138
Mailbox-enabled users
  configuring Internet clients, 505
  creating, 549
  email addresses, modifying, 553
  existing users, designating as mailbox-enabled, 551
  mailbox storage limits, 559
  message restrictions, 557
  recipient limits, 558, 559
  retention period, deleted items, 560
Mailboxes
  adding to mailbox-enabled objects, 151
  administrative models, 535, 537
  configuring, 388–389, 406
  delegating sending permissions, 557
  deleted, reconnecting to new user objects, 294
  deleting, 290, 552, 586
  disabled user accounts, 161
  Exchange 5.5 recipient objects, 134

MAPI-based access, 157
migrating foreign messaging systems to Exchange 2000, 618–619
mixed centralized and distributed management, 539
moving, 552
postmaster mailbox, 161
recovering backed-up mailboxes, 295
replication in mixed-mode environment, 340
retention periods, 292, 293, 560
scalability of Exchange 2000 *vs.* Exchange 5.5, 162
storage limits, 559
synchronization in mixed-mode environment, 340–341
Mail-enabled contacts, 139, 550
Mail-enabled groups
creating, 194, 551
distribution groups, 156, 344–345
optimizing replication traffic, 160
Mail-enabled objects
access control overview, 336
Exchange 2000 overview, 57–58
overview, 138–141, 532
Mail-enabled recipients
email addresses, 554
limiting message size, 560, 561
message restrictions, 561
Mail-enabled users, 153, 156, 550
Maintaining server resources. *See* Resource management; Troubleshooting.
Maintenance. *See also* Monitoring Exchange 2000 Services; Resource management.
database maintenance, 288–289, 313, 528, 582–587
goals, 567–568, 574
maintenance tools, 575–576
messaging server overview, 44
Manage permissions, KM Service, 246
Management areas, implementation planning, 103–104
Management consoles, MMC. *See also Names of specific consoles;* Snap-ins, MMC.
creating, 238
customizing, 426
distributing, 240
overview, 212–213
Taskpad views, 427
Management roles, deployment planning, 68
Management tools, implementation planning, 105
Managing Exchange 2000. *See* System administration.
Managing Exchange 2000 Servers. *See also* Server management.
administrative groups, 225, 226
administrative models, 223–224
client connections, 237
client-server overview, 222–223
domain structure, 225–226
OUs, 225
routing groups, 226
Managing Exchange 2000 Services
administrative tools, 209–210, 211
affinities, 227–228
distribution groups, 192, 195, 227
Event Viewer, 216
Exchange 2000 tools, 213–215
Exchange Monitoring and Status Tool, 213–214
Message Tracking Center, 214, 472
Microsoft Operations Framework, 208
Performance Monitor, 216
policies, 221–222
public folders, 227
Queue Viewer, 214
RTC. *See* Managing RTC Services.
security groups, 192, 195, 227
SLAs, 206
Windows 2000 tools, 216
Managing recipients
administrative models, 218–219
centralized administrative model, 218
Delegation of Control Wizard, 220–221, 334–336, 365
domain structure, 217–218, 220
Exchange Administrative Delegation Wizard, 221
MMC toolsets, 219
OUs, 218
overview, 216
permission management, 220–221, 314
policies, 221–222
Terminal Services, 219
Managing RTC Services
Chat Service, 228–231
IM Service, 231–233
outsourcing, 236
RTC overview, 228

MAPI
installing Outlook and Exchange on same machine, 507
MAPI clients, enabling through firewalls, 778
MAPI-based access to Exchange 2000, 157
message flow architecture, 184
MIME conversions, 319–321, 322
overview, 493–494
queues, monitoring, 581–582
troubleshooting connectivity issues, 591–592
Mapping object attributes, 340–341
MAPS Realtime Blackhole List, 359
Maximum logging level, Event Viewer, 454
Medium logging level, Event Viewer, 454
Member servers, Windows 2000, installing Exchange 2000, 397
Memory
monitoring Memory object, 572–573
optimizing memory usage, 596
system requirements, Exchange 2000, 106–107
virtual memory allocation and monitoring, 577, 596, 600, 604
Merchant, Way of, 3, 765–766
Message Categorizer. *See* Categorizer.
Message flow architecture. *See also* Site topology.
connectors, 445–450
current messaging environment, 436–437
Exchange 5.5 message processing, 455
Exchange 2000 overview, 45
implementation planning, 200
inbound message processing, 183–184, 444–445
intercomponent communication, 62–63, 180–181, 182–183
MAPI messages, 184
message access, 181–182
message tracking, 214, 426, 453, 472
messaging connectors, 445–450
optimizing message routing, 450–452
outbound message processing, 185
planning. *See* Planning routing strategy.
topologies, 442–444
troubleshooting message flow path, 590–593
Message formats
global recipient settings, 129
HTML message bodies, 321, 348
MIME conversions, 319–321, 322, 350
overriding, 348
plain-text message bodies, 321, 348
on POP3 Virtual Servers, 346
S/MIME format, 323
TNEF conversions, 321
Message processing
ETRN command verb, 178, 202, 447
in Exchange 5.5, 455
inbound messages, 183–184, 444–445
outbound message processing, 185
performance baselines, 574
routing overview, 432
troubleshooting message flow path, 590–593
TURN command verb, 178, 202, 447
Message queues. *See* Queues.
Message routing. *See* Routing.
Message sealing, 234, 323
Message settings, 556, 560, 561
Message signing, 234, 323
Message tracking (Message Tracking Center)
configuring, 426
managing Exchange 2000 Services, 214
troubleshooting message routing, 453, 472
Message Transfer Agent. *See* MTA.
Message-based security, 318–323, 350
Messages
content-management software, 323–325, 351, 356, 357
deleting from Information Store, 586
deleting in SMTP queues, 469
external connector failures, correcting, 608
freezing in SMTP queues, 452–453, 469
limiting number in SMTP queues, 605
message restrictions, 561
migrating foreign messaging systems to Exchange 2000, 618–619
Outlook security issues, 270, 327–328, 360
retrieving, 484
troubleshooting mail delivery issues, 589
Messages tab
Chat Communities Properties sheet, 248
Mailbox Store Properties sheet, 406
Messaging Application Programming Interface protocol. *See* MAPI.
Messaging Connectors, 445–446. *See also* Connectors.
Messaging, defined, 42
Messaging interoperability
Active Directory and message system coexistence, 619

connectors supported, 618
migrating foreign systems to Exchange 2000, 618–619
Mobile Information Server, 628–629
MS Mail for PC Networks Connector, 620–622, 631, 633, 634, 635
overview, 617–618
Schedule+ Free/Busy Connector, 621, 634
upgrading to Exchange 2000, 617
viewing installed connectors, 630
Messaging Servers, 42–43, 43–44
Messaging Services
needs assessment, 79, 94
planning.
See Planning Exchange 2000 Services.
Microsoft Exchange 5.5 Administrator Program, 391
Microsoft Exchange Client, 494–495, 505
Microsoft IIS Log File Format, 475
Microsoft Management Console. *See* MMC.
Microsoft Operations Framework, 70, 208
Microsoft Readiness Framework, 70–71
Microsoft Solutions Framework, 70, 208
Middleware, Web Services, 672–673
Migrating to Exchange 2000, 618–619. *See also* ADC tool; Foreign mail system interoperability.
Migration Wizard, 619
MIME content
MAPI conversions, 319–321, 322
message formats, 319–320, 350
message-based security, 318–319
S/MIME format, 323
TNEF conversions, 321
using OWA, 322
MIME protocol
Exchange 2000 network structure and, 176–177
message-based security, 318–323
OWA support, 29
Minimum logging level, Event Viewer, 454
Mirrored volumes, 280
MIS, 628–629
Mixed administrative model
accounts and mailboxes, 539
administrative groups, 537, 538
managing Exchange 2000 Servers, 223, 224
overview, 537
routing groups, 538
mixed-mode environments
groups, creating, 194
legacy recipient objects, 147–148
limitations of, 113
managing routing groups, 441–442
planning routing strategy, 438–439
synchronizing data. *See* ADC tool.
system administration, 529
TCP/IP port numbers for firewalls, 364
troubleshooting mail delivery issues, 589
MMC
console frames, creating, 238
consoles
creating, 238
customizing, 426
distributing, 240
overview, 212–213
Taskpad views, 427
Exchange 2000 overview, 61
overview, 210–211
restricting author mode, 241
restricting snap-in use, 242
server management tools, 105
snap-in tool design, 211–212
MMC Registry key, 240
Mobile Information Server, 628–629, 763
Mobile users. *See* Remote access services.
MOD, 714, 719, 722
Moderated channels, Chat Service, 421
Modification permission, digital dashboards, 682
MOF (Microsoft Operations Framework), 70
Monitoring and Status tool, 50
Monitoring client resources, 568
Monitoring CPU loads, 577, 595
Monitoring Exchange 2000 deployment, 75–77
Monitoring Exchange 2000 Services
Conferencing Server, 595
front-end servers, 595
full-text indexing service, 595
message queues, 578–582
notifications from server monitors, 578, 604
overview, 50
performance baselines, 574
routing groups, 593
server monitors, 577
System Manager snap-in, 576
Monitoring network topology, 568
Monitoring remote services, 219

Monitoring server resources.
  See Resource management.
Monitoring tab, Server Properties sheet, 404
MRF (Microsoft Readiness Framework), 70–71
MS Mail Dirsync protocol, 621–622, 633
MS Mail for PC Networks connector
  Dirsync protocol, 621–622, 633
  establishing mail flow, 631
  installing, 631
  MS Mail MTA, creating, 633
  overview, 620
  Schedule+ Free/Busy Connector, 621, 634
  troubleshooting, 634
MSExchangeMTA object, monitoring, 573
MSF (Microsoft Solutions Framework), 70
MSN Messenger client, 233, 417
MSXML Parser, installing, 769
MTA
  Exchange 2000 overview, 62
  external connector failures, correcting, 608
  monitoring, 573
  MS Mail MTA, creating, 633
  planning Exchange 2000 Services, 207
  resource management, 571
  routing overview, 434
  SMTP and, 176
  troubleshooting mail delivery issues, 589
  X.400 Connector and, 176
Multiple database architecture, 18, 58
Multiple routing groups, 456
Multithreading, 179
Musashi, Miyamoto, 3
MX records, 363, 422

N

Name resolution, 187. *See also* Namespaces.
Named objects, 109–110
Names
  LegacyExchangeDN attribute, 295
  naming standards, 119–120
Namespaces
  ADO object access, 750–751
  domain topology and, 110–111
  naming contexts, 108, 127
  organizational topology and, 110–111
  planning, 109–110, 126
  schema namespaces, WSS, 744
  trees, 113
  trust relationships, 113–114
Naming contexts, 108, 127
Naming standards, 119–120, 120–121
NCSA Common Log File Format, 476
Needs assessment, 78–82
.NET Framework
  ASP.NET, 752
  ASP.NET API, 763–764
  .NET Enterprise Servers, 762
  overview, 760–761, 764–765
  Way of the Merchant, 765–766
  Windows 2000 in, 761
.NET initiative, 5–5
.NET services, 667
NetWare Server, 656.
  See also Novell GroupWise Connector.
Network infrastructure, implementation
  planning, 107–108
Network interface cards, 107
Network Monitor, 50
Network News Transport Protocol, 423, 424,
  491–492, 506
Network structure
  protocols, 175–178
  site links, 189, 201
  site topology, 174
  Windows 2000 *vs.* Exchange 2000, 174–175
Network topology
  monitoring, 568
  needs assessment, 81
  physical topology, 15
  site topology design, 174
New Newsgroup Wizard, 425
New Taskpad View Wizard, 427
Newsgroups, 423, 424, 425, 491–492
NICs, 107
NNTP, 29–30, 423, 424, 491–492, 506
No Access permission, digital dashboards, 682
Nonediting Author role, public folders, 369
Non-Microsoft DNS, 330
Notes client, installing, 638
Notifications from server monitors, 578, 604
Novell GroupWise Connector
  API gateway, configuring, 657, 658
  configuring, 662
  directory synchronization, 627
  DLs, expanding, 659
  external foreign domains, 660

importing directory entries, 664
NetWare Server preparation, 656
NTGateway group, 661
overview, 625–626
Properties sheet, 662–664
NTBACKUP utility, 105
NTDSUTIL utility, 105
NTGateway group, GroupWise Connector, 661

O

Object attributes, mapping, 340–341
ODBC, connecting to data stores, 773
ODBC Logging, 476
Office XP Developer
digital dashboard projects, creating, 692
WSS development tools, 678
Offline address books, 142, 502, 512
Offline backups, 283, 285, 289
Offline connections, Outlook clients, 511
Offline defragmentation, 609
Offline folder stores, 501–502, 511
Offline recovery servers, 295
OLE DB
data providers, 746
Exchange 2000 support, 745–746
One-way connection agreements, 338–339
Online backups, 283, 285, 289, 586
Online discussions. *See* Chat Service; IM Service.
Online services, deployment planning, 79
OnSyncDelete event, 700, 728
OnSyncSave event, 700, 728
OnTimer event, 700, 728
Open Buying on the Internet initiative, 679–680
Open third-party mail relay abuse, 359
Operational framework, deployment planning, 72
Optimization. *See also* Troubleshooting.
databases, 582–587
Information Store, 585–586
least-cost routing, 452
maintenance goals, 567–568
memory usage, 596
message queues, 578–582
message routing, 450–452
monitoring components, 568–569
monitoring hardware resources, 572–573
performance baselines, 574
replication traffic, 160
resource management, 570–572
server monitors, 577
storage groups, 582–587
tools for maintenance and monitoring, 575–576
transaction logs, 586–587, 613
virtual memory allocation and monitoring, 577, 596, 600, 604
Options dialog box, Outlook clients, 498
Organizational objectives, deployment planning, 67–68
Organizational planning, deployment planning, 83
Organizational structure, deployment planning, 80–81, 91
Organizational topology, and namespaces, 110–111
Organizations, naming standards, 119
Other tab, Outlook Options dialog box, 498
OUs
delegating control, 335
domain structure and recipient management, 218, 220
managing Exchange 2000 Servers, 225
recipient objects, 136–137, 143–144
structure, planning, 191
Out Of Office Assistant, 499, 514
Outgoing messages, size limits, 556
Outlook 2000 Team Folders Kit, 708. *See also* Team Folders.
Outlook and Outlook clients
CDO access, 756
client access to Exchange 2000, 86
configuration, 497–499
content management overview, 324
Email Security Update, 327–328, 360
Inbox Assistant, 324, 354
installing with Exchange 2000 Server, 507
offline connections, 511
offline folder stores, 501–502, 511
Out Of Office Assistant, 499, 514
Outlook 97, 495
Outlook 98, 495
Outlook 2000, 495–496, 504–505
Outlook 2002, 495–496
Outlook client overview, 495–496
Outlook Express, 496
Outlook Web Access. *See* OWA.

personal folder stores, 500–501, 510
profiles, 500
public folder access, restricting, 367
Remote Mail feature, 513
roaming user support, 502–503
Rules Wizard, 324, 351, 499, 516
security issues, 270, 327–328, 360
upgrading to Outlook 2000, 504–505
user profiles, 497, 508, 509
versions, 495–496
Outlook Email Security Update, 327–328, 360
Outlook Forms. *See also* Web Forms.
modifying, 723
overview, 707–708
publishing, 724
removing forms from Personal Forms Library, 726
Team Folders
creating, 725
overview, 708–710
Team Folder Solutions, 724
templates, 709–710
Outlook Mobile Access, 628
Outlook Mobile Manager, 629
Outlook Web Access. *See* OWA.
Outsourcing RTC Services, 236
OWA
accessing resources using browsers, 191
administration, 25
browser support, 759, 760
client access to Exchange 2000, 86
deployment, 25
displaying objects, 27
Exchange 2000 overview, 24–27, 47–48
HTTP overview, 486–488
MIME content, 322
new features in Exchange 2000, 745
Outlook client overview, 496
passwords, changing, 770
protocols supported, 27–30
resource management, 571
scalability features, 48
servicing requests, 26
Owner role, public folders, 368

P

/p switch, **ESEUTIL** utility, 584
Parameter ADO object, 749
Passwords
administrative passwords, changing, 245
OWA passwords, changing, 770
password policy, IM Service, 253
Patch files, 284
Performance. *See also* Optimization; Troubleshooting.
baselines, 574
defragmentation, 288–289, 313–314, 583–585, 609
message queues, 578–582
monitoring components, 568–569
server monitors, 577
tools for maintenance and monitoring, 575–576
Performance Monitor, 216
Performance tuning. *See* Optimization.
Permissions and permission management
assigning to administrative groups, 169
Delegation of Control Wizard, 220–221, 334–336, 365
digital dashboards, 682–683
Exchange Administrative Delegation Wizard, 221
File System Digital Dashboard, 694
Global Address List views, 336
groups and group scopes, 344
managing recipients, 220–221
public folder views, 337
public folders, 343
sending permissions, delegating, 557
System Manager snap-in, 314, 367
Web Parts, 682–683
workflow event sinks, 728
Personal folder stores, 500–501, 510. *See also* Public folder stores.
Personal Forms Library, 726
Personal information, email security, 541
Physical network structure
protocols, 175–178
site links, 189, 201
site topology, 174
Windows 2000 *vs.* Exchange 2000, 174–175
Pilot studies, 86–87, 91, 102–103

PIMs. *See also* Outlook and Outlook clients.
CDO access, 757
remote access, 628
Pipelining, 177
PKI. *See also* Key Management Service.
CAs, 243, 268, 323
message-based security, 318
overview, 234
session-based security, 318
S/MIME format, 323
Plain text messages, POP3 clients, 321, 348
Planning Exchange 2000
deployment. *See* Deployment planning.
implementation.
See Implementation planning.
routing. *See* Planning routing strategy.
services.
See Planning Exchange 2000 Services.
Planning Exchange 2000 Services
administrative tools, 209–210, 211
Exchange 2000 components, 207, 390–391
Exchange 2000 integration with Windows 2000, 207–208
Microsoft Solutions Framework, 208
service level agreements. *See* SLAs.
Planning objectives, 99–101
Planning routing strategy
administrative models, 458, 459, 536
current messaging environment, 436–437
link state routing, 463
message flow architecture, 444–445
message flow topologies, 442–444
messaging connectors, 445–450
mixed-mode environments, 438–439
multiple routing groups, 456
optimizing message routing, 450–452
overview, 199
public folders, 200, 440–441, 457–458
replication traffic, 199
RGMs, selecting, 459
routing groups, 439–442
single routing groups, 455
Policies
centralized policy management, 539
data recovery policy, 311
Group Policy, 263–265, 306
implementation planning overview, 117
mailbox store policy, 543
managing Exchange 2000 Services, 221–222
password policy, IM Service, 253
public store policy, 545
recipient policies, 118, 130, 165, 221–222, 530, 547
system. *See* System policies.
system administration, 529
verifying, 548
POP3
configuring Virtual Servers, 506
message formats, 346
MIME conversions, 319–321, 322
overview, 484
OWA support, 28
plain text *vs.* HTML messages, 321, 348
Virtual Servers, access control, 519
Pop-up consoles, 780
Ports and port numbers
disabling ports for security purposes, 275
Exchange 5.5 and Exchange 2000, 331, 333
firewalls, 364
protocols, 266
Trojan horses, 332
Virtual Servers, 301
Post Office Protocol Version 3. *See* POP3.
Post Office tab, Lotus cc:Mail Connector Properties sheet, 650
Postmaster mailbox, 161
Potential recipients, 137
Preferences tab, Outlook Options dialog box, 498
Presentation layer, workflow applications, 710–711
Printing workflow diagrams, 740
Private keys, 268
Private visibility setting, 249
Proactive tools, 213, 216
Problem management, deployment planning, 77–78
Problem statement, deployment planning, 68–69
Process applications, isolating, 771
Process flows, CDO access, 756–757
Process model, deployment planning, 70–72
Process object, monitoring, 573
Processors
monitoring CPU usage, 577, 595
system requirements, Exchange 2000, 106–107
Product challenges, Exchange 2000, 60

Product strategies, Exchange 2000, 56–57
Product strengths, Exchange 2000, 57–59
Profanity Filter, Chat Service, 249
Profiles, Outlook clients
configuring, 509
forcing user selection of, 508
overview, 497, 500
Project management approach, implementation planning, 98–99
Project management, deployment steps, 88. *See also* Deployment planning.
Project scope, deployment planning, 70
Prompting for connection string arguments, 775
Property ADO object, 749
Property stores. *See* EDB files.
Proposed solution, deployment planning, 69
Protocol configuration and management, 47
Protocol events, workflow processes, 717
Protocol hosting, 46
Protocol logging, 453, 475
Protocol management, 528
Protocol Services, implementation planning, 104
Protocols. *See also Names of specific protocols.*
global recipient settings, 130
Internet protocols, 483
port numbers, 266, 331, 333
Windows 2000 *vs.* Exchange 2000, 175–178
Proxy addressing schemes, removing, 130
Proxy Servers, 233
Proxy Servers, configuring, 689
Proxycfg.exe utility, 689
Public folder servers, deployment planning, 84
Public Folder Store Properties sheet, 410
Public folder stores, 282, 377. *See also* Personal folder stores; Public folders.
Public folder trees, 409, 533
Public folders
access control, 369
administrative needs assessment, 82
affinities, 121–122, 227–228, 533
configuring, 410
connection agreements, 342
creating, 410
deployment planning, 80, 95
Exchange 5.5 recipient objects, 135
hierarchy, 121
home servers, 412
implementation planning, 120–122
interoperability, 341–343
lower-level folders, 95
managing Exchange 2000 Services, 227
naming standards, 120–121
needs assessment, 80
permissions, 343
referrals, 440–441, 457–458
replicas, 440–441, 457–458
replication, 122, 340, 413, 532–533
replication traffic, 200
restricting access, 367
roles, 368–369
routing groups and, 440–441
server management, 532–533
synchronization in mixed-mode environment, 340–341
top-level folders, 95
views, 337
workflow folders, 713, 730, 731
Public keys, 268
Public Store, configuring, 404
Public store policy, 545
Public visibility setting, 249
Public-key infrastructure. *See* PKI.
Published information, global recipient settings, 130
Publishing Author role, public folders, 369
Publishing Editor role, public folders, 368
Publishing Outlook Forms, 724

Q

Quarantine list, third-party mail relay abuse, 359
Queue Viewer
deleting messages, 469
displaying SMTP queues, 468
Exchange 2000 overview, 50
freezing messages, 469
managing Exchange 2000 Services, 214
monitoring message queues, 578–582
troubleshooting message routing, 452, 468
Queues
message queues, monitoring, 578–582
SMTP queues
freezing messages, 452–453, 469
limiting number of messages, 605
managing, 469, 470, 607
monitoring, 581–582
troubleshooting mail delivery issues, 589
X.400 queues, monitoring, 578, 581–582

Quotas
global recipient settings, 129
recipient objects, 163

R

RAID-0+1 configuration, 282, 283, 311
RAID-1 configuration, 280, 282, 283, 311
RAID-2 configuration, 282
RAID-3 configuration, 282
RAID-4 configuration, 282
RAID-5 configuration, 281, 282, 311
RAID-6 configuration, 282
RAID configurations
basic disks, 280
dynamic disks, 281–283
fault tolerance overview, 281–283
hardware-level RAID, 280
planning, 310
Raw directories, Exchange 2000, 768
Reactive tools, 213, 216
Read Only permission, digital dashboards, 682
Read-ahead caches, 283
Realtime communication, 54–55
Receive events, workflow processes, 715, 716
Recipient containers. *See* OUs.
Recipient management
administrative roles, 116
delegating sending permissions, 557
deleting mailboxes, 552
email addresses, 553, 554, 555, 557
forwarding addresses, 558
global recipient settings, 129
hiding recipients, 130
implementation planning, 118–119, 128
limiting message size, 560, 561
mailbox storage limits, 559
mailbox-enabled users, 549, 551
mail-enabled contacts, 139, 550
mail-enabled groups, 551
mail-enabled users, 550
message restrictions, 561
message settings, 556
moving mailboxes, 552
overview, 531–532, 548
recipient limits, 558, 559
recipient policy, 130, 165, 547
retention period, deleted items, 560
system administration, 531–532
Recipient objects
administrative groups, 141
administrative models, 145–147
contacts, 139, 550
Exchange 5.5. *See also* OUs.
list of objects, 134–135
nested containers, 135–136
overview, 136
GC Servers and, 144
legacy recipients, 147–149
mailbox-enabled objects, 137–138
mail-enabled objects, 138–141
naming standards, 119
offline address books, 142
OUs, 143–144
routing groups, 141–142
storage groups, 142–143
storage limits, 163
updating, 115, 167
Recipient policies
creating, 547
defining, 130
implementation planning, 118
managing Exchange 2000 Services, 221–222
overview, 165, 547
removing, 130
server management, 530
Recipient Update Service, 115, 167
Recordset ADO object, 749, 758, 764, 776
Recovering from system failure. *See* Disaster recovery.
Redirector object, monitoring, 573
Reducing risk in Exchange 2000 deployment. *See* Risk management.
Redundancy. *See* Fault tolerance.
Referrals, public folders, 227–228, 440–441, 457
Registered channels, Chat Service, 229, 421
Registry, creating Emergency Repair Disk, 239
Registry key changes
MMC
distributing consoles, 240
restricting author mode, 241
restricting snap-in use, 242
schema write operations, enabling, 400
SMTP queues, limits on, 605
Relaying third-party mail, 359
Reliability. *See* Fault tolerance.
Remote access services.
See also SMTP Virtual Servers.

email security, 540
external network security, 265–267
IMAP4, 485
Mobile Information Server, 628–629
needs assessment, 79
offline address book, 512
offline folder stores, 501–502
roaming user support, 502–503
Remote Mail feature, Outlook 2000, 513
Remote server administration. *See also* MMC.
Terminal Services, 219
Replicas, public folders, 440–441, 457
Replication
legacy recipient objects, 147–148
mailboxes, 340
mixed-mode environments. *See* ADC tool.
public folders, 122, 413, 532–533
replication traffic, 160, 199, 200
site links, 189, 201
source and destination containers, 373
Replication (Policy) tab, Public Store Policy Properties sheet, 546
Replication traffic
GC attributes, 199
message flow between sites, 200
routing strategies, 199
Request ASP object, 752
Resource management.
See also Troubleshooting.
Active Directory, 571
configuration change management, 575
databases, maintaining and optimizing, 571, 582–587
defragmentation, 288–289, 313–314, 583–585, 609
hardware configuration, 570
Information Store, 585–586
maintenance goals, 567–568
memory usage optimization, 596
message queues, maintaining and optimizing, 578–582
monitoring components, 568–569
monitoring hardware resources, 572–573
MTA, 571
OWA configuration, 571
performance baselines, 574
server monitors, 577
SMTP protocol, 571
storage groups, maintaining and optimizing, 582–587
tools for maintenance and monitoring, 575–576
transaction logs, 586–587, 613
virtual memory allocation and monitoring, 577, 596, 600, 604
WSS configuration, 571
Resources, WSS
events, 675–676, 700
overview, 673, 674–675
schema, 674
workflow event sinks, 700, 714
Response ASP object, 752, 777
Restoring backed-up data.
See also Backups and restoration.
database consistency, maintaining, 288–289, 313
database stores, 296
mailbox stores, 49, 290
offline backups, 283, 285, 289
offline recovery servers, 295
online backups, 283, 285, 289
planning restoration, 287
recovering backed-up mailboxes, 295
retention periods, 292, 293, 560
RestrictAuthorMode Registry key, 240
RestrictToPermittedSnapins Registry key, 242
Retention periods, 292, 293, 560
Reviewer role, public folders, 369
RGCs
creating, 463
destination bridgehead addresses, resolving, 465
overview, 435, 539–540
planning routing strategy, 448–449
RGC Delivery Option, configuring, 564
RGMs, 186, 459
Risk analysis, deployment planning, 69, 89
Risk management
contingency countermeasures, 74–75
contingency management overview, 73, 92
disaster-recovery plan, 93
Roaming user support, 502–503
Roles
administrative, 116, 335, 367
public folders, 368–369
Root CAs, 323
Routers, IM Service, 415
Routing
administrative needs assessment, 82
centralized administrative model, 539

components overview, 432–435
Exchange 5.5 routing, 438–439
inbound message processing, 183–184, 444–445
least-cost routing, 452
link state routing, 463
Lotus Notes Connector, configuring, 643
message tracking, 214, 426, 453, 472
messaging connectors, 445–450
mixed-mode environments, 438–439
optimizing, 450–452
outbound message processing, 185
Routing engine, 180
Routing Group Connectors. *See* RGCs.
Routing group masters. *See* RGMs.
Routing groups
administrative models, 458, 459, 534, 536
connectivity between Exchange Servers, 527
group expansion, 187
link state routing, 187–188
managing, 441–442
managing Exchange 2000 Servers, 226
message flow topologies, 442–444
mixed centralized and distributed management, 538
mixed-mode environments, 441–442
monitoring and troubleshooting, 593
moving servers between routing groups, 462
multiple routing groups, 456
naming standards, 119
optimizing message routing, 450–452
overview, 185, 186, 526
planning routing strategy, 437, 439–442
public folder referrals and replicas, 440–441, 457
recipient objects, 141–142
Routing Group Connectors (RGCs), 463
routing group masters (RGMs), 186, 459, 461
routing overview, 434–435
routing strategies, 199
single routing groups, 455
system administration, 526–527
Windows 2000 sites and, 439–440
Routing Servers, IM Service, 231–232
RPCPing, 592
RPCs, compared to SMTP, 175
RTC Servers, deployment planning, 84
RTC Services
Chat. *See* Chat Service.
components, 391
implementation planning, 123–124
Instant Messaging. *See* IM Service.
outsourcing, 236
RTC overview, 32–36, 228
Rules Wizard, 324, 351, 499, 516
RUS, 115, 167

S

%s placeholder, recipient policy, 167
/s switch, **ESEUTIL** utility, 584
SANs, 84
Scalability
Exchange 2000 overview, 52–53
Exchange 2000 *vs.* Exchange 5.5, 162
implementation planning, 118
messaging server overview, 43
needs assessment, 80
OWA features, 48
Schedule+ Free/Busy connector, 621, 634
Schema Master role, 398
Schema Update Allowed Registry key, 400
Schemas
naming context, 128
in raw Exchange 2000 directories, 768
schema namespaces, 744
schema write operations, 400
WSS, 46, 674, 744
Scopes, group, 117, 125, 131, 140, 192, 343–344
Scripts
ASP. *See* ASP scripts.
debugging, enabling, 737
workflow. *See* Workflow scripts.
Secret visibility setting, 248
Secure channels, Chat Service, 229–230
Security. *See also* Disaster recovery; Key Management Service.
ActiveX controls, 271
authentication
external network security, 267
IM Service, 232
Kerberos authentication, 51
methods (list), 303
security overview, 317
SMTP Virtual Servers, 302
trust relationships, 113–114
bastion hosts, 274
command-line utilities, 220

content-management software, 323–325, 351, 356, 357
Delegation of Control Wizard, 334–336, 365
demilitarized zones, 273–274
digital dashboards, 682–683, 694
disaster prevention, 269–270
email security, 540–541
encryption, 234
Exchange 2000 integration with Windows 2000, 262
Exchange 2000 overview, 50–52
external networks, 265–267
File System Digital Dashboard, 694
firewalls, 274
Global Address List views, 336
HTML code issues, 270–271
internal networks, 263–264
KM Service. *See* Key Management Service.
message sealing, 234
message signing, 234
message-based security, 318–323
messaging server overview, 44
MIME protocol, 318–323
network security overview, 262
online services, security ramifications, 79
Outlook/Outlook 2000, 270, 327–328, 360
overview, 317–318
permission management, 220–221
ports, disabling, 275
public folder access control, 367, 369
public folder views, 337
public-key infrastructure, 234
remote network access, 265–267
Security Analysis and Configuration snap-in, 269, 308
services, disabling, 275
S/MIME protocol, 318, 323
SMTP Virtual Servers, 299, 302, 303
System Manager snap-in, 314, 367
viruses and virus control, 325–328
vulnerabilities, system
  account vulnerability, Exchange 2000, 273
  ActiveX controls, 271
  demilitarized zones, 273–274
  denial-of-service attacks, 272–273
  HTML code, 270–271
  IIS/Exchange 2000 security flaws, 271–272
  Outlook security, 270, 327–328, 360
  third-party mail relay abuse, 359
  viruses and virus control, 270–271
Security Analysis and Configuration snap-in, 269, 308
Security descriptors, 336
Security groups
  converting distribution groups, 369
  implementation planning, 116–117, 131, 195
  mail-enabling, 156
  managing Exchange 2000 Services, 227
  overview, 140, 192, 195, 343
  server management overview, 530–531
Security tab
  Mailbox Store Properties sheet, 406
  Outlook Options dialog box, 498
  System Manager snap-in, 314
Sending permissions, delegating, 557
Server deployment
  client access to Exchange 2000, 86
  Clustering Services, 85–86
  deployment planning, 83, 85
  types of servers (list), 84–85
Server management
  administrative tools, 105, 528–529
  database maintenance, 528
  distribution groups, 192, 195, 530–531
  mixed-mode server environments, 529
  overview, 524
  policies overview, 529
  protocol management, 528
  public folders, 532–533
  recipient management, 548
  recipient policies, 165, 530
  RGCs, 539–540
  security groups, 192, 195, 530–531
  server policy, 543
  system administration, 527–529
  system policies, 529–530, 542
Server monitors
  default monitor, 577–578
  notifications, 578, 604
  overview, 577
  virtual memory, monitoring, 600, 604
Server policy, creating, 543
Server resources. *See also* Troubleshooting.
  databases, maintaining and optimizing, 571, 582–587
  Information Store, maintaining and optimizing, 585–586

message queues, maintaining and optimizing, 578–582
resource management, 570–572
storage groups, maintaining and optimizing, 582–587
transaction logs, 586–587, 613
Server roles, 287
Servers
bastion hosts, 274
GC Server sizing, 198
moving between routing groups, 462
naming standards, 119
virtual. *See* Virtual Servers.
Server-side key recovery, 235
ServerXMLHTTP object, 689
Service failures
contingency countermeasures, 74–75
contingency management, 72–74, 92
risk analysis, 69, 89
risk management, 73, 74–75, 92, 93
Service level agreements. *See* SLAs.
Service management, deployment planning, 75
Service Packs
external connector failures, 608
running Backup utility, 286
Session ASP object, 752, 772
Session-based security, 318
SGs. *See* Storage groups.
Shared data, knowledge management, 669
Shared keys, 234
Shared script procedures, 737
SharePoint Portal Servers, 701
Simple Mail Transfer Protocol. *See* SMTP.
Simple Object Access Protocol, 670
Simple volumes, 280, 281
Single-master domain model, 217
Site boundaries, 195
Site links, 189, 201
Site topology.
See also Message flow architecture.
enterprise organization and, 172–174
GC Servers, 196–199
message flow between sites, 200
physical network structure, 174
routing groups, 185–188
routing strategies, 199
site boundaries, 195
site links, 189, 201
Windows 2000 *vs.* Exchange 2000, 174–175
Sites and Services snap-in, 212, 213
Sites, Windows 2000, 439–440
SIZE command, 178
SLAs
contingency management, 73, 92
cost/benefit analysis, 90
maintenance goals, 567–568, 574
overview, 566
performance baselines, 574
planning Exchange 2000 Services, 206
S/MIME protocol, 176–177, 318, 323
SMTP
compared to RPCs, 175
compared to X.400 Connectors, 175–176
configuring Virtual Servers, 506, 517
connectors. *See* SMTP Connectors.
DNS configuration, 379
ETRN command verb, 178, 202, 447
Exchange 2000 overview, 62
Exchange 5.5 *vs.* Exchange 2000, 178
Internet connectivity overview, 378
mail gateway configuration, 378
MIME protocol, 318–323
optimizing message routing, 450–452
overview, 488–489
OWA support, 29
postmaster mailbox, 161
queues. *See* SMTP queues.
RGCs, 539–540
routing overview, 432–435
sending email in ASP scripts, 778
troubleshooting message flow path, 590–593
TURN command verb, 178, 202, 447
Virtual Servers. *See* SMTP Virtual Servers.
SMTP Connectors
bridgehead addresses, resolving, 463
installing, 562
optimizing message routing, 450–452
planning routing strategy, 446–448
Properties pages, 563
SMTP format, global recipient settings, 129
SMTP protocol, 571
SMTP queues
deleting messages, 469
displaying in Queue Viewer, 468
freezing messages, 469
limiting number of messages, 605
managing, 469, 470, 607
monitoring, 581–582

SMTP Virtual Servers
additional Virtual Servers, 378, 422
authentication, 302
configuring, 506, 517
connections, restricting, 303
creating, 299, 378, 422
Exchange 5.5 *vs.* Exchange 2000, 179
protocol logging, 475
Smurf denial-of-service attacks, 273
Snap-ins, MMC. *See also Names of specific snap-ins;* MMC.
creating, 238
restricting snap-in use, 242
snap-in tool design, 211–212
SOAP, 670
Software environment, needs assessment, 82
Source containers for replication, 373
Spam
email security, 540
prevention, 325, 358
Spanned volumes, 280, 281
Speaking restrictions, chat communities, 230, 249
Spelling tab, Outlook Options dialog box, 498
Spool leak denial-of-service attacks, 273
SQL Server 2000, 763
SRS files, 277–278
SRV records
DNS queries, 328–329
IM Service, 35, 416
non-Microsoft DNS Service, 330
SSL, 318
Stacheldraht denial-of-service attacks, 273
Standalone root CAs, 243
Standalone subordinate CAs, 243
Standard primary zones, DNS, 330
Standard secondary zones, DNS, 330
States, workflow processes
adding actions to states, 727
adding and modifying, 722, 727, 733
assigning to events, 715–716
captions, 734
defined, 715
deleting, 735
labeling, 734
Static IP addresses for Exchange 2000 Servers, 362
STM files
database storage overview, 47
ESE architecture, 277–278
MIME conversions, 320, 322
Storage Area Networks, 84
Storage groups
circular logging, 612
configuring, 404
defragmenting, 288–289, 313–314, 583–585, 609
ESE architecture, 277–278
Exchange 2000 overview, 62
maintaining, 582–587
memory usage optimization, 596
optimizing, 582–587
overview, 377
planning Exchange 2000 Services, 207
RAID configurations, planning, 310
recipient objects, 142–143
restoring backed up data, 287–288
Storage limits
global recipient settings, 129
recipient objects, 163
Storage services, implementation planning, 104
Storage space, system requirements, 95
Store drivers
inbound message processing, 445
routing overview, 435
Transport Core components, 180
Store module, digital dashboards, 684
STORE.EXE. *See* Information Store.
Storing collaborative information. *See* WSS.
Streaming media files. *See* STM files.
Striped volumes, 281
Subordinate CAs, 323
Subsystems, CDO, 755–756
Success entries, workflow scripts, 737
Support objectives, deployment planning, 68
Supporting Exchange 2000 deployment
change management, 75–77
contingency management, 72–74, 92
Help Desk, 76–77, 93
problem management, 77–78
service management, 75
Symmetric keys, 234
SYN flood denial-of-service attacks, 273
Synchronization
foreign mail systems. *See* Directory synchronization.
mailboxes, 340–341
mixed-mode environments. *See* ADC tool.

Synchronous events, WSS, 676, 717, 718, 728
Synchronous replication, 200
System administration
  administrative groups, 525
  administrative models, 525, 533–535, 533–539
  administrative tools, 528–529
  connection schedules, 564
  connectivity between Exchange Servers, 527
  database maintenance, 528
  delegating sending permissions, 557
  distributed administration and management, 536–537
  distribution groups, 192, 195, 530–531
  email addresses, 553, 554, 555, 557
  email security, 540–541
  Exchange features, enabling and disabling, 561
  mailboxes
    deleting, 552
    moving, 552
    storage limits, 559
  message settings, 556
  mixed centralized and distributed management, 537–539
  mixed-mode server environments, 529
  overview, 524
  policies overview, 529
  protocol management, 528
  public folders, 532–533
  recipient management, 531–532, 548
  recipient policies, 165, 530
  RGCs, 539–540, 564
  routing groups, 526–527
  security groups, 192, 195, 530–531
  server management, 527–529
  SMTP Connectors, installing, 562, 563
  system policies, 529–530, 542
System Attendant
  configuring, 402
  Exchange 2000 overview, 62
  planning Exchange 2000 Services, 207
System failure, recovering from. *See* Disaster recovery.
System management tools, 391
System Manager snap-in
  assigning administrative roles, 367
  Exchange 2000 overview, 47
  monitoring Exchange 2000 Services, 576
  overview, 527
  permission management, 314, 367
  Queue Viewer, 468, 578–582
  Routing Group Connectors, creating, 463
  routing groups, creating, 461
  Security tab, displaying, 314
  server monitors, 577–578
  servers, moving between routing groups, 462
  SMTP queues, 469, 470, 607
  system management overview, 391, 527
  viewing administrative groups, 170
  virtual memory, monitoring, 600, 604
System Monitor, 529
System policies
  applying policies, 548
  groups and, 226
  mailbox store policy, 543
  public store policy, 545
  recipient policy, 165, 547
  server management overview, 529–530, 542
  server policy, 543
  System Policies folder, 542
  verifying policies, 548
System queues, displaying in Queue Viewer, 468
System requirements, 95, 106–107
System resources, managing. *See* Resource management.
System state data, 285, 287

T

/t switch, **ESEUTIL** utility, 584
Tape drives, 107
Taskpad views, MMC consoles, 427
TCP ports, 331, 332, 333. *See also* Ports and port numbers.
Team Folders
  creating, 725
  overview, 708–710
  Team Folder Solutions, 724
  templates, 709–710
Team Folders Wizard, 709
Technical support
  deployment planning, 76–77
  Help Desk, 76–77, 93
  problem management, 77–78
Technician, Way of, 3
Templates, Team Folders, 709–710
Terminal Services, 219
Third-party mail relay abuse, 359

Threats, defined, 89
TLS command, 178
TNEF format, 321
Tools
  administrative. *See* Administrative tools.
  development. *See* Development tools.
  MMC. *See* MMC.
Top-level domains, 112–113
Top-level public folders, 95
Topologies
  Active Directory topology, 61
  current network topology assessment, 81
  domain topology and namespaces, 110–111
  Load Simulator topology, 430
  message flow architecture, 442–444
  network topology, 81, 174, 568
  organizational topology and namespaces, 110–111
  physical topology, 15
  site. *See* Site topology.
Tracking logs, 453
Transactions, 718
Transformation documents, 760
Transitions, workflow processes
  adding and modifying, 735, 736
  captions, 734
  defined, 715
  overview, 714
Transport Core, 179–181
Transport events, workflow processes, 717
Transport Neutral Encapsulation Format, 321
Transportation services, implementation planning, 104
Trees
  GC Servers, 114–115
  namespaces, 110, 113–114, 126
Trigger events, workflow processes, 717
Trojan horses, 326–327, 332. *See also* Viruses and virus control.
Troubleshooting
  Active Directory components, 593–594
  connectivity, 588–593
  deleting messages, 469
  Dirsync protocol, 635
  domain controllers, 593
  external connector failures, 608
  freezing messages, 469
  GC Servers, 593
  IM Service, 251
  mail delivery issues, 589
  message flow, 590–593
  message routing, 452–454, 472, 475
  messaging server overview, 43
  MS Mail for PC Networks Connector, 634
  routing groups, 593
  security access errors, File System Digital Dashboard, 695
  Security tab, System Manager Console snap-in, 314
  steps in troubleshooting, 587–588
Troubleshooting tools
  connectivity issues, 592
  diagnostic logging, 50, 403, 454, 478
  Event Viewer, 454
  message tracking (Message Tracking Center), 214, 426, 453, 472
  protocol logging, 453, 475
  Queue Viewer, 452, 468, 469
  RPCPing, 592
  WinRoute.exe, 592–593
Trust relationships, 113–114
Tuning. *See* Optimization.
TURN command verb, 178, 202, 447
Two-way connection agreements, 338–339

U

UDP ports, 331, 332, 333. *See also* Ports and port numbers.
Unattended installation, Exchange 2000, 397
Unfreeze All Messages option, SMTP queues, 607
Universal distribution groups
  converting to security groups, 369
  mail-enabled groups, 344–345
  overview, 344
Universal groups, 160, 193, 343–344
Universal security groups
  converting distribution groups, 369
  mail-enabled groups, 344–345
  overview, 140, 344
Unlodctr command, 429
Unsolicited commercial or bulk email, 325, 358, 540
Upgrading to Exchange 2000
  foreign mail system connectors, 617
  mailboxes, creating, 389
  synchronizing data. *See* ADC tool.
  X.400 Connectors, 450

Upgrading to Outlook 2000, 504–505
URLs
ADO object access, 750–751
syntax, 109–110
Usage levels, performance baselines, 574
User accounts
account vulnerability, Exchange 2000, 273
administrative models, 535, 537, 539
disabled user account mailboxes, 161
mailbox-enabled objects, 138
migrating foreign messaging systems to Exchange 2000, 618–619
User connection agreements, 340
User interfaces, workflow processes, 713
User management, administrative needs assessment, 82
User objectives, deployment planning, 68
User profiles, Outlook clients
configuring, 509
forcing user selection of, 508
overview, 497, 500
Users
delegating control, 335, 365
enabling for IM, 416
enrolling, 246, 255
Exchange features, enabling and disabling, 561
mail-enabled object overview, 139, 140
Users and Computers snap-in, 213, 528, 576

V

/V switch, **ESEUTIL** utility, 610
VBScript, 719–720
Verifying policies, 548
Vertical scalability, 80, 118
Video conferencing servers, 84
Viewing raw Exchange 2000 directories, 768
Viewing workflow diagrams, 740
Views
Global Address List views, 336
modifying using Outlook interface, 723
public folder views, 337
Virtual machines, 763–764
Virtual memory, 577, 596, 600, 604
Virtual Servers
clusters and Cluster Services, 19, 85–86, 278–279, 397
configuring, 506
IM Service, 231–232, 415
IP addresses, 301, 303
NNTP Service, 424
overview, 506
POP3, 519
port numbers, 301
SMTP Virtual Servers
authentication, configuring, 302
configuring, 506, 517
connections, restricting, 303
creating, 299, 378, 422
Viruses and virus control
Outlook security, 270, 327–328, 360
security overview, 270–271, 317
virus propagation, 326–327
virus-scanning API, 326
virus-scanning software, 325–326, 327
Vision statement, deployment planning
corporate objectives, 67–68
gap analysis, 70
problem statement, 68–69
project scope, 70
proposed solution, 69
risk analysis, 69
VRFY command, 178
Vulnerabilities, system
account vulnerability, Exchange 2000, 273
ActiveX controls, 271
demilitarized zones, 273–274
denial-of-service attacks, 272–273
HTML code, 270–271
IIS/Exchange 2000 security flaws, 271–272
Outlook security, 270, 327–328, 360
third-party mail relay abuse, 359
viruses and virus control, 270–271
Vulnerability, defined, 89

W

Warning conditions, server monitors, 578
Way of the Craftsman, 3
Way of the Merchant, 3, 765–766
Way of the Technician, 3
W3C Extended Log File Format, 476
WDE. *See* Workflow Designer for Exchange.
Web controls, ASP.NET, 764
Web folders, 46, 693
Web Forms, 677–678, 764.
See also Outlook Forms.

Web Part Builder, 696, 698
Web Parts
  access control, 682–683
  adding to digital dashboards, 693, 698
  building inline, 697
  COM+ components, 685
  creating digital dashboards, 699
  design considerations, 683–684, 687–688
  designing, 698
  Properties sheets, 691
  Web Part Builder, 696, 698
Web portals, 679
Web Services. *See also* WSS.
  architecture, 671–672
  knowledge management overview, 669–671
  platform requirements, 672–673
Web services Description Language, 670
Web Storage System. *See* WSS.
Web store. *See* WSS.
WebDAV, 182, 674
Well-known port numbers, Trojan horses, 332
Windows 2000
  integration with Exchange 2000, 207–208, 262
  member servers, installing Exchange 2000, 397
  in .NET Framework, 761
  services, monitoring, 578
  sites, 439–440
  tools, 216
Windows 2000 ADC tool. *See* ADC tool.
Windows OS, roaming user support, 502–503
WinRoute.exe, 592
Workflow applications
  business logic layer, 711
  design guidelines, 712
  development tools, 711–712
  overview, 711, 712–713
  presentation layer, 710–711
  public folders, creating, 730, 731
  running, 730
  testing, 741
  WDE 2000, 713
  workflow folders, 713
  WSS events, 676–677
Workflow Design Surface, 722
Workflow Designer for Exchange
  overview, 676–677, 719
  states, adding and modifying, 722, 727
  workflow applications, creating, 713
  workflow processes, 714, 726, 733
  workflow scripts, 720
Workflow diagrams
  adding states, 727, 733
  changing display, 739
  printing, 740
Workflow engine, 719, 755–756
Workflow event sinks
  permissions, 728
  registering, 700, 771
  in workflow processes, 714, 717–718
Workflow folders, 713
Workflow process events
  assigning state to, 715–716
  defined, 715
  order of evaluation, 717
  protocol events, 717
  transport events, 717
  trigger events, 717
Workflow processes
  action tables, 714
  activating, 739
  changing diagram display, 739
  COM+ roles, 729
  components, 721
  copying, 738
  creating, 726, 731
  deleting, 736
  designing, 733
  events, 715–716
  overview, 713, 714–715, 720–721
  states. *See* Workflow states.
  transitions, 714, 734, 735, 736
  user interfaces, 713
  Workflow Design Surface, 722
Workflow scripts
  creating shared script procedures, 737
  debugging, enabling, 737
  overview, 717, 719–720
  success entries, enabling, 737
Workflow states
  adding actions to states, 727
  adding and modifying, 722, 733
  assigning to events, 715–716
  captions, 734
  defined, 715
  deleting, 735
  labeling, 734

Worms, 326–327.
See also Viruses and virus control.
Write-back caches, 283
WSDL, 670
WSS. *See also* Workflow applications.
development tools, 678
events. *See* WSS events.
interaction with Internet protocols, 492
knowledge management tools, 667
overview, 20–24, 31–32, 45, 744
resource management, 571
resources, 673, 674–675
schema, 674
SharePoint Portal Servers, opening, 701
Web Forms overview, 677–678
Web storage instances, creating, 690
WebDAV, 32, 674
WSS events
event sinks, 700, 714, 728, 771
overview, 675–676, 717–718
workflow applications, 676–677
WSS folders, 700, 714, 717–718, 771

X

X.400 Connectors
legacy Exchange Servers, 175–176
planning routing strategy, 449–450, 466
upgrading to Exchange 2000, 450
X.400 queues, monitoring, 578, 581–582
/X switch, **ESEUTIL** utility, 610
XML
ADO access to data providers, 758
MSXML Parser, installing, 769
overview, 758–759
transformation documents, 760
XML scripting, 758

Z

ZDESTT, 162
Ziff Davis Email Server Test Tool, 162
Zones, DNS, 330, 331